Small Arms Of The World

A BASIC MANUAL OF SMALL ARMS

a basic manual of

small arms

SMALL ARMS of the WORLD

EDWARD CLINTON EZELL

**A completely new and revised version of the
classic work by W. H. B. Smith**

11th REVISED EDITION

STACKPOLE BOOKS, Harrisburg

ARMS AND ARMOUR PRESS, London

SMALL ARMS OF THE WORLD
Copyright © 1977 by
The Stackpole Company
Eleventh edition
Published by
STACKPOLE BOOKS
Cameron and Kelker Streets
P.O. Box 1831
Harrisburg, Pa. 17105

Published simultaneously in Don Mills, Ontario, Canada by
Thomas Nelson & Sons, Ltd.

Distributed by
ARMS & ARMOUR PRESS
2-6 Hampstead High Street
London NW3 1QQ
Great Britain

Printed in the U.S.A.

This new edition of *Small Arms of the World* represents at once a partial departure from recent versions and a return to the basic manual concept of earlier editions. Thirty-four years have passed since W. H. B. Smith copyrighted the first *Basic Manual of Military Small Arms* (December 1943), and the small arms of the world have changed significantly since that time. After consulting the publishers, this editor decided that some significant alterations were needed to acquaint the reader with the small arms scene today and in the process give him a look at the evolution of current generation small arms. Starting from the assumption that the average reader will be more conversant with firearms of the period before 1945 and relying upon the increased availability of books and other printed material on older small arms, we have concentrated on weapons development since the Second World War in Part I of this edition. Part II reflects an attempt to return to the basic manual. As a result, more attention is given developmental

Preface

weapons in Part I; Part II is primarily devoted to discussion of standard small arms. We hope this division of material will help the reader understand where the current small arms came from (Part I) and how the standard issue weapons of the world operate and are assembled/disassembled for field maintenance (Part II).

Since each edition of *Small Arms of the World* reflects changing conditions, the current one updates earlier versions. But no one volume of *Small Arms* completely supplants the previous ones. In fact, the serious student of infantry weapons should study all editions. In Part I of the eleventh edition, the reader will find both metric and English measurements given for weights, dimensions, and projectile velocities. Only inch/foot/pound specifications are used in Part II. This partial conversion reflects the status of the metric system in the United States today. It is likely that subsequent editions of *Small Arms of the World* will contain metric measurements only, since that is the trend in the world of small arms. For example, when the US Army let a contract for prototypes of the XM235 Squad Automatic Weapon in February 1977, it called for all drawings and specifications to be made in the metric system. As the world changes, so must this publication.

As in the past, the editor encourages readers to comment on the text and illustrations. Photographs or data on old and new weapons, suggestions for areas to be covered, corrections of errors and other proposals for improving this book are always welcome. Please address all correspondence to the editor in care of the publisher at P.O. Box 1831, Harrisburg, PA 17105. Insofar as it is possible, correspondence will receive the editor's personal attention, and replies will be made.

EDWARD CLINTON EZELL

Walter Harold Black Smith, 1901–1959
Joseph Edward Smith, 1921–1976

Over the years, many individuals, organizations, and business firms have contributed to the preparation of the ten preceding editions of *Small Arms of the World.* This list is devoted to those who assisted in preparing the eleventh edition.

Acknowledgments

United States:

Harold E. Johnson, US Army Foreign Science and Technology Center, Charlottesville, VA

Thomas B. Nelson, Replica Models, Inc., Alexandria, VA

Robert E. Roy, David A. Behrendt, and George Curtis, Colt Firearms, Hartford, CT

James B. Hughes, Deep River Armory, Houston, TX

Office of the Secretary of the Army:
> Martin R. Hoffman, former Secretary of the Army
> Major Donald E. Nowland, Military Assistant to the Secretary of the Army

US Army Development and Readiness Command:
> Joe Penton, Information Office

US Army Armament Materiel Readiness Command, Rock Island, IL.
> Richard Dorbeck
> Dorrell Garrison
> Richard Maguire
> Colonel J. N. Payne
> Elaine Pospishal
> Truman Strobridge

US Army Armament Research and Development Command, Picatinny Arsenal, Dover, NJ:
> Lt. Col. Bob B. Lukens, SAW Project Manager, Small Caliber Weapons Systems Laboratory

US Navy Surface Weapons Laboratory, Silver Spring, MD:
> L. H. Dreisonstok

Jerry Lee Elmore, Houston, TX

J. P. Harahan, History Office, Strategic Air Command, USAF, formerly of the History Office, US Army Armament Materiel Readiness Command

R. G. Jinks, Smith & Wesson, Springfield, MA

Edward J. Klein, EJK Development Corp., Houston, TX

Robert Mellichamp, Houston, TX

C. M. Roberts, Maremont Corp., Saco, ME

Russel S. Robinson, Tucson, AZ

Eugene M. Stoner and Ann Paulsen, ARES, Inc., Port Clinton, OH

Steve Vogel and James Triggs, Sturm, Ruger Co., Southport, CT

Richard S. Winter and Carl Ring, Interarms, Alexandria, VA

William H. Woodin, Tucson, AZ

Australia:

Major J. B. Wilson

Austria:

Steyr-Daimler-Puch, Steyr

Belgium:

Claude Gaier, Chief, Information Service, Fabrique Nationale, Liege

Czechoslovakia:

Antonin Reha, Publicity Manager, Merkuria Foreign Trade Corp., Prague

France:

Col. J. P. Lepreux
Groupment Industriel des Armaments Terrestres, Saint-Cloud

West Germany: Heckler & Koch, Oberndorf
J. P. Sauer & Sohn, Eckernforde
Carl Walther, Sportwaffenfabrik, Ulm

Israel: Zvi Eyal, Ministry of Defense

Japan: Masami Tokoi, Tokyo

Norway: H. Kjeldaas, Kongsberg Vapenfabrikk, Kongsberg
Lt. Col. Birger Setsaas, Norwegian Army, Oslo

Sweden: G. L. M. Kjellgren, Interdynamic, Stockholm

Switzerland: SIG Neuhausen am Rheinfall
H. Ditesheim, Waffenfabrik, Bern

USSR: Mikhail Timofyevich Kalashnikov, Izhvesk Machine Factory, Urdmurt, Khazak ASSR

United Kingdom (Britain): Maj. F. W. A. Hobart (deceased)
Maj. B. B. Keen, Sterling Armament Co., Ltd., Dagenham, Essex
Maj. Peter Labbett, Croyden, Surrey
Maj. R. J. M. Mosse, Ministry of Defence, London
Herbert Woodend, Pattern Room, Royal Small Arms Factory, Enfield

I also wish to acknowledge the tireless reading, editing, and typing of text, both old and new, done by my wife, Linda. She was more than a good sport about lost weekends and clutter on the dining room table.

Finally, Vaclav "Jack" Krcma, Willowdale, Ontario, Canada, whose photographs have contributed to this and earlier editions.

E. C. E.

Contents

Contents

Part II   A Basic Manual of Current Weapons

Contents

Contents

PART

1

Historical

1 Rifle and Carbine Development Since 1945

When the Second World War began in 1939, only the Soviet Union and United States—a nonbelligerent—had made firm commitments to the production of self-loading rifles. At the end of the war, the M1 (Garand) Rifle was the only semiautomatic weapon to have successfully withstood the tests of the battlefield. As of September 1945, Springfield Armory and Winchester had delivered 4,024,034 M1 Rifles. Although the Soviets appear to have made greater use of the SVT-38 (Tokarev) Rifle than previously thought, they relied more heavily on the bolt action M1891 rifle and submachine gun than on their semiautomatic rifles. After World War II, bolt action rifles were relegated to secondary status as most of the world's major armies began to search about for their own solution to the self-loading rifle problem.

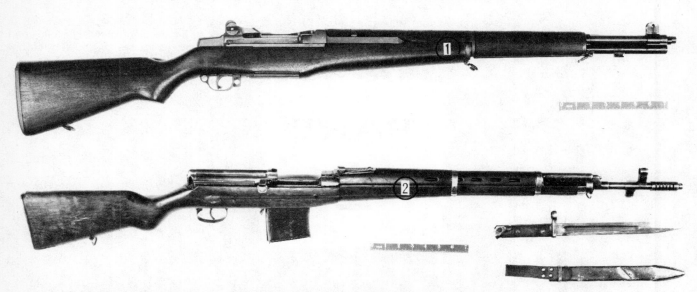

1) US Rifle, Caliber .30, M1—eight-shot clip; and 2) USSR *Samozariadnyia Vintovka Tokareva Obrazets 1938G* (SVT-38) 7.62 × 54Rmm—ten-shot magazine. The M1 Rifle was produced from 1936 to 1945 and again during the Korean conflict of the 1950s. The SVT-38 was modified in 1940, and both semiautomatic (SVT-40) and selective fire (AVT-40) versions were produced during World War II.

In spite of more than thirty years of rapid scientific and technological development in the field of military armaments, the standard weapon of the world's infantrymen is still the rifle. Immediately following the Second World War, many military commentators argued that the foot soldier was obsolete. They expected him to be replaced by tactical nuclear weapons and automated battlefields. A succession of military encounters in Korea, Vietnam and the Middle East, not to mention insurgencies and counterinsurgencies fought around the globe in the same period, have proven the infantrymen to be the match of their colleagues who use more sophisticated arms.

At the end of the 1939–1945 war, several important trends were obvious in the small arms of the world. First, the rapid movement of the battlefield, generally typified by the advance of infantry supported by tanks and other armored fighting vehicles, stood in direct contrast to the stalemated battle front of the 1914–1918 conflict. Portability and rapidity of fire were required in all classes of weapons—rifles, submachine guns and machine guns. The German *Wehrmacht* and the Soviet Red Army were notable in their efforts to produce large quantities of pistol caliber submachine guns to provide the desired massed firepower to accompany the offensive thrust of their armored forces, but the striking power of such weapons was limited to close ranges—usually 50–100 meters. Beyond those ranges, all armies during the Second World War relied upon rifles and machine guns firing "full power" cartridges dating from either the last decades of the 19th century or the first decades of this century. World War I had confirmed the desire to have cartridges that were reliably accurate and lethal to 1200 meters and beyond. In both the European and Asian theaters of the 1939–1945 war, the ranges at which effective small arms fire was delivered were usually under 350 meters. Thus, one pressure on weapons designers was the desire of infantry tacticians to acquire small arms that combined the rapid, massed and shocking power of the submachine gun with the lethality of the standard infantry rifle cartridge.

A second fact of life brought home to military planners by World War II was the logistical nightmare created when one's forces had small arms of various types and calibers. The *Wehrmacht* was the worst example. While the German Ordnance Corps struggled mightily to issue only caliber 7.92 × 57 mm rifles and machine guns to their front line troops, the variety of weapons chambered for that cartridge was staggering. Each weapon type required a separate spare parts inventory and special training. British and French troops had similar headaches. They started the war with their own national patterns of small arms, but after the evacuation of Dunkirk and the fall of France, American weapons came to play an increasingly important role in the Allied war effort.

Late in the war, the Germans introduced a new class of small arms, the *Sturmgewehr*—or assault rifle, as this class of weapons has been designated in the post-1939–1945 war era. This weapon fired a shortened 7.92 mm cartridge (7.92 × 33), with an average velocity of approximately 640 meters per second (m.p.s.) (2100 feet per second [f.p.s.]) versus 840 m.p.s. (2750 f.p.s.) for the standard 7.92 mm round fired from Mauser Kar. 98k. Projectile weight was reduced from 12.8 grams (197.5 grains) to 8.1 grams (125 grains). Although not as lethal as the longer range rifle cartridge, the 7.92 mm *Kurz* was far more ef-

fective than the standard 9mm Parabellum pistol cartridge used in submachine guns by the *Wehrmacht*—muzzle velocity, 381 m.p.s. (1250 f.p.s.) for a 7.4-gram (115-grain) projectile. Experimentation with the *Kurz* cartridge led the German army in 1944/45 to plan to replace all existing bolt action and self-loading (semiautomatic) rifles with the MP43/44, *StG 44* series of selective fire assault rifles. However, this plan was thwarted by the crippling effect of the Allied land and air offensives on the German production and supply system. Nevertheless, the German experiment had a profound effect on the post-war thinking of American, Belgian, British, Soviet, Spanish and Swiss small arms designers. Captain H. B. C. Pollard, an English intelligence officer, commented on the virtues of the 7.92 × 33mm cartridge in a 1945 Allied intelligence report: "This is a wholly admirable cartridge which may well be the prototype of the rifle cartridge of the future." He continued his praise, "while as effective for military purposes as the old 8mm Mauser German Army Service Cartridge, [it] is only two-thirds the size and two-thirds the weight. In other words, a man can carry twice the amount of ammunition into action."

As a consequence of the search for rifles with greater firepower and lighter weight during the past thirty years, many new rifles have been proposed, dozens have been tested and a few have become standard weapons, replacing the Second World War generation of small arms. Three basic calibers dominate the scene today—7.62 × 51mm NATO caliber, 7.62 × 39 M43 (Soviet) caliber and 5.56 × 45mm caliber. While each can trace its origins to the assault rifle concept, each of these groups of rifles reflects a particular technical/historic trend in small arms development and as such is described by caliber in this chapter.

2.0 inches (51mm)

POST-WAR RIFLE CARTRIDGES COMPARED WITH THE 7.92MM KURZ AND M1911 .45 CALIBER CARTRIDGES

| 7.62 × 51mm NATO | .280/30 (7mm) UK | 7.62 × 45mm M52 Czech | 7.62 × 39mm M43 USSR | 7.92 × 33mm PP 43 Germany | .45 (11.5mm) USA |

Two World War II German self-loading rifles. Top, *Gewehr 41 (W)* and bottom, *Gewehr 43*. Both weapons fired the standard 7.92 × 57mm cartridge.

Typical *Sturmgewehr*, the German MP 44, which fired the 7.92 × 33 cartridge.

NATO CALIBER RIFLES

The end of the Second World War found the Atlantic Allies armed with an incredible pot pourri of small arms. At war's end, the United States, the United Kingdom, France and Canada all began to cast about for new infantry weapons. High on the list was a new rifle. Nationalism, differences in opinion about rifle and ammunition specifications and the desire to standardize weapons among the old allies created a muddled situation that lasted for the better part of a decade, popularly known as the "great rifle controversy."

During the struggle with the Axis powers, the British employed several models of the Short Magazine Lee Enfield (SMLE) Rifle. While this had been the basic pattern for their service rifle since 1902, the desire for a self-loading rifle went back to the pre-1914 period. The successful development of the No. 4 Rifle in the 1930s (an updated SMLE) set back the effort to obtain a self-loading rifle. Some experimentation toward that end was taken during World War II with the Belgian SAFN in 7.92 × 57 (called the 7.92 S.L.E.M.1), but no change was seriously contemplated as long as the war continued.

At the end of the hostilities, the Ministry of Supply created the "Small Arms Ideal Calibre Panel" and assigned it the task of developing a new infantry rifle cartridge. The British sought the lightest rifle and ammunition combination that would be consistent with firing comfort and effectiveness at the reduced maximum range of 600 meters. Commenting on this shortened range, one member of the development team said, "It was recognized that the old .303 over-killed at rifle ranges." They were seeking an "intermediate power" cartridge to be used in an assault-type rifle.

Dr. Richard Beeching, Deputy Chief of the Armaments Design Establishment, and his associates carried out the basic ballistic studies for the "Ideal Calibre Panel," which included an experimental determination of the optimum caliber, muzzle velocity and external and internal ballistics. This work, without equal at the time, led to the conclusion that the ideal caliber was .270.

Preliminary talks with American Ordnance representatives led Beeching's staff to increase the caliber to .276, later designated .280, although the diameter of the projectile was not actually altered. In the summer of 1947, Beeching's panel submitted its classified findings in a formal report. The British Army team, dispatched to the United States with this document, encountered for the first time American plans for the development of a lightweight .30 caliber rifle. A difference in calibers was just the first hurdle on the path toward a common rifle cartridge.

At first, the controversy over caliber was difficult to understand, since the desire for an "intermediate power" cartridge was sparked by a common admiration for the 7.92 × 33 *Kurz* round that the Germans employed in their *Sturmgewehr* series. But the Americans displayed an ambivalence in their goals for a new rifle/ammunition system. They wanted the firepower of the *Sturmgewehr,* but they also wanted to keep the long range of their older .30-06 (7.62 × 63) cartridge. As one official statement phrased it:

> The Army is firmly opposed to the adoption of any less effective small caliber cartridge for use in either its present rifle, or in new weapons being developed. . . . Battle experience has proved beyond question the effectiveness of the present rifle ammunition, and there have been no changes in combat tactics which would justify a reduction of rifle caliber and power.

In the spring of 1951, the British Labour Party announced the adoption of the .280 E.M.2 Rifle, and the rifle controversy in the UK divided along party lines. The Labour Party stood for national integrity at the risk of disunity in the NATO alliance (formed in 1949). The Conservatives urged international cooperation based upon the relative power position of the UK in NATO.

Top: Rifle, .280 E.M.2. Bottom: Rifle No. 4 Mark 1. The No. 4 Rifle fired an 11.3-gram (174-grain) projectile at 751 m/s (2465 f.p.s.) from a 592mm (23.3-inch) barrel; while the E.M.2 fired an 8.4-gram (140-grain) projectile at 736 m/s (2415 f.p.s.) from a 622mm (24.5-inch) barrel. Overall length of the E.M.2 was kept short by its bull pup design. The magazine and receiver group are to the rear of the pistol grip, thus permitting the use of a full length barrel in a shorter weapon: E.M.2 914mm (36 inches) vs No. 4 1079mm (42.5 inches).

Stefan K. Janson demonstrating the E.M.2 Rifle he designed at the Royal Small Arms Factory, Enfield.

FABRIQUE NATIONALE
FUSIL AUTOMATIQUE LÉGÈR (FAL)

FN's *Fusil Automatique Légèr* was one of the basic NATO caliber weapons to emerge from the "rifle controversy" of the 1950s. Designers at FN began work on a self-loading rifle before World War II; Dieudonne J. Saive was the principal engineer when the German army invaded Belgium. In 1940, he and several of his associates went to the UK where they continued their work on the rifle at the Royal Small Arms Factory, Enfield. After the war, the rifle was manufactured at FN. Designated the ABL (*Arme Belgique Légèr*) and SAFN (*Saive Automatique, FN*), it was produced in 7mm, .30-06 and 7.92 calibers.

Building upon his experience with the SAFN, Saive designed a prototype assault rifle that fired the 7.92 × 33mm *Kurz* cartridge. Demonstrated early in 1948, these early FALs were very close to being in concept ideal assault rifles. The short cartridge with its moderate recoil permitted the construction of a compact and relatively light weapon. These initial models were subsequently replaced by prototypes chambered for the British .280 (7mm) cartridge. Two variants of the .280 FAL were developed—a bull pup design and one conventionally stocked. When the US Army rejected the UK cartridge, Saive and Ernest Vervier redesigned the FAL to fire the American experimental 7.62 × 51mm cartridge. During this evolution in design, the rifle gained weight and grew in length. The American, British and Canadian armies dropped the full automatic fire requirement because the weapon was no longer controllable when fired automatically. As ultimately adopted by more than 50 nations, the basic rifle is essentially an advanced semiautomatic rifle with a 20-shot magazine. The heavy barrelled version adopted by several countries as a light squad automatic weapon, replacing older weapons such as the BREN, is neither an assault rifle nor a good light machine gun. Australia's L2A1 heavy barrel FAL, used by several Commonwealth nations, has a "bang, bang, jam" phenomena. Instead of automatic fire, it fires two rounds, and then experiences a failure to feed.

Despite its shortcomings (length, weight and recoil), the FAL has been an exceedingly popular weapon. Once the British discovered that the US Army did not like the E.M.2 Rifle but that there were some American officers who thought the FAL was a good weapon, the British became strong proponents of the FAL. The Belgian weapon was tested extensively by the NATO armies between 1951 and 1956. Two experimental lots of the FAL were manufactured in the United States—Harrington & Richardson (500) and High Standard (13). While the US Army ultimately adopted its own design, the 7.62 × 51mm M14 Rifle, instead of the foreign FAL, the Belgian rifle has seen wide use throughout the world and has been produced in larger quantities than any other NATO caliber rifle since 1945.

The latter party asked if Britain were being realistic in expecting the United States with its proportionally larger commitments and greater population to bend to the whims of the British on the caliber of the next American rifle.

By August 1951, the rifle controversy had embroiled the major members of the alliance. The Canadians, in particular, who had been stoically awaiting a solution of the disagreement, began to grow more and more concerned about producing a third cartridge. They were already manufacturing cartridges for both British and American rifles. They did not want to increase the logistical difficulties made evident by the Korean conflict. As a consequence of the Canadian desire for a resolution to the NATO ammunition question, Brooke Claxton, Canada's Defense Minister, called for a four-power conference between representatives of Canada, the US, the UK and France. The meeting resolved nothing. A standard cartridge, the American Cal. .30 T65E3 emerged subsequently as the standard round in 1956. A standard rifle was never to be.

Early FAL prototype chambered for the 7.92 × 33mm *Kurz* cartridge.

SPRINGFIELD ARMORY - ORDNANCE CORPS
CHARACTERISTICS
RIFLE CAL . . 30, T44 & T48(FN) (LIGHT BARREL)

T44

T48

CHARACTERISTICS	M1	T44	T48 (FN)
WEIGHT - BASIC RIFLE (w/Empty Mag.-Less Sling)	9.6 #	8.7 #	9.7 #
WEIGHT - RIFLE READY TO FIRE (Fully Loaded- w/Sling)	10.3 # (8 Rds)	10.0 # (20 Rds)	11.0 # (20 Rds)
LENGTH - w/FLASH HIDER	43.6″ (w/o F.H.)	44.25″	44.5″
MUZZLE VELOCITY	2800	2800	2800
WEIGHT - AMMUNITION (20 Rds)	1.18 #	1.04 #	1.04 #
WEIGHT - BAYONET	.88 #	.70 #	0.63 #
WEIGHT - GRENADE LAUNCHER	.81 #	.31 #	0.34 #

Springfield Armory photograph comparing the American T44 (Prototype M14 Rifle) and the FN FAL (T48) as built for tests in the United States.

The FN FAL is also called: the SLR, for self-loading rifle; L1A1, by the UK and some Commonwealth nations; the *Gewehr 1,* by the *Bundeswehr* (West Germany); the *Sturmgewehr 58,* by the Austrians; the CA1, by the Canadians; and the 1A SL, by the Indian Army.

COUNTRIES USING THE FN FAL IN THEIR ARMED FORCES

Argentina (* Fabrica Militar, Rosario)
Austria (* Steyr-Daimler-Puch)
Australia (* Commonwealth Small Arms
  Factory, Lithgow)
Bangladesh
Barbados
Belgium (* Fabrique Nationale, Liege)
Brazil
Burundi
Cambodia, Khmer Republic
Canada (* Canadian Arsenals Ltd.)
Chile*
Congo, Republic of
Cuba
Dominican Republic
Dubai
Ecuador
Gambia
Germany-Federal Republic (obsolete
  1959)
Greece
Guyana
India (* Ishapore)
Indonesia
Ireland, Eire
Israel (* Israeli Military Industries)
Jamaica
Jordan
Kenya

Kuwait
Lebanon
Liberia
Libyan Arab Republic
Luxembourg
Malawi
Malaysia
Mexico
Morocco
Mozambique
Muscat and Oman
Nepal
Netherlands
New Zealand
Panama
Paraguay
Peru
Portugal
Qatar
Ras Al Kahimah
Rhodesia
Rwanda
Singapore, Republic of
South Africa, Republic of (* Pretoria)
Syria
Thailand
United Kingdom (* BSA and RSAF Enfield)
Venezuela

*Denotes countries that have manufactured their own FALs. See Belgian chapter in Part II for the variations in the *Fabrique Nationale*-produced FALs.

US RIFLE, 7.62mm M14

The American M14 (T44E4 in prototype form) was the major competitor against the FAL in the NATO trials of the 1950s. Designer John Garand had begun work on an automatic version of the M1 Rifle before the Second World War ended. This series, called T20, was constructed in a limited number of prototypes at Springfield Armory, Springfield, Massachusetts. A different fire control mechanism was developed for the Garand by the Remington Arms Company, and that experimental series was called the T22 and T27. Plans for the production of 100,000 T20E2 Rifles in caliber .30-06 (7.62 × 63) were terminated with the August 1945 end of the war in the Pacific.

After the war, the "Army Ground Forces Equipment Review Board Preliminary Board Study" called for a 3.2-kilogram (7-lb.) .30 caliber selective fire (automatic and semiautomatic) rifle that could replace the M1 Rifle, the Browning Automatic Rifle (M1918A2) and all the existing sniper weapons. Subsequently, the US Army altered this requirement so that the new rifle could also be used in place of versions of the carbine and all the submachine guns then in use. Three basic weapons came from all this effort: the T25, designed by Earle M. Harvey; the T28, developed by Cyril A. Moore from the unfinished Mauser *Sturmgewehr 45;* and the unconventional T31, designed by John Garand. Only the T25 (later redesignated the T47) got beyond the very limited prototype stage. Building upon design studies conducted during 1942–1944, Earle Harvey had started work on his rifle before the official specifications were laid down in 1946. The first T25s were test fired in 1948. Despite promise, this design fell victim to politics within the US Army. After a series of trials and at least one proposal that it be adopted as the replacement for the M1 Rifle, the T25 was dropped from contention following tests by the Infantry at Fort Benning, Georgia, in 1952. Of four candidate rifles, the FN FAL finished first; the new Springfield entry (T44) came in a poor second; and the T25 and British E.M.2 were eliminated from consideration.

John Garand in his tool room at Springfield Armory holding an M1 Rifle (ca 1943).

Caliber .30 T20 Rifle.

Caliber .30 T20E2 Rifle.

US Rifle caliber .30 T22.

Caliber .30 Rifle T22E2.

US caliber .30 T27 Rifle.

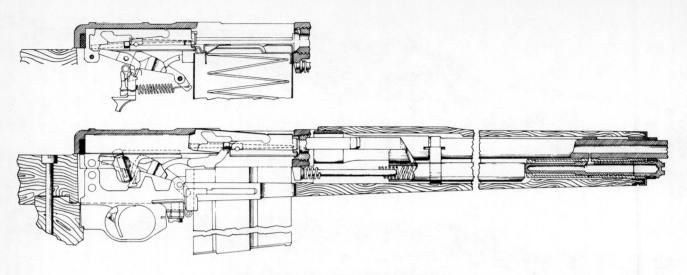

DETAIL SKETCH OF THE T25 RIFLE MECHANISM.
Top: Bolt in the recoil position. Bottom: Bolt in locked position. Note the manner in which the bolt hinges.

Caliber .30 T28 Rifle.

T-31

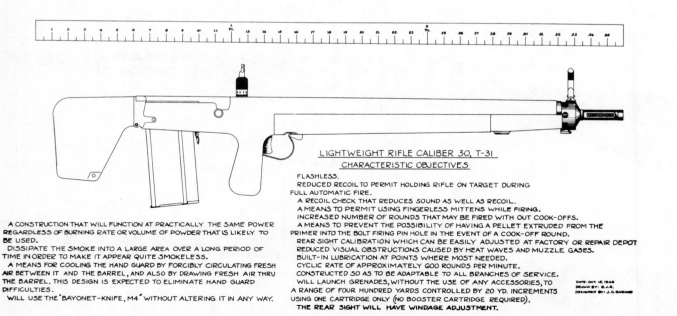

LIGHTWEIGHT RIFLE CALIBER 30, T-31
CHARACTERISTIC OBJECTIVES

FLASHLESS.
REDUCED RECOIL TO PERMIT HOLDING RIFLE ON TARGET DURING FULL AUTOMATIC FIRE.
A RECOIL CHECK THAT REDUCES SOUND AS WELL AS RECOIL.
A MEANS TO PERMIT USING FINGERLESS MITTENS WHILE FIRING.
INCREASED NUMBER OF ROUNDS THAT MAY BE FIRED WITH OUT COOK-OFFS.
A MEANS TO PREVENT THE POSSIBILITY OF HAVING A PELLET EXTRUDED FROM THE PRIMER INTO THE BOLT FIRING PIN HOLE IN THE EVENT OF A COOK-OFF ROUND.
REAR SIGHT CALIBRATION WHICH CAN BE EASILY ADJUSTED AT FACTORY OR REPAIR DEPOT
REDUCED VISUAL OBSTRUCTIONS CAUSED BY HEAT WAVES AND MUZZLE GASES.
BUILT-IN LUBRICATION AT POINTS WHERE MOST NEEDED.
CYCLIC RATE OF APPROXIMATELY 600 ROUNDS PER MINUTE.
CONSTRUCTED SO AS TO BE ADAPTABLE TO ALL BRANCHES OF SERVICE.
WILL LAUNCH GRENADES, WITHOUT THE USE OF ANY ACCESSORIES, TO A RANGE OF FOUR HUNDRED YARDS CONTROLLED BY 20 YD. INCREMENTS USING ONE CARTRIDGE ONLY (NO BOOSTER CARTRIDGE REQUIRED).
THE REAR SIGHT WILL HAVE WINDAGE ADJUSTMENT.

A CONSTRUCTION THAT WILL FUNCTION AT PRACTICALLY THE SAME POWER REGARDLESS OF BURNING RATE OR VOLUME OF POWDER THAT IS LIKELY TO BE USED.
DISSIPATE THE SMOKE INTO A LARGE AREA OVER A LONG PERIOD OF TIME IN ORDER TO MAKE IT APPEAR QUITE SMOKELESS.
A MEANS FOR COOLING THE HAND GUARD BY FORCIBLY CIRCULATING FRESH AIR BETWEEN IT AND THE BARREL, AND ALSO BY DRAWING FRESH AIR THRU THE BARREL. THIS DESIGN IS EXPECTED TO ELIMINATE HAND GUARD DIFFICULTIES.
WILL USE THE "BAYONET-KNIFE, M4" WITHOUT ALTERING IT IN ANY WAY.

DATE: OCT. 12, 1948
DRAWN BY: B.J.R.
DESIGNED BY: J.C. GARAND

John Garand's proposal for the .30 caliber, T31 Rifle (October 1948).

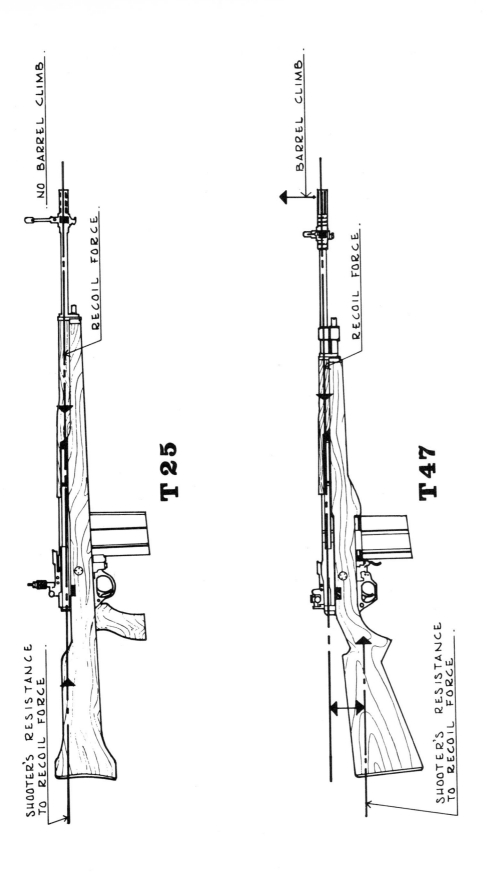

NO BARREL CLIMB.

RECOIL FORCE.

T25

SHOOTER'S RESISTANCE TO RECOIL FORCE.

BARREL CLIMB.

RECOIL FORCE.

T47

SHOOTER'S RESISTANCE TO RECOIL FORCE.

Recoil has always been one of the serious headaches facing designers. Early in the development of the T25 Rifle, it became apparent that the .30 Caliber Light Rifle Cartridge (7.62 × 51mm) was too powerful to be used in a 3.2-kg (7-lb.) rifle. The T25 was equipped with a "straight-in-line" stock to lessen the effect of recoil. Early tests of rifles with this type of stock indicated that it was an advance over conventional stocks. Although functional, this type of stock was rejected because it did not look functional, and it was replaced by a "drop" stock of more familiar form. The T47, as the restocked rifle was called, proved uncontrollable during automatic fire.

Earle M. Harvey, Chief of Small Arms Development at Springfield Armory in the late 1950s and early 1960s, shown here receiving an award from the Commanding Officer of the Armory, Col. O. E. Hurlbut in 1958.

and political flack finally cleared, the United States Army adopted the T44E4 on 1 May 1957 as the US Rifle, 7.62mm, M14, and the T44E5 (heavy barrel version) as the M15. The latter was never produced in quantity, and on 17 December 1959 was declared obsolete. Subsequently, Captain Durward Gosney of the US Army Infantry Board designed a version of the M14 to overcome three specific problems associated with automatic fire—(1) excessive dispersion of bullets, even when fired by an expert rifleman; (2) excessive recoil; and (3) muzzle climb. Gosney's alterations included an "in-line" stock, front and rear pistol grips and a recoil brake that fastened over the standard flash-hider. Combined, these elements made the rifle more manageable during automatic fire. Although subsequently adopted as the M14A1, this weapon was still too light (5.8 kg [12.75 lb.]) to be used as a suitable replacement for the M1918A2 Browning Automatic Rifle (8.8 kg [19.4 lb.]).

Springfield's T44 was essentially a lightened T20E2, or "product improved" M1 Rifle. Lloyd Corbett at the Armory modified the T20E2 by adding a lightweight barrel (T36, November 1949) and adapting the receiver of the weapon so that it would function properly with the shorter T65E3 (7.62 × 51mm) cartridge. As tested in 1951–1952, this weapon (now called the T44) was really a makeshift item that should not have been expected to compete successfully with the more fully developed FAL and T25. When it did perform satisfactorily for a weapon with such a limited development history, the Army decided to press for its improvement. This was only after a Board of Infantry Officers had in August 1952 recommended the limited procurement of the FAL for extensive field trials. During the next five years, the FN FAL and a series of constantly improved T44s were tested, retested and tested again in a wide variety of field conditions—tropical to arctic. After the gunsmoke

M14A1 Muzzle compensator.

US Rifle, 7.62mm M14.

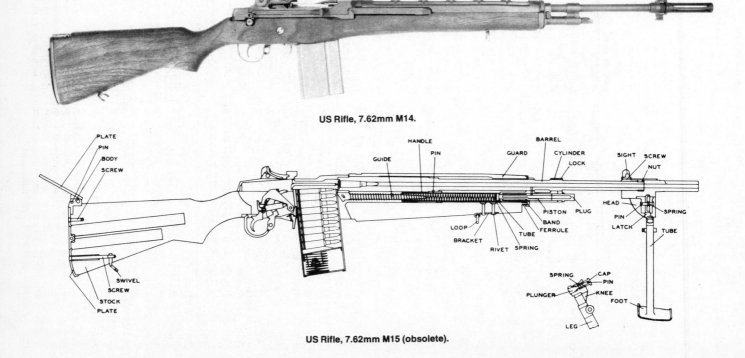

US Rifle, 7.62mm M15 (obsolete).

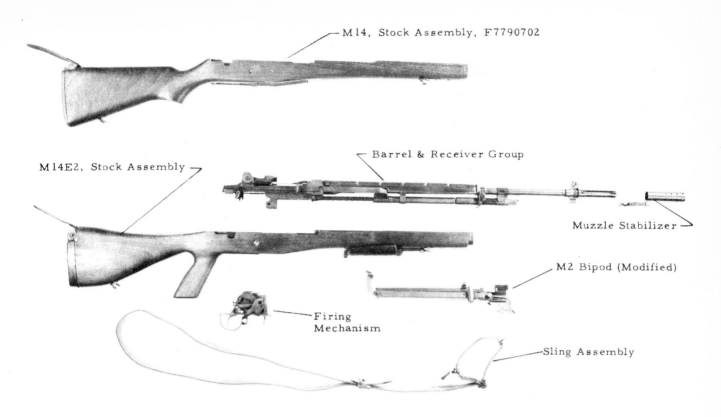

M14, Stock Assembly, F7790702

M14E2, Stock Assembly

Barrel & Receiver Group

Muzzle Stabilizer

M2 Bipod (Modified)

Firing Mechanism

Sling Assembly

Comparison of M14 and M14A1 (M14E2 in prototype) Rifle stocks.

After a tortuous five years of production, Robert S. McNamara, US Secretary of Defense, terminated manufacture of the M14 in 1963. The production version of the M14 was fabricated at: Springfield Armory (167,100), Winchester Division Olin Corporation (356,501), Harrington & Richardson (537,582) and Thompson-Ramo-Woolridge, Inc. (319,691). In 1967, surplus M14 production tooling was sold to the Republic of China (Taiwan). Since 1968, the Taiwanese have been producing that rifle as the Type 57 Rifle (i.e., 57th year since the establishment of the Republic of China in 1911).

NATO CALIBER VERSIONS OF THE US M1 RIFLE

The American experimental rifle program that led to the development of the M14 Rifle also demonstrated the feasibility of converting the standard M1 Garand to fire the NATO cartridge. The first tests of altered M1s were conducted in 1948, and they indicated that the slightly different case taper of the T65E3 cartridge case caused the new experimental case to stick in the standard eightshot M1 clip. To solve this problem, Springfield Armory engineers increased the gas port diameter from 2.15mm (.085 in) to 2.22mm (.0875 in). While this increased the power to overcome the sluggishness of the altered rifle, it also increased the strain on the other components. A new barrel was required for the shorter 7.62 × 51mm cartridge, as was a 6.3-gram (.224-oz) steel filler block at the front of the receiver. Experiments with the T35, as this converted M1 was designated, continued through the early 1950s. For various reasons, notably the manufacture of the M14 Rifle, no large alteration of M1 Rifles was undertaken by the US prior to 1963, when the Navy embarked upon such a program.

When Defense Secretary McNamara terminated production of the M14, the Navy did not have enough NATO caliber rifles to equip its shore units. The Bureau of Naval Weapons settled upon a special chamber bushing conceived and patented by Commander Richard F. Haley and a civilian Navy employee, James O'Conner. A steel sleeve just under 25mm (1 in) long, this bushing provided for the difference between the .30-06 (7.62 × 63mm) and 7.62 × 51mm cartridges. The external dimensions equalled the former cartridge, whereas the internal measurements matched the shoulder and neck of the NATO cartridge. The bushing was seated in the barrel and secured by firing two eight-shot clips. In the process of developing this conversion, the H. P. White Laboratories rediscovered the necessity of having a filler block to assure proper feeding of the shorter cartridges into the barrel. This time molded plastic was substituted for steel.

Tests during the summer of 1964 by the US Army Test and Evaluation Command of 10 M1E14 Rifles, converted by the American Machine and Foundry Company (AMF), York, Pennsylvania, indicated that under prolonged firing bushings were ejected randomly. Marine Corps tests indicated the same problem. While a new bushing was subsequently developed at the Weapons Production Engineering Center, Naval Depot, Crane, Indiana, the Navy also decided to purchase new NATO caliber barrels from Harrington & Richardson for 8,750 M1 Rifles. AMF altered 17,050 with the first model bushing and 5,000 with the new bushing. Harrington & Richardson used the new bushing in modifying 12,250 M1s. The grand total was 30,050 weapons. Congressional critics later questioned the economic wisdom of the Navy program, but it was carried out at a time when there were too few M14s and M16s to go around. All rifles converted in the Navy effort were marked "7.62 NATO" on the left side of the receiver.

While Fabrique Nationale also devised a conversion process for the M1 Rifle, Beretta of Italy went even further and developed an updated NATO caliber M1, the BM59. Early in the 1950s, Beretta began production of the M1 Rifle with technical support from the US. The first rifles went to the Italian Army in 1952. Later, Denmark and Indonesia purchased M1s from the Italian company. More than 100,000 Garands had been produced when Beretta decided to develop a modernized version of that rifle in the NATO caliber. Studies in this direction began in 1958–1959. Domenico Salza and Vittorio Valle were the two key

figures responsible for carrying out this project. Many variants were developed—most in prototype form only—with the "BM59 Mark Ital" being adopted by the Italian Army in 1962. That weapon had a Beretta-designed selective fire mechanism—full and semiautomatic—and used detachable 20-shot magazines instead of the Garand eight-shot clip. Further details on variants can be found in Chapter 28. Indonesia and Morocco have produced the BM59 with technical assistance from Beretta. Nigerian plans to produce the rifle appear to have been thwarted by the late civil war.

Total US production of the M1 Rifle between 1936 and 1957 was 6,034,228.

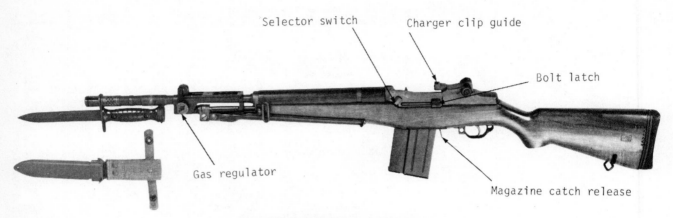

Beretta Mark 1 Ital. *BM59 Versione Normale.*

BM59 Versione speciale per Paracadutisti **with stock folded and compensator/grenade launcher removed.**

ARMIES USING THE M1 IN .30-06 (7.62 × 63mm)

Austria*	Korea
Brazil*	Liberia
Republic of China (Taiwan)	Mexico
Cyprus	Norway
Denmark (Beretta)	Pakistan
Ethiopia	Panama
Greece	Philippines
Guatemala	Thailand
Haiti	Turkey
Indonesia*	USA*
Iran	Vietnam (status unknown)

*Denotes secondary or obsolete.

CETME, G-3 AND RELATED ROLLER LOCK RIFLES

A whole family of rifles grew out of work done in 1944–1945 at the *Mauserwerke.* As part of the late Nazi war effort to produce an inexpensive but reliable weapon, engineers at Orberndorf am Neckar developed a delayed blow-back mechanism, using a two-piece bolt with a roller locking system, which provided the

necessary delay in opening. This design was not fully developed in 1945, and incomplete weapons were captured by the Allies. The weapon had several designations: StG 45(M), Gerat 06H, MP45(M). (Operational details are presented in Chapter 20 under the G3 Rifle.) As noted above, the American designer C. A. Moore used this concept in his T28 Rifle.

Automatisches Gewehr G 3, Kal. 7,62 mm × 51

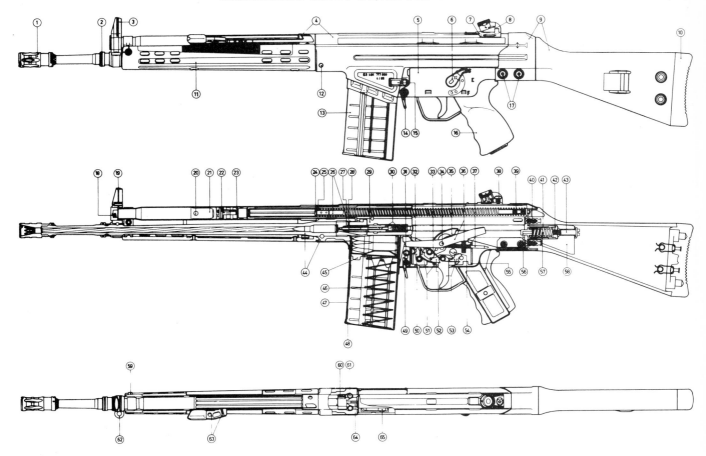

G3 Automatic Rifle, 7.62mm NATO:

1. Flash suppressor/ grenade launcher
2. Snap ring
3. Front sight holder
4. Receiver and operating housing
5. Grip assembly
6. Safety
7. Sight base
8. Rotary rear sight
9. Back plate with buttstock
10. Butt plate
11. Handguard
12. Cylindrical pin
13. Magazine
14. Grip assembly locking pin
15. Magazine catch
16. Grip
17. Buttstock locking pins
18. Cap
19. Front sight
20. Stop pin
21. Stop abutment
22. Operating handle spindle
23. Operating handle support
24. Stop pin
25. Recoil spring guide ring
26. Recoil spring tube with recoil spring
27. Bolt head
28. Clamping sleeve and holder for locking roller
29. Bolt body with recoil spring tube
30. Firing pin with firing pin spring
31. Contact piece
32. Release lever
33. Elbow spring for trigger
34. Ejector spindle
35. Hammer
36. Ejector with spring
37. Pressure shank and spring
38. Fixing screw
39. Stop pin for spring guide
40. Countersunk screw
41. Buffer housing
42. Buffer closure
43. Screw for buffer
44. Barrel with barrel extension
45.-48. Magazine assembly
49. Magazine release lever
50. Catch
51. Elbow spring with roller
52. Sear
53. Trigger
54. Safety pin
55. Trigger assembly
56. Buffer pin
57. Buffer spring
58. Support for buffer housing
59. Hanguard locking pin
60. Extractor with spring
61. Locking roller
62. Eyebolt
63. Operating handle with elbow spring
64. Locking piece
65. Bolt head locking lever

The Mauser engineer Ludwig Vorgrimmler went to France after World War II to work on his roller lock mechanism. While at the French armament center at Mulhouse, he produced two breech mechanisms designed for the American .30 carbine cartridge (7.62 × 33).

In the early 1950s, Vorgrimmler went to Spain where he worked with other German and Spanish engineers at the government *Centro de Estudios Tecnicos de Materiales Especiales* (CETME) in Madrid. Without the immediate pressures of war, the former Mauser engineers were able to give considerable attention to weapons design and ammunition considerations. Included in their efforts was the creation of a 7.9 × 40mm cartridge that had an elongated and very light projectile—6.8 grams (105 grains)—with a muzzle velocity of 800 m.p.s. (2,625 f.p.s.). By 1952, the first prototypes of the CETME Automatic Rifle were ready for testing. After two years of experimentation, the Spanish Government began to look for a company to assist them in establishing a factory for rifle production.

In March 1954, Heckler & Koch was invited by the Spanish to attend discussions concerning the advanced development and preparation for manufacture of the CETME Rifle.

Heckler & Koch GMBH, Oberndorf am Neckar, was established in 1949. The founders of the firm had been executive engineers in the *Mauserwerke* at Oberndorf. Most of the key engineers, foremen and skilled machinists had worked for the Mauser factory, which was dismantled at the end of the war. Germany ordered the first 400 rifles in 1956, and they were produced by Heckler & Koch in the NATO caliber, 7.62 × 51mm. In 1958, Spain adopted the improved CETME Rifle, which fired a reduced power version of the NATO cartridge. The following year, the *Bundeswehr* adopted the weapon as the *Automatisches Gewehr G3, Kal. 7.62mm × 51*. The G3 replaced the FAL, which had been used as the G1. A key element in the decision to adopt the G3 was the inability of the German Government to work out a satisfactory licensing agreement with Fabrique Nationale for production of the FAL.

Spanish CETME 7.92mm Assault Rifle, the prototype CETME.

THE FOLLOWING COUNTRIES USE THE G-3 RIFLE:

Abu Dhabi	Dominican Republic	Nigeria	Sharjah
Bolivia	Dubai	Norway* (Kongsberg	Spain* (CETME)
Brazil*	El Salvador	Vapenfabrikk)	Sudan
Burma	Germany-Federal	Pakistan*	Sweden* (FFV)
Chad	Republic*	Peru	Tanzania
Chile	Ghana	Philippines	Thailand
Colombia	Indonesia	Portugal*	Turkey
Denmark	Iran*	Qatar	Uganda
	Jordan	Saudi Arabia	Zambia
	Kenya		

*Denotes local manufacture of the rifle.

The French arms factory SAV-CIE. and the Royal Small Arms Factory, Enfield, are manufacturing the G-3 for Heckler & Koch as subcontractors.

Current manufacture H&K G3A3.

ARMALITE AR-10 AND AR-16 RIFLES

The Armalite Division of the Fairchild Engine and Airplane Corporation was established in October 1954, for the express purpose of developing new military firearms using the latest advancements in plastics and non-ferrous metals. While the Armalite firm has gone through several reorganizations, its small development facility has always been located in Costa Mesa, California. Eugene M. Stoner was the key designer with the firm in the early years, while Robert Fremont supervised prototype manufacture and L. James Sullivan oversaw the routine drafting work. Several weapons were undertaken prior to the work on an assault rifle, including:

AR-1—7.62 NATO parasniper rifle, extremely lightweight, using a Mauser-type bolt action mechanism. Only prototypes were built in 1954.

AR-3—7.62 NATO self-loader designed by Stoner into which he incorporated an aluminum receiver, fiberglass stock and a multiple lug locking system of the type later found in the AR-10.

AR-5—.22 Hornet caliber survival rifle developed for the US Air Force and officially designated the MA-1.

AR-7—.22 long rifle self-loader, which comes apart so that the barrel and receiver could be stored in the synthetic stock. Developed in 1959–1960, this rifle is still marketed under the commercial name "Explorer."

AR-9—12 gage (18.5mm) self-loading shotgun with aluminum barrel and receiver, weighing only 2.27 kg (5 lb.). Developed in 1955, it never was produced in quantities.

Work was begun on the AR-10 before Stoner joined the firm. By mid-1956, the Fairchild organization was actively promoting that rifle, depite the fact that it was still in the early stages of development. A third version of the AR-10, with a titanium barrel surrounded with an aluminum jacket, was tested by Springfield Armory in 1956 on the eve of the adoption of the M14 Rifle. When the composite barrel ruptured during the endurance test, there were severe recriminations; the Armalite people thought that their weapon had been mistreated because they were given less than favorable treatment in the report prepared on the test. Subsequently, Stoner, with the assistance of Springfield Armory, designed a new barrel for the AR-10 made of conventional barrel steel.

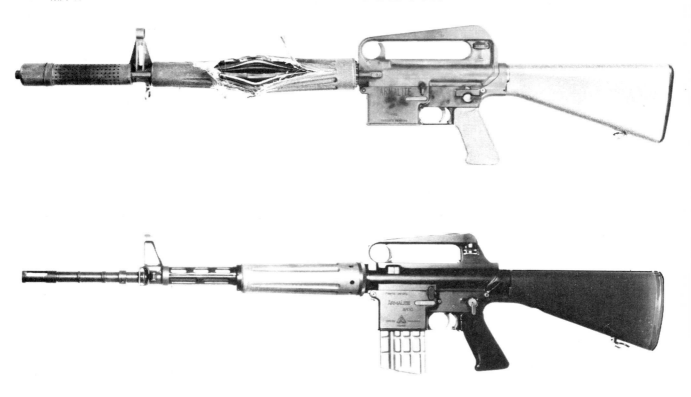

Top: Early Armalite AR-10 with burst barrel. Bottom: AR-10 as manufactured by Artillerie-Inrichtingen.

At about the same time, Richard H. Boutelle, president of Fairchild, was searching for a manufacturing facility that could produce the AR-10. Ultimately, as part of a Fairchild-Fokker of Holland deal, an agreement was worked out where Artillerie-Inrichtingen, a government owned company in Zaandam, Netherlands, would manufacture the rifle. The weapon was reworked, and the newer A-I version was tested by several countries, including the Netherlands and Austria. Delayed acquisition of

tooling with which to produce the AR-10 and political considerations kept the weapon from being adopted by a major military power. Small lots of the rifle were sold to Nicaragua and the Sudan by Interarms, to the Burmese Army by Cooper-Macdonald and to the Portuguese Army by Artillerie-Inrichtingen. Due to chaotic conditions at Artillerie-Inrichtingen, production was suspended sometime in 1959–1960. Twelve hundred rifles had been delivered to the Portuguese by that time. The real significance, however, of the AR-10 is that it led to the AR-15, which after several modifications was adopted by the US Army as the 5.56mm M16/M16A1 Rifles (see section on 5.56 × 45mm rifles).

The AR-16 was another 7.62 NATO caliber rifle designed at Armalite. This weapon appeared following the separation of the company from Fairchild and the departure of the Stoner design team. Whereas the AR-10 utilized aluminum forgings for the upper and lower receivers, the AR-16 was made of sheet metal stampings after the fashion of the German *Sturmgewehr*. Development work went on from 1959 to 1961 but was suspended in favor of a scaled-down version of the AR-16 in 5.56mm. That latter rifle, the AR-18, is discussed later under the 5.56 × 45mm rifles.

A final weapon deserves mention here since it is related in design concept to the other Armalite rifles. The Stoner 62 weapons system, built at the Cadillac Gage Division of Excello Corporation in Warren, Michigan, was another Stoner product. After he left Armalite, Stoner decided that a multipurpose family of weapons could be developed around a common set of basic parts. The Stoner 62 system was an attempt to create a rifle and machine gun family in the NATO caliber. He terminated work on that system when the popularity of the 5.56mm cartridge became apparent. His 5.56 × 45mm Stoner 63 system is also discussed below.

Armalite AR-16 Rifle with folding stock.

SWISS SIG RIFLES 510 AND 542

The Schweizerische Industrie-Gesellschaft at Neuhausen am Rheinfall has been one of the primary sources of sophisticated, precision, self-loading rifles. If anything, their products have tended to be of too high a quality and too expensive to manufacture until recent years. A commercial firm in competition with the government owned Waffenfabrik, Bern, SIG has been very successful in designing weapons but less so in selling them outside Switzerland. Their sales problems have been due in part to the restrictive export policies of the Swiss Government.

SIG and the Waffenfabrik, Bern, experimented with many designs in the 1940s. The government arsenal designed rifles

similar to the German FG-42, to fire intermediate size cartridges in 7.65 and 7.5mm. Shortly after World War II, SIG introduced the SK-46, a gas-operated self-loader designed for such full power cartridges as the 7.5 × 55.5mm Swiss or 7.92 × 57mm German. In this design, the operating gases were tapped close to the chamber, and the gas cylinder and piston were positioned to the side of the receiver. The bolt was of the tipping variety with the locking surface located in the upper portion of the receiver. Externally it resembled the straight-pull Schmidt-Rubin Rifle.

SIG subsequently introduced the AK53, a gas-operated selective fire assault rifle. The *Automat Karabin 1953* employed an

SIG SK46 Rifle.

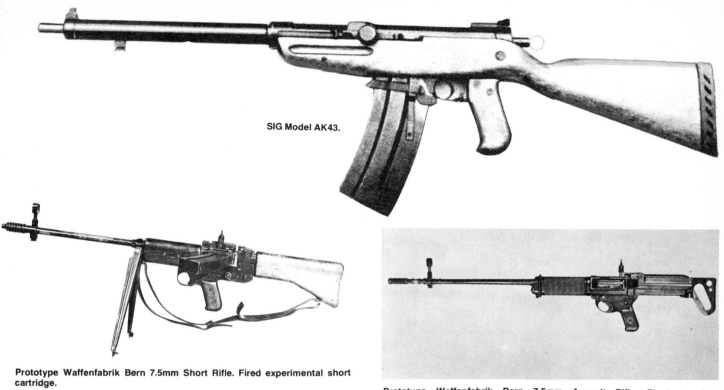

SIG Model AK43.

Prototype Waffenfabrik Bern 7.5mm Short Rifle. Fired experimental short cartridge.

Prototype Waffenfabrik Bern 7.5mm Assault Rifle. Fired standard 7.5 × 55.5mm cartridge.

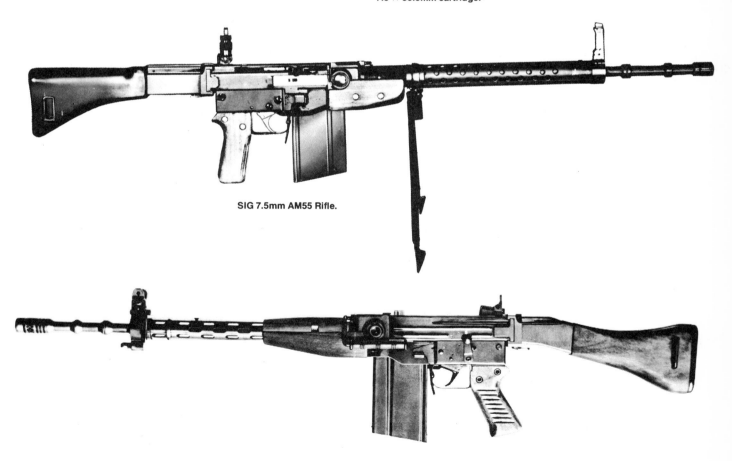

SIG 7.5mm AM55 Rifle.

7.62mm NATO SIG Type SG510-4.

unusual action in which the barrel moved forward and the fired cartridge case was ejected at the end of the forward cycle. With this system, a low cyclic rate of about 300 shots per minute was obtained, making the weapon manageable even though it fired the standard 7.5mm Swiss cartridge. This weapon was never put into large scale production.

In the mid-1950s, SIG introduced a new rifle, the AM 55. Subsequently known as the *Sturmgewehr 57* (StG 57) in Swiss Army terminology and SIG 510 in commercial form, it is one additional permutation of the Mauser *Sturmgewehr 45* retarded roller lock breech mechanism. SIG's version was worked out by Rudolf Amsler, the company's technical director. Several 510 series rifles exist:

510-0 Swiss Army version in 7.5 × 55.5mm.
510-1 Commercial in any standard caliber.
510-2 Commercial lightweight.
510-3 Commercial in any intermediate caliber; e.g., 7.62 × 39 Soviet.
510-4 Commercial in 7.62 × 51 NATO. This weapon has in effect superseded the 510-1.

Although there have been alterations in stock design since 1955, the basic rifle mechanism remains essentially the same. There is no 520 series, but SIG later introduced a 530 series chambered to fire the 5.56 × 45mm cartridge. This weapon incorporated improvements in sheet metal stamping and substituted plastics for wood and metal, but the operating mechanism is still essentially the same as in the 510 Rifles.

Since the early 1970s, SIG has introduced the 540 family of rifles. The 540 and 543 are available in prototype form only, chambered for the 5.56 × 45mm cartridge; limited production runs have been made for the 542 Rifle in 7.62 NATO. Outwardly, these rifles bear a strong resemblance to the 530 series, but internally they are quite different. Whereas the 530-1 has a roller locked bolt, the 540 Rifles have a rotating bolt, which is cammed into and out of the locked position by a cam machined into the bolt carrier. The bolt carrier arrangement is quite similar in concept to the Soviet Kalashnikov family of weapons. Unlike the AK, where the rear part of the piston assembly is machined as an integral element of the bolt carrier, on the SIG 540 Rifles the rear end of the piston fits a hole in the bolt carrier, and the operating handle holds it in place by sliding through a slot into the side of the carrier.

Following the current trend in European small arms design, these rifles have a combined flash suppressor/grenade launcher assembly attached to the barrel; they fire three-shot bursts in addition to full and semiautomatic, and they can be supplied with bipod and fixed or folding buttstock.

SIG 530-1 5.56mm Rifle with bayonet.

5.56mm SIG, Assault Rifle SG 543 short version with folding butt and 20 rounds magazine.

JAPANESE TYPE 64 RIFLE

While the Japanese Ground Self Defense Forces still use the US M1 Rifle, re-equipment is underway with the Type 64 Rifle, developed by the Howa Machinery Company, Ltd., Nagoya. This weapon, known as the R6E in prototype form, was designed to be used with a reduced charge NATO cartridge.

The goal of the designers was to create a standard caliber weapon that could be fired comfortably by their smaller-in-stature troops. A lavender bullet tip coloration indicates the reduced power rifle loading. When full power NATO cartridges are used, the gas regulator can be set to a smaller orifice to prevent overpowering the weapon. As with the U.S. M14 Rifle, the gas system can be closed off completely for launching grenades from the combination muzzle brake/grenade launcher. The Type 64 has a folding shoulder rest fitted to the top of the butt stock, and all rifles are fitted with bipods.

7.62mm R6A Rifle; one of the prototypes of the Type 64 Rifle.

FRENCH 7.5 × 54mm M1949/56 RIFLES

France was a major Western nation that did not adopt the 7.62 NATO cartridge. After participating in the NATO trials of the early 1950s and their subsequent withdrawal from the North Atlantic Alliance, the French decided to keep their older standard cartridge. Both their 1949/56 series of rifles and the FR-F1 Sniper Rifle fire the 7.5mm M1929 cartridge. These weapons are described in Chapter 18.

PROTOTYPE NONPRODUCTION NATO CALIBER RIFLES

Several NATO caliber rifles never got beyond the prototype stage. Among these, the 4.81-kg (10.6-lb.) Madsen Light Auto Rifle of Danish design is the most notable. Similar in operating mechanism to the Kalashnikov, it was not produced due to the success of the G3 and to the fact that the Dansk Industri Syndicat (Madsen) went out of the small arms business since it could not compete successfully with other European manufacturers.

Madsen 7.62 mm NATO Light Automatic Rifle with tubular steel stock.

The Luigi Franchi LF-59 Rifle is a 4.3-kg (9.5-lb.) selective fire weapon quite similar in design to the FN FAL. It has a tipping bolt like the FAL, and the magazines are interchangeable. The piston is attached to the bolt carrier, and the recoil spring is mounted in a tube that telescopes from the rear of the carrier. Steel stampings constitute the receiver, and plastics are used for the stocks of later prototypes. To make the rifle manageable during full automatic fire, the design embodies a rate reducer, producing a cyclic rate of 610-630 shots per minute. This weapon was intended to be a companion piece to the 9mm LF-57 submachine gun and .30 caliber carbine LF-58.

Luigi Franchi weapons. Top, LF - 59 Rifle. Middle, LF - 58 Carbine. Bottom, LF - 57 Submachine Gun.

The Dominican Republic produced in prototype form only the Model 1962 Rifle.

Tactically speaking, none of the 7.62 × 51mm NATO caliber rifles can be called true assault rifles. All of the major weapons in this caliber tend to be too heavy and cumbersome for easy maneuvering in the field. More significant, the recoil produced by the cartridge makes weapons such as the FAL and the M14 all but uncontrollable during bursts of automatic fire. As a consequence, most M14s were issued without the selector switch for automatic fire, and many FALs were produced as semiautomatics only. Whereas the next American rifle, the M16, would come closer to the assault rifle ideal, the Soviets, utilizing an intermediate power cartridge, had already introduced a true assault rifle.

7.62 × 39mm M43 (SOVIET) CALIBER RIFLES

Assault rifles as a concept were not a new idea in the Soviet Union. Vladimir Gregoryevich Federov (also spelled Fyodorov) after considerable experimentation introduced his *Avtomaticheskaya Vintovka Federova, 1916g* (Federov 1916 Automatic Rifle) during World War I. He utilized the 6.5 × 50.5SR Japanese cartridge instead of the larger and more powerful rimmed 7.62 × 54R cartridge used in the 1891 Mosin Nagant Rifle, since the Japanese round was better suited for use in a rapid firing rifle. Approximately 3200 M1916 *Avtomats* were fabricated at the Sestroretsk Weapons Factory before the 1917 revolution intervened. These rifles were used toward the end of the 1914–1918 war and during the Russo-Finnish war of 1939–1940.

During the interwar years, the Soviets experimented extensively with self-loading rifles, but for some reason they returned to the 7.62 × 54R cartridge, defeating the lessons learned during World War I. Just as the Americans dropped the .276 cartridge in the 1920s to pacify the twin gods of "standard issue caliber" and "markmanship tradition," the Soviets returned to their old cartridge. Both S. G. Simonov and F. W. Tokarev produced self-loaders to fire the 7.62mm rimmed cartridge. The *Avtomaticheskaya Vintovka Simonova Obrazets 1936g* (AVS36, Automatic Rifle Simonov) recoiled badly, had poor parts durability and demonstrated feeding and extraction difficulties. In 1938, the Red Army adopted a new model of Tokarev's design, the *Samozariadnya Vintovka Tokareva Obrazets 1938g,* SVT38. Tokarev, known for his automatic pistol and his modifications to the Soviet Maxim machine guns, had evolved a rifle bolt mechanism that was quite similar to that which was later used in the FAL. Federov, Simonov and Tokarev weapons

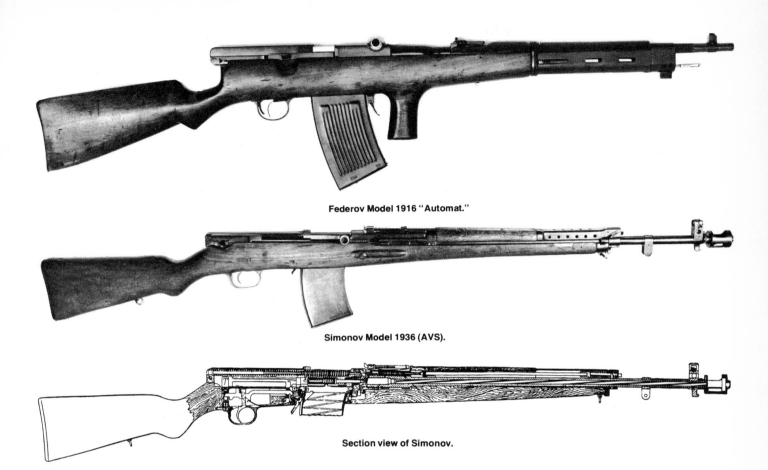

Federov Model 1916 "Automat."

Simonov Model 1936 (AVS).

Section view of Simonov.

were all used during the winter war with Finland. As some of the parts of the SVT38 proved fragile, Tokarev modified his design and produced the SVT40. The most obvious differences between the two models was the use of a one-piece stock and the placement of the cleaning rod beneath the barrel. In the SVT38, a two-piece stock was used, and the cleaning rod fit a groove along the right side of the stock.

SKS45—SAMOZARIDNYA KARABINA SIMONOVA OBRAZETS 1945g

Although the Tokarev rifles were widely used throughout the 1939–1945 war, the Soviets made greater use of the submachine gun than any other country. Infantry massed with large armored units found the firepower of the PPSh41 and PPS43 submachine guns extremely effective. Out of this experience came the requirement for an *Avtomat,* an assault rifle. N. M. Elizarov and B. V. Semin developed an intermediate cartridge, the M43 7.62 × 39mm, for this purpose. Ironically, the first

adopted weapon to fire this cartridge was the SKS45 self-loading carbine. Scaled down from the 14.5 × 111.8mm PTRS self-loading antitank rifle and the 7.62 × 54Rmm SKS41 this 10-shot Simonov weapon represented an anachronism. Despite its large scale production, the SKS did not fit the Motorized Infantry/Armored Fighting Vehicle tactic that was evolving within the Soviet Union. First field tested in the latter days of World War II, it was adopted as a standard weapon in 1945. The SKS is a secondary weapon in most Warsaw Pact countries today.

COUNTRIES MANUFACTURING THE SKS

USSR
East Germany—*Karabiner-S*
PRC—Type 56 Carbine
North Korea—Type 63 Carbine
Yugoslavia—M59/66 Rifle

Soviet SKS45 self-loading carbine.

THE SOVIET 7.62mm AK ASSAULT RIFLE

A new generation of Soviet small arms emerged from the mind and later the design bureau of Mikhail Timofeyevich Kalashnikov. While on convalescent leave from the Tank Corps due to serious wounds received in the battle of Brausk in the fall of 1941, Kalashnikov turned his attentions to small arms design. In 1942, he produced a submachine gun, but it could not compete with such designs as A. I. Sudayev's, which was adopted as the PPS43. Early in 1944, he began work on a turning bolt carbine firing the 7.62 × 39mm cartridge, but little came of that design either. By early 1946, Kalashnikov had completed yet another weapon. Later adopted as the *Avtomat Kalashnikova 1947g* (AK47), this weapon was a true assault rifle.

M. T. Kalashnikov 1919—; designer of the AK47, AKM, RPK, PK and SVD—the latter is a product of the design bureau he heads up at the Izhvesk Machine Factory, Urdmurt, Kazakhstan, USSR.

Even though it was in the 4.3-kg (9.5-lb.) class, unloaded, the AK47 proved to be a highly dependable, highly manageable automatic weapon. This success did not come overnight. A stamped steel receiver model built in the late 1940s and early 1950s did not prove to be durable enough. The machined steel receiver model commonly encountered is actually the third version manufactured by the Soviets. The second model can be distinguished by the angular metal fitting into which the butt stock was mounted. That attachment was in turn pinned to the rear of the receiver. Versions one and two were still in the Soviet inventory in 1952. In addition to the Soviet Union, the People's Republic of China, East Germany, Poland, Bulgaria, Romania, North Korea, Hungary and Yugoslavia have manufactured the AK47. Finland has produced the weapon in modified form, the M60 and M62, while the Israeli Galil 5.56mm Rifle is a derivative design. The initial production PRC Type 56 (with Chinese markings on the selector) is identical to the third Soviet version, but late production Type 56s have permanently attached folding spike bayonets. The PRC Type 56-1 assault rifle is similar to the Soviet folding stock model, but it has prominent rivets in the arms of the stock.

Poland has produced a special grenade launching version, the PMK-DGN-60, to which is attached the 20mm diameter LON-1 grenade launcher. This variant has a gas cutoff valve added to the gas cylinder, a special grenade sight that fastens to the standard rear sight, a recoil absorbing butt pad, a latch added to the recoil spring and a special 10-shot magazine, which will take only the grenade blanks.

Yugoslavia has produced three variations of the AK47—M64 with a longer 508-mm (20-in) barrel and fixed wooden stock; M64A (later redesignated the M70) with a standard 414-mm (16.3-in) barrel and fixed wooden stock; and the M64B (M70A) with standard barrel and folding stock. All models are fitted with a folding grenade launching sight, a muzzle compensator and (unique among AK47s) a bolt hold-open device that catches the bolt in the recoil position after the last cartridge in the magazine has been fired. Finland's M60/M62 series has a special flash suppressor/bayonet mount, front sight mounted on the gas cylinder, aperture, plastic forearm and tubular fixed butt stock. East German AK47s do not have cleaning rods under the barrel or a recess in the butt for cleaning tools. Except for these specific differences and the selector markings, all Eurasian AK47s are similar. Operational and field stripping details are presented in Chapter 43.

Introduction of the modernized Kalashnikov assault rifle (*Modernizirovannyi Automat Kalashnikova,* AKM) in 1959 reflected a shift from the forged and machined receiver to an improved stamped sheet metal construction. The weight of the AKM, 3.15 kg (6.9 lbs.), is about two-thirds that of the AK47. Otherwise, the AK47 and the AKM are mechanically identical, except that the AKM has a cyclic rate reducer in its trigger mechanism, which slightly slows down the automatic firing cycle from the 600 shots per minute of the AK47. Recognition features of the AKM are the sheet metal receiver with a small magazine guide dimple pressed into each side, the grasping rails on the forestock, the ribbed receiver cover, the bayonet lug and the absence of vent holes in the gas tube. AKMs have been produced by the USSR, East Germany, Poland, Hungary, Romania and North Korea. The North Korean weapon does not have a rate reducer. Some late model AKMs are fitted with muzzle compensators. The Kalashnikov series has probably been produced in larger numbers than any other modern small arm; total production has been estimated to be between 30 and 50 million.

COUNTRIES USING THE SKS AND AK FAMILY BUT NOT MANUFACTURING THEM DOMESTICALLY

Afghanistan	SKS & AK
Albania	SKS & AK
Chile	AK only
Congo, People's Republic	SKS & AK
Cuba	AK only
Indonesia	SKS & AK
Iraq	SKS & AK
Laos	SKS & AK
Lebanon (para-military forces)	SKS & AK
Mongolia	SKS & AK
Morocco	SKS & AK
Pakistan	AK (PRC) only
Syria	AK only
United Arab Republic (Egypt)	SKS & AK
Vietnam, Socialist Republic of	SKS & AK
Yemen, People's Democratic Republic	SKS & AK

First model Kalashnikov with stamped steel receiver.

Second (bottom) and third (top) versions of the AK47. Note differences indicated by numbers in the photograph.

GRENADE LAUNCHING SIGHT

LOCK ON DRIVING SPRING GUIDE

GRENADE LAUNCHER

RECOIL BOOT

SPECIAL SHORT MAGAZINE

GAS VENT

Polish PMK-DGN6O grenade-launching rifle.

GRENADE LAUNCHING SIGHT

COMPENSATOR

Yugoslav M64B.

APERTURE REAR SIGHT

FRONT SIGHT

FLASH SUPPRESSOR/BAYONET MOUNT

Finnish Valmet M60.

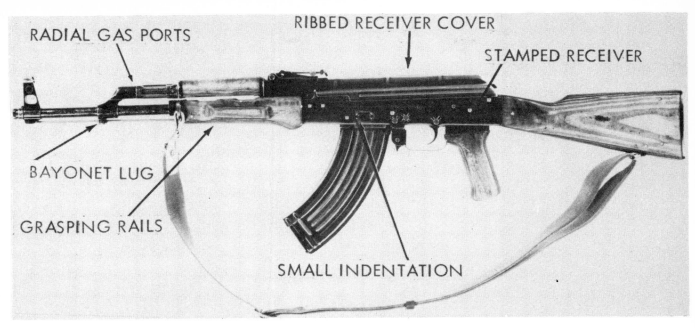

RADIAL GAS PORTS

RIBBED RECEIVER COVER

STAMPED RECEIVER

BAYONET LUG

GRASPING RAILS

SMALL INDENTATION

Soviet AKM.

PLASTIC HAND GUARD

SOLID, UNLAMINATED WOOD

PLASTIC REAR GRIP

East German MPiKM assault rifle.

LAMINATED WOOD

LAMINATED WOOD
PISTOL GRIP/FOREARM

PLASTIC

Romanian AKM.

Upper or Full Auto Symbol	Lower or Semi Auto Symbol	Producer	Native Name or Remarks
AB	О Д	Soviet	AK-47, AKM and AKMS
AB	Е Д	Bulgaria	AK-47 and AKM
C	P	Poland	PMK, PMK-DGN, KbK AK
D	E	E. Germany	MPK, MPiKmS - Rifles do not have cleaning rods MPiKM and MPiKMS have cleaning rods
FA	FF	Romania	Has "S" at top for safe position
连	单	Communist China	Early Production
L	D	Communist China	Type 56 and 56-1 Assault Rifle (Late Production)
∞	1	Hungary	
...	.	Finland	RYNNAKOKIVAARI - applies to M60 and M62
자ㄴ	ㄷㄴ	North Korea	Types 58 and 68 Assault Rifle
R	J	Yugoslavia	M64 series - has U at top for safe position
30	1	Czechoslovakia	M58 Assault Rifle

Kalashnikov assault rifle selector markings.

Accompanying photos and illustrations in chapters on countries producing the various Kalashnikov models give a better understanding of model variations.

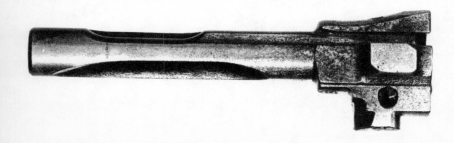

The picture illustrates the bolt and bolt carrier relationship (top), while the one below illustrates the AK bolt and the U.S. M1 Carbine bolt, for size comparison.

CZECHOSLOVAK RIFLES

Czechoslovakia has always been a fertile source of small arms. After World War II, the Czech military adopted the Vzor (Model) 52 self-loading carbine chambered for their own 7.62 × 45mm cartridge. Beginning in 1957, many of these carbines were altered to fire the 7.62 × 39mm cartridge, VZ52/57 (M52/57). While obsolete in Czechoslovakia, the M52 and M52/57 carbines have been shipped and sold to third world nations. These weapons are unusual in that they employ a unique concentric gas cylinder, which surrounds the barrel, and

the gas operating mechanism is composed of a bearing mounted on the barrel, a gas port in the barrel, a sliding gas cylinder sleeve positioned over the bearing, a connecting se-micylinder and an actuator. Upon firing the cartridge, gases force the gas cylinder sleeve, connector and actuator to the rear, an action which in turn forces the bolt and bolt carrier to the rear. In concept, this gas system is similar to the German *MKb42(W) Sturgewehr.* The major complaint with this weapon has been its weight, 4.5 kg (9.8 lbs.), and its somewhat fragile side folding bayonet.

Czech Model 52 Rifle.

Subsequently, the Czechoslovakian Army adopted the VZ58 (M58) assault rifle, which was also a domestic design. This weapon exists in two forms—the M58P with conventional fixed stock and the M58V with folding metal stock. Early production weapons had wooden forearms, pistol grips and, in the case of

the M58P, butt stocks. These components are made of a wood fiber/plastic composition material in more recently fabricated weapons. While some of these rifles have been sold abroad, the Czechs are the major user of this design.

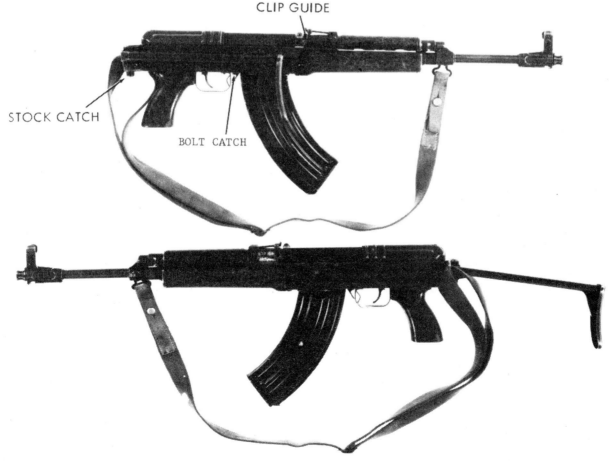

Folding stock version of Model 58.

CHINESE TYPE 68 RIFLE

The Type 68 Rifle, adopted by the People's Republic of China, is yet another basic pattern selective fire weapon adopted in the M43 7.62 × 39mm caliber. This small arm represents a divergence from the assault rifle tactical concept as it has emerged among the Warsaw Pact countries. Evidently, the People's Liberation Army tacticians decided that its army would not be engaging in the massive armored infantry types of conflicts envisaged for potential European conflicts. Therefore, they adopted a selective fire rifle, the barrel being the same length as the SKS, with a 15-shot magazine, five shots more than the SKS but half the capacity of the AK family. Two versions of the rifle exist. The earlier model has a receiver machined from a steel forging, while the later model has a stamped steel receiver, identifiable by the large rivets at each side of the

receiver. There are other minor differences apparent when the weapons are compared.

In the Type 68, the bolt and bolt carrier have evolved from the Kalashnikov design. A major difference lies in the separation of the gas piston and the bolt carrier. The piston rod acts as a tappet against the face of the bolt carrier in a fashion reminiscent of the SKS and SVT 38/40 designs. Unlike the SKS or the AK, the Type 68 has a two-position gas regulator. A permanently attached spike bayonet similar to the Type 56 carbine and Type 56 assault rifle and an under-the-barrel cleaning rod are standard fixtures. As issued, the Type 68 Rifle has a bolt stop to hold the bolt open after the last shot has been fired. Unless the stop is altered, only the 15-shot magazine will fit; if the stop is ground down, the rifle will also accept the 30-round AK-type magazines.

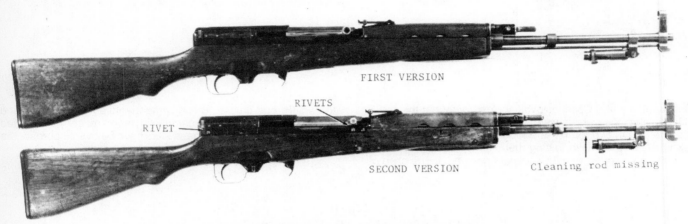

First and second models of the PRC Type 68 selective fire rifles.

MISCELLANEOUS M43 7.62 × 39mm CALIBER RIFLES

In the past two decades several 7.62 × 39 rifles have been produced in limited quantities to appeal to those nations that might have received small arms from the Soviet Bloc. These include the RH-4, made in prototype by Rheinmettal Wehrtechnik

of Dusseldorf, West Germany, the HK32 by Heckler & Koch and the SIG 510-3. Only the Egyptians attempted a design for domestic consumption. That rifle, the Rashid, was made in very limited numbers and was a rework of the Ljungman Model 42 Rifle, which has been produced in Egypt (United Arab Republic) as the 7.92 × 57mm Hakim Rifle.

Rheinmetall 7.62mm RH4 Rifle with wood stock.

RH4 Rifle with retractable metal stock.

5.56 × 45mm CALIBER RIFLES

The United States Army Continental Army Command made an important departure from traditional small arms development in 1957 when it sought commercial assistance in the development of a 5.56mm (.223 in.) military rifle—due to dissatisfaction among many senior military officers with the M14 Rifle and the 7.62 × 51mm cartridge. An adequate understanding of the 5.56mm rifle story is impossible without a brief look at three small arms projects—SALVO, SPIW and SAWS. SALVO studies conducted by the Operations Research Office (ORO) at

Johns Hopkins University and supported by several contractors gave the impetus for the development of the M16 Rifle. Failure of the radical SPIW (Special Purpose Individual Weapon) concept assured the M16 a permanent place in the US Army's arsenal, and the Small Arms Weapons Study (SAWS), 1966-1967, judged the M16 to be the best small caliber rifle available.

ORO had been created by the US Army in 1948 to analytically study a number of problems associated with ground weapons in the nuclear era. One of ORO's early projects was ALCLAD, a search for better infantry body armor. As that study progressed, ORO and Army specialists discovered just how little was known about how individuals were wounded in combat. ORO looked into several questions regarding the manner in which soldiers were struck by rifle projectiles and shell fragments. Among them were the frequency and distribution of such hits, the types of wounds incurred in combat and the average ranges at which wounds were inflicted. Answers to these questions were obtained by evaluating over three million casualty reports for World Wars I and II, as well as data from the Korean conflict. ORO's investigations revealed that in the overall picture aimed rifle fire did not seem to have any more important role in creating casualities than randomly fired shots. Marksmanship was not as

important as volume. For Army officers raised on a traditional diet of carefully aimed rifle fire, this conclusion was heretical, but analysis proved it valid.

ORO's second important conclusion was equally disturbing to the traditionalists. Whereas effective rifle fire had been occasionally delivered at 1200 meters during the 1914–1918 war in the trenches, World War II and Korean war experience indicated that the rifle was seldom effectively employed beyond 300 meters. Even when expert riflemen tried to use their weapons at greater ranges, they discovered that terrain features usually prevented accurate long distance firing. Finally, statistical data indicated that most rifle kills were made at less than 100 meters. These revelations called for some new thinking in rifle design.

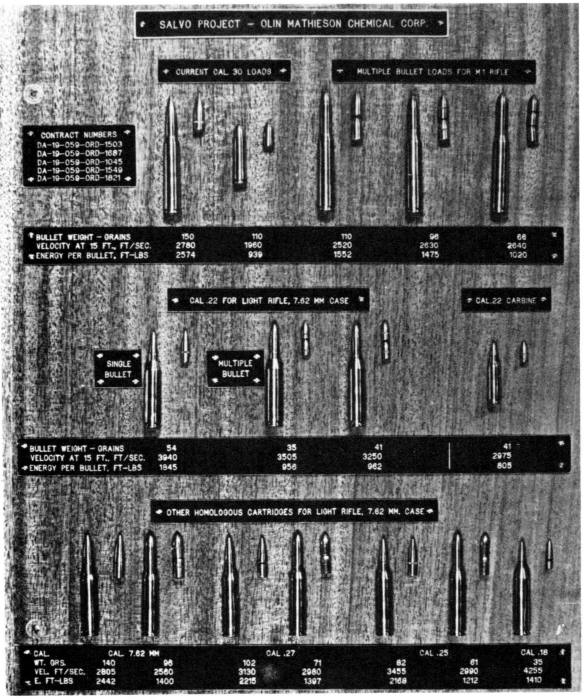

Display board showing some of the basic cartridges tested during Project SALVO.

One fruitful approach appeared to be the development of a light recoil weapon firing a salvo of small caliber projectiles with a controlled dispersion pattern. While Project SALVO was taking form, US ordnance officers were telling their British counterparts that the UK .280 cartridge was too small, but SALVO was considering projectiles as small as 4.2mm (.17 in.).

After following the SALVO work for several years, the Continental Army Command (CONARC) decided to sponsor the development of a .22 caliber military rifle. CONARC commanding officer William G. Wyman asked Winchester and Armalite to develop a high velocity 5.56mm rifle. From the outset, the Armalite AR-15 was more popular than the Winchester design. Even Ralph Clarkson, the designer of the Winchester .224 Lightweight Military Rifle (patterned after the M1 Rifle and M1

Carbine), had to admit that the AR-15 had unmistakable "sex appeal." A Springfield Armory contender designed by A. J. Lizza did not get very far either. In fact, ordnance personnel opposed to the small caliber concept forbade the Armory, an Ordnance Corps facility, to participate in CONARC's heretical program.

CONARC specifications for a 5.56mm rifle called for full and automatic fire, a 20-shot magazine, a loaded weight of 2.7 kg (6 lbs.) and penetration of both sides of a standard Army helmet at 500 meters. If possible, the engineers were to keep the trajectory flatter than that of the 7.62mm NATO cartridge. The desire to use the rifle at ranges up to 500 meters indicated a compromise between the SALVO studies and conventional rifle thinking current in the US Army.

US lightweight rifles, 1957: Top, Winchester .224 Lightweight Military Rifle. Middle, Armalite .223 AR-15. Bottom, Springfield Armory .224 Rifle.

M16 RIFLE

Stoner's AR-15 was designed around a slightly enlarged version of the Remington .222 cartridge case. That alteration permitted him to propel a 3.6-gram (55-grain) bullet at 1005 m.p.s. (3300 f.p.s.). The weapon itself was an eclectic design. As other designers before him, Stoner chose the best from earlier designs. For the locking system, he chose a design quite similar in concept to that of the Johnson Semiautomatic Rifle of the 1940s. He also used an "in-line" stock to aide manageability during automatic fire. That stock arrangement permitted him to place the recoil buffer in a tube that ran the length of the stock. A tube type gas system was employed to convey the gas from a port under the front sight, along the top of the barrel and into a space in the bolt carrier assembly.

There were a number of other features reminiscent of earlier weapons, such as the hinged upper and lower receiver mechanism, similar to the FN FAL; the rear sight in the carrying handle, a la the British E.M.2; and the ejection port dust cover, which followed the pattern established in the MP44 Sturmgewehr. Stoner's achievement in the AR-15 was the combination of all these ideas into an attractive, lethal package that weighed only 3 kg (6.7 lbs.).

In December 1959, Colt Firearms acquired the manufacturing and marketing rights to the AR-15 from Armalite. But selling the rifle proved to be a tough task. Although many people liked the weapon, the Army Ordnance staff was opposed to it. But in 1962, in an end run around the Army, Colt was able to get the Department of Defense's Advanced Research Project Agency

(ARPA) to test 1,000 weapons in its Vietnam-oriented Project Agile. ARPA's enthusiastic report led to additional studies by the Department of Defense and the Department of the Army. Despite strong Army opposition, Defense Secretary McNamara ordered 85,000 M16 Rifles for Vietnam and 19,000 for the Air Force. From this beginning, the AR-15 became the M16, and ultimately the M16A1.

Resistance to the adoption of the AR-15/M16 led to serious problems in 1967. Congressional and Department of Defense investigations disclosed that the weapon had been issued without proper operational and maintenance training to some troops and that totally inadequate supplies of cleaning equipment had been provided to the men in the field. Combined with an ammunition/rifle mismatch and the highly corrosive nature of the humid jungle regions of Southeast Asia, this lack of training and cleaning materials led to serious problems. But after training programs were established, cleaning supplies made available and modifications made to the rifle, the M16 performed reliably.

Major changes to the rifle included a new buffer mechanism to slow the rate of fire, which was greater with ball type propellants than with the IMR propellants for which the weapon had been designed. A chrome plated chamber—later followed by a chrome plated barrel—solved the rusty chamber problem, which had in turn caused failures to extract. Today (1977) the M16/M16A1 Rifle has become the basic rifle for the United States Army. It was also produced by General Motors and Harrington & Richardson during the Vietnam era; Colt continues to manufacture the rifle for the Army. In addition, with US State Department approval, Singapore, the Philippines and South Korea also produce the weapon under license from Colt.

By the end of 1976, Colt had produced some 3,440,106 M16 Rifles. Harrington & Richardson and General Motors had produced 250,000 each. Total AR15 production through 1976 was 68,211. Of the Colt production, 3,135,227 M16s had gone to the US government and 304,879 had been sold overseas.

M16A1 with 30–shot magazine and old style buttstock.

While the validity of the 5.56 × 45mm ammunition as a military cartridge is still a matter of military debate and while this subject may or may not be settled within NATO by the rifle ammunition trials that are scheduled to begin in the spring of 1977, several European and American companies have developed and marketed rifles in this caliber.

Flechettes: Top, typical rifle version. Bottom, shotgun type.

SPIW AND SAWS

Before turning to the European 5.56 × 45mm rifles, some mention needs to be made of two other US Army projects—SPIW and SAWS. The former was an attempt to "leapfrog" ahead in small arms development. The latter was a full scale field evaluation of existing small arms.

The Special Purpose Individual Weapon (SPIW) grew out of experimentation by the US Ordnance Corps and Aircraft Armaments Inc. (AAI) with high velocity steel darts called flechettes. Irwin R. Barr pioneered work on flechettes at AAI and proposed a whole range of such projectiles in a February 1951 report. In 1952, AAI produced a 12 gage shotgun shell loaded with flechettes for the Office of Naval Research. A later version was tested by the Army as part of the Project SALVO tests. Large dispersion patterns and limited range led Barr and his AAI colleagues to turn to single flechettes supported by sabots, fired sequentially from a rifle type weapon. After nearly a decade of energetic promotion of the flechette concept by AAI, the US Army decided in March 1962 to develop a Special Purpose Individual Weapon that would combine the flechette projectile with

the 40mm grenade cartridge, which emerged from another project called NIBLICK. (See Chapter 45 for more on grenade launcher development.)

In February 1963, contracts for SPIW type weapons were let to AAI, Harrington & Richardson, the Winchester Division of Olin and Springfield Armory with delivery of the prototypes due in February of the next year. This incredibly short development time proved impractical, and although firing models were delivered and tested in 1964, SPIW became a long, drawn out project. After the first rounds of testing, the Harrington & Richardson and Winchester SPIWs were eliminated. Later, the Springfield weapon was dropped following the Armory's closing. Work continued on the AAI model, redesignated the XM19. In 1973, the Army announced that the XM19 could not be made to meet military requirements. A modified and simplified XM19 was tested as the XM70, but for practical purposes the single flechette concept is moribund in the US. No one disputes the lethal nature of these little steel arrows (Witness the multiple flechette artillery projectiles used with devastating effect in Vietnam.), but the SPIW concept died due to complex technical,

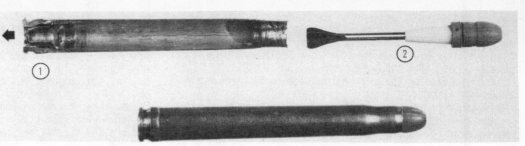

From left to right: M193 5.56 × 45mm; XM110 5.6 × 52.8mm flechette, M59 7.62 × 51mm NATO.

Late version flechette round (XM645) showing (1) primer piston and (2) flechette with sabot.

First Springfield Armory SP1W (1964).

AAI SP1W (1964).

Winchester SP1W (1964).

Harrington & Richardson SP1W (1964).

Springfield Armory SP1W (1966).

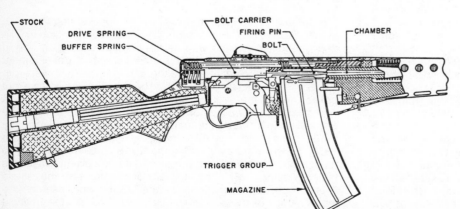

STOCK

DRIVE SPRING

BUFFER SPRING

BOLT CARRIER

FIRING PIN

BOLT

CHAMBER

TRIGGER GROUP

MAGAZINE

AAI XM19 primer actuated SP1W.

economic and political problems.

In 1964, General Harold K. Johnson, Army Chief of Staff, instituted a comprehensive program to review the major small arms being used and under development. This Small Arms Weapons Systems (SAWS) study was to determine which weapons were most suited for the Army's tactical missions during the years 1967–1980. After more than 18 months of investigation and the preparation of several dozen reports, the SAWS study was completed, and the Chief of Staff's office reviewed the SAWS recommendations, the requirements of the Vietnam war and the state of SPIW development. The Secretary of the Army submitted the Chief of Staff's report to the Secretary of Defense on 17 December 1966. The major suggestions were as follows. First, rifle procurement in the "forseeable" future should be limited to the M16 Rifle. Second, steps should be taken to permit "early replacement" of the M1s and BARs in the Army's inventory. Third, planning over the long term should be based upon the replacement of the M14 with the M16. Fourth, an additional

production source for the M16 should be provided in the 1968 budget. And finally, "an active and broadened research and development program should be conducted to bring about further major improvements in the Army's small arms."

In his cover memorandum, the Secretary of the Army made several significant comments about the Chief of Staff's recommendations. He concluded that M16 type weapons were "generally superior for Army combat use." Second, "The current SPIW program is unlikely to result in a satisfactory competitive weapon as early as previously forecast." The Secretary's memo also suggested that some changes might be necessary in the M16, especially the propellant used in the .223 cartridge. These thoughts were passed on to the Secretary of Defense with a request for approval. After considerably more internal debate, Secretary McNamara decided that the Army would use the M16 as its primary rifle but that the M14 would also continue to be considered a standard weapon.

Top to bottom: HK33, HK33K *(kurz)* and HK 53.

HK33

Heckler and Koch began work on the delayed roller-locked HK33 Rifle in 1963. After a series of modifications, this scaled-down version of the G3 was put into modest production in 1968. Major purchasers of the HK33 include the Brazilian Air Force (15,000), the Malaysian Army (5,000) and the Thai Army. In

addition, the Malaysians have assembled 30,000 domestically, and the Thais are manufacturing the rifle at a factory set up for them by Heckler and Koch. There is also a short-barrelled version of this weapon called the HK53, which is designed for use as a submachine gun.

In addition to the M16 and HK33, several other 5.56 weapons have been developed and manufactured in various quantities.

STONER 63 SYSTEM

Gene Stoner, after he left Colt where he had worked as a consultant, joined forces with Cadillac Gage Corporation of suburban Detroit to develop a family of small arms built around a number of common assemblies and parts. Once again, he was assisted by Robert Fremont and James Sullivan. As noted above, Stoner built his 62 system around the 7.62mm NATO cartridge; in the 63 system he turned to the 5.56 × 45mm cartridge. Fully matured, the system consisted of six weapons—a rifle, a carbine, two light machine guns (magazine or belt feed), a medium machine gun and a fixed (tank) machine gun. To adequately power the machine guns in the system and to assure reliable belt feed, Stoner used a long stroke piston system instead of the gas tube arrangement utilized in the M16. The rifle (called the XM22 by the US Army) and the carbine (XM23) fired from a

closed bolt, with selective fire. The magazines were mounted below the receiver. The machine guns (The belt fed version was tested by the Army as the XM207 and by the Navy as the MK23.) all fired from an open bolt. (See Chapter 2 for more details.) During the mid-1960s, the Stoner 63 system was tested several times by the US military, after which numerous improvements were made based upon their experiments. Only the MK23 was used to any extent in combat, by Navy SEAL teams.

Although Cadillac Gage granted a manufacturing license to Mauser-IWK who later transferred their rights to NWM of the Netherlands, the Stoner system never became popular. In the US, the M16 was too deeply entrenched for the Stoner to make much headway, and in Europe there were several competing designs. The Stoner 63 system was a good concept, but the timing—an important factor—was not auspicious. It was, therefore, never successfully marketed.

XM22E1 Rifle (Stoner 63) Field stripped.

ARMALITE AR-18

A scaled-down version of the AR-16, the AR-18, never met military requirements successfully. Throughout its testing history, it had a bad record for parts breakage and feeding difficul-

ties. Since Armalite never developed their own production capabilities, they gave a production license to Howa Machinery Company of Japan in 1967. Military sales to the US military were frustrated by American-Japanese treaty agreements that prohibited Japan from selling military equipment to belligerent na-

Armalite AR-18 Rifle.

tions. The Japanese decided that under this arrangement the rifles could not be sold to the US because this country was engaged in the Vietnam conflict.

In 1974, Armalite and Sterling Ltd. of England concluded a production agreement whereby the AR-18 and the commercial semiautomatic version (AR-180) would be manufactured in the UK. Production began in 1975.

STERLING LIGHT AUTOMATIC RIFLE

Before starting production of the AR-18, Sterling's chief designer, Frank Waters, designed a rotating bolt, gas operated rifle to fire the 5.56mm cartridge. There appear to be no plans to produce this rifle.

BERETTA AR70/.223.

Beretta and SIG began a study of 5.56mm rifles in 1963. After a number of years, the two companies terminated their joint development effort. In 1968, Vittorio Valle at Beretta began work anew, and the Italian firm introduced the AR70/.223 in 1970. At one point in the early 1970s, Beretta negotiated with Colt to produce the M16 in Italy. When these discussions proved fruitless, they began to market the AR70/.223 more agressively. In this weapon, the designers decided in favor of a conventional gas piston and recoil spring system located above the barrel. After looking at existing locking systems, they adapted the twin lug used in the M1 Carbine and Kalashnikov weapons. Following the pattern of the Soviet AKM rifles, Beretta engineers welded a sleeve into the forward portion of the stamped steel receiver. That sleeve contained locking recesses for the lugs on the bolt.

The only major sale of the Beretta rifle has been to Malaysia (5,000 in 1972; Malaysia also purchased the same number of M16s and HK33s). It would appear that Beretta has abandoned the effort to produce and sell this weapon.

SIG 530 AND 540 RIFLES

As an outgrowth of their joint effort with Beretta in the early 1960s, SIG introduced the 530 series. Unlike their Italian counterparts, the Swiss used a roller lock mechanism evolved from the 510 series. In the 5.56mm rifle, the rollers are actually a locking system instead of a delay system as in the 510 series and the Heckler and Koch weapons. Only limited numbers have been fabricated with few sales.

The latest SIG series, the 540 and 543, represent a departure from the roller lock breech mechanism and a turn to the rotating bolt mechanism. While strikingly similar to the Beretta AR70/.223, the breech mechanism of the 540 series is actually closer to the Kalashnikov family. (See discussion above.)

FN CAL

Fabrique Nationale introduced the *Carbine Automatique Leger* in 1966. While this rifle looks like a smaller version of the FAL, it uses a different bolt than its predecessor. (For more details, see Chapter 9.) Made in very limited quantities, the CAL design embodied a three-shot burst feature in addition to automatic and single fire. The future of the CAL is uncertain.

GALIL ASSAULT RIFLE

During the past decade, the FN FAL produced by Israeli Military Industries (IMI) has been the basic rifle in the Israel Defense Force's (IDF's) inventory. The performance of the FAL did not satisfy Israeli military officers during the Six-Day War of 1967, due to malfunctions caused by desert sands and the "bang, bang, jam" malfunction of the heavy barrelled automatic version. Following the war, the IDF tested the M16, the Stoner 63, the HK33 and a native rifle designed by Lt. Col. Uziel Gal, the designer of the UZI submachine gun. All these weapons fired the US 5.56 × 45mm cartridge.

The standard weapon against which the 5.56mm weapons were judged was the AK47. That weapon had performed almost flawlessly in the hands of Israel's adversaries, and it was that performance that the IDF wished to equal or surpass. Tests that ensued were among the most stringent ever conducted for small arms. Indeed, in the effort to simulate the rigors of desert warfare, the battle hardened Golani Brigade did everything they could to destroy the weapons given them. In nearly every case, they succeeded. IDF authorities decided that the best weapon for their purposes was the AK47.

Israeli Galil (Blashnikov before he changed his name) worked up a 5.56mm version of the Kalashnikov rifle, using a barrel, bolt face parts and magazines from the Stoner system. The resulting weapon showed excellent promise. Meanwhile, IMI personnel learned from an executive officer of Interarms in the US that Valmet in Finland was producing a copy of the AK47 called the M62. After modifying samples of the M62 purchased from Interarms, IMI, at the direction of Yaacov Lior, head of the small arms branch, purchased unmarked Valmet M62 receivers and mated them to barrel blanks procured from Colt. A modified Stoner magazine was also developed. IMI has produced a hybrid weapon of promise. A folding stock version borrowed the butt assembly from the FAL. The extent of Israeli production of this rifle is unknown, but IMI has offered it for overseas sales, and deliveries have been started on an order from Guatemala.

RUGER MINI-14

Sturm, Ruger and Company introduced the Mini-14 in 1972. As its name suggests, it borrows many characteristics from the NATO caliber M14 Rifle, but there are several differences. It is not simply a scaled-down version of the US military rifle. While Ruger kept the wooden stock, the pattern of which has become a company trademark, the M14 type receiver is fabricated from an investment casting, instead of being machined from a forging. A short barrel, selective fire, folding stock variant—the AC-556K—was introduced in late 1976. Although the resulting product has considerable eye appeal, tests in the Philippines, France and elsewhere indicate that it presently is best suited for use as a police weapon.

MAS 5.56 RIFLE

The French arms factory at St. Etienne—part of the state armament group *(Groupement Industriel des Armaments Terrestres)*—has introduced its own rifle with a bullpup configuration, the MAS, making it one of the shortest weapons in the current crop of 5.56mm assault rifles. The delayed blowback mechanism is also unique among current 5.56mm rifles. (Addi-

Beretta AR70/.223

S1G 530-1.

FN CAL.

STOCK PIVOT

REAR SIGHT

OPERATING HANDLE

RIGHT SELECTOR LEVER

BIPOD

Israeli Galil.

AC-556K version of the Ruger Mini–14.

MAS 5.56mm Rifle.

MKS Rifle.

tional details are given in Chapter 18.) For several years, the French possessed a license to manufacture the HK33. In July 1977 the French General Staff announced the standardization of the MAS rifle and have placed an initial order for 236,000 with GIAT. The first weapons will be issued to the French armed forces in 1979.

MKS RIFLE AND CARBINE

Available only in prototype versions, the MKS is a product of Interdynamic AB of Stockholm. Both rifle and carbine versions have been designed to date. The MKS has a rotary bolt mechanism and gas operation. Following the lead set by the French MAS, the designers of the MKS have sought to produce a lightweight and extremely compact weapon. Interdynamics has indicated that the company is waiting for a decision on the NATO ammunition question before committing themselves to large scale production.

VALMET M71

This is essentially a reworked version of the M62 (Kalashnikov) design, chambered for the 5.56mm cartridge. Sales appear to be limited to a semiautomatic commercial version—the M71S—marketed by Interarms.

5.56mm RIFLE COMPARATIVE DATA (STANDARD MODELS W/O MAGAZINES)

	Barrel length mm (inches)	Overall length mm (inches)	Weight kg (pounds)	Average muzzle velocity m.p.s. (f.p.s.)
M16A1	500.0 (20.0)	975.0 (39.0)	2.900 (6.5)	991.25 (3250)
AR-18	456.3 (18.25)	909.4 (36.375)	3.200 (7.0)	979.05 (3210)
Stoner Rifle (XM22)	500.0 (20.0)	1006.3 (40.25)	3.600 (7.9)	991.25 (3250)
Stoner Carbine (XM23)	392.5 (15.7)	896.9 (35.875)	3.465 (7.7)	915.00 (3000)
HK33A2	383.8 (15.35)	905.5 (36.22)	3.474 (7.72)	960.75 (3150)
AR70/.223	442.5 (17.7)	925.0 (37)	3.400 (7.5)	969.90 (3180)
SIG 530	385.0 (15.4)	937.5 (37.5)	3.261 (7.2)	869.25 (2850)
SIG 540	460.0 (18.4)	950.0 (38)	3.260 (7.17)	980.00 (3214.4)
Ruger Mini-14	462.5 (18.5)	931.3 (37.25)	2.900 (6.4)	979.05 (3210)
MAS 5.56	440.0 (17.6)	750.0 (30)	3.150 (6.9)	960.00 (3148.8)
MKS Rifle	467.0 (18.7)	868.0 (34.7)	2.750 (6.05)	975.00 (3198)
U.K. 4.85 Individual Weapon	510.3 (20.41)	757.5 (30.3)	3.090 (6.875)	900.36 (2952)
Galil	460.0 (18.4)	970.0 (38.8)	3.900 (8.58)	980.00 (321.4)

UK 4.85 × 49mm Individual weapon.

RIFLES—A 1977 STATUS REPORT

Rifle development today is a dynamic industry in a state of flux. The 1977–1980 ammunition/weapons trials conducted by NATO may lead to a resolution of the 30-year-old caliber controversy. The 5.56mm is not necessarily the cartridge of the future. For example, the British introduced a 4.85mm rifle in 1976. And Heckler and Koch has produced a prototype rifle, the HK36, in 4.6 × 36mm and a new weapon that uses 4.75mm caseless ammunition. However, there does seem to be considerable evidence that the 5.56 × 45mm cartridge is here to stay for some time. The US Army is concentrating on new versions of that cartridge—the XM777 and XM778, described in the next chapter. Too many M16s have been produced for the 5.56mm round to be abandoned very easily. But as long as designers invent new weapons and cartridges and NATO remains undecided on a standard cartridge, the world of rifles will continue to experience change and confusion.

As for trends in Western rifles, it would appear that the light, rapid firing, small caliber assault rifle is the wave of the future. Politics and salesmanship will determine the exact nature of the next generation of rifles as much as analytical studies in the late 1950s influenced the emergence of current 5.56mm weapons.

Although the Soviet Union and its Warsaw Pact allies seem committed to the 7.62 × 39mm cartridge, there are rumors of a new small caliber 5.6mm rifle that fires a semi-caseless cartridge from a large-capacity drum. Validity of these stories has yet to be confirmed.

The future of the 7.62 × 51mm NATO cartridge is unclear. It is likely that the 1977–1980 trials will favor a smaller rifle caliber. Despite experiments with 6.0mm and 5.56mm machine guns, however, the larger cartridge (7.62 × 51mm) will be utilized for many years as a machine gun cartridge.

2 Machine Gun Development Since 1945

Machine guns can be as confusing a topic as rifles. Armed forces have used machine guns in varying roles since the beginning of this century, and during the past three decades the old distinctions among light, medium and heavy machine guns have blurred considerably. Before the 1939–1945 war, weapons like the UK Vickers and the US Browning, chambered for their respective rifle cartridges, were called heavy machine guns because they were just that. They were used as base-of-fire weapons in essentially fixed positions. The mobile battle fronts of World War II saw these heavy guns become obsolete, as portability became the key consideration in machine gun development. Today, the term light machine gun (LMG) usually refers to a magazine-fed weapon, while medium machine guns (MMG) are generally belt-fed. This distinction can be bewildering when a belt-fed machine gun (e.g., the XM235) is actually lighter than the M1918A2 Browning Automatic Rifle of WWII days. The machine guns discussed in this chapter will be described according to caliber family, dropping the former LMG/MMG distinctions. Differentiation between infantry and armored fighting vehicle versions will be maintained. To the three basic rifle calibers discussed in Chapter 1, we will add one—the 7.62 × 54R round used in Soviet machine guns.

NATO CALIBER MACHINE GUNS

MG42 AND M60

In addition to the search for a standard rifle, NATO has also looked for a common machine gun. That effort has been just as unsuccessful. As a consequence, there are several major machine guns in the hands of NATO soldiers. The oldest pattern is the UK NATO caliber version of the Bren Gun—the L4 series. Next is the German MG3, an updated version of the WWII MG42 described in Chapter 20. This highly popular weapon is used by Austria, Chile, Denmark, West Germany, Iran, Italy, Norway, Portugal, Spain and Turkey. The MG42/MG3 design has had an impact on American machine gun design as well, its feed mechanism being found in a modified form on the US M60 Machine Gun. After WWII, the US Ordnance Corps undertook a machine gun development program. Out of two designs (the T52 developed by Bridge Tool & Die Co. and the T161 developed by the Inland Division of General Motors), the US Army and its contractors produced an American gun with a heavy Germanic accent. In addition to the MG42 feed system, the M60 had a modified version of the *Fallschirmjäger Gewehr* (FG42) operating mechanism. Whereas the FG42 was equipped to provide either automatic or semiautomatic fire, the M60 is full automatic only. On the other hand, its low cyclic rate allows the gunner to squeeze off single shots without too much difficulty. Standardized in February 1957 as a companion piece to the new NATO caliber rifle (M14), the M60 was produced on a pilot line basis at Springfield Armory and has been subsequently manufactured on a large scale by Maremont Corporation in Saco, Maine (185,000). Australia is also a user of the M60. The Nationalist Chinese Government on Taiwan currently produces the M60 machine gun with US-provided machinery, blueprints etc.

The M60 was the first US machine gun to have a true quick barrel change. A new version, the M60E1, was introduced after a few years to permit even easier barrel removal and to decrease the number of parts. This weapon differs from the M60 as follows. (1) The barrel does not have the bipod or gas cylinder attached to it; they are attached to the gas cylinder tube. (2) The bipod is attached semi-permanently to the rear of the gas cylinder. (3) The gas cylinder has been simplified and has no threads; it has a U-shaped key to retain the gas cylinder extension. (4) The operating rod guide tube has a lug that retains the gas cylinder and bipod on the weapon and eliminates the gas cylinder nut. (5) The modified spool type gas piston has no holes. (6) The modified rear sight has the lateral adjustment increased by 20 mils. (7) The modified die-cast feed cover eliminates parts and allows the cover to be closed whether the bolt is in the forward or cocked position. (8) The modified feed tray eliminates parts. (9) The magazine hanger fitted to the left side of the weapon eliminates parts and can be used with either a modified magazine or a modified bandolier. (10) The new die-cast forearm eliminates parts and eases changing the barrel because the absence of a forearm cover allows the carrying handle to be fitted to the barrel. (11) The sling swivels have been relocated to the left side of the forearm and the top rear of the buttstock, improving the ease with which the weapon can be carried. (12) The carrying handle has been increased in diameter.

The infantry versions of the M60 are considerably lighter than the M1919A6 Browning Machine Guns of WWII vintage—10.5 kg (23.1 lbs.) versus 14.74 kg (32.5 lbs.), and only slightly greater than the 20-shot M1918A2 BAR, which weighed 8.8 kg (19.4 lbs.). Other models of the M60 include the M60C and M60D. Both of these weapons are used in aircraft armament roles. The M60C, with the stock removed, is remotely charged and fired. The M60D, which has spade grips and a trigger at the rear of the weapon, has been used as a door gun on US helicopters. And finally, there is the M60E2, which is used as a fixed (coaxial)* tank machine gun by the US Marine Corps. This gun has a barrel extension and a gas evacuator tube protruding beyond the gas cylinder. The evacuator system carries the gun smoke forward and out of the armored vehicle. A modified M60E2 used in the Mechanized Infantry Combat Vehicle as its interim armament is designated the XM238.

M73/M219

Two weapons were developed in the 1950s to answer a June 1951 call for a new NATO caliber tank gun—the T153 (M37), an interim modification of the M1919A4, and the T197, which was to become the standard armor machine gun, designed by Richard Colby and Jack Lockhead at Springfield Armory. However, in June 1953, the T197 project was suspended until 1956. Several malfunctions, including the tendency of fired car-

MAGAZINE ADAPTER SCREW

BAR TYPE FLASH SUPPRESSOR

FOLDING OPERATING HANDLE

UK L4A1 Bren Gun, 7.62 × 51mm NATO.

Rheinmettal MG3, 7.62 × 51mm NATO.

US M60 Machine Gun, 7.62 × 51mm NATO.

tridges to jam in between the buffer and the lever that actuated the cartridge rammer, had bedeviled the developmental guns. When testing was resumed in June 1957, some functioning problems still showed up. After further research and development work, on 14 May 1959, the T197E2 was standardized as the M73. From 1960 to 1965, Springfield Armory was the sole production source for this weapon.

When problems continued with the M73, Armory engineers began a product improvement program; the M73E1 was the result of their effort. It had fewer parts, a fixed ejector and was easier to clear when it jammed. In December 1970, the M73E1

was standardized and redesignated the M219, since its parts could not be interchanged with the M73. Approximately 13,500 M73/M219s were produced by General Electric and Rock Island Arsenal. The designers sought to provide the following characteristics in the improved weapon: short receiver length, feeding from either side, capability for barrel change from within the armored vehicle, top cover hinged from either side, absence of smoke and fumes, and easy dismounting. Despite continued efforts by GE and Rock Island to improve the performance of their machine guns (Over 40 modifications were made between 1959 and 1974.), the armed forces were never happy

The first post-1945 generation of United States Machine Guns showing relative sizes, feed directions and ejection patterns.

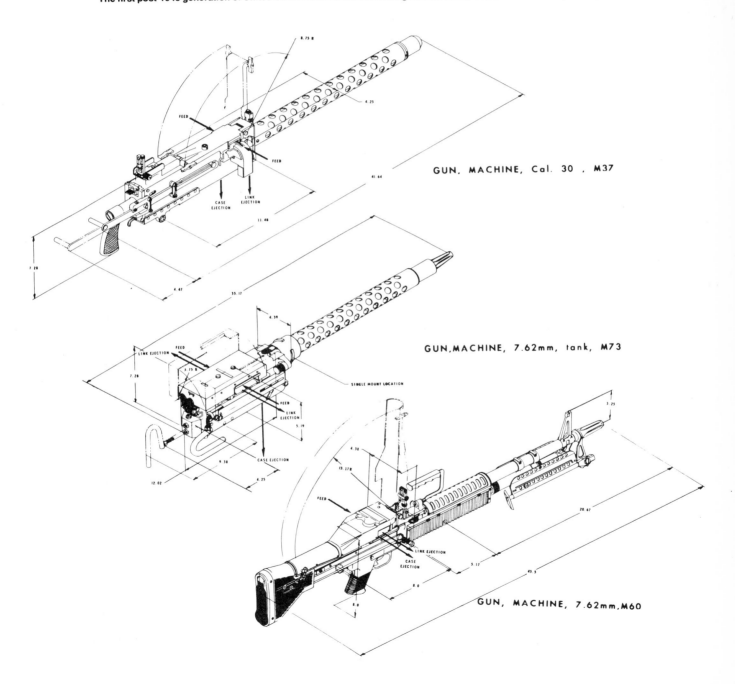

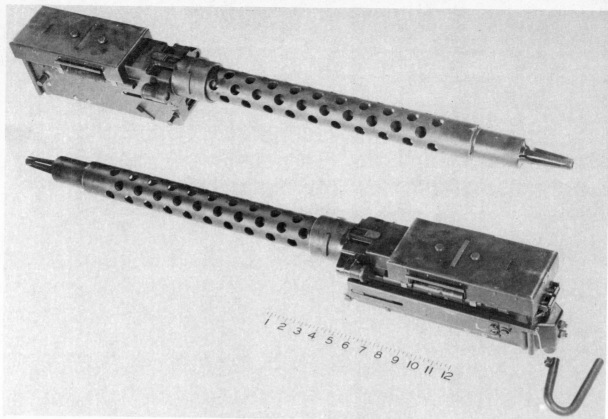

US M73 Machine Gun, 7.62 × 51mm NATO.

with it. When the Israeli Armored Corps had serious problems (the major one being the failure to extract empty shells when the extractor broke off parts of the cartridge rims) with the M73/M219 during the Yom Kippur war of 1973, the US Army began to look for a replacement.

MAG58

Besides the M60, M60E2 and M73/M219, six "off-the-shelf" foreign weapons were thoroughly examined to determine their suitability as replacements for the M219—the French *Mle. 1952 AAT NF1,* the Belgian Fabrique Nationale *Mitrailleuse a gas 58* (MAG58 or GPMG), the UK L8A1 (British version of the MAG58), the Canadian C1 (M1919A4 converted to 7.62mm NATO by Canadian Arsenals Ltd.), the German MG3 and the Soviet Kalashnikov-designed PKM. Beginning in 1974, a series of tests were carried out in two phases (Development Test and Operational Test phase II [DT/OTII] and later DT/OTIII). Operational evaluation of the three US guns was carried out at the Fort Knox Armor Center. Technical laboratory examinations, including test stand firings, were conducted at Aberdeen Proving Grounds for all nine weapons.

Two criteria were given special consideration. These were the so-called Mean Rounds Between Stoppages (MRBS) and Mean Rounds Between Failures (MRBF). The difference between a stoppage and a failure was defined in terms of the time the gun was out of action. Stoppages were less than a minute, while failures jammed the weapon for over a minute or were the result of parts breakage. After a careful test, the machine guns were ranked in order of superiority of performance:

1. M60E2	4. PKM	7. AAT52
2. MAG58	5. L8A1	8. M219
3. M219	6. MG3	9. C1

In March 1975, US Army authorities held a meeting on the coaxial armor machine gun and decided the following. Production and product improvements of the M219 should be terminated; shortcomings in the M60E2 should be corrected; and a new round of tests should be readied. At the end of March, the Army purchased 10 production model coaxial guns from FN. By that time, the Belgian firm and its licensees had manufactured over 700,000 MAGs, which had an operational system similar to US Browning Automatic Rifles. Fewer modifications were necessary to the Belgian weapon to make it fit the coaxial role, and the major alteration involved adding a cocking cable with a return spring. The standard gas regulator was replaced by a special unit that did not have any vents. A different flash suppressor was mounted on the barrels in some versions purchased in Europe. Whereas the barrel extension of the M60E2 protruded through the protective turret mantlet, the MAG barrel was hidden. Gas evacuation was provided by the flash suppressor. The tank version of the MAG could more readily be adapted to ground use by fitting a buttstock and mounting the gun on a lightweight tripod. A final advantage was its ability (with minor parts changeout) to use either the US M13 links or the German DM6 continuous link belts.

The final evaluation phase (DT/OTIII) was divided into three parts—technical testing (parts functioning and operational utilization), human engineering testing (interface between weapon and operator/tank) and RAM-D testing (Reliability, Availability, Maintainability-Durability). The last element, durability and ruggedness, was given the greatest weight in the subsequent evaluations. All of the Maremont M60s displayed a remarkable life span—over 100,000 rounds were fired without any parts problems. FN's guns began to show rivet breakages in the receiver at about 70,000 rounds, but they remained serviceable until well over 90,000 rounds. In the reliability test, the MAG was superior as the following indicates:

Type	No. of rounds fired	MRBS	MRBF
M60E2	50,000	846	1,699
MAG58	50,000	2,962	6,442
Minimum specified		850	2,675
Minimum desired		1,750	5,500

As a result of the US trials at Aberdeen Proving Ground and Fort Carson, Colorado, the MAG has been adopted as the M240 machine gun for eventual use in all American armored fighting vehicles (M60A1, M60A2, M48, M551, MICV and XM1). On 14 January 1977, the US Army and Fabrique Nationale signed a contract for 10,000 M240 machine guns. Subsequently, an American producer will fabricate metric dimensioned M240s from a Technical Data Package provided by FN. The Belgian company will receive a royalty payment on all American made M240s, just as Colt is paid for each M16 Rifle that is made outside their own factory. Early M240s will be installed in the Mechanized Infantry Combat Vehicles (MICVs). Later, the new machine gun will be used in place of the M73/M219, which will be phased out. The US Marine Corps will use the M60E2 in their M60A1 tanks. Over 45 nations currently include the various models of the MAG in their armed forces' inventories.

The process by which the M240 was selected may well set the tone for future NATO standardization efforts. For the first time, the US Army will utilize a foreign designed infantry/tank weapon. This test program was a far cry from the emotionally charged rifle standardization attempt. Fabrique Nationale and other arms manufacturers hope that the adoption of the M240 will set a precedent for the future and thus give real significance to the NATO ammunition trials.

E. Vervier holding a production model of the MAG58 Machine Gun he designed for FN.

US M60E2 (top) and FN MAG58 [US M240] (bottom) to approximately the same scale.

AAT52

At the end of World War II, the French set out to develop an inexpensive and reliable general purpose machine gun (GPMG). The delayed-blowback *Arme Automatique Transformable Mle. 52* was the product of their search. Fabricated from semi-cylindrical stamped steel shells welded together, the AAT52 is available in standard French 7.5 × 54mm and 7.62mm NATO. The latter is called the *AAT 7.62 NF1*. Since it can be fitted with either a light or heavy barrel, the AAT is a true GPMG. A heavy barrel model (without stock or sights) is used as a coaxial gun in armored fighting vehicles. While this tank version was well received by US field and test personnel, it did not perform as reliably as the MAG.

French *AAT Mle. 52*, 7.5 × 54mm.

MISCELLANEOUS 7.62 × 51mm NATO MACHINE GUNS

HK21A1. See Chapter 20.

HK11. See Chapter 20.

MG710-1 on bipod with drum magazine. See Chapter 41.

SIG 7.62mm NATO 710-3 Machine Gun.

Japanese Type 62. See Chapter 29.

MISCELLANEOUS 7.62 × 51mm MACHINE GUNS

In addition to the above, there are five other NATO caliber machine guns of note. First, there is the Heckler & Koch HK21, which is a belt-fed version of the G-3 Rifle. Presently, the NATO caliber version (Some 7.62 × 39mm and 5.56 × 45mm guns have been made.) is in production, and the weapon is being used by the Portugese armed forces. Second, is the Type 62, adopted by the Japanese Ground Self Defense Forces in 1962. Although somewhat complex in its operating mechanism, the Type 62 has an excellent reputation for reliability and accuracy. A third NATO caliber gun is the Czech M59N, which is a re-

worked version of their 7.62 × 54Rmm weapon. No large sales of this weapon have been made. SIG has developed the 710-3 machine gun, which fires the NATO cartridge. It is a spinoff from the Mauser MG45 developed toward the end of the Second World War. Although this gun is available for sale, to date there have been no sizeable purchases. Finally, the Maremont Corporation Universal Machine Gun was designed to replace the M60 in the ground role and the M73/M219 in the tank role. The recent adoption of the MAG(M240) probably means that the Maremont UMG will never be sold in large numbers. Indeed, the future of NATO caliber machine guns is unclear as the alliance members move forward with tests of 5.56 × 45mm weapons.

Czech M59N, 7.62 × 51mm NATO Machine Gun. See Chapter 14.

Maremont Corporation's 7.62 × 51mm NATO Prototype Universal Machine Gun.

5.56 × 45mm CALIBER MACHINE GUNS

CMG-2

Colt was the first company to experiment with a 5.56mm machine gun. Their idea was to produce a companion weapon for the M16 Rifle. Early entries into this field were a heavy barrel magazine-fed Colt Automatic Rifle (CAR) and a belt-fed machine gun version of the AR-15. Colt engineers, under the direction of Robert E. Roy, subsequently turned their attention to the development of a true machine gun. The CMG-1 was the fruit of their labor. Using M16 components where possible, this gun was dropped in favor of a completely new design, the Colt Machine Gun-2 (CMG-2), designed and developed by two Colt employees, Henry J. Tatro and George F. Curtis. The US Army tested the first models of the CMG-2 in the fall of 1969. Official reaction to the gun was that it did not have great enough range (even with the improved 4.4-gram [68-grain] projectile) and that it could not yield a high enough rate of sustained fire. This report, dated December 1969, came at a time when the Army was formulating the characteristics for a new Squad Automatic Weapon (See SAW below.), and there was some evidence that the 800-meter range for helmet penetration and tracer visibility later specified were in part the result of prejudice against the 5.56 × 45mm cartridge.

Tatro and Curtis borrowed a number of design concepts from earlier guns for incorporation into the CMG-2. The forward moving pistol grip as cocking mechanism was taken from the Czechs, who have used it in the ZB50, M52 and M59 machine guns. The gas system is essentially the same as the American M60. An M52 type belt feed mechanism was employed and ejection accomplished by a Lewis gun type spring loaded striker, which ejects spent rounds downward out of the gun. The CMG-2 has been ready on the shelf for production since December 1972, but no orders large enough to warrant production have been forthcoming.

Robert E. Roy firing early belt-fed AR-15—note ejected cases which are circled.

CMG-1 mounted on mock-up of a Colt 20mm gun turret. (June 1966)

Later version of belt-fed, heavy barrel AR-15.

STONER 63

Part of the system described in Chapter 45, the Stoner machine guns have also been a system in search for a major market. Despite the fact that the XM207 has been extensively tested by the US Army and was used by the US Navy SEAL teams as the MK23 in Vietnam, the Stoner machine guns have never been well received by the American military. Test reports indicate that the major strike against the weapon has been its unreliable performance under adverse conditions. Navy SEAL teams, who made a virtual ritual of preventive maintenance, were completely sold on the Stoner, but Army officials opposed it because they knew that the average infantry soldier could not be expected to lavish such careful attention on his machine gun. They wanted a soldier-proof weapon. Also, Stoner ran into the same prejudice against a 5.56 × 45mm machine gun in 1968–

D. A. Behrendt, Colt technical representative, with CMG-2.

1972 as had Colt. Until the Army resolved the ammunition question, both the CMG-2 and Stoner were at a disadvantage. Once the ammunition question was settled, the Army had its own candidate weapons.

Colt CMG-2, 5.56 × 45mm Machine Gun.

Early Stoner 63, 5.56 × 45mm Machine Gun.

Eugene M. Stoner, designer of the M16 Rifle and the Stoner 63 system.

5.56mm Stoner 63 Fixed Machine Gun. Firing solenoid shown as attached to receiver.

Stoner XM207E1, 5.56 × 45mm Machine Gun field stripped.

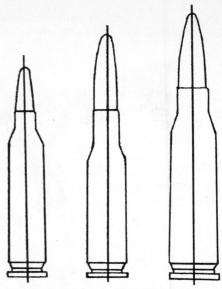

Comparative sizes: 5.56 × 45mm and 7.62 × 51mm NATO with 6.0 × 45mm SAW (Approximately full size).

HECKLER & KOCH 5.56

As yet one more element in their program to fully exploit the roller lock breech mechanism developed in the G3 rifle, Heckler & Koch has developed magazine- and belt-fed (HK13 and HK21) 5.56 × 45mm machine guns. These weapons are essentially the same as the G3 in basic operating principles, and they are described more fully in Chapter 20.

US SQUAD AUTOMATIC WEAPON (SAW) PROGRAM

At the outset, this project explored a large number of current weapons, product improvement proposals and conceptual designs that might possibly have satisfied the squad automatic weapon requirement for the 1980s. Over 1000 different configurations were considered in calibers ranging from 5.56mm to 7.62mm. A new 6.0 × 45mm cartridge was the result of a joint user/developer decision; no current or product improved cartridge could meet the desired characteristics. The new SAW round projected a long 6.8-gram (105-grain) projectile at 747 m.p.s. (2450 f.p.s.). While this velocity was considerably lower than the 990 m.p.s. (3250 f.p.s.) of the M16 cartridge, the projectile weight was nearly double (M16 round = 3.5 grams). A larger diameter projectile had been selected by the US Army research and development engineers at Rock Island Arsenal so that they could produce a reliable tracer projectile. The desired military performance was a fully visible trace in bright daylight to a range of 800 meters plus. In addition, the ball ammunition program sought increased hard target penetration at 800 meters; that is, the equivalent of at least helmet penetration as a measure of defeating hard targets.

After 20 months of preliminary work, during which the performance and dimensional specifications of the cartridge were decided, the Department of the Army issued a "Materiel Need" for a Squad Automatic Weapon, Light Machine Gun, on 8 March 1972. That document, which filled the role of "Military Characteristics" formerly issued by the Army, spelled out in detail the specifications for the weapon. Two contracts were let for the development of prototype weapons—to Maremont Corporation (XM233) and to Philco-Ford Corporation (now Ford Aerospace and Communication Corporation) (XM234). Rodman Laboratory engineers* under the direction of Curtis D. Johnson developed a

third entrant for the tests. That weapon was designated the XM235. After a little more than two years, a Development Test and Operational Test I (engineering and user tests) were concluded in December 1974. In addition to the three SAW candidates, the 5.56mm HK23A-1 belt-fed machine gun, the FN Minimi 5.56mm belt-fed machine gun and the heavy barrelled M16 were tested. The standard M16 was the yardstick against which all the other guns were measured. H&K's entry, after rough handling by testing personnel, allegedly did not meet safety requirements. Other HD23A-1s have been tested by the US Navy without any problems. The Heavy Barreled M16 was also dropped at this time. The latter had a limited magazine capacity—30 shots, versus the 200-round self-contained belt capacity called for in the Materiel Need. The FN Minimi machine gun, however, performed quite well.

Fabrique Nationale's 5.56 × 45mm machine gun was another product of the fertile mind of Ernest Vervier. Introduced late in 1974, this gun looked like a conventional machine gun, and it had a wood stock, which endeared it to traditional infantrymen who had grown weary of fiberglass and other synthetics. One strike against the Minimi was its 5.56 × 45mm caliber. Another was the fact that it fired a special 63-grain projectile. Thus, its ammunition was not interchangeable with either the M16 or the three SAW entries. But performance was the key factor, and the Minimi was as reliable as the XM233, XM234 and XM235.

Lt. Col. Bob B. Lukens, SAW Project Manager at Rock Island Arsenal, prepared an extensive trade-off study in which he evaluated the various weapons. At about the same time, the Department of the Army held a review of the SAW project, calling for a redirection of the effort. The 6.0mm cartridge would mean the introduction of a third type of ammunition into the US inventory. In discontinuing 6.0mm development, the Department of the Army asked the weapon designers to evaluate alternatives in 5.56mm and 7.62mm NATO. Materiel Development and Readiness Command (DARCOM) personnel were asked to consider the possibilities of amending the Materiel Need and to think over the international, i.e., NATO, implications of any decisions.

*The team included L. D. Antwiler, L. C. McFarland, A. R. Meyer, F. J. Skahill, D. L. White, K. L. Witwer and R. L. Wulff.

XM233 Maremont Corporation, 6.0 × 45mm SAW.

XM234 Ford Aerospace and Communication Corp., 6.0 × 45mm SAW.

XM235 US Army, Rodman Laboratory, Rock Island, Illinois, 6.0 × 45mm SAW.

5.56 × 45mm Version of the Rodman Laboratory SAW. Compare with one on preceding page.

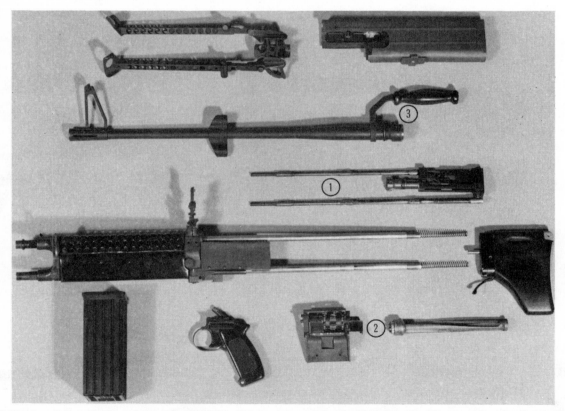

Field stripped view of Rodman Laboratory SAW. Note (1) twin pistons and bolt carrier assembly, (2) long cam for operating the belt feed, and (3) quick change barrel assembly.

Joint studies by DARCOM and the Training and Doctrine Command (TRADOC), which represented the infantry, led to the selection of the 5.56 × 45mm round. This cartridge would permit the development of a machine gun that would not weigh more than 9.53 kg (21 lbs.) when loaded with 200 rounds of ammunition. In February 1976, TRADOC, commanded by General William E. DePuy, decided to go for improved 5.56 projectiles fired from the XM235 (Rodman-RIA) and the FN Minimi. General DePuy wanted a platoon size comparative test of the two weapons, in which they would be measured against the M16

and the M60 machine gun. The new cartridges were the XM777 (ball) and the XM778 (tracer). Whereas the former had better hard target penetration due to design changes discussed below, the tracer round almost met the 800-meter requirement.

In June 1976, after a special In Process Review (IPR), DARCOM and TRADOC went to the Department of the Army with the following recommendations. (1) Modify the Materiel Need to reflect the change to 5.56mm and, (2) reduce the over-800-meter requirement to up to 800 meters. The Department of the Army approved the revised Materiel Need in October 1976.

DA APPROVED REVISED MATERIEL NEED HIGHLIGHTS
(OCT 76)

Characteristic	System Requirement
Operator	One-Man
Weight	Light-Weight (21 Lbs Max)
Reliability	≥ M60 Machine Gun
Sustained Fire Rate	Machine Gun Role
Ammunition Capacity	100 & 200 Round Containers
Range (Point and Area Targets)	0 to 800 Meters

DARCOM then issued a prototype manufacturing request for a proposal to produce 18 XM235 SAWs. Maremont and Ford Aerospace and Communication were the competing bidders. Ford won the competition and on 3 February 1977 signed a contract with the Army.

Meanwhile, a budget cut in December 1976 complicated the picture. The Army was left with only enough to build the 18 prototypes. There was not even money left in the budget for testing. Army officials are currently looking for some agency or other source of funds to underwrite the tests. The Infantry Center is hoping that FN will produce enough lightened Minimis (Their entry was about .68 kg over the weight limit.) for comparison testing. But FN will have to do so at their own expense. The Marine Corps was to fund the building and testing of two different heavy barrelled M16s. One of these utilized a Ballistics Research Laboratory, Aberdeen Proving Ground, version of the Soviet RPK drum magazine. The Infantry did not like that magazine (only 80–100-round capacity) because it was hard to reload and it sat to one side of the rifle, making it cant. The infantry preferred belted ammunition and weapons that had a barrel change capability. The second Marine Corps candidate for an "interim SAW" was produced by WAK Inc. of Medway, Ohio. This latter gun modified by Maxwell Atchisson used a heavy barrel, stronger buffer and special muzzle compensator. In addition, the rifle fired from an open bolt to aid cooling and prevent cookoffs in the over heated barrels. The 30-shot magazines were held side by side with a special metal clip, the Tri-Mag. In March 1977, the Marine Corps decided not to pursue the Heavy barrelled M16 project. There will be no interim SAW.

A 5.56mm ammunition improvement program has been a major part of the redirected XM235 Squad Automatic Weapon project. Its objectives are:

(1) Improved hard target effectiveness without a reduction in its performance against unprotected targets.
(2) Improved daylight tracer range.
(3) Maintenance of ammunition commonality with the M16 Rifle.

The performance goals of the XM777 and XM778 ammunition are:

(1) Helmet penetration at 800 meters.
(2) Same effective probability of incapacitation given a hit (P(i)H) as the M193 5.56mm cartridge.
(3) A tracer range between 700 and 800 meters in the worst possible daylight conditions.

The XM777 projectile has the same ballistics as the M193 ball round except that it contains a 0.29-gram (4.5-grain) steel insert at the tip of the full metal jacket. This use of an insert came about as the result of considerable experimentation by Frankford Arsenal and BRL ammunition specialists. That insert yielded significantly increased penetration of lightly armored targets. The overall weight of the projectile was reduced by .03 gram (.5 grain) for a weight of 3.53 grams (54.5 grains). In the tracer projectile, XM778, a deeper cavity was provided for this pyrotechnic mix. This cavity and a modified tracer compound with more burning increments produced a much improved daylight tracing range. An additional result of the improved 5.56 ammunition program has been a better trajectory match for the XM777 and XM778 than existed previously for the ball (M193) and tracer (M196) projectiles. The new projectiles follow nearly the same flight path. Currently, they are the US candidate cartridges in the NATO ammunition trials.

Although it is impossible to predict which squad weapon the US Army will adopt, it is safe to say that American soldiers will one day carry a belt-fed 9.5-kg (21-lb.) class machine gun with its own self-contained ammunition supply. This projection reflects the continued trend toward infantry weapons of lighter weight and greater firepower.

Fabrique Nationale, 5.56 × 45mm Minimi Machine Gun.

7.62 × 39mm M43 SOVIET CALIBER MACHINE GUNS

RDP AND RPK

The Soviets too have sought companion weapons for their Kalashnikov series of assault rifles. The 7.62 × 39mm *Ruchnoi* Pulemet Degtyareva* (RPD) evolved from earlier designs by Vasily Alexseyevich Degtyarev (See Chapter 43). Although work was begun on the RPD in 1943, production did not start until after the end of the 1939–1945 conflict. During its service life, several variants of this belt-fed gun were manufactured. The main differences among the five major variants are:

(1) First model: Cup type gas piston; no dust cover; straight reciprocating handle; right-hand windage knob. Most first version guns now have a cylinder sleeve fitted to the gas spigot, so that their gas mechanism resembles the later versions, and have a sliding dust cover fitted over the operating handle slot.

(2) Second model: Plunger type gas piston; no dust covers; straight reciprocating operating handle; left-hand windage knob. Some second version guns have had a sliding dust cover similar to the ones fitted to the first version guns; others have had a bracket riveted to the side of the receiver to accept a nonreciprocating operating handle. This latter type may have a handle that folds upward like the later model RPDs or one that folds forward.

(3) Third model (also PRC Type 56): As for second version, but has dust covers on feed mechanism and has folding nonreciprocating operating handle.

(4) Fourth model (RPDM): As for third version, but with longer gas cylinder, additional roller on piston slide and buffer in butt.

(5) Fifth model (PRC Type 56-1): As for fourth version, but with folding magazine bracket/dust cover and cleaning rod (sectional) carried in butt.

Top, first model RPD. Bottom, second and subsequent models.

These changes have no effect on the gun's operation and very little effect upon its functioning. The RPD has also been manufactured in the People's Republic of China as the Type 56 and Type 56-1 light machine guns and in North Korea as the Type 62 light machine gun. These latter types can be identified by the Chinese or Korean markings on their feed covers.

PRC Type 56 Light Machine Gun
(Copy of Soviet *Ruchnoi Pulemet Degtyareva*) 7.62 × 39mm.

*Ruchnoi or the prefix "R" is used by the Soviets to denote shoulder-fired or light machine gun. *Stankovy* or the prefix "S" denotes mounted guns; i.e., on a tripod or vehicle mount.

Now obsolete in the Warsaw Pact, the RPD is still used by some military forces in Southeast Asia and Africa.

Sometime in the early 1960s (before 1964), the Soviet Red Army adopted the *Ruchnoi Pulemet Kalashnikova* (RPK). Lighter than its predecessor, the RPD (4.99 kg vs. 7.1 kg [11 lbs. vs. 15.6 lbs]), the RPK is intended for use as a squad level support weapon. Given the absence of a barrel change capability, this adaptation of the AKM with longer and heavier barrel, must be used for relatively short bursts of fire. Sustained fire greater than 80 shots per minute would likely lead to cook-offs since the weapon fires from a closed bolt. Equipped with 40-shot magazines and/or 75-round drums, the RPK can provide the squad with a significant level of support firepower. When needed, the RPK can use standard 30-shot AK magazines because all these feed devices are interchangeable. An attractive and popular weapon, the RPK has also been manufactured by the Soviets with a side folding stock (RPKS). For a time, the North Vietnamese produced a heavy barrel gun using an AK47 type machined receiver and the standard RPK 75-round magazine. The Vietnamese weapon was designated the TUL-1. Yugoslavia's M65A and M65B (quick change barrel) are also designed to be used in the same manner as the RPK.

CZECH M52-M59

The Czech Model 52 machine gun was adopted as a companion to the Model 52 Rifle. Originally chambered for the 7.62 × 45mm cartridge, it was later altered to fire the Soviet M43 round and redesignated the Model 52/57. While an extremely sophisticated weapon using a large number of stampings, it was probably too sophisticated for modern armed forces. It has been replaced by the M59 universal GPMG. The M59 borrowed several design features from its predecessor. It has also been simplified to make it less complicated and easier to manufacture. Whereas the M52 can be fed by either box magazine or linked belt, the larger 7.62 × 54Rmm M59 is belt-fed only. As indicated above, the M59N is chambered for the NATO cartridge.

Seventy-five-shot RPK magazine.

CZECH URZ

Introduced in 1970 by Cekoslovenska Zbrojovka, Strakonice, the URZ system (universal small arms) was the East European answer to the Stoner system. It consists of an automatic rifle, light machine gun, medium machine gun and tank machine gun. It would seem that the first two weapons use the 7.62 × 39mm cartridge, while the latter two fire the 7.62 × 54Rmm round. Beyond that, limited data is available, but apparently the system is based upon the M59 design. Furthermore, it is likely that the URZ system has been designed for the export market.

Soviet *Ruchnoi Pulemet Kalashnikova* (RPK) with 75-shot magazine.

Soviet RPK with 40-shot magazine.

Vietnamese TUL-1, 7.62 × 39mm Machine Gun.

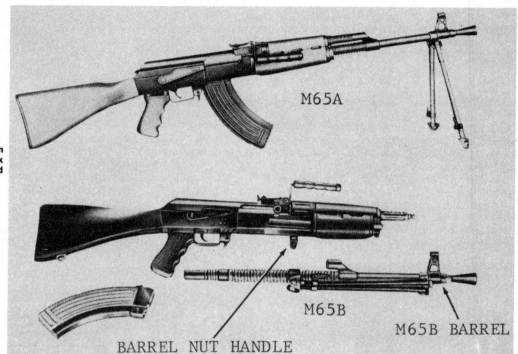

Yugoslav M65A and M65B, 7.62 × 39mm Machine Guns. The latter has a quick change barrel. These weapons are issued with the standard 30-shot magazines.

Czech M52 Machine Gun. Originally produced in 7.62 × 45mm, these guns were subsequently altered to fire the Soviet 7.62 × 39mm cartridge. They were redesignated Model 52/57. They can use either a box magazine (as shown) or a non-disintegrating belt.

7.62 × 54Rmm SOVIET CALIBER MACHINE GUNS

DEGTYAREV MG

Soviet tacticians continue to favor their Model 1891 rimmed cartridge for their base-of-fire weapons. The Soviets have upgraded the infantry machine guns several times since the Degtyarev DP was first manufactured in 1933 (See Chapter 43 for full details.) A. I. Shilin modernized the Degtyarev in 1946 by placing the recoil spring in a straight line with the recoiling parts of the operating mechanism instead of under the barrel and by adding a pistol grip. The weapon was redesignated DPM ("M" for modified). The one major shortcoming of the Degtyarev weapon was its horizontal 49-shot magazine. More reliable when loaded with 47 cartridges, that magazine severely limited the amount of fire that could be delivered. Toward the end of World War II, Shilin, P. P. Polyakov and A. A. Dubinin devised a belt-fed mechanism for the gun. As standardized in 1946, the RP46 could use either a 250-shot continuous metallic belt or, with a change of the top cover, a flat drum during an assault. Called the "Company" machine gun, it was designed for utilization as a base-of-fire weapon; that is, as a medium rather than light machine gun. Although the Red Army adopted this weapon, it has been more widely used by the PRC (Type 58) and North Korea (Type 64). The RPD described above was the final development in the Degtyarev series.

Soviet DP, 7.62 × 54Rmm Machine Gun.

Soviet DPM, 7.62 × 54Rmm Machine Gun.

Soviet RP46, 7.62 × 54Rmm Company Machine Gun.

GORYUNOV MG

A heavy 7.62 × 54Rmm Degtyarev machine gun, the M1939 never worked satisfactorily. It was replaced by the SG43 designed by Pytor Maximovich Goryunov. Primarily used as a fixed gun, the Goryunov was often found mounted on tanks, armored personnel carriers and earthwork emplacements. Whereas the SG43 was only .6 kg heavier than the RP46, its barrel weighed 4.8 kg (vs. 3.2 kg for the Degtyarev barrel). This extra weight in the barrel permitted the weapon to provide more sustained bursts of fire without overheating. All SG43 models (Six different versions are described in Chapter 43.) use the same 250-shot belt as the RP46. SG43s will still be found in use by Warsaw Pact armed forces and in the inventories of nations receiving aid from the Soviet Union and her allies, but the PK series is rapidly displacing the Goryunovs.

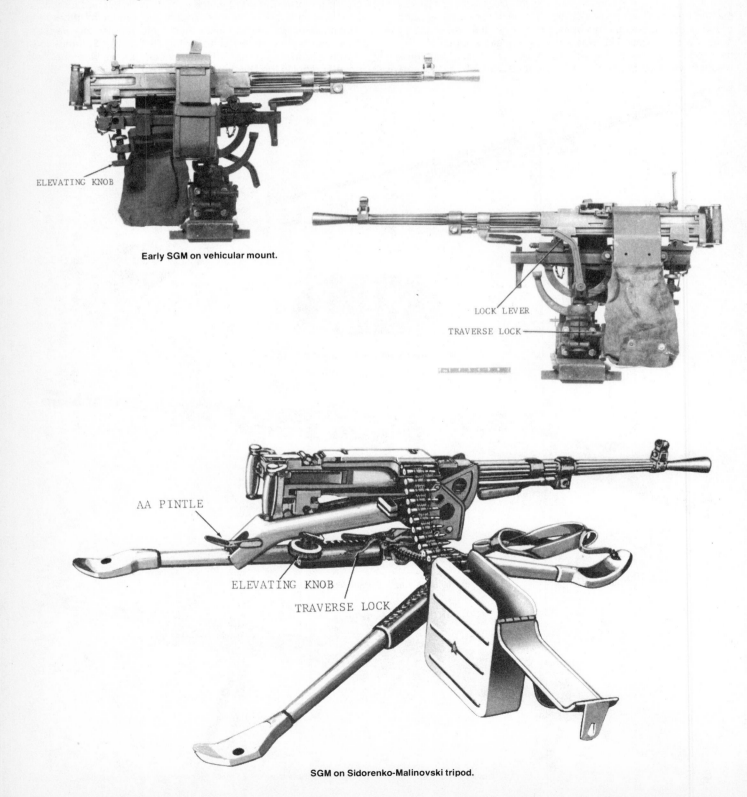

ELEVATING KNOB

Early SGM on vehicular mount.

LOCK LEVER

TRAVERSE LOCK

AA PINTLE

ELEVATING KNOB

TRAVERSE LOCK

SGM on Sidorenko-Malinovski tripod.

KALASHNIKOV PK SERIES

M. T. Kalashnikov's design bureau has produced yet another excellent weapon in the *Pulemet Kalashnikova*. As the Soviet Union's entry in the GPMG category, the PK borrows a number of components and concepts from earlier weapons. The bolt and bolt carrier are from the AK series and for purposes of a machine gun inverted, with the gas piston mounted below the barrel instead of on top as in Kalashnikov assault rifles. For feeding the standard belt, the cartridge gripper of the Goryunov was incorporated into the PK. The Goryunov barrel change system was also borrowed. In the feed mechanism, the idea of using the piston to power the feed pawls comes from the Czech M52. Finally, the trigger mechanism is an adaptation of the one used on the RPD. This weapon has an excellent record for reliability. During the US search for an M219 replacement, a rebarrelled PK (changed from 7.62 × 54Rmm to 7.62 × 51 NATO) came in fourth. That performance has impressed many American and European technical people.

When the PK first came to the notice of Western intelligence specialists in 1964, it was assumed that the PK would just replace the RP46 Company machine gun. But Kalashnikov's design bureau has shown considerable ingenuity and flexibility. Six variants currently exist.

(1) PK: The basic gun with a heavy, fluted barrel; stamped and machined feed mechanism components; a plain butt plate without shoulder rest; weight = 8.9 kg (19.8 lbs.).

(2) PKS: The basic gun mounted on a ground tripod; can be converted for use against aircraft; weight = 7.4 kg (16.5 lbs.).

(3) PKT: Coaxial version designed for armored applications. Sights, stock, bipod and trigger mechanism have been removed. A longer, heavier and smooth barrel was fitted, and a solenoid was employed to the back of the receiver to permit remote triggering. An emergency manual trigger and safety were also incorporated in the design.

(4) PKM: Modernized or product-improved version; feed cover made entirely from stamped parts. A folding shoulder rest was added to the stock. Weight reduced by about .6 kg (1.3 lbs.).

(5) PKMS: Tripod-mounted PKM.

(6) PKB: Tripod mounted PKM in which the stock and pistol grip have been removed and in their place a set of spade grips substituted and a center thumb operated trigger installed. Quite similar to the SGMB (See Chapter 43.). The PKB is used on armored personnel carriers such as the BRDM, BTR50 and BTR60.

Introduction of the PK machine gun family gives Kalashnikov-designed shoulder weapons a virtual monopoly in the USSR. Even the Dragunov Sniper Rifle (SVD) is a variant of the AK design. Mikhail Timofeyevich Kalashnikov must, therefore, be added to the roll of the world's preeminent weapons designers. Only 58 years old in 1977, Kalashnikov will likely be an important source of small arms concepts for many years to come.

PRC TYPE 67

The PRC Type 67 machine gun is a genuinely eclectic design, which will likely replace both the Type 53 (Soviet SG43) and Type 58 (Soviet RP46) machine guns. This new Chinese weapon borrows design concepts from several earlier weapons—the DP trigger, the Czech ZB30 bolt and piston, a modified Maxim type feed, the SG43 quick change barrel, an RPD type gas regulator, and a Czech M59 push-out type belt.

NOTE APPROVED FIRING POSITION

PKS

FRONT MOUNTING POINT

REAR MOUNTING POINT

AA ADAPTOR

ELEVATING MECHANISM

LEG CLAMP

BELT BOX

PKS, 7.62 × 54Rmm Machine Gun on ground mount.

The Type 67 still employs the 7.62 × 54Rmm cartridge. Although far from revolutionary in design, the new Chinese gun will likely provide reliable service since it is based upon well tested design elements.

Kalashnikov PKM Machine Gun.

12.7mm (.50 CALIBER) MACHINE GUNS

There are three basic 12.7mm (.50) caliber guns in use today—the US M2, the US M85 and the USSR DShK-38 series.

M2 AND M85

The American .50 caliber M2 machine gun was developed by John M. Browning at the end of World War I. After a series of early water cooled, aircraft and tank models were tested in the 1920s, an improved version was adopted in 1933 as the M2 Browning water cooled machine gun. Subsequent models (.50 M2 aircraft gun and M2 heavy barrel gun) using the same receiver were adopted by the Army. During the Second World War, nearly two million M2 guns of all variations were produced. The last M2s were manufactured in 1946, and despite their in-

credible record of reliability many of the remaining ones are showing signs of age. Toward the end of 1976, the US Army took steps to begin making the M2 once again. An initial contract for several thousand M2 machine guns, incorporating all the changes made over the past 44 years, will be awarded in 1977. The success of the M2, plus the fact that it has not been supplanted for some specific purposes, is a tribute to Browning's design talents.

Although the M2 is an excellent weapon, it is too large for contemporary applications in armored vehicles. After World War II, there was considerable experimentation with .50 caliber tank guns. The T175 series was the most successful design, largely due to its reasonably short receiver. AAI produced several versions of this weapon, and in June 1959 the T175E2 was standardized as the M85 caliber .50 Tank Machine Gun. This gun has been produced by General Electric, Springfield Armory and Rock Island Arsenal. The M85 will continue to be the standard American coaxial .50 caliber machine gun, and the M2 will be used in other roles; for example, as a flexibly mounted gun on armored fighting vehicles. Just over 10,000 M85s have been produced.

DShK38 AND M38/46

The Soviet DShK38 was the product of V. A. Degtyarev (basic gun design) and Georgii Semyonovich Shpagin (feed mechanism). Shpagin is better known for his work on the PPSh41 submachine gun. Shpagin's feed system for the 12.7mm was a rotary-type, in which successive cartridges were removed from the links, fed through a feed plate and then pushed into the chamber by the forward traveling bolt. Since this process was somewhat complicated, there were frequent stoppages with the DShK38 in combat. After the 1939–1945 war, the Soviets introduced the simplified M38/46, which had a scaled-up shuttle type mechanism of the kind found on the RP46. Parts do not interchange between the DShK46 and the M38/46. These guns are still widely used, and a PRC copy of the M38/46 (Type 54 HMG) has also been manufactured in large quantities. It should be noted that American .50 caliber guns fire a 12.7 × 90mm cartridge, while the Soviet guns use a 12.7 × 108mm round.

John Moses Browning, the most successful arms inventor in history.

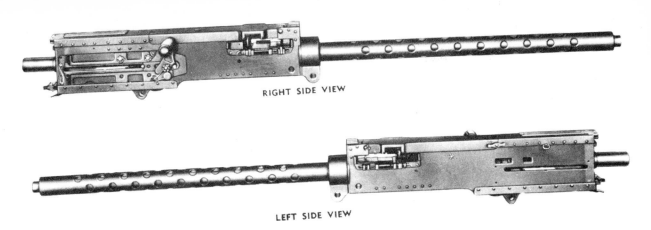

RIGHT SIDE VIEW

LEFT SIDE VIEW

US Aircraft Version of the .50 Caliber Browning Machine Gun.

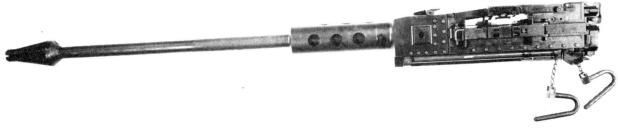

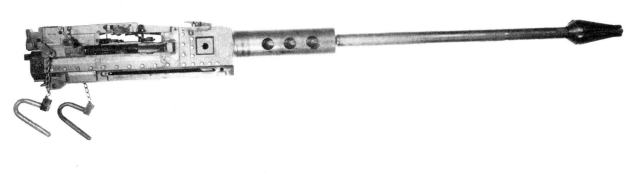

Current US .50 Caliber Tank Machine Gun, M85.

Soviet 12.7mm DShK Machine Gun.

MACHINE GUNS—A 1977 STATUS REPORT

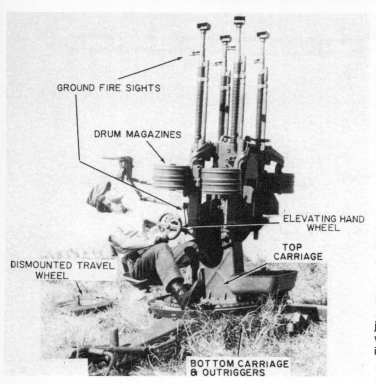

GROUND FIRE SIGHTS

DRUM MAGAZINES

ELEVATING HAND WHEEL

TOP CARRIAGE

DISMOUNTED TRAVEL WHEEL

BOTTOM CARRIAGE & OUTRIGGERS

Czechoslovak Quad-mounted M54 12.7mm Machine Guns. These guns are a copy of the Soviet Model 1938/46.

It would appear that NATO and the Warsaw Pact will both use three machine gun calibers in the future—5.56 × 45mm (or a variation on this theme) or 7.62 × 39mm, at the squad level; 7.62 × 51mm NATO or 7.62 × 54Rmm, as a base-of-fire weapon at the platoon level or as a coaxial weapon; and 12.7mm or larger (e.g., the Soviet 14.7mm), for armored personnel carriers and tanks. NATO seems committed to experimentation with a small caliber, belt-fed machine gun, and it is not yet clear how that weapon will be integrated into the squad. Nor is it understood how such a weapon will affect the use of the rifle. Ammunition tests will likely continue, with efforts being made to increase the number of target hits per shot. One concept tried in Vietnam by the US Navy was the .50–.30 Salvo Squeeze Bore, developed by Russell S. Robinson and marketed by Colt. In the Salvo Squeeze Bore, five .50 (12.7mm) projectiles were fired from a modified M2 Browning with each round fired. As the projectiles entered a special muzzle attachment, they were swaged to .30 (7.62mm) caliber. In the swaging process, their velocity was increased with the lead projectile having a muzzle velocity of about 930 m.p.s. (3050 f.p.s.). Extremely effective against personnel and lightly clad targets, this ammunition demonstrated considerable promise. Equally significant have been tests with sabotted, depleted uranium flechettes fired from .50 (12.7mm) and 20mm guns. These very low radioactive projectiles exhibit a thermal and chemical reaction upon contact with armor plate that gives them an increased penetrating and incendiary effect over standard armor piercing and incendiary projectiles. While much of this experimentation with new ammunition is still confined to the laboratory, it is apparent that increased kills and incapacitation will be associated with the next generation of machine guns.

US Army Quad-mounted .50 Caliber M2 Machine Guns installed on flat-bed of a truck.

3 Submachine Gun Development Since 1945

The introduction of assault rifles and the increased portability of infantry machine guns have diminished the tactical role of submachine guns. Made by the millions during the Second World War, weapons such as the US M1 Thompson, UK Sten, Soviet PPSh41 and PPS42/43 and German MP38/40 are now considered obsolete. In many instances, thousands upon thousands of these submachine guns lie idle in warehouses. Even though new Sten guns might be available at a modest price from surplus stocks, potential customers seek the M16 or AKM. Not only are they more modern, powerful weapons, they also represent a status symbol—they are the current issue weapons of the two "super powers."

Despite the fact that the submachine gun is a weapon-type in search of a mission, this class of small arms continues to be very popular with designers, students of firearms, police and security forces. Two major subdivisions of submachine guns exist today—those firing full power pistol cartridges (7.62 × 25mm, 9 × 19mm Parabellum, .45 ACP [11.43 × 23mm]) and those firing the less powerful pocket pistol cartridges (.32 ACP [7.65 × 17mm], .380 ACP [9 × 17mm], 9 × 18mm Makarov). In a break with tradition but in an effort to limit confusion, we have designated the former "submachine guns" and the latter "machine pistols" in the discussion that follows. Formerly, the British called submachine guns "machine carbines," but today they also use the American term.

A third category of weapons is sometimes labeled submachine gun but is in reality a short barrelled rifle firing rifle cartridges; e.g., the Colt XM177 series and the Heckler & Koch 53, which are chambered for the 5.56 × 45mm cartridge, or the Hungarian AMD version of the 7.62 × 39mm AKM. In performance, these weapons fall between the submachine gun and the assault rifle. Their most singular feature is their extremely loud report, the result of the shortened barrel. Despite its popularity, the Colt XM177E2 is no longer a standard issue weapon in the US Army.

By the end of the 1939–1945 war, the designers of submachine guns had evolved several basic types. By far the most popular has been the simple blow back operated weapon. In these submachine guns, the heavy reciprocating bolt once released by pressing the trigger moves forward stripping the cartridge from the magazine and detonating the cartridge primer as the bolt comes in contact with it when the round is seated in the chamber. Recoil energies and gas pressure from the fired cartridge provide the necessary force to drive the heavy bolt to the rear. The firing cycle repeats itself until the trigger is released and the sear stops the bolt from moving forward. Two good examples of the blow back submachine gun are the American M3A1 and the British Sten. First introduced in December 1942 as the M3, the updated and improved M3A1 is still in service with United States armored forces. (See Chapter 45.) The Sten gun, production of which began in 1941, was one of the simplest and least expensive shoulder weapons ever manufactured. (See Chapter 10.)

More complex are those submachine guns that fire from a closed or locked bolt. A post-war period example of this type of weapon is the Heckler & Koch MP5(HK54). Extending its family of delayed roller locked weapons, Heckler & Koch has marketed for several years this 9mm Parabellum submachine gun, which is based upon a number of standard components used in H&K rifles and machine guns. (See Chapter 20.)

Some representative models of current issue submachine guns and machine pistols are illustrated below.

The caliber .45 M3A1 Submachine Gun with flash hider is one of the few World War II era weapons still standard with US forces. It is issued as a personal defense weapon for armored fighting vehicle crews.

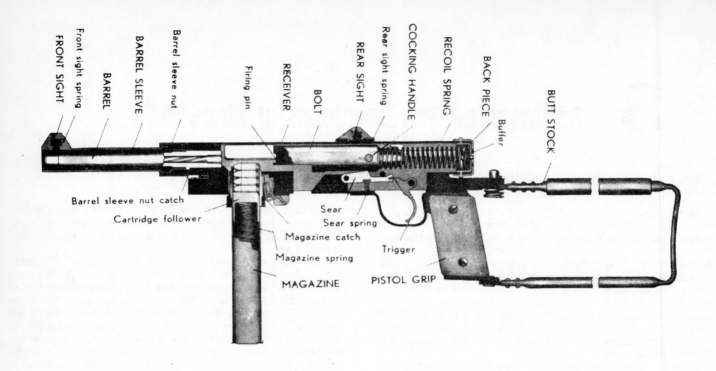

FRONT SIGHT
Front sight spring
BARREL
BARREL SLEEVE
Barrel sleeve nut
Firing pin
RECEIVER
BOLT
REAR SIGHT
Rear sight spring
COCKING HANDLE
RECOIL SPRING
BACK PIECE
Buffer
BUTT STOCK

Barrel sleeve nut catch
Cartridge follower
Magazine catch
Magazine spring
MAGAZINE
Sear
Sear spring
Trigger
PISTOL GRIP

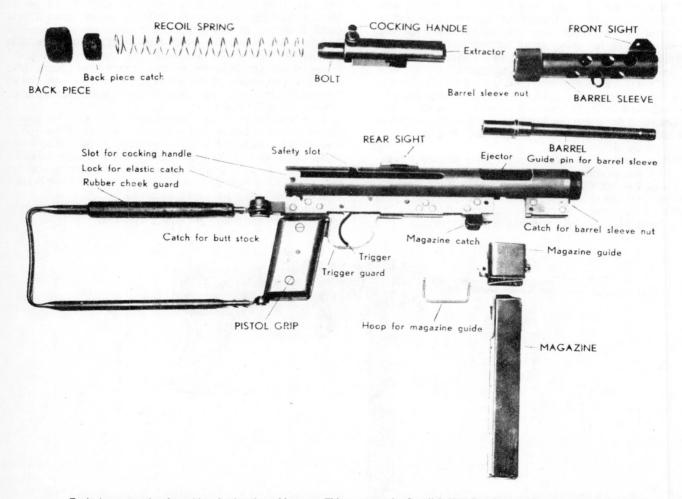

RECOIL SPRING
Back piece catch
BACK PIECE

COCKING HANDLE
Extractor
BOLT

FRONT SIGHT
Barrel sleeve nut
BARREL SLEEVE

Slot for cocking handle
Lock for elastic catch
Rubber cheek guard
Catch for butt stock
PISTOL GRIP

Safety slot
REAR SIGHT
Ejector
Trigger
Trigger guard
Magazine catch
Hoop for magazine guide

BARREL
Guide pin for barrel sleeve
Catch for barrel sleeve nut
Magazine guide
MAGAZINE

Typical construction for a blow back submachine gun. This weapon, the Swedish M45 Carl Gustaf, has been one of the more popular post-World War II submachine guns.

Czech Model 24 7.62 × 25mm Submachine Gun.

Shortly after the Second World War, the Czech arms factory at Uherský Brod introduced a new submachine gun (two different models in 9mm Parabellum—M23 and M25—and two in 7.62 × 25mm—M24 and M26) that had a significant impact on the subsequent design of such weapons. Whereas earlier blowback submachine guns had relatively short barrels in an effort to keep the overall length of the weapons to a manageable size (The M3A1 had a 203-mm [8-in.] barrel.), this new Czech design had a significantly longer barrel—284mm (11.18 in.). Overall length of the Model 25 and 26 folding stock versions was only 445mm (17.5 in.) versus 579mm (22.8 in.) for the M3A1, when the stocks for both weapons were retracted. The designers relied upon a simple design trick to achieve this result. They extended a large part of the barrel into the receiver and machined the bolt in such a fashion that it had a recess for the barrel. When the bolt was forward, it telescoped the rear 159mm (6.25 in.) of the barrel. In addition, the designers included an ejection port in the bolt, as well as in the receiver. When the bolt is in the closed or cocked position, the ejection port in the receiver is closed; thus, in effect, the weapon has nearly full time protection from the entry of dust and other foreign particles. A distinctive feature of this gun is the location of the magazine in the pistol grip. (See Chapter 14).

While this weapon was only produced for a limited time (About 100,000 were manufactured.), the telescoping bolt concept influenced several subsequent designs—notably the Israeli Uzi and the Steyr-Daimler-Puch Model 69 9mm Parabellum Submachine Gun.

Israeli 9mm Parabellum Uzi Submachine Gun with folding stock.

Students of modern small arms generally agree that the Uzi is the best submachine gun ever devised. That consensus, unusual in the world of small arms, is ample testimony to the creative talents of Uziel Gal, the designer of this weapon. First manufactured in 1951 by Israeli Military Industries for the Israeli Defense Forces and subsequently produced under license by Fabrique Nationale, the Uzi has been purchased by several countries, including West Germany, Haiti, Iran, the Netherlands, Panama, Peru and Venezuela. Many police forces use the Uzi for special applications, including the US Secret Service, whose agents carry the Uzi during their Presidential protection assignments. As with the majority of blowback submachine guns, the Uzi fires from an open bolt. Gal made extensive use of sheet metal stampings and heat-resistant plastics. The barrel, which is held in position by a threaded locking nut, can be quickly changed. The Israeli Defense Forces have even experimented with Colt's Salvo Squeeze Bore ammunition, which contains three projectiles that are reduced from 9mm (.357 in.) to 7.62 mm (.30 in.) in a special tapered smooth bore attachment for the Uzi. The Uzi has a 254-mm (10-in.) barrel and an overall length, with the stock retracted, of 440mm (17.32 in.); it weighs 3.5 kg (7.72 lbs.).

Current Uzi submachine guns in the Israeli service are designated the No. 2, Mark A. In West Germany, they are called the MP2. As with several of the newer blowback type submachine guns, the Uzi has a grip safety, making it much safer to handle than older weapons, e.g., the Sten, M3A1 and MP40. The Uzi cannot discharge accidentally when dropped because the grip safety locks the sear mechanism, preventing the rearward movement of the bolt and subsequent firing (as illustrated). Special cuts in the bolt also prevent accidental discharge if the shooter's hand slips from the cocking knob before the bolt is pulled fully to the rear in the cocked position. (See Chapter 27).

Uziel Gal

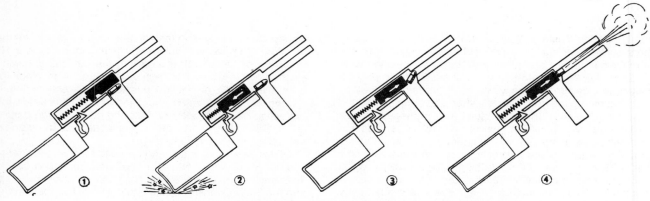

Diagram showing accidental discharge of blowback submachine gun without bolt lock.

Steyr Model 69 9mm Parabellum Submachine Gun.

The Steyr M69 submachine gun, designed by a team led by Hugo Stowasser, follows in the tradition of the Czech and Israeli weapons. Generally, it is a much simpler design than the Uzi. The 254-mm (10-in.) barrel is rifled on the Steyr cold forging equipment. All the processes used to produce this weapon are designed to keep the cost to a minimum. This submachine gun is currently a standard weapon with the Austrian Armed Forces (see Chapter 8).

Other submachine gun designs embodying the telescoping bolt concept include the standard issue Argentine PA3-DM, the Australian Kokoda (prototype), the Mexican Mendoza HM-3 (limited production) and the US Maxwell Atchisson M1957. Before going bankrupt in 1976, Military Armaments Corporation in the US produced the M10 (.45 ACP and 9mm Parabellum) and the M11 (.380 ACP) submachine guns. These weapons, designed by Gordon B. Ingram, were extremely compact and lightweight. Because of the light bolt, these guns had an extremely high rate of fire. The .45 caliber M10 had a cyclic rate of nearly 1200 rounds per minute, whereas the M3A1 has a cyclic rate of about 450 rounds per minute. Both the M10 and M11 were designed to be used with the Sionics noise suppressor. Early in 1977, RPB Industries of Atlanta, Georgia, began production of the M10 and M11 submachine guns on a limited basis.

9mm Ingram Model 10 Submachine Gun.

Among the conventional submachine guns currently in service are the following:

Sterling 9mm: Britain (L2A2, Chapter 10), Barbados, Canada, Dubai, Ghana, India, Jamaica, Lebanon, Malawi, Malaysia, Nepal, Oman, Singapore, Tunisia.

Beretta M12 9mm: Italy (Chapter 28), Bahrain, Gabon, Indonesia, Italy, Libya, Nigeria, Venezuela.

Madsen Model 50 9mm and .45 ACP: (Chapter 15), Brazil, Chile, Columbia, Ireland, Paraguay, Thailand.

MAT49 9mm: France (Chapter 18), Lebanon, Morocco, Vietnam (modified to fire 7.62 × 25mm).

M3A1: US (Chapter 45), Nationalist China, Greece, Guatemala, Iran, Turkey.

Other basic submachine gun types are described in the country by country chapters of Part II.

A typical model of the Sterling type 9mm Parabellum Submachine gun. (See Chapter 10.)

Australian F1 9mm Parabellum Submachine Gun. (See Chapter 11.)

Walther MPL (L = long barrel) 9mm Parabellum introduced in 1963. This weapon has been sold commercially for police use. (See Chapter 20.)

Disassembled view of HK54 adopted by West German border patrol as the MP5. Note the easily interchanged fixed and retractable butt stocks. (See Chapter 20.)

ment. Given the limited power of the cartridge and the weapon's high cyclic rate, this gun is best suited as a personal defense weapon rather than as an offensive weapon. In addition to the Czech Army and Internal Security Forces, the Skorpion has been sold by the Czech export firm Omnipol to a number of African nations. (See Chapter 14.)

World War 1 Mauser pistol converted to caliber 9mm Parabellum and fitted with detachable shoulder stock and holster. Experimental models were full auto. After the war the design was also issued commercially with a full auto switch. This design is too light for practical true submachine gun use.

Poland, too, has developed a high rate of fire machine pistol. Designed by Professor Wilniewczyc, the Wz63 (Model 63) fires the Soviet 9 × 18mm Makarov cartridge. Unlike the Skorpion, which fires from a closed bolt, the Wz63 fires from an open bolt as do conventional submachine guns. The combination of open bolt operation and high rate of fire (probably greater than the specified 600 rounds per minute) causes this weapon to be generally inaccurate. Although best suited as a personal defense weapon, the Polish armed forces issue this weapon to parachute troops as well as to armored fighting vehicle crews. (See Chapter 36.)

Fully automatic pistols were first used during World War I, but in Eastern Europe several new machine pistols have been introduced since World War II. The Czech Model 61 (Skorpion) was one of the earliest models. Designed by Miroslav Rybář at the Zbrojovka Brno Factory, this miniature weapon can be fired on either full automatic or single-shot. The Skorpion, chambered for the 7.65 Browning (.32 ACP) cartridge, has a 10- or 20-shot curved box magazine and fires at a high rate of fire—in excess of 850 rounds per minute. It is available with a silencer attach-

For a time, the Soviet Armed Forces used the Stechkin Automatic Pistol. Equipped with a wooden shoulder stock/holster, this weapon was similar in concept to the World War I Mauser automatic pistol. The Stechkin fired the 9 × 18mm Makarov cartridge at a rate of approximately 750 rounds per minute. It, too, proved uncontrollable during automatic fire. While the Stechkin is now obsolete in the Soviet Union, it may still be found in the hands of some specialized troops. (See Chapter 43.)

MACHINE PISTOL CHARACTERISTICS

	Model 61	Wz63	Stechkin
Caliber:	7.65 × 17	9 × 18	9 × 18
Overall length:	508mm (20 in.)	610mm (24 in.) (approx.)	558mm (22 in.) (approx.)
Stock extended:			
Stock retracted:	269mm (10.6 in.)	333mm (13.1 in.)	226mm (8.8 in.)
or removed:	112mm (4.41 in.)	152mm (6.0 in.)	127mm (5.0 in.)
Barrel length:	1.55 kg (3.42 lbs.)	1.80 kg (3.97 lbs.)	1.02 kg (2.25 lbs.)
Weight:	Blowback	Blowback	Blowback
Operation:	10- or 20-shot	15- or 25-shot	20-shot
Magazine capacity:	305 m.p.s. (1000 f.p.s.)	325 m.p.s. (1066 f.p.s.)	340 m.p.s. (1115 f.p.s.)
Muzzle velocity:			

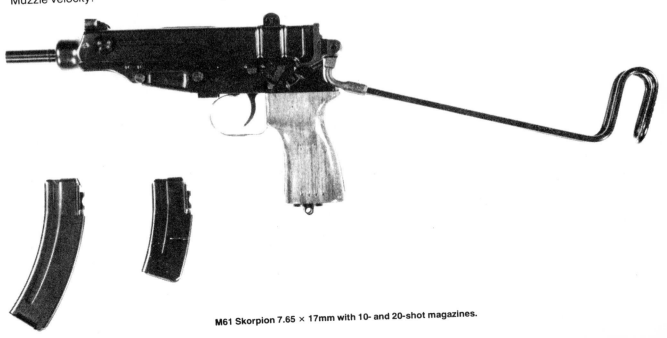

M61 Skorpion 7.65 × 17mm with 10- and 20-shot magazines.

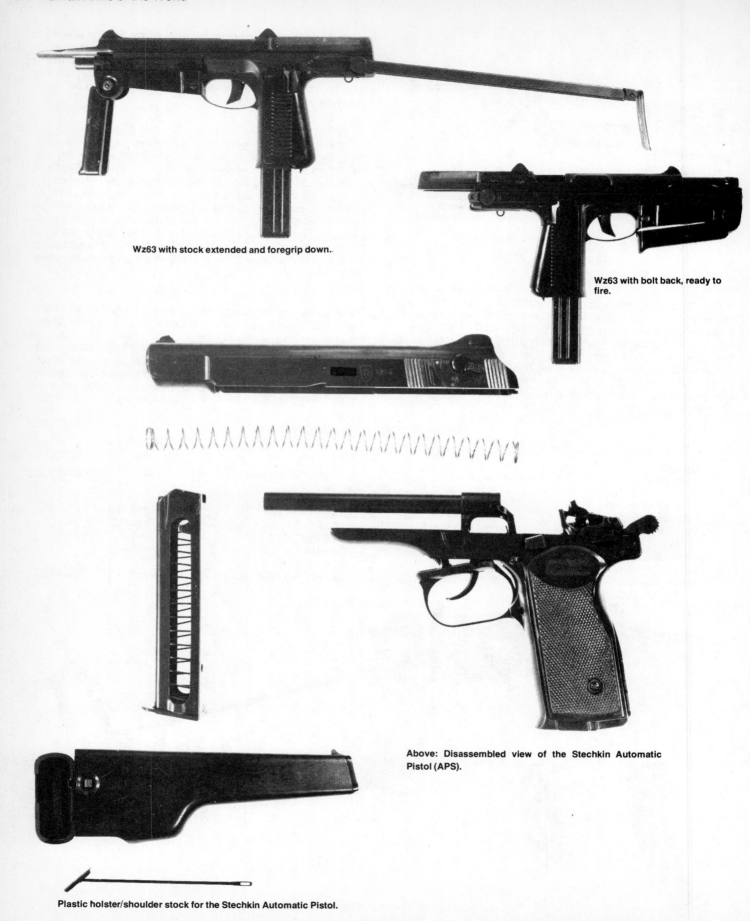

Wz63 with stock extended and foregrip down.

Wz63 with bolt back, ready to fire.

Above: Disassembled view of the Stechkin Automatic Pistol (APS).

Plastic holster/shoulder stock for the Stechkin Automatic Pistol.

Early in the 1970s, Heckler & Koch of West Germany introduced the 9mm Parabellum VP70 automatic pistol. When used without the plastic shoulder stock, it will fire only semiautomatically; when the stock is attached, it will fire automatically (2200 rounds per minute) or in three-shot bursts. Even with the shoulder stock, the VP70 is a relatively light weapon (1.6 kg [3.5 lbs.] when loaded with 18 rounds) due to the use of plastics for the basic pistol frame. Despite the use of non-traditional synthetics and the high cyclic rate, Heckler & Koch predicts a 30,000-round life span for this weapon. (See Chapter 20.)

SUBMACHINE GUNS— A 1977 STATUS REPORT

Although the traditional submachine gun role has been diminished by the introduction of lightweight assault rifles, these fast-firing weapons are still used widely by paramilitary, security and police forces in situations where a rifle would be too cumbersome or too powerful for safe use. Machine pistols are now quite often found filling roles formerly assigned to handguns. In fact, many military arms designers now speak in terms of personal defense weapons, as a consequence of the blurring of the formerly clear distinctions between machine pistols and handguns. A good example of the confusion that exists is Colt's arm gun developed for the US Air Force. For want of a better nomenclature, Colt has called this weapon the "Lightweight Rifle/Submachine Gun," which is chambered for a caliber .221 IMP cartridge. That round produces a velocity of 732 m.p.s. (2400 f.p.s.), falling between the 390 m.p.s. (1280 f.p.s.) of the Sterling L2A2 and the 1000 m.p.s. (3250 f.p.s.) of the M16 Rifle. As development of small caliber assault rifles, on the one hand,

Lightweight Rifle/Submachine Gun
in Firing Position

and development of personal defense weapons, on the other hand, continues, the role of submachine guns will likely continue to be restricted. Nevertheless, millions of submachine guns have been manufactured, and they will probably continue to see service. If not as the standard equipment of organized armed forces, they will be utilized by insurgents and terrorists since they are relatively compact and use ammunition that is readily available.

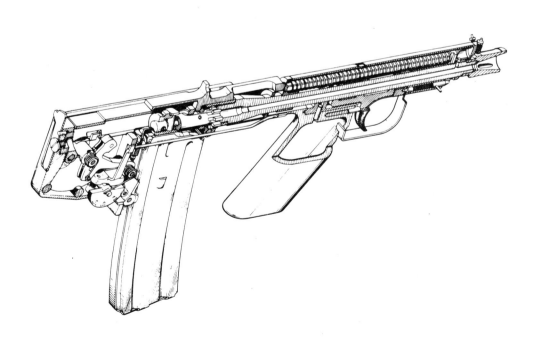

When Colt engineers began their design of an "arm gun," based upon a concept proposed by Dale M. Davis of the Air Force Armament Laboratory at Eglin Air Force Base, they started with the 9mm Parabellum cartridge. After completing one firing prototype, they discovered that they could use a much more powerful cartridge and include an automatic fire feature that would give an airman the equivalent of an assault rifle in a much smaller and more compact unit. Weapons such as this may someday be used for personal defense in place of both submachine guns and handguns.

Colt Industries 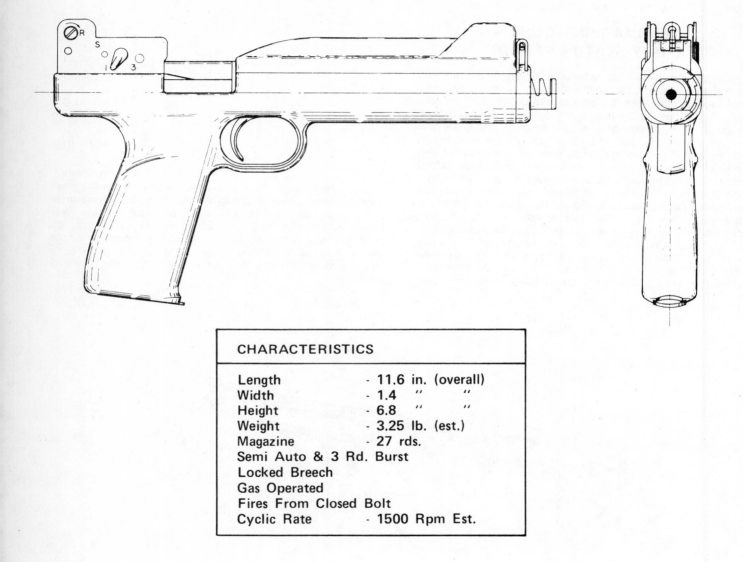 **Colt's Military Arms Division**

CHARACTERISTICS

Length	- 11.6 in. (overall)
Width	- 1.4 '' ''
Height	- 6.8 '' ''
Weight	- 3.25 lb. (est.)
Magazine	- 27 rds.

Semi Auto & 3 Rd. Burst
Locked Breech
Gas Operated
Fires From Closed Bolt

Cyclic Rate	- 1500 Rpm Est.

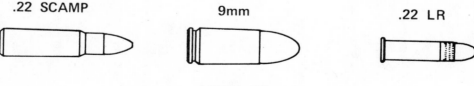

.22 SCAMP   9mm   .22 LR

ACTUAL SIZE

The Colt SCAMP (Small Caliber Machine Pistol) was designed in the early 1970s as a personal defense weapon with the equivalent lethality of a 9mm Parabellum weapon but with less recoil. Prototypes of the SCAMP fired a 2.6-gram (40-grain) .22 caliber projectile at 640 m.p.s. (2100 f.p.s.), producing a muzzle energy nearly as great as the 9mm Parabellum. SCAMP was manageable even with its high rate of fire. The US Army subsequently experimented with similar weapons as part of the Personal Defense Weapons Program.

4 Handgun Developments Since 1945

Unlike the rapid changes that occurred in rifles and machine guns, many older model handguns are still in service. Two of the major designs—the M1935 Browning High Power *(Grande Puissance)* and the M1911A1—are the product of John M. Browning's fertile imagination. The former, while known by many different names, is essentially the same weapon as introduced by Fabrique Nationale in 1935. More than two dozen nations have adopted this 9mm Parabellum pistol, and Argentina, Belgium, Canada, India, Indonesia and the United Kingdom have produced it. The American M1911A1 .45 caliber pistol is still the standard sidearm in the US Army after 66 years of continuous service. A dozen or more armies include this Browning design in their inventory, and it has been used by at least twice that many armed forces in the past. The Tula-Tokarev 1933 (TT33) Pistol formerly used by the Soviet Armed Forces is a Browning derivative, and it is still found in the hands of many officers around the world from Afghanistan to Yugoslavia. One other design of World War II vintage that is still standard issue in at least six armies is the post-war version (P1) of the 9mm Walther P38. Presently, this sidearm is manufactured by Carl Walther in West Germany and by Steyr-Daimler-Puch in Austria.

A number of new pistols have been introduced since 1945. Clearly, the trend has been away from revolvers and toward a limited number of calibers for self-loading pistols. By far, the most popular cartridge is the 9×19mm Parabellum cartridge, which was introduced in 1902 and adopted by the German Navy in 1904 and by the German Army in 1908. Second, in terms of popular usage, is the US .45 ACP (11.43×23mm) cartridge, introduced by John Browning in 1905 and adopted by the US Army in 1911. The Soviet 7.62×25mm cartridge (a variant of the 1896 7.63 Mauser pistol round) was previously widely used for both pistols and submachine guns. Since 1945, it has gradually been supplanted by the less powerful 9×18mm Makarov cartridge. The .32 caliber (7.65×17mm) Browning cartridge is the other major round used for some smaller pocket pistols. Almost without exception, these are the four basic self-loading cartridges used today. While it would be impossible to cover all the handguns developed since World War II, the text that follows covers some of the major pistols in current service. Additional handguns are described in the country by country chapters of Part II.

Indonesian-made Browning High-Power 9mm Pistol.

Colt-made M1911A1 .45 ACP Pistol.

Current manufacture Walther P1 9mm Parabellum Pistol.

9mm PARABELLUM HANDGUNS

CZECH MODEL 1975 PISTOL

Since the end of World War II, the Czechs have introduced several new self-loading pistols. The best known is the Model 1952 7.62 × 25mm pistol. (See Chapter 14.) In 1975, the Czech export agency Merkuria announced the availability of a new 9mm Parabellum self-loading pistol manufactured by the Ceska Zbrojovka factory at Strakonice. In adding this pistol to their current offerings, CZ borrowed the Browning operating principle. In fact, the weapon looks like a cross between the Browning High-Power and Smith & Wesson's Model 39. Its magazine capacity is 15 rounds, two more than the High-Power. The Model 1975 is unique for a Warsaw Pact country in that it is chambered for 9mm Parabellum instead of 7.62 × 25mm or 9 × 18mm Makarov. Undoubtedly intended for the international market, the Model 1975 has been produced in two versions—commercial and military. (See Chapter 14.)

Ceska Zbrojovka's Model 1975 9mm Parabellum Pistol.

FRENCH MAB P15 PISTOL

The French military arms establishments have also introduced two 9mm Parabellum pistols since 1945. The best known, the MAS 1950, was designed at the *Manufacture d'Armes Automatiques St. Etienne.* This weapon was an updated version of the M1935 Pistol, chambered for the more powerful 9 × 19mm instead of the older and less lethal French 7.65 × 20mm cartridge. Whereas the M1935 and MAS 1950 were basically variations of the Browning design, the MAB P15 is a different design, worked out by the engineers at the *Manufacture d'Armes Automatiques Bayone.* The P15 employs a hesitation lock that retards the rearward thrust of the slide after a cartridge has been fired. A cam lug machined onto the barrel interacts with a cam groove in the slide, slowing its recoil. The cam groove in the slide causes the barrel to rotate, and the interplay between the slide and the barrel delays the rearward motion until the gas pressure from the fired round has been reduced to a safe level.

The MAB P15 is so designated because of its 15-shot magazine capacity. As with the Browning High-Power and the Czech Model 1975, the large capacity magazine makes the grip quite thick; all of these pistols are a handful. A P-8 (eight-shot) and F-1 target version are also marketed commercially.

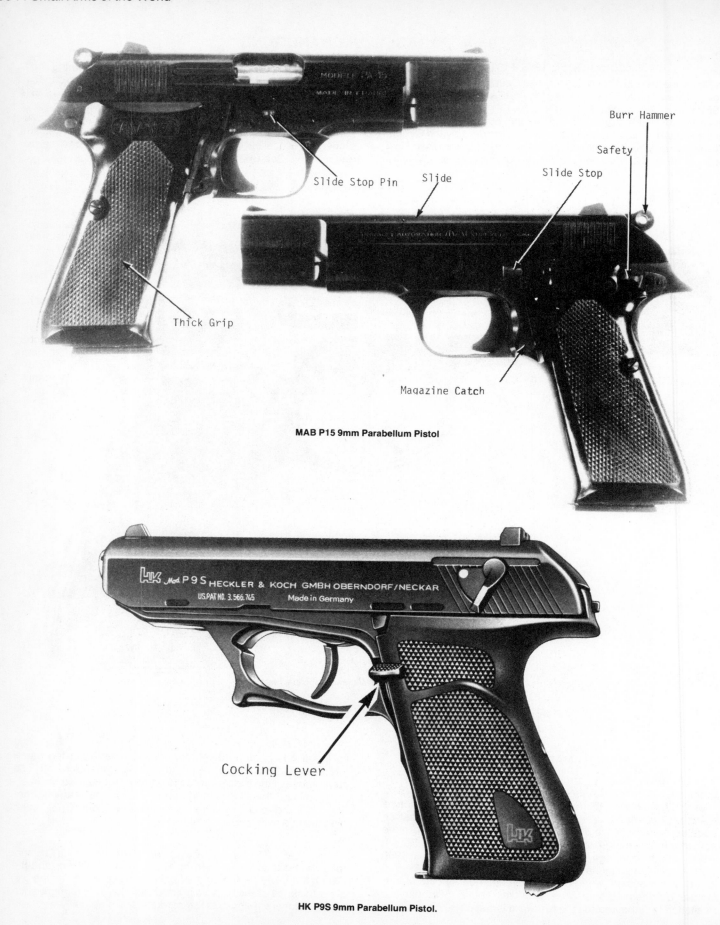

MAB P15 9mm Parabellum Pistol

HK P9S 9mm Parabellum Pistol.

GERMAN HECKLER & KOCH P9 AND P9S PISTOLS

Although the Walther P1 (P38) continues to enjoy extraordinary popularity, the German firm of Heckler & Koch has introduced two 9mm Parabellum pistols recently—the selective fire VP70, mentioned in the preceding chapter, and the series P9 and P9S. The latter differ only in their trigger mechanisms; the P9 is a single action, and the P9S is a double action. Both models have internal hammers that can be cocked by an external lever near the trigger guard on the left side of the receiver. In further exploiting their roller lock retarded blowback breech mechanism (G3 and HK33 Rifles and HK54 Submachine Gun), Heckler & Koch has designed a weapon that is unique for two reasons—its locking system and its wide use of stamped metal parts and plastic components. The receiver consists of a light stamped steel shell encased in molded plastic. Other features, such as the polygonal rifling, are described in Chapter 20. Magazine capacity of the P9 series is nine shots.

ITALIAN BERETTA MODEL 1951 PISTOL

Although one of the older post-war designs, the Beretta Model 1951 9mm Parabellum has enjoyed considerable popularity since its introduction. In addition to being the standard handgun of the Italian Army, it is also used by the Israeli Defense Forces, the Egyptian Army and the Nigerian police force. The swing wedge shaped locking block type locking system is described in Chapter 28. This pistol has an eight-shot magazine.

SWISS SIG-SAUER P220 PISTOL

For nearly three decades, the Schweizerische Industrie-Gesellschaft (SIG) P210 Pistol has been considered the finest machined handgun in the world. Starting with Charles Petter's concepts for an improved Browning-Colt design that first emerged as the French M1935, SIG engineers produced a sidearm made as precisely as a Swiss watch. As the Model 49, the P210 has been the standard Swiss Army pistol for most of the post-war period. Recently, SIG teamed up with the old-line German firm J. P. Sauer & Sohn of Eckenforde to produce two new pistols—the P220 and the P230. These pistols were designed by SIG engineers and are being manufactured by Sauer. The major reason for this across-the-border cooperation is the increasingly stringent Swiss export laws for small arms. While also advertised in US .45 caliber, the P220 is basically a 9mm Parabellum pistol, and the P230 is a modern pocket automatic, produced in 7.65 × 17mm and 9 × 17mm (.380 ACP). The Swiss Army announced the adoption of the P220 as the Model 75. To gradually replace the M49, 10,000 P220s have been ordered.

SIG-Sauer's P220 is unique in several respects, but one of its most notable features is the large utilization of stamped steel parts. While SIG was long regarded the last bastion of machined steel components, the P220 is a modern handgun in all aspects, including the techniques used to fabricate its stamped steel slide, slide release lever, trigger, trigger rod, decocking lever, lanyard loop and magazine catch. Although the new manufacturing processes make the pistol cheaper to manufacture, it is still a high quality weapon. (See Chapter 41.)

Assembled and disassembled views of the SIG-Sauer P220 9mm Parabellum Pistol.

US 9mm PISTOLS

In the West, the United States remains the odd country out. After 66 consecutive years of service, the standard US self-loading pistol continues to be the .45 caliber M1911A1. During the early 1950s, the US Army investigated the possibility of adopting a 9mm Parabellum pistol. That effort, however, was stopped when the Department of the Army decided it would be uneconomical to change calibers with so many .45 caliber pistols in service. The Smith & Wesson Model 39 pistol evolved from designs tested by the Army during the 1950s, and it has been widely marketed as a police sidearm. The Navy used some Model 39s as silenced weapons during the Vietnam conflict. (See Chapter 5.)

In the late 1960s when the US Army was searching for a new pistol to be issued to officers of General rank, Colt proposed a variation of their 9mm Commander pistol to replace the old .32 and .380 ACP pistols. The Army ultimately adopted a modified M1911A1 .45 caliber pistol, the M15, which borrowed many features from the National Match Pistols developed during the past 20 years at first Springfield Armory and later Rock Island Arsenal.

Other 9mm designs, such as the Colt 1970 Stainless Steel Military Pistol, have died in the development stages due to a lack of interest. There is a low priority program to develop a new personal defense weapon, but it will not likely lead to a new standard American Army handgun for many years to come.

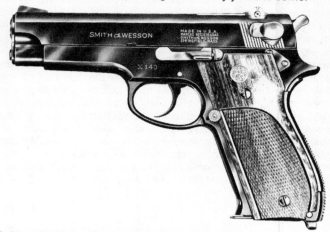

Smith and Wesson 9mm auto pistol. This is the military model with double-action trigger. Barrel 102mm (4 ins.). Overall 188mm (7.4 ins.). Weight with light alloy frame .79 kg (28 oz.).

SPRINGFIELD ARMORY - ORDNANCE CORPS

M1911A1, CAL..45

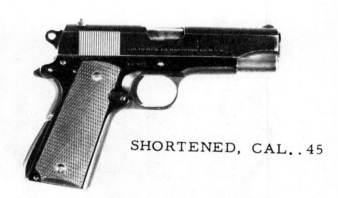

SHORTENED, CAL..45

SHORTENED, 9MM

T-4, 9MM

T-3, 9MM

LIGHTWEIGHT PISTOL DEVELOPMENTS (ALUMINUM ALLOY FRAMES)

Collection of some of the experimental pistols tested by Springfield Armory in the early 1950s. All of these pistols with the exception of the T-3 were Colt developments. The T-3 was designed by High-Standard Arms Company engineers.

SPRINGFIELD ARMORY - ORDNANCE CORPS

T-3, 9MM

X-100, 9MM

LIGHTWEIGHT PISTOL DEVELOPMENT
(ALUMINUM ALLOY FRAMES)

High Standard T-3 and Smith & Wesson experimental pre-M39 pistol, which were tested by the US Army in the early 1950s.

CHARACTERISTICS OF M1969

Caliber: 9mm Parabellum.
Barrel length: 104 mm (4.1 in.).
Weight: 1.02 kg (36 oz.) (w/magazine & empty).
Trigger pull: 2.04 to 2.95 kg (4½ to 6½ lbs.).
Stocks: American walnut.
Finish: Can be Colt's Standard Blue, Royal Blue or Nickel.
Accuracy: Capable of 100% on silouhette targets at 50 meters.
Design criteria: Same as government specifications utilized by the 1911 Service Pistol.
Magazine capacity: 8 rounds.
Advantages:
   —All steel construction; therefore, it can be subjected to all 9mm ammunition regardless of its manufacture.
   —Basic components, such as trigger, hammer, sear, disconnector, magazine catch, main spring & housing, etc., are standard Model 1911A1 parts.

Colt General Officers Pistol M1969, 9mm Parabellum.

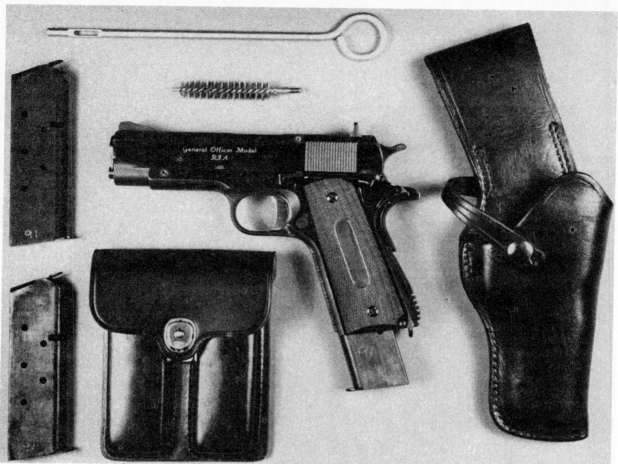

M15 General Officers .45 caliber Pistol with accessories.

M15 General Officers Pistol, standard issue since 1972.

Comparison of:

	M15 General Officers Pistol	M1911A1
Caliber:	.45.	.45.
System of operation:	Recoil.	Recoil.
Length overall:	200mm (7.875 in.).	219mm (8.62 in.).
Barrel length:	108mm (4.25 in.).	127mm (5 in.).
Feed device:	7-shot box magazine.	7-shot box magazine.
Sights: Front:	NM type blade.	Blade.
Rear:	NM type square notch.	Square notch.
Weight:	1.02 kg (2.25 lbs.)	1.1 kg (2.43 lbs.).

9 × 18mm MAKAROV HANDGUNS

As part of the overall introduction of new small arms in the post-World War II period, the Soviets have added a new sidearm to their inventory, the *Pistolet Makarova,* chambered for the 9 × 18mm cartridge. That cartridge is slightly more powerful than the older .380 ACP (9mm *Kurz*) round that was common in the West before 1945, but it is less lethal than the 9 × 19mm Parabellum. Part of the reduced lethality is due to the lower ve-locity of the Makarov round, 335 m.p.s., compared to the 350 m.p.s. of the Parabellum. But the projectile of the Soviet car-tridge is also somewhat lighter—6.9 grams (106 grains) versus 7.5 grams (115 grains). The Makarov type pistols have been manufactured in the USSR (as the PM), in the German Demo-cratic Republic (as the Pistole M) and in the People's Republic of China (as the Type 59). It has been widely distributed in allied countries, as well. For additional details, see Chapter 43.

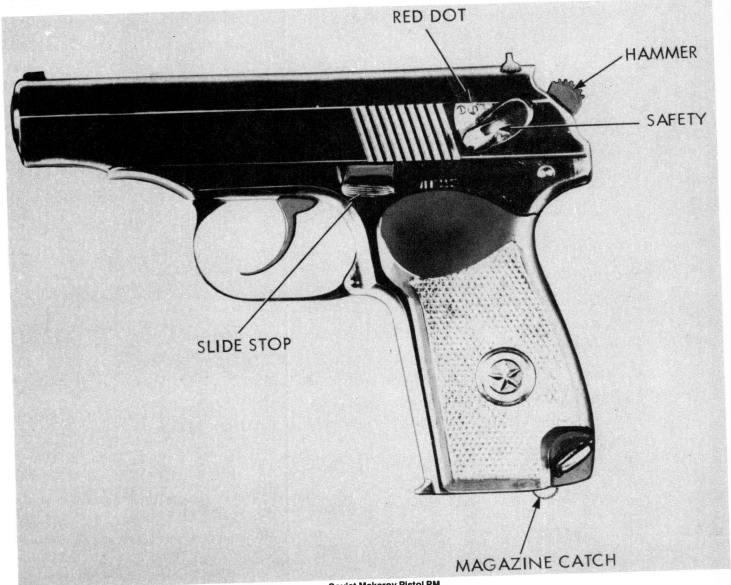

Soviet Makarov Pistol PM.

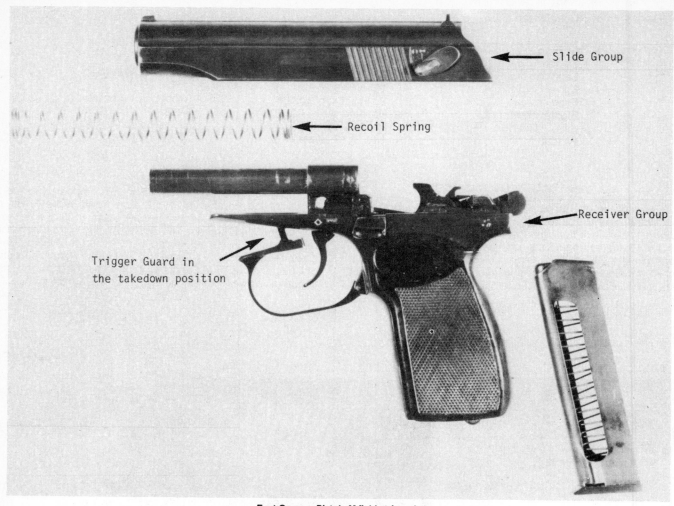

East German *Pistole M* field stripped.

The Polish Armed Forces use another design, the P64, that combines some design features from the Makarov and the Walther PP series of pistols. As with its Soviet counterpart, the P64 is a simple blowback mechanism. It has a six-shot magazine capacity, while the Makarov magazine holds eight rounds. Neither of these pistols are offensive weapons; rather they are small, compact personal defense weapons. (See Chapter 36.)

Perhaps the most unusual development in recent years was the North Korean resurrection of the Browning 1900 pistol as their Type 1964. Chambered for the 7.65 × 17mm (.32 ACP) cartridge, this weapon appears to have been intended for clandestine operations as it has often been found fitted with a silencer. (See Chapter 34.)

HANDGUNS—A 1977 STATUS REPORT

As does the submachine gun, the handgun appears to be entering a period of transition. With the exception of the US with their .45 caliber pistols, most armies seem to be moving toward the 9mm diameter bullet. Soviet developments indicate that they no longer consider a high power pistol to be an essential item in their arsenal. Evidently, they view the 9mm Makarov pistol the last resort in personal defense, the assault rifle being the first line of personal protection.

With the introduction of lighter rifles, most Western armies also are less concerned with handguns. Often a status symbol,

for example, the US General Officer Pistol, the handgun will only be used in combat when all else fails. Other new weapons, such as the Firing Port Weapon (Chapter 5), will likely diminish even further the importance of handguns. Newer concepts of Personal Defense Weapons, for example, the Colt SCAMP and Lightweight Rifle/Submachine Gun arm gun (described in Chapter 3), may lead to even further dimunition of the handgun role. The small caliber, high velocity assault rifle concept has initiated a period of change that will alter the entire world of small arms in the next several decades.

5 Special Purpose Weapons Development Since 1945

Changes in the nature of conventional combat since the end of World War II have produced a number of special purpose small arms. This chapter looks at three categories—sniper rifles, firing port weapons and silenced weapons.

SNIPER RIFLES

At the end of World War II, most of the world's major armies had special models of their standard service rifle that had been adapted for use by snipers. The basic modification was the addition of a telescopic sight and scope mount, and when possible specially selected components, such as barrels and stocks were chosen to yield a more accurate rifle. The M1C and M1D rifles equipped with telescopic sights replaced the older M1903A4

sniper rifle during the Second World War. In the Soviet Army, both the Model 1891/1930 Mosin bolt action rifle and the Tokarev SVT40 self-loading rifle were modified for sniper use. Since 1945, considerable work has been done in both the East and the West to develop newer sniping rifles. A look at current American and Soviet sniper weapons will give the reader a better idea of post-war developments.

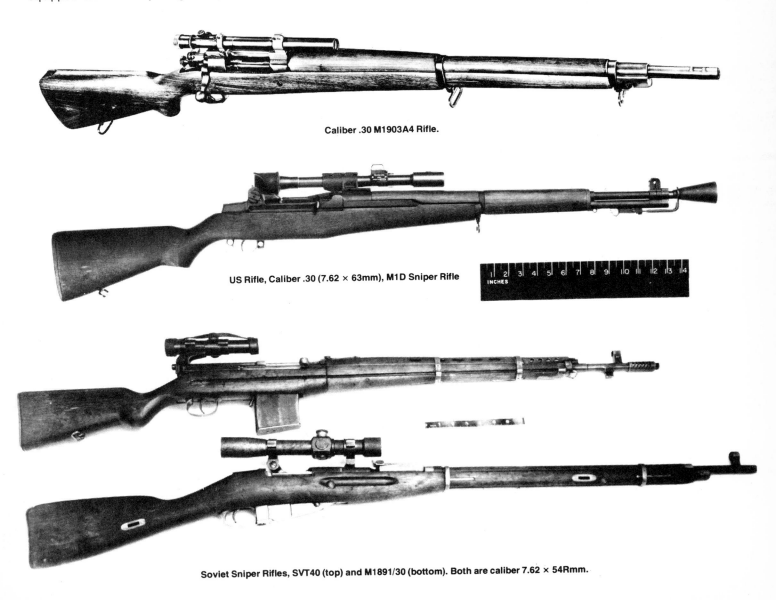

Caliber .30 M1903A4 Rifle.

US Rifle, Caliber .30 (7.62 × 63mm), M1D Sniper Rifle

Soviet Sniper Rifles, SVT40 (top) and M1891/30 (bottom). Both are caliber 7.62 × 54Rmm.

Close-up view of Soviet M1891/30 telescopic scope and mount.

Close-up of Soviet SVT40 telescopic scope and mount.

UNITED STATES SNIPER RIFLES

The long war in Vietnam with its peculiar absence of a stationary or continuous battle front meant that the enemy could literally appear anywhere allied forces were stationed. Snipers equipped with accurized rifles proved to be an excellent addition to the defensive armament of a variety of types of military installations. In September 1968, the Department of the Army directed the Army Materiel Command to provide 1,800 accurized M14 Rifles equipped with the Adjustable Ranging Telescope (ART) designed by James Leatherwood to US forces in Vietnam as ENSURE Requirement 240 (*E*xpediting *N*on *S*tandard *U*rgent *R*equirements for *E*quipment). Standards for the accurized rifle were defined by the US Army Markmanship Training Unit at Fort Benning, Georgia. Telescope specifications were prescribed by Frankford Arsenal based on the Leatherwood design evolved at the US Army Limited War Laboratory. The first 65 weapons shipped to Vietnam came from the Limited War Laboratory. All M14 Rifles were manufactured with the provision for attaching a scope mount directly to the left side of the receiver. Thus, theoretically any M14 in service could be equipped with a telescopic sight in a matter of minutes. But the

Army wanted specially selected and very accurate examples fine tuned for sniping. Subsequently, 300 National Match M14s were fitted with M84 telescopes (the M1D scope) and sent to Vietnam on a high priority basis. At Rock Island Arsenal, 1,435 M14NM Rifles were converted to XM21 sniper rifle configuration to complete the total number of 1,800 required by ENSURE 240. At the end of December 1975, the XM21 was standardized as the M21 Sniper Rifle.

In the course of the work on the XM21, the Small Arms Systems Laboratory at Rock Island did an additional evaluation of contemporary sniper rifles to determine the characteristics for a Future Army Sniper Rifle System. The weapons tested included the XM21, the Marine Corps M40 7.62 × 51mm (Remington Model 700 bolt action rifle), the French FRF1 7.62 × 51mm Sniper Rifle (Chapter 18) and the Steyr-Mannlicher Scharfshutzengewehr (SSG) 7.62 × 51mm sniper rifle (Chapter 8). All of these weapons provided excellent accuracy at sniping ranges. The Small Arms Systems Laboratory at Rock Island carried out some experimentation with product improved versions of the M14/M21 Rifle, during which alternative gas systems and stock configurations were tested. With the winding

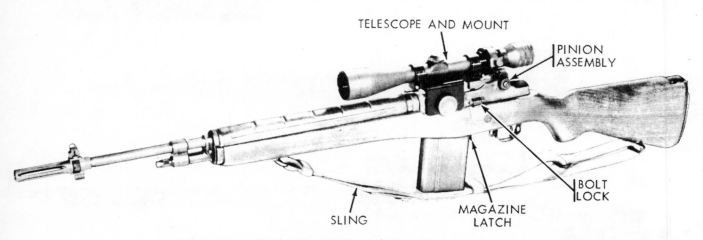

Rifle, Sniper, 7.62-MM, XM21, w/adjustable ranging telescope and mount, sling and controls – left front view.

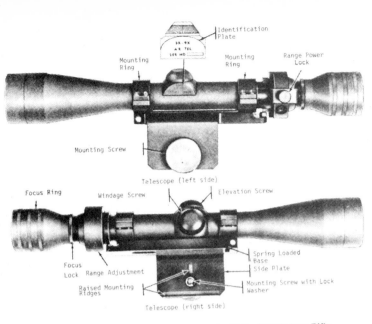

Adjustable Ranging Telescope as used with the M21 Sniper Rifle.

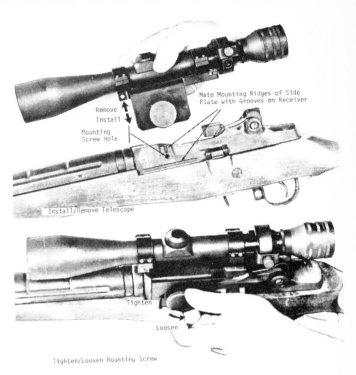

Installation and removal of ART and mount.

down of American participation in the war in Indochina, work on newer sniper rifle concepts was terminated. Current US sniper rifles include the M21 and M1C for the Army and the M40 for the Marine Corps.

The telescopic sight used on the M21 deserves some comment. Having variable power magnification—3 to 9—the scope is intended for adjustable ranging between 300 and 900 meters. When set on 3 power and aimed at a target 300 meters distant, the two vertical marks above and below the cross hairs (stadia) mark out a distance of 762mm (30 in.), the approximate distance between the average infantryman's belt buckle and the top of his helmet. By bracketing those features in the stadia on the average human target, the sniper can place the cross hairs at the midpoint of the target's chest. If the range is greater than 300 meters, the magnification ring on the scope is used to increase the size of the image until once again the two vertical stadia rest on the belt and helmet of the target. This adjustable ranging feature removed much of the guesswork from aiming at a target. It thus increased markedly the lethality of the rifle/telescope combination. This ART scope has been ballistically matched with the US M118 NATO match ammunition.

M21 Sniper Rifle with Adjustable Ranging Telescope.

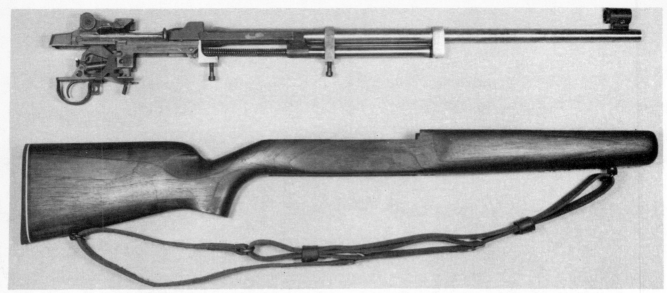

Prototype for an improved M14 National Match Rifle. Note heavy target type barrel, modified gas system, target type stock and two point screw down bedding mounts.

TEST FIXTURE , 7.62 mm
XM21 , MODIFIED

Prototype for an improved M21 Sniper Rifle. Note bullpup type stock, heavy barrel and modified gas system.

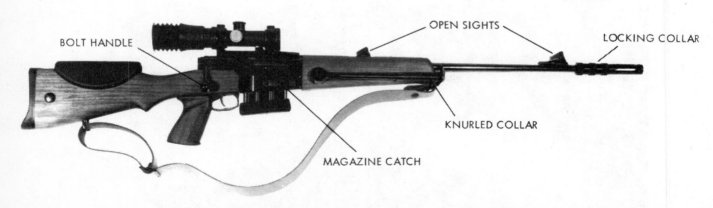

French FR-F1 Sniper Rifle. Available in both 7.5 × 55.5mm and 7.62 × 51mm NATO.

Steyr-Daimler-Puch 7.62 × 51mm NATO *Scharfshutzengewehr* **(SSG).**

Heckler & Koch 7.62 × 51mm NATO G3SG/1 Sniping Rifle. Note set trigger.

HK33SG/1 5.56 × 45mm Sniper Rifle with set trigger.

HK33A2ZF. Standard 5.56 × 45mm Rifle with telescope but no set trigger.

SOVIET DRAGUNOV SNIPER RIFLE

The Soviet Union adopted a new self-loading sniper rifle in 1963, designed by sporting rifle specialist Yevgeniy Fyedorovich Dragunov. Called the *Samozaridnyia Vintovka Dragunova* (SVD), this 10-shot weapon chambered for the full power 7.62 × 54R cartridge is an evolution of the Kalashnikov operating mechanism. Unlike the AK and PK weapons, the Dragunov does not use a long stroke piston system. That type of gas system tends to be rather heavy for a large caliber rifle, and the motion of that mass during the firing cycle changes the rifle's center of gravity, which in turn reduces the accuracy of the rifle. In the Dragunov, the designer employed a short stroke piston system. The piston, which is separate from the bolt carrier, delivers its impulse to the carrier, which then moves to the rear. The remainder of the operating sequence is quite similar to the Kalashnikov assault rifle. A commercial Soviet rifle, the *Medved* ("Bear"), embodies the basic operating mechanism of the SVD.

While not as sophisticated as the American ART scope, the Soviet PSO-1 telescope, nevertheless, contains some unique features. A range finder scale located in the lower left of the telescope is graduated to the height of a man 1702mm (67 in.). By placing the horizontal line at the foot of the target and following the curved line to the head of the target, one can estimate the range in hundreds of meters. There are alternative aiming marks on the reticle for ranges above 1,000 meters. In addition, the PSO-1 scope has a battery powered element that will illuminate the reticle under poor visibility conditions. And finally, the scope has an infrared detecting filter that can be used at night to detect infrared night vision devices. This filter can also be used with an external infrared spot light to help illuminate targets. (See Chapter 43.)

MISCELLANEOUS SNIPER RIFLES

In addition to the standard Austrian, French, US and Soviet sniper rifles, Fabrique Nationale has produced a new weapon that is essentially a highly accurate Mauser bolt action rifle. FN formerly manufactured a sniper version of the FAL. Heckler & Koch produce a sniper version of the G3, the G3SG/1, which is used by German police forces. This weapon has a special set trigger unit that permits more precise adjustment of the trigger pull. The British use a 7.62 × 51mm NATO caliber version of the older Lee Enfield. This weapon, the L42A1, is essentially a reworked version of the No. 4 Rifle. Other older weapons, such as the Australian Spartco M44 Sniper Rifle, may still be found in use, but most have been out of production for some time.

Soviet *Samozaridnyia Vintovka Dragunova* (SVD) 7.62 × 54Rmm Sniper Rifle.

Close-up View of the Soviet SVD Receiver and telescopic sight.

FIRING PORT WEAPONS

Introduction of the Armored Personnel Carrier (APC) as a means of transporting infantry troops has led to the development of modified small arms that can be fired from the inside of the APC. During the 1939–1945 conflict, both Allied and Axis forces discovered the vulnerability of armored fighting vehicles to individuals with hand carried explosive charges. During that war, the German *Wehrmacht* experimented with a special curved barrel attachment (Krummlauf) for the *Sturmgewehr 43,* developed by the Unterluss Laboratory of Rheinmetall-Borsig. Equipped with this barrel and a periscopic sight, the tank crew could fire the *Stg 43* and keep opposing forces off the vehicle's back.

More recently, the US and the USSR have begun using Armored Personnel Carriers. The newer ones include a provision whereby the infantrymen inside can fire out of the vehicle. The Soviets introduced a folding stock version of the modernized Kalashnikov assault rifle—the AKMS—which can be fired through special ports in the sides of vehicles such as the BRDM APC. Cadillac Gage's XM706 Commando Armored Car had firing ports and vision blocks so that the Stoner 63 rifle or carbine could be fired from inside the squad compartment. Passengers could thereby provide perimeter defense for the vehicle. Combat experience demonstrated that conventional weapons produced high levels of carbon monoxide and gun smoke that were both dangerous and discomfiting for the individuals inside the vehicle.

Heckler & Koch's MICV Firing Port Weapon (Modified HK53).

The HK54 9mm Parabellum Submachine Gun mounted in Heckler & Koch's combination vision block/firing port.

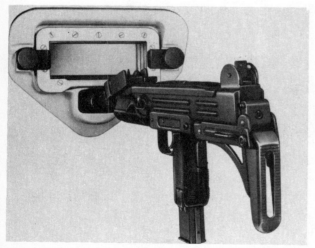

UZI Submachine Gun adapted to HK's vision block/firing port.

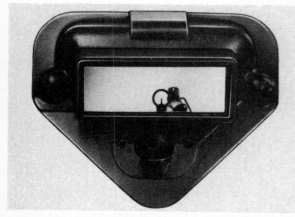

External view of HK vision block/firing port. Note ball swivel joint.

As a result of these experiences and the requirement for a Firing Port Weapon (FPW) for the XM723 Mechanized Infantry Combat Vehicle (MICV), the Small Arms Systems Laboratory at Rock Island began in 1972 to work on weapons modified so that the gas system would exhaust the operating gases outside the squad compartment. Because of the high cyclic rate requested, the weapons fired from an open bolt. In addition, test weapons were fitted with a barrel sleeve that in turn permitted the weapon to be mounted in the ball and socket mount in the side of the MICV. Two 5.56mm candidates, a modified M16A1 and a modified HK33, and a control weapon, the M3A1 submachine gun, were subjected to a Development Test/Operational Test I. After these tests, a Concept Validation In-Process Review was held in May 1974. The modified M16A1 was selected for advanced development and was designated the XM231.

As a consequence of the DT/I testing, two weapon performance areas (reliability and hit probability) were singled out for further study. The XM231, which then had a 279-mm (11.0-in.) barrel, had a cyclic rate of about 1,050 shots per minute. Experimentation indicated that a reduction of the rate of fire down to 200 rounds per minute improved the probability of hits. However, the overall shock power of six weapons (two on each side and two to the rear), each firing away at over a thousand shots per minute, was sacrificed. Additional study indicated that hit probability could be increased by using all tracer ammunition. In the reliability field, extractors were improved and bolts were modified to reduce incidence of bolt fractures that accompanied the high rate of fire. A DT/OT II was run in late 1976 and early 1977. The XM231s used in the Operational Test/II were equipped with a short handguard, flip-up sights and a M3A1 type collapsible wire buttstock for use as a dismounted weapon. These additions are only expected to permit the weapon to be used as a Personal Defense Weapon when all other means of defense have failed. Some weapons specialists opposed these additions because the XM231 Firing Port Weapon is not really suited for use as a shoulder fired weapon. In April 1977, the XM231 had the following characteristics:

Caliber: 5.56 × 45mm.
System of operation: Gas, modified M16A1 type.
Length overall: 699mm (27.5 in.)
Barrel length: 368mm (14.5 in.) (w/o suppressor).
Feed device: 30-round M16A1 box magazine.
Weight: 3.9 kg (8.5 lbs.).
Cyclic rate: 950–1000 r.p.m.

Standardization of this weapon can be expected in the next couple of years.

XM231 Firing Port Weapon with stock collapsed. Note modified buffer.

Flip-up Front Sight

Stock Catch Release

Firing Port Mounting Point

Short Handguard

XM231 Firing Port Weapon with stock extended.

SILENCED WEAPONS

While silenced weapons have generally been regarded as the armament of secret agents and Hollywood film script writers, a substantial number of silenced weapons have been developed since 1945 for use by specialized military forces. During the 1939–1945 war, the M3A1 and Sten submachine guns were among the leading weapons fitted with silencers, but they were still noisy due to the movement of the open bolt. Less well known were the Mark I Hand Firing Device and the Sleeve Gun. The former was made in both 7.65mm (.32 ACP) and 9mm, while the latter was produced in 7.65mm only. These weapons, issued to US Office of Strategic Services and British Special Operations Executive personnel, had silenced mechanisms as well as silenced projectiles. Since that time, developments have

taken two approaches. First is the true silencer, used with reduced velocity projectiles so that there is no sonic boom as the projectile breaks the sound barrier (335 m.p.s. [1100 f.p.s.]). Second are the noise suppressors, such as the muzzle device used on the Colt XM177E1 and XM177E2 carbines; another suppressor confuses the source of the sound, typified by the Sionics suppressor formerly marketed by Military Armaments Corporation. It should be noted that silenced weapons and silencers are classified as registerable and transfer taxable items under Title II of the US Gun Control Act of 1968.

A review of some of the major developments is all that is possible in this volume.

Two World War II silenced pistols: Top, the Mark I Hand Firing Device (also known as the Welrod). Bottom, the Sleeve Gun. Both weapons fired the .32 Colt (7.65 × 17) Pistol Cartridge.

Czech 7.65mm Model 27 Pistol of wartime manufacture; this pistol has special barrel to be used with silencer.

PEOPLE'S REPUBLIC OF CHINA

The PRC has developed two silenced pistols and a silenced submachine gun since the early 1960s. The Type 64 Silenced Pistol is intended as an assassination weapon. It can be either manually operated or shot as a self-loader. When the complete effect of the silencer is desired, the slide can be locked shut so that it will not recoil open when the pistol is fired. A special 7.65 × 17mm cartridge similar to but not interchangeable with the semi-rimmed .32 ACP round is used with this pistol. Overall length of the Type 64 is 330mm (13 in.), and it weighs 1.27 kg (2.8 lbs.).

A newer and improved version of the Type 64—the Type 67— has been introduced. The basic action and caliber has been retained, and a new tubular silencer has supplanted the older and more ungainly Type 64 suppressor.

Disassembled view of the PRC Type 64 Silenced Pistol.

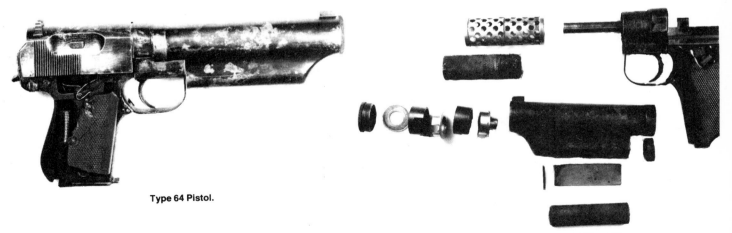

Type 64 Pistol.

Internal view of Type 64 Pistol Silencer.

There is also a Chinese-designed and manufactured silenced submachine gun, the Type 64, that has seen service in recent years. The basic bolt mechanism was borrowed from the Soviet PPS43; the trigger mechanism was patterned after the British Bren gun. The silencer is of the basic Maxim type with a larger tube surrounding a vented barrel. The length of the barrel is 203mm (8 in.), and the length of the tube is 368mm (14.5 in.).

The forward portion of the silencer has a 165-mm (6.5-in.) stack of baffles to help reduce the sound. Chambered for the 7.62 × 25mm cartridge, this weapon has a muzzle velocity of 512 m.p.s. (1681 f.p.s.) and a cyclic rate of 1315 rounds per minute. Together, these two elements keep the gun from being an effectively silenced weapon. Reportedly, the Type 64 is no longer in service.

BRITAIN

During World War II, the British issued three different silenced versions of the Sten gun—Mark IIS, Mark IVA and Mark VI. In 1964, George W. Patchett devised a silenced version of the Sterling Submachine Gun that was adopted by the British Army as the L34A1 Submachine Gun. Sterling markets a commercial model for police use as the Mark 5. The accompanying illustration shows the internal construction of the Sterling silencer. Loaded, the L34A1 weighs 4.31 kg (9.5 lbs.).

Sterling Armament Company's Mark 5 Silenced 9mm Parabellum Submachine Gun.

THE OPERATION OF THE SILENCER. To silence a firearm effectively it is necessary not only to silence the noise of the discharge but also to ensure that the bullet leaves the weapon at below the speed of sound (1088 feet per sec/332 metres per sec, in still air), to eliminate the 'crack' caused by the bullet passing through the sound barrier. This is achieved by diverting some of the gases propelling the bullet through 72 small holes drilled into the rifling of the barrel. The diverted gases pass into the diffuser tube, through the holes in the tube into the expanded metal wrap and are contained by the silencer casing. These gases are dissipated partially through holes in the front barrel support and partially by returning to the barrel. By the time the bullet leaves the barrel most of the column of gas has been broken up.

The gases emerging from the barrel and front barrel support are subjected to a swirling motion imparted by the spiral diffuser before passing into the front expansion chamber where the leading gases are deflected backwards by the special internal profile of the front cap.

The bullet leaves the weapon at a subsonic velocity of approximately 1000 feet per sec (308 metres per sec) and is followed by a smooth silenced flow of gas.

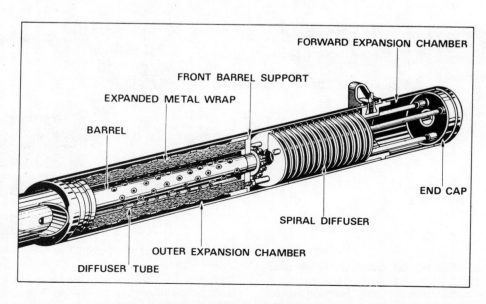

Description of Sterling Submachine Gun Silencer Assembly.

CZECHOSLOVAKIA

The M61 Skorpion has been issued with a silencer attachment that likely is only moderately effective given the high cyclic rate of this weapon.

GERMANY

Both the Walther MPL and Heckler & Koch HK54 submachine guns have been offered with silencers. In the case of the Walther, the silencer is an attachment.

Heckler & Koch's MP5SD2 is a more extensively modified weapon. Like the Chinese Type 64 submachine gun, the MP5SD2 has a vented barrel surrounded by an outer jacket into which the propellant gases can expand. Inside the jacket, there is a helix, which slows the gases down. Both the projectile and the gases exit at subsonic velocities. Loaded, this weapon weighs around 3.14 kg (6.9 lbs.), depending on the stock configuration.

Assembled and disassembled views of the HK MP5SD2 Silenced Submachine Gun.

NORTH KOREA

As noted in Chapter 4, the North Koreans adopted a copy of the Model 1900 Browning Pistol as their 7.62mm Type 64. A version of this weapon has been adapted as a silenced pistol.

North Korean Type 64 Silenced Pistol.

UNITED STATES

During the Vietnam conflict, the US Navy sponsored development of a silenced pistol for use by its SEAL Teams (Sea, Air and Land). Nicknamed the "Hush-Puppy" because of its intended function of killing enemy watch dogs, this modified version of the steel framed Smith & Wesson Model 39 Pistol was put to other clandestine uses as well. Called the Mark 22, Mod. O Pistol by the Navy, the Hush-Puppy had a slide lock to keep the mechanism closed and silent while firing. It fired a special green tipped 9mm Parabellum projectile weighing 10.2 grams (158 grains) that yielded a muzzle velocity of 274 m.p.s. (900 f.p.s.), below the speed of sound. Use of standard supersonic ammunition quickly degrades the effectiveness of the silencer insert. With subsonic ammunition, an insert is good for about 30 rounds; with standard velocity cartridges the insert may have to be replaced after six shots. Official Navy designation for the silencer is Mark 3, Mod. O. Ammunition and replacement silencer parts are supplied as Accessory Kit MK26, Mod. O. Each accessory kit includes 24 9mm Pistol Cartridges MK144, Mod. O and one silencer tube insert.

All the work on the Model 39 Hush-Puppy was carried out by Smith & Wesson before the end of 1968. Subsequently, Smith & Wesson provided two prototype 13-shot pistols made from stainless steel. These weapons were improved to overcome problems such as extractor breakages, which had been experienced with the Model 39. This modified pistol in a slightly different form was later commercially marketed as the Model 59 Smith & Wesson 9mm Parabellum Pistol.

SCALE INCHES

US Navy Mark 22, Mod. O Silenced 9mm Parabellum Pistol with holster.

WOX–13A
9 MM PISTOL

WOX–1A GUN
SILENCER

SHOULDER
STOCK

SCALE INCHES

Mark 22, Mod. O Pistol (Experimental Designation WOX-13A) with shoulder stock.

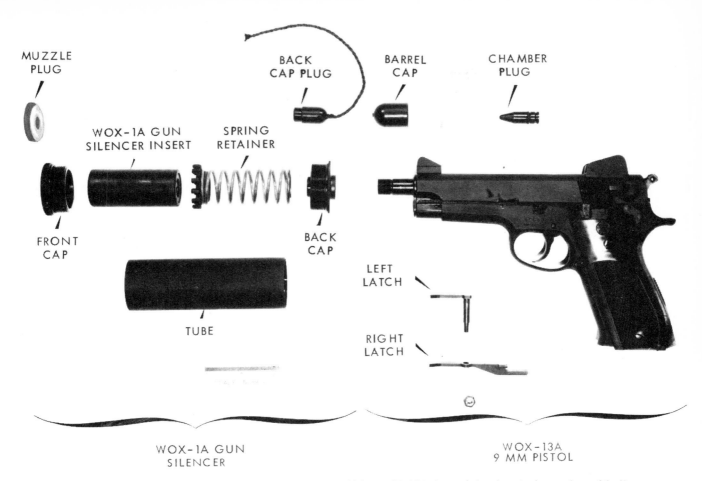

MUZZLE PLUG

BACK CAP PLUG

BARREL CAP

CHAMBER PLUG

WOX-1A GUN SILENCER INSERT

SPRING RETAINER

FRONT CAP

BACK CAP

TUBE

LEFT LATCH

RIGHT LATCH

WOX-1A GUN SILENCER

WOX-13A 9 MM PISTOL

Mark 22, Mod. O Pistol equipped with special caps and plugs, which permitted it to be carried underwater by members of the Navy SEAL Teams.

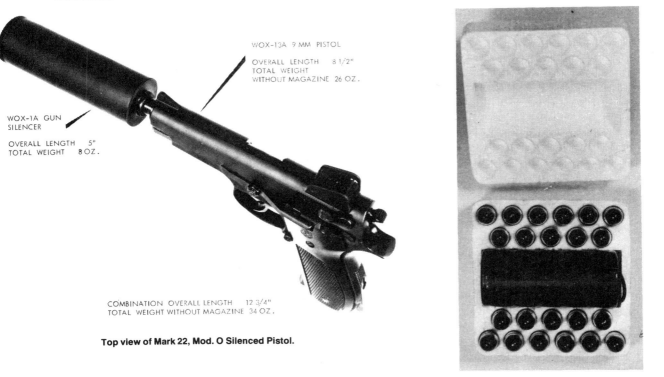

WOX-13A 9 MM PISTOL

OVERALL LENGTH 8 1/2"
TOTAL WEIGHT
WITHOUT MAGAZINE 26 OZ.

WOX-1A GUN SILENCER

OVERALL LENGTH 5"
TOTAL WEIGHT 8 OZ.

COMBINATION OVERALL LENGTH 12 3/4"
TOTAL WEIGHT WITHOUT MAGAZINE 34 OZ.

Top view of Mark 22, Mod. O Silenced Pistol.

Mark 26, Mod. O Accessory Kit.

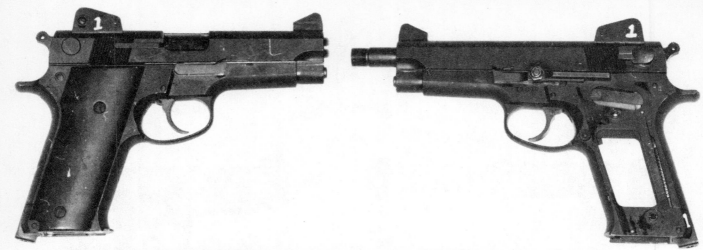

Experimental 15-shot Smith & Wesson Pistol developed for the US Navy. A later version was marketed as the Model 59. In this prototype, note lock on both sides of the slide.

Experimental M16A1 (Note modified upper receiver.) fitted with Sionics Noise Suppressor.

An unofficial, but nevertheless interesting, development is the M10 and M11 Submachine Guns mentioned in Chapter 3. Military Armaments Corporation, while in business, offered both weapons with their own Sionics noise suppressors. The accompanying illustrations show the M11 compared with the Uzi and the interior construction of the Sionics suppressor.

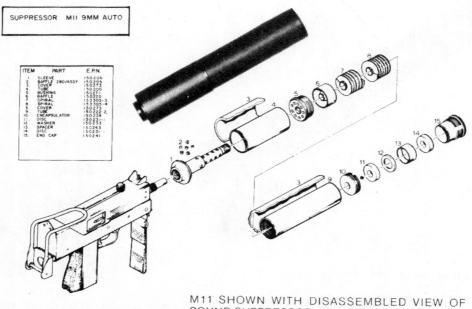

M11 SHOWN WITH DISASSEMBLED VIEW OF
SOUND SUPPRESSOR (SILENCER).

M11

WITH

Loaded 32 round magazine

COMPARISON SHOWS SIZE AND POTENTIAL FIRE- POWER OF M11 WHEN COMPARED TO CONVENTIONAL SUBMACHINE GUNS.

TECHNICAL SPECIFICATIONS FOR M11:

INCHES

Length without stock	8.75 (222 MM)
Length stock extended	18.11 (460 MM)
Barrel length	5.06 (129 MM)
Weight gun with empty magazine	3.50 lbs (1.57 Kg)
Type of fire	Selected semi-automatic or full automatic.
Cyclic rate of fire	Approx. 1200 rounds per minute.
Front sight	Protected post.
Rear sight	Fixed aperture for 50 meters.
Safety arrangements	Two manually operated "safe" positions for locking bolt in open or closed position.

The retracting knob will lock the bolt in closed position by rotating the knob 90 degrees.

The weapon employs blowback operation and fires the .380 ACP (9mm Kurz) cartridge.

A second safety is located to the side and slightly forward of the trigger guard on the right hand side of the weapon. Pulling the safety lever to the rear locks the bolt in open or closed position.

M21 Sniper Rifle with Sionics Noise Suppressor.

PART 2

A Basic Manual of Current Weapons

6
Argentina

The Argentine Army is currently equipped with the 7.62mm NATO FN FAL rifle, manufactured at the Fabrica Militar de Armes Portatiles Domingo Matheu at Rosario, Santa Fe. The heavy barrel version of this weapon is also produced at Rosario. The current standard pistol is the 9mm Browning High Power, made at Rosario. Formerly, the caliber .45 M1916 and M1927 automatic pistols, copies of the Colt M1911 and M1911A1 respectively were standard. The FN 7.62mm NATO MAG machine gun is replacing the 7.65mm Browning light and heavy machine guns, which were standard for many years, as were a few 7.65mm Madsen machine guns. The caliber .50 Browning machine gun is the standard weapon used on armored vehicles. The 9mm P.A.M. 1 and P.A.M. 2, Rosario products, are standard submachine guns.

The Argentine police use the following: 7.65mm M1891 carbine, Star full automatic pistol, Israeli UZI submachine gun, US Caliber .45 M1928A1 and M1 Thompson.

ARGENTINE PISTOLS

Argentina has manufactured copies of the caliber .45 Colt M1911 and M1911A1, called the M1916 and M1927 respectively.

ARGENTINE BALLESTER MOLINA PISTOL

The firm "HAFDASA" of Buenos Aires manufactured the Ballester Molina and Ballester Rigand pistols. This firm is no longer in business, and the pistols are no longer being manufactured. The Ballester Molina caliber .45 pistol is still in wide use as it was manufactured in quantity during World War II.

The Ballester Molina is a slightly modified copy of the Colt .45 M1911A1 pistol. Loading, firing and functioning of the pistol are the same as for the US pistol.

Characteristics of the Ballester Molina

Caliber: 45 M1911 automatic pistol cartridge.
System of operation: Recoil, semiautomatic fire only.
Weight, empty: 2.25 lbs.
Length, overall: 8.5 in.

Barrel length: 5 in.
Feed device: 7-round, single column, detachable box magazine.
Sights: Front, blade; rear, notched bar.
Muzzle velocity: 830 f.p.s.

Major Differences Between the Ballester Molina and the Colt M1911A1

Hammer strut: The hammer strut is much smaller than that of the US M1911A1. It is 0.75 inches in length and 0.158 inches in diameter.

Firing pin stop: The firing pin stop is not recessed on the sides, as it is on the US models.

Safety lock: The safety lock is redesigned and the pin is larger in diameter than the safety lock pin on the US model.

Mainspring housing: The mainspring housing, although arched as in the US Model M1911A1, is an integral part of the receiver.

Trigger: The Argentine pistol has a pivoting trigger. An extension from the trigger, along the right side, cams the disconnector and engages the sear.

Argentine caliber .45 M1927 pistol

Caliber .45 Ballester Molina pistol.

Magazine and magazine catch: The magazines are interchangeable. The magazine catch is located in the same place as the catch on the US M1911A1. The assembly of the catch is somewhat different, but it operates in the same manner as the US model.

Slide: There is no slide stop disassembly notch as on the US models.

Field Stripping the Ballester Molina

Disassembly is the same as for the US M1911A1, except that the pin for the hammer and the sear must be driven out. The trigger is held by a trigger pin. Upon removing the trigger and the trigger extension, the disconnector can be removed downward. After the sear has been removed, the main spring can be removed.

Argentine 7.65mm M1905 pistol.

7.65mm M1905 MANNLICHER PISTOL

This was formerly the Argentine service pistol, and quantities of them were sold to surplus arms dealers in the US. The pistol was developed at Steyr and introduced commercially in 1901. The weapon is essentially a blowback-operated type and is loaded with a stripper type clip (charger) from the top. The weapon can be unloaded from the top by pulling the slide to the rear and pulling down the catch on the right side of the pistol.

Characteristics of the 7.65mm M1905 Mannlicher Pistol

Caliber: 7.65mm Mannlicher (called 7.63mm Mannlicher in Austria).
System of operation: Blowback with slight retardation.
Weight: 2 lbs.
Length overall: 9.62 in.
Barrel length: 6.31 in.
Feed device: 8 round non-detachable box magazine.
Sights: Front, blade; rear, notch.
Muzzle velocity: approx. 1025 f.p.s.

ARGENTINE RIFLES

RIFLES IN USE

The M1891 Argentine Mauser is quite similar to the 7.65mm M1890 Turkish Mauser. The M1909 Mauser is a slight modification of the German Gewehr 98 (rifle 98).

The M1891 Carbine is still used as a police weapon, but the rifles are obsolete. The FN 7.62mm NATO FAL rifle and the 7.62mm NATO heavy-barrel rifles are now standard.

Characteristics of the M1891 and M1909 Argentine Mausers

	M1891	M1909
Caliber:	7.65mm rimless.	7.65mm rimless.
System of operation:	Manually operated bolt action.	Manually operated bolt action.
Length, overall:	48.6 in.	49 in.
Barrel length:	29.1 in.	29.1 in.
Feed device:	5-round, single column, box magazine.	5-round, staggered-row box magazine.
Sights: Front	Barleycorn.	Barleycorn.
Rear	Leaf.	Tangent leaf.
Muzzle velocity: (w/spitzer-pointed ball)	2755 f.p.s.	2755 f.p.s.
Weight (empty):	8.58 lbs.	9.2 lbs.

7.65mm Model 1891 Argentine Mauser.

7.65mm Model 1909 Argentine Mauser.

ARGENTINE CARBINES

Argentina has had a number of 7.65mm Mauser carbines in service. The Model 1891 carbine is stocked to the muzzle, has a 17.6 inch barrel and is 37 inches overall. There are two versions, one with and one without bayonet lug. There are four common versions of the Model 1909 carbine. The cavalry carbine is stocked to the muzzle. Some cavalry carbines have bayonet lugs and others do not. The Engineer carbine has a typical military stock and a bayonet stud, which protrudes horizontally from the upper band like that of the German Mauser 98. A carbine similar to the Engineer carbine, sometimes called the Mountain carbine, has a bayonet stud, which protrudes vertically in front of and below the upper band.

A large number of these weapons have been converted into sporters in Argentina.

ARGENTINE SUBMACHINE GUNS

NEW MODELS

The Fabrica Militar de Armas Portatiles at Rosario is currently producing a new submachine gun designated the PA3-DM. Available in both fixed and collapsible stock versions, this gun has a bolt that telescopes the rear portion of the 285-mm (11.4-in.) barrel and a magazine well in the pistol grip, similar to the Israeli UZI.

THE "MEMS" SUBMACHINE GUNS

The firm of Armas & Equipos S.R.L. located in Cordoba, Argentina, has developed a series of light, easily manufactured submachine guns. These are the Models 52/58, 52/60, AR 163 and 67. All are generally similar in design being conventional blow-back operated guns making extensive use of stamping and fabrications in their design. The Model 67 is advertised as being particularly suitable as a counter-insurgency weapon because of its relative simplicity and ease of manufacture. All parts, excepting the barrel, are made with low tolerances. The barrels have microgroove rifling.

OLDER MODELS

The older guns in Argentina are the Ballester Molina caliber .45 Type C3, the Halcon caliber .45 M1946, the Halcon caliber .45 M1943, the P.A.M. 1, a 9mm copy of the US M3A1 made at the government arsenal at Rosario and the 9mm Ballester Rigaud and HAFDASA C-4. The P.A.M. 2 is also made at Rosario. With the exception of the P.A.M. 2, it is believed that all the older Argentine submachine guns are out of production. The characteristics of Argentine submachine guns follow:

Argentine 9mm Parabellum "MEMS" Model 52/60 Submachine Gun.

Argentine 9mm Parabellum "MEMS" Model AR63 Submachine Gun.

Argentine 9mm Parabellum "MEMS" Model 52/58 Submachine Gun.

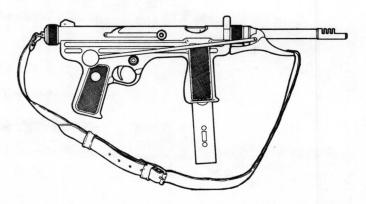

Argentine 9mm Parabellum "MEMS" Model 67 Submachine Gun.

CHARACTERISTICS OF ARGENTINE SUBMACHINE GUNS

Weapon	Caliber	Type of operation	Overall length	Feed device	Barrel length	Cyclic rate	Muzzle velocity	Weight
Ballester Molina C3	.45	Blowback selective fire	33.2 in.	40-round detachable staggered box magazine	12.62 in.	500-600 rpm	900 fps	8.6 lbs.
Halcon M1943	.45	Blowback selective fire	33.40 in.	17-or 30-round detachable, staggered box magazine	11.5 in. W/ compensator	700 rpm	950 fps	10.45 lbs.
Halcon M1946	.45	Blowback selective fire	Stock folded; 24.4 in. Stock extended: 31.1 in.	17-or 30-round detachable, staggered box magazine	6 in.	700 rpm	920 fps	8.90 lbs.
Hafdasa C-4	9mm Parabellum	Blowback selective fire	Stock folded: 21 in. Stock extended: 31.2 in.	30-round detachable, in-line box magazine	7.75 in.	600 rpm	1200 fps	7 lbs.
Halcon M.L. 57	9mm Parabellum	Blowback selective fire	Stock folded: 21 in. Stock extended: 30.7 in.	40-round detachable, staggered box magazine	8.86 in.	520 rpm	1200 fps (approx.)	6.95 lbs.
P.A.M. 1	9mm Parabellum	Blowback full automatic	Stock folded: 21.2 in. Stock extended: 28.6 in.	30-round detachable, in-line box magazine	7.9 in.	450 rpm	1200 fps (approx.)	6.6 lbs.
Model 52/58	9mm Parabellum	Blowback full automatic	Stock extended: 35.2 in.	40-round detachable, staggered box magazine	12 in. (approx.)	750-800 rpm	1200 fps (approx.)	6.8 lbs.
Model 52/60	9mm Parabellum	Blowback selective fire	Stock extended: 35 in.	40-round detachable, staggered box magazine	12 in. (approx.)	750-600 rpm	1200 fps (approx.)	6.8 lbs.
Model AR 163	9mm Parabellum	Blowback selective	Stock extended: 35 in.	40-round detachable, staggered box magazine	12 in. (approx.)	750-800 rpm	1200 fps (approx.)	6.8 lbs.
MEMS M67	9mm Parabellum	Blowback selective	Stock folded: 25.6 in. Stock extended: 34.7 in.	40-round detachable, staggered row magazine	7.9 in.	750-800 rpm	1100 fps (approx.)	6.1 lbs.
PA3-DM	9mm Parabellum	Blowback selective	Stock folded: 20.6 in. Stock extended: 27.3 in.	25-round detachable, staggered magazine	11.4 in.	650 rpm	1312 fps (approx.)	7.6 lbs.

7

Australia

With the establishment of the government rifle factory at Lithgow in 1912, Australia began to manufacture rifles. Production of the caliber .303 Rifle No. 1 Mark III* continued until 1955. While they never adopted the No. 4 rifle, a lightweight modification of the No. 1 rifle, called the Rifle No. 6 (Aust), was developed at Lithgow during World War II, but it was not produced in quantity. Lithgow and its feeder plants produced a total of 640,000 Lee Enfields before the end of manufacture. Today, Australia uses the 7.62mm NATO FN FAL rifles as modified by the UK (L1A1). A few US 5.56mm M16 rifles have been tested by Australian forces.

The Australians have shown considerable design interest in submachine guns; the Austen, Owen and current issue F1A1 are described below.

Other current issue weapons include the US 7.62mm NATO M60 machine gun, the Bren gun converted to 7.62mm NATO and the Caliber .50 Browning machine guns.

AUSTRALIAN SUBMACHINE GUNS

Australia has produced a number of native submachine gun designs. The Austen and the Owen were developed during World War II and were considered excellent designs for their time.

THE AUSTEN SUBMACHINE GUNS

These guns were made by Diecasters Ltd. and W. T. Carmichael of Melbourne. About 20,000 guns were made during World War II. Although the Austen resembles the British Sten externally, internally it resembles the German MP 38 and MP 40 (Schmeisser). The Austen has the same telescoping type cover over its recoil spring and firing pin assembly as do the MP 38 and MP 40.

Australlian 9mm Austen Mark I Submachine Gun, no longer being made.

Characteristics of the Mark I Austen

Caliber: 9mm Parabellum.
System of operation: Blowback, selective fire.
Length overall: Stock fixed: 33.25 in.
               Stock folded: 22 in.
Barrel length: 7.8 in.
Weight: 9.2 lbs.
Feed device: 32-round, detachable, staggered row box magazine.
Sights; Front: Barley corn.
        Rear: Aperture set for 100 yards.
Muzzle velocity: Approx. 1280 f.p.s.
Cyclic rate: 500-550 r.p.m.

How the Austen Gun Works

Follow standard procedures for the Sten gun or the Schmeisser MP38/MP40.

Loading and Firing the Austen

Standard blowback submachine gun. See Sten gun or Schmeisser MP38/MP40 for detailed description.

THE MARK II AUSTEN SUBMACHINE GUN

A later version of the Austen machine carbine was also introduced. This design, known as the Mark II, resembles the original in outward appearance but differs radically in construction.

The receiver consists of two pieces of cast aluminum and represents an endeavor on the part of the designers to speed up production and at the same time provide a sturdy weapon.

The receiver may be separated when stripping the weapon by pushing a button just ahead of the front hand grip on the left side, then pulling back on the rear grip. The rear section of the receiver containing the trigger mechanism will come straight back out of its joint with the front section.

The barrel rests in the front section of the aluminum receiver,

while a cylindrical steel bolt travel-piece acts as a barrel extension. It is attached to the barrel but extends back into the rear section of the aluminum receiver. Both the barrel extension and the rear of the receiver are cut away to permit travel of the cocking handle to be unimpeded. Note that the bolt travels back and forth in this steel barrel extension—at no time does it come in touch with the aluminum receiver shell. The customary Sten type push-through button is provided to give single-shot or full automatic fire.

As the tube in which the bolt travels is of heavy steel and is partly enclosed in and cushioned by the aluminum receiver, injury to or deformation of the travel tube is not as likely to occur as in submachine guns made from straight steel stampings. The bolt and recoil spring tube, as in the Mark I Model, follow the Schmeisser design.

Field Stripping the Mark I Austen

Push down on stock locking plunger and bend the stock down out of line with the rear of the gun.

With the left thumb, press in on the head of the spring tube protruding through the back of the gun. With the right hand, grasp the stock firmly and

slide it down out of its locking groove in the rear of the receiver. Lift out the buffer cap.

Pull back the cocking handle, which will bring the recoil and buffer spring tube back and pull the telescoping tube out of the receiver.

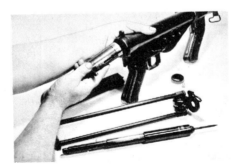

Now pull the bolt back out of the gun. The extractor may be punched out of the bolt if necessary.

With the fingers of the left hand, pull back the barrel nut catch against its spring tension (it is at the front end of the magazine housing on the left side of the gun), and with the right hand unscrew the barrel casing and barrel nut to the right.

Pull the barrel nut and casing forward out of the receiver. Pull barrel straight forward out of the receiver.

This completes field stripping.

THE OWEN SUBMACHINE GUN

Over 40,000 Owen submachine guns were made by Lysaghts Newcastle Works, New Castle, South Wales, Australia, during World War II. The Owen is somewhat unusual in having a top-mounted magazine, like the current F1A1, and a quick-change barrel. The ease of barrel removal is of help in maintenance of the weapon, but is not intended for change in battle as are the quick change barrels of machine guns.

Characteristics of the Owen Mark I

Caliber: 9mm Parabellum.
System of operation: Blowback, selective fire.
Length overall: 31.8 in.
Barrel length: 9.8 in.
Weight: 9.37 lbs.
Feed device: 30-round, detachable staggered row, box magazine.
Sights; Front: Off-set barley corn.
      Rear: Off-set aperture.
Muzzle velocity: Approx. 1300 f.p.s.
Cyclic rate: 800 r.p.m.

How to Load and Fire the Owen

When a loaded magazine is inserted in the housing on top of the receiver and pushed in until it locks, pulling the cocking handle back until the bolt is caught and held by the sear leaves the gun ready for firing. The gun may be set to fire a shot for each pull of the trigger or for full automatic fire as long as the trigger is held and cartridges feed.

It will be noted that the barrel is equipped with a compensator at the muzzle to help hold the gun down when firing, with radial cooling surfaces near the breech end. The barrel catch releases the barrel and front grip for speedy removal under favorable conditions.

The operating spring and guide are mounted in standard fashion in the head of the bolt and within the receiver tunnel, where they are retained by the cap at the rear.

The metal skeleton stock is easily removed by pressing the spring held catch mounted within its forward section.

How the Owen Works

When a loaded magazine is in position and the bolt is withdrawn to its fullest extent, if the change lever is set for single-shot fire, pressure on the trigger forces the rear end of the sear out of contact with the bolt. As the operating spring starts to drive the bolt forward, the bent on the front end of the sear slips over the bent on the trigger permitting the sear to return to its former position under action of the sear spring. This leaves it free to engage and hold the bolt when it returns to the rear.

As the bolt is driven forward by the operating spring, either the right or the left upper feed piece machined in the bolt strikes the base of the first cartridge in the magazine and drives it straight ahead through the opening in the front end of the magazine lips.

The bullet nose is guided by the barrel feed into the chamber as the rear of the cartridge clears the lips of the magazine. As the cartridge enters the chamber, it lines up with the bolt, enabling the head of the cartridge to seat in the base of the bolt head recess, in which the firing pin is machined.

The cartridge comes to rest when the front end of the case stops against the square shoulder at the front end of the chamber. As the cartridge comes to rest, the bolt continues forward to drive the firing pin against the primer and discharge the cartridge. At this time, the extractor is sprung over the groove in the cartridge case.

The gases generated in the cartridge case drive the light bullet forward and exert rearward pressure through the base of the cartridge case to the base of the bolt head. The bolt starts to the rear, but in view of the much greater weight of the moving parts and the spring tension in relation to the comparatively light bullet weight, the action does not open appreciably until the bullet has left the muzzle. By this time, the breech pressure has dropped to a safe limit.

When the bullet emerges from the muzzle, the gas behind it expands in the compensator.

The pressure wave thus created thrusts downward against the solid lower half of the compensator while the gases expanding upward strike against the inclined surfaces cut into the compensator to result in a forward and downward thrust at the muzzle end. This tends to hold the muzzle down during automatic fire.

(Note that the compensator merely acts to stabilize the gun. It has nothing whatever to do with the functioning of the weapon itself.)

As the bolt starts to the rear, the empty cartridge case is held in the bolt face gripped by the extractor. When it clears the chamber far enough, the upper face of the cartridge strikes the ejector (which in the Owen is a part of the rear magazine wall). The empty shell is hurled out the ejection opening, which in this weapon is in the lower part of the receiver tube.

The bolt continues to travel to the rear in a straight line pressing the operating spring behind it until the rear face of the bolt is stopped against the receiver plug.

In this weapon, the cocking handle and the cocking bolt are permitted to travel still further to the rear in the slotted hole provided for the bolt pin in the head of the cocking bolt. This action prevents a sudden shock on the bolt pin.

At this point, the main spring is at practically full compression, and it halts further rearward movement.

The sear spring forces the sear up to catch in the underside of the bolt, holding it ready for the next shot.

Trigger action. There are three projections on the trigger in the Owen that can engage with the sear. The upper projection

Owen 9mm Submachine Gun, no longer being made.

Owen 9mm Submachine Gun, magazine removed.

locks the sear from rising if the change lever is set at the safe position. The central projection forms a bent, which is accurately located from the trigger axis. When the change lever is adjusted to the single-shot position, the rise of the trigger is strictly limited assuring that the sear will hold the bolt back on its first rearward movement. The lower projection engages the underface of the sear and carries one end of the trigger spring. It permits continuous fire.

The three surfaces on the change lever are in a circle and in turn engage the top of the trigger to limit the distance of rise. Thus on "safe," the trigger is locked; on "single shot," the rise of the trigger being limited, only one shot can be fired until the trigger is released and pulled back again; and on automatic fire the trigger is permitted full movement, which permits the bolt to shuttle back and forth so long as cartridges are fed into the chamber and the trigger is kept depressed.

Special Note on the Owen

Two other varieties of this gun were issued. The first is called the "Mark I Wood Butt" type. This is a lightened version of the Mark I in which some of the metal is cut away from the receiver behind the rear grip and which is provided with a wooden butt.

The second type of Owen is the Mark II. In this type, the shape of the receiver to the rear of the rear hand grip is still further modified, resulting in a weight with butt and empty magazine of only eight pounds and three ounces; without the butt it is only eight pounds. The trigger assembly differs from the Mark I.

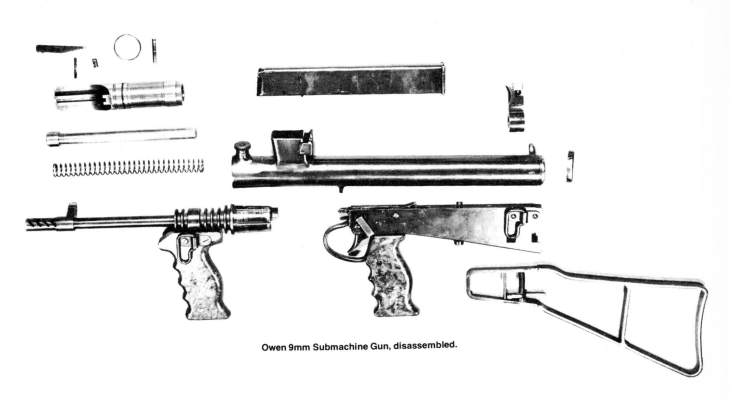

Owen 9mm Submachine Gun, disassembled.

9mm SUBMACHINE GUN F1 (AUST)

Australia has been the most prolific designer of submachine guns among the Dominions of the British Commonwealth. In a desire to secure a weapon with the reliability of the Owen, but lighter in weight, with lower rate of fire, and easier to produce, the Australians designed the F1. (The weapon was called the X3 while in development.)

Characteristics of the F1 (Aust) Submachine Gun

Caliber: 9mm Parabellum.
System of operation: Blowback, automatic fire only.
Weight, loaded with bayonet: 9.88 lbs.
Length, overall: 28.12 in.
Feed device: 34-round staggered detachable box magazine.
Sights: Front: Blade mounted on the right side of magazine guide.
Rear: Aperture in stamped leaf type sight.
Muzzle velocity: Approx. 1300 f.p.s.
Cyclic rate: 600 r.p.m.

How the F1 Works

The F1 has a separate cocking handle and cover that do not reciprocate with the bolt during firing. The pistol grip and butt plate are the same as those used on the Australian-made FN L1A1 rifle. The top loading magazine of the F1 is the same as that used on the British L2A3 and the Canadian C1 (the Sterling or Patchett submachine gun). The weapon has a bayonet lug on the left side.

Loading and Firing the F1

Pull cocking handle to the rear. Insert a loaded magazine in the guide on top of the receiver. Press trigger, and the weapon will fire. To put the weapon on safe, push safety catch located on the left side of the pistol grip to down position; word "Safe" will be exposed.

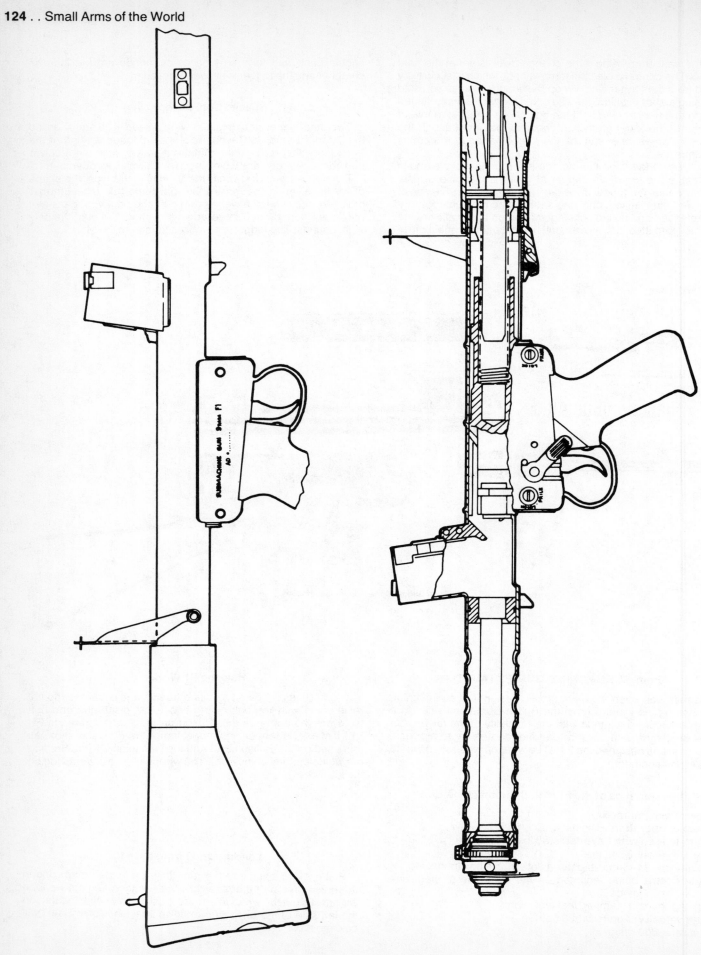

SUBMACHINE GUN 9mm F1
No ....

Australian F1 9mm Parabellum Submachine Gun.

Right side of the F1, bayonet fixed.

AUSTRALIAN MACHINE GUNS

The Lithgow plant was expanded and tooled to produce the caliber .303 Vickers Machine Gun Mark I between 1925 and 1930. Tooling for the caliber .303 Bren Gun was done in 1938-39. Production of machine guns at Lithgow during World War II amounted to over 12,000 Vickers and 17,000 Bren guns.

Australia adopted the US 7.62mm NATO M60 general purpose machine gun in the late fifties. The caliber .50 Browning gun is also used.

Vickers .303 Machine Gun Mark I

8 Austria

The Austrian Army uses the FN 7.62mm NATO "FAL" rifle (StG58), which is made under license at Steyr. They also use the 9mm Walther P 38 pistol and the 7.62mm Model 42/59 machine gun made by Rheinmetall.

After the signing of the Austrian peace treaty, the new Austrian Army was initially equipped with US, British and Soviet arms. These weapons have been either disposed of or relegated to reserve status.

AUSTRIAN PISTOLS

Steyr Daimler Puch is again making pocket pistols; however, no pistol of Austrian design is receiving any significant military usage in the world today.

AUSTRIAN ROTH STEYR 8mm PISTOL M1907

This pistol was used by the Austrians in World War I. It was produced by the Oesterreichische Waffenfabrik (Steyr) and by the Fegyvergyr in Budapest. The design of the pistol is based on patents issued to George Roth, G. Krnka and K. Krnka. Limited quantities of these pistols were apparently used in World War II.

Characteristics of Roth Steyr 8mm Pistol M 1907

Caliber: 8mm Roth Steyr, 8mm Steyr M7
System of operation: Recoil.
Feed device: 10-round in line non-removable magazine.
Muzzle velocity: 1045 f.p.s.
Barrel length: 5.1 in.
Overall length: 9.1 in.
Sights: Blade with notch.

Special Feature of Roth Steyr

This weapon was originally designed for use by cavalry. The recoil of the weapon ejects the empty case and strips a new cartridge into the firing chamber as in other automatic pistols. However, it does not cock in the regular fashion. The striker is drawn back and released to fire the cartridge by pulling the trigger, exactly as in hammerless revolvers. This makes the weapon safe to handle but difficult to shoot accurately.

Both pistol and cartridge are generally considered obsolete.

9mm STEYR PISTOL M12

The Steyr Model 12 Pistol was the most widely used of the various pistols used by the Austro-Hungarian forces in World War I. It was also used by Romania and by Germany (in 9mm Parabellum) to a limited extent. There is considerable confusion over the correct nomenclature for this pistol; many call it the Model 1911 or M 11, others call it the Model 1912 or M 12. Both designations are correct—the commercial designation for the weapon is Model 1911; the official Austrian Army nomenclature for the pistol was Selbstlade Pistol M 12. The pistol is also called the Steyr Hahn. During World War II, the Germans rebarreled a number of these weapons for the 9mm Parabellum Cartridge. These weapons can be identified by the "08" stamped on the slide.

Although there were about 250,000 of these pistols made, they are no longer used as service pistols anywhere in the world and have not been made since 1919.

Austrian Roth-Steyr 8mm Pistol M1907

Austrian 9mm Steyr Pistol M12.

Characteristics of 9mm Steyr Pistol M12

Caliber: 9mm Steyr.

Feed device: 8-round. Located in handle; cartridges must be stripped into it from the top of the pistol.

Capacity: 8 cartridges.

Muzzle velocity: 1112 f.p.s.

Barrel length: 5.2 in.

Overall length: 8.5 in.

Weight: 2.12 lbs.

Sights: Blade with notch.

Locked: By cam ribs on barrel, which lock in cam slots on inside of top of slide. As bullet passes down barrel, barrel tends to twist to the right. As barrel and slide move to the rear under recoil, cam rib twists barrel to the left and opens lock permitting slide to continue backward and function the action.

Type of fire: Single-shot only.

Magazine loading arrangement: Clip guide on top of slide permits insertion of loaded clip when action is opened.

Position of slide when last shot is fired: Open.

Safeties: (a) A thumb safety somewhat like that on the Colt .45 Automatic will be found on the left side of the pistol just below the hammer. Turning this up into its notch in the slide makes the pistol safe. (b) An automatic disconnector on the right side of the pistol under the slide prevents this pistol from being fired until the action is wholly closed.

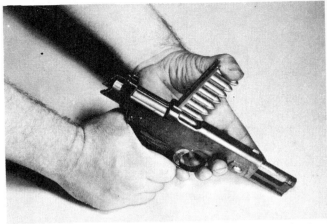

Stripping in a clip of cartridges—loading the Steyr M12 9mm pistol.

M12 Steyr chambered for 9mm Parabellum cartridge, stamped "08" on slide.

Austrian 9mm Steyr Pistol M12—field-stripped.

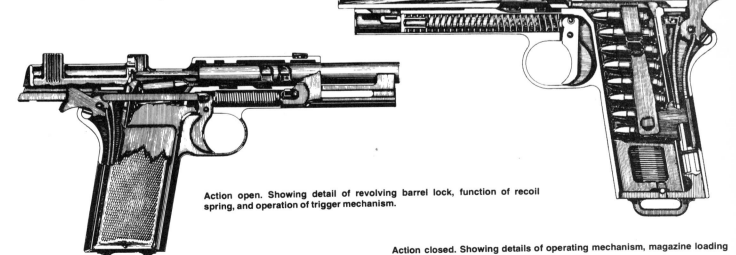

Action open. Showing detail of revolving barrel lock, function of recoil spring, and operation of trigger mechanism.

Action closed. Showing details of operating mechanism, magazine loading and release, and revolving barrel lock.

AUSTRIAN RIFLES

The current Austrian service rifle is the 7.62mm FN FAL. Military rifles of Austrian design have not seen use since the end of World War II. The most commonly used was the Mannlicher straight-pull design.

Austria-Hungary was apparently prepared to drop the straight-pull Mannlicher in favor of the 98 Mauser design in 1914. The 7mm Model 1914 rifle is a rare specimen, having the pointed type pistol grip and bands as found on the earlier Mannlicher. The Model 29 was Mauser made by Steyr for export; a quantity were made for the German Air Force during World War II and are marked G29/40 on the left side of the receiver. The receiver ring is marked 660—which was the numerical code for the Steyr plant.

AUSTRIAN MANNLICHER SERVICE RIFLES

None of the Austrian Mannlicher service rifles are used in significant quantity in active military service anywhere today. They were used extensively in World Wars I and II, however, and still exist in large numbers in the hands of collectors. A short description of each model follows.

11mm Rifle Model 1885 (Repetier Gewehr M85)

This was the first magazine rifle to be used by the Austro-Hungarian Empire. The M85 has a straight-pull non-rotating bolt, which is locked by a block pivoted from the underside of the rear section of the bolt. This block abuts against a shoulder in the receiver when in the locked position. The Model 85 introduced the Mannlicher magazine system in which the clip is inserted into the magazine of the rifle and functions as a part of the magazine—as does the clip of the US M1 rifle. The Model 85 was chambered for the 11mm M77 cartridge and was not made in significant quantity. Its design led directly to the next of the Mannlichers.

11mm Rifle Model 1886 (Repetier Gewehr M86)

The M86 is similar in most respects to the M85. It is the first of the Austrian service rifles to introduce the feature of the clip dropping out of the bottom of the magazine when the last round is chambered. The 11mm cartridge was improved with the introduction of this rifle, and as a result it had better ballistics than the M85. The sights of the M86, as the M85 and all other Austrian weapons until after World War I, are graduated in "Paces" (one pace equals 29.53 inches), a term similar to the "Arshin" formerly used as a Russian standard of measurement. Approximately 90,000 M86 rifles were made by Steyr.

8mm Rifle Model 1888 (Repetier Gewehr M88)

The M88 is chambered for the black-powder M88 cartridge, and its rear sight is graduated for that cartridge; with these exceptions it is the same as the M86.

8mm Rifle Model 1888–90 (Repetier Gewehr M88-90)

In 1890 the Austrian 8 x 50mm cartridge with smokeless powder charge was introduced. The sights of the M88 rifle were modified for the new and more powerful cartridge by the addition of new graduation scales, which were engraved on plates and attached to the sides of the sights. Rifles thus modified are called M88–90.

8mm Carbine Model 1890 (Repetier Carabiner M90)

This weapon introduced the straight-pull bolt with rotating bolt to the Austrian Service. Although Mannlicher had introduced a rotating straight-pull bolt in 1884, it was not very successful and was never made in quantity. The bolt is of two-piece design. The bolt handle and bolt body are one piece; mounted within the bolt body is the bolt shaft or bolt cylinder. The locking lugs are mounted on the head of the bolt cylinder, and the bolt cylinder rotates within the bolt body during the locking and unlocking process. This bolt system is used with all the later Austrian straight-pull bolt-action Mannlichers and, since it provides for frontal locking, is considered by many to be a stronger system than that of the Models 84, 86 and 88. The magazine system adopted with the M86 is used in the M90 carbine and the later rifles. The M90 carbine has no handguard, and the sight swivels are mounted on the left side of the stock; it is not fitted for a bayonet, and the cocking piece is round. All later models have a thumb-shaped cocking piece. The M90 carbine is a relatively rare piece these days.

8mm Rifle Model 1895 (Repetier Gewehr M95)

This weapon, which was made at Budapest as well as Steyr, was the principal Austro-Hungarian rifle of World War I. The M95 rifle was made in tremendous quantities.

8mm Carbine Model 1895 (Repetier Carabiner M95)

The carbine version of the M95 rifle, in addition to its short length, can be distinguished by the following: (1) sling swivels on side of stock only; (2) no provision for bayonet lug; and (3) no stacking hook.

8mm Short Rifle M1895 (Repetier Stutzen M95)

The M95 "Stutzen" is frequently confused with the M95 carbine. It apparently was designed for use by special troops, i.e. Engineer, Signal, etc., and not for Cavalry, since it is fitted with a bayonet stud and has sling swivels fitted to the underside as well as the side. This weapon also has a stacking hook, which screws into the upper band. When the rifle is fired with bayonet fixed, a blade on top of the bayonet barrel ring is used as the front sight to compensate for changes in center of impact due to the weight of the bayonet on the barrel.

MODIFIED AUSTRIAN SERVICE RIFLES

The Austro-Hungarian Empire, as a loser in World War I, had to provide large amounts of war material to the Allies. Among those countries that benefited from the Austrian war booty were: Italy, Yugoslavia and Greece. Italy used large quantities of the M88-90 and M95 series weapons in World War I without modification and made large quantities of the 8 x 50mm cartridges for those rifles.

Yugoslav 7.92mm M95

Yugoslavia converted many of the M95 weapons to 7.92mm. These weapons can be distinguished by the addition of the stamped letter "M" after "M95," which is on the top of the receiver. These rifles have a clip permanently fixed in their magazine and therefore can be loaded with the standard Mauser five-round charger.

7.92mm M95/24

These rifles were apparently used by Bulgaria. They have the markings "/24" stamped on the receiver after the "M95." They are generally similar to the Yugoslav M95M in their magazine arrangements.

Conversion of M88-90 to 7.92mm

This rifle is believed to have been used by Greece. The barrel has been shortened and a wooden handguard added (the Austrians frequently used a laced canvas handguard on the M88 and M88-90).

Mannlicher service rifles showing (top to bottom) M88 8mm Rifle, M95 8mm Rifle, and M95 8mm Short Rifle "Stutzen."

Austrian M1888 and 1888-90. Note engagement of clip catch above clip projection Locking block is wedged down into locking position in the receiver.

Bolt of the 8mm M90 Carbine.

8mm M95 Stutzen Converted to 8 × 56mm

There are two versions of this weapon extant. The Austrian version appeared in 1930 with the adoption of the Model 30 (8 × 56mm) cartridge. The Model 30 was a large-rimmed cartridge with a pointed bullet—*Spitzgeschoss*—and therefore, a letter "S", twelve millimeters high, was stamped on the receiver to distinguish it from the unconverted weapons. These weapons were used considerably by the German police in World War II, and steel-cased Austrian-made ammunition, bearing the date 1938 plus the German Eagle and Swastika marking, has been found in quantity. In 1931, the 8 × 56mm cartridge was adopted by Hungary, who called it the 31M (Model 31). The Hungarians had large quantities of M95 "Stutzen" on hand and converted many of these to the 31M cartridge; these weapons can be distinguished by the letter "H" stamped on the receiver. It should be noted that M95 rifles rebarreled for the 8 × 56mm cartridge—the M30 or M31—cannot be used with the old conical-nosed 8 × 56mm cartridge. Although both are rimmed, the 8 × 56mm is considerably longer and more powerful—these cartridges are definitely NOT interchangeable. Both the Austrian and Hungarian conversions require special clips.

AMMUNITION FOR AUSTRIAN MANNLICHER SERVICE RIFLES

The 11mm M77 Austrian cartridge is a typical black-powder cartridge. Although it was once made in the United States, it is now basically a collector's item, as is the 8mm M88 black-powder loaded cartridge. The 8mm M90 and its slightly improved version, the M93, may be encountered in quantity on occasion, but it should be born in mind that all military loads are at least 20 years old and all the above rifles chambered for this cartridge require a special clip to be used as magazine loaders. The situation is the same for the 8 × 56mm (M30 or M31) cartridge. This cartridge has not, to the writer's knowledge, been manufactured for 20 years.

The conversions that are chambered for the 7.92mm cartridge present a far simpler problem. They do not require special clips, and the 7.92mm (8mm Mauser) cartridge is available in quantity both in military and sporting configurations. A word of warning is in order, however; 7.92mm cartridges can be found with pressures up to 55,000 p.s.i. The Model 88-90 converted to 7.92mm was built to take a maximum pressure of about 40,000 p.s.i.; therefore, shooting this weapon with some of the military and commercial cartridges currently available could be EX-

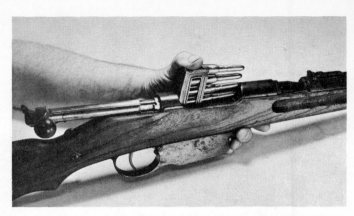

Note that both clip and cartridges are inserted into the magazine when loading the Steyr-Mannlicher Model 95 series 8mm rifles.

TREMELY HAZARDOUS! Shooting any of these weapons unless previously checked by a reliable gunsmith can be hazardous, especially if the weapon shows any signs of hard usage.

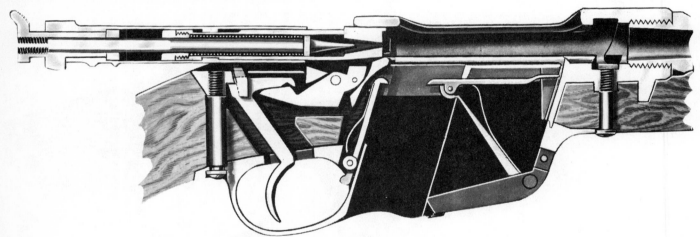

Austrian Model 95 Mannlicher straight-pull section and mechanism.

CHARACTERISTICS OF AUSTRIAN STRAIGHT PULL MANNLICHER SERVICE RIFLES

Weapon	Method of locking	Overall length	Barrel length	Feed device	Sights	Muzzle velocity	Weight
Rifle: 11 mm M86	Wedge	52 in.	31.75 in	5-round, single column, fixed box magazine	Front: Barley corn Rear: V notched tangent with long range side sight	1610 f.p.s.	10 lbs.
Rifle: 8mm M88	Wedge	50.38 in.	30.14 in.	5-round, single column, fixed box magazine	Front: Barley corn Rear: V notched tangent with long range side sight	1750 f.p.s.	9.7 lbs.
Rifle: 8mm M88/90	Wedge	50.38 in.	30.14 in.	5-round, single column, fixed box magazine	Front: Barley corn Rear: V notched tangent with long ranged side sight	2115 f.p.s.	9.7 lbs.
Carbine: 8mm M90	Frontal locking lugs	39.5 in.	19.5 in.	5-round, single column, fixed box magazine	Front: Barley corn Rear: V notched tangent	1900 f.p.s.	6.9 lbs. (approx.)
Rifle: 8mm M95	Frontal locking lugs	50 in.	30.12 in.	5-round, single column, fixed box magazine	Front: Barleycorn Rear: Leaf	2030 f.p.s.	8.31 lbs.
Short Rifle: 8mm M95	Frontal locking lugs	39.5 in.	19.65 in.	5-round, single column, fixed box magazine	Front: Barleycorn Rear: Leaf	1900 f.p.s.	7.5 lbs.
Carbine: 8mm M95	Frontal locking lugs	39.5	19.65 in.	5-round, single column, fixed box magazine	Front: Barleycorn Rear: Leaf	1900 f.p.s.	7 lbs. (approx.)

STEYR 7.62mm NATO MODEL SSG RIFLE

Steyr Daimler Puch has developed a rifle based on their post war bolt action system. This rifle has been adopted by the Austrian Army as a sniper rifle. It has a heavy, cold hammered barrel. The bolt has six rear-mounted locking lugs. Steyr claims ten round 2.75-inch groups with this rifle at 300 meters.

May also be fitted with Walther micrometer rear and hooded front sight with changeable inserts.

Characteristics of the Steyr Model SSG Rifle

Caliber: 7.62mm NATO
System of operation: Bolt action
Weight (w/o telescope): 10.25 lbs.
Length overall: 45 in.
Barrel length: 25.6 in.
Feed mechanism: 5-round, removable rotary
Sights: Front: (w/telescope) hooded post
Rear: (w/telescope) notch
Muzzle Velocity: 2800 f.p.s.

Steyr 7.62mm NATO Model SSG Rifle.

AUSTRIAN SUBMACHINE GUNS

THE AUSTRIAN MP34 SUBMACHINE GUN

Although Austria did little if anything in the line of submachine guns, they did have one gun that attained fairly wide usage during World War II. The MP34 is commonly known as the Steyr Solothurn and is a product of German design worked out at Waffenfabrik Solothurn A.G. of Solothurn, Switzerland, a Swiss plant owned by Rheinmetall of Germany, during the period when German military arms development was restricted by the Versailles Treaty.

The MP34 was taken over by the Germans when they took over Austria in 1938 and was called by the Germans MP34 (Ö)–Maschinen Pistole 34 Österreich-, (Österreich meaning Austrian). The weapon was widely used by German police and rear area units. The weapon in various modifications was offered commercially and was also used by Chile, El Salvador, Bolivia and Uruguay. It was used, in extremely limited quantities, by the Japanese in 7.63mm Mauser. The commercial designation for the weapon is Sl-100. It is probable that all the MP34s used by Austria were made by Steyr, as from 1930 on the gun was known as the Steyr Solothurn and the two concerns had a joint marketing arrangement.

It should be noted that the MP34 as used by the Austrian Army was chambered for the 9mm Mauser cartridge. It was used by the Austrian police in 9mm Steyr; both calibers were found in German service or police units. It may also be found chambered for the 9mm Parabellum cartridge.

Characteristics of Austrian MP34 Submachine Gun

Caliber: 9mm Mauser (Army Model).
System of operation: Blowback.
Weight loaded: 9.87 lbs.
Length overall: 33.5 in.
Barrel length: 7.80 in.
Feed mechanism: 32-round detachable, staggered box magazine.
Sights: Front: Barley corn.
Rear: Tangent with "V" notch graduated from 50–500 meters in 50-meter increments.
Muzzle velocity: 1360 f.p.s. (For 9mm Mauser).
Cyclic rate of fire: 500 rounds per minute.

Unusual Features of MP34

The weapon is typical of the period in which it was made in that it is heavy and expensive, being made of heavy forgings. The only unusual feature is the magazine loader, which is machined into the magazine housing. The magazine is inserted into the underside of the magazine housing and is then loaded with ten-round chargers—stripper clips—through the opening in the top of the magazine housing.

Austrian 9mm Model 34 Steyr Solothurn Submachine Gun.

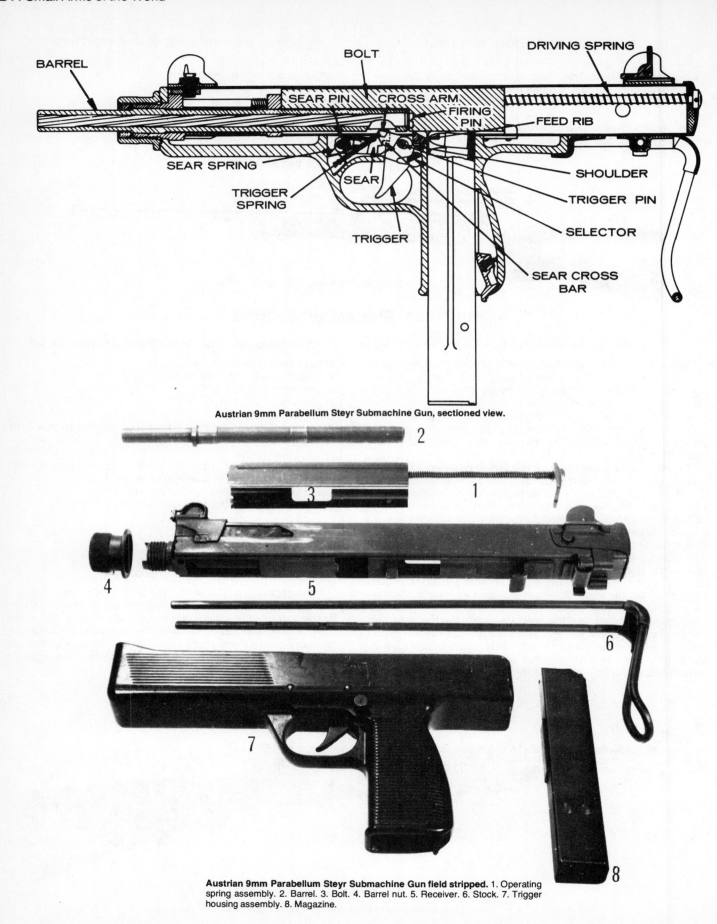

BARREL

BOLT

DRIVING SPRING

SEAR PIN

CROSS ARM

FIRING PIN

FEED RIB

SEAR SPRING

SEAR

SHOULDER

TRIGGER SPRING

TRIGGER PIN

TRIGGER

SELECTOR

SEAR CROSS BAR

Austrian 9mm Parabellum Steyr Submachine Gun, sectioned view.

Austrian 9mm Parabellum Steyr Submachine Gun field stripped. 1. Operating spring assembly. 2. Barrel. 3. Bolt. 4. Barrel nut. 5. Receiver. 6. Stock. 7. Trigger housing assembly. 8. Magazine.

STEYR SUBMACHINE GUN

Steyr Daimler Puch has developed a new submachine gun chambered for the 9mm Parabellum cartridge. This is the first military weapon to be developed in Austria since the 1930s.

The Steyr submachine gun is a compact weapon, resembling the Israeli UZI in several respects. Like the UZI, it has a long barrel and a short overall length, accomplished by having a bolt that telescopes the barrel for about 2/3rds of the barrel length.

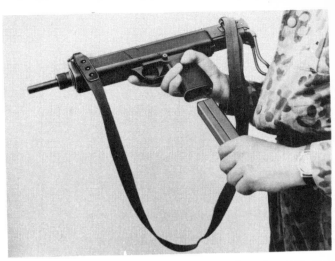

Austrian 9mm Parabellum Steyr Submachine Gun, inserting magazine.

Steyr 9mm Parabellum Submachine Gun.

Characteristics of the Steyr Submachine Gun

Caliber: 9mm Parabellum
System of operation: blowback, selective fire
Weight: 6 lbs.
Length overall:
  stock retracted: 18 in.
  stock extended: 25 in.
Barrel length: 10.2 in.
Feed mechanism: 25- or 32-round detachable staggered row box magazine.
Sights—front: post with protecting ears
       rear: "L" w/apertures set for 100 and 200 meters
Muzzle velocity: approx. 1350 f.p.s.
Cyclic rate: 550 r.p.m.

Description of the mechanism of the Steyr Submachine Gun

The Steyr, as most submachine guns, fires from an open bolt. Pressure on the trigger, which pulls the trigger half of its length of travel, produces semi-automatic fire; pulling the trigger all the way to the rear produces automatic fire. As with the UZI, the ejection post is open only when the bolt moves to the rear with the fired case and on its return to the closed position. The push-button type safety is located on the left side of the trigger housing above and to the rear of the trigger. The magazine catch is located at the bottom rear of the pistol grip. The magazine well is in the pistol grip as on the UZI. There is a cocking safety that prevents the bolt from closing and firing if it slips in cocking. The weapon is easily field stripped. The barrel is moved by depressing the barrel catch lock at the right top front of the receiver and unscrewing the barrel nut. The receiver cover is desengaged by pushing in on a catch at the top rear of the receiver. Before attempting disassembly, the stock must be in the fixed position.

AUSTRIAN MACHINE GUNS

The Austro-Hungarian Empire used the Schwarzlose machine gun in several models. The Schwarzlose, in addition to being used in Austria, was also used in Sweden (6.5mm Model 14), in the Netherlands (08, 08/13 and 08/15), in Czechoslovakia (7.92mm) and in Italy in the form of Austrian war booty (8mm). The Schwartzlose is not in active use in any country, country, and it is doubtful if this weapon will ever see active service again.

AUSTRIAN 8mm MODEL 30S MACHINE GUN

This weapon was adopted by the Austrians in 1930 and was among the materiel taken from Austria by the Germans after the annexation of Austria. A similar weapon designated as the 31M (Model 31) was adopted by Hungary in 1931. Both guns were marketed by Waffenfabrik Solothurn A.G., a Swiss plant owned by Rheinmetall-Borsig A.G. They were developed from the designs of Louis Stange, a Rheinmetall engineer. Assembling and marketing the gun by Solothurn was a neat dodge by the

Austrian Schwarzlose 8mm Machine Gun M07/12.

Germans to avoid Versailles Treaty restrictions. The gun was offered first in 7.92mm as the Solothurn Model 29. In addition to being adopted by the Austrians and Hungarians as ground guns, the weapon, slightly modified, was adopted in 7.92mm by the Germans as a fixed aircraft gun, the MG15, and as a flexible aircraft gun, the MG17.

9 Belgium

The Belgian Army is currently equipped with the following small arms: the 9mm Parabellum Browning FN G. P. (High Power) pistol; the 9mm Parabellum Vigneron M2 submachine gun; the 7.62mm NATO FN FAL rifle; the 7.62mm NATO FN MAG general-purpose machine gun; and the caliber .50 Browning machine gun.

The Belgian Army was stripped of weapons during World War II and for a period after World War II was equipped mainly with British weapons, i.e., Lee Enfields, Vickers and Bren guns. Re-equipment with FN-made weapons started very rapidly; a caliber .30-06 bolt-action Mauser was among the first of the weapons of native origin to be issued to Belgian troops. The .30-06 FN-made Browning machine gun and the .30-06 FN M1949 self-loading rifle were also issued. The Mausers have been sold, and the other weapons are presumably held in reserve.

THE FN PLANT

Fabrique Nationale d'Armes de Guerre (FN) of Herstal lez Liege is the major designer of successful small arms still in service in the Western World today. The FN Browning G.P. (Grande Puissance—High Power) pistol is used in many countries, as is the FN FAL rifle and the MAG machine gun. FN-made Browning pistols of .32 and .380 caliber, as well as FN-made Browning machine guns, automatic rifles and the FN commercial weapons, are found throughout the Western World.

The FN organization was founded in 1889 by a combine of Liege interests and Ludwig Loewe and Co. of Berlin to manufacture the Model 1889 Mauser rifle for the Belgian government. The company had a stroke of luck early in the present century when John Browning—upset over his financial arrangements with Winchester—and, according to a many times told story, more than a little bit annoyed at having to cool his heels in the anteroom of a prominent American gun manufacturer waiting to see some now unknown dignitary who had unfortunately died the night before, decided to take the design of his now renowned long recoil operated shotgun to Liege and to FN. Thus began a close relationship with the outstanding genius of American gun designers, which ended with his death in 1926 in Belgium. Browning brought more than his automatic shotgun to FN. They also produced his automatic pistols—the M1900, M1903, M1906 (.25 automatic), M1907, M1910, M1922 and the M1935 (the High Power). They produced his commercial semiautomatic rifle and after World War I produced the Browning Automatic Rifle and Browning machine gun, which Browning had developed for his native land during the war. Although John M. Browning is generally known in the US, especially to those who have used his weapons in service, in Europe his name is a household word for automatic pistol. It should be noted that Browning designs similar to those produced and marketed by FN in the Eastern Hemisphere were produced and marketed by American manufacturers in the Western Hemisphere. Colt produced in one form or another successful Browning pistol designs including the still standard US Army caliber .45 Colt automatic pistol. Colt also produced the automatic weapons, Remington and Savage-Stevens produced the shotguns, and of course, Winchester continued manufacture of many of the earlier rifles and is still producing the famed .30-30 Model 94 carbine.

FN, in addition to producing the Browning automatic rifle and Browning machine guns (water cooled, air cooled, aircraft and heavy), began producing Mauser bolt-action rifles based on the Model 98 action in 1924. These weapons were quite successful, and modified forms of these military Mausers were in production as late as 1964 for small Middle Eastern countries that could not afford the more modern semiautomatic and automatic rifles. FN and the Zbrojovka Brno plant of Czechoslovakia had the world's Mauser military rifle market to themselves to a great extent during the period 1924 to 1938; the Belgians, being extremely astute businessmen in addition to manufacturing a fine product, got at least their share of the business. (There is actually no real difference in the quality of the products made by the two concerns during this period; they are among the finest quality military rifles ever built.)

World War II found Belgium again an occupied country. The Germans continued manufacture of weapons suited to their ammunition system, i.e. the 7.92mm Mauser carbine, the 9mm Parabellum High Power pistol (called Pistol 640(b) by the Germans), the 9mm Browning short (.380 ACP) M1922 (called pistol 626(b) by the Germans) and various weapon parts. The weapons made during World War II are not equal in quality to the pre- or post-war products.

Fortunately the FN plant was not destroyed by Allied air strikes or by the Germans when they departed in late 1944. The plant was able to set up rapidly for the manufacture of Browning automatic rifle and Browning machine-gun parts for the US Army. At the conclusion of hostilities, FN got a large contract to rebuild a large number of US weapons in Europe. The first postwar weapon they put on the market was actually designed prior to the war by D. Saive. It was the FN self-loading rifle, known variously as the ABL, SAFN or Model 1949. This rifle was followed by the Type D Browning Auto rifle, the FAL rifle and its heavy barrel version and the MAG machine gun.

BELGIAN PISTOLS

MODELS 1900, 1903, 1910 AND 1922

The M1900 7.65mm (.32 ACP) FN Browning Pistol

This pistol had limited use as a military pistol. It is the first of John Browning's automatic pistols produced in quantity by FN. A blowback-operated pistol, it is of somewhat unusual design in that the recoil spring is mounted in a separate tunnel above the barrel. This pistol and its earlier versions—the Model 1898 and Model 1899, which were made in very limited quantity—introduced the 7.65mm Browning cartridge, or .32 ACP cartridge as it is known in the US. This cartridge was apparently designed by Winchester with the assistance of Browning. Copies of the M1900 may be encountered in the Orient with various weird markings, which are attempts of Chinese counterfeiters of the pistol to reproduce the FN markings.

The M1903 9mm FN Browning Pistol

This handgun is a blowback-operated pistol similar in operation and construction to the Colt caliber .32 and .380 pocket model automatics, which appeared during the same period. This pistol was quite extensively used as a military automatic but is no longer used as a service pistol and has not been produced

FN Browning M1903 9mm automatic pistol.

for many years. This weapon is chambered for the 9mm Browning long cartridge, which has not been manufactured in the US for many years.

The M1903 Browning was a standard service pistol in Sweden (pistol M/07), Belgium, Denmark, the Netherlands and Turkey.

The M1910 FN Browning Pistol

This weapon may be found chambered for either the 7.65mm (.32 ACP) or 9mm Browning Short (.380 ACP) cartridge. It is still manufactured and is distributed in the US by the Browning Arms Co. of St Louis. This blowback-operated pistol is basically an improvement on the Model 1903 and has been extensively used abroad as a police pistol. It has also had some use as a limited standard service pistol.

The M1922 FN Browning Pistol

This is basically an enlarged Model 1910. It has been made in caliber .32 ACP and caliber .380 ACP and is blowback operated.

This pistol, frequently called the Model 10/22, was apparently designed with an eye to the military market and was adopted as a service pistol by several countries including the Netherlands, Yugoslavia and Belgium. Its manufacture in both calibers was continued by the Germans during the occupation of Belgium. Specimens of the pistol bearing the German Waffenamt stamps (eagle over Swastika with letters Waa) are not of good quality and should be avoided except as collectors' items.

FN Browning M1910 Pistol.

FN Browning M1922 Pistol.

THE 9mm FN BROWNING HIGH POWER PISTOL

The FN Browning High Power is one of the most extensively used military pistols in the world today. It is also widely distributed as a commercial weapon. This pistol was the last developed by John Browning and first appeared in prototype form in 1926. It was introduced to the market in 1935 in two forms—an "Ordinary Model" with fixed sights; and an "Adjustable Rear Sight Model," which had a tangent type rear sight graduated to 500 meters and a slotted grip for attachment of a wooden shoulder stock. This shoulder stock is attached to a leather holster in contrast to the all wooden shoulder-stock holsters made for the Canadian-made FN Browning pistols No. 1 mark 1 and No. 1* during World War II. The High Power, which is called the G.P. *(Grande Puissance)* in Belgium, uses the Browning Colt parallel ruler system of locking but is considerably simplified in many was in comparison with the US caliber .45 Model 1911.

The High Power has been or is being used as a service pistol by Belgium, Lithuania, Denmark, the Netherlands, Nationalist China, Canada, the United Kingdom, Romania and other countries. It was manufactured by the John Inglis Company of Toronto, Ontario, during World War II. (For further information see under Canada.) Large quantities were manufactured for the Germans during the occupation of Belgium; the High Power was used as a first-line weapon by the Germans because of its caliber, 9mm Parabellum. During the post-war period, the pistol has been manufactured in the Indonesian arsenal at Bandung on the island of Java. The pistol in commercial form is distributed in the US by the Browning Arms Co.

The following are some of the nomenclatures that have been or are being used for the High Power in various countries:

Belgium: Pistolet Automatique Browning Modele a Grande Puissance (GP).
Canada, UK: Pistol, Browning, FN, 9mm HP No. 1, Marks 1 and 1.* and No. 2, Marks 1 and 1.*
Denmark: 9mm Pistol M/46.
Germany: *Pistole 640 (b).*
Indonesia: Pindad PiA 9-mm
Netherlands: *Pistool,* 9mm Browning, FN, GP.

Characteristics of the FN Browning High Power Pistol

Caliber: 9mm Parabellum.
System of operation: recoil, semiautomatic.
Magazine: Box type, double line staggered. Capacity 13 cartridges.
Muzzle velocity: 1040 to 1500 feet per second depending on type and manufacture of ammunition.
Barrel length: 4.75 in.
Overall length: 8 in.
Weight: 1.9 lbs.

FN Browning 9mm High Power pistol, standard model.

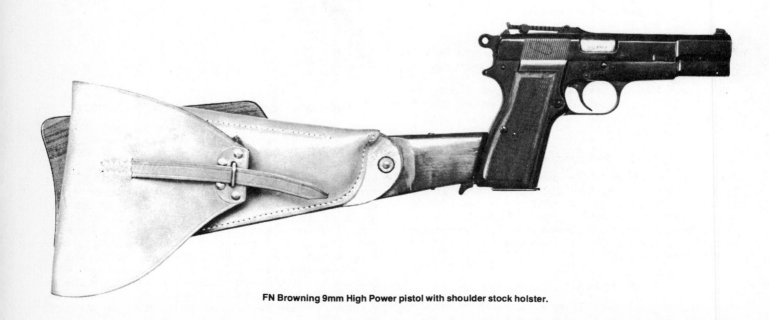

FN Browning 9mm High Power pistol with shoulder stock holster.

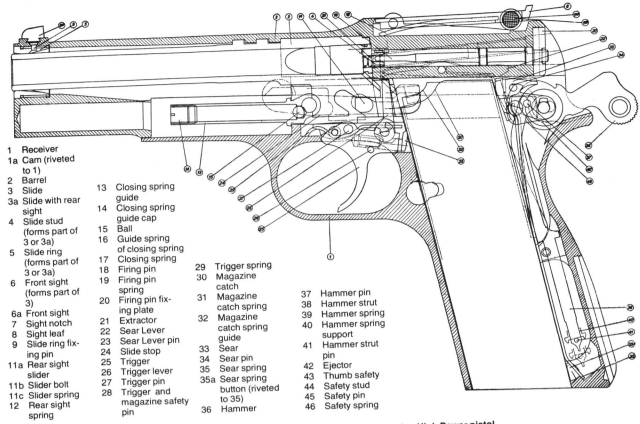

1	Receiver		
1a	Cam (riveted to 1)		
2	Barrel		
3	Slide		
3a	Slide with rear sight		
4	Slide stud (forms part of 3 or 3a)		
5	Slide ring (forms part of 3 or 3a)		
6	Front sight (forms part of 3)		
6a	Front sight		
7	Sight notch		
8	Sight leaf		
9	Slide ring fixing pin		
11a	Rear sight slider		
11b	Slider bolt		
11c	Slider spring		
12	Rear sight spring		

13	Closing spring guide
14	Closing spring guide cap
15	Ball
16	Guide spring of closing spring
17	Closing spring
18	Firing pin
19	Firing pin spring
20	Firing pin fixing plate
21	Extractor
22	Sear Lever
23	Sear Lever pin
24	Slide stop
25	Trigger
26	Trigger lever
27	Trigger pin
28	Trigger and magazine safety pin

29	Trigger spring
30	Magazine catch
31	Magazine catch spring
32	Magazine catch spring guide
33	Sear
34	Sear pin
35	Sear spring
35a	Sear spring button (riveted to 35)
36	Hammer

37	Hammer pin
38	Hammer strut
39	Hammer spring
40	Hammer spring support
41	Hammer strut pin
42	Ejector
43	Thumb safety
44	Safety stud
45	Safety pin
46	Safety spring

Section view and parts listing—FN Browning High Power pistol

Field Stripping the High Power Browning

Pull slide back and push thumb safety up into the second notch.

Press magazine catch and withdraw magazine.

Push pin from right side of receiver and lift out the pin and slide stop unit.

Holding firmly to the slide, depress the safety catch and permit the slide assembly to go forward and off the receiver runners.

Holding slide assembly upside down, pull recoil spring toward the muzzle and lift it out of engagement. Remove it and the spring.

Remove barrel from rear of slide.

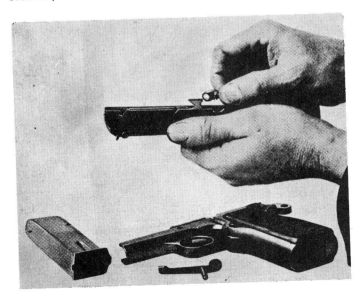

Field stripping the Browning High Power.

Description of the Mechanism of the Browning High Power

The use of a double-row staggered magazine gives greater magazine capacity but at the same time necessarily increases the thickness of the grip. This additional width, together with an arched lower section of the handle section of the receiver, gives the pistol better than usual instinctive pointing qualities.

While in general the design follows that of the Colt .45 Automatic, in detail it is quite different. The positive hammer safety is positioned as in the US service pistol. When it is forced up into its notch in the slide, a projection on its lower side fits at the rear of the sear to prevent the release of the hammer.

The slide stop, which is forced up by the magazine follower to hold the pistol open when the last shot has been fired, and the button magazine release both follow the standard Browning form. No grip safety is provided.

Other features include a magazine safety. When the magazine is withdrawn, the safety spring forces this safety out, swinging the trigger lever forward out of engagement with the sear. Inserting a magazine presses the safety against its spring tension and swings the trigger lever back and under the sear to permit finger pressure to be transmitted.

CAUTION. Many of these pistols made for the Germans in World War II had the magazine safety removed.

In place of the Colt stirrup-type trigger, this weapon is fitted with a comfortable trigger, which, when pressed, forces a trigger lever upward. This rotates the sear lever, which acts upon the sear arm, causing it in turn to swivel and release the hammer.

Unless the slide is fully forward and the barrel securely locked to it, this sear lever remains at the rear, and the trigger lever cannot act upon it. This acts as a positive disconnector to prevent the weapon from being fired. Should the trigger be held back after a shot has been fired, the trigger lever is retained in raised position but is also forced forward by the sear lever on the forward motion of the slide. This prevents the trigger lever from acting upon either the sear or the sear lever, and so the hammer cannot fall until the trigger is permitted to move to its normal forward position. Thus, only one shot is possible on each pull of the trigger.

The slide in particular is an improvement over the original Browning design. Its forward end has only one opening, that for the barrel. The front of the slide below the muzzle opening is solid, doing away with the weak barrel bushing of previous models. The recoil spring and its guide seat in the hollow below the barrel, and the head of the guide sets into the barrel nose (or lock) where it is securely retained by the transverse slide stop pin.

The barrel lock is also improved. While it retains the basic Browning locking idea (that of ribs on top of the barrel fitting into corresponding grooves inside the slide at the moment of firing), this new Browning does away with the swinging link and pin used in the US service pistol. It provides instead a "barrel nose," which is part of the barrel forging itself. This barrel nose is placed directly below the heavily reinforced chamber section and has a guiding slot that is controlled by a cam machined into the receiver. This arrangement gives a much more rigid barrel support and permits simplification of the recoil spring system.

How the Browning High Power Pistol Works

At the moment of discharge, the barrel is locked securely to the slide as the top-locking ribs engage in the locking slots in the slide. As the slide starts back in recoil carrying the barrel with it and the bullet leaves the barrel, the sear lever is disconnected from the trigger lever.

As the barrel pressure drops to safe limits, the lower section of the notch of the barrel nose contacts the cam in the receiver, and the rear end of the barrel is thus drawn down until its ribs are free from the locking slots. At this point, the rearward barrel movement is stopped as the barrel nose brings up sharply against its receiver stop.

The slide continues on backwards, riding over the hammer to cock it. The extractor claw carries the empty cartridge case back until it strikes the ejector and is tossed out of the pistol. Meanwhile the recoil spring is compressed around its guide. Rearward motion of the slide stops when its lower part strikes against the forward end of the receiver.

For the return motion, the recoil spring pushes the slide forward to strip the top cartridge from the magazine into the chamber. The breech end of the slide strikes the barrel; under the action of the cam in the receiver acting against the upper part of the barrel nose notch, the rear of the barrel is brought up into locking position, and its ribs fit firmly into their slots in the slide.

The trigger, sear and hammer mechanisms hook up properly, and the pistol is ready for the next pull of the trigger.

The FN Hi-Power is now being made with a side-mounted pivoting extractor. The spring loaded extractor lies in a cut in the slide behind the ejection port and is visible from the outside, rather than being mounted in a hole cut through from the rear of the slide to the slide breech face.

BELGIAN RIFLES

The story of modern Belgian rifles begins with the 7.65mm M1889 Mauser, which is considered the first of the Modern Mauser rifles. FN began the manufacture of Mauser 98 type military rifles and carbines around 1924 and still produces them to a limited extent. The principal military rifle produced in Belgium at the present time is the FN FAL rifle. FN is the only currect producer of military rifles in Belgium; the government arsenal Fabrique d'Armes de L'Etat no longer manufactures military rifles.

BELGIAN SERVICE BOLT-ACTION RIFLES AND CARBINES

Belgium adopted what might be called the first of the modern Mauser rifles in 1889. The 7.65mm M1889 Belgian Mauser was the first Mauser to have a solid bolt body bored from the rear with locking lugs at the head of the bolt. The Model 1889 was also the first rifle to use the Mauser type charger (stripper clip). This type of rifle was used by Belgium until 1935 when a rifle generally similar to the German Kar 98K was adopted.

7.65mm Rifle M1889. Long barreled, with metal jacket covering barrel to serve as handguard; straight bolt handle; single line magazine protrudes below stock, magazine not normally detached.

The Model 1889 series were made by FN, Fabrique d'Armes de L'Etat, Hopkins and Allen of Norwich, Conn., and an arms plant established by Belgian refugees in Birmingham, England. The 1889 series were made for loads of about 39,000 P.S.I. pressure and should not be used with higher-powered loads.

7.65mm Rifle M1935. This rifle has the 98 Mauser bolt system and flush magazine. Except for bands, the front sight guard and sling swivels are the same as the German 7.92mm Kar 98K.

7.65mm Rifle M1936. Sometimes called the Model 89/36, this rifle was converted from the M1889 rifle. The barrel is partially covered with a wooden handguard, the tubular metal handguard being removed. An upper band and front sight guard similar to that of the Model 1935 rifle are used. The bolt system has been altered by the fitting of a bolt sleeve similar to that of

Top to Bottom: 7.65mm M1889 Rifle, 7.65mm M1889 Carbine, M1924 FN Mauser-system rifle, M1924 Carbine.

the 98 and a new 98 type cocking piece firing pin system.

Caliber .30 FN Rifle M1924/30. Used in limited quantity by the Belgian Army after World War II, it is standard Model 98 type. This rifle is also known as the M1930; both model designations given are FN designations. In every mechanical respect, they are duplicates of the German and Czech Service rifles, and the descriptions of mechanisms given for those arms cover the FN line as well. Model modifications are minor and deal with externals.

Most Mauser military actions are based on the same receiver and bolt. The standard 7mm, 7.65mm and 7.9mm Mauser cartridges were developed by Paul Mauser to permit simplicity of conversion, as well as low cost design. Thus, the machinery that in time of peace made 7mm rifles for South America could be readily converted to 7.9mm German Service when needed.

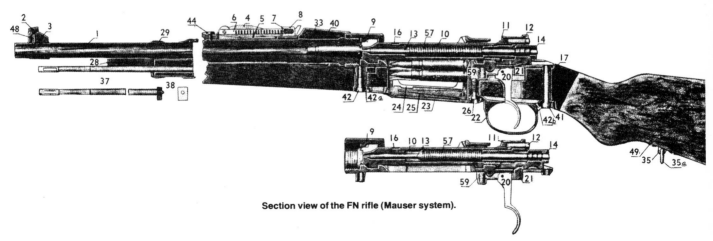

Section view of the FN rifle (Mauser system).

1. Barrel.	13. Firing pin.	29. Upper band.
2. Front sight.	14. Cocking piece.	37. Cleaning rod.
3. Front sight ring.	16. Extractor ring.	38. Cleaning rod stop.
4. Rear sight bed ring.	17. Bolt stop.	40. Handguard.
5. Rear sight spring.	20. Trigger.	41. Trigger guard screw (rear).
6. Rear sight tangent.	21. Trigger bar.	42. Trigger guard screw (front).
7. Spring pawl.	22. Trigger guard.	42a. Check screw of front trigger guard screw.
8. Sight slide.	23. Magazine cover plate.	42b. Check screw of rear trigger guard screw.
9. Body.	24. Magazine platform.	44. Rear sight bed screw.
10. Bolt.	25. Magazine spring.	48. Front sight ring screw.
11. Bolt plug.	26. Magazine cover plate catch.	57. Firing pin spring.
12. Safety wing.	28. Bayonet attachment.	59. Trigger bar spring.

Characteristics of M1924 Rifles in Caliber 7mm, 7.65mm or 7.9mm

Length of rifle without bayonet: 43.3 in.
Length of rifle with bayonet: 58.2 in.
Length of barrel: 23.2 in.
Weight without bayonet: 8.5 lbs.
Number of cartridges in magazine: 5.

The Model 1924 and 1924/30 rifles and carbines were made for Argentina, Belgium, Bolivia, Brazil, Chile, China, Columbia, Costa Rica, Ecuador, Iran, Liberia, Lithuania, Luxembourg,

Mexico, Paraguay, Peru, Turkey, Uruguay, Venezuela, Yemen and Yugoslavia.

Characteristics of M1924 Carbines in Caliber 7mm, 7.65mm or 7.9mm

Length of carbine: 37.4 in.
Length of barrel: 17.3 in
Weight of carbine: 7.3 lbs.
Number of cartridges in magazine: 5.
Lowest rear sight graduation in meters: 200.
Highest rear sight graduation in meters: 1400.

Caliber .30 FN Mauser rifle as made after W. W. II.

CHARACTERISTICS OF PRE-WORLD WAR II BELGIAN SERVICE BOLT-ACTION RIFLES AND CARBINES

	Rifle M1889	Carbine M1889*	Rifle M1935	Rifle M1936
Caliber:	7.65mm Mauser.	7.65mm Mauser.	7.65mm Mauser.	7.65mm Mauser.
Overall length:	50.13 in.	41.16 in.	43.6 in.	Approx. 43 in.
Barrel length:	30.69 in.	21.65 in.	23.5 in.	23.7 in.
Feed device:	5-round in line box magazine.	5-round in line box magazine.	5-round staggered box magazine.	5-round in line box magazine.
Sights: Front:	Barley corn.	Barley corn.	Barley corn.	Barley corn.
Sights: Rear:	V notch, leaf sight.	V notch, leaf sight.	V notch, tangent.	V notch, tangent.
Muzzle velocity: (at date of adoption)	2034 f.p.s.	1900 f.p.s. (approx).	2755 f.p.s.	2378 f.p.s.
Weight:	8.88 lbs.	7.75 lbs.	9. lbs.	8.7 lbs. (approx).

*The other three carbines vary in detail.

BELGIAN AUTOMATIC RIFLES

FUSIL AUTOMATIQUE MODELE 49 (FN SELF-LOADING RIFLE-SAFN)

Prior to World War II, Dieudonne Saive developed a gas operated rifle that was intended to replace the bolt-action Mausers of the Belgian Army and also to be offered to the armies of the world as a replacement for their bolt-action rifles. It should be remembered that only the US and USSR had adopted semiautomatic rifles as the standard shoulder weapon at that time. The occupation of Belgium by the Germans in 1940 halted work on the self-loading rifle, and it did not appear on the world market until the end of World War II. The rifle was offered in caliber .30, 7mm, 7.65mm and 7.92mm and was adopted by Belgium in caliber .30 model 1949, Egypt in 7.92mm, the former Netherlands East Indies in caliber .30, Brazil in caliber .30, Venezuela in 7mm (model 49), Luxembourg in caliber .30, Argentina in 7.65mm., the former Belgian Congo in caliber .30, and Columbia in caliber .30.

The tilting bolt of this rifle locks on a bar set in the bottom of the receiver, cammed into and out of the locked position by cam slots on the bolt carrier in engagement with lugs on the rear of the bolt. This bolt system is essentially the same as that of the Soviet Tokarev rifles and the FN FAL rifle. Specimens of this rifle were made that had selective fire capability.

This rifle is frequently referred to as the ABL or SAFN. ABL (*Arme Belgique*) is the marking found on the rifles made for the Belgian government; SAFN stands for semiautomatic FN.

Characteristics of FN Self-loading Rifle (SAFN)

Caliber: .30 M2, 7mm, 7.65mm, and 7.92mm Mauser.
System of operation: Gas, semiautomatic.
Feed device: Projecting steel box. Capacity 10 cartridges. Loaded single shot or from 5-shot clip.
Barrel length: 23.2 in.
Overall length: 43.7 in.
Weight: 9.48 lbs.
Sights: Front, shielded post; rear, tangent.

Operation: Tappet driving back through hole in receiver above line of barrel strikes bolt carrier and starts it to the rear until pressure has dropped. At unlocking point, the housing is machined to cam the bolt up a ramp at its rear end, thus allowing the carrier and bolt to travel to the rear with the bolt carrying the cartridge case in its face, held by the extractor, until it strikes the ejector and is tossed out of the weapon. Recoil springs compressed during this motion start the housing and bolt forward at the end of the recoil stroke. Upon closing, as the cartridge is chambered and the bolt face is against the breech face

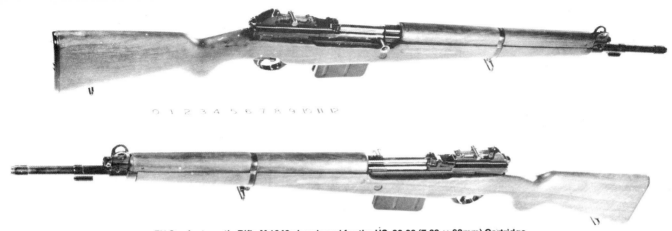

FN Semiautomatic Rifle M 1949 chambered for the US .30-06 (7.62 × 63mm) Cartridge.

of the barrel, the housing still has continuing forward movement, which enables it, through its machined surfaces, to depress the rear of the bolt into its locking recess with the rear locking surface at the top of the ramp.

How the FN Self-Loader Works

The hammer mechanism in the design is an adaptation of the familiar John Browning hammer hook system as used originally in his automatic shotgun. Variations of this design are encountered in most sporting arms of successful types today, and a minor variant of it is used in the United States Rifle M1 and the Carbine M1.

The hammer hook system is so designed that during recoil the rear upper hook on the hammer is engaged automatically to prevent full automatic fire. When the trigger is deliberately released, the upper hook (or sear) releases; the hammer spring reacts, but the forward holding sear, which is at a lower level than the automatic holding one, grips a lower cut or hook in the hammer. One innovation in the design (which has, however, appeared on German rifles, notably of Walther commercial design) is that the hammer spring guide is designed to protrude slightly below the line of the trigger guard when the hammer is in cocked position. It is remembered that the hammer is concealed in this type of weapon. The FN design permits the holder of the weapon to tell by sight or touch if the hammer is cocked as evidenced by the protruding nose of the mainspring guide.

The safety system also includes a variation of the one utilized in the Garand in that the bolt housing or carrier is so designed that it interferes with the hammer striking the firing pin until both the bolt is locked and the housing itself is in its forward position. Thus, if the housing is not completely closed while the hammer may fall, it can only strike the rear of the housing and cannot fire the cartridge in the chamber. In such an instance, it is necessary to pull back the cocking handle to recock the arm before it can be fired. The firing pin is automatically retracted by a return spring after being driven forward to fire.

The face of the bolt is slotted to allow it to travel back over the ejector, which also helps to serve as a travel guide. As the proper motion nears the end of the recoil stroke, the ejector is far enough out from the face of the bolt so that it can pivot the cartridge out of the gun.

The manual safety is on the right side of the trigger guard and is in the form of a turning lever with a half round block, which not only locks the trigger to prevent any movement but also drops its bar down far enough to interfere with the trigger finger being inserted into the trigger guard as a warning that the safety is applied.

A study of the detail drawings will disclose all the salient features and show the resemblance to the Russian designs in particular. While this is a beautifully constructed rifle, the very nature and quality of the workmanship in it make it a relatively costly one to produce.

How to Load and Fire the FN Self-Loading Rifle

Apply safety by pushing down, and pull bolt operating handle completely to the rear. Bolt will remain to the rear, and two 5-round chargers can be loaded into the magazine in a manner similar to that used when loading a Mauser or Springfield rifle. Pull bolt slightly to the rear and release; the bolt will run forward and chamber a cartridge. The magazine may also be loaded by inserting the cartridges one by one in the magazine. Disengage safety by pushing it back up away from the rear of the trigger. Pressure on the trigger will fire the rifle, and for each individual pull of the trigger a round will be fired until the magazine is exhausted.

How to Field Strip the FN Self-Loading Rifle

At the rear of the receiver is a locking key that seats on the rear end of the operating spring guide, which protrudes through the rear end of the receiver. Making sure that the bolt is forward, turn locking key 180° upward, push receiver cover forward against the pressure of the operating spring lifting rear end of cover to release it from the guide track in the receiver. Pull cover to the rear and remove cover and operating spring assembly. Pull bolt operating handle to the rear until the bolt carrier guides are in line with clearance cut in receiver track. Lift front end of bolt carrier/bolt assembly and remove from receiver. Remove bolt from the receiver. The piston and piston spring are removed by depressing the gas cylinder plug, located at the front of the gas cylinder tube under the front sight, and rotating it 90°. It can then be removed, tilting the rifle forward will cause the gas piston and spring to slide forward and out of the gas cylinder tube. The magazine can be removed by pushing up the magazine catch with the point of a bullet or some similarly shaped object. The amount of gas let into the rifle can be regulated. Remove gas cylinder plug; then remove front end cap screw and front end cap. Remove front hand guard by swinging its front end upwards. The gas adjusting sleeve can be turned by inserting a bullet or pointed instrument in the holes in its body. To increase gas pressure, screw the sleeve forward; to decrease the gas pressure, screw the sleeve to the rear.

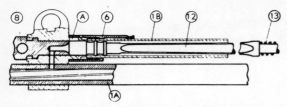

(1) Gas action. May be sealed off by turning nut. Standard gas port top of barrel bleeds gas into cylinder to drive piston back on tappet principle as for German Kar. 43.

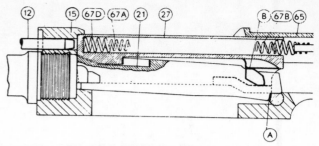

(2) Unlocking action. Bolt locked. Tappet hits bolt carrier starting it back. Spring returns piston to battery. Slide has initial free movement before camming action starts.

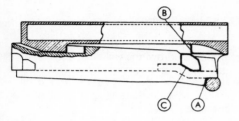

(3) Cams on carrier raise bolt out of receiver engagement as with Russian Tokarev rifle.

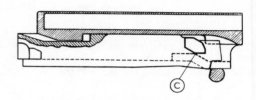

(4) Bolt and carrier go back. Hammer is ridden down to cock. Recoil spring compressed in standard fashion.

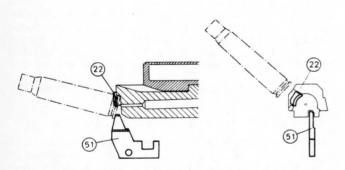

(5) Near end of recoil stroke, the cartridge case held by the extractor hits the ejector and is tossed out of the rifle.

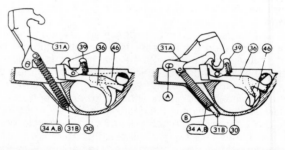

(6) Left-Hammer and mechanism in fired position. On recoil, hammer hook will be engaged Browning-style on rear sear to prevent firing until trigger is released. Right-Hammer held by forward sear ready for firing. Mainspring guide pin projects as signal that hammer is cocked. Walther system.

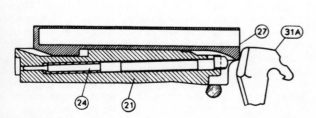

(7) Safety feature. If action is not locked, hammer will hit carrier instead of firing pin.

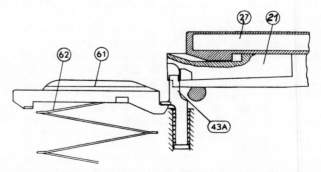

(8) Magazine follower pushed up plunger to hold bolt open when last shot is fired.

Operation of the FN Semiautomatic Rifle.

FUSIL AUTOMATIQUE LÉGÈR (FAL)–FN LIGHT AUTOMATIC RIFLE

Characteristics of FN Light Automatic Rifle (FAL)

Caliber: 7.62mm NATO.
Weight w/empty magazine: 9.06 lbs.
Overall length: 40 in.
Barrel length: 21 in.
Method of operation: Gas, selective fire.
Feeding: From detachable box magazine, staggered 20-round capacity.

Sights: Front; Hooded post. Rear aperture graduated in 100 meter steps to 600 meters.
Cyclic rate of fire: 650 to 700 per minute. Most of the weapons in service throughout the world are only used as semiautomatic weapons.

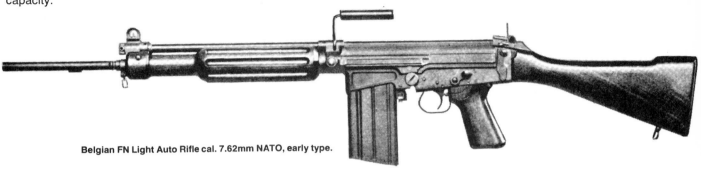

Belgian FN Light Auto Rifle cal. 7.62mm NATO, early type.

FN 7.62mm NATO FAL Rifle, 1964 pattern with plastic stock, handguard and pistol grip.

FN 7.62mm NATO FAL Paratroop Rifle, stock extended.

Heavy barrel version of the FN 7.62mm FAL. This rifle is in service in Israel and Peru, among other countries. It is used as squad automatic weapon. A modified version of this weapon is manufactured in Australia and Canada.

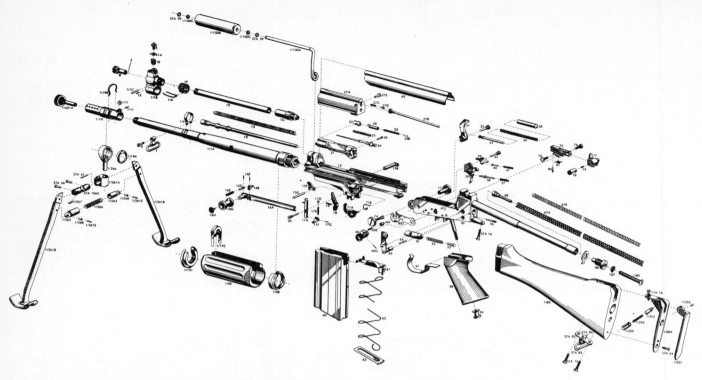

FN Heavy-barrel Automatic Rifle as made for South Africa. Caliber 7.62mm.

How the FAL Works

Pull cocking handle on left side of receiver to rear as in BAR. This leaves the right hand on the pistol grip ready for firing. The cocking handle does not move during firing, again as in the case of the BAR. This removes danger to the firer's face and does not interfere with aiming.

If there is an empty magazine in the rifle at the end of the cocking handle's stroke, the bolt is held open automatically. A loaded magazine is inserted in the magazine housing and pushed in until the retaining catch secures it.

Pressing the release stud on the left side near the magazine catch releases the bolt, which is driven forward by its compressed return spring.

This return spring is housed in the butt. It acts on the bolt carrier through a rod pivoted at its rear face. As the bolt moves forward, its feed face strips the top round from the magazine in standard fashion and thrusts it up the ramp into the barrel chamber, where the extractor engages the cannelure in the case. The gun is now ready for firing.

Firing the FAL

The change lever on the left side of the receiver may be set for "safe," "single shot" or "full automatic" fire. The positions are widely spaced deliberately so that in the dark one can tell by sense of touch the position of the change lever.

If the change lever is set for single shot fire, pressure on the trigger releases the hammer to strike the rear face of the firing pin and fire the cartridge. Since the weapon fires from a closed breech, there is no such disturbance of aim as occurs in weapons like the submachine gun and the Browning machine rifle, where the mass of the breech mechanism moves forward with the pull on the trigger.

The operation is the standard gas system whose reliability has long been established for this type of weapon. Part of the gases following the bullet down the barrel pass through the port into the forward section of the gas cylinder. A gas regulator, previously adjusted, provides sufficient gas to satisfactorily operate

the piston, which is driven back to function the mechanism. Remaining gas passes to the open air through holes in the gas cylinder.

The piston, acting on the tappet principle, is driven to the rear in its tube on top of the barrel. It strikes the bolt carrier and pushes it to the rear.

Ramps machined into the bolt carrier engage a cam on the bolt after the bullet has emerged from the barrel and the pressure has dropped to safe limits. The bolt is cam lifted out of engagement with its locking shoulder in the receiver—this unlocks the action.

The bolt carrier and bolt now travel together to the rear. They ride down the hammer to cock it.

During rearward motion of the bolt, the extractor has carried the empty case out of the chamber with it. The case strikes the ejector and is thrown out the right side of the gun.

After the piston tappet strikes the bolt carrier and imparts the necessary impetus to it, during which travel the spring around the piston has been compressed, the spring operates to return the piston to forward (battery) position. The return spring within the butt is fully compressed during rearward movement of the bolt and carrier in standard fashion. At the end of the recoil stroke, the compressed spring reasserts itself and working through it connecting rod thrusts the bolt and carrier forward. The bolt strips a cartridge from the magazine and chambers it and stops against the face of the barrel. The bolt carrier, which still has continuing movement under thrust from the recoil spring guide and spring, works through the cam and ramps to force the rear locking end of the bolt down its locking recess in the receiver. At the end of the movement of the carrier, it is resting against the receiver above the line of the chamber where it is in line with the rear end of the piston tappet. The extractor, of course, snaps over the cannelure of the cartridge as the bolt chambers the cartridge.

When the change lever is set for automatic firing, the operation is identical with that already described except that the hammer is automatically released to continue fire until pressure on the trigger is released.

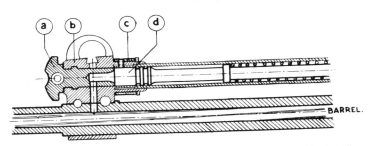

Gas plug (a) is positioned in end of gas cylinder (b). It may be turned to shut off gas when using rifle for grenade launching or as a straight-pull rifle. Gas regulator (c). Head of gas piston (d).

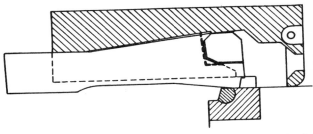

Bolt and carrier reach end of stroke. Case hits ejector. Return spring in butt is fully compressed.

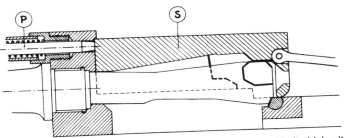

Piston driven back by gas hits movable carrier above locked bolt, driving it back and compressing return spring.

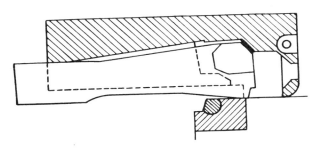

Spring starts carrier and bolt forward. Bolt picks up top cartridge in magazine and starts it toward chamber.

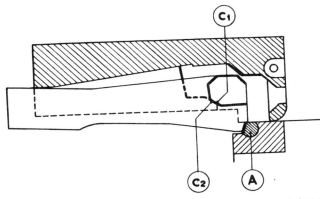

Ramps in the carrier engage cam (CI) on bolt as bullet leaves barrel, thus raising the rear of bolt out of its locking seat (A) in the receiver.

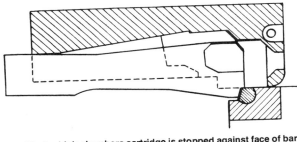

Face of bolt which chambers cartridge is stopped against face of barrel. Carrier is still driven forward, until it cams bolt down into its locking seat in the receiver.

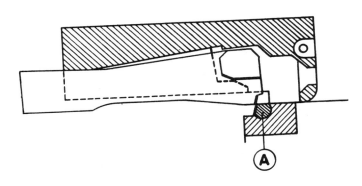

Carrier and bolt travel back together. Piston tappet spring returns piston. Bolt rotates and cocks hammer. Extractor withdraws fired case.

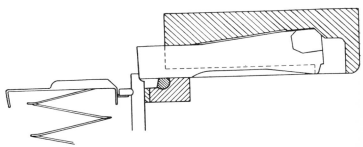

When last shot has been fired, the magazine follower forces a holding plunger up in front of the bolt to hold the action open.

FAL Hold-Open Device

The pin to hold the bolt in rear position when the magazine is empty is mounted in the receiver to the right of the ejector.

It is in the form of a heavy plunger, which is elevated by a nib on the rear of the magazine follower through a small pin working in a slot.

In rest position, this plunger is held down by its spring. However, when the magazine follower rises as the last cartridge is fired, upward pressure of the heavy magazine spring overcomes the lighter spring attached to the pin, and the pin is thrust upwards. The plunger is thereby raised to its complete height and projects into the forward path of the bolt.

When a full magazine is inserted in the gun, drawing the bolt slightly to the rear allows the plunger spring to react and lower the plunger, and the bolt driven by the recoil spring now moves forward to chamber a cartridge.

FAL Trigger Operation

Turning the change lever on the left side of the receiver to the safe position turns a stud into position at the extreme rear of the trigger to lock it mechanically. In this position, trigger movement is impossible.

When the change lever is set for single shot fire, the stud is turned into position to clear the rear of the trigger and to permit a pull on the trigger to draw the tip of the sear attached to the trigger down out of engagement with the hammer notch to release the hammer for firing. There are actually two sears—the rear or firing sear that connects hammer and trigger during single-shot operation and the front or safety sear. This safety sear performs two functions. It blocks the hammer to prevent it from falling except when the bolt and the bolt carrier are fully home. It is struck by the bolt carrier at the final movement of closing travel when it releases the hammer so the firing sear may be operated on single-shot operation to release the trigger, or so the hammer may fire in full automatic fashion if the firing sear is out of engagement due to the automatic fire control being set on the change lever.

The entire operation is extremely simple mechanically and a

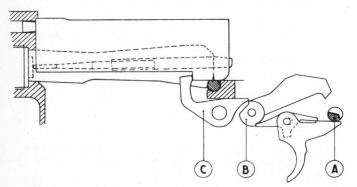

Gun with safety, applied. Change-lever stud (A) is locking trigger to prevent movement.

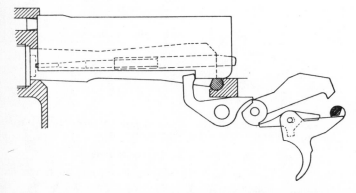

Change-lever stud set for single-shot fire. Pressure on trigger will free sear from hammer contact, but as the rifle action opens, the safety sear will hold the hammer until finger pressure is released.

study of the drawings accompanying the explanation will clearly demonstrate all the mechanical features involved.

The ejector is mounted in the receiver and serves as a guide in its slot in the lower side of the bolt. At the end of the recoil stroke, the cartridge case strikes the ejector as the bolt passes slightly past the nose of the ejector to hurl the empty case out of the gun.

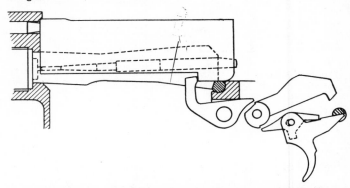

Lever is set for full-auto fire. Sear is out of engagement except when the trigger is released. Safety sear controls firing to prevent premature discharge.

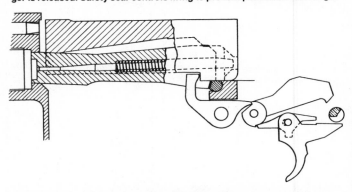

The safety sear mechanism is released by blow of the carrier as it goes home after bolt is locked, thus freeing the hammer to fire.

FAL Gas Regulator

A gas regulator and gas plug control the quantity of gas permitted to reach the piston. The gas plug A is fixed into the end of the gas cylinder B. This plug has two positions. One permits full access of the gas from the barrel directly to the gas cylinder. The other when turned through 180 degrees blocks off all entry of gas. In this condition, the arm will not function automatically. In this condition, however, it can be operated manually as a straight-pull bolt-action rifle. In other words, pulling the cocking handle back and releasing it will load and cock the gun ready for firing. After firing, another full pull to the rear and release of the cocking handle will eject the empty case and load a new round ready for another pull.

In this closed position, the arm may be used as a grenade launcher, since automatic action is not desired for such a purpose.

A gas regulator C consists of a shroud around the end of the gas cylinder. Unscrewing allows gas to escape.

This system of gas regulation by exhaust keeps fouling of the piston to an absolute minimum and allows regulation of power.

The gas cylinder is placed above the barrel. The center of gravity of the weapon is in line with the axis of the barrel. As a result, the recoil does not tend to pull the weapon upwards as much as many semiautomatic rifles.

FAL Field Stripping

Stripping and assembling this weapon for normal maintenance and repairs is done without the aid of tools.

With the magazine removed, the release catch at the rear of the top of the receiver is pressed, and the body of the gun is hinged exactly as in the case of the familiar shotgun. The entire bolt and gas operating assembly may now be withdrawn as a unit from the open rear of the receiver. The extractor and firing pin (the normal breakage points in any automatic design) may be withdrawn in a matter of seconds and replaced. All parts are self-contained. There are no loose springs, guides, screws or pins to be removed during this operation. The recoil spring is retained within the butt when the gun is opened for field stripping. When the assembly is returned to the receiver, the guide rod at the end of the bolt, resting against the compression plug in front of the butt, serves to compress the spring housed within when the action is cocked or in recoil motion.

For all practical purposes, no further stripping of this arm is necessary.

Belgian FN Light Auto Rifle. Operating parts removed. Field strip without tools.

FAL Carrying Handle

A special folding carrying handle is provided above and forward of the magazine housing. This handle is placed at the center of gravity to make the arm easy to carry in rapid advances. It may also be used as a carrying handle for marching and general field order. It can be quickly turned down out of the line of sight and out of the way.

The grip of pistol type design behind the triggerguard aids greatly in stabilizing fire, and since all operations of loading and cocking and change lever adjusting are done on the left side of the receiver full control of the arm may be maintained at all times. In addition, of course, this pistol grip gives the weapon the advantage of ease of operation for firing at waist level under appropriate conditions. The forestock is designed for comfort and secure control as a normal left hand hold for shoulder firing or waist firing.

As special accessories, a muzzle brake and flash hider are available. A grenade launcher is also part of the accessory equipment as is a special bayonet and a detachable folding bipod mount.

FAL Further Dismounting

Remove the magazine. Draw the cocking lever to the rear and check that the chamber is empty. Move the cocking handle back to free the bolt and allow it to go forward to locked closed position.

Push down the butt locking lever on the left rear side of the reciever as far as it will go. Simultaneously push the butt itself downwards. The butt will pivot together with the lower receiver section. This allows the arm to open as in the familiar case of the hinged-frame shotgun.

Pull back the spring rod attached to the bolt; this will pull the bolt and carrier assembly to the rear out of the gun.

Slide the receiver cover to the rear off the receiver.

Lift the front end of the bolt while pressing it forward into the carrier and continue lifting the front end to raise the rear gently out of carrier contact against the pressure of the firing pin spring.

Push out the cross retaining pin while holding onto the rear of the firing pin, and the pressure of its spring will force it out of its housing.

Insert the nose of a bullet under the extractor and pry outwards and upwards to withdraw the extractor.

The gas plug can be removed if desired and a rod passed through the gas cylinder to clean fouling.

The gas plug can be turned with the nose of a bullet for removal. This permits removal of the piston and spring from the gas cylinder. While there are very few remaining parts, and additional stripping of the firing mechanism can be done easily, it is not normally done by the average soldier.

FN 7.62mm FAL Rifle with low-mounted scope.

FN 7.62mm NATO FAL Rifle with high-mounted scope.

VARIATIONS AMONG SOME FN LIGHT AUTOMATIC RIFLES PRODUCED AT FN.

	Barrel 1. Smooth muzzle 2. Threaded muzzle 3. Threaded muzzle for combined grenade launcher/flash suppressor	Flash suppressor 1. Without 2. With 3. Combined with grenade launcher	Bayonet 1. Flash suppressor type or normal 2. Tubular type 3. Without	Extractor in 1. One piece 2. Two pieces	Butt stock 1. Without front socket 2. With front socket	Butt plate 1. Without butt trap 2. With butt trap	Handguard 1. Wood 2. Metal 3. Molded material	Bipod 1. Without 2. With	Loading 1. Without charger (Stripper clip) 2. With charger
Austria	3	3	3	2	2	2	2	2	1
Belgium	1	1	1	2	2	1	3	1	2
Cambodia	1	1	1	2	2	1	3	1	1
Chile	2	2	1	2	2	1	3	1	1
Ecuador	2	2	1	2	2	1	3	1	1
Indonesia	1	1	1	2	1	2	1	1	1
Ireland	2	3	2	2	2	2	3	1	1
Israel	1	1	1	1	1	1	1	1	1
Kuwait	1	1	1	2	1	2	1	1	1
Libya	1	1	1	2	2	1	3	1	1
Luxembourg	1	1	1	1	1	2	1	1	2
Netherlands	3	3	2	2	2	1	2	2	1
Paraguay	1	1	1	2	1	2	1	1	1
Peru	1	1	1	2	2	2	1	1	1
Portugal	1	1	1	2	2	1	3	1	1
Qatar	1	1	1	1 & 2	1	2	1	1	1
Santo Domingo	1	1	1	2	1	1	1	1	1
South Africa	1	1	2	2	2	1	3	1	1
Syria	1	1	1	1	1	2	1	1	1
West Germany	1	2	3	2	1	2	2	2	1
Venezuela	2	2	3	1	1	1	1	1	1

There are other variations; as for example, the British-produced L1A1 and the Canadian-produced C1A1.

Identification of FALs can be puzzling. Several modifications can aid in determining the origin of particular FALs. The West German G-1, the Austrian StG58 and the Dutch FAL all have a lightweight, folding metal bipod as part of their metal forestock; the British L1A1 and the Indian Ishapore rifles, capable of semiautomatic fire only, have zigzag dirt clearance cuts in the bolt carriers, folding operating handles and enlarged magazine catches and selectors. In addition, the FAL is found with or without flash suppressors, with different types of bolt covers and with forearms of different styles. It is often difficult to identify the original purchaser of a FAL unless the rifle is stamped with an identifying seal or crest.

CARBINE AUTOMATIQUE LÉGÈR (CAL)—LIGHT AUTOMATIC CARBINE, 5.56mm

As long ago as 1963, FN was working on a military rifle for the 5.56mm (.223) cartridge. At that time, they were considering scaling down the FAL from 7.62mm to 5.56mm and did build some FAL prototype rifles chambered for the 5.56mm cartridge. The CAL—Carbine Automatique Léger, or light automatic carbine—does resemble the FAL externally in its overall configuration. The FAL has a tilting bolt system, but the bolt of the CAL rotates to lock and unlock. The bolt head has an interrupted screw type locking mechanism. There are two sets—top and bottom—of buttress type lugs, which are inclined at an angle to the axis of the bolt body. This inclination provides for slow initial extraction, i.e., an initial loosening of the case in the chamber before the case is withdrawn from the chamber.

Characteristics of the "CAL"

Caliber: 5.56mm
System of operation: gas, selective fire
Length overall: 38.6 in.
Barrel length: 18.4 in.
Feed device: 20-round, detachable, staggered row box magazine
Sights: Front: protected post
      Rear: "L" with apertures
Muzzle velocity: 3182 f.p.s.
Weight: 7.3 lbs. loaded w/light alloy magazine
Cyclic rate of fire: approx. 750-800 r.p.m.

Description of the CAL

The CAL makes extensive use of steel stampings—the forend, receiver and magazine and trigger housing are all of stamped construction. The rotating bolt, described above, locks into a barrel extension keeping the strain on the receiver to a minimum. The barrel is locked in the receiver by a nut that is slipped over the front end of the barrel and is screwed onto a thread near the breech-end of the barrel, bearing against the conical surface at the front of the receiver. The gas system is basically the same as that of the FAL; the spring loaded piston strikes the bolt carrier and then returns to its forward position; a cam slot cut in the top and side of the bolt carrier cams a stud on the bolt causing it to rotate into and out of the locked position. The trigger mechanism has a 3-round burst selector in addition to the provisions for full and semiautomatic fire. If the safety/selector lever is set on the figure 3, the weapon will fire three rounds and cease fire until the trigger is pulled again.

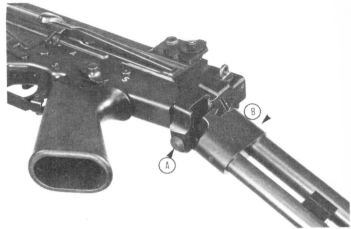

Detailed view of folding stock. Push release (A) upwards and push stock assembly (B) downwards. Fold the stock along the left side of the rifle.

FN 5.56mm *Carbine Automatique Légèr* (CAL).

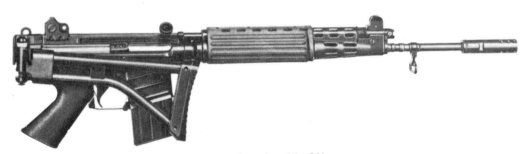

Folding stock version of the CAL.

Release of the magazine can be accomplished without removing the hand from the pistol grip.

CAL fitted with telescopic sight. Note also the three position selector: Safe, single shot, three shot burst and automatic fire.

Field Stripping the FN CAL

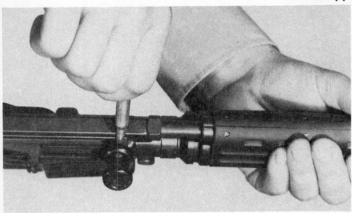

Draw the operating handle to the right and, if necessary, use a cartridge to pry the handle outward.

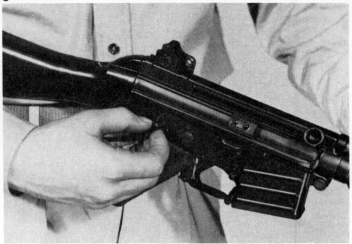

From left to right, press out the take down spring, and then swing open the two halves of the receiver. Pull the operating handle to the rear, remove it and elevate the muzzle, thus allowing the bolt to slide out the rear of the receiver.

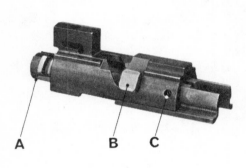

Take hold of the bolt carrier and push the bolt (A) fully to the rear. In this position, the lock pin (B) is in its low and rear position and the retaining pin can be seen

in hole at (C). Using the drift pin from the assembly kit push out the firing pin retention pin.

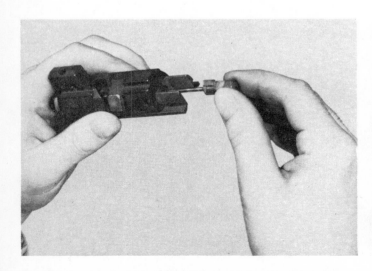

Withdraw firing pin.

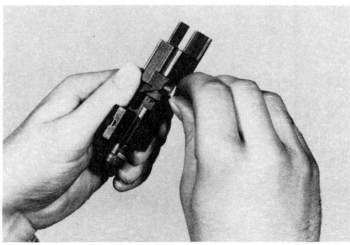

Remove lock pin.

Remove the piston and its spring from the gas cylinder, tapping lightly, if necessary. Lean the piston head against something fairly hard; compress the return spring. Remove the clips from the piston rod and then remove the spring from the rod.

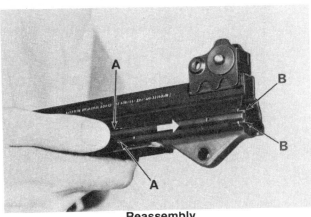

Reassembly

Assembly is done in the opposite order. Certain precautions must be observed. In reassembling the ejector, make certain that the four securing lugs, two in front (A) **and two at the rear** (B) **of the ejector housing, are correctly positioned facing the corresponding lugs in the receiver. Then slide the ejector housing forward. It must be fully forward so that the rear part does not project at the rear of the receiver when the two halves are closed. The remainder of the assembly steps are the opposite of disassembly.**

THE MODEL 30 BROWNING AUTOMATIC RIFLE

FN produced the Browning Automatic rifle for Chile, China, Belgium and other countries before World War II. Most of these weapons were variations of the Model 30 and were similar to the U.S. Model 1918A1 BAR. The Model 30 can be distinguished from the US issue BAR by the magazine and ejection port covers, the separate pistol grip, the ribbed barrel (the U.S. M1922 BAR had a ribbed barrel, but few of these were made), the shape of the fore-end and the dome-shaped gas regulator. Some Model 30 rifles were made with quick change barrels, and all could be mounted on a special tripod made by FN. The Model 30 was made in the following calibers: 7mm, 7.65mm and 7.92mm. The Model 30 Browning automatic rifle is an obsolescent weapon and is not likely to be found in the hands of troops today.

BROWNING AUTOMATIC RIFLE TYPE D

After World War II, FN introduced the Type D Browning automatic rifle. This weapon features major improvements not found in other versions of the BAR. The Type D has a quick change barrel and a rate-reducing mechanism as do several other versions of the BAR. It is the only version of the BAR, however, to have a rapid method of field stripping. The stock is hinged, and by removal of the trigger guard assembly pin and butt access pin the piston slide and bolt assembly can, be removed. The recoil (operating) spring of the Type D is mounted in the butt rather than in the piston slide assembly, as it is in the US BAR. A clockwork type rate reducer is used with the Type D rather than the buffer type found on the US Browning Automatic Rifle M1918A2. The Type D was purchased by Egypt in 7.92mm during the reign of King Farouk and by Belgium in caliber .30-06.

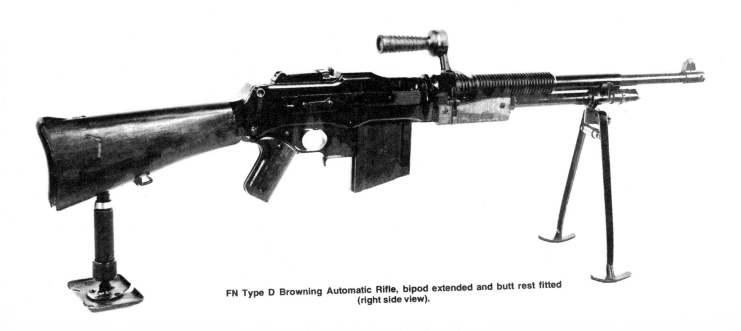

FN Type D Browning Automatic Rifle, bipod extended and butt rest fitted
(right side view).

BELGIAN SUBMACHINE GUNS

Belgium used the Schmeisser MP 28 II prior to World War II. This 9mm parabellum weapon is described in some detail under Germany. The postwar Belgian Army used the Vigneron M2 submachine gun. A number of other submachine guns have been developed and/or produced in Belgium since World War II. Outstanding among these is the FN-produced UZI, which is of Israeli design and is covered in detail under that country. FN designed and produced a 9mm parabellum submachine gun prior to the UZI, but it was not a very successful design.

Repousemetal of Belgium developed an interesting weapon in 9mm called the RAN submachine gun. It has an internal cooling system, which uses the bolt as a pneumatic ram to force air through a system of helical grooves around the barrel. It was produced in limited quantities in several versions, including one with a folding bayonet. Another departure from conventional submachine gun design was in the fitting of a bipod to one model. The value of a bipod on a weapon firing 9mm parabellum ammunition is questionable because of the limited accurate range of this, or any other, pistol cartridge.

Several other submachine guns—basically modified Sten guns have been developed in Belgium since World War II.

THE VIGNERON M2 SUBMACHINE GUN

The Vigneron is a conventional post World War II submachine gun of stamped construction. Loading and firing of the weapon are basically the same as for the British Sten except that it has a grip safety that must be squeezed to fire the gun and a selector on the left side of the weapon that can be set on semiautomatic, automatic fire or safe. The grip safety prevents accidental discharge if the gun is dropped with a loaded magazine in place and the bolt in the forward position.

The Belgian 9mm Vigneron M2 Submachine Gun.

FN 9mm UZI submachine gun.

Characteristics of the Vigneron M2 Submachine Gun

System of operation: Blowback selective fire.
Weight loaded: 8.74 lbs.
Length overall: 34.9 in. w/stock extended 24 in. w/stock telescoped.
Barrel length: 12 in.
Feed device: 32-round, detachable, staggered box magazine.
Sights: Front: Blade.
       Rear: Nonadjustable aperture.
Muzzle velocity: 1224 f.p.s.
Cyclic rate of fire: 600 r.p.m.

How to Field Strip The Vigneron M2

Remove magazine and check chamber for a cartridge. Unscrew the receiver cap at rear of receiver and remove the bolt. Unscrew barrel nut on front of receiver and remove the barrel. Further disassembly is not recommended. Reassembly is performed by reversing the above steps.

BELGIAN MACHINE GUNS

The Lewis gun, which was probably the outstanding light machine gun of World War I, was first manufactured in Belgium circa 1913 by "Armes Automatique Lewis" in Liege. It was first encountered by the Germans in the hands of Belgian troops, and they called it "the Belgian rattle snake." The last part may be legend, but in any event the Belgians appreciated the value of automatic fire power that was truly mobile.

As has already been mentioned, FN produced Browning machine guns prior to World War II, and has produced the caliber .30 Browning aircooled for the Belgian Army after World War II. These weapons were sold world-wide, and among the purchasers were Argentina, China, Thailand, the Netherlands, Greece and Belgium. They are no longer in production.

The MAG field stripped.

The 7.62mm FN MAG machine gun as currently made on new model tripod
Note smooth barrel.

Section view of FN MAG machine gun.

MITRAILLEUSE A GAS (MAG)—GENERAL PURPOSE MACHINE GUN

The MAG is another development of FN, and like most of the products of that concern it demonstrates first-class engineering ability. The gun combines the operating system of the Browning automatic rifle (BAR) with a belt feed mechanism similar to that of the German MG 42. The bolt mechanism of the BAR has been changed in the MAG so that it locks on the bottom of the receiver, rather than on the top as with the BAR. It has a chrome-plated and stellite-lined bore and chamber in its quick change barrel. The MAG, like the German World War II guns and the U.S. M60, is designed to be used on a bipod as a light machine gun and on a tripod as a heavy machine gun. Its rate of fire can be adjusted through the use of its gas regulator from a low cyclic rate of 700 rounds per minute to a high cyclic rate of 1000 rounds per minute.

Characteristics of MAG Machine Gun

Caliber: Has been made in 7.62mm NATO and 6.5 Swedish.
System of operation: Gas, automatic only.
Weight, w/butt and bipod: 23.92 lbs.
Weight, w/o butt and bipod: 22.22 lbs.
Weight of FN tripod: 22 lbs. (constructed of aluminum alloy).
Length, overall: 49.21 in. w/flash suppressor.
Barrel length: 21.44 in.
Feed mechanism: Link belt. (Nondisintegrating push-out type links similar to those used on the MG 34 and MG 42 or US M13 disintegrating links may be used.)
Sights: Front: Folding type with blade, or type adjustable for height.
Rear: Combined battle-sight peep and leaf with notch; peep adjustable to 800 meters and leaf adjustable to 1800 meters.
Muzzle velocity: 2800 f.p.s. (approx.) 7.62mm NATO ball cartridge.
Cyclic rate of fire: 700 to 1000 r.p.m.

How to Load and Fire the MAG

Pull the operating handle to the rear; since the MAG fires from an open bolt, the slide and bolt will remain to the rear. Push the button type safety mounted in the pistol grip from the left side, so that the letter "S" is exposed on the right side. Open cover by pressing cover catch at rear of cover. Lay cartridge belt on feedway so that the first cartridge abuts against the cartridge stop. Close cover securely and push safety button from right to left. Squeeze trigger and the weapon will fire.

Loading the MAG.

How the MAG Works

Essentially, the operation of the MAG is the same as that of the Browning automatic rifle, with the exception of its belt feeding mechanism and bottom receiver locking. A stud mounted on the top of the bolt operates in a track in the belt feed lever, which moves the belt feed slide back and forth, pulling cartridges into position for ramming by the bolt. The trigger mechanism of this weapon is much simpler than that of the BAR. No rate-reducing mechanism is used with this gun.

Field Stripping the MAG

Open the cover and check to insure that the weapon is not loaded. Push in on stock catch located on front underside of butt and slide butt up and off the receiver. Push in on recoil spring rod and disengage it from the bottom of receiver; remove recoil spring assembly (recoil spring and rod are packaged unit). Pull operating handle to the rear, and the slide and bolt will move to the rear. Grasp slide and bolt assembly by the slide post and withdraw assembly from the receiver. Remove link pin; the link, bolt lock and bolt can be removed from the slide. To remove the pistol grip, pull out the retaining pin from the right side. To remove the cover and the feed tray, pull out the cover pin from the right side. To remove barrel, push barrel lock in (barrel lock is located at left front of receiver), move the barrel handle to the left so that it is in the vertical position and pull barrel straight out. No further disassembly is recommended.

Reverse the above procedure to reassemble the weapon. When reassembling the bolt slide assembly to the receiver, the head of the bolt must be supported so that the forward grooves on the bolt engage the mating ridges on the sides of the receiver.

Special Note on the MAG

The MAG can be used with any rifle cartridge that has the same base dimension as the 7.92mm Mauser; this includes 7.62mm NATO, simply by changing the barrel. The butt and bipod can be removed from the gun for use in transport vehicles or tanks. The weapon can be used on the tripod with the butt removed.

The MAG has proven to be quite a popular machine gun and has been purchased by the following countries: Argentina, Belgium, Cuba, Ecuador, India, Israel, Kuwait, Libya, New Zealand, the Netherlands, Northern Rhodesia, Peru, Quatar, Ruanda, Sierra Leone, Southern Rhodesia, South Africa, Sweden, Tanganyika, Uganda, the United Kingdom (Great Britain) and Venezuela. With the exception of Sweden, which chose 6.5mm, all countries adopted the gun in 7.62mm NATO. It is probable that the Swedish guns will also be converted to this caliber in the future. The MAG (machine gun, general purpose L7A1) is being manufactured at the Royal Small Arms Factory at Enfield Lock.

The Belgian FN General Purpose Machine Gun. Type MAG.

(1) Removing butt assembly.

(2) Disengaging recoil spring rod.

(3) Removing recoil spring assembly.

(4) Removing bolt, piston and slide.

(5) Removing bolt lock and link.

(6) Removing extractor.

(7) Bolt and slide components.

(8) Removing grip trigger assembly.

(9) Removing cover.

(12) Removing feed plate.

(11) Cover assembly.

(10) Removing barrel.

(13) Replacing barrel.

(14) Drawing barrel to rear.

(15) Adjusting gas cylinder aperture.

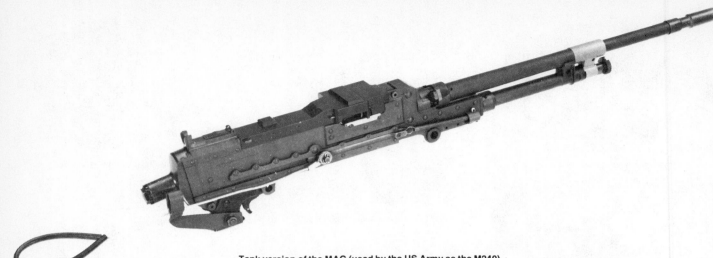

Tank version of the MAG (used by the US Army as the M240).

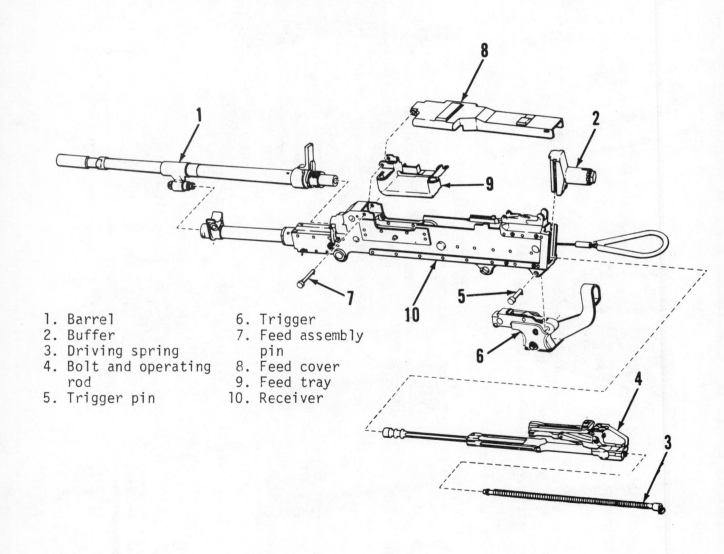

1. Barrel
2. Buffer
3. Driving spring
4. Bolt and operating rod
5. Trigger pin
6. Trigger
7. Feed assembly pin
8. Feed cover
9. Feed tray
10. Receiver

Disassembled view of MAG (M240).

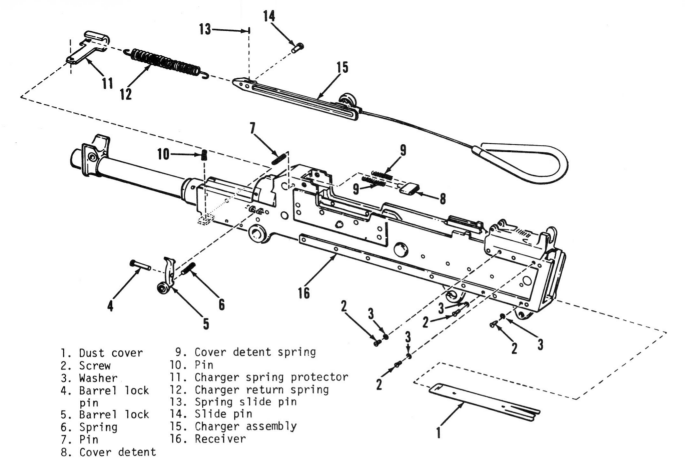

1. Dust cover
2. Screw
3. Washer
4. Barrel lock pin
5. Barrel lock
6. Spring
7. Pin
8. Cover detent
9. Cover detent spring
10. Pin
11. Charger spring protector
12. Charger return spring
13. Spring slide pin
14. Slide pin
15. Charger assembly
16. Receiver

MAG (M240) Receiver Assembly.

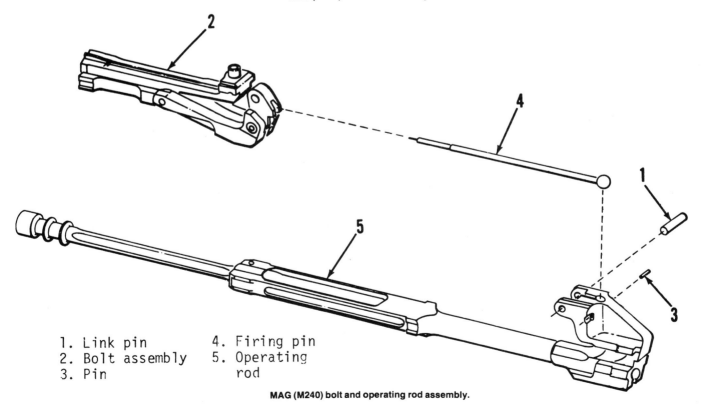

1. Link pin
2. Bolt assembly
3. Pin
4. Firing pin
5. Operating rod

MAG (M240) bolt and operating rod assembly.

10

Britain (United Kingdom) and the British Commonwealth

It is no longer realistic to attempt to collect under Britain all weapons in use in the British Commonwealth, since many of the member nations have taken an independent course. This independence in weaponry should not be too surprising, inasmuch as the United Kingdom does not dictate to the members of the Commonwealth what weapons they will or will not adopt. In the past, these nations have usually adopted the same weapons as the UK, because in most cases (but not all) they were members of defense treaties with the UK and their political, social and economic orientation would put them on the same side as the UK in any major war. Since World War II, however, the defense arrangements have tended to be more general and include nations outside the Commonwealth, notably the United States. It is therefore likely that the future will see many American weapons added to those that are already standard in the British Commonwealth.

The standard small arms in the British Army are the 9mm Browning FN H.P. pistol in its various marks, the 7.62mm rifle L1A1, the 9mm submachine gun L2A3, the 7.62mm/L7A1 general purpose machine gun and the caliber .50 Browning machine gun. Some caliber .30 Browning M1919A5 and M37 machine guns are still in service on various armored vehicles.

The United Kingdom has procured quantities of Colt 5.56mm (.223) AR 15 rifles for use by forces that might have to operate in tropical climates. The 7.62mm NATO L4A2 Bren gun has been continued in service with Infantry in the Far East and is used by other branches of the Army on a world-wide basis.

A separate chapter is given each to Australia, Canada, India and New Zealand.

BRITISH SMALL ARMS NOMENCLATURE

The model-designation procedures of the UK are somewhat involved and can be confusing. Prior to World War I, British model designations for small arms were comprised of the word Mark followed by a Roman numeral, e.g., Mark I, Mark II. Two exceptions to this form of designation were the Pattern 13, which was an experimental cal. .276 rifle tested in 1913, and the Pattern 14, which was made in cal. .303 as the production version of the Pattern 13.

Between World Wars I and II, rifles and pistols were given number designations in addition to mark designations. Thus the Rifle Mark III SMLE became Rifle No. 1 Mark III SMLE, and the Pattern 14 became the Rifle No. 3 Mark I. Toward the end of World War II, the British began using Arabic numerals for both the number and mark designations. An additional complication was the star symbol (*), which was frequently found tacked to the end of everything else, e.g., Rifle No. 4 Mark 1*. This star indicates a minor modification from the Mark design.

Since the early fifties, weapons entering the British service have received an L designation, and modifications have been indicated by an A, as in L2A3. The L stands for "Land service." Older weapons that have been considerably modified, such as the Brens rebarreled for the 7.62mm NATO cartridge, also receive an L designation, as do (in most cases) United States weapons adopted as standard or limited standard by the UK.

A revolver is usually called a "pistol" by the British.

BRITISH PISTOLS AND REVOLVERS

The British army was the last major army in the world to use the revolver as a standard service weapon. Lieutenant Winston Churchill of the 21st Lancers used a personally procured Mauser Automatic against the Dervishes at the battle of Omdurman in the Sudan in 1898 and carried the same weapon during his stint as a war correspondent in the Boer War. This put Sir Winston Churchill approximately fifty years ahead of his country's army. After World War II, in which the caliber .38 Enfield revolvers were standard (Webley, Smith and Wesson and Colt revolvers and Canadian-made Browning, Webley, Colt, Star and various other automatic pistols were also used), the UK ran a series of pistol tests. These tests confirmed that a 9mm Parabellum automatic pistol was the best service arm, and the Canadian-made Browning FN H.P. pistol was adopted as standard. Troops were equipped with pistols on hand, which had been used by British paratroop and commando units during the war.

The United Kingdom purchased a quantity of 9mm Parabellum Browning Hi-Power pistols for the RAF from FN. These are the latest type with extractors mounted on the slides and two-piece barrels. They are called Pistol 9mm L9A1 by the British.

WEBLEY REVOLVERS

The British Government used Webley revolvers as standard or limited standard for 60 years. The Mark I was adopted in November 1887, and the last of the standard Webley revolvers, the No. 1 Mark VI, was declared obsolete in 1947. All the standard British issue Webley revolvers were caliber .455, and all were similar in design. The Webley is a top breaking revolver, locked by a heavy stirrup type barrel catch. The first five Marks have "birds head" type grips, and the Mark VI has a square grip. The Mark VI (called No. 1 Mark VI after 1927), which was adopted in May 1915, was made in the greatest quantity, over 300,000 of these revolvers having been made by Webley & Scott at Birmingham during World War I. A quantity of the Mark VI were also made at Enfield Lock after World War I.

After World War I, the British decided that .455 was too heavy for the most effective use and after tests decided upon the use

Webley .455 Mark V pistol, 6-inch barrel pattern introduced in 1915.

The .38 Webley Mark IV. Used during World War II.

of a caliber .38 cartridge based on the .38 Smith & Wesson cartridge case. Webley designed a new pistol using many of the features of their commercial Mark III caliber .38 revolver. The design was taken over by Royal Small Arms Factory and as completed was not compatible with the Webley pistol; parts are not interchangeable. The Webley Mark IV caliber .38 revolver was adopted as limited standard in World War II.

THE WEBLEY .455 "PISTOL" NO. 1 MARK VI

Although this revolver has been obsolete in Great Britain since 1947, it is widely distributed throughout the British Commonwealth and former British territories.

Characteristics of Webley .455 Pistol No. 1 Mark VI

Caliber: .455 Webley.
System of operation: Single or double-action, top break revolver.
Weight: 2.37 lbs.
Length: overall: 11.25 in.
Barrel: 6 in.
Feed device: Cylinder with 6 chambers.
Sights: Front: Blade.
      Rear: Notch.
Muzzle velocity: 620 f.p.s.
NOTE: Some No. 1 Mark VI revolvers have been rechambered for the caliber .45 Colt automatic cartridge. These revolvers use the three-round clip used with the Colt and Smith & Wesson Model 1917 revolvers.

Loading and Firing the Webley Mark VI

Push forward on the curved tail of the pivoted barrel catch, which is on the left side of the revolver just below the hammer. As the catch is pushed, it pivots on its screw drawing the upper latching end back over the barrel strap, freeing the barrel to be tipped down on its hinge. As the barrel is bent down, the extractor will rise on its stem until the revolver is fully opened, at which

Webley .455 Pistol No. 1 Mark VI.

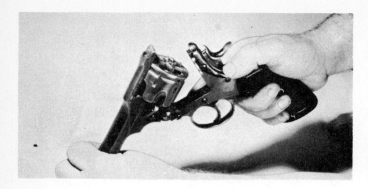

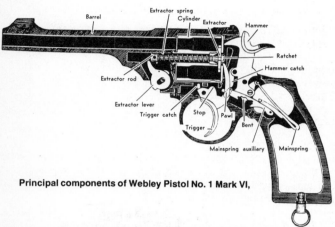

Principal components of Webley Pistol No. 1 Mark VI,

point the extractor under the influence of its spring will slip back into its place in the cylinder.

Now load the six chambers. With a little practice this may be done two chambers at a time. If the cylinder is to be only partly loaded, remember that the cylinder revolves clockwise; and that the first cartridge must be to the left of the chamber in direct line with the hammer nose when the weapon is closed. Cocking the hammer automatically turns the cylinder the distance of one chamber.

Now turn barrel and loaded cylinder up to the fullest extent. The heavy catch will automatically be sprung over the barrel strap and lock it securely.

If you have time, and accuracy is desired, always pull back the hammer with the thumb to full cock for each shot. For close quarters or emergency firing, drawing the trigger straight back will raise the hammer to full cock and turn the cylinder and trip the hammer, completing the firing. It is necessary to release the pressure on the trigger after each shot to permit the mechanism to engage for the next shot. Accurate shooting except at close range is difficult when shooting double action.

Field Stripping the Webley Mark VI

The only stripping necessary and recommended for this revolver is removing the cylinder. The bottom screw at the extreme forward end on the left side of the receiver is the cylinder catch retaining screw. Unscrew this. Now push the bottom of the cylinder catch retainer directly above the screw upwards. This will depress the rear of the catch and permit the cylinder to be lifted out.

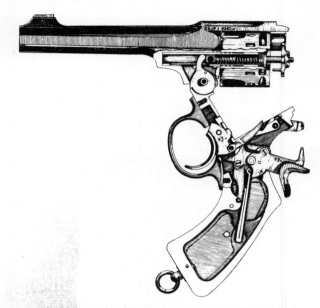

Action open showing details of extraction and locking.

To extract cartridges, break the revolver and push barrel down.

Caliber .22 L.R. version of the Webley Pistol No. 1 Mark VI, which was used by the British for training.

ENFIELD REVOLVERS

As noted previously, the British government and Webley & Scott parted company on uniformity of design in 1926 when the No. 2 Mark 1 Enfield pistol was in prototype form. The No. 2 Mark 1 had many of the best features of the .455 Webley Mark VI and in addition had a movable firing pin mounted on the hammer (all the earlier Webley government revolvers had a fixed hammer nose type firing pin) and a removable side plate. These features had appeared in the commercial .38 Webley Mark III.

The revolver, called Pistol .38 No. 2 Mark 1, was produced from 1927 to 1938; it was officially adopted on 2 June 1932. On 22 June 1938, the first modification of this revolver—the No. 2 Mark 1*—was introduced. The modification consisted of the removal of the spur and the single-action cocking notch on the hammer. The No. 2 Mark 1* can therefore only be used double-action. Since this requires lifting of the hammer, firing and rotation of the cylinder by the pulling of the trigger, the trigger pull is very hard. As a result, this revolver is of very limited accurate range. In 1942, another Model was introduced, the pistol No. 2 Mark 1**. This model has no hammer safety stop. As originally issued, the No. 2 Mark 1 had Mark 1 walnut grips of rather square configuration; at a later date Mark 2 black bakelite or walnut grips with thumb recesses were adopted. These are usually seen on the No. 2 Mark 1* and Mark 1** but may occasionally be seen on the No. 2 Mark 1 as well.

Complete revolvers were made by Enfield and by Albion Motors at Glasgow. Singer Sewing Machine of Great Britain made parts, which were assembled into complete revolvers at Enfield. In 1957, the Enfield revolvers were dropped as standard and replaced by the FN Browning Hi-Power automatic. These revolvers are still in extensive use in former British territories and are considered a reserve weapon in the United Kingdom.

The Enfield revolver, as the Mark IV Webley, uses the British .380 (or .38), revolver cartridge. It can also be used with commercial US caliber .38 Smith & Wesson ammunition (not S&W special) but will have a tendency to shoot high with this ammunition, since the issue front sight is set for the heavier British Mark 2 caliber .38 bullet. Higher sight blades can be obtained from arms dealers in the UK, or the blade can be built up by brazing.

Characteristics of Enfield Revolver

Caliber: .38, .380 in. revolver, .38 S&W, .38 Webley.
System of operation: No. 2 Mark 1 single or double action, No. 2 Mark 1* and No. 2 Mark 1** double action only.

Weight: 1.58 lbs. [1]
Length, overall: 10.25 in.
Barrel length: 5 in.
Feed device: Cylinder with 6 chambers.
Sights: Front: Blade.
   Rear: Square notch.
Muzzle velocity: 600.

[1]No. 2 Mark 1* and No. 2 Mark 1** weigh about an ounce less.

Loading and Firing the Enfield

Loading and firing the Enfield Mark 1 are accomplished exactly as in the Webley Mark VI. The Mark 1* is handled in the same manner, except that it can be used only double-action. The barrel latch is the same as on the Mark VI.

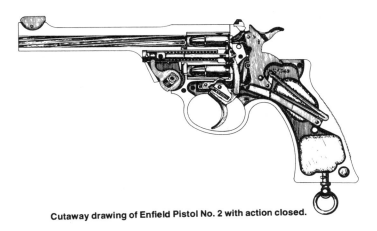

Action open, showing details of extraction and cocking.

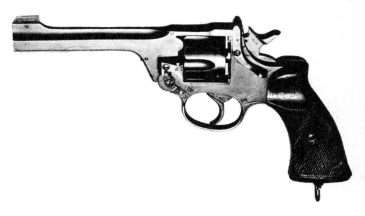

Enfield .38 Pistol No. 2 Mark I with Mark II grips.

Cutaway drawing of Enfield Pistol No. 2 with action closed.

Enfield .380 Pistol No. 2 Mark I*.

Field Stripping the Enfield

Unscrew cam lever fixing screw. Push barrel catch to open pistol and remove the cylinder.

Unscrew the stock and side plate screws on the left side of the weapon; remove the stock and the side plate.

All parts are now exposed and further dismounting is not recommended except by a competent armorer, as springs and parts may be injured unless properly handled.

SUBSTITUTE STANDARD AND NON-STANDARD BRITISH PISTOLS AND REVOLVERS

In both World War I and World War II, Great Britain found it necessary to obtain automatic pistols and revolvers abroad.

During World War I, Smith & Wesson and Colt made large quantities of caliber .455 revolvers for Britain. Although there were a number of models supplied, the most common models were the Colt New Service and the Smith & Wesson Mark II Hand Ejector, of which 73,650 were supplied to the UK and Canada. Colt caliber .32, .38, .45 and .455 automatic pistols were also purchased by the UK, and many of these weapons have since come back to the US with British proof and broad arrow (signifying government ownership) marks on all major components. Approximately 10,000 .455 M1911 Colt automatics were supplied to the UK during World War I. After the war, these pistols were issued to the R.A.F., and most bear the markings of that organization.

During World War II, the US supplied Great Britain with 20,000 Colt and Smith & Wesson caliber .45 Model 1917 revolvers after Dunkirk. Large quantities of Smith & Wesson .38/200 K200 revolvers and Colt .45 Model M1911A1 automatics were supplied under Lend-Lease. Apparently in 1940, the UK purchased every type of pistol that had any military potential, as they also procured quantities of Smith & Wesson K-38 target revolvers. Ballester Molina caliber .45 automatics were purchased from Argentina, and Star (among other) automatics were purchased from Spain. Since World War II, the United Kingdom has disposed of all of these nonstandard weapons, mainly by sale to surplus arms dealers.

BRITISH SMITH & WESSON .38 PISTOL

Characteristics of British S&W .38 Pistol

Caliber: British Service .380 inch. Also .38 S & W, 148- or 200-grain bullet. (Note: British Service Ammunition has metal jacketed bullet).

Cylinder: 6 chambers.

Muzzle velocity: 600 feet per second with British Service Ammunition.

Barrel length: 5 in.

Overall length: 10.2 in.

Weight: 1.81 lbs.

Sights: Front, blade. Rear, square notch.

Other data: Essentially the same in operation and stripping as the United States Smith & Wesson .45 1917 Revolver. This revolver is almost identical to the S & W Military and Police Model.

Note: This revolver, which in British terminology is called a pistol, will not handle the .38 Smith & Wesson Special type cartridges. It will handle the shorter and wider .38 S & W type. This cartridge is known in England as the Webley .380 inch. These weapons are considered obsolescent in the UK at present.

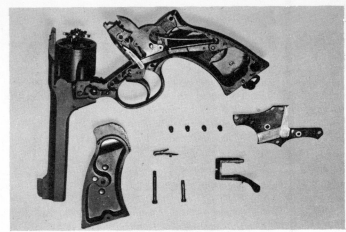

The Enfield No. 2 Mark I* field stripped.

British Smith & Wesson .38 Pistol (.38/200).

Hammer back, showing details of lockwork and front and rear cylinder locking mechanism.

Hammer down, cylinder swung out to show details of extraction. Sideplate cut away to show detail of thumb lock.

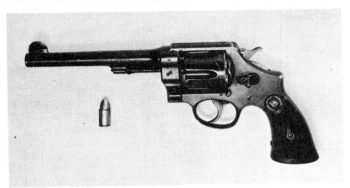

Smith & Wesson .455 Mark II (hand-ejector).

British Colt .455 Automatic Pistol.

BRITISH COLT .455 AUTOMATIC PISTOL

The standard United States .45 pistol cartridge may be used in this weapon. However, the .455 cartridge will not chamber in the .45 service pistol.

This one way interchangeability of ammunition is occasioned by the fact that the actual bullet diameter of the US .45 Auto cartridge is .4515 inch; while that of the .455 Webley S. L. is actually .455 inch. Thus, while the smaller diameter .45 will chamber in the .455, the reverse is not true. The caliber .455 will be found stamped on the right side of the receiver in this weapon.

THE .455 WEBLEY AUTOMATIC PISTOL

The Webley Automatic pistol was standard issue in the Royal Navy from 1912 until the end of World War II. There are two basic models, the Mark 1 and the Mark 1 No. 2. The Mark 1 No. 2 has a different type rear sight than the Mark 1 and has a different type manual safety. During World War I, some .455 Webley automatics were fitted with shoulder stocks to be used by the Royal Flying Corps.

Characteristics of British Webley Automatic Pistol

Caliber: .455 Webley automatic.
System of operation: Recoil operated
Weight: 2.43 lbs.
Length, overall: 8.5 in.
Barrel length: 5 in.
Feed device: 7-round, in line detachable box magazine.
Sights: Front: Blade.
        Rear: Mark 1 fixed notch, Mark 1 No. 2 adjustable.
Muzzle velocity: 710 f.p.s.

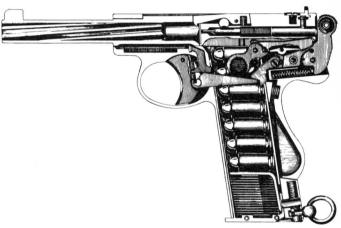

Webley automatic pistol—action closed.

Action open and cutaway to show mainspring and sear.

Webley .455 Automatic Mark I.

Special feature: Magazine is provided with two catch notches in the magazine, one above the other. Push the magazine all the way in and the catch will lock in the lower notch leaving the pistol ready for magazine fire. If the magazine is pushed only part way in so that the catch locks in the upper notch, the pistol can be loaded with single cartridges inserted through the open breech; and action closed by pressing slide release catch. After each shot thus fired, the slide will remain open ready for the next cartridge. Meanwhile the magazine remains loaded in the handle held in reserve. To achieve magazine fire, it is only necessary to push the magazine in until it catches in the second lock notch.

BRITISH RIFLES AND CARBINES

The current standard British Service rifle is the 7.62mm L1A1. Quantities of the No. 4 Mark 2, Mark 1/2 and Mark 1/3 rifle may be held for Naval use and in reserve.

BRITISH BOLT ACTION MILITARY RIFLES FROM 1888 TO 1951

The British and Canadian governments have disposed of most of their bolt action rifles since World War II. The caliber .22 No. 7, No. 8 and No. 9 rifles are still used as training rifles. The No. 1, Mark III and Mark III* and the No. 4 Mark I, I* and II are still extensively used throughout the former British territories and in a few other countries such as Greece. The greater percentage of these rifles have been sold on the US market.

The bolt action rifles that follow are not all of the various models that have been used by Great Britain by any means; they are the most common. As with pistols, Britain has had to import rifles during both world wars to meet military requirements. During World War I, contracts were let with Remington Arms, Ilion, N.Y.; Remington Arms, Eddystone, Pa.; and Winchester for the production of the .303 Pattern 14 (Rifle No. 3 Mark I*). This rifle was continued in manufacture for the United States in caliber .30-06 as the U.S. Rifle M1917. Although large quantities of Pattern 14 rifles were made, they were apparently used on the battle front in very limited quantities and principally as sniper rifles.

During World War II, the British were desperately short of rifles, especially in 1940–41, due to losses at Dunkirk and temporary loss of industrial plants due to bombing. In order to make up for these losses, Canada gave the UK 70,000 Ross rifles, and the United States supplied 785,000 caliber .30 M1917 Enfield rifles out of United States war reserve stocks, at a price of $7.50 per rifle. The British government contracted with Remington Arms to produce caliber .303 Springfield M1903 rifles; this contract was later taken over by the US government. Stevens Arms of Chicopee, Massachusetts, produced over one million No. 4 Mark I and Mark I* rifles for Great Britain. All contracts let with US manufacturers were supervised by the US government after the introduction of Lend-Lease in 1941. The Ross, M1917 Enfield and Springfield M1903 rifles were used by Home Guard units and have since been disposed of by the British government.

Safety Measures and Inspection Criteria

British rifles are usually well made and, if in good condition, are safe enough. Rifles of earlier marks than the Long Lee Enfield Mark I should not be used with the Mark 7 or other heavily loaded cartridges. The No. 4 and later rifles, if they are in good condition, will safely use any .303 cartridge loaded for rifles. Some United States commercial ammunition is not loaded too heavily in cal. .303 and will not bother any of the Long Lee Enfields or later weapons. Wherever there is any doubt about safety, the weapon should not be fired until checked by a reliable gunsmith.

As an aid to gunsmiths and others who will undoubtedly encounter many British Lee Enfield rifles in the future, some of the inspection criteria for the weapons are listed below.

Headspace. Since the .303 is a rimmed cartridge, headspace is measured from the rear face of the barrel to the face of the bolt. The headspace of the .303 rifle should not exceed .074 inch, although—as a wartime measure—a maximum of 0.80 inch was allowed. Minimum headspace is .064 inch.

Barrel gaging. The bore diameter should be from .301 to .304 inch in a new barrel. To gage a used barrel, plug gages from .303 to .310 inch should be used. The .303 gage should run through the barrel; the .307 gage should not run through the barrel. The .308 gage should not enter the muzzle more than .25 inch, and the .310 gage should not enter the breech more than .25 inch.

Firing pin protrusion. The high for firing pin protrusion for the No. 1's is .055 inch, and the low is .050 inch. The high for the No. 4's and No. 5's is .050 inch, and the low is .040 inch.

Trigger pull. The first pull or slack should be from 3 to 4 pounds. The second pull should be from 5 to 6 pounds. To increase or decrease the trigger pull weight, alter the angle of the cocking piece sear notch.

Buttstock lengths. Butts for the No. 1 rifles were made in long and short lengths, and during World War I a special short butt called the Bantam was made. These butts will be marked "L," "S" or "B" on the top of the stock, approximately one inch from the butt plate tang. Butts for the No. 4 and No. 5 rifles come in long, short and normal lengths.

In passing, it is worth noting that the .303 British and .303 Savage are not the same cartridge and are not interchangeable. The .303 British, as currently loaded by one American cartridge manufacturer, has a 215-grain bullet with a muzzle velocity of 2,180 feet per second. This is quite close to the loading of the British Mark 6 cal. .303 cartridge, which had a 215-grain bullet with a velocity of 2,060 feet per second. The Mark 6 cartridge was used with the Long Lee Enfields and the early No. 1s.

The Cal. .303 Lee Metford Rifles and Carbines

Rifle, Magazine, Lee Metford Mark I. Adopted December 1888. Was the first British production Lee. Chambered for the cal. .303 black-powder loaded cartridge. Had an eight-round magazine and a full-length cleaning rod.

Rifle, Magazine, Lee Metford Mark I*. Adopted January 1892. Was a conversion of the Mark I; the sights were changed from "Lewes" and "Welsh" pattern to barleycorn front and V-notch rear sight.

Rifle, Magazine, Lee Metford Mark II. Adopted April 1892. Was the first of the series to be fitted with a 10-round magazine. The bolt was modified, and the outside contour of the barrel was changed. A half-length cleaning rod was fitted to the gun, and the brass marking disk on the buttstock was omitted.

Carbine, Magazine, Lee Metford Mark I. Adopted 1894.

Rifle, Magazine, Lee Metford Mark II*. Adopted 1895. Had a safety catch added to the bolt. (Previous marks had a half-cock notch on the cocking piece as their only safety.)

The Cal. .303 Lee Enfield Rifles and Carbines

Rifle, Magazine, Lee Enfield Mark I. Adopted November 1895. Had the deep Enfield rifling, rather than the shallow Metford rifling used on previous marks. The sights were also modified.

Rifle, Magazine, Lee Enfield Mark I*. Adopted 1899. Had no cleaning rod mounted in the stock.

Carbine, Magazine, Lee Enfield Mark I. Adopted 1896. Same as Lee Metford carbine except for rifling.

Carbine, Magazine, Lee Enfield Mark I*. Same as the Mark I carbine but has no cleaning rod and no sling bar in the left side of the butt.

Carbine, Magazine, Lee Enfield, RIC Model. Adopted in 1905 when 10,000 of this model were made up from Lee Enfield Carbines. The carbine nose cap was removed and the stock cut back and slimmed down to take an upper band with bayonet stud to fit the pattern 88 knife bayonet. These carbines were made up for the Royal Irish Constabulary-RIC, which was disbanded in 1922.

Lee Metford Mark I.

Lee Metford Mark II.

Lee Metford Mark II*.

Rifle, Charger Loading, Long Lee Enfield Mark I*.

Lee Enfield Carbine Mark I.

Lee Enfield .303 RIC Carbine; a conversion of the Standard Carbine.

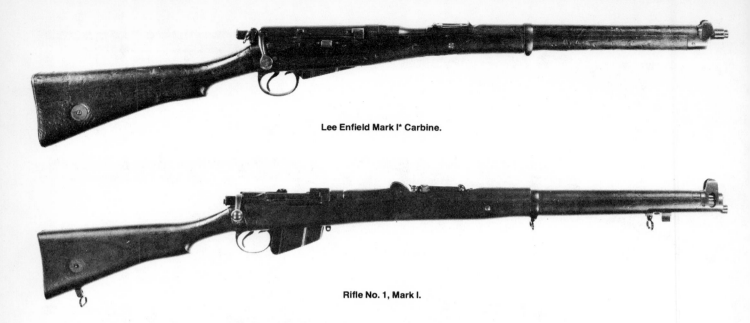

Lee Enfield Mark I* Carbine.

Rifle No. 1, Mark I.

Rifle No. 1, Short Magazine, Lee Enfield Mark I. Adopted December 1902. Was the first of the short rifles (SMLE). Was stocked to the muzzle and charger loaded. The right side charger guide is on the bolt head, and the left charger guide is on the receiver. Has a V-notch rear sight with adjustable windage and a barleycorn front sight. Was the first of what later came to be called the No. 1 series of rifles.

Rifle, No. 1, Short Magazine, Lee Enfield Mark II (CNVD). Essentially the same as the SMLE No. 1 Mark I, but was converted from earlier Mark II and Mark II* Lee Metford's and Long Lee Enfield's.

Rifle No. 1, Short Magazine, Lee Enfield Mark I*. A minor variant of the SMLE No. 1 Mark I.

Rifle No. 1, Short Magazine, Lee Enfield Mark II*. A minor variant of the No. 1 Mark II SMLE.

Rifle No. 1, Short Magazine, Lee Enfield Mark III. Adopted January 1907. Was the backbone of the British Army in World War I, and was also used extensively in World War II. Is still in use in many of the areas of the British Commonwealth today.

Rifle No. 1, Short Magazine, Lee Enfield Mark IV (CNVD). Adopted July 1907. Basically the same as the No. 1 Mark III; converted from Long Lee Metford's and Long Lee Enfield's.

Rifle, Charger Loading, Long Lee Metford Mark II. Was converted to charger loading in 1907 for use of the Territorial Army, and converted to rifle charger loading Lee Enfield Mark I* in 1909. Few of these were made.

Rifle, Charger Loading, Long Lee Enfield Mark I. A 1907 conversion of early marks of Long Lee Enfield to charger load-ing. The Mark I* version is more common. A large number of these weapons were used by British forces in the early days of World War I.

Rifle No. 1, Short Magazine, Lee Enfield Mark III*. Was adopted during World War I and made in very large quantities. Is still in widespread use throughout the world. Does not have the long-range side sights of the Mark III and earlier marks, and does not have a magazine cutoff.

The Royal Ordnance Small Arms Factory at Enfield Lock made over 2 million of this model and the No. 1 Mark III during World War I. During the same period, B.S.A. made 1,601,608 and L.S.A. made several hundred thousand. This rifle was last manufactured in the UK by B.S.A. in 1943. The Australian arsenal at Lithgow and the Indian plant at Ishapore manufactured the Mark III* after the adoption of the No. 4. Lithgow produced 415,800 from 1939 to 1955 when production was switched to the FN rifle.

Rifle No. 1, Short Magazine, Lee Enfield Mark V. Appeared around 1922. The rear sight is mounted on the receiver bridge, and an additional stock band is mounted to the rear of the nose cap.

Rifle No. 1, Short Magazine, Lee Enfield Mark VI. Was developed in the period 1924–1930. Was the forerunner of the No. 4 rifles. Had rear sight on the receiver bridge. Had a lighter nose cap, heavier barrel and smaller bolt head than the earlier marks. Had cut-off, and left receiver wall is cut low as the Mark III.

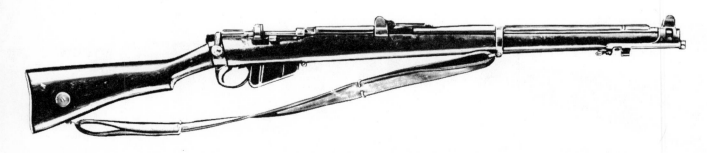

Rifle No. 1, Mark III.

Rifle No. 1, Mark III*.

Rifle No. 1, Mark V.

Rifle No. 1, Mark VI.

Rifle No. 4 Mark 1. Originally appeared in 1931. Was finely made, and was generally similar to the No. 1 Mark VI except that it had a heavier receiver. Was redesigned for mass production around 1939 and became, with the No. 4 Mark 1*, the British "work horse" of World War II. Stamped bands were used, and various manufacturing shortcuts were taken to increase production. Three different marks of rear sights may be found on this weapon, ranging from a finely machined adjustable leaf to a simple L-type. Many of these weapons are still in service in the British Commonwealth and in former British territories.

Rifle No. 4 Mark 1*. Was the North American production version of the No. 4 Mark 1. The principal difference was that the bolthead catch, which was situated behind the receiver bridge on the No. 4 Mark 1 (and earlier Marks), was eliminated on the No. 4 Mark 1*, and a cutout on the bolt head track was used for bolt removal. Over five million No. 4 rifles were made during World War II in the UK, Canada and the United States (Stevens Arms). Australia did not adopt the No. 4 but continued production of the No. 1 Mark III* at Lithgow during World War II.

Canadian Rifle No. 4 Mark I* (light weight). This weapon was produced at the Canadian arsenal at Long Branch in prototype form. It has a one-piece stock, and its trigger is pinned to

the receiver. Weight about 6¾ pounds. Barrel length about 23 inches. Overall length about 42½ inches. Receiver wail cut down and stock inletted to reduce weight. Sporting type Hawkins rubber buttplate. Micrometer sights with peep battle sight. Sight adjustable in clicks and 100-yard steps from 100 to 1300 yards. This arm may be used for grenade launching. Has a Mauser type trigger.

Rifle No. 4 Mark 2. Was developed at the end of World War II. Differed from the earlier marks by having its trigger pinned to the receiver rather than to the trigger guard.

Rifle No. 4 Mark 1(T) and No. 4 Mark 1* (T). Are the sniper versions of the No. 4. Are fitted with scope mounts on the left side of the receiver and have a wooden cheek rest screwed to the butt. The No. 32 telescope is used on these weapons. There are also sniper versions of the No. 1 and No. 3 rifles (Pattern 14). The Canadians also used the No. 4 Mark 1*(T) with the Telescope C No. 67 Mark 1.

Rifle No. 4 Mark 1/2 and Rifle No. 4 Mark 1/3: These are conversions of the No. 4 Mark I and No. 4 Mark I* respectively to the pattern of the No. 4 Mark II. These rifles, like the No. 4 Mark II, are still in extensive use and are probably held as reserve weapons by the UK.

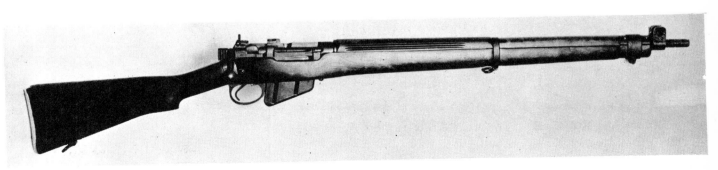

British Rifle No. 4 Mark I*.

Canadian Rifle No. 4 Mark I* (lightweight).

British Rifle No. 5 Mark I* (jungle carbine).

Rifle No. 4 Mark I (T).

Rifle No. 5 Mark I Appeared toward the end of World War II. Was a lightweight weapon, and was commonly called the jungle carbine. Has a lightened and shortened barrel, which is fitted with a flash hider. Fore-end has been cut back and rounded, giving weapon the appearance of a sporting rifle. A rubber recoil pad is fitted to the butt.

Rifle No. 6(Aust). Appeared only as prototype; 18-inch barrel version of No. 1. Developed at Lithgow.

The Cal. .22 Rifles

Cal. .22 R.F. Short Rifle Mark I. Adopted in 1907. This rifle is a conversion of the Lee Metford Mark I rifle; it is approximately the same length as the SMLE. Sights are an adjustable blade front sight and a tangent type rear sight with adjustment for windage.

Cal. .22 R.F. Long Rifle Mark II. Adopted in 1911. Conversion of Long Lee Enfield to .22 rimfire. The Mark I pattern of .22 R.F. long rifles was converted from Long Lee Metfords.

Cal. .22 R.F. Short Rifle Mark I*. Conversion to .22 rimfire in shortened form of Lee Metford Mark I*. Mark II of this pattern was converted from Lee Metford Mark II.

Cal. .22 R.F. Short Rifle Mark III. Adopted in 1912—this is a

conversion of SMLE Marks II and II* to .22 rimfire. A number of different patterns of Lee were converted during World War I to .22 caliber rimfire. Some were fitted with new barrels, and others had their .303 barrels bored out and a caliber .22 liner inserted. The .22 R.F. pattern 1914 had "conveyors"—cartridge adaptors or auxillary cartridges, which fed through .303 magazines.

Rifle No. 2 Mark IV. Is a conversion of cal. .303 SMLE's to cal. .22. Some have new .22 barrels, and some were "Parker Rifled," i.e., a .22 liner was placed in a bored-out .303 barrel. A special bolt head was made for these rifles.

Rifle No. 2 Mark IV*. A variant of the No. 2 Mark IV.

Rifle No. 7. Developed at Long Branch; single shot version of No. 4 Mark I*. Called Rifle "C" No. 7, .22 in Mark I. Also has been made by B.S.A. with a 5-shot magazine.

Rifle No. 8 Mark 1. Two variations of this rifle were developed simultaneously. They were called the Infantry Model and the Match Model and differed principally in sights and length of barrel. The Infantry Model has sights similar to the No. 4 rifle and a shorter barrel than the Match Model. The Match Model, in addition to the longer barrel, has match type sights. The Infantry Model was adopted in 1950 as the Rifle No. 8 Mark 1.

Rifle No. 9. Converted to .22 by Parker Hale from No. 4 rifles, single shot.

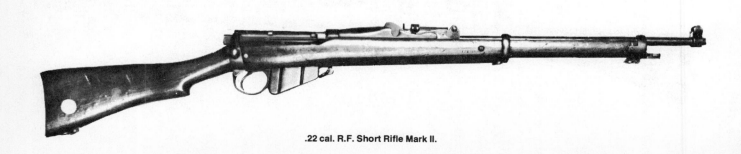

.22 cal. R.F. Short Rifle Mark II.

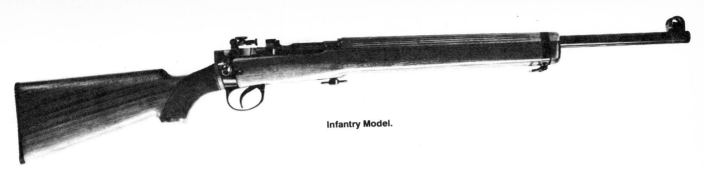

Infantry Model.

Conversion of No. 4 Rifles to 7.62mm NATO. The Royal Small Arms Factory at Enfield Lock has developed a conversion kit for the No. 4 rifles to convert them to use the 7.62mm NATO cartridge. This kit consists of a new barrel, extractor, magazine, charger guide liner, front sight block fixing pin and a barrel breeching washer. This kit can be fitted to an existing No. 4 rifle with normal armorers tools and certain special purpose tools, i.e. a special drift, a taper pin reamer, a breeching gage etc.

Model designations have been assigned to converted rifles as follows: .303 Rifle No. 4 Mark I becomes 7.62mm Rifle L8A4; .303 Rifle No. 4 Mark I* becomes 7.62mm Rifle L8A5; .303 Rifle No. 4 Mark 1/2 becomes 7.62mm Rifle L8A2; .303 Rifle No. 4 Mark 1/3 becomes 7.62mm Rifle L8A3; .303 Rifle No. 4 Mark II becomes 7.62mm Rifle L8A1. A conversion kit also exists for the Rifle No. 5.

B.S.A. has also developed a conversion kit for the No. 4 rifles.

7.62mm Rifle L39A1 is a conversion of the No. 4 MK 1/2 or 2 to 7.62mm NATO using a heavy barrel. A special hand guard is fitted, and the fore-end is cut back in sporting style so that its forward end is just beyond the lower band. A standard No. 4 butt stock is used. This rifle is designed for competitive shooting within the British services. A front sight base is provided, but no front sight or rear sight is provided. Units are supposed to supply their own and a variety of sights are available. The L39A1 uses a 10-round box magazine, but the magazine, which is .303, serves only as a loading platform. The barrel is 27.5 inches long and overall length is 46.5 inches. The trigger pull is lighter than that of the No. 4. L39A1; weighs 9.75 pounds.

7.62mm Rifle L42A1 is the current standard sniper rifle. It has a heavy 7.62mm NATO barrel and the fore-end is cut back the same as the L39A1. Receivers from No. 4 Mark 1 (T) or Mark 1* (T) are used for this rifle. The magazine of the L42A1 is designed for 7.62mm NATO catridges and has a capacity of 10 rounds. The butt stock has the same type "screw on" wooden check piece as used with the No. 4 Mark 1 (T). The left side of the receiver has a telescope bracket for the telescope No. 32 Mark 3. A leaf type rear sight and a protected blade type front sight are also used.

The Envoy, a 7.62mm match rifle conversion of the No. 4, is also being produced by the Royal Small Arms Factory. This rifle has a swaged, heavy free floating barrel and a full pistol grip type butt stock. It is somewhat similar to the L39A1 and L42A1 but more finely finished and has a match type tunnel front sight and match type aperture rear sight fitted.

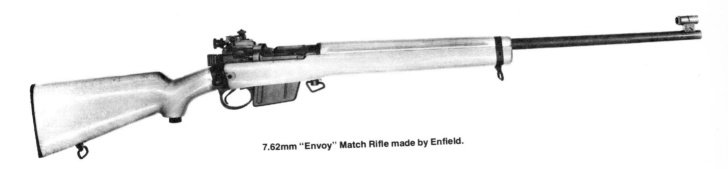

7.62mm "Envoy" Match Rifle made by Enfield.

Loading and Firing Lee Enfield Rifles

Turn bolt handle up as far as it will go and pull it straight back to the limit of travel.

Insert loaded clip in the clip guide in the receiver and strip the cartridges down into the magazine. Remove the empty clip. Insert a second clip, push these cartridges down and remove clip. This will leave the magazine fully charged with 10 cartridges.

Pushing bolt handle fully forward and down loads the firing chamber, cocks, and locks ready for firing with a pull of the trigger.

Unless weapon is to be fired immediately, pull the thumb rocker on the left rear of the receiver to "Safe."

Replacing bolt, No. 1 Lee Enfield Rifle.

Field Stripping Lee Enfield Rifles

Remove magazine. This may be done by pushing in or pulling up, as different rifles may require, the magazine catch located in the forward end of the triggerguard. This will release the heavy sheet steel box, which may be withdrawn from the bottom of the receiver.

Removing the magazine follower and its spring is simply done. Hold the magazine, open end up, and push the rear of the magazine follower down inside the casing. This will permit you to ease the front end of the follower up and out of the casing and remove it and the spring.

In order to remove the bolt, it is first necessary to rock forward the safety catch just above the rear end of the triggerguard, on the left side of the rifle. Then turn the bolt handle up and turn it back as far as it will go. Catch your right forefinger under the head of the bolt. Pull the bolt head up until it is released from its spring catch. Then withdraw it straight to the rear.

Field Stripping for Rifle No. 4 Mark I*. The No. 4 Mark I* rifle has a different method of removal of the bolt from the rifle than do the other Lee Enfield rifles. On the bolt head track—right side of receiver—there is a cut-out; draw bolt back until bolt head is over this cut-out; then lift bolt head straight up and draw bolt out of rifle.

Note on Replacing Bolt. These bolts are not interchangeable, and the number on the bolt should always be checked against the number on the rifle when there has been any possibility of substituting another bolt. Before inserting the bolt, be sure that the head is fully screwed home, and that the cocking piece lines up with the lug on the underside of the bolt. Insert the bolt in the boltway and thrust it forward, and then pull it back as far as it will go until the head touches the resistance shoulders and force the bolt head down over the spring retaining catch. Then push it forward to the forward position. Turn down bolt handle and press trigger.

How the Lee Enfield Rifle Works

Starting with the rifle loaded and cocked, the action is as follows. When the trigger is pressed, it draws down the sear until the sear nose reaches the bottom of the full bent. (This provides the first pull or slack, which is a feature of the best military rifles.) As the trigger pressure continues, the upper part of the sear is drawn still further down until the sear nose clears the bent allowing the cocking piece on the striker to be driven forward by the compressed mainspring. The striker nose, or firing pin, passes through a hole in the face of the bolt head and discharges the cartridge in the firing chamber.

Special Note on the Lee Enfield System. The locking system on this rifle makes it the fastest operating bolt action rifle in the world. The abrupt turning action of the Mauser system will not permit it to attain a speed of operation possible with the Lee Enfield.

This rifle, since it has no locking recesses cut into the receiver, is much easier to clean than the Mauser type and functions well under all battle conditions.

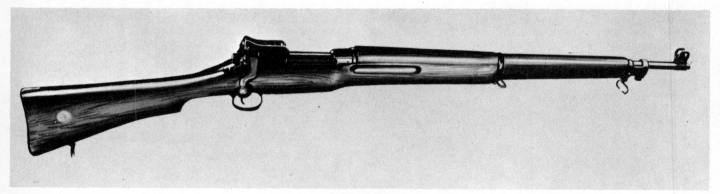

Pattern 14 Rifle.

The Mauser Type Rifles

Pattern 13 (P-13). Tested in 1913. Was a modified Mauser (it cocked on the forward stroke of the bolt), chambered for a large cal. .276 cartridge. The cartridge was remarkably similar to the Canadian cal. .280 Ross cartridge. The rifle was made in comparatively small numbers for field trials.

Pattern 14 (P-14). Was the production model of the P-13. Was made in the United States in cal. .303 for the UK during World War I. The weapon was classed as limited standard in the British Army and except for sniping was not too widely used. Upon the entrance of the United States into World War I, the design was changed to U.S. Cal. .30, and the weapon was produced as the U.S. rifle, cal. .30, M1917 and was commonly known as the Enfield. Between World Wars I and II, the British changed the nomenclature of the P-14 to Rifle No. 3 Mark I.

Pattern 14 Sniper Rifles. The P-14 was extensively used as a sniper rifle in World War I. The two basic patterns were the P-14 (T) and the P-14 (T) A. The former has a Pattern 1918 telescope adjustable for range and windage, and the latter has an Aldis telescope adjustable for range only. In 1926, when all British small arms were given number designations, these weapons were renamed the Rifle No. 3 Mark I* (T) and Rifle No. 3 Mark I* (T) A, respectively.

Springfield .303. This rifle, which apparently has no official nomenclature, is a modification of the U.S. M1903 designed by Remington Arms at the request of Great Britain in 1941. Production of the Springfield rifle by Remington Arms during World War II was initially—until Sept 1941—set up for a British contract. The .303 version was made only as a prototype and development on this rifle stopped in September 1941. The type "C" stock was used with the pistol grip modified to the Enfield type; the bolt face, extractor, follower and magazine were modified to fit the .303 cartridge. The receiver bridge was lengthened. The "L" type rear sight was similar to the Mark 2 sight used on the No. 4s. Note that the bayonet mounting lugs are on the barrel as with the No. 4.

BRITISH SELF-LOADING RIFLES

Basic satisfaction with the SMLE family of bolt action rifles, production demands imposed by World Wars I and II and the cost of converting to new patterns were all factors that caused the British Ministry of Defence to proceed slowly with the development, testing and adoption of a self-loading rifle. Many models were tested in the 1930s and 1940s, but none were adopted. In the 1950s, the British undertook an extensive ammunition and rifle development effort (see discussion in Chapter I), but due to political and economic considerations they finally settled on the FN FAL (light automatic rifle) and designated it the L1A1. This rifle has been manufactured at both the Royal Small Arms Factory, Enfield Lock (RSAF), and the Birmingham Small Arms Company (B.S.A.).

The British version has been modified in a few components, but basically the weapon is the same as that covered in the chapter on Belgium. Cuts have been added to the bolt carrier to serve as gathering places for dirt and dust that might otherwise enter the action. These cuts are deep enough so that a good deal of foreign matter can accumulate in them without impairing the normal functioning of the weapon. The L1A1 fires the 7.62 x 51mm NATO cartridge.

UK 4.85mm SMALL ARMS SYSTEM

After several years of renewed experimentation with small caliber ammunition, the British have selected a 4.85mm diameter for their Individual and Light Support Weapons, which will be the UK contenders in the NATO trials. As noted in Chapter 1, both are of bull pup design, and 80% of the parts interchange between the two weapons. An armorer's kit permits the weapons the be altered so that left-handed soldiers can use them. The Light Support Weapon differs from the Individual Weapon in that it has a longer and heavier barrel, 30-shot versus 20-shot magazine and a bipod. It cannot be used for grenade launching, whereas the Individual Weapon can. Both weapons are equipped with a four-power optical sight evolved from the current UK issue Sight Unit Small Arms Trilux.

Characteristics of the L1A1
(British Version of the FN NATO Light Rifle)

System of operation: Gas, semiautomatic fire only (can be modified to selective fire).
Weight, loaded: 10.48 lbs.
Length, overall: 44.5 in.
Barrel length: 21 in.
Feed device: 20-round, detachable, staggered box magazine.
Sights: Front: Post w/protecting ears.
       Rear: Aperture, adjustable from 200 to 600 yd.
Muzzle velocity: 2800 f.p.s.

Characteristics of the Individual Weapon

System of operation: Gas; single-shot and automatic burst.
Weight, loaded: 9.1 lbs.
Length, overall: 30.3 in.
Barrel length: 20.4 in. (including Flash Hider).
Feed device: 20-round magazine; 30-round available.
Sight: Optical sight, x4.
Muzzle velocity: 2952 f.p.s.

Characteristics of the Light Support Weapon

System of operation: Gas; single-shot and automatic burst.
Weight, loaded: 11 lbs., 9.5 oz.
Length, overall: 35.4 in.
Barrel length: 25.4 in. (including Flash Hider).
Feed device: 30-round magazine; 20-round available.
Sight: Optical sight, x4.
Muzzle velocity: 3051 f.p.s.

UK 4.85 × 49mm Individual Weapon.

UK 4.85 × 49mm Light Support Weapon designed for the automatic rifle/light machine gun role.

The UK 4.85 × 49mm weapons in the field. To the left the infantryman holds the Individual Weapon. To the right the soldier is aiming the Light Support Weapon.

CHARACTERISTICS OF BRITISH BOLT ACTION RIFLES AND CARBINES

	Lee Metford Rifle Mark I*	Lee Metford Rifle Mark II	Lee Metford Carbine Mark I	Lee Enfield Rifle Mark I
Caliber	.303	.303	.303	.303
Overall length	49.85 in	49.85 in	40 in	49.5 in
Barrel length	30.19 in	30.19 in	20.75 in	30.19 in
Feed device	8 rd detachable Box w/cut-off	10 rd detachable box w/cut-off	6 rd detachable box w/cut-off	10 rd detachable box w/cut-off
Sights: Front	Barley corn	Barley corn	Barley corn w/ protecting ears	Barley corn.
Rear	Vertical leaf and ramp	Vertical leaf and ramp	Vertical leaf and ramp	Vertical leaf and ramp
Muzzle velocity (at date of adoption)	2000 FPS	2000 FPS	1940 FPS	2060 FPS
Weight	10.43 lbs.	10.18 lbs	7.43 lbs	9.25 lbs

	Pattern 14 Rifle (Rifle No. 3 MKI*)	Short Lee Enfield Rifle Mark I (Rifle No 1 SMLE MK 1)	Short Lee Enfield Rifle Mark III (Rifle No 1 SMLE MK 3)	Short Lee Enfield Rifle Mark III* (Rifle No 1 SMLE MK 3*)
Caliber	.303	.303	.303	.303
Overall length	46.25 in	44.5 in	44.5 in	44.5 in
Barrel length	26 in	25.19 in	25.19 in	25.19 in
Feed device	5 rd integral magazine	10 rd detachable box w/cut-off	10 rd detachable box w/cut-off	10 rd detachable box
Sights: Front	Blade w/ protecting ears	Barley Corn w/ protecting ears	Blade w/ protecting ears	Blade w/ protecting ears
Rear	Vertical leaf w/ aperture battle sight, long range side sights	Tangent leaf w/notch long range side sights	Tangent leaf w/notch long range side sights	Tangent leaf w/notch
Muzzle velocity (at date of adoption)	Apprx 2500 FPS	2060 FPS	2060 FPS	2440 FPS
Weight	9.62 lbs	8.12 lbs	8.62 lbs	8.62 lbs

	Rifle No 2 Mark 4	Rifle No 4 Mark 1	Rifle No 5 Mark 1	Rifle No 8 Mark 1
Caliber	.22	.303	.303	.22
Overall length	44.5 in	44.5 in	39.5 in	41.05 in
Barrel length	25.2 in	25.2 in	18.7 in	23.3 in
Feed device	Single shot	10 rd detachable box	10 rd detachable box	Single shot
Sights: Front	Blade w/ protecting ears	Blade w/ protecting ears	Blade w/ protecting ears	Blade w/ protecting ears
Rear	Tangent leaf w/notch	Vertical leaf w/ aperture battle sight or L type	Vertical leaf w/ aperture battle sight	Vertical leaf w/ aperture battle sight
Muzzle velocity (at date of adoption)	1050 FPS	2440 FPS	2400 FPS	1050 FPS
Weight	9.19 lbs	8.8 lbs	7.15 lbs	8.87 lbs

Characteristics are listed only for the principal models.
Lengths are with normal butt.

BRITISH SUBMACHINE GUNS

Although B.S.A. had developed a number of modifications of the Thompson Submachine Gun during the 1920s, the British Army did not show much interest in submachine guns until after World War II started. In 1940, large contracts were let for the manufacture of the caliber .45 Thompson Submachine gun M1928A1 by the Auto Ordnance Corporation of Bridgeport, Conn.

Britain was desperate for weapons at this time, and a limited quantity of the 9mm Parabellum Smith & Wesson semiautomatic carbines were purchased. These guns, which were very finely made and very expensive, wound up in the hands of the Royal Navy.

During World War II, the Lanchester and Sten guns were designed and produced. A number of other submachine guns were produced in prototype form. Among these was the Patchett, developed by the Sterling Engineering Company; in considerably modified form it is the L2A3, the current standard British submachine gun.

British 9mm Welgun, produced in limited quantities.

Right side of the Lanchester 9mm Mark I submachine gun, bolt cooked ready for firing. Note recoil spring compressed around end of firing pin unit, which protrudes from rear of bolt. Ejection port is exposed.

THE LANCHESTER MARK I

This submachine gun was designed by G.H. Lanchester; it was manufactured by the Sterling Engineering Company, the same firm that developed the L2A3. The design of the Lanchester is based on that of the German MP 28 II. The selector lever is positioned differently than that of the MP 28 II, and the Lanchester has a bayonet boss and stud for the Mark I (Pattern 1907) bayonet.

The Lanchester is a typical pre-World War II submachine gun in that it is of heavy construction and is relatively expensive and difficult to manufacture. The Mark 1, a selective fire weapon, was introduced in 1941. Later in the war a model appeared capable of automatic fire only—the Mark 1*. The Lanchester was used by the British Navy and is now obsolete.

THE STEN GUNS

The Stens, which are variously known as the "plumbers delight," the "Woolworth gun" and sometimes unflatteringly as the

"Stench gun," introduced a new era in submachine gun design and manufacture. The Stens filled the need of the United Kingdom for an easily made, cheap weapon that did not require a large usage of scarce machine tools in their manufacture. Although the early Stens had many shortcomings, they were just as effective in killing people as were more expensive weapons. They have been given the greatest flattery by being copied in Germany, China, Argentina, Belgium and Indonesia.

The Stens were made by the millions by a number of basic manufacturers who in turn were supported by a number of subcontractors. In the United Kingdom, the primary producers were B.S.A. and the Royal Ordnance Factory at Fazakerley. B.S.A. made over 400,000 Stens at a special plant at Tysely; some were made at their Shirley plant prior to September 1941. As subcontractors, B.S.A. had firms that made cheap jewelry, lawn mowers, hardware, children's scooters and the engineering department of a brewery among others. The gun was also extensively made in Canada.

The basic Sten gun was developed at Enfield by R.V. Shep-

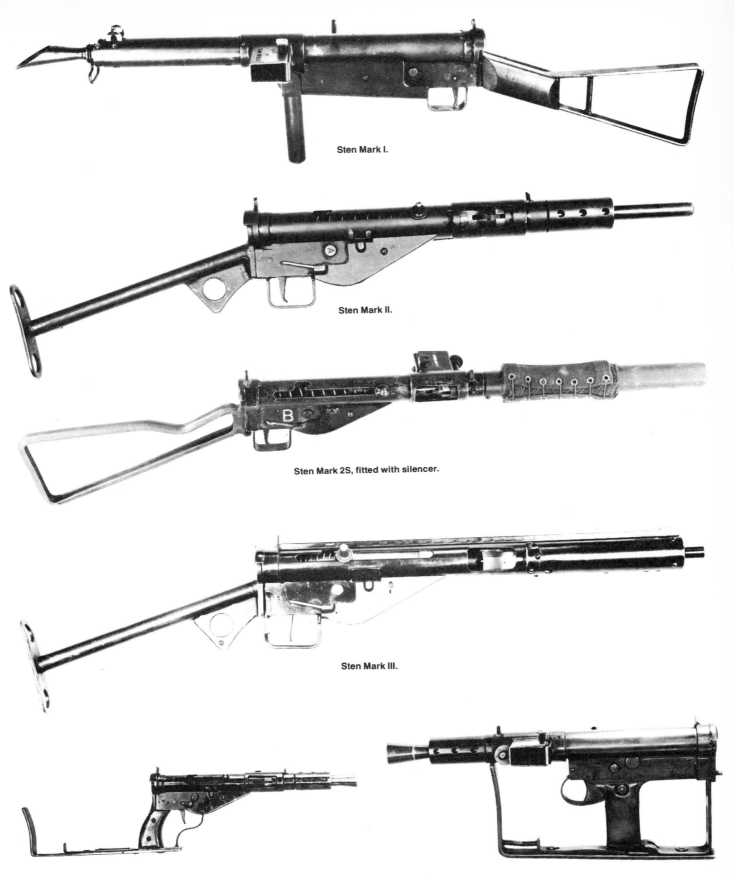

Sten Mark I.

Sten Mark II.

Sten Mark 2S, fitted with silencer.

Sten Mark III.

Sten Mark IV, Model A, with stock fixed.

Sten Mark IV, Model B, with stock folded.

perd and H.J. Turpin, and its name is derived from the first letters of their last names and the first two letters of Enfield. In addition to being used by the troops of the British Commonwealth, the Sten was dropped in large numbers into occupied Europe during World War II. The later model Stens are still in extensive use throughout the world, but the Stens are no longer used as standard weapons by the United Kingdom.

Sten Mark I

Adopted in 1941, the Mark I has a complete barrel jacket, a flash hider, a wooden fore-end and a vertical fore grip which can be folded up under the barrel jacket. Two basic butt stocks are used with this weapon—the No. 1 Mark I, made of steel with a wooden piece in its forward section. The No. 2 Mark II stock is made of tubular steel and does not have the wooden brace.

Sten Mark I*

A simplification of Mark I without flash hider and wooden fore-end. A stamped steel housing replaces the fore-end. Most of the Mark I* guns do not have a wooden fore grip.

Sten Mark II

The weapon differs from the Mark I only in externals. The barrel and barrel jacket were shortened; the design of the bolt handle was altered, and a simplified buttstock was issued with this gun. The Mark II may be found with a number of different buttstocks as may all of the Sten guns. Butt stocks are interchangeable among the various models. The Mark II Sten magazine housing can be turned on the axis of the receiver so that it acts as a dust cover for the magazine and ejection ports.

Sten Mark II S

This weapon is the Mark II with a shorter barrel, silencer, a lighter bolt and a shorter recoil spring. The weapon should only be used semiautomatic, as automatic fire burns out the silencer very rapidly.

Sten Mark III

The barrel of the Mark III is not detachable as are those of other models. The receiver and barrel jacket are made of one welded steel tube, and the magazine housing is welded to the receiver. The Mark III is probably the most cheaply made of the Sten guns.

Sten Mark IV

This weapon was made in two models—A and B—but very few were manufactured—about 2,000 total. The Mark IV was designed for special units and is a very compact weapon. The Model A has a pistol grip and trigger just to the rear of the magazine port whereas the Model B has the pistol grip and trigger at the rear of the receiver as do the other Stens and has the same type trigger assembly cover as does the Mark II. Both weapons have a flash hider and a very short barrel.

Sten Mark V

This is the last basic design of Sten and was the standard Sten until the adoption of the Sterling (Patchett) in 1953. The Mark V has a number of features not found on most of the earlier Stens. These are: a wooden pistol grip, a wooden stock, a front sight with protective ears (same as that of the Rifle No. 4 Mark 1), the barrel has lugs for the No. 7 Mark I and the No. 4 Mark II bayonet. Early specimens had a wooden vertical fore grip.

Sten Mark VI

This weapon is the Mark V fitted with a shortened barrel and a silencer. As with the Mark II S, automatic fire is discouraged.

Loading and Firing Sten Guns

A small special hand loader is provided as part of the equipment of every Sten gun. This is very helpful as compressing cartridges in this magazine is quite difficult due to the cartridge capacity and heavy spring.

The loader is clamped over the mouth of the magazine. The ring is pulled down as illustrated and a cartridge inserted into the mouth of the loader.

The ring is then lifted up to force the cartridge down and back under the magazine lips. It is then brought down to permit insertion of the next cartridge.

Insert loaded magazine, bullets pointing forward, into magazine housing on left side of gun just ahead of forward end of cocking handle slot. Push in until magazine locks with a click.

Pull back cocking handle and turn down into safety slot if the model is Mark I. (If model is Mark II, III, or V, the safety slot is up—so turn cocking handle up into slot.)

When ready to fire, turn cocking handle out of the safety slot.

Directly under the safety slot is a button passing through the gun from side to side. (a) If you wish to fire one shot with each pull of the trigger, push the button from the left side. (It is marked "R," meaning "Repetition.") (b) If you wish to fire full automatic, push the button through on the right side of the gun where it is marked "A," meaning "Automatic."

Note. To remove magazine press down with the left thumb on the magazine catch (which is at the rear of the magazine housing), and at the same time grasp and pull the magazine out with the fingers of the left hand.

Sten Mark V, early type with fore-grip.

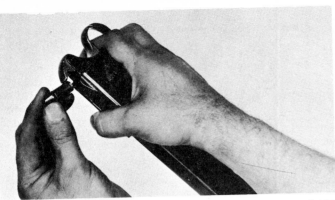
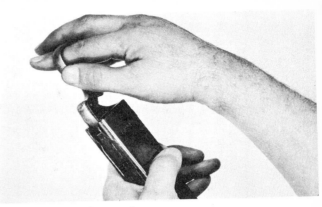

Using special Sten gun magazine loading accessory. Ring down at left to permit cartridge insertion; ring raised up at right to force cartridge down into the magazine.

Field Stripping Sten Guns

Press in the stud on the return spring housing to clear hole and slide butt down out of its slots.

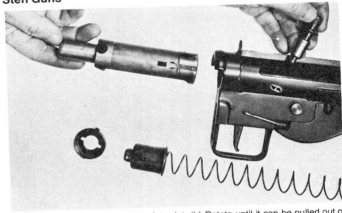

(a) Pull cocking handle back to safety slot. (b) Rotate until it can be pulled out of breechblock. (c) Tip up gun and slide out breechblock.

Press in on stud and spring cap and twist to the left to unlock lugs. Ease out spring cap, return spring and return-spring housing and remove.

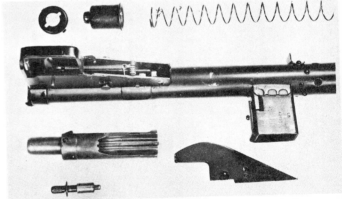

Weapon disassembled showing trigger and feeding mechanism.

How the Sten Gun Works

A loaded magazine being inserted in the magazine housing until it locks, the cocking handle is then pulled back to the cocked position, compressing the return spring.

When the trigger is pressed, the heavy breech block is freed and driven forward by the return spring. Feed ribs on the breech block strip the top cartridge from between the lips of the magazine and drive it into the chamber. The extractor, which is attached to the breechblock, snaps into the cannelure in the car-

tridge case and the firing pin strikes the cartridge primer exploding the powder.

The inertia of the heavy breech block and spring in forward motion keeps the breech closed until the bullet has left the barrel and the breech pressure has dropped to safe limits.

The remaining pressure drives the empty cartridge case and moving parts to the rear. The case strikes against the ejector and is hurled out of the gun. The magazine spring pushes the next cartridge in line for feeding.

CHARACTERISTICS OF BRITISH WORLD WAR II SUBMACHINE GUNS

	Lanchester Mark I	Sten Mark I	Sten Mark II	Sten Mark II S	Sten Mark III	Sten Mark IV (Model A)	Sten Mark IV (Model B)	Sten Mark V
Caliber[1]:	9mm.	9mm.	9mm.	9mm.	9mm.	9mm.	9mm.	9mm.
System of operation:	Blowback, selective fire.	Blowback, selective fire.	Blowback, selective fire.	Blowback, selective fire.	Blowback, selective fire.	Blowback, selective fire.	Blowback, selective fire.	Blowback, selective fire.
Overall length:	33.5 in.	35.25 in.	30 in.	37 in.	30 in.	Stock extended 27.5 in. Stock folded 17.5 in.	24.5 in. 17.5 in.	30 in.
Barrel length:	7.9 in.	7.75 in.	7.75 in.	3.61 in.	7.75 in.	3.85 in.	3.85 in.	7.8 in.
Feed device:	50-rd. box magazine.	32-rd. box magazine.	32-rd. box magazine.	32-rd. box magazine.	32-rd. box magazine.	32-rd. box magazine.	32-rd. box magazine.	32-rd. box magazine.
Sights: Front:	Barleycorn.	Barleycorn.	Barleycorn.	Barleycorn.	Barleycorn.	Barleycorn.	Barleycorn.	Barleycorn.
Rear:	Tangent, adj. to 600 yds.	Fixed. Aperture.[2]	Fixed. Aperture.	Fixed. Aperture.	Fixed. Aperture.	Fixed. Aperture.	Fixed. Aperture.	Fixed. Aperture.
Muzzle velocity:	1280 f.p.s.	1280 f.p.s.	1280 f.p.s.	[3]	1280 f.p.s.	Approx 1200 f.p.s.	Approx 1200 f.p.s.	1280 f.p.s.
Cyclic rate:	575–600 r.p.m.	540 r.p.m.	540 r.p.m.		540 r.p.m.	575 r.p.m.	575 r.p.m.	575 r.p.m.
Weight:	9.62 lb.	7.8 lb.	6.62 lb.	7.48 lb.	7 lb.	7.5 lb.	7.5 lb.	8.5 lb.

Notes:
1. All weapons on this chart, use the 9mm Parabellum cartridge.
2. The fixed aperture sight on all of the Sten guns is set for 100 yds.
3. This silenced version was equipped with a bronze bolt. It was not intended to fired automatically.

THE STERLING (PATCHETT) GUN

This weapon was developed by G.W. Patchett toward the end of World War II at the Sterling Engineering Co., Dagenham, Essex. The weapon was tested by the United Kingdom as the "Patchett" in several different forms and was chosen for extensive field test after the competitive trials held around 1949. It was issued in limited quantities in 1951 and in a modified form was issued as Submachine Gun L2A1 in 1953. The current standard model is the L2A3. The Sterling has been adopted by New Zealand, Canada, India and a number of other countries in addition to the United Kingdom. In addition to the selective fire military version of the Sterling, there is also a semiautomatic version called the Sterling Police Carbine. This weapon was sold quite extensively to planters in Kenya during the Mau Mau uprising.

Principal components of the Sten gun.

Patchett Machine Carbine

The original gun was considerably different than the weapons in service today. The buttstock was made of heavy flat steel stripping and was of different design than the later weapons. The fire selector/safety is on the front of the trigger housing as opposed to its position on the left top of the pistol grip on the later guns. The overall impression of the weapon is that it is much heavier than the later guns.

L2A1 Submachine Gun

The basic difference between this weapon and the later L2A2 is that the L2A1 had parts—grip screw and cocking (bolt) handle—that could be used for the removal of the barrel screws, and the inner block of the bolt had an extension for removal of the extractor pin.

9mm Sterling Police Carbine Mark 4.

L2A2 Submachine Gun

Parts were not used as stripping tools; a forward finger guard was added; the rear sight was modified by repositioning of the sight flip-over lever and increasing the size of the 100-yard aperture. The butt was strengthened, a fouling plunger added to the bolt to prevent improper assembly and the chamber modified to feed under adverse conditions.

British 9mm Submachine Gun L2A1.

L2A3 Submachine Gun

This is the standard service gun and differs from the L2A2 as follows: rear sight flip lever has been deleted; the butt has again been redesigned and made as a complete stamping rather than as a fabrication with the butt plate indexing and the position along barrel jacket changed. The chamber was modified to the NATO standard and the trigger guard made removable. The previous model had a special Arctic trigger, which was mounted on the trigger guard. An early model of the Sterling Gun had a folding bayonet; all later models have a bayonet boss and stud for a knife type bayonet.

Characteristics of L2A3

System of operation: Blowback, selective fire.
Weight: Unloaded, w/o bayonet: 6 lbs.
    Loaded, w/bayonet: 8.25 lbs.
Overall length: Stock extended: 28 in.
    Stock folded: 19 in.

The L2A3—field stripped.

L2A3—stock folded.

Barrel length: 7.8 in.
Feed device: 34-round, detachable, staggered box magazine.
Sights: Front: Blade w/protecting ears.
      Rear: Flip-type aperture, graduated for 100 and 200 yd.
Muzzle velocity: 1280 f.p.s. w/British 9mm service ball.
Cyclic rate: 550 r.p.m.

How to Load and Fire the L2A3

Pull the cocking handle to the rear; the bolt will remain to the rear since the weapon fires from an open bolt. Engage the safety by turning the change lever (located on the left side of the pistol grip) to the letter "S." Insert a loaded magazine in the magazine guide, checking to insure that it locks in place. Move change lever to letter "R" for semiautomatic fire or letter "A" for automatic fire. Squeeze the trigger and the weapon will fire.

Field Stripping the L2A3

Elementary Stripping. Before stripping, insure that the weapon is not loaded and remove sling if fitted. Set change lever to "A"; place butt in the folded position and bolt forward.

To Remove Return Spring and Bolt. Press back-cap catch for full depth. Push back-cap forward and rotate counter-clockwise until locking lugs disengage from locking recesses. Remove back-cap and draw cocking handle to rear of weapon. Lift cocking handle outward and withdraw return spring assembly from rear of receiver. Remove bolt from rear of receiver. Reassemble in reverse order. The spring-loaded fouling pin will prevent misassembly, since the cocking handle cannot be inserted until this pin is pushed forward by the center pin on the spring assembly. This ensures that the cocking handle must pass through the hole in the center pin.

To Remove Trigger Group. With a small coin or the rim of a cartridge, turn the slot in the head of the trigger group retaining pin until it is in line with the word "FREE" on the right side of the pistol grip. With the nose of a bullet or the blunt end of the cocking handle, push the trigger group retaining pin out and remove. Press the trigger, and pull the trigger group toward rear of weapon, disengaging it from the step in underside of barrel case; then swing front of trigger group out and remove from receiver.

Note: Elementary stripping does not include any further stripping of trigger group.

Assembly

Assemble in the reverse order of stripping.

Applied Safety. When the weapon is cocked, and the change lever is set at the safe position "S," the inner arm of the change lever is positioned directly under the short arm of the tripping lever. When the trigger is pressed, the sear cradle and sear cannot be depressed because the short arm of the tripping lever is held immovable by the inner arm of the change lever.

When the bolt is forward, and the change lever is set at the safe position, the weapon cannot be cocked because the sear is engaged in the safety slot at the rear of the bolt, and the sear cannot be depressed because it is held immovable as described in the previous paragraph.

The Butt Mechanism. To open butt, hold the weapon with the left hand near the rear sight, with the barrel pointing toward the ground. Pull the butt plate outward with the right hand to release the butt catch, and swing the butt to the rear of the weapon. With the thumb of the left hand, press the back-cap catch and snap the butt into engagement with the lugs on the back-cap. Open the butt frame to form a triangle, and the butt catch will engage, to lock.

To close butt, release the butt plate catch and collapse the triangle by pushing the tubular member into the frame. With the thumb of the left hand, press the back-cap catch; at the same time, push the back-cap forward and swing the butt away from the back-cap. Pivot the butt to its folded position, swing the butt plate out to operate the butt catch, to engage in the barrel casing, then fold the butt plate flat to lock in position.

L34A1 Submachine Gun

This weapon is a silenced version of L2A3. The barrel jacket is covered by a silencer casing, which is supported by front and rear supports. The barrel has gas escape holes throughout its length and is threaded at the muzzle. The barrel has a metal wrap and diffuser tube; the extension tube extends beyond the silencer casing and barrel. Beyond the barrel is a spiral diffuser; this is a series of discs and is held in place by tie rods that run from the end cap at the muzzle to the front support. The spiral diffuser has a hole through its center to allow passage of the bullet. L34A1 uses the standard British 9mm Parabellum cartridge.

British 9mm L34A1 Submachine Gun.

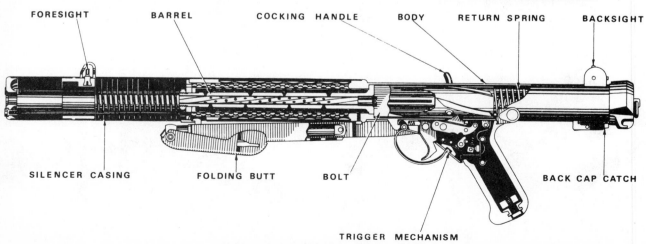

Section view of L34A1 Silenced Submachine Gun.

THE FORWARD ACTION

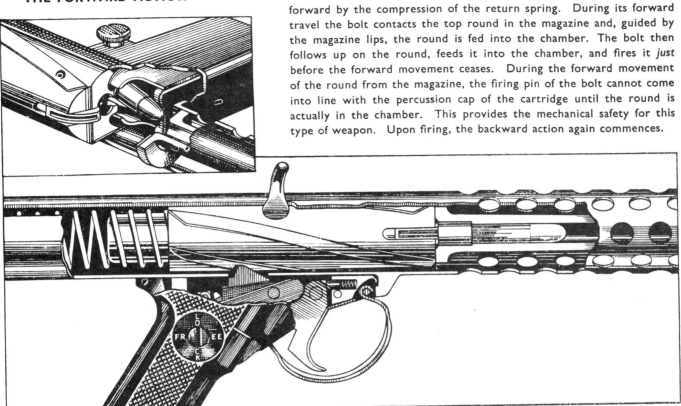

When the bolt reaches the limit of its backward travel it is forced forward by the compression of the return spring. During its forward travel the bolt contacts the top round in the magazine and, guided by the magazine lips, the round is fed into the chamber. The bolt then follows up on the round, feeds it into the chamber, and fires it *just* before the forward movement ceases. During the forward movement of the round from the magazine, the firing pin of the bolt cannot come into line with the percussion cap of the cartridge until the round is actually in the chamber. This provides the mechanical safety for this type of weapon. Upon firing, the backward action again commences.

THE BACKWARD ACTION

When the cartridge is fired the propellant gases exert an equal pressure against both the bullet and the cartridge case, the latter being supported by the bolt and the compression of the return spring. The gas pressure accelerates the bullet also the cartridge case and bolt in opposite directions and as the weight of the bullet is considerably less than that of the combined weight of the cartridge case and bolt, the bullet attains a much greater velocity than that of the cartridge case and bolt. When the bullet clears the muzzle all have reached their maximum velocities but the cartridge case has not yet cleared from the chamber, thus preventing the gases escaping from the breech. The cartridge case does not clear the breech until the gases behind the bullet have dispersed into the air, ensuring that pressures are down to safe limits before the breech is unsealed.

The bolt is now being decelerated by the compression of the return spring.

The empty cartridge case, held against the face of the bolt by the extractor, is carried back until it strikes the ejector and is ejected through the opening on the right side of the weapon.

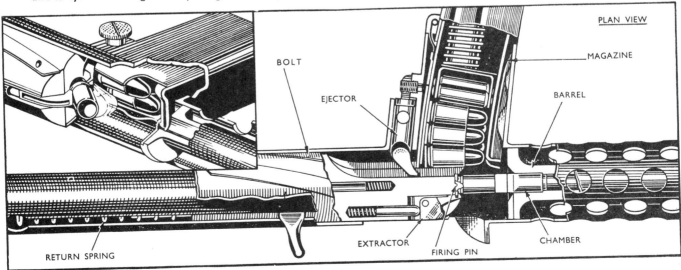

How the L2A3 Works

Characteristics

Caliber: 9mm Parabellum
System of operation: blowback, selective fire
Weight: approx. 8 lbs.
Overall length: Stock extended: 34 in.
             Stock folded: 26 in.
Barrel length: 7.8 in.
Feed device: 34-round, detachable, staggered row, box magazine

Sights: Front: blade w/protecting ears
        Rear: "L" type w/apertures
Muzzle velocity: approx. 1200 f.p.s.
Cyclic rate: 550 r.p.m.

Special Note on British Submachine Guns

Prior to the mid-fifties the United Kingdom called submachine guns "Machine Carbines," since that time they have adopted the same terminology as the US, but in Britain it is slightly differently arranged—"Sub-machine gun."

BRITISH MACHINE GUNS

Britain adopted her first true machine gun—the .450 Maxim—around 1891, and the Maxim in one form or another was used by British forces until quite recently. During World War I, the .303 Vickers, the .303 Lewis and the .303 Hotchkiss were the main machine guns. Between the wars, the British looked for a replacement for the Lewis gun; the replacement was found when the Bren gun was adopted in 1935. Manufacture of the Bren started slowly, however, and did not really gain volume until World War II started.

As with all other small arms, Britain was short of machine guns during World War II, and 87,000 machine guns from US war reserves were sold to Britain in 1940. The following weapons—all caliber .30—were in the 1940 shipments:

    1,157 M1917 Lewis ground guns
    7,071 M1915 Vickers ground guns
    2,602 M1918 Marlin tank guns
  15,638 M1917 Marlin aircraft guns
    5,124 Vickers aircraft guns
  38,040 Lewis aircraft guns
  10,000 M1917 Browning ground guns

These guns were used by the Home Guard and to some extent by the Merchant Marine, who used the stripped-down Lewis for defense against low level air attack. British forces in the field used the Mark 1 Vickers, the Bren, the Besa and, to a limited extent, the Vickers gas operated Mark 1, which, although designed as an aircraft gun, was used as a vehicular gun. All the rifle caliber machine guns used in the field were caliber .303 except for the 7.92mm Besas.

After World War II, Britain looked for a new machine gun to replace the Vickers and, if possible, the Bren. Although the Vickers was a reliable and proven weapon, it was overly heavy and bulky and not as tactically flexible as modern general purpose machine guns. Two of the guns tested by the UK were the B.S.A. general purpose machine gun and the Enfield-developed X11E2. In basic design, both of these guns are quite similar, based on that of the ZB26-Bren family of weapons, excepting

Prototype B.S.A. 7.62mm NATO General Purpose Machine Gun on tripod.

the fact that they are belt-fed rather than magazing-fed.

After extensive trials conducted around 1957, the UK decided to adopt the FN 7.62mm NATO MAG machine gun. According to accounts appearing in British papers at the time, the MAG was adopted because it was the best available gun then in production. For reasons of economy the British Government did not want to pay at that time for the industrial engineering and tooling up necessary with the developmental British weapons. Be that as it may, the MAG, which was tested as the X15E2, was adopted as the L7A1 machine gun.

Lewis Mark I Machine Gun, caliber .303.

THE LEWIS MACHINE GUN

First produced in quantity in Belgium, the Lewis gun was the principal light machine gun of the British Army in World War I and was used by the Home Guard and Merchant Marine (for defense against low-level air attack) in World War II. It was also used—in caliber .30—by the US Marine Corps and Navy until World War II. The US gunboat Panay, which was sunk by Japanese bombers in China during 1937, had Lewis guns as part of its antiaircraft armament as did many other US naval vessels.

The Lewis was made in large quantities during World War I, and a few were assembled by Savage Arms early in World War II. B.S.A. made 145,397 guns at Small Heath; Savage Arms Corporation of Utica, N.Y., produced Lewis guns for the UK and Canada and produced 2,500 caliber .30 and 1,050 caliber .303 ground guns for the US. In addition to the ground guns, large numbers of aircraft guns were made as well.

The basic ground gun is the Mark I; during World War I a number of different model ground guns were made, but all were converted to Mark I after the war. The Lewis gun, in one form or another, was used by France, the Netherlands, Norway, Japan, Imperial Russia, Belgium, Portugal, Italy, Honduras and Nicaragua, in addition to the US and the British Commonwealth.

Characteristics of Mark I Lewis Gun

Caliber: .303 British.
System of operation: Gas, automatic fire only.
Weight: 27 lbs.
Length, overall: 50.5 in.
Barrel length: 26.04 in.
Feed device: 47-round drum magazine, a 97-round drum designed for aircraft use also exists.
Sights: Front: Barley corn.
          Rear: Leaf w/aperture.
Muzzle velocity: 2440 f.p.s.

During World War II, many of the caliber .30 aircraft Lewis guns that were sold to the UK by the US were converted to ground use for the Home Guard. An aperture sight fixed for 400 yards was mounted on the rear aircraft gun sight base and either the standard ground gun wooden butt or a steel skeleton stock with wooden cheek rest were substituted for the aircraft type spade grip. They initially had no mounts and were to be laid over walls or fired from the hip; a non-telescoping bipod was later issued. During the same time, a number of British ground guns were modified for antiaircraft use on ships. The radiator casing and radiator were removed, the butt shortened by two inches, a forward hand grip added and a light steel guard fitted over the gas cylinder.

British .303 Vickers Machine Gun Mark I on tripod, Mark IVB, with ammunition box and steam condensing assembly.

THE VICKERS MACHINE GUN

The Vickers, originally called the Vickers Maxim, was adopted by Great Britain in 1912. It was their principal heavy rifle-caliber machine gun in both world wars and was a standard weapon until the adoption of the L7A1 general purpose machine gun in the early sixties. The Vickers, which is a modified Maxim gun, has the reputation of being one of the most reliable and rugged machine guns ever built. The weapons used by the UK were made by Vickers at Crayford, Kent, in both ground and aircraft versions. The US had bought some Colt-made Maxims—the Model 1904—in very limited quantities prior to World War I. Colt tooled up to produce the Vickers in World War I; and in caliber .30, it was adopted as the US Machine Gun Model 1915. Due to the emergence of the Browning in 1917 and the limited quantities of Vickers Colt was able to produce (it was a difficult gun to make), US troops received few Vickers ground guns during

World War I. Those on hand in 1940 were sold to the UK and were used by the Home Guard. These caliber .30 weapons had a red stripe painted on the receiver, the mouth of the feed block and on the side lever, to distinguish them from the .303 Vickers. The UK made all the Vickers ground guns needed for their forces in both wars.

The weapon can be found with two different water jackets (barrel casings): a corrugated type and a smooth-surfaced type. The smooth-surfaced type is made of slightly heavier metal than the corrugated type. The feed block bodies may be made of either steel, gun metal (bronze) or gun metal with steel strips.

The Vickers may still be found in use throughout the former British territories and is probably still held in reserve in the United Kingdom. It is likely to be found in service in various odd areas of the world for some years to come.

Characteristics of Vickers Machine Gun

Caliber: .303 British, Mark 8z ball normally used.
System of operation: Recoil with gas boost from muzzle booster, automatic only.
Weight:
gun w/o water—33 lbs.
gun w/water—Approx. 40 lbs.
tripod—50 lbs.
Overall length: 43 in.
Barrel length: 28.4 in.
Feed device: 250-round canvas belt.
Sights: Front: Hooded blade.
      Rear: Leaf with aperture, 400 yard battle sight.
Muzzle velocity: 2440 f.p.s.
Cyclic rate: 450-550 r.p.m.

Because of the differences in the barrel erosion characteristics of the .303 Mark 7 ball (cordite loaded) and .303 Mark 7z or .303 Mark 8z ball (single-base nitrocellulose loaded), barrels should be used with either the Mark 7 round or the others—not both. British experience in World War II indicates barrels that have been used with Mark 7 cartridges should NEVER be used with Mark 7z or Mark 8z cartridges for OVERHEAD fire because of erratic wear pattern.

Loading the Vickers Gun

Under normal firing conditions, the rear leg of the tripod will be aligned with target. The gunner sits behind the gun to the rear of this leg with his legs on either side of the tripod. The knees are drawn up slightly so that the elbows can rest on the inside of his thighs while his hands grasp the traversing handle.

Proper Hand Position. Both thumbs are rested lightly on the thumb trigger. The forefingers are wrapped around the top of the handle. The second fingers are placed underneath the ring safety catch. The other two fingers of each hand grasp the traversing handles firmly but without strain.

To Load. See that ammunition box is placed on right side of gun directly below the feed block.

If the gun is equipped with a shutter, open the shutter.

Pass the brass tag-end of the belt through the feed block from the right side and grasp it firmly with the left hand.

With the right hand, pull the crank handle back on its roller as far as it will go, and while holding it in that position pull the belt sharply through the feed block with the left hand as far as it will go.

Release the crank handle and let it fly forward under the influence of the spring. This action grips the first cartridge firmly between upper and lower portions of a gib at the top of the extractor. Now pull the crank handle back on its roller once again. Give the belt another sharp tug to the left as far as it will go, and again let the crank handle fly forward under the influence of the

spring. This action withdraws the cartridge from the belt, places it in the chamber ready for firing and grips the next cartridge by the gib in the upper part of the extractor.

The gun is now cocked and ready to fire, whenever the safety catch is lifted and the trigger pushed in.

Note on Unloading. Because of the method of feeding, safely unloading this weapon requires special consideration. Without touching the belt, pull the crank handle back onto the roller as far as it will go and release it.

Again pull the crank handle back as far as it will go and permit it to fly forward. The first motion of the crank handle extracts the cartridge from the firing chamber and drops or ejects it through the bottom of the gun. The cartridge in the feed block is withdrawn for positioning by this movement and is fed into the chamber, but as the belt is not moved across no new cartridge is gripped by the top of the extractor. Thus when the crank handle is run back for the second time, the second live cartridge is dropped through the bottom of the gun, leaving the firing mechanism empty.

With the left hand, raise the finger plate of the bottom pawls and simultaneously push down the top pawl by squeezing the pawl grips. Keeping the pawls disengaged, pull the belt out of the block to the right. The pawls hold the belt in position in the feed block, the top pawls being behind the first cartridge and the bottom pawls behind the second. During recoil of the gun, the top pawls feed the cartridge into position while the bottom ones prevent any backward lash of the belt; thus, it is necessary to release the pawls from their position before the belt can be pulled out of the gun.

Illustrating correct hand position for firing.

Firing the Vickers Gun

With forefingers wrapped over the top of the traversing handle, raise the safety catch with the second fingers of the hands, wrap the other fingers around the traversing handles and with both thumbs press in on the thumb trigger.

The gun will now fire as long as the trigger is kept pushed in and cartridges are fed into the gun. Releasing either trigger or safety will stop the gun.

Remember that this gun is supported by the tripod and that the hands are intended only for use in firing. Thus, no particular effort is required on the part of the gunner.

How the Vickers Gun Works

Starting with the gun loaded and cocked, the action is as follows. The safety catch is normally held down by a spring that also holds the firing lever to the rear. This catch prevents any forward movement of the firing lever to the rear. This catch prevents any forward movement of the firing lever while it is in safe position. When this catch is raised by the second finger, it clears the way for the thumb piece of the firing lever to push the lower end of the trigger bar forward. The trigger bar lever is engaged with the trigger bar in the rear cover, and as the lever moves back it draws the trigger bar to the rear also.

The forward end of the trigger bar is in engagement with the trigger situated in the lock, and as the trigger moves to the rear, it releases the striker, contained in the lock, from its spring, and the striker is driven forward to fire the cartridge in the chamber.

When the cartridge fires, the bullet is driven down the barrel, and the locked barrel and locking mechanism start rearward.

As the bullet leaves the barrel, the gases behind it expand in the muzzle attachment. Some of these gases strike against a cone, which surrounds the muzzle, and rebound to strike the front face of the muzzle cap cup, fastened over the muzzle.

Thus it will be seen that the rearward action of this gun is brought about by two forces: (1) by recoil (the rearward thrust of gases in the barrel against the cartridge case and the lock as the bullet is forced ahead); and (2) by the effect of the rebounding gases after the bullet has left the muzzle, giving an added backward push against the muzzle cup.

On the rear of the left side plate is a protruding metal box. A powerful fusee spring is attached to the front end of this box. The rear end of the box is locked to the body of the gun. At the front end of this box is the fusee, which is attached to the fusee spring. The rear of this spring, being attached to the fusee, can be drawn straight backwards, extending the spring and storing up energy to provide the return movement of the action. The recoil forces the tail of the crank handle to roll against its roller and rotate the crank, which is attached to the fusee. This winds the fusee chain and extends the fusee spring while the lock is traveling to the rear. The sharp backward thrust caused by the recoil forces the lock, crank and crank handle to move back as the crank handle continues to roll against the roller.

While the mechanism is moving backward, a stud on the bottom lever of the feed block located in a recess in a prolongation of the left side plate is forced to the rear, taking with it the bottom lever, which being connected with the top lever carries the bottom one over to the right, thus causing the feed block slide to move over to the right. This movement causes the top pawls in the feed block to drive to the right and slip over and behind the next cartridge in the belt, which is being held in place by the bottom pawl.

Meanwhile the lock has been moving backwards. The extractor attached to it removes the loaded cartridge from the belt at the same time it draws the empty cartridge case from the chamber. Horns on this extractor ride along the top of solid cams in the breech casing sides, and as the cartridge is drawn clear of the belt, the horns clear the ends of these cams. Rims in the rear cover force the extractor downward and bring the live cartridge into line with the chamber. During this downward movement of the extractor, the empty cartridge case usually drops out. If it fails to, it will be ejected during the forward movement of the extractor. The loaded cartridge is held firmly in position in the extractor by the gib, which has a bottom projection to prevent the cartridge from slipping down out of the extractor face.

During recoil, the backward rotation of the crank moves the connecting rod and side lever head upwards. The side lever head bears on the tail of the tumbler and rotates it, thrusting the firing pin to the rear.

Further rotation of the tumbler in the lock completely withdraws the firing pin as the long arm of the lock spring bears against the projection of the pin. Thus the lock spring is compressed until the trigger nose, forced by the short arm of the lock spring, is pushed over the bent of the tumbler. The firing pin is withdrawn still farther until the sear spring forces the bent of the sear into the bent of the firing pin, which thus holds it in cocked position.

It should be noted that in this weapon part of the action attributable to backward movement is actually to start some parts forward. The crank handle, continuing to roll against the roller during recoil movement, actually starts the recoiling portions forward while the lock is still moving backwards.

Return Movement of the Action. The force of the recoil having expended itself, the stretched fusee spring now reasserts itself, unwinds the fusee chain, moves the link to rotate the crank in the forward direction and forces the connecting rod and side lever head to drive the lock forward.

The stud of the bottom lever of the feed block is carried forward in its recess in the prolongation of the side plate, moves the bottom lever of the feed block forward, thus causing the top lever and the slide to move over to the left. As the pawls move and are gripping the next cartridge in the belt, the loaded cartridge is moved into position against the cartridge stops, ready to be gripped by the extractor on the next rearward movement.

As the lock is driven forward, the extractor supported by the gib is carrying the cartridge into the firing chamber.

The extractor is now raised, and its levers are pushed by the side levers; the gib is depressed against its spring, thus letting go its hold of the cartridge as the round is chambered and the gib is forced back into the face of the extractor.

The upper end of the extractor slips up around the rim of the cartridge in the feed block, and the gib is pushed forward by its spring to grip the head of the cartridge to place it in proper position in the extractor when the next rearward motion of the lock will draw it out of the feed block. Springs located in the side plates engage in slots in the side of the extractor to hold it in its highest position to prevent it from falling should there be no cartridges left in the belt.

If the empty cartridge case has not dropped off the extractor face, it is ejected as the extractor rises during the forward movement by striking against the ejection feeding in the barrel casing.

When the lock approaches its fully forward position, its side lever head is forced slightly below the horizontal by the connection rod. It now depresses the sear, disengaging it from the firing pin and allowing the firing pin to move forward slightly so that the trigger nose engages the bent in the tumbler.

If pressure on the thumb pieces in maintained for automatic fire, the trigger nose is held clear of the bent in the tumbler. The firing pin is free to spring forward under compression of the lock spring when the sear is depressed by the side lever head. However, it should be noted that the depression of the sear is so arranged that the firing pin cannot possibly be released until the lock is fully home and in firing position.

Locking Principle. This gun is locked securely at the moment of firing by a toggle joint. This is the principle developed by Hiram Maxim. The Vickers gun is a modification of the Maxim gun. This locking principle was used in Maxim guns throughout the world, notably in Germany and in Russia.

The simplest way to explain this principle is to compare it with the human knee.

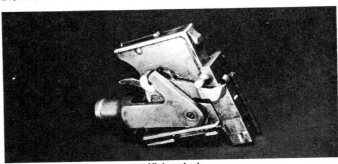

Vickers lock.

When in firing position, the lock on the Vickers gun fits securely against the firing chamber. Now picture the human foot with the heel held firmly in the position of this lock against the head of the cartridge. Pivoted to the lock is the connection rod, a heavy metal bar, thrust straight forward. This connection rod is like the lower part of the leg, but it can buckle at the ankle where it joins the foot. The crank is attached to the connection rod by a hinge pin and extends to the rear. This crank forms a bending knee where it joins the connection rod; it resembles the upper part of the human leg. However, the knee in this mechanical device is actually below the line of the connection rod and crank.

This crank is rigidly supported from below by the inside plates of the weapon, and pressure applied to it by the side levers, during the opening movement of the recoil, merely presses the crank down harder on the plates.

Attached to the crank is a crank handle which travels back with it, and after the gun has recoiled far enough to permit the bullet to leave the barrel, the tail on the lower side of this handle is forced back in contact with a roller, which causes the crank handle to rotate upwards. This raises the axis of the crank pin and permits the knee-like joint to buckle. (Thus, as the human foot is driven backwards, pressure applied to the underside of the knee will buckle the knee but draw the foot straight back.)

The connection rod is locked securely by a twisting motion inside the side lever head, which projects beyond the lower rear end of the lock. As the connection rod buckles, it naturally raises the side lever head with it, and this raises a tumbler, which cocks the lock.

Field Stripping the Vickers Machine Gun

At the rear of the gun above the safety is the rear cover catch. It is held in place by a spring. Push up on the catch and raise the cover up as far as it will go. Now pull back the crank handle against the tension

of the fusee spring. Hold it firmly. Reach inside the gun and lift out the lock, which is fastened to the connection rod. Now twist the lock on the connection rod about one-third of a turn to the right, to release it from

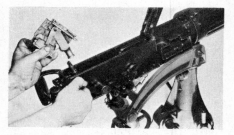

the connection rod, which in its turn is connected to the crank. Lift the lock out, ease the crank handle home under the tension of the fusee spring. Then close the cover.

Turn the cover latch (on the forward end of the cover on the left side of the gun) up to the left as far as it will go. This releases the front cover which should now be raised as high as it will go.

Now lift complete feed block directly up and out of the gun. Go to the forward end of the gun. Pull out the split pin and twist the outer casing through about one-sixth of a turn. It can now be pulled off to the front. The muzzle cup and the front cone may also be unscrewed and removed. (The gland and packing

should be removed only if absolutely necessary.)

Grasping the front end of the spring box with the left hand, push forward on the rear end with the right hand until the hooks which fasten the box at front end and rear can be sprung out of their studs. Disconnect the box from the gun and unhook the fusee spring

from the fusee. The fusee may now be turned until its lugs are free, and then it can be withdrawn with its chain from the left.

Now lift the rear cover and unscrew the large key pin protruding from the left side at the rear of the gun. Pull this pin out to the left, and it will permit the handles and their enclosed mechanism to be swung down to a horizontal position. Slides that travel in the body at the rear may now be pulled straight out. The right slide carries the roller with it. Now pull the crank handle stem directly to the rear, which will withdraw the crank together with the right and left inside plates and the barrel. Disconnect the right and left side plates from the crank and the barrel. This completes field stripping.

Further Notes on Stripping the Vickers Gun

As this is one of the world's basic machine gun types, a more detailed explanation of stripping should be of value. An understanding of the Vickers is particularly helpful in understanding all the German and Russian type Maxim guns.

Stripping the Lock. The lock is cocked as it comes out of the gun. Should it not be, due to having been snapped when withdrawn, it may be cocked by raising the side lever head.

A split pin with a bushing fastens the combined side lever head and side levers to the lock casing. Force these out. The side levers and the extractor and extractor levers may now be removed.

The tumbler, the finger-like projection protruding from the locked casing just above the side lever, is fastened by an axis pin. Push this lever out and remove the tumbler. Now push down the tail of the sear, which will release the lock spring.

Push out the trigger axis pin (the tip of the trigger protrudes from the top of the lock) and the trigger and lock spring may be removed.

Push downward on the sear and remove the firing pin and the sear and sear pin.

The gib may be removed by pushing out its spring cover and removing spring and gib.

To Assemble the Lock. First insert the sear with spring downward, making sure that the sear jaws engage with the sear pivot.

Next insert the firing pin in its groove. Then replace the tumbler and fasten it with its tumbler axis pin.

Insert the trigger; fasten it by the trigger axis pin.

Replacing the gib and its spring and cover in position on the extractor, slide the assembled extractor from the bottom up in the guides in the locked casing.

Replace the extractor levers and side levers and fasten with the bushing and pin.

With sear held down by side lever head, pull back the trigger and press down the tumbler. Now insert the lock spring with its long arm facing toward the extractor and force it down and home.

The firing pin must be released only when the extractor is up in the casing as far as it will go; as only at this point is it lined up so that it will pass through the hole in the extractor. The pin will be injured if it strikes against a solid steel surface in the extractor.

Stripping the Feed Block. The split pin holds the top and bottom block together, and this must be forced out to permit separating the top and the bottom levers.

Pull out the slide with the top pawls and springs. They may be removed from the slide.

Now pull out the bottom pawl axis pin, which will permit removal of the bottom pawl and spring.

Assembling the Feed Block. Reverse the above procedure.

Adjusting the Vickers Gun

The most important adjustment on a machine gun of this type is the head space. This is the correct space between the end of the barrel at the firing chamber and the face of the lock. Should this space be too great, the head of the cartridge will not be held firmly during the moment of high breech pressure. This may bulge the cartridge case so that extraction will be extremely hard, or it may rip the head completely off the cartridge case, resulting in an even more serious jam.

On the other hand, if there is insufficient head space, the lock cannot go forward completely and as a result the side lever head on the lock will not push the sear down far enough to permit the gun to fire.

To Adjust Head Space. Remove the lock and the fusee spring.

Place crank handle in vertical position. Put the No. 1 washer on the outer face of the adjusting nut, making sure that the nut is tight. Now replace the lock in the rear position.

Reach up from below the breech and insert a dummy round or the correct armorer's gauge in the extractor over the firing pin hole, and raise the extractor to its highest point with the fingers. (Use a live cartridge only under suitable range conditions as this is a dangerous operation.)

Make sure that recoiling portions are all locked fully forward and guide the round or gauge into the firing chamber.

Rotate the crank handle forward while guiding the cartridge into the chamber.

Aside from the pressure necessary to compress the sear, a slight check will be felt when the crank handle reaches the check lever if the connecting rod is adjusted to the proper length to give the correct test space.

If no check is left, separate No. 1 or No. 2 washers should be added as required to the outer face of the adjusting nut to provide the correct length.

When the correct length has been ascertained, the washers are assembled permanently on the shoulder of the connecting rod and secured by its nut. (This is done by unscrewing and removing the nut with a combination tool, placing the washers on the connecting rod, and replacing and screwing up the adjusting nut on the washer.)

Tests should be made to be sure that adjustment has been done correctly before completing assembly.

Water Glands. To prevent the cooling water from leaking out of the casing, glands are provided at the muzzle end and oiled asbestos packing wound in a cannelure cut around the breech end of the barrel.

If water leaks at the rear or breech end, empty the casing and then strip the weapon to remove the barrel. A piece of oil soaked asbestos string is then wound into the cannelure of the barrel and pressed in with the point of a screw driver until the cannelure is full. Now oil this packing and smooth it down until it is flush with the barrel, then reassemble the weapon.

Should water leak at the muzzle, stand the gun up on its traversing handles and remove the muzzle attachment together with the cup and unscrew the muzzle gland.

Remove the asbestos string packing, reoil it and wind it loosely around the barrel, pushing it in with a punch or piece of wood. Then screw the gland on as tightly as possible by hand.

This should stop the leakage and yet permit the recoiling portions to move freely.

Cooling System. Whenever it is at all possible, the barrel casing should be kept full during the firing period. The water will boil after firing two belts. It evaporates at the rate of one and a half pints for every 500 rounds, or two belts, if fired continuously. If 2000 rounds are fired, casing will require refilling.

Weighing the Recoiling Portions. Remove the fusee spring and put the crank handle in almost vertical position. Now place the loop of the spring balance on the crank shaft and draw it slowly to the rear. The weight should not exceed 4 lbs. If more than 4 lbs. is required to remove the recoiling portions, it indicates that the packing is pressing too hard on the barrel, and the gland nut must be removed and one or two strands taken out of the asbestos.

To Check Weight of Fusee Spring. Remove the lock and place the loop of the spring balance over the top of the crank handle. Stand to the left of the gun and press down the check lever with the left hand; and with the right pull the balance vertically upwards. When the crank handle begins to move, the weight should be between 7 and 9 lbs.

If necessary to adjust it, wind the vice pin at the forward end of the fusee spring box on the left side of the gun. Six clicks turning from right to left increases the weight one pound; while six clicks turning from left to right decreases the weight one pound.

Improper adjustment of the fusee spring will jam the weapon.

THE BESA TANK MACHINE GUNS

The Besa guns were developed by B.S.A. from the Czech ZB53 (Model 37) machine gun and were used by the UK for tank armament. In 1936, B.S.A. signed an agreement with Zbrojovka Brno allowing them to manufacture the 7.92 ZB53. In April 1938, the War Office placed its first order for the gun, and in 1939 production commenced. B.S.A. soon discovered, however, that considerable modification would have to be made to the gun if it was to be capable of mass production; the modified gun was called the Besa. B.S.A. made 59,322 7.92mm Besa guns during World War II.

The Besa was produced in four different models: Mark 1, Mark 2, Mark 3 and Mark 3*. These weapons differ in minor details, but principally in that the Mark 1 and Mark 2 have two rates of automatic fire, which can be selected by moving the selector lever at the left rear of the receiver ("L" is for low rate and "H" is for high rate), and the Mark 3 and 3* guns have only one rate of fire.

The Besa guns have one unusual feature; although they are gas operated they have a recoiling barrel. The cartridge is chambered and fired before the recoiling barrel is completely in the battery position (fully forward). The recoil of the firing cartridge, therefore, must overcome the inertia of the forward-moving barrel. This action helps in buffing the bolt and reduces the shock on the weapon and the mounting when firing.

The Besa is no longer a standard weapon in Britain, having been replaced by the Browning caliber .30. It may still be found, however, on some of the older armored vehicles. The Besa tank gun is still widely used on older British armored vehicles throughout the British Commonwealth and former British Territories.

Besa 7.92mm Mark 2 Machine Gun.

Characteristics of the Besa Tank Machine Gun

Caliber: 7.92mm.
System of operation: Gas, automatic only.
Weight: Mark 1 47 lbs.
          Mark 2 48 lbs.
          Mark 3 54 lbs.
          Mark 3* 53.5 lbs.
Overall length: 43.5 in.
Barrel length: 29 in.
Feed device: 225-round link or metal and (canvas) belt.
Sights: None fitted to gun, telescopic sights used on vehicles.
Muzzle velocity: 2,700 f.p.s.
Cyclic rate: MK 1 MK 2 - 450-750 r.p.m.
          MK 3 MK 3* - 450 r.p.m.

Loading and Firing the Besa

The trigger guard is part of a heavy steel unit called the trigger guard body. Press forward on the cocking catch thumbpiece, which is mounted on the left side of the trigger guard body, to disengage the cocking catch in a recess in the underside of the receiver. Be careful not to touch the trigger.

Push the trigger guard body forward, and the sear will click into engagement in a bent in the piston extension.

Still keeping the finger away from the trigger and holding firmly to the pistol grip, pull the trigger guard body back with a quick motion. This withdraws the working parts and compresses the return spring. The operating parts will be held to the rear by the sear, which is now engaged in the bent of the piston extension. The cocking catch engages in a recess in the underside of the receiver and locks the trigger guard in firing position.

Push the tab-end of the belt through the feed block from the right side and pull through to the left as far as possible. This places the first cartridge in line with the chamber, bullet pointing downwards. The weapon is now ready to fire.

The pistol grip of the trigger guard body in this weapon is fitted with a grip safety somewhat like the one on the Colt .45 automatic. With finger on trigger, compress the hand to push in the safety catch lever. This will rotate the safety catch to the rear until it clears the underside of the sear; as the trigger is pressed, the sear is pulled out of the bent of the piston extension permitting the return spring to force the working parts forward. The gun will fire as long as the trigger is held back and the safety catch lever is kept depressed. The gun will stay open between shots when trigger is released.

Note: When the belt is emptied, it is expelled from the gun, but the action will go forward to close on an empty chamber.

Unloading the Besa

Release feed pawl depressor lever, which will free the feed pawl from engagement with the belt. Open cover to release retaining pawl, which permits engagement with belt links.

Lift out the belt. Close the cover, lower the depressor lever and ease the working parts forward.

Field Stripping the Besa

See that the gun is cocked.

Pull the barrel retainer carrying handle up about half an inch and push it forward until it rests on the ramp.

Press in the cover catch, push the carrying handle straight forward, then strike the handle with the palm of the hand to bring it to the upright position.

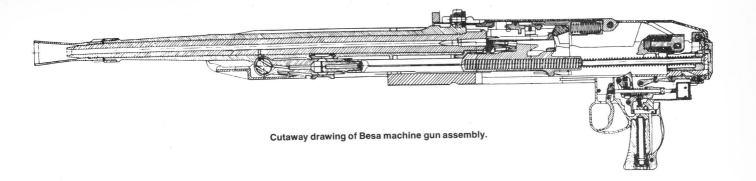

Cutaway drawing of Besa machine gun assembly.

Lift the rear of the barrel until it clears the barrel extension, then ease it forward. This frees the slides on the barrel sleeve from their guides in the body and permits the barrel to be pulled out.

Remove the body cover. Pull the cover locking pin out as far as it will go, press in on the cover catch and lift the cover. Raise it until it can be lifted out of the body (receiver).

Press in the catch on the belt guide and lift it out of the receiver. Lift out the feed block and remove the feed slide.

The breech block may now be lifted out.

Now pull the exposed accelerator arm and plunger cap outwards, pull up the crank arm and lift out the accelerator.

Maintain downward pressure on the barrel extension with the left hand and ease the working parts forward. Pull the trigger guard to the rear.

Push the return spring guide block ahead until it clears the guides in the receiver, then lift it up. The guide lock and return spring may now all be removed.

Grasp piston with the right hand and the rear end of the barrel extension with the left and lift both pieces out, then slide out the piston.

The feed lever may now be inclined inward and lifted out of the weapon.

At the rear of the receiver is the trigger guard catch. Raise this and press the trigger guard easily to the rear to its fullest extent. Then release the trigger, jerk back on the trigger guard till it clears the gun and then lower the catch.

Field Assembly, Besa Machine Gun

Reverse the stripping procedure. Start by replacing the trigger guard, and make sure that it is in its normal position. In replacing feed lever, check that the upper arm is slightly to the right so it will engage correctly its stud with the groove in the piston.

In assembling barrel extension and piston, take care that the upper flange on the piston engages in the lower groove in extension. Work piston backwards and forwards when inserted to be sure that stud on lower arm of feed lever is properly engaged with piston extension groove.

Place return spring in piston, and while holding the spring firmly place the guide rod in the spring, push forward until the rod enters the piston extension. Then press the guide lock down into the receiver and release the pressure. This will permit the spring to position the guide lock properly.

Hold the barrel extension down with the left hand while cocking the gun with the right and replace accelerator, breech block, feed block body and feed slide assembly. Be sure that the stud on the feed slide engages in the slot of the upper arm of the feed lever belt guide.

When replacing the body cover, check that the cover bearings engage properly with the body trunnions.

Barrel Replacement

Keeping rear end of the barrel elevated, insert the slides on the barrel sleeve in the guides on the body. Then draw the barrel to the rear until the flanges at the breech end of the barrel are just above the grooves in the barrel extension. Then lower the barrel into the barrel extension, push the carrying handle over to the right until it rests on the ramp; strike it back sharply with the palm of the hand and push the handle down to lock the barrel.

THE BREN LIGHT MACHINE GUNS

As previously noted, the Bren was developed from the Czech 7.92mm ZB26 by Enfield and ZB in the mid-thirties. Production of the gun started at Enfield in 1937. Most of the production capabilities of Enfield were used to produce Bren guns during World War II. The Bren was also made by Inglis in Canada, both in .303 for British and Canadian service and in 7.92mm for the Chinese Nationalists. By 1943, Canada was making 60% of the Bren guns.

The Bren was one of the best light machine guns of World War II and is still considered a fine gun. The Bren converted to 7.62mm NATO models L4A2, L4A4 and L4A6 is still in service with all British troops except Infantry throughout the world and is used by British Infantry in Asia. There are still many .303 Brens in use throughout the world. ZB produced the Bren at Brno for commercial sale, and the gun was listed in some of their early post-World War II catalogs. It was called the ZGB by the Czechs.

Types of Bren Guns

Bren Light Machine Gun Mark 1. The Mark 1 has a radial type sight, and the butt is shaped differently from the later models. Early versions had a wooden handle, which was hinged under the butt.

Bren Light Machine Gun Mark 1 (M). This weapon was only manufactured in Canada and differs from the Mark 1 in the following ways: the bipod legs do not telescope, the gas vent in the barrel has been enlarged, and the stock has been simplified by the removal of the shoulder support (butt strap), simplification of the butt plate and removal of the butt plate buffer spring.

Bren Light Machine Gun Mark 2. This weapon was made in both the UK and Canada. It has the simplified butt and a leaf type rear sight.

Bren Light Machine Gun Mark 3. The Mark 3 has been lightened and has a shorter barrel.

CHARACTERISTICS OF BREN CAL. .303 LIGHT MACHINE GUNS

	Mark 1	Mark 2	Mark 3	Mark 4
System of operation	Gas, selective fire.	Gas, selective fire.	Gas, selective fire.	Gas, selective fire.
Overall length	45.5 in.	45.6 in.	42.6 in.	42.9 in.
Barrel length	25 in.	25 in.	22.25 in.	22.25 in.
Feed device	30-round box or 100-round drum.	30-round box or 100-round drum.	30-round box.	30-round box.
Sights:				
Front	Blade w/ears.	Blade w/ears.	Blade w/ears.	Blade w/ears.
Rear	Aperture w/radial drum.	Leaf w/aperture.	Leaf w/aperture.	Leaf w/aperture.
Muzzle velocity				
w/MK 7 ball	2,440 fps.	2,440 fps.	Approx 2,400 fps.	Approx 2,400 fps.
Cyclic rate	500 rpm.	540 rpm.	480 rpm.	520 rpm.
Weight of barrel	6.28 lbs.	6.46 lbs.	5.09 lbs.	5 lbs.
Weight of gun	22.12 lbs.	23.18 lbs.	19.3 lbs.	19.14 lbs.

Bren. .303 Light Machine Gun Mark 1.

Bren Light Machine Gun Mark 4. The butt assembly of the Mark 4 differs in minor details from the Mark 2 butt used with the Mark 2 and 3 guns. There have been other minor changes as well.

Bren Light Machine Gun L4A2. This weapon is a conversion of the later model Brens to 7.62mm NATO. A new magazine, bolt and barrel are used with this gun. The receiver has been modified to ensure feeding of the 7.62mm cartridge. The barrel has a prong type flash suppressor.

L4A2 Bren 7.62mm NATO.

Mark 3 Bren.

Loading and Firing the Bren

To load the magazine by hand: The magazine is rested on the thigh or some solid object and cartridges placed in the magazine as for ordinary automatic pistol. They should be inserted with the right hand, and pressed down into place with the thumb of the left hand. Unlike the United States cartridge, the British service cartridge had a rim. In inserting cartridges in magazine, therefore, care must be taken to see that the rim of each cartridge is placed in front of the round already in the magazine. If rim gets behind rim, jams will inevitably result.

Magazine Filler. Push the magazine into the mouth of the filler and swing the filling lever as far as it will go to the left. Fill the hopper and push the filling lever over to the right and back to its limit 6 times; this will put 30 rounds into the magazine. If the filler is the small hand type, push magazine in until the magazine catch engages, and then insert a loaded cartridge charger (or clip as it is called in the United States) into the mouth of the filler over the head of the magazine. See that the tip of the operating lever is against the topmost cartridge and push down slowly and firmly with the operating lever.

Note on Magazine. While the magazine capacity is 30, it is better practice to use 27 or 28 cartridges so as not to strain the magazine spring.

The magazine opening on top of the receiver is fitted with a sliding cover; push this opening cover forward as far as it will go.

Holding the magazine mouth downward in the right hand, insert the lip at the front end into the magazine opening and hook it there; then press downward the rear of the magazine until the magazine catch engages on the magazine rim.

Draw the cocking handle back as far as it will go to cock the action and push it forward again. If weapon has a folding cocking handle, fold it over.

Set the change lever on the left side of the receiver at the desired position of "Automatic," "Safe" or "R" for single shot.

Note on Ejection. A cover over the ejection opening will automatically spring open when the trigger is pulled to permit ejection of empty cartridge case.

Caution: Always remember that gun fires from an open bolt. The bolt should never be permitted to go forward while there is a magazine in the gun unless you intend it to fire. The magazine must be removed first, and the action eased forward second in unloading the weapon.

Field Stripping the Bren

Be sure there is no magazine in the gun and all moving parts are forward.

The body locking pin passes through the receiver from right to left directly under the aperture of the rear sight. Push it with the point of a bullet from the left side and withdraw it from the right.

Grasp the back sight drum firmly with the left hand, and with the right pull back the butt group as far as possible. The return spring rod, which is housed in the butt, will now protrude from the butt through the buffer.

With the thumb and forefinger of the left hand, pull the return spring rod to the left out of line with the piston, and with the right

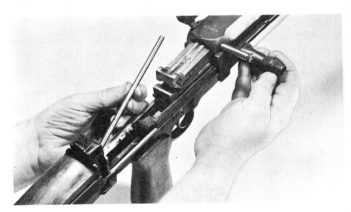

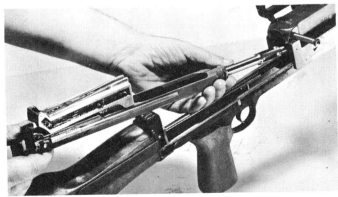

hand pull the cocking handle back with a rapid motion. The piston and breechblock will now come out of the receiver and may be removed from the gun.

The claws at the front end of the breechblock are in engagement with grooves on the piston, and if the breechblock is slid to

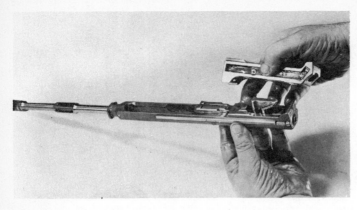

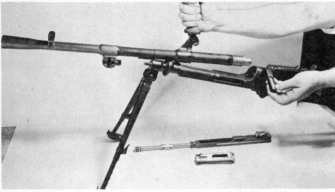

the rear it can be lifted out of this engagement and removed.

The barrel nut catch lies on the side of the barrel just ahead of the magazine opening. Force in the spring catch on its underside and lift the barrel nut catch as far as it will go, which will free the barrel for removal.

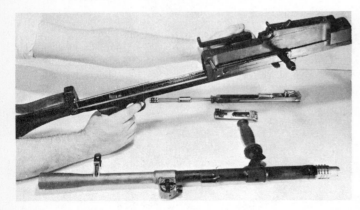

Grasp the rear sight drum firmly with the left hand and with the right hand pull directly back on the butt. The entire butt group may now be removed.

The barrel nut may be removed by lifting the catch as far as it will go and pushing down the small stud in front of the magazine opening cover. The barrel nut is then lifted out vertically.

Now lift the front of the body with the right hand and with the left pull the left leg of the bipod as far forward as possible—slide bipod sleeve off the front end of the gas cylinder.

Notes on Assembling. Reverse the stripping order.

In replacing bipod take care the mount is fully home.

In Mark 1 guns check that the stop on the left of the forward end of the butt group is in front of the barrel nut catch before lowering the catch.

In replacing barrel on Mark 1, make sure the long groove underneath between gas block and carrying handle engages properly with stud on top of receiver.

Be sure the barrel nut catch is fully locked and catch has engaged on rib in the body or receiver.

When replacing breechblock on piston, slide the claws down into the groove as far forward as possible and then let the tail of the breechblock drop.

When inserting the assembled breechblock and piston, make sure that the breechblock is fully forward and that the two are pushed into the receiver before attempting to push forward the butt group.

Be sure that the return spring rod engages in a recess for it in the end of the piston when the butt group is being pushed forward.

Gas Regulator. The gas regulator is mounted on the barrel near the muzzle. It faces to the left. The correct setting is usually the No. 2 size. There are four different ports. Lifting the retainer pin permits the gas regulator to be turned to increase the size of the port. Should the gun become sluggish in action, the gas regulator is altered to the next larger hole to increase the amount of pressure available.

How the Bren Gun Works

Starting with the gun loaded and cocked the action is as follows. If the change lever is set at "R", pressing the trigger pulls a connecting tripping lever, which in its turn draws down the sear out of engagement with the pin on the piston. This action also compresses the coil sear spring. The compressed return spring, situated in the butt, pushes the rod forward, and this in turn pushes against the seat in the piston driving the piston forward, carrying with it the locking and firing mechanism.

Showing change-lever for Safe, Automatic, or Single-shot fire settings.

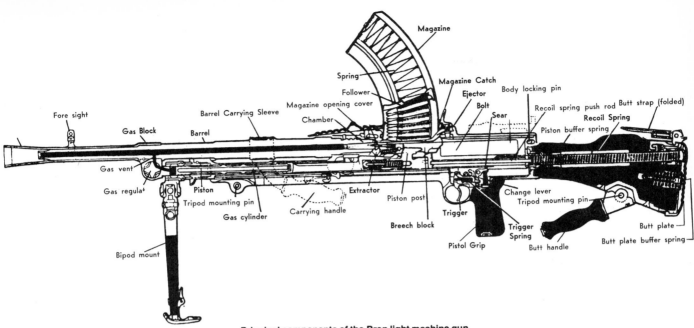

Principal components of the Bren light machine gun.

Meanwhile the sear spring pushes the sear back into place. The breechblock mounted on the top of the piston is carried forward, and the feed piece strikes the base of the first round in the magazine and forces it forward out of lips of the magazine and into the chamber, with the extractor slipping over the rim. The rear end of the breechblock is cammed up into a locking recess in the top of the receiver as the cartridge is properly chambered; in its final move the piston post drives the firing pin against the primer of the cartridge, exploding it.

As the bullet passes over the small gas vent cut in the barrel, a short distance from the muzzle, a small amount of gas under high pressure passes through the vent and through the gas regulator (where the size of the port selected determines the amount of gas to be let in) and escapes into a well where it expands with a hammerlike thrust against the piston. As the piston is driven back in its cylinder, the gas can now escape through holes provided for it.

Meanwhile the sudden thrust on the piston drives it back and

Bren gun on antiaircraft mount.

forces the return spring rod back into the butt where the return spring is compressed, this action being finally stopped by the piston buffer.

The empty cartridge case, gripped by the extractor and carried to the rear in the face of the breechblock, strikes its face against the base of the ejector and is hurled downward through the ejection slot in the piston and out of the weapon. During this rearward action, the upper locking surfaces of the breechblock are forced down into line, so that in its final movement, the piston and breechblock travel together in a straight line.

Note: The buffer spring is in the butt below the line of the return spring.

The Bren Tripod Mark 2 and 2/1

A tripod was issued for use with the Bren light machine gun. Approximately one tripod was issued for every three guns. The tripod is of Czech design and is basically the same as that used with the Czech ZB26 and ZB30 machine guns. A modified form of this tripod is used with the Chinese copy of the US 57mm recoiless rifle.

Details of tripod mount.

THE L7A1 MACHINE GUN

The L7A1 is the British version of the FN MAG 7.62mm NATO machine gun. Enfield has made a few changes in the FN design, particularly in the barrel. In addition, Enfield has developed a tripod for use in the sustained fire role.

Originally a heavy barrel with Stellite liner was to be produced for this gun to use on its role as a tripod mounted sustained fire weapon. Due to manufacturing difficulties, this project was dropped, and L7A1 uses the light barrel in both light and heavy machine gun roles.

Characteristics of L7A1 Machine Gun

Caliber: 7.62mm NATO.
System of operation: Gas, automatic only.
Overall length: 49.7 in.
Barrel length: W/flash suppressor 24.75 in.
Feed device: Disintegrating link belt.
Sights: Front: Protected blade.
  Rear: Peep battle sight of tangent type and leaf.
Weight of gun: 24 lbs. with light barrel.
Weight of tripod L4A1: 29 lbs.
Muzzle velocity: 2800 f.p.s.
Cyclic rate: 700 to 900 r.p.m.

This weapon has been adopted by the UK for use as a tank machine gun to replace the caliber .30 Browning.

7.62mm Machine Gun L7A1 on L4A1 tripod. The gun shown has a grooved barrel which was developed only in prototype form.

ground gun. It is basically an L8 with barrel from L7. It may also be found with butt, bipod and trigger group from L7.

L19A1: This weapon has an 8-pound barrel; it has not been issued to troops.

L7A1 7.62mm Machine Gun on bipod.

The L7A1 is being modified so that it will have a sear with double nose with slide notched to match. Other versions of this weapon are as follows:

L7A2: has attachment for 50-round belt box on left side of the receiver, double feed pawls and double bent sear with slide machined to match.

L8A1: This is a tank gun; the barrel has a fume extractor—bore evacuator—incorporated. It has a three-position, non-venting gas regulator, and the trigger is designed for use with a solenoid. It has a folding pistol grip for emergency manual operation, and a feed pawl depressor is fitted. It is used on the "Chieftain" tank.

L20: This is an experimental version of the L8 for use in aircraft gun pods. It is capable of left or right feed. It has a hybrid barrel assembly having the L8 gas regulator on the L7 barrel. The front sight and the carrying handle have been removed from the barrel.

L37A1: This gun is a mixture of L7 and L8 components produced to make a gun for armored vehicles other than "Chieftain", which can be removed and used as a normal

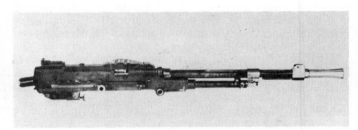

7.62mm Tank Machine Gun L8A1.

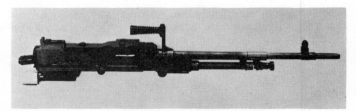

British 7.62mm Machine Gun L20.

US MACHINE GUNS IN BRITISH SERVICE

The United Kindom has adopted the US Browning caliber .50 M2 heavy barrel machine gun, which they call the L1A1. The caliber .30 Browning M1919A4 and 1919A5 machine guns are also used on armored vehicles.

The .30 caliber Brownings in service are called the L3A1 Fixed, L3A2 Flexible, L3A3 and L3A4.

OTHER COMMONWEALTH MEMBERS

South Africa, which is no longer a member of the Commonwealth, is producing the 7.62mm NATO L1A1 (British FN FAL) rifle at Pretoria. South Africa has also adopted the 7.62mm

NATO FN MAG general purpose machine gun, as have Zambia, Southern Rhodesia, Tanzania, Uganda and Sierra Leone.

Canada 11

Canada uses the 9mm FN Hi-Power pistol of native manufacture. The Canadians also use rifles 7.62mm NATO C1A1 and C2A1, the Canadian counterparts of the FN FAL and its heavy barrel version, respectively. These rifles were considerably modified from the original FN design by the Canadian government arsenal at Long Branch, Ontario, where they are manufactured. Canada was the first country to put the FN in mass production and the first member of NATO to have its regular army completely equipped with 7.62 weapons.

Canada has adopted the British 9mm Sterling (Patchett) submachine gun in slightly modified form as the submachine gun C4. The standard machine gun in Canada is the 7.62mm NATO C1. This gun is a converted caliber .30 Browning Model 1919A4. Bren guns and other .30 caliber Browning guns may be held in reserve stocks. The caliber .50 Browning M2 H.B. machine gun is also standard in Canada.

CANADIAN PISTOLS

Canada used the British service pistol, the Webley .455 Pistol No. 1, Mark VI to some extent in World War I. However, they extensively used Colt and Smith & Wesson revolvers and Colt automatics. Canada was the first member of the British Commonwealth to adopt and produce a truly modern automatic pistol. The Canadian-made 9mm Parabellum Browning Hi-Power pistol is standard in Canada and in the United Kingdom. This weapon was supplied to the UK during World War II to arm Commandos and paratroop divisions. The pistol was originally put into production for the Chinese Nationalist Army.

THE CANADIAN HI-POWER BROWNING PISTOL

The John Inglis Company of Toronto, Ontario, produced the 9mm Parabellum Browning Hi-Power pistols in several models for the Canadian and Chinese Nationalist Governments during World War II.

Pistol, Browning, FN 9mm, HP, No. 1 Mark 1

The butt is machined for a shoulder-stock holster, and a tangent leaf rear sight graduated from 50 to 500 meters is fitted.

Pistol, Browning, FN, 9mm, HP, No. 1 Mark 1*

Also machined for a shoulder-stock holster, but the height of the ejector has been increased, and the tangent-type rear sight (similar to the No. 1, Mark 1) has been machined to accommodate the increased height of the Mark 2 ejector. The extractor also differs and cannot be interchanged with the Mark 1 extractor.

Pistol, Browning, FN, 9mm, HP, No. 2 Mark 1

Not machined for shoulder stock holster, it has a smaller ejector and a notched, fixed rear sight. Uses Mark 1 extractor and Mark 1 ejector.

Pistol, Browning, FN, 9mm, HP, No. 2 Mark 1*

Same as No. 2 Mark 1, except for ejector and extractor. Uses extractor Mark 2 and ejector Mark 2 for which slide clearance is machined.

There are two models—Mark 1 and 2—of hammer and link for these pistols; however, these are interchangeable. The wooden shoulder-stock holster is no longer in common use; these pistols are used now as "one-hand" weapons.

Canadian Browning FN 9mm HP No. 2 Mark 1.

Right side of the No. 2 Mark 1.

Canadian lightweight version of the 9mm Browning FN Hi-Power pistol.

Canadian caliber .45 NAACO "Brigadier" pistol.

The characteristics of the Canadian Browning FN HP pistol are basically the same as those of this pistol as produced in Belgium and given in the chapter on Belgium.

POST-WAR CANADIAN PISTOLS

After World War II, a number of pistol tests were conducted in Canada, the UK and US. Among the competitors was a lightweight version of the Canadian Hi-Power.

This pistol has lightening cuts on both sides of the slide. The pistol tests turned out to be of little consequence since economics and logistics—the quantity of weapons and ammunition on hand and tooled for—dictated that pistols in hand would be used.

The Brigadier .45 Pistol

NAACO—the North American Arms Corporation of Canada—developed a caliber .45 pistol called the "Brigadier." This pistol is a modified Browning Hi-Power chambered for a new caliber .45 cartridge of considerably more power than the .45 automatic cartridge.

It should be noted that the "Brigadier" has its safety catch on the slide where it blocks the firing pin rather than on the receiver as does the Browning (and the Colt.)

CANADIAN RIFLES

BRIEF HISTORICAL SUMMARY

Canada had a rifle of native origin for part of World War I—the Ross in its various models. The Ross was dropped as standard in 1916, and the British Short Magazine Lee Enfield Mark III (Rifle No. I Mark III) was adopted. The US bought 20,000 Ross rifles from Canada in 1917 for training purposes. The Lee Enfield No. 1 rifles were used between World Wars I and II, and Canada adopted the No. 4 rifle at about the same time as the UK Long Branch tooled up to produce the No. 4 early in World War II and produced a total of 952,000, of which the greater part by far were No. 4 Mark 1*

ROSS RIFLES

Description of Weapons

Although Ross rifles have not been used as first-line weapons since mid-World War I, there are still a fairly large number of them in circulation among collectors and sportsmen. There are two basic variations of the .303 Ross and a number of minor variations to the basic types; all are straight pull bolt actions. The Mark II, which is frequently called the Model 1905, has solid bolt locking lugs and the Harris type magazine. This magazine, which is flush with the stock, cannot be loaded with chargers. There is a magazine lifter thumb lever on the right side of the rifle ahead of the receiver. The Mark II may be found with tangent type sight or with leaf type sight. A cut-off projects into the forward part of the trigger guard. The Mark III has several variations in rear sights and front sights. The Mark III is frequently called the M1910. It is easily distinguished from the Mark II by its magazine, which protrudes below the stock. The Mark III magazine can be loaded with a charger, and the Mark III cut-off is mounted at the left rear of the receiver in the same position as that on the US Springfield M1903. It also functions the same as that of the Springfield. The Mark III has locking lugs with interrupted screw thread.

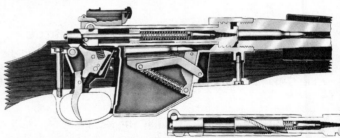

Representative Canadian Ross straight pull rifle and bolt in section to show operation.

Special Note on the Ross Rifles

The Ross rifles are well made of good materials, but they had several serious design defects that caused their abandonment as an infantry weapon by Canada in 1916. The action is suitable for sporting rifles but was found eminently unsuited for the mud of Flanders. In an attempt to make up for the poor extracting qualities of these weapons when dirty, the chamber was relieved slightly. This makes the Ross a rather poor rifle for a hand loader, since cases are badly stretched on firing.

The most serious problem with the Ross for the modern shooter is the fact that on most models the bolt can be reassembled wrong and yet be put in the weapon, it may then fire a cartridge in an unlocked condition with resulting **serious injury, if not death,** to the shooter. The bolt is assembled wrong if the distance between the bolt head and the bolt sleeve is less than one inch when the bolt is withdrawn from the rifle (bolt in unlocked posture). The bolt is exceedingly difficult to disassemble and reassemble, and it is best to take it to a gunsmith if in doubt.

Caliber .303 Canada Ross rifles. From top down: Mark III, Mark II*, Mark II, and the Mark III*.

Bolt of the Ross M1910 Mark III Rifle at left and that of the Ross M1905 Mark I Rifle right.

7.62mm AUTOMATIC RIFLES FN C1 AND C1A1

Canada was among the first to adopt the FN FAL rifle and was the first to mass produce the weapon. Prior to the adoption of the production model (the C1), Canada, as well as the UK, tested a number of experimental models. The Ex 1 model was quite similar to the British-adopted L1A1 in that it could not be fed with chargers and had a rear sight with a fixed-size aperture.

The EX 2 could not be fed with chargers either but had an optical sight similar to that of the British E.M. 2 rifle. Both rifles had barrels without flash suppressors.

Similar rifles were tested by the UK as rifle 7.62mm, FN BR X8E1, Type A (iron sight type), and rifle 7.62mm, FN BR, X8E2, Type B (optical sight type.) Canada made additional modifications and adopted the rifle 7.62mm FN (C1) in June 1955.

The obvious external differences between the C1 and most other versions of the FN FAL family are the rear sight and the charger guide, which allows feeding of the magazine when in the rifle with five-round chargers.

The sight of the C1 is similar to that found on some sporting rifles. A disc containing five differently sized apertures is held in a frame. The edge of the disc is serrated for ease of turning; a flick of the disc turns up the range aperture desired from 200 to 600 yards. The range for which the aperture is set is indicated by numbers from 2 to 6, which are visible in the lower part of the sight. The sight can be folded when not in use.

Characteristics of C1 and C1A1 Rifles

Caliber: 7.62mm NATO.
System of operation: Gas, semiautomatic only.
Overall length: 44.75 in.
Barrel length: 21 in.
Weight: 9.4 lbs.
Feed device: 20-round, detachable, staggered row. Box, can be fed with 5-round chargers.
Sights: Front: Protected post.
Rear: Revolving disc with apertures.
Muzzle velocity: 2,750 f.p.s.

Experimental 7.62mm FN FAL Rifle CDN EX 1.

Experimental 7.62mm FN FAL rifle CDN EX 2.

Canadian 7.62mm Rifle FN C1.

Receiver detail of 7.62mm Rifle FN C1.

Rear sight of 7.62mm FN C1 Rifle.

7.62mm Rifle FN C1A1.

Modification of C1—the C1A1

The C1 was modified slightly around 1959; the modification is called: rifle 7.62mm FN C1A1. The principal modifications were in the firing pin, which was altered to two-piece configuration, and a new plastic carrying handle, which replaced the wooden type.

Presumably C1 rifles in service will be converted to C1A1 rifles. Both C1 and C1A1 have prong-type flash suppressors fitted to the muzzle of the barrel.

7.62mm AUTOMATIC RIFLE FN C2

Characteristics of 7.62mm Automatic Rifle FN C2

Caliber: 7.62mm NATO.
Weight loaded: (30-round magazine); 15.25 lbs.
Overall length: (normal butt): 44.75 in.
Barrel length: 21 in.
Feed device: 20 or 30 round box magazine.
Sights: Front: Protected post.
        Rear: Tangent w/aperture graduated from 200-1000 yds.
Muzzle velocity: 2800 f.p.s.
Cyclic rate of fire: 675-750 r.p.m.

The C2 is the heavy-barreled, selective-fire version of the Canadian semiautomatic FN rifle C1. The method of operation and field strip of the C2 are similar to that of the C1. C2 like C1 has a prong-type flash suppressor and can be fitted with a bayonet or grenade launcher. The bipod legs are fitted with wooden strips, allowing the bipod to be used as a fore-end when in the folded position. Differences between the C2 and C1 rifles other than noted above are as follows:

a. The rear sight of C2 is different.
b. C2 has a bipod.
c. C2 has no handguard.
d. C2 change lever has 3 positions: safe, semiautomatic and automatic fire.
e. C2 gas block assembly includes a mounting for the bipod.

This weapon, the Canadian squad automatic weapon, has the advantage of using most of the components of the basic rifle including magazines.

C2 is, like C1, made at the Canadian government small arms plant at Long Branch, Ontario.

7.62mm AUTOMATIC RIFLE FN C2A1

About 1960, C2A1—a modification of C2—was adopted. C2A1, like C1A1, has a two-piece firing pin and a plastic carrying handle. C2A1 is about one-quarter pound lighter than C2. As with all of the Canadian FN rifles, C2A1 can be fitted with any of three lengths of buttstock; normal, long, and short.

7.62mm Rifle C2 with bipod fixed.

Receiver detail of FN C2 Rifle.

CANADIAN SUBMACHINE GUNS

Modified Mark 2 Sten

In addition to the Sten gun, which was produced in tremendous quantities during World War II, a good deal of design work was carried out at Long Branch Arsenal by Anton Rosciszewski with improved versions of that submachine gun.

The trigger is curved at the top and the bottom; pressure on the top of the trigger produces automatic fire, and pressure on the bottom produces semiautomatic fire. This feature is not unique, for it is essentially the same feature used on the German MG 13 and other weapons; it is unusual for a Sten. The other unusual feature is the operation of the magazine. The reciprocal action of the bolt works the magazine through a spring and plunger linkage. This method of feed control ensures a constant feed pressure on the cartridge thereby cutting down feed stoppages resulting from the irregular spring pressure frequently experienced with conventional magazines.

Experimental Rosciszewski Model 2

In 1945, Mr. Rosciszewski developed another submachine gun called the Model 2.

This weapon used the same type trigger mechanism as the modified Sten but had several different features. The magazine is parallel to the barrel, and therefore the cartridges must go through an arc of 90° to feed into the chamber. The breech block activates the cartridge lifter strut, which pivots the cartridge lifter through 90°. The bolt is also different in that is has a forward extension, similar to that of the German G3 rifle, which rides in a tunnel over the barrel and to which the bolt handle is attached.

Canada has adopted the Sterling (Patchett) submachine gun as submachine C4. The Canadian Sterling differs in minor details from the L2A3.

Long Branch Arsenal

The Long Branch Arsenal was organized in 1940 at Long Branch Ontario, a suburb of Toronto, as "Small Arms Ltd." On 1 January 1946, it was taken over by Canadian Arsenals Ltd., a government-owned corporation, and renamed Small Arms Division. The principal product in World War II was the No. 4 Mark I* rifle.

Experimental Rosciszewski Model 2 submachine gun.

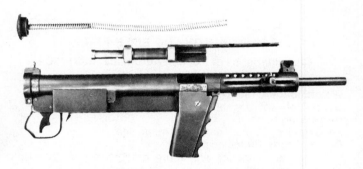

Experimental Model 2 submachine gun—field-stripped.

CANADIAN MACHINE GUNS

Canada used the .303 Lewis and Vickers guns in World War II. In World War II, the John Inglis firm in Toronto manufactured large quantities of .303 Mark 1 (M) and Mark 2 Bren guns. In addition, Inglis made substantial quantities of 7.92mm Mark 2 Brens for the Nationalist Chinese. A few .30-06 Brens were made, apparently for experimental work.

The Canadian forces engaged in the Korean conflict were mainly supplied with US weapons in order to simplify the logistics problem. In addition, Canada had considerable stocks of caliber .30 Browning guns, mainly from vehicles, left over from World War II. Canada ran tests of several 7.62mm NATO machine guns during the fifties and decided to convert existing stocks of caliber .30 Browning Model 1919A4 machine guns for 7.62mm NATO. The converted gun is the 7.62mm NATO C1 machine gun.

7.62mm NATO C1 Machine Gun

The C1 is supplied in fixed, for vehicular mounting, and flexible, for infantry, versions. In external appearance it differs very little from the US caliber .30 Browning M1919A4. In the ground role, it is used on a light tripod. The principal differences between the 1919A4 and the C1 are the barrel and the feed mechanism. The feed mechanism of the Browning was originally designed for a "pull out" type belt or metallic link. The feed mechanism of the C1 has been modified so that a "push through" type link—the US M13—can be used with a "pull out" type mechanism. The front barrel bearing plug has also been modified to give the action more gas boost in order to provide more power to extract cartridges from the links. A link guide has been installed on the feedway, and a short round stop has been fitted to the receiver in front of the feedway.

In addition to these and several other minor changes, two spring loaded ball bearings have been added to the T slot of the bolt. They prevent rounds from sliding completely through the T slot. The cartridge extractor has also been modified by removal of the ejector finger, spring and pin; the rear sight leaf has been engraved with new graduations in meters to match the ballistics of the 7.62mm NATO round.

12 Free China: "The Republic of China" (on Taiwan)

The Chinese Nationalist Army usually used the term "Type" rather than "Model" for the nomenclature of weapons. The Chinese character for "Type" can be translated as "SHIH" or "SHIKI" and is the same as that used by the Japanese. Since a type designation may be followed by a model designation to indicate a modification (as with the old Japanese system, for example, the Type 34 Model 1), Chinese markings on weapons must be carefully examined to secure the proper nomenclature. On many (but not all) Chinese Nationalist weapons, the Type designation indicates the date of adoption of the weapon in number of years since the Chinese revolution—1911. Thus the Type 36 submachine gun was adopted in 1947; the Type 41 light machinegun was adopted in 1952. The People's Republic of China, however, uses the calendar year designation, i.e., 51 for 1951, etc.

Although for a period of time Nationalist China and the People's Liberation Army used the same types of small arms, this picture has changed considerably since the Korean war. During World War II, the Chinese Nationalists received large quantities of small arms from the United States. After World War II, the Chinese Nationalists started production of some US-type weapons on the mainland of China and also took over Japanese ordnance plants in the Manchurian area. The production of Japanese weapons was continued, as was the production of Japanese small arms ammunition. However, in an effort to standardize on ammunition, some of the Japanese weapons were rebarreled or made for 7.92mm cartridges.

Thus, at the time the Chinese Nationalists were forced to leave the mainland, they had weapons chambered for a multitude of different calibers. Since the Nationalist Army has been on Taiwan (Formosa), it has been able to standardize its weapons and simplify its supply problems. At present, the Nationalist Army uses US M1903 and M1 Rifles. They have manufactured a modification of the Bren in .30-06, and they are currently producing the US M14 Rifle and M60 Machine Gun on tooling provided by the US.

CHINESE PISTOLS

As with all other small arms, the Chinese had a wide collection of pistols. The Mauser in 7.63mm was a great favorite, and Chinese-made copies of the Mauser in cal. .45 have been encountered. During World War II, the United States supplied the Chinese with cal. .45 M1911A1 automatics, with Colt and Smith & Wesson M1917 revolvers, as well as some cal. .38 revolvers. The Canadians supplied the Chinese with the 9mm Browning Hi-Power pistol made by John Inglis in Toronto.

Chinese 9mm FN Browning Hi-Power pistol with shoulder stock holster attached.

CHINESE RIFLES

The pre-World War II Republic of China had many rifles in service. The oldest was probably the Type 88, or Hanyang rifle as it was called from its place of manufacture. This weapon is a copy of the German M1888 rifle, large quantities of which were sold to China by Germany after the Germans adopted the Model 98 rifle. This rifle is chambered for the old 7.92mm × 57mm rimless cartridge and has a .318 bore rather than the .323 bore of the 98 and later 7.92mm weapons. Therefore, this weapon should not be used with 7.92mm × 57mm IS (sometimes called JS) ammunition. The Chinese issued a special conical-nosed ball cartridge for this weapon. It should also be noted that Chinese weapons of pre-World War II manufacture are widely variable in quality of materials and construction. Chinese weapons manufactured since World War II are, so far as can be determined, made of first-class materials and show fine workmanship. Other Chinese rifles of this period are:

7.92mm Belgian FN M1924 and M1930 rifles, and Chinese copies.

7.92mm Czechoslovak Brno M1924 rifles, and Chinese copies.

The Mauser 7.92mm "Standard Model," a Mauser export model copied by the Chinese in 1935, is called the "Generalissimo" or "Chiang Kai Shek" model. This model is now called the type 79 by the PRC. All these weapons were used by PRC troops in Korea.

The 7.62mm NATO Type 57 Rifle

The Chinese Nationalists manufacture a copy of the US M14 rifle called the Type 57 (1968). This rifle varies only in minor details from the US made rifle. The most noticeable difference is the shape of the stock immediately behind the receiver. The Chinese made rifle has a more pronounced flat surface immediately behind the rear of the receiver than does the US rifle.

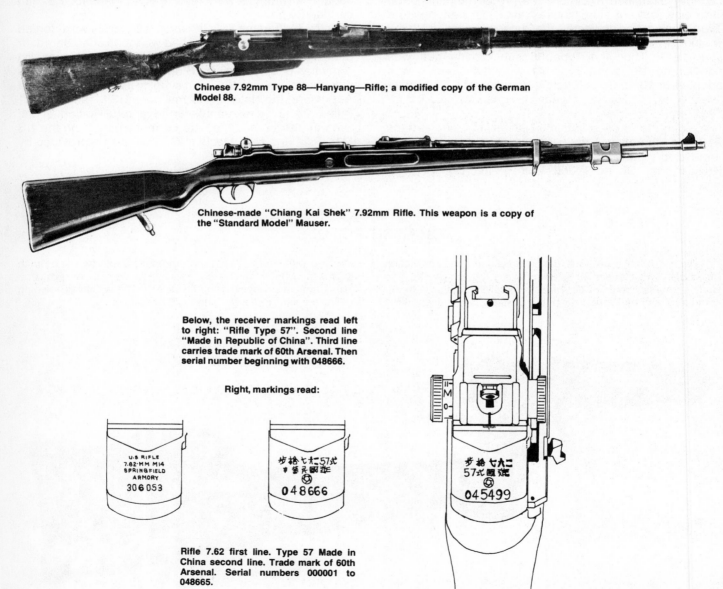

Chinese 7.92mm Type 88—Hanyang—Rifle; a modified copy of the German Model 88.

Chinese-made "Chiang Kai Shek" 7.92mm Rifle. This weapon is a copy of the "Standard Model" Mauser.

Below, the receiver markings read left to right: "Rifle Type 57". Second line "Made in Republic of China". Third line carries trade mark of 60th Arsenal. Then serial number beginning with 048666.

Right, markings read:

U·S RIFLE
7.62·MM M14
SPRINGFIELD
ARMORY
306053

步槍七九二57式
中華民國造
048666

步槍七九二
57式國造
045499

Rifle 7.62 first line. Type 57 Made in China second line. Trade mark of 60th Arsenal. Serial numbers 000001 to 048665.

CHINESE SUBMACHINE GUNS

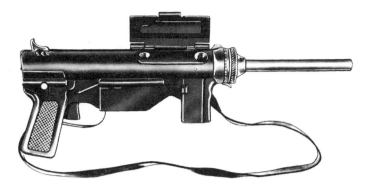

Type 36 submachine gun. A caliber .45 Chinese-made copy of the US M3A1 submachine gun. Similar weapons in 9mm Parabellum were made by the Chinese.

Caliber .45 submachine gun, based on design of Japanese Type 2, believed to be of Chinese manufacture.

The most common submachine guns in the Chinese Army prior to and during World War II were:

All the models of the US Thompson in cal. .45 (frequently called 11mm by the Chinese) plus a Chinese-made copy of the 1928 Thompson.

The US M3 and M3A1, and a Chinese copy of the M3A1 called the Type 36, in cal. .45, and Type 37 in 9mm Parabellum.

British Stens chambered for the 9mm Parabellum cartridge. The Chinese also made some copies of these.

The Thompson, the M3A1 and the Type 36 are still in use in the Chinese Nationalist Army.

CHINESE MACHINE GUNS

The Chinese used a wide variety of machine guns prior to and during World War II. Most of these weapons again appeared in Korea during the early stages of the Chinese Communist commitment. The most common weapons were:

The Chinese-made Type 24 heavy machine gun. This 7.92mm weapon is a modification of the German Maxim Model 08 (MG 08).

Czechoslovak- and Chinese-made 7.92mm ZB 26 and ZB30 light machine guns. These weapons were called Type 26 and Type 30 by the Chinese.

Swiss SIG-made KE 7 light machine guns in 7.92mm caliber.

Danish Madsen-made 7.92mm light machine guns.

Chinese-made 7.92mm Maxim aircooled machine guns.

French-made Hotchkiss M1914 heavy and Model II light machine guns in 7.92mm caliber.

Colt- and FN-made Browning automatic rifles, also chambered for the 7.92mm cartridge. There apparently were not too many of these.

Colt- and FN-made Browning watercooled machine guns in 7.92mm. These were also apparently in short supply.

Chinese-made Type 41 light machine gun. Bren-modified for US caliber .30.

7.92mm Bren guns Mk. 2, made in Canada for the Chinese during World War II.

The list given above is by no means complete. When one considers purchases, Lend-Lease, war booty, etc., the Chinese Army was a gun collector's paradise and an ammunition supply officer's nightmare. All the standard United States machine guns and most of the standard British machine guns were in wide use before the end of World War II. The 7.62mm NATO M60 machine gun made in Taiwan is now the standard machine gun of the Nationalist Chinese Army.

"The People's Republic of China" (on Chinese mainland)

13

At the conclusion of World War II, the People's Republic inherited large quantities of Japanese weapons from the Soviets, who had taken them in Manchuria. During the Chinese civil war, they captured materiel from the Chinese Nationalists, including large quantities of US weapons. When the PRC entered the Korean conflict, they had far more Chinese, Japanese and US equipment in the battle area than Soviet materiel. By war's end they were well along the road to standardizing Soviet small arms for their troops.

During the past two decades, they have put a number of those Soviet weapons into production, using their own year of adoption model designations. For example, the PPSh-41 was adopted by the PRC as the Type 50. The M1944 Mosin Nagant carbine was put into production as the Type 50. The DPM light machine gun was called the Type 53. In recent years, the PRC has begun to manufacture a new series of domestically developed small arms. Among these weapons are the 7.62 × 39mm Type 68 rifle, the 7.62 × 54Rmm Type 67 light machine gun and the 7.62 × 25mm Type 64 submachine gun, a silenced weapon.

SERVICE WEAPONS OF THE PEOPLE'S LIBERATION ARMY

The Chinese Communist army is currently equipped with Chinese-made copies of Soviet small arms as follows:

Soviet 7.62mm TT M 1933 Pistol, **Type 51 Pistol.**
Soviet 7.62mm AK-47 assault rifle, **Type 56 assault rifle.**
Soviet 7.62mm SKS carbine, **Type 56 carbine.**
Soviet 7.62mm RPD light machine gun, **Type 56 machine gun.**
Soviet 7.62mm DPM light machine gun, **Type 53 light machine gun.**
Soviet 7.62mm RP-46 light machine gun, **Type 58 light machine gun.**
Soviet 7.62mm SG-43 heavy machine gun, **Type 53 heavy machine gun.**
Soviet 7.62mm SGM heavy machine gun, **Type 57 heavy machine gun.**
Soviet 12.7 mm DShK M1938/46 heavy machine gun, **Type 54 heavy machine gun.**

Many of the older model Soviet weapons covered later in this text are still in use, and many of these weapons, as well as some of the smaller newer weapons listed above, were shipped to Vietnam.

Type 50 7.62mm submachine gun, a copy of the Soviet PPSh M1941.

7.62mm Type 53 carbine.

7.62mm Chinese Tokarev pistol Type 51, a copy of Soviet TT M1933 Tokarev.

First Model Type 56 Chinese Assault Rifle.

Type 56-1 Assault Rifle.

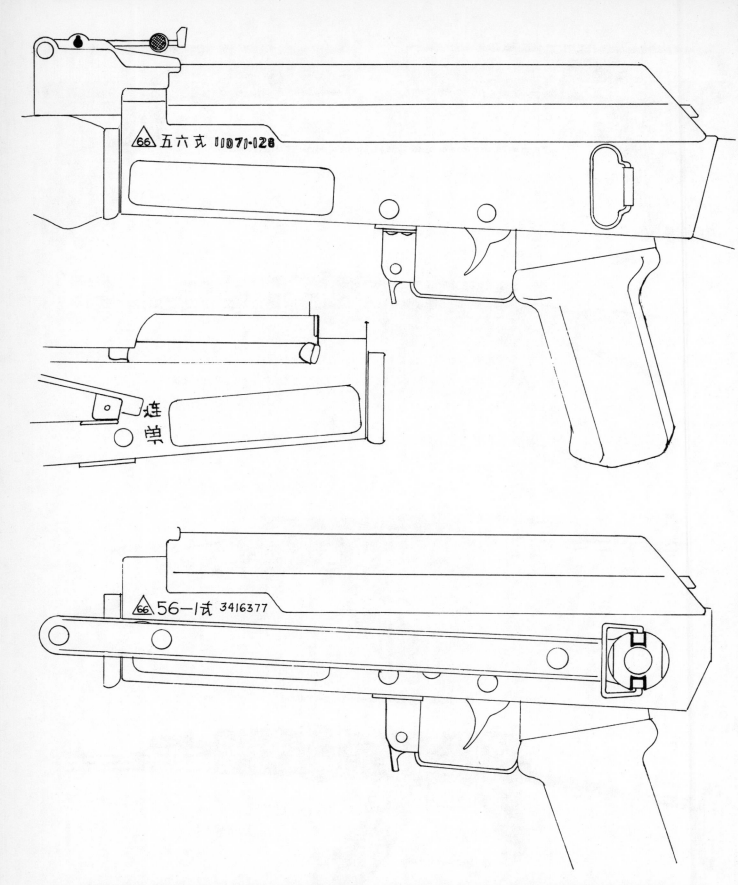

PRC Type 56 Rifle markings. Top, early type 56 with Chinese selector markings. Bottom, Type 56-1, which has L&D selector markings.

Late model Type 56 Chinese Assault Rifle with folding spike bayonet. Chinese selector markings have been replaced by "L" for full auto and "D" for semiautomatic fire.

Close-up of Type 56 Assault Rifle spike bayonet in folded position.

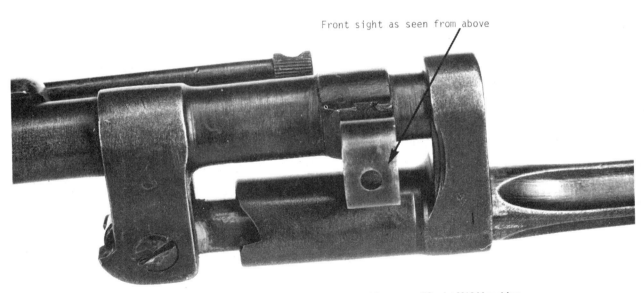

Front sight as seen from above

Top view of side mounted folding bayonet on Type 53 carbine copy of Soviet M1944 carbine.

CHINESE MODIFICATIONS OF SOVIET DESIGNED WEAPONS

The Chinese have modified several of the Soviet weapons that they manufacture. The standard Soviet 7.62mm AK assault rifle, manufactured in China as the Type 56, has a removable knife type bayonet. While they still use the Type 56, they also make a modification, which has a folding type, cruciform section bayonet attached to the under section of the front sight base.

The Chinese are also making the 7.62mm Type 56 Carbine (copy of the Soviet SKS) with a folding bayonet.

The 7.62mm Type 53, which is a copy of the Soviet 7.62mm M1944 Mosin Nagant carbine, has appeared with a rifle grenade launcher. The launcher is of the removable type and has a clamp type lock that engages behind the front sight in a manner similar to the US M7 and M8 rifle grenade launchers. When the rifle grenade launcher is attached, the folding bayonet cannot be fixed.

CHINESE 7.62mm TYPE 68 RIFLE

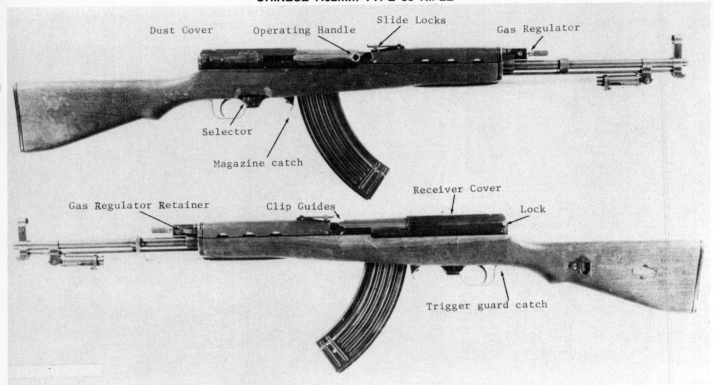

Right and left side views of Type 68 Rifle.

The Type 68 is a native Chinese designed selective fire weapon. Externally it resembles the Soviet SKS carbine modified to use a detachable box magazine. Internally it is quite different; the bolt and bolt carrier mechanism are basically the same as that of the AK, but the piston is a separate piece. The Type 68 is made in two different versions, one having a stamped steel receiver and the other having a machined steel receiver. Unlike the SKS or the AK, the Type 68 has a gas regulator whose retainer is mounted on the left of the gas cylinder beyond the hand guard. The amount of gas fed into the gas cylinder tube can be regulated by pressing the retainer in until it disengages from the hand guard and then rotating the retainer down until it can be pulled out of the gas cylinder. The gas regulator has indicator holes that correspond to the size of the gas ports in the regulator; the indicator hole that is closest to the barrel shows how much gas is being fed to the action.

Characteristics of the Type 68 Rifle

Caliber: 7.62mm (7.62 × 39)
System of operation: gas, selective fire
Weight: 7.7 lbs.
Length overall: 40.5 in.
Barrel length: 20.5 in.
Feed device: 15-round, staggered row, detachable box magazine
Sights: Front: hooded post
      Rear: tangent with notch
Muzzle velocity: 2395 f.p.s.
Cyclic rate: 750 r.p.m.

How to Load and Fire the Type 68

The Type 68 rifle can be loaded either with SKS type chargers (stripper clips) or by removing the magazine and loading the car-tridges into it individually. Pulling the operating handle to the rear with a loaded magazine in place will chamber a cartridge. The combination safety/selector lever is on the right side of the rifle in front of the trigger guard. The figure "O" setting is used to put the rifle on safe; the figure 1 setting is used for semi-automatic fire, and the figure 2 setting is used for automatic fire. The bolt remains open after the last round is fired.

How to Field Strip the Type 68

Clear the weapon, press in the lock at the left rear of the receiver and pull the cover rearward off the receiver. If the rifle has a machined receiver, pull the driving spring guide up and out of its seat in the rear of the receiver and remove the driving spring assembly. If the rifle has a stamped receiver, press in lock and push the driving spring and its guide forward until it is clear of its seat. Ease the spring forward; then remove it. Pull the operating handle rearward while keeping downward pressure on the bolt carrier. When the bolt carrier is about one inch from the rear of the receiver, it can be lifted up and out of the receiver. The bolt is removed from the carrier by pushing it to the rear, turning the bolt head and pulling it forward and out of the carrier.

The gas regulator has to be removed in order to remove the gas piston and its spring. It can be removed by turning its retainer down as explained earlier. Lower the muzzle and the gas cylinder, and its spring will slide out. The hand guard can then be slid forward off the gas cylinder. The heat shield, which may be found on the gas cylinder, can be slid to the rear and removed.

The trigger guard catch is at the rear of the trigger guard. Rotate it, and the trigger group is disengaged; the trigger guard can now be pulled free of the rifle. Swing the bayonet downward, and the stock can be disengaged from the barrel and receiver. Reassemble in reverse order.

How the Type 68 Works

The bolt action of the Type 68 operates in a manner similar to that of the Soviet AK assault rifle (Type 56), with the exception that the gas piston is separate from the bolt carrier and therefore impinges against the bolt carrier. The trigger mechanism has three sears. The automatic sear is located in front of the hammer and is actuated by the bolt carrier. The trigger sear is to the right behind the hammer, and the semiautomatic sear is to the right. The trigger sear always moves when the trigger is pressed, but the semiautomatic sear functions only when the selector is set at 1. Since the Type 68 fires from a closed bolt, the automatic sear has been tripped by the bolt carrier on loading, and only the trigger sear holds the hammer cocked. When the trigger is pressed, the trigger sear releases the hammer firing

the weapon. As the bolt carrier moves to the rear, it pushes the hammer rearward and releases the automatic sear to hold the hammer in cocked position until the bolt carrier returns fully forward, at which time the full automatic sear releases the hammer and the rifle fires again and will continue to fire until the trigger is released or the magazine emptied. The above happens when the selector lever is set on the figure 2. When the selector lever is set on the figure 1, the selector releases the semiautomatic sear, which is then controlled by the trigger. When the trigger is pressed, it causes the trigger sear to release the hammer and allows the semiautomatic sear to move to a position where it can catch the hammer; therefore, the trigger must be pressed for each shot. If the selector is set at 0, the selector blocks movement of the trigger sear and prevents release of the hammer.

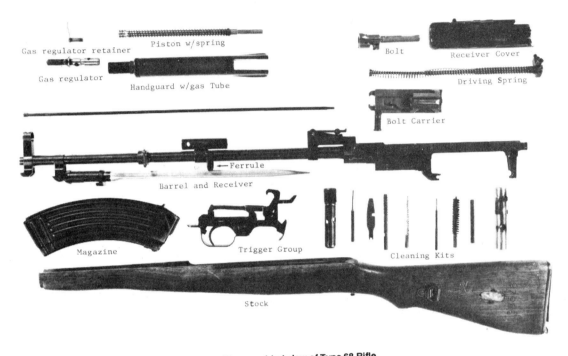

Disassembled view of Type 68 Rifle.

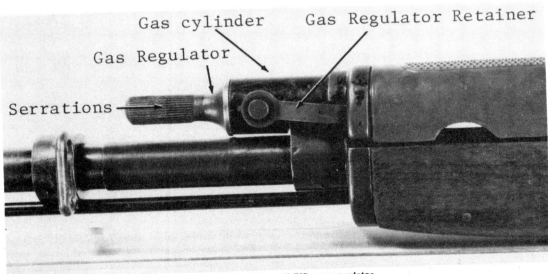

Detailed view of Type 68 Rifle gas regulator.

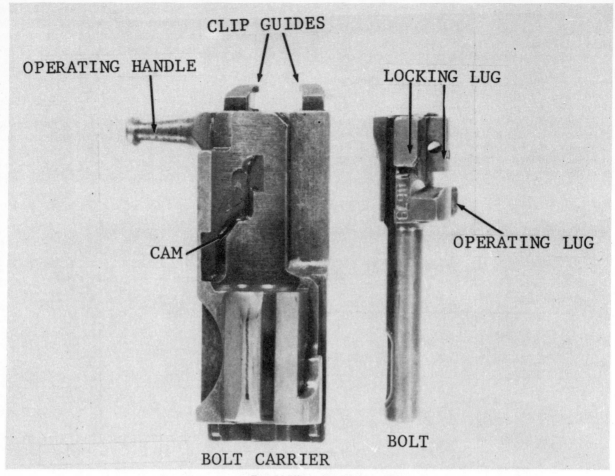

Type 68 Rifle bolt assembly.

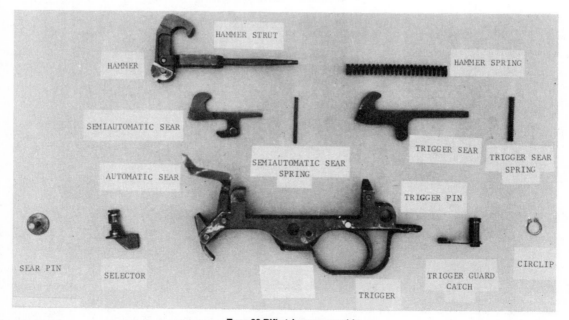

Type 68 Rifle trigger assembly.

Note: The type 68 Rifle has a bolt stop to hold the bolt open after firing the last cartridge in the magazine. If the bolt stop is ground down the standard Type 56 Rifle (AK47) type magazines can be used as well.

THE CHINESE TYPE 67 MACHINE GUN

The Type 67 is a rather odd combination of a number of other weapons, some relatively new and some quite old. The bolt mechanism is like that of the Czech ZB30 light machine gun; the trigger mechanism is like that of the Soviet DP; the quick change barrel is like that of the Soviet SG43, and the feed is modeled on the old Maxim gun. The rear sight of the Type 67 is similar to that of the Czech Type 59 machine gun but has a permanently fixed AA rear sight post on its top. A removable speed ring type AA front sight is mounted at the front of the receiver. The Soviet style stock of the Type 67 is made of plastic. The Type 67 also has the screw type headspace adjustment feature of the Soviet SGM machine gun.

The Type 67 is chambered for the 7.62mm × 54mm rimmed cartridge and can be used either on a bipod or a tripod. The tripod can be used for AA fire as well as ground fire.

The 7.62mm Type 67 machine gun will probably replace both the Type 53 light machine gun and the Type 58 company machine gun.

Characteristics of the Type 67 Machine Gun

Caliber: 7.62mm (7.62 × 54).
System of operation: gas, automatic fire only.
Weight: 21.8 lbs.
Length overall: 45 in.
Barrel length: 23.5 in.
Feed device: 100 round metallic link belt.
Sights: Front: protected post.
        Rear. leaf.
Muzzle velocity: 2,650 f.p.s.
Cyclic rate: 600 – 700 r.p.m.

How to Load and Fire the Type 67

Load the feed belt by placing a cartridge over the link opening, so that the rim of the cartridge is just ahead of the turned down tab on the link. Press the cartridge into the link; the tab must be behind the cartridge base.

Press the cover latch to one side and allow the feed cover to swing open. Unfold the operating handle until it points downward at a 45-degree angle; pull it fully to the rear, then return it fully forward. Place the cartridge belt on the feed tray with the first round in the feedtray slot. Close the cover. The gun is now loaded and ready to fire! If the gun is not to be immediately fired, render it safe by rotating the safety forward. Prior to firing, lift the rear sight to its vertical position and set it for the proper range (calibrated in hundreds of meters). For elevation, up to 1000 meters, one click = 25 meters; beyond 1000 meters, one click = 20 meters. Turn the right hand knob to change windage; each click changes bullet impact about 25mm (1 inch) for each 100 meters.

To fire, rotate safety to rear, aim and fire. The gun will continue to operate as long as the trigger is pressed and cartridges are in the belt. Best results are obtained firing short bursts of five to eight rounds. The bolt will remain open between bursts and will close on an empty chamber when the last shot has been fired.

To clear or unload the Type 67, reverse the steps for loading. Inspect the chamber to insure that it is clear.

Should the barrel overheat during firing, it may be removed and a cool one substituted. To change barrels, press the cover catch and open the feed cover. Press the barrel lock to the left as far as possible. Use the carrying handle and pull the barrel forward, out of the gun. Insert the spare barrel into the receiver, insuring that the gas cylinder enters the gas cylinder tube. Press the barrel lock in, fully to the right. (Note: There is a screw adjustment on the barrel lock to compensate for wear. This should only be adjusted by an armorer.) Close the cover. Adjust the gas regulator if the gun becomes sluggish during firing. See Soviet RPD regulator description for details.

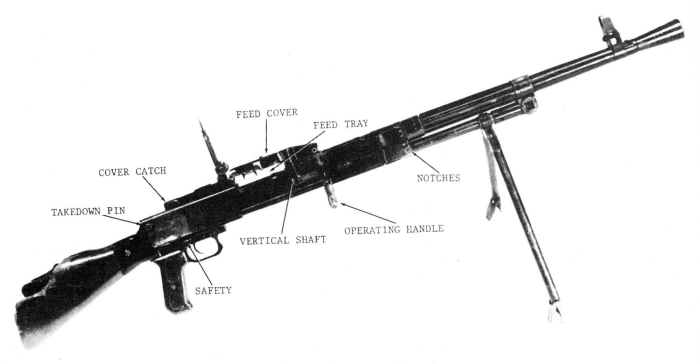

Key features of PRC Type 67 Machine Gun.

How to Field Strip the Type 67

Clear the gun, but do not close the cover or fold the operating handle. Remove the barrel. Press the take-down pin out to the right as far as possible, then pull the stock and trigger group straight to the rear until it comes free. Remove the driving spring and guide. Pull the operating handle rearward; this will move the gas piston, slide and bolt to the rear where they can be removed. Lift the bolt off the slide. Pull the operating handle until it comes clear of the receiver. Unscrew the gas regulator screw and push the regulator to the right until it comes out of its recess in the barrel. (Note: Further disassembly is neither necessary nor desirable.)

To reassemble, first insert the regulator into its recess until the "1" notch lines up with the index pin. Screw the gas regulator screw into the regulator, finger tight. Slide the operating handle onto the lower grooves in the receiver and push the unit as far forward as possible. Place the bolt over the hammer post of the slide and move the bolt forward as far as possible. Insert the bolt and slide, piston leading, into the receiver and press them firmly forward. Insert the driving spring into its tunnel in the slide and then insert the guide into the driving spring. Start the stock and trigger group onto the lower grooves of the receiver until the driving spring guide touches the rear wall. Do not kink the driving spring as you shove the stock and trigger group fully forward. Push the takedown pin fully into the receiver. Insert the barrel, close the cover and fold the operating handle.

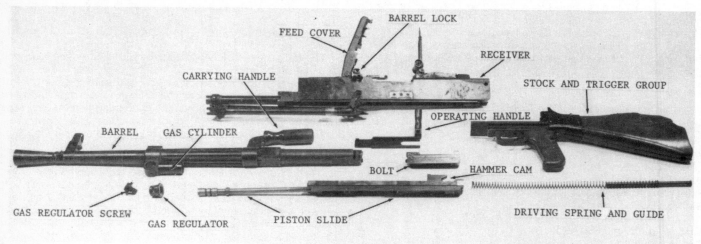

Disassembled view of Type 67 Machine Gun.

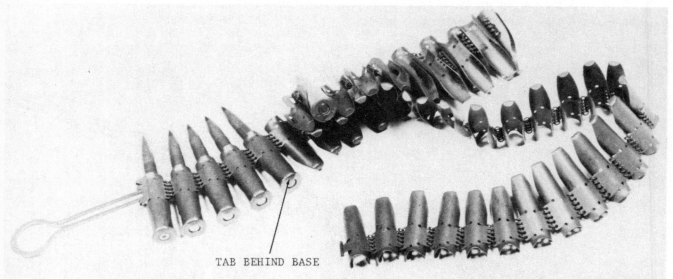

Feed belt for Type 67 Machine Gun.

CHINESE MILITIA WEAPONS

The Chinese have a "People's Militia," which numbers in the millions. This militia, which is a part-time local-defense type force, is armed with an amazing variety of small arms. Apparently the Chinese never scrap or throw away a weapon. Among the weapons still used are Japanese 6.5mm Type 38 rifles made at Shansi and Shenyang arsenals and called Type 65, 7.92mm Mauser "Standard" models—same as Chinese Na-tionalist "Generalissimo" model—called Type 79, the Japanese Type 99 7.7mm rifle—also found in 7.92mm—US caliber .30 rifles and carbines of all models since the M1903, all the pre-World War II and World War II Japanese machine guns, German 7.92mm MG 34s and US, British, Chinese and German submachine guns. The effectiveness of this force from a logistical point of view is, to put it mildly, dubious.

14
Czechoslovakia

Czechoslovakia is entering her third post-World War II generation in some categories of small arms. The current small arms are the 7.62mm Model 52 pistol, the 7.65mm Model 61 submachine gun, the 7.62mm Model 58 assault rifle, the 7.62mm Model 54 sniper rifle, the 7.62mm Model 52/57 light machine gun, the 7.62mm Model 59 general purpose machine gun and the Czech-made 12.7mm DShK M1938/46 heavy machine gun. All these weapons with the exception of the DShK are of native design. The 9mm Models 23 and 25 and the 7.62mm Models 24 and 26 submachine guns are no longer standard and, like the now also obsolescent 7.62mm Models 52 rifle and machine gun, have been exported in large quantities.

All weapons now in service use standard Soviet type ammunition—the 7.62mm M43 (called M57 in Czecho-slovakia) for assault rifle and light machine gun; and the 7.62mm rimmed for the Model 59 machine gun and 12.7mm for the DShK. An exception is the Model 61 submachine gun, which uses the 7.65mm—.32 Colt ACP cartridge. The Czech-designed 7.62mm Model 52 cartridge is no longer standard.

A word on Czech nomenclature: The Czech word for Model is Vzor. This word is usually abbreviated to "VZ" in markings on Czech weapons and has frequently been picked up in English language publications as part of the nomenclature, as per example "Light Machine Gun Model VZ 26." This of course is the same as saying "Model Model"; in the following text the English term "Model" is used for "VZ" wherever applicable.

CZECHOSLOVAK PISTOLS

Czechoslovakia has developed a number of automatic pistols of generally good design. The first Czech designed and made service automatic, the 9mm Short (.380 ACP) Model 22, was actually based on the German Nickl design and was produced to a limited extent by Mauser as well as by Ceska Stan Zbrojovka, Brno. This pistol has a rotating locked barrel somewhat similar to the M12 Austrian Steyr pistol. The Model 22 was apparently made in very limited quantity and was soon followed by the Model 24, which has a slightly modified locking and firing mechanism. This pistol was made in considerable quantity, and production apparently continued until 1937.

The 7.65mm Model 27 was the last of this series of Czech pistols. Originally made in Prague by Ceska Zbrojovka, like the Model 24, manufacture was carried on after World War II at Strakonice until 1950 or '51. During the German occupation of Czechoslovakia, the name of the plant in Prague was changed to Böhmische Waffenfabrik A.G., and pistols made there during the period between the seizure of Czechoslovakia and the beginning of World War II bear that marking. Pistols made during the war are marked "fnh." The Ceska Zbrojovka marking was resumed after the war; after 1948 (the time of the Communist take-over) the words "Narodni Podnik" (People's Factory or Cooperative Enterprise) were added. Although the M24 and the M27 are externally quite similar, the M27 is a blowback operated arm, while the M24, like the M22, is recoil operated.

In 1938, Ceska Zbrojovka, commonly known as CZ, introduced a new pistol, the 9mm Short (.380 ACP) Model 38, for the Czech Army. This weapon was designed by Frantisek Myška and was considerably different than the earlier designs. The trigger mechanism is double-action, and the barrel is permanently mounted in a collar that is hinged to the front of the receiver. The Germans called this pistol the Model 39(t).

Since-World War II, the Czechs have produced several pistols that have military or police application.

The 7.65mm M1950 is basically a modified copy of the Walther PP and was designed as a police weapon and for com-mercial sale. The 7.62mm Model 52 is entirely different from the earlier Czech pistols; it fires a heavily-loaded cartridge and utilizes a unique locking system for a pistol. The Model 52 is the current Czech service pistol. A number of pocket automatics, target pistols and a target revolver chambered for the .38 special cartridge are also currently made in Czechoslovakia.

CZECH 9mm SHORT M22 PISTOL

This pistol is the first of the series of Nickl designs made by the Czechs. The pistol was made on license from Mauser. Mauser submitted a modified form of this pistol chambered for the 9mm Parabellum cartridge to the German Army during the thirties for consideration in the tests, which resulted in the Germans adopting the P38. The Model 22 and its successor, the Model 24, are somewhat unusual in that they are locked-breech pistols, using a relatively low-powered cartridge.

How to Load and Fire the Model 22 Pistol

The magazine catch is on the base of the receiver (frame) grip at the rear; pulling this to the rear releases the magazine. The magazine is loaded round by round and then inserted smartly into the grip until the magazine catch snaps into place. Pull the slide to the rear and release; this will chamber a cartridge, and the weapon is now loaded. Pressure on the trigger will cause the weapon to fire; pressure must be applied for each shot. On firing the last round, the slide will move to the rear and stay open. When the magazine is removed, the slide will run forward. The safety is on the left side and is similar to that of the M1910 Mauser pistol (Mauser M1910 9mm short magazines can be used in this pistol). A lever is pushed down to put the pistol on safe; pressing the button below releases the safety.

Field Stripping the Model 22 Pistol

With empty magazine in gun, pull slide to rear. Slide will remain in position; push down on dismounting catch on side of receiver over front of trigger guard. Remove magazine and slide may then be moved forward and lifted off the receiver. The barrel can then be removed by turning barrel bushing 30°; bushing can then be pulled off slide and barrel. Pull barrel out of slide. No further disassembly is recommended. Reassemble by reversing the above procedure.

How the Model 22 Pistol Works

Pressure on the trigger causes the trigger and its spring-loaded bearing piece to operate the extension sear, which in turn operates the hammer. The hammer strikes the inertia-type spring-loaded firing pin, causing it to strike the primer of the cartridge, thereby firing the cartridge. The barrel and slide are rigidly locked by two rectangular lugs on either side of the barrel engaging in recesses in the side walls of the slide. A helical-portion camming lug on the barrel underside rides in a corresponding helical groove in a rigidly pinned block on the upper surface of the receiver. Upon functioning of the cartridge, the barrel is rotating clockwise through 22°, causing disengagement of the lugs and permitting further recoil of the slide. Recoil of the slide compresses against the recoil spring mounted on its guide, which passes through the helical camming block below the barrel. During recoil, the extractor, mounted in the slide, has withdrawn the fired case, which is ejected by the ejector, which is mounted over the rear of the magazine well. The slide returns forward under the pressure of the compressed recoil spring and strips a cartridge from the magazine, feeding it into the chamber. Pressure on the trigger again will repeat the above process.

Disconnection—prevention of full automatic fire—is accomplished by the camming down of the trigger-bearing surface so that it cannot contact the trigger extension. The disconnector is mounted in a recess in the slide on the left side.

THE CZECH 9mm SHORT PISTOL MODEL 24

The Model 24 is also a locked-breech pistol and is generally similar to the Model 22.
The pistols vary in the following details:

Locking action: A stopping stud is provided on the under side of the barrel ahead of the helical lug. This stud butts against the helical camming block to act as a stop during recoil. The helical lug is widened and the camming block is machined so that is can be assembled without regard to position. The block of the M1922 has an arrow to indicate assembly position.

Magazine: A magazine safety has been added, which blocks trigger motion and prevents firing the weapon without a magazine in place.

Trigger mechanism: The trigger bearing piece is incorporated into the trigger extension where it serves as a disconnector, and the separate disconnector is no longer used. The trigger extension is loaded with a coil spring rather than a wire form spring, and the trigger mounting and pin differ.

Other parts: The hammer spring is separate from the magazine spring, the former being retained by a screw.

Earlier types have one-piece, unchecked wood grips; later types have one-piece, checked molded-plastic grip with CZ insignia.

Czech 9mm Model 22 Pistol.

THE CZECH 7.65mm M27 PISTOL

The Model 27 was made in the largest quantity of all the pre-World War II Czech automatic pistols. It was extensively used by the Germans, who called it Pistol 27(t), during World War II.

The Model 27 differs from the Models 22 and 24 in caliber and in being blowback operated. The barrel is not rigidly fixed to the receiver as in many blowback operated pistols, such as the Walther PP, but is removable in a fashion similar to the Colt .32 and .380 pocket automatics.

During the course of the war, various simplifications in manufacture were introduced by the Germans. Pistols that bear the marking "fnh" were made with the following modifications: Trigger extension bar, safety, safety release, magazine release and firing pin retaining plate are stamped; magazine catch can be used as lanyard loop, and the retaining screw on side plate is eliminated.

Czech 7.65mm M27 Pistol of post-1948 manufacture.

Side plate on left side is relatively flat, retained by a small screw; 1922 has no screw but has a step projecting from its lower edge to close off the trigger mounting.

The slide rib is matted, and the frame and slide show different machining. A variant of this pistol with a 10-round rather than an 8-round magazine has been reported.

Loading, firing and field stripping of the Model 24 are essentially the same as that of the Model 22.

Manufacture of the pistol was continued by CZ after the war. The modifications made during the war were retained for the most part, and initially the old type Czech markings were used. After 1948, however, the "Narodni Podnik" marking was added.

As can be noted from the photograph, finish is extremely rough, especially for a weapon intended for export as indicated by the marking "made in Czechoslovakia."

The Model 27 is loaded, fired and field stripped in a manner similar to the earlier models with one exception: the barrel is held in place by parallel ribs (similar to Colt pocket pistols) and must be rotated to be removed from the slide.

Czech 9mm Short Model 38 Pistol.

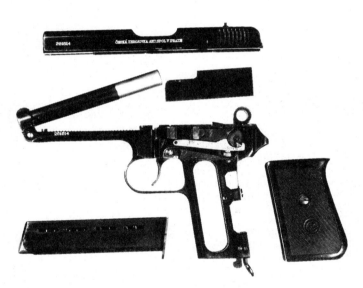

Czech 9mm Short Model 38 Pistol—field-stripped.

THE CZECH 9mm SHORT M38 PISTOL

This pistol was not made in the quantity of the earlier models; it was used by the Germans as Pistole Modell 39(t). There are a number of variations of this pistol and some are fitted with safety catch. Essentially the pistol has the Model 22, 24, 27, trigger mechanism modified to double-action and ordinary blowback operation.

Field Stripping the Model 38 Pistol

Remove magazine, push dismounting catch on left side of receiver above trigger, pull slide to the rear and up. Barrel may be lifted on hinge for cleaning and side plate may be removed for cleaning trigger mechanism. No further disassembly is recommended. To assemble, reverse procedure.

CHARACTERISTICS OF PRE-WORLD WAR II CZECH PISTOLS

	Model 22	Model 24	Model 27	Model 38
Caliber:	9mm Short*	9mm Short*	7.65mm†	9mm Short*
System of operation:	Recoil, semi-automatic only.	Recoil, semi-automatic only.	Blowback, semi-automatic only.	Blowback, semi-automatic only.
Weight:	1.37 lb.	1.5 lb.	1.56 lb.	2 lb.
Length overall:	6 in.	6 in.	6.3 in.	7.8 in.
Barrel length:	3.44 in.	3.56 in.	3.9 in.	4.7 in.
Feed device:	8-round in line. Detachable box. magazine.	8-round in line. Detachable box. magazine.	8-round in line. Detachable box. magazine.	8-round in line. Detachable box magazine.
Muzzle velocity:	984 f.p.s.	984 f.p.s.	919 f.p.s.	1,000 f.p.s.
Sights: Front:	Blade.	Blade.	Blade.	Blade.
Rear:	V notch.	V notch.	V notch.	V notch.

* same as .380 A.C.P.   † same as .32 A.C.P.

POST–1945 CZECH PISTOLS

CZECH 9mm PARABELLUM MODEL 47 PISTOL

The Model 47 was apparently made only in prototype form. It combines the double-action trigger mechanism of the Model 38 with the Browning-Petter locking mechanism.

Czech 9mm Model 47 Pistol.

CZECH 7.65mm M1950 PISTOL

Characteristics, 7.65mm M1950 Pistol

System of operation: Blowback, semiautomatic fire only.
Weight, unloaded, w/magazine: 1.5 lbs.
Length, overall: 6.8 in.
Barrel length: 3.8 in.
Feed device: 8 round removable box magazine.
Muzzle velocity: 919 f.p.s.
Sights: Front: Blade.
     Rear: Round notch.

The M1950 is no longer used as a service pistol in Czechoslovakia but is probably still used as a police weapon. It is chambered for the 7.65mm automatic pistol cartridge (cal. .32 ACP). Specimens have been examined and appear to be of good quality manufacture, but there is nothing unusual about the design of the weapon.

Czech 7.65mm M1950 Pistol.

7.62mm ZKP524 PISTOL

This pistol, chambered for the 7.62mm rimless pistol cartridge, was developed by Francis and Joseph Koucky. It is a recoil operated pistol using the basic Browning type action and has an 8-round magazine. It was produced only as a prototype and was probably designed in competition with the Model 52, which was adopted as the Czech service pistol.

Czech 7.62mm ZKP 524 Automatic Pistol.

How to Load and Fire the M1950 Pistol

Remove magazine from pistol grip by depressing the release button on left side of receiver and pulling magazine out. Fill magazine with eight cartridges. Insert magazine in the well in pistol grip. Draw slide smartly to the rear and release. With the safety off, the trigger may now be squeezed, and the weapon will fire; when the trigger is released, it may be squeezed to fire again. This process may be repeated till the weapon is empty.

The safety of the M1950 operates like that of the Walther PP and PPK. The M1950 is a double action pistol; with a cartridge in the chamber and the hammer in the down position, pulling the trigger to the rear will cause the hammer to rise and fall, firing the weapon.

How the M1950 Pistol Works

In its functioning, the M1950 pistol is generally similar to the Walther PP and PPK.

How to Field Strip the M1950 Pistol

The dismounting button is pushed, and the slide is pulled to the rear as far as it will go. The rear end of the slide is then drawn upwards, and the slide is pushed forward and off the weapon. The recoil spring, which encircles the barrel, can be removed. The barrel is fixed to the receiver and should not be removed. No further disassembly is recommended. Reverse the procedure to reassemble the weapon.

CZECH 7.62mm MODEL 52 PISTOL

The Czechoslovaks have used several types of service pistols since the conclusion of World War II. The 7.62mm Model 52 is the current service weapon.

The Model 52 pistol is a native Czechoslovak design, which has borrowed its locking system from the German MG42 machine gun. The pistol is chambered for the Czechoslovak-made version of the Soviet 7.62mm Type P pistol cartridge, which the Czechoslovaks call the Model 48. The Soviet and Czechoslovak cartridges are interchangeable with the 7.63mm Mauser but are considerably hotter loadings than are the United States commercial loadings of this cartridge. For this reason, the functioning of Soviet and Czechoslovak weapons with commercially loaded 7.63mm cartridges is, at best, marginal. The Czechoslovak cartridge has a particularly heavy loading, being about 20% heavier than the Soviet.

Characteristics of 7.62mm Model 52 Pistol

Caliber: 7.62mm pistol cartridge.
System of operation: Recoil, semiautomatic fire only.
Weight, loaded: 2.31 lbs.
Length, overall: 8.25 in.
Barrel length: 4.71 in.
Feed device: 8-round removable box magazine.
Muzzle velocity: 1600 f.p.s.
Sights: Front: Blade.
Rear: Square notch.

Czech 7.62mm Model 52 Pistol: 1. Takedown catch; 2. Spring retaining clamp holding grips in place; 3. Safety; 4. Magazine catch release; and 5. Slide stop.

How to Load and Fire the Model 52 Pistol

Remove the magazine by forcing to the rear the magazine catch, which is located at the bottom rear of the grip. Load the magazine with eight cartridges; insert magazine in well in pistol grip. Draw slide smartly to the rear, and release; the weapon is now loaded. With the safety in the "fire" position, squeeze the trigger and the weapon will fire; after the trigger is released, it can be squeezed again to fire the pistol. This sequence can be repeated until the weapon is empty. The slide remains to the rear on the last shot. The slide cannot be released from the outside of the weapon as can that of the United States M1911A1 automatic pistol. The slide must be drawn to the rear before it will release. The Model 52's safety is mounted on the left rear of the receiver and has three positions; the lowest position is "fire," and the middle and topmost positions are "safe." The Model 52 is not a double-action automatic. The hammer, if it is in the down position with a cartridge in the chamber, must be manually cocked before the weapon can be fired.

Field Stripping the Model 52 Pistol

The slide-dismounting catches at the front of the trigger guard are pulled down, and the slide assembly is pushed forward until it can be drawn straight up, to the rear and off the receiver. With the slide in an upside down position, the barrel can be removed from the slide by pushing the roller cam and barrel forward so that the rollers clear their locking recesses. (To force the barrel forward, a screwdriver or a punch must be inserted in the hole in the roller cam.) Then the breech end of the barrel can be swung upward, clear of the slide, after which the barrel can be removed toward the rear of the slide. This process is very difficult and must be performed carefully, because the barrel, while being withdrawn, is under the pressure of the partly compressed recoil spring.

How the Model 52 Pistol Works

Loading. A loaded magazine is inserted in the magazine well in the grip of the receiver. The slide is drawn to the rear, cocking the hammer, and then released. As it moves forward, the slide forces a cartridge out of the lips of the magazine, up the bullet ramp, and into the chamber. The claw of the extractor, which is mounted on the right side of the slide behind the ejection port, slips over the rim of the cartridge.

Firing. Pulling the trigger to the rear draws forward the trigger bar, which is pinned to the trigger. If the slide is now in battery position (locking the weapon), the trigger bar pulls the sear ahead, allowing the hammer to snap forward under the pressure of the mainspring. The hammer strikes the firing pin and then rebounds to a position out of contact. The firing pin in turn strikes the primer of the cartridge and causes the cartridge to explode.

Operation of the Slide Group. Both the barrel and the slide, which are locked together by the roller bearings, move to the rear for three-sixteenths of an inch. During this period, the roller bearings are locked in their recesses in the slide and in the barrel lug (located under the barrel) by the thick center section of the roller cam. The roller cam, a sleeve-like piece which encircles the barrel ahead of the barrel lug, has a tongue-shaped section that extends through a longitudinal groove cut in the underside of the barrel lug. The roller cam is kept from going to the rear by another lug, which is located in the mid-section of the receiver, forward of the bullet ramp. When the narrowed section of the roller cam tongue lines up with the roller bearings and their locking slot in the barrel lug, the roller bearings are cammed completely into the cutout portion of the barrel lug by the edges of the roller bearing recesses in the slide. The gun is now unlocked.

When the barrel and slide have traveled three-sixteenths of

an inch to the rear, the barrel is stopped by the abutment of the barrel lug against the forward edge of the bullet ramp of the receiver. The slide continues to the rear and compresses the recoil spring, which is mounted on the barrel between the roller cam and the front of the slide.

The cartridge case, which is held by the extractor, goes rearward with the slide until it hits the ejector. The ejector, mounted on the sear pin on the left rear side of the receiver, then throws the case out the ejection port.

The lower front of the slide abuts against the receiver, and the compressed recoil spring forces the slide back into battery position. As the moving slide picks up the next round from the magazine and pushes it into the chamber, the extractor claw slips over the rim of the cartridge and engages the extractor groove. The roller bearings are cammed out of their position in the cutout of the barrel lug and into the locking recesses of the slide. They are then held in the locked position (i.e., half in the slide and half in the cutout of the barrel lug) by the wide central portion of the roller cam.

If the trigger is pulled again, the process is repeated. After the last shot is fired, the slide is held to the rear by the slide stop, which is mounted on the left side of the receiver, and which engages a cutout on the underside of the slide.

Operation of the Receiver Group. The spur-type trigger is attached to the trigger bar, which disengages the sear from the hammer when the trigger is pulled to the rear. On the top side of the trigger bar, near the center, is a lug that serves as a means of disconnection. When the trigger is pulled, this lug rises into a cutout portion in the right rear underside of the slide. If the weapon is not fully locked, however, the trigger bar lug will strike the underside of the slide rather than the cutout portion; thus prevented from rising, the trigger bar will be unable to contact the sear, and the weapon will not fire.

Pulling the trigger also causes an arm of the sear to rise and force up the spring-loaded firing pin lock, which is mounted in the feed rib of the slide. A portion of the firing pin lock is seated in a semicircular notch cut in the inertia-type firing pin, near its head, and both locks the firing pin in and cams it back from the primer when the slide and barrel start to move to the rear. The forcing of the firing pin lock upward by the sear arm allows the firing pin to move forward when struck by the hammer. Rearward movement of the slide disengages the firing pin lock from the sear arm, allowing the firing pin lock to come down, under the pressure of its spring, and to cam the firing pin rearward out of engagement with the cartridge primer.

The hammer is the rebound type. The sear engages the rebound notch of the hammer, which then cannot move forward to strike the firing pin unless the trigger is pulled to the rear.

The safety, which is mounted on the left rear side of the receiver, has three positions. Its lower position is "fire"; in this position, the safety does not engage the hammer or the trigger mechanism. Its central position, indicated by a red dot, is "safe"; when pushed upward to cover the red dot, the safety blocks rearward movement of the trigger bar and engages the rebound notch of the hammer, preventing its forward movement. With the safety in this position, not only can the hammer be locked, but the slide can be drawn to the rear, permitting the unloading of the chamber. With hammer cocked, the safety may be pushed all the way up to its top position, which also is a "safe." The hammer will fall, but, restrained by the safety stud, which enters the rebound notch, cannot strike the firing pin.

The mainspring is mounted on the mainspring strut, which is positioned to the rear of the magazine well of the receiver. The mainspring exerts pressure upon the hammer when the hammer is cocked. It also presses against the magazine catch, mounted at the bottom rear side of the receiver, in the rear of the magazine well, thus enabling the catch to hold the magazine firmly in place.

Commercial version of the CZ 9mm Parabellum Model 75 Pistol.

CZ 9mm PARABELLUM MODEL 75 PISTOL

More details are presented in Chapter 4.

Characteristics of CZ 9mm Parabellum Model 75 Pistol

Caliber: 9mm Parabellum.
System of operation: Recoil; semiautomatic fire only.
Length, overall: 8 in.
Barrel length: 4.72 in.
Weight, w/ empty magazine: 2.2 lbs.
Feed device: 15-round removable box magazine.
Muzzle velocity: 1214 f.p.s.
Sights: Front: Blade.
       Rear: Square notch.

Military version of the M75 Pistol.

CZECH RIFLES

When the Republic of Czechoslovakia was founded in 1919, it continued to use for a short time the Austro-Hungarian Mannlicher M1895 rifles.

In 1924 Ceskoslovenska Zbrojovka Brno—"ZB"—began the production of Mauser rifles for the Czech Army and for export. The Czechs, in competition with the Belgians of FN, took over a goodly part of the military rifle arms trade of the world.

All the Mausers produced by ZB were based on the M98 action. The models produced were: the Rifle 98/22, Rifle 98/29, Short Rifle 98/29, Carbine 12/33 and the rifle Model 24. The rifle Model 24 was adopted by Czechoslovakia and is covered in detail later in this chapter; the 98/29 weapons are covered in detail under Iran. The 98/22 differs from the 98/29 mainly in the use of front sight guards—"Sight ears"—on the 98/29. The 98/22 was used by Turkey, among other countries. Romania, Guatemala, Yugoslavia and China used the Model 24 rifle in addition to Czechoslovakia. Model 24(t) was the German Army designation for the Czech Mauser, and eleven divisions of the

German Army were equipped with it and other Czech weapons in September 1939 when World War II began.

Czechoslovakia also adopted the 16/33 Carbine, which has a small diameter receiver ring, as the Model 33 rifle. This weapon was kept in production at ZB during World War II with minor modifications as the 33/40 and was issued to German paratroops and mountain troops. During the war, the production of the Model 24 was gradually changed so that the rifles that were being produced at the end of the war were actually Kar 98ks. Those rifles marked 24(t) differ from the standard Model 24 in having a cup type butt plate, a firing pin disassembly disk on the buttstock and a slot through the buttstock for the sling. As finally produced at ZB, the Mauser rifle has a stamped oversize trigger guard, firing pin dismounting hole in the butt plate, slotted buttstock, German-type stamped bands and modified gas escape holes in the bolt. This rifle was produced until circa 1950 and was sold to Israel and Pakistan. It is actually the Kar 98k in its last production version.

Czech 7.92mm Model 24 (VZ 24).

THE 7.92mm CZECH MODEL 24 RIFLE

The Model 24 Rifle was the standard Czech rifle prior to World War II and as previously stated was widely used by Germany and other countries. It uses the basic Mauser 98 action and differs from the German Kar 98k mainly in fittings, having a full length handguard, sling swivels on both the side and underside of the stock and a straight bolt handle.

Characteristics of the 7.92mm Czech Model 24 Rifle

Caliber: 7.92mm.
System of operation: Bolt action, manually operated.
Weight: 8.98 lbs.
Length overall: 43.3 in.

Barrel length: 23.2 in.
Feed mechanism: 5-round staggered row, non-detachable box magazine.
Sights: Front: Barley corn.
　　　　Rear: Tangent graduated from 300-2000 meters by 100-meter steps.
Muzzle velocity: 2700 f.p.s.

Dismounting and Assembling the Bolt, M24

Before removing the bolt from the receiver, turn the safety catch into its central position between its safe and fire position, i.e., with the wing turned upwards. The bolt can be removed from the receiver only when the bolt stop is moved to the side with a slight pressure, whereby the groove in the receiver is (fig. 1) opened to permit bolt passage.

Turn the bolt sleeve to the left, then the latter with the safety catch, the cocking piece and the firing pin may easily be separated from the bolt. While removing these parts, the main spring is still in a state of compression (fig. 2).

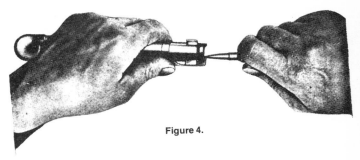

Figure 1.

For further dismounting, put the striker with its point turned downward against a convenient bearing (for this purpose a hole is provided in the stock sleeve) (fig. 3). Press home the main spring until the cocking piece can be turned 90°, remove the latter and, in releasing the pressure of the spring, take out the firing pin. The safety catch may be dismounted by turning the wing to the right side.

Figure 4.

To remove the bolt sleeve lock, pull it into a position of 90°, where its spindle can be turned in the notch of the bolt lock.

To remove the extractor, pull it to the side with the help of a solid object (for instance with a cartridge) till it disengages the dovetail before the bolt lug (fig. 4). Then turn it to an angle of 90°, and, holding it against a table edge, draw it out of the groove of the extractor ring (fig. 5).

The extractor ring of the bolt should not be dismounted. The extractor and the bolt sleeve lock should seldom be removed.

The assembling is done in the opposite order. Mount the extractor on the extractor ring until it can be turned and engaged in the groove of the bolt. Put into the bolt lock the bolt sleeve lock spring, then the bolt sleeve lock itself, and turn 90°. Place the main spring on the firing pin, place the safety catch into the bolt sleeve, and compress the main spring, just enough to insert the cocking piece, and turn 90°. The bolt sleeve, thus assembled, is screwed on the bolt. Now the bolt can be pushed into the receiver. When doing so, it is not necessary to push aside the bolt stop, for it disengages itself by the pressure on the bolt.

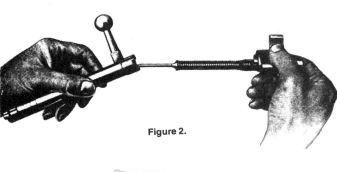

Figure 2.

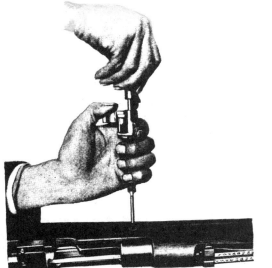

Figure 3.

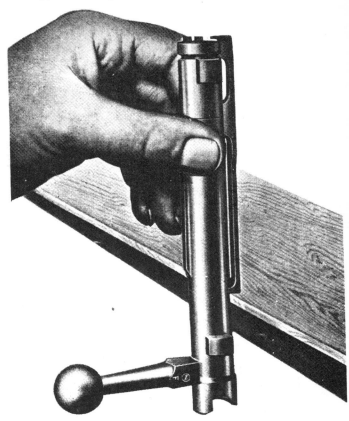

Figure 5.

CZECH SEMIAUTOMATIC RIFLES

The first truly Czech semiautomatic rifle was probably the Netsch, developed at CZ between 1922–24. This 7.92mm rifle was gas operated with a drum magazine. The ZH 29 was the first Czech rifle of this category to become well known and exported in any quantity. The design is credited by the Czechs to Emmanuel Holek of ZB. This rifle, chambered for the .276 Pedersen cartridge, was tested by the United States at Aberdeen Proving Ground in 1929.

This rifle was used by Ethiopia and Thailand to a limited extent.

Characteristics of Czech ZH29

Caliber: 7.92mm.
System of operation: Gas, semiautomatic fire (specimens capable of full automatic fire have been reported).
Weight: Approx. 10 lbs.
Length overall: 45.5 in.
Barrel length: 21.5 in.
Feed mechanism: 10- or 25-round, detachable box magazine.
Sights: Front: Protected blade.
      Rear: Tangent leaf adjustable from 100–1400 meters.
Muzzle velocity: Approx. 2650 f.p.s.

An unusual feature of the ZH 29 is the aluminum cooling jacket fitted over the barrel and gas cylinder ahead of the wooden hand guard. This is an interesting commentary on the military concepts of the time since it indicates that the designer thought that in normal battle usage the rifle would be fired frequently enough in one fight to require such a gadget for cooling. The sad and bloody experiences of the last forty years indicate that most fire fights are short and sharp and that heating is only a major problem with automatic support weapons. Far more handguards are burned off in proving ground and user tests than in battle! The main purpose of the handguard over the barrel today is to prevent burning of the hand in the very remote and rare possibility of a bayonet fight after a fire fight.

The CZ Model 38 was designed by Vaclav Polanka and Jan Kratochil. This gas operated rifle was made in 7.62mm and 7.92mm and was tested in the Soviet Union. It broke open like a shotgun for disassembly in a manner somewhat similar to the current FN FAL. The hinge point is beneath the forward portion of the receiver.

The ZK381 was developed by Joseph Koucky and is also a gas operated box magazine-fed weapon. This weapon was tested by the USSR in August 1938, by France in February 1939 and by Great Britain in approximately the same period.

In 1939, Joseph and Francis Koucky brought out another rifle with the ZK391. The ZK391 more closely resembles the ZK420 series than do any of the earlier Czech semiautomatic rifles. In 1943, a modification of this rifle was manufactured in limited quantities in Cremona, Italy. The ZK391 was tested by Denmark in 1946.

THE CZECH 7.92mm ZK420 RIFLE

The ZK420 design was produced by Josef and Frantisek Koucky in 1942 and went through a number of modifications until the final model—the ZK420S—appeared after World War II. As originally made, the ZK420 had Mauser-type bands and bayonet stud and a full-length type stock. The magazine was not removable and was loaded with chargers. In 1946, the first modification of this design appeared; the 1946 version has a sporter-type stock, a removable magazine, and in general resembles the ZK420S. The outstanding external differences between the 1946 Model and the ZK420S are the configuration of the magazine and the prominent safety catch lever—as that of the US M1 rifle—on the ZK420S. The latter rifle appeared between 1947 and 1950 and was the last of the series.

The ZK420 series of rifles received extensive testing abroad. The 1942 and 1946 Models were tested by Denmark, and the 1946 Model was tested by the United Kingdom, Sweden, Ethiopia, Egypt, Israel and Switzerland. A version of the ZK420S with permanently attached bayonet was made for Israel for test purposes. The 1946 Model was made in 7.92mm, 7mm, .30-06 and 7.5mm Swiss. It is somewhat surprising that the Czech Army never adopted this weapon, since it was extensively developed and certainly advertised throughout the world; the ZK420 appears in a post-1948 ZB catalog. The design in certain features, i.e. bolt and gas system, appear to be at least equal to, if not superior to, that of the rifle finally adopted—the Model 52. The ZK420 series weapons are, however, generally heavier designs and undoubtedly much more expensive to manufacture than is the Model 52.

Characteristics of the ZK420S Rifle

Caliber: 7.92mm.
System of operation: Gas, semiautomatic fire only.
Weight: 10.58 lbs.
Length overall: 41.73 in.
Barrel length: 21.65 in.
Feed mechanism: 10-round, double staggered row, detachable box magazine.
Sights: Front: Hooded post.
      Rear: Notched tangent with ramp.
Muzzle velocity: Approx. 2700 f.p.s.

The ZK420S has a trigger mechanism similar to the US M1, as do the later Czech M52 and M52/57 rifles. The bolt mechanism of this weapon bears a superficial resemblance to that of the US M1, but it actually more closely resembles the Soviet AK47. The body or shaft of the one-piece bolt is enclosed by the bolt carrier and is cammed by a camway within the bolt carrier. The head of the bolt bears the locking lugs and protrudes forward of the bolt carrier.

In 1942 the Koucky's brought out another rifle called the ZK425. This gas operated rifle has a very neat outward appearance. It was tested in Denmark in 1946. The last of this series of rifles, the ZK472, is also gas operated. It has a 10- or 15-round box magazine and is chambered for an "intermediate" sized 7.5mm cartridge. The ZK472 is 39.4 inches long, and the barrel is 20.5 inches long. The muzzle velocity is 2526 feet per second.

Czech 7.92mm ZK 381 Semiautomatic Rifle

Czech CZ 38 Semiautomatic Rifle

Czech 7.92mm Model ZK-420S

Czech ZH 29 Semiautomatic Rifle.

CZECH 7.62mm MODEL 52 RIFLE

Characteristics of 7.62mm Model 52

Caliber: 7.62mm, Czechoslovak Model 52.
System of operation: Gas, semiautomatic fire only.
Weight, loaded: 9.8 lbs.
Length, overall: 39.37 in.
Barrel length: 20.66 in.
Feed mechanism: 10-round, double staggered, detachable box magazine (loaded with 5-round chargers).
Sights: Front: Hooded blade (removable hood).
      Rear: Notched tangent with curved ramp.
Muzzle velocity: 2440 f.p.s.

The Model 52 is chambered for the Czechoslovak 7.62mm Model 52 cartridge. Its design is a combination of several older designs added to a few native ideas. The gas system is generally similar to that of the German MKb 42W and some of the earlier Walther commercial semiautomatic rifle designs. The trigger mechanism is similar to that of the United States M1 rifle. The bolt appears to be a native design; it is somewhat unusual in that it is a tipping bolt design with frontal locking lugs. For the first time, the Czechoslovaks put a nondetachable bayonet on one of their rifles. The Model 52 makes fairly extensive use of stampings, but, all in all, the design is hardly revolutionary and in some respects is not too remarkable considering the date it appeared—1952.

The Czechs have issued a slightly modified version of the 52 rifle called the Model 52/57, chambered for the Soviet designed 7.62mm M43 cartridge. The Model 52 and Model 52/57 rifle are no longer standard in the Czech Army.

How to Load and Fire the Model 52 Rifle

Pull the operating handle all the way to the rear; since the weapon has a bolt-holding-open device, the bolt and carrier will remain open. Insert the end of a five-round charger in the charger (clip) guide at the front of the receiver cover and force the cartridges down into the magazine with the thumb of the left hand. Repeat this process with another five-round charger; then draw the operating handle slightly to the rear and release. The bolt and carrier will run home, chambering a cartridge. The weapon is now loaded and, with safety off, the trigger will cause it to fire. The trigger must be released after each shot. The safety is similar to that on the United States M1 rifle. When the safety is forward the rifle will fire; when the safety is drawn to the rear, the weapon is on "safe."

Field Stripping the Model 52 Rifle

The magazine is released by pressing forward on the magazine lever. After clearing the weapon to assure that the chamber is empty, disassemble the receiver cover—carefully, as the driving spring is always compressed. Push the receiver cover forward until the side rails are out of the receiver slots. Lift the cover slightly and slide back along the top of the receiver until the driving spring snaps down. Hold bolt carrier to the right and slide it to the rear until it reaches the disassembly notch. Remove bolt carrier and bolt. To remove bolt from bolt carrier, slide bolt to the rear and press down the front end until it is disengaged from the bolt carrier.

Czechoslovak 7.62mm Model 52 Semiautomatic Rifle.

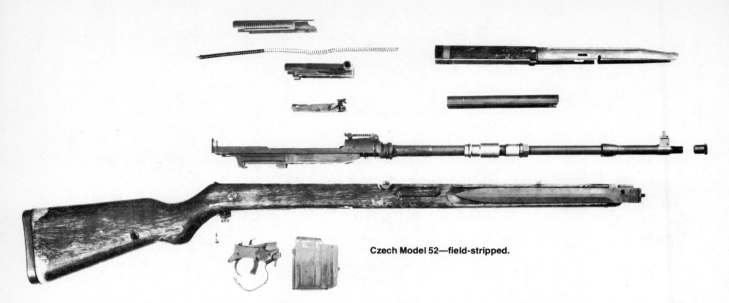

Czech Model 52—field-stripped.

Slide the bolt forward out of the carrier. After applying the safety, remove the trigger housing group by forcing the rear of the trigger guard back and rotating it downward. (Disassembly is difficult, as the rear of the trigger guard is hard to grasp and pull to the rear to disengage guard from housing.) Slide the trigger housing group forward and downward. Remove the handguard over the barrel by depressing ears on each side of the stock at the rear end of the handguard. If the barrel and receiver assembly is to be removed from the stock, depress plunger visible through hole in bayonet and slide the barrel sleeve forward. Assemble in the reverse order.

How the Model 52 Rifle Works

The magazine is loaded and the operating handle is pulled to the rearmost position, compressing the driving spring, and released. The driving spring drives the bolt carrier and bolt forward. The top round is stripped from the magazine and chambered during the forward stroke of the bolt. As the bolt chambers the round, the extractor enters the extractor groove of the cartridge case. Locking occurs during the last 0.3 of an inch of bolt carrier travel, when the bolt locking lugs are cammed down into the receiver locks. The weapon can now be fired by pulling the trigger, which releases the hammer. The hammer strikes the firing pin to fire the round. After firing, powder gases pass through the gas port and enter the gas chamber formed by the gas sleeves and barrel. The gases cause the actuator to strike the bolt carrier. Momentum of the bolt carrier unlocks the action and carries the bolt to the rearmost position, compressing the driving spring. During the bolt recoil stroke, the extractor pulls the cartridge case back with the bolt until ejection occurs as the ejector strikes a lug in the rear of the receiver recess. The driving spring returns the bolt carrier and bolt to battery to complete one cycle of fire.

CZECH 7.62mm MODEL 58 ASSAULT RIFLE

In 1958, a new weapon, the 7.62mm Model 58 assault rifle, appeared. This rifle, a gas-operated selective fire weapon, replaced the Model 52/57 and the 7.62mm Model 24 and 26 submachine guns in the Czech Army.

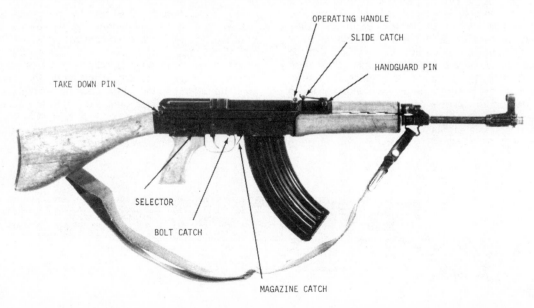

Czech 7.62mm Model 58P Assault Rifle with wooden stock.

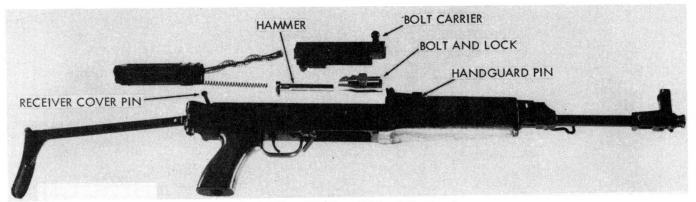

Czech 7.62mm M58P Assault Rifle—field-stripped.

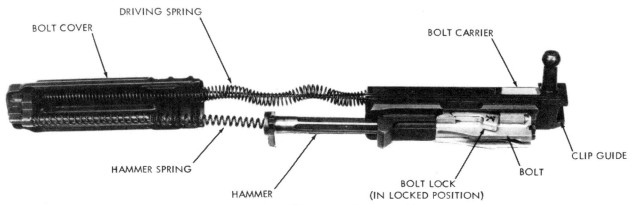

Model 58 hammer and bolt assembly.

Characteristics of Model 58 Assault Rifle

Caliber: 7.62, uses Czech copy of Soviet M1943 rimless cartridge.
System of operation: Gas, selective fire.
Weight, loaded:
  Wooden stock version: 8.75 lbs.
  Metal stock version: 8.75 lbs.
  Weight, empty: 7.31 lbs.
Length, overall:
  Wooden stock version: 33 in.
  Metal stock version, stock folded: 25 in.
  Metal stock version, stock fixed: 33 in.
Barrel length: 15.8 in.
Feed mechanism: 30-round, staggered column, detachable box magazine.
Sights:
  Front: Protected post.
  Rear: Tangent leaf, adjustable in 100-meter increments from 100 to 800 meters.
Cyclic rate: 700-800 r.p.m.
Muzzle velocity: 2300 f.p.s.

The Model 58 assault rifle is the standard shoulder weapon of the Czech Army. It is similar in concept and in external appearance to the Soviet AK47 but is quite different internally. Its outstanding characteristic is its light weight, but this is of dubious value considering its use in automatic fire from the shoulder. Lighter arms rise more rapidly in automatic fire than do heavier arms, even if they do have a straight-line stock configuration as does the Model 58.

The Model 58 may be found with wooden stock and handguards, plastic stock and handguards or with folding steel stock. The version of the Model 58 with fixed stock is called the Model 58P; the version of the Model 58 with folding metal stock is called the Model 58V.

How to Load and Fire the Model 58 Assault Rifle

Push magazine catch in front of trigger guard forward and remove magazine. Fill magazine with cartridges and insert in magazine well. Set safety on safe by turning safety-selector lever to the safe position. Pull operating handle to the rear and release; a cartridge will be chambered. The selector has two fire positions; up for semiautomatic fire and midway for automatic fire; push safety-selector lever to position desired, and the weapon will fire. When last round is fired, the bolt will remain open.

Field Stripping the Model 58 Assault Rifle

Remove magazine and check chamber to insure that weapon is not loaded. Press the trigger to release hammer if cocked. Pull cover assembly retaining pin, mounted at rear of receiver cover, to the right and remove receiver cover. Move bolt and bolt carrier assembly to the rear and lift it up and out of the receiver. Rotate the hammer-striker approximately ⅛ turn counterclockwise and withdraw to the rear so that the bolt carrier, bolt assembly and locking lugs are separated. Pull handguard retaining pin, located at front of rear sight base to the right and remove handguard by lifting up its rear portion and withdrawing it to the rear. Pull the piston to the rear and pull the piston head up so that piston and piston return spring can be removed. Reassemble by reversing the above procedure.

How the Model 58 Assault Rifle Works

Unlike most weapons of this type, the Model 58 does not have a rotating hammer—it has a linear travel hammer firing pin. Pressure on the trigger causes the sear (there are two sears—semiautomatic and automatic) to release the hammer and fire the cartridge. Gas from the cartridge is tapped off at the gas port into the gas cylinder, and it moves the gas piston to the rear at high speed; the rear end of the spring-loaded piston protrudes through the rear sight base and strikes the top front of the bolt carrier. The bolt carrier moves to the rear, camming the bolt lugs out of their locking recesses in the receiver and compressing the operating spring. The extractor in the face of the bolt withdraws the empty cartridge case, which is ejected out of the weapon.

The operating spring forces the bolt and bolt carrier forward, and the bolt picks up a cartridge from the magazine and chambers it. If the weapon is set on automatic, the automatic sear will remain disengaged—assuming pressure is continued on the trigger—and the weapon will fire again. If the weapon is set on semiautomatic fire, the semiautomatic sear will rise and hold the hammer to the rear until pressure is released on the trigger and the trigger is pressed again.

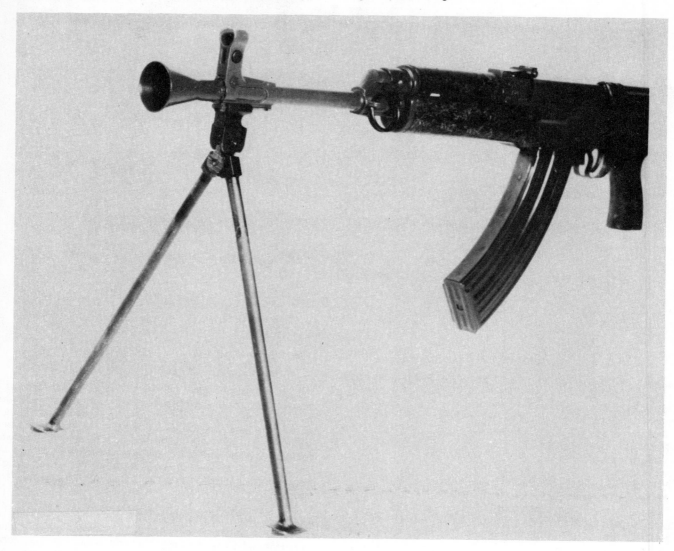

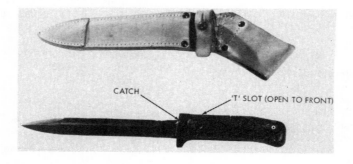

CATCH 'T' SLOT (OPEN TO FRONT)

CZECH SUBMACHINE GUNS

The Czechoslovaks have come out with a large number of submachine gun designs since World War II. Most of these designs appeared only in prototype form and were intended for overseas sales. Among these were the ZK466, CZ247, ZB47 and ZK476. These weapons are not used by the Czechoslovak Army. Before the Communists took over Czechoslovakia, her army used the 9mm Parabellum as the service cartridge for pistols and submachine guns. Two submachine guns chambered for that cartridge were adopted by the Czechoslovak Army: the Model 23 and the Model 25 submachine guns. After the adoption of the Soviet 7.62mm pistol cartridge by the Czechoslovaks, two weapons similar to the Models 23 and 25, but chambered for the 7.62mm pistol cartridge, were produced, the Model 24 and the Model 26. These weapons have been replaced, for most purposes, by the Model 58 assault rifle and in some cases by the 7.65mm Model 61 submachine gun.

ZK466 9mm Submachine Gun.

ZK476 9mm Submachine Gun.

Czech 9mm ZK383 Submachine Gun with bipod fixed.

THE CZECH ZK383 SUBMACHINE GUN

The ZK383 was designed and produced in some quantity prior to World War II and was carried in a post-1948 ZB catalog. The weapon was designed by Josef and Frantisek Koucky and was produced in three slightly different designs. The basic ZK383 has a folding bipod attached and was used by Bulgaria and several South American countries. It was continued in production at ZB (then called Waffenwerke Brunn by the Germans) and was apparently used by the Waffen S.S. to some extent during the war. The ZK383P was developed for police use and does not have a bipod or a removable barrel like the other models.

The ZK383H is the third variation of this weapon and differs mainly in having a folding-type magazine housing fitted to the bottom of the weapon rather than to the left side as with the other models.

Characteristics of the ZK383

Caliber: 9mm Parabellum.
System of operation: Blowback, selective fire.
Length overall: 34.4 in.
Barrel length: 12.8 in.
Weight: 9.6 lbs.
Sights: Front: Protected blade.
    Rear: V-notch tangent graduated from 100-800 meters.
Feed mechanism: 30-round detachable, staggered row box magazine.
Muzzle velocity: approx. 1400 f.p.s.
Cyclic rate: 500 r.p.m., normal; 700 r.p.m., accelerated.

The bolt of this weapon has a six-ounce removable block. Removal of this block provides the higher rate of fire.

THE CZECH MODEL 23 AND MODEL 25 SUBMACHINE GUNS

Characteristics of Models 23 and 25

Caliber: 9mm Parabellum.
Weight, M23, loaded: 8 lbs.; with 24-round magazine. 8.4 lbs., with 40-round magazine.
M25, loaded: 8.7 lbs. with 24-round magazine. 9.0 lbs., with 40-round magazine.

Length, overall: 27 in. for Model 23 and Model 25 with stock extended; 17.5 in. for Model 25 with stock folded.
Barrel length: 11.2 in.
Feed Mechanism: 24-round or 40-round detachable, staggered, box magazine.
Sights: Front: Hooded barleycorn.
        Rear: V-notch on rotary base; adjustable for 100, 200, 300, and 400 meters.
Muzzle velocity: 1470 f.p.s.
Cyclic rate of fire: 600–650 rounds per minute.

How to Load and Fire the Model 23 and Model 25 Submachine Guns

Draw the operating handle to the rear. The weapon fires from an open bolt, and therefore the bolt will remain to the rear. Insert a loaded magazine in the well of the pistol grip. Squeeze the trigger. If the trigger is pulled about halfway to the rear, the weapon will fire single shots with occasional doubles. If the trigger is pulled all the way to the rear, the weapon will fire automatically until it is empty or until the trigger is released. To remove the magazine, pull the magazine catch (located at the bottom rear of the pistol grip) to the rear, and pull the magazine down and out of the weapon. The safety blocks the rear of the trigger, and also locks the bolt. To put the weapon on SAFE, push the safety lever to the right.

Czech 9mm Model 23 Submachine Gun.

The Model 23 and Model 25 are basically the same weapon, but the Model 23 has a wooden stock, and the Model 25 has a folding metal stock. The weapons have several outstanding features and are good examples of modern submachine gun construction. They share most of their unusual features with the Israeli UZI submachine gun. Among these features are:

The magazine well is in the pistol grip. This gives the magazine far better support than is normally obtained with a submachine gun.

The guns have a very short overall length in comparison to their barrel length. This is made possible by a hollow bolt, which telescopes the rear 6 ⅛ inches of the barrel. Only a 1 ⅞-inch length of the 8-inch bolt is solid; the remainder is hollowed out to telescope the barrel.

The trigger mechanism on the Czechoslovak weapons is so designed that a short pull on the trigger gives semiautomatic fire, while pulling the trigger all the way to the rear gives full automatic fire.

The ejection port is closed at all times to the entry of dirt, except when the weapon is ejecting.

These weapons also have an unusually simple method of disassembly and assembly.

Field Stripping the Model 23 and Model 25 Submachine Guns

Disassembly of Weapon. Remove magazine. Push forward on button in center of receiver barrel jacket cap; at the same time, turn cap ⅛ turn to right or left and remove to the rear.

Slide bolt assembly rearward by means of the operating handle.

Pull trigger, and slide bolt assembly to the rear, out of receiver/barrel-jacket assembly.

Use bolt assembly as tool to loosen barrel locking nut. Place bolt assembly around barrel, with slots at front of bolt engaging lugs of barrel locking nut. Unscrew locking nut by turning bolt counterclockwise.

Pull barrel forward from receiver/barrel-jacket assembly.

To unfasten stock, remove screw holding the metal neck of stock to the stock support. To remove from receiver/barrel-jacket assembly, pull stock to the rear and left.

Use same procedure for Model 23.

Disassembly of magazine. Through the rectangular opening in magazine base, depress flat metal stop; slide flat metal base cover to the rear, thereby releasing magazine spring. Withdraw spring and cartridge follower through bottom of magazine.

Assembly. Assembly is accomplished by performing the steps for disassembly in reverse order.

Czech 9mm Model 25 Submachine Gun.

How the Model 23 and Model 25 Submachine Guns Work

Chambering. With the bolt in rearward position, the trigger is pulled. This depresses the sear, releasing the bolt. The operating spring drives the bolt forward. The lower edge of the bolt face strips a round from the magazine and forces it forward into the chamber.

Locking. No locking step takes place, since the weapon is of the straight blowback type.

Firing. Firing occurs when the operating spring drives the bolt forward against the chambered round, and the fixed firing pin strikes the primer.

Extraction. The extractor engages in the extraction groove of the round as it is chambered. When blowback drives the bolt rearward, the extractor pulls the cartridge case out of the chamber.

Ejection. When the cartridge case (held by the recoiling bolt) clears the chamber, it strikes the tip of the stationary ejecting rod and pivots to the right. Simultaneously, the ejection ports of the bolt and receiver move into alignment, allowing the cartridge case to be thrown clear of the weapon.

Cocking. Since the gun fires only from an open bolt, it is cocked by moving the bolt rearward until the sear engages the sear notch in the bolt, thus holding the bolt to the rear against pressure of the operating spring. Cocking may be accomplished either manually or, when firing, by blowback.

Semiautomatic Fire. The sear assembly is pivoted at the front and contains a spring-loaded plunger extending to the rear. The trigger, which is pivoted at the rear, has a forward projection that rests on the sear plunger. As the trigger is pulled, its projection bears against the sear notch in the bolt. The bolt then moves forward to chamber and fire the round. As the trigger is pulled beyond the point at which the bolt is released, the trigger projection rotates out of engagement with the sear plunger, thus allowing the sear to rise under pressure of the sear spring. Upon firing, the bolt is blown back to the rear until the sear engages the sear notch in the bolt.

NOTE. Since no positive disconnector is provided, a slow squeeze on the trigger can result in short bursts.

Full Automatic Fire. In full automatic fire, the trigger is pulled all the way to the rear, beyond the semiautomatic fire position. A projection on the trigger now engages the sear directly, disengaging it from the bolt and allowing full automatic fire until the trigger is released or the magazine emptied.

7.62mm Replacement for 9mm Models 23 and 25

The 7.62mm submachine gun, which replaced the 9mm Models 23 and 25 in the Czechoslovak Army, is basically the same as the Models 23 and 25. A few minor changes have been made, but function, loading, firing, assembly and disassembly remain the same. The major change is the chambering of the weapons for the 7.62mm pistol cartridge. The heavy loading of the Czechoslovak-made 7.62mm pistol cartridge gives the weapons a velocity that falls in the class of the United States M1 and M2 carbines.

Characteristics of 7.62mm Submachine Gun Model 24

System of operation: Blowback, selective fire.
Length, overall: 27 in.
Barrel length: 11.2 in.

Model 25 field-stripped.

Feed mechanism: 32-round detachable, staggered-box magazine.
Sights: Front: Hooded blade.
      Rear: Square notch on rotary base, adjustable for 100, 200, 300, and 400 meters.
Muzzle velocity: 1800 f.p.s.
Cyclic rate of fire: 600–650 r.p.m.
Weight, loaded: 8.8 lbs.

Note that only the weight and overall length with stock folded will be different for the version with metal stock.

THE CZECH MODEL 61 SUBMACHINE GUN (SKORPION)

This weapon might be described as a "machine pistol" since it is designed to be fired from one hand as well as from the shoulder. It could be considered the Czech equivalent of the Soviet Stechkin machine pistol or the M1932 Mauser. It uses a relatively low powered cartridge, the 7.65mm Browning short or the .32 ACP as it is called in the United States, and is relatively easy to control in full automatic fire from the shoulder because of that fact. As a matter of interest, the .32 ACP cartridge as loaded in the United States has less muzzle energy than the .22 Long Rifle cartridge in high velocity loads. With a weapon of the M61 type, however, there is a possibility of obtaining multiple hits on a target.

Characteristics of Model 61 Submachine Gun

Caliber: 7.65mm (.32 ACP).
System of operation: Blowback, selective fire.
Length overall: With stock fixed: 20.55 in.
                With stock folded: 10.62 in.
Barrel length: 4.5 in.
Weight: 2.87 lbs.
Sights: Front: Protected post.
      Rear: Flip-over notch graduated for 75 and 150 meters.
Feed Device: 10- or 20-round detachable staggered row box magazine.

Muzzle velocity: 1040 f.p.s.
Cyclic rate: 750 r.p.m.

Special Note on Czechoslovak Submachine Guns

The Czechoslovak 9mm Models 23 and 25 submachine guns, as well as the 7.62mm submachine guns, have a magazine filler built into the right side of their plastic fore-ends. The ammunition for these weapons is packed in 8-round chargers (clips). The charger is laid base down in the guide slot of the magazine filler, with the weapon on its left side. The empty magazine is then pushed down the guide, mouth forward (toward the muzzle of the weapon), and the cartridges are stripped into the magazine.

How to Load and Fire the Model 61 Submachine Gun

The magazine can be removed by pressing the button located on the left side of the receiver in front of the trigger guard. Pull bolt to rear; bolt operating knobs are on both sides of the receiver. Set the weapon on safe by pushing the safety-selector lever, located over the pistol grip on the left side of the receiver, down to its central position. Insert a loaded magazine and set safety-selector lever for type of fire desired—forward for automatic fire—to "20" and to the rear for semiautomatic fire to "1." Press trigger and weapon will fire; bolt remains open on the last shot.

Field Stripping the Model 61 Submachine Gun

Remove magazine and pull bolt to the rear to clear gun. Fix shoulder stock. Push out pin—at lower front of the receiver—to the left. Pull receiver forward and hinge upward; remove bolt operating knobs. Remove bolt and operating springs assembly. Further disassembly is not recommended. Reassemble by reversing above procedure.

How the Model 61 Submachine Gun Works

This weapon is a pure blowback, i.e., the cartridge is held in place during firing by the weight of the bolt and the recoil spring. The rate reducer, used to lower the cyclic rate, is a hook at the

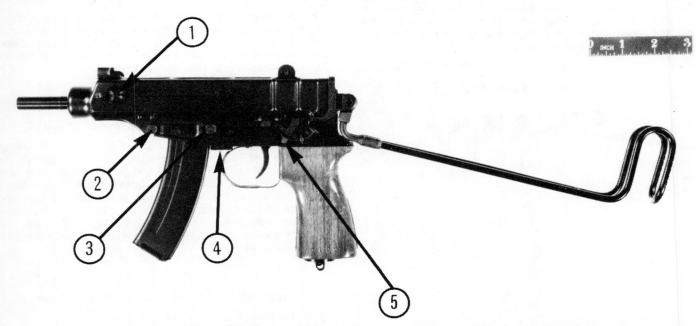

Czech 7.65mm Model 61 Submachine Gun with stock fixed. 1. Cocking knob; 2. Takedown pin; 3. Magazine catch; 4. Bolt stop; and 5. Selector lever.

rear of the receiver, which holds the bolt to the rear momentarily after each shot. This hook is released by pressure from a spring loaded tripper-plunger mounted in the pistol grip. As the bolt comes to the rear, it cams down this tripper-plunger compressing its spring. The tripper-plunger and spring are mounted in a tube and the tripper-plunger travels a considerable distance down the tube before it is pushed up by the spring, causing the hook to tip up and release the bolt. This system, which is quite similar to that used on the Soviet Stechkin machine pistol, has the effect of reducing the cyclic rate of fire. The bolt telescopes

the barrel as in the earlier Model 23 series submachine guns but is square in configuration like the Israeli UZI, rather than round like the Model 23.

Special Note on Model 61 Submachine Gun

There is a silencer available for this weapon that should be effective due to the relatively low velocity of the bullet fired. Luminescent night sights are also available.

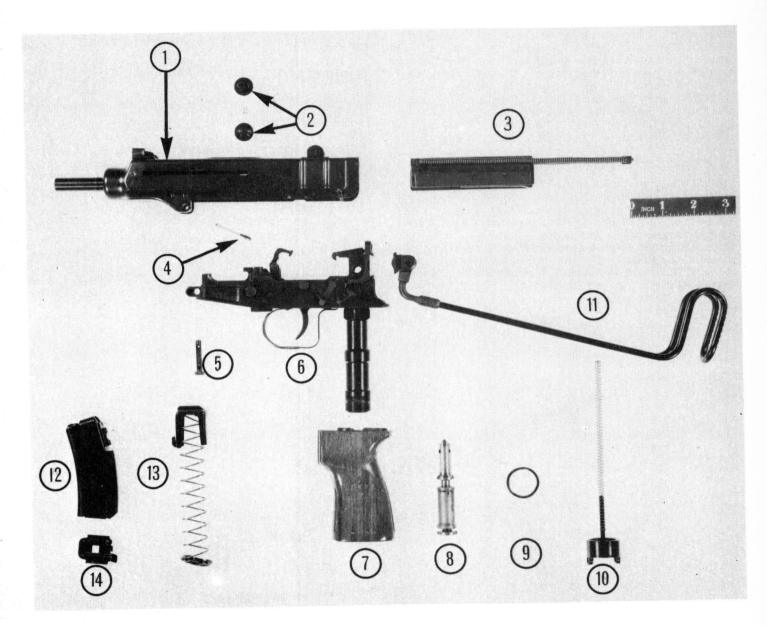

Czech 7.65mm Model 61 Submachine Gun. View of weapon disassembled into sub-groups. 1. Receiver with barrel. **2.** Cocking knobs. **3.** Bolt assembly with operating springs. **4.** Hinge pin retaining spring and plunger. **5.** Hinge pin. **6.** Pistol grip assembly. **7.** Pistol grip. **8.** Actuator assembly. **9.** Pistol grip cap spring washer. **10.** Pistol grip cap and actuator spring. **11.** Stock assembly. **12.** 10-shot magazine body. **13.** Magazine follower and spring. **14.** Magazine floorplate.

CZECH MACHINE GUNS

Czechoslovakia has been a prolific producer of machine gun designs since the early twenties. The famed ZB26 (Model 26 light machine gun) is still used extensively throughout the world, as is the ZB30 and ZB53 (Model 37 heavy machine gun). The British Bren was developed from the ZB series of light machine guns and still has an excellent reputation as a light machine gun.

Since World War II, the Czechs have come out with several new machine gun designs. The Model 52, a rather versatile weapon, originally replaced the 7.92mm Model 26 as the standard light machine gun. The Model 52 is chambered for the Czech 7.62mm Model 52 cartridge, but a later modification, the Model 52/57, is chambered for the Czech copy of the Soviet 7.62mm M1943 cartridge. The Czechs abandoned the 7.92mm Model 37 as a heavy machine gun and used the Soviet 7.62mm Goryunov for awhile; this weapon has now been replaced by a new "Universal," i.e., general purpose machine gun, the 7.62mm Model 59. The 15mm Model 38 (ZB60) used prior to the war, and by the Germans during World War II, has been replaced by the Soviet designed 12.7mm DShK M38/46, which is used on vehicles and on a Czech-designed quadruple mount.

CZECH ZB26 and ZB30 MACHINE GUNS

In 1924, Vaclav Holek introduced a belt-fed light machine gun. In the same year, he modified the weapon; it was called the Praga Model 24. This weapon is now known as the ZB26 (although it is frequently still called the Model 24 in Czechoslovakia; the gun is stamped VZ26) and was one of the most popular light machine guns in the world. The Model 26, Model 30 and Model 30J were used in 24 countries throughout the world. Models 26 and 30 have been manufactured in China, the Model 30 in Iran and Romania, and the Model 30J in Yugoslavia. All three models were carried in a post-1948 ZB catalog.

Characteristics of ZB26 Machine Gun

Caliber: 7.92mm.
System of operation: Gas, selective fire.
Length overall: 45.8 in.
Barrel length: 23.7 in.
Weight loaded: 21.28 lbs.
Sights: Front: Protected blade.
      Rear: Radial tangent.
Feed device: 20-round, detachable staggered row box magazine.
Muzzle velocity: 2500 f.p.s.
Cyclic rate: 550 r.p.m.

These weapons can be mounted on a tripod similar to that of the Bren Gun.

Loading and Firing the ZB26

Pull back the bolt handle to cock the bolt and then push the handle forward. Pull back magazine cover and insert loaded magazine mouth end first. Push down until it locks. For semiautomatic fire move the selector on the left side of the trigger group to the rear; for full auto fire, push it forward. When the selector is in the vertical position, it acts as a safety.

Field Stripping the ZB26

Push out receiver locking pin and withdraw the frame group. The slide, bolt and gas piston will now come out the rear of the receiver.

Release the barrel nut catch and lift up to the right as far as it will go. This releases the barrel, which may now be slid off to the front.

Push the butt plate catch and remove the two buffer springs.

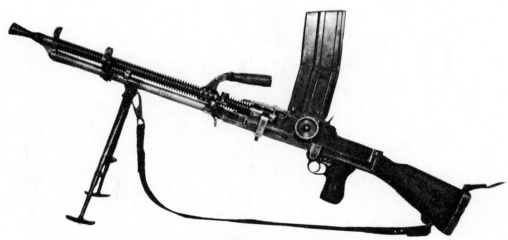

ZB26 (Brno) L.M.G. The magazine is a special oversized one.

Differences Between the ZB26 and ZB30

Outwardly, the two weapons are almost identical. The bolt of the ZB26 does not ride on the piston post as does that of the ZB30 (and the Bren). It is cammed into the locked position by a built-up rear section of the piston/slide assembly but does not "sit" on the post. The ZB30J is similar to the ZB30 but has a knurled section on its barrel to the rear and just in front of the carrying handle.

7.92mm ZB30 L.M.G. of Czech manufacture.

CZECH MODEL 52 LIGHT MACHINE GUN

The Model 52 light machine gun is also chambered for the Czechoslovak 7.62mm Model 52 "intermediate-sized" cartridge. The weapon can be fed from a belt or a box magazine without changing feed covers. When fed from the belt, the feed is similar to that of the Czechoslovak Model 37 heavy machine gun; when fed from the magazine, it is similar to that of the ZB26. The weapon makes extensive use of stampings and is, all told, a very sophisticated weapon. Possibly its greatest shortcoming is that it may be too sophisticated; in general, it can be said that the simplest weapons give the best performance in the field. Although the Model 52 is a well-designed weapon, it is not particularly simple.

A slightly modified version of the model 52 light machine gun, chambered for the Soviet designed 7.62mm M43 cartridge, was adopted in 1957 as the Model 52/57.

Characteristics of M52 Machine Gun

System of operation: Gas, selective fire.
Length, overall: 41 in.
Barrel length: 21.3 in.
Feed mechanism: 25-round box magazine, or 100-round nondisintegrating link belt (push-out type link.)
Sights: Front: Blade with removable hood.
 Rear: U-notch, adjustable for elevation and windage, graduated from 200 to 1200 meters.
Muzzle velocity: 2450 f.p.s.
Cyclic rate of fire: 1140 r.p.m. with belt, 900 r.p.m. with box magazine (approx).
Weight without belt or magazine, with bipod: 17.6 lbs.

Czech 7.62mm Model 52 Light Machine Gun with magazine feed. Note: 1. Magazine release; 2. Magazine feedway cover in open position; and 3. Gas regulator, lever with position indicator is located on left side of the gun.

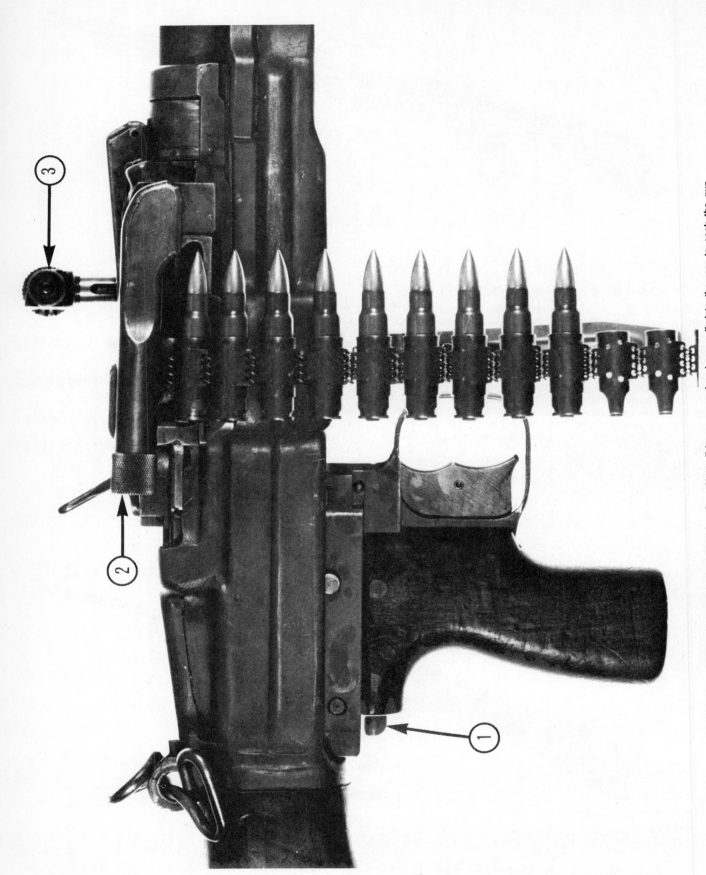

Czech 7.62mm Model 52 belt-fed Light Machine Gun. Note: Trigger group has been pulled to the rear to cock the gun.
1. Safety lever in fire position; 2. Belt feed cover lever; 3. Rear sight.

How to Load and Fire the Model 52 Light Machine Gun

Cock the gun by pressing down on the lug which protrudes from the safety (on top left side of pistol grip) and pull pistol grip to the rear. The bolt will remain to the rear since this weapon fires from an open bolt. If the pistol grip is in the rearward position, press down on the lug and push the pistol grip forward until the slide is engaged by the sear; then pull the pistol grip rearward until the pistol grip catches on the rear lock.

To load the gun with a belt of ammunition, push upward on the feed-way cover. Lay the first cartridge in the belt between the belt holding pawls, and close and lock the cover. The link ejection port cover must be in its raised position or belt movement will be blocked.

To load the gun for magazine fire, press forward on the magazine feed port latch, allowing the cover to spring forward. Invert the magazine and insert it in the magazine opening until the latch engages the magazine. The belt feedway cover and the link ejection port cover should be closed. Pressure on the bottom half moon of the trigger will produce automatic fire; pressure on the top half moon of the trigger will produce semiautomatic fire. To put the weapon on safe, push the safety lever (located on top left side of the pistol grip) down.

Czech Model 52 with box magazine.

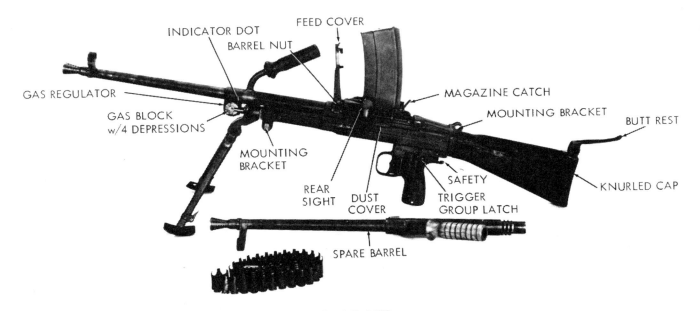

Czech Model 52.

Field Stripping the Model 52 Light Machine Gun

Driving Spring and Rod. The driving spring is retained by a cap with internal bayonet-type slots that engage projections of the spring tube within the stock. To remove the spring assembly, press in on the cap, turn it counterclockwise to disengage the slots, and withdraw the spring and rod from the stock.

Barrel and Bipod. Press forward on the magazine feed port latch, allowing the cover to spring open. Using the cover as a handle, turn the barrel lock clockwise and draw the barrel forward out of the receiver. Turn the bipod assembly to disengage its key, and remove the bipod from the weapon housing.

Receiver Assembly, Bolt Carrier and Bolt. The receiver, bolt carrier and bolt are removed simultaneously. Draw the bolt carrier rearward so that the piston is located slightly to the rear of the gas chamber in the receiver housing. Lift up on the front end of the receiver and remove the receiver, bolt carrier and bolt from the weapon. Remove the bolt carrier and bolt through the rear of the receiver.

Trigger Mechanism Assembly. Depress the pistol grip lock lever and push forward on the pistol grip. Slide the trigger mechanism assembly out of the front end of its slot in the weapon housing. Unhook the dust cover from the rear of the trigger mechanism housing.

Reassembly. Reassemble the weapon by reversing the procedure described above.

Adjustment of Gas Cylinder. There are four gas port openings that may be selected to vary the power of the weapon. To change the port setting, the barrel must first be removed from the gun as described above. To change port setting, turn the gas regulator until the desired port is aligned with the barrel gas port. The ports are identified by different-size indents in the quadrants formed by the crossed cylinder locking slots on the left side of the regulator. Alignment of one of these indents with the indent in the cylinder body selects the appropriate port size.

How the Model 52-Light Machine Gun Works

When the gun is fired, gas from the barrel is bled through a port into the gas cylinder and into the gas chamber at the front of the receiver housing. The expanding gas operates on the gas piston to force the bolt carrier rearward in recoil. For a short distance, the bolt carrier travels alone. This short period is followed by an unlocking period, during which the rear of the bolt rotates downward out of engagement with the receiver locking abutments. Upon completion of unlocking, the bolt is carried to the rear by the carrier, the spent cartridge is extracted from the barrel, and the case is ejected forward.

Upon completion of recoil, the residual energy of the bolt and bolt carrier is absorbed by a recoil plate at the rear of the receiver housing, and the bolt carrier moves forward under the force of the compressed driving spring in the stock. If the gun is being fired semiautomatically, the sear will engage the carrier and hold it until the trigger is again pressed. When the trigger is pressed, the carrier will move forward; as the rear of the carrier clears the sear, it will depress the disconnector, releasing the sear so that it can again be in position to engage the carrier.

Feeding takes place on the counterrecoil stroke of the bolt and bolt carrier. The cartridge to be fed is held in the center of the feedway by the belt holding pawl or by the pressure of the magazine spring, depending upon the type of feed being used. The forward-moving bolt strikes the lower edge of the cartridge rim, stripping it from the belt link or magazine lips. The nose of the cartridge is depressed by a ramp in the receiver breech ring, and, as the bolt continues forward, the ramp depresses the rear of the cartridge seating the rim between the extractor claws.

Special Note on the Czech Model 52-Light Machine Gun

This weapon has many very interesting features. Because of its ability to feed from either a box magazine or a belt, without changing feed components, it has a great deal of tactical flexibility. Its trigger mechanism, while hardly new in concept (the double half moon trigger can be traced back at least as far as World War I), adds considerably to the weapon. The use of a large stamped receiver housing with a much smaller machined receiver within the housing also is advantageous from an industrial point of view. It should be noted, however, that the machined receiver is quite a complex piece from a manufacturing point of view. Dirt may be kept out of the Model 52 by closing the feed and link ejection port covers, and by pulling the pistol grip forward and locking it by engaging the safety. When the weapon is ready to fire, however, the bottom of the receiver is open to dust and dirt.

The bolt is carried on a post on the slide/piston assembly in a fashion similar to that of ZB26 or the Bren gun, but it does not lock like these guns. The two locking lugs on the rear of the bolt ride in cut-outs in the receiver and are locked in the side of the receiver.

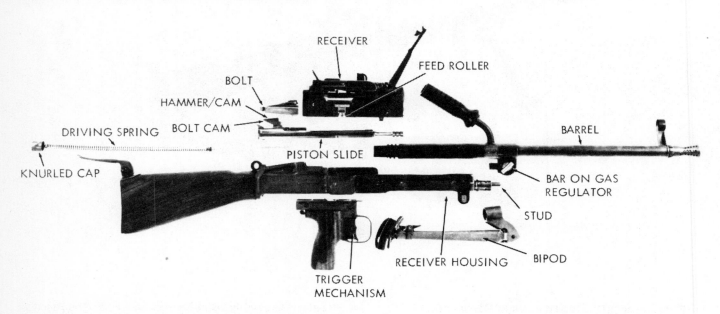

THE CZECH MODEL 59 MACHINE GUN

The Model 59 is called a "Universal" machine gun by the Czechs. This basically means that it is a general purpose machine gun, similar to the US M60, which is used on a bipod as a light machine gun and on a tripod as a heavy machine gun. The Model 59 comes equipped with heavy and light barrels, which are used in its heavy gun and light gun roles, respectively.

Characteristics of the Model 59

Caliber: 7.62mm rimmed (7.62mm Russian).
System of operation: Gas, automatic only.
Length overall: W/heavy barrel: 47.9 in.
W/light barrel: 43.9 in.
Barrel length:
  Heavy: 27.3 in. w/flash hider.
  Light: 23.3 in. w/flash hider.

Model 59 Machine Gun with telescopic sight.

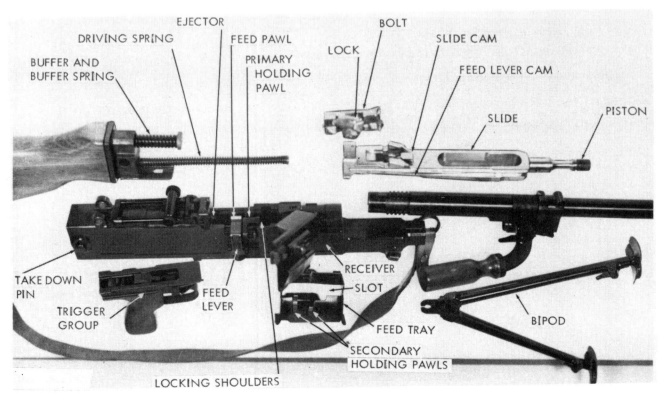

Model 59, field stripped.

Weight: W/heavy barrel on tripod, 42.4 lbs.
W/light barrel on bipod, 19.1 lbs.
Feed device: 50-round, non-disintegrating metallic link belt.
Muzzle velocity: W/heavy barrel: 2723 f.p.s.
W/light barrel: 2657 f.p.s.
Cyclic rate: 700-800 r.p.m.

When used with the light barrel, this weapon is called the Model 59L.

How to Load and Fire the Model 59 Machine Gun

The linked cartridges come in 50-round, non-disintegrating link belts; five of these belts are usually joined together for use with the weapon when it is used on the tripod. When used as a light machine gun—on bipod—a box with a 50-round belt may be attached to the side of the receiver. The cover is opened, and the belt—open side of links down—is laid on the feedway from right to left; close cover. If bolt is forward, push lug, which protrudes from the safety mounted on left rear side of the pistol grip/trigger group, down; pull the trigger and push pistol grip as far forward as it will go, release the trigger then draw to the rear. The belt may be inserted whether the bolt is in the forward or rearward position. If the trigger is pulled, the weapon will now fire. To put gun on "safe", push safety lever down. The gas cylinder block has four ports and can be adjusted as required for reliable operation.

Field Stripping the Model 59 Machine Gun

Check to insure weapon is not loaded and let bolt forward. Remove barrel by opening cover and turning one quarter turn to the right and pulling barrel forward out of the receiver. Push pin at middle rear of receiver from left to right. **Bolt must be forward so that tension on recoil spring is released.** Remove butt; recoil spring and buffer spring are mounted in the butt. Withdraw slide/pistol assembly and bolt assembly from the rear of the receiver by pulling pistol grip to the rear. Pistol grip/trigger assembly will also come off the receiver. The feed plate can be lifted up off the receiver. Reassemble in reverse order.

How the Model 59 Machine Gun Works

With a belt in the feedway and the bolt in the rear position, pressure on the trigger causes the sear to disengage from its notch in the rear underside of the slide/piston assembly. The slide/piston assembly with the bolt is forced forward by the compressed recoil spring (operating spring) and strips a cartridge out of the belt forward and downward into the chamber. The bolt lock is cammed into the locked position by cam rails on the receiver and the piston post continuing its travel a short distance further engages the striker causing it to strike the cartridge primer functioning the cartridge. Gas from the cartridge is drawn off through the gas port in the barrel and travels through the gas cylinder impinging on the piston head driving the piston/slide assembly to the rear. Rearward movement of the piston/slide cams the bolt lock up out of the locked position and the bolt starts moving to the rear with the empty cartridge case; the ejector knocks the case downward out of the bottom of the gun.

Feeding is achieved through the operation of a cam surface on the slide against the belt feed pawl, which is mounted on the right side of the receiver. At the bottom of the feed pawl, is a roller that contacts the cam surface on the slide causing the pawl to go in and out, i.e., move from right to left, in relation to the side of the receiver. Movement of the feed pawl pulls the linked rounds in one at a time. The pawl engages the linked cartridge as the slide/piston moves to the rear and is then moved to the left on the forward run of the bolt. The cartridge is held in place by the spring loaded belt-feed pawl.

Special Note on the Czech Model 59 Machine Gun

The Model 59 is one of a series of "universal" or general purpose machine guns which have appeared only since World War II. It is used on a tripod as a heavy machine gun or on a bipod as a light machine gun. In Czech service, it is used with a heavy barrel for tripod use and light barrel for bipod use, and a medium weight barrel is advertised as well in trade brochures. The weapon has been made in 7.62mm NATO, in which caliber it is called the Model 59N, to attract sales to non-Communist nations. Barrels, gas piston, gas cylinder block and bolt are chrome plated. There are spring loaded dust covers over the feed, link ejection and case ejection ports. The case ejection port cover is opened and closed by pulling the trigger.

The Model 59 is an interesting gun in many ways. There is no major feature of the weapon that is new in concept. The feed mechanism is basically the same as that of the pre-World War II ZB37 and is also used for belt feed in the Model 52.

The cocking mechanism is also similar to that of the ZB-37 and exactly the same as that of the Model 52. The bolt mechanism is a modification of the basic ZB-26, ZB-37, Model 52; the separate bolt locking lug piece is similar to that used on the Czech Model 58 Assault rifle. The method of barrel removal is the same as that of the Model 52 machine gun. A notable feature of the Model 59 as opposed to the previous Model 52 is the comparatively small number of stampings or fabrications used in its manufacture. The receiver is a milled forging, and most other parts of the weapon except the feed plate and dust covers seem to be forgings as well. The design is basically good, but as pointed out above, hardly novel.

Czech 7.62mm Model 59 Machine Gun without bipod.

CZECH MACHINE GUN MODEL 37 (ZB53)

The Model 37 heavy machine gun has been extensively manufactured for export. The military designation for the gun is Model 37 (ZB37); the commerical designation is Model 53 (ZB53).

The Model 37 is an air-cooled, gas-operated weapon with selective slow (500 r.p.m.) and fast (700 r.p.m.) rates of fire. It is fed from the right side by a metal belt of either 100- or 200-round capacity. By use of an attachment to the Model 45 tripod, it can be quickly adapted to antiaircraft fire.

This weapon was the forerunner of the British-made Besa tank machine gun. The main functioning features of the Model 37 are the same as those given for the Besa machine gun, which can be found in the chapter on Britain.

Czechoslovakian Heavy Machine Gun Model 37 (ZB 53).

Characteristics of the Model 37

Caliber: 7.92mm.
System of operation: Gas operated, two cyclic rates of fire.
Weight: 41.8 lbs.
Length, overall: 43.5 in.
Barrel length: 26.7 in.
Sights: Front: Blade with guard.
       Rear: Folding, leaf, graduated from 300 to 2000 meters in 100-meter increments, fixed 200-meter battle sight.
Cyclic rate: 450-550 r.p.m. or 700 r.p.m.
Feed device: Metallic link belt, 100- or 200-round capacity.
Muzzle velocity: 2600 f.p.s. (approx.).

Model 37 with smooth barrel.

CZECH 12.7mm QUAD DShK M1938/46 HEAVY MACHINE GUN (M54)

This weapon consists of four Czechoslovak-made (but Soviet-designed) DShK M 1938/46 heavy machine guns on a Czechoslovak-designed, two wheeled antiaircraft mount. (The DShK machine gun is covered in detail in the chapter on the USSR.) The weight of the complete equipment is 1411 pounds, and the mount is capable of 360-degree traverse and 90-degree elevation.

THE CZECH "URZ" WEAPONS FAMILY

Czechoslovakia has come out with a new weapons family called the "URZ" — which translates to Universal Small Arms — which, in concept, appears to be modeled on the Stoner 63 system. A common receiver system is used for an automatic rifle (AP), a light machine gun (LK), a heavy machine gun (TK) and a tank machine gun (T).

The automatic rifle (AP) has a lighter barrel than the other models. A grenade launcher is built onto the end of the barrel and a grenade launcher sight is attached to the rear of the front sight. It uses a fifty-round, light alloy drum type magazine. It can be used with the telescopic sight normally used with the heavy machine gun TK. The AP takes a bayonet.

The light machine gun LK has a heavier barrel than the AP rifle, a folding bayonet, and a chrome lined barrel. It also uses the 50-round drum magazine.

The heavy machine gun TK is actually the light machine gun LK with a belt type feeder mounted on a tripod and normally using a telescopic sight. This weapon is fed with a 250-round metallic link belt.

The Tank machine gun T is intended for use on vehicles and aircraft. It is belt-fed and fired by the use of a solenoid.

CHARACTERISTICS OF URZ WEAPONS FAMILY

	Rifle AP	LMG LK	Hvy MG TK	Tank MGT
Caliber:			---------7.62mm---------	
System of operation:			----gas, selective fire----	
Length overall:	39.2 in.	39.2	47.2 in.	34.5 in.
Weight: (less magazine)	8.62 lb.	11.5 lb.	24:3 lb. w/tripod mount	12.6 lb.
Feed device:	50 rd drum	50 rd drum	250 rd belt	250 rd belt
Muzzle velocity:			-----2625 f.p.s.-----	
Cyclic rate:	800 r.p.m.	800 r.p.m.	800 r.p.m.	1100 r.p.m.

The URZ weapons family as advertised is not chambered for the 7.62mm "intermediate" sized Czech Model 57 (Soviet Model 43) cartridge. It is advertised for cartridges of the size and muzzle energy of the 7.62mm NATO or the Soviet rimmed 7.62 × 54mm cartridges. This does not necessarily mean that the Czechs intend to adopt this type of system themselves. Czechoslovakia is a large exporter of arms to many countries outside the Warsaw Pact, and the URZ family is probably intended for this trade.

15
Denmark

The Danish Army currently uses the small arms listed below. Shown for each weapon is: (1) its common name; (2) its Danish nomenclature; and (3) the chapter in this book where the weapon is covered in detail.

(1) The 9mm FN Browning Hi-Power Pistol; (2) 9mm P M/46; (3) see Belgium.

(1) 9mm SIG Pistol 47/8; (2) 9mm P M/49; (3) see Switzerland.

(1) 9mm Suomi Submachine Gun; (2) 9mm Mp M/41; (3) see Finland.

(1) 9mm 37-39 Suomi Submachine Gun; (2) 9mm Mp M/44 (37); (3) see Sweden.

(1) 9mm Hovea Submachine Gun M/49; (2) 9mm Mp M/49; (3) see Denmark.

(1) 7.62mm NATO Rifle G3; (2) 7.62mm G M/66; (3) see West Germany.

(1) .30 cal. Rifle M1; (2) 7.62mm G M/50; (3) see US.

(1) .30 cal. Rifle M1917; (2) 7.62mm G M/53 (17); (3) see US.

(1) 7.62mm NATO MG 42/59 (MG 1); (2) 7.62mm Mg/62; (3) see West Germany.

(1) .30 cal. Madsen M48 Machine Gun; (2) 7.62mm Mg M/48; (3) see Denmark. (Note. The characteristics for the M48 Madsen machine gun are basically the same as those for the M1950, given later in this chapter. Operating characteristics are the same.)

(1) .30 cal. SIG M50 Machine Gun; (2) 7.62mm Mg M/51; (3) see Switzerland.

(1) .30 cal. M1919A4 Machine Gun; (2) 7.62mm Mg M/52-1 (19); (3) see US.

(1) .30 cal. M1919A5 Machine Gun; (2) 7.62mm Mg M/52-11 (19); (3) see US.

(1) .50 cal. M2 Browning Heavy Barrel; (2) 12.7mm Mg M/50; (3) see US.

(1) 7.62mm NATO MG42 (MG42/59); (3) see Germany.

DANISH PISTOLS

The Danish Army, which had previously used the Gasser revolver, adopted the Bergmann Bayard automatic pistol Model 1908 in 1911, calling it the Model 1910. This pistol is a slightly modified version of the Bergmann 1903, which was made at the Bergmann plant in Germany. The Model 1908 was made by Anciens Etablissements Pieper of Herstal, Belgium. The weapon was used by Greece and Spain; pistols used by Denmark were made in Belgium or, after 1922, in Denmark.

In 1922, the pistol was slightly changed and the model designation altered to Model 1910/21. All original Model 1910/21 pistols—a total of 2204—were made at the Army Arsenal. Between 1922 and 1935 the 4840 Belgian-made pistols were converted to the 1910/21 pattern.

In 1940, Denmark decided to adopt the 9mm Parabellum FN Hi-Power Browning pistol. A few pistols were delivered to Denmark before it was invaded by the Germans. In 1946, the order was re-instituted, and 1577 pistols were purchased. The Hi-Power is called the Model 46 by the Danes. Among the weapons that the Danish Brigade (troops who had been maintained in Sweden during the war) brought back with them, were Swedish Model 40 Lahti pistols. These pistols were called Model 40S by the Danes. In 1948, Denmark adopted the Swiss S.I.G. 9mm Parabellum Model 47/8, which they call the pistol Model 49. This is the current standard Danish service pistol.

Danish 9mm Model 1910 Pistol.

DANISH 9mm M1910/21 PISTOL

The Model 1910/21 is a recoil-operated weapon of heavy construction. It is chambered for the 9mm Bergmann-Bayard cartridge (in Spain where it is still used, this cartridge is called the 9mm Largo), which is quite similar to the Austrian 9mm Steyr

Danish 9mm Model 1910/21 Pistol converted from Model 1910.

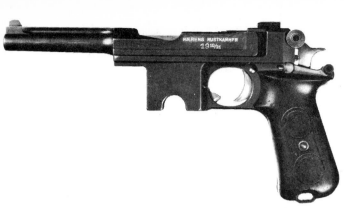

Danish 9mm Model 1910/21 Pistol as made in Denmark; magazine has been removed.

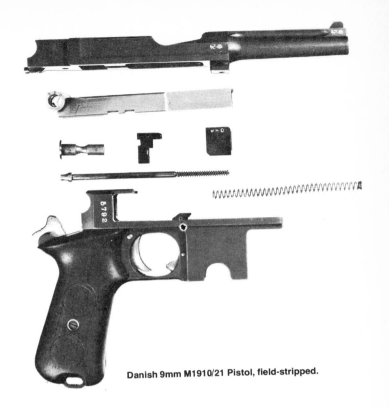

Danish 9mm M1910/21 Pistol, field-stripped.

cartridge and the US Super .38 automatic pistol cartridge. It is not made in the United States.

These pistols are quite heavy, weighing about 2.25 pounds, and have a relatively short barrel—about four inches—in comparison to their overall length of about 10 inches. There are six-, eight-and ten-round magazines for these weapons.

One of the strongest and most powerful pistols ever made, the Model 1910/21 incorporates good materials and fine workmanship with a positive lock. However, the design is clumsy and bulky and should be considered obsolete.

DANISH RIFLES

Denmark was the first country to adopt the Krag Jorgensen—in 1889—and continued to use this weapon, in a series of models, through World War II. After the war, Denmark was supplied with US, British and Swedish rifles, and eventually the US caliber .30 M1 was adopted as standard. Recently the German 7.62mm NATO G3 has been adopted, and this rifle will replace all others in the Danish service.

The Danish Home Guard was equipped with Swedish 6.5mm M94, M96 and M38 carbines and rifles until 1953, when these weapons were returned to Sweden. The Home Guard was then issued US caliber .30 M1917 (Enfield) rifles, called Model 53 by the Danes, and US M1 rifles. During World War II, the Danish sporting rifle firm of Schultz and Larsen produced a police carbine (the Model 1942) for the 8mm Danish cartridge. This rifle has four locking lugs on the bolt like the current Schultz and Larsen sporters and a box magazine, which protrudes below the level of the stock.

In 1896, the Danish Navy and Coast Guard adopted the Madsen M1896 recoil operated semiautomatic rifle. Denmark, therefore, was probably the first country to use a semiautomatic service rifle.

DANISH KRAG RIFLES

Denmark was the first country to adopt the rifle developed by Krag and Jorgensen. This weapon in slightly modified form was later adopted by the United States and Norway. The principal points of difference between the Danish and the Norwegian and US Krags are: the loading gate swings out horizontally on the Danish weapon, on the US and Norwegian Krags the loading gate swings down to open and is pushed up to close; the Danish 1889 rifle and several of the carbine models have a metal barrel jacket, the US and Norwegian Krags use wooden handguards. All Danish Krags were chambered for the 8mm rimmed cartridge.

Danish Madsen M1896 Semiautomatic Rifle

Danish 8mm Rifle Model 1889/10

Characteristics of M1889 Rifle

Caliber: 8mm Danish Krag rimmed.
System of operation: Manually operated bolt.
Length overall: 52.28 in.
Barrel length: 32.78 in.
Weight: 9.5 lbs.
Feed device: 5-round in-line magazine, loaded singly through side gate.
Sights: Front: Barley corn.
      Rear: Leaf, can be used as tangent with leaf down.
Muzzle velocity: 1968 f.p.s. w/M1889 ball.
                 2460 f.p.s. w/M1908 ball.

Danish Krag Models

Rifle M1889. This weapon, whose characteristics are given above, is typical of its period in having a long barrel and stock without pistol grip. As noted above, a metal handguard encircles the barrel in a fashion similar to that of the Belgian M1889 rifle. As originally issued, this rifle had no safety catch; a half-cock notch on the cocking piece—firing pin assembly—served this purpose. In 1910, this weapon was modified by the addition of a manual safety, which was placed on the left side of the receiver just behind the closed bolt handle.

8mm Infantry Carbine M1889. Introduced in 1924, this weapon also has a metal barrel jacket and a stud for a bayonet. A tangent-type rear sight is used on this weapon rather than the leaf-type rear sight of the rifle. This carbine has the stamp "F," i.e., *Fodfolk* or Infantry, before the serial number. Overall length is 43.3 inches with a barrel length of 24 inches; the carbine weighs 8.8 pounds. A horizontal-type bolt handle is used.

8mm Artillery Carbine M1889. This carbine was also introduced in 1924. It is generally similar to the Infantry carbine, but it has a turned-down bolt handle, a triangular upper sling swivel and a stud on the left side of the stock. This stud was used to hang the carbine from a leather hanger worn on the gunner's back.

8mm Engineer Carbine M1889. The Engineer carbine was also introduced in 1889. It has a wooden handguard, and the barrel was shortened to 23.6 inches to accommodate the muzzle cap of the Cavalry Rifle M1889. The letter "I" is found before the serial number.

Cavalry Rifle M1889. This weapon was introduced in 1914. The rear sling swivel is mounted on the left side just ahead of the trigger guard. It has a straight-bolt handle and a mounting stud similar to that of the M1889 cavalry carbine on the left side of the stock. The letter "R" is found before the serial number. This rifle is not fitted for a bayonet.

Sniper Rifle M1928. This is an alteration of the rifle M1889 and has a heavier barrel with wooden handguard, a sporting type stock with pistol grip, a turned-down bolt handle, micrometer-type rear sight and a hooded target type front sight. This rifle, which resembles the US caliber .30 Style "T" rifle in general configuration, weighs 11.7 pounds and is 46 inches in length with a 26.3-inch barrel.

8mm M1889 Artillery Carbine, 8mm M1889 Cavalry Rifle and 8mm M1928 Sniper Rifle.

DANSK INDUSTRI SYNDICAT (MADSEN)

After over 60 years of manufacturing weapons of fine quality, Dansk Industri Syndicat—DISA (or Madsen, as it is commonly known)—the manufacturers of the Madsen gun, are out of the small arms business. This company has produced many outstanding weapons and has had much influence on arms design since the early 1900s. DISA fell victim to the East-West arms trade which has seen the USSR and USA dominate small arms sales through competitive prices and subsidized military assistance programs. Of equal impact has been the fact that many nations, which formerly purchased Madsen products, now manufacture their own small arms.

DISA has in recent years continued to design small arms accessories. For example, the firm developed tripods for both the Belgian MAG and the German MG-1. The latter has been adopted by the West German Army.

Madsen Post-War Rifles

Dansk Industri Syndicat developed a number of rifles since World War II. None of these developments were commercially successful.

The Danish M47 Rifle

The Model 47 bolt-action rifle was designed primarily for the smaller races of the world. It weighs about 7.5 pounds and is fitted with a rubber recoil pad. Owing to the availability of large stocks of World War II surplus rifles at very low prices, it was sold in limited quantities only to Columbia.

The Ljungman Rifle

The Ljungman made by Madsen differs from the Swedish and Egyptian varieties of this weapon in one important respect. In the Swedish and Egyptian versions of this rifle, the gas blows through a straight gas cylinder directly against the bolt carrier. In the Madsen-made gun, the gas cylinder is coiled around the barrel; therefore the gas has further to travel before it contacts the bolt carrier. This had the tendency to cool the gas before it hits the bolt carrier and to reduce the thrust of the gas, thereby making the action less abrupt. Possibly because the Ljungman is basically an expensive and rather heavy weapon, this rifle was not a commercial success.

Danish Madsen .30 caliber Model 47 Bolt Action Rifle as supplied to Colombia.

Madsen-made Ljungman semiautomatic rifle.

Madsen 7.62mm NATO Light Automatic Rifle with tubular steel stock.

Madsen 7.62mm NATO Light Automatic Rifle with wooden stock.

MADSEN LIGHT AUTOMATIC RIFLE

Characteristics of Madsen Light Automatic Rifle

Caliber: 7.62mm NATO.
System of operation: Gas, selective fire.
Weight w/loaded magazine: 10.6 lbs.
Length, overall: 42.3 in.
Barrel length: 21.1 in.
Feed device: 20-round detachable, staggered box magazine.
Sights: Front—Hooded blade.
      Rear—Aperture, graduated from 100 to 600 meters.
Muzzle velocity: Approx. 2650 f.p.s.
Cyclic rate: 550-600 rounds per minute.

This weapon currently exists in prototype form only. Extensive use is made of lightweight materials in its construction. Aluminum alloy is used in the receiver, receiver cover, trigger guard, rear sight, magazine and bipod.

How to Load and Fire the Madsen Light Automatic Rifle. Insert a loaded magazine into the magazine port and push home until locked by the magazine catch. Cock the weapon by pulling the operating handle to the rear as far as it will go, release the handle, and let it run forward. The weapon is now cocked and ready to fire. The safety selector lever can be set on safe, semiautomatic or automatic as desired.

Special Note on the Madsen Automatic Rifle. The Madsen has its return spring mounted above the barrel and circles the piston rod, thus it pulls the bolt forward into battery position rather than pushes it forward as with most weapons. The bolt is similar to that of the Soviet AK-47 in that it rotates to lock and is rotated by means of a lug on the bolt operating in a cam in the bolt carrier. However, the piston rod of the Madsen is not permanently attached to the bolt carrier as with the AK. The piston rod of the Madsen has a ball-shaped end, which fits in a cut-out in the bolt carrier. The trigger mechanism of the Madsen is similar to that of the AK. The Madsen has a grenade launcher built into the end of the barrel. It can also be easily fitted with a bipod and a telescopic sight. There are two versions of the weapon: one with a tubular metal stock and one with a wooden stock.

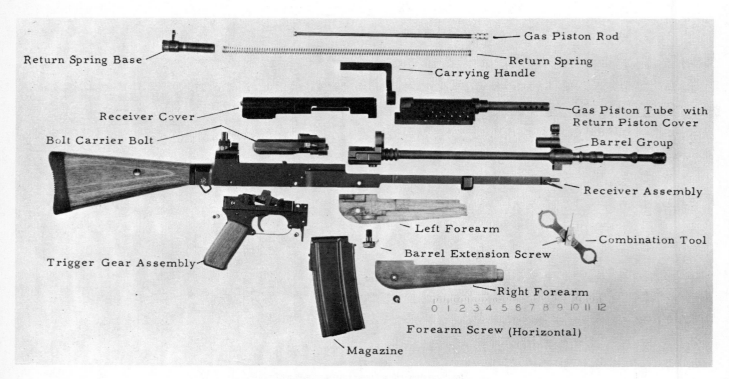

Madsen 7.62mm NATO Light Automatic Rifle, field-stripped.

DANISH SUBMACHINE GUNS

The standard submachine gun of the Danish Army is the 9mm M49 "Hovea." However, several versions—Finnish and Swedish—of the 9mm Suomi are used as well. DISA has developed several submachine guns since World War II. The initial postwar submachine developed by Madsen was the Model 45; although it had several interesting features, it was not a success. The Model 1946 and its successors, the Model 50 and Model 53, have been fairly extensively manufactured and are in use in a number of countries throughout the world.

DANISH MADSEN SUBMACHINE GUN MODEL 1945

While this gun has been rendered obsolete by the improved 1946 and later patterns, it is worthy of some attention because of a few original design factors that may have some future application in other arms.

Madsen Model 1950 Submachine Gun. One of the finest examples of modern, low cost, fast production stamped designs. Also made in Brazil in caliber .45 A.C.P.

Characteristics of M1945

Caliber: 9mm Parabellum.
Magazine: Standard box. 50 cartridges mounted below receiver.
Overall length: 31.5 in.
Weight, excluding magazine: 7.1 lbs.
Operation: Blowback. Standard general operation but unusual inertia movements added, selective fire.
Cyclic rate of fire: About 800 r.p.m.
Special feature: Safety pin lock on firing pin.

Despite the fact that this arm uses a rifle type wooden stock and fore-end, the designers achieved the extremely light weight for a submachine gun of only 7.1 pounds.

A cocking cover over the barrel breech in the form of a slide (not unlike that of the typical automatic pistol design) has serrated sides forward of the magazine. Cocking, instead of by customary handle, is by withdrawing this member, which travels with the true breechblock in recoil. The recoil spring is positioned around the barrel below this sliding cover member. Utilization of this spring position, together with the sliding cover, was used to supplement the inertia and mass of a light breechblock, to thereby achieve minimum weight.

In an endeavor to produce a safety factor to overcome accidental discharge during slamming of the breechblock when the gun is dropped or violently put aside, a sear interrupter was introduced in this model. The striker can move forward through the breechblock to fire only when the trigger is depressing the sear. Dropping the weapon will not cause accidental firing.

The spring position around the barrel, of course, subjects the spring to considerable heat under continuous fire, inevitably producing crystallization and spring breakage.

MADSEN M1950 SUBMACHINE GUN

Characteristics of M1950

Caliber: 9mm Parabellum.
System of operation: blowback, automatic fire only.
Magazine: 32-round detachable straight line box.
Weight: 7.6 lbs., excluding magazine.
Overall length: 30.71 in. with folding butt extended.
Barrel length: 7.87 in.
Muzzle velocity: approx. 1200 f.p.s.
Cyclic rate: 500-550 r.p.m.

Construction and Design, M1950

This is one of the most unusual submachine gun designs ever produced. The gun is designed to lend itself to high-speed production at extremely low cost.

Because of its unusual design, we will consider it here in considerable detail. The construction itself is most ingenious. The receiver (or frame) is flat. It is divided vertically in longitudinal section and is hinged at the rear. The pistol grip and magazine guide are a simple stamping.

The barrel is fastened to the receiver by a locking nut which when unscrewed and thrust forward permits the entire left side of the receiver to be folded back exposing the right side in which all the moving parts are housed. The barrel may be lifted out for immediate replacement or for cooling. While this system of design has been applied in Europe to revolvers in the past, this is the first production example of the application of the design principle to the submachine gun. It permits not only simplified manufacture but extreme ease of fitting and assembly.

The stock is a folding metal skeleton design permitting the gun to be used easily either from the shoulder or from the hip.

The stock when folded does not interfere with access to the trigger. The sling swivel positions on the left side of the gun are designed to permit the weapon to be slung across the chest for immediate use at a moment's notice.

A very unusual factor, yet one of extreme simplicity, is the special automatic safety provided. This is a lever positioned to the rear of the magazine housing. When firing, the normal manner of gripping an arm of this type is with the right hand about the grip and the left hand around the magazine or magazine housing. In this position, the firer's left hand in this new design also embraces the safety lever. Should he release this grip at any time, or should he stumble and lose control of it, the lever automatically blocks the path of the breechblock so that it cannot chamber a cartridge from the magazine for firing. Pulling the cocking handle all the way back will put the gun back in readiness for operation.

The receiver is composed of two nearly identical sections of stamped sheet steel. The pistol grip and magazine housing are formed as sections of these individual halves of the receiver. The two frame sections are hinged at the rear. At the front they are secured to the barrel by the barrel bearing nut.

The left side of the receiver serves as an actual cover for the right section in which the moving members are housed. The sling swivels and sights are on the left-hand half. The front sight is positioned at the forward end of the receiver instead of on the barrel, thus eliminating need for accurate barrel positioning, since barrel locking ridges are cylindrical. It is a standard blade design and may be adjusted laterally for windage. The rear sight positioned at the rear of the receiver section is a fixed aperture sight. The gun is sighted in at a practical hundred meters range. While the sighting radius is relatively short, it is still adequate.

A projecting rib at the forward end of the left section of the receiver serves as the ejector. The right side of the receiver is pierced for the ejection port.

Except for the barrel, which is detachable by merely unscrewing its nut, all the other operating parts are housed in the right hand side of the receiver.

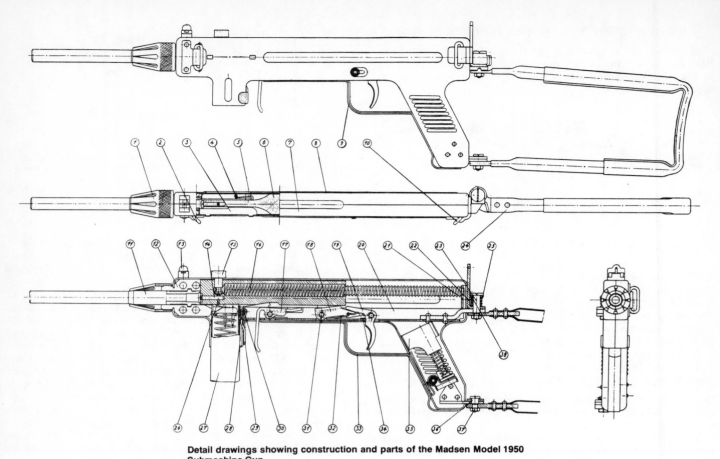

Detail drawings showing construction and parts of the Madsen Model 1950 Submachine Gun.

1. Barrel-bearing nut	11. Barrel	21. Return spring guide (complete)	31. Trigger rod pin
2. Sling swivel	12. Barrel bearing	22. Rear sight plate	32. Trigger rod spring
3. Ejector	13. Front sight	23. Shoulder piece bolt (upper)	33. Trigger guard
4. Extractor pin	14. Firing pin	24. Shoulder piece	34. Trigger spring
5. Extractor	15. Cocking handle	25. Shoulder piece spring	35. Magazine loading apparatus
6. Breechblock	16. Return spring	26. Firing pin rivet	36. Shoulder piece bolt (lower)
7. Frame half (left)	17. Breech block retainer	27. Magazine	37. Shoulder piece bolt nut
8. Frame half (right)	18. Trigger rod	28. Magazine catch pin	38. Shoulder piece lock
9. Safety catch	19. Trigger	29. Magazine catch	
10. Sling swivel	20. Trigger plate	30. Magazine catch spring	

The Barrel. No radiating rings or cooling flanges are provided. The barrel is a smooth taper screw machine or lathe-turned unit and is quite light. Because of interchangeability factors, the heavier barrel is not considered essential, though for hard military usage a heavy or flanged barrel could readily be provided.

The breech section of the barrel is housed in the forward breech section of the receiver. It is furnished with an external rib which fits into corresponding grooves in both frame halves to prevent the barrel from moving forward or rearward. A groove cut in the rear of the chamber section of the barrel mates with the ejector rib in the left section of the receiver. This positively prevents any barrel rotation when assembled.

Breechblock. This rectangular unit reciprocates inside the receiver on the flat bottom wall of the right receiver section. The firing pin is an integral part of the breechblock for complete simplicity. The extractor at the front right side section of the breechblock is secured with an elementary vertical pin.

Cocking Handle. This is a separate member, inserted in the top of the breechblock and fastened by a cross pin. It travels in a slot in the top of the frame between the two halves.

Trigger Mechanism. This is positioned at the bottom of the right receiver section. The unit consists simply of the trigger and arm, the trigger rod, and their respective springs. The rod (or sear member) is thrust upwards by its spring to catch in a notch in the bottom of the breechblock when in cocked position. The trigger arm projects down through the opening in the bottom of the right frame section, where it is protected by the trigger guard.

Safety Catch. This is at the bottom of the frame. It can be locked only when the breechblock is cocked. Pushing back the catch in its short travel slot in the left side of the frame effectively locks the trigger rod in position to prevent any movement of the breechblock.

Magazine. Box design holding 32 cartridges. This is inserted in standard fashion into the magazine housing from below. The magazine retaining catch is in the rear wall of the housing. Pushing the catch backwards releases the magazine. The magazine may be inserted when the breechblock is open or closed. However, if the breechblock is in closed position, more force must be applied to insert the magazine as it must be thrust up enough for the top cartridge (which presses against the underside of the breechblock) to be thrust further down into the magazine itself.

Buttstock. This is a skeleton folding butt of steel tubing partly

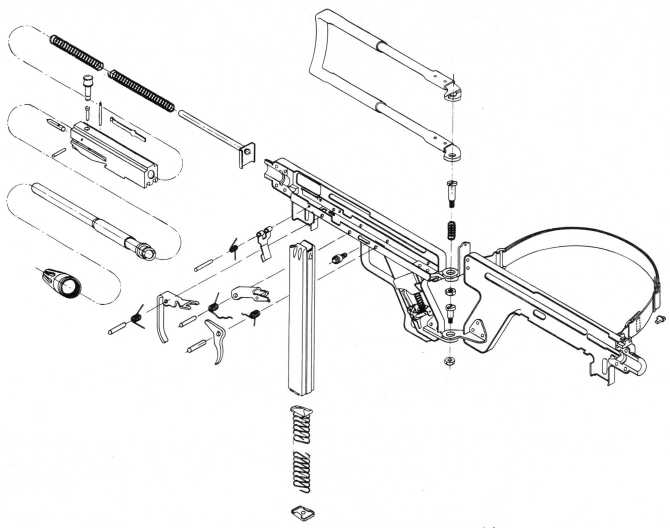

Detail exploded view of the Madsen Model 1950 Submachine Gun as made in Denmark.

leather covered for comfort. It is hinged to the rear end of the right section of the receiver, its lower hinge being behind the pistol grip. In both open and closed positions the stock is held by a notch and a lug in the hinge. A slight jerk will free it to be moved to either position. However, a lock on the upper shoulder piece bolt allows it be securely locked into extended position if desired. When folded forward, it lies along the right side of the frame to make a very compact fold, without interfering with the use of the arm in any way.

Dismounting and Reassembling the M1950

To Dismount. Press the release catch and remove the magazine. Fold the shoulder piece. Ease the breechblock to forward position if it is not already there. Unscrew the barrel bearing nut and slide forward. Place the gun on its right side. Pull the front wing swivel with the right hand while holding the left hand pressing against the barrel. This will raise the left receiver section, freeing the barrel. Withdraw the barrel.

Press the base of the return spring forward and upwards. This will allow it to be withdrawn from the breechblock. Lift the breechblock up and out. No further disassembly is normally required. The magazine bottom may be slid out to remove the spring and follower, although this too is not commonly necessary. Reassembly is merely reversal of this procedure.

Special Note. This gun in Caliber .45 is currently being made in Brazil under Madsen license. Many of the design and manufacturing features lend themselves readily to application to other small arms designs.

Operation of M1950

A magazine is inserted in the housing and thrust in until the magazine catch secures it. The cocking handle on top of the breechblock is drawn to the full rear position to compress the recoil spring. At the end of the stroke, the trigger rod spring thrusts the rod up to catch in its notch in the under side of the breechblock. The safety catch may be pushed to lock the rod into the breechblock if desired. Otherwise the weapon is now ready to fire on pull of the trigger.

Firing. Pressing the trigger causes it to pivot, and its forward arm moves the attached trigger rod down out of contact with the breechblock. The compressed recoil spring drives the breechblock ahead. If the left hand is not supporting both the magazine housing and the safety lever behind it, the breechblock will be halted before striking the cartridge in the

Brazilian cal. .45. Similar to the Danish Madsen Model 1946 except for caliber. Presented to Gen. J. Lawton Collins, then Chief of Staff, US Army by the Brazilian Minister of War. This gun is manufactured by INA in Brazil. Its bolt handle is on the right side rather than on the top.

Danish Madsen Model 1953 9mm Submachine Gun.

magazine lips.

Assuming that the supporting hand is pressing in the safety catch towards the magazine housing, the breechblock impelled by the recoil spring is free to move ahead, since the upper section of the safety lever is not in its path. Its feed face strips the

SAFETY

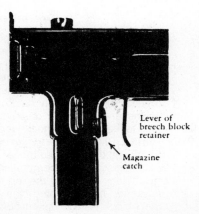

Lever of breech block retainer

Magazine catch

The breech block retainer serves to prevent a round from being fired accidentally owing to an incomplete cocking motion or as a result of a shock to the gun if dropped or laid down hard. — It does not require any attention, however, to release the breech block retainer, because the correct grip for firing the gun, whether kneeling, standing, sitting or prone, is with left hand firmly round the magazine housing, the thumb in the most natural way pressing against the downward lever of the breech block retainer, and with the right hand round the pistol grip.

top cartridge from between the lips of the magazine and drives it into the chamber. The nose of the bullet is guided by the barrel feed section of the breech into the chamber as the rear section of the cartridge clears the magazine lips. When the cartridge enters the chamber, it lines up with the firing pin, which is fixed in the face of the breechblock. The firing pin strikes the cartridge primer while still moving forward. At the same time the extractor on the right side of the breechblock springs over the cannelure in the cartridge case.

In this quite standard practice for submachine guns, the heavy breechblock and spring members are still moving forward at the actual instant of firing before the chambering is really complete. This serves as an additional inertia factor to offset the recoil of the discharge.

DANISH MADSEN SUBMACHINE GUN M1953

This is a newer model of the submachine gun Model 1946. This weapon was changed in 1950, and again in 1953. This model is called the M53.

The M53 is very similar to the 1950 Model, but it has incorporated several improvements. The most noticeable, at first glance, is the design of the magazine, which is curved instead of being straight as on the 1946 and 1950 models. The curved

Hovea Submachine Gun M49.

magazine is considered a better design for feeding purposes.

Another new feature in the M53 submachine gun is that the barrel bearing nut now screws onto the barrel, rather than onto the front of the receiver as on the M46 and M50 models. This feature gives the M53 added strength and stability for the barrel. The bolt has also been streamlined to aid in better functioning.

If desired, the weapon can be supplied with a removable barrel jacket to which a special short bayonet can be fixed. All the Madsen models can be made with or without selection-fire features.

The characteristics and field stripping are the same for this weapon as for the 1950 model given earlier in this chapter.

Hovea 9mm Submachine Gun M1949

This weapon, commonly called the Hovea, was developed by Husqvarna in Sweden. It is similar in construction to the Swedish M45 submachine gun. Functioning, disassembly and assembly are similar to that described under the Swedish 9mm M45 submachine gun.

Characteristics of Hovea 9mm Submachine Gun M1949

Caliber: 9mm Parabellum
System of operation: Blowback.
Weight: 8.9 lbs. (loaded).
Length, overall: 31.8 in. (w/stock extended)
                21.6 in. (w/stock folded)
Barrel length: 8.4 in.
Feed device: 35-round detachable, staggered, box magazine
Sights; Front: Hooded post.
       Rear: L-type with setting for 100 and 200 meters
Muzzle velocity: 1263 f.p.s.
Cyclic rate: 600 r.p.m.

DANISH MACHINE GUN

Denmark has used various models of the Madsen machine gun since 1904 in the standard light gun versions and in aircraft versions as well as heavy (20mm) guns of this design. After World War II, the Danish Army was equipped with British .303 Bren guns, Swedish 6.5mm Model 37 Browning guns and US caliber .30 M1919A4 and A5 and caliber .50 M2 Browning Heavy Barrel machine guns. In 1948, Denmark adopted the last of the true Madsens in caliber .30, and in 1950 they adopted the SIG 50 as the Model 50 in caliber .30. Recently Denmark adopted the German 7.62mm NATO MG1 (MG 42/59) as standard and also adopted the DISA Model F 197 tripod mount for this gun.

THE MADSEN MACHINE GUN

The Madsen machine guns have been among the most popular in the world since their introduction in the early 1900s. They have world-wide distribution and will continue to be encountered in service for many years. There are many variations of this gun in existence, but all operate basically in the same way. The Madsen is an expensive gun to manufacture and requires quality ammunition for reliability of function. These factors limited its use among the major powers during the world wars. In 1926, the Madsen was issued in a water-cooled version; a quantity of these weapons were sold to Chile. The Madsen has been sold to 34 countries in a dozen different calibers.

Loading and Firing the Madsen

Like the Chatellerault and the Bren guns, the Madsen uses a top-loading magazine. This requires the sights to be set off to the side of the gun. The magazine is arc-shaped, for use with rimmed cartridges, which cannot lie flat on top of each other.

Pull the cocking handle back as far as it will go and release it.

Put the forward end of the magazine into the forward end of the magazine opening and lower the rear end down into place, snapping it down until it locks. Now set the selector on the left side of the receiver above the trigger in the fire position. **Note:** Remember that this weapon fires as the bolt goes forward, and no attempt should ever be made to let the action go forward while there is a magazine mounted on top of the gun.

How the Madsen Gun Works

This gun fits into a subdivision of functioning principles known as the "long barrel recoil type." In the short recoil types, the barrel moves backward a less distance than the length of the case.

In the long recoil type, the breech has to move back far enough to permit feeding up the entire cartridge in one operation. This is done by the barrel going forward while the lock is held back until the cartridge has partly entered the chamber. In this type of action, the rate of fire is much lower than in the short recoil.

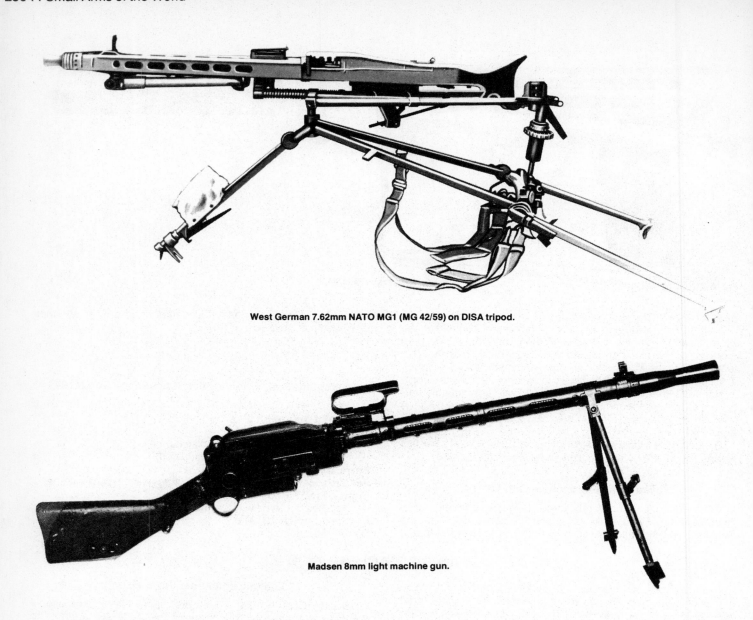

West German 7.62mm NATO MG1 (MG 42/59) on DISA tripod.

Madsen 8mm light machine gun.

Starting with the gun cocked and in firing position, the action is as follows: As the trigger is pressed, the spring below it is compressed while the trigger nose is pulled down out of the bent of the recoil lever. This permits the recoil spring in the butt to force the lever downward, and, as it is engaged in the rear of the breech mechanism, it thrusts the recoiling parts forward. As the recoiling mechanism nears forward position, the recoil arm is still up somewhat. The hump on the recoil lever now bears on the side of the sear and forces the sear downward. The nose of the sear is thus relieved from the bent of the firing lever and compresses the sear spring. The firing lever is now forced downward by its spring and strikes the tail of the hammer. The front of the hammer drives the firing pin forward to explode the cartridge in the firing chamber. A coiled spring around the firing pin, which is compressed by the hammer movement, pulls the firing pin back into the face of the breech block as the cartridge is fired.

As the recoiling parts are thrust forward by the recoil lever spring, a circular stud in the lower part of the breech block, work-ing in the guide grooves of a switch plate fitted to the nonrecoil-ing portion of the receiver, strikes the rear of the center block in the plate and so guides the breech block downward, leaving the chamber ready for the cartridge to be inserted. As the stud continues forward, it strikes the lower cam surface of the switch plate causing the breech block to rise and close the breech. Now the stud is lined up with the horizontal slot in the switch plate, down which it travels during the final half-inch forward motion, securely locking the breech.

Also during the forward thrust of the recoiling parts, an arm is forced up by a cam on the left side of the receiver, forcing out-wards the distributor against the tension of its spring and permit-ting the first cartridge from the magazine, which was resting on the distributor to drop into the magazine opening.

Meanwhile the front surface of the rear claw of the feed arm engages with the rear surface of the feed arm actuating block, thus rotating the feed arm forward. The arm strikes the head of the cartridge in its seat against the left flange of the breech block, pushing it ahead into the chamber. The rear claw of the

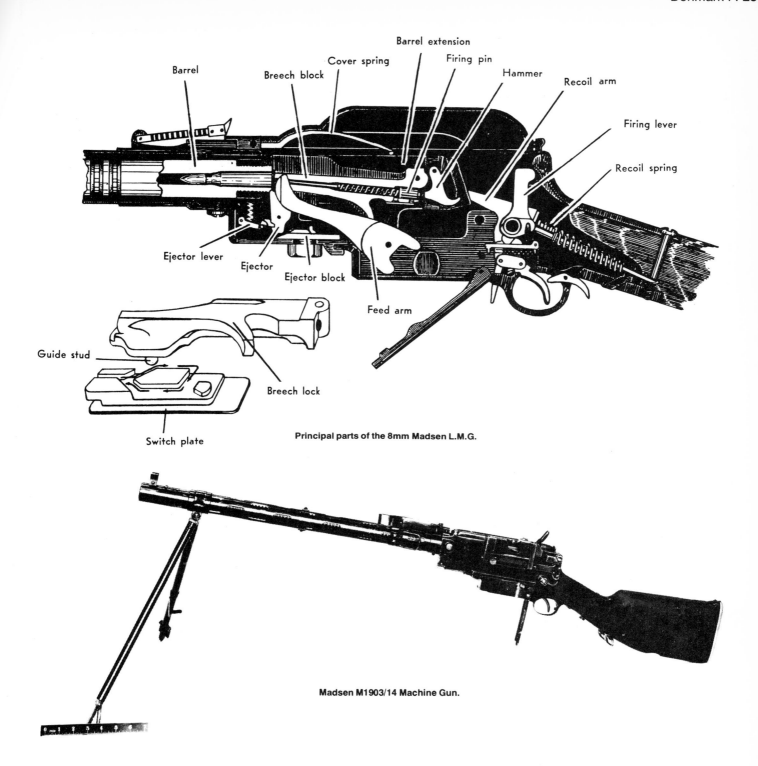

Principal parts of the 8mm Madsen L.M.G.

Madsen M1903/14 Machine Gun.

feed arm rises up to the rear surface of the feed arm actuating block and travels along its upper surface. The bottom of the rear claw, now being above the feed arm actuating block, moves the cartridge in the chamber to allow the breech block to rise. It also prevents any rebound of the feed arm.

As the forward action starts, the ejector is positioned alongside the rear of the ejector block. As the recoiling parts go forward, a stud on the ejector lever rides down the sloping cam and forces an ejector downward on its spring, thus bringing the lever in contact with the tail of the ejector. As soon as the breech block starts to rise, the tail of the ejector is clear of the ejector block and is raised in position by its lever. As the breech closes, the ejector is able to rise to the vertical under the influence of the ejector lever spring and falls in place just below the chamber with its hook below the rim of the cartridge.

Note that in this type of gun the cartridge is not set into the chamber by the breech block, and until the front of the breech block rises to a complete locking position, the hammer, firing pin and cartridge are not in alignment, therefore, there can be no accidental discharge during feeding.

Return Movement of the Action. At the breech, the barrel is joined to the breech block casing in which are the hinged breech blocks. These three units recoil together, with the breech remaining closed and locked for about ½". This sudden rearward thrust forces the firing lever up as it is struck by the rear of the breech mechanism and frees it from the hammer, permitting the hammer to pivot back and the firing pin to be withdrawn by the firing pin spring. The guide stud is now passed out of the horizontal groove and travels up the upper cam of the switch plate, which pivots the breech block upwards at its nose to permit ejection. The extra stud travels along the top of the cam, and the cover spring then forces the front of the breech block downward, compelling the stud to drop out of the rear stud of the switch plate.

Note: This gun has no individual extractor. The ejector pulls the empty cartridge out of the chamber and hurls it from the gun.

With the first movement to the rear, the inclined slope in the front of the ejector block raises the ejector, which is held in vertical position by its lever engaged in a recess in the bottom of the ejector. From the influence of this separate movement, a hook on the ejector catches the rim of the empty cartridge case, and the bottom of the ejector lies on top of the front flats of the ejector block.

The stud on the ejector lever runs up the sloping cam on the left of the ejector block to compress the ejector lever spring. This also disengages the ejector lever from the ejector, allowing the ejector tail to be tripped forward by the step on the ejector block, and as the ejector is pivoted about its center, the tripping motion of the tail forces the hook to the rear, pulling the empty cartridge case out and hurling it from the bottom of the gun.

An ejection guide on the breech block guides the empty cartridge case as it is hurled out. The ejector lever stud now rests above the sloping cam holding the ejector levers upwards and

free of the ejector, which lies on top of the rear flap of the ejector block beneath the breech block. During the recoil movement, the distributor arm rides down its cam and rotates the distributor inwards and downwards under the influence of the spring. This places the cartridges in the feedway against the left flange of the breech block. Meanwhile, the rear surface of the front feed arm claw engages with the front face of the feed arm actuating block and rotates the feed arm backwards. The bottom of the front claw now rides along the top of the feed arm block, preventing rebound of the feed arm.

Further Note on Recoil System. Some Madsens are fitted with a so-called "recoil increaser," which forms a choke at the muzzle. By reversing the two parts of the increaser, the rear portion forms a collar that forces the gasses escaping at the muzzle to rebound onto the barrel, giving additional thrust to the rearward action. This speeds the gun up greatly.

When the gun is cocked, the claws of the feed arm automatically open the ejector cover. It must be closed by hand on cease fire.

Field Stripping the Madsen

Remove magazine from gun and ease recoiling parts forward.

Lift the locking bolt lever into vertical position and withdraw it to the left.

Push the butt to the right front while gripping the receiver with the left hand; then remove the butt.

Holding forefinger of right hand ahead of feed arm axis bar, with the hand draw back barrel and breech mechanism.

Pull out the barrel. Remove barrel very carefully as it is easy to damage the front end ring. This barrel ring is one of the weak points in the weapon. Handle it carefully.

Remove the breech block bolt.

Pull feed arm to the rear. Lift the front, and lower the end of the breech block; then pivot the front up to vertical position, when the feed arm may be eased forward and lifted out of the block.

Further dismounting need not be attempted.

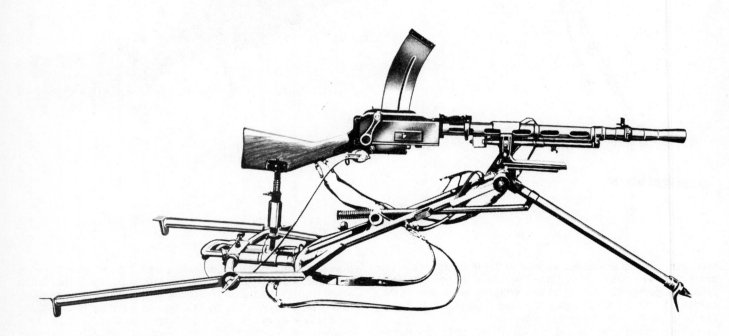

Madsen Model 1950 mounted on tripod.

DANISH MADSEN MACHINE GUN M1950

Characteristics of the Madsen Machine Gun Model 1950

Caliber: Advertised for any rifle cartridge, usually found in .30-06.
System of operation: Recoil, selective fire.
Length overall: 45.9 in.
Barrel length: 18.8 in.
Weight: 22 lbs.
Feed device: 30-round, detachable box magazine.
Sights: Front: Blade.
    Rear: Tangent, graduated from 200-1800 meters.
Muzzle velocity: Approx. 2700 f.p.s. w/.30-06.
Cyclic rate: 400 r.p.m.

Special Note on Operating Characteristics of M1950

The operating characteristics of the Model 1950 Madsen machine gun, except for minor variations as required by feed alterations in some instances, are the same as described previously.

This model, while recoil operated on the Madsen principle, is a modification of the earlier production. The change is in the barrel removal. This may be removed without the use of tools or without removing any component parts.

This Madsen may be fired from the bipod with or without the shoulder stock. It may also be fired from a light tripod, which is convertible to an antiaircraft high-angle fire mount. In addition, it may be fired from the shoulder by the rifleman in kneeling, standing, or prone positions.

Madsen Model 1950 mounted on bipod with flash hider and top mounted magazine.

Distribution of Madsen Machine Guns

As a matter of record, background on the distribution of Madsen machine guns may be of interest. The models are listed by country in which used.

Argentina. Madsen machine guns Models 1910, 1925, 1926, 1928, 1931 and 1935. Most in calibers 7.65mm Mauser.

Bolivia. Model 1925. Caliber 7.65mm Mauser.

Brazil. Models 1908, 1913, 1916, 1925, 1928, 1932, 1934, 1935 and 1936, in calibers 7mm Mauser and 1946 Model machine gun in caliber .30-06.

Bulgaria. Models 1915 and 1927. Caliber 8mm (8 × 50R);

Chile. Models 1923, 1925, 1926 water cooled, 1928 and 1940. Most in caliber 7mm Mauser. Model 1946 in caliber .30-06.

China. Models 1916, 1930 and 1937. All in the standard caliber 7.92mm Mauser.

Czechoslovakia. Models 1922 and 1923. Caliber 7.92mm German.

Denmark. Models 1904, 1916, 1919, 1924, 1939 in caliber 8mm and Model 1948 in caliber .30-06

El Salvador. Models 1951 in caliber .30-06 and Model 1934 in caliber 7mm Mauser.

Esthonia. Models 1925 and 1937 in caliber .303 British.

Ethiopia. Models 1907, 1910, 1934 and 1935. All in caliber 7.92mm.

Finland. Models 1910, 1920, 1921, and 1923. Most in caliber 7.62mm Russian.

France. Models 1915, 1919, 1922 and 1924. All in caliber 8mm Lebel.

Germany. Models 1941, 1942 in caliber 7.92mm.

Great Britain. Models 1915, 1919, 1929, 1931 and 1939 in caliber .303 British.

Holland. Models 1919, 1923, 1926, 1927, 1934, 1938 and 1939. All in caliber 6.5mm Dutch.

Honduras. Models 1937 and 1939 in caliber 7mm Mauser.

Hungary. Models 1925 and 1943 in caliber 7.92mm.

Indonesia. Model 1950 in caliber .30-06.

Italy. Models 1908, 1910, 1925 and 1930 in caliber 6.5mm Italian.

Lithuania. Model 1923. Caliber 7.92mm.

Mexico. Models 1911 and 1934. Caliber 7mm Mauser.

Norway. Models 1914 and 1918. Caliber 6.5mm Mauser.

Pakistan. Model 1947. Caliber .303 British.

Paraguay. Model 1926. Caliber 7.65mm Mauser.

Peru. Model 1929. Caliber 7.65mm Mauser.

Portugal. Models 1930, 1936 and 1952. Caliber 7.7mm. Also in Portugal, Models 1936, 1940 and 1947 in caliber 7.92mm.

Russia. Models 1904 and 1915 in caliber 7.62mm Mosin-Nagant, Russian.

Spain. Model 1907 and 1922 in caliber 7mm Mauser.

Sweden. Models 1906, 1914 and 1921. Caliber 6.5mm Mauser.

Thailand. Models 1925, 1930, 1934, 1939, 1947 and 1949. Caliber 8mm and Model 1951 in caliber .30-06.

Turkey. Models 1925, 1926, 1935 and 1937. Caliber 7.92mm.

Uruguay. Model 1937. Caliber 7mm Mauser.

Yugoslavia. Various in caliber 7.92mm.

MADSEN/SAETTER RIFLE-CALIBER MACHINE GUN

The Madsen/Saetter machine gun is belt-fed and gas operated. It is usually mounted on a light field tripod but can be fired from a bipod or from the hip. The gun is, in appearance and design, a modern weapon, embodying all the experience gained during the last few years in the development of machine guns. The component parts are easily mass produced by punching, turning and precision casting without detracting from reliability and durability.

The Madsen/Saetter machine gun has gone through three changes. These three models are the Mk I, Mk II and Mk III. The Mk III was not completely developed until 1959. The Mk III is more reliable and shorter than the Mk I or Mk II. Madsen also made a tank machine gun model that has no buttstock and no bipod. The return spring is placed round the gas piston. A special "lightweight" tripod is made for this weapon for use outside the tank.

Characteristics of Madsen/Saetter Machine Gun

Caliber: Any military rimless cartridge from 6.5mm to 8mm.

System of operation: Gas operated, full automatic fire only.

Weight: 25.6 lbs. w/heavy barrel.

Weight of tripod: 36.2 lbs.

Length, overall: 48 in.

Barrel length: 26 in.

Feed device: By non-disintegrating metallic belts of 50 rounds, which can be joined to any desired length. The weapon can also be supplied with two box magazines that fasten to the receiver directly below the action; one magazine holds 50 rounds, and the other holds 100 rounds, in metal link belts. The feed system used on this weapon is a copy of the German MG42.

Sights: Front: Barley corn.

      Rear: Open, with graduations up to 1200 meters.

Muzzle velocity: Standard for ammunition employed.

Cyclic rate: 700 to 1000 r.p.m.

Field Stripping the Madsen/Saetter

Insure that the chamber is empty by opening the feed cover, and pull back the cocking handle.

To remove the buttstock, seize the pistol grip with one hand, and, with the thumb, press the trigger gear housing latch. The buttstock, now released, should be turned 90 degrees with the other hand, and pulled to the rear.

To remove the triggerguard housing, the cocking handle should be pulled fully back, and then pushed forward again. This brings the bolt carrier to the rear. The triggerguard housing can now be turned downward and taken out of engagement.

To remove the gas piston: when the bolt assembly is in its rearmost position, the gas piston head is just outside a clearance at the end of the receiver and can be withdrawn.

To remove the bolt, let it slide to the rear, out of the receiver.

To remove the barrel, turn the barrel handle forward until it is free.

To strip the bolt assembly, press out the bolt carrier pin, pull back the action head, and remove components.

To assemble, follow the above instructions in reverse order.

The Madsen/Saetter light machine gun in caliber .30 is used by and manufactured in Indonesia.

Dansk Industri Syndicat developed a new version of the rifle caliber Madsen/Saetter. The Mark IV is shorter and lighter than the earlier Marks and is used with a lighter tripod. Like the earlier Marks, it can be made for any rimless cartridge from 6.5mm to 7.92mm and, of course, for the US cal. .30 rifle and machine gun cartridge. Any of the Madsen/Saetter machine guns can be easily modified to use disintegrating metallic links.

The Danish Madsen/Saetter machine gun (rifle caliber).

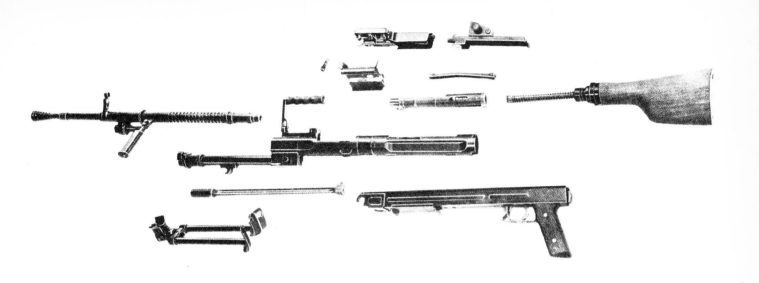

Stripped view of early model 7.62mm Madsen/Saetter.

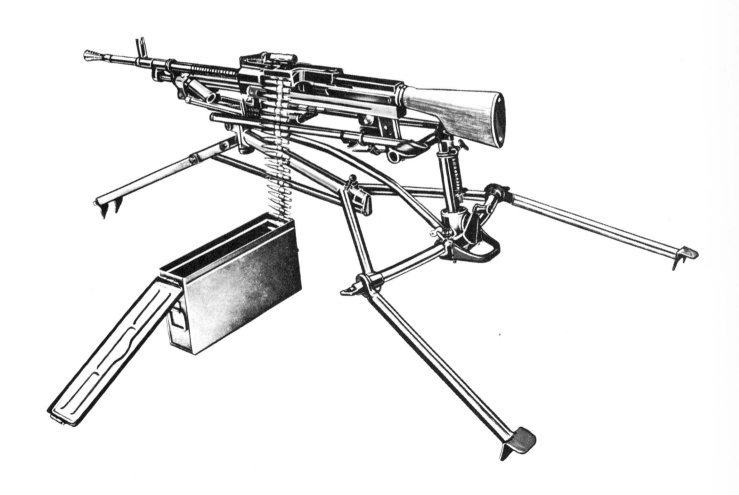

Madsen/Saetter 7.62mm NATO Machine Gun on tripod.

MADSEN/SAETTER 7.62mm TANK MACHINE GUN

This is a version of the rifle caliber Madsen/Saetter made specifically for use on tanks and armored vehicles. It can also be used as a ground gun on a tripod. The arrangement of the gas cylinder and piston is interesting. As with the Soviet RPD light machine gun, there is a definite air gap between the gas cylinder and piston when the gun is cocked. This gap serves a useful purpose during functioning—a good deal of the gas bled through the gas port into the gas cylinder is dissipated into the atmosphere after it has served to force the piston to the rear. This has several advantages in that it results in less build-up of carbon in the gas cylinder and piston tube, and, of special importance in a tank machine gun, it cuts down the amount of "operating" gas filters back into the receiver and thereby into the tank.

Characteristics of Madsen/Saetter Tank Machine Gun

Caliber: 7.62mm NATO (can be made in other calibers).
System of operation: Gas.
Weight: 22.3 lbs.
Length, overall: 38.2 in.
Barrel length w/flash hider: 22.2 in.
Sights: Front: Protected blade.
      Rear: Tangent with V-notch.
Feed Device: Non-disintegrating 50-round metallic link belt, which can be joined to other belts.

    The weapons can be built to use disintegrating links of the M13 (US) type. Belt is normally contained in a box attached to left side of receiver.
Muzzle velocity: 2800 f.p.s.
Cyclic rate: 700-800 r.p.m.

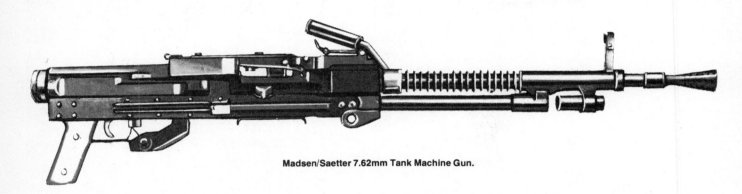

Madsen/Saetter 7.62mm Tank Machine Gun.

DANISH MADSEN/SAETTER CAL. .50 MACHINE GUN

This caliber .50 weapon exists only in prototype form. This machine gun utilizes the same basic system and design features as the Madsen/Saetter rifle-caliber machine gun, with the exception of the mounting. The cal. .50 weapon can be adapted for special mounts, for use in armored cars and tanks or for antiaircraft or antipersonnel use.

There are two types of mounts for this weapon. One serves a dual purpose, as it can be set up for antiaircraft fire, or, with the addition of rubber wheels, can be towed and used against troops on the ground. This mount is generally similar in principle to that of the Soviet DShK M1938/45 heavy machine gun mount, which serves the same dual role.

The other mount used is a light tripod for use on the ground or on armored vehicles.

Characteristics of Madsen Cal. .50 Machine Gun

Caliber: Cal. .50 (12.7mm).
System of operation: Gas operated, full automatic fire only.
Weight: 61.7 lbs.
Length, overall: 64 in.
Barrel length: 39.4 in.
Feed device: 50-round non-disintegrating metallic link belts; box magazine holding 50 rounds may be attached to left side of receiver.
Sights: Open sights for ground use; special antiaircraft sights are used when set up for antiaircraft fire.
Muzzle velocity: Standard for cal. .50 ammunition.
Cyclic rate: 1000 r.p.m.

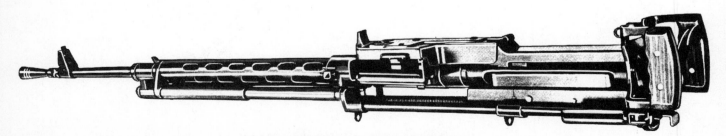

Danish Madsen/Saetter caliber .50 machine gun.

16

Dominican Republic

The Dominican Army has a wide variety of small arms, but within the past several years has attempted to standardize by selling some of the older weapons. Colt caliber .45 M1911 Pistols, FN Browning 9mm Hi-Power Pistols, and Colt and Smith & Wesson caliber .38 revolvers are used. The caliber .30 Cristobal Carbine Model 2 is used in large quantities. The 7mm M1908 Mauser rifle is being replaced by the 7.62mm NATO FN FAL and the 7.62mm NATO G3 rifles.

The most common machine guns are the Browning caliber .30 M1919A4 and M1917A1, and the caliber .50 Browning M2 HB and M2 water cooled. There are also some 7mm Madsen guns in service.

DOMINICAN AUTOMATIC CARBINE CRISTOBAL MODEL 2

The Dominican Republic manufactures an automatic carbine chambered for the US cal. .30 carbine cartridge. This weapon is called the automatic carbine Cristobal Model 2 by the Dominicans. The weapon is produced in a plant that has been run with the help of technicians from P. Beretta of Italy and Hungary; it is, therefore, not too surprising that the Model 2 has some striking similarities in outward appearance to the Beretta submachine guns. Internally, however, there are some significant differences. The Beretta Model 38-series submachine guns are blowback operated; the Model 2 Cristobal carbine is a delayed blowback.

How to Load and Fire the Cristobal Model 2

Insert a loaded magazine in the magazine well. Pull the handle on the right side of the receiver to the rear. The bolt will remain to the rear, since this weapon fires from an open bolt. Push the handle forward—it does not reciprocate with the forward and rearward movements of the bolt. If the forward trigger is pulled, the weapon will fire single shots; if the rear trigger is pulled, the weapon will produce automatic fire. To put the weapon on safe, pull the lever mounted on the left side of the receiver to the rear. The safety blocks the sear and the triggers and prevents rearward movement of the bolt. This weapon has no bolt-holding-open device, and therefore the bolt must be pulled to the rear every time a new magazine is loaded.

How to Field Strip the Cristobal Model 2

Remove the magazine by pushing the magazine catch forward. Press in the receiver cap lock and turn the receiver cap, removing it from the rear of the receiver. The recoil spring and the bolt can now be removed from the receiver. The bolt can be disassembled by removing the cross pin at its forward part and slipping off the inertia lock. No further disassembly is recommended. To reassemble the weapon, perform the above steps in reverse order.

Characteristics of the Cristobal Model 2

Caliber: Cal. .30 (US M1 carbine cartridge.)
System of operation: Delayed blowback, selective fire.
Weight, w/o magazine: 7.75 lbs.
Length, overall: 37.2 in.
Barrel length: 16.1 in.
Feed device: 25- or 30-round, detachable, staggered-row box magazine.
Sights: Front: Hooded blade.
      Rear: Notch with elevator.
Muzzle velocity: 1875 f.p.s.
Cyclic rate: 580 r.p.m.

How the Cristobal Model 2 Works

The trigger mechanism of this weapon is similar to that of the Beretta Model 38-series of weapons. The bolt consists of two main parts: the bolt body and a heavy part called the striker. These parts are joined by a two-armed inertia lever seated in the rear end of the bolt proper. The upper long arm of the movable inertia lever engages the striker, and the lower short arm of the lever projects down from the bolt. When the bolt is closed, the short arm of the inertia lever stands before a stationary shoulder firmly attached to the bottom of the receiver. When a round is fired, the gases thrust rearward on the cartridge case base, which pushes back against the face of the bolt. Before the bolt can open, however, its inertia must be overcome. When the bolt begins to move rearward, the lower arm of the inertia lever (which could be called an inertia lock) bears against the bottom shoulder of the receiver. The rearward movement of the bolt then causes rearward rotation of the inertia lever, swinging the bottom arm up and out of engagement with the receiver and forcing the upper arm back against the heavy striker. It is claimed that this system of delayed opening offers as great a resistance to the cartridge thrust as that of a bolt three to five times heavier than the one used with this weapon. During the

Caliber .30 Cristobal Model 2 Automatic Carbine.

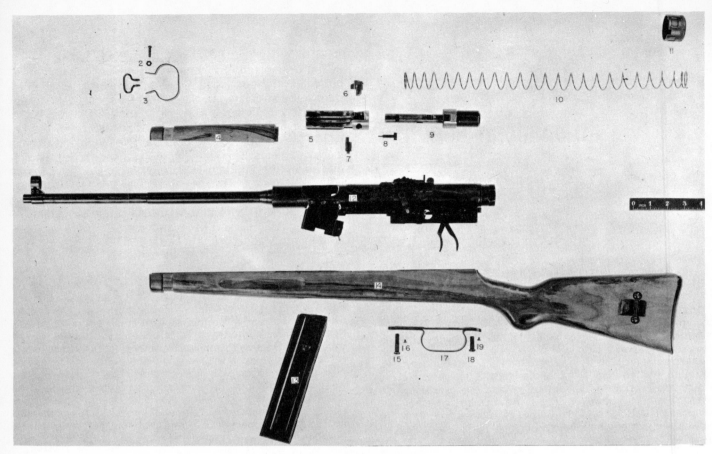

Cristobal carbine, stripped.

closing of the bolt, another lateral arm of the inertia lever slides on the receiver wall, and retains the inertia lever and the striker in a cocked position long enough for the bolt to run fully home. When the bolt is fully closed, the lateral arm of the inertia lever moves above a slot in the receiver wall, permitting forward rotation of the lever by the striker and the firing of the round. The inertia lever therefore prevents the weapon from firing before the bolt is fully closed.

DOMINICAN CARTRIDGES

The Dominican Republic also manufactures its own cal. .30 rifle and carbine cartridges. These are loaded with Berdan primers, rather than the Boxer type used in the United States and Canada.

DOMINICAN CAL. .30 AUTOMATIC CARBINE M1962

A new model of the Cristobal carbine has been developed. The Model 1962 Automatic carbine may be found either with a fixed wooden stock or a folding metal stock. Its loading, firing, field stripping and functioning are the same as those of the Cristobal Model 2. The main difference in construction, other than the folding steel stock, is the use of a perforated metal barrel jacket on the Model 1962 weapons.

Characteristics of the M1962 Automatic Carbine

Caliber: Cal. .30 (US M1 carbine cartridge).
System of operation: Delayed blowback, selective fire.

Weight, loaded:
  W/wooden stock—8.7 lbs.
  W/wooden steel stock—8.2 lbs.
Length, overall:
  W/Wooden stock—34.1 in.
  W/steel stock extended—37 in.
  W/steel stock folded—25.6 in.
Barrel length: 12.2 in.
Feed device: 30-round, detachable, staggered-row box magazine.
Sights: Front: Protected blade.
          Rear: L type
Muzzle velocity: 1870 f.p.s.

DOMINICAN 7.62mm AUTOMATIC RIFLE MODEL 1962

The Model 1962 automatic rifle combines the gas system of the US M14 rifle with the bolt mechanism of the FN light automatic rifle. This weapon was apparently made only as a prototype.

Characteristics of the M1962 Automatic Rifle

Caliber: 7.62mm NATO.
System of operation: Gas, selective fire.
Weight loaded: 10.4 lbs.
Length, overall: 42.5 in.
Barrel length: 21.3 in.
Feed device: 20-round, detachable, staggered row box magazine.
Muzzle velocity: 2700 f.p.s.

Dominican caliber .30 Automatic Carbine Model 1962 with folding metal stock.

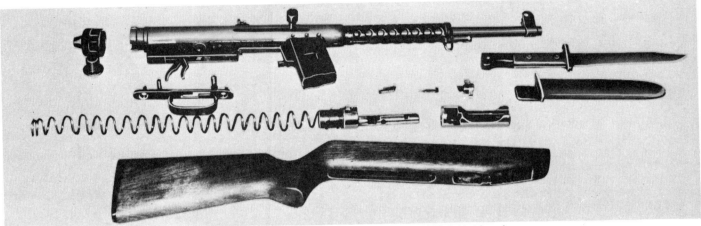

Dominican caliber .30 Automatic Carbine Model 1962, field stripped.

Dominican 7.62mm Automatic Rifle Model 1962.

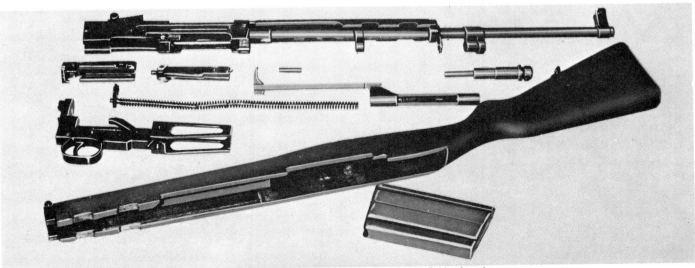

Dominican 7.62mm Automatic Rifle Model 1962, field stripped.

Finland

17

Finland uses the 9mm Lahti pistol Model L35. The 9mm M31 and Model 44 Suomi submachine gun may still be found but will probably be replaced by the 7.62mm Model 60 and 62 assault rifles.

The Finns adopted the 7.62mm Soviet M1943 "intermediate"-size cartridge and the Model 60 assault rifle and Model 62 assault rifle to replace their bolt-action 7.62mm Mosin-Nagant rifles and carbines. These weapons, like the older Finnish machine guns, are chambered for the 7.62mm Russian rimmed cartridge. The 7.62mm Lahti Saloranta light machine gun is being replaced by the Model 62 light machine gun, which is chambered for the Soviet 7.62mm M1943 cartridge.

FINNISH PISTOLS

THE FINNISH 9mm LAHTI PISTOL MODEL L-35

In 1935, the Lahti pistol was adopted; this pistol was made by VKT at Jyvaskyla, Finland. (Earlier, in 1923, Finland had adopted the 7.65mm Luger.)

The Finnish Lahti pistol was issued in several variations. The principal difference is in the lock retaining spring; the Lahti uses a yoke-type lock. Early models have a lock retaining spring, but later models do not have this part.

The Finnish Lahti is essentially the same as the Swedish Model 40 Lahti, which is described in detail under Sweden. The principal differences are as follows:

a. The Swedish weapon does not have the lock retaining spring; in this respect it is similar to the Finnish pistols of later manufacture.

b. The Swedish pistol does not have the loaded chamber indicator, which is mounted on the top of the Finnish pistol.

c. The recoil spring is assembled differently on the Swedish weapon. It is assembled on a rod plugged through the grip frame, on a projection of the grip frame that passes into the bolt cavity.

d. The grips of the Finnish pistol are marked "VKT"; those of the Swedish pistol have the trademark of Husqvarna Vapenfabrik of Husqvarna, Sweden.

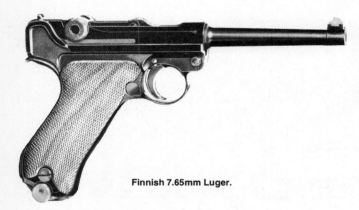

Finnish 7.65mm Luger.

The 9mm Lahti pistol (left side).

The 9mm Lahti pistol (right side).

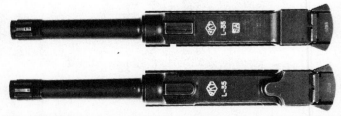

Top of Finnish Lahti of late manufacture (above) with no provision for lock retaining spring; the top of a Finnish Lahti of early manufacture (below) with lock retaining spring. Note larger bulge on top of the latter frame.

FINNISH RIFLES

Former Finnish service rifles were all based on the Russian 1891 Mosin Nagant action. The Finnish models of the Mosin Nagant vary from the Russian mainly in sights, stocks, fittings, etc. In general it can be said that the Finnish-made weapons are of higher quality manufacture than the Russian weapons.

Various Finnish service rifles chambered for the 7.62mm rimmed cartridge are the Model 91 Carbine, Model 27 Rifle, Model 28 Rifle, Model 28-30 Rifle, Model 30 Rifle and the Model 39 Rifle. The Model 62 assault rifle is now standard.

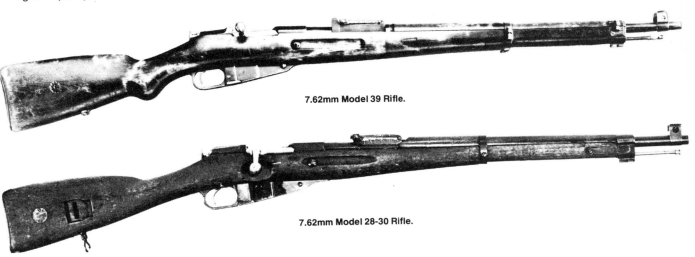

7.62mm Model 39 Rifle.

7.62mm Model 28-30 Rifle.

FINNISH 7.62mm M60 ASSAULT RIFLE

Characteristics of M60 Assault Rifle

Caliber: 7.62mm; uses copy of Soviet M34 rimless.
System of operation: Gas, selective fire.
Weight, loaded: 9 lbs.
Length, overall: 36 in.
Barrel length: 16.5 in.
Feed device: 30-round detachable, staggered box magazine.
Sights: Front: Hooded post.
      Rear: Tangent w/aperture.
Cyclic rate: 650 r.p.m.
Muzzle velocity: 2362 f.p.s.

Finnish 7.62mm M60 Assault Rifle.

FINNISH 7.62mm M62 ASSAULT RIFLE

The Model 62 Assault Rifle is a more recent version of the M60 Assault Rifle. A conventional trigger guard is used, and the plastic stock has been improved. Finland now makes the Model 62 assault rifle with a stamped steel receiver similar to that of the Soviet AKM. It can also be found with a wooden stock.

FINNISH 5.56mm M71 ASSAULT RIFLE

Characteristics of M71 Assault Rifle

Caliber: 5.56mm (.223).
System of operation: Gas, selective fire.
Weight, loaded: 9 lbs.
Length, overall: 36.25 in.
Length, barrel: 16.5 in.
Feed device: 30-round detachable, staggered box magazine.
Sights: Front: Hooded post.
      Rear: Tangent w/aperture.
Cyclic rate: n.a.
Muzzle velocity: approx. 3050 f.p.s.

Both the M60 and the M62 are products of Valmet. In recent years, a semiautomatic version (M62/S) has been marketed in the US by INTERARMS.

This weapon is a modified copy of the Soviet AK-47. Loading and firing, field stripping and functioning are the same as described under that weapon in the chapter on the USSR.

The fore-end and pistol grip of the M60 are made of plastic, and the weapon has a tubular steel stock. The rear sight is mounted on the receiver cover rather than on the receiver, as on the AK. An unusual feature of the weapon is that it does not have a full trigger guard; a post protrudes downward from the receiver and blocks the trigger from the front. This allows easy use of the weapon with heavy winter mittens. The bayonet of the M60 and its manner of mounting are different from that of the Soviet AK47.

Finnish 7.62mm M60 Assault Rifle, field stripped.

Finnish 7.62mm M62 Assault Rifle without magazine.

Finnish 7.62mm M62 Assault Rifle, bayonet fixed.

Finnish M71S in 5.56× 45mm. Note stamped steel receiver.

FINNISH SUBMACHINE GUNS

Although the Finns have used a number of submachine guns and made a modified copy of the Soviet PPS43, the story of the submachine gun in Finland is really the story of the Suomi. The Suomi was developed at Tikkakosi O/Y, Sakara, Finland.

THE FINNISH SUOMI SUBMACHINE GUN

The Suomi has been made in a number of different models and is still used extensively. In Finland the weapon is used in two models: the Model 31 and Model 44; both are chambered for the 9mm Parabellum cartridge. The Suomi was also used in Sweden where, as made in Sweden, it was known as the Model 37-39 and as imported from Finland, it was called the Model 37-39F. In Switzerland, where the gun was made by Hispano-Suiza and at the Waffenfabrik, Bern, the gun is known as the Model 43/44. In Denmark the Suomi has been made by Madsen, and the Swedish Model 37-39 version of the gun is still in limited use as the Model 44 (37).

Loading and Firing the Suomi

A loaded magazine is inserted below into the magazine housing and pressed up until it locks. The cocking handle protrudes from the rear of the weapon under the milled recoil spring cap. Grip it firmly, pull back to the rear to compress the bolt spring and cock the bolt, and allow to run forward under the influence of its own spring. Pressure on the trigger will now fire the weapon. The bolt will stay back between shots. When a continuous burst of fire is required, maintain a firm stiff pressure.

A delayed blowback version of the Suomi chambered for a rimmed 7.62mm "intermediate-sized" cartridge was made in very limited quantity.

Characteristics of Model 31 Suomi

Caliber: 9mm Parabellum.
System of operation: Blowback, selective fire.
Length overall: 34 in.
Barrel length: 12.62 in.
Weight: 11.31 lbs. w/ empty 50-round box magazine.
Feed device: 70-round drum, 25 or 50-round box magazine.
Sights: Front: Blade.
        Rear: Tangent graduated from 100-500 meters.
Cyclic rate: 800-900 r.p.m.
Muzzle velocity: Approx 1300 f.p.s.

Field Stripping the Suomi

At the rear of the receiver is a heavy milled cap. Unscrew this cap and ease out the housing recoil spring guide, and recoil spring.

Drawing back on the cocking handle will now pull the bolt back for removal from the weapon.

Finnish Suomi 9mm submachine gun.

9mm Suomi submachine gun, field stripped.

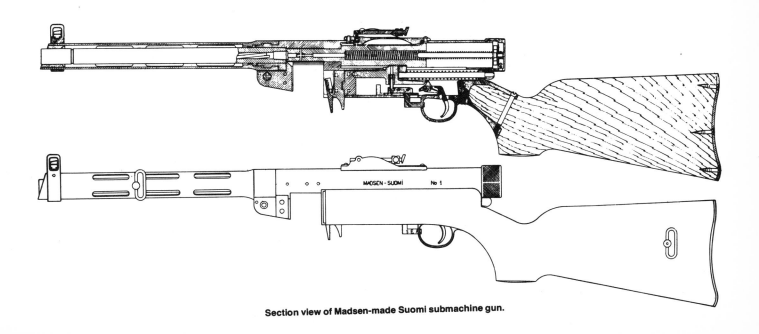

Section view of Madsen-made Suomi submachine gun.

FINNISH MACHINE GUNS

The Finns used three 7.62mm heavy machine guns. Apparently, all were Maxim types; their model designations were Model 09, Model 21 and Model 32.

The light machine gun formerly used was the Model 26 Lahti Saloranta. Although this weapon was developed for international sale and was advertised as being suitable for any service caliber, so far as known it has only been made in 7.62mm caliber for the Finnish Army and in 7.92mm for the Chinese prior to World War II.

FINNISH LAHTI SALORANTA LIGHT MACHINE GUN

The Model 26 was one of the first of the post-World War I "true" light machine gun types. It was considered a noteworthy gun at its time of development and, although somewhat lacking in adaptability as compared with the post-World War II guns, is still a basically sound weapon.

Characteristics of the Model 26 Lahti Saloranta

Caliber: 7.62mm rimmed.
System of operation: Recoil, selective fire.
Weight, w/loaded 20-rd. magazine: 23 lbs.
Length, overall: 46.5 in.
Feed device: 20-round box, or 75-round drum.
Cyclic rate: 500 r.p.m.
Muzzle velocity: 2625 f.p.s.

How to Load and Fire the Model 26 Lahti Saloranta

Pull the operating handle to the rear, insert a loaded magazine in the magazine port (when using the box magazine) and set the selector on the type of fire desired. Squeeze the trigger and the weapon will fire. The Model 26 fires from an open bolt.

Finnish 7.62mm Model 32 Heavy Machine Gun.

The 7.62mm Model 26 Lahti Saloranta Light Machine Gun.

To attach the 75-round drum magazine to the gun, remove the magazine support and push the magazine up into position until the holding latch clicks. To remove the barrel, turn the lever 180 degrees. This releases the catch holding the butt to the receiver. Lift the receiver cover and the barrel, barrel extension, and bolt can be lifted out as a unit. Usually the complete unit is replaced.

How the Model 26 Lahti Saloranta Works

Two distinct feed systems are available with this gun. A spring loaded clip which holds 25 cartridges may be used. The alternate is a flat drum magazine mounted below the gun with a capacity of 75 rounds.

Maximum rate of fire is normally set at 500 per minute.

In the Lahti the bolt is automatically held to the rear after the trigger has been released. The effect of this is to keep the action open to prevent a round in the chamber cooking off. This also, of course, permits air circulation through the barrel for cooling purposes.

The barrel is removed by turning the dismounting lever 180 degrees to release the catch, which holds the buttstock to the receiver. The receiver cover is lifted, and the barrel extension together with the barrel and bolt are then pulled out to the rear in a manner not unlike that of the Swiss Furrer.

When using the flat 75-shot drum, the magazine support is removed and the drum is pushed up until its holding catch snaps

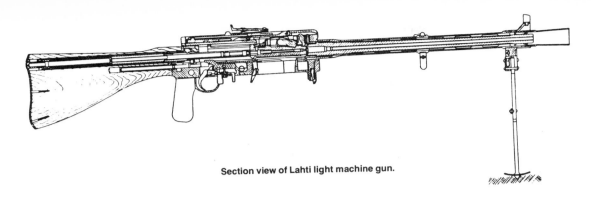

Section view of Lahti light machine gun.

into place. The operating handle on the right is pulled all the way to the rear. The springloaded sear rises to catch the notch in the bottom of the bolt and holds it back. The arm is now cocked and ready to fire. Setting the selector from safe to automatic fire prepares it for action.

As the trigger is pulled, the sear is freed from the bolt. The bolt is driven ahead by the compressed operating spring. A feed rib machined into the top of the bolt pushes the first round out of the lips of the magazine and toward the chamber.

The bolt seats behind the cartridge when about one-half inch from final position, and the claw extractor snaps over the case.

Simultaneously the bolt locking piece is cammed downwards into its locking notch in the bolt. This releases the holding catch, which has been preventing the barrel and extension from moving forward.

The locked barrel with its extension and the bolt start the final movement ahead. When it nears complete battery position, a pivoting pin in the bolt body, which has been blocking the firing pin, hits a ramp in the receiver and is pushed up out of the way to permit the firing pin to be released and go forward to fire the cartridge.

Again rather on the Furrer principle, we find the timing such that the recoil starts before the forward moving locked parts strike the receiver. This buffing action eases the recoil and makes for smoother functioning.

During the recoil stroke, the parts are locked together for about one-half inch of travel. At that point, the stud on the bolt lock engages a cam in the receiver to lift it out of its locking recess there.

The bolt is allowed a rearward motion of a few thousandths of an inch before complete unlocking sets in, thereby permitting the extractor to loosen the cartridge before the gas pressure affects it directly. (This allows the extractor to break the gas seal.

The cartridge is thereby entirely loosened in primary extraction at this point.)

As the gun fires, energy is transferred from the recoiling barrel to the bolt through an accelerator, which pivots to speed the bolt to the rear while the extractor withdraws the empty cartridge case until its rim hits the solid ejector and is knocked out the ejection port to the right.

The firing pin is withdrawn during the initial recoil movement. The firing pin sear in the top of the bolt drops in front of a circular projection over the body of the pin. As the bolt is released from locking, the barrel and barrel extension are hald rearward by the holding catch. The compressed operating spring is ready at the end of the stroke to return the members if the trigger is on full automatic.

FINNISH 7.62mm M60 LIGHT MACHINE GUN

The M60 is used on a bipod or on a light weight tripod. The weapon has a prong-type flash suppressor and a tubular steel stock. Like the M60 Assault rifle, it has a bar in front of the trigger in lieu of a conventional trigger guard. The ammunition container is hung on the right side of the receiver, allowing easy movement of the gun with ammunition by one man.

Characteristics of Model 60

Caliber: 7.62mm uses copy of Soviet M43 rimless.
System of operation: Gas.
Weight: 16.8 lbs.
Feed device: 100-round non-disintegrating metallic link belt.
Sights: Front—Hooded post.
　　　　Rear— Tangent leaf.
Cyclic rate: 1050 r.p.m.

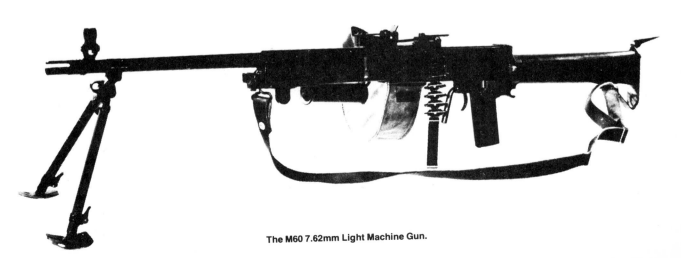

The M60 7.62mm Light Machine Gun.

18 France

The 9mm Parabellum M1950 pistol is the standard service pistol. The standard service rifle is the 7.5mm M1949/56; M1949 rifles are also in service. The 9mm M1949 (MAT 49) submachine gun is standard, as is the 7.5mm general purpose machine gun, Model 52 (AAT52). The 7.5mm M1924 M29 light machine gun (called an automatic rifle by the French) is still used extensively, as is the US caliber .50 Browning M2 HB machine gun. As this book went to press, the French have announced the purchase of an initial 236,000 MAS 5.56mm assault rifles.

FRENCH SERVICE PISTOLS

The French Army during World War I was equipped with the 8mm Model 1892 revolver and the 11mm Model 1873 revolver. During this war, extensive purchases were made of 7.65mm (.32 ACP) Star and Ruby automatics from Spain. Numbers of the above weapons were still in service during World War II.

Between the wars, the French developed two automatic pistols that were quite similar, the 7.65mm M1935A and M1935S. These pistols were developed for the 7.65mm long cartridge which is much like the caliber .30 cartridge developed for the US Pedersen device of 1918.

The M1935 pistols are based on the patents of C. Petter of SACM and are essentially modifications of Browning recoil-operated pistols. These pistols were used throughout World War II, supplemented by earlier weapons and the US caliber .45 M1911 and M1911A1 pistols, plus some British pistols. There were sufficient M1935 pistols in stock for them to be used extensively by the French Government Forces during the 1945-54 fighting in Indo-China. They are not to be found in quantity with French forces at present.

French 7.65 Long M1935A Pistol.

THE FRENCH M1935 PISTOLS

The Model 1935A and 1935S pistols are quite similar in design and differ principally in method of locking. The Model 1935A has two lugs on the upper surface of the barrel that lock into mating grooves in the slide in a fashion similar to the US Colt M1911A1. The M1935S, on the other hand, has a step machined on the top of the barrel at a point slightly ahead of the chamber, this step locks into a cut-out section in the slide.

They were made at Chatellerault (MAC), Saint Etienne (MAS), Tulle (MAT), Société Alsacienne de Construction Mecanique (SACM), and Société d'Applications Générales Electriqueset Méchaniques (SAGEM).

Characteristics of the Model 1935 Pistols

	Model 1935A	Model 1935S
Caliber:	7.65mm long.	7.65mm long.
System of operation:	Recoil operated, semiautomatic.	
Length overall:	7.6 in.	7.4 in.
Barrel length:	4.3 in.	4.1 in.
Weight:	1.62 lbs.	1.75 lbs.
Feed device:	8-round, detachable, in-line box magazine.	
Sights: Front:	Blade.	Blade.
Rear:	Rounded notch.	Rounded notch.
Muzzle velocity:	1132 f.p.s.	1132 f.p.s.

French 7.65mm Long M1935A Pistol, field stripped.

Loading, firing, and field stripping of these pistols is essentially the same as that of the US caliber .45 M1911A1 or the 9mm M1950. These pistols have packaged hammer, main spring and sear assemblies that can be removed after the slide is dismounted from the receiver.

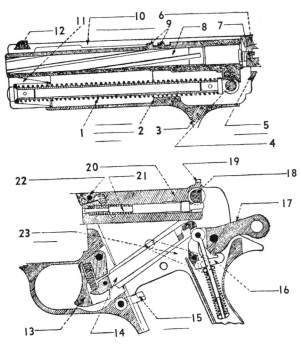

French Pistolet 1935A (Drawing from French Manual).

1. Recoil spring.
2. Receiver stop.
3. Receiver.
4. Barrel pivot pin.
5. Barrel stop.
6. Loading indicator.
7. Face of breechblock.
8. Barrel.
9. Dual barrel locking lugs.
10. Slide-breechblock unit.
11. Front of slide.
12. Front sight.
13. Trigger.
14. Trigger bar.
15. Magazine catch.
16. Sear.
17. Hammer.
18. Manual Safety.
19. Rear sight.
20. Breech section of slide.
21. Firing pin.
22. Loading indicator.
23. Magazine safety.

French 7.65mm Long M1935S Pistol.

FRENCH 9mm PISTOL M1950

The M1950 pistol is similar in most respects to the US cal. .45 Colt automatic. It is a much better made and more lethal weapon than any of the earlier French pistols.

Characteristics of the M1950 Pistol

Caliber: 9mm Parabellum.
System of operation: Recoil, semi-automatic fire only.
Weight: 1.8 lbs.

Length, overall: 7.6 in.
Barrel length: 4.4 in.
Feed device: 9-round, single-column, detachable box magazine.
Sights: Front: Tapered post.
      Rear: U-notch; the top of the slide has a matted ramp.
Muzzle velocity: 1156 f.p.s.

M1950 field stripped.

How to Load and Fire the M1950 Pistol

The M1950 pistol is loaded and fired the same as the US M1911A1 cal. .45 automatic pistol. However, it cannot be fired with the magazine removed. A loaded-chamber indicator is mounted in the slide. The safety catch is mounted on the left rear of the slide.

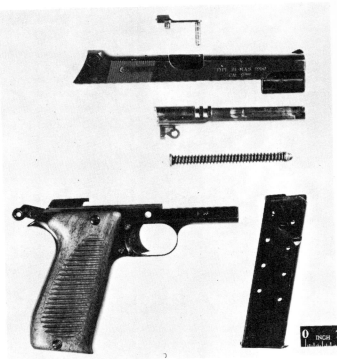

French 9mm M1950 Pistol.

How to Field Strip the M1950 Pistol

Field stripping is the same as for the US .45, with the following exceptions:

SLIDE

CAM LUG

SLIDE STOP

SEAT LUG BARREL SEAT

BARREL

SLIDE STOP PIN

EJECTOR

DRIVING SPRING GUIDE DRIVING SPRING

RECEIVER

MAGAZINE →

Field stripped view of P15S.

French 9mm MAB P15S Pistol as produced by Manufacture d'Armes Automatiques, Bayonne.

There is no barrel bushing and recoil spring plug; the recoil spring is dismounted after the slide has been removed from the receiver.

The hammer, its spring and lever and the sear assembly are contained in a housing that can be lifted out as one piece when the slide is removed.

How the M1950 Pistol Works

The functioning of the M1950 pistol is essentially the same as that of the US service automatic.

Special Note on the M1950 Pistol

The M1950 pistol incorporates most features of the M1935 French pistols and has a few changes borrowed elsewhere. The safety on the slide was used in the M1935A and M1935S; it blocks the hammer from the firing pin. The internal mounting of the recoil spring is used on practically all the Browning and modified Browning-design pistols in service today except the US cal. .45 and those pistols that are direct copies of the US cal. .45.

PISTOLS 9mm MAB P-15, P-8 and F 1

This family of pistols is used by the French Armed Forces and has been sold commercially around the world. The P-15 and P-8 pistols, with 15- and 8-round magazines respectively, have a standard blued exterior, while the PAP Mle F 1 has a parkerized finish and special sights suitable for competition shooting.

Characteristics of the Model F 1

Caliber: 9mm Parabellum.
System of operation: Recoil operated, semi-automatic.
Length overall: 9.64 in.
Barrel length: 6 in.
Weight: 2.43 lbs.
Feed device: 15-round staggered row, detachable box magazine.
Sights: Front: Blade.
    Rear: Notch adjustable for elevation and windage.
Muzzle velocity: Approx. 1200 f.p.s.

French 9mm Parabellum Model F 1.

French-made Walther PPK, caliber .380. This pistol was made by Manhurin in France before Walther postwar resumption of manufacture. It was not used as a French service pistol and is no longer being made in France. It is currently manufactured in Germany.

How to Load and Fire the Model F 1 Pistol

The Model F 1 is loaded and fired in the same manner as the US caliber .45 M1911A1 pistol. The pistol has a magazine safety and cannot be fired with the magazine removed.

How to Field Strip the Model F 1 Pistol

The Model F 1 is field stripped in a manner similar to that of the French 9mm M1950 except that it has a barrel bushing. The barrel bushing is removed by pressing in on the barrel bushing catch, a spring loaded detent mounted on the under side of the muzzle end of the slide, and unscrewing the barrel bushing.

How the Model F 1 Works

The F 1 has a rotating barrel type locking mechanism. The barrel has lugs mounted on its top and bottom that engage a cut-out section in the top of the slide and a cam track cut in a locking piece mounted in the receiver. This piece is held in place in the receiver by the pin portion of the slide stop in a manner reminiscent of the Mexican Obregon pistol; the recoil spring guide rod and recoil spring are mounted on the front portion of the piece. Rearward movement of the slide on firing causes the bottom lug to rotate in the camway of the receiver locking piece, thereby rotating the locking lug on top of the barrel out of its locked position allowing the slide to continue its travel to the rear with the empty cartridge case gripped in the slide mounted extractor. The ejector, mounted on the right side of the receiver, engages the base of the case and forces the case out of the ejection port. At the same time, the slide is forcing the externally mounted hammer to the rear causing the hammer to engage the sear and remain to the rear in cocked position. Rearward movement of the slide has compressed the recoil spring, and the slide reaches its limit of rearward travel; the spring forces the slide forward. The slide, during its forward movement, strips a cartridge from the magazine and feeds it into the chamber. The cam slot in the receiver locking piece begins camming the barrel around so that the locking lug on the barrel is engaged in its recess in the slide when the slide is in its forward position. Pressure on the trigger will fire the pistol again and the whole process is repeated for each separate pull of the trigger until the magazine is empty.

FRENCH BOLT-ACTION RIFLES AND CARBINES

The French developed the first modern small-bore magazine rifle—the Lebel—in 1886. In 1890 they dropped the tubular magazine of the Lebel for the Mannlicher-type magazine of the Berthier rifles and carbines. The Lebel and the Mannlicher Berthier rifles and carbines were the standard service weapons of the French Army until the thirties. An interesting fact is that, during the early part of World War I, France purchased considerable quantities of the single-shot rolling block Remington rifle, chambered for the 8mm Lebel cartridge. Remington also produced 8mm M1907/15 rifles for the French during World War I.

The French realized that the 8mm Lebel cartridge had several outstanding shortcomings—for example, a peculiar shape and rim, which made feeding in automatic weapons difficult—and soon after World War I, developed a new 7.5mm rimless cartridge, the Model 1924. The Model 1924 was quite similar to the 7.92mm Mauser; so similar, in fact, that a number of accidents occurred when people used 7.92mm cartridges in 7.5mm weapons. (The Model 1924 light machine gun was in limited service at this time.) In 1929, the French shortened the case of the 7.5mm cartridge and produced the M1929 cartridge, which is still the principal rifle cartridge of the French Army. A number of prototype bolt-action rifles were made for this cartridge, the principal rifle being the M1932. A modification of this rifle, the Model 1936, was adopted and is still used extensively in France and former French territories. Several modifications of this rifle—the M1936 CR39 and M1936 M51—also exist. At approximately the same time, France, having huge stocks of World War I materiel on hand, began to modify and convert some of the older bolt-action arms on hand. Many of the 8mm Model

1907/15 rifles were altered and rebarreled with 7.5mm barrels. A modification of the 8mm Lebel rifle M1886 M93 was also produced—the 8mm M1886 M93 R35—during this period.

During World War II, the Free French Army was provided with over 69,000 US caliber .30 M1903 and M1917 bolt-action rifles and Browning Automatic rifles.

FRENCH RIFLES AND CARBINES OF PRE-WORLD WAR II DESIGN

The older French rifles are still commonly encountered in Middle Eastern areas and among collectors in the United States. Therefore, coverage on them has been expanded to include a table of characteristics of the various models, and a few words have been added to explain the major differences among the various categories of these weapons. See table.

BOLT-ACTION CATEGORIES

Basically, the bolt-action French rifles and carbines can be broken down into three categories: (1) the M1886; (2) the M1890; and (3) the M1932 and its production model, the M1936.

The M1886 (Commonly Called the Lebel)

This rifle was introduced in 1886 to use a new 8mm cartridge loaded with the then revolutionary smokeless powder of Paul Vielle.

FRENCH RIFLES AND CARBINES OF PRE-WORLD WAR II DESIGN

Weapon	System of Operation	Overall Length	Barrel Length	Feed Device	Sights	Muzzle Velocity	Weight
Rifle: 8mm M1886 M93	Manually operated 2-piece bolt	51.3 in.	31.4 in.	8-rd tubular magazine	Front: Notched blade Rear: Leaf	2380 f.p.s.	9.35 lb.
Rifle: 8mm M1886 M93R35	Manually operated 2-piece bolt	37.64 in.	17.7 in.	3-rd tubular magazine	Front: Notched blade Rear: Leaf	2080 f.p.s.	7.84 lb.
Carbine: 8mm M1890	Manually operated 2-piece bolt	37.2 in.	17.7 in.	3-rd Mannlicher-type, integral, in-line magazine	Front: Blade Rear: Leaf	2080 f.p.s.	6.83 lb.
Mousquetoon 8mm M1892.	Manually operated 2-piece bolt	37.2 in.	17.7 in.	3-rd Mannlicher-type, integral, in-line magazine	Front: Blade Rear: Leaf	2080 f.p.s.	6.8 lb.
Rifle: 8mm M1902 "Indo-China Model"	Manually operated 2-piece bolt	38.6 in.	24.8 in.	3-rd Mannlicher-type, integral, in-line magazine	Front: Blade Rear: Leaf	2180 f.p.s.	7.9 lb.
Rifle: 8mm M1907 "Colonial Model"	Manually operated 2-piece bolt	52 in.	31.4 in.	3-rd Mannlicher-type, integral, in-line magazine	Front: Blade Rear: Leaf	2380 f.p.s.	8.6 lb.
Rifle: 8mm M1907/15	Manually operated 2-piece bolt	51.42 in.	31.4 in.	3-rd Mannlicher-type, integral, in-line magazine	Front: Notched blade Rear: Leaf	2380 f.p.s.	8.38 lb.
Rifle: 8mm M1916	Manually operated 2-piece bolt	51.42 in.	31.4 in.	5-rd Mannlicher-type, integral, in-line magazine	Front: Notched blade Rear: Leaf	2380 f.p.s.	9.25 lb.
Carbine: 8mm M1916	Manually operated 2-piece bolt	37.2 in.	17.7 in.	5-rd Mannlicher-type, integral, in-line magazine	Front: Blade Rear: Leaf	2080 f.p.s.	.7.17 lb.
Rifle: 7.5mm M1907/15 M34	Manually operated 2-piece bolt	43.2 in.	22.8 in.	5-rd integral, staggered-row, box magazine	Front: Blade Rear: Leaf	2700 f.p.s.	7.85 lb.
Rifle: 7.5mm M1932	Prototype of M1936, made in limited quantities						
Rifle: 7.5mm M1936	Manually operated 1-piece bolt	40.13 in.	22.6 in.	5-rd integral, staggered row, box magazine	Front: Barley-corn w/guards Rear: Ramp w/aperture	2700 f.p.s.	8.29 lb.
Rifle: 7.5mm M1936 CR39	Manually operated 1-piece bolt	Stock extended 34.9 in. Stock folded: 24.3 in.	17.7 in.	5-rd integral, staggered-row, box magazine	Front: Barley-corn w/guards Rear: Ramp w/aperture	2700 f.p.s.	8 lb. (approx.)

The Lebel bolt is quite similar to that of the 11mm Gras rifle Model 1874, and the feed mechanism is similar to the 11mm Model 1878 Kropatschek rifle used by the French Navy.

The M1886 is the parent of all modern small-bore military rifles. It was slightly modified in 1893 by strengthening the receiver, boring a gas-escape hole in the bolt, changing the rear sight mounting and leaf, and adding a stacking hook to the upper band. It was still in limited service in World War II, while numerous modified rifles were built around many spare parts of the old 86/93.

This is a turn-bolt action rifle of conventional design. The magazine is a tube in the forestock below the barrel, being loaded through the open action. The bolt is a two-piece design with a long detachable bolt head, which carries the dual locking lugs.

To remove the bolt, the action must be opened. A holding screw is then removed from a projecting strap on top of the bolt body. The bolt body can then be pulled out of the receiver, leaving the bolt head in the boltway ahead of the receiver bridge.

The head can then be picked out of the boltway. Primary extraction is given as the bolt handle is lifted by the projecting bolt strap working against a cam face in a long overhang on the top of receiver.

As the bolt is withdrawn, it operates an elevator, which raises a cartridge in its trough and lines it up with the bolt. A hook on the bottom of the elevator trough blocks the cartridge in the magazine tube at this point. When the cartridge is chambered, the bolt motion lowers the elevator trough, permitting the magazine spring in the tube to force the next cartridge into the trough ready to be raised on the following rearward bolt stroke.

Modification—1886 M93 R35

This carbine modification was issued in 1935. It is merely a shorter form with different furniture and smaller magazine. Model number is on receiver.

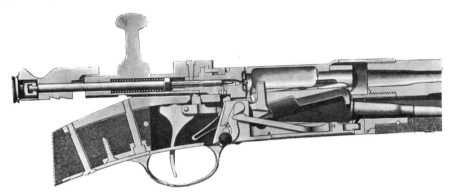

Section of French 1886 (Lebel). Tube repeating rifle showing operating system.

French 8mm Rifle Model 1886 M93.

MANNLICHER BERTHIER CARBINES AND MODIFICATIONS

French 8mm Carbine M1892

This is one of the first Berthier arms. Bolt is two-piece type with removable head as in the earlier Lebel tube loader (1886). It is modified, however, to feed from a Mannlicher-type fixed box magazine.

Cartridges for these arms come in Mannlicher-style clips, which are inserted in the receiver with the cartridges to form a part of the magazine action. Clips fall out bottom of receiver when last cartridge has been chambered. The three-round models use the Model 1892 clip; five round models use the Model 1916 clip.

All the Mannlicher Berthier carbines (1890, 1892, 1916) were modified in 1927. Modification consisted of removing cleaning rods and adding a stacking swivel.

French 8mm Fusil, M1907/15/34 and M1916

The French drawing (next page) shows details of Fusil (Rifle) 1916. The hinged magazine plate is opened to show how clip is dropped out of magazine when empty. Bolt has been thrust forward far enough to strip cartridge out of clip and guide bullet into chamber. This is a turn bolt rifle. This design uses the Mannlicher-clip loading system.

The 07/15 design was modified in 1934 to handle the 7.5mm rimless cartridge developed in 1929 for light machine guns. The changeover included replacing the old Mannlicher type magazine with a standard 5-shot Mauser type. Cartridges may be loaded into the magazine at any time, staggering from side to side in regular Mauser fashion. The detachable bolt head locks with two heavy lugs into a solid receiver section behind the cartridge head. The Mauser magazine permitting the use of cartridges without clips is an important feature.

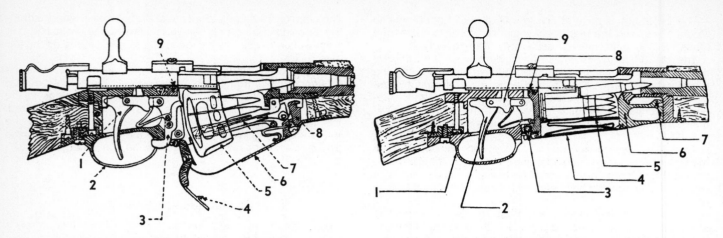

French Fusil 1916 (Drawing from French Manual).

French Fusil 07/15 M34 (Drawing from French Manual).

1. Trigger	6. Magazine bottom
2. Trigger guard	7. Follower
3. Clip catch	8. Follower support
4. Magazine plate	9. Ejector
5. Mannlicher-type clip	

1. Trigger guard	5. Follower
2. Trigger	6. and 7. Forward magazine section
3. Magazine plate lock	8. Ejector
4. Bottom plate	9. Sear

Typical 8mm M1892 Carbine as modified in 1927; 3-round capacity.

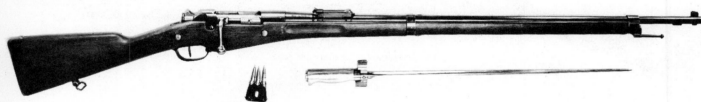

8mm Fusil 1907/15.

8mm Rifle Model 1916, 5-round capacity.

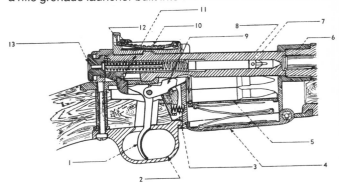

THE FRENCH MAS 1936 RIFLE

The M1936 is a 7.5mm caliber rifle with modified Mauser magazine. Action is shown ready for trigger pull. Note that dual locking lugs are engaged in recesses within the receiver bridge directly above the trigger. Placing the lugs this far back from the chamber permits a short bolt stroke but results in a rifle locking design weaker than the conventional Mauser front-lug type.

This turn bolt rifle has a modified Mauser magazine with quick removable bottom plate. Primary extraction is by action of bolt handle extension working against a cam in the receiver bridge.

The breech locking system of this rifle is somewhat different than the Mauser. Dual lugs at the rear of the bolt body turn into seatings in the receiver bridge as the handle is turned down. No manual safety.

Locking lugs are on rear of bolt cylinder near handle knob; they lock into receiver bridge to rear of magazine. Note cam shape of left face of receiver bridge, which affords leverage for primary extraction cam on modified Mauser system. Rifle is loaded with Mauser-type charger clip. Note cuts in receiver for finger pressing cartridges into magazine. This is necessary because of large bolt diameter.

The 7.5mm M1936 CR39 is the same as the Model 1936 but has a folding aluminum buttstock.

A post-war version of the M1936, the 7.5mm M1936 M51, has a rifle grenade launcher built into the muzzle end of the barrel.

French Fusil 1936 (Drawing from French Manual).

1. Trigger
2. Triggerguard
3. Sear spring
4. Magazine bottom plate
5. Magazine follower
6. Barrel
7. Bolt
8. Firing pin
9. Ejector & Bolt stop unit
10. Receiver bridge
11. Sear
12. Peep sight
13. Cocking piece head.

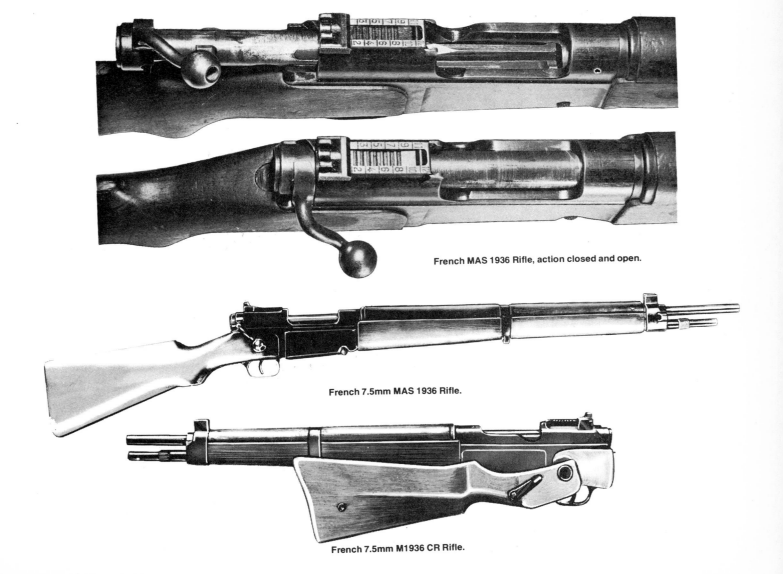

French MAS 1936 Rifle, action closed and open.

French 7.5mm MAS 1936 Rifle.

French 7.5mm M1936 CR Rifle.

THE 7.5mm MODEL F 1 RIFLE

The *Fusil a Repetition Modele F 1* (Repeating rifle Model F1) is produced at MAS (St. Etienne) exclusively for the French Army around a modification of the now obsolete MAS 1936 Rifle. It is manufactured in three variations: (1) *Tireur d'Elite* (sniper); (2) *Tir Sportif* (target); and (3) *Grande Chasse* (hunting). The first has a 3.8-power telescopic sight and a non-adjustable 100-meter open sight (with luminous dots for use under poor lighting conditions). The second has metallic type target sights. The hunting version has an APX Model 804 telescopic sight. Only the sniper's rifle is equipped with a bipod. All versions have a muzzle brake/flash suppressor. The length of the butt stock can be adjusted by adding or removing spacers between the end of the stock and the rubber recoil pad.

Characteristics of the 7.5mm Model F 1 Rifle

Caliber: 7.5mm
System of operation: Manually operated bolt action
Length overall: 44.8 in.
Barrel length: 22.8 in.
Feed device: 10-round, staggered row, detachable box magazine.
Sights: Front: Tunnel type.
       Rear: Telescope or micrometer.
Weight: 9.9 lbs.
Muzzle velocity: Approx. 2700 f.p.s.

This rifle has been made in 7.62mm NATO as well as 7.5mm French. The French claim that this rifle will consistently group 10 rounds into a circle smaller than 7.8 inches at 200 meters when used with good ammunition.

SAFETY

MAGAZINE RELEASE

Comparison of MAS 1936 and FR-F1 Rifle receivers. Note the new safety and magazine release on the FR–F1 Sniper's Rifle.

Left side view of FR–F1 Sniper's Rifle.

FRENCH SEMIAUTOMATIC RIFLES

France started working on semiautomatic rifles with the Clair brothers developments circa 1888. A total of 15 different prototype rifles were made between 1897 and 1911. These weapons were developed by a number of French military establishments in great secrecy and were developed for a number of different cartridges; 6mm, 6.5mm, 7mm, 8mm, and 8.5mm. Gas-operated, short-recoil and long-recoil types were represented among these weapons. Seven of the weapons were given extensive test.

In 1910, the STA8 rifle—also known as the A6 rifle—developed by Monsieur Meunier at the Technical Section of Artillery (Section Technique De L'Artillerie) was adopted. Manufacture was started in 1913, but was stopped by World War I. The STA8 rifle was long-recoil operated and chambered for a 7mm rimless cartridge.

The adoption of the automatic rifle Model 1915 CSRG slowed development of semiautomatic rifles, but requirements from the front soon resulted in the adoption of the 8mm M1917 rifle.

THE FRENCH MODEL 1917 and MODEL 1918 SEMIAUTOMATIC RIFLES

The 8mm Model 1917 rifle is also known as the R.S.C. for Ribeyrolle, Sutter and Chauchat who worked on the design. Although the rifle is commonly known as the Saint Etienne in the United States, it is probable that much of the development work was done at Puteaux. The 1917 was adopted in May 1916, and mass production began in April 1917. Components were made at Manufacture d'armes de Paris, Chatellerault, Tulle and Saint Etienne. The weapons were assembled at Saint Etienne; a total of 86,333 were made.

Service use indicated many deficiencies, and broken parts were numerous. There were also complaints about the excessive weight. As a result, the 8mm Model 1918 rifle was developed. A modification of the 1917, it did not get into active service during World War I, since manufacture did not begin until November 1918.

Characteristics of the Model 1917 and Model 1918 Rifles

	Model 1917	Model 1918
Caliber:	8mm Lebel.	8mm Lebel.
System of operation:	Gas, semiautomatic.	Gas, semiautomatic.
Overall length:	52.4 in.	44.1 in.
Barrel length:	31.4 in.	23.1 in.
Weight:	11.6 lbs.	10.5 lbs.
Feed device:	5-round, non-detachable, in-line box magazine.	
Sights: Front:	Blade.	Blade.
Rear:	Leaf.	Leaf.
Muzzle velocity:	2380 f.p.s.	2180 f.p.s.

Operation of 8mm Semiautomatic Rifles M1917 and M1918

The operation of both of these rifles is basically the same. The piston is attached to an operating rod, which is attached in turn to the bolt carrier. The bolt, which has an interrupted thread-type head (multiple) lug, rides in spiral splines in the bolt carrier (the bolt carrier could also be considered the bolt body of a two-piece bolt).

Five-round Mannlicher type clips are used to feed these weapons. The clips remain in the action (as with the US M1 rifles) and are necessary for semiautomatic fire. The Model 1917 uses a special clip, and the Model 1918 uses the standard French 8mm Model 1916 clip, which is also used with the Model 1916 Berthier bolt-action rifles.

In 1935, both of these rifles were converted into manually-operated straight-pull rifles by the welding of a block under the gas port. Their model designations in this form are Rifle Model 1917-1935 and Modele 1918-1935. Both rifles are obsolete.

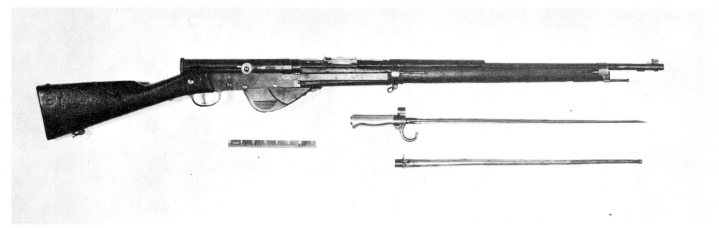

French 8mm Semiautomatic Rifle Model 1917.

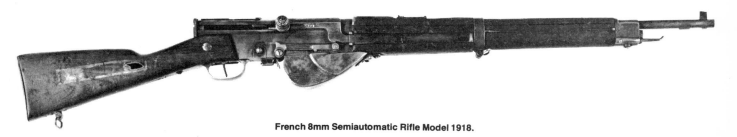

French 8mm Semiautomatic Rifle Model 1918.

THE MODEL 1949 AND 1949/56 RIFLES

Little real effort seems to have been expended in France between the wars on semiautomatic rifles. In 1944, a semiautomatic rifle was produced at Saint Etienne—the 7.5mm MAS44. This rifle was further developed into the Model 1949. The current standard rifle, the Model 1949/56, is a modification of the Model 1949.

These gas-operated weapons show considerable designing skill. They are relatively simple in operation and are very easy to strip and clean. They use a tilting bolt system and have no moving parts in the gas system. The forward part of the barrel is used as a grenade launcher on both models, and both have built-in grenade launcher sights. On the M1949, the grenade launcher sight is on the left front side of the fore-end; on the M1949/56, the grenade launcher sights are on top of the barrel, to the rear of the front rifle sight. Both of these weapons have two-piece stocks, as did the M1936 series of weapons. The M1949 does not use a bayonet, but the M1949/56 does.

Characteristics of M1949 and M1949/56

	M1949	M1949/56
Caliber:	7.5mm French M1929 cartridge, for both models.	
System of operation:	Gas, semiautomatic fire only, for both models	
Weight:	10.4 lbs.	8.6 lb. w/o magazine.
Length, overall:	43.3 in.	43.4 in.
Barrel length:	22.8 in.	20.7 in.
Feed device:	10-round, detachable, staggered-row box magazine, normally loaded with 5-round chargers: for both models.	
Sights: Front:	Blade w/protecting ears, for both models.	
Rear:	Ramp w/aperture, for both models.	
Muzzle velocity:	2705 f.p.s.	2700 f.p.s.

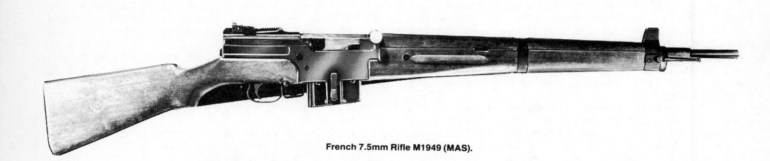

French 7.5mm Rifle M1949 (MAS).

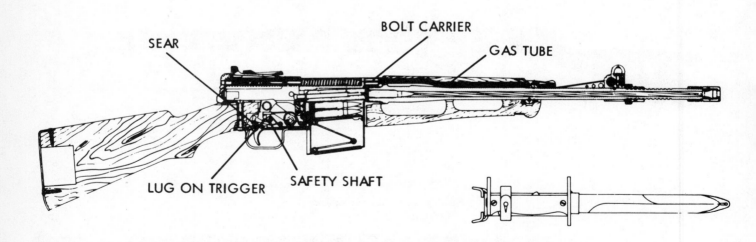

Sectioned view of M49/56.

How to Load and Fire the M1949-Series Rifles

The weapon can be loaded by pulling the operating handle to the rear and filling the magazine, using chargers (clips) in a manner similar to that used with the US M1903 rifle, or the magazine may be removed (note that the magazine catch is a part of the magazine, not of the weapon) and then filled by hand. If the bolt is to the rear, it will require a short rearward jerk to release the bolt latch—the bolt remains open after the last round is fired—allowing the bolt to go forward and chamber a cartridge. If the bolt is forward, it will have to be pulled to the rear and released. The safety is located at the right front side of the trigger-guard. Upon firing the last shot, the bolt will remain open.

How to Field Strip the M1949-Series Rifles

Remove magazine by depressing magazine catch on right side of magazine and pulling magazine down and out of the receiver. Release receiver cover by depressing the latch, located at the rear of the receiver; push the cover forward slightly and lift it from its grooves in the receiver. **CAUTION:** The bolt must be in the forward position before attempting to remove the receiver cover. (When the bolt is to the rear, the recoil spring, which is housed in the receiver cover, is compressed.) The bolt and bolt carrier can now be lifted out of the receiver. The trigger group can be removed by removal of one screw. No further disassembly is recommended.

To reassemble the weapon perform the above steps in reverse.

How the M1949-Series Rifles Work

When a cartridge is fired, propellent gas is tapped off through the gas port in the barrel. This gas blows back through the gas tube directly into a hole in the top face of the bolt carrier. The gas tube protrudes a small distance, so that a portion of it actually enters the bolt carrier. The bolt carrier moves to the rear, and after a slight "dwell" time the bolt is cammed up and out of its locked position in the bottom of the receiver and starts to travel back with the bolt carrier. The ejector is a pin type that protrudes from the face of the bolt like that of the US M1 rifle; it ejects the spent case when the case mouth clears the face of the barrel. The trigger mechanism is quite similar to that of the US M1 rifle and operates in a similar fashion. The bolt and bolt carrier compress the recoil spring, which decompresses at the end of their travel and returns the bolt and carrier to the battery position. On the return of the bolt and its carrier, the bolt strips the top cartridge from the magazine and feeds it into the chamber. The bolt carrier cams the lugs of the bolt down, and the rear end of the bolt is brought down into engagement with the locking bar in the bottom of the receiver. The weapon is ready to fire again.

Special Note on the M1949-Series Rifles

The gas system of the M1949-series rifles is similar to that of the Swedish Ljungman Model 42. Its tilting bolt (or propped breech, as it is sometimes called) has been used in a great number of systems, e.g., the Tokarev, the FN, the Ljungman, and so on. These weapons are an illustration of the fact that a good modern weapon can be produced by selectively choosing from proven past designs and modifying them to suit the need.

Both of these weapons have mounting grooves, cut on the left side of the receivers, for the mounting of telescopic sights.

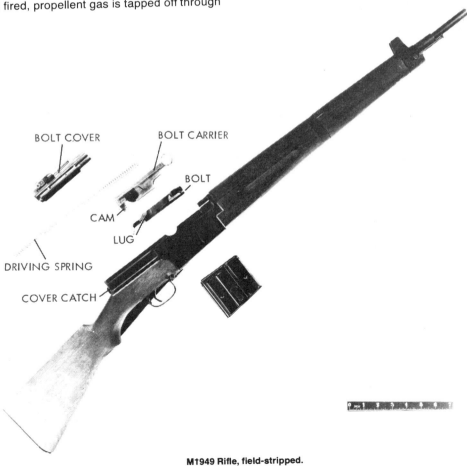

M1949 Rifle, field-stripped.

FRENCH SEMIAUTOMATIC CARBINES

French 7.65mm Carbine MAS 1949.

French .30 cal. MAC 1949 Carbine.

During the forties, several carbines were developed by Saint Etienne (MAS) and Chatellerault (MAC). The 7.65mm MAS 1949 carbine is chambered for a French developed 7.65mm "intermediate-sized" cartridge. This cartridge appeared to be modeled on the German 7.92mm short (PP43) cartridge. The MAS49 carbine has a folding stock.

The MAC 1949 carbine was chambered for the US caliber .30 carbine cartridge and bears a superficial resemblance to the US carbine. Internally this weapon is quite different from the US carbine, since the MAC 1949 is a delayed blowback operated weapon. Both of these weapons appeared only in prototype form.

FRENCH AUTOMATIC RIFLES

FUSIL AUTOMATIQUE MAS 5.56mm

As indicated in Chapter 1, this rifle represents the French Army's debut into the world of 5.56mm automatic weapons.

Characteristics of MAS 5.56mm Rifle

Caliber: 5.56mm
System of operation: Delayed blowback.

Weight: 7.5 lbs., w/o magazine.
Length, overall: 29.8 in.
Barrel length: 19.2 in.
Feed device: 25-round box magazine.
Sights: Front: Blade.
          Rear: Aperture 0-300 meters.
Cyclic rate: 900–1000 r.p.m., and 3-shot bursts.
Muzzle velocity: 3150 f.p.s.

FRENCH SUBMACHINE GUNS

France used the German 9mm Parabellum Vollmer Erma submachine gun to a limited extent prior to 1941. French development of a native submachine gun began at MAS (Saint Etienne) during the thirties. In 1935, the first of the MAS weapons developed for the 7.65mm long pistol cartridge appeared. This weapon, called the 7.65mm L Type SE-MAS 1935, was quite similar to the later and more common MAS 1938.

The 7.65mm long MAS 1938 was the standard French submachine gun until 1949. It is still in wide use with French police forces. After World War II, submachine gun development was very active in France. The Hotchkiss firm developed a submachine gun that had some overseas sales and limited service use in Indo-China.

Characteristics of the Model 1938 Submachine Gun

Caliber: 7.65mm Long.
System of operation: Blowback, automatic fire only.
Length overall: 24.8 in.
Barrel length: 8.8 in.
Weight: 6.3 lbs.
Feed device: 32-round, detachable staggered row, box magazine.
Sights: Front: Block with notch.
   Rear: Two folding leaves, 100 and 200 meter.
Muzzle velocity: Approx. 1200 f.p.s.
Cyclic rate: 700 r.p.m.

THE FRENCH MODEL 1938 SUBMACHINE GUN

The 7.65mm Long Model 1938 submachine gun, or MAS 38 as it is commonly known, is a relatively simple blowback-operated weapon. It does have a few unusual features, however: the use of a folding trigger for a safety and the angular travel of the bolt.

How the MAS Model 38 Operates

A hinged cover seals the mouth of the magazine housing in the bottom of the receiver in this weapon when the magazine is withdrawn. Pushing this forward on its hinge opens the mouth of the housing and permits insertion of a loaded magazine from the bottom. The magazine is pushed in until it locks in standard fashion.

When the bolt handle on the right side of the receiver is pulled to the rear, it draws the bolt back and presses the recoil spring behind it, which extends from the rear of the receiver down into a steel tube inside the shoulder stock. When the bolt has been drawn back far enough, it rides over the sear, which is then forced up by its spring to catch in the bent or notch in the underside of the bolt and hold it open ready for firing.

Pressure on the trigger will now withdraw the sear from the bolt and permit the compressed recoil spring to drive the bolt up the slightly inclined surface machined into the receiver, stripping a cartridge from the magazine and thrusting it into the chamber.

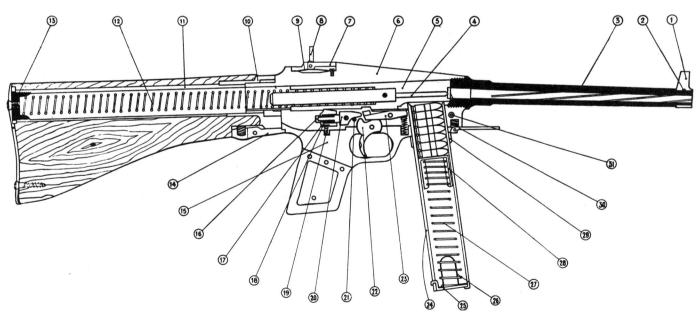

MAS 1938 Submachine Gun (Drawing from French Manual).

1. Front sight.
2. Fixing pin.
3. Barrel.
4. Striker.
5. Breechblock (bolt).
6. Receiver.
7. Rear sight leaf, down position.
8. Rear sight leaf, up.
9. Spring.
10. Recoil spring tube bridge.
11. Recoil spring tube.
12. Recoil (or operating) spring.
13. Tube butt cap.
14. Takedown lever.
15. Grip.
16. Sear nose.
17. Sear.
18. Sear buffer seat.
19. Sear spring.
20. Sear bar.
21. Stop pin.
22. Trigger.
23. Safety lever.
24. Magazine.
25. Floorplate.
26. Spring guide.
27. Spring.
28. Follower.
29. Magazine stop.
30. Opening plate (used to close magazine opening when magazine is withdrawn).
31. Magazine release.

French 7.65mm Model 1938 Submachine Gun.

Notes on the MAS Model 38

The bolt is not a true cylindrical piece moving in a straight line as in most submachine guns. It has a somewhat tilted face to permit it to bring up flush with the head of the cartridge as it is chambered, while the main body of the bolt is at an angle to the bore; this tends to give the effect of a hesitation action.

Just how practical this system is is open to question, in view of the fact that even with a low-powered cartridge and a comparatively light bolt, the recoil action is somewhat stiff. The bolt not only travels to the rear in the receiver but actually passes down the tube inside the stock itself. During rearward movement, the extractor withdraws the empty case and strikes it against the ejector, which is part of the fastening pin to which the forward sling swivel is attached. The empty case is ejected from the port on the right hand side of the receiver.

The sliding cover over the bolt opening or ejection port should be pulled further to the rear after the weapon has been cocked so that it will not have to be carried forward by the bolt in forward travel. This is a full automatic weapon in which the action will continue to function so long as the trigger is held back. When the trigger is released, a spring will force the sear up to catch and hold the bolt to the rear. The weapon fires from an open bolt.

The sights are rough and are of a rather impractical design. The rear sight consists of two separate leaves, which fold down into the top of the receiver. One aperture is for one hundred meters, and the other is for two hundred meters. The front sight is offset to the left and is too clumsy to permit anything but typical submachine gun burst fire.

Note that this weapon cannot be fired when the shoulder stock is removed. Additional travel of the bolt inside the tube in the stock is necessary to function the weapon.

Magazine. The magazine catch, which is pressed in to release the magazine for withdrawal from the receiver, is on the left side of the housing. The magazine itself may be dismounted by pushing the protruding rib at the lower front end of the box. This will tilt the floor plate so that it can be slid out rear end first. The zigzag spring and the follower may be withdrawn from the magazine box.

Design. An unusual safety is incorporated in this weapon. When the trigger is pushed forward, it folds up and hence cannot be pressed. Thus, if the bolt is cocked, the weapon cannot be fired until the trigger is deliberately unfolded. On the other hand, if the bolt is in forward position and the chamber empty, pushing the trigger forward will force a catch up into a hole in the bolt and prevent the bolt handle from being pulled back to open the weapon.

Field Stripping the MAS

Push in the spring buttstock catch at the under side of the forward end of the stock and, as it releases, twist the butt to the right.

Ease the butt and the recoil or operating spring out of the receiver.

Pressing the trigger will lower the sear and permit the triggerguard unit to be withdrawn from its guide in the receiver.

Pull back the bolt handle, which will bring the bolt to the rear when it and the recoil spring may be withdrawn from the receiver.

THE FRENCH MODEL 1949 SUBMACHINE GUN

The M1949 submachine gun, which was built by Tulle (MAT), has a very good reputation with French troops. It has a telescoping steel stock and magazine, which folds up under the gun when not in use; this makes the weapon very handy for armored or airborne troops. The M1949 also has a grip safety and an ejection port cover. The grip safety prevents the gun from firing when accidentally dropped, and the ejection port cover helps to keep dirt out of the internal mechanism of the gun.

Characteristics of the M1949 Submachine Gun

Caliber: 9mm Parabellum.
System of operation: Blowback, automatic fire only.
Length, overall:
  Stock extended: 28 in.
  Stock retracted: 18.3 in.
Barrel length: 9.05 in.
Feed device: 32-round, detachable, staggered-row box magazine.
Sights: Front: Hooded blade.
      Rear: L-Type w/apertures for 100 and 200 meters.
Muzzle velocity: 1237 f.p.s.
Cyclic rate: 600 r.p.m.
Weight, loaded: 9.41 lbs.

How to Load and Fire the M1949 (MAT 49) Submachine Gun

Insert a loaded magazine in the well of the magazine housing; if the housing is in the horizontal position, swing it down to the vertical, making sure that the lock located on the underside of

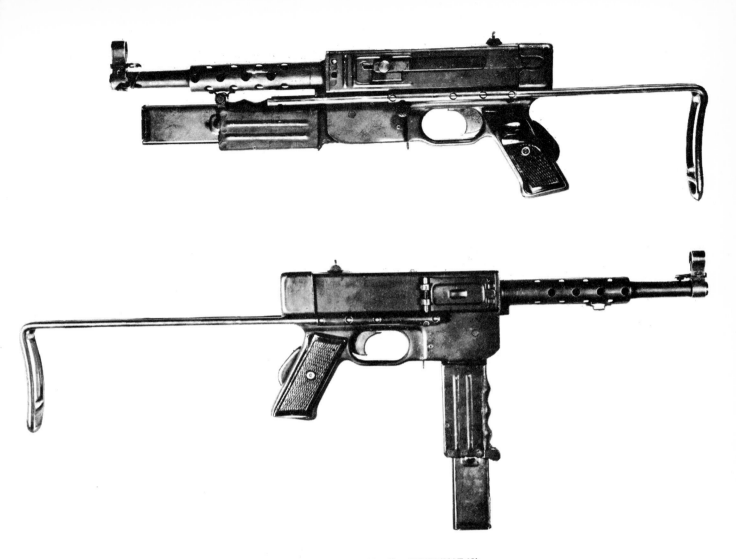

French 9mm Submachine Gun M1949 (MAT 49).

the trigger housing engages the magazine housing. Pull the cocking handle, located on the left side of the receiver, to the rear. The bolt will remain to the rear, since this weapon fires from an open bolt. Push the cocking handle to its forward position. Squeeze the grip safety with the rear of the hand, pull the trigger, and the weapon will fire. To remove the magazine, engage the magazine catch located at the bottom rear of the magazine housing. To lift the magazine housing and magazine into the horizontal position under the barrel depress the lock located on the underside of the trigger housing and swing the magazine up till the lug at the forward end of the housing engages the clip on the underside of the barrel jacket. To change the position of—or remove—the stock, depress the catch located on the left side of the trigger housing.

How to Field Strip the M1949 (MAT 49) Submachine Gun

Remove the magazine and clear weapon. Pull trigger and let

bolt go forward. Press the knurled bar located on the rear section of the barrel jacket to the rear. The barrel and receiver assembly can now be pulled upward and forward off the frame. The operating spring and bolt can be removed from the rear of the receiver. Further disassembly is not recommended.

Special Note on the M1949 (MAT 49) Submachine Gun

The M1949 submachine gun is composed mainly of steel stampings. Since its functioning is basically the same as that of any other blowback-operated submachine gun, no extended coverage on functioning is given. The ejection port cover is automatically opened by the forward or rearward movement of the bolt.

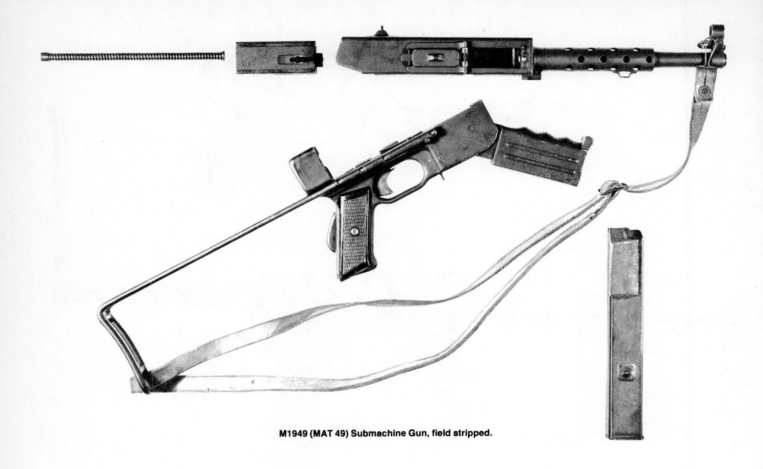

M1949 (MAT 49) Submachine Gun, field stripped.

FRENCH MACHINE GUNS

France adopted her first true machine gun in 1897—the Hotchkiss. Other guns soon followed: the Models 1900 and 1914 heavy Hotchkiss, 09/13 light Hotchkiss (Benét-Mercié) and the arsenal-designed guns—Puteaux of 1905 and the Saint Etienne of 1907 and its modification, the 1907 T. The Lewis gun was used as an aircraft gun, as was the Darne. The Hotchkiss was also made in 11mm during the war.

THE FRENCH MODEL 1915 LIGHT MACHINE GUN C.S.R.G.

Although this weapon is called an automatic rifle by the French, it is usually considered a machine gun in the United States. This weapon was developed by Chauchat, Sutter and Ribeyrolle at Puteaux from the prototype APX 1910 rifle. Some American publications indicate that Chauchat, Ribeyrolle and Sutter were members of the commission that approved the weapon; French publications indicate that they actually worked on the design.

This weapon is long-recoil operated and is of rather poor manufacture, but it was a wartime product and built by a number of subcontractors, who shipped parts to a central plant for assembly. You could consider it a World War I Sten gun insofar as manufacture is concerned. The main problem was that it was not as reliable in performance as the Sten.

Characteristics of the Model 1915 Light Machine Gun

Caliber: 8mm Lebel.
System of operation: Long recoil, selective fire.
Length overall: 45.2 in.
Barrel length: 18.5 in.
Weight: 20 lbs. w/bipod.
Feed device: 20-round, detachable, in-line crescent shaped magazine.
Sights: Front: Blade.
          Rear: Tangent with notch.
Muzzle velocity: 2300 f.p.s.
Cyclic rate: 240 r.p.m.

FRENCH CAL. .30 M1918 LIGHT MACHINE GUN, C.S.R.G.

United States forces used the C.S.R.G., commonly called the Chauchat (or, by the Doughboys, the "Shosho") during World War I. The United States purchased 15,988 of these weapons in 8mm and 19,241 in caliber .30-06. The .30-06 weapons were made by the French specifically for the United States Army and have a straight 16-round box magazine rather than the crescent-shaped magazine required by the rim and taper of the French 8mm cartridge.

The C.S.R.G. was adopted by Belgium in 7.65mm after World War I and by Greece, where it was called the Gladiator, in 8mm Lebel. It was used to some extent in World War II as well. This weapon is called the Chauchard in England.

Chauchat 8mm Light Machine Gun Model 1915, C.S.R.G. (called Fusil Mitrailleur Chauchat Sutter Ribeyrolle-Gladiator).

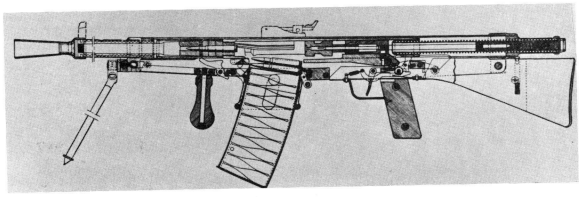

French US .30-06 version of Chauchat M.G. in section to show operation known as US Model 1918.

THE FRENCH MODEL 1914 HOTCHKISS MACHINE GUN

The 1914 Hotchkiss was the principal machine gun of the French Army in World War I and was also still in service by the French Army until the fall of France in 1940. The Hotchkiss appeared again, to a very limited extent, during the French campaign in Indo-China (Vietnam). Although a rather heavy and bulky gun, the 1914 Hotchkiss had a good reputation for reliable performance.

Characteristics of the Model 1914 Hotchkiss

Caliber: 8mm Lebel.
System of operation: Gas, automatic fire only.
Length overall: Approx. 51.6 in.
Barrel length: 31 in.
Weight: Gun, 55.7lbs; tripod, 60 lbs.
Feed device: 24- and 30-round strip or 250-round belt consisting of articulated strips.
Sights: Front: Blade.
　　　　Rear: V-notch.
Muzzle velocity: 2325 f.p.s. w/ball 1932N.
Cyclic rate: 450-500 r.p.m.

This weapon was used by twelve US divisions in France in 1918. A total of 5,255 of these machine guns were procured from France for the United States Army. Most of the guns used by US troops were converted to caliber .30-06.

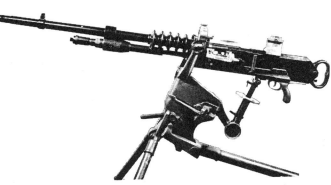

The French 1914 model Hotchkiss, caliber 8mm French.

THE FRENCH MODEL 1924 M29 LIGHT MACHINE GUN

This weapon is called an automatic rifle by the French and is used as a squad automatic weapon. It has had extensive combat use and is a very popular weapon with French troops. The basic design, except for the top mounted magazine and the double trigger, is quite similar to the US Browning Automatic rifle Model 1918. The original gun, the Model 1924, was issued chambered for the 7.5mm Model 24 cartridge. When the cartridge was shortened, the machine gun was modified to chamber the new cartridge and designated Model 1924 M29. This weapon may be found in any of the former French colonies or mandates.

Characteristics of the Model 1924 M29

Caliber: 7.5mm French.
System of operation: Gas, selective fire.
Length overall: 42.6 in.
Barrel length: 19.7 in.
Weight: 24.51 lbs. w/bipod.
Feed device: 25-round, detachable, staggered row, box magazine.
Sights: Front: Blade.
      Rear: Tangent.
Muzzle velocity: 2590 f.p.s.
Cyclic rate: 550 r.p.m.

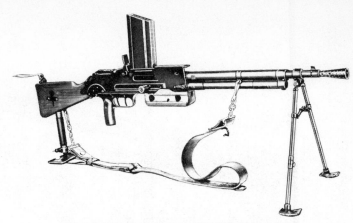

French Chatellerault 7.5mm 1924 M29 Machine Gun.

Trigger guard assembly will now swing forward on hinge. Pushing first in, then out, unhook front end and remove.

Field Stripping the M1924/29

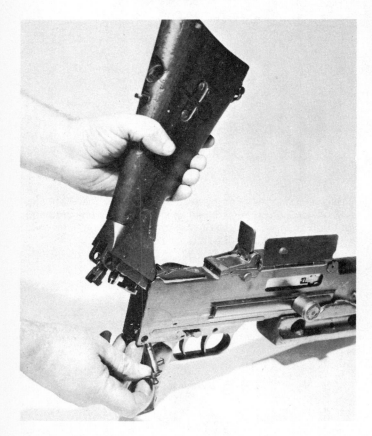

At lower right side of receiver is a retaining pin. Remove it; this permits the rear of the buttstock to be hinged up and back, when it can be lifted out of receiver.

Pulling head of ejector out of its slot will permit it to be removed from the rear. Remove recoil spring and guide.

Withdraw bolt and piston with slide out of receiver.

Gas cylinder tube lock is at lower front of receiver. Turn it to "O" mark on receiver, then raise rear end of tube. Tube can now be pulled out of receiver. Barrel lock is on upper front of receiver. Turn it to "O" and unscrew barrel to right.

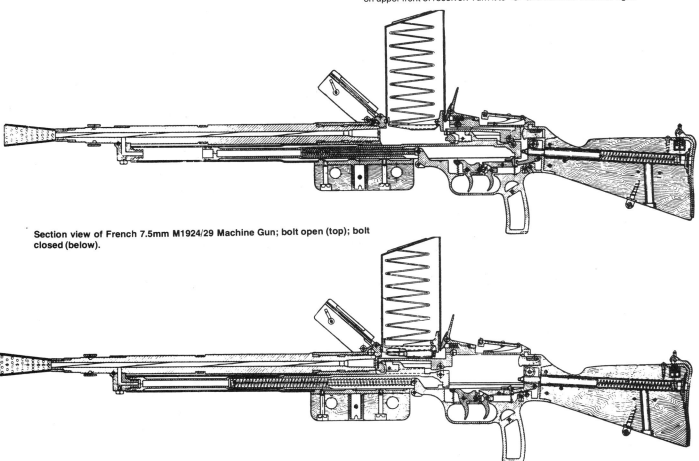

Section view of French 7.5mm M1924/29 Machine Gun; bolt open (top); bolt closed (below).

Loading and Firing the M1924/29

A loaded magazine is inserted vertically in the top of the gun. The magazine opening is fitted with a dust cover, which must be hinged up and forward to expose the magazine opening. The magazine release catch is positioned at the rear opening. Pressing it forward will release the magazine to be lifted out with the hand that is operating the catch.

Pull back the cocking handle to cock the weapon and compress the mainspring. Safety lever on the trigger guard may be used to lock the weapon in this position.

If front trigger is pulled, pressure will be exerted on the sear to release the bolt to fly forward and fire the cartridge stripped out of the magazine by the bolt in its forward travel. If the second trigger is pulled, the sear will not engage as long as the trigger is held back, and the weapon will continue to fire full automatic.

How the Model 1924/29 Works

Starting with the gun loaded and cocked, the action is as follows: If the first trigger is pulled, it pushes up the forward tip of the sear, bending down the rear end against the tension of the sear spring and pulling it out of the bent in the slide. The slide carries the striker in the front of its face. The slide and piston form a single unit; the bolt is fastened by a swinging link pin to the rear end of the slide. As the slide goes forward, pulled by the compressed recoil spring, carrying the moving components with it, the feed rib on top of the bolt passes between the lips of the magazine and strips a cartridge out. The extractor is forced over the base of the cartridge by the magazine spring, bringing the cartridge to proper feeding position in the bolt face.

As the forward motion nears its completion, the front end of the bolt stops against an abutment in the receiver. The rear end of the bolt, fastened on a rotating link to the slide, is now lifted up as the forward-moving slide rotates the link about the pins and locks firmly in locking recess in the top of the receiver (somewhat like the Browning Automatic Rifle).

The slide, which carries the striker, continues to move ahead during the period of link rotation, and the pin passes through its hole in the face of the bolt and strikes the cartridge now locked in the firing chamber.

Return Movement of the Action, M1924/29

Gas escaping through the port as the bullet passes over it (a short distance from the muzzle) passes through the gas cylinder and expands violently against the cup end of the piston in standard Hotchkiss fashion. As the piston starts back under the impact of the thrust, the gas escapes through slots in the gas cylinder tube. The piston, slide and link go back while the bolt is still securely locked.

Then as the dangerous period of pressure is passed, the rearward moving slide pulling on the bottom of the swinging link rotates it down, drawing with it the locked rear end of the bolt. As the movement continues, the bolt moves back in straight line with the other parts, carrying the empty cartridge case in the extractor. This case strikes the ejector and is expelled from the gun.

In semiautomatic fire, the rearward movement is completed as the end of the slide strikes the buffer sear release attached to the sear mechanism, causing a rebounding action, which catches the sear in the side to hold it back, while the back end of the bolt strikes the buffer absorbing shock through a coil spring. In automatic fire, of course, the sear cannot engage, and the slide goes forward immediately.

An interesting development in this weapon is an actuator in the buttstock used to check the rate of fire.

A plunger rod rides in a tube with a spring behind the rod. The front end of this rod passes through a hole into the receiver in line with the slide and touches a sear trip attached to the sear mechanism. This device adds resistance to recoil and increases the time between shots, as the sear is held in engagement longer than usual.

FRENCH MODEL 1931A MACHINE GUN

The French 7.5mm tank and fortress machine gun M1931A was adapted for use on the US cal. 30 M2 tripod because of French post-war shortage of machine guns. This weapon is still in use on French-made armored vehicles. Since it is likely to be encountered by some of the readers of this book, it will be covered in detail even though it is not a post-war weapon.

The M1931A machine gun is the tank and fortress version of the French 7.5mm M1924/29 light machine gun. The weapon has a very heavy barrel, since it is designed for a high rate of sustained fire and does not have a quick change barrel. Two magazines can be used with the gun—a box type or a large drum, which fastens to the side of the gun.

Characteristics of M1931A Machine Gun

Caliber: 7.5mm M1929 French rimless.
System of operation: Gas, automatic fire only.
Lenght, overall: 40.5 in. w/flash hider.
Weight, empty: 27.48 lbs.
Weight of Mounts:
  Tripod M2: 16.22 lbs.
  Tripod M1945: 32.15 lbs.
Barrel length: 23.5 in.
Feed device: 36-round, detachable, staggered-row box magazine or 150-round drum magazine.
Sights: Front: Blade.
       Rear: Tangent leaf w/open notch.
Muzzle Velocity: 2750 f.p.s.
Cyclic Rate: 750 r.p.m.

How to Load and Fire the M1931A Machine Gun

Cock the gun by pulling the operating handle to the rear. If the box magazine is to be used, rotate it into the feed fixture on the right side of the gun, so that the lug on the magazine engages in the recess in the fixture. Then pull the magazine toward the rear of the gun, so that the rear of it is locked in place in the feedway. Pull the trigger, and the weapon will fire. This weapon fires from an open bolt and has no safety. To load the drum-type magazine, fit the magazine on the projection of the receiver, which is just ahead of the feedway. A stud to the rear of the projection serves an an index when assembling the magazine to the gun. Firing is carried on in the same way with the drum as with the box magazine. To remove the box magazine, engage the magazine catch and swing the magazine forward and out. To remove the drum magazine, pull the handle on the outside of the drum, and pull the magazine straight off. When this gun is unloaded, using either magazine, there may be a round in the feedway, unless all the rounds have been fired. To clear the gun, the round must be pushed forward so that it falls free inside the receiver and out the bottom of the gun. USE EXTREME CARE IN UNLOADING THE GUN! DO NOT ALLOW ANYONE TO GET IN FRONT OF THE GUN!

French 7.5mm Machine Gun M1931A on US M2 tripod.

How to Field Strip the M1931A Machine Gun

Check to see that the weapon is not loaded. Depress the springloaded catch in the rear of the backplate. Rotate the lock 90 degrees, and remove the recoil spring and guide. Remove screw at the lower rear of the receiver; a lever attached to the screw assists in its removal. Remove the backplate; the trigger housing and recoiling parts can then be removed. No further disassembly is recommended.

To reassemble the weapon, perform the above steps in reverse order.

How the M1931A Machine Gun Works

The piston and gas cylinder are similar to those on the M1924 M29 light machine gun. However, because the M1931A ejects through the bottom of the receiver, the piston assembly is cut away to permit cases or complete rounds to pass through. The operating spring is positioned at the rear of the piston assembly, with only a small portion of it inside the piston. Locking is accomplished in the same manner as on the M1924 M29 light machine gun. A spring-loaded lever, positioned in the right side of the bolt, engages the base of the cartridge case for feeding and firing. The ejector operates in a groove in the top of the bolt. The firing pin operates inside the bolt but is held rigidly to a projection on the rear of the piston assembly.

Special Note on the M1931A Machine Gun

The M1931A cannot be considered an up-to-date machine gun for use either as a tank gun or as a ground gun. It probably will be replaced by the M1952 machine gun in armored vehicles, as well as in the ground role.

FRENCH MODEL 52 MACHINE GUN

The M1952 is called the *Arme Automatique Transformable* (AAT) by the French, since it is designed to be used as both a heavy and light machine gun. The weapon can be used as a light machine gun with a light barrel, a bipod and a butt support. It can also be used as a heavy machine gun on the US M2 tripod with a French adapter. This gun has been made in 7.62mm NATO caliber for test and for export.

How to Load and Fire the M1952 (AAT Mle. 52) Machine Gun

Pull the operating handle to the rear, cocking the weapon. Push the cover catch forward and open the cover; lay the belt on the feedway, so that the first cartridge in the belt is positioned against the cartridge stop. Close the cover and press the trigger; the weapon will fire. An alternate method is to feed the loading tab of the belt into the feed port on the left side of the gun, and pull it through to the right until a cartridge clicks into position. Then pull the charging handle to the rear and fire. The weapon fires from an open bolt.

Characteristics of the Model 52 Machine Gun

Caliber: 7.5mm French M1929 rimless.
System of operation: Delayed blowback, full automatic fire only.
Length, overall:
  Stock extended: 45.9 in.
  Stock retracted: 38.6 in.
Barrel length (Quick-change barrel):
  Heavy barrel, w/o flash hider: 23.6 in.
  Light barrel, w/o flash hider: 19.3 in.
Feed device: 50-round, metallic, nondisintegrating link belt; when used as a light gun, a box containing one link belt section is hung on the side of the receiver.
Sights: Front: Barley corn
      Rear: Tangent leaf w/U-notch.
Muzzle velocity: 2690 f.p.s.
Cyclic rate: 700 r.p.m. (approx.).
Weight, w/light barrel: 21.7 lbs.
      w/heavy barrel: 23.28 lbs.

BARREL CLAMP

French 7.5mm Model 1952 On US M2 tripod.

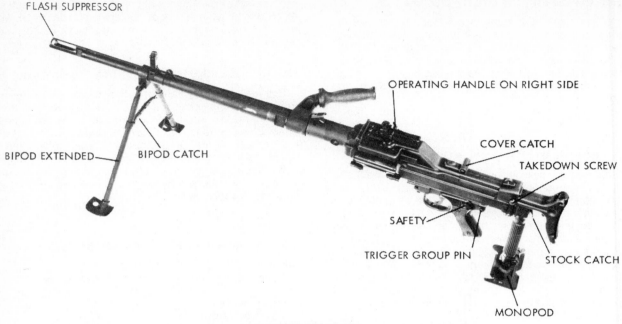

AA52 Light Machine Gun.

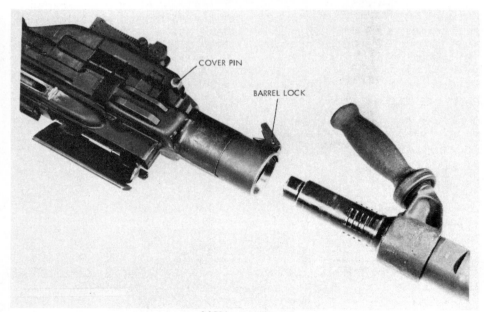

AA52 barrel release.

How to Field Strip the M1952 (AAT Mle. 52) Machine Gun

With the stock in the extended position, press down on the stock bolt lever to remove the two stock bolts; then pull the butt to the rear and remove. Unscrew and remove the assembly pin. Pull back the bolt assembly by swinging it up. Pull the cocking handle to the rear. Remove the recoil spring and the recoil spring guide; then remove the bolt assembly by sliding it out the rear. Remove the trigger guard retaining pin and disengage the trigger guard from the receiver. Pull back the barrel catch with the left hand and, with the right hand, twist the carrying handle 1/6th turn to the right; then pull the barrel forward. Put the cover and the feed plate at a 90-degree angle from the receiver and remove the cover pin. Separate the bolt head by moving the head forward and up. Remove the firing pin and the bolt lock from the bolt.

To reassemble the weapon, perform the above steps in reverse order.

How the M1952 (AAT Mle. 52) Works

The delayed-blowback bolt system of the M1952 machine gun is similar in principle to that of the Spanish CETME assault rifle and the Swiss Model 57 assault rifle. The bolt is in two pieces—a head and a body; the head is much smaller than the body. Instead of using two roller bearings for locks, as do the Spanish and Swiss weapons, the M1952 employs a locking lever. The bolt head cannot move to the rear until the pressure is high enough to cause the locking lever to start opening and, in turn,

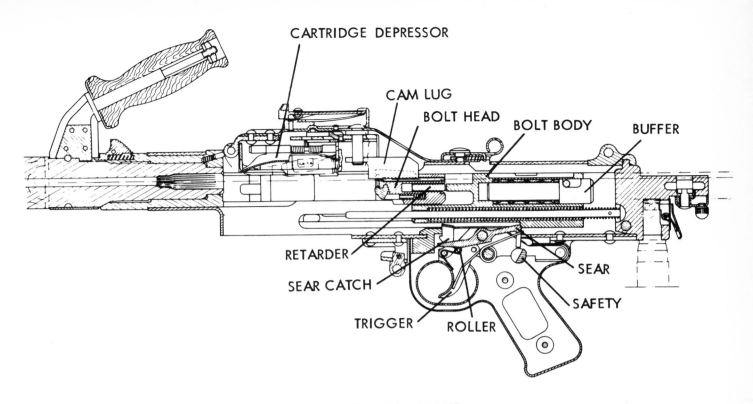

CARTRIDGE DEPRESSOR

CAM LUG

BOLT HEAD

BOLT BODY

BUFFER

RETARDER

SEAR CATCH

SEAR

SAFETY

TRIGGER

ROLLER

Section view of French 7.5mm Model 52.

force back the bolt body and firing pin. This weapon also uses a partially fluted chamber, to make up for its lack of slow initial extraction. The feed system appears to be quite similar to that of the MG42.

Special Note on the M1952 (AAT Mle. 52)

The M1952 machine gun is quite an interesting design; it represents a great departure from pre-World War II French practice. This machine gun has replaced the M1924 M29 as the squad automatic weapon, since the French refer to the gun as a "fusil Mitrailleur" (automatic rifle) when it is used in the light role on a bipod. On the subject of squad (or "section," as the British refer to squad) automatic weapons, it is interesting to note that the US, Belgium, France and Sweden call their squad-level guns "automatic rifles." Most other countries call them "light machine guns"—e.g., the Bren, the RPD, etc.

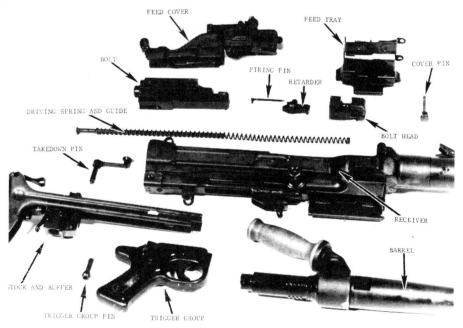

FEED COVER

FEED TRAY

COVER PIN

BOLT

FIRING PIN

RETARDER

DRIVING SPRING AND GUIDE

BOLT HEAD

TAKEDOWN PIN

RECEIVER

BARREL

STOCK AND BUFFER

TRIGGER GROUP PIN

TRIGGER GROUP

Disassembled view of AAT (Mle. 52).

19

East Germany: "German Democratic Republic"

The East German Army is currently equipped with most of the Soviet post-war small arms. The 9mm Makarov pistol and 9mm Stechkin machine pistol are used as are the 7.62mm AK47 and AKM assault rifles and the 7.62mm RPD and 7.62mm RPK light machine guns. The 7.62mm RP46 light machine gun and 7.62mm SG43 and SGM heavy machine guns are in service as well as the 12.7mm DShK M1938/46.

The 7.62mm General Purpose PK/PKS machine gun is now in service in the East German Army and will probably eventually replace the 7.62mm RP 46, SG 43 and SGM machine guns in that Army.

Some of the pre-world War II and World War II Soviet weapons such as the 7.62mm PPSh M1941 submachine gun and the 7.62mm DT and DTM machine guns are still in service with border guards and armored forces respectively (on older armed vehicles).

The workers militia is armed with German World War II weapons such as the 7.92mm Kar 98K and the 7.92mm MP44. They also have older weapons. The East

Germans manufacture or have manufactured the 9mm Makarov pistol, the 7.62mm AK 47 and AKM assault rifles, the 7.62mm SKS carbine and the RPK light machine gun. The arms plant in the Suhl area are in production manufacturing sporting arms in addition to military arms.

The East Germans use slightly different nomenclature for the Soviet weapons than do the Soviets. The usual procedure is to use the first letter of the designer's name tacked on to the German abbreviation of the weapon type. Thus the AK 47 assault rifle with wooden stock is the MPi K and with folding stock it is the MPi KmS. The AKM is the MPi KM, the RPK is the LMG K, the RPD is the LMG D, etc.

Some of the Soviet designed weapons manufactured in East Germany differ in minor detail from those made in the USSR. The Soviet made AK47 and SKS have cleaning rods mounted under their barrels; the cleaning rods are not carried on the East German-made weapons.

East German copy of 9mm Soviet Makarov pistol.

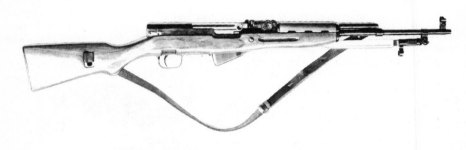

East German 7.62mm copy of Soviet SKS carbine. Note that sling is mounted similar to Kar 98k and that no cleaning rod is carried under barrel.

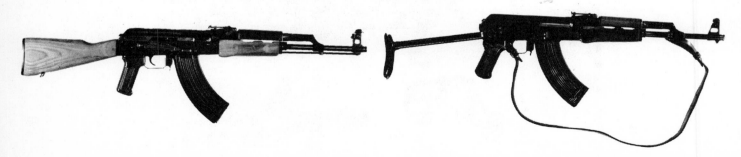

East German 7.62 MPi KM (AKM).

East German 7.62mm MPiK (AK-47) Assault Rifle with folding stock.

20 West Germany: "Federal Republic of Germany"

The West German Army uses the following small arms:
9mm Walther P38 pistol called P1;
9mm Israeli UZI submachine gun;
7.62mm Rifle G3A3, G3A4 and G3A3ZF;
7.62mm NATO machine gun Model 42/59 MG3.

US caliber .50 Browning guns are also in service, particularly on armored vehicles.

The West German Army when originally organized was armed mainly with US small arms. Most of these weapons are no longer in service.

WEST GERMAN PISTOLS

WALTHER PISTOLS

The P1 (P38) is made at the new Walther plant at Ulm. It is essentially the same as the P38 of World War II, which is covered in detail in the next chapter, German World War II weapons.

Walther is again producing the PP and PPK pistols in three calibers.

West German 9mm P38 of current manufacture. The P-1 of the West German Army.

HECKLER AND KOCH VP70 MACHINE PISTOL

The HK VP70 is a rather unusual weapon in that it is a normal blowback operated pistol when used without its shoulder stock holster and when the shoulder stock holster is fitted it can be used as a full automatic weapon to fire 3 round bursts. The change lever that accomplishes this is mounted on the shoulder stock holster. It operates through a toggle lever, mounted on the top front of the shoulder stock holster, which goes through a slot in the top rear of the pistol receiver. Another somewhat unusual feature is that this pistol fires double action only; for this reason it is not normally fitted with a safety.

Characteristics

Caliber: 9mm Parabellum
System of operation: blowback, selective fire-3-round bursts.
Weight: w/o stock: 2.5 lbs. loaded
w/stock: 3.5 lbs. loaded

Length, overall: w/o stock 8 in.
w/stock 21.5 in.
Feed device: 18-round, detachable, staggered row
Sights: Front: blade
Rear: square notch
Muzzle velocity: 1,180 f.p.s.
Cyclic rate: 2,200 r.p.m.

Loading and Firing the VP70

When the VP70 is used without the shoulder stock holster, it is loaded and fired much like any other self-loading pistol. A loaded magazine is inserted and the slide pulled to the rear and released, chambering a cartridge. Pressure on the trigger will fire the weapon, one round for each separate pull of the trigger. When the VP70 is fired with the shoulder stock holster attached,

Heckler and Koch 9mm VP 70 Pistol.

the selector switch on the left, top front of the shoulder stock determines the mode of fire. If the selector is put on the figure 1, one round is fired for each squeeze of the trigger; if the selector is put on 3, three rounds are fired for each squeeze of the trigger. As pointed out previously, this weapon has no safety catch although Heckler and Koch advise that they can fit it with one if desired. The magazine catch is at the bottom rear of the grip.

Field Stripping of the VP70

Remove magazine and pull slide back to insure that pistol is empty. Release slide and pull the retaining catch, located just to the rear of the trigger guard bow, down and pull the slide to the rear. Lift the slide off upward and to the rear and guide it forward and off the barrel.

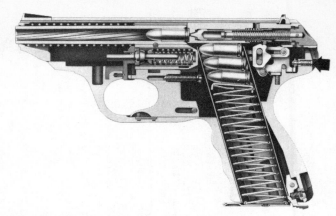

Sectioned view of VP70. Note arrow indicating selector mechanism which is actuated by the attachment of the holster stock.

Disassembled view of HK VP70 Pistol.

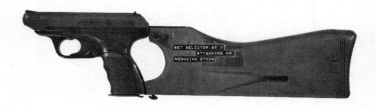

Heckler and Koch 9mm Parabellum Model V70 machine pistol with shoulder-stock-holster attached.

Available commercially as VP70Z without the full automatic feature.

HECKLER AND KOCH 9mm PISTOL MODEL P9 AND P9S

Heckler and Koch has developed a new self-loading pistol chambered for the 9mm Parabellum cartridge. The P9 uses the same type roller locking system as the G3 rifle series. This pistol makes extensive use of stampings in its manufacture. It has a pin type indicator, which shows that the pistol is cocked. This pin protrudes from the rear of the receiver. The loaded chamber indicator is mounted above and to the rear of the chamber somewhat like that of the Luger. The P9 has a cocking lever mounted on the left side of the receiver. The safety is mounted on the left side of the slide; it operates by blocking the firing pin. The pistol can be cocked or unloaded with the safety in the "on" position.

The only difference between the P9 and P9S is that the former has a single action trigger, and the P9S has a double action trigger.

Heckler and Koch 9mm Parabellum Model P9 Pistol.

Characteristics of the P9

Caliber: 9mm Parabellum
System of operation: delayed blowback
Weight: 1.93 lbs.
Length overall: 7.5 in.
Barrel length: 4 in.
Feed device: 9-round in-line detachable box magazine
Sights: Front: blade
Rear: square notch
Muzzle velocity: 1180 f.p.s.

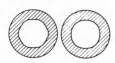

Polygon barrel
As opposed to the grooves and lands of conventional barrels, the bore of the polygon barrel has a highly rounded, rectangular profile. This results in better seating of the bullet in the bore and reduced gas cutting, thereby providing higher penetration power, extremely long service life, and is easy to clean.

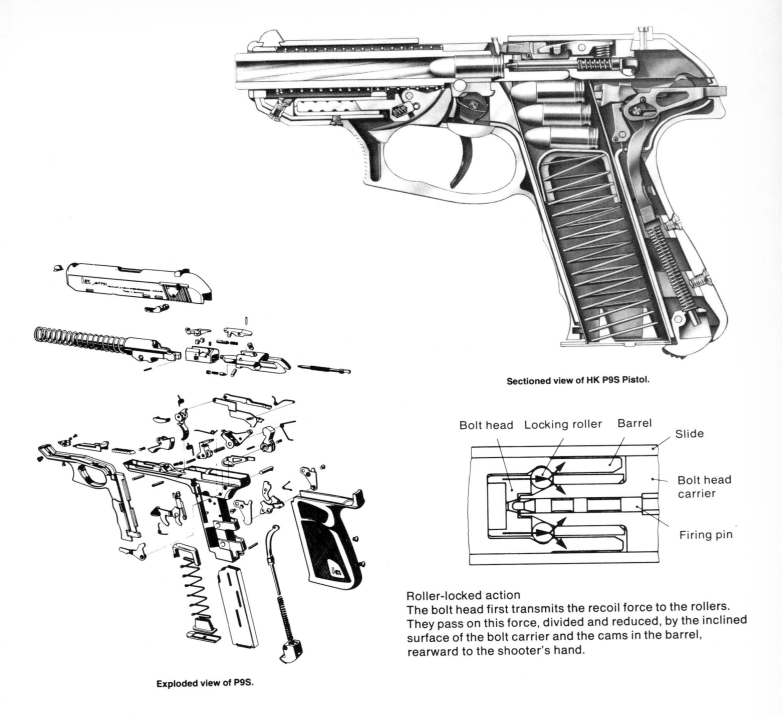

Sectioned view of HK P9S Pistol.

Bolt head   Locking roller   Barrel

Slide

Bolt head
carrier

Firing pin

Roller-locked action
The bolt head first transmits the recoil force to the rollers.
They pass on this force, divided and reduced, by the inclined
surface of the bolt carrier and the cams in the barrel,
rearward to the shooter's hand.

Exploded view of P9S.

Disassembly and Assembly

Clear the pistol, but do not insert the magazine. Press the takedown lever into the trigger guard and push the slide forward; then lift the slide up and off the receiver. Press the barrel forward in the slide against the force of the driving spring until the rear of the barrel can be lifted up and out of the slide. Remove the driving spring. Normally no further disassembly is required, but if desired, the bolt can be removed from the slide. To do so, insert one of the barrel extensions into the slide, just forward of the bolt carrier, and press the barrel down to release the bolt lever. Press the bolt forward, off the bolt carrier. No further disassembly should be attempted.

To reassemble the pistol, place the bolt into the slide with its extractor or rounded side toward the ejection port and start it onto the bolt carrier. Use the barrel extension to depress the bolt lever and push the bolt fully onto the bolt carrier. Remove the bolt extension and push the bolt forward until it clicks into place. Insert the barrel with driving spring into the slide (driving spring first), and insure that the spring is seated in its recess around the inner front of the slide. Rotate the barrel so that its rounded side is toward the ejection port; then press the barrel forward into the slide, against the force of the driving spring, until the barrel seats into the slide. Ease the barrel rearward so that the extensions fit alongside the bolt. Place the slide on the receiver so that the indentations in the slide are aligned with the cutaways in the receiver; then pull the slide rearward and release it. The pistol is ready to be loaded like any other automatic pistol.

WEST GERMAN RIFLES

The West Germans were initially equipped with US M1 rifles. They then purchased a quantity of FN 7.62mm NATO FAL rifles, which they called Rifle G1.

Beginning in 1959, the *Bundeswehr* began replacing the G1 with the G3, which had evolved through the Spanish CETME Rifle from the StG 45(M), as described in Chapter 1. Rheinmettal Wehrtechnik of Dusseldorf and Heckler & Koch have produced the G3 for the West German Government. In addition, Heckler & Koch has produced a number of variants of the G3 in the NATO, 7.62 × 39mm and 5.56 × 45mm calibers for the world market.

WEST GERMAN RIFLE 7.62mm G3

Characteristics of the G3

Caliber: 7.62mm NATO.
System of operation: Delayed blowback, selective fire.
Weight (loaded w/o bipod): 9.9 lbs.
Length, overall: 40.2 in.
Barrel length: 17.7 in.
Feed device: 20-round, detachable, staggered-row box magazine.
Sights: Front: Hooded post.
Rear: L type
Muzzle velocity: 2624 f.p.s.
Cyclic rate: 500-600 r.p.m.

Automatic rifle G3 caliber 7.62 mm × 51 NATO

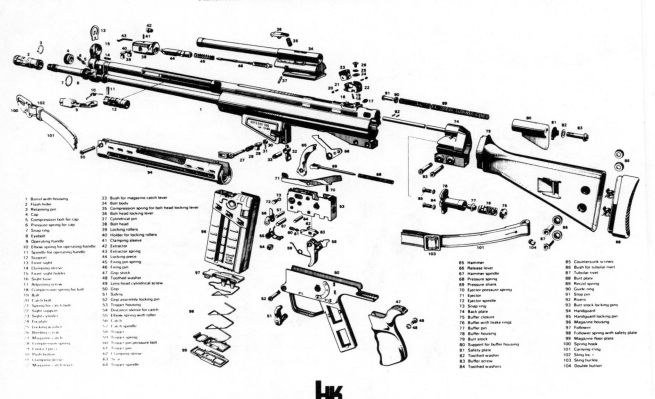

1 Barrel with housing	33 Bush for magazine catch lever
2 Flash hider	34 Bolt body
3 Retaining pin	35 Compression spring for bolt head locking lever
4 Cap	36 Bolt head locking lever
5 Compression bolt for cap	37 Cylindrical pin
6 Pressure spring for cap	38 Bolt head
7 Snap ring	39 Locking rollers
8 Eyebolt	40 Holder for locking rollers
9 Operating handle	41 Clamping sleeve
10 Elbow spring for operating handle	42 Extractor
11 Spindle for operating handle	43 Extractor spring
12 Support	44 Locking piece
13 Front sight	45 Firing pin spring
14 Clamping sleeve	46 Firing pin
15 Front sight holder	47 Grip stock
16 Sight base	48 Toothed washer
17 Adjusting screw	49 Lens head cylindrical screw
18 Compression spring for ball	50 Grip
19 Ball	51 Safety
20 Catch bolt	52 Grip assembly locking pin
21 Spring for catch bolt	53 Trigger housing
22 Sight support	54 Distance sleeve for catch
23 Sight cylinder	55 Elbow spring with roller
24 Tin plate	56 Catch
25 Locking washer	57 Catch spindle
26 Bushing screw	58 Trigger
27 Magazine catch	59 Trigger spring
28 Compression spring	60 Trigger pin pressure bolt
29 Guide piece	61 Trigger pin
30 Push button	62 Clamping sleeve
31 Clamping sleeve	63 Sear
32 Magazine catch lever	64 Trigger spindle

65 Hammer	85 Countersunk screws
66 Release lever	86 Bush for tubular rivet
67 Hammer spindle	87 Tubular rivet
68 Pressure spring	88 Butt plate
69 Pressure shank	89 Recoil spring
70 Ejector pressure spring	90 Guide ring
71 Ejector	91 Stop pin
72 Ejector spindle	92 Rivets
73 Snap ring	93 Butt stock locking pins
74 Back plate	94 Handguard
75 Buffer closure	95 Handguard locking pin
76 Buffer with brake rings	96 Magazine housing
77 Buffer pin	97 Follower
78 Buffer housing	98 Follower spring with safety plate
79 Butt stock	99 Magazine floor plate
80 Support for buffer housing	100 Spring hook
81 Safety plate	101 Carrying sling
82 Toothed washer	102 Sling lock
83 Buffer screw	103 Sling buckle
84 Toothed washers	104 Double button

HECKLER & KOCH GMBH OBERNDORF NECKAR · GERMANY

How the G3 Works

The G3 Rifle is a delayed blowback weapon. The rearward thrust of the cartridge case, upon firing, drives the bolt mechanism to the rear, but the rearward movement is delayed by the mechanical arrangement of the two-piece bolt until the chamber pressure has dropped to a safe limit. Rearward movement of the cartridge case is facilitated by flutes cut into the chamber. These flutes allow propellant gases to leak rearward along the cartridge case, providing a film of gas upon which the mouth of the cartridge floats. Cases fired in the G3 (and other weapons such as the Tokarev rifles) are readily identified by the sharply defined gas marks that extend along the neck for about half of the length of the case. When the G3 is ready to fire, a cartridge is chambered; the locking piece in the bolt cams the locking rollers into their recesses, and the hammer is released and strikes the firing pin, which fires the cartridge. The gas pressure drives the cartridge case rearward, and this movement is resisted by the bolt, whose locking rollers are seated in the locking piece attached to the barrel.

Automatisches Gewehr G3

Kal. 7,62 mm x 51

Vorgang im Verschluß

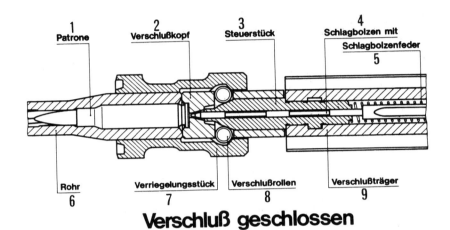

Verschluß geschlossen

Rifle loaded and locked

1. Cartridge
2. Bolt-head
3. Locking piece (or locking cam)
4. Firing pin
5. Firing pin spring
6. Barrel
7. Barrel extension
8. Locking rollers
9. Bolt body (or carrier)

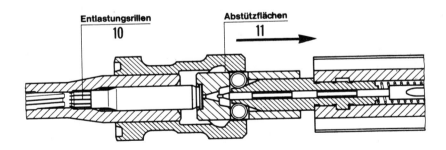

Verschluß geöffnet

Rifle unlocked

10. Fluted chamber
11. Supporting (or cam surface)

HECKLER & KOCH GMBH OBERNDORF-NECKAR · GERMANY

Operating mechanism of G3 Rifle.

The rearward thrust of the case is sufficient to start the bolt to the rear; this causes the rollers to be forced out of their seats. As they move, the rollers ride on the cam surface of the locking cam (locking piece) and force it rearward; because the cam is locked to the heavy bolt carriers, the bolt carrier is also forced to the rear against the driving spring. The delay, occasioned by the rollers resisting camming the heavy bolt to the rear, allows time for the bullet to leave the muzzle and the pressure to drop to a safe level. Inertia developed and the residual pressure still thrusting the bolt rearward provide sufficient energy to drive the bolt fully to the rear, to compress the driving spring and to cock the hammer.

The extractor pulls the fired case from the chamber and holds it to the bolt face. The rear end of the ejector is struck by the recoiling bolt carrier; this causes the ejector to pivot so that its front end enters the bottom of the bolt head. As the bolt continues to recoil, the cartridge case strikes the ejector, pivots about the extractor and is expelled from the rifle.

The bolt carrier strikes the buffer at the front of the butt stock and stops. The driving spring then drives the carrier forward, and the bolt head forces the top cartridge out of the magazine and into the chamber. The extractor snaps into the cartridge groove, and the forward movement of the bolt head stops when it hits the end of the barrel. The carrier has a lock to keep the bolt head locked forward; this is now tripped by a lug in the receiver. The carrier continues forward, and the locking piece, which travels with the carrier, forces the locking rollers into their recesses.

The rifle's trigger mechanism is similar to that of the FN FAL. The hammer, powered by a coil spring and plunger, is held cocked by a sear that can move back and forth in relation to the trigger. When the hammer is cocked, pressure on the trigger is transmitted to the rear end of the sear through the trigger lever. This causes the front of the sear to move down and release the hammer, which under pressure of its spring, swings forward and strikes the firing pin. Upon firing, the recoiling bolt carrier rocks the hammer back into the cocked position.

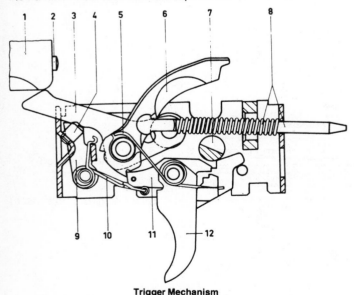

Trigger Mechanism

Initial Position at "S" = Safe

1. Bolt head carrier
2. Firing pin
3. Release lever
4. Anvil for hammer
5. Trigger spring
6. Hammer
7. Safety pin
8. Pressure shank with compression spring for hammer
9. Catch
10. Elbow spring with roller
11. Sear
12. Trigger

When the selector is set for semiautomatic fire—"E"— a cutaway section on the selector shaft limits the upward movement of the trigger lug. When the trigger is pressed and the hammer is released, the sear spring forces the front of the sear forward and upward. As the bolt carrier returns forward, the hammer starts to move forward, and the sear mates with a notch on the hammer. When the strong hammer spring overcomes the weaker sear spring, the sear is forced to the rear against the trigger lever to hold the hammer cocked. By releasing the trigger, the lever is lowered, and the hammer spring, working through the hammer, forces the sear rearward over the lever. Pressure on the trigger will now move the sear and fire another shot.

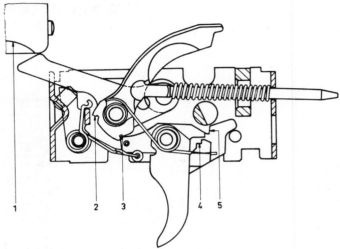

Selective fire lever at "E" = single fire

1. Cam surface
2. Notch for burst
3. Notch for single fire
4. Notch for the sear
5. Recess for single fire

When the selector is set for automatic fire—"F"—the trigger can rise to its highest point, and the nose of the sear is depressed far enough so that the sear cannot reengage the hammer. The automatic sear holds the hammer cocked, and as the bolt carrier completes its forward travel, it depresses the automatic sear lever; this in turn moves the automatic sear out of engagement with the hammer. The hammer swings forward to fire, and this cycle is repeated until the trigger is released. The sear can then rise, intercept the hammer and interrupt the firing cycle.

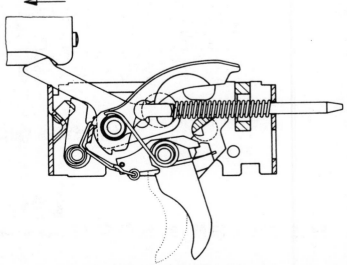

Function in Position "F" = Burst

When set at safe—"S"—the selector places a solid section of its shaft over the trigger lever. This prevents the trigger from moving enough to disengage the sear from the hammer and keeps the rifle from firing.

There are two automatic safeties incorporated into the design of the G3—the automatic sear and the locking piece. If the bolt mechanism is not fully forward, the automatic sear will continue to hold the hammer and prevent firing. The locking piece, unless it is fully forward and holding the locking rollers fully outward, will prevent the firing pin from protruding through the bolt face; thus, the weapon cannot fire unless the bolt is fully locked.

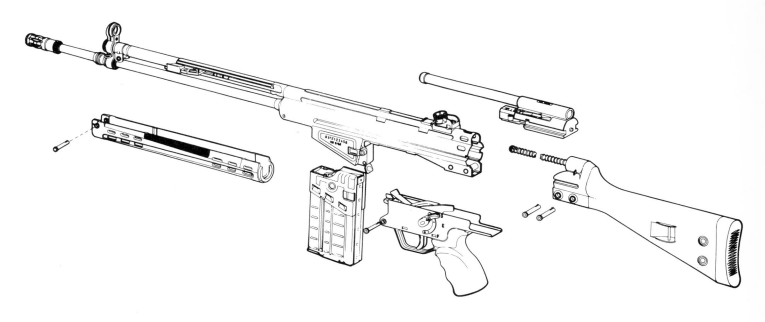

Field stripped G3 Rifle.

Field Stripping

To disassemble the G3, clear the chamber and do not press the trigger or reinsert the magazine. Set the selector to safe—"S". Remove the takedown pins from the butt stock and pull the stock and driving spring to the rear. Allow the trigger group to hand down on its front pin. Pull the operating handle to the rear and point the muzzle upward until the bolt assembly can be grasped and pulled to the rear. Turn the bolt head 90 degrees to the right and pull it forward out of the carrier. Turn the locking piece until its lug clears the carrier; then remove the locking piece, the firing pin and the spring.

No further disassembly is necessary or advisable.

To reassemble the G3, insert the locking piece and the firing pin with its spring into the bolt head. Insure that the lug on the locking piece is aligned with the rounded side of the bolt head. Place the bolt head (bolt face down) on a firm surface and place the bolt carrier on the assembled bolt head/locking piece unit. Turn the bolt head slightly to the left; pull it forward about 1/4 inch, and then rotate it fully to the left. If the bolt head is pushed back into the carrier, the rollers will lock outward, and the bolt cannot be assembled into the rifle. If this happens, swing the trigger group down on its pin. Reverse the bolt unit and insert it into the receiver as far as possible. Strike the projecting driving spring tubular housing (on the bolt carrier) a sharp blow. This will cause the rollers to retract into the bolt, and the entire unit will go farther into the receiver. Remove the reversed bolt unit and proceed as in the following paragraph.

Insure that the locking rollers are flush with sides of the bolt head; then insert the complete bolt assembly into the receiver and point the muzzle down; the bolt will slide forward. Swing the trigger group up into place; then slide the butt over the rear of the receiver and insure that the driving spring enters its recess in the bolt carrier. Remove the takedown pins from their storage holes and replace them in the receiver. Insert the magazine, rotate the selector off safe and press the trigger. Replace the magazine.

Barrel with Receiver, Cocking Lever Mechanism and Sights

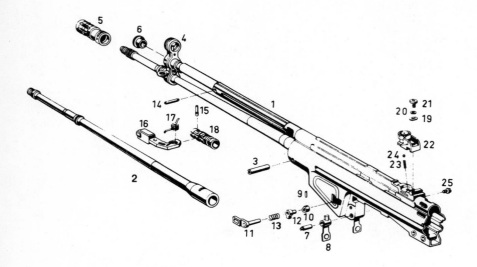

1. Barrel with receiver, cocking lever housing, front sight holder and magazine release lever
2. Barrel
3. Barrel fixing pin
4. Front sight holder
5. Flash suppressor
6. Cap
7. Bush for magazine release lever
8. Magazine release lever
9. Retaining pin
10. Contact button for magazine catch
11. Magazine catch
12. Contact piece for magazine catch
13. Contact spring for magazine catch
14. Pin for stop abutment
15. Axis pin for cocking lever
16. Cocking lever
17. Cocking lever elbow spring
18. Cocking lever support
19. Fix plate for rear sight support
20. Lock washer
21. Binding screw
22. Rotary rear sight
23. Spring for ball catch
24. Ball
25. Adjusting screw

Bolt Assembly

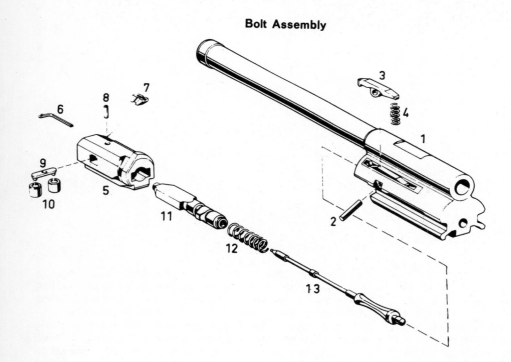

1. Bolt head carrier
2. Cylindrical pin
3. Locking lever
4. Compression spring
5. Bolt head
6. Extractor spring
7. Extractor
8. Cylindrical pin
9. Holder for locking rollers
10. Locking rollers
11. Locking piece
12. Firing pin spring
13. Firing pin

The 7.62mm NATO G3 rifle as originally made for West Germany has a flip over type sight and wooden butt. The G3A1 has a folding type stock and flip over sight. The G3A2 has a rotating type rear sight; the current weapon being manufactured is the G3A3. It has a rotating type rear sight, a modified front sight guard and a prong type flash suppressor. G3A4 is similar, but has a retractable type stock, and G3AZF is the G3A3 with a scope mounted for sniping.

VARIATIONS OF THE G3 RIFLE

Heckler and Koch has produced assault rifle versions of the G3 rifle in caliber .223 (model HK33 and HK33K) 7.62X39 Soviet M1943 cartridge (Model HK32 and 32K).

Semiautomatic versions of the G3 are sold as the HK 91A2 (standard stock) and HK 91A3 (retractable stock); the 5.56mm HK33 is marketed as the HK 93A2 and HK 93A3.

CHARACTERISTICS OF FOUR G3 VARIATIONS

	HK33	**HK33K**	**HK32**	**HK32K**
Caliber:	.233	.233	7.62 × 39mm.	7.62 ×39mm.
Barrel length:	15.35 in.	12.4 in.	15.35 in.	13.6 in.
Length overall:	36.1 in.	Stock retracted, 24.4 in.	36.1 in.	Stock retracted, 25.6 in.
		Stock extended, 32.7 in.		Stock extended, 33.9 in.
Weight:	6.6 lb.	6.6 lb.	6.6 lb.	6.6 lb.
Magazine capacity:	20rounds.	40 rounds.	30 rounds.	30 rounds.
Cyclic rate:	600 r.p.m.	600 r.p.m.	600 r.p.m.	600 r.p.m.
Muzzle velocity:	3182 f.p.s.	3018 f.p.s.	2560 f.p.s.	2493 f.p.s.

All the above rifles operate the same as the G3.

West German G3A3 Rifle.

Back Plate with Rigid Butt Stock

1. Butt stock
2. Butt plate
3. Buffer screw
4. Lock washer
5. Safety plate
6. Tubular rivets
7. Bush for tubular rivet
8. Back plate with recoil spring guide tube
9. Recoil spring
10. Guide ring
11. Stop pin
12. Rivets
13. Buffer assembly
14. Locking screw
15. Lock washer
16. Locking pins

1. Butt stock
2. Back plate
3. Recoil spring
4. Guide ring
5. Stop pin
6. Rivets
7. Buffer bolt
8. Buffer spring
9. Buffer screw
10. Spring loaded latch
11. Cover
12. Gripping lever
13. Locking ring with spring
14. Spring ring
15. Locking pins

Back Plate with Retractable Butt Stock

Heckler and Koch 5.56mm HK 33KA1 Rifle.

WEST GERMAN SUBMACHINE GUNS

The standard submachine gun of the West German Army is the Israeli-designed UZI, but a number of native West German designs have appeared since the late fifties. Mauser, Walther, Heckler & Koch, Anschütz and Erma have all prepared designs. These weapons have mainly appeared in prototype form and are usually made of stampings and are of short length.

DUX 53

The DUX 53 is a weapon designed at the Oviedo Arsenal in Spain by W. Daugs and L. Vorgrimmler, based on the design of the Finnish 9mm Model 44 submachine gun, which in turn was based on the Soviet PPS M1943. A quantity of these weapons was manufactured for the West German Border Police. This weapon and various modifications made by Mauser and Anschütz were tested by the West German Army during the mid-fifties.

THE WALTHER SUBMACHINE GUN

The Walther submachine gun was introduced in 1963. There are two basic versions of this gun: the MPL (long model), and the MPK, (short model). The Walther is made mainly of steel stampings, with a folding steel stock that can be folded to either side. The bolt is guided through the receiver by a guide rod mounted in the receiver above the bolt face.

The safety lever on the Walther gun is fitted on both sides of the receiver.

9mm Parabellum Walther MPL submachine gun with stock extended.

Characteristics of the Walther Submachine Gun

	MPL	MPK
Caliber:	--------------9mm Parabellum----------------	
System of operation:	Blowback, full automatic only*	
Length overall: w/stock extended	29.42 in.	25.96 in.
w/stock folded	18.1 in.	14.75 in.
Barrel length:	10.25 in.	6.75 in.
Weight:	6.62 lbs.	6.27 lbs.
Feed device:	32-round, staggered row, detachable box magazine.	
Sights: Front:	--------------Protected blade----------------	
Rear:	Flip over, notch for 75m and aperture for 125m. ------------------------	
Muzzle velocity:	Approx.	Approx.
	1370 f.p.s.	1250 f.p.s.
Cyclic rate:	--------------550 r.p.m. ------------------------	

*Can be made selective fire in special order.

Cutaway view of the Walther submachine gun showing the weapon ready to fire.

9mm Parabellum MPL (top) and MPK (bottom) submachine guns.

THE HECKLER AND KOCH HK54
(MP5)SUBMACHINE GUN

The HK 54 is the submachine gun version of the G3 rifle. It is, as the G3 rifle, a delayed blowback operated weapon that fires from a closed bolt. There is a theory that delayed blowback submachine guns have less vibration and rise than blowback operated submachine guns. On the other hand, they are more complex and usually more expensive.

A finer degree of accuracy can be obtained with a gun that fires from a closed bolt, since the only disturbing influence on "hold" is the forward movement of a light hammer and/or firing pin as opposed to the forward movement of a heavy bolt. The "lock time" (the period from trigger/sear release to ignition of primer) is also less on a weapon that fires from a closed bolt than on a weapon that fires from an open bolt; the other side of the coin in this case, however, is the "cook-off" problem. Automatic fire heats up a weapon rather rapidly, and a point is reached when the temperature of the chamber will cause cartridges to function spontaneously. Some designs have solved this problem by firing from an open bolt in automatic fire and from a closed bolt in semiautomatic fire, as is done by the 7.92mm FG42 German World War II paratroop rifle and the US

Johnson.

Many parts of the HK54 are common to the G3 rifle.

Characteristics of the HK54 Submachine Gun

Caliber: 9mm Parabellum.
System of operation: Delayed blowback, selective fire.
Length overall: w/fixed stock, 26 in.
          w/retractable stock fixed, 26 in.
          w/retractable stock retracted, 19.3 in.
Barrel length: 8.85 in.
Weight: 5.5 lbs.
Feed device: 30-round, detachable box magazine.
Sights: Front: Post.
       Rear: Flip-type w/"U" notch.
Muzzle velocity: Approx. 1312 f.p.s.
Cyclic rate: 600 r.p.m.

The West German Border Police have adopted the HK54, which with fixed stock is called the MP5 and with retractable metal stock is called the MP5A1. A later version of this weapon with modified front sight, rotating rear sight and modified front section of barrel is called the MP5A2 with fixed stock and MP5A3 with retractable metal stock.

HK MP5A2 (top) and MP5A3 (bottom) as used by the West German Border Guards.

Maschinenpistole 9 mm × 19
· MP 5 A 2 ·

Tafel IVa

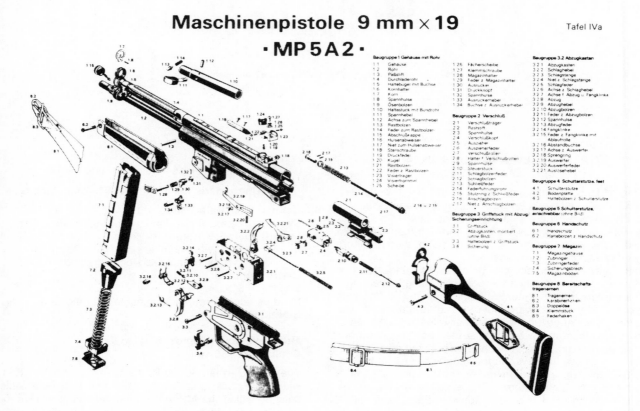

Baugruppe 1 Gehäuse mit Rohr

1.1 Gehäuse
1.2 Rohr
1.3 Paßstift
1.4 Durchladerohr
1.5 Haltebügel mit Buchse
1.6 Kornhalter
1.7 Korn
1.8 Spannhülse
1.9 Ösenbolzen
1.10 Haltestück mit Bundrohr
1.11 Spannhebel
1.12 Achse zum Spannhebel
1.13 Rastbolzen
1.14 Feder zum Rastbolzen
1.15 Abschlußkappe
1.16 Hülsenabweiser
1.17 Niet zum Hülsenabweiser
1.18 Stellschraube
1.19 Druckfeder
1.20 Kugel
1.21 Rastbolzen
1.22 Feder z. Rastbolzen
1.23 Visierträger
1.24 Visiertrommel
1.25 Scheibe

1.26 Fächerscheibe
1.27 Klemmschraube
1.28 Magazinhalter
1.29 Feder z. Magazinhalter
1.30 Ausrücker
1.31 Druckknopf
1.32 Spannhülse
1.33 Ausrückerhebel
1.34 Buchse f. Ausrückerhebel

Baugruppe 2 Verschluß

2.1 Verschlußträger
2.2 Raststift
2.3 Spannhülse
2.4 Verschlußkopf
2.5 Auszieher
2.6 Auszieherfeder
2.7 Verschlußrollen
2.8 Halter f. Verschlußrollen
2.9 Spannhülse
2.10 Steuerstück
2.11 Schlagbolzenfeder
2.12 Schlagbolzen
2.13 Schließfeder
2.14 Federführungsrohr
2.15 Stützrg z. Schließfeder
2.16 Anschlagbolzen
2.17 Niet z. Anschlagbolzen

Baugruppe 3 Griffstück mit Abzug-/Sicherungseinrichtung

3.1 Griffstück
3.2 Abzugkasten, montiert (ohne Bild)
3.3 Haltebolzen z. Griffstück
3.4 Sicherung

Baugruppe 3.2 Abzugkasten

3.2.1 Abzugkasten
3.2.2 Schlaghebel
3.2.3 Schlagstange
3.2.4 Niet z. Schlagstange
3.2.5 Schlagfeder
3.2.6 Achse z. Schlaghebel
3.2.7 Achse f. Abzug u. Fangklinke
3.2.8 Abzug
3.2.9 Abzughebel
3.2.10 Abzugbolzen
3.2.11 Feder z. Abzugbolzen
3.2.12 Spannhülse
3.2.13 Abzugfeder
3.2.14 Fangklinke
3.2.15 Feder z. Fangklinke mit Ablaufrolle
3.2.16 Abstandbuchse
3.2.17 Achse z. Auswerfer
3.2.18 Sprengring
3.2.19 Auswerfer
3.2.20 Auswerferfeder
3.2.21 Auslösehebel

Baugruppe 4 Schulterstütze, fest

4.1 Schulterstütze
4.2 Bodenplatte
4.3 Haltebolzen z. Schulterstütze

Baugruppe 5 Schulterstütze, anschiebbar (ohne Bild)

Baugruppe 6 Handschutz

6.1 Handschutz
6.2 Haltebolzen z. Handschutz

Baugruppe 7 Magazin

7.1 Magazingehäuse
7.2 Zubringer
7.3 Zubringerfeder
7.4 Sicherungsblech
7.5 Magazinboden

Baugruppe 8 Bereitschafts-trageriemen

8.1 Trageriemen
8.2 Karabinerhaken
8.3 Doppelöse
8.4 Klemmstück
8.5 Federhaken

WEST GERMAN MACHINE GUNS

WEST GERMAN 7.62mm MG42/MG3.

The Bundeswehr uses updated MG42s chambered for the NATO cartridge. These weapons are discussed in Chapters 1 and 21. During the past decade Heckler and Koch has developed a series of machine guns based upon the roller lock mechanism of the G3 rifle.

THE HECKLER AND KOCH MODEL 11, 12, 13, 21, 21A1 AND 23 MACHINE GUNS

These weapons are variations on the basic G3 design guns. The Model 11 can be fed with either a saddle drum magazine or a box magazine and is chambered for the 7.62mm NATO cartridge. The Model's 12 and 13 are the same as the Model 11 but are chambered for the Soviet 7.62 X 39mm and the 5.56mm (.223) cartridges, respectively. Models 12 and 13 are also somewhat lighter than the Model 11.

The Model 21 is belt fed but can also, with a special adaptor, use a box magazine. The Model 21 may be chambered for the 7.62mm NATO, 7.62 X 39mm or 5.56mm (.233) cartridges. The Model 21A, which has been adopted by Sweden, differs from the Model 21 in having a hinged rather than a removable feed tray. A reduced weight 5.56mm (.223) version of the Model 21A is the Model 23.

All of the above weapons have quick change barrels. Rear sights are usually of the radial type, but the rotating type aperture, as on the G3A3 rifle, may also be found.

All of these weapons fire from a closed bolt, and all have a quick change barrel. Many of the components of these weapons are interchangeable with the components of the G3 rifle. The concept of having a weapon system consisting of a number of weapons of basically similar construction with different application, i.e. individual weapon, squad automatic weapon and (in some cases) support machine gun, has become quite popular. This type of weapon system design has a definite advantage from a training and logistical point of view but frequently has some technical drawbacks. Briefly, gun design is a series of tradeoffs; what one gains in one area one loses in another, and there is no weapon in any category that is better than all other weapons of its type in all characteristics.

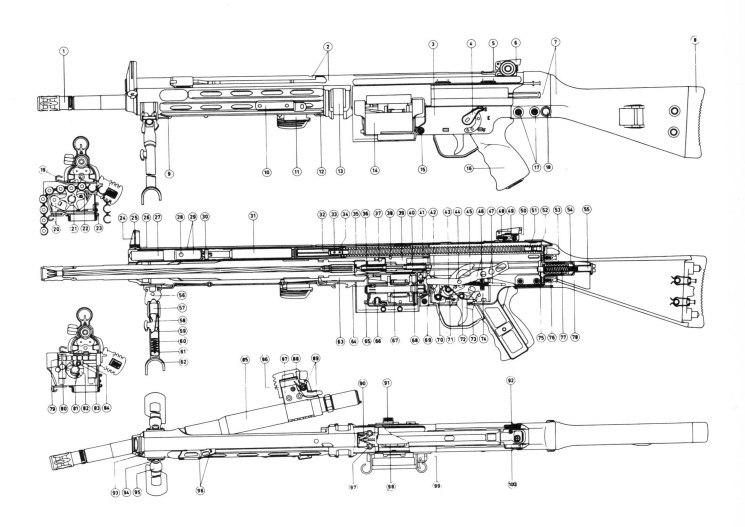

Schematic view of HK21 Machine Gun; note especially that bottom drawing shows the quick barrel change feature.

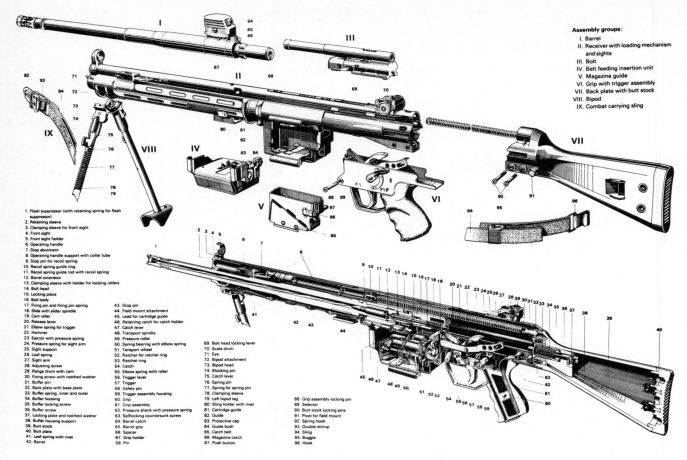

Assembly groups:
  I. Barrel
 II. Receiver with loading mechanism and sights
III. Bolt
 IV. Belt feeding insertion unit
  V. Magazine guide
 VI. Grip with trigger assembly
VII. Back plate with butt stock
VIII. Bipod
 IX. Combat carrying sling

1. Flash suppressor (with retaining spring for flash suppressor)
2. Retaining spring
3. Clamping sleeve for front sight
4. Front sight
5. Front sight holder
6. Operating handle
7. Stop abutment
8. Operating handle support with collar tube
9. Stop pin for recoil spring
10. Recoil spring guide ring
11. Recoil spring guide rod with recoil spring
12. Barrel extension
13. Clamping sleeve with holder for locking rollers
14. Bolt head
15. Locking piece
16. Bolt body
17. Firing pin and firing pin spring
18. Slide with slider spindle
19. Cam roller
20. Release lever
21. Elbow spring for trigger
22. Hammer
23. Ejector with pressure spring
24. Pressure spring for sight arm
25. Sight support
26. Leaf spring
27. Sight arm
28. Adjusting screw
29. Range drum with cam
30. Fixing screw with toothed washer
31. Buffer pin
32. Back plate with base plate
33. Buffer spring, inner and outer
34. Buffer housing
35. Buffer locking screw
36. Buffer screw
37. Locking plate and toothed washer
38. Buffer housing support
39. Butt stock
40. Butt plate
41. Leaf spring with rivet
42. Barrel

43. Stop pin
44. Field mount attachment
45. Lead for cartridge guide
46. Retaining catch for catch holder
47. Catch lever
48. Transport spindle
49. Pressure roller
50. Spring bearing with elbow spring
51. Transport wheel
52. Ratchet for ratchet ring
53. Ratchet ring
54. Catch
55. Elbow spring with roller
56. Trigger lever
57. Trigger
58. Safety pin
59. Trigger assembly housing
60. Grip
61. Grip assembly
62. Pressure shank with pressure spring
63. Selflocking countersunk screw
64. Barrel catch
65. Barrel grip
66. Spacer
67. Grip holder
68. Pin

69. Bolt head locking lever
70. Scale drum
71. Eye
72. Bipod attachment
73. Bipod head
74. Blocking pin
75. Catch lever
76. Spring pin
77. Spring for spring pin
78. Clamping sleeve
79. Left bipod leg
80. Sling holder with rivet
81. Cartridge guide
82. Guide
83. Protective cap
84. Guide bush
85. Catch bolt
86. Magazine catch
87. Push button

88. Grip assembly locking pin
89. Selector
90. Butt stock locking pins
91. Pivot for field mount
92. Spring hook
93. Double stirrup
94. Sling
95. Buggle
96. Hook

Exploded and section view of HK 7.62mm NATO HK21 Machine Gun. This weapon has been adopted by Portugal.

CHARACTERISTICS OF THE HECKLER AND KOCH MACHINE GUNS

Model:	HK11	HK21	HK13
Caliber:	7.62mm NATO	7.62mm NATO	.223
System of operation:	--	Delayed blowback, selective fire	--
Length overall:	40.15 in.	40.1 in.	38.6 in.
Barrel length:	17.71 in.	22.63 in.	22.13 in.
Weight w/o magazine:	15 lbs.	14.7 lbs. w/o bipod.	8 lbs.
Feed device:	80-round saddle drum or 20-round box	Metallic link belt.	100-round detachable drum or 20-round detachable box magazine
Sights: Front:	--Protected post--		
Rear:	------------------------------Rotary rear with V notch and apertures------------------------------		
Cyclic rate:	850 r.p.m.	750 r.p.m.	600 r.p.m.
Muzzle velocity:	2589 f.p.s.	2625 f.p.s.	3248 f.p.s.

Heckler and Koch .223 HK 13 Machine Gun.

Germany manufactured over 13 million small arms during World War II. In addition, they used tremendous quantities of captured arms and arms made in occupied countries. There were never sufficient numbers of standard German small arms on hand at any time during World War II to arm all German forces. Even at the beginning of the war, 11 divisions of the German Army were armed with Czech small arms.

As a result of the continual shortage, the Germans used a great variety of small arms. However, they did standardize to the extent that all front-line units used weapons chambered for standard service cartridges; they also had the highest priority for standard service weapons. Service and police units and other German war organizations used whatever was available.

Considered standard during World War II were the following: the 9mm Walther P38 service pistol (the 9mm Luger 08 was a substitute standard); the 9mm MP38 and MP40 submachine guns; the 7.92mm Mauser Kar98K and 7.92mm G33/40 and semiautomatic Kar43 rifles; and the 7.92mm MG42 machine gun, which became standard at the end of the war, replacing the MG34.

German World War II Small Arms
21

GERMAN PISTOLS

A total of twenty-seven different models of German designed and made pistols (not including caliber .22 pistols) were approved for service use by the German forces between 1914 and 1945. Only a few models were ever purchased in quantity. These pistols were in 6.35mm (.25ACP), 7.65mm (.32 ACP), 9mm short (.380 ACP), 9mm Parabellum, 7.65mm Luger (caliber .30 Luger) and 7.63mm Mauser.

Toward the end of World War II, Walther and Mauser developed 9mm Parabellum pistols composed mainly of steel stampings, which were to be used to arm the Volksturm. This was a Home Guard type organization composed of those males too old or too young or too infirm for the regular armed forces or those having essential jobs in civilian industry. Both designs were disapproved by the German Army Ordnance Office.

Because of the large number of different types of pistols used by the German Army, only those that were used in large quantities will be covered in detail in this book. The Germans also used many foreign pistols, of which some were captured and some were made in occupied countries. The most common among these were the Polish 9mm Parabellum, Radom M1935, the FN Hi-Power, the Czech 7.65mm Model 27, the Czech 9mm short Model 38, the Hungarian 7.65mm Model 37 and the Belgian 7.65mm and 9mm short FN Browning Model 1922.

The pistol on the left has a special safety feature not embodied in the P-38, through otherwise the pistols are much alike. The P-38 is the mass production version of the Walther HP. Firing pins of the pattern pictured in the left photo are commercial safety types. In these, the pin is retracted to prevent the hammer from reaching it.

THE 9mm P38 PISTOL

The P38 was developed by the Waffenfabrik, Carl Walther at Zella Mehlis Thuringia. It is descended from a double-action 9mm Parabellum pistol developed around 1935 that used the double-action system introduced with the Walther PP pistol in 1929. In 1937, the Walther HP Heeres (Army) pistol appeared on the commercial market. In addition to 9mm Parabellum, the HP was made in caliber .45 and Super .38. The Heeres pistol has a rectangular section firing pin, a machined slide stop as opposed to the fabricated type used on the P38, anvil surface hammer and different type grip pieces (usually checkered wood).

The P38 was adopted in 1938. As originally made for the German Army, it bore the Walther marking. During the war, German code letters were used to identify the manufacturers: "ac" for Walther, "cyq" for Spree werke, "byf" and "svw" for Mauser, "dov" for Brunn (Brno) and "ch" for FN, which manufactured approximately 3500 sets of components. About one million P38s were made during World War II.

A considerable impression was made on US personnel by the double-action feature of the P38. While not a new concept, Walther introduced it in 1929 with the PP and it was used on earlier pistols—it was apparently almost unknown in the US. The value of the double-action feature is somewhat exaggerated. If a man is in battle and carrying a pistol, he will have it in his hand cocked; the main advantage of the double-action feature is the possibility of striking a defective primer a second blow with a pull of the trigger. Even with wartime ammunition, defective primers are rare, and the long trigger pull through with double action, if used for all first shots (the P38 hammer can be cocked and the weapon fired single-action), will have a tendency to impair accuracy. There is a safety advantage to the double action when carrying a pistol with a cartridge in the chamber, but single-action automatics, like the US .45 M1911A1 with inertia-type firing pins, can be carried with the hammer down on a loaded chamber with safety if reasonable precautions are taken.

The P38 was used by Sweden, who called it P39. It saw some use in France, East Germany and in some of the Soviet satellites for a time after World War II.

The Walther "Armee" pistol is a hammerless version of the Walther HP made for commercial sale prior to World War II. It was made for the 9mm Parabellum cartridge, and a few were made in caliber .45 for sale in the US. One variant of the "Armee" pistol has been reported with a duraluminum receiver.

Loading and Firing the P38. Load and insert magazine in handle as is customary in all automatic pistols of this general design.

Draw back the slide, which will ride over the head of the hammer, and cock it, meanwhile compressing the recoil springs and permitting a cartridge in the magazine to rise in line with the breechblock. Release the slide and let it go forward under the influence of the recoil springs.

If the safety catch has been in the "Fire" position during the backward movement of the slide, then the hammer will remain at full cock, and the pistol is now ready for immediate firing.

If the safety catch was in the "Safe" position when the slide was retracted, then the chamber will load but the hammer will go forward safely to its resting place. The pistol cannot be fired now

9mm Parabellum Walther of early manufacture.

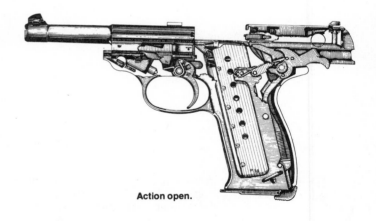

Action open.

Protruding pin (arrow) on the P-38 indicates a loaded chamber.

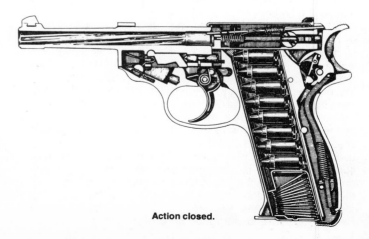

Action closed.

as the safety is locking the firing pin. However, if you now move the safety catch, the hammer may be cocked by the thumb, or the pistol may be fired by pulling straight back on the trigger bringing the double action factor into play.

Warning. Applying the thumb safety when hammer is cocked automatically locks the firing pin and then drops the hammer on it. In case of a defective or crystallized safety, the pistol may fire accidentally. It is not advisable to use this hammer lowering device on a loaded chamber with pistols of late World War II manufacture.

Field Stripping the P38

(1) Set the safety catch in the "safe" position and pull the slide back over the empty magazine, so that the inside catch on the slide stop will be forced up by the magazine follower and hold the slide open. Then remove the magazine.

(2) At the front end of the frame below the receiver is a lever-type locking pin. Turn this down and around as far as it will go.

(3) Hold the slide under control with the left hand and with the right thumb push down the slide stop. Now press the trigger and pull the barrel and slide directly forward in their runners on the receiver, sliding them out of the guides.

(4) Now turn barrel and slide upside down. A small locking plunger will be seen at the rear of the barrel assembly. Push the plunger and spring out the white metal locking cam block.

(5) Now slide barrel directly ahead out of slide. Lock will come forward with barrel.

(6) Push forward and up on locking cam block and lift it out of its recess. This completes field stripping.

(7) Top to bottom, left: Slide, barrel, lock, magazine. Top to bottom, right: Receiver, stock.

Note on Assembly of P38

Reverse stripping procedure.

When replacing locking block, be sure that its lugs are in line with the wide ribs on both sides of the barrel.

Insert barrel assembly as far as it will go into slide, then push the locking block into its locked position.

Hammer must be uncocked, and the ejector and the safety mechanism levers pushed down to prevent them from catching on the rear end of the slide.

With safety catch at "safe" position, hold the locking block in the locked barrel position, and push the slide and barrel onto the receiver in the guide. Force the slide all the way back against the tension of the springs and raise the stop to catch and retain the slide in the open position.

Turn the locking lever around on its pin as far as it will go to its original position. Press the slide stop and permit the slide to run home. Insert magazine.

Special Note on the P38 Pistol

When the pistol is loaded with a cartridge in the chamber, a floating pin protrudes from the slide above the hammer. A glance, or (in the dark) a touch, will always tell whether the chamber is loaded, making it unnecessary to pull back the slide as in other pistols.

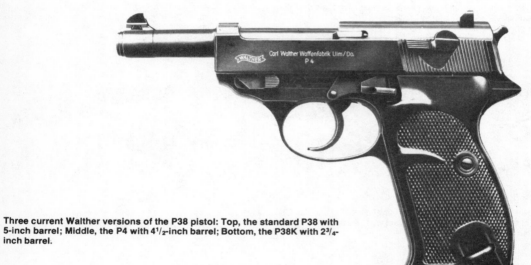

Three current Walther versions of the P38 pistol: Top, the standard P38 with 5-inch barrel; Middle, the P4 with 4$\frac{1}{2}$-inch barrel; Bottom, the P38K with 2$\frac{3}{4}$-inch barrel.

The Walther PPKS in .380 ACP. This variant of the PP and PPK family was devised for Interarms to meet current US import regulations.

THE 9mm LUGER (PO8)

The Luger is one of the best known pistols in the world, and there are several excellent books in English that deal with this pistol in detail far beyond the scope of this book. The Luger was first adopted as a service pistol by Switzerland in 1900; this model was chambered for the bottle-necked 7.65mm (called caliber .30 Luger in the US) Luger cartridge. The 9mm Parabellum cartridge version, which introduced the most widely-used pistol and submachine gun cartridge in the world, appeared in 1902 and was adopted by the German Navy in 1904. In 1908, it was adopted by the German Army and remained the standard service pistol until 1938. There were over 400,000 Lugers manufactured for the German Army after the adoption of the P38, and manufacture was continued until 1943. There are at least thirty-five different variations of the Luger in existence, including numerous variations of the basic PO8 used by the German Army.

The Luger was manufactured in Germany by Deutsch Waffen und Munitions fabriken (DWM), Simson, Krieghoff, Erfurt Arsenal and Mauser. It has also been manufactured by Vickers in England for the Dutch government and by the Swiss government arsenal at Bern for the Swiss government. Total Lugers manufactured is unknown, but it is probably at least two million and possibly considerably more.

The Luger is a fine-hanging pistol, very pleasant to shoot, and it introduced an exceptionally fine cartridge, the 9mm Parabellum. It is not, however, a standard pistol in any major country today because it is prone to stoppages if mud or sand gets into the action.

The Navy Luger and long-barreled 1908 type (frequently called the Model 1914, Artillery, or Model 1917) were also used in German service. The Navy Luger has a six-inch barrel, adjustable rear sight and is ridged for a wooden shoulder-stock holster. The long-barreled 1908 has an eight-inch barrel and a tangent-type rear sight and was frequently issued with the 32-round "Snail" magazine. The latter type appeared toward the end of World War I and is made of PO8 components except for barrel and sights.

Many Lugers have their grips ridged for shoulder-stock holsters, and the following facts should be brought to the attention of US collectors. Possession of a pistol that is ridged or slotted for a shoulder stock and the stock that fits the pistol requires

German 9mm Parabellum Model 08 Pistol (Luger PO8).

under US firearms laws that the weapon be registered with the Bureau of Alcohol, Tobacco and Firearms, US Treasury Department, the branch of the goverment that registers submachine guns and machine guns and enforces Federal Firearms laws. Failure to register this type of weapon can result in fine or imprisonment and at a minimum considerable trouble and embarrassment. It should be noted that in addition to the Federal statutes, most states have similar laws.

To Load 32-Shot Magazines

This magazine was issued during World War I. Each magazine comes with a filler. The lever must be wound against the tension of the magazine spring and locked into position by means of a spring loaded catch. The loading tool is slid over the mouth end of the magazine, and by a pumping action the cartridges are forced downward into the magazine. The magazine must be loaded cautiously since the lever is under heavy spring tension and if released it can do serious damage to the fingers.

(Note: this magazine is also used in the early model of the MP 18l Submachine Gun.)

The Long PO8 Luger with shoulder stock attachment and 32-shot magazine.

Field Stripping the P08 Luger

(1) Holding pistol in right hand press muzzle down firmly on a hard surface about 1/2 inch to release tension on the recoil spring. With the tension removed, the thumb catch on the sideplate may now be turned down to a vertical position.

(2) Now lift out the sideplate.

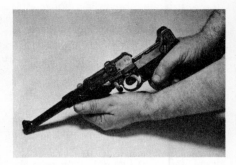

(3) Slide the complete barrel and toggle assembly directly to the front and out of the receiver.

(4) Buckle the toggle slightly to relieve tension and extract retaining pin on the left hand side.

(5) Now pull toggle assembly, breechblock containing firing pin and extractor directly back in their guide and out of the frame. No further dismounting is necessary nor recommended.

Note on Reassembling. Merely reverse stripping procedure. Take care hook suspended from rear of the toggle assembly drops into proper place, which is in front of the inclined ramps. Also note that when replacing the side plate, the tongue on the rear end must be inserted in the recess in the receiver and the projecting section of the trigger bar must fall into the proper slot at the top of the trigger.

Instructions for Loading and Firing the Luger

(1) To extract magazine: Press magazine release stud near trigger on left hand side and withdraw magazine from butt of pistol. To load magazine: Hold magazine firmly in left hand. Pull down stud attached to magazine platform. This will compress spring and permit cartridge to be dropped into the magazine.

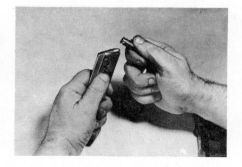

(2) To load chamber: Holding pistol pointed down toward ground with right hand, grip the milled knobs on the toggle and pull up and back as far as the breechblock will go. This compresses the recoil spring in the grip and permits the first cartridge in the magazine to rise in line with the breechblock.

(3) Release grip and spring will force breechblock back into locked position driving a cartridge into the chamber.

(4) To set thumb safety: Pull thumbpiece back and down. This will expose the German word "Gesichert," "Made safe." At the same time a flat solid steel piece will be seen to rise directly in front of the milled knob on the toggle. This locks the sear so the weapon cannot be fired.

(5) Breechblock stop: When the last cartridge has been fired, the stud of the magazine follower will force the catch up and hold the breech open with toggle joint buckled. Reloading from open breech: (a) Remove empty magazine. (b) Replace with loaded magazine. (c) Pull back on milled surfaces and permit breechblock to drive forward loading chamber.

How the Pistol (Luger) 08 Works

Starting with the pistol loaded and cocked, the action is as follows: The trigger being pressed, a connecting piece forces back a pin, which presses out a spring-retaining lock, permitting the striker to go forward and fire the cartridge in the chamber. (The involved trigger system of this pistol is one of its greatest weaknesses.) As the bullet goes forward down the barrel, the barrel and the recoiling mechanism locked together move backwards about half an inch. There is a toggle joint behind the breechblock, which functions exactly as a human knee. A strong pin at the rear fastens this toggle securely to the barrel extension. At the point where the breech pressure has dropped to safe limits, the center part of this toggle joint strikes against a sloping part of the frame, buckling the toggle exactly as a human knee but continuing to draw the breech block in a direct line in its guide in the barrel extension. During this opening movement, a short coil spring, which drives the firing pin and is situated inside the breech block, is compressed, caught and held by the sear. The extractor, fitted in the top front of the breech block, pulls the empty cartridge case back until it strikes an ejector piece and is hurled out of the pistol. A small coil spring snaps the extractor back into place. As the toggle joint buckles upward, a hook lever hanging from its pin and hooked under claws attached to the recoil spring in the grip, compresses the recoil spring, storing up energy for the return movement of the action. The magazine spring forces a cartridge up into line with the breech block. A shoulder below the rear end of the barrel contacts a shoulder in the receiver in front of the magazine space stopping further travel. The rearward motion is now complete.

Return Movement of the Action. The compressed recoil spring pulls down against the hook lever drawing down the bent toggle exactly as a bent knee straightens out when one stands up. This forward action drives the attached breech block straight ahead in its guide and strips the top cartridge out of the magazine and into the chamber. The extractor springs over the head of the cartridge and locks in the cannelure of the cartridge case. This raises the height of the extractor so that it is above the face of the breech block. Looking at the extractor—or touching it if in the dark—tells if the chamber is loaded. The breech block and the two levers of the toggle are now in a straight line, and the axis of the toggle is slightly below the other axes. The pistol is thus securely locked. The sear now connects with the trigger mechanism, trigger spring pushes trigger into place, and pistol is ready for the next shot.

How the Thumb Safety Works. While the normal method of applying the thumb safety on this pistol is to push it back and down, there are models in which the procedure is the exact reverse. When the pistol is on safe, a flat steel piece attached to thumb piece is forced up out of the receiver on the left-hand side just above the stock. This prevents the outward expansion of springs that lock the striker back in firing position.

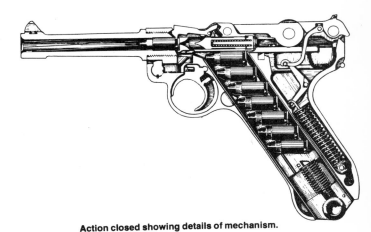

Action closed showing details of mechanism.

Action open, showing recoil spring hook-up.

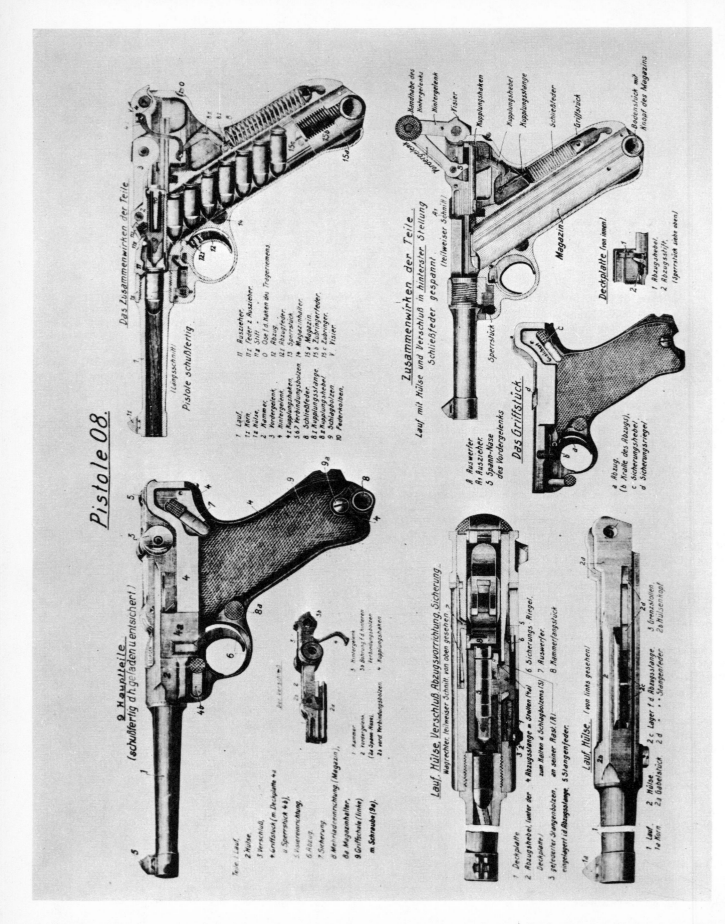

Pistole 08.

Das Zusammenwirken der Teile

Pistole schußfertig

(Längsschnitt)

1 Lauf.
1a Korn.
1b Hülse.
2 Kammer.
3 Vordergelenk.
4 Hintergelenk.
4+1 Kupplungshaken.
5/6 7 Verbindungsbolzen.
8 Schließfeder.
8 I Kupplungsstange.
8 a Kupplungshebel.
9 Schlagbolzen.
10 Federkolben.

11 Auszieher.
11:1 Feder z. Auszieher.
11a Stift .
0 Öse i.d. Haken des Trägeriemens.
12 Abzug.
12:1 Abzugfeder.
13 Sperrstück.
14 Magazinhalter.
15 a Magazin.
15 b Zubringerfeder.
15 c Zubringer.
V Visier.

2 Hauptteile

(schußfertig d.h. geladen u entsichert!)

Teile 1 Lauf.
2 Hülse.
3 Verschluß.
+ Griffstück (m. Deckplatte +a
a Sperrstück +b).
5 Visiereinrichtung.
6 Abzug.
7 Sicherung.
8a Magazinhalter.
9 Abladevorrichtung (Magazin).
8a Magazinhalter.
9 Griffschale (linke)
m Schraube (9a).

1 Kammer.
2 Vordergelenk.
2a verst Verbindungsbolzen.

3 Hintergelenk.
3b Bohrung f.d. hinteren
Verbindungsbolzen
+ Kupplungshaken.

Zusammenwirken der Teile

Lauf mit Hülse und Verschluß in hinterster Stellung
Schließfeder gespannt A1
(teilweiser Schnitt)

Handhabe des
Hintergelenks
Hintergelenk
Visier
Kupplungshaken
Kupplungshebel
Kupplungsstange
Schließfeder
Griffstück
Bodenstück mit
Knopf des Magazins

Magazin

Sperrstück

Deckplatte (von innen!)

1 Abzugshebel
2 Abzugsstift.
(Sperrstück siehe oben)

R Auswerfer.
R₁ Auszieher.
5 Spann-Nase
des Vordergelenks

Das Griffstück

a Abzug.
(b Kralle des Abzugs).
c Sicherungshebel.
d Sicherungsriegel.

Lauf, Hülse, Verschluß Abzugsvorrichtung, Sicherung
Wagrechter, (teilweiser Schnitt von oben gesehen.)

1 Deckplatte
2 Abzugshebel, (unter der
Deckplatte)
3 getrennter Stangenbolzen,
eingelagert id Abzugstange.

4 Abzugstange = Stollen (hai
zum Halten d Schlagbolzens (9)
an seiner Rast. (R!)
5 Stangenfeder.

6 Sicherungs Riegel.
7 Auswerfer
8 Kammerfangstück

Lauf Hülse (von links gesehen.)

1 Lauf.
1a Korn.
2 Hülse.
2a Gabelstück
2b

2c Lager f. d Abzugsstange
2d + + Stangenfeder

2e Grenzstollen
2e Hülsenkopf

3 Grenzstollen

THE MAUSER MILITARY MODEL

The Mauser was one of the first successful automatic pistols to appear but was never used by any power in the massive quantities of the Luger, P38, Colt M1911, Tokarev or Browning Hi-Power. The Mauser has usually been the substitute standard pistol, probably because it is basically a rather expensive and somewhat awkward weapon. It does not have the natural pointing qualities of the Luger or the ruggedness under poor environmental conditions of the Colt Browning pistols. Granting all this, it is an interesting weapon and represents a stage in the development of the modern self-loading pistol.

The Mauser pistol first appeared in 1895, and with it appeared the bottle-necked 7.63mm (caliber .30 Mauser) cartridge. The cartridge became more popular than the pistol, as it was adopted in slightly modified form by the USSR as their standard pistol and submachine gun (7.62mm Type P) cartridge from 1930 to the late 1940s and is still extensively used by the Soviet Bloc. At least thirty models of this pistol have been made, and it is beyond the scope of the book to cover them all.

In addition to being made in 7.63mm, the Mauser was made in 9mm Mauser and, for the German Army during World War I, in

German Mauser 7.63mm Automatic, Model 1912.

Mauser 7.63mm Model 1932 Selective Fire Pistol.

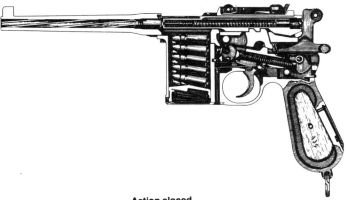

Action closed.

Action open and side cut away to show details of cocking mechanism.

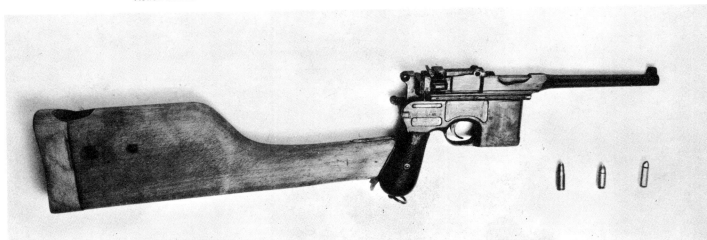

The Mauser 7.63mm automatic pistol with shoulder stock holster.

Loading and Firing the Mauser

(1) Grasp bolt wings firmly and draw bolt straight to the rear as far as it will go. The magazine follower will rise and hold the bolt open.

(2) Now insert a loaded clip in the clip guide directly in front of the rear sight. Exert firm even pressure with thumb and strip cartridges down into the magazine.

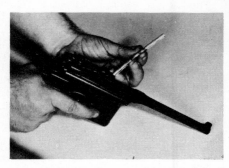

(3) Now pull clip straight up out of pistol. The bolt will run forward and load the chamber the instant the clip is withdrawn.

(4) Unless pistol is to be fired immediately, set the thumb safety by rocking it forward as far as it will go. Thumb safety may be easily released by pulling back slightly on hammer and tilting pistol up and back.

Field Stripping the Mauser

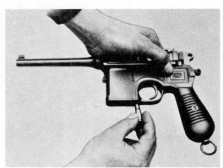

(1) To dismount magazine: Insert nose of a bullet in hole in magazine base plate and push up lock stud. With tension thus removed, slide plate forward slightly. It may now be eased out together with magazine spring and magazine follower.

(2) Cock the hammer. Using a cartridge clip, or screwdriver, press up the catch just below the base of the hammer and pull back barrel.

(3) Now withdraw barrel, barrel extension, and hammer mechanism clear of the receiver.

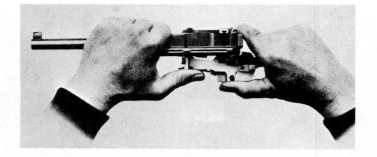

(4) Lift hammer mechanism out of barrel extension.

9mm Parabellum. The 9mm Mauser cartridge is a rather large cartridge, not interchangeable with any other 9mm cartridge. Copies of the Mauser have been made in Spain and China. Some of the Chinese copies have been in .45 caliber.

The 1912 Mauser was issued in 9mm Parabellum during World War II, equipped with shoulder stock, and was called Model 1916. A large figure "9" is branded on each grip piece of this weapon. The 7.63mm Model 1932, (commercial designation Model 712) was used by the German security units during World War II. This model of the Mauser has a detachable magazine—10- and 20-shot magazines are used—but it can also be loaded with 10-round stripper clips from the top of the receiver. It is a selective-fire weapon. The 7.63mm Mauser cartridge was made for German service use with steel cased cartridges during World War II; this would indicate that there was a considerable quantity of 7.63mm Mauser pistols in service at that time.

Mauser 7.65mm Model 1914 Pistol.

MAUSER MODEL 1910 PISTOL

The 1910 Mauser was extensively used as a pistol for service troops during World War I and was used, among others, by SS police units during World War II. The Mauser 1910 was very widely distributed through commercial channels. It is a straight blowback weapon, which has only one really unusual feature. When the last shot is fired, the slide remains open and the insertion of a magazine—after removal of the magazine originally in the weapon—whether loaded or empty causes the slide stop to release the slide and lets it return to the closed position, chambering a cartridge in the process (if a loaded magazine was inserted). The slide will also remain open if it is drawn manually to the rear with an empty magazine in the gun.

In 1934, Mauser modified the 1910. The modification consisted principally of various changes in components to ease manufacture, substitution of stampings for machined parts etc., and the use of streamlined type grips.

Magazine catch is in the bottom of the butt and must be pushed back to release the magazine.

When loaded magazine has been inserted in handle, slide is drawn fully to the rear exactly as in the case of the Colt automatic pistol and then permitted to run forward under the influence of the compressed recoil spring. The indicator pin protrudes from the rear of the breech block when the pistol is cocked, giving warning that the weapon is dangerous.

Pressing down on the milled thumb catch on the left side of the pistol just back of the trigger, sets the pistol as "safe." To release this safety, press in the small button directly below the thumb piece.

Mauser 7.65mm Model HSc Pistol.

Loading and Firing the Mauser HSc Pistol

The slide is pulled back its full length to cock the hammer and permit the magazine spring to force a cartridge up to the feed way. This movement also cocks the hammer. Releasing the slide permits the recoil spring, which is wrapped around the barrel, to pull the slide forward and load the firing chamber.

When the last shot has been fired, the magazine follower holds the slide open as a notice. When the magazine is removed, and then reinserted, the slide goes forward automatically.

A positive magazine safety is incorporated in this weapon. When the magazine is withdrawn, the trigger cannot be pulled.

A positive disconnector prevents more than one shot being fired for each pull of the trigger.

The action, being a straight blowback, permits the weapon to be a comparatively simple design, as no locking mechanism is necessary to shoot this low-power cartridge.

The exposed hammer may be lowered with the thumb. When it is necessary to fire, a pull on the trigger will function the hammer in the same general way that it does in a double-action revolver.

MAUSER MODEL HSc PISTOL

This pistol was frequently called the Mauser *Pistole neuer Art* (M.n.A.), or Mauser new-type pistol by the Germans. The design was produced in the late thirties and was intended for military, police, and service use. The weapon was widely used by German service and police units during World War II and although the finish varies depending on date of manufacture, it is, generally speaking, a well-designed weapon of good manufacture.

The HSc is a double-action pistol; an enlarged version, the 9mm parabellum HSv, was Mauser's entry in the German service pistol tests of the late thirties, which resulted in the selection of the Walther P38 as the German service pistol.

Field Stripping the HSc Mauser

Set the safety lever at the "Safe" position. Push the small spring supported piece inside the trigger guard directly in front of the trigger. While maintaining this pressure, push the slide forward a short distance.

Move the slide slightly backward. It may then be lifted up and off the receiver.

The barrel may be pushed forward against tension of the recoil spring and lifted up and out of the slide.

Removing the stock screws and lifting off the stocks exposes the firing mechanism.

THE SAUER MODEL 38 PISTOL

The Model 38 is a double-action pistol with internal hammer. It was a very popular weapon with the Germans and has several good features. Like the Walthers, it has a loaded-chamber indicator, which projects from the rear of the slide when the cartridge is in the chamber.

Field Stripping the Model 38 Sauer

When the magazine is removed, the weapon cannot be fired. The thumb safety not only blocks the hammer when it is applied, but pushes it back out of engagement with the sear.

The double-action firing system is one of the best developed. It utilizes a minimum of springs and is entirely enclosed.

One unique feature is an exposed cocking lever that does not move with the action. When the weapon has been loaded and cocked by a movement of the slide, pressing down on this lever will safely lower the hammer so that a cartridge may be carried in the firing chamber in complete safety. Pulling straight through on the trigger will cock and trip the hammer to fire the cartridge. However, pressure on the cocking lever will also recock the hammer should it be desirable to take more deliberate aim.

Sauer 7.65mm Pistol Model 38.

Action closed.

Action open.

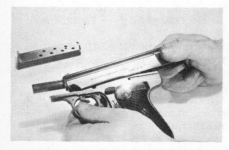

Pull down the locking latch in front and above the trigger. Draw the slide back to its full extent, lifting upward as you draw.

Let the disengaged slide move forward and push it off the barrel.

Recoil spring may be drawn off the barrel. Removing the grips exposes all working parts for attention. No further stripping need be done.

THE WALTHER PP AND PPK PISTOLS

These pistols are among the best known in the world and were made in large quantities for German service use and commercial sale. The Model PP *(Polizei Pistole)* was introduced in 1929, and the PPK *(Polizei Pistole Kurz),* a shorter version of the PP, was introduced in 1931. Both were originally chambered for the 7.65mm (.32 ACP) cartridge, but caliber .22, 6.35mm (.25 ACP) and 9mm short (.380 ACP) versions were also produced.

The PP and PPK had considerable influence on pistol design in Germany prior to World War II and throughout the rest of the world since. Copies of the PP have been made in Turkey (Kirikkale), Hungary (M48) and under license in France (Manurhin) since World War II. The PP and PPK may have been the first production pistols made with lightweight alloy receivers, since they were on the market with light receivers during the thirties. The PP and PPK are currently being made by Carl Walther at Ulm a/d, West Germany.

The Model PP was approved for German service use in 9mm short as well as 7.65mm. Some PP pistols made during World War II do not have the pin-type loaded chamber indicator, which normally protrudes from the rear of the slide.

How to Load and Fire the PP and PPK

The magazine is removed by pressing the magazine catch on the left side behind the trigger guard. Fill magazine with cartridges and insert smartly in grip. Push safety catch—on left rear of slide—down; pull slide to the rear and release. Push safety up into the off position, and pistol is ready to fire double action by pulling through on trigger. If a lighter trigger pull is desired, cock hammer and then press trigger. The slide will remain open on the last shot. It can be released on a new loaded magazine by pulling it slightly to the rear and releasing. The hammer will be cocked, and the pistol can be fired by pressure on the trigger or by applying the safety, in which case the hammer will fall and remain in the down position.

How the PP and PPK Work

These are blowback pistols of advanced design with external hammers, double-action triggers and positive manual safeties.

The recoil spring is positioned around the barrel. When the slide is drawn back over the top of a loaded magazine in standard automatic pistol fashion, the rear of the slide runs over and cocks the hammer. The recoil spring is compressed between a shoulder in the front end of the shaped slide (which surrounds the barrel muzzle) and the receiver abutment into which the barrel is secured. Releasing the slide permits the spring to pull it for-

Walther 7.65mm Model PPK Pistol.

ward. The breechblock face of the slide chambers a cartridge from the top of the magazine. The extractor claw in the right side of the breechblock is snapped into cartridge engagement by its spring.

Pulling the trigger will cause an attached trigger bar to draw the sear out of engagement with the hammer to fire the cartridge.

When the chamber is loaded, the front end of a floating pin in the slide is raised. The rear end of the pin projects from the rear of the slide. If this pin can be seen or felt, the chamber is loaded.

Safety Systems. A special hammer block of steel prevents any forward hammer movement until the trigger is deliberately pulled. When the trigger bar pulls the upper section of the rotating sear, a nose on the sear raises the hammer block until it is opposite a cut in the hammer face. Only at this point can the hammer fall far enough to hit the firing pin.

The firing pin is the spring-loaded type, shorter than the length of its stroke. Its spring pulls it back into the breechblock as soon as its forward drive is halted.

The rearward thrust of the gas within the cartridge case drives the slide to the rear to extract and eject and reload in standard blowback fashion.

Disconnector. The opening movement of the slide runs over and forces down a section of the trigger bar. This disconnects the trigger bar from effective sear contact. Until the trigger is released permitting the spring to force it ahead into firing position, the trigger bar attached to the trigger cannot rise into a slide undercut. Only when it can rise in this undercut can the trigger bar tip draw the sear out of engagement to let the hammer fall.

Thus one pull is necessary for each shot fired.

Walther 7.65mm Model PP Pistol.

Representative blowback type. The German Walther PP Pistol.

PPK stripped; hammer is cocked. Pull on trigger will draw trigger bar ahead to disengage sear from hammer. Pulling trigger guard down lowers slide locking lug seen under barrel.

CHARACTERISTICS OF GERMAN WORLD WAR II SERVICE PISTOLS

	P38	P08	Mauser Model 1932	Mauser Model 1910
Caliber:	9mm Parabellum.	9mm Parabellum.	7.63mm.	7.65mm.
System of operation:	Recoil, semi-automatic.	Recoil, semi-automatic.	Recoil, selective fire.	Blowback, semi-automatic.
Length overall:	8.6 in.	8.75 in.	11.75 in. w/o stock. 25.5 in. w/stock.	6.2 in.
Barrel length:	4.9 in.	4.06 in.	5.63 in.	3.4 in.
Weight:	2.1 lb.	1.93 lb.	2.93 lb. w/o stock. 3.93 lb. w/stock.	1.3 lb.
Feed device:	8-round, in-line, detachable box magazine.	8-round in-line, detachable box magazine.	10-or 20-round, staggered row, detachable box magazine.	8-round, in-line, detachable box magazine.
Sights: Front	Blade.	Blade.	Blade.	Blade.
Rear:	Rounded notch.	V notch.	Tangent leaf.	Round notch.
Muzzle velocity:	1115 f.p.s.	1050 f.p.s.	1575 f.p.s.	950 f.p.s.
Status:	Army Standard.	Army Limited Standard.	Police and S.S. use.	Army and Police use.

*Also made in 9mm short (.380 ACP)

CHARACTERISTICS OF GERMAN WORLD WAR II SERVICE PISTOLS, Continued

	Mauser HSc	Sauer Model 38	Walther PP	Walther PPK
Caliber:	7.65mm.	7.65mm.	7.65mm*.	7.65mm*.
System of operation:	Blowback, automatic.	Blowback, semiautomatic.	Blowback, semiautomatic.	Blowback, semiautomatic.
Length overall:	6.5 in.	6.3 in.	6.8 in.	6.1 in.
Barrel length:	3.4 in.	3.5 in.	3.9 in.	3.4 in.
Weight:	1.3 lb.	1.56 lb.	1.5 lb.	1.25 lb.
Feed device:	8-round, in-line, detachable box magazine.	8-round, in-line, detachable box magazine.	8-round, in-line, detachable box magazine.	7-round, in-line, detachable box magazine.
Sights: Front:	Blade.	Blade.	Blade.	Blade.
Rear:	Round notch.	Round notch.	Round notch.	Round notch.
Muzzle velocity:	950 f.p.s.	920 f.p.s.	948 f.p.s.	919 f.p.s.
Status:	Army and Police use.	Army and Police use.	Army and Police use.	Army and Police use.

GERMAN WORLD WAR II RIFLES

The Germans used a great variety of rifles during World War II, but only a few were of German manufacture and considered standard by the German Army. The 7.92mm (called 7.9mm by the Germans) Mauser Kar 98k was the most widely used standard rifle; none of the semiautomatic rifles were ever made in the quantity of the bolt action Kar 98k. The German plan of 1944/45 was to replace the bolt action and semiautomatic rifles with the selective-fire assault rifles of the MP43/44, StG44 series; the conclusion of the war prevented the fulfillment of this plan.

Many of the older German rifles such as the 11mm Mauser Models 1871, 1871/84, Model 98, 98a and the Model 88 were used by *Volksturm* (Home Guard Units), as were large quantities of captured weapons. Some weapons originally of foreign origin were adopted by the Germans, such as the bolt-action Model 33/40, which was basically a slight modification of the Czech Model 33 Carbine, and the Model 98/40, which was an alteration of the Hungarian Model 35 Rifle. Many other foreign rifles were not adopted or standardized in the American sense of the term but were used in quantity, such as the Czech and FN Model 24 Mausers and the numerous varieties of these found in Romania, Yugoslavia, Greece and Bulgaria. It is probable that at least one-third of the rifles brought back to the United States by returning soldiers and referred to as German service rifles are not German at all but in all probability were used by the Germans in one fashion or another. Even the 6.5mm Norwegian Model 1894 Krag was made in limited quantities for the Germans, and some Italian Model 38 Mannlicher Carcano rifles were, around 1943, made in 7.92mm for the Germans. The Polish 7.92mm Model 29 Mauser was also used extensively.

The Germans never seemed, until it was too late, to appreciate the advantage of semiautomatic rifles. They had used two semiautomatic rifles early in World War I—the Mexican-designed, Swiss-made 7mm Mondragon called the Aircraft self-loading carbine Model 1915 and the Mauser 7.92mm aircraft self-loading carbine, both of which were used by the Germans as aircraft guns before their aircraft were fitted with machine guns. A full-stocked version of the Mauser aircraft rifle, the 7.92mm Model 1916, was issued in limited quantities during the war.

Mauser had developed semiautomatic designs as early as 1898. Walther also produced a semiautomatic rifle prior to World War II. Still, the German Army adopted a modified 98 Mauser bolt-action rifle (the Kar 98k) in 1935, one year before the United States adopted the semiautomatic M1 rifle. This dim spot in German weapons technology may have been due to their accent on the machine gun, an area in which they were very advanced indeed.

Desperate measures were taken during the war to make up for the shortage of rifle fire power. A high percentage of each squad was equipped with submachine guns. The 7.92mm Rifle 41(M) and Rifle 41(W) were made in small quantity and were not very successful. The 7.92mm Model 43 Rifle was made in larger quantity but too late to have any real effect on the battlefield.

While the German Ordnance engineers did not exploit the self-loading rifle concept with their characteristic astuteness, they were the first to develop the idea of the comparatively light-weight assault rifle, which would replace the rifle and submachine gun. Development of an "intermediate" sized cartridge was started in Germany prior to World War II, but the conclusion of the war in 1945 prevented the Germans from putting their plan into fruition.

THE 11mm MAUSER MODEL 1871 AND 1871/84 RIFLES

These rifles were not used by any German Army units during World War II but were issued to the Home Guard. The Model 1871 was the first Mauser rifle to be adopted by any country and is a single-shot, black-powder weapon.

The Model 1871/84 is basically the same as the Model 1871 but has a nine-round tubular magazine. The Model 1871, 1871/84 and all their variations use a two-piece bolt. The 11mm Model 71 black powder cartridge, which has a round-nosed bullet, and the 11mm Model 71/84 black-powder cartridge, which has a flat-nosed bullet, were developed for use with these weapons. The Model 1871 rifle was widely used in China for many years and was one of the principal weapons of the Chinese during the Boxer rebellion in 1900. They were also still in wide use by German African colonial troops during World War I.

THE 7.92mm MODEL 1888 RIFLES AND CARBINES

The adoption of the 8mm Lebel, using smokeless powder cartridges, by the French in 1886 caused the Germans to search for a suitable counter weapon. The 7.92mm Model 1888 rifle and carbine were the German answer to the Lebel.

This rifle is frequently called a Mauser and also a Mannlicher; it was actually developed by a German Army Commission and combines the magazine of the Mannlicher with bolt features of the Mauser Model 1871/84. With the introduction of the Model 1888, Germany introduced the 7.92mm cartridge. The 7.92×57mm Model 88 cartridge had the same case as found in this cartridge today but had a .318-inch bullet, as opposed to the current .323-inch bullet (the "S" bullet, which was introduced circa 1904-05). Many of these rifles were modified later to use the larger-sized bullet, but as a matter of course the 1888 pattern weapons should not be used with current 7.92mm cartridges. In addition to the bore diameter problem, the chamber pressure of currently available 7.92mm cartridges, especially military rounds, far exceeds that for which the Model 1888 weapons were made.

The Model 1888 uses a five-round Mannlicher clip, which can be loaded with either side down, unlike the Mannlicher 1886 clip, which had to be loaded from one end only. The clip functions as part of the magazine and drops out the bottom of the protruding magazine box when the last round has been chambered.

The Model 1888 rifle and carbine and the Model 1891 rifle do not have wooden handguards. They have a sheet metal barrel jacket, which covers the barrel from the receiver to the muzzle. Theoretically this barrel jacket provided for better accuracy since it prevented the changes in center of impact frequently caused by the change of bearing on barrels of wooden stocks and handguards, as a result of humidity, etc. In actual practice, the metal barrel jacket suffered from many shortcomings; it was easily dented, water would seep into the joints and rust both the jacket and the outer portion of the barrel, and it was expensive and difficult to replace.

The Model 1888 was made in a rifle version and a carbine version; a carbine with stacking hook was introduced in 1891—for some reason this carbine was called Rifle Model 1891.

Numbers of these weapons were modified by Germany at a later date. There were three basic modifications:

(1). Some were fitted with a plunger and spring to eject the clip out of the top of the magazine after the last round was ejected in a fashion similar to that used

German 11mm Mauser Model 1871/84 Rifle.

German Gew 88.

M1888 sectioned to show locking, firing, and magazine systems. Magazine loaded. Bolt-head is detachable. Note relationship of locking lug seats to the face of the breech. Also see magazine follower driving cartridges up between clip walls. This is the Mannlicher clip system.

by the US M1 rifle. The clip ejection slot in the bottom of the magazine was covered.

(2.) Some were modified to use the charger used with the Model 98 rifle by milling a charger guide on the upper front end of the receiver guide and fitting a spring-loaded cartridge retaining rib on the upper side of the magazine.

(3.) Many were modified by relieving the chamber neck and forcing cone (lead) to use the "S" (.323 inch) bullet. These weapons are stamped "S" on the receiver.

The various modifications are called 88/05, 88/14 and 88S.

The Model 1888 was made at the German arsenals and by Ludwig Loewe, Haenel, Schilling and Steyr. This rifle was used to some extent by Austria during World War I. China bought many 1888 pattern weapons from Germany and made a modified copy, the Type 88 or "Hanyang" rifle. Yugoslavia and Ethiopia also used the Model 1888 in limited quantities.

THE 7.92mm MODEL 98 AND ITS VARIATIONS

Model 98 Rifle (Gew 98)

The rifle 98 *(Gewehr 98)*, introduced in 1898, is the most successful bolt-action design ever produced. In one form or another, the 98 action has been used by most of the countries of the world since 1898. As originally produced in Germany, the 7.92mm Model 98 rifle had the smaller sized (.318) bore of the Model 88 rifle; in 1903 the rifles were altered to use the larger diameter "S" bullet, and bore diameter was set at .323. At the same time, the rear sight was modified to match the ballistics of the "S" bullet.

The rifle 98 was the principal rifle of the German Army in World War I, and a number of variations of the rifle appeared during that war. One of the first was the 98 rifle with turned-down bolt handle used by bicycle troops. Sights were again modified to reduce the battle sight setting from 400 meters to 150 meters; the marking disc on the left side of the buttstock was replaced with a washer type disc used to assist in disassembly of the firing pin. A variant of the 98 (the Model 18) with a sliding breech cover similar in concept to that of the British Lee Metford and the Japanese Type 38 rifle, with detachable 5-, 10- and 25-round box magazines, was developed toward the end of World War I.

The Model 98/17 also had a bolt cover and a sqaure shoulder on the follower to prevent closing the bolt on an empty magazine in the heat of action. The 98/17 had a 100-meter sight setting.

The Model 98 rifle also appeared in a caliber .22 training version, which was made from the standard 98 by fitting a liner in the barrel. Some Model 98 rifles were fitted with tangent-type rear sights.

Model 98 Carbine (Kar 98)

The original Model 98 carbine was apparently never made in quantity since, unlike the Model 98 rifle, it is a rare item these days, and photographs of German troops in World War I rarely show this weapon in evidence. The rear sight is similar to that of the Model 98 rifle, and it has a peculiar stock and band arrangement. The stock runs to the muzzle as with the Model 88 carbine and 91 rifle, but is reduced in diameter at a point about six inches to the rear where a lower band, similar to the upper band of the 98 rifle, complete with bayonet mounting bar is fitted.

Model 98a Carbine (Kar 98a)

Originally called Kar98, this was the most popular carbine version of the Model 98 in World War I, and it had limited usage in World War II. The Carbine 98a appeared in 1904 and was made in tremendous quantities until approximately 1918. It has been claimed that the appearance of the Mark I Short Magazine Lee

Enfield in 1903 and the Springfield of the same year influenced the Germans in the adoption of this weapon. In any event, it is of handy size and was very popular with German troops. It introduced the tangent-type sight in the 98 series and was sighted for the "S" bullet as first issued. The prominent stacking hook, jointed upper band, front sight guard and full length handguards distinguish this weapon from the other German Mauser Service weapons. This weapon served as the model for the Polish Model 98 carbine.

Model 98b Carbine (Kar 98B)

This rifle, although designated a carbine, has the same length as the 98 rifle, but it has a turned-down bolt handle and a tangent sight like that of the Kar 98a, which is graduated for SS (heavy ball) bullet.

Model 98k Carbine (Kar 98k)

This weapon was the standard rifle of the German Army in World War II and has been made in tremendous quantities. It was adopted by Germany in 1935 and has many of the features of the commercial Mauser "Standard Model." The "k" in "98k" stands for *kurz*, meaning "short," and which is somewhat surprising since it is longer than the original Kar98 and about the same length as the Kar98a. Kar 98k has a half-length handguard, a tangent-type rear sight, turned down bolt handle and a hole bored through the stock in lieu of rear sling swivel (the Kar 98 and Kar 98a also have this feature).

In addition to the normal wooden furniture, Kar 98k has been issued with laminated and wooden stocks. Kar98k may still be found in service in various places in the world, and rebuilt specimens of this weapon were taken from the Viet Cong in South Vietnam. The Kar98k was made without bayonet mounting bar and with stamped bands in 1944–45.

Rifle 33/40 (Gew 33/40)

The nomenclature of this weapon is an example of the inconsistency of German nomenclature—this weapon is one of the shortest barreled Mausers used by the Germans, yet it is called a rifle. The 33/40 is the German version (made at Brno in occupied Czechoslovakia) of the Czech Model 33 carbine. It is distinguished by its light weight (the receiver has lightening cuts), short length and the extension of the shoe-type butt plate on the right side of the butt. It was used by German mountain and paratroop divisions, and because of its light weight and short barrel has a very sharp blast and heavy recoil. A folding-stock version of this rifle was made in limited quantity.

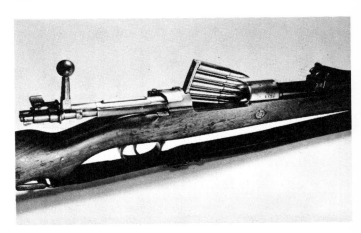

The Kar 98k is clip-loaded.

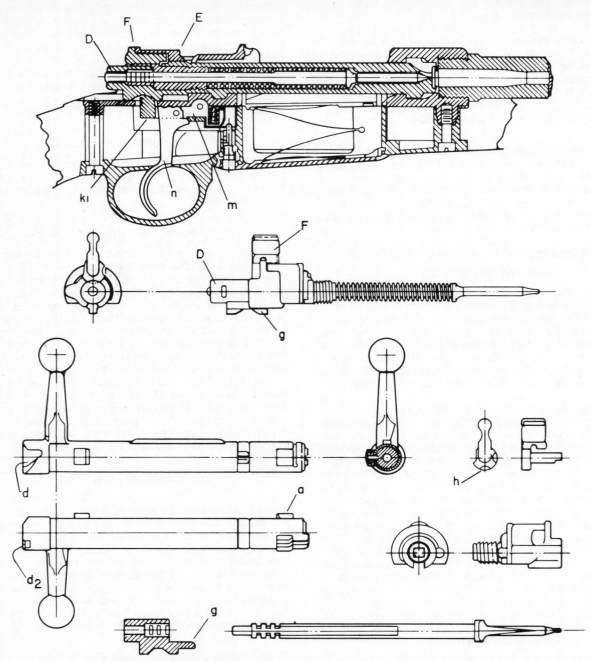

SCHEMATIC VIEW OF STANDARD MAUSER 98 OPERATING MECHANISM.

Functioning

a. The Mauser 98 is manually operated; all actions necessary to remove the fired cartridge case from the chamber and reload with a fresh cartridge are performed by the manipulation of the rifle's mechanism by the shooter.

b. As the bolt handle is turned upward, a cam in the rear of the bolt (d) forces the firing pin nut and firing pin rearward, compressing the firing spring. The root of the handle also cams against the receiver to provide powerful leverage for initial extraction of the fired cartridge. The firing pin unit has a lug on its underside which overrides the sear when the handle is turned fully up.

c. By drawing the bolt to the rear, the empty cartridge is removed from the chamber by action of the extractor. The extractor holds cartridge against the bolt face until it strikes the ejector (housed in the left rear of the receiver). The ejector pivots the cartridge about the extractor and expels it from the rifle.

d. The zigzag magazine spring has forced a fresh cartridge up, under the receiver feed lips. As the bolt is shoved forward, it pushes the cartridge out of the magazine, and the cartridge rides up the bolt face under the extractor. The locking lugs (a) are reseated in their abutments in the receiver by rotating the bolt handle

downward.

e. The trigger (n) is pinned to the sear (m) and has two humps on its top where it bears against the bottom of the receiver. When the trigger is pressed, the front hump (closest to the pin) acts as a lever to move the sear down. At this stage, the trigger pull has been very light, but as the second hump at the rear of the trigger contacts the receiver, a definite stop is felt and increased trigger pressure is necessary to completely disengage the sear from the lug on the firing pin nut. When these disengage, the firing pin spring drives the firing pin forward and fires the cartridge.

f. This rifle has two safety features: the manual safety and an automatic safety. The manual safety is operated by swinging it to the left; this interposes a solid portion of the safety (f) in front of the firing pin nut and cams the nut slightly rearward, off the sear. At the same time, a section of the safety shaft rotates into a fore-and-aft cut (d2) in the rear of the bolt; this locks the bolt closed. The automatic safety is the cocking cam (g and d) in the bolt; if the bolt is not completely locked, the cam on the firing pin nut will force the bolt closed by engaging the cam in the bolt. These cams prevent the firing pin from going completely home unless the bolt is rotated to a fully locked position.

7.92mm Model 98 Rifle and Model 98a Carbine.

The Kar 98b.

7.92mm Kar 98k.

The Gew 33/40.

Folding stock version of Gew 33/40.

The Gew 98/40.

The VG 1.

The VK98.

Caliber .22 DSM34 Rifle.

Caliber .22 KKW rifles.

Rifle 40k (Gew40k)

This weapon was apparently made in very limited quantity. It is a short weapon with a smaller trigger guard than the Kar98k. It also has a hole through the bolt handle and does not have a lower band.

Field Stripping the Mauser Carbine 98k

To remove bolt, proceed as for US Rifle Model 1917. With rifle cocked and safety lever vertical, half way between safe and locked position, pull out near end of bolt stop on left side of receiver and draw bolt straight out to the rear.

To dismount bolt, proceed as for Springfield.

To remove magazine mechanism, same as for Springfield.

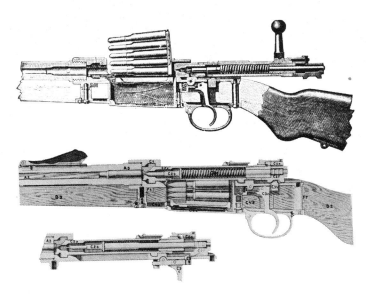

Kar 98k sectioned to show details of locking, firing and magazine systems.

Note position of dual forward locking lugs, which assure maximum support to case head at instant of firing.

The 98/40 Rifle (Gew 98/40)

The 7.92mm 98/40 is not a Mauser. It is based on the design of the 8mm Model 1935 Hungarian Rifle. The 98/40 was made only in Hungary by the Danuvia Arms Works. The 98/40 has a two-piece Mannlicher-type bolt, staggered row box magazine, which is flush with the bottom of the stock, and a two-piece stock similar to that of the Lee Enfield.

The Hungarian Model 43 rifle is quite similar to the 98/40, but the 98/40 can be distinguished from the Model 43 by the bayonet mounting bar under the barrel and the sling mounting slit drilled through the buttstock.

GERMAN VOLKSSTURM RIFLES

Volkssturm Gewehr 1 (VG1)

The 7.92 VG1 was a last ditch weapon made in a number of shops during the closing days of World War II. It has a crudely-made bolt and stock and uses the magazine of the semiautomatic Model 43 rifle.

Firing the VG1 can be a risky affair, since they were made at the low point of German manufacture in World War II.

Volkssturm Karabiner 98 (VK98)

The 7.92mm VK98 uses the Model 98 action combined with miscellaneous barrels from old German and foreign Mausers. The stock is very crude and is of unfinished, unseasoned wood. Most of these weapons are single shot, but some were fitted with the semiautomatic Model 43 rifle magazine.

GERMAN TRAINING RIFLES

The Germans used a number of rifles for training, including service rifles such as the Model 98 rifle converted to caliber .22; it had a conversion unit that could be easily inserted into a service rifle to convert it to .22 caliber; they had similar devices to convert the pistol 08.

They also had two caliber .22 training rifles: the Sport Model 34 and the Small Caliber KKW.

The German Sport Model 34 (DSM34)

This single-shot rifle, which was sold commercially in addition to its military use, was made by most of the standard German rifle makers, i.e., Mauser, Walther, Simson, etc. It has military-type sights and a sling, which is mounted on the left side as was done on the Kar 98k.

The Small Caliber Rifle (KKW)

This rifle is also single shot but is about ½ pound heavier than the DSM34. It has the same type bands as the Kar 98 k and has a slightly improved action as compared to the DSM34.

THE 7.92mm MODEL 41(W) SEMIAUTOMATIC RIFLE (GEW41(W))

In 1941, Mauser and Walther both introduced semiautomatic rifles, which were issued in limited quantities to the German Army and used in what was apparently a competitive combat trial. The Walther Model 41(W) was the more successful of the two designs, since it was developed into the Model 43 rifle, which was made in considerable quantity. The 41(W) is quite similar to the Model 43 except for the gas system. The bolt of the Model 41(W) has locking flaps, which are pushed into the locked position by the forward movement of the firing pin and are cammed out of the locked position by the rearward movement of the bolt carrier and the firing pin.

The gas system is a modification of the Bang system. A muzzle cone traps gas, which rebounds against a piston, forcing it to the rear. The piston in turn forces an operating rod to the rear and the operating rod forces the bolt carrier to the rear, thereby unlocking the bolt. The 41(W) has a fixed magazine and is loaded with two five-round chargers. This weapon is a finely-machined weapon and is much better made than the Model 43. There are specimens of this rifle stamped G41. They do not have a bolt-release catch.

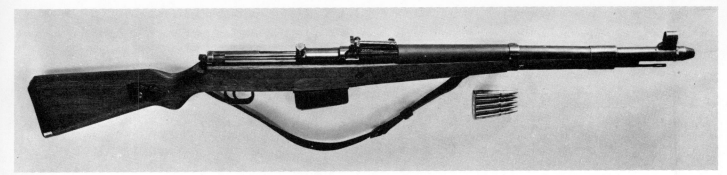

Gew 41(W), right side, bolt closed.

The Gew 41 (above) and the Gew 41(W) (Below).

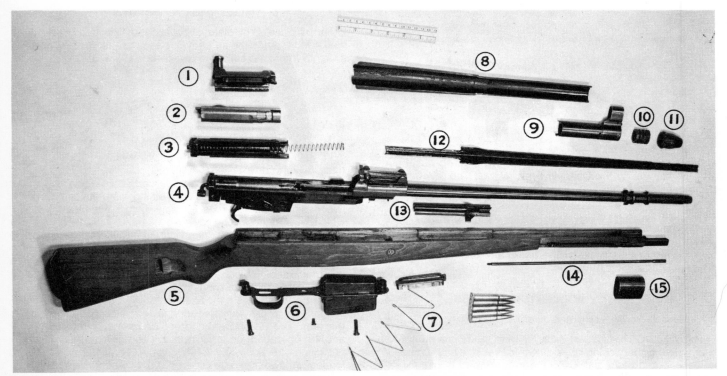

Detailed stripping to show gas and locking systems.
1. Bolt carrier. 2. Bolt. 3. Bolt housing with buffer and recoil springs. 4. Receiver and barrel assembly. 5. Stock. 6. Trigger guard and magazine.

7. Magazine follower and spring. 8. Forearm. 9. Gas cylinder. 10. Gas piston. 11. Gas cone. 12. Operating rod. 13. Operating rod trough and spring. 14. Cleaning rod. 15. Front band.

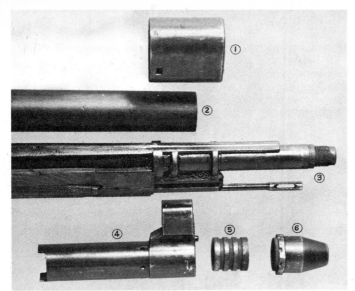

Gas operating assembly, Gew 41(W).
1. Front band lock. 2. Plastic handguard. 3. Barrel threaded for blast cone. Flat operating rod on top of barrel. 4. Operating rod cover which fits over barrel. 5. Piston which mounts around barrel and floats inside operating rod cover. 6. Blast cone which screws on barrel and traps gas to force floating piston back against operating rod.

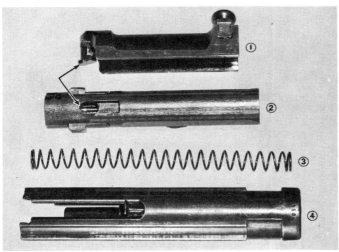

Details of bolt assembly.
1. Bolt carrier. Note projection at front end which seats in top of bolt and when driven back functions the firing-pin carrier to unlock the bolt. 2. Bolt complete with two lugs in locked position. Note firing pin housed inside carrier within the bolt. 3. Operating and recoil spring, which seats inside the hollow bolt. 4. Stamped bolt housing guides the travel of the bolt.

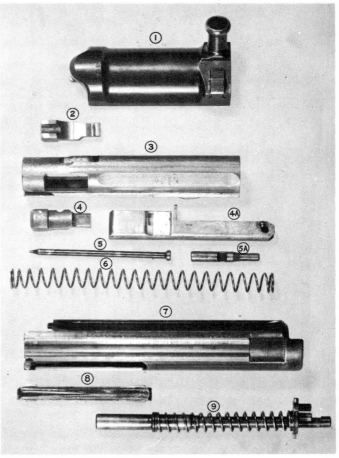

Details of bolt assembly, Gew 41(W).
1. Bolt carrier. Note projection on front end at left for pulling back firing-pin housing. Note bolt handle at upper right and carrier lock in line with it. 2. Bolt lock right side. 3. Detail of bolt. Note slot in left side to receiver bolt lock. Also cut in top to receive bolt carrier projection. Also note cam-face at lower right of bolt body which serves to cock the hammer by riding over and depressing it. 4. Left side bolt lock and 4A. Hollow firing-pin housing. 5. Firing-pin and 5A. Firing-pin extension which are inserted in the housing. Extension is retained by pin at rear of housing. 6. Recoil or operating spring. 7. Bolt housing. 8. Sliding cover for housing. 9. Recoil spring guide with secondary or buffer spring affixed. Right end of this rod projects through bolt housing. The two lugs lock in slot in the receiver to hold the bolt assembly securely in place.

Top receiver details, Gew 41(W).
1. Mauser tangent sight. 2. Operating rod forced through slot to indicate its position. 3. Bolt carrier fully retracted and manually locked by pushing bolt carrier lock to the right. Magazine cannot be loaded until this has been manually locked. 4. Bolt assembly rests inside the carrier. 5. The arm projecting from the rear of the receiver and turned up to the right is the safety which positively blocks sear action. Swinging it over to the extreme left sets it in the firing position.

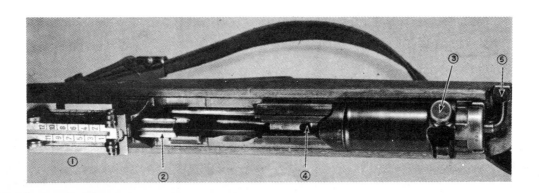

THE 7.92mm MODEL 41(M) (GEW41(M)) SEMIAUTOMATIC RIFLE

The 41(M), a Mauser development, was not a very successful design, and was abandoned in 1943. Apparently there were not very many of these rifles made, as they are comparatively rare today. The 41(M), like the 41(W), draws its operating gas at the muzzle. The gas rebounds from a muzzle cone and strikes a piston mounted under the barrel. The piston forces back an operating rod, which is connected to the rear section of the two-piece bolt. The rear section of the bolt pulls the front section backward, causing the frontally-mounted bolt locking lugs to be cammed out of their locking recesses in the receiver.

The 41(M) has an operating handle which has the same appearance as a bolt handle on a manually-operated bolt-action rifle and is operated in much the same manner, but it does not reciprocate with the action when the weapon is fired. The magazine of the 41(M) is fixed and loaded with two five-round chargers.

Gew 41(M), showing bolt open and gas cylinder and gas trap removed.

Bolt cover open. Showing detail of bolt and recoil spring. This is the Gew 41(M). It employs a turning bolt-head for locking.

Kar 43.

THE 7.92mm MODEL 43 SEMIAUTOMATIC RIFLE (G43)

In the *Gewehr 43 (G43)*, which is basically the same as the *Karbiner 43* or Kar43, Walther combined the bolt mechanism of the Model 41(W) with a gas system quite similar to that of the Soviet M1940 Tokarev rifle. G43 was made in large quantities, and a number of variations may be found among these rifles. The hand guard may be of wood or plastic, and the bolt carrier latch, which locks the bolt carrier and bolt to the rear, may be on the left or right side of the bolt carrier, or may not exist at all.

The G43 is very roughly made of many stampings, castings and forgings, which are machined only where necessary. All G43 rifles have a scope mounting to be used with the 1 ½ power ZF41 scope. The G43 has a detachable ten round magazine, which can be loaded while in the weapon with two five-round chargers.

The G43 was used to a limited extent by the Czech Army for a few years after World War II.

How the *Gewehr 43* Works

This rifle has a gas vent drilled in the barrel about 12 ½ inches back from the muzzle. It is on top of the barrel and leads into a

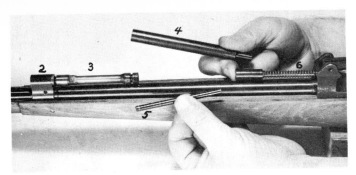

Gas piston operation.
2. Gas chamber above port in barrel into which gas escapes as bullet travels down barrel. 3. Gas cylinder screwed on. 4. Outside gas piston just pulled off the gas cylinder. 5. Connecting tappet piece. When piston is in place over cylinder, the front end of this tappet piece seats in the recess in the front end of the moving piston while its rear seats in the base of the operating rod. 6. Operating rod and spring being held to permit removal of gas piston and tappet.

gas chamber rising above the barrel, which is fitted with a cylinder to receive a very short piston.

As the bullet passes the gas vent in the barrel, a portion of the gas enters the port and expands in the cylinder driving back the short piston violently.

This piston, acting on the tappet principle, strikes the operating rod, which extends backward into the receiver. As the end of this rod passes through a hole drilled in the receiver above the line of the bolt, the thrust imparted to it is transmitted to the bolt carrier on top of the bolt. Meanwhile a spring around the operating rod is compressed to provide energy to return the rod to its forward position.

At the start of its rearward travel, the bolt carrier moves independently, leaving the weapon securely locked until the pressure has dropped. The slide carries the firing pin housing back independently of the bolt at this point also.

After a short travel, the slide and firing pin housing attached to the bolt pick up the bolt. The firing pin housing is so constructed that it cams in two locking lugs, drawing them out of their seats

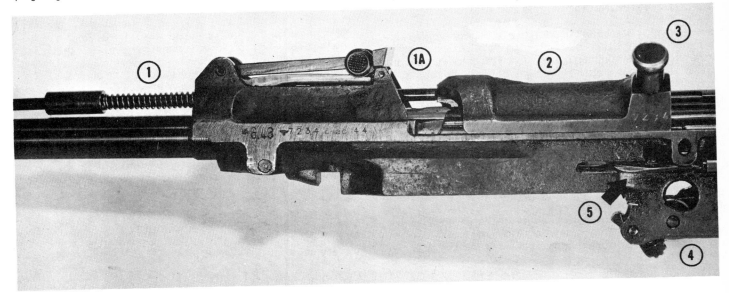

Details of operating rod system, Gew 43.
1. Operating rod being driven to the rear. As it passes though the hole in the receiver above the line of the bore, the spring around it is compressed to store up energy for the forward movement. 1-A. Rear end of operating rod moving back to drive the bolt carrier to the rear. 2. Bolt slide moving back in its tracks. Finger on its

underside will carry the firing-pin carrier to cam the bolt locks in so that the bolt may be unlocked and travel back to the rear. 3. Bolt handle used for cocking weapon. 4. Magazine release catch. 5. Ejector. (Note that the receiver and the bolt carrier are steel castings.)

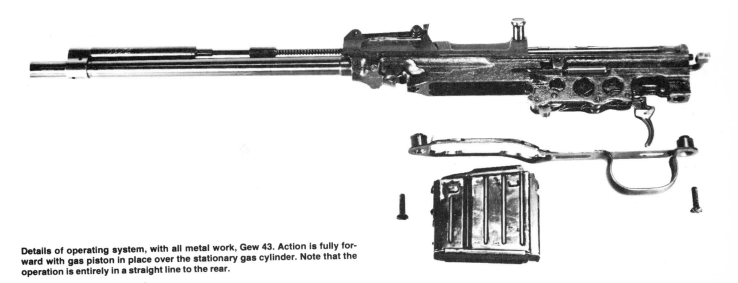

Details of operating system, with all metal work, Gew 43. Action is fully forward with gas piston in place over the stationary gas cylinder. Note that the operation is entirely in a straight line to the rear.

in the receiver walls and into the surface of the bolt.

From this point on, the parts travel to the rear together extracting and ejecting the empty shell and compressing the recoil spring around its guide.

Forward Movement of the G43 Action. The recoil spring compressed around its guide now exerts a forward thrust against the bolt assembly. The bolt strips a cartridge from the magazine and chambers it, the extractor set in the face of the bolt snapping into the extracting groove of the cartridge as it is chambered.

As the bolt reaches its fully forward position, it stops against the face of the chamber. The spring still exerts forward pressure and drives the firing pin housing straight ahead independently of the bolt. This is so constructed that it forces the locking lugs, which are loosely set into each side of the bolt, out into the receiver walls in a fashion not unlike that of the Russian Degtyarev light machine gun.

When the bolt is fully home in forward position, the carrier mounted on top of it is forced still farther forward into its niche in the receiver, where it rests against the operating rod hole.

When the trigger is pressed, the sear is rotated away from the hammer (which has been ridden over and cocked by the rearward motion of the bolt). The hammer spring drives the hammer forward to strike the firing pin extension. This in turn strikes the firing pin and drives it against the primer to fire the cartridge in the chamber.

THE 7.92mm PARATROOP RIFLE MODEL 42 (FG42)

One of the most interesting German World War II rifles from a design point of view—the Paratroop Rifle (FG 42)—was not adopted by the Army. It was adopted by the Air Force (*Luftwaffe*), who controlled the airborne divisions. The FG42 is a very impressive rifle from many points of view and lives on to some extent in the operating mechanism of the US M60 machine gun.

The *Fallschirmjäger Gewehr (FG42)* was developed by Rheinmetall-Borsig at the request of the German Air Force. It has been reported that only 5,000 of these rifles were made. FG42 had the following good features:

(1) Straight-line stock configuration and muzzle-brake compensator to assist in holding down the weapon in automatic fire from the shoulder.

(2) Reduction of recoil by use of a recoil-spring sliding shoulder-stock system.

(3) The weapon fires from a closed bolt in semiautomatic fire and from an open bolt in automatic fire—this solves the "cook off" problem.

FG42 was designed to replace the rifle, machine gun in the light role, and the submachine gun.

The bolt mechanism of the FG42 was copied from that of the Lewis gun, but a standard multiple coil recoil spring is used rather than the clock work type spring used with the Lewis Gun. The FG42-type bolt mechanism is currently used in the US M60 machine gun. The trigger mechanism is cleverly designed and features a swivel mounted sear, which can be moved left or right to engage the semiautomatic or automatic sear notch.

A short gas pistol rod is used with this weapon; the operating handle is connected to the piston rod, which also has a stud to operate the bolt. The stud operates in a camway in the bolt, rotating it into and out of the locked position. FG42 has a spike-type bayonet, which is carried in under the barrel point reversed when not fixed, in a manner similar to that of the French MAS36 rifle. A light stamped bipod, which failed in US tests of the rifle at Aberdeen Proving Ground during World War II, is also used with this weapon.

Some of these rifles are fitted with a stamped steel stock, and others have a wooden stock. All things considered, FG42 was one of the most interesting of the German World War II designs. It did not introduce any revolutionary design principles, but it did combine a number of previously uncombined principles to produce an advanced selective-fire weapon for full-size rifle cartridges. The first US weapon patterned on the FG42 was the 7.92mm T44 light machine gun. This weapon was rather unusual; it is belt-fed—it uses the MG42 type belt-feed mechanism—but the feed cover is mounted on the side of the receiver so that the belt feeds in a vertical position rather than horizontally as is usual. This weapon was developed by the Bridge Tool and Die Manufacturing Corp. under contract with the Ordnance Corps.

It should be noted that several authoritative publications credit the design of FG42 to the Heinrich Krieghoff Plant of Suhl, Saxony, but German publications credit it to Rheinmettal.

German 7.92mm *Fallschirmjaeger Gewehr 42* automatic rifle with steel butt.

7.92mm FG42 with wooden stock.

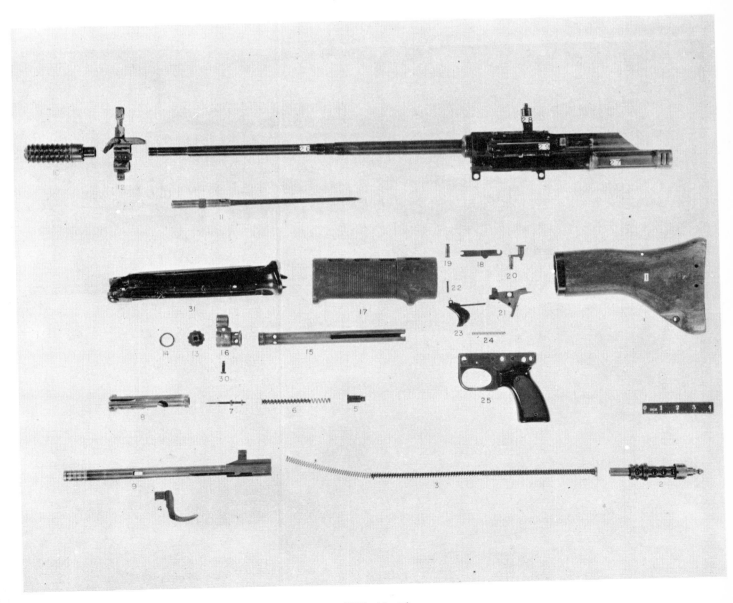

FG42, stripped.

German 7.92mm VG1-5.

THE 7.92mm VG1-5 SEMIAUTOMATIC RIFLE

The *Volkssturm Gewehr 1-5* is a rather unusual weapon in many ways. The first unusual thing about the rifle is that it was never apparently approved by the *Waffenamt* (Ordnance Office) in Berlin and does not bear the usual government acceptance stamps. The VG1-5 was put into production at a time when control was crumbling in Germany, and the Nazis had given the local *Gauleiters* authority to draw up contracts for arming the *Volkssturm* in their own districts with whatever weapons they could beg, borrow or steal.

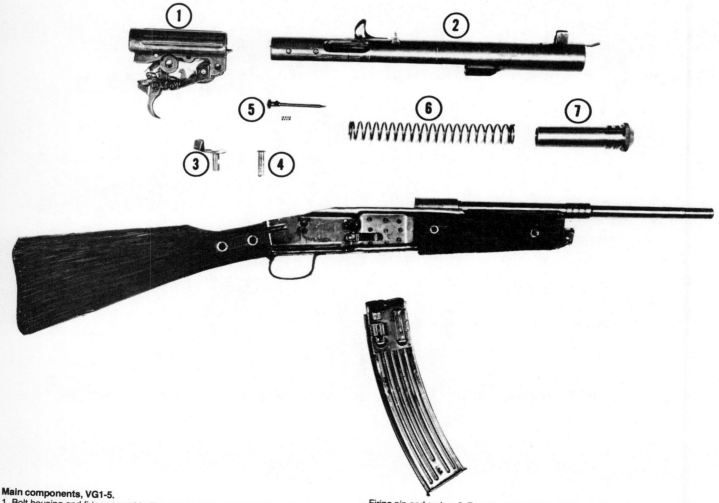

Main components, VG1-5.

1. Bolt housing and firing assembly. The bolt and slide assembly can move back in this housing when it is in place in the receiver. 2. Bolt and slide assembly. The bolt is riveted into the rear of this hollow sliding member. 3. Safety. 4. Retainer pin. 5. Firing pin and spring. 6. Recoil spring. 7. Gas chamber which locks inside front end of slide when the latter is in place around the barrel. Barrel, stock and receiver assemblies; note slide stop abutment on barrel at forward end of the forearm. Standard MP44 magazine for 7.92mm Short cartridge.

Considering this somewhat dubious ancestry, VG1-5 has some rather good design features. The weapon was designed and produced by the Gustloffwerke at Suhl and was apparently made in limited quantity. Stampings are extensively used in this weapon; the wooden furniture is left rough, and machining is of very simple type.

How the VG1-5 Operates

A standard MP 43-44 magazine loaded with 30 cartridges is inserted in the magazine housing from below and pushed in until it locks.

The bolt handle, which is a heavy steel piece riveted to the left side of the housing, is pulled back. This draws all the moving members to the rear, and the bolt rides over and compresses and cocks the hammer, which is held by a simple sear arrangement.

When the bolt handle is released, the compressed recoil spring pushes the members forward and strips a cartridge from the magazine into the firing chamber, where the extractor grips it as it seats.

Pressure on the trigger is communicated through the sear to release the hammer, which flies forward to strike the firing pin and discharge the cartridge.

As the bullet travels down the barrel, it passes over the 4 gas ports about 2½ inches before reaching the muzzle. Thus it will be seen that gas escapes from the barrel into the space between the removable sleeve and the housing to exert a forward thrust as the bullet continues out of the muzzle. The sleeve is shaped to insure that most of the gas thrust will be exerted toward the concave forward end.

As this is a retarded blowback weapon without a lock, the recoil force of gas against the head of the cartridge case drives the action to the rear. However, the thrust has to overcome not only the inertia and weight of moving parts as in the standard blowbacks but also the forward action of the gases, which have expanded in the moving housing. This check system delays the opening of the action long enough to permit the use of a cartridge so powerful that normally a locking device would be required to permit its use.

Rearward action ejects, recocks and reloads in standard semiautomatic fashion.

THE GERMAN STURMGEWEHR SERIES

The Germans had decided after World War I that their 7.92 × 57mm cartridge was overly powerful for shoulder weapons. Analysis of the average ranges at which rifles were commonly used and the marksmanship capabilities of the average soldier, especially under the stress of battle, led them to the conclusion that a cartridge with considerably less ballistic potential than the 7.92 × 57mm would be adequate and in addition would result in shorter, generally lighter weapons, allow the soldier to carry more cartridges on his person, cause less fatigue from recoil and result in a considerable saving of materials in the manufacture of propellents, cartridge cases and bullets.

The German requirement was solidified in 1934, and prototype cartridges were produced by Gustav Genschow, Rheinisch Wesphalische Sprengstoff (RWS) and Polte. Polte was given the development contract in 1938 and produced the "7.9mm Infanterie Kurz Patrone" by 1941. This cartridge had a case 33mm long with 24.6 grains of propellent as opposed to the 57mm case and 45-50 grains of propellent of the standard full-size 7.92mm rifle cartridge.

To parallel the cartridge development, Haenel was awarded a contract in 1938 for development of a weapon for these cartridges. Hugo Schmeisser of Haenel produced a gas-operated weapon for the 7.92mm Kurz cartridge by 1940, and 50 specimens of the prototype were produced by July 1942. Walther started development of the weapon for the cartridge in 1940, basing their design upon that of an earlier semiautomatic rifle of their conception—the GA115.

Machine Carbine MKb42(H) and Machine Carbine MKb42(W)

Both the Haenel and Walther designs were produced in limited quantity—approximately 7,800 of each—as machine carbines (Maschinen Karabiner), designated MKb42(H) and MKb42(W), respectively. They were extensively used on the Russian front, and the Haenel design proved superior to that of Walther.

The Walther design MKb42(W) has a somewhat unusual gas system, which was carried on in the design of the Czech Model 52 rifle. Rather than the conventional gas tube, usually found on gas-operated rifles, the gas in this design is confined by a steel jacket around the barrel and drives a piston, which encircles the barrel, and an operating sleeve. There are two gas ports in the barrel, and the bolt is operated by the sleeve. The bolt has frontal locking lugs.

Differences Between MKb42(H) and MP43

The Haenel MKb42(H) is generally similar in internal design to the MP43 series of weapons. The principal differences between

Walther 7.92mm GA115 semiautomatic rifle.

7.92mm MKb42(W).

the MKb42(H) and the MP43 series of weapons are as follows:

(1) The piston of the MKb42(H) is longer than that of the MP43 and is mounted in a separate tube, divided by a visible air space above the barrel. In the MP43, the piston rides in a tunnel immediately above the barrel.

(2) There is a cut-out for the bolt handle on the receiver of the MKb42(H); this cut-out is not present on the MP43.

(3) MKb42(H) has a bayonet lug (its prototype does not). MP43 does not have a bayonet lug.

There are also differences in the stock, fittings, etc.

MP43.

The MP43, MP43/1, MP44, and StG44 Assault Rifles

Schmeisser reworked the MKb42(H) in the spring of 1943, and the MP43, 44 series of weapons was born. This was a significant event in current military small arms history, since it introduced for the first time, in large quantities, the concept of the selective fire assault rifle chambered for the "intermediate" - sized cartridge.

The MP43 was adopted by the Waffenamt as a standard weapon and after 1944 was scheduled to replace the rifle, submachine gun and light machine gun in the infantry squad. By February 1944, production of this weapon had risen to about 5,000 per month. Producers of this family of weapons were Hanenel, Mauser and Erma; at least seven subcontractors made components. The term "family" as it refers to these weapons means the MP43, MP43/1, MP44 and StG44. All are essentially the same weapon; minor differences are as follows:

(1) MP43/1 is the same as MP43 but has a screw on type grenade launcher rather than the clamp on type used with MP43.

(2) There is no apparent reason for the change in nomenclature from MP43/1 to MP44. Most MP43/1 rifles have the V-type

telescope mounting bracket on the right side of the receiver; some MP44s have this bracket, but no MP43s have been found with the bracket.

The change in nomenclature to StG44 was politically inspired, but "Assault Rifle" (StG Sturmgewehr) is more truly descriptive of the role of the weapon than is "Submachine Gun" or "Machine Pistol" (MP-*Maschinen Pistole*).

The StG44(P) and StG44(V) were experimental versions of StG44; they had 90° curved and 40° curved barrels, respectively. Both were rejected by the Waffenamt.

Field Stripping the MP43—MP44 Series

A spring-held pin passes through the receiver and stock from the right. Pull this out from the right side.

The stock may now be withdrawn exposing the recoil spring.

Press the trigger and swing the trigger guard and all its contained units (these are not dismountable) down on its hinge.

Pull back the bolt handle. This will bring back the recoil spring, bolt, bolt carrier and the piston for removal.

With the small steel tool found in the butt trap inserted in the hole of the gas cup protruding from the casing at the front end, the gas cup may be unscrewed and withdrawn. The cylinder

Main Components, MP44.
.1 Receiver lock pin. 2. Push-through firing control switch. 3. Thumb safety, in off position. 4. Trigger housing pivot pin. 5. Magazine release catch. 6. Magazine housing. 7. Bolt handle.

may now be cleaned without difficulty.

The bolt may be lifted off the bolt carrier, and the extractor and firing pin removed.

Loading and Firing the MP43-44

There is a trap in the top of the stock on this weapon. A special magazine filler will be found in the hollow.

Place this filler in the mouth of the magazine. Insert cartridges, and then force them directly down with thumb pressure. The magazine will hold 30.

Pull bolt handle to compress recoil spring and cock the hammer and let it fly forward. It will pick up the top cartridge from the magazine and load it into the chamber. The dust cover will open automatically.

Push safety up unless weapon is to be fired at once. If it is left down, pressing the trigger will fire a single shot or full automatic fire depending on which way the control button has been pushed through the receiver.

How the MP43-MP44 Weapons Work

When the trigger is pressed, the hammer is released to strike the inertia firing pin. This is a wedge-shaped pin that does not have a conventional spring. It is primer retracted.

As the bullet passes the gas port in the barrel, it expands into the gas chamber or cup screwed into the housing around the barrel and on top of it.

The gas impinges on a piston somewhat resembling the old Lewis piston and drives it to the rear. In the start of its rearward travel, the piston (which has attached to it by a fixed pin the bolt carrier) can move without interfering with the secure locking of the weapon. A gas vent in the top of the casing permits the gas to escape as the gas end of the piston clears it.

After a short rearward travel the bolt carrier hook picks up the separate bolt member, mounted below it, and pulls it down and back to perform the unlocking action.

The recoil spring is mounted behind the bolt extending back to the stock. This spring is compressed as the moving members travel to the rear to extract and eject the empty case in normal fashion and to cock the hammer.

This weapon is fitted with a disconnector.

THE StG45(M) AND OTHER PROTOTYPES

Development of assault rifles by the various arms companies in Germany became very active after adoption of the MP43 series. One disadvantage of the early assault rifles was their weight; they are quite heavy in relation to the muzzle energy of the 7.92mm short cartridge. There was also a continual effort at this time to simplify weapons from the manufacturing point of view and from the point of view of saving on materials.

Gustloff Werke, Haenel, Mauser and possibly Erma all developed prototypes, and although none were accepted, the Mauser weapon had a great influence on future weapon developments. The Mauser development, originally called *GerätO6(H),* was a delayed blowback weapon weighing only 8.18 pounds, as opposed to the over 11 pounds of the StG44. The original *GerätO6(H)* had a combination of gas and blowback operation, but the gas element of operation was dropped in the final design.

The StG45(M) introduced the delayed blowback with roller bearings now used in the Spanish CETME, West German G3, the Swiss StuG57 and in modified form in the French Model 52 machine gun. The construction of this bolt is explained in detail under the G3 Rifle in Chapter 20.

MP44 field-stripped. Note that the gas piston, operating rod, operating handle, spring guide, bolt camming and locking units are actually only two units. A pin secures the rod section to the rear operating section. The bolt is a separate unit.

7.92mm StG45(M) Assault Rifle.

StG45(M), stripped.

CHARACTERISTICS OF GERMAN BOLT-ACTION RIFLES AND CARBINES.

	Rifle 1888	Carbine 1888	Rifle 1891	Rifle 98	Carbine 98
Caliber:	7.92mm.	7.92mm.	7.92mm.	7.92mm.	7.92mm.
Length overall:	48.91 in.	37.4 in.	37.3 in.	49.2 in.	37.4 in.
Barrel length:	29.1 in.	17.6 in.	17.6 in.	29.1 in.	16.9 in.
Feed device:	5-round in-line, fixed, box magazine.	5-round, in-line, fixed, box magazine.	5-round, in-line, fixed, box magazine.	5-round, staggered row, fixed, box magazine.	5-round, staggered row, fixed, box magazine.
Sights: Front:	Barley corn.	Barley corn.	Barley corn.	Barley corn.	Barley corn.
Rear:	Leaves with V notch.	Leaves with V notch.	Leaves with V notch.	Bridge type tangent or tangent leaf, V notch.	Bridge type tangent w/V notch.
Muzzle velocity: (at date of adoption)	2099 f.p.s.	1935 f.p.s.	1935 f.p.s.	2099 f.p.s.	590 m/s.
Weight:	8.56 lb.	6.88 lb.	6.8 lb.	8.81 lb.	Approx. 7.5 lb.

CHARACTERISTICS OF GERMAN BOLT-ACTION RIFLES AND CARBINES (Cont'd)

	Carbine 98a	Carbine 98b	Carbine 98k	Rifle 40k	Rifle 33/40
Caliber:	7.92mm	7.92mm	7.92mm	7.92mm	7.92mm
Length overall:	43.3 in.	49.2 in.	43.6 in.	39.1 in.	39.1 in.
Barrel length:	23.6 in.	29.1 in.	23.6 in.	19.2 in.	19.29 in.
Feed device:	5-round, staggered, fixed, box magazine.	5-round, staggered, fixed, box magazine.	5-round, staggered, fixed, box magazine.	5-round, staggered, fixed, box magazine.	5-round, staggered, fixed, box magazine.
Sights: Front:	Barley corn.	Barley corn.	Barley corn.	Barley corn.	Barley corn.
Rear:	Tangent w/V notch.	Tangent w/V notch.	Tangent w/V notch.	Tangent w/V notch.	Tangent w/V notch.
Muzzle velocity: (at date of adoption)	2853 f.p.s.	2574 f.p.s.	2476 f.p.s.	Approx 2400 f.p.s.	Approx 2400 f.p.s.
Weight:	8 lb.	9 lb.	8.6 lb.	8.3 lb.	7.9 lb.

CHARACTERISTICS OF GERMAN BOLT-ACTION RIFLES AND CARBINES (Cont'd)

	Rifle 98/40	VGI	VK98	DSM34	KKW
Caliber:	7.92mm.	7.92mm.	7.92mm.	Cal. .22 L.R.	Cal. .22 L.R.
Length overall:	43.6 in.	43 in.	40.6 in.	43.3 in.	43.7 in.
Barrel length:	23.6 in.	23.2 in.	20.8 in.	25.98 in.	25.98 in.
Feed device:	5-round staggered row, fixed, box magazine.	10-round staggered row, detachable, box magazine.	Mostly single shot.	Single shot.	Single shot.
Sights: Front:	Barley corn.	Post.	Barley corn.	Barley corn.	Barley corn.
Rear:	Tangent with V notch.	V notch.	V notch.	Tangent with V notch.	Tangent with V notch.
Muzzle velocity: (at date of adoption)	2476 f.p.s.	2476 f.p.s.	2400 f.p.s. (approx)	1500 f.p.s. (approx)	1500 f.p.s. (approx)
Weight:	8.9 lb.	8.3 lb.	6.9 lb.	7.7 lb.	8.6 lb.

CHARACTERISTICS OF GERMAN WORLD WAR II SEMIAUTOMATIC AND SELECTIVE FIRE RIFLES

	Rifle 41(M)	Rifle 41(W)**	Rifle 43***	FG42	VG1-5
Caliber:	7.92 × 57mm.	7.92 × 57mm.	7.92mm × 57mm.	7.92 × 57mm.	7.92mm Kurz (short)
System of operation:	Gas, semi-automatic only.	Gas, semi-automatic only.	Gas, semi-automatic only.	Gas, selective fire.	Delayed blowback, semiautomatic only.
Overall length:	46.25 in.	44.25 in.	44 in.	37 in.	35 in.
Barrel length:	21.75 in.	21.5 in.	21.62 in.	19.75 in.	14.75 in.
Feed device:	Fixed, 10-round*, staggered row, box magazine	Fixed, 10-round, staggered row, box magazine.	Detachable, 10-round, staggered row, box magazine.	Detachable, 20-round, staggered row, box magazine.	Detachable, 30-round, staggered row, box magazine.
Sights: Front:	Barley corn.	Barley corn.		Barley corn on folding base.	Fixed post.
Rear:	Tangent leaf w/U notch.	Tangent leaf w/U notch.	Tangent leaf.	Aperture on folding base.	Non-adjustable U notch.
Muzzle velocity:	Approx 2550 f.p.s.	Approx 2550 f.p.s.	Approx 2550 f.p.s.	Approx 2500 f.p.s.	2163 f.p.s.
Cyclic rate:	—	—	—	750-800 r.p.m.	—
Weight:	11.25 lb.	11.08 lb.	Approx 9.5 lb.	9.93 lb.	10.18. lb.

*The magazine can be removed, but is not easily removable for reloading.
**This weapon is also called Rifle 41 (SG41).
***This weapon may be marked G43 or K43.

CHARACTERISTICS OF GERMAN WORLD WAR II SEMIAUTOMATIC AND SELECTIVE FIRE RIFLES (Cont'd)

	MKb42(W)	MKb42(H)	StG44	StG45(M)
Caliber:	7.92mm Kurz.	7.92mm Kurz.	7.92mm Kurz (PP43 m.e.).	7.92mm Kurz (PP43 m.e.).
System of operation:	Gas, selective fire.	Gas, selective fire.	Gas, selective fire.	Delayed blowback, selective fire.
Overall length:	36.75 in.	37 in.	37 in.	35.15 in.
Barrel length:	16.1 in.	14.37 in.	16.5 in.	15.75 in.
Feed device:	Detachable, 30-round, staggered row, box magazine.	Detachable, 30-round, staggered row, box magazine.	Detachable, 30-round, staggered row, box magazine.	Detachable, 30-round, staggered row, box magazine.
Sights: Front:	Hooded barley corn.	Hooded barley corn.	Hooded barley corn.	Hooded barley corn.
Rear:	Tangent w/U notch.	Tangent w/U notch.	Tangent w/U notch.	Tangent w/U notch.
Muzzle velocity:	2132 f.p.s.	Approx 2100 f.p.s.	2132 f.p.s.	Approx 2100 f.p.s.
Cyclic rate:	600 r.p.m.	500 r.p.m.	500 r.p.m.	350-450 r.p.m.
Weight:	9.75 lb.	11.06 lb.	11.5 lb.	8.18 lb.

GERMAN SUBMACHINE GUNS

GERMAN MODELS AND
MODIFICATIONS OF FOREIGN MODELS

The first German submachine gun was the Bergmann 9mm MP18I which appeared in 1918. This blowback-operated submachine gun was fed with the 32-round "snail"-type magazine developed for the Luger pistol. The MP18I was designed by Hugo Schmeisser, who was by far the best-known of the German submachine gun designers.

The weapon was introduced into battle during the last part of World War I; about 35,000 were made before the war ended. Many of these weapons were used by the German civil police after the war. The MP18I was modified after the war by removing the magazine housing for the "snail"-type magazine and fitting a magazine housing for a box-type magazine. This modification was done by Haenel.

Further modification resulted in the MP28II, which was also produced by Haenel. The 28II has selective fire and a tangent type rear sight. This weapon was extensively used by German police, to include SS Police units, but was never officially adopted by the German Army. This does not mean that army personnel did not use the weapon at one time or another; as with all other small arms, the German Army used almost anything it could get. The MP28II was manufactured in Belgium by Pieper and was adopted by the Belgian Army as the *Mitraillete Model 34.* It was also used by Bolivia, in addition to several other South American countries.

The next German submachine gun produced in quantity was the Bergmann 9mm 34/I. This gun, unlike the earlier Bergmanns, was not designed by Hugo Schmeisser. The prototypes of this gun were made in Denmark, circa 1932; production of the weapon in Germany was at the Walther plant in Zella Mehlis, since Bergmann did not have production facilities. This weapon was not adopted by the German Army but was exported on a limited scale. The Model 34/I can be distinguished by its bolt handle—which resembles, and is operated in a fashion similar

to a manually operated bolt-action rifle—and its trigger mechanism. The weapon has two triggers; pressure on the outer trigger produces semiautomatic fire until the inner trigger is engaged, at which time the weapon fires automatically. The Model 34/I was produced in long barrel and short barrel versions.

The 9mm Model 35/I is a modified Model 34/I. This weapon was produced during World War II for the SS by Junker and Ruh. German police manuals of this period refer to this weapon as the Model 35. The Model 35/I was adopted by Ethiopia and Sweden, which called the weapon the "M/39."

The Erfurter Werkzeug and Maschinenfabrik "Erma Werke" of Erfurt produced a submachine gun designed by Heinrich Vollmer; it had fairly wide distribution as the Vollmer Erma. The most common model is called the EMP or MPE. Versions of the Erma were sold to France, Mexico and Yugoslavia. This weapon, as well as many of the earlier German submachine guns, was extensively used in the Spanish Civil War. The Erma submachine gun MPE was used by the German police and Waffen SS Units; it was never adopted by the German Army.

This first submachine gun to be adopted by the German Army after the MP18I was the 9mm MP38. The MP38 and its successor the MP 40 were developed by the Erma Werke at the request of the German Army. Although the weapon is commonly called a "Schmeisser," Hugo Schmeisser had little if any connection with its design. The Haenel firm, of which Schmeisser was general manager, was among the producers of the weapon during the war, and Schmeisser developed the MP41, a modification of the MP40. The MP38 and 40 were the standard submachine guns of the German Army during World War II, and over a million of these weapons were made.

During the war several new designs of submachine guns were produced by the Germans in rather limited quantities. In general,

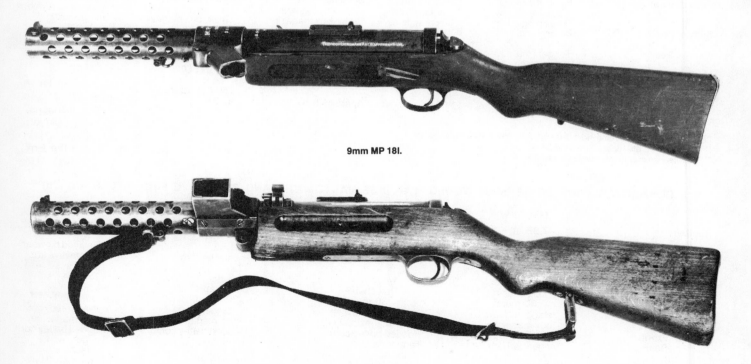

9mm MP 18I.

9mm MP18I, modified.

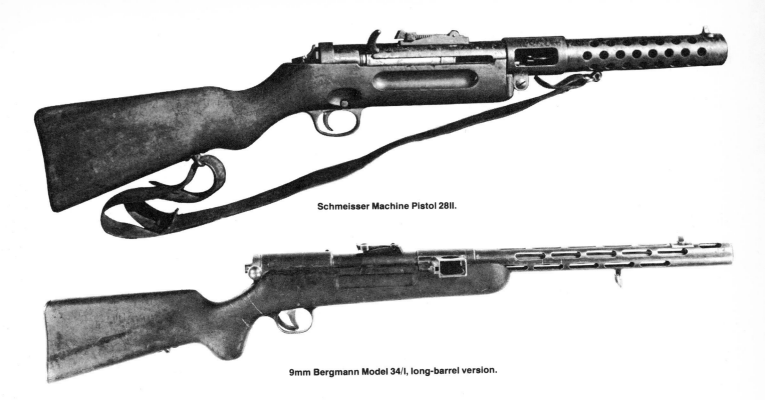

Schmeisser Machine Pistol 28II.

9mm Bergmann Model 34/I, long-barrel version.

their development seemed to be an attempt to produce a cheap, easily-made submachine gun in order to conserve materials and manufacturing facilities.

There are indications, however, that the Mauser-made copy of the British Mark II Sten may have been intended for some clandestine use, since even the British markings were copied. This weapon is called the *Gerät Potsdam.*

The MP3008 is also a copy of the Sten, produced by Mauser and six other firms. This weapon, which appeared in a number of versions, was intended for *Volkssturm* use. Production did not begin until the closing months of the war.

The EMP44 was developed by Erma Werke; it is a relatively simply made weapon consisting mainly of welded steel tubing. It appears to have been made only as a prototype and was probably designed for special use.

The Germans modified a number of Soviet PPSh M1941 submachine guns for their own use by altering them to use the MP38 and 40 magazine and fitting them with 9mm Parabellum barrels. In addition, the Germans used other foreign-made weapons. The Italian 9mm Beretta Model 38/42 was made for the German Army with German markings and acceptance

stamps. The Steyr Solothurn submachine gun adopted by Austria was used by the Germans as the MP34 (Ö). Weapons produced prior to 1939 are chambered for the 9mm Mauser cartridge; those produced during 1939 and 1940 were chambered for the 9mm Parabellum cartridge. The Austrian Police used the MP34, to use the Austrian nomenclature, in a version chambered for the 9mm Steyr cartridge; these weapons were used to some extent by the German *Ordnungs polizei.*

The 9mm Model 38, Model 40 and Model 41 Submachine Gun (MP38, 40 and 41)

The MP38 was the first submachine gun developed for the German Army since the MP18I of World War I. Although the design has been credited to Schmeisser in many publications, it was probably designed by Erma; first production was carried on at that plant. The telescoping, multi-piece recoil spring and firing pin assembly were developed from those used with the Erma submachine gun. The MP38 was made from 1938 to 1940 at the Erma plant.

Erma 9mm Machine Pistol (EMP).

The plastic receiver housing and aluminum frame and folding steel stock of the MP38 were unique, and the design of this weapon had considerable influence on later submachine guns. The receiver of the MP38 is made of steel tubing.

The MP38 had one serious deficiency—which is shared by most submachine guns—it was not completely safe to handle. The only safety, a cut-out in the receiver into which the bolt handle locked when the gun was cocked, did not allow the gun to be carried safely with the bolt forward and a loaded magazine in the gun. If the gun received a severe jolt, such as falling on its breech end, the bolt could bounce back far enough to pick a round up from the magazine and fire. The MP38 was modified to remedy this defect by the fitting of a two-piece bolt handle and the cutting of a slot above the front of the bolt receiver track to lock the bolt in the forward position. This modification was called the MP38/40.

The MP38 was somewhat expensive to manufacture and the weapon was re-engineered to cut down the use of expensive tooling. The weapon produced as the result of this redesign was called the MP40, which differs from the MP38 in the following: new ejector, magazine release assembly, receiver (ribbing eliminated), grip frame of the MP38 is cast aluminum while that of the MP40 is formed, and the stamped middle tube of the recoil spring assembly is drawn and pinched on the MP40. There are numerous other minor differences. MP40 was made in much larger quantities than was the MP38 and was manufactured by Steyr, Haenel and Erma with the assistance of a number of subcontractors. Over 1,000,000 MP40s were made from 1940 to 1944.

There were several modifications of the MP40. The most common modification of the MP40 has a stamped, ribbed magazine housing and uses the two-piece bolt handle. This weapon, which apparently was called MP40/I, is far more common than the MP40 itself. A rarer modification is the MP40/II, which is fitted with a magazine housing to accommodate two magazines. The magazines are held in a sliding housing arranged to allow each magazine to feed in turn.

The MP41 was developed at Haenel by Schmeisser. It was made in very limited numbers and it was not used by the German Army or Police; it may have been made for export. MP41 has the receiver and barrel assembly and bolt assembly of the MP40, but the stock and trigger mechanism are modeled on that of the MP28II.

Loading and Firing the MP38

Six spare magazines and a special magazine loader are issued in a web haversack with each one of these guns. The loader is a simple lever device with an attached housing into which the magazine is inserted. Snapping a cartridge into the top of the housing and pushing down firmly on the lever loads the individual cartridge into the magazine. This motion is repeated until the magazine is filled. If no loader is available, cartridges may be inserted by the normal procedure for loading automatic pistol magazines; leverage for inserting the last few cartridges may be exerted by pressure of both thumbs, once the cartridge has been seated.

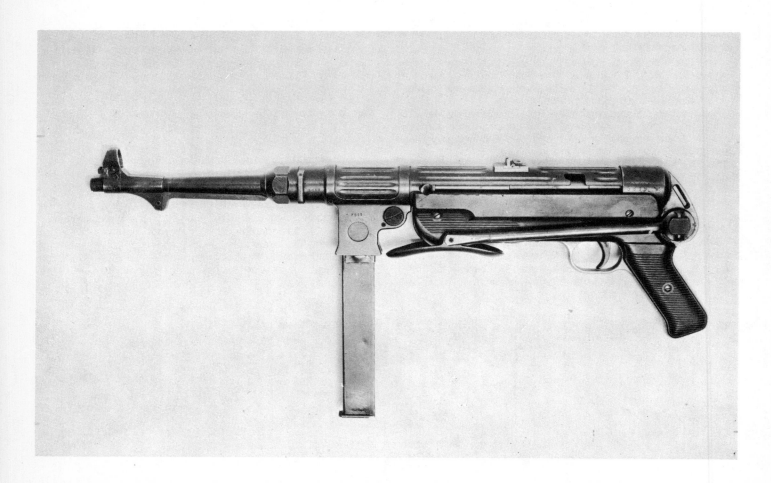

German 9mm Model 38 Machine Pistol.

9mm MP41.

Loading the MP38/40

 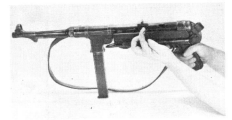 

Insert loaded magazine from below into the magazine housing and push up until it locks. Note: a stud on the outside of the magazine will prevent it from going in beyond the proper length.

Warning: always remember that this weapon fires when the bolt goes forward! Never, therefore, let the bolt go home while the loaded magazine is in position. Unless you wish to fire the weapon, always remove the magazine before easing the bolt home.

Whenever possible, always use this weapon as a carbine. To do this, press the catch stud as indicated. This will release catch and permit you to unfold the stock and turn the butt piece down into proper place for firing from the shoulder.

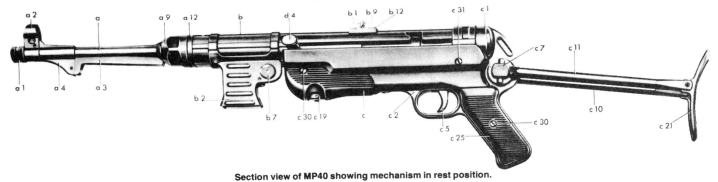

Section view of MP40 showing mechanism in rest position.

CHARACTERISTICS OF GERMAN SERVICE SUBMACHINE GUNS

	MP18I	MP38	MP40	MP40II	MP41
Caliber:	9mm Parabellum.	9mm Parabellum.	9mm Parabellum.	9mm Parabellum.	9mm Parabellum.
System of Operation:	Blowback, full automatic only.	Blowback, full automatic only.	Blowback, full automatic only.	Blowback, full automatic only.	Blowback. Selective fire.
Length:					
Stock extended:	32.1 in.	32.8 in.	32.8 in.	32.8 in.	34 in.
Stock folded:	—	24.8 in.	24.8 in.	24.8 in.	—
Barrel length:	7.88 in.	9.9 in.	9.9 in.	9.9 in.	9.9 in.
Feed device:	32-round, "snail" drum type, detachable, box magazine.	32-round, detachable staggered row, box magazine.	32-round, detachable, staggered row, box magazine.	64 rounds in 2 detachable staggered box magazines.	32-round, detachable, staggered row, box magazine.
Sights: Front:	Barley corn.	Hooded barley corn.	Hooded barley corn.	Hooded barley corn.	Hooded barley corn.
Rear:	Notched flip-over leaf.	Notched flip-over leaf.	Notched flip-over leaf.	Notched flip-over leaf.	Notched flip-over leaf.
Weight:	9.2 lbs.	9.5 lbs.	8.87 lbs.	10 lbs.	8.15 lbs.
Cyclic rate:	350-450 r.p.m.	500 r.p.m.	500 r.p.m.	500 r.p.m.	500 r.p.m.
Muzzle velocity:	Approx 1250 f.p.s.	Approx 1300 f.p.s.	Approx 1300 f.p.s.	Approx 1300 f.p.s.	Approx 1300 f.p.s.

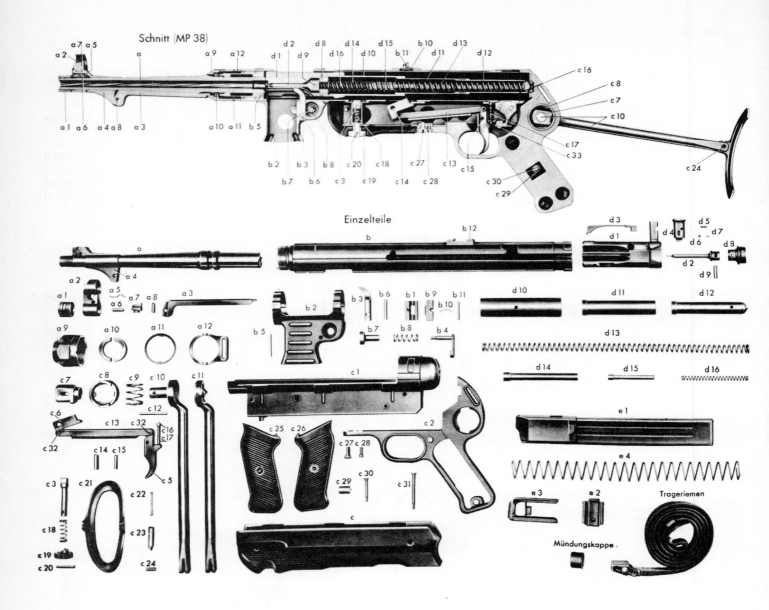

Schnitt (MP 38)

Einzelteile

Trageriemen

Mündungskappe

a2	Front cap cover	a1	Barrel cap	a1	Barrel cap
d10	Recoil spring tube large	a6	Cover retainer	a2	Front sight cover
a7	Front sight	a4	Barrel jacket	a3	Resting bar
a5	Front sight retainer	a8	Resting bar pin	a9	Barrel nut
a	Barrel	a3	Resting and retracting bar	a12	Collar
a9	Barrel nut	a10	Barrel nut washer	b	Chamber cover
a12	Collar	a11	Barrel threads	b2	Magazine guide
d1	Bolt	b2	Magazine guide	b7	Magazine release cap
d2	Firing pin	b7	Magazine release cap	d4	Bolt handle
d9	Firing pin retaining pin	b3	Magazine release screw	b1	and b9 Rear sight leaves
d8	Recoil spring tube end	b6	Washer	b12	Rear sight base
d14	Recoil spring	c3	Receiver lock	c31	Lock frame screw
d10	Recoil spring tube large	c20	Receiver lock screw retainer	c1	Buffer housing
d15	Recoil guide	c19	Receiver lock screw	c7	Stock release button
b10	and b11 Rear sight leaf spring	c18	Receiver lock spring	c10	and c11 Stock arms
d11	Recoil spring second tube	c14	Sear	c21	Shoulder piece
d13	Buffer spring	c27	and c28 Frame screws	c30	Fore-end Screw
d12	Buffer spring tube	c13	Sear lever	c19	Dismounting screw
c10	Stock arm	c15	Trigger axis screw	c	Fore-end
c7	Stock pivot	c17	and c16 Trigger spring	c2	Trigger guard
c8	Stock release	c29	and c30 Grip screws	c5	Trigger
c24	Shoulder piece pivot	a	Barrel	c25	Pistol grip
				c30	Grip screw

How the MP38 Works

The loaded magazine inserted from below is held securely in place by the magazine lock. The firing pin is attached to the forward end of the telescoping housing. It passes through the hole in the center of the bolt, while the abutment behind it lodges into the head of the bolt recess. As the bolt is drawn back by its handle, or forced back by the functioning cartridge, it telescopes the three-piece recoil spring housing (which carries the firing pin) and compresses the recoil spring inside the telescope. The rear of the recoil spring housing rests against the inside of the rounded buffer end of the frame, which is securely locked to the receiver.

When the bolt is in the fully cocked position, the sear locks into the bottom of the bolt and connects with the trigger. Pressing the trigger depresses the sear and permits the bolt to run forward under the influence of the recoil spring acting through the telescopic section to force the bolt forward.

As the feed ribs on the bottom of the bolt strip the top round from the magazine and push it into the firing chamber, the face of the extractor set in the bolt blocks the base of the cartridge. When the cartridge is fully seated, the further forward movement of the bolt pushes the heavy extractor to snap it into the extracting groove. At the same time, the bolt face strikes against the base of the cartridge. The firing pin, a separate unit from bolt, is under the pressure of the recoil spring and functions in the same manner as a fixed firing pin—it protrudes at all times. This pin now strikes the cartridge and discharges it.

During the backward action, the extractor hook withdraws the empty cartridge case, carrying it back until it strikes against the ejector and is ejected. This cycle of operation continues as long as the trigger is held back and there are cartridges left in the magazine.

Field Stripping the MP38/40

(1) After extracting the magazine, and seeing that the bolt is in its forward position, pull out the receiver lock against the tension of the spring and twist it to keep it locked in the outward position. (This stud is on the bottom of the frame at its forward end.)

(2) While pressing the trigger with the right forefinger, hold firmly to the magazine housing with the left hand, then twist the pistol grip to the right, about 80°; this will revolve the entire frame assembly and the components.

(3) Now draw the frame group back and out of the receiver.

(4) Draw back slightly on cocking handle. This will bring out a telescoping tube inside which is the recoil spring, and at the front of which is the firing pin. Remove this unit.

(5) Now draw straight back on the cocking handle which is a part of the bolt and withdraw the bolt from the receiver. No further stripping is required.

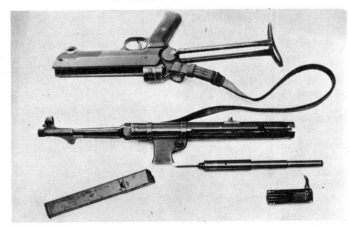

MP40 dismounted, complete field strip.

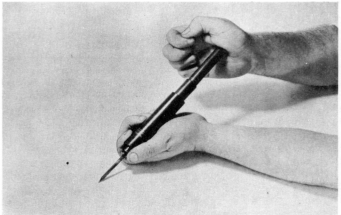

Recoil spring housing, showing firing pin and telescoping of tube.

GERMAN MACHINE GUNS

Germany adopted the Maxim gun about 1899 and in 1908 produced the Maxim gun, which may have the doubtful honor of killing more people than any other military instrument designed by man; it was certainly the most murderous weapon of World War I. The 7.92mm Model 1908 Maxim machine gun (MG08) was the standard German heavy machine gun of World War I and was made in tremendous quantities. A water-cooled weapon, it operated essentially the same as the British Vickers described in detail in the chapter on Britain. It is unlikely that it will be found in service in any country at present.

Although the MG08 was a very effective weapon, it was also quite heavy on the sleigh-type mount used during World War I, and a lightened version, the Model 08/15 (MG08/15), was introduced. The 08/15 is fitted with a shoulder stock, bipod, modified receiver and barrel jacket; its ammunition belt is carried on a reel type drum magazine mounted on the side of the receiver. Its operation is the same as that of the MG08.

7.92mm MG08.

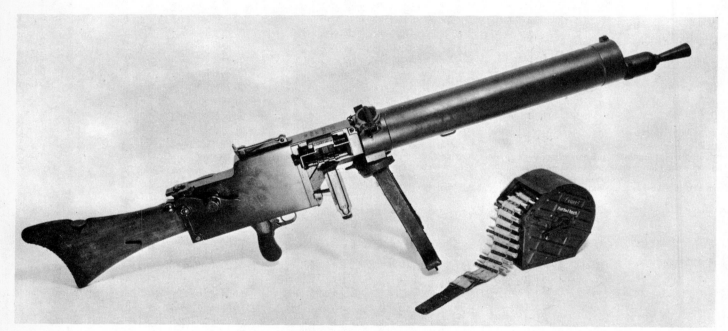

Maxim 7.92mm MG08/15 (light MG).

The MG08/15 was adapted for aircraft use by fitting it with a ventilated type barrel jacket in place of the water jacket. This gun and the Parabellum, a modified Maxim, were the principal German aircraft guns of World War I. Toward the close of the war, the MG08/18 appeared; this was essentially a ground version of the aircraft 80/15, being air cooled with a ventilated barrel jacket.

Machine gun development and production in Germany after World War I was restrained by the Versailles Treaty, but the Germans managed to "keep their hand in" through development done by German-owned firms in foreign countries. None of the ground gun designs produced by foreign firms—Waffenfabrik Solothurn is the principal example—were adopted by the German Army, but they did add to the German capability in that they gave them an experience factor in translating military requirements into design that might otherwise have been lost.

The 7.92mm MG13 was adopted as a standard machine gun by the German Army about 1932. MG13 was made up from Dreyse M1918 water-cooled light machine guns that had been manufactured in the last year of the war, Simson of Suhl doing the work. These weapons existed in very limited numbers and

were apparently all sold to Portugal in 1938. The Mauser-developed MG34 was the first true general purpose machine gun made in quantity, i.e., a gun that is used on a bipod as a light machine gun and on a tripod as a heavy machine gun. MG34 was made in very large quantities and was the standard 7.92mm ground machine gun during World War II until the adoption of the MG42. An aircraft version of MG34, MG81, was also developed and made in quantity. MG81 differed from MG34 principally in its high rate of fire—1000-2000 rounds per minute—and its lack of a semiautomatic capability.

Solothurn had developed a gun called MG29, rejected by Germany but adopted in improved form by Austria as the 8mm Model 30 and by Hungary as the 8mm Model 31. Rheinmetall developed two 7.92mm aircraft guns using the basic operating system of the MG30—the MG17 fixed gun and the MG15 flexible gun. Late in World War II, MG15 was fitted with an improvised stock and a bipod and used as a ground gun. One other German aircraft machine gun, the MG151, was modified for use as a ground machine gun and was found mounted on the US caliber .50 machine gun tripod.

The most famous of all German World War II machine guns is the 7.92mm MG42. This weapon, now chambered for the 7.62mm NATO cartridge, is the current standard machine gun of the West German Army. Like the MG34, MG42 is a dual-purpose machine gun and might be considered something of a pace setter in its method of manufacture. The weapon is composed mainly of stampings, and its barrel change system, and feed and locking mechanisms have had considerable influence on post-war machine gun design.

At the close of the war, a delayed blowback machine gun—the MG45 or MG42V—was under development at Mauser. This weapon utilized the same type of bolt mechanism as the prototype StG45(M) assault rifle; the feed mechanism and barrel change was the same as that of the MG42. The SIG MG710-1 is quite similar to the MG45.

As with all other weapons, Germany used foreign machine guns to some extent. Rear area and police units were likely to be found armed with any type of machine gun for which there was sufficient ammunition on hand. The Czech ZB26 and ZB30 were continued in production at Brno after the plant was taken over by the Germans until it was tooled up to produce MG34. The ZB53 (Model 37) was also widely used by the Germans, particularly on vehicles. These Czech guns were considered as limited standard by the Germans, and manuals concerning their usage and maintenance were issued by the German Army.

THE MG34

This weapon was designed by Mauser at the direction of the Waffenamt. It was the first modern general purpose machine gun to be produced in large quantities. The design of MG34 incorporated many of the best features of previously developed weapons and had some outstanding features of its own. Among these were: A good method for changing barrels; a simple method of field stripping, major components being held together with bayonet-type catches; a high impact plastic stock; and a combined recoil booster, flash hider and barrel bearing.

The trigger mechanism of the MG34 is similar to that of the MG13 in that the trigger is pulled at the top for semiautomatic fire and at the bottom for automatic fire. MG34 is frequently confused with the Solothurn MG30. The Solothurn gun is based on patents of Louis Stange, a Rheinmettal engineer. The locking mechanism of the MG30 is a rotating ring, which locks the barrel and bolt together, while in the MG34 the bolt head rotates and locks into a barrel extension, which is permanently attached to the barrel. Stange's design undoubtedly did influence MG34, but it is different.

Various modifications of the basic MG34 were produced during World War II. These modifications and the ways in which they differ from the basic MG34 are as follows:

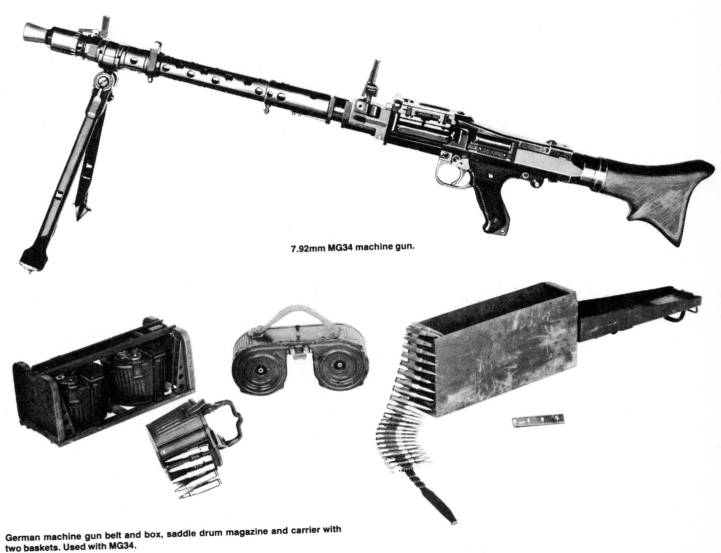

7.92mm MG34 machine gun.

German machine gun belt and box, saddle drum magazine and carrier with two baskets. Used with MG34.

MG34 (modified) has a heavier barrel jacket than MG34, developed for use in armored vehicles.

MG34S and MG34/41: (1) Are several inches shorter than MG34 and have shorter barrels; fire automatic only and have a simple spur-type trigger and simpler trigger mechanism; have a larger buffer; the diameter of the barrel at the muzzle is increased in order to give more surface for the gas trapped in the recoil booster to bear against; the firing pin nut on the rear of the bolt has been eliminated; and minor changes in the feed system.

MG34 has been used since World War II by the Czechs, the Israelis and the French; MG34s have been captured from the Viet Cong in South Vietnam. Of interest is the fact that the United States Army had the MG34 analyzed by the Savage Arms Corporation during World War II. Savage concluded that the weapon would require the use of considerable numbers of machine tools in its manufacture, at a time when machine tools were in short supply; therefore, further investigation was discontinued. MG34 can be cranky on occasion, and the Germans have admitted that it took quite a while to work the bugs out of the weapon when it was first issued. One of the basic problems with the weapon is that it is too finely made, with very close fitting parts. Automatic weapons that have operating parts designed to work with plenty of play operate much better under adverse conditions of dust and mud, since they have plenty of space in which the dirt can lie without causing a malfunction.

Loading and Firing the MG34

A machine is provided but is not needed to load this form of belt. The belt consists of a series of individual metal links, joined

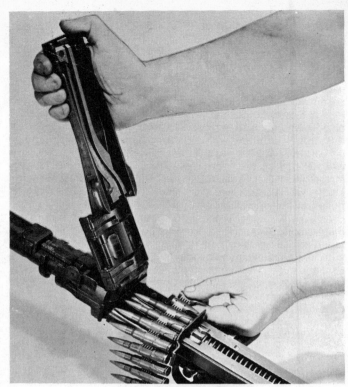

Loading the MG34 Machine Gun.

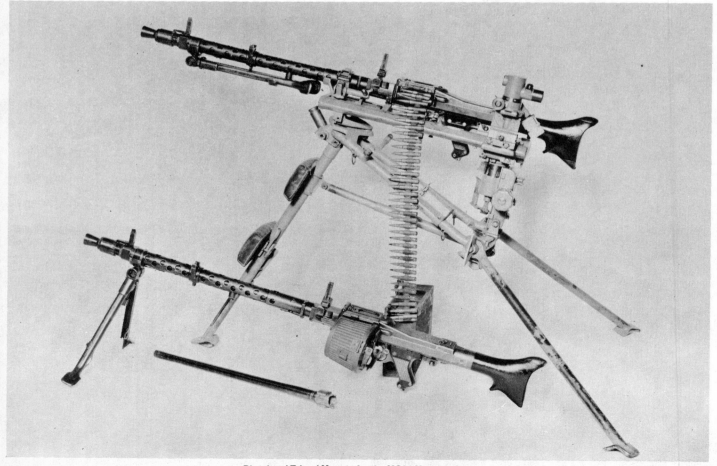

Bipod and Tripod Mounts for the MG34 Machine Gun.

together by small pieces of coiled wire. These links are shaped much like an ordinary pencil clip. Press the cartridge down into the clip so that the spring sides fasten around the cartridge and retain it. A nib at the end of the clip will spring into the cannelure of the cartridge and hold it in the correct position. It will be evident that in this form of belt there can be no malfunction of the type common to web belts, which may expand when wet, and to brass-studded belts, which must pass through a complicated feed mechanism.

In the 50-round drums, the loaded belt is inserted in the drum, being wound around the center piece.

The 75-round, saddle type drums do not use a belt. The drum itself contains the cartridges. The springs force them around into position, one coming alternately from each side.

Tabs are provided on the end of each belt. If several sections are being fastened together, or if no tab is available, then the first two or three cartridges should be removed from the metal belt.

Insert the feeding end of the belt in the feedway on the left side of the receiver, and pull through as far as it will go.

Warning: Unlike the Browning and the Vickers, the belt on this gun lies on top of the cartridges as they pass through the feed block. An alternate way of loading is to push forward the cover catch (which is on top of the receiver at the rear of the gun) and lift the feed cover to vertical position. The belt may then be laid in the feedway; make sure that the first cartridge rests against the stop on the right side of the guide. Close the cover and snap it down in place.

Pull back the cocking handle as far as it will go and the bolt will be caught and held in rearward position by the sear. Now push the cocking handle forward as far as it will go. If this is not done, it will be carried forward as the bolt moves to the front, and this additional weight may cause malfunctioning.

Pressing the upper part of the trigger will now fire a single shot. Pressing the lower part of the trigger will fire the weapon automatically.

NOTE: If the cocking handle will not come back, it indicates that the safety is on. Move the lever to the "Fire" position.

Firing with the 50-Round Drum. Press the catch on the sliding cover of the drum and open the cover so that the tag end of the belt can be pulled out. Insert the tag of the belt in the feedway as for the ordinary belt. The narrow end of the belt is the front end. Engage the hook on the front end with the lug on the rear end of the lower part of the feed plate. Now swing the rear end of the drum around until the spring catch engages with the lug on the rear end of the feedway. Pulling back the cocking handle now leaves the weapon ready for firing.

Firing with the 75-Round Saddle Drum. With this drum the feed cover is removed and a magazine holder is substituted. The feed plate is also removed. Belts are not used in this type of feed. The drum is placed directly over the magazine holder ahead of the trigger guard. Its center piece pushes down the dust cover in the magazine holder. A spring catch at the top center of the connecting piece can be pressed to release the drum and a hand-strap is provided to lift it off the gun.

How the MG34 Works

Starting with the gun loaded and cocked, the action is as follows: Pressing the trigger pulls the sear out of its bent in the bolt and allows it to go forward under the thrust of the compressed recoil spring located in the butt.

A feed piece on the top of the bolt strikes the base of the cartridge in line and pushes it from the belt toward the firing chamber. The feed arm is hollow and is operated by a stud on the top rear end of the bolt, which rides in this hollow groove and causes the feed pawl to push the next cartridge in the direction of the firing chamber.

As the bolt continues forward, two inner rollers on its head

MG34 on AA tripod.

strike two cams on a cam sleeve and rotate the head of the bolt from left to right so that threads on the bolt engage threads on the cam sleeve; this effectively locks the bolt to the barrel.

As the cartridge chambers, the extractor in the bolt face slips over the cannelure of the cartridge. Meanwhile the rear of the bolt continues forward, tripping the firing pin lever and allowing the firing pin to go forward through the face of the bolt to strike the primer. The forward movement of the bolt is stopped when a shoulder on its right front side strikes the cocking handle stop, which is in its forward position at the end of its slot. Just before the cartridge is fired, a locking catch on the bolt engages behind the outer roller on the right side of the head of the bolt.

Return Movement of the Action. This gun is fitted at the muzzle with a recoil increaser somewhat resembling that operating on the Vickers gun.

As the bullet leaves the barrel, part of the gas pressure behind it expands in the muzzle attachment and rebounds against the cone to give additional backward thrust to the barrel. This action, together with the rearward thrust of the gas in the firing chamber against the head of the empty cartridge case, which transmits it to the bolt, starts the action to the rear.

Barrel and bolt start back, firmly locked together during the period of high pressure. After a backward travel of about 3/16'', the outer rollers on the bolt head again engage with the two cam faces in the forward end of the receiver, thus forcing the bolt head to rotate from right to left, thereby unlocking the bolt from the barrel.

The rearward motion of the barrel is stopped as soon as the

Field Stripping the MG34

(1) Order of stripping: Push the spring catch at the extreme rear of the cover on top of the receiver and lift the cover to a vertical position. Push the cover hinge pin from the right and lift out the cover. The feed block may be lifted off.

(2) The butt catch is on the underside of the receiver a few inches behind the pistol grip. Press this up with the left thumb. With the right hand, turn the butt a quarter-turn left or right. (Note: the bolt should be in forward position when this stripping motion is being done. Otherwise, the very powerful recoil spring cannot be controlled.) The recoil spring will now force the butt out of the receiver. Now remove the recoil spring.

(3) Pull the cocking handle back with a quick motion. (A jerking motion is required here because the action in releasing the bolt twists the barrel extension and the barrel. Watch that the bolt and its carrier do not fly out the back of the receiver.)

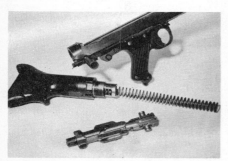

(4) Bolt and carrier may now be removed.

(5) Pressing the locking catch on left of receiver, below and behind rear sight, twist receiver from left to right until it clears the barrel casing. Raise the muzzle and slide the barrel out of the casing. A hinge pin catch will be found on the underside of the barrel casing, near its end and to the right. Press this up and while maintaining pressure twist the receiver, left to right, until it has completed a half-turn. It may now be pulled out to the rear.

(6) A catch will be found in front of the foresight. Lifting this permits you to unscrew the flash hider over the muzzle. Inside it is a mouthpiece and a recoil cone. Remove them. The trigger assembly is locked to the receiver by two automatic locking pins. Pinching the split ends together permits them to be pulled out. (Removal of this assembly is not recommended without suitable tools.)

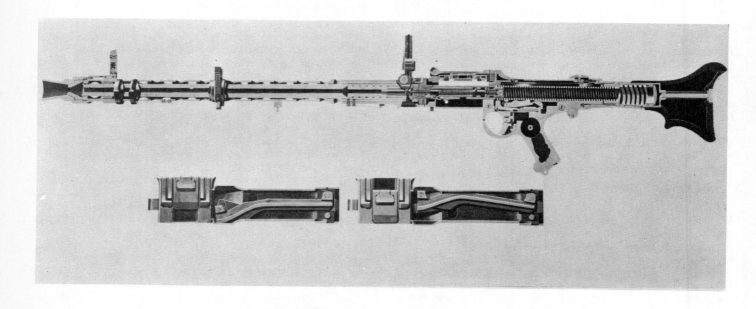

Section view of MG34.

unlocking operation is completed, when its cam sleeve strikes against shoulders in the front end of the receiver.

The stud riding straight to the rear on the bolt, its head caught in the groove in the feed arm above it, twists the feed arm, which forces the feed pawl slide to move back, and permits the feed pawl to lock behind the next cartridge in the belt.

The empty case, being drawn from the firing chamber by the extractor in the face of the bolt, is struck by the ejector and hurled out of the gun. The ejector is a pin in the top of the bolt; during the backward movement of the bolt the rear end of this pin strikes against a stop, which forces the front end through its hole in the bolt to hit the base of the empty cartridge case. The ejection is downward. The end of the breech block carrier strikes against the buffer, the compression of the recoil spring is completed, and, if the semi-automatic portion of the trigger is being pulled, the bolt will stop open, engaged from below by the sear forced up by its spring. If the automatic trigger is being pressed, the firing cycle will be completed and continued as long as there are any cartridges left in the belt.

MG42

After nearly three years of combat, the German Army adopted a new machine gun, the MG42. The MG42's design borrowed concepts from several sources. For example, the quick barrel change mechanism (necessary because of the weapon's cyclic rate of fire, 1200 rounds per minute) was an improvement on the Italian Breda machine gun, and the recoil operated locking system was an adaptation of a mechanism devised by Edward Stecke of Warsaw. Reportedly, a mockup of the Stecke gun was captured by the *Wehrmacht* in 1939. Dr. Grunow of Johannus Grossfuss was responsible for incorporating all the various ideas into a single, new weapon, which was made largely from metal stampings and pressings, the first machine gun to be so made. Its design and adoption cut down on machine tool usage during the war years. Since then, the practice of using stampings has become much more common. The MG42's feed mechanism has also been very successful, having been employed in the design of the American M60 machine gun, among others.

During the Second World War, the following factories produced the MG42: Johannus Grossfuss Mettal-und Locierwarenfabrik, Doblen, Saxony; Mauserwerke, Berlin; Maget, Berlin; Gustlof Co.; Suhl Waffenfabrik, Suhl; and Steyr Daimeler Puch A. G., Vienna. In the post-war period, Rheinmettal, Dusseldorf, has been the basic producer of the updated MG42/59 for the *Bundeswehr*. To date, over 180,000 of these new guns have been manufactured by the German firm alone.

The first post-war MG42/59 machine guns (MG1s), used primarily by West German Border Patrols, were chambered for 7.92 × 57 cartridges. Since then, several modifications have been made by Rheinmettal.

The MG34 stripped.

—The MG1A1, converted to 7.62 × 51mm NATO, has a hard chrome plated barrel. The sight has been corrected for the NATO cartridge and the trigger mechanism slightly modified.

—The receiver of the MG1A2 has been modified and case ejection port widened. A heavier bolt has been utilized that reduces the rate of fire to 700–900 shots per minute. The MG1A2 can be used with either the German nondisintegrating link belt or the American M13 disintegrating link belt. The cocking stud on the cocking slide has been shortened and the buffer, recoil booster and flash hider modified. The barrel is similar to the MG1, but the barrel guide sleeve (front barrel bearing) has been modified. This model has been adopted by Italy.

—The MG1A3, with a modified sight, has a barrel similar to the MG1A1's. An additional stud has been added to the bolt housing and other minor modifications made to the bolt, belt-feed lever and feed mechanism. The trigger mechanism has been changed and trigger pull tightened. The stock has been modified in the dimension of the sleeve, which threads on to the buffer.

—Also modified have been the butt plate, mounting screw, bipod, recoil booster and flash hider, which was made in one piece. The barrel and barrel bearing have been chrome plated.

—The current model of this machine gun being used in West Germany in the MG3, which differs in minor details from earlier models. The most noticeable differences are the addition of an anti-aircraft sight in front of the rear sight, the shape of the barrel booster flash hider unit and the fact that the gun can use DMI nondisintegrating belts, DM6 disintegrating belts and US M13 links.

—There are two bolts and two buffers for the MG1 series guns. Use of the light bolt, called V550 (weighing 550 grams) by Rheinmettal, and the Type N buffer produces a cyclic rate of 100–1300 rounds per minute. Use of the heavy bolt, called V950 (weighing 950 grams), and the Type R buffer produces a cyclic rate of 700–900 rounds per minute.

In the post-war period, in addition to the *Bundeswehr,* the Austrian, Chilean, Danish, Iranian, Italian, Norwegian, Portugese, Spanish and Turkish armed forces have been major users of this NATO caliber machine gun. Yugoslavia has built its own version of the MG42 in the older 7.92 × 57mm caliber.

Diagrammatic view of MG42 feed mechanism taken from G. M. Chinn, *The Machine Gun.*

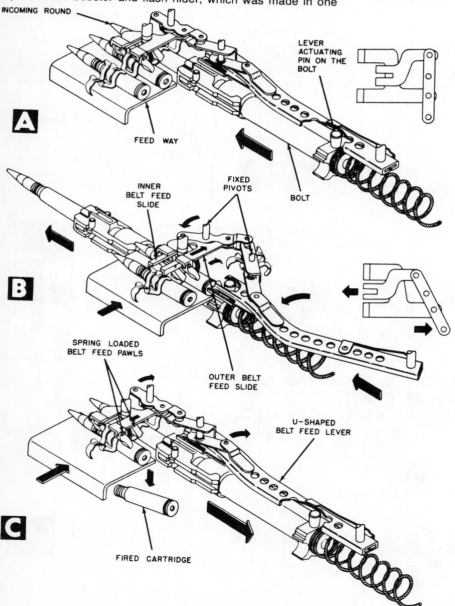

INCOMING ROUND

LEVER ACTUATING PIN ON THE BOLT

A

FEED WAY

INNER BELT FEED SLIDE

FIXED PIVOTS

BOLT

B

SPRING LOADED BELT FEED PAWLS

OUTER BELT FEED SLIDE

U-SHAPED BELT FEED LEVER

C

FIRED CARTRIDGE

Pin on Bolt Actuates Belt Feed Lever.

Unless gun is to be used immediately, set the safety. On this gun the safety is just above the pistol grip. Push the botton from the right side and it sets the safety. Push the button from the left as far as it will go and the gun is ready to fire.

NOTES ON UNLOADING. Unloading this gun is a very simple operation. First pull back the cocking handle as far as it will go. Then set the safety. Push forward the cover catch and raise the cover as high as it will go. Lift the belt out of the gun.

It is not good practice to permit the bolt to go home on an empty chamber. Always hold the cocking handle firmly while pressing the trigger and ease the bolt into forward position.

Note that there is a spring cover over the ejection opening in these guns. It flies open when the trigger is pressed. On "Cease Fire" always push it shut. This will keep dirt and dust out of the mechanism.

How the MG42 Works

In general this gun follows the operating detail of the MG34.

However, an entirely new design of bolt and locking mechanism is employed. The barrel and bolt in this gun travel back in a straight line during the period of recoil. There is no turning action.

A heavy barrel extension is screwed onto the chamber end of the barrel. In its sides are slots into which cams are machined. As the bolt goes forward, a movable locking stud on each side of the front end of the bolt strikes a corresponding cam in the barrel extension. This forces locking lugs out and into slots in the barrel extension as the face of the bolt comes flush with the base of the cartridge in the firing chamber. The extractor slips over the base of the cartridge. The firing pin, mounted in the rear of the bolt assembly, is driven forward to explode the cartridge. Note that a stud, driving from the top of this rear bolt assembly, travels in a groove in the curved feed arm and shuttles the feed across and back to operate the feed mechanism.

During the recoil movement, barrel extension and bolt are firmly locked together during the moment of high breech pressure. Then as the barrel extension and barrel are stopped in rearward travel, the studs on the bolt head are cammed out by the camming surfaces on the barrel extension, and the locking lugs are thus withdrawn from their seats in the barrel extension permitting rearward direct line motion in the action. This action is patterned after a simple pile-driver, the bolt resembling the pile-driver hammer being pulled up (or out) to its full extent, then the gripping surfaces being cammed out to release it.

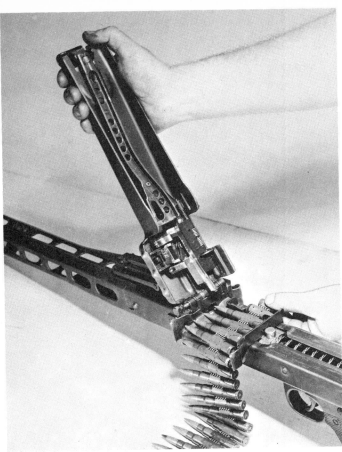

MG42, feed cover open.

Loading and Firing the MG42

To Load: (As for MG34). Feed cover may be open or closed. Be sure that the first cartridge rests against the stop on the right side of the feed guide.

Pull back cocking handle on left side of gun as far as it will go. The bolt will stay open. Then shove the cocking handle fully forward until it clicks.

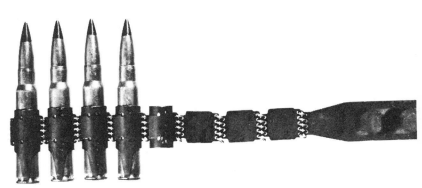

German metal belt showing detail of cartridges, locking system and tab.

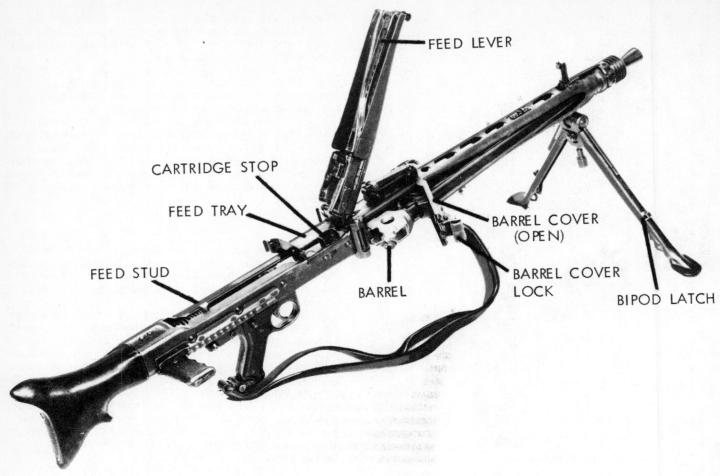

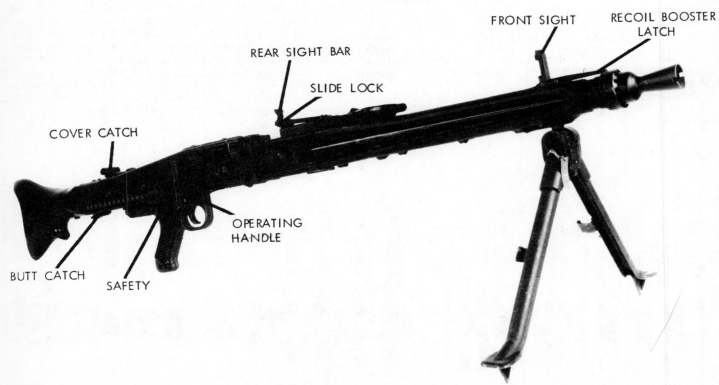

Major features of MG42 (top) and MG 42/59 (MG1) (bottom).

Field Stripping the MG42

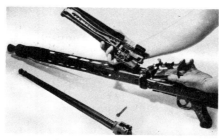

(1) In general field stripping this gun is similar to the MG34. There are, however, some few differences. To remove barrel: It is first necessary to cock the weapon. This is done by pulling back the cocking handle. Then thrust forward and outward on the heavy release catch jutting out from the rear of the barrel extension on the right hand side of the gun, below the feed block. This draws the rear of the barrel out of its seat and permits it to be drawn from the rear of the gun.

(2) The feed resembles the MG34. Push forward the feed cover catch on top of the gun near the stock and lift the cover. Pull out the feed cover hinge-pin and remove the feed block from the gun. Dismounting this is very simple.

(3) Remove buttstock, same as for MG34. Be sure bolt is in forward position before removing buttstock. Catch is on the underside of the stock. Push it and twist the butt a quarter turn, right or left.

(4) Remove buffer and recoil spring. As in the MG34, the housing catch is on the rear end of the receiver, just back of the pistol grip. Press the catch and control the buffer housing that moves away from the receiver under tension of the powerful spring. Remove the bolt. Press the trigger and strike the cocking handle a sharp rearward blow. This will drive the bolt to the open rear of the receiver where it may be withdrawn. No further stripping is normally necessary.

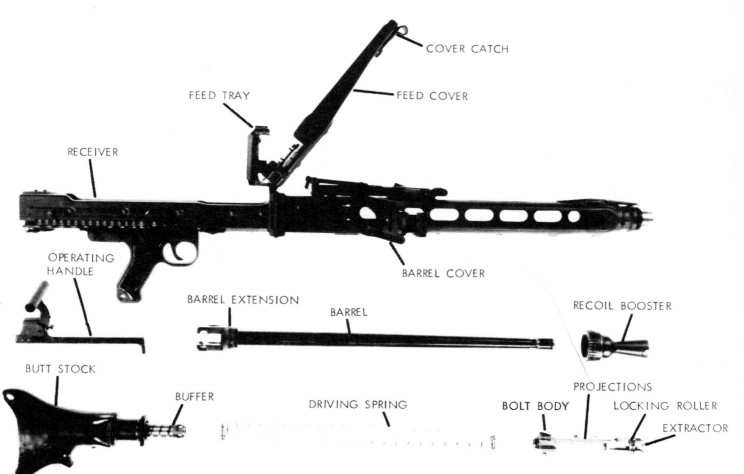

Post–war MG 42/59.

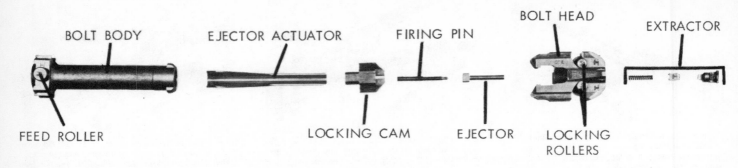

BOLT BODY   EJECTOR ACTUATOR   FIRING PIN   BOLT HEAD   EXTRACTOR

FEED ROLLER   LOCKING CAM   EJECTOR   LOCKING ROLLERS

Disassembled MG42 Bolt.

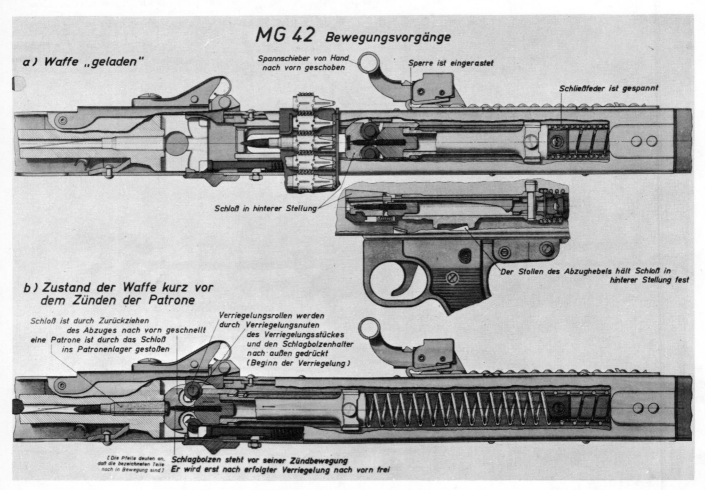

MG 42 Bewegungsvorgänge

a) Waffe „geladen"

Spannschieber von Hand nach vorn geschoben

Sperre ist eingerastet

Schließfeder ist gespannt

Schloß in hinterer Stellung

Der Stollen des Abzughebels hält Schloß in hinterer Stellung fest

b) Zustand der Waffe kurz vor dem Zünden der Patrone

Schloß ist durch Zurückziehen des Abzuges nach vorn geschnellt eine Patrone ist durch das Schloß ins Patronenlager gestoßen

Verriegelungsrollen werden durch Verriegelungsnuten des Verriegelungsstückes und den Schlagbolzenhalter nach außen gedrückt (Beginn der Verriegelung)

(Die Pfeile deuten an, daß die bezeichneten Teile nach in Bewegung sind)

Schlagbolzen steht vor seiner Zündbewegung Er wird erst nach erfolgter Verriegelung nach vorn frei

Views of MG42 mechanism showing bolt feeding into chamber, bolt unlocked.

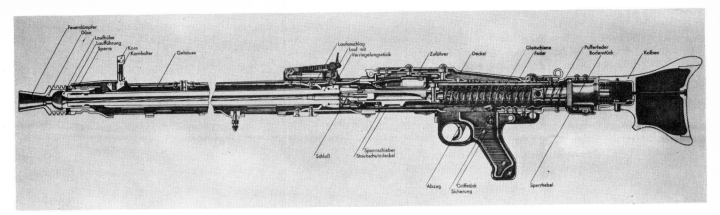

Phantom drawing showing all operating parts in full closed position. View of left side. Nomenclature, left to right, top. 1. Flash hider. 2. Barrel mouth. 3, 4, and 5. Blast cone assembly. 6 and 7. Front sight and spring. 8. Housing. 9. Barrel retainer. 10 and 11. Barrel and barrel locks. 12. Feed. 13. Cover. 14 and 15. Recoil spring and guide. 16. Buffer spring. 17 and 18. Butt assembly and butt. Left to right, bottom: 1. Lock. 2. Bolt. 3. Bolt extension. 4. Trigger. 5. Safety. 6. Grip. 7. Buffer release.

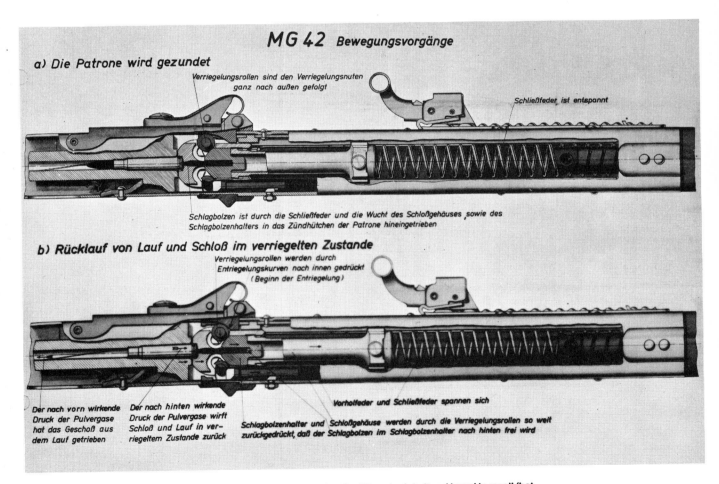

Section view of MG42 cartridge fired (top view); bolt and barrel in recoil (bottom).

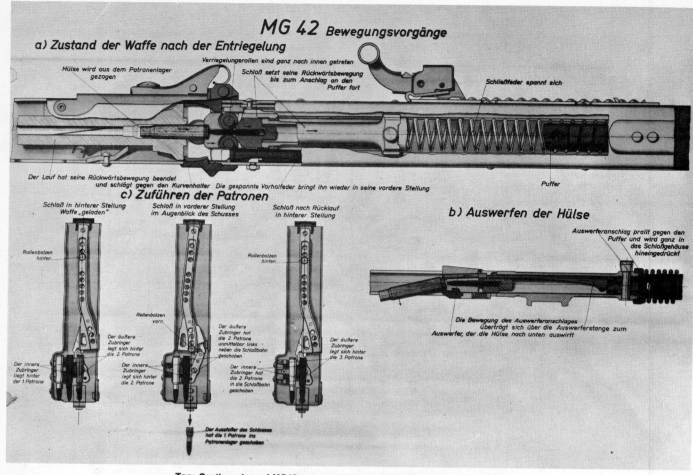

MG 42 Bewegungsvorgänge

a) Zustand der Waffe nach der Entriegelung

Hülse wird aus dem Patronenlager gezogen

Verriegelungsrollen sind ganz nach innen getreten

Schloß setzt seine Rückwärtsbewegung bis zum Anschlag an den Puffer fort

Schließfeder spannt sich

Der Lauf hat seine Rückwärtsbewegung beendet und schlägt gegen den Kurvenhalter Die gespannte Vorholfeder bringt ihn wieder in seine vordere Stellung

Puffer

c) Zuführen der Patronen

Schloß in hinterer Stellung Waffe „geladen"

Schloß in vorderer Stellung im Augenblick des Schusses

Schloß nach Rücklauf in hinterer Stellung

b) Auswerfen der Hülse

Auswerferanschlag prallt gegen den Puffer und wird ganz in das Schloßgehäuse hineingedrückt

Rollenbolzen hinten

Rollenbolzen hinten

Rollenbolzen vorn

Der äußere Zubringer hat die 2. Patrone unmittelbar links neben die Schloßbahn geschoben

Der äußere Zubringer legt sich hinter die 2. Patrone

Der innere Zubringer legt sich hinter die 2. Patrone

Der äußere Zubringer legt sich hinter die 3. Patrone

Der innere Zubringer liegt hinter der 1. Patrone

Der innere Zubringer hat die 2. Patrone in die Schloßbahn geschoben

Die Bewegung des Auswerferanschlages überträgt sich über die Auswerferstange zum Auswerfer, der die Hülse nach unten auswirft

Der Ausstoßer des Schlosses hat die 1. Patrone ins Patronenlager geschoben

Top: Section view of MG42, gun unlocked, cartridge being withdrawn from chamber by bolt. Bottom left: View showing movement of belt feed mechanism. Bottom right: View shows action of ejector.

STANDARD GERMAN ARMY MACHINE GUNS

	MG08	MG08/15	MG13	MG34*	MG42
Caliber:	7.92mm.	7.92mm.	7.92mm	7.92mm	7.92mm.
System of operation:	Recoil, automatic only.	Recoil, automatic only.	Recoil, selective fire.	Recoil, selective fire.	Recoil, automatic only.
Length overall: (gun only)	46.25 in.	Approx 57 in.	Approx 57 in.	48 in.	48 in.
Barrel length:	28.25 in.	28.25 in.	28.25 in.	24.6 in.	21 in.
Cooling:	Water.	Water.	Air.	Air.	Air.
Feed device:	100- and 250-round fabric belt.	50-, 100-, & 250-round fabric belt. Can be used with spool type container with 50-round belt or with ordinary ammo can.	25-round box magazine or 75-round saddle drum.	50-round non-disintegrating belt, linked together to form 250-round belt. 50-round belt drum. 75-round saddle drum.	50-round non-disintegrating belt usually joined into 250-round belt, 50-round drum.
Sights: Front:	Barley corn.	Barley corn.	Folding barley corn.	Folding barley corn.	Folding barley corn.
Rear:	Folding leaf w/v notch.	Tangent leaf w/V notch.	Tangent leaf w/V notch.	Leaf w/V notch.	Tangent w/V notch.
Muzzle velocity:	2750 f.p.s. (S ball)	2750 f.p.s. (S ball)	2750 f.p.s.(S ball)	Approx 2500 f.p.s. (sS ball)	2480 f.p.s. (sS ball)
Cyclic rate:	400-500 r.p.m.	400-500 r.p.m.	750 r.p.m.	800-900 r.p.m.	1100-1200 r.p.m.
Weight of gun:	40.5 lb.	31 lb.	26.4 lb. w/bipod.	26.5 lb. w/bipod	25.5 lb. w/bipod.
Weight of mount:	83 lb. sled mount. 65.5 lb. tripod mount.	51 lb.	Approx 25 lb.	42.3 lb.	42.3 lb.

*Data is given for basic MG34; other versions vary as follows:
MG34S and MG34/41—automatic fire only.
Overall length: approx 46 in.
Barrel length: approx 22 in.

22 Greece

The Greek Army is currently equipped with a mixture of US and British service arms. The Greeks lost a great number of their small arms during World War II. The British supplied the Greek Army in their fight against the Communists until the Americans started their military assistance in 1947. British caliber .38 and .455 revolvers, the No. 2 9mm Browning Hi-Power, caliber .303 No. 4 rifles and Bren and Vickers guns are in service. US weapons include the caliber .45 M1911A1 pistols, caliber .30 M1 rifles, M1918A2 Browning automatic rifles and the caliber .30 and .50 Browning machine guns.

GREEK PISTOLS

Greece has developed no native designs in pistols and has used a wide variety of pistols in the past, including the 9mm M1903 Bergmann Bayard and various models of the Browning.

GREEK RIFLES AND CARBINES

MANNLICHER SCHOENAUER 6.5mm 1903 RIFLE

The Greeks adopted the Mannlicher Schoenauer rifle in 6.5mm in 1903. This rifle combines the Mannlicher two-piece rotating bolt with the rotating spool type magazine developed by Otto Schoenauer. This system is still used in the sporting type Steyr rifles made currently, and the 6.5 x 54 Greek cartridge is still popular throughout most of the world as a sporting cartridge.

A modification of the 1903 model, the 1903/14, was adopted in 1914. Differences between the two models are relatively minor and are principally in the graduations on the rear sight, shape of grasping grooves on the stock and in the length and ease of removal of the handguards.

The Greek Army lost many of these weapons during the first World War and as part of the reparations for that war received a mixed batch of Austrian Mannlicher rifles as well as some Turkish Mausers. During that war, the Greeks were supplied with a number of French weapons, including French 8mm Lebel and Mannlicher Berthier rifles.

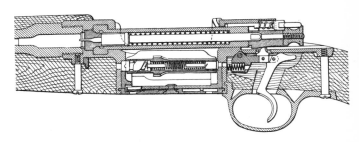

Section of rifle with action closed. Note position of locking lugs in rear of bolt head.

6.5mm Model 1903/14 Carbine.

6.5mm Mannlicher Schoenauer M1903/14 Rifle.

OTHER GREEK SHOULDER ARMS

The Greeks had a number of Austrian 8mm M1888/90 and 8mm M1895 rifles converted to 7.92mm. The Model 1895 conversion was called the model 95/24. In 1930, the Greeks adopted the Model 1924 FN Mauser in 7.92mm, which they called the Model 30. This rifle is covered in detail under Belgium.

Shortly before the beginning of World War II, the Greek Powder Company announced that it was developing an automatic rifle. This gas-operated 7.92mm weapon was apparently never produced in quantity. It weighed 9.1 lbs, was 35.4 inches long, with a 15.74-inch barrel and a cyclic rate of 750 rounds per minute.

GREEK SERVICE RIFLES AND CARBINES

	M1903 Rifle	M1903 Carbine	M95/24	M1930
Caliber:	6.5mm.	6.5mm.	7.92mm.	7.92mm.
System of operation:	Turn bolt.	Turn bolt.	Straight-pull bolt.	Turn bolt.
Overall length:	48.3 in.	40.3 in.	39.5 in.	43.3 in.
Barrel length:	28.5 in.	20.5 in.	19.6 in.	23.2 in.
Feed device:	5-round, revolving spool, non-detachable box magazine.	5-round revolving spool, non-detachable box magazine.	5-round, in line* non-detachable box magazine.	5-round staggered row, non-detachable box magazine.
Sights:				
Front:	Barley corn.	Barley corn	Barley corn.	Barley corn.
Rear:	Tangent with 'V' notch.	Tangent with "V" notch.	Leaf with 'V' notch.	Tangent with 'V' notch.
Weight:	8.31 lbs.	Approx. 8 lbs.	6.8 lbs.	8.5 lbs.
Muzzle velocity:	2225 f.p.s.	Approx 2125 f.p.s.	Approx. 2410 f.p.s.	2500 f.p.s.

*Magazine is charger fed; charger does not remain in magazine.

Prototype 7.92mm automatic rifle.

GREEK MACHINE GUNS

The Greek Army was equipped with the French 8mm Saint Etienne M1907 heavy machine gun and the 8mm C.S.R.G. Model 1915 light machine gun during and immediately after World War I. For some peculiar reason, the 8mm Lebel cartridge was called the 7.8mm cartridge in Greece. The German Maxim MG08 in 7.92mm was among the captured weapons used by the Greeks. During World War II, the Greeks captured all types of Italian machine guns as well as all other types of Italian small arms.

23
Hungary

The Hungarian Army is currently equipped with copies and/or modified copies of Soviet World War II and post-war small arms. The service pistol is the 7.62mm Model 48, a Hungarian copy of the Soviet 7.62mm TT33 Tokarev. The service rifle is a modified copy of the 7.62mm AK made in Hungary. Service machine guns include the 7.62mm RPD, 7.62mm SGM, and the 12.7mm DShK M1938/46. There are probably still Hungarian-made 7.62mm Model 48 submachine guns (copy of Soviet PPSh M1941) and Hungarian-made 7.62mm Model 48 rifles (copy of the Soviet 7.62mm M1891/30 rifle) and some of the old Degtyarev series machine guns still in service.

HUNGARIAN SERVICE PISTOLS

THE HUNGARIAN 7.65mm FROMMER STOP PISTOL MODEL 19

Hungary was, until 1918, part of the Austro-Hungarian Empire and in general used the standard weapons of that empire. Because of local development capabilities, and probably local politics, the Hungarians used a different pistol during World War I than the rest of the empire forces. This pistol was the 7.65mm (.32 ACP) Model 19 Frommer Stop pistol. This long recoil-operated pistol was developed in 1912 and used by the Hungarian police and service forces after World War I. A 9mm (.380 ACP) version, which, according to some authorities, was never issued as a military weapon, appeared some time between 1916 and 1919. The designation Model 19 for the 7.65mm Frommer is rather unusual since the weapon appeared in 1912 and was adopted by the Hungarian Army (Honved) prior to World War I, but official Hungarian documents indicate that this is the correct designation. The Frommer Stop was manufactured by Fegyvergyan at Budapest. It is basically not a good design, is somewhat delicate for a service weapon and was reportedly not popular

Frommer M1939. Caliber .380. Obsolete in Hungary.

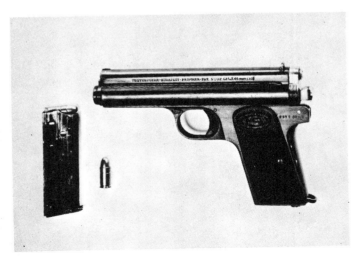

Frommer 7.65mm Automatic, Model 19.

9mm Model 29 Pistol.

with Hungarian troops. The complication of a long recoil system is absolutely wasted on relatively low-powered cartridges, which can be adequately handled by a simple blowback action. A later 9mm (.380 ACP) version of this pistol is marked "1939M". This was apparently not a service weapon, and the purpose for which it was made is not apparent.

THE HUNGARIAN 7.65mm (AND 9mm) PISTOL MODEL 37

In 1929, the Hungarians adopted a modified Browning blowback design, the 9mm (.380 ACP) Model 29. This weapon has an internal bolt assembly fixed to the slide rather than having the bolt (breech) portion machined in the rear of the slide. This weapon was apparently made in very limited quantity and is overly complicated, as is the Frommer Stop.

A version of the Model 29 with a conventional slide appeared in 1937. The Model 37 is a conventional blowback pistol chambered for both the 7.65mm (.32 ACP) and the 9mm (.380 ACP). The Model 37 was made in large quantities for the Hungarian Army and is probably the most common Hungarian pistol in the US today.

During World War II, Hungary became—for all practical purposes—a satellite of Germany. Hungarian arms plants produced large quantities of weapons for the Germans. Among

7.65mm Model 48 Pistol.

these weapons was the Model 37 pistol in 7.65mm. The weapon, as made for the Germans, bears German acceptance markings and the three-letter manufacturers code "jhv." The weapons manufactured for the Germans have, in addition to the grip safety fitted to the earlier-made Model 37 pistols, a plate-type safety mounted on the left side of the receiver.

THE HUNGARIAN 7.62mm PISTOL MODEL 48

After World War II, a modified copy of the German 7.65mm Walther PP was introduced in Hungary. This pistol, which has a loaded chamber indicator over the chamber rather than at the rear of the slide as does the Walther, is called the Model 48 by the Hungarians. It is not a military weapon but is used by police and has been sold commercially in 9mm (.380 ACP) as the "Walam." These pistols are three-quarters of an inch longer than the PP.

Loading, firing and field stripping these pistols is the same as for German Walther PP and PPK.

The current Hungarian service pistol, the 7.62mm Model 48, is a copy of the Soviet 7.62mm TT33 and is loaded, fired and field stripped as is that pistol. An aluminum frame version has been introduced and designated the M60. It has been issued to Hungarian military forces.

9mm Model 37 Pistol.

7.65mm Model 37 Pistol made for the Germans.

9mm Walam 48 Pistol.

The Model 48 field stripped.

Hungarian 7.62mm Model 48, a copy of Soviet TT M33.

9mm Tokagypt 58 Pistol.

CHARACTERISTICS OF HUNGARIAN SERVICE PISTOLS

	Frommer Stop Model 19	7.65mm Model 48	9mm Model 37	7.62mm Model 48
Caliber:	7.65mm (ACP).	7.65mm (.32 ACP).	9mm (.380 ACP)*	7.62mm.
System of operation:	Long recoil, semiautomatic.	Blowback, semi-automatic.	Blowback, semi-automatic.	Recoil, semi-automatic.
Overall length:	6.5 in.	7 in.	6.8 in.	7.68 in.
Barrel length:	3.8 in.	3.94 in.	3.9 in.	4.57 in.
Feed device:	7-round, in line detachable, box magazine.	8-round, in line detachable, box magazine.	7-round, in line detachable, box magazine.	8-round, in line detachable, box magazine.
Sights:				
Front:	Blade.	Blade.	Blade.	Blade.
Rear:	V notch.	U notch.	V notch.	U notch.
Weight:	1.31 lbs.	1.92 lbs.	1.62 lbs.	1.88 lbs.
Muzzle velocity:	920 f.p.s.	920 f.p.s.	984 f.p.s.	1,378 f.p.s.

*Also made in 7.65mm (.32 ACP)

THE TOKAGYPT 58

The Tokagypt 58 was reportedly developed for the Egyptian police. It is a modified copy of the Tokarev TT33 chambered for the 9mm Parabellum cartridge. A safety catch has been added to the basic Tokarev design, which is fitted on the left top side of the receiver.

In addition, a plastic wrap-around type one-piece grip and a finger support on the magazine are found on this pistol. It is not a Hungarian service pistol.

9mm Tokagypt 58, field stripped.

HUNGARIAN RIFLES

HUNGARIAN 8mm STUTZEN RIFLE MODEL 31

The Hungarians were equipped during World War I with various models of the straight pull 8mm Steyr rifle chambered for the 8mm M93 cartridge. After the adoption of the 8 x 56mm rimmed M31 cartridge, a number of the 8mm M95 short rifles (the Stutzen) were modified to take this cartridge. This rifle is called the Model 31 and is identified by a letter "H," 5/16 of an inch high, stamped on the barrel or receiver.

HUNGARIAN 8mm RIFLE MODEL 35

In 1935 a turn-bolt Mannlicher type was adopted, the Model 35, chambered for the 8mm Model 31 cartridge. The Model 35 has a two-piece bolt with the bolt handle positioned ahead of the receiver bridge when the bolt is forward. The magazine is an in-line type, which protrudes below the line of the stock. The Model 35 has a two-piece stock similar in concept to the British Lee Enfield.

HUNGARIAN 7.92mm RIFLE MODEL 43

In 1940, the Model 35 was redesigned for German use. The caliber was changed to 7.92mm, a staggered row Mauser type box magazine flush with the stock was fitted and German type bands and bayonet lug were used on this rifle, which was called the Model 98/40 by the Germans. In 1943, Hungary adopted the 7.92mm cartridge and started issue of a slightly modified 98/40—the Model 43—to the Hungarian Army. This rifle differs from the 98/40 principally in its bands and fittings, i.e., bayonet lug, sling swivels, etc.

HUNGARIAN 7.62mm RIFLE MODEL 48 (COPY OF SOVIET MOSIN NAGANT)

The conclusion of the war found Hungary disarmed. The Hungarian Army was equipped with Soviet 7.62mm Mosin Nagant rifles and carbines. Some copies of these weapons were made in Hungary and called Model 48. Within the past decade, the post-war Soviet rifles and carbines have been adopted, and both the 7.62mm SKS carbine and 7.62mm AK assault rifle have been made in Hungary.

HUNGARIAN 7.62mm MODIFIED SOVIET AKM RIFLE

Recently the Hungarians have adopted a modification of the 7.62mm AKM. This rifle has a plastic stock and pistol grips and a metal hand guard. The forward pistol grip is grasped during fire rather than the hand guard or the magazine. It has no top hand guard. This weapon is loaded, fired and field stripped in a manner similar to the Soviet AKM.

HUNGARIAN AMD ASSAULT RIFLE

The Hungarians have come out with another variation of the AKM. The AMD has a short barrel with a large muzzle brake. It has a single strut steel folding stock. The plastic fore grip and the metal forend are the same as those on the standard Hungarian modification of the AKM. Because of the relatively low energy of the 7.62 x 39mm cartridge, recoil with this weapon is probably not excessive, but the muzzle blast is probably very high. The AMD is 33.5 inches long with stock fixed and 23.5 inches long when the stock is folded. The barrel is 12.6 inches long.

Hungarian 7.62mm Model AMD Assault Rifle

HUNGARIAN SERVICE RIFLES

	Model 31	Model 35	Model 43	Model 48	Modified AKM
Caliber:	8 x 56mm.	8 x 56mm.	7.92mm.	7.62 Mosin Nagant.	7.62 M43
System of operation:	Straight pull bolt	Turn bolt.	Turn bolt.	Turn bolt.	Gas, selective fire.
Overall length:	39.5 in.	43.7 in.	43 in.	48.5 in.	34.25 in.
Barrel length:	19.65 in.	23.6 in.	23.8 in.	28.7 in.	16.34 in.
Feed device:	5-round single column, fixed box magazine.	5-round single column, fixed box magazine.	5-round staggered row, fixed box magazine.	5-round single column, fixed box magazine.	30-round staggered row, detachable box magazine.
Sights:					
Front:	Barley corn.	Hooded barley corn.	Barley corn.	Hooded post.	Protected post.
Rear:	Leaf with notch.	Tangent with notch.	Tangent with notch.	Tangent with notch.	Tangent with notch.
Weight:	7.5 lbs.	8.9 lbs.	8.6 lbs.	8.7 lbs.	Approx. 10.7 lbs.
Muzzle velocity:	Approx. 2300 f.p.s.	2395 f.p.s.	Approx. 2480 f.p.s. (SS ball)	2800 f.p.s.	2329 f.p.s.
Cyclic rate:					600 r.p.m.

Hungarian 7.92mm Model 43 Rifle.

The 8mm Model 35 Rifle.

Hungarian modification of 7.62mm AKM Assault Rifle.

HUNGARIAN SUBMACHINE GUNS

HUNGARIAN 9mm SUBMACHINE GUN MODEL 39

A native-designed submachine gun was produced in Hungary in the late thirties and adopted in 1939. The design of this weapon, which is chambered for the 9mm Mauser cartridge, is credited to Pal D. Kiraly and resembles in many respects the SIG (Swiss) MKMO submachine gun. Kiraly was concerned with the design of the Dominican Cristobal carbine; the bolt design of the Cristobal is similar to that of the Model 39. The folding

magazine system of the Model 39 is similar to that of the SIG MKMO.

The standard Model 39 submachine gun has a one-piece stock; a version with a folding wooden butt was produced as the Model 39/A. Both the Model 39 and 39/A were produced in very limited numbers. The fire selector /safety is the circular cap located on the rear of the receiver, operated by rotating the cap to align with one of the three settings:-'E' for semiautomatic fire, 'S' for automatic fire and 'Z' for safe.

9mm Mauser Model 39 Submachine Gun.

HUNGARIAN 9mm SUBMACHINE GUN MODEL 43

The Model 43, which was made in much larger quantity than the Model 39, is essentially the same as the Model 39 but has a folding metal stock. The folding stock has wooden strips on the side of the metal stock frame. The magazine of the Model 43 is canted slightly forward when in the fixed position as opposed to the straight vertical position of the Model 39 magazine, and the barrel of the Model 43 is approximately three inches shorter than the Model 39. The magazines of the Models 39 and 43 are not interchangeable.

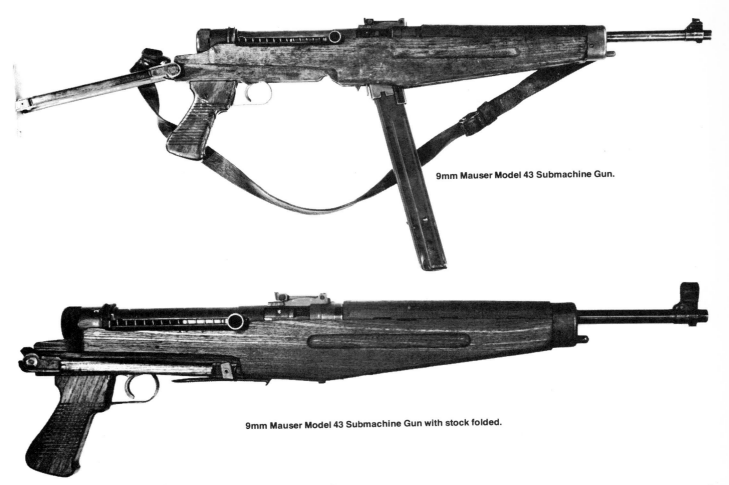

9mm Mauser Model 43 Submachine Gun.

9mm Mauser Model 43 Submachine Gun with stock folded.

HUNGARIAN 7.62mm SUBMACHINE GUN MODEL 48
(COPY OF SOVIET PPSh M1941)

After World War II, the Hungarians were supplied with Soviet weapons and manufactured a copy of the Soviet 7.62mm PPSh M1941 as the Model 48. A submachine gun intended basically for police purposes, known as the Model 54, was also produced.

Currently the submachine gun is used as a reserve weapon or as a Border Patrol weapon in Hungary. As with other Warsaw Pact nations, the assault rifle is replacing the submachine gun in the Army.

Model 48 7.62mm Submachine Gun.

CHARACTERISTICS OF HUNGARIAN SUBMACHINE GUNS

	Model 39	Model 43	Model 48
Caliber:	9mm Mauser.	9mm Mauser.	7.62mm.
System of operation:	Delayed blowback, selective fire.	Delayed blowback, selective fire.	Blowback, selective fire.
Overall length:	41.25 in.	Stock extended: 37.5 in. Stock folded: 29.5 in.	33.15 in.
Barrel length:	19.65 in.	16.7 inches	10.63 inches
Feed Device:	40-round, staggered row, detachable box magazine.	40-round, staggered row, detachable box magazine.	71-round drum or 35-round detachable box magazine.
Sights:			
Front:	Barley corn.	Barley corn.	Hooded post.
Rear:	Tangent with V notch.	Tangent with V notch.	L type.
Weight:	8.2 lbs.	8 lbs.	11.9 lbs. with loaded drum magazine.
Muzzle velocity:	1475 f.p.s.	1450 f.p.s.	1640 f.p.s.
Cyclic rate:	750 r.p.m.	750 r.p.m.	700-900 r.p.m.

HUNGARIAN MACHINE GUNS

8mm Model 31 Machine Gun.

The Hungarian Army, after the foundation of a separate Hungary in 1919, was equipped with the 8mm Schwarzlose 07/12 heavy machine gun. Hungary followed the lead of Austria in adopting the Solothurn machine gun developed by Louis Stange. The Hungarian gun was chambered for the 8mm Model 31 cartridge (8 x 56 R) and was called the Model 31. The gun has the same characteristics as the Model 30.

Some Schwarzlose machine guns were modified to use the 8mm Model 31 cartridge; they are called the Model 7/31. The Hungarians also produced an aircraft gun chambered for the Model 31 cartridge, which was called the Model 34/AM. During World War II, the Hungarians changed their machine gun caliber at the same time as they changed caliber with rifles—in 1943. The Hungarian Model 43 machine gun is essentially the same as the Model 31 but is chambered for the 7.92mm cartridge.

As with all their other weapons, the Hungarians were equipped with Soviet machine guns after World War II. Initially they adopted the older Soviet weapons, such as the 7.62mm DP, DPM and DTM machine guns. They currently use the 7.62mm RPD, 7.62mm SGM and 12.7mm DShK 38/46. All these weapons are covered in detail in the chapter on the Soviet Union.

India

24

The Indian Army is mainly armed with British type service weapons. The 7.62mm FN FAL rifle in the L1A1 version (British) is now standard, as is the 9mm Sterling submachine gun. The Sterling is called the SAF in India and is made at Cawnpore. The Indians have Vickers Berthier, Bren and Browning light machine guns and Vickers heavy machine guns, but these weapons will be replaced by the 7.62mm FN MAG general purpose machine gun.

INDIAN RIFLES

The government small arms factory at Ishapore has been making rifles for a considerable time and produced the Lee Enfield No. 1 Mark III* through World War II. The Ishapore rifles varied in minor details from the rifle as made in the United Kingdom, frequently having no stacking swivels, the stacking swivel mounting lug being left solid. Ishapore made 692,587 Mark III* rifles during World War II. India is now producing the 7.62mm rifle L1A1 (British FN FAL).

INDIAN MACHINE GUNS

India produced 8,357 machine guns during World War II and was preparing to produce Bren Guns at a new factory at Hyderabad when the war ended. The current standard Indian machine gun is the 7.62mm FN MAG general purpose gun. The standard machine gun of the Indian Army during World War II was the Vickers Berthier.

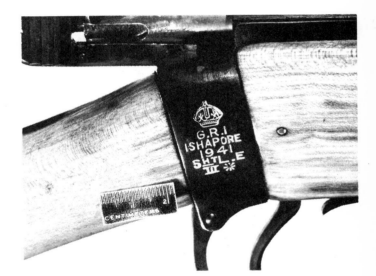

Marking on Short Lee Enfield No. 1 Mark III* made at Ishapore.

INDIAN CAL. .303 VICKERS BERTHIER MACHINE GUN

During the period between World Wars I and II, the Indian Army, then a semi-autonomous branch of the British Army, adopted the cal. .303 Vickers Berthier Light Machine Gun Mark III. This weapon is still in limited use in India. It is quite similar in construction and external appearance to the Bren. The main differences between the Bren and the Berthier lie in the breechblock, the feed, the holding-open device, the gas cylinder arrangement, the barrel change and the sights.

Characteristics of Vickers Berthier Machine Gun

Caliber: .303 British.
Weight, loaded: 24.4 lbs.
Overall length: 45.5 in.
Barrel length: 23.9 in.
Feed mechanism: 30-round, detachable, staggered box magazine.
Sights: Front: Hooded blade.
      Rear: Leaf.
Muzzle velocity: 2400 f.p.s. w/Mk 7 ball (approx).

Caliber .303 Vickers Berthier Mark III.

Indonesia has an unusually large variety of service small arms, from a diverse number of sources. The US caliber .45 M1911A1, the 9mm FN Hi-Power Browning, the 7.62mm Tokarev and various models of the Walther are some of the pistols used by the Indonesians. Rifles and carbines used include the caliber .30 M1 rifle, caliber .30 M1 carbine, the caliber .30 M1918A2 Browning automatic rifle, the caliber .30 FN semiautomatic rifle (the M1949), the 7.62mm G3 rifle, 7.62mm M59 rifle, the Soviet 7.62mm AK47 assault rifle, the Soviet 7.62 SKS carbine, the British caliber .303 No. 1 and No. 4 rifles and the 7.92mm Kar98k. The submachine guns in service include the 9mm Beretta, 9mm Sten, 9mm M1950 Madsen, the Swedish 9mm M45 Carl Gustaf, the caliber .45 Thompson, the 9mm Owen and the Czech 7.62mm M24 and M26. The standard machine gun is the caliber .30 Madsen Mark II, which is made in Indonesia. The caliber .30 Browning guns, the caliber .303 Bren and Vickers guns, the 7.62 Degtyarev and Goryunov and the 12.7mm DShK M1938/46 are also used.

25 Indonesia

INDONESIAN RIFLES

The Indonesians had considerable quantities of Dutch 6.5mm Mannlicher M1895 rifles and carbines, and caliber .303 rifles, at the conclusion of their rebellion against the Dutch. A number of Mannlicher carbines were rebarreled for the .303 cartridge for the Dutch forces during World War II in the then Dutch East Indies. The fall of the Netherlands in 1940 cut off their supply of 6.5mm ammunition. At a later date the Indonesian Army started to standardize on caliber .30 weapons, the principal weapon being the US M1 rifle. The Indonesians purchased some of these from Beretta in Italy and from US sources. Purchases were also made of Soviet 7.62mm AK-47 assault rifles and SKS carbines. The Indonesians have converted some of their M1 rifles to the 7.62mm NATO BM59 (a Beretta design).

INDONESIAN SUBMACHINE GUNS

A number of prototype 9mm Parabellum submachine guns were developed by the Indonesians. None were made in quantity.

Late models of the 9mm Parabellum Beretta submachine gun are currently manufactured in Indonesia.

9mm PM Model VIII, 1957.

26

Iran (Persia)

While the Iranian Armed Forces continue to use many US small arms, the Government now produces the G3 Rifle and MG1A1 under license. It has also made purchases of the UZI submachine gun in recent years.

IRANIAN RIFLES

Iran adopted the Czech ZB 7.92mm Model 98/29 short rifle and the Model 98/29 carbine as the Model 1309 and Model 1317 (Moslem calendar years), respectively. The Christian calendar years for these are 1930 and 1938. The rifles were originally made in Czechoslovakia, but the Iranian arsenal produced them as well. Production at the Iranian arsenal probably started during World War II, since Czech supplies were shut off during the war.

The Iranians developed a modification of the Model 1930 short rifle, the Model 1949 (Model 1328 by the Moslem calendar); the Model 1949 differs from the Model 1930 only in bands and sling swivels. These rifles are loaded, fired and field stripped in the same manner as the Czech Model 24 rifle, which is covered in the chapter on Czechoslovakia.

Iranian 7.92mm Model 1938 Rifle.

Iranian 7.92mm Model 1930 Short Rifle.

CHARACTERISTICS OF IRANIAN RIFLES

	1938 Rifle	1930 Short Rifle
Caliber:	7.92mm.	7.92mm
System of operation:	Manually operated turning bolt action.	Manually operated turning bolt action.
Weight:	9.1 lbs.	8.4 lbs.
Length overall:	49.2 in.	38 in.
Barrel length:	29.13 in.	17.91 in.
Feed device:	5-rd, staggered row. non-detachable box magazine.	5-rd, staggered row, non-detachable box magazine.
Sights: Front:	Protected barley corn.	Protected barley corn.
Sights: Rear:	Tangent with V-notch, grad. from 100-2000m.	Tangent with V-notch, grad. from 100-2000m.
Muzzle velocity:	Approx. 2800 f.p.s.	Approx. 2600 f.p.s.

Iranian 7.92mm Model 1949 Short Rifle.

IRANIAN SUBMACHINE GUNS

Iran currently has quantities of US caliber .45 M3A1 submachine guns. Iran has also produced copies of the Soviet 7.62mm PPSh M1941 submachine gun. The Iranians began producing the gun during World War II for the Soviets on a contract basis and continued to produce the weapon for their own use. Characteristics of the weapon are the same as those given in the chapter on the Soviet Union.

IRANIAN MACHINE GUNS

The Iranians currently have US caliber .30 and .50 Browning machine guns. They also have the Czech ZB30 machine gun, made in Iran. This weapon was originally manufactured in 7.92mm but is currently used by the Iranians in cal. .30. Characteristics, loading firing, and field stripping of this weapon are basically the same as those given for the ZB30 in the chapter on Czechoslovakia.

Iranian copy of Soviet PPSh M1941 Submachine Gun.

Iranian 7.92mm Model 30 Light Machine Gun.

Israel

The current Israeli service weapons are: the Beretta 9mm M1951 pistol, the 7.62mm NATO FN FAL rifle and the heavy barrel version of the FAL, the 9mm UZI submachine gun and the 7.62 NATO FN general purpose machine gun. The FN Browning Automatic Rifle Type D is also used. Israel has developed a new 5.56mm Rifle, the Galil, which will replace the FALs and the Browning automatic rifle. Older weapons that may still be in limited service or reserve are the 7.62mm Kar 98k, and various caliber .38 and .455 British pistols. The US caliber .30 and caliber .50 Browning machine guns are in service on various armored vehicles.

27

ISRAELI PISTOLS

The Israelis had a variety of pistols at the time of the foundation of the State. For the most part these were caliber .38 and caliber .455 Enfield and Webley revolvers, but there were odd quantities of 9mm FN Browning Hi-power, Luger and P38 automatics as well. The Israelis developed a modified copy of the Smith & Wesson Military and Police pistol, which is unusual in that it is chambered for the 9mm Parabellum cartridge. This rimless cartridge requires the use of two three-shot clips similar to those used with the US caliber .45 Colt and Smith & Wesson service revolvers. This revolver, which bears Israeli Security Forces markings, is basically a police weapon. The Israelis use the 9mm Parabellum M1951 Beretta pistol as their standard military service pistol. This pistol is covered in detail in the chapter on Italy.

ISRAELI RIFLES

The Israelis were originally equipped mainly with British caliber .303 No. 1 and No. 4 rifles. About 1948, purchases were made of 7.92mm Kar 98k rifles of both World War II German and post-war Czech manufacture. Because of the procurement of 7.92mm machine guns at the same time, the 7.92mm cartridge was adopted as standard. Towards the end of the 50s Israel standardized the 7.62mm NATO cartridge and adopted the FN FAL rifle and the heavy barrel version of this weapon. Israel has converted her 7.92mm Kar 98K Mausers to 7.62mm NATO.

THE ISRAELI 5.56mm GALIL RIFLE

Israel's new rifle, the Galil, was first issued to troops in May 1973. The design lineage of the Galil is described in Chapter I under the 5.56 × 45mm rifles.

The Galil has a folding type steel stock and a bipod that folds between the hand-guards when not in use. It also has a grenade launcher on the end of the barrel. The cyclic rate has been reported as 650 rounds per minute.

The Israelis have announced that the Galil is to be used to replace the FAL and the heavy barrel FAL; it therefore has quite a heavy barrel.

galil assault rifle

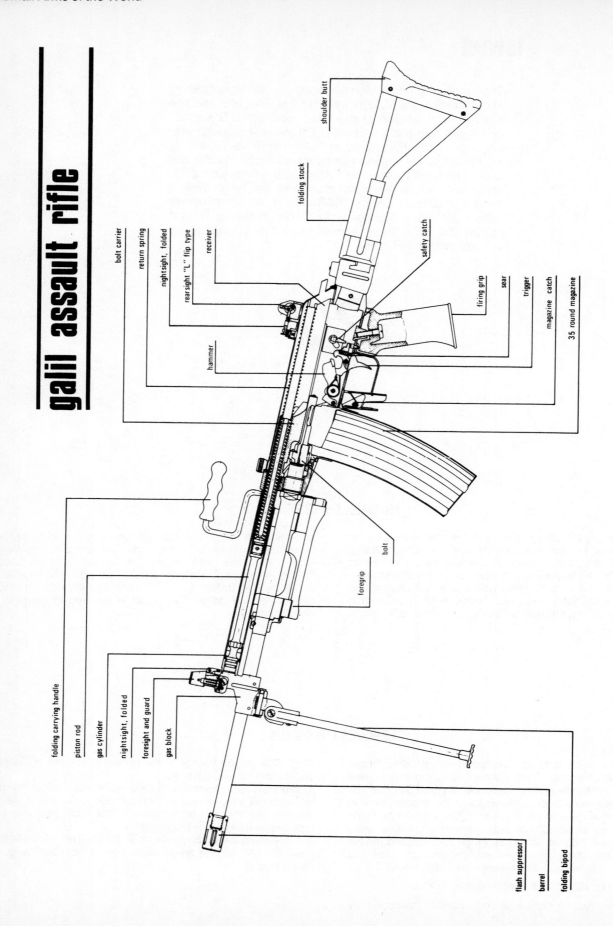

shoulder butt

folding stock

safety catch

bolt carrier

return spring

nightsight, folded

rearsight "L" flip type

receiver

firing grip

sear

trigger

magazine catch

35 round magazine

hammer

bolt

foregrip

folding carrying handle

piston rod

gas cylinder

nightsight, folded

foresight and guard

gas block

flash suppressor

barrel

folding bipod

How to Load and Fire the Galil

Follow the procedures outlined for the Kalashnikov assault rifles in Chapter 43.

Field Stripping the Galil

Follow the procedures outlined for the Kalashnikov assault rifles in Chapter 43.

UNIQUE DESIGN FEATURES OF THE ISRAELI GALIL RIFLE

FOLDING STOCK VERSION OF THE GALIL RIFLE.

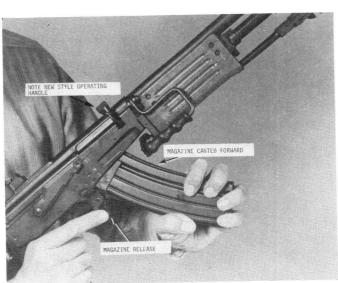

NOTE NEW STYLE OPERATING HANDLE

MAGAZINE CANTED FORWARD

MAGAZINE RELEASE

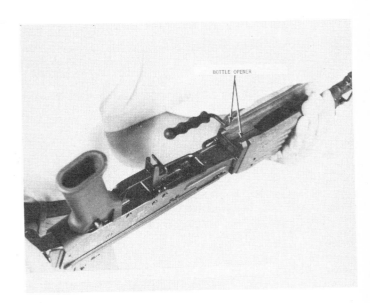

BOTTLE OPENER

BUILT-IN BARBED WIRE CUTTER
(PART OF BIPOD MECHANISM)

FLIP UP ILLUMINATED SIGHT ELEMENT FOR NIGHT USE

Disassembled view of Galil 5.56mm Rifle.

The Galil Rifle has been produced in two versions—assault rifle/light machine gun and short assault rifle. With the exception of barrel length, both weapons are essentially the same.

Characteristics of Galil 5.56mm Rifle

Caliber: 5.56mm.
System of operation: Gas, Kalashnikov type.
Weight: 7.7 to 8.6 lbs.
Length, overall:
  w/stock extended, short barrel: 32.3 in.
  w/stock extended, long barrel: 38.2 in.
  w/stock folded, short barrel: 23.6 in.
  w/stock folded, long barrel: 29.1 in.
Barrel length: short barrel: 13.0 in.
             long barrel: 18.1 in.
Feed devices: 35- and 50-shot magazines.
Sights: Front: Post sight set for 100 meters.
      Rear: "L" flip type aperture.
Muzzle velocity: Short barrel: 3010 f.p.s.
             Long barrel: 3215 f.p.s.
Cyclic rate: Approx. 650 r.p.m.

REMOVAL OF GALIL GAS PISTON AND GAS PISTON HOUSING ASSEMBLY.

Galil 5.56mm Rifle.

ISRAELI SUBMACHINE GUNS

The Israelis used the 9mm Sten in its various configurations in their early fighting with the British and the Arab States; some German 9mm MP40s were also procured from Central Europe. With the development of a native submachine gun—the UZI—Israel made her greatest impression on the small arms world.

THE ISRAELI 9mm UZI SUBMACHINE GUN

There are several different models of the UZI. The early model guns had a wooden stock and a wooden or fiber fore-end and pistol grip. The model with folding steel stock and plastic fore-end followed soon after the introduction of the gun, circa 1952. About 1960, the UZI was again modified, and a larger bolt-retracting handle was fitted and the fire-selector/safety modified. The model supplied to West Germany has the bolt-handle track in the receiver cover serrated to prevent forward movement of the bolt if accidentally released during retraction. The bolt-retraction handle of the UZI does not reciprocate with the bolt.

The UZI is named for Major Uziel Gal, its developer. It is the standard submachine gun of the Israeli Army and also has been sold to other countries. In basic operating principles, the UZI is quite similar to the Czech ZK 476 and its descendants, the Czech Models 23 and 25 submachine guns. As far back as 1945, the UK had an experimental gun with a bolt that telescoped the barrel—the telescoping bolt is a feature common to all of these weapons and to the Beretta Model 12 as well.

The UZI is a very well-made gun, and its performance leaves little to be desired. FN of Belgium is now marketing this weapon in Europe.

Characteristics of the UZI Submachine Gun

Caliber: 9mm Parabellum.
System of operation: Blowback, selective fire.
Weight: 8.9 lbs. w/loaded 25-round magazine and metal butt.
　　　　8.8 lbs. w/loaded 25-round magazine and wooden butt.
Length, overall: 25.2 in. (wooden-butt model, and metal-butt weapon with stock extended). The length of the metal-butt model with the stock folded is 17.9 in., and the length of the wooden-butt model with the butt removed is 17.3 in.
Barrel length: 10.2 in.
Feed device: 25-round, 32-round or 40-round, detachable, staggered box magazine.
Sights: Front: Truncated cone w/protecting ears.
　　　　Rear: L-type w/setting for 100 and 200 yards.
Muzzle velocity: 1310 f.p.s. w/8-gram 9mm Parabellum bullet.
Cyclic rate: 650 r.p.m.

How to Load and Fire the UZI

Insert a loaded magazine in the magazine well located in the pistol grip. Pull the cocking handle, located on the top of the receiver, to the rear. The UZI fires from an open bolt, and the bolt will remain to the rear. To fire single shots, set the change lever, located on the top left side of the pistol grip, to the letter R (this is the mid-position). To fire automatic fire, set the change lever at the letter A (this is the forward position). To put the weapon on safe, set the change lever at S (this is the rear position). Pressure on the trigger will fire the weapon, if the change lever is set on semiautomatic or automatic fire positions. The grip safety must be squeezed when firing the weapon.

How the UZI Works

With the exception of the trigger mechanism, the functioning of the UZI is quite similar to that of the Czech Model 23 submachine gun. (See Chapter 14.)

9mm Parabellum Israeli revolver showing 3-round clip.

Israeli 9mm UZI Submachine Gun with wooden stock.

Field Stripping the UZI

To release the cover, press the catch in front of the rear sight housing to the rear. Raise the cover and remove it from the receiver. Raise the bolt from the front; when its forward part is completely disengaged, withdraw it from the receiver together with the recoil spring, giving the whole assembly a short pull forward. To remove the extractor, take out its retaining pin. Press in the lock of the barrel retaining nut; unscrew the nut and withdraw the barrel. Take out the split pin and the sleeve in which it is housed, and remove the trigger group and pistol grip from the assembly. To strip the folding metal butt, unscrew the hexagonal head of the nut retaining the butt (the nut is located in the rear of the receiver). To remove the wooden butt, press in the butt retaining catch, and pull the butt to the rear. No further disassembly is recommended.

To reassemble the weapon, follow the above procedure in reverse order.

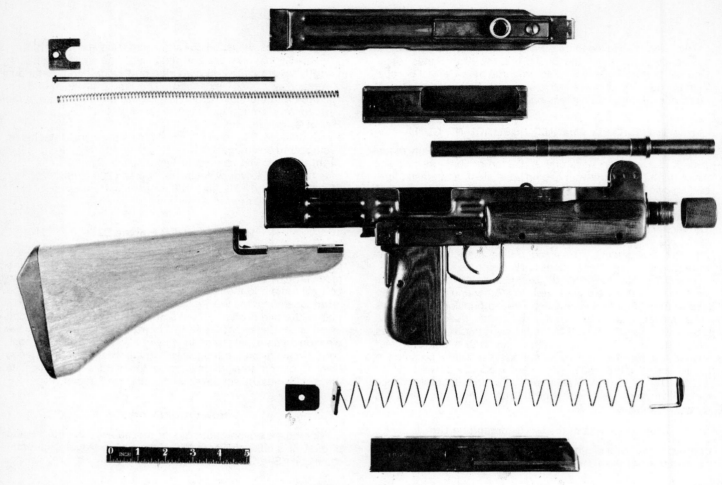

UZI field stripped.

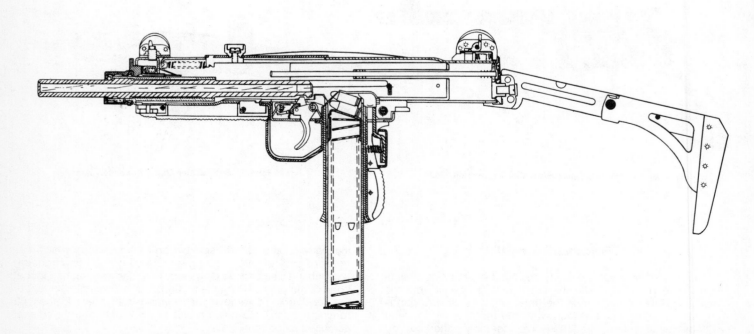

Section view, UZI 9mm submachine gun.

28
Italy

Current standard Italian service small arms are the 9mm Parabellum Pistol M1951, the 9mm Parabellum Beretta Model 4 submachine gun, the 7.62mm NATO BM59 Mod I and the 7.62mm NATO MG42/59 machine gun. All these weapons are currently manufactured in Italy and are of post-World War II design or modifications of pre-war or World War II weapons.

Other weapons in limited use are as follows:-9mm (.380 ACP) Beretta M1934 pistol, earlier models of the 9mm Parabellum Beretta submachine gun, the caliber .30 and caliber .50 Browning machine guns (used mainly on armored vehicles), the 8mm Breda Model 37 machine gun, caliber .30 Browning Automatic rifle M1918A2 and caliber .303 Bren guns.

ITALIAN SERVICE PISTOLS

ITALIAN SERVICE PISTOLS, 1889 to 1951

The Italians have had a number of service pistols since World War I, and the long use in service of some of them is rather surprising.

The Model 1889 Glisenti revolver is a double-action Chamelot Delvigne design revolver, loaded through a loading gate on the right side. These weapons were made in small shops and will be found with brass frames, cast steel frames, forged steel frames and even frames made of copper plates brazed together. The M1889 may be found with a folding trigger and no trigger guard, and is also found with a conventional spur trigger and trigger guard. The manufacture of these revolvers continued through the 1920's, and the use of these weapons by the Italians in World War II would be equivalent to the US use of the caliber .45 Model 1873 (Frontier Model) revolver in the same conflict.

The above would suggest that the pistol development in Italy was comatose, but such was not the case. The Brixia automatic pistol appeared in Italy around 1906, and (although it is reported of Swiss origin, developed from patents of Haensler and Roch) it was first manufactured by Metellurgica Bresciana Tempini at Brescia, Italy. This weapon, which is chambered for a low-powered version of the 9mm Parabellum cartridge, was, with slight modification, adopted as the 9mm Model 1910 Glisenti service pistol. The Glisenti is a retarded blowback pistol, using the 9mm (sometimes called 8.9mm) M1910 cartridge. This cartridge is dimensionally interchangeable with the 9mm Parabellum cartridge. There are differences of opinion as to whether or not the higher standard loadings of the 9mm Parabellum cartridge should be used with this pistol, but the outstanding authorities agree that use of the standard loads of 9mm Parabellum in the Glisenti is not advisable. The Italian Government apparently agreed with this course as well, since their 9mm Parabellum loads for the M1938 Beretta submachine gun are stamped M938, probably to prevent their usage in the Glisenti. The Glisenti cartridge has a truncated conical bullet as opposed to the conical nosed bullet used with the 1938 and later Beretta submachine guns.

In 1915, the first Beretta automatic pistol was introduced into Italian service. As of this date, Beretta designed and made automatic pistols are still the standard service pistol in Italy. The most widely distributed Model 1915 is chambered for the 7.65mm cartridge and is a hammerless blowback operated pistol.

A model of the 1915 chambered for the 9mm Glisenti cartridge was also produced; this weapon differs from the 7.65mm

10.35mm Revolver M1889.

Glisenti 9mm 1910 Automatic.

only in minor details such as checked wood grips, the positioning of the ejector, the functioning of the magazine as a slide stop and the presence of a small mechanical safety at the rear of the receiver, which can be engaged when the slide is to the rear.

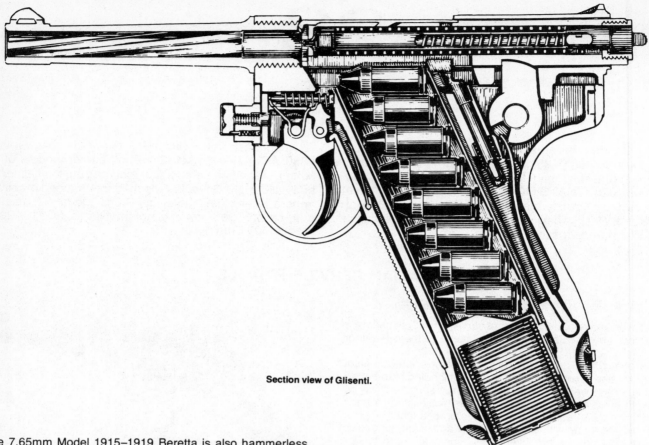

Section view of Glisenti.

The 7.65mm Model 1915–1919 Beretta is also hammerless but resembles the later Berettas in many respects, such as the larger portion cut out on the top of the slide and the barrel mounting, a grooved block under the chamber, which slides into channels machined in the receiver ahead of the magazine well. This pistol was apparently not issued to the Army, but the specimen shown bears Naval markings.

In 1923, another Beretta was introduced, chambered for the 9mm Glisenti cartridge. The Model 1923 was the first service Beretta to have an external hammer and is, in other respects, the same as the Model 1915–1919. These pistols were used by the Italian Army in limited quantities.

A later Beretta, which closely resembles the well-known Model 1934, is the 7.65mm Model 1931. This pistol has a straighter grip than the Model 34 and issue was limited to the Italian Navy.

The 9mm *corto* (.380 ACP) Model 34 Beretta is probably the best known of the Italian automatic pistols and was one of the best Italian weapons in World War II. It is still used by Italian forces to some extent and is manufactured for commercial sale as the "Cougar." The Model 1934 has also been made in 7.65mm. The 9mm Parabellum Model 1951 is the current standard service pistol. If is the first Beretta pistol with a positively locked breech and utilizes full-powered 9mm Parabellum cartridges. It is sold commercially as the Beretta Brigadier.

THE 9mm BERETTA PISTOL MODEL 1934

The Model 1934 is a very finely-made weapon and was very popular with the Italian Army during World War II, as well as with US troops who managed to acquire them. Specimens marked "RE" *(Regio Esercito)* or "Royal Army" were Italian Army issue; other specimens may be found with the marking "PS," which indicates police or *carabinieri* issue. The Italian service designation for the .380 ACP cartridge is 9mm Model 34.

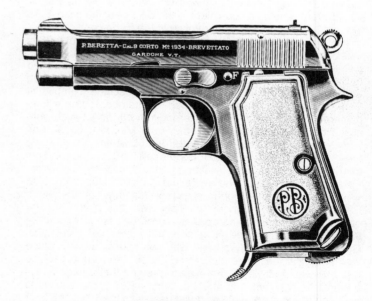

9mm (.380 ACP) Model 1934 Beretta.

Loading and Firing the M1934 Beretta

Load magazine exactly as for Colt automatic pistol. Insert in handle and push in until it locks.

Draw back slide exactly as for Colt automatic. Release slide and let it drive forward pushing cartridge into firing chamber and closing pistol.

Push safety catch around into locking position unless weapon is to be fired.
(Note: The exposed hammer may be let down gently on the firing pin if care is taken and the operation is done with both hands. It may also be set at half-cock.)

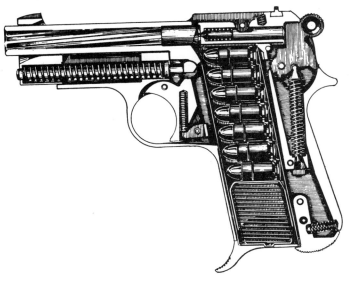

Action closed, showing detail of firing mechanism.

Action open, showing operation of recoil and feeding mechanism.

Field Stripping the M1934 Beretta

(1) With magazine out of weapon, pull back slide as far as it will go; hold it with right hand, and with left thumb push safety catch up into locking notch in underside of slide.

(2) Now push straight back on barrel with palm of hand. This will free barrel from its locking recess.

(3) Pull barrel straight back and up, drawing it out of the slide as shown.

(4) Push slide, recoil spring and recoil spring guide straight forward off the receiver. Spring and guide may now be removed from their seats. Safety locking stud may also be lifted out now. No further dismounting is necessary with this pistol.

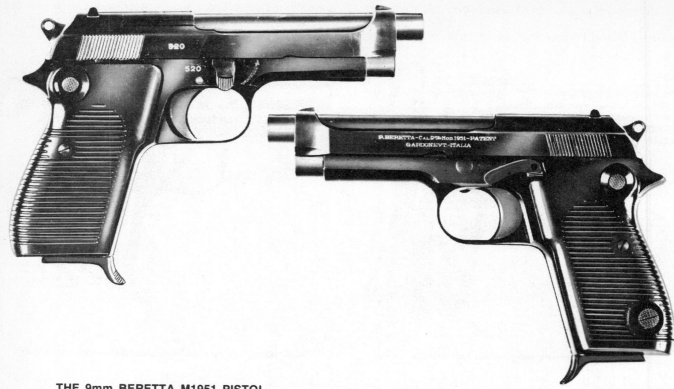

THE 9mm BERETTA M1951 PISTOL

The interesting 9mm M1951 Beretta pistol has been adopted by the Italian Army and Navy and is also used by the Israeli and Egyptian Defense Forces. It is a very well-made weapon and has many interesting features. It is made with an aluminum alloy or steel receiver. The weapon, which fires the 9mm Parabellum cartridge, also is known as the Model 951.

How to Load and Fire the M1951 Pistol

The magazine is loaded the same as any single-column pistol magazine. Insert loaded magazine in magazine well located in pistol grip. Pull the slide sharply to the rear, and release; the slide will run home and chamber a cartridge. The weapon may now be fired by squeezing the trigger. The safety is a button type mounted at the top rear of the grip; to put the weapon on "safe," push the button from right to left. The M1951 is not a double action weapon. With a cartridge in the chamber and the hammer down, the weapon must be manually cocked before it will fire.

How the M1951 Pistol Works

Loading, Cocking and Chambering. A magazine containing eight rounds is inserted into the bottom of the grip section of the receiver. The slide is drawn to the rear by hand; it forces the hammer downward and to the rear. The full-cock notch of the hammer engages the nose of the sear, and the hammer remains in its rearward position. When the slide is released, it goes forward under the pressure of the recoil spring. The slide feed rib forces a round from the magazine into the chamber of the barrel.

Locking. As the slide goes forward, the locking wedge is cammed into its locked position in the locking grooves of the slide by the cam surfaces on the receiver. The locking mechanism of this pistol is similar to that of the Walther Pistole 38, covered in the chapter on Germany in World War II.

Firing. When the trigger is pulled, the trigger bar is forced to the rear. The trigger bar pushes the disconnector up into the disconnector notch in the slide. If the weapon is not completely

locked, the disconnector will be held down by the slide and will force the trigger bar down and out of contact with the trigger (this arrangement is similar to that of the M1934 Beretta). When the weapon is locked, the trigger bar forces the sear backward against the pressure of the sear spring; the hammer then disengages itself from the sear and moves forward under the pressure of the hammer spring. The hammer strikes the firing pin, forcing it forward against the pressure of the firing pin spring. The firing pin strikes the primer of the cartridge and immediately rebounds under the pressure of the firing pin spring. The M1951 is not a double-action pistol; if a misfire occurs, the hammer must be recocked manually.

Unlocking. The barrel and slide recoil together for a distance of one-half inch; then the unlocking plunger on the rear barrel lug abuts against the receiver and, moving forward, forces the locking wedge out of the locking grooves in the slide and down into the cammed surface on the receiver. Having been disconnected from the barrel, the slide (with the empty cartridge case gripped by the extractor) moves to the rear for an additional two inches, cocking the hammer in the process. The cartridge case is knocked out of the grip of the extractor claw, and out of the pistol, by the nose of the ejector. When the last round is fired, the slide stop is forced up by the magazine follower and holds the slide to the rear.

Field Stripping the M1951 Pistol

Remove magazine by pushing the magazine catch inward.

Draw the slide to the rear and align the dismounting latch with the dismounting notch of the slide.

Push the dismounting latch upward, toward the muzzle end of the pistol.

Pull the slide group forward and off the receiver.

Pull the recoil spring and guide assembly slightly to the rear, and remove it from its position in the slide.

Push the barrel backward and withdraw it from the rear of the slide.

No further disassembly is recommended.

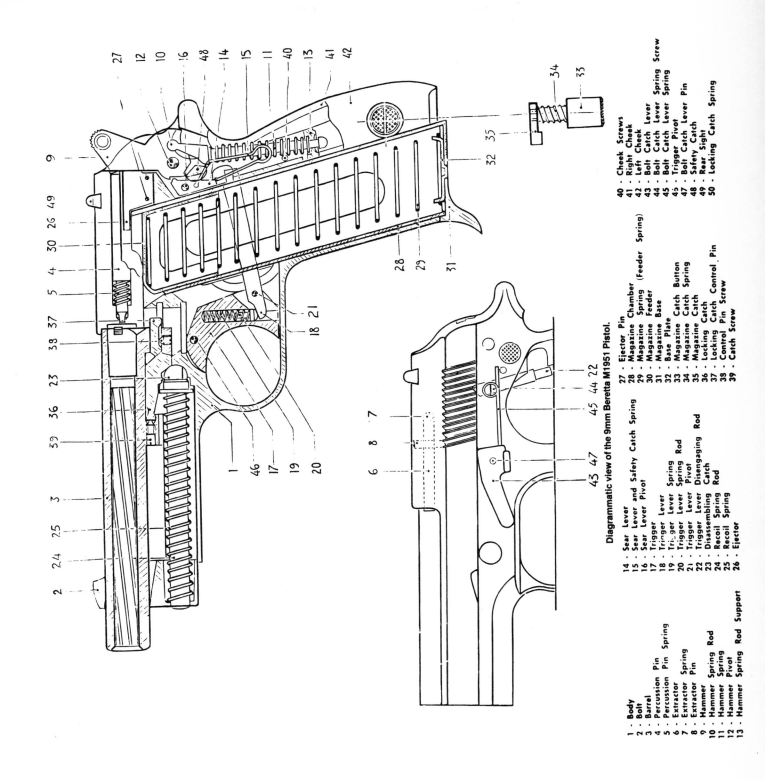

Diagrammatic view of the 9mm Beretta M1951 Pistol.

1 - Body
2 - Bolt
3 - Barrel
4 - Percussion Pin
5 - Percussion Pin Spring
6 - Extractor
7 - Extractor Spring
8 - Extractor Pin
9 - Hammer
10 - Hammer Spring Rod
11 - Hammer Spring
12 - Hammer Pivot
13 - Hammer Spring Rod Support

14 - Sear Lever
15 - Sear Lever and Safety Catch Spring
16 - Sear Lever Pivot
17 - Trigger
18 - Trigger Lever
19 - Trigger Lever Spring
20 - Trigger Lever Spring Rod
21 - Trigger Lever Pivot
22 - Trigger Lever Disengaging Rod
23 - Disassembling Catch
24 - Recoil Spring Rod
25 - Recoil Spring
26 - Ejector

27 - Ejector Pin
28 - Magazine Chamber
29 - Magazine Spring (Feeder Spring)
30 - Magazine Feeder
31 - Magazine Base
32 - Base Plate
33 - Magazine Catch Button
34 - Magazine Catch Spring
35 - Magazine Catch
36 - Locking Catch
37 - Locking Catch Control Pin
38 - Control Pin Screw
39 - Catch Screw

40 - Cheek Screws
41 - Right Cheek
42 - Left Cheek
43 - Bolt Catch Lever
44 - Bolt Catch Lever Spring Screw
45 - Bolt Catch Lever Spring
47 - Trigger Pivot
48 - Bolt Catch Lever Pin
49 - Safety Catch
50 - Rear Sight
50 - Locking Catch Spring

Selective Fire Beretta M1951A

Beretta has come out with a selective fire version of the Model 1951. This pistol, which is called the Model 951 "A Raffica," has a longer barrel, 4.92 inches, and uses 10-or 15-round magazines. It has a folding, vertical fore grip mounted at the front end of the receiver and a selector switch mounted on the right of the receiver above and behind the trigger. This weapon weighs 4.6 pounds loaded.

9mm Parabellum Sosso Pistol Model 1941

This pistol was developed in 1936 by Guilio Sosso. The Sosso is a recoil operated, double action weapon, unusual in one major respect. It takes nineteen cartridges, fed by a chain link belt within the magazine. The cartridges are placed into carriers within the magazines, and the belt is driven by the action. FNA— Fabrica Nazionale d' Armi—tooled up to produce these pistols, and a few were produced. Most were confiscated by the Germans, as was the tooling, after the Italian surrender in 1943. This, unfortunately for the Italians, was the fate of many of their World War II arms developments.

M1951 field stripped.

CHARACTERISTICS OF ITALIAN SERVICE PISTOLS

	Model 1889	Model 1910	Model 1915	Model 1915
Caliber:	10.35mm (10.4mm).	9mm Glisenti (M910).	7.65mm.*	9mm Glisenti (M910).
System of operation:	Double-action revolver	Delayed blowback, semiautomatic	Blowback, semi-automatic.	Blowback, semi-automatic.
Length overall:	10.25 in.	8.1 in.	6 in.	6.75 in.
Barrel length:	5.25 in.	3.9 in.	3.4 in.	3.75 in.
Feed device:	6-round revolving cylinder.	7-round in-line detachable, box magazine.	7-round in-line detachable, box magazine.	7-round in-line detachable, box magazine.
Sights:				
Front:	Bead.	Barley corn.	Blade.	Blade.
Rear:	V notch.	V notch.	V notch.	V notch.
Weight:	2.2 lb.	1.87 lb.	1.25 lb.	2 lb.
Muzzle velocity:	Approx 840 f.p.s.	1050 f.p.s.	Approx 960 f.p.s.	Approx 1035 f.p.s.

*.32 ACP.

CHARACTERISTICS OF ITALIAN SERVICE PISTOLS (CONT'D)

	Model 1915-19	Model 1923	Model 1934	Model 1951
Caliber:	7.65mm.*	9mm Glisenti (M910).	9mm Corto.**	9mm Parabellum (M1938).
System of operation:	Blowback, semi-automatic.	Blowback, semi-automatic.	Blowback, semi-automatic.	Recoil, semi-automatic.
Length overall:	6 in.	6.2 in.	6 in.	8 in.
Barrel length:	3.4 in.	3.88 in.	3.5 in.	4.51 in.
Feed device:	8-round in-line detached, box magazine.	8-round in-line detachable, box magazine.	7-round in-line detachable, box magazine.	8-round in-line detachable, box magazine.
Sights: Front:	Blade.	Blade.	Blade.	Blade.
Rear:	V Notch,	V notch.	V notch.	V Notch,
Weight:	1.31 lb.	1.87 lb.	1.25 lb.	1.93 lb.***
Muzzle velocity:	Approx 960 f.p.s.	Approx 1035 f.p.s.	970 f.p.s.	1182 f.p.s.

*.32 ACP.
**.380 ACP.
***1.57 lb. with aluminum receiver.

ITALIAN RIFLES

The Italian Army was equipped with a number of different types of rifles prior to and during World War II. Considering everything, the Italian Army was the poorest armed of the major powers in World War II. The 6.5mm M1891 Mannlicher Carcano and its various 6.5mm and 7.35mm variants were the principal weapons, but numerous 8mm M1889 and 1895 Mannlicher rifles, received as war booty from the first war, and even some ancient Vetterli Vitali rifles, rebarreled for 6.5mm rifle, were used.

THE MANNLICHER CARCANO RIFLE

The Mannlicher Carcano, also known occasionally as the Mauser Paravicino, is a modified Mauser. It has a Mauser type one-piece bolt with frontal locking lugs, but, unlike most Mausers, the bolt handle is in front of the receiver bridge when locked. The magazine is a Mannlicher in-line type, fed with a six-round clip, which stays in the magazine until the last round is chambered.

There have been a number of rumors passed around about the safety of the Mannlicher Carcano rifle. When in good condition and used with the proper ammunition, it is as safe as any other military rifle.

The Carcano was developed at the Italian Government arsenal at Turin by M. Carcano. Early models have gain twist rifling, i.e., the twist of the rifling gradually increases toward the muzzle. In 1938, the 7.35mm cartridge was introduced, and a rifle and two carbines chambered for this cartridge were adopted.

Upon Italy's entrance into World War II in 1940, the 6.5mm caliber was re-introduced, and all Mannlicher Carcano's manufactured from that date on were chambered for the 6.5mm cartridge. In addition, many of the 7.35mm weapons already in existence were rebarreled for 6.5mm.

The Mannlicher Carcano was made in limited numbers in 7.92mm, apparently for the Germans, toward the close of World War II. These rifles were apparently made in very limited quantities.

Italian Semi-automatic and Automatic Rifles

Italy's experiences with semi-automatic rifles before World War II were discouraging for several reasons. First, the military was short on the funds necessary for rifle development. Second, Italy always seemed to be on the brink of another war when the military was considering a new weapon. A self-loading rifle was patented in 1905 by Filippo Genovesi, and three years later the Italian Government bought the rights to manufacture the weapon. Production was suspended in 1912 when the weapon failed to perform satisfactorily in the desert sands of Libya. Another rifle developed by Lt. Col. Amasigo Cei-Rigotti was re-jected because the recoiling parts moved too violently. Development lagged until after World War I, when the Italian Army set forward the requirement for a selective fire rifle. The Government arsenal at Terni in 1921 developed an automatic carbine chambered for the new 7.35mm cartridge. A year later the arms factory in Rome also produced an automatic weapon in the same caliber. A Government commission ran a trial of these weapons, plus submachine guns by Fiat and Ansaldo and a semiautomatic carbine by Beretta. The latter three weapons were rejected because they were chambered for the 9mm Gilsenti cartridge, which was designed for pistol use and could not meet the requirement for accurate fire at 600 meters. The commission decided that the Terni weapon was best, but they did not favor the 7.35mm cartridge. Subsequently, it was rechambered for the 6.5mm round and called the Model 1921/28.

Several other rifles were developed in this period. Bethel Abiel Revelli, who had developed the Fiat machine gun, produced a rifle in 1928. Also there was the Brixa 1931, a Model 1891 Rifle modified to semiautomatic fire and two recoil operated Berettas—the Model 1931 (6.5mm) and the Model 1937 (7.35mm). Breda's Model 1935 GP selective fire rifle was ultimately adopted in 7mm by Costa Rica. With all these rifles available, the inevitable competitive trials were held in 1937. Weapons tested included two self-loaders from Terni, the Breda C.R.5, the recoil operated Scotti Model X, the Pavesi—F.N.A., a self-loader from the National Arms Plant at Bresica—the SI/S.T.A.R. and the Revelli Manifatturo Armaguerra recoil operated rifle (later called the Model 1939, designed by the son of the above named Revelli). When the commission's tests were completed in 1939, it was decided that none of the rifles met all the requirements. The Revelli was judged to be the best of the lot, but manufacture was never begun in earnest because of the continuing 6.5mm vs 7.35mm controversy and the necessity to manufacture other standard weapons.

In 1952, the Italian Army began receiving M1 Rifles manufactured by Beretta and Breda. The BM family of rifles firing the 7.62 × 51mm NATO round is the current standard weapon. M1s converted to the NATO caliber are also in reserve stocks.

THE BERETTA BM59 SERIES OF RIFLES

After a series of prototypes, the basic design of the Beretta conversion emerged as the BM59, which used an M1-type stock and was generally similar externally to the Garand, except for the 20-round magazine, charger guide and the new handguard and gas cylinder arrangement.

BM59D was produced with a straight-in-line stock (with pistol grip) and a rate reducer to facilitate control during full automatic fire.

BM59GL was basically the same as the BM59, except that it had an integral grenade launcher and grenade launcher sight.

6.5mm Mannlicher Carcano Model 38 Carbine with attached grenade launcher. When the grenade launcher is used, the bolt is removed from the rifle and used in the launcher.

Representative Italian rifles. 1. Model 1891 Rifle. 2. Model 91TS Carbine. 3. Model 91 Carbine. 4. Model 1941 Rifle. 5. Model 91/24 Carbine. 6. Model 38(7.35mm). 7. Model 38TS (7.35mm) Carbine. 8. Model 38 (7.35mm) Carbine. 9. Model 1938 Rifle (caliber 6.5mm). 10. Model Youth Rifle (Moscheto) Ballila, caliber special 6.5mm. Barrel 14.43''. (Weapon does not fire ball cartridges.)

6.5mm Beretta Model 1931 Semiautomatic Rifle.

6.5mm Beretta Model 1931 Semiautomatic Rifle, field stripped.

6.5mm Scotti Brescia Model X Rifle.

6.5mm Model 1935 GP Breda Rifle.

7.35mm Beretta Model 1937 Semiautomatic Rifle.

Beretta 7.62mm NATO BM59 Rifle.

Beretta 7.62mm NATO BM59D Rifle. Stock changed and bipod attached.

Beretta 7.62mm NATO BM59GL Rifle. Permanently attached grenade launcher and grenade sights.

7.62mm NATO BM59 Mark I Rifle.

7.62mm NATO BM59 Mark I Rifle (Modified).

7.62mm NATO BM59 Mark II modified with winter trigger.

7.62mm NATO BM59 Mark III with folding stock.

7.62mm NATO BM59 Mark III (modified).

BM60CB was offered by Beretta in 1960 with a burst control feature.

Subsequently, Beretta revised the designations for these rifles:

The BM59 Mark "I" and Mark "I"-A

The "I" in these designations stands for "Italian" since these are the weapons adopted by the Italian Government. They are also known as the BM59 Mark Ital and Ital-A rifles. These rifles are equipped with bipods, and grenade launchers and differ from each other mainly in their stocks. The Mark "I"-A is for paratroops and armored troop use.

Loading and Firing the BM59 Mark "I" and Mark "I"-A. Pull operating handle to the rear, locking the weapon. Put safety, located in forward part of trigger guard, on safe by pushing rearwards. Insert a loaded magazine in the magazine well and pull upward and to the rear until the magazine catch engages. If there is already a magazine in the weapon it can be loaded by five-round chargers (stripper clips). Set the selector, located on the far left side of the receiver, on "A" for automatic fire, or "S" for semiautomatic fire. Disengage the safety and press the trigger to fire the weapon. This weapon has a winter trigger, which can be used when heavy gloves are required. It can be swung down into position.

Field Stripping the BM59 Mark "I" and Mark "I"-A

This rifle is field stripped in a manner similar to the US M1 rifle, which is covered in detail in the chapter on the US.

BERETTA .223 MODEL 70/.223 ASSAULT RIFLE

Beretta has developed a selective fire rifle chambered for the 5.56mm cartridge. It resembles the SIG Model 530-1 externally, but the field stripped view indicates that there are significant differences in design. The Model 70/.223 has a combination grenade launcher/flash suppressor built into the barrel. The grenade launcher sight is positioned behind the front sight, pivoting on the front sight base as with those versions of the BM59 that have grenade launchers. There are variations in the weapon: the 70/.223 SC and the 70/.223 LM in addition to the basic 70/.223 AR. They vary in length and weight, the SC having a folding stock and the LM (Light Machine Gun) having a bipod and carrying handle.

Carabina per truppe speciali BERETTA mod. 70/.223 SC con baionetta
Special troops carbine BERETTA mod. 70/.223 SC with bayonet

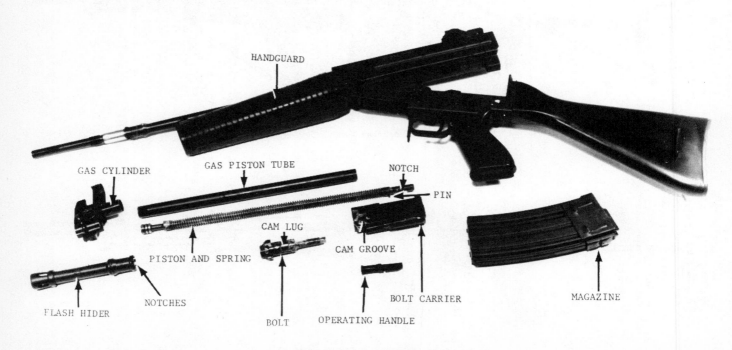

Field stripped view of the AR70/.223.

Luigi Franchi 7.62mm NATO LF 59 Rifle

The LF 59 is a selective fire weapon quite similar to the FN FAL in design. The magazine of the LF 59 is interchangable with that of the FAL and has a tipping bolt as does the FAL. The bolt carrier of the LF 59, however, is attached to the piston, and the recoil spring is mounted in a telescoping tube protruding from the back of the bolt carrier. The stock of the fixed stock model is made of plastic. The receiver is made principally of stampings. Both fixed and folding stock models were made only as prototypes. The LF 59 has a rate reducer.

Luigi Franchi Caliber .30 LF58 Carbine

The LF 58 is a selective fire weapon chambered for the caliber .30 carbine cartridge. The magazine of this weapon is interchangeable with that of the US caliber .30 carbine. Like the LF 59, it is made principally of stampings. The bolt is different from that of the LF 59 in that it has two plates that cam the bolt in to and out of the locked position by action on lugs mounted on the bolt carrier. The LF 58 has a rate reducer, which reduces the cyclic rate from 720-740 rounds per minute to 375 rounds per minute. This weapon has also been made for the Soviet 7.62 × 39mm (M43) cartridge. In all versions it was made only as a prototype.

Beretta Caliber .30 Carbine P30 Model 781

Beretta has produced a gas operated selective fire carbine chambered for the US caliber .30 carbine cartridge. The Beretta weapon is quite similar in outer appearance to the US carbine but is quite different internally. The bolt is of the tipping type and locks against the top of the receiver. There are two triggers; the front trigger produces semiautomatic fire, and the rear trigger provides full automatic fire. In addition to the fixed wooden stock version of this weapon, there is a folding steel stock model. The Beretta carbine is in service in Morocco and is being produced there. This weapon, designed around 1957, was one of the last designs of Tullio Marangoni, who developed most of Beretta's automatic weapons.

Luigi Franchi 7.62mm NATO LF59 Rifle, field stripped.

Luigi Franchi 7.62mm NATO LF59 Rifle.

Luigi Franchi 7.62mm NATO LF59 Rifle with folding stock.

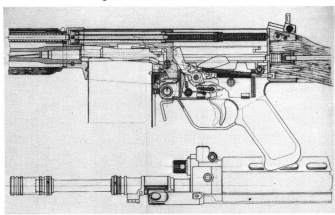

Section view of action of LF59 Rifle.

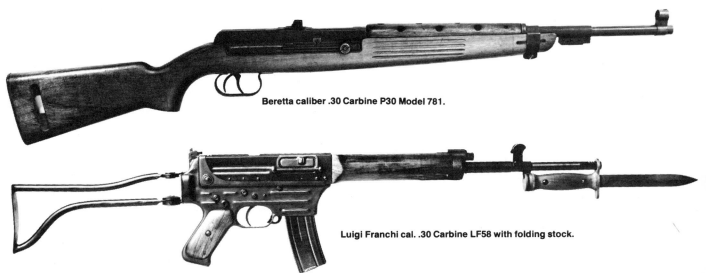

Beretta caliber .30 Carbine P30 Model 781.

Luigi Franchi cal. .30 Carbine LF58 with folding stock.

CHARACTERISTICS OF MANNLICHER CARCANO BOLT-ACTION RIFLES AND CARBINES

	Rifle M1891	Carbine M1891	Carbine M1891 TS	Carbine M1891/24
Caliber:	6.5mm	6.5mm	6.5mm	6.5mm.
Overall length:	50.8 in.	36.2 in.	36.2 in.	36.2 in.
Barrel length:	30.7 in.	17.7 in.	17.7 in.	17.7 in.
Feed device:	6-round in line non-detachable box magazine	6-round in line non-detachable box magazine.	6-round in line non-detachable box magazine.	6-round in line non-detachable box magazine.
Sights: Front:	Barleycorn.	Barleycorn.	Barleycorn.	Barleycorn.
Rear:	Tangent w/V notch graduated from 500-2000 M; leaf turned over for battle sight.	Tangent w/V notch graduated from 500-1500 M; leaf turned over for battle sight.	Tangent w/V notch graduated from 500-1500 M; leaf turned over for battle sight.	Tangent w/V notch graduated from 500-1500 M; leaf turned over for battle sight.
Weight:	8.6 lbs.	6.6 lbs.	6.9 lbs.	6.9 lbs.
Muzzle velocity:	2395 f.p.s.	2297 f.p.s.	2297 f.p.s.	2297 f.p.s.
Remarks:	Basic rifle, straight bolt handle, uses knife type bayonet.	Bayonet permanently attached, bolt handle bent.	Uses knife-type bayonet, bolt handle bent.	Uses knife-type bayonet, bolt handle bent, except for lower band the same as M1891 TS carbine.

	Rifle M1938	Carbine M1938	Carbine M1938TS	Rifle M1941
Caliber:	7.35mm.	7.35mm.	7.35mm	6.5mm.
Overall length:	40.2 in.	36.2 in.	36.2 in.	46.1 in.
Barrel length:	20.9 in.	17.7 in.	17.7 in.	27.2 in.
Feed device:	6-round in line non-detachable box magazine.	6-round in line non-detachable box magazine.	6-round in line non-detachable box magazine.	6-round in line non-detachable box magazine.
Sights: Front:	Barleycorn.	Barleycorn.	Barleycorn.	Barleycorn.
Rear:	Fixed.	Fixed.	Fixed.	Tangent w/V notch graduated from 300-1000 M; leaf turned over for battle sight.
Weight:	7.5 lbs.	6.5 lbs.	6.8 lbs.	8.21 lbs.
Muzzle velocity:	2482 f.p.s.	Approx. 2400 f.p.s.	Approx. 2400 f.p.s.	Approx. 2360 f.p.s.
Remarks:	First of Italian rifles chambered for 7.35mm cartridge, bolt handle bent. Some have knife-type folding bayonet which can be carried folded on rifle or removed.	7.35mm version of M1891 carbine, has permanently attached folding bayonet, bolt handle bent.	7.35mm version of M1891/24 carbine, uses knife-type bayonet, bolt handle bent.	Basically the same as the Rifle M1891 except for length and rear sight.

	Rifle M1938	Carbine M1938	Carbine M1938 TS
Caliber:	6.5mm.	6.5mm.	6.5mm.
Overall length:	40.2 in.	36.2 in.	36.2 in.
Barrel length:	20.9 in.	17.7 in.	17.7 in.
Feed device:	6-round in line non-detachable box magazine.	6-round in line non-detachable box magazine.	6-round in line non-detachable box magazine.
Sights: Front:	Barleycorn.	Barleycorn.	Barleycorn.
Rear:	Fixed.	Fixed.	Fixed.
Weight:	7.6 lbs.	6.6 lbs.	6.9 lbs.
Muzzle velocity:	2320 f.p.s.	2297 f.p.s.	2297 f.p.s.
Remarks:	6.5mm version of 7.35 mm Rifle M1938, made after beginning of World War II.	6.5mm version of 7.35mm Carbine M1938, made after beginning of World War II.	6.5mm version of 7.35mm Carbine M1938 TS, made after beginning of World War II

Notes: (1) All the pre-World War II 6.5mm weapons have right-hand gain twist (progressive) 19.25 to 8.25; 7.35mm weapons have constant right-hand 10-inch twist. (2) All weapons use 6-round Mannlicher type clips. (3) Some of the Model 1938 weapons were made in 7.92 × 57mm Mauser for the Germans during World War II. (4) Caliber is marked on sight base of all 1938 series weapons.

CHARACTERISTICS OF THE BERETTA BM59 RIFLES

	BM59	BM59D	BM59GL	Mark I	Mark II	Mark III	Mark IV	Mark Ital
Caliber:	7.62mm NATO							
System of operation:	Gas, selective fire.							
Length overall:	37.2 in.	37.2 in.	43 in.	39.4 in.	48.9 in.*	48.9 in.	42.5 in.	43.1 in.
Barrel length:	17.7 in.	17.7 in.	21 in.	17.7 in.	17.7 in.	17.7 in.	21 in.	19.3 in.
Feed device:	20-round, detachable box magazine							
Sights: Front:	Protected blade							
Rear:	Aperture, adjustable for windage & elevation							
Weight:	8.15 lbs.	9 lbs.	9 lbs.	8.9 lbs.	8.9 lbs.	8.9 lbs.	12 lbs.	10.4 lbs.
Cyclic rate:	750 r.p.m.							
Muzzle velocity:	2620 f.p.s.	2620 f.p.s.	2730 f.p.s.	2620 f.p.s.	2620 f.p.s.	2620 f.p.s.	2730 f.p.s.	2700 f.p.s.

*29.5 in. with stock folded.

CHARACTERISTICS OF THE BERETTA .223 MODEL 70/.223 RIFLES

	70/.223 AR	70/.223 SC	70/.223 LM
Caliber:		.223 (5.56mm)	
System of operation:		gas, selective fire	
Length overall: w/stock fixed:	37.6"	37.8"	37.6"
Length overall: w/stock folded:		28.8"	
Barrel length:		17.8"	
Feed device:		30-round, staggered row, detachable box magazine	
Sights: Front:		protected post	
Rear:		aperture adjustable for 100, 250 and 400 meters	
Weight:	8 lb.	8.5 lb.	8.9 lb.
Cyclic rate:	630 r.p.m.	630 r.p.m.	600 r.p.m.
Muzzle velocity:		3,180 f.p.s.	

	LF 59	LF 58	P30 M781
Caliber:	7.62mm NATO	cal. .30 carbine	cal. .30 carbine
System of operation:		gas, selective fire	
Weight:	9.5 lb.	7.5 lb.	6.5 lb.
Length overall stock fixed:	40.5 in.	36.4 in.	37.3 in.
stock folded:	31.7 in.	27.5 in.	approx. 27 in.
Barrel length:	20.9 in.	16.9 in.	17.7 in.
Feed device:	20-round, detachable staggered box magazine	30-round, detachable staggered box magazine	30-round, detachable staggered box magazine
Sights: Front:	protected blade	hooded blade	protected blade
Rear:	aperture	rotary aperture	"L" adjustable for windage
Muzzle velocity:	2690 f.p.s.	1900 f.p.s.	1950 f.p.s.
Cyclic rate:	610-630 r.p.m.	375 r.p.m.	550 r.p.m.

ITALIAN SUBMACHINE GUNS

Italy was the first country to adopt a submachine gun—the 9mm Villar Perosa of 1915. The Villar Perosa as originally produced had no stock and was mounted in dual sets. The weapon was fired with thumb type triggers, similar to those used on machine guns. It was mounted, usually with a shield, on motorcycle side cars, aircraft and on various types of tripods and bipods. At a later date, a stock was added to the gun, and it became a selective-fire individual weapon. The Villar Perosa and all other early Italian submachine guns were chambered for the 9mm Glisenti cartridge—basically a low-powered 9mm Parabellum cartridge.

Beretta produced a modified copy of the Villar Perosa in 1918 and produced a selective-fire weapon called the Beretta Moschetto Automatico, or the M1918 - 1930.

The Model 1918 Beretta was retarded blowback as was the Villar Perosa and was designed by Tullio Marengoni, who designed all the Beretta submachine guns until the late 1950s.

The 9mm Parabellum Model 1938A Beretta was the first of a series of very well-designed finely-made weapons, which were widely distributed in other countries in addition to Italy. The Beretta Model 38A and 38/42 were considered the finest Italian

9mm O.V.P. Submachine Gun.

9mm Beretta Model 1918 Submachine Gun.

9mm Beretta Model 1918-30 Submachine Gun.

Italian Beretta 9mm Submachine Gun Model 38A.

small arms in service in World War II. The first Model Beretta 38 had longitudinal slots in the barrel jacket as opposed to holes in the barrel jackets of later production. Some Model 38As had folding bayonets, and early production had bayonet lugs for the mounting of a removable knife type bayonet.

The early Model 38A did not have the push-through type full automatic safety located behind the full automatic trigger and had a dual port compensator rather than the multi-slotted compensator found on later models. The most common variation of the Model 38A was without bayonet or bayonet lug, and with a multi-slotted compensator.

This model was sold to Romania and Argentina and was made in tremendous quantities for the Italian Army. The Model 38A was produced to some extent after World War II, and in

1949 a modification of the weapon, using the cross bolt safety mounted in the stock as used with the Model 38/49 (Model 4), was produced in limited quantity. Although it has generally been considered that the fixed firing pin was introduced with the Model 38/42, late Model 38As with a fixed firing pin were apparently made. It is quite possible that these weapons were made after the introduction of the Model 38/42, since the Model 38A was made as late as 1950.

The Beretta 9mm Parabellum Model 38/42 is basically a simplified Model 38A; the barrel jacket is not used with the 38/42, and all Model 38/42s have a fixed firing pin. The 38/42 uses a stamped receiver and magazine housing and has a fluted barrel (early production). Models of the 38/42 with smooth barrel are called 38/43 by Beretta. There are three distinctly different

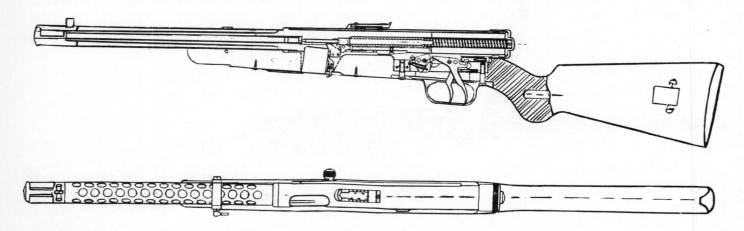

Diagram of the Model 38A from official Italian manual.

Beretta Model 38/42 Submachine Gun, fluted barrel.

models of the 38/42 - 38/43, and an additional similar weapon, the 38/44, has a shorter bolt but does not have the operating spring guide found on the earlier Berettas. This can be noted by the absence of the recoil spring guide rod head protruding through the cap on the end of the receiver. The external differences can be noted in the pictures below. Pakistan, Iraq and Costa Rica purchased Model 38/44 submachine guns.

An unusual Beretta Model 38A submachine gun, which apparently appeared in prototype form, has an aluminum barrel jacket rather than the multi-perforated barrel jacket. Another Beretta, which appeared only in prototype form, was the Model 1. This weapon was developed prior to the Model 38/42 and has a folding stock similar to that of the German MP38; it was apparently an expensive gun to make and was dropped in favor of the Model 38/42. A gun called the 38/44 Special by Beretta closely resembles the Model 1 but does not have the fluted barrel of the Model 1 and does have a cross bolt type safety mounted in the fore-arm. This weapon is also called the Model 2.

The Model 38/49, also known as the Model 4, is the current standard submachine gun and is covered in detail separately. The Model 5 Beretta submachine gun is basically the same as the Model 38/49 except that it has a grip safety located in the fore-end.

The Model 5 was introduced in 1957. Another weapon somewhat similar in appearance to the Model 2, and also made only as a prototype, is the Model 4. The Model 4 has a grip safety and a sliding-wire type stock similar to that on the US M3 submachine gun. The weapon illustrated below is similar to the Model 4 but has a wooden fore-end. This weapon is described as a modified 38/44 by Beretta.

Throughout the 1950s, Beretta developed a number of prototype guns, including the Model 6 (1953) and the Model 10 (1957), which were steps in the development of their latest gun, the 9mm Model 12. The Model 12 has a bolt that telescopes the barrel in a fashion similar to the Czech Model 23 and the Israeli UZI. The Model 12 has been adopted by the Italian Government and is covered in detail later in this chapter.

There were other submachine guns developed in Italy in addition to those developed by Beretta, although Beretta has been the most prolific developer. The Fabbrica Nazionale d'Armi of Brescia developed a submachine gun manufactured in limited quantities during the war. This weapon, called the FN A-B Model 1943, is rather unusual for the time in which it was made, since it is machined out of steel forgings. It has a single strut folding steel stock, and the magazine can be folded up under the barrel jacket when not in use. The combination muzzle brake compensator resembles that used on the Soviet PPSh41 submachine gun. The Model 1943 is a retarded blowback, selective-fire weapon. Reportedly 7,000 of these weapons were made for the Italian Army.

The TZ45 is another 9mm Parabellum submachine gun manufactured in limited quantities toward the end of the war. It was designed by Toni and Zorzoli Giandoso in about 1944. The TZ45 is a relatively crudely-made weapon and has a grip safety fitted behind the magazine housing in a fashion similar to the later model Madsen submachine guns. The TZ45 was adopted in a modified form by Burma after the war. It is manufactured in Burma, where it is called the BA52.

The Bernardelli firm produced a modified copy of the Beretta Model 38/42, a few of which were made in 1948 and 1949. This weapon, called the VB, was well made but had no unusual features.

Fabbrica Nazionale d'Armi developed a gun in the 1950s called the X4. The X4 was composed almost entirely of stampings, has a sheet steel retracting slide, which partially surrounds the receiver and is used to retract the bolt. A shorter version of the X4 called the X5, which had a barrel just over 4.5 inches long, was brought out in the mid 1950s.

The firm of Luigi Franchi has also brought out a family of submachine guns called the LF57. The LF57 is another weapon composed mainly of stampings and is of relatively short length. It is 16.52 inches overall with stock folded, using an 8.1 inch barrel. A semiautomatic only version of this weapon with 16-inch barrel was also offered for sale.

9mm Beretta Model 38/44 Special (Model 2).

9mm TZ45.

9mm F.N.A.-B Model 1943.

9mm Bernardelli Model VB Submachine Gun.

9mm Semiautomatic Model LF-57.

9mm F.N.A. Model X-4.

Beretta 9mm Model 38/49 Submachine Gun.

THE 9mm BERETTA MODEL 38/49 SUBMACHINE GUN MODEL 4

The Model 38/49 is one of the standard submachine guns of the Italian Army. It is a modification of the Model 38/44; like this weapon, it has no recoil spring guide and a fixed firing pin. The principal difference between the two weapons is the use of a cross-bolt type safety, which is mounted in the stock above the front of the trigger guard.

The 38/49 was sold to Costa Rica, Egypt (with folding bayonet), Yemen, Tunisia, West Germany, Indonesia, Thailand and the Dominican Republic.

How to Load and Fire the Model 38/49

Insert a loaded magazine into the magazine port. Pull bolt retracting handle (located on the right side of the receiver) to the rear and cock the bolt. Push forward retracting handle (it does not reciprocate with the bolt). The safety is engaged by pushing in from the left side. Pressure on the forward trigger will produce semi-automatic fire and pressure on the rear trigger will produce automatic fire.

How to Field Strip the Model 38/49

Remove the magazine and check weapon to insure that a cartridge has not remained in the chamber. Twist the receiver cap one quarter-turn to the left and remove with the operating spring assembly. The bolt may now be pulled to the rear and withdrawn from the rear of the receiver. Further disassembly is not recommended. To assemble, reverse the above procedure.

Beretta 9mm Model 12 Submachine Gun.

Beretta Model 12—field stripped.

THE 9mm BERETTA MODEL 12 SUBMACHINE GUN

The Model 12 comes in both folding metal stock and detachable wooden stock models. As previously pointed out, this weapon has a bolt that telescopes the barrel for about three-quarters of the length of the bolt. The weapon therefore appears to have a much shorter barrel than it really has. An excellent feature of the weapon is that the grooves extend the length of the receiver. The grooves serve as dirt catchers and allow operation even with a considerable amount of dirt in the action. The Model 12 has a grip safety.

How to Load and Fire the Model 12

Remove magazine, if an empty magazine is in the weapon, by pushing magazine catch located at the bottom front of the trigger guard forward and (after pulling magazine down and out of the magazine guide) insert loaded magazine and pull bolt retracting handle, located on the left side of the receiver to the rear. The manual safety is a push button located above the grip; to put the weapon on safe, push the button from left to right. The fire selector is also of the push-button type, located ahead of the pistol grip. Pushing the button in from the left sets the weapon for semi-automatic; pushing the button from the right produces automatic fire. Push manual safety button from right to left, select type of fire desired, and press trigger.

How to Field Strip the Model 12

Remove the magazine. Pull barrel-locking-nut catch down and unscrew the nut at front of receiver. The barrel and bolt can be removed from the front of the receiver. Push in catch on receiver cap (rear of receiver) and screw off receiver cap. The operating spring can be removed from the rear of the receiver. No further disassembly is recommended.

CHARACTERISTICS OF ITALIAN SERVICE SUBMACHINE GUNS

	Villar Perosa Model 1915	Villar Perosa (O.V.P.)	Beretta Model 1918	Beretta Model 1938A	Beretta Model 1938/42
Caliber:	9mm Glisenti.	9mm Glisenti.	9mm Glisenti.	9mm Parabellum.	9mm Parabellum.
System of operation:	Retarded blowback, full automatic.	Retarded blowback, selective fire.	Retarded blowback.	Blowback, selective fire.	Blowback, selective fire.
Overall length:	21 in.	35.5 in.	33.5 in.	37.25 in.	31.5 in.
Barrel length:	12.56 in.	11 in.	12.5 in.	12.4 in.	8.4 in.
Feed device:	25-round, staggered row, detachable, box magazine.	25-round, staggered row, detachable, box magazine.	25-round, staggered row, detachable, box magazine.	10, 20, 30, or 40-round, staggered column, detachable, box magazine.	20- or 40-round, detachable, staggered row, box magazine.
Sights: Front:	None on some, aperture cut into brace between barrels.	Blade.	Blade.	Blade.	Blade.
Rear:	Y shaped-plate with notch.	U notch.	V notch.	Tangent with V notch.	"L" type flip over with U notch.
Weight:	14.30 lb. for twin gun.	Approx 8 lb.	7.2 lb.	9.25 lb.	7.2 lb.
Cyclic rate:	1200 r.p.m.	900 r.p.m.	900 r.p.m.	600 r.p.m.	550 r.p.m.
Muzzle velocity:	1312 f.p.s.	1250 f.p.s.	1275 f.p.s.	1378 f.p.s.	1250 f.p.s.

CHARACTERISTICS OF ITALIAN SERVICE SUBMACHINE GUNS (Cont'd)

	Beretta Model 38/49 (Model 4)	FN A-B Model 1943	TZ 45	Beretta Model 12
Caliber:	9mm Parabellum.	9mm Parabellum.	9mm Parabellum.	9mm Parabellum.
System of operation:	Blowback, selective fire.	Retarded blowback, selective fire.	Blowback, selective fire.	Blowback, selective fire.
Overall length:	31.5 in.	Stock fixed: 31.1 in. Stock folded: 20.7 in.	Stock fixed: 33.5 in. Stock folded: 21.5 in.	Stock fixed: 25.39 in. Stock folded: 16.43 in.
Barrel length:	8.4 in.	7.8 in.	9 in.	7.9 in.
Feed device:	20-and 40-round, detachable, staggered row, box magazine.	20-and 40-round, detachable, staggered row, box magazine.	20- and 40-round, detachable, staggered row, box magazine.	20-, 30-, & 40-round staggered row, detachable, box magazine.
Sights: Front:	Blade.	Blade.	Post.	Blade.
Rear:	"L" type flip over with U notch.	V notch.	Aperture.	"L" flip over with U notch.
Weight:	7.2 lb.	7.06 lb.	7.2 lb.	6.6 lb.
Cyclic rate:	550 r.p.m.	400 r.p.m.	550 r.p.m.	550 r.p.m.
Muzzle velocity:	1250 f.p.s.	1225 f.p.s.	1265 f.p.s.	1250 f.p.s.

ITALIAN MACHINE GUNS

Italy adopted the Maxim gun in 1906 and used two models chambered for the 6.5mm cartridge, the Model 1906 and Model 1911. Apparently few of these guns were made, as they rarely appear in photos of Italian troops in World War I. The 6.5mm watercooled Revelli Model 1914 was the first Italian-designed gun to appear on the scene in quantity. This retarded blowback gun was unusual in that it was fed with a magazine composed of ten compartments, each holding five rounds. To provide for the lack of slow initial extraction—a slight bolt turning movement to loosen the case before extraction to the rear begins—the cartridge cases were lubricated by an oil pump built into the receiver. The Revelli was manufactured by Fiat and is frequently known by that name.

During World War I, Italy purchased quantities of the Colt Model 1914, Browning "potato digger" in 6.5mm to supplement their machine gun supply. The French supplied the Italians with large quantities of the M1907 F St. Etienne heavy machine gun chambered for the 8mm Lebel cartridge. At the conclusion of World War I, the Italians received tremendous quantities of 8mm (8 × 50R) Schwarzlose Model 1907/12 from the Austrians as part of their share of war reparations. These weapons were still used by the Italians in World War II.

The Breda 6.5mm Model 1924 was one of the first Italian light machine guns. It is, except in details such as the stock and use of a thumb-operated trigger, basically the same as the 6.5mm Model 1930 Breda. The Model 1930 was the standard Italian light machine gun in World War II. A few thousand of the Model 1924 Breda were made, as well as a few thousand 6.5mm Fiat SAFAT light machine guns—a light version of the Revelli Model 1914. A number of machine guns never made in quantity (such as the Brixia) were introduced during the twenties and thirties.

The 6.5mm Model 1930 Breda was an unusual weapon in many respects. It is a retarded (delayed) blowback-operated gun with recoiling barrel, as is the Model 1914 Revelli. This weapon has a massive bolt with multiple-locking lugs and an oil pump, which lubricates the cartridges prior to chambering. The magazine is permanently attached to the side of the gun and is swung forward to be loaded with a 20-round horse-shoe type charger. The chargers may be brass or cardboard.

This weapon was among the first to be introduced with a quick change barrel. All in all, the Breda Model 30 was hardly a satisfactory weapon. Any weapon that requires lubricated cases will

Model 1914 Revelli (Fiat) 6.5mm Machine Gun.

Colt 6.5mm Model 1914.

6.5mm Breda Model 1924 Light Machine Gun.

be unreliable in sandy or dusty conditions, because the lubricant will pick up the foreign matter and introduce it into the action. This weapon was sold in 7.92mm to Portugal and Lithuania. It was made in limited quantities in 7.35mm as the Model 38 for Italy.

In 1931, the 13.2mm Breda antiaircraft and tank machine gun appeared. This weapon, unlike earlier Italian machine guns, had nothing in its design that would make it "peculiar" from a machine-gun point of view. The 13.2mm Model 31 was a conventional, gas-operated, magazine-fed gun and was the first step in the development of the best Italian developed machine gun—the 8mm Model 37.

The 8mm Model 37 Breda, although it had some peculiar features, was by far the best of the Italian machine guns used in World War II. A gas-operated gun, it is fed by feed trays from which the cartridge is pushed into the chamber and into which the empty cartridge case is reinserted before the feed tray is ejected. The reason for this tidy arrangement is rather mysterious. The Breda Model 37 was a very reliable weapon, used in many varying climatic conditions with good results. The Model

37 was used after World War II, and there was some discussion about converting the weapon to caliber .30, but this idea was apparently dropped since there is a Model 55 tracer cartridge for the weapon. Although the weapon is gas operated, the cartridges are lubricated by an oil pump since no provision is made for slow initial extraction. The Breda has been replaced in the Italian service by the 7.62mm NATO MG 42/59. The Breda Model 37 was made for Portugal in 7.92mm and is known as the Model 1938.

In 1938, a tank version of the Model 37, chambered for the same Breda 8mm Model 35 cartridge, fed by a top-mounted box magazine, was introduced and adopted.

Aircraft versions of the Breda in 7.7mm (.303 British), 7.92mm and 12.7mm were also produced. The 12.7mm gun was also produced as an antiaircraft gun. The Italian government used the 7.7mm and 12.7mm versions of this gun. It might be pertinent to point out that the Italians used seven different machine-gun cartridges during World War II, in addition to four different pistol and submachine gun cartridges.

8mm Breda Model 37 Heavy Machine Gun.

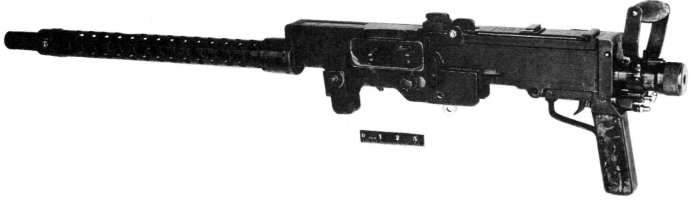

7.7mm Breda Aircraft Gun.

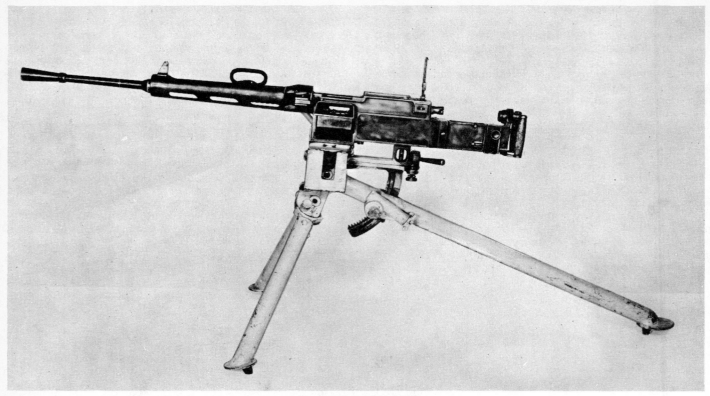

8mm Fiat (Revelli) Model 35.

The Fiat (Revelli) Model 1935 8mm heavy machine gun is essentially a modified Revelli Model 1914; many of the Model 35 Fiats were actually converted Model 1914 weapons. Some of the weapons were of new manufacture. The Model 1935 is air cooled and has a fluted chamber rather than an oil pump (it was also a retarded blowback). It was fed by a non-disintegrating belt rather than by the compartmented magazine of the Model 1914. The Model 35 was not a very successful gun; it was actually worse than the Model 1914. The ammunition still required lubrication for proper function, and the weapon, unlike the Model 1914, fired from a closed bolt with resultant "cook-offs" after periods of sustained fire. This weapon as the 1914 had an

operating rod that reciprocated outside to buff against a pad mounted on the front of the back plate. This made clearing a gun with a cartridge in a hot barrel a hazardous proposition and may account for the nickname it received during World War II—the "knucklebuster."

After World War II, Italy was supplied with American and British machine guns. The current standard Italian machine gun is the 7.62mm NATO MG42/59, called the *Mitragliatrice Leggere 42/59* in Italy. This weapon is covered in detail in the chapter on Germany. The MG42/59 is currently being manufactured in Italy.

ITALIAN SERVICE MACHINE GUNS

	Model 1914 Revelli	Model 1930 Breda*	8mm Breda Model 37	8mm Fiat (Revelli) Model 35
Caliber:	6.5mm.	6.5mm.	------------8mm (Italian Model 35 Cartridge) ------------	
System of operation:	Delayed blowback, selective fire.	Delayed blowback, automatic only.	Gas, automatic only.	Delayed blowback, selective fire.
Length overall:	46.5 in.	48.5 in.	50 in.	49.75 in.
Barrel length:	25.75 in.	20.5 in.	Approx. 25 in.	25.75 in.
Feed device:	50-round "mouse-trap" type magazine.	20-round, non-detachable magazine, fed by changers.	20-round strip.	300-round non-disintegrating belt.
Sights: Front:	--Barley corn --			
Rear:	--Leaf --			
Weight:	37.5 lb. (less water) tripod—49.5 lb.	22.75 lb.	42.8 lb.	39.75 lb.
			Tripod—41.5 lb.	Tripod—41.5 lb.
Cyclic rate:	450-500 r.p.m.	450-500 r.p.m.	450 r.p.m.	500 r.p.m.
Muzzle velocity:	2080 r.p.s.	2063 f.p.s.	2600 f.p.s.	2600 f.p.s.

*7.35mm Model 38 has essentially the same characteristics.

29

Japan

The Japanese Ground Self-Defense Forces (JGSDF) were initially equipped completely with United States World War II type small arms. For the most part, they still use these weapons. US caliber .45 Model 1911A1 pistols, M3A1 submachine guns, US caliber .30 M1 and M2 carbines, caliber .30 M1 rifles, Model 1918A2 Browning Automatic rifles, US caliber .30 and caliber .50 Browning machine guns are all in service. In addition, however, the caliber 7.62mm NATO Type 64 rifle and caliber 7.62mm NATO Type 62 light machine gun, of Japanese manufacture, have been introduced.

JAPANESE PISTOLS

The firm of Shin Chuo Kogyo K.K. (New Central Industrial Co. Ltd. of Tokyo) has developed a number of pistols since World War II. These are: a modified copy of the US caliber .45 M1911A1, called the Type 57 New Nambu; a smaller caliber .32 automatic, the Type 57B New Nambu; and a caliber .38 special revolver similar to the Smith & Wesson, which is called the New Nambu Type 58.

JAPANESE 9mm TYPE 57 NEW NAMBU AUTOMATIC PISTOL

Characteristics of Type 57 Pistol

Caliber: 9mm Parabellum (also made in .45 cal.).
System of Operation: Recoil operated, semiautomatic only.
Weight: 2.12 lbs.
Length, overall: 7.8 in.
Barrel length: 4.6 in.
Feed device: 8-round, single line, detachable box magazine.
Muzzle Velocity: 1148 f.p.s.

This weapon, called the "New Nambu," is a modified copy of the US M1911 automatic pistol. It does not have a grip safety and has its magazine catch mounted on the bottom of the grip, but is otherwise much the same as the US pistol.

Loading, firing, field stripping and functioning are the same as the US M1911 pistol with the exception of the features noted above.

CAL. .32 TYPE 57B NEW NAMBU AUTOMATIC PISTOL

Characteristics

Caliber: .32 ACP (7.65mm Browning).
System of operation: Blowback, semi-automatic only.
Weight: 1.3 lbs.
Length, overall: 6.3 in.
Feed device: 8-round, detachable in-line box magazine.

This weapon is also called a New Nambu. It is basically a Browning type blowback pistol and loading, firing, field stripping and functioning are the same as the Browning M1910 pistol.

A modification of the Model 57, the Model 57A, has been introduced by Shin Chuo Kogyo and differs from the Model 57 in having a button type magazine catch on the left rear of the grip near the bottom, larger stocks, slightly different shaped receiver and slide stop. Although there were indications that the Japanese Self Defense Forces were going to adopt the Model 57, it was produced only as a prototype. The Model 57A also appeared only in prototype form. It is likely that the Model 57A in time will replace the .45 M1911A1 automatic.

9mm Parabellum Model 57A "New Nambu" Pistol.

JAPANESE RIFLES

THE 7.62mm NATO TYPE 64 RIFLE

How to Load and Fire the Type 64 Rifle

The magazine can be removed, if in weapon, by pushing in on the magazine catch, located behind the magazine port, and pulling magazine down and out. The safety/selector switch is located over the trigger on the right-hand side of the receiver. Insert a loaded magazine in the magazine port, pushing up until the magazine catch engages. Select type of fire desired and pull operating handle—top front of receiver—to the rear and release it, chambering a cartridge.

Characteristics of the Type 64 Rifle

Caliber: 7.62mm NATO.
System of operation: Gas, selective fire.
Length overall: 38.97 in.
Barrel length: 17.71 in.
Feed device: 20-round, detachable, box magazine.
Sights: Front: Hooded folding blade.
    Rear: Folding aperture adjustable for windage.

Weight: 9.5 lbs. w/o magazine.
Cyclic rate: 450-500 r.p.m.
Muzzle velocity: 2650 f.p.s. with full-charge cartridge.
    2347 f.p.s. with reduced-charge cartridge.

Disassembly and Assembly

Clear the rifle but leave the hammer cocked and do not insert the magazine. Set the selector off safe and fold the bipod or sights.

Pull the takedown pin to the right; then lift up the rear end of the receiver cover until the cover comes off. Pull the driving spring out of the bolt carrier; then pull the carrier to the rear until it can be lifted out of the receiver. Lift the bolt out of the receiver.

No further disassembly is necessary or desirable.

To reassemble, first place the bolt onto the rear of the receiver with the leveled end up and to the rear. Place the bolt carrier over the bolt so that the cam on the bolt carrier mates with the cam cuts in the bolt. Move the carrier slightly back and forth until the carrier seats into the receiver. Push the bolt and carrier fully forward. Insert the driving spring into the bolt carrier.

7.62mm Type 64 Rifle.

Place the receiver cover onto the receiver so that the projections on the cover fit into their recesses and the driving spring seats in the cover. Push the takedown pin back into place. Clear the weapon.

Note on Method of Operation

The bolt of the Type 64 is of the tipping type and is held by a bolt carrier, which cams it down into and up out of the locked position in a fashion quite similar to that of the Soviet 7.62mm SKS carbine. The bolt carrier is forced to the rear by a piston rod mounted above the barrel; the pistol is spring loaded and returns to the battery position after firing. The operating spring and guide, which return the bolt to the locked position, are mounted in a tunnel in the top of the bolt carrier.

JAPANESE SUBMACHINE GUNS

SHIN CHUO KOGYO SUBMACHINE GUN

This is a conventional 9mm Parabellum blowback operated, selective fire weapon with folding steel stock.

Note that this gun has a grip safety attached to the magazine housing in a manner similar to that of the Madsen and the Italian TOZ. The ejection port has a cover similar to the US M3A1 submachine gun.

Characteristics of the Shin Chuo Kogyo Submachine Gun

Caliber: 9mm Parabellum

System of operation: Blowback
Length overall: Stock folded—30 inches
                Stock fixed—19.75 inches
Barrel length: 6 or 7.3 inches
Feed device: 30-round, detachable box magazine
Sights: Front: Hooded post
        Rear: "L" type, graduated for 100 and 200 meters
Weight: 8.8 lbs., loaded
Cyclic rate: 600 r.p.m.
Muzzle velocity: 1181 or 1220 f.p.s.

9mm Parabellum Shin Chuo Kogyo Submachine Gun.

JAPANESE MACHINE GUNS

Requirements for a general purpose machine gun to replace the caliber .30 Browning M1919A4 and M1917A1 machine guns were laid down by the JGSDF in 1956. The current gun, the 7.62mm NATO Type 62, is the end result of this requirement. The gun was developed by Nittoku Metal Industry Co. and represents an improvement on the third prototype developed.

THE 7.62mm NATO TYPE 62 MACHINE GUN

The Type 62 is a general purpose gun, i.e., it is used as a light machine gun on a bipod and a heavy machine gun on a tripod. The gun can be used either with full charge 7.62mm NATO cartridge or the reduced charge 7.62mm NATO. It uses the US M13 metallic link. When used on the US M2 tripod, a buffer unit is placed on the mount. There are no really unusual features to this weapon, but it is a basically good design and is of quality manufacture.

The Type 62 has a quick change barrel fitted with a prong-type flash suppressor.

7.62mm NATO Type 62 Machine Gun.

Characteristics of the 7.62mm NATO Type 62 Machine Gun

Caliber: 7.62mm NATO.
System of operation: Gas, automatic fire only.
Length overall: 47.3 in.
Barrel length: 23.6 in.
Feed device: Disintegrating metallic link belt.
Sights: Front: Hooded blade.
      Rear: Folding leaf with aperture, adjustable for windage.

Weight: 23.6 lbs.
Cyclic rate: 650 r.p.m. with full-charge cartridges.
600 r.p.m. with reduced-charge cartridges.
Muzzle velocity: 2800 f.p.s. with full-charge cartridges.
2530 f.p.s. with reduced-charge cartridges.

Loading and Firing the Type 62 Machine Gun

If the bolt is to the rear, pull trigger and allow bolt to run forward. Insert end link of belt into feedway so that feed pawls grasp the link. Pull bolt retracting handle, located on the right side of the receiver down and to the rear and then return it forward. The safety is located on the trigger guard; when forward, it is on "fire" and when to the rear it is on "safe." Push safety forward and press trigger. The gun will fire. The gun may also be loaded by opening the cover and laying the belt on the feedway.

How to Field Strip the Type 62 Machine Gun

Open cover and pull bolt to rear to insure that there are no cartridges in the weapon. Close cover and allow bolt to run forward. Push stock retaining pin out of the receiver to the left. Remove stock assembly with recoil spring guide, and buffer assembly from rear of receiver. Raise the cover, releasing the barrel-locking plunger, draw bolt handle fully to the rear, and remove. Draw slide and bolt assembly from the rear of the receiver. Align carrying handle dismounting stud with dismounting notch in barrel-locking ring; push barrel-locking plunger rearward and turn carrying handle until dismounting guide lines are aligned, then pull barrel forward out of the receiver. Remove gas piston return spring from receiver. Assemble in reverse order.

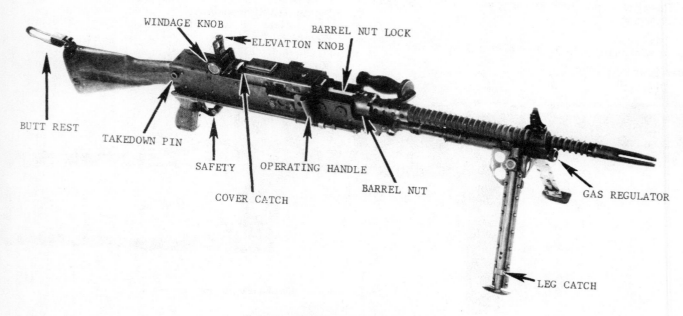

Japanese 7.62 NATO Type 62 Machine Gun.

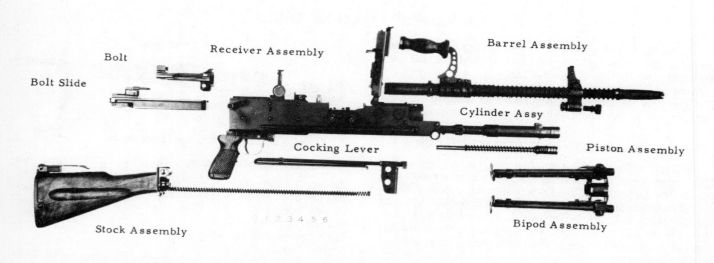

Field stripped view of Type 62 Machine Gun.

30

Imperial Japanese World War II Weapons

The Imperial Japanese Forces had a heterogenous assortment of weapons during World War II, especially in their collection of automatic weapons. Japan, like Italy, was caught in the midst of a change of rifle and machine gun calibers when the war began. This added considerably to the logistic problems of a country that was using four different rifle caliber cartridges in machine guns. The Japanese had also adopted the German 7.92mm MG15 aircraft gun as the Type 98 and a 12.7mm aircraft gun.

One of the basic reasons for this assortment of so many calibers was the fact that the Army, Navy and Air Force had all proceeded independently, adopting whatever caliber they wanted. No higher authority had forced standardization. In addition, captured materiel was used; thus 7.92mm FN-made Browning Automatic Rifles captured from the Chinese were used against United States forces in the Philippines. Other captured weapons included: Czech-and Chinese-made 7.92mm ZB26 and ZB30 light machine guns; Dutch 6.5mm Madsen guns; British caliber .303 Bren and Lewis guns; and various Dutch, British and Chinese rifles.

Japanese World War II weapons are no longer standard in the armies of any major power. Their future use is doubtful since, unlike the standard German World War II small arms, they are not chambered for cartridges still manufactured extensively. Limited manufacture of Japanese rifle and machine-gun ammunition was carried on in mainland China as late as the Korean War.

JAPANESE PISTOLS

The Japanese Army adopted a 9mm revolver, the Type 26, in 1893. This weapon is a break-open type similar to the Smith & Wessons of the period but has lock work similar to the Austrian Rast and Gasser. This revolver is unusual in two respects: it is double-action only (like the later models of the .38 Enfield); and is chambered for a "one-of-a-kind" 9mm rimmed pistol cartridge. Although this revolver was replaced as the standard arm by an automatic in 1925, it was used in quantity during World War II. The only good feature about the weapon is a hinged side plate, which allows for easy exposure of the lock work.

The Nambu 8mm automatic pistol, which appeared in 1904, introduced the bottle-necked 8mm Japanese pistol cartridge.

The Nambu was never a standard Japanese service arm, but it was used by Japanese troops during World War II and also exported. The pistol was developed by Colonel Kijiro Nambu and manufactured by the Kayoba Factory Co. Ltd.

The 1904 Nambu is a recoil-operated weapon fitted with a grip safety mounted on the front of the grip below the trigger guard. This weapon is usually found with a slot cut in the rear of the pistol grip to accommodate a shoulder-stock holster. A smaller version of this weapon chambered for a 7mm bottle-necked cartridge is known as the "Baby Nambu." This was apparently a nonstandard weapon although it may have had limited issue in the Air Force. The "Baby Nambu" has a "V"-notch type rear sight, rather than the ramp-type rear sight of the 8mm Nambu.

In 1925, a modified form of the 8mm 1904 Nambu pistol was adopted by the Japanese Army as its standard pistol. The principal differences between the 1925 Nambu, called Type 14 by the Japanese and the 1904 arm are as follows:

(1) The 1904 Model has a grip safety, the Type 14 has a manual safety.
(2) The 1904 Model has no magazine safety, the Type 14 does.
(3) The 1904 Model has a tangent-type sight, the Type 14 has a fixed notch.

A modification of the Type 14 appeared somewhat later. This modified pistol is easily distinguishable from the early Type 14 pistols by its enlarged trigger guard, which allows use with heavily-gloved hands. Additional modifications are: (1) the firing pin spring guide is less elaborate than that of the early Type 14; and (2) the modified pistol has a spring mounted on the lower front of the grip, which engages a cut-out in the magazine to hold it more securely in place. Although the magazines of the early Type 25s do not have the cut-out for the spring, they will function in the modified type 14 pistols.

Japanese Revolver 9mm Type 26 (1893).

8mm Nambu Pistol, 1904 Type and 7mm Baby Nambu.

8mm Nambu Type 14 Pistol.

Modified 8mm Type 14 Pistol.

In 1934, a new 8mm pistol was introduced in Japan. This weapon was apparently intended principally for export sale but was used as a service pistol during World War II. This pistol, called the Type 94, is mainly distinguished by having an externally-mounted extension bar sear; it is recoil operated; most specimens show evidence of poor manufacture.

In 1942, work was started on the design of a simplified pistol chambered for the 8mm pistol cartridge. The result of this work was the Type II pistol, approximately 500 being made at Nagoya Arsenal by the end of the war. Although this weapon has been reported as being recoil operated, stripped views indicate that it is blowback operated. In any event, if any are in existence today, they are collectors' items.

Japanese Type 14 (1925) with magazine loaded and action in full forward position.

8mm Type 94 Pistol.

CHARACTERISTICS OF JAPANESE WORLD WAR II PISTOLS

	Type 26	Type 14	Type 94	1904 Nambu*	"Baby Nambu"
Caliber:	9mm.	8mm.	8mm.	8mm.	7mm.
System of operation:	Double-action only, revolver.	Recoil operated semiautomatic.	Recoil operated semiautomatic.	Recoil, semi-automatic.	Recoil, semi-automatic.
Length overall:	9.4 in.	9 in.	7.2 in.	9 in.	6.75 in.
Barrel length:	4.7 in.	4.7 in.	3.8 in.	4.7 in.	3.25 in.
Feed device:	6-round revolving cylinder.	8-round, in-line detachable box magazine.	6-round, in-line detachable box magazine.	8-round, in-line detachable box magazine.	7-round, in-line detachable box magazine.
Sights: Front:	Rounded inverted V.	Barley corn.	Barley corn.	Barley corn.	Barley corn.
Rear:	"V" notch.	Undercut notch.	Square notch.	Tangent w/notch.	"V" notch.
Weight:	2 lb.	2 lb.	1.68 lb.	1.93 lb.	1.43 lb.
Muzzle velocity:	634 f.p.s.	1065 f.p.s.	1000 f.p.s.	1065 f.p.s.	1050 f.p.s.

*Although these pistols were apparently never service pistols, they were used by Japanese Forces.

JAPANESE RIFLES

The first rifle of Japanese design to appear was the Type 13 11mm Murata, a single-shot bolt-action weapon. The Murata was followed by the 8mm Type 20 (1887) rifle and Type 27 Carbine. These were magazine arms chambered for an 8mm cartridge of Japanese design. In 1897, the first Arisaka rifle, the 6.5mm Type 30, appeared and became the standard Japanese rifle in the Russo-Japanese War of 1904–05. A carbine version of this weapon was developed in the same year. The Type 30 introduced to Japan the Mauser action in a modified form and the 6.5mm semi-rimmed cartridge.

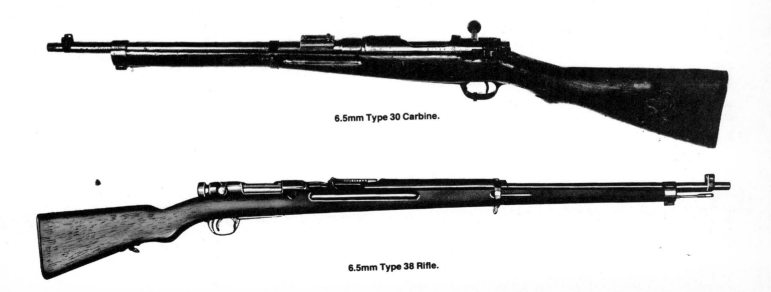

6.5mm Type 30 Carbine.

6.5mm Type 38 Rifle.

6.5mm Type 38 Carbine with hinged stock.

6.5mm Type 44 Carbine.

6.5mm Type 97 Sniper Rifle.

The 6.5mm Type 38 (M1905) was one of the two principal rifles used during World War II. The Type 38 differs from the 98 Mauser action only in the firing pin safety arrangement. The Type 38 has a large knob on the rear of the bolt, which is pushed in and rotated to put the weapon on "safe," rather than the flag-type safety mounted on the bolt sleeve as on the Mauser. The Type 38 also has a sliding bolt cover similar to that of the Lee Metford, but this bolt cover was usually removed from rifles by soldiers in the field because of the amount of noise they made in operation.

The Arisaka cocks on forward movement of the bolt in a fashion similar to that of the Enfield. The Type 38 carbine is a shortened version of the rifle and has a bayonet lug for the standard knife bayonet. A number of type 38 carbines were converted for paratroop use by the fitting of a hinged buttstock.

In 1911, the Type 44 Carbine was introduced; this weapon differs from the Type 38 Carbine in having a permanently attached folding bayonet.

In 1937, a sniping version of the 6.5mm Type 38 rifle—the Type 97—was adopted.

A rifle that was used to some extent by the Japanese Forces but remains very much a mystery is the 6.5mm so-called Type "I" rifle. This rifle, which uses the standard Japanese 6.5mm cartridge, has a Mannlicher Carcano action and a Mauser type magazine. The stock is of typical Japanese two-piece type; i.e., the lower half of the butt and pistol grip is a separate piece pinned and glued to the body of the stock. These rifles were apparently made in Italy, but why the Japanese purchased them is unknown.

Japanese experiences in China showed the need for a cartridge more powerful than the 6.5mm. A 7.7mm semi-rimmed cartridge was already in service with the Type 92 (1932) heavy machine guns. A rimless version of this cartridge was developed for use in rifles. Four trial rifles were submitted, including one each from Nagoya and Kokura arsenals. Several models were patterned after the Type 38 and Type 44 carbines, but tests indicated that the recoil of these weapons was excessive for the short-statured Japanese soldiers. A decision was made to develop a short rifle for cavalry and special troops and a long rifle for infantry. In 1939, the second series of tests was run at Futsu Proving Ground, and the Nagoya designed Rifle "Plan No. 1," which was similar to the Type 38, was adopted. A third series of tests, to dispose of accuracy "bugs" and to check out improved ammunition, was completed, and the Type 99 rifles were adopted in mid-1939. In 1942, a Type 99 rifle with four-power scope was introduced for sniper use.

The Type 99 has the sliding bolt cover of the Type 38 but in addition has a folding wire monopod that can be used to support the rifle when firing from the prone position or from a support. The rear sight has folding antiaircraft lead arms, which can be extended out to 90° at each side of the sight leaf when the weapon is used against aircraft.

In 1943, a substitute Type 99 was introduced made of inferior materials, without bolt cover, sling swivels or chrome-plated bores. The rifles have fixed rear sights. It is inadvisable to fire them, since they can be dangerous. On the subject of material and the strength of actions, tests conducted after World War II showed that the 6.5mm Type 38 action was stronger than the

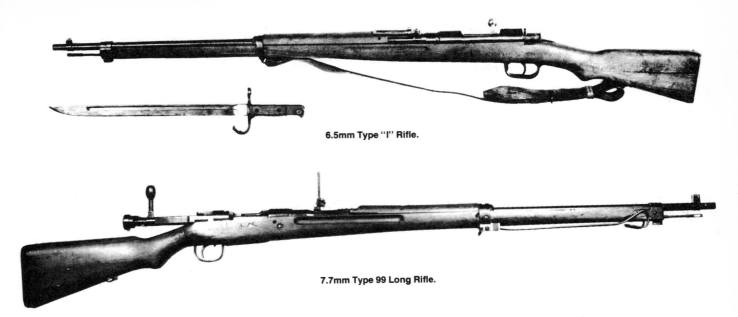

6.5mm Type "I" Rifle.

7.7mm Type 99 Long Rifle.

US Springfield, 1917 Enfield or German Mauser action.

A take-down version of the Type 99 with interrupted screw-type dismounting was introduced in 1942. The barrel of this rifle had a tendency to loosen in service, and further work in this area was done by Japanese Ordnance. The result was the Type 2 takedown rifle with a barrel-locking mechanism similar to that used on some machine guns. A locking key goes through the receiver and engages a slot in the barrel.

Although Japan started experiments with semiautomatic rifles in 1922, no semiautomatic rifle was produced for use in World War II. At the time, the United States was considering adopting the Pedersen rifle in caliber .276; a few copies of this rifle, fitted with a rotary magazine, were made in Japan.

There were many requests from the Japanese Forces in the field during World War II for a semiautomatic rifle to counter the US M1 rifle. The Japanese Navy produced in 1945 a modified copy of the US M1 rifle chambered for the 7.7mm cartridge. This weapon, called the Type 5, used a 10-round box magazine loaded with two 5-round chargers rather than the 8-round en bloc type clip of the M1.

Type 99 rear sight, showing AA lead arms.

Numerous difficulties were encountered with the rifle, principally because of the low quality materials then available. Only about twenty rifles were made.

The Type 99 Short Rifle (above) and Type 2 Take-down Rifle (below), both 7.7mm.

Japanese copy of U.S. Pedersen semiautomatic rifle.

7.7mm Type 5 Semiautomatic Rifle, Japanese copy of the M1.

CHARACTERISTICS OF JAPANESE WORLD WAR II RIFLES

	Type 38 Rifle	Type 38 Carbine	Type 44 Carbine	Type 97 Rifle
Caliber:	6.5mm.	6.5mm.	6.5mm.	6.5mm.
System of operation:	Turn bolt.	Turn bolt.	Turn bolt.	Turn bolt.
Length overall:	50.2 in.	34.2 in.	38.5 in.	50.2 in.
Barrel length:	31.4 in.	19.9 in.	19.2 in.	31.4 in.
Feed device:	5-round, nondetachable, staggered row, box magazine.	5-round, nondetachable, staggered row, box magazine.	5-round, nondetachable, staggered row, box magazine.	5-round, nondetachable, staggered row, box magazine.
Sights: Front:	Barley corn with protecting ears.	Barley corn with protecting ears.	Barley corn with protecting ears.	(Same as Type 38 plus 2.5X scope.)
Rear:	Leaf.	Leaf.	Leaf.	
Weight:	9.25 lb.	7.3 lb.	8.9 lb.	11.2 lb. w/scope.
Muzzle velocity:	2400 f.p.s.	Approx. 2300 f.p.s.	Approx 2300 f.p.s.	2400 f.p.s.

	Type 99 Long Rifle		Type 99 Short Rifle		Type 2 Rifle
Caliber:	7.7mm Type 99.		7.7mm Type 99.		7.7mm Type 99.
System of operation:	Turn bolt.		Turn bolt.		Turn bolt.
Length overall:	50 in.		43.9 in.		43.9 in.
Barrel length:	31.4 in.		25.8 in.		25.8 in.
Feed device:	5-round nondetachable, staggered row, box magazine		5-round nondetachable, staggered row, box magazine.		5-round nondetachable staggered row, box magazine.
Sights: Front:	Barley corn with protecting ears.		Barley corn with protecting ears.		Barley corn with protecting ears.
Rear:	Leaf.		Leaf*.		Leaf.
Weight:	9.1 lb.		8.6 lb.		8.9 lb.
Muzzle velocity:	2390 f.p.s.		Approx 2360 f.p.s.		Approx 2360 f.p.s.

*Late production models of this rifle may be found with a fixed notch type rear sight.

JAPANESE SUBMACHINE GUNS

The Japanese did little in the line of submachine gun development until the thirties. They purchased quantities of Bergmann submachine guns manufactured by SIG in Switzerland during the 1920s. These weapons, which were basically the same as the MP 18 I modified to use a box magazine, are chambered for the 7.63mm Mauser cartridge. A bayonet mounting bar was added to the weapon to take the standard rifle bayonet. These weapons were apparently mainly used by the Japanese Special Landing Forces (Marines) and were encountered during the Bataan campaign by American and Filipino forces.

Japanese Ordnance authorities and the Nambu firm developed two prototype model submachine guns: the Type I, chambered for the standard Japanese 8mm pistol cartridge using a 50-round magazine, and the Type II, chambered for 6.5mm with a newly developed bullet using a 30-round magazine. Type I was tested in 1930 and 1937, and the results were promising but indicated that further development work was required. The Type II design was entirely unsatisfactory and was dropped. In August 1937, an improved Type I was submitted to the Cavalry School; tests indicated that more development work was required. In April 1939, the Nambu firm submitted a design for an improved Type I. Testing indicated that with little improvement this weapon, called Type III, was generally satisfactory. The improved weapon, called Type IIIB was approved for issue and adopted as the 8mm Type 100 (1940).

The Type 100 was issued initially to paratroopers, but by 1944 there were demands from the infantry for submachine guns. The Type 100 may be found fitted with a bipod and comes in three basic types:
(1) Type 100 with fixed stock and bayonet lug bar; some of these are fitted with a compensator.
(2) Type 100 with folding stock and bayonet lug bar.
(3) Type 100, circa 1944, with fixed stock, bayonet lug on barrel jacket, compensator, and fixed aperture-type rear sight.

Time caught up with the Japanese on submachine guns. The Type 100 was never really satisfactory, possibly because the Japanese had the concept of an automatic rifle in mind while working on the design rather than the concept of a submachine gun as understood by most other countries.

Prototype development continued during the war, and the 8mm Type II was discovered by United States personnel in Japan after the war was over. The 8mm Type II was a step in the right direction insofar as weight and length were concerned. It also had one unusual feature borrowed from the 1926 Finnish Suomi, an airlock-type buffer/piston arrangement, which can be used to regulate the cyclic rate.

A special air lock is provided to accomplish this. The lock is at the rear of the receiver. As the bolt is blown back, it is secured to an extension arm on the piston of the air lock. An escape valve can be set to allow the air compressed within the lock to escape at different rates. By thus speeding or slowing down the travel rate of the bolt, the cyclic rate of fire can be increased or decreased.

CHARACTERISTICS OF JAPANESE WORLD WAR II SUBMACHINE GUNS

	Bergmann 1920	Type 100	Type 100 (1944 version)
Caliber:	7.63mm.	8mm.	8mm.
System of operation:		-----Blowback, automatic only-----	
Length overall:	32 in.	w/stock extended: 34 in.*	36 in.
		w/stock folded: 22.2 in.	
Barrel length:	8 in.	9 in.	9.2 in.
Feed device:	50-round, staggered row, detachable box magazine.	30-round, staggered row, detachable box magazine.	30-round, staggered row, detachable box magazine.
Sights: Front:	Barley corn.	Barley corn with protecting ears.	Barley corn.
Rear:	Tangent with notch.	Tangent with notch.	Fixed aperture set for 100 meters.
Weight:	Approx 9.5 lb.	7.3 lb.	8.5 lb.
Muzzle velocity:	Approx 1350 f.p.s.	Approx 1100 f.p.s.	Approx 1100 f.p.s.
Cyclic rate:	600 r.p.m.	450 r.p.m.	800 r.p.m.

8mm Type II Submachine Gun.

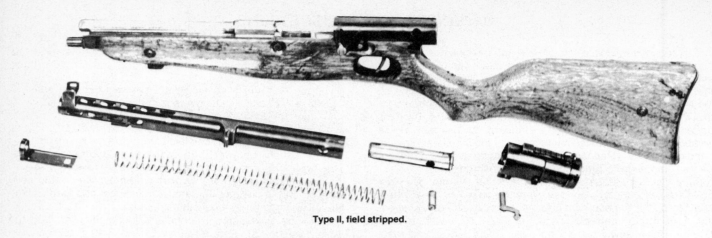

Type II, field stripped.

JAPANESE MACHINE GUNS

The Japanese adopted the Hotchkiss gun at the time of the Russo-Japanese War (1904–05) and also adopted the later 1914 Hotchkiss in a modified form. Both models were chambered for the 6.5mm cartridge, which left something to be desired insofar as long-range performance was concerned, but the initial adoption of the Hotchkiss set the tone for Japanese machine gun development for many years to come.

The Type 3 (1914) is a modified Hotchkiss 1914 developed by General Nambu. Like all later Nambu/Hotchkiss machine guns, it has a gravity-fed oil reservoir, which, through a spring-loaded lubricator, oiled all cartridges before they were fed into the chamber. The Nambus also differ from the Hotchkiss in the

method of ejection. They use the ejection system of the Lewis gun.

During World War II, a modification of the Type 3 was encountered; the modified gun was lighter, and the barrel could be removed more rapidly than on the original Type 3. The 6.5mm Type 11 was introduced in 1922 and is designed basically for use as a light machine gun, although it was also used on a tripod.

An unusual feature of the Type 11 is the feed hopper, which is fed with six 5-round chargers (stripper clips). The chargers are the same as those used with the 6.5mm Arisaka rifle.

6.5mm Type 3 (1914) Machine Gun.

The Type 11 also appeared in a tank version called the Type 91 (1931). The Type 91 has a telescope mount and a larger feed hopper than the Type 11.

The 7.7mm Type 97 (1937) tank gun was the other standard Japanese tank machine gun of World War II. The Type 97 is a copy of the Czech ZB26 as an examination of the stripped view will show.

The Type 97, although a better tank gun than the Type 91,

was not completely satisfactory because it was magazine-fed— hardly an ideal method of feeding a rifle caliber tank machine gun. Research was started during the war to develop a belt-fed gun with a high rate of fire.

A Browning type gun, developed from the Japanese aircraft Browning, was to be introduced as the 7.7mm Tank machine gun Type 4, but the conclusion of the war prevented its introduction.

6.5mm Type 11 on tripod.

Feed mechanism of Type 11 Machine Gun.

Japanese machine gun development was very chaotic since guns were developed by the Army, Navy and for aircraft without any apparent coordination. (The reader will have to forgive the skipping back and forth throughout the text from one type of machine gun to another, but this is apparently what happened in Japanese Ordnance circles at the time. One thing is quite obvious—the Japanese pre-war military had no true appreciation of the logistic difficulties they would encounter in an "all-out" war.)

As pointed out previously, the 6.5mm cartridge was not a good performer at long range, and in 1932 the Japanese introduced a new cartridge—the 7.7mm semi-rimmed Type 92 cartridge—and a new weapon chambered for this cartridge—the Type 92 Heavy Machine gun. This weapon is essentially an improved Type 3 and was the most widely-used Japanese heavy machine gun in World War II.

There is nothing very unusual about the Type 92. As with all the Japanese heavy machine guns, the mount is built to be carried by means of pipes fitted to each of the front legs and with a single fork type pipe fitted to the rear leg. This allows two men to carry the gun and mount in firing position relatively rapidly over limited distances.

The need of a further lightened modification of the Type 92 was recognized by 1937, and a requirement was laid down for a gun and mount weighing less than 88 pounds, with a type of mount easily carried by two men. In March 1940, the first prototype was tested and found unsatisfactory. In June 1940, a second model was tested and with modifications was found to be suitable for service. A modified Type 92 mount was issued with the gun, which was adopted as the Type 1 in November 1942. In addition to being lighter than the Type 92, the barrel of the Type 1 can be removed more easily than that of the Type 92. The Type 1, unlike the Type 92, which can use the semi-rimless Type 92 or the rimless Type 99 cartridges, only uses the Type 99 cartridge.

In 1936, the 6.5mm Type 96 machine gun was introduced. This weapon represented a great improvement over the Type 11. The Type 96 does not have a cartridge oiler on the gun, has a quick change barrel and is box magazine-fed. The weapon is frequently found with a 2.5 power telescope mounted on the receiver. The cartridges for the Type 96 are oiled when loaded into the magazine by an oiler built into the magazine loader. Both the Type 11 and Type 96 lacked built in slow initial extraction and therefore required oiled cartridges.

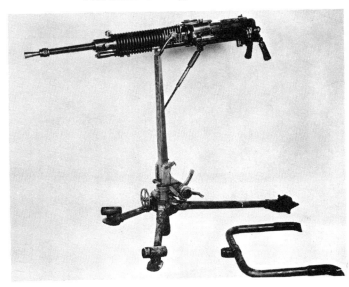

7.7mm Type 92 on an AA mount.

6.5mm Type 91 Tank Gun, fitted with bipod for ground use.

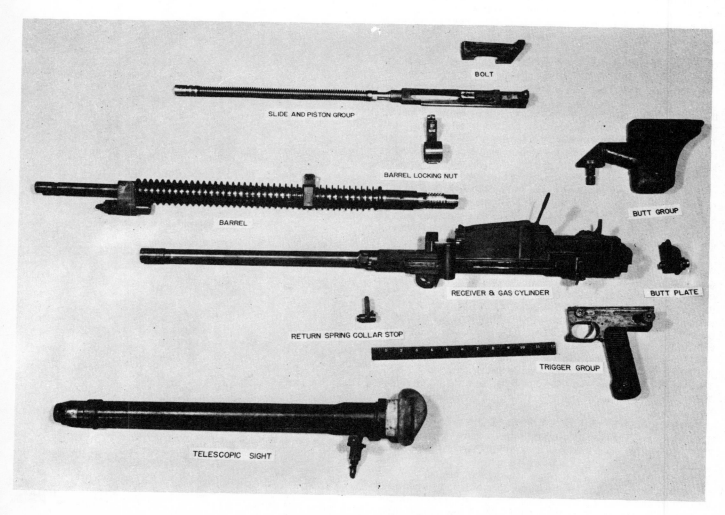

7.7mm Type 97 Tank Gun, stripped.

The Type 99 (1939) light machine gun was designed to obviate the necessity for lubricated cartridges. The barrel lock has a head space adjustment nut, and machining of the critical components was held to closer tolerances than with early guns. The Type 99 came into being because of the need for a light machine gun chambered for the 7.7mm rimless Type 99 cartridge. Four different types of prototype guns were built. Type 1 was modeled on the Type 96 light machine gun. Type 2 was a lightened version of the Type 92 with shoulder stock, bipod and quick change barrel. Type 3 was similar to the Type 97 Tank gun, and Type 4 was another light variation of the Type 92 heavy machine gun. The requirement was for a weapon weighing not more than 24.7 pounds with sights graduated to 1500 meters. A flash hider was also required since the muzzle flash of the 7.7mm cartridge was much greater than that of the 6.5mm cartridge. The modified Type 96 prototype was chosen and adopted as the 7.7mm Type 99.

A paratrooper version of the Type 99 machine gun was built at the Nagoya Arsenal in 1943. This weapon was easily broken down into barrel and receiver group, buttstock, barrel and piston and could be rapidly assembled.

The Japanese Navy and Navy Air Corps used the Lewis gun in ground and air versions. These were chambered for 7.7mm rimmed cartridges, the same as the caliber .303 British cartridge. Both guns are called Type 92; note the complication of having two ground machine guns that use different cartridges called by the same model designation. This situation was due to the almost complete lack of coordination between the Army and Navy Ordnance authorities.

The Japanese copied a number of foreign weapons to use as aircraft guns and in one case produced the Browning in a larger caliber—20mm—than it was produced elsewhere. The Japanese also purchased specimens and the right to manufacture a number of German aircraft machine guns, which they made in 7.92mm, including the MG15 called Type 98. The British Vickers aircraft gun was copied as the 7.7mm (.303 British) Type 89. A Japanese copy of the US caliber .50 Browning chambered for the Japanese 12.7mm cartridge was also quite common. This weapon was called the Type 1.

The Japanese also produced various types of blowback operated training machine guns that do not seem to conform to any set pattern. At least five different variations were found in Korea. They are all rather delicate in construction probably intended for use with a reduced-charge cartridge.

Japanese 7.7mm Heavy Machine Gun, Type I. Standard cartridge strip which is fed into gun from the left side is shown in foreground.

CHARACTERISTICS OF JAPANESE WORLD WAR II ARMY MACHINE GUNS

	Type 3	Type 11	Type 92	Type 96	Type 99
Caliber:	6.5mm.	6.5mm.	7.7mm Type 92 or 99.	6.5mm.	7.7mm Type 99.
System of operation:	Gas, automatic only.	Gas, automatic only.	Gas, automatic only.	Gas, automatic only.	Gas, automatic only.
Length overall:	Approx 47 in.	43.5 in.	45.5 in.	41.5 in.	46.75 in.
Barrel length:	Approx 29 in.	19 in.	Approx 29 in.	21.7 in.	Approx 21.5 in.
Feed device:	30-round strip.	30-round hopper.	30-round strip.	30-round staggered row, detachable, box magazine.	30-round staggered row, detachable, box magazine.
Sights: Front:	Barley corn with protecting ears.	Barley corn with protecting ears.	Barley corn with protecting ears.	Barley corn with protecting ears.	Barley corn with protecting ears.
Rear:	Folding ring A.A. sight and tangent with aperture.	Tangent with "V" notch.	Tangent with aperture or telescope.	Radial wheel tangent with aperture.	Radial wheel tangent with aperture.
Weight:	122 lb. w/tripod.	22.5 lb.	122 lb. w/tripod.	20 lb.	23 lb.
Muzzle velocity:	2434 f.p.s.	Approx 2300 f.p.s.	Approx 2400 f.p.s.	Approx 2400 f.p.s.	Approx 2350 f.p.s.
Cyclic rate:	450-500 r.p.m.	500 r.p.m.	450-500 r.p.m.	550 r.p.m.	850 r.p.m.

All barrel lengths include flash hider length.

Japanese 7.7mm Light Machine Gun Type 99 (1939).

6.5mm Type 96 Light Machine Gun.

CHARACTERISTICS OF JAPANESE WORLD WAR II ARMY MACHINE GUNS (Cont'd)

	Type 1	Type 91	Type 97	Type 93
Caliber:	7.7mm Type 99.	6.5mm.	7.7mm Type 99.	13.2mm.
System of operation:	Gas, automatic only.	Gas, automatic only.	Gas, automatic only.	Gas, automatic only.
Length overall:	42.4 in.	33 in.	46.5 in. w/stock.	95 in. (approx).
Barrel length:	23.2 in.	19.2 in.	28 in.	65 in.
Feed device:	30-round strip.	Hopper.	30-round staggered row, detachable, box magazine.	30-round staggered row, detachable, box magazine.
Sights: Front:	Barley corn with protecting ears.	Barley corn with protecting ears.	1.5X scope.	Barley corn with protecting ears.
Rear:	Tangent with aperture.	Tangent with "V" notch and telescope.		Leaf and speed ring type A.A.
Weight:	70 lb. w/tripod.	22.4 lb.	24.5 lb.	Approx 213 lb. w/tripod.
Muzzle velocity:	Approx 2400 f.p.s.	Approx 2300 f.p.s.	Approx 2400 f.p.s.	2210 f.p.s.
Cyclic rate:	550 r.p.m.	500 r.p.m.	500 r.p.m.	450-480 r.p.m.

All barrel lengths include flash hider length.

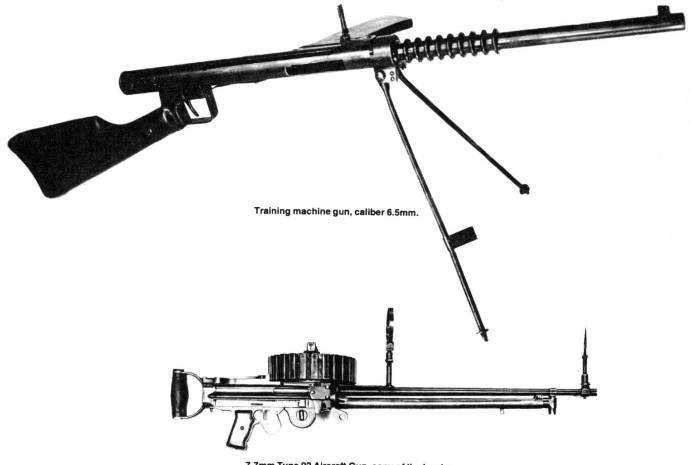

Training machine gun, caliber 6.5mm.

7.7mm Type 92 Aircraft Gun, copy of the Lewis.

JAPANESE WORLD WAR II SMALL ARMS AMMUNITION

As the reader must realize, the Japanese small arms ammunition situation during World War II bordered on anarchy. Although outside the scope of this book, it should be noted that a similar situation existed in the mortar and artillery ammunition areas as well.

In the pistol and submachine gun area, things were simple; there were only two cartridges; the 9mm Type 26 revolver cartridge and the 8mm Type 14 pistol and submachine gun cartridge. But real anarchy reigned in the rifle and machine gun ammunition situation. The rifle and machine gun cartridges used by the Japanese Army, Navy and Air elements in World War II are listed below, together with the weapons in which they were used.

Cartridge	Type of Rim	Using Weapons
6.5mm Type 38	Semi-rimmed	Type 38 and 97 rifle, Type 38 and 44 carbine. Type 3, 11, 91, 96, and 38 (Hotchkiss) machine guns.
7.7mm Type 92	Semi-rimmed	Type 92 machine gun (Army).
7.7mm Type 99	Rimless	Type 99 and 2 rifle, Type 92, 99, 1 and 97 machine guns.
7.7 Type 92 (Navy only, copy of .303 British)	Rimmed	Type 89, Type 92, and Type 97 Navy machine guns.
7.92mm.	Rimless	Type 98 and 100 machine guns, Type 1 (Navy copy of Type 98).
12.7mm	Semi-rimmed	Type 1 (HO-103) machine gun.
13.2mm Type 93	Rimless	Type 93 and Type 3 machine guns.

Mexico

The Mexican Army is currently armed with caliber .45 Colt automatic pistols. The .45 caliber Obregon is now relatively rare. Mexico has purchased 7.62mm NATO FN FAL rifles and 7.62mm NATO FN MAG machine guns. The caliber .30 M1954 and various US caliber .30 rifles and carbines may still be in service as may the caliber .30 Mendoza light machine gun and various models of the Browning machine gun.

Older weapons such as the 7mm Model 1936 rifle and the 7mm Model 1934 light machine gun may be held in reserve.

31

MEXICAN SERVICE PISTOLS

Development of pistols in Mexico has been rather limited. Only one military pistol of native design has been produced in any significant quantity. This weapon, the caliber .45 Obregon, is no longer manufactured, mainly because the cost per weapon was high. Mexico, because of it's proximity to the United States, has closely followed the United States in pistol development. The standard United States military and commercial pistols are well known in Mexico, and American and Mexican-made ammunition is readily available for these pistols. The Colt Model 1911A1 automatic pistol in caliber .45 and super .38 is widely used by the Mexican Armed Forces and Federal Police.

Caliber .45 Obregon pistol

THE CALIBER .45 OBREGON PISTOL

Characteristics of Obregon Pistol

Caliber: .45 Model 1911 (11.43mm).
System of operation: Recoil, semiautomatic.
Length overall: Approx. 8.5 in.
Barrel length: Approx. 5 in.
Feed device: 7-round, in-line, detachable box magazine.
Sights: Front: Blade.
       Rear: Dove-tailed bar with notch.
Weight: Approx. 2.5 lbs.
Muzzle velocity: 830 f.p.s.

How to Load and Fire the Obregon Pistol

This pistol is loaded and fired in a manner similar to that of the US Caliber .45 M1911A1, which is covered in detail in the chapter on the United States.

How to Field Strip the Obregon

Field stripping is essentially the same as that for the US M1911A1 with the exception of the barrel unlocking cam, which is held in place by the combination slide stop safety. The unlocking cam will be removed during field stripping and must be reinserted with the cam surface up so that it will engage the camming lug of the barrel.

Caliber .45 Obregon pistol, field stripped.

How the Obregon Works

The locking design on the Obregon system differs radically from the Browning. As the slide moves to the rear, an unlocking cam on the underside of the barrel moves in the locking sleeve camcut causing the barrel to rotate after initial locked short travel with the slide, until its top lugs pass out of engagement with their locking slots in the underside of slide. There is, of course, no downward hinging movement of the barrel as in the Colt-Browning practice.

The functioning of the mechanism, except for the breech locking, is quite similar to that of the conventional Browning pattern. The locking system is a Steyr-Hahn variant.

This pistol was made for the Mexican Army in caliber 11.43mm (.45 Colt ACP). Its general manufacture and design are a credit to its national origin. The pistol has a slide stop to hold it open on the last shot. This weapon is no longer in manufacture.

MEXICAN RIFLES

Mexico adopted a 7mm Mauser in 1895; this rifle is almost identical to the Spanish 7mm Mauser Model 1893. In 1902, another 7mm Mauser was adopted; this rifle has the Model 98 type action. Except for the action, the M1895 and M1902 are almost identical. In 1912, another 7mm Mauser was purchased by Mexico. The Model 1912 is similar to the German Rifle Model 98 but has a tangent type rear sight and a longer handguard than does the Model 98.

7mm Model 1902 Mauser Rifle.

7mm Model 1936 Rifle.

Caliber .30 M1954 Rifle.

During the Mexican revolution, an extended period that began about 1910 and ended about 1920, Mexico secured arms from many sources. At this time, the Mexican Arisaka (the Japanese Type 38 rifle) was purchased from Japan. These are 7mm weapons with the Mexican escutcheon stamped on the receiver. They are relatively rare. In 1936, a Mauser of Mexican design was introduced. The 7mm Model 1936 externally resembles the Springfield Model 1930A1, having a Springfield type cocking piece, bands and stacking swivel, but the action is of the Mauser "short" type. The Model 1936 is of Mexican manufacture and is very well made.

The Model 1954 rifle is patterned on the Springfield Model 1903A3 but also uses the Mauser-type action, i.e., one-piece firing pin. The stock is made of laminated plywood. A carbine version of this weapon, which is chambered for the .30-06 cartridge, has also been reported.

THE MEXICAN MONDRAGON SEMIAUTOMATIC RIFLE

A number of semiautomatic rifles have also been produced in Mexico, the best known being the Mondragon, one of the earliest reasonably successful semiautomatic rifles of military pattern. It was invented by the Mexican General Mondragon in 1908. Manufacture of the weapon, which was a gas operated locked breech rifle, was undertaken in Switzerland by the Schweizerische Industrie Gesellschaft. When World War I broke out, these rifles were shipped to Germany. They did not stand up well in trench service but were among the earliest rifles issued to observers in aircraft as the Model 1915 before the introduction of the machine gun.

The Mondragon was gas operated from a port near the muzzle. The mechanism was actuated by the gas piston driven back by the expanding gas in the cylinder. While complicated and heavy by modern standards, the Mondragon was a very serious attempt at early semiautomatic rifle production.

7mm M1908 Mondragon Semiautomatic Rifle. This rifle was produced by SIG in Switzerland.

CHARACTERISTICS OF MEXICAN RIFLES

	Model 1895	Model 1902	Model 1912	Model 1936	Model 1954
Caliber:	7mm.	7mm.	7mm.	7mm.	.30-06.
System of operation:	Turn bolt.	Turn bolt.	Turn bolt.	Turn bolt.	Turn bolt.
Length overall:	48.6 in.	49.2 in.	49.1 in.	42.9 in.	Approx 48 in.
Barrel length:	29.1 in.	29.1 in.	29.1 in.	19.29 in.	24 in.
Feed device:	-- 5-round, non-detachable, staggered row box magazine--				
Sights: Front :	Barley corn.	Barley corn.	Barley corn.	Hooded barley corn.	Hooded barley corn.
Rear:	Leaf.	Leaf.	Tangent	Tangent w/"V" notch.	Ramp type aperture.
Weight:	8.8 lb.	8.8 lb.	9 lb..	8.3 lb.	Approx 9 lb.
Muzzle velocity:	Approx 2300 f.p.s.	Approx 2300 f.p.s.	Approx 2300 f.p.s.	Approx 2600 f.p.s.	Approx 2800 f.p.s.

MEXICAN SUBMACHINE GUNS

Mexico has used various models of the caliber 45 Thompson submachine gun, and the noted Mexican small arms designer Rafael Mendoza developed a series of simple lightweight submachine guns during the 1950s. These weapons have been made in caliber .45, .38 super and 9mm Parabellum and have limited use in the Mexican service.

MEXICAN MACHINE GUNS

Mexico has used a number of foreign-developed machine guns and developed a number of her own. The Mexicans have used the 7mm Model 1911 and 1934 Madsen guns, the 7mm Model 1896 Hotchkiss gun, the 7mm Browning Model 1919 and 7mm Colt guns.

MEXICAN MENDOZA MACHINE GUNS

In the early 1930s Rafael Mendoza, then working at the Mexican National Arms factory, developed a gas operated light machine gun, which was standardized in the Mexican Army as the Model C-1934.

While the gun itself utilizes principles already established by the Hotchkiss and Lewis guns, it possesses a number of unique developments of its own. The Lewis type action is improved with the incorporation of a double cam slot, which helps to equalize the torque. Locking friction is materially reduced thereby.

While the gas cylinder is modeled somewhat after the Hotchkiss, the piston system of the Hotchkiss is not employed. The gas assembly is in the form of a cup-shaped projection on the barrel. Within it is housed a short piston. The operating stroke is very short, and at its limit the gases are dissipated openly into the air, thereby reversing the operation of the typical gas mechanism of this sort. A firing switch on the left side of the

7mm Light Machine Gun Model C-1934.

receiver forward of the trigger guard may be set for full or semiautomatic fire in the standard manner.

The cocking handle projects from the left side and is placed well forward. The gun fires from an open bolt position. A special firing pin is provided that carries a firing tip at each end. In the event of firing pin breakage, it is necessary only to reverse the pin to continue firing.

The ejector is an integral part of the hold-back assembly. The quick-change barrel is not threaded. As a result, no provision is made for head spacing.

When the gun is cocked, the barrel latch at the forward end of the receiver can be pressed in. A large lug, which holds the barrel to the receiver, is thereby freed. The barrel can then be pulled forward out of the receiver.

The rear of the barrel is slotted to permit the locking key to pass through. This key, of course, passes through corresponding receiver slots and is retained by the retaining pin.

A three-corner stop on the magazine follower rises above the lips of the magazine into the receiver as the magazine is emptied. This interferes with the movement of the hold-back pawl. Insertion of the loaded magazine releases the rear sear and allows the bolt to move forward enough to engage a notch in the actuator. Pulling the trigger releases the sear. The operating parts are driven ahead by the tension of the operating spring. The bolt face passes over the double column magazine and drives the first cartridge ahead. The extractor cams itself over the cannelure of the cartridge.

As the cylindrical bolt chambers the round and stops, the light locking lugs on the bolt are in line with the fixed lugs. The bolt extension is still three-fourths of an inch from firing and is continuing forward. It rotates the bolt, locking it firmly to the receiver.

The gas port is about 11 inches from the breech end of the barrel. When the bullet passes over it, gas is released into the piston area. The bolt extension starts rearward some three-fourths of an inch before its lug hits the cam in the bolt slot. The firing pin is started backward with the actuator. Continuing rearward movement unlocks the bolt and carries it to the rear.

Mendoza developed a number of other machine guns, some of which have been produced in limited quantity. Early in World War II a modified version of the Model C-1934, was produced. This weapon was designed for use as a light machine gun on a bipod or as a heavy machine gun on a tripod. This weapon was apparently not introduced into Mexican service.

In 1945, Mendoza introduced another light machine gun chambered for the .30-06 cartridge. This weapon is basically an improved Model C-1934 and has the same type quick-change barrel as the Model C-1934, but has a different receiver configuration and a multi-perforated muzzle brake.

The caliber .30 RM-2 is another Mendoza design. It has been especially designed for easy and low cost manufacture.

While it does not have the quick removal barrel feature of the earlier model, it stresses a very simple, rapid and effective takedown. Pressing the release catch at the rear of the receiver allows the gun to be broken on its hinge much in the manner of the Belgian FN automatic rifle. The gas piston and slide with recoil spring and the few operating components may be withdrawn from the rear of the gun. The unusual Mendoza feature of reversible firing pin again appears in this new design but in improved form. In the event of firing pin breakage in the field (a relatively weak point in any machine gun), merely dropping the rear of the gun will allow the mechanism to be drawn back far enough to lift the bolt off the piston slide. The firing pin has a firing point at each end. If one should be broken, merely withdrawing and reversing the pin and reinstalling it in the bolt prepares the gun for firing again.

CHARACTERISTICS OF MEXICAN MACHINE GUNS

	Model C1934	Model RM2
Caliber:	7mm.	.30-06.
System of operation:	gas, selective fire.	gas, selective fire.
Length overall:	46. in.	43.3 in.
Barrel length:	Approx 25 in.	24 in.
Feed device:	--------------20-round, detachable box magazine ---------------------	
Sights: Front:	Hooded barley corn.	Hooded barley corn.
Rear:	Adjustable aperture.	Adjustable aperture.
Weight:	18.5 lb.	14.1 lb.
Muzzle velocity:	Approx 2700 f.p.s.	Approx 2750 f.p.s.
Cyclic rate:	400-500 r.p.m	600 r.p.m.

Mexican Mendoza Model RM-2 Light Machine Gun, caliber .30-06.

Mexican RM-2, field stripped.

32
Netherlands

The standard small arms of the Netherlands Army are as follows: the 9mm Browning, FN Hi-Power pistol, the 7.62mm NATO FN FAL rifle, the 9MM UZI M61 submachine gun and the 7.62mm NATO FN MAG general purpose machine gun. The US caliber .30 and .50 Browning machine guns are still in service on armored vehicles. The Netherlands were furnished with American and British small arms after World War II.

NETHERLANDS SERVICE PISTOLS

The Netherlands Army adopted a 9.4mm service revolver in 1873, which was, with minor modifications, used as late as World War II, especially in the former Dutch East Indies. Prior to World War I, the Netherlands adopted the M1903 Browning 9mm Long pistol and in the early 1920s adopted the 9mm (.380 ACP) Browning M1922 pistol, which they called Pistool M25 No. 2. The Netherlands also used the 9mm Parabellum Luger, some of German pre-war manufacture similar to the P-08, and approximately 9,000 of Vickers (British) production usually called the Model 1920. Whether or not these particular pistols were made by or assembled by Vickers is a controversial question.

The 9mm Parabellum FN Hi-Power pistol was adopted by the Netherlands after World War II.

NETHERLANDS SERVICE RIFLES

The Netherlands adopted the 6.5mm Mannlicher rimmed cartridge and rifle in 1895. The Netherlands Mannlicher is a turn-bolt type, using the standard 5-round Mannlicher type clip, which is loaded in the weapon and drops out when the last round is chambered. The Dutch Mannlicher is basically the same as the Romanian Model 1893 Mannlicher.

Seven carbine versions of this weapon exist, including a model with folding bayonet for gendarmerie use. These carbines vary only in minor details, such as position of sling swivels and length of handguards. The Model 95 No. 1 O.M. carbine has a sporter type stock and uses an old type triangular bayonet. The Model 95 No. 1 N.M., Model 95 No. 3 O.M., Model 95 No. 3 N.M., Model 95 No. 4 O.M. and Model 95 No. 4 N.M. all use knife type bayonets. An unusual feature of the carbines is that most models have a wooden piece covering the left side of the magazine. This piece is glued and doweled to the stock. The No. 3 O.M. and No. 3 N.M. carbines have handguards that extend beyond the stock, almost to the muzzle. Many of these 6.5mm Mannlicher carbines were converted to caliber .303 British by the Indonesians in the early 1950s.

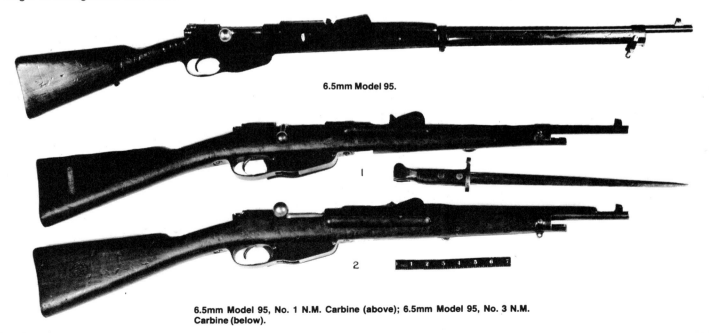

6.5mm Model 95.

6.5mm Model 95, No. 1 N.M. Carbine (above); 6.5mm Model 95, No. 3 N.M. Carbine (below).

6.5mm Model 95, No. 4 N.M. Carbine.

FN 7.62mm NATO Light Automatic Rifle as made for the Netherlands.

These weapons are no longer in service in the Netherlands.

In 1917, a version of the Model 95 rifle chambered for the 7.92mm rimmed cartridge was introduced. This weapon was made in very limited quantity.

In 1940, the Netherlands government purchased quantities of the .30-06 Johnson semiautomatic rifle for the East Indies Forces and the Royal Netherlands Navy. These rifles are called the Model 1941. The United States and Great Britain supplied the Netherlands with caliber .30 M1 rifles and caliber .303 Lee Enfield rifles. The Netherlands also purchased a quantity of caliber .30 FN bolt action carbines for police use. About 1960, the 7.62mm NATO FN FAL rifle was adopted. The Netherlands version of the FAL has metal handguards, a folding bipod and protecting ears on the rear sight. The Dutch has also made several modifications in the bolt of the FAL since adopting the weapon.

The government arsenal Artillerie Inrichtingen manufactured the 7.62mm NATO AR-10 rifle in limited quantities on a contract basis. This weapon was never adopted by the Dutch Army.

NETHERLANDS MACHINE GUNS

The Dutch adopted the Schwarzlose machine gun in 7.92mm rimmed in 1908. This weapon is basically the same as the Austrian 07/12 Schwarzlose and was used by the Dutch Army during World War II. The Dutch were also one of the largest users of the Madsen, having used the Model 1919, 1923, 1926, 1927, 1934, 1938 and 1939—all chambered for the 6.5mm cartridge. The Dutch also adopted the Lewis gun in 6.5mm in 1920. These weapons are not as frequently encountered as are the Dutch Madsens. The Vickers Model 1918 was also purchased in 7.92mm.

After World War II, the Dutch received United States Browning guns and British Bren guns. After extensive tests, the 7.62mm NATO FN MAG machine gun was adopted in the early sixties.

8mm Model 8 Machine Gun.

6.5mm Model 20, Lewis gun.

33
New Zealand

New Zealand forces have always been equipped with British pattern arms, made in the UK, in Australia (Lithgow) or locally. The pistols used have been the caliber .455 Webley Marks V and VI and the Enfield caliber .38 revolvers (No. 2 Marks 1, 1* and 1**). Rifles used in the past have been the No. 1 Mark III and III*. The current rifle is the 7.62mm NATO L1A1 (FN FAL) as made at Lithgow. Submachine guns have been produced in New Zealand. Approximately 10,000 Sten and 2000 Charlton machine guns were made in New Zealand during World War II. The Charlton is a native design.

It should be noted that, in the area of submachine guns and machine guns, New Zealand has conformed more closely to the United Kingdom than to Australia. New Zealand has adopted the 9mm Parabellum L2A3 (Sterling submachine gun)—the standard submachine gun in the United Kingdom—and the FN-developed 7.62mm NATO MAG general purpose machine gun. The MAG, in modified form, is the L7A1 general purpose machine gun in the United Kingdom, and the version of the MAG used in New Zealand is probably the same as the British gun.

THE CHARLTON .303 LIGHT MACHINE GUN AND RIFLE

Philip Charlton, a New Zealander, developed a design for converting the Lee Enfield rifle into a selective fire weapon. He was issued a patent in 1941 and, due to the shortage of automatic weapons, work commenced on the conversion of old long Lee Enfields on hand into Charlton machine guns. A plant was established in Hastings, New Zealand, to carry out this conversion. Approximately 2000 Long Lee Enfields had been converted when production ceased. The Charlton weighed 16.5 pounds and had a cyclic rate of fire of about 700 rounds per minute. It is a gas operated weapon fed with a 30-round magazine but could use the standard 10-round Lee Enfield magazine as well.

Essentially the conversion consisted of fitting a cylinder on the right side of the weapon originating at a point approximately midpoint of the barrel and extending beyond the rear of the action. This cylinder acted as a gas cylinder in its forward part and a piston tube for the remainder. The piston rod is attached to a slide which has an inclined cam that operates on the bolt handle stub pulling it to the rear and opening the action. A spring attached to the lower portion of the piston is mounted in a cylinder below the gas cylinder and returns the slide and piston forward. The standard Lee trigger mechanism has been modified by the addition of a disconnector system. A selector is mounted behind the trigger and engages the trigger. Setting it on safe prevents rearward movement of the trigger, setting it on "R" allows the trigger to rotate far enough to the rear to allow single shots to be fired and setting it on "A" lets the trigger come fully to the rear producing full automatic fire.

A hinged cover is place over the action to protect it from dirt, and a circular fin assembly, to assist in cooling the barrel, is placed over the rear half of the barrel. The semi-pistol grip of the Lee Enfield is cut away, and a full pistol grip is mounted to the rear of the trigger guard. A heavy flash hider with protected front sight is mounted on the front end of the barrel. Australia also converted several thousand Lee Enfields to the Charlton design. The work in Australia was done by the Electrolux Company.

An earlier effort of Charlton's was the conversion of the .303 Rifle No. 1 Mark 3* to a semiautomatic rifle. This design was tested by the United Kingdom but not adopted.

Charlton conversion of .303 Rifle No. 1 SMLE Mark 3*.

34

North Korea

The North Korean army was originally equipped with Soviet World War II weapons such as the 7.62mm Tokarev pistol, the 7.62mm M1944 carbine and M1891/30 rifle, the 7.62mm DP and DPM machine guns, the 7.62mm Maxim machine gun and the 12.7mm DShK M1938 machine gun. North Korea made the 7.62mm PPSh M1941 Submachine gun during the Korean war.

North Korea, however, is now equipped with more modern arms, most of which are of native manufacture. The 7.62mm Model 68 pistol is standard, and the 7.62mm Model 68 assault rifle is a copy of the Soviet AKM, The 7.62mm SKS carbine, RPD light machine gun and the 7.62mm TUL-1 light machine gun are all used, as is the 12.7mm DShK M1938/46.

NORTH KOREAN 7.62mm TYPE 68 PISTOL

The Type 68 is a North Korean variation of the Soviet Tokarev TT M1933 pistol. The Type 68 is shorter than the Tokarev and is considerably different in internal construction. The Tokarev, like the Colt M1911, uses a link to pull down the barrel in unlocking. The Type 68 uses the cam type barrel lug as used on the Hi-Power Browning. The magazine catch on the Type 68 has been relocated to the bottom rear of the grip, as opposed to the button type catch on the upper receiver of the Tokarev. The method of holding in the firing pin has also been changed. The same 7.62mm cartridge is used in both pistols.

Characteristics of the Type 68 Pistol

Caliber: 7.62mm
System of operation: Recoil operated, semiautomatic only
Weight: 1.75 lbs.
Length overall: 7.3 in.
Barrel length: 4.25 in.
Feed device: 8 round, in line, detachable box magazine.
Sights: Front: Blade
      Rear: Square notch
Muzzle velocity: 1295 f.p.s.

North Korean 7.62mm Type 58 Assault Rifle without magazine.

NORTH KOREAN 7.65mm TYPE 64 PISTOL

This pistol can be best explained as a mystery; it is a copy of the Model 1900 Browning. The mystery is why the North Koreans brought out this rather ancient piece of ordnance. A version of this pistol with silencer has a shortened slide and fine thread on the barrel of the attachment of a silencer.

NORTH KOREAN 7.62mm TYPE 58 ASSAULT RIFLE

The Type 58 is a copy of the AK and comes in both wooden stocked and folding steel stocked versions. It does not appear to be as finely finished as AKs manufactured in other countries.

NORTH KOREAN 7.62mm TYPE 68 ASSAULT RIFLE

This weapon is a copy of the Soviet AKM. It does not have the rate reducer found on the AKM. It uses the standard 7.62 × 39mm "intermediate" sized cartridge.

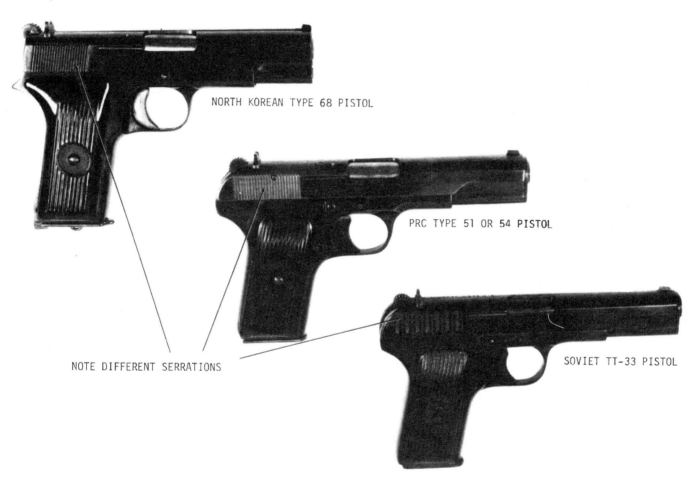

NORTH KOREAN TYPE 68 PISTOL

PRC TYPE 51 OR 54 PISTOL

SOVIET TT-33 PISTOL

NOTE DIFFERENT SERRATIONS

Comparative photo showing differences among North Korean Type 68, PRC Type 51/54 and Soviet Tokarev Pistols.

North Korean 7.65mm Type 64 Pistol.

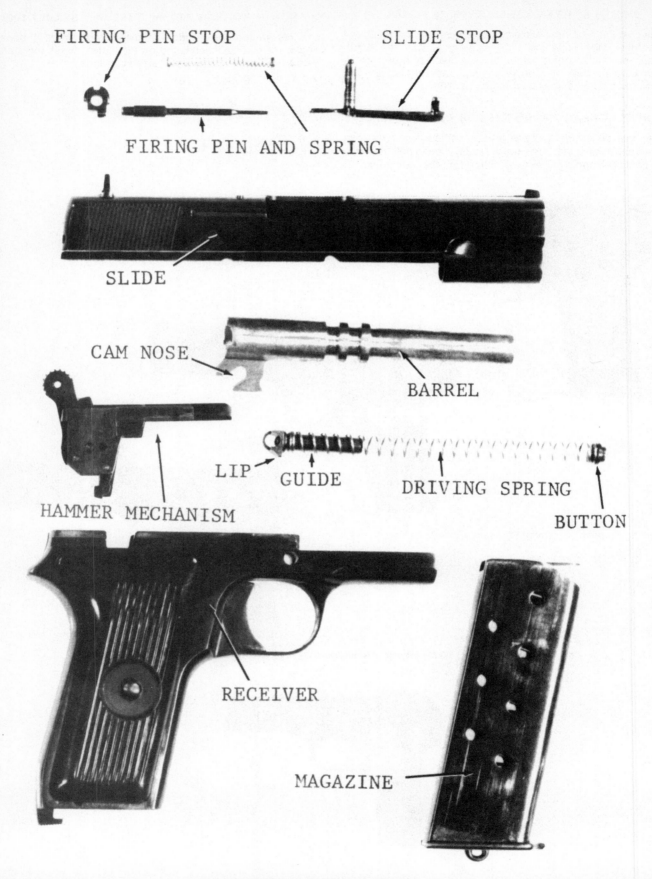

FIRING PIN STOP

SLIDE STOP

FIRING PIN AND SPRING

SLIDE

CAM NOSE

BARREL

HAMMER MECHANISM

LIP

GUIDE

DRIVING SPRING

BUTTON

RECEIVER

MAGAZINE

Field stripped view of North Korean Type 68 Pistol.

35 Norway

The Norwegian Army is currently equipped with the following weapons: caliber .45 Model 1914 and caliber .45 Model 1911A1 pistols and various submachine guns including the caliber .45 Thompson, the caliber .45 M3A1 and 9mm Parabellum Sten guns. The caliber 7.62mm NATO G3 rifle is standard, but US caliber .30 M1 rifles, 7.92mm Kar98k and British Lee Enfield rifles are probably still held. US caliber .30 Browning guns, Browning automatic rifles and British Bren caliber .303 Bren guns were furnished to Norway after World War II. The US caliber .50 Browning machine gun is also used. Norway has adopted the 7.62mm NATO MG 42/59 machine gun as standard.

NORWEGIAN SERVICE PISTOLS

Norway adopted a single-action Nagant revolver in 1883, but apparently only 794 of the weapons were procured. In 1893, the 7.5mm Model 1893 Nagant revolver was adopted. This weapon, which is basically the same as the Russian 7.62mm Model 1895 Nagant, was the standard pistol until the adoption of the caliber .45 Model 1914 pistol. The Model 1914 is basically the same as the US caliber .45 M1911 Colt pistol except for the external shape of the slide stop.

The first 300 caliber .45 pistols were procured by Norway from Colt and are unmodified Model 1911s. All of the Model 1914 arms were made at the Norwegian government arsenal at Kongsberg. Since World War II, Norway has obtained quantities of caliber .45 Model 1911A1 automatics from the United States.

In the period after World War II, considerable quantities of 9mm P-08 Luger and P-38 pistols were used by the Norwegian forces.

Norwegian caliber .45 Model 1914 Automatic Pistol.

NORWEGIAN RIFLES AND CARBINES

Norway adopted the Krag Jorgensen rifle, chambered for the 6.5 × 55mm rimless Mauser cartridge, in 1894, and this rifle and its carbine versions were used by the Norwegian Army until the majority of the weapons were lost to the Germans in World War II. Some Model 1894 rifles were made at Steyr, but the majority were made by Kongsberg. A few were made during the German occupation; these bear German *Waffenamt* inspection stamps.

THE NORWEGIAN KRAG

The Norwegian Krag is generally similar to the US caliber .30 Krag but does not have a cutoff. As with the Krag, there is a single frontally-mounted locking lug. It has been stated many times that the Krag action is not suitable for high-pressure cartridges, but the Norwegian Krag was made after World War II (for a limited period of time) chambered for the 7.92 × 57mm cartridge—hardly a low pressured cartridge. This is mainly a matter of metallurgy—Norwegian Krags produced since World War I are obviously made of steel alloys that are better than those used in the United States Krag, which was made from 1892–1902 when metallurgy was not too precise.

Distinctive Details of Norwegian Rifles and Carbines

The various models of rifles and carbines can be distinguished by the following characteristics:

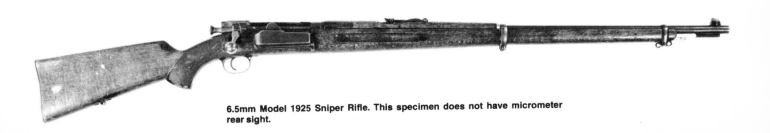

6.5mm Model 1925 Sniper Rifle. This specimen does not have micrometer rear sight.

Rifle Model 1894. Stock with pistol grip, half-length cleaning rod mounted in forward part of stock; bayonet lug mounted under the barrel and a half-length handguard is fitted.

Sniper Rifle Model 1923. Full-length stock with full checked pistol grip; full-length handguard, wide upper band/ nose cap with bayonet lug, micrometer type rear sight. The rifle is marked M/1894.

Sniper Rifle Model 1925. Basically the same as the Rifle Model 1894, but has checked full pistol grip, micrometer type rear sight, marked M/25.

Sniper Rifle Model 1930. Has sporter type stock with checked full pistol grip, heavy barrel, no bayonet lug, micrometer rear sight, marked M/1894/30.

Carbine Model 1895. Sporter type stock, no bayonet lug, similar in appearance to the United States Krag carbine.

Carbine Model 1897. Same as the Model 1895 carbine, but butt swivel is positioned further toward the rear of the butt.

Carbine Model 1904. Full stock with pistol grip and full length handguard, no bayonet lug.

Carbine Model 1907. Basically the same as the Model 1904, but sling swivels are positioned on rear band and on the butt.

6.5mm Carbine Model 1912. Stocked to the muzzle with full-length handguard, similar to the Sniper Rifle Model 1923. Has bayonet lug mounted on combination upper band nose cap.

After World War II, the Norwegian Army had few Norwegian Krags but many German 7.92mm Mauser Kar98ks. American and British rifles were also supplied. In 1959, a caliber .30-06 heavy barrel modification of the Mauser with sporter-type stock and micrometer sight was produced for the Norwegian National Rifle Association. A few Krags were produced after the war, but costs were prohibitively high, and there was no intention to equip the armed forces with the Krag, since it can hardly be considered a modern rifle.

In 1964, the Norwegians adopted the West German 7.62mm NATO G3 rifle, and that rifle is now in production at Kongsberg Vapenfabrik. The Norwegians modified the G3 slightly; in early models the bolt operating handle was removed, and the bolt was pulled to the rear by means of a finger hole, as in the US M3A1 submachine gun. A semiautomatic sniper model with telescope has also been adopted. Kongsberg currently manufactures the standard G3 for domestic consumption and sale to West Germany.

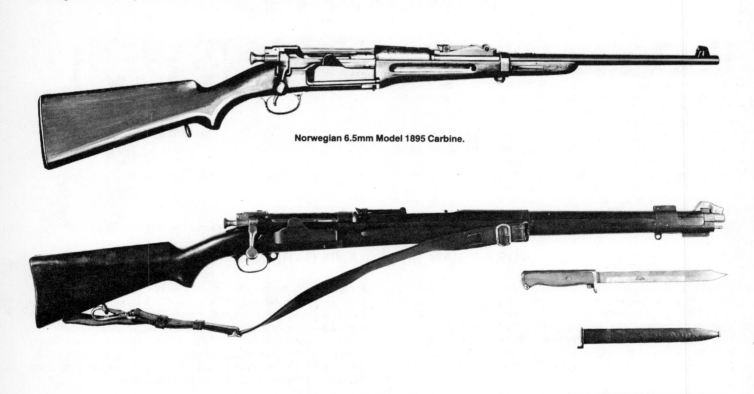

Norwegian 6.5mm Model 1895 Carbine.

Carbine Model 1912, caliber 6.5mm.

CHARACTERISTICS OF NORWEGIAN RIFLES AND CARBINES

	Rifle M1894	Sniper Rifle Model 1923	Sniper Rifle Model 1925	Sniper Rifle Model 1930
Caliber:	6.5 × 55mm.	6.5mm × 55mm.	6.5mm × 55mm.	6.5 × 55mm.
System of operation:	Turn bolt.	Turn bolt.	Turn bolt.	Turn bolt.
Length overall:	49.9 in.	Approx 44 in.	49.7 in.	48 in.
Barrel length:	29.9 in.	Approx 24 in.	30 in.	29.5 in.
Feed device:	5-round horizontal box.	5-round horizontal box.	5-round horizontal box.	5-round horizontal box.
Sights: Front:	Barley corn.	Barley corn.	Barley corn.	Hooded barley corn.
Rear:	Tangent.	Micrometer with aperture.	Micrometer with aperture.	Micrometer with aperture.
Weight:	9.38 lb.	Approx 9 lb.	9.9 lb.	11.46 lb.
Muzzle velocity:	Approx 2625 f.p.s.	Approx 2600 f.p.s.	Approx 2625 f.p.s.	Approx 2625 f.p.s.
Cyclic rate:	-----------	-----------	-----------	-----------

CHARACTERISTICS OF NORWEGIAN RIFLES AND CARBINES (Cont'd)

	Carbine M1895	Carbine M1904	Carbine M1912	G-3
Caliber:	6.5 × 55mm.	6.5 × 55mm.	6.5 × 55mm.	7.62mm NATO.
System of operation:	Turn bolt.	Turn bolt.	Turn bolt.	Gas, selective fire.
Length overall:	40 in.	40 in.	43.6 in.	40.2 in.
Barrel length:	20.5 in.	20.5 in.	24 in.	17.7 in.
Feed device:	5-round horizontal box.	5-round horizontal box.	5-round horizontal box.	20-round staggered row box magazine.
Sights: Front:	Barley corn.	Barley corn.	Barley corn.	Hooded post.
Rear:	Tangent.	Tangent.	Tangent.	Aperture.
Weight:	7.5 lb.	8.4 lb.	8.8 lb.	2624 f.p.s.
Muzzle velocity:	Approx 2575 f.p.s.	Approx 2575 f.p.s.	2600 f.p.s.	500-600 r.p.m.
Cyclic rate:	-----------	-----------	-------------------	

Two current models of the 7.62 × 51mm NATO AG3 manufactured at the Kongsberg Vapenfabrik in Norway.

NORWEGIAN MACHINE GUNS

Norway adopted the Hotchkiss gun chambered for the 6.5mm cartridge in 1911 and also used the 6.5mm Model 1914 and 1918 Madsen guns. The Browning water cooled machine gun was also used and called the Model 29. This weapon is similar to the Colt M38B machine gun.

After World War II, Norway obtained American caliber .30 Browning guns and British machine guns and also used the 7.92mm MG34 and MG42 machine guns. The 7.62mm NATO MG42/59 machine gun is now standard in Norway, where it is called the LMG3.

36

The Polish Army is currently mainly equipped with Soviet designed weapons. Pistols used include the Polish 9mm Model 64, the Soviet 9mm Makarov and the Polish 9mm Model 63 Machine Pistol. The Soviet-designed, Polish-made 7.62mm AK and AKM assault rifles and 7.62mm SVD sniper rifles are used as are the 7.62mm RPK, RPD,

Poland

PK/PKS and PKT machine guns.

The 7.62mm SGM machine gun and its tank version, the SGMT, are still used as is the 7.62mm RP-46 light machine gun. The 12.7mm DShK M1938/46 is used on vehicles.

Older Soviet weapons such as the 7.62mm Model 1944 carbine, the 7.62mm PPSh M1941 submachine gun, the 7.62mm DPM and SG43 machine guns, as well as the Polish 7.62mm M43/52 submachine gun, may still be encountered.

POLISH PISTOLS

THE POLISH 9mm MODEL 35 ("RADOM") PISTOL

A modification of the Colt Browning locked-breech pistol was designed by the Poles at the Fabryka Broni Radom, a government arms plant. The design is credited to P. Wilniewczyc and J. Skrzypinski. This 9mm Parabellum weapon, called the Vis Model 35, or more popularly the Radom, was the Polish service pistol at the time of WW II, and the Germans continued its manufacture after they occupied Poland. The Model 35 Radom locks and unlocks in a manner quite similar to that of the Browning FN Hi-Power pistol, in that it has a nose forged on the rear underside of the barrel. This serves as a cam to pull the barrel down out of the locked position, rather than using the barrel link as with the US Colt Model 1911 pistol.

As manufactured for the Polish forces, the weapon has the firing pin retracting device mounted on the left rear of the slide and a slide lock, which appears to be a safety, mounted on the left rear side of the receiver. Most of the pistols manufactured during the German occupation do not have the slide lock. The firing pin retracting device is used to lower the hammer on a loaded chamber. This weapon, although it has a grip safety, does not have the conventional Colt-Browning manual-safety catch. The slide lock is used to lock the slide to the rear to assist in field

stripping. Pistols manufactured prior to the German occupation are very well made and are marked on the slide with the Polish eagle and Polish markings. The Model 35s manufactured for the Germans are of much rougher construction and bear the German *Waffenamt* proof marks. The Radom Model 35 is no longer in service in any Army.

Manufacture of the 7.62mm Tokarev Model TT M1933 was begun in Poland after World War II; this pistol is being replaced by the 9mm Makarov (PM) pistol and the 9mm Stechkin (APS) machine pistol. Characteristics of these weapons will be found in the chapter on the USSR.

Characteristics of Model 1935 Pistol

Caliber: 9mm Parabellum.
System of operation: Recoil, semiautomatic.
Length overall: 7.8 in.
Barrel length: 4.7 in.
Feed device: 8-round, in line, detachable box magazine.
Sights: Front: Blade.
        Rear: "V" notch.
Weight: 2.25 lbs.
Muzzle velocity: Approx. 1150 f.p.s.

9mm Model 35 Pistol manufactured for the Polish Army.

9mm Model 35 Pistol manufactured for the Germans without slide lock.

THE POLISH 9mm MODEL 64 PISTOL

This double action, blowback operated pistol is smaller in size than the Soviet Makarov pistol but is chambered for the same 9mm cartridge. In some respects, it seems to resemble the Walther PPK more than it does the Makarov, as for example the trigger bar linkage system and the internally mounted slide stop. The system, however, is actually different than either the Makarov or the Walther.

Polish 9mm Model 64 Pistol.

Characteristics of 9mm Model 64 Pistol

Caliber: 9mm Makarov
System of operation: Blowback, semi-automatic only
Length overall: 6.1 in.
Barrel length: 3.3 in.
Feed device: 8-round, in-line, detachable box magazine
Sights: Front: Blade
          Rear: Notch
Weight: 1.5 lbs.
Muzzle velocity: 1017 f.p.s.

The Model 64 is disassembled in a manner similar to that of the Walther PP and PPK. The magazine catch is at the bottom rear of the grip, and the safety catch is mounted on the slide and is pushed down to engage. In this position, it blocks the firing pin.

Polish 9mm Model 64 field stripped.

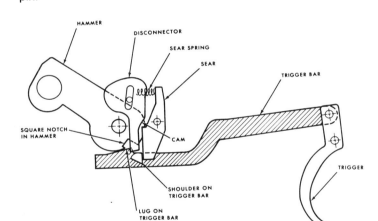

Polish 9mm Model 64 trigger linkage.

POLISH 9mm MODEL 63 MACHINE PISTOL

This weapon is similar to the Soviet 9mm Stechkin and the Czech 7.65mm M61 "Skorpion" machine pistols in concept. It is a selective fire weapon, which can be used as a pistol or as a shoulder weapon. It is seemingly intended for issue to junior officers in combat units and to armored troops.

Characteristics of 9mm Model 63 Machine Pistol

Caliber: 9mm Makarov
System of operation: Blowback, automatic only
Length overall: w/folded stock—13.1 in.
Feed device: 15- and 25-round, detachable box magazines
Sights: Front: Blade.
          Rear: "L" type
Weight: 3.96 lbs.
Muzzle velocity: 1065 f.p.s.
Cyclic rate: 600 r.p.m.

Polish 9mm Model 63 Machine Pistol.

This weapon has a sliding type metal shoulder stock used in conjunction with a vertical fore grip. When the stock is in the retracted position and the vertical fore grip is pushed up, it extends beyond the muzzle of the weapon; the weapon can be carried in a holster and fired with one hand. The butt plate portion of the shoulder stock folds up under the rear of the receiver.

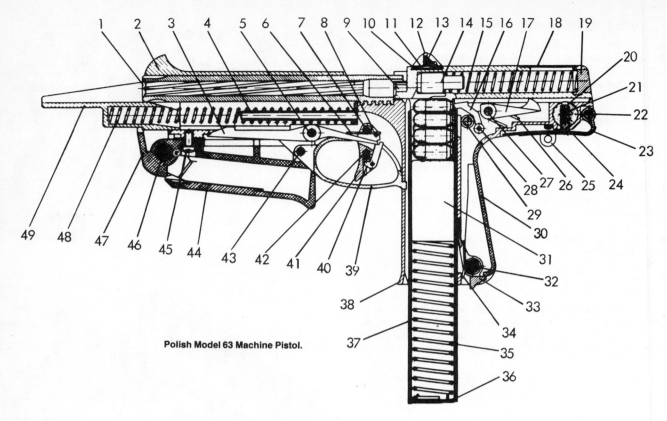

Polish Model 63 Machine Pistol.

1. Barrel	11. Sight spring	21. Butt-latch spring	30. Stock	40. Trigger-catch lever
2. Front sight	12. Rear sight	22. Butt-plate pin	31. Magazine follower	41. Trigger catch
3. Trigger lever	13. Rear sight pin	23. Butt plate	32. Magazine-catch pin	42. Trigger-catch-leaver spring
4. Recoil-spring guide	14. Retarder	24. Butt latch	33. Magazine catch	43. Back screw
5. Trigger-lever pin	15. Retard spring	25. Lanyard loop	34. Magazine-catch spring	44. Grip
6. Trigger spring	16. Slide stop	26. Retarder-lever spring	35. Magazine spring	45. Front screw
7.,8. Trigger pins	17. Retarder lever	27. Retarder-lever pin	36. Magazine cover	46. Grip catch
9. Firing pin	18. Bearing latch	28. Slide-stop axis	37. Magazine body	47. Frame
10. Sight-leaf	19. Bearing	29. Safety-lock	38. Pistol grip	48. Recoil spring
	20. Grip mount		39. Trigger guard	49. Compensator

POLISH SUBMACHINE GUNS

The Poles were supplied with the Soviet 7.62mm PPSh M1941 and PPS M1943 submachine guns. They developed a variation of the PPS M1943, which was manufactured in Poland.

THE POLISH 7.62mm M1943/52 SUBMACHINE GUN

The M1943/52 submachine gun is a modification of the Soviet PPS M1943. Its characteristics are basically the same as those of the Soviet weapon, except that it has a wooden stock and is reportedly capable of semiautomatic as well as automatic fire.

Special Note on the Polish M1943/52

Loading, firing, functioning and disassembly of this weapon are the same as for the Soviet 7.62mm submachine gun PPS M1943.

Characteristics of M1943/52 Submachine Gun

System of operation: Blowback, selective fire.
Length, overall: 32.72 in.
Barrel length: 9.45 in.
Feed device: 35-round, detachable staggered box magazine.

Polish 7.62 M1943/52 Submachine Gun.

Sights: Front: Flat-topped post, adjustable for elevation and windage.
      Rear: L-type, open V-notch with setting for 100 and 200 meters.
Muzzle velocity: 1640 f.p.s. w/Soviet 7.62mm Type P pistol cartridge.
Cyclic rate: 600 r.p.m.
Weight: 8 lbs.

POLISH RIFLES AND CARBINES

When Poland gained her freedom after World War I, stocks of Russian 7.62mm M1891 rifles and carbines and 7.92mm Mauser 98 carbines and rifles were available to them.

POLISH—PRODUCED RIFLES

The first rifle produced by the Poles contained features of both Russian and German design. The Polish 7.92mm Model 91/98/25 rifle has the Russian Mosin Nagant action but Mauser-type bands and fittings. The bolt head has been modified to use the 7.92mm cartridge.

The manufacture of Mauser rifles and carbines started at the Warsaw Arsenal soon after World War I. The Polish 7.92mm Karabin 98a is basically the same as the later German rifle 98. Similarly, the Polish Karabinek 98 is basically the same as the German Kar 98a.

The 7.92mm Karabin 29 is a variant of the Czech Model 24, differing from the Czech weapon mainly in location of the sling swivels and the front sight.

After World War II, the Poles were initially equipped with various models of the Soviet 7.62mm Mosin Nagant rifle and carbine. The Poles now produce the Soviet-designed 7.62mm AKM assualt rifle. The characteristics of these weapons are covered in the chapter on the USSR.

7.92mm Model 91/98/25 Rifle

CHARACTERISTICS OF POLISH RIFLES

	Rifle 91/98/25	Rifle 98a	Carbine 98	Rifle 29
Caliber:	7.92mm			
System of operation:	Turn bolt			
Length overall:	43.3 in.	49.2 in.	43.3 in.	43.4 in.
Barrel length:	23.6 in.	29.1 in.	23.6 in.	23.6 in.
Feed device:	5-round in-line, non-detachable box magazine.	5-round staggered row non-detachable box magazine.	5-round staggered row non-detachable box magazine.	5-round staggered row non-detachable box magazine.
Sights: Front:	Barley corn.	Barley corn.	Barley corn with protecting ears.	Barley corn with protecting ears.
Rear:	Leaf.	Tangent.	Tangent.	Tangent.
Weight:	8.16 lb.	9 lb.	8 lb.	9 lb.
Muzzle velocity:	Approx 2470 f.p.s.	Approx 2570 f.p.s.	Approx 2470 f.p.s.	Approx 2470 f.p.s.

7.92mm Carbine Model 98.

7.92mm Model 29 Rifle.

POLISH 7.62mm AK ASSAULT RIFLE WITH GRENADE LAUNCHER

This weapon is a modification of the AK made in Poland fitted with a rifle grenade launcher. It has been called the PMK-DGN and also the KbKg Model 1960.

The grenade launcher, which is not the same size as those used in the NATO countries, is screwed onto the threaded end of the barrel and locked in place by the spring loaded plunger mounted in front sight base of the AK. A valve is fitted into the right side of the gas cylinder to allow shutting off the gas from the gas port of the barrel when firing grenades. The grenade launcher sight is mounted on the hand-guard retaining pin. A heavy rubber recoil pad is attached to the stock with straps and

Polish 7.62mm AK Assault Rifle with Grenade launcher (PMK-DGN or KbKg M1960)

a special ten-round magazine is used when launching grenades from this rifle. This magazine has a filler block in it that prevents it from being used with bulleted cartridges.

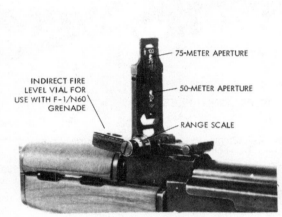

(a) FOR 50- AND 75-METER FIRING (LEAF DOWN)

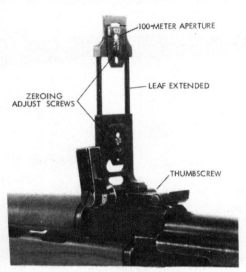

(b) FOR 50- AND 100-METER FIRING (LEAF UP)

Polish PMK–DGN grenade launcher sights.

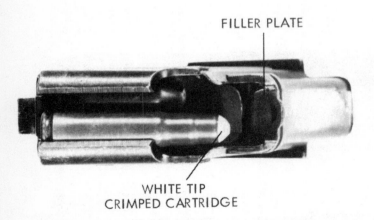

Special 10–shot magazine with filler block to prevent use of ball cartridges.

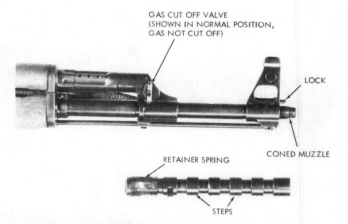

Polish PMK–DGN grenade launcher and gas cut–off valve.

POLISH MACHINE GUNS

The Poles used a 7.92mm water-cooled Browning Machine Gun, which they called the Model 30. They had previously adopted a 7.92mm version of the Browning automatic rifle in 1928. The Polish Browning guns are basically the same as those used by the United States. They are no longer in use in the Polish Army.

37

Portugal

Portugal recently secured military small arms from many sources in the West. Most Portuguese service arms are procured from abroad, but the 7.62mm NATO Rifle M961—German G3 rifle—and the 9mm Model 48 F.B.P. submachine gun are made at the Portuguese government arms plant, Fabrica de Braco de Prata. Because of the large variety of weapons in service in Portugal, only those which are unique in Portugal are covered in any detail. The 7.62mm NATO MG42/59 and the HK21 machine guns are among the more recent weapons procured.

PORTUGUESE SMALL ARMS IN WORLD WAR II

During the period preceding World War II and during the war, Portugal procured a large number of different types of small arms from Germany and Great Britain. There were still some quantities of the older Portuguese weapons in service as well. As a result, Portugal holds a somewhat varied collection of small arms in various calibers.

Among the weapons used by Portugal are the following:

Pistols: 7.65mm Savage M/908 and M/915, 9mm M/43 Parabellum (Luger), 9mm M/908 Parabellum (Luger).

Rifles: 7.92mm Mauser M/937 (same as Kar. 98k).
Cal. 303 Lee Enfield M/917 (same as SMLE MkIII and III*).
Portugal has adopted the German G3 (CETME)assault rifle in 7.62mm NATO caliber as standard. The Portuguese call this weapon Rifle 7.62mm M/961. The 7.62mm NATO FN FAL rifle is also used.

Submachine Guns: 9mm M1934 Bergmann, 9mm M/43 (Sten), 9mm Model 48 F.B.P., 9mm M/42 (Schmeisser).

Machine Guns: Cal. .303 Lewis M/917 (same as British Mark I Lewis).
Cal. .303 Vickers M/917 (same as British MK 1 Vickers).
7.92mm Breda M/938 (Breda M1937 in 7.92mm).
7.92 Madsen M/940.
Cal. .303 M/931 (Vickers Berthier).
7.92mm Dreyse M/938 (same as German MG 13).
Cal. .303 M/43 (Bren).
Cal. .303 M/930 (Madsen).

PORTUGUESE PISTOLS

The only pistol used by the Portuguese not used by any other country was the 7.65mm (.32 ACP) Savage M1907 and M1915 pistols, called the M/908 and M/915 pistols by the Portuguese. Although these pistols have been or are being disposed of by the Portuguese government, they are interesting weapons and bear some description.

The Savage Model 1907 is based on the patents of E. H. Searle, first issued in 1904. The weapon is delayed blowback and has an action similar in some respects to the Model 12 Steyr. A lug on the top of the barrel is butted against a cam surface on the top underside of the slide. The cam surface is initially angled and then parallel to the axis of the bore, causing the barrel to rotate, delaying the action slightly, although the system starts opening from the moment of firing. The M/908 has a rounded and notched cocking lever, which has the appearance of and is mounted in the position of a hammer. The striker of the Savage pistols is spring loaded and is released by the sear. The cocking lever does not strike the firing pin as does the hammer

7.65mm Model 915 Pistol.

in the Colt Browning design. The cocking lever of the M/908 should not be let down with a cartridge in the chamber.

PORTUGUESE 7.65mm M/915 PISTOL

The M/915 differs from the M/908 mainly in that it has a spur type cocking lever rather than the rounded type used on the M/908. The M/915 has a greater number of grasping grooves to assist in pulling the slide to the rear than does the M/908. The spur-type cocking lever was introduced in the Savage commercial pistols in 1917. The Model 908 is 6.5 inches overall with a 3.8-inch barrel and weighs 1.2 pounds. It has a 10-round, staggered row, box magazine. Characteristics of the Model 915 are generally similar.

PORTUGUESE RIFLES

PORTUGUESE 6.5mm M1904 MAUSER-VERGUEIRO RIFLE

The only rifle used by Portugal that is unique to that country is the 6.5mm Model 1904 Mauser-Vergueiro. This weapon is somewhat peculiar in that its bolt handle seats ahead of the receiver bridge, like that of the Mannlicher or the Italian Mannlicher Carcano, rather than behind the receiver bridge as with most Mausers. The Model 1904 also has a separate bolt head;

the trigger mechanism, bolt stop and ejector are of Mauser 98 type, but this weapon has no bolt sleeve; therefore the safety is attached to the cocking piece.

These rifles were all made by D.W.M. and originally chambered for the 6.5 × 58mm cartridge, which was used only as a military cartridge by Portugal. During the thirties, some of these weapons were converted to 7.92mm. This rifle is not likely to be found in service at present.

Model 1904 6.5mm Rifle.

PORTUGUESE SUBMACHINE GUN

The 9mm Parabellum Model 43 F.B.P. is the only submachine gun of Portuguese design in service with the Portuguese army. All other weapons in service are covered under their country of origin.

THE 9mm MODEL 48 F.B.P.

There are no unusual features in the design of this weapon. It has a massive bolt and a telescoping operating spring assembly as originated by Erma and made famous by the MP38 and MP40. This weapon is made in Portugal.

Characteristics of the Model 48 F.B.P.

Caliber: 9mm Parabellum.
System of operation: Blowback, automatic only.
Weight, empty: 8.2 lbs.
Length overall: Stock extended, 32 in.; stock folded: 25 in.
Barrel length: 9.8 in.
Sights: Front: Blade.
  Rear: Fixed aperture graduated for 100 meters.
Feed device: 32-round, detachable staggered row, box magazine.
Muzzle velocity: 2600 f.p.s. (approx).
Cyclic rate: 500 r.p.m.

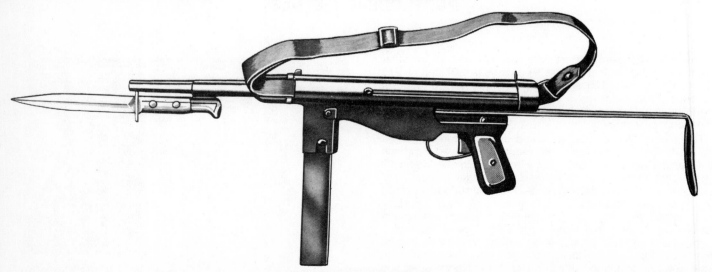

9mm Model 48 F.B.P. Submachine Gun.

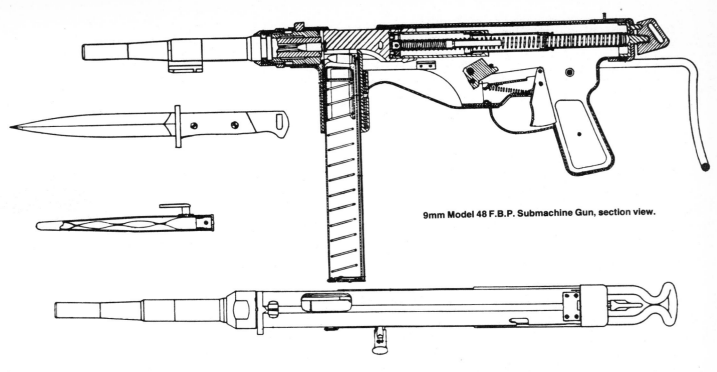

9mm Model 48 F.B.P. Submachine Gun, section view.

PORTUGUESE MACHINE GUNS

There are no machine guns in service in the Portuguese Army of Portuguese origin. The 7.92mm M/938 is not covered in detail under Germany, its country of origin; therefore, some details on this weapon are given here.

THE 7.92mm M/938 MACHINE GUN

This weapon is the German MG13, which was sold by Germany to Portugal in 1938. It was used as the standard German light machine gun until the adoption of the MG34. The weapon is a modified Dreyse M1918.

Characteristics of M/938 Machine Gun

Caliber: 7.92mm.
System of operation: Recoil, selective fire.

Weight: 26.4 lbs.
Length, overall: 57 in. (approx).
Barrel length: 28.25 in.
Sights: Front: Folding blade.
         Rear: Tangent leaf.
Cyclic rate: 750 r.p.m.
Feed device: 25-round box magazine or 75-round saddle drum.
Muzzle velocity: 2600 f.p.s. (approx).

Special Note on the M/938 Machine Gun

It should be noted that this weapon uses two features also found on the later MG34; the trigger with two half-moon sections, which are used for either automatic or semiautomatic fire, depending on whether the bottom or the top section of the trigger is squeezed; and the saddle drum magazine. (However, the mounting of the saddle drum on the MG34 is different.)

Portuguese 7.92mm M/938 Machine Gun.

The Romanian Army is currently equipped with Soviet service weapons or Romanian copies of these weapons. The 7.62mm Tokarev TT33 and other Soviet service pistols are used, as are the 7.62mm SKS carbine and the 7.62mm AKM assault rifle. Machine guns in use include the 7.62mm RPD light machine gun, the 7.62mm RP46 light machine gun, the 7.62mm SGM and SG43 heavy machine guns and the 12.7mm DShK M1938/46 heavy machine gun.

Older Soviet weapons such as the 7.62mm PPSh M1941 submachine gun, the 7.62mm Model 1944 Mosin-Nagant carbine, and the 7.62mm DP and DPM light machine guns may still be found.

38 Romania

ROMANIAN PISTOLS

The principal pistols in service in the Romanian Army prior to World War II were the Austrian 9mm Model 12 Steyr and the 9mm FN Browning Hi-Power. Since World War II, the 7.62mm Tokarev TT M1933 and other Soviet pistols have been used.

ROMANIAN RIFLES

In 1892, Romania adopted a 6.5mm Mannlicher Rifle. The Romanian 6.5mm cartridge is the same as that used by the Dutch and is known as the 6.5mm Model 93 or the 6.5 × 53mm R. The Romanian Mannlicher is a turn-bolt type with typical removable bolt head and clip-loading magazine with a clip that functions as part of the magazine, as with the US M1 rifle.

The 1892 and Model 1893 Mannlicher rifles differ only in sight graduations, position of the ejector (on the bolt on the Model 1892 and on the receiver on the Model 1893) and in the presence of a stacking rod on the left side of the upper band of the Model 1893.

The Model 1893 rifle differs from the Dutch Model 1895 only in minor details. A carbine version of the Mannlicher was also used by the Romanians.

After World War I, Romania obtained considerable quantities of French equipment, including 8mm Mannlicher Berthier rifles and carbines. The 7.92mm Czech Model 24 rifle and Austrian 8mm Model 1895 rifles and carbines were also in service. The Model 24 was manufactured in Romania. The Romanian Army was initially equipped with various models of the Soviet 7.62mm Mosin Nagant rifles. The Soviet 7.62mm SKS carbine and 7.62mm AK assault rifle are the current standard rifles. Characteristics of the rifles other than the Romanian Mannlicher are given under country of origin.

Romania now manufactures a modified copy of the Soviet 7.62mm AKM. The Romanian AKM has a vertical fore grip that extends downward from the fore-end.

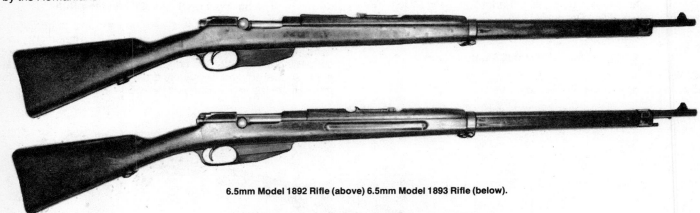

6.5mm Model 1892 Rifle (above) 6.5mm Model 1893 Rifle (below).

CHARACTERISTICS OF ROMANIAN RIFLES

	Rifle M1892	Rifle M1893	Carbine M1893
Caliber:	6.5 × 53mmR.	6.5 × 53mm R.	6.5 × 53mm R.
System of operation:	Turn bolt.	Turn bolt.	Turn bolt.
Length overall:	48.3 in.	48.3 in.	37.5 in.
Barrel length:	28.5 in.	28.6 in.	17.7 in.
Feed device:	5-round, in-line, non-detachable box magazine		
Sights: Front:	Barley corn.	Barley corn.	Barley corn.
Rear:	Leaf.	Leaf.	Leaf.
Weight:	8.9 lb.	9 lb.	7.25 lb.
Muzzle velocity:	Approx. 2400 f.p.s.	Approx. 2400 f.p.s.	Approx. 2325 f.p.s.

Romanian modification of 7.62mm AKM Assault Rifle.

ROMANIAN SUBMACHINE GUNS

Prior to World War II, the Romanian government purchased 9mm Parabellum Model 1938A Beretta submachine guns and during the war purchased 9mm Parabellum Beretta 38/42 submachine guns.

THE 9mm MODEL 1941 ORITA SUBMACHINE GUN

The only notable weapon of Romanian design that was used during World War II was the Orita submachine gun. This weapon has been replaced by Soviet weapons in Romania at the present time but is covered as a matter of interest.

There is also a version of the Orita submachine gun with a folding metal stock.

Characteristics of Model 1941 Orita Submachine Gun

Caliber: 9mm Parabelum.
System of operation: Blowback, selective fire.
Weight, loaded: 8.8 lbs.
Length, overall: 35.2 in.
Barrel length: 11.3 in.
Feed device: 32-round, staggered row, detachable box magazine.
Sights: Front: Hooded blade.
    Rear: Open V, adjustable, graduated from 100 to 500 meters.
Muzzle velocity: 1280 f.p.s.
Cyclic rate of fire: 400 r.p.m.

Romanian 9mm Orita submachine gun.

ROMANIAN MACHINE GUNS

The Romanians used a rather mixed collection of machine guns prior to World War II. The French 8mm Model 1915 light machine gun (Chauchats), 8mm Model 1914 Hotchkiss, Schwarzlose 8mm Model 1907/12 and the 7.92mm Czech ZB30 were all used. The ZB30 was made in Romania at Cugir.

There were probably other types of machine guns in service, as well.

Spain

The Spanish Army is equipped with the following weapons: the 9mm Super Star pistol, the 9mm Star Model Z45 submachine gun, the Star 9mm Model Z-62 submachine gun, the 7.92mm Model 43 rifle, the 7.62mm NATO Model 1916 carbine, the 7.62mm NATO Model 58 assault rifle, the 7.62mm NATO FAO59 light machine gun, the 7.92 mm FAO light machine gun and the 7.92mm ALFA 1944 heavy machine gun. Spain also adopted the 7.62mm NATO MG 42/59. A quantity has been purchased from Rheinmettal, and series manufacture is being carried on at Oviedo. The US caliber .30 and .50 Browning machine guns are in use on US armored vehicles in the Spanish Army.

39

SPANISH PISTOLS

The first automatic pistol adopted by Spain was the 9mm Campo Giro Model 1913. This pistol was chambered for the 9mm Bergmann Bayard cartridge, which is called the 9mm Largo in Spain. The Campo Giro was the basic model of the well-known Astra pistol. It is basically a blowback operated pistol with a very heavy recoil spring wrapped around the barrel; it is the product of Unceta and Company, originally of Eibar. The pistol was modified slightly in 1916 and issued as the Model 1913-16.

In 1921, the Astra Model 400 (commercial designation), which had the official Spanish government designation of Model 1921, was adopted. The Astra 400 is a most unusual pistol in that it will chamber and fire the following cartridges: 9mm Largo, 9mm Parabellum, 9mm Steyr, 9mm Browning long and the .38 super automatic cartridge. The military issue pistol has wooden grips and does not have the full commercial markings. The commercial Astra 400 has hard rubber grips, commercial markings, and many of the small components are nickeled or chromed. The commercial model was sold widely throughout the world.

A later model, the 9mm Parabellum Astra Model 600, never used as a Spanish service weapon, was made in limited quantities for the Germans during World War II; it differs from the Model 400 only in minor details. A post-World War II version of the 9mm Parabellum Model 600—the Condor—has been introduced by Astra. This pistol, although not a standard service pistol, is easily adaptable for such use. Unlike the earlier Astra Models 400 and 600, it has an external hammer.

Unceta and Company produced a copy of the 7.63mm Mauser military model pistol after World War I, several of which were selective-fire weapons. The semiautomatic Astra Model

9mm Model 1921 Astra Pistol.

9mm Astra Condor Pistol.

9mm Campo Giro Model 1913-1916.

900 is a copy of the Mauser, with shoulder-stock holster. The Model 902, also known as the Model "F", is a selective-fire weapon, generally similar to the Model 1932 Mauser. These weapons have been used by police and gendarmerie units throughout the world, but they were not used as Spanish service pistols.

At this point, a bit of history relating to the manufacture of Spanish pistols between World Wars I and II is in order. Many "job shop" copies of standard Smith & Wesson revolvers and cheap blowback automatics were made in Spain during the twenties and early thirties. These weapons were frequently made of poor materials; they are commonly known as Spanish "booby traps" and gave Spanish-made arms a poor name.

9mm Largo Llama Pistol Mark IX.

9mm Astra Model 400 Pistol (above); 9mm Parabellum Model 600 Pistol. (below).

Caliber .32 Llama Pistol.

7.63mm Astra Model 902 in shoulder stock holster.

7.63mm Star Pistol Carbine Model "A".

7.63mm Astra Model 902 with shoulder stock holster attached.

Spanish "Star" Automatic Pistol, caliber .45, Model M.

Unceta, the manufacturers of Astra pistols; Gabilondo, the manufacturers of Ruby revolvers and Llama pistols; and Star Bonifacio Echeverria S.A. all made quality weapons throughout this period and still do. World War II and large military export orders brought tighter proof laws to Spain. Only good quality weapons are exported currently.

The "Llama" pistol made by Gabilondo is basically a copy of the US caliber .45 Model 1911 Colt automatic in the heavier calibers and blowback edition of the Colt Model 1911 in the lighter calibers, i.e., caliber .22, .32 and .380. Differences between these pistols and the Colt are superficial. The Llama has had limited Spanish military use in caliber 9mm Largo but has been mainly a police and commercial weapon. Like the Astra and the Star, the Llama has been used as a substitute standard wartime pistol by countries other than Spain.

Star Bonifacio Echeverria S.A., of Eibar, has produced a number of military type pistols, some of which have been used as substitute standard in foreign armies and several of which have been used by the Spanish Army as regulation weapons. The Star, in the higher-powered models, is similar to the US .45 Model 1911 but does not have a grip safety.

During the twenties, Star introduced the caliber 7.63mm Pistol Carbine Model "A". This weapon was adapted for use with a shoulder-stock holster and fitted with a tangent type rear sight. There are two versions of this pistol: one with a five-inch barrel and one with a 6.5-inch barrel. It was never adopted as a standard service pistol.

The 9mm Largo Star Model "A" pistol was adopted as a Spanish standard pistol prior to World War II. This pistol, chambered for the 9mm Parabellum cartridge, was purchased by a number of governments during World War II. This pistol was made in very large quantities and is quite common throughout the world.

A selective-fire version of the Model "A" was produced during

the thirties as the Model "M". This weapon was made in caliber .45 and possibly in other calibers as well. It was sold to Nicaragua in limited quantities. Cyclic rate is reported to be 800 rounds per minute. The selector switch is mounted on the right side of the slide. The selective-fire feature of this weapon is very impracticable, since the weapon is impossible to control in automatic fire.

As with the Llama, a number of simple blowback versions of the "Star" in calibers .22, .32 and .380 were and are being produced. Many of these models outwardly resemble the US .45 Colt Model 1911.

SPANISH 9mm SUPER STAR PISTOL

The Super Star is the standard Spanish service pistol. Although it outwardly resembles the US caliber .45 M1911A1 pistol, the locking mechanism resembles that of the FN Browning Hi-Power. The barrel is cammed into and out of its locked position in the receiver by the action of the slide stop pin on a cam-way cut in a lug on the rear underside of the barrel.

The Super Star is field stripped by pushing down and forward on the dismounting lever mounted on the right side of the receiver. The slide, with barrel and recoil spring plug, can then be slid off the receiver from the front. After the slide is removed from the receiver, the recoil spring with guide, recoil spring plug and barrel bushing can be removed from the slide. The Super Star has a pivoting trigger rather than the sliding trigger of the US M1911A1. There is no grip safety on the Super Star. This pistol is of good design and construction and is sold commercially in caliber .380, Super .38 automatic and 9mm Parabellum.

Spanish 9mm Super Star Pistol.

SPANISH SERVICE PISTOLS

	Campo Grio Model 1913-16	Model 1921 Astra	Super Star	Star Model "A"
Caliber:	9mm Largo.	9mm Largo.*	9mm Largo.	9mm Largo.
System of operation:	Blowback, semiautomatic.	Blowback, semiautomatic.	Recoil, semiautomatic.	Recoil, semiautomatic.
Length overall:	9.7 in.	8.7 in.	8.03 in.	7.95 in.
Barrel length:	6.7 in.	5.9 in.	5.25 in.	5 in.
Feed device:	8-round, in line, detachable box magazine.	8-round, in line, detachable box magazine.	9-round, in line, detachable box magazine.	8-round, in line, detachable box magazine.
Sights: Front:	Blade.	Blade.	Blade.	Blade.
Rear:	"U" notch.	Square notch.	"V" notch.	"V" notch.
Weight:	2.1 lb.	2.1 lb.	2.21 lb.	2.21 lb.
Muzzle velocity:	Approx 1210 f.p.s.	Approx. 1210 f.p.s.	Approx. 1200 f.p.s.	Approx. 1200 f.p.s.

*This weapon will also chamber and fire: the 9mm Steyr, 9mm Parabellum, .38 Super Auto, and the 9mm Browning Long.

Section view of M1893 Mauser.

7mm M1893 Short Rifle.

7mm Model 1916 Short Rifle.

7.92mm "Standard Model" Mauser.

7.92mm Model 1943 Rifle.

SPANISH RIFLES

Spain adopted its first Mauser in 1891, chambered for the 7.65mm Mauser cartridge. A rifle and carbine version of this weapon, closely resembling the Argentine Model 1891, were each produced. A considerable quantity of these weapons, especially the carbines, were captured by United States troops in Cuba during the Spanish-American War. The 1891 has an in-line type magazine, which protrudes below the stock. The 1892 Mauser adopted by Spain introduced the 7mm cartridge and the non-rotating extractor attached to the bolt by a collar, which is found on later Mausers and the US Springfield Model 1903.

The most famous and most significant of the Spanish Mausers was the 7mm Model 1893. The Model 1893 introduced the integral staggered-row box magazine used in all future Mausers. The Model 1893 also had a simplified safety lock and an improved bolt stop. A carbine version of this weapon is the 7mm Model 1895, which is stocked to the muzzle as was the fashion with Mauser carbines in those days.

The Model 1893 bolt does not have a third or safety lug or the enlarged shield on the bolt sleeve, as does the Model 98 bolt and bolt sleeve. A number of variations of the Model 1893, in addition to the Model 1895 carbine, were made.

A short rifle version of the Model 1893, and a 1916 short rifle, were also issued. The Model 1916 short rifle was made in very large quantities during the Spanish Civil war. Stocks of 7mm M1893 rifles and 7mm M1916 short rifles on hand were converted to 7.62mm NATO, probably for issue to reserve forces.

During the Spanish Civil war, large quantities of French, Soviet, Italian and German rifles came into Spain. The "Standard Model" Mauser was among the weapons procured by Spain at this time. It was chambered for the 7.92mm cartridge, the standard rifle and machine-gun service cartridge, until 1957.

In 1943, Spain adopted a modified copy of the German 7.92mm Kar 98k, which in the Spanish service is called the Model 1943. This rifle has been replaced by the 7.62mm NATO CETME Model 58 assault rifle, which was adopted in September 1957.

Spanish 7mm Model 1893 Mauser Rifle.

THE 7.62mm NATO CETME MODEL 58 ASSAULT RIFLE

CETME, the Centro de Estudios Tecnicos de Materials Especiales, a Spanish government research establishment, has produced a number of interesting weapon designs, but the CETME assault rifle is by far the most successful of their efforts. See Chapter 1 for further background.

How to Load and Fire the CETME Assault Rifle

Insert a loaded magazine in the magazine well. Pull the operating handle located on the left side of the operating rod (above the barrel) to the rear and release it. If the selector lever has been set on the letter "T," the bolt will run home, chambering a cartridge, and the weapon will fire single rounds when the trigger is pulled. If the selector has been set on the letter "R," the bolt will remain to the rear when cocked. When the trigger is pulled, the weapon will deliver automatic fire. The CETME commences semiautomatic fire from a closed bolt and automatic fire from an open bolt. The operating handle does not reciprocate with the bolt. To put the weapon on SAFE, set the selector lever on the letter "S."

How to Field Strip the CETME Assault Rifle

Remove the magazine by pushing on the magazine catch. Remove the two pins at the rear of the pistol grip-trigger assembly and pull off the stock to the rear. Pull the operating handle to the rear and remove the bolt assembly. No further disassembly is recommended. To reassemble the weapon, perform the above steps in reverse order.

How the CETME Assault Rifle Works

The bolt in this weapon is composed of two major parts: the head and the rear section. The head, which contains the locking rollers, is considerably smaller than the rear section, which contains the firing pin. The two bolt sections are joined together so that they can move horizontally with respect to each other. The large rear section of the bolt has a nose end that is pointed to fit in the head of the bolt. When the bolt runs home, this nose end enters the head of the bolt and cams the locking rollers into their locking recesses in the receiver. When the cartridge is fired, the pressure on the base of the cartridge, after a period of time, forces the locking rollers back against the nose of the rear bolt section. The rear bolt section, which is held in position only by the energy of the recoil spring, starts to the rear. The bolt is unlocked and the firing pin drawn to the rear, away from the primer, by the rearward movement of the rear bolt section.

Special Note on the CETME Assault Rifle

The CETME assault rifle is worthy of note in several respects. It is composed mainly of stampings, and CETME claims that the weapon can be made in a total working time of nine hours in series manufacture. There are fewer than twenty parts that require machining. The weapon is fitted with a bipod, which, when folded, serves as a fore-end. When supported on the bipod, the gun can be used as a squad automatic weapon. There is, however, one unfortunate aspect to the delayed-blowback system, and this applies to other weapons as well as to the CETME. The system makes no allowance for slow initial extraction, i.e., for a small turning or a short rearward movement of the bolt to loosen up the spent case before it is withdrawn from the receiver. Delayed-blowback action bolts start to the rear with considerable velocity when the pressure arrives at their opening

CETME field stripped.

Section view of CETME.

"**Sport**" **model of 7.6mm NATO CETME Assault Rifle; fires semiautomatic only.**

level. Therefore, delayed-blowback weapons depend on lubricated (oiled) cases, as with the Schwarzlose and Breda Model 30, or on fluted chambers, to make up for their lack of slow initial extraction. Lubricating prevents the case from expanding fully against the walls of the chamber and a fluted chamber allows the forward part of the case to float on gas and therefore not expand completely to the walls of the chamber. Without lubricated cases or fluted chambers (the degree of fluting varies from three-quarters the length of the chamber to only the length of the neck and shoulder), a delayed-blowback may pull the base off the case in extraction. These weapons must therefore be designed around brass cartridges of a certain hardness. If a weapon with a fluted chamber is used with brass considerably softer than that for which it was designed, the brass may be engraved by the flutes, and the bolt may lose enough kinetic energy in extracting the case to prevent it from going into full recoil, with resultant feed jams. It is probable, however, that a delayed blowback designed around the softest brass likely to be encountered in service will do very well with all sorts of brass, hard or soft. Delayed-blowback weapons do not usually give any trouble with steel cases.

Specimens of the CETME assault rifle have also been made of the Soviet 7.62mm M1943 "intermediate-sized" cartridge.

CHARACTERISTICS OF SPANISH RIFLES

	Model 1893	Model 1893 Short Rifle	Model 1895 Carbine	Model 1916 Short Rifle
Caliber:	7mm.	7mm.	7mm.	7mm.
System of operation:	Turn bolt.	Turn bolt.	Turn bolt.	Turn bolt.
Length overall:	48.6 in.	41.3 in.	37 in.	40.9 in.
Barrel length:	29.1 in.	21.75 in.	17.56 in.	Approx 23.6 in.
Feed device:	5-round, staggered row, non-detachable, box magazine.	5-round, staggered row, non-detachable, box magazine.	5-round, staggered row, non-detachable, box magazine.	5-round, staggered row, non-detachable, box magazine.
Sights: Front:	Barley corn.	Barley corn.	Barley corn w/ears.	Barley corn w/ears.
Rear:	Leaf.	Leaf.	Leaf.	Tangent.
Weight:	8.8 lb.	8.3 lb.	7.5 lb.	8.4 lb.
Muzzle velocity:	2650 f.p.s.	Approx 2650 f.p.s.	Approx 2575 f.p.s.	Approx 2625 f.p.s.
Cyclic rate:	--------------	--------------	--------------	--------------

CHARACTERISTICS OF SPANISH RIFLES (Cont'd)

	Mauser Standard Rifle	Model 1943	CETME Model 58
Caliber:	7.92mm.	7.92mm.	7.62mm NATO.
System of operation:	Turn bolt.	Turn bolt.	Delayed blowback selective fire.
Length overall:	43.6 in.	43.7 in.	39.37 in.
Barrel length:	23.62 in.	Approx 23.7 in.	Approx 17 in.
Feed device:	5-round, staggered row, non-detachable, box magazine.	5-round, staggered row, non-detachable, box magazine.	20-round, staggered row, detachable, box magazine.
Sights: Front:	Barley corn.	Barley corn.	Hooded blade.
Rear:	Tangent.	Tangent.	Tangent.
Weight:	8.8 lb.	8.8 lb.	11.32 lb.
Muzzle velocity:	2360 f.p.s.	2360 f.p.s.	2493 f.p.s.
Cyclic rate:	--------------	--------------	600 r.p.m.

SPANISH SUBMACHINE GUNS

A considerable number of submachine guns have been developed in Spain, and copies of foreign submachine guns have been made, as well. Prior to World War II, a modified copy of the Bergmann MP 28 II, chambered for the 9mm Largo (Bergmann Bayard), was made in Spain in limited numbers. This weapon is distinguishable from the Standard MP28II by its oversized bolt handle, sling swivels and the brass trigger guard and magazine housing.

The Spaniards also manufactured a modified copy of the Vollmer Erma chambered for the 9mm Largo cartridge, which they called the Model 1941/44. The weapon was made at La Coruna until the mid-fifties. The principal difference between the German-produced weapon and the Spanish-produced weapon is that the Spanish weapon has a completely different type of safety from that used on the German weapon.

The Star firm designed a series of submachine guns in the mid-thirties known as the SI35, RU35 and TN35. The SI35 had an adjustable cyclic rate of fire, 300 or 700 rounds per minute. The RU35 has a cyclic rate of 300 rounds per minute and the TN35 has a cyclic rate of 700 rounds per minute. A limited number of the SI35 and RU35 guns were used in the Spanish Civil war, but the weapon was never standard in the Spanish Army.

The Star TN35 was tested by the United States as the "Atlantic" submachine gun in 1942 but was not found acceptable for service. The British and Germans also apparently tested guns of this series but were not interested. All activity on these guns ceased about 1942.

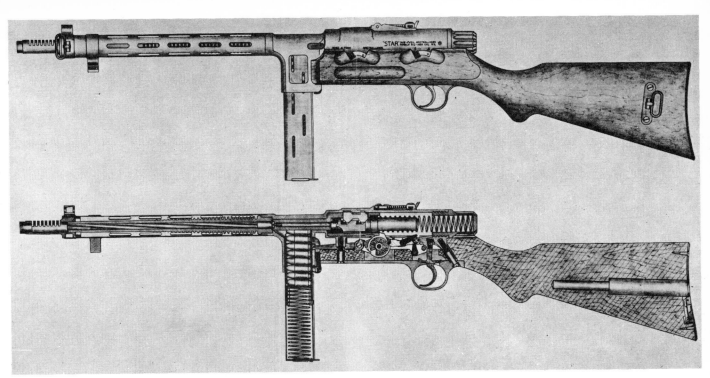

9mm Star Model R.U.-1935 Submachine Gun.

Star 9mm Z45 Submachine Gun.

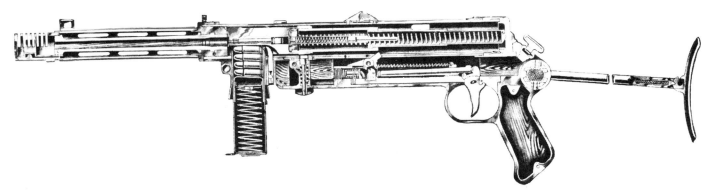

Section view of the Star Z45.

CHARACTERISTICS OF SPANISH SERVICE SUBMACHINE GUNS

	Model Z-45	Parinco Model 3R	A.D.A.S.A. Model 1953	Star Model Z-62
Caliber:	9mm Largo.	9mm Largo.	9mm Largo or 9mm Parabellum.	9mm Largo, also made in 9mm Parabellum.
System of operation:	Blowback, selective fire.	Blowback, selective fire.	Blowback, selective fire.	Blowback, selective fire.
Length overall:				
Stock extended:	33.1 in.	31.4 in.	31.9 in.	27.6 in.
Stock folded:	23 in.	24.4 in.	24 in.	18.9 in.
Barrel length:	7.9 in.	10 in.	9.85 in.	7.9 in.
Feed device:	30-round, staggered-row detachable box magazine.	32-round, staggered row detachable box magazine.	30-round in-line, detachable box magazine.	20-, 30- or 40-round. detachable box magazine.
Sights: Front:	Blade w/protecting ears.	Blade.	Hooded blade.	Blade
Rear:	L-type w/notch	Notch.	L-type w/notch.	"L" w/apertures for 100 and 200 meters
Weight:	10 lb. (loaded).	6.8 lb.	7 lb.	6.3 lb w/empty 30-round magazine
Muzzle velocity:	1250 f.p.s.	Approx. 1270 f.p.s.	Approx. 1270 f.p.s.	Approx. 1200-1800 f.p.s.
Cyclic rate:	450 r.p.m.	600 r.p.m.	600 r.p.m.	550 r.p.m.

The Labora 1938, sometimes known as the Fontbernat, is another Spanish designed submachine gun that was made in limited quanitites during the Spanish Civil war. Other than being made out of expensive machined material during a war and having a push-button type selector, the Labora has no unusual or unique features. In 1953, another submachine gun developed by CETME was introduced. This weapon, known as the A.D.A.S.A. Model 1953, will fire either the 9mm Largo cartridge or the 9mm Parabellum. The weapon resembles the Soviet PPS M1943 and was apparently made in very limited quantity for the Spanish Air Force.

In 1959, the Parinco Model 3R was patented. This is another blowback-operated weapon that has appeared in several forms. The Parinco has a plastic frame and trigger housing and a grip safety. The trigger group can be rotated on a pin mounted behind the magazine housing and swung down away from the receiver for maintenance and cleaning. The Parinco has been made in 9mm Parabellum and 9mm Largo.

The standard submachine gun of the Spanish Army is the Star Model Z45, which is modeled on the MP40 and differs from that weapon only in the following:

(1) The bolt handle of the Z45 is on the right rather than on the left as on the MP40.

(2) The Z45 has a metal barrel jacket; the MP40 has none.

(3) The barrel and jacket of the Z45 can be removed rapidly by twisting the compensator. The barrel of the MP40 is not easily removable.

(4) The Z45 is a selective-fire weapon; the MP40 has only automatic fire capability.

(5) The Z45 has wooden grips and handguard; the grips and handguard of the MP40 are plastic.

The Z45 has been made with a fixed wooden stock in addition to the more common folding steel stock.

The Z45 has been supplied to Chile, Cuba, Portugal and Saudi Arabia.

Star has developed a later weapon, the Z62, which is a very compact weapon with a tubular steel combined barrel jacket/receiver similar to the British L2A3 Sterling submachine gun.

Characteristics are limited to current Spanish service submachine guns of Spanish origin; other submachine guns used by Spain are covered under country of origin.

THE STAR Z-62 SUBMACHINE GUN

This weapon has been adopted by the *Guardia Civil* and the Army of Spain. It has a number of interesting features and is a considerable improvement over the Z-45 in lightness and and bulk, safety, maintenance and reliability under rigorous service conditions, i.e. sand, mud etc.

How to Load and Fire the Z-62

The magazine is loaded in the normal fashion. If the weapon has a magazine in place, it can be removed by depressing the magazine catch, which is on the left side of the magazine housing. Insert loaded magazine in magazine housing as far as it will go. Unlock—pull rearward—the cocking handle located on the left forward side of the barrel jacket. Pull cocking handle completely to the rear and release. The cocking handle will return to the forward position, fold and lock itself to the barrel jacket. The weapon is now cocked and ready to fire; pressure on the lower part of the trigger produces semiautomatic fire, and pressure on the top of the trigger produces automatic fire. To put the weapon on "safe", push the safety button, located in the upper section of the pistol grip, from right to left. This blocks the sear with the bolt in either open or closed (battery) position. If the bolt is forward when the safety is engaged, it cannot be drawn to the rear.

9mm Star Model Z-62 Submachine Gun.

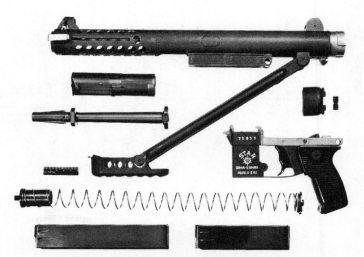

9mm Star Model Z-62 Submarine Gun field stripped.

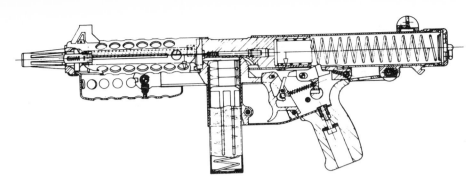

Sectional view of 9mm Star Model Z-62 Submachine Gun.

How to Field Strip the Z-62

Remove the magazine as described above. Push the recoil spring stop, which protrudes through the middle of the receiver cap, in and rotate the receiver cap either way until it disengages from its mounting lugs on the receiver. Carefully remove cap—which is under the tension of the operating spring—and withdraw recoil spring with recoil spring stop and guide. Point the weapon downward and draw cocking handle to the rear; release cocking handle, tilt gun up and the bolt will slide out the rear. The pistol grip/frame can be removed by pushing out the pin mounted at the top rear. The stock must be fixed before the pistol grip/frame can be removed. After the pin, which has a ball type retaining catch, has been removed, the pistol grip/frame can be swung down and disengaged from its mounting in the lower front of the receiver. Grasp barrel at the muzzle and rotate it clockwise a quarter of a turn and tilt the weapon down and slightly to the right. Let the barrel slide back and out of the receiver, ensuring that the "U" shaped notch below the breech is in line with the bolt guide lugs on the inner right face of the receiver.

How the Z-62 Works

The Z-62 is a blowback operated gun and in most respects is conventional enough. It does however have some unusual fea-tures which are very interesting. Most submachine guns are potentially dangerous if dropped when the bolt is forward and a loaded magazine is in place. Unless the bolt is locked in place by a grip safety or manual safety, the bolt may go to the rear just far enough to pick up and fire a cartridge. The Z-62 has solved this problem in an unusual way. In the bolt, behind the spring loaded firing pin, are mounted a hammer and a spring loaded inertia bolt safety. The hammer engages the firing pin when a rod-shaped piece, called the tripping lever, engages the hammer. The tripping lever protrudes through the bolt, and when the bolt engages the rear of the barrel it is forced rearward striking the hammer, which pivots and strikes the firing pin driving it forward to function the cartridge. The bolt inertia safety, which is mounted on the same pin as the hammer, is pushed outward into a recess in the receiver/barrel jacket when the bolt is forward. This prevents the bolt from coming to the rear if the weapon is dropped. The tripping lever disengages this lock at the same time as it strikes the hammer, thereby preventing it from interfering with rearward movement of the bolt after firing.

The spring loaded cocking handle and slide assembly do not reciprocate with the bolt, and the automatic folding of the cocking handle makes for ease of handling during firing. Considering everything, the Z-62 is a very well made gun and should be easy to maintain in the field.

SPANISH MACHINE GUNS

The Spaniards adopted the 7mm Hotchkiss machine gun in 1907 and later adopted the Model 1914, similar to the French Model 1914, also in 7mm. The 7mm light Hotchkiss Model II, also called the Model 1922, was adopted by Spain as were the Madsen in 1907 and 1922 models.

During the Spanish Civil war, large quantities of foreign machine guns were shipped into Spain. Among these were French Hotchkiss guns, Soviet 7.62mm Maxim Tokarev, Maxim Ko-leshnikov, and DP machine guns, Czech 7.92mm ZB26, ZB30, and ZB53 (Model 37) machine guns, and various German and Italian machine guns. The Spaniards started the manufacture of a copy of the Czech ZB26 at the Fabrica de Armas de Oviedo chambered for the 7.92mm cartridge and called it the FAO. This weapon was modified to belt feed and rebarreled for the 7.62mm NATO cartridge and is called the FAO Model 59. It is used on a tripod as well as on a bipod. The weapon uses a drum fitted to the left side, which holds a 50-round belt.

Spain developed the 7.92mm ALFA Model 1944 heavy machine gun to replace the somewhat motley collection of heavy machine guns she had previously collected. A later version of the ALFA, the Model 55, is chambered for the 7.62mm NATO cartridge. The Model 55 is shorter than the Model 1944, has a ribbed barrel and has a lighter tripod but is otherwise much the same as the Model 1944. It is probable that all these weapons will be replaced by the 7.62mm NATO MG 42/59.

THE 7.92mm ALFA MACHINE GUN MODEL 1944

The ALFA resembles the Breda Model 1937 in some respects. A quantity of these weapons were exported to Egypt prior to 1952.

7mm Model 1922 Hotchkiss Light Machine Gun. This specimen is missing a pistol grip.

How to Load and Fire the Alfa Machine Gun

Pull the charging handle to the rear, and release; it will return to its forward position. Insert the end tab of the belt in the feed port on the left side of the receiver, and pull it through the ejection port on the right side of the receiver. Lift the safety lever from the trigger and press the trigger. The weapon will fire; when the trigger is released, the safety lever will again snap into place.

How to Field Strip the Alfa

Cock the gun, to permit the operating rod to clear the gas-port collar. Remove the knurled handle of the barrel latch from the locking recess in the receiver and rotate the latch to lock the handle in the upper locking recess. This operation will permit the barrel to pass through the groove cut in the barrel latch, and will also retract the operating rod housing tube out of the gas chamber.

Grasp the barrel handle and rotate the barrel to the right until it is arrested by the stop in the receiver. At this point the interrupted thread will disengage, and the barrel can be pulled forward and out of the receiver.

To remove the feeder mechanism support, grasp the support retainer key (linchpin) by its handle, and slide it back out of the keyway in the support. Remove the support by pulling it out the left side of the receiver.

To remove the operating spring and guide, release the operating rod by firing the trigger. Press the head of the guide rod and rotate it a quarter-turn to the left, so that the keys on the rod will be in line with the keyways on the backplate. The operating rod spring will force both the rod and spring through the hole, facilitating its removal.

To remove the backplate, remove the backplate retainer pin. If the backplate does not drop out, hit it with a wooden or fiber hammer. The backplate will slide out of the grooves in the receiver.

To remove the sear housing, pull the housing back out of the receiver.

To remove the charging handle, pull the handle back to the end of the slot and then to the right, away from the receiver.

To remove the operating rod and bolt assembly (removal of the charging handle leaves the operating rod partly out of the receiver), a slight pull is necessary. To disassemble the bolt from the operating rod, retract the bolt until the locking block engages the cam on the operating rod, and raise the bolt out of its seat.

To remove the ejector, index the ejector 90 degrees and pull out of the receiver.

To reassemble the weapon, reverse the above procedures.

How the Alfa Works

When the cartridge is fired, the pressure of the propellent gases drives the bullet down the bore. As soon as the projectile passes the gas port in the barrel, a portion of the propellent gases will flow through the opening in the regulator and into the gas cylinder. The gases impinge on the piston, driving the operating rod to the rear and compressing the operating rod spring.

As the operating rod moves to the rear, it withdraws the firing pin from the primer and continues until the ramp raises the locking block. The locking block unlocks, and the operating rod and bolt continue to the rear together. Since the spent case is held by the extractor, it is withdrawn from the chamber and carried backward until the base of the case strikes the ejector blade. The blade deflects the case against the rubber deflection pad on the right side of the receiver, and ejects it through the ejection port.

As the operating rod retracts, the lug on the operating rod frees the lower arm of the belt feed lever which, being spring loaded, drags the belt-feed slide from left to right, placing a new cartridge in feeding position before the chamber. The bolt is locked in position before the chamber. The bolt is locked in position by the action of a lug (at the forward end of the central part of the operating rod) resting against the lower arm of the belt feed lever.

The backward motion of the operating rod is limited by the striking of its rear end against the buffer spring.

7.62mm NATO FAO Model 59 Light Machine Gun.

7.92mm FAO Light Machine Gun.

Spanish 7.92mm Alfa Machine Gun M1944.

CHARACTERISTICS OF SPANISH SERVICE MACHINE GUNS

	FAO Model 59	ALFA Model 1944	ALFA Model 55
Caliber:	7.62mm NATO.	7.92mm.	7.62mm NATO.
System of operation:	Gas, automatic only.	Gas, selective fire.	Gas, selective fire.
Length overall:	43.3 in.	Approx. 57 in. (gun).	43.4 in. (gun).
Barrel length:	21.8 in.	29.53 in.	Approx. 24 in.
Feed device:	50-round, metallic link belt, loaded in drum.	100-round, metallic link belt, loaded in drum.	100-round metallic link belt, loaded in drum.
Sights: Front:	Hooded blade.	Blade.	Blade.
Rear:	Radial tangent.	Leaf.	Leaf.
Weight:	Approx. 20 lb.	28.66 lb.	28.6 lb.
Tripod weight:	14.3 lb.	59.5 lb.	59.52 lb.
Muzzle velocity:	Approx. 2800 f.p.s.	2493 f.p.s.	2825 f.p.s.
Cyclic rate:	650 r.p.m.	780 r.p.m.	780 r.p.m.

40

The Swedish Army is currently equipped with the following weapons: 9mm Lahti Model 1940 Pistol, the 9mm Model 45 submachine gun, the 6.5mm Rifle AG42, the 6.5mm Sniper rifle Model 41, the 7.62mm NATO rifle AK4 (modified copy of West German G-3), the 6.5mm or 8mm Model 36 Browning machine gun and the 7.62mm NATO FN Model 58 general purpose machine gun. Sweden has adopted the Heckler and Koch 7.62mm Model 21A light machine gun.

Sweden

SWEDISH PISTOLS

The Swedes adopted a 7.5mm Nagant revolver known as the Model 87. These revolvers remained in limited service until after World War II. Sweden brought the FN 9mm Browning Long M1903 automatic pistol into service as the Model 07. This relatively low-powered, blowback operated pistol was the standard service pistol until the adoption of the 9mm Parabellum Lahti M40 pistol in 1940. A limited number of 9mm Walther P38 pistols were purchased in 1939 and are known in Sweden as the Model 39. The principal Swedish pistol has been the Lahti Model 40.

SWEDISH 9mm LAHTI MODEL 1940 PISTOL

This pistol is basically the same as the Finnish Model 1935 Lahti but differs slightly from the later designed Finnish Lahti in the mounting of the recoil spring. The Model 40 has its grip grooved for a shoulder stock. The Swedish Lahti was manufactured at the Husqvarna Vapenfabrik A.B.

How the Model 40 Works

This pistol is a strange composite of features of the Luger and the Bergmann-Bayard, with several individual characteristics.

As with the Luger, the barrel is screwed into a slide. This slide, however, is enclosed except for an ejection port on the right side and an emergence cut for the breechblock at the rear.

The exterior appearance somewhat resembles the Luger, the pitch of the grip being very much like it.

The takedown also somewhat resembles the Luger. When the breechblock is back, a dismounting lever above the trigger can be turned to release the assemblies. The barrel and breechblock assemblies will then come off the receiver runners to the front.

The recoil spring is positioned in a tunnel in the rear of the separate breechblock. The head of the recoil spring guide rod projects from the rear of the breechblock.

Wings with finger grips are machined at the sides of the rear of the breechblock to permit pulling back for loading.

The breechblock travels in the slide. A surface is machined on its under face to force back and ride over an internal hammer. The firing pin is mounted in a sloped tunnel in the forward section of the breechblock below the recoil spring position.

The breech lock is a separate removable unit. It is housed in the bulge in the extreme rear of the slide. When the pistol is locked, the locking piece is in its slide recesses on right and left and is also in engagement (its inner surfaces) with cuts in the breechblock. During rearward and forward movement, cam

9mm Parabellum Model 40 Pistol.

faces on the sides of the locking piece are utilized to raise and lower the lock out of and into breechblock engagement.

Magazine is the familiar box type. It has a follower button as in the Luger to make loading easier. The button actuates a pivoted stop when the magazine is empty, to hold the action open.

The trigger is pivoted. It has a bar crossing the grip that transmits the pull on the trigger to release the sear. The internal hammer has the conventional hammer strut, which compresses the coil mainspring below it in the handle. The magazine release catch works off the mainspring.

An unusual device is the accelerator in the forward end of the receiver. It is the Browning MG pivoted type. When barrel travel halts, the barrel flips up the point of the accelerator to deliver an accelerating blow to the breechblock to speed up its rearward movement.

The safety is a positive mechanical block, which forces the sear into locked engagement with the hammer notch, making it impossible for the hammer to rotate.

Loading and Firing the Model 40

Grasp wings of breechblock and pull back over loaded magazine. Release breechblock and let recoil spring drive breechblock ahead to chamber a cartridge.

When magazine is empty, breechblock will be held back. Insert a loaded magazine. Pull back slightly on breechblock wings to release the catch and let the breechblock go forward to load.

Field Stripping the Model 40

Pull the breechblock back over empty magazine. Remove magazine. Turn down dismounting lever above trigger. Pull back breechblock to free it from stop. Ease assemblies forward off receiver. Remove breechblock from slide.

Note. Do not unscrew barrel unless necessary.

Removing stocks will give access to firing mechanism if necessary.

Characteristics of the Model 40

Caliber: 9mm Parabellum.
System of operation: Recoil operated, semiautomatic.
Length overall: 10.7 in.
Barrel length: 5.5 in.
Feed device: 8-round in-line detachable box magazine.
Sights: Front: Barley corn.
Rear: "U" notch.
Weight: 2.4 lbs.
Muzzle velocity: Approx. 1250 f.p.s.

SWEDISH RIFLES AND CARBINES

The Swedes adopted a 6.5mm Mauser carbine in 1894. This short and light weapon is now obsolete in the Swedish Army. Its action is the same as the M96 rifle. The M96 is a very accurate weapon for a military rifle, and very good shooting can be done with it, if it is in good condition and if a micrometer rear sight is fitted to the receiver. The Model 38 is a conversion of the M96, into a shorter and lighter weapon. A sniper version of this weapon, called the Model 41, is fitted with a telescope that is also called the Model 41.

The Swedes also used another shoulder weapon, the 8mm M40 rifle. This weapon is a German-produced Kar. 98k rebarreled for the Swedish 8mm × 63mm Bofors M1932 machine gun cartridge. The weapon is fitted with a muzzle brake and has a four-round magazine. It is no longer in Swedish service.

SWEDISH 6.5mm LJUNGMAN SEMIAUTOMATIC RIFLE

In 1942, Sweden adopted the 6.5mm Ljungman semiautomatic rifle. This weapon is called the AG42B by the Swedes. As originally issued, it was called AG42 but after some slight modifications was designated the AG42B. The Ljungman has been manufactured in Egypt in caliber 7.92mm.

The Ljungman gas system is unusual in that it seeks to avoid the use of an intermediary thrusting piston for its actuation.

As the weapon is fired and the bullet passes by the gas port about one-third of the distance from the muzzle, gas is tapped off through a hole into the gas cylinder on top of the barrel in standard fashion. The gas is directed back through the gas cylinder where it impinges upon an extension of the bolt carrier whose forward end passes into a mating receiver cut.

The gas thus delivers its thrust directly to the face of the bolt carrier itself.

The bolt carrier has the customary short free travel in its guides in the receiver, during which time the bolt itself, lying below the carrier, is locked securely to the receiver by lugs at its rear end, being depressed into corresponding receiver cuts.

As the gas pressure drops with the passing of the bullet out of the barrel, cam faces on the bolt carrier engage the bolt and elevate its rear section out of locking engagement. At this point, the bolt and carrier with the empty cartridge case gripped in the face of the extractor travel to the rear to compress the recoil springs in the receiver behind the bolt carrier. During the recoil stroke, the magazine follower and spring elevate the next cartridge into line for feeding. The bolt and carrier at end of stroke move ahead under the thrust of the counter recoiling spring. The top cartridge is stripped from the magazine and fed up the ramp into the chamber. The extractor snaps into the cannelure of the cartridge case. At this point, where the bolt face is halted against the breech face of the barrel, the bolt carrier still has forward travel under the impetus of the spring behind it. Its cam faces thrust the rear of the bolt down into locking recesses in the receiver. The bolt carrier continues forward as a free member from this point. The front face of the bolt carrier rides into a cup-shaped port in the receiver, which forms the emergence port for the gas at the next discharge.

The rifle is equipped with bayonet. The muzzle brake built into the rifle by slotting across the top of the barrel serves to hold the muzzle down to some degree during firing.

The gas system of the Ljungman, in which the gas blows directly back upon the bolt or the bolt carrier, is also used in the French M1949 and M1949/56 and in the United States (Stoner-developed) AR-10 and AR-15 rifles. The Ljungman never replaced the Mauser in Swedish service and was issued on a basis of several per squad.

In 1965, Sweden adopted the 7.62mm NATO G3 rifle with some modifications. The rifle that is to replace the AG42B, the Mausers and the Model 37 Browning automatic rifle will be made at the government Carl Gustafs Stads plant at Eskilstuna and at the Husqvarna firm. The Swedish rifle, which is called the AK4, has a plastic handguard and stock, a modified magazine, and has an aperture type rear sight. The detailed characteristics of the G3 rifle are given in the chapter on West Germany.

CHARACTERISTICS OF SWEDISH RIFLES AND CARBINES

	Model 94 Carbine	Model 96 Rifle	Model 38 Rifle
Caliber:	6.5 × 55mm.	6.5 × 55mm.	6.5 × 55mm.
System of operation:	Turn bolt.	Turn bolt.	Turn bolt.
Length overall:	37.6 in.	49.6 in.	44.1 in.
Barrel length:	17.7 in.	29.1 in.	23.6 in.
Feed device:	5-round, staggered row, non-detachable, box magazine.	5-round, staggered row, non-detachable, box magazine.	5-round, staggered row, non-detachable, box magazine.
Sight: Front:	Barley corn.	Barley corn.	Barley corn.
Rear:	Leaf.	Leaf.	Leaf.
Weight:	7.6 lb.	9.1 lb.	8.5 lb.
Muzzle velocity:	2313 f.p.s.	2625 f.p.s.	2460 f.p.s.

6.5mm Model 94 Carbine.

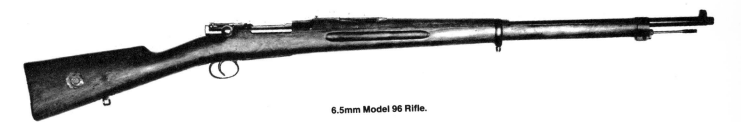

6.5mm Model 96 Rifle.

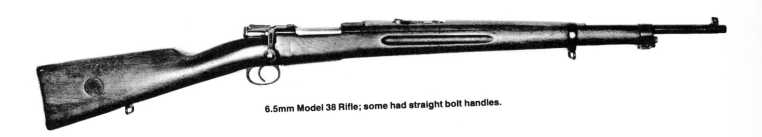

6.5mm Model 38 Rifle; some had straight bolt handles.

8mm Model 40 Rifle. Note muzzle brake.

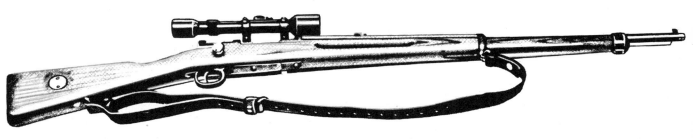

6.5mm Model 41 Rifle. Note scope.

CHARACTERISTICS OF SWEDISH RIFLES AND CARBINES (Cont'd)

	Model 40 Rifle	Model 41 Rifle	Model 42B Rifle
Caliber:	8 × 63mm.	6.5 × 55mm.	6.5 × 55mm.
System of operation:	Turn bolt.	Turn bolt.	Gas-operated, semiautomatic.
Length overall:	Approx 49.2 in.	49.6 in.	47.8 in.
Barrel length:	Approx 29.1 in.	29.1 in.	24.5 in.
Feed device:	4-round, staggered row, non-detachable, box magazine.	5-round, staggered row, non-detachable, box magazine.	10-round, staggered row, non-detachable, box magazine.
Sights: Front:	Barley corn.	3X or 4X telescopic.	Hooded post.
Rear:	Tangent.		Tangent.
Weight:	Approx. 9.5 lb.	11.1 lb.	10.4 lb.
Muzzle velocity:	2428 f.p.s.	2625 f.p.s.	2460 f.p.s.

SWEDISH AUTOMATIC RIFLES

SWEDISH 6.5mm AUTOMATIC RIFLE MODEL 21

Sweden adopted the Browning automatic rifle in 1921, at which time she bought a quantity of these weapons from Colt. The M1921 is now obsolete in Sweden. The weapon is quite similar to the US M1918 BAR except that it has a separate pistol grip and dust covers for the ejection port and the magazine well.

Characteristics of M21

Caliber: 6.5mm × 55mm Mauser rimless cartridge.
System of operation: Gas, selective fire.
Weight: 19.2 lbs.
Length, overall: 44 in. (approx.).
Barrel length: 26.4 in.
Feed device: 20-round, detachable box magazine.
Sights: Front: Blade.
Rear: Leaf w/notch.
Muzzle velocity: 2460 f.p.s. (approx.).
Cyclic rate: 500 r.p.m.

SWEDISH 6.5mm AUTOMATIC RIFLE MODEL 37

Characteristics of Model 37

Caliber: 6.5mm.
System of operation: Gas, selective fire.
Weight: 20.9 lbs.
Length, overall: 46.1 in.
Barrel length: 24 in. (approx.).
Feed device: 20-round, detachable, staggered-row box magazine.
Sights: Front: Hooded blade.
Rear: Leaf w/aperture graduated to 1200 meters, aperture battle sight.
Muzzle velocity: 2460 f.p.s. (approx.).
Cyclic rate: 480 r.p.m.

This modification of the Browning Automatic rifle was developed by the Swedish government arsenal, Carl Gustaf State Arms Factory. It will probably be replaced in the Swedish Army by the 6.5mm Model 58 machine gun.

6.5mm Model 37 Automatic Rifle.

How to Load and Fire the Model 37

Cock the weapon by pulling the operating handle completely to the rear—push operating handle back to the forward position. The bolt will remain open, since the weapon fires from an open bolt. The safety selector lever is on the left side of the receiver at the top of the pistol grip. Settings are marked "P"-semiautomatic fire; "A"—full automatic fire; and "S"—safety. Insert loaded magazine in magazine well in underside of receiver. If the trigger is pulled and safety selector is set on "P" or "A", the weapon will fire.

Barrel Change. Beginning with an empty weapon, cock gun; push barrel latch (located at top left front of receiver) to the rear. Lift carrying handle and turn ¼ turn to the right. Pull barrel out.

Field Stripping the Model 37

Remove the trigger guard retaining pin, located at left forward end of trigger guard. Pull pistol grip backward and upward and remove. The recoil spring guide bears against the rear of the slide; gently push it back and disengage it from the slide. Line up the hammer pin with the holes in the side of the receiver and with the hole in the operating lever. Push hammer pin out from left to right. Remove operating lever by pulling straight back and remove hammer from the receiver. Push out bolt guide with screwdriver blade and remove bolt link, bolt lock and bolt. Push barrel latch to rear and remove as described above. Remove gas cylinder retaining pin at forward left side of receiver and slide gas cylinder and bipod straight ahead. Pull slide and gas piston assembly out of receiver.

To reassemble the weapon, reverse the above procedure.

How the Model 37 Works

The Model 37 works basically the same as the US Browning Automatic Rifle M1918 covered in the chapter on the United States. The recoil spring in the Model 37 is located in the butt as with the F.N. Type D Browning Automatic Rifle.

SWEDISH SUBMACHINE GUNS

The Swedish Army has used a number of submachine guns in the past twenty years. The US-made Thompson was used in limited numbers by the Swedes as the 11mm M40, and the Finnish-designed Suomi was used in two versions, the Model 37-39 and the Model 37-39F. The 9mm Bergmann M34 was used as the Model 39.

THE SWEDISH 9mm CARL GUSTAF SUBMACHINE GUN MODEL 45

The 9mm Model 45 (commonly known as the Carl Gustaf) is the current standard submachine gun in the Swedish Army. This weapon has also been produced in Egypt. It was designed and is produced in Sweden at the Carl Gustafs Stads Gevärsfaktori in Eskilstuna. All submachine guns in service fire the 9mm Parabellum cartridge.

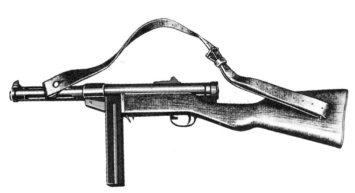

9mm Model 37-39 Submachine Gun.

Characteristics of M45 Submachine Gun

Caliber: 9mm Parabellum
Magazine: Detachable box, staggered dual line.
Magazine capacity: 36 cartridges.
Overall length: w/stock extended: 31.8 in.
                          w/stock folded: 21.7 in.
Barrel length: 8 in.
Weight: 9.25 lbs. (loaded).
Cyclic rate of fire: 550 to 600 per minute.
Type of fire: Automatic.
Operation: Elementary blowback. Actuation of bolt mechanism is by projection of spent case.
Sights: Front: Protected post.
         Rear: L type.
Muzzle velocity: 1200 f.p.s.

How to Load and Fire the Model 45

Pull bolt handle to the rear; bolt and bolt handle will remain to the rear since the gun fires from an open bolt. The weapon can be put on safe when the gun is cocked by pulling the bolt handle beyond the sear and engaging it in the cutout section above the bolt handle track of the receiver. Insert magazine, take weapon off safe, pull trigger, and weapon will fire. To put the weapon on safe with the bolt forward, push down on bolt handle.

How to Field Strip the Model 45

Remove magazine; bolt should be forward. Depress catch in center of the receiver cap (rear of receiver), turn receiver cap slightly counter clockwise, and cap will come off. Remove recoil spring and bolt. Push in on barrel jacket nut catch with a drift and unscrew barrel jacket nut. Remove barrel jacket and barrel. To reassemble, carry out in reverse the steps outlined above.

9mm Model 37-39F Submachine Gun.

Swedish 9mm M45 Submachine Gun with fixed magazine guide, stock fixed.

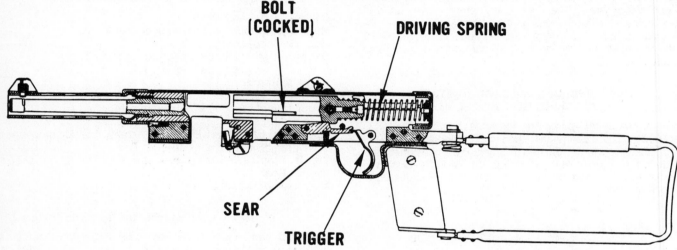

**BOLT
(COCKED)**

DRIVING SPRING

SEAR

TRIGGER

Section view of M45 9mm Submachine Gun.

Special Note on the Model 45

There have been at least three different variations of this weapon since it first appeared in 1945. The variations are in the barrel jacket and magazine guide. Some of the M45s have a re-movable magazine guide. When the guide is removed, the weapon can be used with the thicker Suomi submachine gun magazine. The weapon is principally made of stampings and has a folding steel stock.

SWEDISH MACHINE GUNS

The Swedish Army has a collection of various types of machine guns in use at present, but most, if not all, of these weapons will probably be replaced by the Model 58. The Model 58 is the Belgian FN Type MAG and is covered in detail in the chapter on Belgium. The Schwarzlose in 6.5mm, Model 14 and Model 14-29 was used by Sweden; this weapon is believed to be out of service at present. A series of rifle-caliber Browning guns is used, chambered for either the 6.5mm cartridge or the 8mm M1932 cartridge (8mm × 63mm). The Model 36 is a water-cooled gun, and the Model 42 is an air-cooled gun. Both of these guns are similar in loading, firing, functioning and field stripping to the US cal. .30 Browning guns, although they have a somewhat higher cyclic rate of fire. The Czech-made ZB26 light machine gun in caliber 6.5mm was also used in Sweden as the Model 39. The German-made Knorr Brense in 6.5mm was also used in limited numbers as the Model 40.

6.5mm MODEL 36 AND MODEL 42B MACHINE GUNS

The Swedish Brownings are basically the same as the United States caliber .30 Brownings. The Model 36 is a water-cooled gun similar to the United States Model 1917A1, and the Model 42B is an air-cooled gun similar to the United States Model 1919A6; it can be used on a bipod with a shoulder stock. As originally made, this weapon was called the Model 42. The Swedish Brownings use spade type grips rather than the pistol type of the United States Brownings. A Model 39 aircraft Browning gun was also used.

The loading, firing, field stripping and functioning of the Swedish Brownings are essentially the same as those of the United States Brownings.

The Swiss Army uses the following small arms: the 9mm Parabellum Model 49 and Model 75 Pistols, the 7.5mm Model 31 Rifle, the 7.5mm Model 55 Sniper Rifle, the 7.5mm Model 57 Assault Rifle and the 7.5mm Model 51 General Purpose Machine Gun. The turret type version of the US cal. 50 M2 Heavy Barrel Machine Gun is also used.

Older weapons, such as the 9mm Parabellum Model 43/44 Submachine Gun, the 7.5mm Model 11 Carbine and the 7.5mm Model 25 Light Machine Gun, may also be found in some units, but they are obsolete.

41
Switzerland

SWISS PISTOLS

7.5mm Model 1882/29 Pistol.

7.65mm Luger cartridge (called caliber .30 Luger in the United States) and has a grip safety. In 1906, a modification of this pistol was adopted, the Model 1906, which differs from the Model 1900 in its extractor, firing pin, recoil spring and in various minor details. Another Luger was adopted by Switzerland in 1929; this weapon may be called the Model 1906/29 or Model 1929. This weapon has a different side plate and take-down catch than the Model 1906 and differs from that model in other minor points. The 1929 modifications were designed by Waffenfabrik Bern, and the weapons were manufactured at that government arsenal.

Model 1929, 7.65mm Swiss Luger.

The Swiss adopted a 7.5mm revolver in 1882; this double-action weapon was modified in 1929 and the model designation changed to Model 1882/29. Although these revolvers are no longer in service, they remained a service weapon of the Swiss Army for an extraordinarily long time.

In 1900, Switzerland adopted the first military production model Luger. The Swiss Model 1900 Luger is chambered for the

7.65mm Model 1900 Luger.

THE SIG P210

The Schweizerische Industrie-Gesellschaft (SIG) Neuhausen am Rheinfall, Switzerland, obtained a license for the Petter System (see Chapter 18) and their P210 pistol was based upon that modified Browning concept. Development of the P210 continued over many years (1938–1946) and included the 9mm SIG Model 44/16 as one of the prototypes in that series. In 1949,

Selfloading Pistol Neuhausen Model 44/16.
Locked breech, small exposed hammer. Thumb safety and bottom magazine release. Magazine capacity 16 cartridges. Calibre 9 mm Parabellum (Luger). This was a forerunner of the SP 47/8 (9 mm Model 49) and only very few specimens of this weapon were made.

the P210 (formerly designated the SP47/8) replaced the Swiss Luger Model 29 as the official service weapon of the Swiss Army. In 1975, the *Pistole 49* was replaced by the *Pistole 75* (or SIG-Sauer P220). Nearly 200,000 *Pistole 49* were made for the Swiss Army, most are still in use, and SIG still offers the P210 commercially. The P210 has been used by the Danish Army and the West German Border Guard *(Bundesgrenzschutz)*.

Design and Construction

The P210 *(Pistole 49)* has several features common with other handguns derived from the basic Browning concept. A nose on the underside of the barrel is slotted to permit the slide stop pin to pass through, locking it firmly to the receiver. During recoil, the barrel and slide are firmly locked together for approximately $1/4$ inch of travel. At this point, the cam slot in the locking nose below the barrel, working against the transverse slide stop pin, serves to cam the barrel down to draw its locking lugs out of their engaging seats in the underside of the breech of the slide.

This weapon is beautifully made in the finest Swiss tradition. Because of the care taken in fitting the barrel, it demonstrates considerable accuracy.

The takedown is quite simple. In general, it follows the standard Colt-Browning procedure except for the firing mechanism.

How to Field Strip the Model 49

Hold pistol in right hand. Push magazine catch at bottom of butt with left thumb and withdraw magazine.

Grip right hand around rear of receiver and slide and draw slide back about ½ inch. With finger of left hand, push slide stop from right side. Withdraw slide stop from left. This can be done when the thumb piece is lined up with its dismounting notch in the slide.

Ease slide, barrel and recoil spring forward.

Grip hammer with thumb and forefinger and work free and up out of receiver. This unit carries the hammer, disconnector, sear and mainspring with its guide compression rod. These may be dismounted if desired, but this is not necessary.

Press recoil spring guide forward from rear and lift out. Spring is captive on its guide rod and will not come loose.

Grip barrel lug and work barrel slightly back and up when it can be lifted out of the slide.

Firing pin may be removed if desired by pushing in on its head and drawing stop down out of slide cut as in Colt Govt. .45.

9mm SIG Pistol P210-2, Swiss Army Model 49, this pistol was formerly called the SP47/8 by SIG.

How the P210 Operates

A loaded magazine is inserted in the butt in standard fashion and pushed in until the catch holds it. The slide is then withdrawn to the full length of its recoil stroke to allow magazine spring to force a cartridge up in line for chambering. Releasing the slide permits the compressed recoil spring to drive the slide forward for chambering and locking.

Applying the thumb safety, which is in a particularly advantageous position for easy operation, locks both the trigger and the trigger bar to prevent firing. This design does not have an automatic grip safety, but it does have, however, the automatic disconnector mechanism which is also standard for the Colt-Browning design. If the slide is not fully forward and the barrel not fully locked into position, the slide is automatically depressing the disconnector, which in turn is pushing the trigger bar down out of possible contact with the trigger. When the slide is fully forward and locked, the spring can force the disconnector up into its cut in the underside of the slide. This allows the trigger, the trigger bar and the sear to function for firing. As the action opens, the slide automatically cams the disconnector down, forcing the breakage in the trigger contact so that on forward motion of the slide the chambered cartridge will not fire. Thus the trigger must be definitely released before contact can again be made for firing the next shot.

This design has several features superior to the Colt Government Model. The forward bushing in the receiver is eliminated, resulting in more machining difficulties but in an inherently simpler design. The recoil spring is under tension in position around its guide rod and during disassembly and reassembly functions as a unit. The unlocking lug on the bottom of the barrel affords much more rigidity during the operation of the pistol. This tends, theoretically at least, to make for more accurate shooting than with the swinging link design. Combining most of the firing mechanism in a single unit (as in the case of the Russian Tokarev pistol) results in a considerable simplification of both design and machining.

To convert the pistol from 9mm to 7.65 Parabellum, it is only necessary to replace the recoil spring and the barrel. The magazine and all other elements will function with either cartridge, since the 9mm was developed directly from the bottle-necked 7.65mm.

A special .22 caliber conversion training unit is also available for use with this pistol for practice shooting. It consists of a lighter weight slide, a special barrel with recoil spring and a magazine. This conversion, of course, does not require a locked breech, hence the barrel is not equipped with locking lugs and does not have any movement. Once installed, it is locked in place. The operation is otherwise identical with that of the heavier caliber.

Considerable attention was given to pitch of grip in the design of this pistol. The center of gravity is at about the trigger point. The locking cam system of barrel operation, as opposed to the swinging link system, prevents movement of the barrel out of the firing axis while the bullet is still in the barrel. This together with the lack of a front bushing makes for a much more solid barrel support.

Field stripped view of an early P210 (SP47/8) pistol. Note the removable hammer assembly.

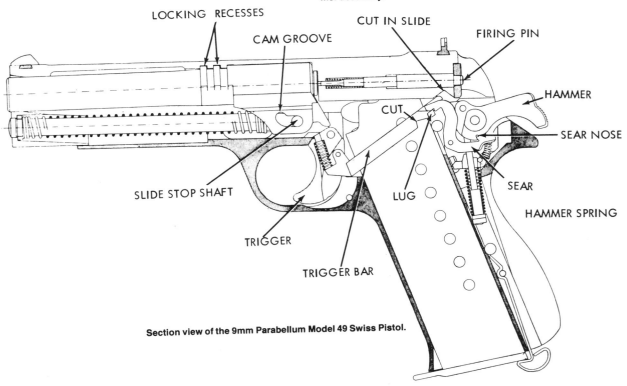

Section view of the 9mm Parabellum Model 49 Swiss Pistol.

M75, 9mm PARABELLUM PISTOL

The latest addition to the Swiss pistol family is the SIG-Sauer P220, which has been adopted as the Model 1975 Pistol by the Swiss Armed Forces. This pistol departs from the standard Browning type action. The blow-back from the detonated cartridge thrusts the barrel and slide to the rear. After these parts have recoiled a distance of about .12 inch, the lock between the barrel and the slide (number 24 in the accompanying illustration) is released; the barrel is swung down and held. In the loading cycle just before reaching the full forward position, the barrel is locked to the slide again. As with many European handguns, this pistol has several safety features. There is a firing pin lock that guarantees absolute safety, even if the loaded weapon is dropped with the hammer cocked. With this feature and the double action mechanism, the designers eliminated the standard manual safety. A de-cocking lever permits hazardless lowering of the hammer into a safety notch without touching the trigger. All these combined features make this pistol an excellent military weapon.

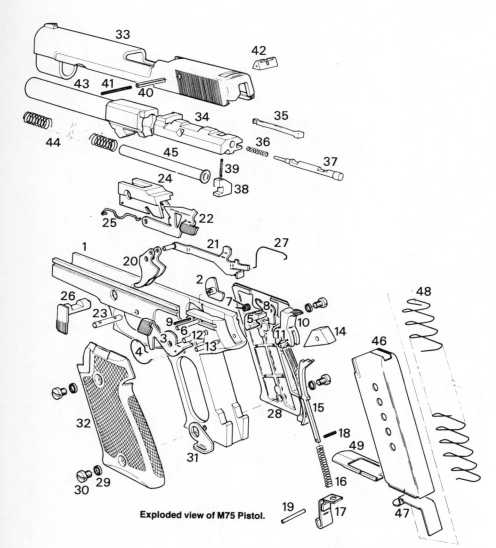

Exploded view of M75 Pistol.

1. Frame
2. De-cocking lever seating
3. De-cocking lever
4. De-cocking lever spring
5. Sear
6. Sear pin
7. Torsion spring for sear
8. Safety lever
9. Spring pin
10. Hammer
11. Hammer pin
12. Hammer axle
13. Pin for stop
14. Stop
15. Hammer spring stirrup
16. Main spring
17. Magazine catch
18. Hammer spring pin
19. Magazine catch pin
20. Trigger
21. Trigger rod
22. Slide catch lever
23. Trigger pin
24. Locking insert
25. Slide catch spring
26. Dismantling lever
27. Trigger spring
28. Right hand grip plate
29. Washer
30. Grip plate screw
31. Strap ring
32. Left hand grip plate
33. Slide
34. Rear insert
35. Extractor
36. Firing pin spring
37. Firing pin
38. Safety slide
39. Safety slide spring
40. Outer spring pin
41. Inner spring pin
42. Rear sight
43. Barrel
44. Recoil spring
45. Recoil spring tube
46. Magazine casing
47. Feeder
48. Magazine spring
49. Magazine base plate

CHARACTERISTICS OF SWISS SERVICE PISTOLS

	Model 1900	Model 1906	Model 1929	Model 49	Model 75
Caliber:	7.65mm Luger.	7.65mm Luger.	7.65mm Luger.	9mm Parabellum.	9mm Parabellum.
System of operation:	Recoil, semiautomatic.	Recoil, semiautomatic.	Recoil, semiautomatic.	Recoil, semiautomatic.	Recoil, semiautomatic.
Length overall:	9.5 in.	9.5 in.	9.5 in.	8.5 in.	7.8 in.
Barrel length:	4.75 in.	4.75 in.	4.75 in.	4.72 in.	4.41 in.
Feed device:	8-round, in-line detachable box magazine.	8-round, in-line detachable box magazine.	8-round, in-line detachable box magazine.	8-round, in-line detachable box magazine.	9-round, in-line detachable box magazine.
Sights: Front:	Blade.	Blade.	Blade.	Blade.	Blade.
Rear:	V-notch.	V-notch.	U-notch.	V-notch.	Square notch.
Weight:	2.25 lbs.	2 lbs. (approx.).	1.98 lbs.	2.14 lbs.	1.94 lbs.
Muzzle velocity:	1200 f.p.s. (approx.).	1200 f.p.s. (approx.).	1200 f.p.s. (approx.).	1150 f.p.s.	1132 f.p.s.

SWISS RIFLES AND CARBINES

SWISS VETTERLI

While Mauser invented the first successful military bolt action, his was not of course the first attempt in the field. The Swiss were actually first in the field to combine the turn bolt and the copper metallic cartridge.

Swiss ordnance men, particularly Frederic Vetterli, had studied closely the American Volcanic and its successful metallic cartridge counterpart, the Henry repeater, as well as the Spencer. They had watched, too, the growing might and arrogance of the Prussian Junkers. They saw Schleswig-Holstein overrun with the aid of the terrible new Dreyse Needle gun; they also saw Austria fall before it, and saw France brace itself for the coming attack, the disaster of 1870–71.

The Swiss set about to devise an arm that might outshoot the German weapon. At this late date, it is difficult to visualize the terror spread by the Dreyse, the first widely used European breechloader. Long before any major European power thought in terms of metallic cartridges, the Swiss actually had a repeater on the drawing boards.

As their whole psychology revolved around defense of their homeland, the rifle-minded Swiss approached the design of their rifle from a far different viewpoint than either the Americans or the other Europeans. Since the American rifle was primarily a hunting or mounted-use arm, US inventors turned in the direction of the lever-action repeater. The typical European military mind outside of Germany thought in terms of better needle guns or conversions to salvage the tremendous stocks of muzzle-loaders. Germany was oversold by the success of the Dreyse, and Mauser had considerable trouble selling his first rifles! Characteristically, once the Prussians adopted the Mauser, they went all out for further development, right up to the day the United States introduced the Garand.

However, a few Swiss and Austrian designers saw the military value of the bolt repeater very early in the game. Since the vertical magazine system of Lee and Mauser and Mannlicher had not yet appeared, and since the successful American systems were tube repeaters, it is understandable that early European magazine design centered around tubes. Basically what the Swiss did was adapt the Henry-Winchester to their needs. They produced an improved rimfire .41 cartridge with copper case. They altered the King loading gate and the Henry cartridge carrier and applied them to turn-bolt actions, which could be better handled prone than could the lever action.

The Federal Assembly of the Swiss Confederation in July and December 1866 officially approved the adoption of the repeating principle. Production of the Vetterli started in 1867, but it took two years to iron out manufacture. In 1871 and 1878, new models were produced at Waffenfabrik Bern. The rifle was used officially until 1889. As issued, it had a 12-shot magazine. The caliber was 10.4mm. With a 313-grain lead bullet, the rifle achieved a muzzle velocity of 1338 feet per second. Maximum range was given at about 3000 meters.

SWISS SCHMIDT RUBIN RIFLES AND CARBINES

The next development of interest in Switzerland was in 1883, when Major Rubin designed a straight-pull bolt system. A special revolving cam turned the locking lugs out of receiver engagement and then brought the bolt back in a straight line to eject when the operating handle was pulled to the rear. Lugs for locking were at the rear of the bolt. A special detachable vertical box magazine was provided. The design was improved through the years as the model 1911 and model 1931. The caliber is 7.5mm Swiss. The Swiss straight-pull has never been imitated elsewhere.

Modifications of the 1889 Schmidt Rubin

M1889/96. The 1889 action was shortened slightly, and the lug system was strengthened.

M97 Cadet Rifle. A single-shot version of the M1889/96 action made for the training of cadets.

Model 89/00 Short Rifle. A special short rifle designed for the use of Fortress Artillery, Signal, Balloon and Bicycle troops. This weapon, which weighs approximately seven pounds, has a lower velocity than the M1889 rifle.

Model 1905 Carbine. Weighs approximately 7.5 pounds; uses the same action as the M1889/96 rifle.

NOTE: None of the above rifles should be used with the more powerfully loaded Model 1911 7.5 × 55mm cartridges.

M1896/11 Rifle. An alteration of the M1889/96 rifle, and some of the carbines, to make them suitable for use with the Model 11 ammunition.

M1911 Rifle. The first of the Schmidt Rubins made specifically for the 7.5mm Model 11 cartridge. The Model 11 cartridge has a much higher pressure than the earlier Swiss cartridges. Therefore the basic 1889 action design had to be modified to handle the new cartridge safely. The locking lugs were relocated from the rear of the locking sleeve to the front of the locking sleeve. The M1896/11 action is similar. The M1911 rifle also had a bolt-holding-open device.

M1911 Carbine. Differs from the M1911 rifle by having a shorter barrel and stock and being lighter. Its rear sight is graduated to 1500 meters, rather than to the rifle's 2000 meters. The M1911 carbine is still in limited use in Switzerland. It can be identified by the red plastic bolt handle knobs.

M1931 Carbine. Commonly known as the K31. This weapon represents the last basic change in the design of the Schmidt Rubin. The basic difference between this weapon and the earlier Schmidt Rubins is the elimination of the long bolt extension. All earlier Schmidt Rubin bolts had a long bolt extension that actually rammed the cartridge into the chamber, supported its base and extracted it from the chamber. It could be considered that this piece was the bolt body. This piece did not rotate in unlocking; the bolt sleeve rotated, instead. The bolt sleeve, a piece that supported the rear of the extension, had the locking lugs. (In

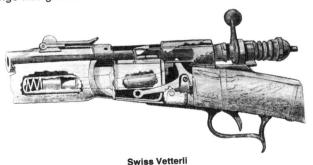

Swiss Vetterli

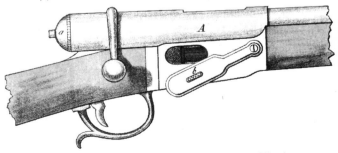

Vetterli Loading Gate, modified from American King type.

Rifle M1911 (above) and Carbine M1911 (below).

Model 31 (K31) Schmidt Rubin. Best of the designs.

Schmidt Rubin bolts. Left: M1889 with locking lugs at rear of sleeve. Center: M1911 with locking lugs at front of sleeve. Right: M31 with locking lugs at front of bolt.

the rifles before 1911, the lugs were at the rear; in the rifles after 1911, at the front.) Thus, an abnormally long receiver was needed for these weapons, and the locking lugs were a long way to the rear of the point where they were actually needed. It was not a very satisfactory design from a military point of view, since it meant a great deal of extra length and weight and still did not offer the best type of bolt support. In the K31, the part formerly considered the bolt sleeve became the bolt body itself, and the locking lugs were mounted at its head in the position where they were most needed. This shortening of the bolt assembly has resulted in a much better weapon, which, although it is about the same overall length as the M1911 carbine, has a barrel 2.5 inches longer (made possible by the shorter receiver). The earlier weapons had their magazines placed a considerable distance in front of the trigger guard, because of the position of the long bolt extension. The magazine of the K31, on the other hand, is immediately ahead of the trigger guard. All in all, the K31 is a vastly superior weapon to the earlier Schmidt Rubins.

Model 31/42 Carbine, K31/42. One of the two sniper versions of the K31. It has a 1.8-power scope permanently built into the left side of the receiver. The head of this scope resembles a periscope, and when in use, is lifted up; when not in use, it is folded down against the side of the carbine. The weapon has a tangent type metallic rear sight, graduated from 100 to 1000 meters.

Model 31/43 Carbine, K31/43. Equipped with a 2.8-power scope mounted like that of the K31/42. Its metallic rear sight is graduated from 100 to 700 meters.

Model 31/55 Sniper Rifle. Note bipod position and telescopic sight.

Model 31/43 Carbine. Periscopic type sight folded behind rear sight.

CHARACTERISTICS OF THE SIGNIFICANT SCHMIDT RUBINS

	M1889 Rifle	M1911 Rifle	M1911 Carbine	M1931 Carbine
Caliber:	7.5mm.	7.54mm.	7.54mm.	7.51mm.
Land diameter:	.295 in.	.2968 in.	.2968 in.	.2956 in.
Weight:	9.8 lb.	10.15 lb.	8.6 lb.	8.83 lb.
Length, overall:	51.25 in.	51.6 in.	43.4 in.	43.5 in.
Barrel length:	30.7 in.	30.7 in.	23.3 in.	25.67 in.
Magazine:	12-rd. detachable box.	6-rd. detachable box.	6-rd. detachable box.	6-rd. detachable box.
Chamber pressure:	38,400 p.s.i.	45,500 p.s.i.	45,500 p.s.i.	45,500 p.s.i.
Muzzle velocity:	2033 f.p.s.	2640 f.p.s.	2490 f.p.s.	2560 f.p.s.

Schmidt Rubin Model 31/55 Sniper Rifle.

Special Note on the Schmidt Rubins

As noted above, there is a considerable difference in the bolt construction of the various models of this weapon. None of the weapons prior to the M1896/11 rifle is considered by the Swiss to be strong enough to use the Swiss Model 11 cartridge. Because of slight differences in bore diameter and rifling, the early rifles will not shoot the Model 11 cartridge very accurately. The early rifles should be used with the Swiss 7.5mm M1890/23 cartridge; this cartridge has a 190-grain, conical-nosed bullet. They should not be used with the Spitzer-pointed Model 11 cartridge, which has a 174 grain bullet.

THE SIG ASSAULT RIFLE *STURMGEWEHR 57*

The selective-fire *Sturmgewehr 57,* Swiss Army designation *Stgw. 57,* has replaced all the Schmidt Rubin Rifles and Carbines in service with the Swiss Army. SIG developed this 7.5mm Swiss (7.5 × 53.5mm) delayed-blowback, roller-locked automatic weapon. More than 600,000 of these rifles have been manufactured to date.

Characteristics of the Model 57

Caliber: 7.5mm (Swiss Model 11 cartridge).
System of operation: Delayed blowback, selective fire.
Weight, empty: 12.32 lb.
Length, overall: 43.4 in.
Barrel length: 23 in., w/muzzle brake.
Feed device: 24-round, detachable, staggered-row box magazine.
Sights: Front: Folding blade, w/protecting ears.
    Rear: Folding aperture, w/micrometer adjustment graduated from 100 to 650 meters.
Muzzle velocity: 2493 f.p.s.
Cyclic rate: 450 to 500 r.p.m.

How to Load and Fire the Model 57

Insert a loaded magazine in the magazine well and pull the operating handle to the rear (the operating handle is located on the right side of the receiver). Release the operating handle, and the bolt will go home, chambering a cartridge. Set the safety selector on the letter "E" if semiautomatic fire is desired, or on the letter "M" if full automatic fire is desired. Pressure on the trigger will fire the weapon. To set the weapon on safe, set the safety selector on the letter "S."

How to Field Strip the Model 57

Remove the magazine by pushing forward the magazine catch, located at the forward end of the trigger quard. Depress the butt retaining catch, located on the forward underside of the butt; turn the butt approximately one-quarter turn to the right, and remove the butt and recoil spring. Pull the operating handle to the rear, and remove the bolt assembly. No further disassembly is recommended.

To reassemble the weapon, perform the above steps in reverse order.

How the Model 57 Works

When the trigger is pulled, the hammer is released and hits the firing lever mounted on the rear of the bolt. The firing lever strikes the firing pin, which hits the primer of the cartridge. The gas pressure forces the base of the cartridge against the head of the two-piece bolt. When a certain pressure has been reached, the locking rollers begin forcing rearward the nose of the rear section of the bolt. The locking rollers are then free to slip back into their recesses in the bolt head, and the weapon unlocks. The bolt travels to the rear, compressing the recoil spring, extracting and ejecting the spent case, and cocking the hammer. The recoil spring drives the bolt forward again, and the bolt picks up and chambers another round. The nose of the rear section of the bolt cams the locking rollers into their locking recesses in the receiver. If the weapon has been set on semiautomatic fire, the trigger must be pulled again. This weapon fires from a closed bolt on both automatic and semiautomatic fire. If the weapon has been set on automatic fire, it will continue to fire as long as the trigger is held to the rear and there are cartridges remaining in the magazine.

Special Note on the Model 57

The Model 57 has many interesting features. Its delayed blowback action is worthy of note. The bolt is composed of two principal parts—the head and the rear section. The head is approximately one-fourth as heavy as the rear section. The head section contains two locking rollers cammed into recesses in the receiver by the nose section of the rear part of the bolt. The principal difference between this weapon and the Spanish CETME assault rifle, insofar as the bolt is concerned, is that the CETME fires from an open bolt on automatic fire. Since this system has no provisions for slow initial extraction, both weapons have fluted chambers to "float" the neck and forward part of the case on gas.

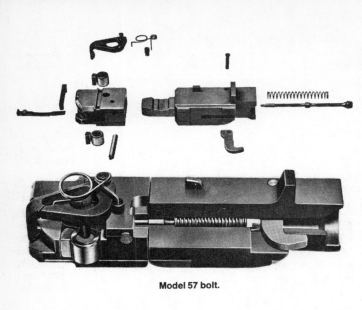

Model 57 field-stripped.

Model 57 bolt.

Swiss 7.5mm Model 57 Assault Rifle.

Model 57 Assault Rifle, left side view, current production.

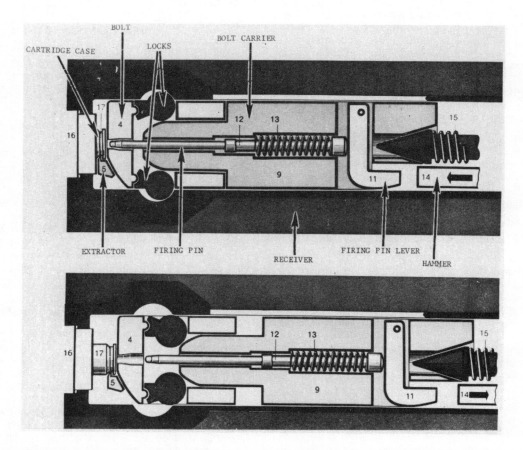

Operation of the Model 57 Roller-locked bolt mechanism. The delay, which results from the time required for the rollers to unseat and force the bolt carrier to the rear, permits the bullet to exit the barrel and the chamber pressures to fall to a safe level.

THE .223 SIG MODEL SG530-1 RIFLE

SIG has developed a new rifle chambered for the .223 (5.56mm) cartridge. This rifle uses a modification of the 7.5mm Model 57 rifle action altered to gas operation. It is made mainly of stampings and fabrications and has a plastic stock, pistol grip and fore-end. In addition to the fixed plastic stock version, there is a folding metal stock version.

Characteristics of the .223 SIG Model SG530-1 Rifle

Caliber: 5.56mm (.223)
System of operation: Gas operated, selective fire
Length overall: w/fixed stock—39.5 in.
w/folding stock, stock folded—30.8 in.
Barrel length: 18.1 in.
Feed device: 30-round, staggered row, detachable box magazine
Sights: Front: Protected post
Rear: Aperture adjustable from 100 to 400 meters
Weight: w/fixed stock—8.35 lbs.
w/folding stock—8.44 lbs.
Cyclic rate: 550-650 r.p.m.
Muzzle velocity: 3150 f.p.s. with US M193 ball cartridge

How to Load and Fire the SG530-1

The magazine catch is immediately to the rear of the magazine; push forward to remove magazine. The magazine is loaded in the normal fashion. Set rifle on safe by turning safety/selector lever, located on the left side of the receiver above the pistol grip, to "S". Insert loaded magazine and pull operating handle, located to the rear of the front sight on the left top side of the gas cylinder tube over the barrel, to the rear and release. The cocking handle will return to its forward position, and the weapon is loaded. If semiautomatic fire is desired, set the safety/selector lever on the number "1"; if automatic fire is desired, set the safety/selector lever on the number "30". Pressure on the trigger will now fire the rifle.

How to Field Strip the SG530-1

Remove magazine. Push receiver catch, located at the top rear of the receiver, in and pivot stock and trigger housing assembly down. The weapon breaks like a shotgun in a fashion

similar to the FN FAL and the US M16A1. Withdraw operating spring assembly, bolt and operating rod/bolt carrier. Remove bolt from bolt carrier. To assemble, perform the above steps in reverse.

How the SG530-1 Works

The SG530-1 is gas operated but uses a roller bearing locking system somewhat similar to the StG 57. The bolt carrier is forced to the rear by the gas piston. This movement pulls the striker, which is mounted on the bolt carrier right behind the bolt, to the rear and allows the firing pin, which holds the roller bearings in their locked position in the receiver, to move to the rear. Thus unlocking occurs after firing; locking occurs when the bolt carrier, under the pressure of the compressed mainspring, forces the firing pin forward camming the locks into locked position.

The receiver of the rifle is grooved for a scope mount that locks into the front of the rear sight base. A prong type flash suppressor is used, and the fore part of the barrel and the flash suppressor can be used as a rifle grenade launcher.

Swiss SIG 5.56mm Model SG530-1 Rifle.

Swiss SIG 5.56mm SG530-1 Rifle with folding butt stock.

Detailed disassembly of the SG530-1 Rifle.

THE SIG MODEL SG540 AND 542 RIFLES

SIG has produced two new rifles—the SG540 chambered for the 5.56mm cartridge and the SG542 chambered for the 7.62mm NATO cartridge. Outwardly these rifles are generally similar in appearance to the SG530-1, but internally they are quite different. The SG530-1 has a roller locked bolt, and the SG540 and 542 rifles have rotating bolts cammed in to and out of the locked position by a cam slot on the bolt carrier. The bolt system is quite similar in concept to that of the AK.

The rear end of the piston fits into a hole in the bolt carrier, held in place by the operating handle, the end of which fits through a slot cut in the side of the bolt carrier.

The 540 series rifles have flash suppressor/grenade launchers attached to their barrels and can be set to fire three round bursts in addition to full automatic and semiautomatic. They can be supplied with bipod and with fixed or folding butt.

CHARACTERISTICS OF THE SIG540 SERIES RIFLES

	SG540	SG542
Caliber:	5.56mm	7.62mm NATO
System of operation:	gas, selective fire	
Weight loaded (20-round magazine):	7.1 lbs.	8 lbs.
Length overall w/stock fixed:	37.5 in.	38.9 in.
w/stock folded:	28.7 in.	30.1 in.
Barrel length:	19.3 in.	19.5 in.
Feed device:	20 or 30-round detachable box magazine	20-round detachable box magazine
Sights: Front:	protected post	
Rear:	rotating drum w/apertures	
Muzzle velocity:	3215 f.p.s.	2690 f.p.s.
Cyclic rate:	650–800 r.p.m.	

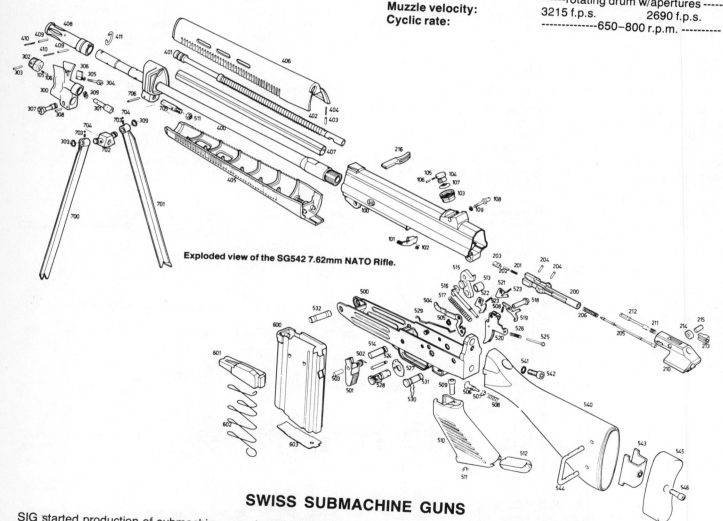

Exploded view of the SG542 7.62mm NATO Rifle.

SWISS SUBMACHINE GUNS

SIG started production of submachine guns in 1920 with the modified Bergmann MP181. Some of these weapons, chambered for the 7.65mm Luger or 7.63mm Mauser cartridge, were sold to Finland, China, and Japan.

Experience with the Bergman led the SIG engineers into a development program of their own, including the:

Automatic carbine (Maschinekarabiner) MKMO Model 1933 with a semi-locked breech for firing the powerful 7.63mm and 9mm Mauser pistol cartridges.

Automatic carbine MKMO Model 1934 with a blowback

mechanism for firing the 7.65mm and 9mm Parabellum cartridges. Both models were available in Military (MKMO) and Police (MKPO) versions.

At the beginning of World War II, the Swiss Army requested SIG and the Waffenfabrik Bern to take part in the development of a new submachine gun. Out of this work came the SIG MP 41 blowback weapon chambered for the 9mm Parabellum cartridge and the Furrer Model 41/44 submachine gun developed by the Waffenfabrik Bern. The latter weapon was adopted by the Swiss Army and SIG terminated work on their MP 41.

All SIG submachine guns are characterized by their "pull-through" trigger whereby a slight squeeze will produce semi-automatic fire and full pressure causes full-automatic fire. A further characteristic of the SIG submachine guns is the forward folding magazines. This latter feature makes them less clumsy to carry and renders the weapon completely safe since there is no possibility of accidental discharge when the magazine is folded forward.

The Swiss 9mm Parabellum Model 41/44 submachine gun was developed by Waffenfabrik Bern and is a most unusual submachine gun in several respects. The weapon is recoil-operated and has a toggle joint action similar to the Model 25 Furrer light machine gun. The vertical fore grip can be folded up under the barrel. It is an extremely expensive weapon to manufacture and unduly complicated. Unlike the Model 41, the Model 41/44 has a bayonet lug.

Swiss 9mm Parabellum Model 41/44 Submachine Gun developed by the Federal Waffenfabrik at Bern.

SIG 9mm Mauser MKMO (MK33) Automatic Carbine.

SIG MP310 9mm Parabellum Submachine Gun.

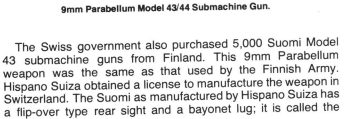

9mm Parabellum Model 43/44 Submachine Gun.

SIG MP310 9mm Parabellum Submachine Gun.

The Swiss government also purchased 5,000 Suomi Model 43 submachine guns from Finland. This 9mm Parabellum weapon was the same as that used by the Finnish Army. Hispano Suiza obtained a license to manufacture the weapon in Switzerland. The Suomi as manufactured by Hispano Suiza has a flip-over type rear sight and a bayonet lug; it is called the MP43/44.

Although the Solothurn (or Steyr Solothurn submachine gun, as it is frequently called) was made in Switzerland, it was of German design. The best known of these weapons was the S1-100. The Steyr Solothurn guns were also made at the Steyr plant in Austria; the Austrian Model 34 submachine gun is a good example of this submachine gun type. The Solothurn was used by Chile, El Salvador, Bolivia, Uruguay, Portugal and reportedly by China and Japan.

In 1944, SIG introduced their MP44, which is basically a modernized version of the MKMS. The Model 44 has a stamped steel fore-end, and is capable of selective fire. The MP46 is basically the same as the MP44 except for some bolt details.

These models were not commercially successful.

The Model 48 was modified by SIG by the fitting of a retractable type steel wire stock and a shorter barrel; the lightened weapon was produced as the Model 48. This weapon was sold to Chile.

Further improvements were made in the Model 48 by SIG and plastics and castings substituted for machined parts. The result is called MP310 by SIG. The Model 310 is capable of selective fire, as are all other SIG submachine guns starting with the MP44, has the folding magazine of the previous models and the retractable wire stock of the Model 48.

The firm of Rexim S.A. of Geneva introduced a submachine gun known as the Rexim FV Mark 4. This weapon, which was made in limited numbers, with many different barrel lengths and several different stocks, is unusual in that it fires from a closed bolt. The Rexim was also made in Spain at the La Coruna arsenal and was offered for sale as the "La Coruna." Although the Rexim is an interesting design, it has not been a very successful one.

SWISS SERVICE SUBMACHINE GUNS

	Model 41/44	Model 43/44
Caliber:	9mm Parabellum.	9mm Parabellum.
System of operation:	Recoil, selective fire.	Blowback, selective fire.
Length overall:	30.5 in.	33.9 in.
Barrel length:	9.8 in.	12.4 in.
Feed device:	40-round, staggered row detachable box magazine.	50-round, in-line, detachable box magazine— has double column divided by central wall.
Sights: Front:	Blade with ears.	Blade.
Rear:	Flip-type w/"U" notch.	Flip-type w/"U" notch.
Weight:	11.4 lb.	10.5 lb.
Muzzle velocity:	1312 f.p.s.	Approx. 1350 f.p.s.
Cyclic rate:	900 r.p.m.	800 r.p.m.

SWISS MACHINE GUNS

Switzerland adopted the Maxim gun in 1894. Later models used were the Model 1900 and Model 1911. The 7.5mm Model 1911 was used as the standard heavy machine gun until 1951.

Colonel Furrer of the Swiss government arms plant at Bern developed the 7.5mm Model 25 light machine gun, also known as the Fusil Furrer. The Model 25 has a toggle-joint action similar to the Luger pistol but which breaks to the side rather than to the top as does the Luger pistol. This weapon was quite impressive in its day but is being replaced by the 7.5mm Model 57 assault rifle. A link belt-fed 13mm aircraft gun version of the Model 25 was also produced.

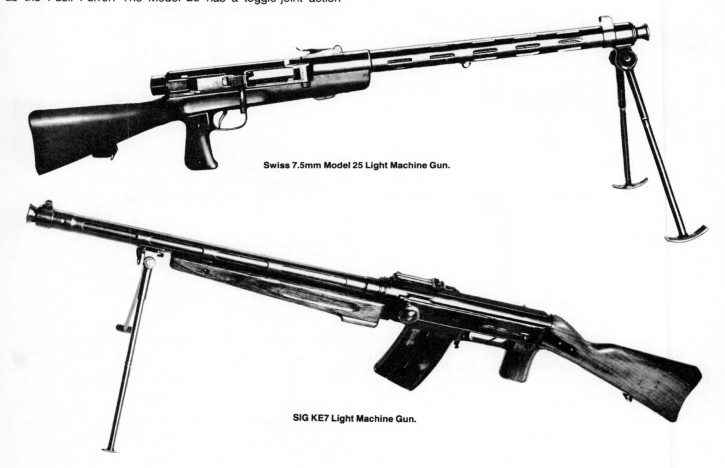

Swiss 7.5mm Model 25 Light Machine Gun.

SIG KE7 Light Machine Gun.

The next machine gun to be developed in Switzerland was a commercial development of SIG—the KE7 light machine gun. This weapon had some success in oversea sales (it was sold to China), but was not adopted by the Swiss government. The KE7 is a recoil-operated gun, which fires from an open bolt. It is selective fire and is relatively light, weighing 17.25 lbs. without magazine.

During the post-war period, the Swiss government arms plant at Bern developed a modified copy of the German MG42 adopted by the Swiss Army as the MG51. The Swiss seem to have defeated much of the purpose of the MG42, however, by making the MG51 mainly out of heavy milled parts rather than stampings. MG51 has locking flaps in its bolt head, which engage locking recesses in the receiver, rather than locking rollers of the MG42. Barrel change and field stripping of the MG51 is generally similar to the MG42.

The Model 1951 General Purpose Machine Gun 7.5mm Swiss developed at the Waffenfabrik Bern. Shown here are three different configurations of the Model 51 as used by the Swiss Armed Forces.

The MG M51 is also used coaxially in tanks. Such guns are fitted with a solenoid type trigger mechanism. The rate of fire for coaxial guns can be adjusted between 500 and 1000 shots per minute.

MG M51 on Bipod with Drum-type Magazine.

MG M51 on Antiaircraft Tripod.

Tripod Mounted MG M51 with Optical Sight. The Swiss still prefer such weapons for prepared defensive positions.

Hispano Suiza Machine Gun, Type HSS808.

Swiss MG50 on bipod. Drum feed. Used as a L.M.G.

Swiss MG50 on tripod, belt feed, as a medium machine gun.

SIG MG710-1 Machine Gun, on tripod.

Hispano Suiza, a well-known manufacturer of aircraft and anti-aircraft cannon, developed a rifle caliber machine gun after World War II. This weapon was not a financial success and was made only as a prototype. It was known as the Type HSS808.

SIG developed a weapon to place in the competition held by the Swiss for a weapon to replace the Model 11 Maxim gun. The SIG Model 50 is a gas-operated weapon designed to be used as a general purpose weapon. It has a quick change barrel and is fed by a non-disintegrating metallic link belt similar to that of the MG42 or by a 50-round drum. This weapon is not used by

SIG MG710-2 Machine Gun.

Switzerland but was adopted by Denmark in caliber .30 as the Model 51 machine gun. It is being replaced in that country by the 7.62mm NATO MG42/59.

After the MG50, SIG developed a series of delayed blowback machine guns using the same locking principles as the Model 57 assault rifle. Originally advertised as the Model 55-1 and 55-2, the first two guns of the series, now called the 710-1 and 710-2, are similar in all respects excepting the barrel, barrel support and the presence of a barrel jacket on the 710-1. The feed mechanism is similar to that of the MG42 and a link belt or a 50-round drum similar to that of MG42 is used.

The SIG MG710-1 is remarkably similar to the MG42V, which was under development in Germany at the close of World War II. The barrel change on this gun is the same as that on MG42.

The SIG 710-2 does not have a barrel jacket, and the barrel is held in the receiver by a bayonet-type joint. The barrel handle is used to change the barrel. The 710-2, as the 710-1, is designed to be used as a general purpose machine gun.

The third weapon in this series is the MG710-3. This weapon has a partial barrel jacket, and the barrel is released for removal by a catch on the top of the barrel jacket. A large barrel-removal handle is fitted to the right side of the barrel and the barrel is pulled to the right and rear to remove. The 710-3 will use a disin-

tegrating or a non-disintegrating link belt. The 710-3 uses more stampings than do the 710-1 and 710-2 and is a bit lighter than those guns. It is advertised for the 7.62mm NATO cartridge only, while the earlier guns were advertised chambered for the 6.5mm, 7.92mm and 7.62mm NATO cartridges.

The SIG MG 710-3 Machine Gun in 7.62mm NATO cartridge weighs 20.5 pounds and is notable for its quick barrel change.

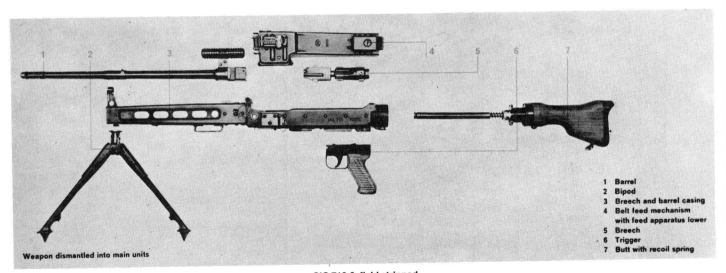

Weapon dismantled into main units

1 Barrel
2 Bipod
3 Breech and barrel casing
4 Belt feed mechanism with feed apparatus lower
5 Breech
6 Trigger
7 Butt with recoil spring

SIG 710-3, field stripped.

CHARACTERISTICS OF SWISS SERVICE MACHINE GUNS

	Model 11 Heavy	Model 25 Light	Model 51
Caliber:	7.5mm.	7.5mm.	7.5mm.
System of operation:	Recoil, automatic only.	Recoil, selective fire.	Recoil, automatic only.
Length overall:	42.4 in.	45.8 in.	50.1 in.
Barrel length:	28.4 in.	23 in.	22.2 in.
Feed device:	250-round web belt.	30-round, staggered row, detachable box magazine.	Non-disintegrating metallic link belt, in 50- and 200-round segments, 50-round drum.
Sights: Front:	Blade.	Blade w/protecting ears.	Folding blade.
Rear:	Leaf.	Tangent w/notch.	Tangent, optical sight used on tripod
Weight:	40.8 lb. (gun only).	23.69 lb w/bipod.	35.3 lb. w/bipod. 57.3 lb. w/tripod.
Muzzle velocity:	2590 f.p.s.	2460 f.p.s.	2460 f.p.s.
Cyclic rate:	Approx. 500 r.p.m.	450 r.p.m.	1000 r.p.m.

42

Turkey

MKE Pistol produced by Makina ve Kimya Endustrisi Kurumu located at Kirikkale, Ankara.

The Turkish Army still has a large assortment of small arms from the World War II era. These include most of the former standard weapons of the US, UK and Germany. As quickly as possible, the Turkish military is replacing these older weapons with the 7.62mm NATO G3 Rifle and MG3 Machine Gun. In addition, the domestically produced pistols are finding their way into the inventory replacing the US M1911A1.

TURKISH PISTOLS

A native-made pistol is the 9mm Kirikkale. This weapon, which is made at the Kirkkale arms factory in Turkey, is a copy of the Walther PP. It is identical to the late commercial-type Walther, except for variations in machining and the finger-rest extension on the removable magazine floor plate. For data on the Walther PP, see the chapter on German World War II materiel. The Kirikkale is chambered for the 9mm Browning short (.380 ACP) or the 7.65mm (.32 ACP) cartridge.

TURKISH RIFLES

Turkey responded very rapidly to the advantages of the military small caliber repeating rifle and adopted a 7.65mm Mauser in 1890—the Model 1890. This rifle, which was chambered for the 7.65mm cartridge introduced with the Belgian Mauser in 1889, has an in-line magazine and bolt similar to the Belgian Model 1889 excepting the buttress threads on the bolt sleeve. The Model 1890 does not have the metal barrel jacket of the Model 1889 and introduced the stepped barrel, which was used in Mausers from that time on.

A number of these rifles were obtained by Yugoslavia after World War I. The Yogoslavs rebarreled with a shorter 7.92mm barrel and fitted a longer handguard. This weapon was called the Model 90T by the Yugoslavs.

The Model 1893 7.65mm Mauser is essentially the same as the 7mm Spanish M1893 Mauser, with the addition of a cutoff to the magazine.

The Model 1903 7.65mm rifle is essentially the same as the German Rifle Model 98 except for the rear sight, hand guard, upper band, longer cocking piece and firing pin and modified bolt stop. There is a carbine Model 1905 and Model 1890 stocked to the muzzle.

During World War I, the Turks were supplied by Germany with many 7.92mm German Mauser rifles and carbines. After the war, Turkey purchased quantities of Czech 7.92mm Model 1924 Mausers and rebarreled many of the earlier 7.65mm rifles and carbines for 7.92mm.

Only the characteristics of rifles designed specifically for Turkey are given. Characteristics of other rifles used by Turkey will be found under country of origin.

CHARACTERISTICS OF TURKISH RIFLES

	Model 1890 Rifle	Model 1893 Rifle	Model 1903 Rifle
Caliber:	7.65mm Mauser.	7.65mm Mauser.	7.65mm Mauser.
System of operation:	Turn bolt.	Turn bolt.	Turn bolt.
Length overall:	48.6 in.	48.6 in.	49 in.
Barrel length:	29.1 in.	29.1 in.	29.1 in.
Feed device:	5-round, in line, non-detachable box magazine.	5-round, staggered row, non-detachable box magazine.	5-round, staggered row, non-detachable box magazine.
Sights: Front:	Barley corn.	Barley corn.	Barley corn.
Rear:	Leaf.	Leaf.	Tangent.
Weight:	8.8 lb.	8.8 lb.	9.2 lb.
Muzzle velocity:	2132 f.p.s.	2132 f.p.s.	2132 f.p.s.

7.65mm Turkish Mauser M1890 Rifle.

7.92mm M90T.

7.65mm Model 1893 Rifle.

7.65mm Model 1903 Rifle.

7.92mm Model 1905 Carbine. This weapon was originally 7.65mm.

Union of Soviet Socialist Republics (USSR) ("Russia")

The Soviets use the following small arms: 9mm Makarov (PM) pistol; 9mm Stechkin (APS) machine pistol; 7.62mm AKM and AK assault rifles; 7.62mm Model SVD Sniper rifle; 7.62mm RPK, RPD and RP-46 light machine guns; 7.62mm PK/PKS machine gun, 7.62mm SGM and SGMB heavy machine guns, 7.62mm DTM, SGMT and PKT tank machine guns; and 12.7mm DShK M1938/46.

The 7.62mm SKS carbine is no longer a standard shoulder weapon but may be found in frontier forces as may the SG43 heavy machine gun. It should be noted

43

that all but the DTM, SG43 and DShK M1938/46 machine guns are of post-World War II origin and that the feed mechanism of the DShK is of post-war origin.

Most of these weapons are in service in Warsaw Pact countries, and many have been exported to non-aligned countries throughout the world.

SOVIET PISTOLS AND REVOLVERS

The Russians adopted the 7.62mm Nagant revolver in 1895. This revolver was produced in both single-action and double-action versions and is somewhat unusual in that the cylinder moves forward before the hammer falls and the forward end of the chamber aligned for fire telescopes the barrel. The cartridge,

Caliber .22 Model R-4 Pistol.

7.62mm Model 1895 Revolver.

which outwardly resembles a blank cartridge, has its bullet seated below the cartridge case mouth. The purpose of these design features is to prevent gas leakage at the joint between the cylinder and barrel. It is doubtful if this complicated system is worth the effort.

Although the Model 1895 was manufactured as late as World War II, it is no longer in military service. A somewhat smaller version of this revolver was made for police use, and a caliber .22 version was made for training purposes.

In 1930, the first model of the 7.62mm TT Tokarev automatic pistol was adopted; a slightly modified version was adopted in 1933. These weapons are no longer in Soviet service, but are widespread throughout the world and are, therefore, covered in detail in this chapter. A caliber .22 training version of the Tokarev called the Model R-3 and a caliber .22 target version called the Model R-4 have also been manufactured.

The 7.62mm Tokarev has been replaced in the Soviet service, and in several Soviet satellites as well, by the 9mm Makarov (PM) pistol and the 9mm Stechkin Machine pistol. These weapons are chambered for a new 9mm cartridge, intermediate in size and power to the 9mm Browning Short (.380 ACP) and the 9mm Parabellum cartridge. It is quite similar to the 9mm Ultra prototype cartridge developed for use in a version of the Walther PP to be used by the Luftwaffe. The 9mm Makarov cartridge has a 94-grain bullet.

The Soviets produced a small 6.35mm (.25 ACP) automatic called the TK (Tula Korovin). This is not a military weapon, but may be used by police and para-military organizations.

Caliber .22 Model R-3 Pistol.

6.35mm TK Pistol.

7.62mm TT M1933 Pistol.

THE 7.62mm TOKAREV TT M1930 AND M1933 PISTOLS

The 7.62mm Tokarev, or Tula Tokarev-TT, was designed by Fedor V. Tokarev. It is a slightly modified Colt-Browning design, notable for its "packaged" type sear and hammer assembly, which is removed as a unit. This type of construction is not unique and has been used in a number of pistols. The TT33 has been manufactured in Hungary as the Model 48 and in China as the Type 51. The Soviet 7.62mm Model 1930 Type P cartridge is almost identical to the 7.63mm Mauser cartridge and is interchangeable with that cartridge.

Description of Tokarev Mechanism

The slide closely resembles the Colt Browning type. However, the barrel bushing, which is inserted in the front end of the slide to support the barrel and retain the recoil spring, is a heavily forged bushing with one large hole for the barrel and a small hole below it in which the steel disc at the end of the recoil spring seats. This is much stronger than the conventional horseshoe shape bushing and plug.

The firing pin unit is retained in the slide by a simple split pin driven through a hole drilled in the slide, the pin passing through

Field Stripping the Tokarev

(1) Insert nose of cartridge through hole in bushing below barrel and compress spring until bushing is free to turn.

(2) Swing bushing up to the right until its locking lugs disengage. Remove it from the slide. Let the recoil spring protrude.

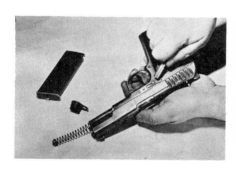

(3) Using a cartridge or the bottom of the magazine, pull back the spring locking clip on the right side of the pistol. This frees the slide-stop pin.

(4) Withdraw the slide-stop barrel-locking pin from the left.

(5) Push the slide and barrel assembly forward out of the guides in the receiver.

(6) Lift the receiver sub-assembly and hammer mechanism out of the receiver.

(8) No further dismounting is normally necessary. However stocks may be removed by reaching inside the handle and turning the metal locking buttons. Firing pin may be removed by punching out split pin from right side of slide. Hammer unit may be completely dismounted by pushing out the three retaining pins. The magazine release catch is a split pin which may be driven out from the right side of the receiver. This permits removing trigger and spring to complete entire disassembly.

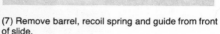

(7) Remove barrel, recoil spring and guide from front of slide.

a slot on top of the firing pin. This pin not only retains the floating firing pin but also determines the distance it can fly forward when struck by the hammer.

The magazine is particularly worthy of note in that it can be easily taken apart for cleaning or repairs. The follower, or platform on which the first cartridge rests, is supported from below by a typical magazine spring. The bottom of this spring, however, rests on a flat platform, which in turn rests on the magazine bottom. The bottom is tongued into grooves in the magazine case, being slid in from the front. It is retained by a small nib on the platform, which protrudes through a hole in the magazine bottom. Pushing this nib in permits the bottom to be pulled forward. The platform, spring and follower can then be removed.

While the barrel locks in the same manner as the Colt Browning, its manufacture has been greatly simplified. Where the Colt has two locking ribs on the top of the barrel only, the TT33 Tokarev locking ribs run entirely around the barrel circumference. The lower sections have no locking function but permit simpler barrel manufacture. They also provide, together with a thickened breech end, a strong support for the high powered cartridge used.

The stocks are of black plastic and require neither screws nor machined-in supports. A pivoted flat spring is riveted on the inner face of each stock. When turned crosswise, each end locks in the frame. Turning the strip disengages it from the frame and permits the stock to be lifted off.

The magazine release catch is a split pin. When punched out, it permits easy removal of the stirrup type trigger and the flat spring in the handle, which acts as the trigger return spring.

The slide stop and barrel locking pin function as in the Colt Browning, but the retaining system has been simplified. Where the pin emerges on the right side of the receiver, a sliding spring

Action open, cut away to show details of recoil system and cocking operation.

clip is provided. When pushed forward, teeth on it engage in notches in the end of the pin. Pulling this back frees the pin to permit removal.

The startling advance of this pistol over all preceding types, however, is in its hammer mechanism. This mechanism, consisting of a simple hammer, sear, disconnector, sear spring and mainspring, is housed in a sub-assembly, which forms part of the receiver and carries part of the slide grooves.

This sub-assembly block has two arms of unequal length. While the outside surfaces line up with the regular receiver guides, the inside surfaces are specially grooved to act as cartridge guides to assure proper feeding as each cartridge is stripped from between the very flat lips of the magazine. The effect of this feature is to make the feeding much more positive, as magazine mouths are normally weak points in feeding systems.

The mainspring is a coil housed inside the hammer itself. Its lower end rests against a pin driven through the housing in the assembly. As the hammer is rocked back by the slide during recoil, this spring is compressed against the supporting pin to provide the energy source for firing the next shot.

The sear, sear spring and disconnector are mounted together on a third pin in the housing. When the slide is fully forward, the disconnector rises into a slot machined for it in the slide housing below the line of the firing pin.

Operation of the Tokarev

When the trigger is pressed, its stirrup forces the flat spring in the handle back to provide energy for returning the trigger to firing position when pressure is released.

The lower end of the disconnector is riding on top of the trigger stirrup while its upper end is in its seat in the breech block. In this position, the sear attached to the disconnector is also in contact with the rear of the trigger stirrups. The trigger forces back against the sear and presses the upper end of the sear out

Action closed, showing details of mainspring in hammer and firing mechanism.

Soviet 9mm Makarov Pistol (PM).

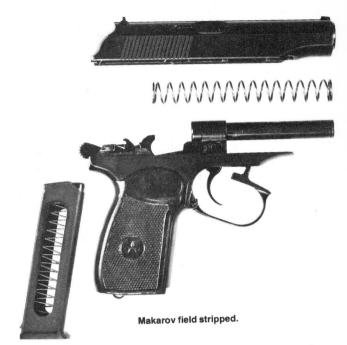

Makarov field stripped.

of its engagement in the second hammer notch. The hammer under the pressure of the compressed spring in it rotates on its axis pin to strike the firing pin and drive it forward to fire the cartridge.

As the slide and barrel under force of the recoil start back, they are locked securely together. As the pressure drops, the barrel swings down on its link to unlock from the slide. The slide continues on backwards to extract and eject in normal fashion.

The slide now forces the hammer back to be caught by the sear. When pressure on the trigger is released so that the disconnector can resume its firing position, the weapon is ready for another shot. The slide has moved forward under tension of the recoil spring below the barrel to strip a cartridge from the top of the magazine.

How TT33 Tokarev Differs From TT30

The 1930 type has a dismountable block assembled into the back edge of the grip frame. This block carries the trigger extension bar operating spring and the disconnector spring. The 1933 type has a solid back edge grip frame with the operating spring

and disconnector spring assembled directly into the grip frame.

The firing system frame of the 1930 type differs from the 1933 frame in its cutouts and general assembly to the grip frame.

The locking lugs of the 1930 type are machined and ground out only on the upper surface of the barrel ahead of the chamber. The lugs on the 1933 type barrel are machined and ground out around the entire circumference of the barrel ahead of the chamber.

The form of the disconnector differs between the two pistols. The 1930 type has a smaller extension bar contacting surface.

THE 9mm MAKAROV (PM) PISTOL

The Makarov, called PM (pistol Makarov) by the Soviets, is a double action, blowback operated self-loading pistol, which out-

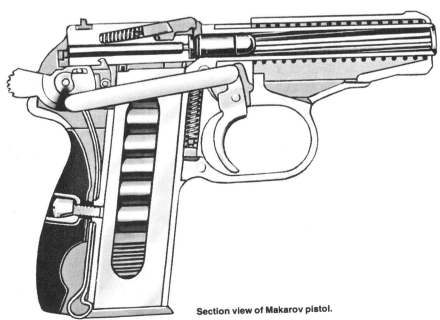

Section view of Makarov pistol.

wardly looks like a scaled up copy of the German Walther PP. The Makarov is quite different in internal design from the Walther. The principal differences are as follows. The Makarov does not have a loaded chamber indicating pin. The PM uses a leaf type main spring; the Walther used a coil spring. The trigger-sear linkage of the Makarov is considerably different than that of the Walther, as is the disconnector. The magazine catch of the Makarov is of the spring type and is at the bottom of the grip. The magazine catch of the Walther is a button type mounted on the left side of the receiver. The Makarov has an externally mounted slide stop; the Walther slide stop is internally mounted and is released by drawing back the slide and allowing it to run forward. The ejector of the Makarov is the back end of the slide stop bar. The safety of the Makarov is pushed up to put it on "Safe" and pushed down to put it on "Fire," which is opposite to that of the Walther. The safety of the Makarov places a bar in front of the hammer and has a lug that positions itself in front of the rear shoulder of the receiver, thereby locking the slide in position and preventing the hammer from being cocked.

Stripping of the Makarov

Pull down the trigger guard; pull the slide to the rear and lift its rear end up; then ease forward the slide and the recoil spring (which encircles the barrel), and remove them from the weapon. Since the Makarov is a blowback-operated weapon, it has a fixed barrel, which should not ordinarily be removed. Further stripping is not recommended.

SOVIET 9mm STECHKIN MACHINE PISTOL (APS)

The Stechkin is a true machine pistol in that it is capable of full automatic and semiautomatic fire. It is equipped with a wooden or plastic holster that can be used as a shoulder stock. The Stechkin, like the Makarov, is blowback in operation, but it is a considerably larger weapon than the Makarov and has considerably more potential as a weapon.

Operation of the Stechkin

The Stechkin is loaded by inserting a loaded magazine into the grip (as with the US cal. .45 M1911A1 automatic pistol), then pulling the slide to the rear and releasing it so that it runs home and chambers a cartridge. The safety selector catch is mounted on the left rear side of the slide, as it is on the Makarov and the Walther PP and PPK pistols. The safety selector catch has three positions. The bottom position is safe, the middle position is semiautomatic fire, and the top position is full automatic fire.

The Stechkin with its shoulder-stock holster attached can hit man-sized targets consistently at ranges of 100 to 150 yards, when it is in the hands of a good shot. This, of course, is in semiautomatic fire. The Stechkin's usable range in full automatic fire probably does not exceed twenty-five yards.

Stechkin, with shoulder stock holster.

Soviet 9mm Stechkin Machine Pistol (APS), stripped.

AUTOMATIC PISTOL STECHKIN (APS) 9 x 18mm

176. АВТОМАТИЧЕСКИЙ ПИСТОЛЕТ

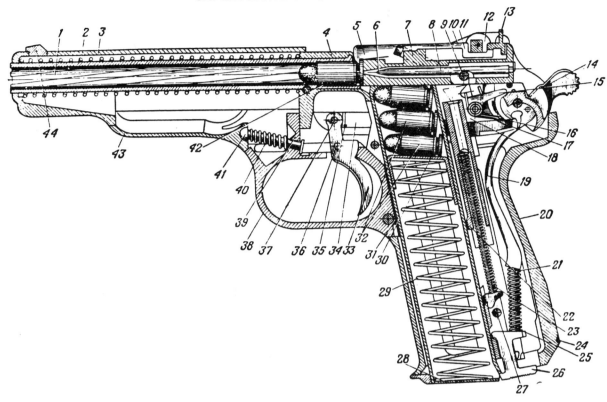

1 ствол
2 возвратная пружина
3 затвор
4 стойка (ствола)
5 выбрасыватель
6 боек
7 пружина выбрасывателя
8 ударник
9 переводчик-предохранитель
10—13 прицел:
11 прицельная планка
12 установочный барабанчик
13 гривка с прорезью;
14 курок
15 шептало
16 пружина шептала
17 разобщитель
18 затворная задержка
19 толкатель
20 рукоятка пистолета
21 боевая пружина
22 замедлитель

23 пружина замедлителя
24 выступ для присоединения кобуры-приклада
25 направляющий стержень боевой пружины
26 защелка магазина
27 отверстие для винта щечек
28 крышка магазина
29 пружина подавателя
30 подаватель
31 корпус магазина
32 пистолетные патроны
33 спусковой крючок
34 спусковая тяга
35 пружина спускового крючка
36 цапфа
37 штифт спускового крючка
38 спусковая скоба
39 стойка (спусковой скобы)
40 пружина стопора
41 стопор
42 патронник с патроном
43 рамка
44 мушка.

1. Barrel
2. Recoil spring
3. Slide
4. Barrel bracket
5. Extractor
6. Firing pin tip
7. Extractor spring
8. Firing pin
9. Safety and fire selector

10.–13. Rear sight mechanism
14. Hammer
15. Sear
16. Sear spring
17. Disconnector
18. Slide stop
19. Hammer strut
20. Pistol grip
21. Mainspring

22. Retarder
23. Retarder spring
24. Stock lug
25. Mainspring guide
26. Magazine catch
27. Grip screw hole
28.–31. Magazine assembly
32. Cartridges
33. Trigger
34. Trigger bar

35. Trigger spring
36. Trigger pin axis
37. Trigger pin
38. Trigger guard
39. Trigger guard post
40.–41. Retainer and spring
42. Chamber with cartridge
43. Receiver
44. Front sight

CHARACTERISTICS OF SOVIET PISTOLS AND REVOLVERS

	Model 1895	TT Model 1933	Makarov (PM)	Stechkin (APS)
Caliber:	7.62mm.	7.62mm.	9mm.	9mm.
System of operation:	Double-action revolver.	Recoil, semiautomatic.	Blowback, semiautomatic.	Blowback, selective fire.
Length overall:	9.06 in.	7.68 in.	6.34 in.	w/shoulder stock—21.25 in. w/o shoulder stock—8.85 in.
Barrel length:	4.33 in.	4.57 in.	3.83 in.	5 in.
Feed device:	7-round cylinder.	8-round, in-line detachable box magazine.	8-round, in-line detachable box magazine.	20-round, staggered row, detachable box magazine.
Sights: Front:	Blade.	Blade.	Blade.	Blade.
Rear:	"U" notch.	"U" notch.	Square notch.	Flip over "L" with notches.
Weight:	1.65 lb.	1.88 lb.	1.56 lb.	w/shoulder stock—3.92 lb. w/o shoulder stock—1.7 lb.
Muzzle velocity:	892 f.p.s.	1378 f.p.s.	1070 f.p.s.	1100 f.p.s.
Cyclic rate:	--------------	--------------	--------------	750 r.p.m.

SOVIET BOLT-ACTION RIFLES AND CARBINES

(Through World War II)

THE MOSIN-NAGANT

The Mosin-Nagant rifle was adopted in 1891 by Imperial Russia. The action of the rifle was developed by Colonel S. I. Mosin of the Imperial Russian Army, and the magazine was developed by Nagant, a Belgian. All Soviet bolt-action military rifles and carbines are Mosin-Nagant weapons, and all are basically similar to the original Mosin-Nagant. These weapons can be considered reasonably effective infantry weapons. Fairly good shooting can be done with them at combat ranges, although their sights do not lend themselves to the finer degrees of accuracy obtained with similar United States weapons. They suffer from an over-complicated bolt but in other respects are relatively simple to service and maintain. The safety, in that it is extremely hard to engage and disengage, represents a shortcoming of the Mosin-Nagant weapons.

The M1891 Mosin-Nagant

The original rifle M1891 was considerably different than later versions of the same model. The original rifle M1891 had no handguard, was fitted with sling swivels instead of the sling slots used on later versions and had a leaf rear sight designed for the old conical-nosed 7.62mm ball cartridge. In 1908, the Spitzer pointed light ball round (which is still used) was introduced, and the rear sight was changed. About this time handguards were added, and the swivels were replaced by sling slots bored in the stock. The original M1891 is now a collector's item. The later versions of the rifle M1891 are obsolete.

The Dragoon Rifle M1891

The Dragoon rifle M1891 was originally developed as a weapon for heavy cavalry. Manufacture of this rifle was discontinued about 1930, when it was replaced by the rifle M1891/30. The Dragoon rifle M1891 is obsolete. Both the M1891 rifle and the Dragoon rifle have hexagonal receivers.

These rifles are all caliber 7.62mm (.30) for rim cartridges. Mechanically they are all basically the same.

The design differs considerably from the Mauser type on which US bolt-action rifles are all built; the following descriptive matter is set down to provide an understanding of the Russian design.

Bolt. The bolt is an entirely original design. It has never been imitated. It is a 2-piece design in which a removable bolt head carries the locking lugs. The two locking lugs engage horizontally in the receiver, the opposite of most types. The bolt head turns with the bolt. If this head is accidentally left out when

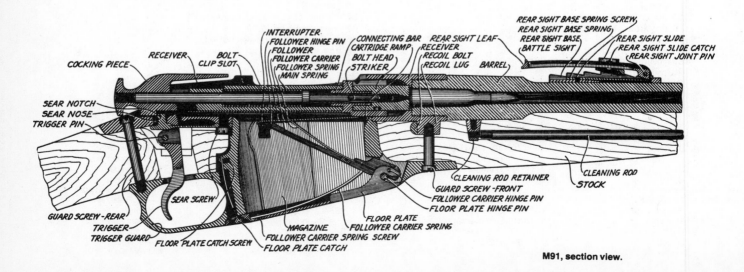

M91, section view.

Export model of the Model 1891 Mosin Nagant made at the Sestroresk Weapons Factory. Note the opened magazine showing the follower and spring.

assembling the rifle, the weapon cannot be fired. The extractor is carried by the bolt head.

A special connecting bar joins the bolt head to the bolt itself. This bar does not turn with the bolt; it is positioned in the underside of the bolt assembly and lies in a receiver cut in the boltway. This bar also acts as a guide for the cocking piece and assists in keeping the bolt securely in the receiver. The bar has a projection rising from its forward end. This projection holds a small hollow cylinder. The rear end of this cylinder nests in the hollow front of the bolt, while the forward end of the cylinder nests in the rear of the bolt head.

The handle is part of the bolt forging. A rib extends forward from the hollowed-out bolt. A cut on the underside of this rib takes the projection on the connecting bar. As the bolt handle is lifted, the connecting bar stays fixed in its groove in the receiver below, but its upper projection in the bolt recess holds the bolt assembly securely together.

A small lug on the front end of the connecting bar fits into a groove inside the bolt head, and a small lug on the rear of the bolt head catches in a recess at the front end of the bolt extension rib. Thus as the bolt turns, the bolt head is compelled to turn with it.

The striker and mainspring are inserted from the front end of the hollow bolt. The rear of the striker passes through a small rear hole in the bolt, and a cocking piece is screwed onto it. A collar at the front end of the striker serves as forward mainspring compression point, and the firing pin end, which is forward of this collar, passes through the hollow cylinder on top of the connecting bar. Flat surfaces on the striker at this point and corresponding surfaces within the cylinder prevent the striker from turning.

Cocking Piece. This is a simple and effective design. When it is screwed onto the end of the striker projecting from the bolt, an upper extension of the cocking piece passes along the top of the bolt and through the cut in the top of the receiver bridge.

A small cocking nose is machined on the rear lower surface of the cocking piece.

Safety. When the cocking piece is pulled back slightly, it draws the attached striker back far enough for the flat surfaces on the striker to pass out of the connecting bar cylinder; at this point the striker and cocking piece can be turned to the left. A lug on the underside of the cocking piece extension is thus turned into a locking recess at the rear end of the bolt.

Hence by pulling back and turning the cocking piece, the following safety results are obtained: (a) The cocking nose on the cocking piece is turned out of contact with the sear—hence a trigger pull cannot affect it. (b) The striker has been turned so that if it were possible for it to slip it could not hit the cartridge primer, because the flat surfaces at its forward end are turned out of line with the corresponding surfaces inside the connecting bar cylinder through which the striker must pass to hit the primer. (c) The lug on the underside of the cocking piece extension is locked into a cut in the rear of the bolt to prevent any forward movement. (d) The long cocking piece extension is turned to the rear of the cut in the receiver bridge and cannot move forward since the receiver bridge is in its path.

Magazine. The magazine is a projecting single-line box holding five rim cartridges. It forms part of the trigger guard. The magazine floor plate hinges forward and is kept closed by a spring catch. When the catch in the floor plate is drawn back, the magazine follower carrier spring forces the plate down and permits removal of cartridges.

As the accompanying drawing shows, the magazine has not merely a follower on which the first cartridge rests, together with its spring, but also a special "follower carrier" and its spring as part of the cartridge lifting system.

Interrupter-Ejector. This unit is also called "distributor-ejector" and "cartridge valve-ejector." No other rifle needs or uses this device.

The interrupter is a specially shaped plate attached to the left side of the receiver. At its rear is a flat spring held to the receiver by a screw. The thin plate section passes through a cut in the receiver wall above the magazine way. A point on this plate acts as ejector.

The interrupter is operated by action of the bolt. It prevents double feeding. When the top cartridge in the magazine has been chambered, the following cartridge cannot rise because the interrupter is holding it down. Only when the bolt is locked and the extractor engaged around the cartridge case head does a cam-shaped groove in the bolt bear against the interrupter and force it out against the interrupter spring. As the holding projection on the interrupter is forced away from the cartridge, the follower spring can push the top cartridge into line to be ready to feed.

When the bolt handle is raised to open the action, the cam groove in the bolt allows a point on the interrupter to enter the magazine and press against the second cartridge from the top.

An ejecting point on the edge of the interrupter is now in line with a groove in the bolt head. Thus, as the bolt is pulled back, the empty case is struck against this point and ejected from the rifle.

Operation. Lifting bolt handle rotates bolt, bolt head and extractor as a unit. A cam cut at the rear of the bolt forces against the cocking nose on the underside of the cocking piece. The cocking piece and striker assembly are forced back, thereby pulling the firing pin point back away from the primer. The mainspring is partly compressed.

The rib extending forward from the bolt proper passes along a special cam surface on the top of the overhanging receiver ring. (The bolt head is entirely enclosed by the receiver ring.) This action forces the entire bolt assembly back to give primary extraction, the rearward thrust beginning as soon as the bolt has turned far enough for the locking lugs on the bolt head to clear their seats in the receiver ring.

The turning bolt operates the interrupter as described, permitting the interrupter spring to force the interrupter in to hold the next to the top cartridge in the magazine and to line up the ejector point.

The short extractor in the bolt head carries the empty case back and strikes it against the ejector. At this point a lug on top of the trigger hits against metal at the end of a groove in the connecting bar. (The bar has been traveling back as part of the bolt assembly, once the rearward action started.) This acts as a bolt stop.

The upright bolt handle passes back through the cut in the receiver bridge on rearward bolt pull.

As the bolt is pushed forward the bolt head starts the cartridge in its path towards the chamber. At the point where the forward extension rib on the bolt hits the cam face in the receiver ring, the sear nose catches and holds the cocking piece nose. The bolt head locking lugs are at the cam grooves leading to their locking seats in the receiver ring.

As the bolt handle is turned down, the locking lugs are forced along their cam grooves. This draws the bolt forward as the bolt head lugs are locked. Since the sear nose is holding the cocking piece back, this forward pull completes compression of the mainspring. The interrupter works as already described to permit the cartridge to rise below the bolt.

The Rifle M1891/30

The rifle M1891/30 is about the same length as the M1891 Dragoon, but it represents many improvements over the Dragoon. The sights used on the M1891/30 are superior to those of the Dragoon, and, because the metric system of measurement was adopted in Russia during this period, the sights of the M1891/30 are calibrated in meters rather than in arshins. (One arshin equals 0.71 meters or 0.78 yards.) Manufacture of the M1891/30 was initiated in 1930. This model was used in large numbers in the Soviet Army, but was replaced by the carbine M1944 as the standard Soviet infantry shoulder weapon at the end of World War II. It is still in use in some of the satellite countries.

The Sniper Rifle M1891/30

The sniper rifle M1891/30, which is basically the M1891/30 adapted for use with a telescope, is still a standard weapon in some satellite armies. The telescopes employed are somewhat similar to those used on United States hunting rifles.

The Carbine M1910

Although Imperial Russia adopted the Mosin-Nagant rifle in 1891, a true carbine did not appear until 1910. The carbine M1910, with its leaf sight and sling slots, had characteristics of both the original and later versions of the rifle M1891. The carbine M1910 has a hexagonal receiver and does not take a bayonet. This model is comparatively rare.

The Carbine M1938

The carbine M1938 replaced the M1910. It is similar in many respects to the rifle M1891/30. It has a tangent-type rear sight, hooded front sight, and rounded receiver. It does not take a bayonet. This model may be encountered in satellite forces, although it is not manufactured at present.

The Carbine M1944

The carbine M1944, introduced during the latter part of World War II, was the last of the Mosin-Nagants. The permanently fixed bayonet folds down along the right side of the carbine stock when not in use. Except for a slightly longer barrel and the addition of the bayonet, the carbine M1944 is identical to the M1938. It is still in use in various Soviet satellites. See Chapter 13 for illustration of PRC copy of M1944 with folding stock.

CHARACTERISTICS OF SOVIET 7.62MM MOSIN-NAGANT BOLT ACTION RIFLES AND CARBINES

	Rifle M1891	Dragoon Rifle M1891	Rifle M1891/30	Sniper Rifle M1891/30	Carbine M1910	Carbine M1938	Carbine M1944
Weight:							
w/o bayonet & sling:	9.62 lb.	8.75 lb.	8.7 lb.	11.3 lb.	7.5 lb.	7.62 lb.	
w/bayonet & sling:	10.63 lb.	9.7 lb.	9.7 lb.		7.7 lb.		8.9 lb.
Length:							
w/o bayonet:	51.37 in.	48.75 in.	48.5 in.	48.5 in.	40 in.	40 in.	40 in. (folded)
w/bayonet:	68.2 in.	65.5 in.	65.4 in.	65.4 in.			52.25 in. (extended)
Barrel length:	31.6 in.	28.8 in.	28.7 in.	28.7 in.	20 in.	20 in.	20.4 in.
Magazine capacity:	5 rounds.	5 rounds.	5 rounds.	5 rounds.	5 rounds.	5 rounds	5 rounds.
Instrumental velocity at 78 ft. w/hvy ball:	2660 f.p.s.	2660 f.p.s.	2660 f.p.s.	2660 f.p.s.	2514 f.p.s.	2514 f.p.s.	2514 f.p.s.
Rate of fire:	8-10 r.p.m.	8-10 r.p.m.	8-10 r.p.m.	8-10 r.p.m.	8-10 r.p.m.	8-10 r.p.m.	8-10 r.p.m.
Maximum sighting range:	3200 arshins (2496 yd.)	3200 arshins (2496 yd.)	2000 meters (2200 yd.)	2000 meters* (2200 yd.)	2000 arshins (1560 yd.)	1000 meters (1100 yd.)	1000 meters (1100 yd.)
Front sight:	Unprotected blade.	Unprotected blade.	Hooded post.	Hooded post.	Unprotected blade.	Hooded post.	Hooded post.
Rear sight:	Leaf.	Leaf.	Tangent.	Tangent.	Leaf.	Tangent.	Tangent.
Ammunition**							

*For iron sights when scope is dismounted. Maximum sighting range for the telescopic sight on this weapon is: PE scope—1400m (1540 yd.); PU scope—1300m (1420 yd.).

**Soviet 7.62mm rifle and ground machine gun rimmed ammunition.

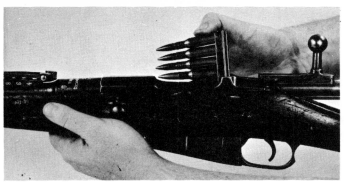

Loading Mosin-Nagant rifle.

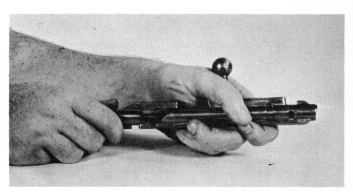

Drawing back cocking piece.

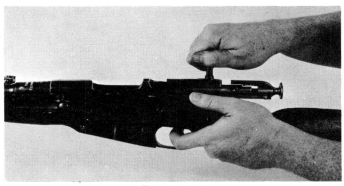

Removing bolt.

bayonets are not provided for this carbine.

The Carbine M1938. Operating instructions for the carbine M1938 are the same as those for the rifle M1891; bayonets are not provided for this carbine.

The Carbine M1944. Operating instructions for the carbine M1944 are the same as those for the rifle M1891; however, this carbine has a nondetachable bayonet, which may be folded or extended by forcing the spring-loaded bayonet tube away from the pivot pin, and then swinging the bayonet to either folded or fixed position.

How to Load and Fire the Mosin-Nagant Rifles and Carbines

The Rifle M1891. To set the safety, draw back the cocking piece and turn it to the left. This prevents the bolt from opening. To put off safe, pull the cocking piece back, turn it to the right and allow it to move forward.

The rifle M1891 is loaded in the same manner as the United States Springfield or any Mauser rifle. Open the bolt, place a clip of cartridges in the clip guides and press the rounds down into the magazine. Close the bolt; the clip will then fall out of the clip guides onto the ground. The weapon is now ready to fire.

To unload the rifle M1891, open the magazine floor plate and remove the cartridges. The magazine floor plate catch is located on the lower rear part of the magazine, forward of the trigger guard. Press the catch rearward; the follower and floor plate will swing down and forward on a pivot pin, and the cartridges will spill out. Open the bolt and extract the round from the chamber.

The M1891 bayonet is attached by a locking ring; if the M1891/30 bayonet is used, a spring-loaded catch holds the bayonet in place.

The Dragoon Rifle M1891. Operating instructions for Dragoon M1891 are the same as for rifle M1891.

The bayonet of the rifle M1891 or M1891/30 is attached to the Dragoon M1891 in the same manner as described for the rifle M1891.

The Rifle M1891/30. Operating instructions for the rifle M1891/30 are the same as those for the rifle M1891.

The bayonet is attached by a spring-loaded catch.

The Sniper rifle M1891/30. Operating instructions for this rifle are the same as those for the rifle M1891. The bayonet for the rifle M1891/30 is attached to the sniper rifle by means of a spring-loaded catch.

The Carbine M1910. Operating instructions for the carbine M1910 are the same as those for the rifle M1891; however,

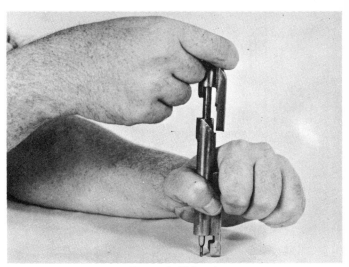

Removal of firing pin.

How to Field Strip the Mosin-Nagant Rifles and Carbines

Open bolt and draw to the rear, pull trigger all the way to the rear and remove bolt from the receiver.

Pull cocking piece to the rear and turn it to the left to relieve the tension of the main spring. Remove bolt head and guide.

Place the firing pin on a solid surface, preferably a block of soft wood, push the bolt body down and unscrew the cocking piece, then remove the firing pin and spring.

The magazine follower can be removed by pushing the magazine floor plate catch, on the bottom of the floor plate just forward of the trigger guard, rearward swinging down the floor plate, follower spring and follower and pressing together, with thumb and forefinger, the follower and floor plate and pulling down to remove them.

Reassembly is in reverse order of disassembly. Care must be exercised when screwing the firing pin into the bolt, that the rear of the firing pin is flush with the cocking piece and that the marks on the rear of the firing pin are aligned with those on the cocking piece in order to assure correct firing pin protrusion.

SOVIET AUTOMATIC and SEMIAUTOMATIC RIFLES and CARBINES

The history of Soviet self-loading rifle and automatic rifle development is detailed in Chapter 1.

TOKAREV 7.62mm SEMIAUTOMATIC RIFLE M1938 (SVT),
7.62mm SEMIAUTOMATIC RIFLE M1940 (SVT) and
7.62mm AUTOMATIC AND SEMIAUTOMATIC RIFLE M1940 (AVT)

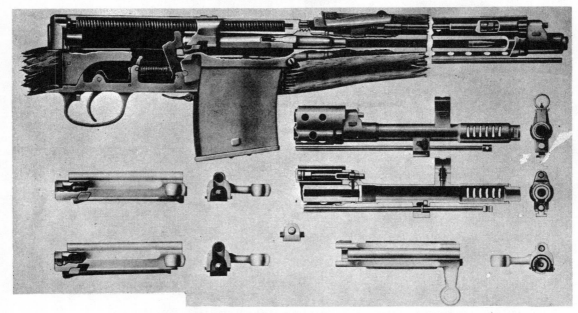

The Russian Tokarev Semiauto Rifle. Phantom view showing action locked at instant of firing. Details show the muzzle brake, gas operation and bolt locking systems.

M1938 7.62mm Tokarev Rifle (SVT), action open.

M1938 Tokarev stock illustrating two–piece construction.

How the M1940 Tokarev Rifle Works

A loaded magazine is inserted in the bottom of the receiver until its catch locks it. The bolt handle is drawn back and released to cock the hammer and strip a cartridge into the firing chamber.

The rear end of the bolt is forced down by the bolt carrier into locking position. The carrier proceeds to ride over projections on the bolt to hold it in the locked position.

When the trigger is pressed, it forces a bar forward to rotate the sear. The sear is fitted vertically in the trigger guard. It now engages a bent in the head of the hammer. The hammer is rotated forward to strike the firing pin and explode the cartridge.

As the bullet passes down the barrel, a portion of the gas escapes through a port drilled in the top of the barrel under the upper section of the wooden fore-end. (The gas regulator has five positions for adjustment.) The expanding gas impinges on the head of the piston rod (which is positioned on top of the barrel) driving it backward for a stroke of about 1½ inches.

The thrust is transmitted to the operating rod, which passes it on to the bolt carrier.

The operating rod is mounted above the barrel, its rear end passing through a hole in the receiver directly above the forward face of the locked bolt and in line with the bolt carrier, which rides on top of the bolt. The operating rod return spring is mounted around the rod itself.

The carrier travels back about ¼ of an inch before unlocking. The bolt travels on back carrying with it the empty cartridge case, which is ejected to the right. It also compresses the dual

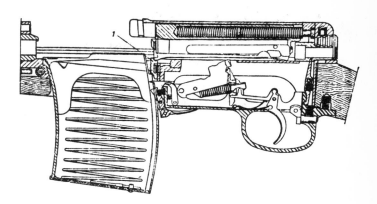

Action open on firing last shot. Recoil spring compressed, hammer cocked, ready for reloading.

springs mounted in the top of the receiver to store up energy for the return motion. At the same time, it forces the hammer to rotate on its axis until it is caught and held by the sear.

When the last shot has been fired, a catch in the bottom center of the bolt way is operated by a projection of the magazine platform and holds the bolt open.

Tokarev 7.62mm M1940 Rifle (SVT).

Field Stripping the Tokarev M1940

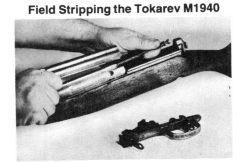

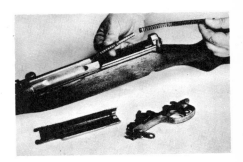

(1) Remove trigger assembly. First turn the thumb latch at the extreme rear of the receiver up to the left as far as it will go. This will expose a cylindrical hole in which the trigger guard locking collar rests. With a screwdriver or a bullet point, push the spring-loaded locking collar in. This will pivot the locking bar in the rear of the receiver and will free the rear end of the trigger guard assembly which may then be removed from the receiver. (Note: when replacing this unit it is necessary that the bolt be back far enough from the chamber so the disconnector is able to rise. Otherwise the front end of the trigger guard unit will not seat in the receiver notches.)

(2) Remove operating spring dust cover. First rest the muzzle of the rifle on the floor, as considerable force must be applied. Then pull the steel cover to the rear of the bolt straight down toward the muzzle. This action will force the buffer and operating springs down inside the bolt, as the buffer guide rod is seated in a groove machined for it at the extreme rear of the cover. When the cover has been pulled down as far as it will go in its guides in the receiver, grasp it firmly with the left hand and squeeze it tightly against the bolt. While retaining this grasp with the left hand, with the thumb of the right hand push the buffer rod down far enough to free its head from the seating in the cover.

(3) Then push it carefully out away from the cover and ease it and the springs up out of the bolt hole. The cover is free to come off at this point. Remove operating and buffer spring assemblies. Holding the protruding buffer spring and rod close to the bolt hole, ease them up and to your right so the rod will clear the rear of the receiver. When all tension is off the springs, the buffer spring and its guide rod may be lifted out of engagement with the hollow operating spring rod. The operating spring and its rod may now be removed from the bolt hole.

(4) Remove the bolt assembly. Pull the bolt handle back slowly until the bolt carrier and the bolt have cleared the magazine well. Then lift up on the bolt handle and continue to pull back and up. At this point the bolt assembly is free of its receiver guides and may be tilted and lifted up out of the receiver. (Note: When re-assembling this unit, the assembly will drop into its receiver tracks at just the one proper point. Do not exert force, but feel for this point if you cannot

locate it immediately.) Remove the bolt from its carrier. Hold the assembly in the palm of the left hand upside down. Place the forefinger over the firing-pin hole and the thumb (of the right hand) over the rear of the firing pin and push the bolt slowly ahead inside the carrier. At the proper point the cam faces on the bolt will mate with the proper surfaces on the bolt carrier and the bolt may then be lifted up out of the carrier. Remove the gas piston. Press in the lock on the front band and push the band forward. This will permit the perforated metal upper cover to be lifted off. The pierced wooden forearm covering the gas piston may then be lifted off. (Note: If it is necessary to remove the stock, unscrew the bolt from the right side of the receiver below the chamber and pull it out. The lower metal fore-end piece may then be removed and the receiver and barrel assemblies lifted out of the stock complete.) Pull the piston back until it clears the face of the gas cylinder over which it is mounted.

(5) Holding the piston at this point, pull the operating rod in which the piston seats back far enough to permit the piston to be lifted off. Then ease the rod forward against the tension of its spring, and remove the rod and its spring from their seating in the receiver below the line of the rear sight. Remove compensator and gas cylinder assembly. Drift the retainer out preferably from the right. The compensator and assembly may then be unscrewed from the barrel and removed.

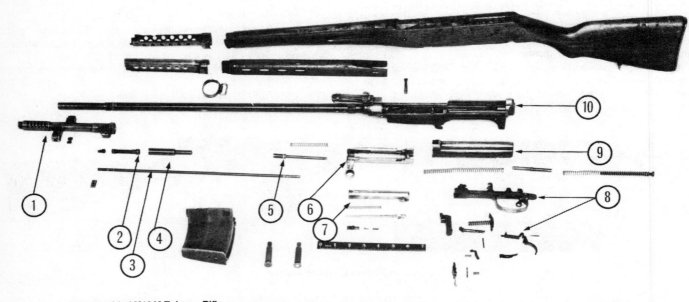

Disassembled M1940 Tokarev Rifle.
1. Muzzle brake, front sight and gas cylinder assembly. 2. Gas cylinder. 3. Operating rod. 4. Gas piston. 5. Operating rod tappet. 6. Bolt carrier. 7. Bolt, disassembled. 8. Trigger group, disassembled. 9. Receiver cover. 10. Barrel and receiver group.

Metal parts removed from stock to show operation of mechanism and dust cover removed. Operating rod is being driven back through hole in the receiver and has pushed bolt carrier back until carrier has unlocked bolt and is carrying it back with it.

CHARACTERISTICS OF SOVIET PRE-WORLD WAR II 7.62mm AUTOMATIC AND SEMIAUTOMATIC RIFLES

	Automatic Rifle M1936	Semiautomatic Rifle M1938	Semiautomatic Rifle M1940	Automatic Rifle M1940	Semiautomatic Sniper Rifle M1940	Semiautomatic Sniper Rifle M1938
Weight:						
w/o bayonet & magazine:	8.93 lb.	8.70 lb.	8.59 lb.	8.35 lb.	9.18 lb.	9.52 lb.
w/bayonet & magazine:	. . . .	10.8 lb.	9.48 lb.	9.24 lb.	. . . .	. . . .
Length:						
w/o bayonet:	48.6 in.	48.1 in.	48.1 in.	48.1 in.	48.1 in.	48.1 in.
w/bayonet:	59.3 in.	60.84 in.	57.1 in.	57.1 in.	57.1 in.	60.84 in.
Barrel length:	24.16 in.	25 in.	24.6 in.	24.6 in.	24.6 in.	25 in.
Magazine capacity:	15 rounds.	10 rounds.	10 rounds.	10 rounds.	10 rounds.	10 rounds.
Instrumental velocity at 78 ft. w/hvy ball:	2519 f.p.s.	2519 f.p.s.	2519 f.p.s.	2519 f.p.s.	2519 f.p.s.	2519 f.p.s.
Rate of fire: (semiautomatic)	30-40 r.p.m.	25 r.p.m.	25 r.p.m.	30-40 r.p.m.	25 r.p.m.	25 r.p.m.
Maximum sighting range:	1500 meters	1500 meters.	1500 meters.	1500 meters	Iron sights: 600 m. (660 yd.) Telescope: 1300 m. (1430 yd.)	Iron sights: 600 m. (660 yd.) Telescope: 1300 m (1430 yd.)
Front sight:	Open guard blade	Hooded post.	Hooded post.	Hooded post.	Hooded post.	Hooded post.
Rear sight:	Tangent.	Tangent.	Tangent.	Tangent.	Tangent and telescope.	Tangent and telescope.
Principle of operation:	Gas.	Gas.	Gas.	Gas.	Gas.	Gas.
Ammunition:	*	*	*	*	*	*

*7.62mm USSR rifle and ground machine gun rimmed ammunition.

POST-WORLD WAR II SOVIET SHOULDER WEAPONS

SOVIET 7.62mm SKS CARBINE

The SKS, like the AK automatic rifle and RPD machine gun, is chambered for the new Soviet "intermediate-sized" M1943 cartridge previously described. Its disassembly is not quite as simple as is the AK's but is still relatively easy. The SKS is distinguished by its folding bayonet, which—unlike earlier Soviet folding bayonets—is of blade section and folds under the weapon rather than to the side of the weapon. The SKS is no longer used in first-line Soviet units.

NOTE: The Soviets call the SKS a carbine because of its short barrel length. It is not intended to be nor is it used as a replacement for the pistol (as the US carbine was designed to be). The SKS was intended to be used as the tactical equivalent to the US M1 or M14.

Field Stripping the SKS

Turn off the safety by rotating it downward. Swing the bayonet upward so that it projects at a 90-degree angle from the muzzle of the rifle. Remove the cleaning rod by disengaging its head from the lugs on the underside of the barrel and pulling the rod forward. Rotate the bayonet downward until it locks in its folded position.

Hold the small of the stock with the left hand and, with the right hand, rotate the receiver cover retaining pin arm (located at the right rear of the receiver) upward; then, pressing on the receiver cover with the thumb of the left hand, move the pin to the right as far as possible, and remove the cover from the receiver. Remove the recoil spring assembly from the bolt carrier. Note

Soviet 7.62mm Simonov Semiautomatic Carbine (SKS).

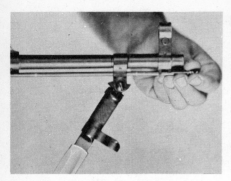

(1) Removing cleaning rod.

(2) Loosening receiver cover retaining pin.

(3) Removing receiver cover.

(4) Removing bolt and bolt carrier.

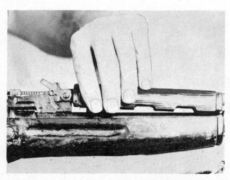

(5) Removing handguard and gas piston assembly.

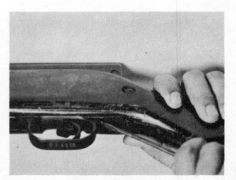

(6) Unlocking trigger guard.

(7) Removing trigger group.

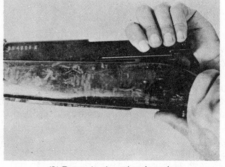

(8) Removing barrel and receiver.

that the recoil spring assembly is, like that of the AK, a packaged unit.

To remove the bolt and bolt carrier from the receiver, pull back on the operating handle; the whole assembly will lift out, and the bolt can be removed from the bolt carrier.

Hold the fore-end of the carbine with the left hand and, with the right hand, rotate the gas cylinder tube lock lever upward (the lock is at the right front side of the rear sight base) until the lock lever lug is stopped by the upper wall of the cutout in the rear sight base. Then the gas cylinder tube and handguard assembly can be slightly raised and pulled rearward off the weapon. The gas piston will slide out of the gas cylinder tube.

To assemble the weapon, follow the above steps in reverse order.

Loading and Firing the SKS

Set the weapon on "Safe" by turning the safety lever up as far as it will go. The safety lever is at the rear of the trigger guard.

Pull the operating handle to the rear as far as it will go; the bolt and bolt carrier will be held to the rear by the bolt-holding-open device. If the cartridges are assembled in the ten-round charger normally used, insert one end of the charger in the charger guide machined into the top forward end of the bolt carrier. Push down on the cartridges with the thumb until all the cartridges are loaded into the magazine; then remove the empty charger guide. Pull back on the operating handle and release it; the bolt and bolt carrier will now go forward and chamber a cartridge. Disengage the safety by turning it down as far as it will go. The rifle is now ready to fire.

If all ten rounds are fired, the bolt and bolt carrier will stay to the rear, leaving the action open for reloading. If only a few rounds are fired and it is desired to unload the weapon, the following procedure should be observed. To the rear of the magazine, on the underside of the weapon, is a catch; pull this catch rearward. The magazine body will now swing downward, and the rounds in the magazine will spill out. The round in the chamber is removed by pulling the operating handle to the rear.

SKS, field stripped.

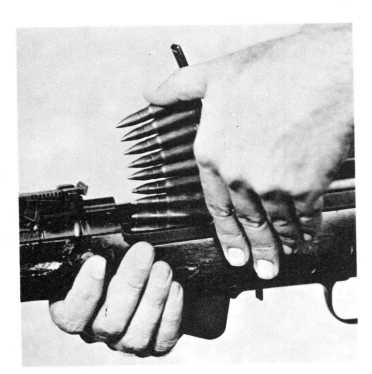

Loading the SKS.

To Fix the Bayonet

To fix the bayonet, the bayonet handle is pulled to the rear, and the bayonet is rotated upward until the bayonet muzzle ring snaps over the muzzle of the weapon. To fold the bayonet, pull the bayonet handle upward until the bayonet muzzle ring clears the muzzle; then swing the bayonet downward and into its groove in the stock.

How the SKS Works.

When the trigger is pressed, the trigger rotates and moves the trigger arm forward. The trigger arm moves the sear forward and disengages it from the hammer. The hammer spring, now being free to expand, rotates the hammer, which strikes the firing pin and drives it through the bolt channel. When the hammer is rotated, the hammer heel lowers the forward end of the disconnector and the forward end of the trigger arm. At this time, the trigger arm is disengaged from the sear, which, under the action of the sear spring, returns to the rear position. The firing pin moves through the bolt channel until the firing pin tip emerges from the bolt face and strikes the primer. After the bullet passes the gas port in the wall of the barrel, the gases enter the gas cylinder, exert pressure on the piston and move the bolt carrier to the rear by means of the piston rod.

The bolt carrier, after traveling a path of eight mm, raises the rear end of the bolt, disengages the bolt locking surface from the receiver lug and brings the bolt to the rear. As the bolt moves to the rear, it extracts the empty cartridge case, which is held in the bolt face by the extractor lug. After traveling a distance of 70 mm, the base of the cartridge case meets the ejector, and the case is ejected from the weapon. In moving to the rear, the bolt carrier, and then the bolt, cocks the hammer. The forward end of the disconnector, under the action of the hammer spring, is raised upward, and the hammer is positioned on the disconnector notch at the same time. The forward end of the trigger arm is located between the base of the trigger guard and the sear. Under the action of the sear spring, the sear, which is in the extreme rear position, is positioned under the hammer cock notch. Under the action of the follower lever spring, the follower positions the next round for the feed rib. The piston, together with the piston rod, pushes the bolt a distance of 20 mm. The bolt thereafter continues by inertia to the extreme rear position, at the same time compressing the recoil spring, and the piston and piston rod return to the forward position under the action of the piston rod spring.

Under the action of the expanding recoil spring, the bolt moves forward, and the bolt feed rib grasps the next round in the magazine and sends it into the chamber. The bolt carrier lowers the rear end of the bolt upon approaching the barrel face, and the bolt locking surface is positioned in front of the receiver locking lug to seal the bore. The bolt, in lowering, depresses the protruding front end of the disconnector, at which time the hammer is disengaged from the disconnector and is then cocked. As it approaches the barrel face, the extractor, which is now sliding along the base of the cartridge case, is forced to the right to grasp the cartridge case rim. The extractor spring is compressed at this time. Under the action of the follower lever spring, the follower raises the next round until it meets the bolt. Before the next round is fired, it is necessary to release the trigger; under the action of the trigger spring, the trigger returns to the forward position, and the front end of the trigger lever is disengaged from the sear and is positioned opposite the sear shoulders.

To fire the next round, it is necessary to press the trigger. The hammer can be released from the cocked position only when the bolt is in the extreme forward position and the bore is completely sealed. If the bolt is in the rear position (on the stop), or if the bore is not completely sealed (bolt in extreme forward position), the forward end of the disconnector is not depressed; the forward end of the trigger lever presses against the guide lugs for the sear in the trigger guard groove, and the hammer cannot be released. If the bolt travels past the locking lug and depresses the forward end of the disconnector and the bolt carrier has not attained the extreme forward position, the weapon still cannot be fired. In this event, the hammer, in moving forward will not strike the firing pin but will strike the vertical surface of the bolt carrier, which cocks the hammer.

THE SOVIET 7.62mm AK ASSAULT RIFLE

The development of this weapon is discussed in Chapter I.

Loading and Firing the AK

The thirty-round magazine is loaded by hand by pressing the cartridges down into the mouth of the magazine with the thumb. Insert the magazine into the underside of the receiver, forward end first; then draw up the rear end of the magazine until a click is heard or until the magazine catch is felt to engage its slot at the rear of the magazine. Pull the operating handle (which protrudes from the right side of the receiver) smartly to the rear and release it. The bolt and bolt carrier will go forward under the pressure of the recoil spring and will chamber a cartridge. To put the weapon on safe, push the safety selector catch (mounted on the right side of the receiver) as far up as it will go. When on safe, the safety selector blocks rearward movement of the

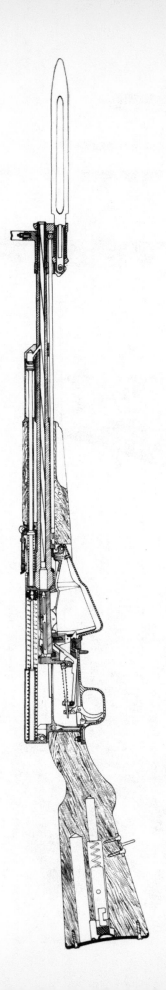

Section drawing of SKS.

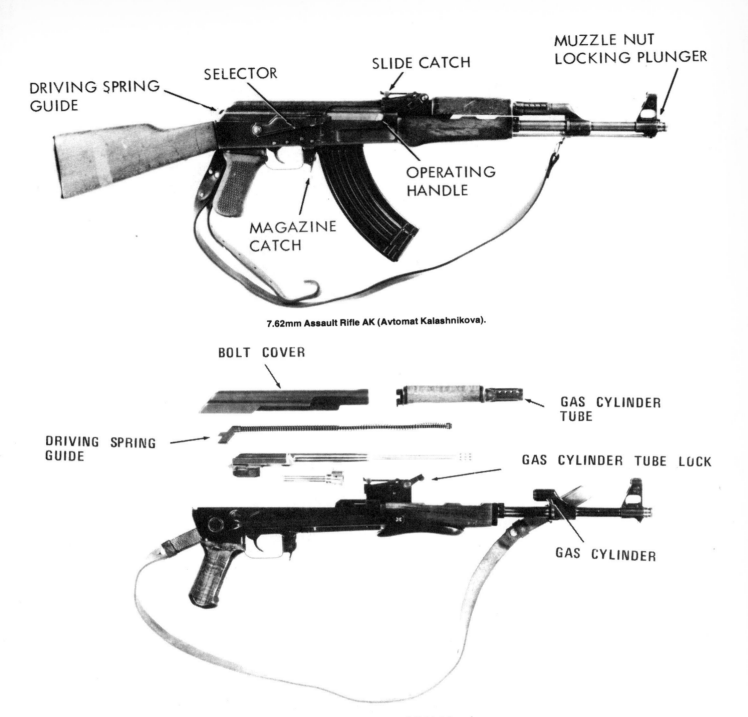

7.62mm Assault Rifle AK (Avtomat Kalashnikova).

DRIVING SPRING GUIDE

SELECTOR

SLIDE CATCH

MUZZLE NUT LOCKING PLUNGER

MAGAZINE CATCH

OPERATING HANDLE

BOLT COVER

GAS CYLINDER TUBE

DRIVING SPRING GUIDE

GAS CYLINDER TUBE LOCK

GAS CYLINDER

AK Rifle with folding stock field stripped.

operating handle and covers a gap to the rear of the bolt carrier. For semiautomatic fire, push the end of the safety selector lever all the way down (so that its forward end is opposite the bottom two Cyrillic letters), aim and squeeze (do not pull) the trigger. For full automatic fire, push the safety selector lever to the middle position marked by the two Cyrillic letters "AB" (which stand for "automatic"). Although the AK is quite heavy, it climbs rapidly in automatic fire; it is therefore necessary to get a good grip on the weapon before squeezing the trigger for automatic fire.

Field Stripping the AK

Remove the magazine and pull the operating handle to the rear to clear weapon of any live ammunition. At the rear of the stamped receiver cover, a serrated catch protrudes; this is the rear end of the recoil spring guide rod. Push the catch in with the finger and at the same time pull the receiver cover upward and backward from the receiver. After removing the receiver cover, push the recoil spring guide forward, so that the bottom rear lug section of the guide clears the dovetail slot at the rear of the receiver. Remove recoil spring. Note that the recoil spring and its guide rod are a packaged unti; i.e., they are held together as one piece by a collar fitted to the end of the guide rod. This is similar to the recoil spring used on the cal. .50 Browning machine gun. The bolt carrier, piston and bolt can now be removed as a unit by pulling them back to the cutout section in the

Loading the AK magazine.

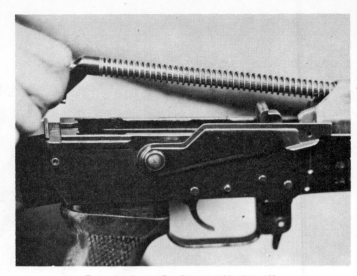

Removing the recoil spring assembly of the AK.

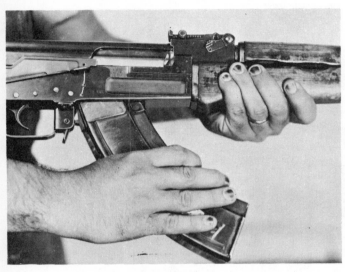

Inserting the AK magazine.

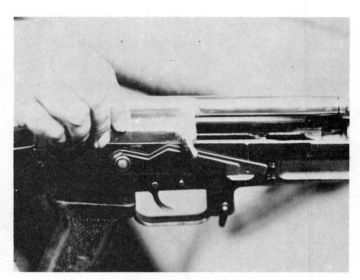

Removing the bolt carrier assembly.

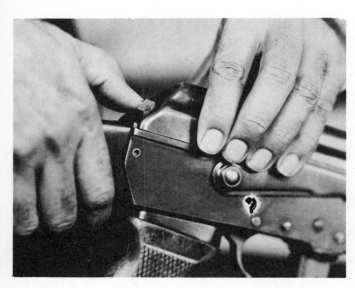

Removing the AK receiver cover.

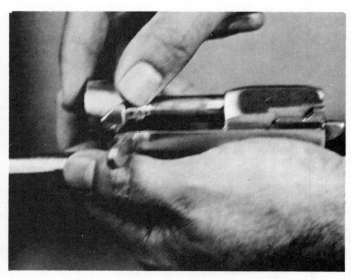

Removing bolt.

receiver track and lifting them upward and rearward. To remove the bolt from the bolt carrier, turn its head so that the guide lug aligns with the cam surface of the bolt carrier, move the bolt as far to rear as possible, rotate the bolt so that the guide lug leaves the camway of the bolt carrier, and pull the bolt forward and out of the bolt carrier. This operation is not as complicated as it seems; the bolt can actually be shaken out of the bolt carrier. Rotate the handguard lock lever (on the forward right side of the rear sight base) upward, and the handguard-piston tube assembly can be lifted out. No further disassembly is recommended.

To assemble the weapon, carry out in reverse the steps outlined above.

How the AK Works

Full Automatic Fire. With the safety selector set on full automatic fire, a cartridge in the chamber (to chamber a cartridge initially, since the AK fires from a closed bolt, it is necessary to pull the operating handle to the rear and release it) and a loaded magazine in the weapon, the following actions occur when the trigger is pulled. The safety selector lug is far enough to the rear to release the rear end of the trigger but stays directly above the rear end of the disconnector. Thus, while the trigger is free to rotate, the safety selector lug prevents the disconnector from rotating. One large multi-stranded spring is used as both hammer spring and trigger spring in the AK.

Semiautomatic Fire. To fire a single round from the rifle, set the weapon for semiautomatic fire by rotating the safety selector as far downward as possible, and then press the trigger.

When the trigger is pressed, the semiautomatic sear and disconnector rotate. The rear end of the sear (which is actually part of the trigger) raises the ends of the hammer-and-trigger spring. As the trigger rotates, the semiautomatic sear releases the hammer cock notch.

The hammer-and-trigger spring rotates the hammer forward, and the hammer strikes the rear end of the firing pin, pushing it forward so that it strikes the primer of the cartridge. The cartridge fires, and gases from the cartridge flow through the gas port in the barrel into the gas cylinder and force the piston and bolt carrier assembly to the rear. As the piston and bolt carrier assembly move to the rear, the recoil spring is compressed. The bevel in the bolt carrier cam acts on the bolt guide lug, rotating the bolt to the left and thereby unlocking the bolt.

After the bolt is unlocked, the bolt carrier and bolt move to the rear together. The bolt carrier rotates the hammer to the rear, compressing the hammer-and-trigger spring. As the hammer rotates, it rotates the disconnector. When the head of the hammer has passed the notch in the disconnector, the disconnector spring forces the disconnector to engage the disconnector notch in the hammer. This holds the hammer at full cock.

The full automatic sear spring rotates the full automatic sear into engagement with the full automatic sear notch in the hammer. The full automatic sear, however, does not hold the hammer in the cocked position, since the disconnector is already performing this function. As the full automatic sear rotates, the upper end of the sear rises to obstruct the passage of the full automatic disconnector.

As the bolt moves to the rear, the extractor pulls the cartridge case from the chamber. When the case strikes the ejector, it is ejected from the receiver.

The top round in the magazine is forced upward by the follower until it is arrested by the magazine flange.

The rearward movement of the bolt carrier and bolt is arrested by the rear wall of the receiver. Forward movement of these parts is caused by the decompression of the recoil spring.

As the bolt carrier moves forward, the top cartridge in the magazine is stripped from the magazine and forced into the chamber.

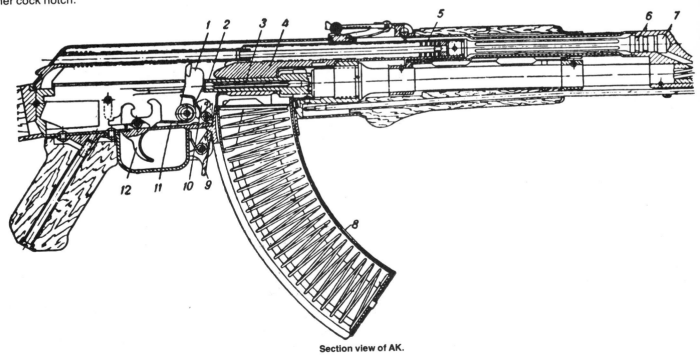

Section view of AK.

1. Hammer
2. Bolt
3. Firing pin
4. Operating rod
5. Recoil spring
6. Gas piston
7. Gas cylinder
8. Magazine
9. Magazine catch
10. Full automatic sear
11. Trigger and hammer spring
12. Trigger

As the bolt approaches the barrel face, the first stage in the rotation of the bolt to the right takes place. At the same time, the extractor engages the extractor groove of the cartridge case. As the bolt carrier moves to the extreme forward position, it produces the final rotation of the bolt to the right, locking the bolt.

After the bolt is locked but while the bolt carrier is still a short distance from the extreme forward position, the full automatic disconnector (which is integral with the bolt carrier) strikes the upper end of the full automatic sear, and rotates the sear forward. This action moves the full automatic sear away from the hammer, so that the hammer will not be prevented from rotating.

The next round is fired by releasing the trigger, and then pressing it again. When the trigger is released, the hammer-and-trigger spring rotates the disconnector and semiautomatic sear to the rear, disengaging the disconnector from the disconnector notch in the hammer. The trigger-and-hammer spring rotates the hammer until the hammer cocknotch engages the semiautomatic sear. This is accompanied by an audible click.

When the trigger is again pressed, the semiautomatic sear releases the hammer cock notch. The hammer once again strikes the firing pin, and the entire operating cycle of the automatic mechanism is repeated.

Automatic Fire. To fire the rifle automatically, set the selector at full automatic fire by rotating the indicator until it is opposite the Cyrillic letters AB on the receiver; press the trigger.

When the trigger is pressed, it rotates on the trigger pin. The disconnector, because it is prevented from rotating by the selector lever, does not engage the disconnector notch in the hammer.

As the trigger rotates, the semiautomatic sear releases the hammer cock notch. The hammer-and-trigger spring rotates the hammer, which strikes the firing pin forcibly. The round is fired. The powder gases act on the gas piston, thrusting the operating rod to the rear, opening the bolt, extracting and ejecting the cartridge case and cocking the hammer.

The full automatic sear engages the full automatic sear notch in the hammer, holding the hammer at full cock.

The top round in the magazine is raised by the follower.

As the bolt carrier and bolt are moved forward by the recoil spring, the round is fed into the chamber, and the bolt is locked.

When the bolt carrier is a short distance from the extreme forward position, the full automatic disconnector strikes the upper end of the full automatic sear and rotates the sear, releasing the hammer. The hammer strikes the firing pin, firing the next round. The entire operating cycle of the automatic mechanism is repeated.

The rifle will continue firing until the last round in the magazine is expended or until the firer releases pressure on the trigger. In the first case, the bolt carrier and bolt will remain in the forward position and the hammer will not be cocked (the AK has no bolt-holding-open device to hold the bolt to the rear after the last round is fired). In the second case, the rifle will be loaded and ready to fire again if the rifleman ceases fire before expending all the rounds in the magazine.

7.62mm AKM Assault Rifle, field stripped.

THE SOVIET 7.62mm AKM ASSAULT RIFLE

The AKM is a modification of the AK and probably will replace the AK in Soviet service. The principal ways in which the AKM differs from the AK are:

(1) The AKM has a stamped steel receiver as opposed to the milled receiver of the AK.

(2) The gas relief holes in the AKM gas cylinder tube are semicircular cutouts at the forward end of the tube, which match similar cutouts in the gas cylinder block. The gas relief holes on the AK are cut into the body of the gas cylinder tube—four on each side.

(3) The AKM has a rate reducer attached to the trigger mechanism; the rate of fire is, however, the same as that of the AK.

(4) The fore-end of the AKM has a beaver-tail configuration, i.e., it bulges out on both sides.

(5) The rear sight leaf of the AKM is graduated to 1000 meters as opposed to the 800-meter graduation on the AK. The AKM uses the sight leaf of the RPK light machine gun.

(6) The AKM stock and fore-end is made of laminated wood; those of the AK are usually made of ordinary beech or birch.

(7) The bolt and bolt carrier of the AKM are parkerized; those of the AK are bright steel.

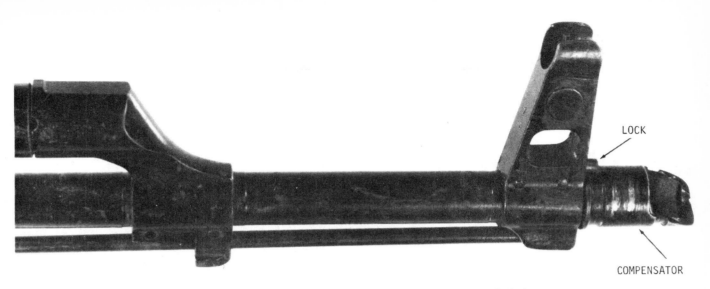

LOCK

COMPENSATOR

AKM screw on muzzle compensator, which is removed by depressing the lock pin.

The AKMS is the folding metal stock version of the AKM. The steel struts of the stock are of stamped steel rather than machined steel as used on the folding stock AK. A short compensator is now frequently seen on the muzzle of the AKM and AKMS. The purpose of the compensator is to hold the barrel down in automatic fire. There is now a light alloy magazine weighing .4 pound available for the AK, AKM series weapons.

The 7.62mm RPK LIGHT MACHINE GUN

The RPK is basically the same as the AKM assault rifle, with longer barrel and a bipod. It uses a 75-round drum magazine, a 40-round box magazine or the 30-round magazine of the AK and AKM. This weapon is replacing the RPD as the squad automatic weapon (base of fire) of the Soviet Army.

Adoption of the RPK by the Soviets eases their logistical and training problems since the RPK uses for the most part the same parts as the AKM and is operated in the same manner.

RPK does not have a quick change barrel, and as a squad automatic weapon it is not designed for long periods of sustained fire.

The 7.62mm RPKS LIGHT MACHINE GUN

The RPKS is a folding stock version of the RPK light machine gun. The stock folds to the left side of the receiver, and although the weapon can be fired with box magazines with the stock folded it is doubtful that the 75-round drum magazine can be used in this model. The RPKS is 40.9 inches long with the stock fixed and approximately 32 inches long with stock folded.

The SOVIET 7.62mm SVD SNIPER RIFLE

The SVD or Dragunov (SVD means Self loading Rifle, Dragunov) rifle is the replacement for the M1891/30 sniper rifle. It is chambered for the 7.62mm rimmed cartridge (7.62 × 53 R). The rifle is fitted with a four-power scope Model PSO-1 and has a somewhat unusual stock in that a large section has been cut out of it immediately to the rear of the pistol grip. This lightens the weight of the rifle considerably. The Dragunov uses an action which closely resembles that of the AK. It has a prong type flash suppressor similar to those used on current US small arms.

How To Load and Fire The SVD

The box magazine is loaded in the normal manner; it is removed from the rifle by pushing the magazine catch—located behind the magazine port—forward and pulling down on the magazine. Insert loaded magazine in the magazine port pushing it upward till it securely locks in place. Pull bolt-operating handle which protrudes from the right side of the receiver to the rear and release, thus chambering a cartridge. The weapon is now loaded and will fire one round for each pull of the trigger until the magazine is empty. The safety is similar to that of the AK/AKM assault rifle and is mounted on the right side of the receiver. To put the rifle on safe, push the lever upwards.

How the SVD Works

The bolt operation of the SVD is essentially the same as that of the AK/AKM in semiautomatic fire. The principal difference is that the SVD has a spring-loaded piston rod, which is a separate assembly; it is not attached to the bolt carrier as is that of the AK/AKM. The trigger mechanism is relatively simple consisting of 12 parts including the fabricated trigger housing/trigger guard. It varies from the AK/AKM trigger mechanism in that, among other things, it does not have a full automatic sear or full automatic disconnector, and it has a separate trigger spring in addition to the hammer spring as opposed to the one spring that performs both functions in the AK/AKM.

Disassembly and Assembly

Clear the SVD but do not set the safety to safe or replace the magazine. Release the telescope sight catch and pull the telescope off the rear. Place the telescope in its carrying case. Remove the cheek pad.

Press the receiver cover catch upward and pull the receiver cover and driving spring upward and off the receiver. Pull the operating handle to the rear; then lift the bolt carrier and bolt out of the rifle. Push the bolt into the bolt carrier until it can be rotated so that the operating lug on the bolt is free of its cam recess in the bolt carrier. Pull the bolt out of the carrier.

Rotate the safety until it is vertical; then pull it to the right out of the receiver. Pull the trigger group out of the receiver.

Press the handguard catch in until it is free of the handguard

Disassembled view of Soviet Dragunov (SVD) Sniping Rifle.

ferrule; then rotate the catch to the right. Push the ferrule forward; then pull the handguard down and out to remove them. It may be necessary to pry tight handguards off the barrel.

Pull the operating rod to the rear against pressure of its spring; then gently move the front of the rod to one side. Pull the piston off the gas block; then ease the operating rod forward and remove it and its spring.

Further disassembly is neither necessary nor desirable.

To reassemble the SVD, first insert the operating rod and its spring in its recess in the rear sight base. Press the rod to one side and slip the piston onto the gas block; then insert the operating rod into the piston.

Slip the rear end of the handguards into their seat, swing the front ends together and push the ferrule to hold the handguards in place. Rotate the ferrule until the handguard catch snaps into place.

Insert the trigger group into its recess in the receiver and when the trigger and receiver are lined up, insert the shaft of the safety into its hole in the receiver. Turn the safety so that its arm is vertical, fully seat the safety into the receiver and then turn it down to its position.

Insert the bolt spindle into the bolt carrier until the operating lug on the bolt can be turned into the cam groove in the bolt carrier. Pull the bolt fully forward in the carrier. Mate the lugs on the bolt carrier with the cutaways in the receiver and insert the bolt carrier and bolt into the receiver; then move them fully forward.

Insert the driving spring into the bolt carrier and while holding the receiver catch up slide the receiver cover onto the receiver.

Replace the cheek pad and while holding the telescope sight catch slide the sight onto its seat from the rear. Replace the magazine, press the trigger and move the safety upward.

The main accessory for the SVD is its PSO-1 telescope. This scope has an illuminated reticle powered by a small dry cell. The battery housing is located at the bottom rear of the telescopic sight mount. To change batteries, press in and rotate the battery housing counterclockwise. Remove the old battery and replace with the same type. The reticle lamp can be replaced by unscrewing its housing and removing the bulb. The reticle light is turned on or off by its switch. The lens cap should always be in place except when actually using the telescope for aiming.

Two covers are issued with each rifle; one is for the telescope sight alone; the other covers the sight and breech of the rifle. A belt pouch is provided for carrying the telescope when dismounted from the rifle, four magazines, a cleaning kit and an extra battery and lamp for the telescopic sight.

If the open sights are to be used, set the rear sight by pressing in the locks on the rear sight slide; then move the slide along the rear sight leaf. The front edge of the slide should be aligned with the numeral that corresponds to the range in hundreds of meters. Use the same sight picture as for firing a pistol.

If the PSO-1 telescopic sight is used, rotate the elevation knob until the figure that corresponds to the range in hundreds of meters is aligned with its index. The range can be fairly accurately determined by use of the range finder located in the lower left of the telescopic reticle. This range finder is graduated to the height of a man (5′7″). Look through the telescope and place the horizontal line at the bottom line of the target. Move the telescope until the upper (curved) line just touches the top of the target's head. The number indicates the range in hundreds of meters; if the target falls between numbers, the remaining distance then must be estimated. When the range is determined and set into the elevation knob, use the point of the top chevron on the reticle as an aiming point. The three lower chevrons are used for firing at 1100, 1200 and 1300 meters with the elevation knob set at 10. The horizontal scale extending out from the sides of the top chevron are used for hasty wind corrections; deliberate changes are made by rotating the windage knob.

For firing when the light is dim, illuminate the reticle by turning on the switch in the telescopic sight mount. If active infrared light sources are believed to be in use by the opponents, set the range drum at "4" and switch the infrared detector into place. Scan the area to the front; if any active infrared light sources are in use, they will appear as orange-red blobs in the telescope. Align the point of the reticle on the light and fire. Turn off the reticle light when not is use to conserve the battery and swing the infrared detector out of the way so that it will be activated by light during the day.

A commercial sporting version of the Dragunov—the "Medved" (bear)—is also available.

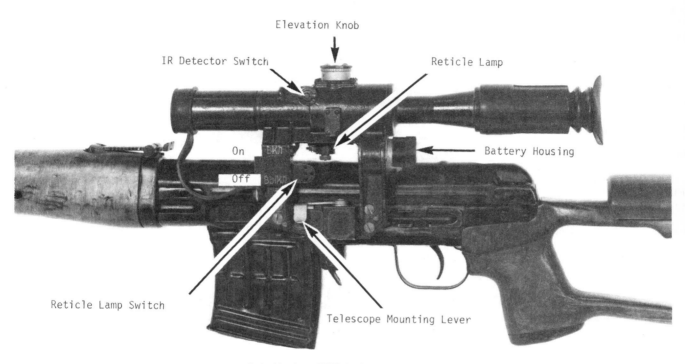

Left side view of PSO-1 telescopic sight.

CHARACTERISTICS OF POST-WORLD WAR II SOVIET RIFLES AND CARBINES

	SKS Carbine	AK Assault Rifle	AKM Assault Rifle	SVD
Caliber:	7.62mm M43 (7.62 × 39mm)	7.62mm M43 (7.62 × 39mm)	7.62mm M43 (7.62 × 39mm)	7.62mm rimmed.
System of Operation:	Gas, semiautomatic.	Gas, selective fire.	Gas, selective fire.	Gas, semiautomatic.
Length overall:	40.16 in.	34.25 in.	34.25 in.	48.2 in.
Barrel length:	20.47 in.	16.34 in.	16.34 in.	24 in.
Feed device:	10-round, staggered row non-detachable box magazine.	30-round, staggered row detachable box magazine.	30-round, staggered row detachable box magazine.	10-round, staggered row detachable box magazine.
Sights: Front:	Hooded post.	Post w/protecting ears.	Post w/protecting ears.	Hooded post.
Rear:	Tangent, graduated to 1000 meters.	Tangent, graduated to 800 meters.	Tangent, graduated to 1000 meters.	Tangent w/notch*
Weight:	8.8 lb.	10.58 lb.	8.87 lb.	9.5 lb.
Muzzle velocity:	2410 f.p.s.	2330 f.p.s.	2330 f.p.s.	2720 f.p.s.
Cyclic rate:	—	600 r.p.m.	600 r.p.m.	—

*Normally fitted with 4-power scope graduated to 1300 meters.

SOVIET SUBMACHINE GUNS

All pre-World War II and World War II Soviet submachine guns were chambered for the Soviet 7.62mm pistol cartridge Type P. Although the two latest types, the PBSh M1941, and the PPS M1943, are still in use in some Warsaw Pact countries, all of these guns are obsolete in the USSR.

THE 7.62mm PPSh SUBMACHINE GUN M1941

Note that the bolt is a very simple machined piece. The recoil spring guide is resting in a hole in the rear of the bolt, with the spring around it, and a plastic buffer at its rear end. This spring arrangement also serves to spring lock the receiver when the weapon is assembled.

Field Stripping The PPSh M1941

Push forward on receiver catch and hinge barrel and barrel casing down.

Draw straight back on bolt handle a short distance, meanwhile exerting an upward pull. The bolt may be lifted out.

Remove recoil spring and buffer.

Barrel is removable from casing. Further dismounting is seldom necessary.

PPSh M1941 with 71-round drum magazine.

7.62mm PPSh M1941, field stripped.

CHARACTERISTICS OF PRE-WORLD WAR II AND WORLD WAR II SOVIET SUBMACHINE GUNS

	PPD Model 1934/38	PPD Model 1940	PPSh Model 1941	PPS Model 1943
Caliber:	7.62mm.	7.62mm.	7.62mm.	7.62mm.
System of operation:	Blowback. Selective fire.	Blowback. Selective fire.	Blowback. Selective fire.	Blowback. Automatic fire only.
Weight: w/loaded drum magazine:	11.5 lb.	11.90 lb.	11.99 lb.	
Weight: w/loaded box magazine:	8.25 lb.		9.26 lb.	7.98 lb.
Length overall:	30.63 in.	30.63 in.	33.15 in.	Stock extended— 32.72 in. Stock folded— 24.25 in.
Barrel length:	10.63 in.	10.63 in.	10.63 in.	9.45 in.
Feed device:	71-rd. drum or 25-rd. box.	71-rd. drum.	71-rd. drum. or 35-rd. box.	35-rd. box.
Sights: Front:	Blade.	Hooded blade.	Hooded post.	Post w/ears.
Rear:	Tangent leaf.	Tangent leaf.	Tangent leaf or L-type.	L-type.
Cyclic rate:	900 r.p.m.	900-1100 r.p.m.	700-900 r.p.m.	650 r.p.m.
Muzzle velocity:	1640 f.p.s.	1640 f.p.s.	1640 f.p.s.	1608 f.p.s.

NOTE: A 1942 version of the PPS M1943 also exists, but differs only in minor details from the Model 1943.

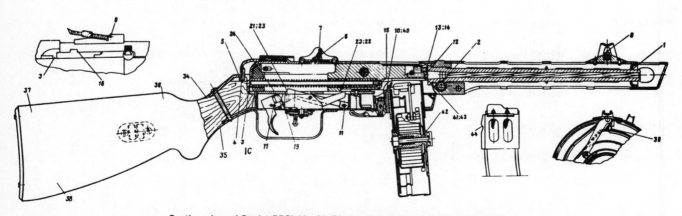

Section view of Soviet PPSh41 with 71-round magazine in place. Upper left drawing illustrates the early type rear sight. Lower right views illustrate differences between the 25-round box magazine and the 71-round drum.

From top down: **M34/38, PPD M1940, PPSh M1941 and PPS M1943.**

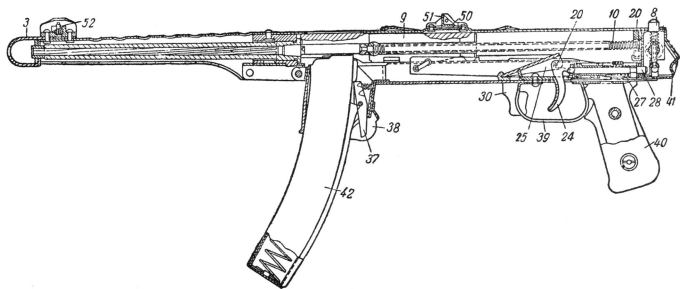

Section view of PPS M1943.
3— Muzzle brake (compensator) 8— Stock release catch 9— Bolt 10— Recoil
spring 20— Buffer 24— Trigger 25— Sear 26— Sear pin 27— Trigger spring 28—
Trigger spring guide 30— Safety 37— Magazine latch 38— Magazine guide 39—
Trigger guard 40— Plastic grip 41— Takedown latch 42— Magazine 50— Rear
sight guard 51— "L" type flip sight 52— Front sight post.

SOVIET MACHINE GUNS

7.62mm Model 1905 Maxim.

Prior to 1900, Imperial Russia adopted the Maxim gun, and Russian troops in the Russo-Japanese War (1904–1905) used Maxims against Japanese Hotchkiss guns. The 7.62mm Model 1905 Maxim was the first machine gun manufactured in Russia. As all the early Maxims, this heavy weapon had numerous brass fittings and a bronze water jacket.

The Imperial government adopted the 7.62mm Model 1902 Madsen as the standard light machine gun. During World War I, the Russians purchased 7.62mm Maxim and Colt Model 1914 (modified Colt Model 1895 "potato digger") machine guns from Colt in the US. They also acquired a considerable number of Lewis guns.

In 1910, the Russians modified the Maxim; the 7.62mm Model 1910 Maxim (SPM) had a ribbed water jacket similar to that of the British Vickers. This weapon, used and manufactured through World War II, was modified by the addition of a tractor type water entry port.

After World War I, the new Soviet Army started developing its own weapons. The 7.62mm Maxim Tokarev and Maxim Koleshnikov were among the first efforts. These air-cooled Maxims fitted with bipods were used in large quantities during the Spanish civil war. The first originally developed Soviet machine gun was the 7.62mm DP—Degtyarev Infantry—which appeared in 1926. The DP introduced the modified Kjellman Frijberg locking system to the Soviets, which is still in service in several machine guns. The DP was the first of a series of Degtyarev machine guns adopted by the Soviet Union. A tank version called the DT may still be found on older Soviet armored vehicles in use among Soviet allies. An aircraft version, the 7.62mm DA, was also produced.

The DP, DT and DA have their operating springs coiled on the piston rod, which is seated under the barrel. The heating of the barrel caused distortion of the spring with resultant malfunctions. During World War II, a modification of the DP—the DPM—was put into service. It is basically the same as the DP, with the recoil spring mounted in a tube that projects to the rear of the receiver. A tank version of this weapon, the DTM, is still in service on pre-1949 Soviet armored vehicles.

A heavy machine gun version of the DP, the 1939 DS, turned out to be a failure in battle, or more properly a failure in the manufacturing plant. The DS was replaced by the Goryunov SG43, a very successful gun still in use in Soviet allied armies. In modified form—SGM, SGMT and SGMB—the SG43 is still in the Soviet Union inventory as a battalion level machine gun, tank machine gun and vehicular machine gun. The Goryunov series does not use the Degtyarev locking system, the bolt of the Goryunov being cammed to the side to lock in a side wall of the receiver.

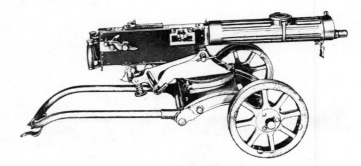

Maxim M1910 Heavy Machine Gun (SPM).

DS M1939 Heavy Machine Gun.

The 12.7mm DShK Model 1938 was the first Soviet heavy caliber machine gun to be produced in quantity. It was preceded by the 12.7mm DK, which appeared around 1934, apparently not a very successful gun. The DShK uses the Degtyarev locking system.

The 7.62mm RPD machine gun is also basically a Degtyarev weapon, having a bolt system generally similar to the earlier Degtyarevs. It is being replaced in Soviet service by the 7.62mm RPK machine gun, similar to the AK assault rifle in most respects.

For further design details, see Chapter 2.

7.62mm DP AND DPM LIGHT MACHINE GUNS

Degtyarev machine gun variations:

DP— infantry light machine gun; 49-shot drum.
DA— aircraft mounted machine gun; DA-2 twin gun mount.
DT— tank mounted; 60-shot drum.
DPM— modernized infantry light machine gun; also PRC Type 53.
DTM— modernized tank gun.
RP46—belt-fed company machine gun; PRC Type 58; North Korean Type 64.

DP, DPM and DTM guns have sliding dust covers over the feed openings at the top of the receivers. DP, DPM and RP46 all have quick change barrels. The tank models do not. All Soviet Degtyarev guns have adjustable gas systems.

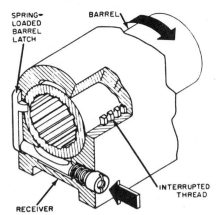

Degtyarev barrel removal.

Tank model of the DP, 7.62 × 54Rmm Machine Gun

Tank model of the DPM, 7.62 × 54Rmm Machine Gun.

Field Stripping The DP

To remove the barrel, pull the cocking handle to the rear to cock the weapon. The barrel locking stud is on the left side near the front of the receiver. Press this stud in, which will release the barrel, then twist the barrel up one quarter turn to the right. Now slide the barrel straight forward out of the receiver.

Both sights are carried on casing. Rear sight base serves as magazine catch.

Flash hider is screwed to barrel. Gas cylinder is just forward of barrel cooling rings. Bolt is shown with right and left side locks and firing pin removed.

Gas piston with operating rod and spring shown attached to bolt carrying slide.

Bipod is easily detachable. Bottom view of magazine to show cartridge feed system. A squeezer-type safety is positioned in

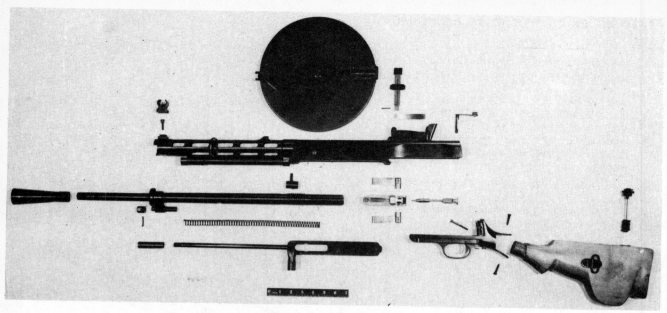

DP Machine Gun field stripped.

the rear of the trigger guard and is automatically pressed in as the fingers tighten around the grip.

Press the trigger and ease the cocking handle forward. Pull out the bolt at the rear of the trigger guard, which leaves the stock and trigger guard free to be turned until the rear of the trigger guard is clear of the receiver. Pull the stock and trigger guard assembly back and out of the receiver.

A small sleeve fits behind the recoil spring at the rear of the gas cylinder tube. Press this forward and twist it to the left; this will free the bolt together with the slide and the gas piston attached to it to be withdrawn at the rear of the receiver.

The bolt may now be lifted from the top of the slide. The firing pin may now be slid out of the rear of the bolt. The bolt locks on each side of the bolt may now be lifted out and the front of the extractor spring raised and pulled forward to permit removal of it and the extractor.

This completes field stripping. Assembling the gun is equally simple and merely calls for reversing the stripping procedure.

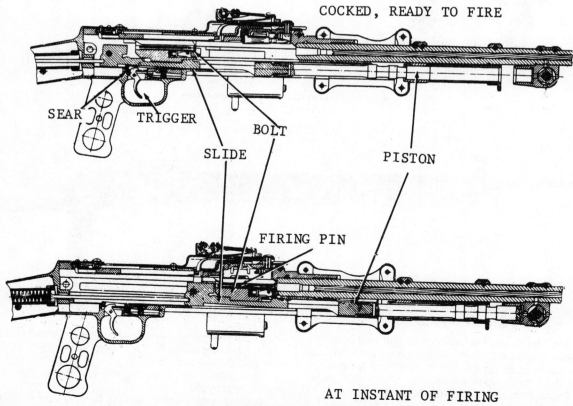

COCKED, READY TO FIRE

SEAR   TRIGGER   BOLT

SLIDE   PISTON

FIRING PIN

AT INSTANT OF FIRING

RPD section view.

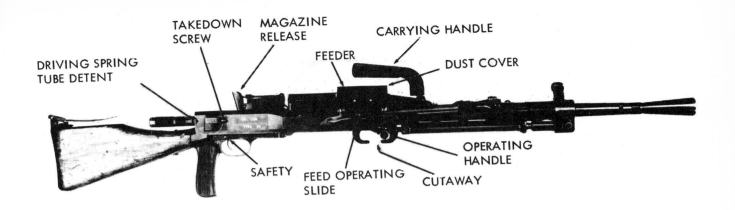

DRIVING SPRING
TUBE DETENT

TAKEDOWN
SCREW

MAGAZINE
RELEASE

FEEDER

CARRYING HANDLE

DUST COVER

OPERATING
HANDLE

SAFETY

FEED OPERATING
SLIDE

CUTAWAY

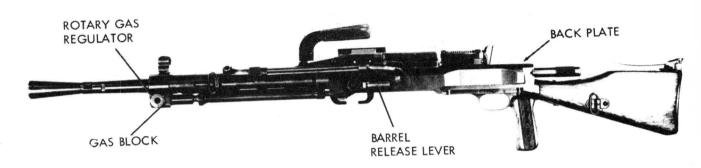

ROTARY GAS
REGULATOR

BACK PLATE

GAS BLOCK

BARREL
RELEASE LEVER

RP46 showing key features.

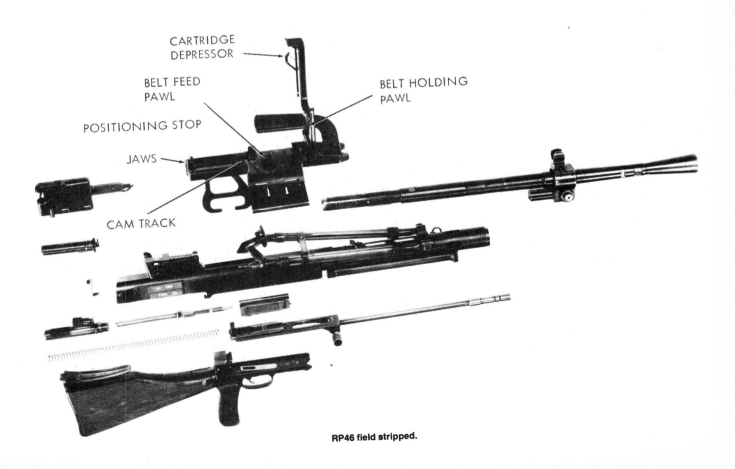

CARTRIDGE
DEPRESSOR

BELT FEED
PAWL

BELT HOLDING
PAWL

POSITIONING STOP

JAWS

CAM TRACK

RP46 field stripped.

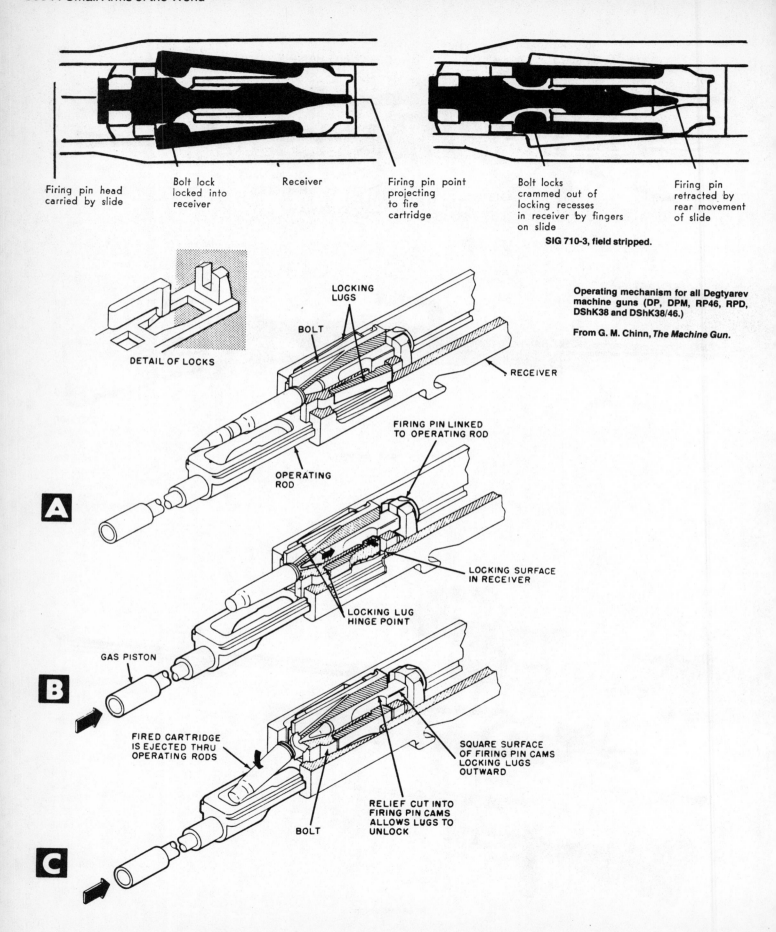

Firing pin head
carried by slide

Bolt lock
locked into
receiver

Receiver

Firing pin point
projecting
to fire
cartridge

Bolt locks
crammed out of
locking recesses
in receiver by fingers
on slide

Firing pin
retracted by
rear movement
of slide

SIG 710-3, field stripped.

Operating mechanism for all Degtyarev machine guns (DP, DPM, RP46, RPD, DShK38 and DShK38/46.)

From G. M. Chinn, *The Machine Gun.*

DETAIL OF LOCKS

LOCKING
LUGS

BOLT

RECEIVER

FIRING PIN LINKED
TO OPERATING ROD

OPERATING
ROD

A

LOCKING SURFACE
IN RECEIVER

LOCKING LUG
HINGE POINT

GAS PISTON

B

FIRED CARTRIDGE
IS EJECTED THRU
OPERATING RODS

SQUARE SURFACE
OF FIRING PIN CAMS
LOCKING LUGS
OUTWARD

RELIEF CUT INTO
FIRING PIN CAMS
ALLOWS LUGS TO
UNLOCK

BOLT

C

Loading and Firing The DP and DPM

The Magazine. This type drum differs radically from the Lewis type. The inner center rotates, while the outer rim is fastened securely to the gun. The cartridges lie in single line around the inside of the pan.

To Prepare for Firing. Mount a loaded magazine on top of the receiver and press firmly down until it is caught by the magazine catch. (The magazine catch is mounted in the front end of the rear sight base.)

Now pull back the cocking handle as far as it will go. It will stay open. Pressing the trigger will now fire the gun. Full automatic fire will ensue as long as the trigger is held down and there are cartridges in the magazine.

Note: A safety catch to the rear of the triggerguard is automatically pressed in as the rifle is gripped ready to fire on the DP; the DPM has a manual safety.

How the DP and DPM Work

A loaded pan magazine is placed on top of the receiver where it engages with a hook on the barrel jacket and is held at the rear by a spring catch, the handle of which forms a guard for the rear sight. The handle on the right side of the gun is drawn back to its full length. This compresses the recoil spring positioned below the barrel; it travels with a rod connecting the gas cup to the slide. This spring is compressed against its lock by a gas cup. The rod moves backwards through the center of this spring and lock.

During this opening movement, unlocking also takes place and the bolt is held open when it is caught by the sear.

Pressing the trigger rotates the sear down and out of its notch in the bottom of the slide. The bolt is carried on top of the slide. The operating rod is attached to the front end of the slide. The compressed spring is now free to pull the moving members forward.

A moving plate inside the fixed magazine pan has brought a cartridge through the medium of a rotor spring into the feed lips in line with the bolt. The bolt strikes this cartridge and drives it ahead into the firing chamber. On each side of the bolt is a loose plate. These plates are flush with the bolt when it is cocked. As the bolt brings up against the face of the cartridge in the chamber and its forward action is stopped, the firing pin is carried still farther ahead by the operating slide on which it is mounted; cams on it force the loose locking plates out into recesses machined into the receiver to accommodate them. The firing pin now discharges the cartridge, with the bolt locked securely to the receiver.

Return Movement of the Action. A small quantity of gas passes through the port in the barrel as the bullet goes over it. This passes into a nozzle attached to the barrel, which directs the expanding gas against the head of a cup that serves in lieu of a piston. The cup walls extend forward about an inch around this nozzle.

The energy from the expanding gas is transmitted through the gas cup at the end of the rod to the attached slide which it starts backward. The first movement of the slide withdraws the firing pin, and from thereon a projection on the bottom of each loose lock plate rides in a cam groove in the slide, camming the projections toward the center. This pulls the locks out of their recesses in the receiver. The slide is then able to carry the bolt straight back extracting and ejecting the empty cartridge case.

THE 7.62mm LIGHT MACHINE GUN MODEL 1946 (RP46)

The RP46 is basically a modification of the 7.62mm DPM light machine gun, which appeared during World War II. The DPM itself was a modification of the DP. While both the DP and DPM were fed by pan type magazines, the RP46 can be fed either by a pan or by the same 250-round nondisintegrating link belt that is used with the 7.62mm Goryunov heavy machine gun.

How to Load and Fire the RP46

Cock gun by pulling operating handle to the rear. Pull rear sight base to the rear and lift cover. Lay belt, open side up, on the feed plate so that the leading round contacts the cartridge stop and close cover. Pull trigger and gun will fire. To unload the gun, pull the rear sight guard to the rear, lift cover, remove belt. If the gun has been fired, there will still be one round in the feed way—remove round. The safety is on when the lever is pointing toward the muzzle.

Field Stripping the RP46

Field stripping of the RP46 is similar to that of the RPD, except that the recoil spring is mounted in a tube which projects out from the right rear side of the receiver. The tube and spring are dismounted by pushing in on the tube lock and turning it to the right, then withdrawing the tube and spring from the receiver. The barrel can be removed by pushing in the latch on the left forward side of the receiver and pulling the barrel out.

How the RP46 Works

The RP46 has the same basic operating system as the other Degtyarev guns (DP, DPM and RPD) and operates the same as they do except for its belt feed mechanism. An ingenious system is used on the RP46 to translate the forward and backward movement of the operating handle into a side-to-side movement of the belt-feed lever. The operating handle on its forward and backward travel operates a double-arm type of feed lever, which transmits this movement to parts in the feed mechanism; these parts in turn transmit the movement to the belt-feed slide. This system is also used on the Soviet 12.7mm DShK M1938/46 machine gun. Insofar as the bolt parts of the Degtyarev weapons are concerned, there is only one major difference among the lot. In DP, DPM and RP46, the firing pin is mounted in the bolt, and the slide post itself serves as a hammer.

THE 7.62mm RPD LIGHT MACHINE GUN

Loading and Firing the RPD

The link belt of the RPD is loaded by pushing the individual rounds into the belt so that the bottom hook-like section of the link snaps into place in the cartridge extractor groove. The two fifty-round sections are joined together by slipping the tongue of the end link on one belt section through the slots of the starting link on the other belt section. A cartridge is then inserted, locking the two belt sections together.

The belt is then rolled into a tight circle and fitted into the stamped metal drum. The drum is fitted on the weapon by sliding its top dovetail on the mating surfaces that protrude under the forward part of the receiver. The belt loading tab should be protruding from the spring-loaded trap door of the drum, so that it can be inserted in the receiver. The drum is locked in place by pulling down the lock on the underside of the receiver; this lock keeps the drum from moving backwards off the gun during fire.

Cock the gun by pulling operating handle to the rear. On older guns, which have the non-folding operating handle, the handle will remain to the rear. On the newer type guns, which have the folding type operating handle, the handle should be pushed forward after pulling to the rear.

Open the cover by pushing forward on cover latch and lifting the cover. Lay belt on feedway so that the leading cartridge lies

RPD Light Machine Gun, right side.

beside the cartridge stop. Close cover.

If the trigger is squeezed, the weapon will now fire. The safety catch is located on the right side of the pistol grip butt group, immediately above the trigger. When the catch is forward of the trigger the gun is on safe; to put the gun on fire, rotate the catch to the rear position.

To unload the gun, lift the cover by pushing forward on the cover catch located at the rear of the cover. Lift the link belt out and snap the cover shut.

Field Stripping the RPD

Turn the butt trap cover so that it is at right angles to the buttstock. Place a screwdriver in the top hole in the stock, and turn

the recoil spring plug one quarter turn; this will release the plug and the recoil spring and recoil spring guide. Withdraw the recoil spring and its guide from the gun. The entire butt and pistol grip group can then be removed by forcing out the butt retaining pin, which is located in the lower rear section of the receiver. When the retaining pin is pulled out as far as it will go, slide the butt group rearward till it separates from the receiver. Pull the operating handle to the rear until the cutout point on the handle track is reached. Pull out the operating handle. The bolt, slide and piston assembly can now be withdrawn from the rear of the receiver. The bolt and bolt locks can now be lifted from the slide. Lift the cover; the belt feed lever assembly and the belt feed slide can

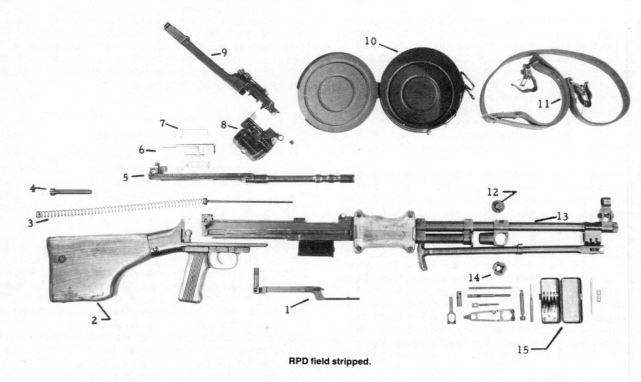

RPD field stripped.

1. Operating handle	6. Bolt	11. Sling
2. Butt stock	7. Bolt locking flap	12. Gas regulator screw
3. Driving spring and rod	8. Feed tray	13. Barrel
4. Driving spring guide	9. Feed cover	14. Gas regulator
5. Operating slide and piston	10. Drum (open)	15. Combination tool kit

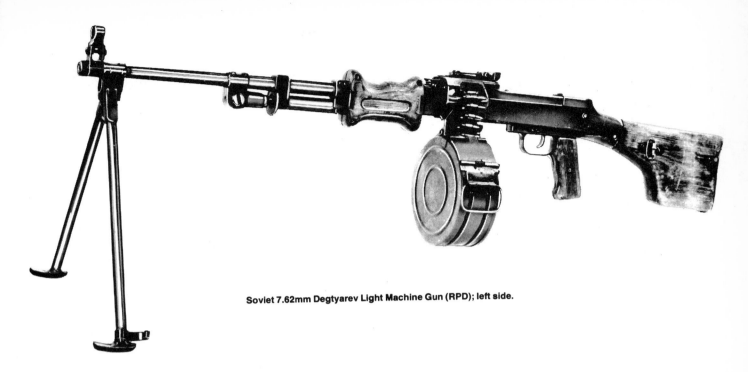

Soviet 7.62mm Degtyarev Light Machine Gun (RPD); left side.

be removed by pinching together with a pliers the split pin located at the right front of the cover. When the end of the pin is compressed, its locking collar can be removed, and all the belt feed components can be removed. Like many other gas-operated weapons, such as the US and FN Browning automatic rifles and the British Bren guns, the gas cylinder of the RPD can be easily adjusted. To adjust the gas cylinder of the RPD to obtain a different size of orifice, a special wrench is used.

To reassemble the weapon, perform the above steps in reverse order.

How the RPD Works

With the belt loaded in the gun and the bolt group to the rear, the trigger is pulled. The trigger pulls the sear down from its engagement in the sear notch on the underside of the slide. The slide piston assembly with the bolt goes forward under the pressure of the decompressing recoil spring. The slide post stud, which operates in the track of the belt feed lever, moves the belt feed lever, which in turn moves the belt feed slide over, indexing the cartridge so that the top of the bolt can engage the cartridge and strip it forward out of the link and downward into the chamber. The locking flaps mounted on the sides of the bolt are cammed out into their locking surfaces in the receiver by the rearward movement of the bolt on the slide, when the bolt abuts the barrel. The outward movement of the locking flaps allows the slide post to strike the rear end of the firing pin, which in turn strikes the primer of the cartridge. Gas from the cartridge enters the gas port in the barrel and forces the piston and slide assembly to the rear. The bolt is also drawn to the rear, and its locking flaps are withdrawn into their unlocked position when the slide post has moved a slight distance to the rear. As the bolt goes to the rear, it carries the empty cartridge case in its face until the ejector strikes the upper part of the rim and knocks the case downward and out of the gun. If the trigger is held to the rear, this process will repeat itself until the 100-round belt is expended. The links are forced out the right side of the receiver by the left-to-right movement of the belt feed slide; when the first fifty rounds are fired, the first fifty-round link belt section falls out of the gun.

Special Note on the RPD

Although there is nothing new in the design of the RPD, the weapon is rather remarkable for its simplicity. There are indications that the weapon/cartridge combination has only marginal operating power.

7.62mm SG43 and SGM HEAVY MACHINE GUNS

Six versions of the Goryunov machine gun have been produced:

SG43— smooth barrel; sear attached to driving spring guide; plain barrel lock; no dust covers; operating handle between spade grips.

SG43M— SGMB type barrel lock and dust covers.

SGM— splined barrel; separate sear housing; micrometer barrel lock; no dust covers (on early production models); operating handle on right side.

SGMT— tank version of SGM with solenoid mounted on the backplate.

SGMB— similar to SGM with dust covers over feedway ports, feed slide and ejection port; SGMB also has semicircular flanges on the lower front of its receiver for mounting on the cradle inside the armored vehicle.

Hungarian General Purpose Version— extensively modified SGM, to fill machine gun role similar to PK GPMG; this model has pistol-grip trigger mechanism and RPD type butt stock; is fired from bipid; resembles PK in outward appearance.

How to Load and Fire the Goryunov

To load the Goryunov, open the top cover by pushing forward the cover latch. Insert the link belt on the feedway, placing the rim of the cartridge in the jaws of the feed carrier. Close the cover and pull the operating handle to the rear as far as it will go. The operating handle of the SG43 is at the rear underside of the gun, under the spade grips. After the operating handle has been

SG43, 7.62 × 54mm Machine Gun. Note rear cocking handle (arrow).

SG43M, 7.62 × 54mm Machine Gun. Note dust cover (arrow).

SGM, 7.62 × 54Rmm Machine Gun.

SGMB, 7.62 × 54Rmm Machine Gun on wheeled mount.

retracted, it should be pushed forward again; the bolt remains to the rear since the Goryunov fires from an open bolt. Raise the safety lock with the left thumb and press the upper end of the trigger with the right thumb. The weapon will now fire and will continue to fire until the trigger is released. The weapon can be unloaded by raising the top cover and lifting out the link belt. NOTE: On the SGM, the operating handle projects from the right underside of the gun.

Field Stripping the Goryunov

Open the top cover by pushing the cover catch forward; then lift the feed cover slightly and remove the feed carrier. Move the cover and feed cover to the vertical position. On the SGM, lift the rear sight leaf and with a punch, push out the backplate catch

pin and move the catch backward; turn the backplate one quarter-turn to the right, and remove it from the receiver; remove the recoil spring and recoil spring guide. Remove the trigger mechanism from the receiver. Move the slide rearward with the operating handle until the bolt emerges from the receiver; grasp the bolt and slide and remove them from the receiver. Lift the bolt up and out of the slide. Move the operating handle rearward until it rests against the rear clamp of the receiver, and, turning it upward, separate it from the receiver. Move the plate covering the lower opening of the receiver to the rear and remove it from the receiver. Move the belt feed slide to the right and withdraw it from the receiver. To remove the barrel, press on the barrel lock with the thumb, moving the lock as far to the left as it will go; then, grasping the barrel handle, pull the barrel forward and remove it from the receiver.

No further disassembly is recommended. To reassemble the weapon, reverse the above procedure.

The field stripping of the SG43 differs in that the backplate is removed by pulling out its retaining pin, which is located at the bottom rear of the receiver.

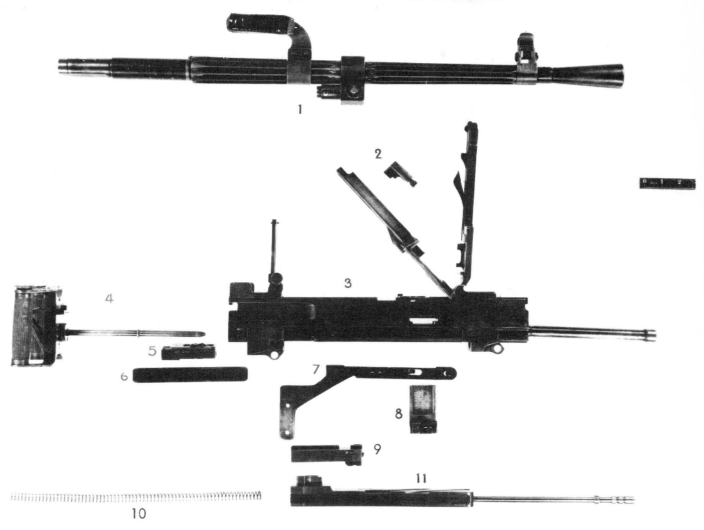

SGM, 7.62 × 54Rmm, Machine Gun, field stripped.

1. Barrel
2. Cartridge gripper
3. Receiver
4. Back plate
5. Sear unit
6. Dust cover
7. Operating handle
8. Feed slide
9. Bolt
10. Driving spring
11. Slide and piston

How the Goryunov Works

In loading, the belt is positioned in the feedway with the cover raised, so that the spring-loaded holders of the feed carrier engage the rim of the first round. The cover is closed and the operating parts retracted by means of the handle provided. The gun is then ready for firing. The feed carrier, which reciprocates in the feed tray (feed cover), operates in a notch in the top of the bolt. As the bolt is retracted, the feed carrier withdraws the cartridge from the belt. A belt holding pawl is located in the cover. The belt feed slide, reciprocating in a cut in the receiver, operates on a cam of the operating slide.

The gun fires from the open bolt position. The bolt is held to the rear by the sear, which is a part of the backplate assembly. The trigger operates through a connector to disengage the sear from the bolt. When the bolt is released, it is driven forward under the energy of the compressed driving spring, which operates against the operating slide. As the round is pushed forward by the bolt, it is forced downward, out of the carrier, and

into the feeding tray. From the feeding tray, the round enters the chamber. As the bolt approaches its forward position, a cam on the operating slide forces the rear of the bolt 3/16 of an inch to the right and into a recess in the receiver. The head of the bolt is recessed at an angle with the center of the bolt to give normal support to the base of the round in firing. As the round is chambered, the spring-loaded extractor, which is located in the left side of the bolt and is pivoted on a pin on the right side of its center, is forced over the rim of the round. After the bolt has been forced into the locked position, the slide moves forward to contact the firing pin. The firing pin strikes the primer, causing ignition of the round.

As the bullet is forced from the barrel by the expanding powder gas, some gas passes through the gas port in the barrel and impinges upon the piston attached to the slide, forcing it to the rear. The slide assembly moves independently of the bolt for a fraction of an inch. At this point, the bolt is forced out of engagement in the receiver and is drawn to the rear.

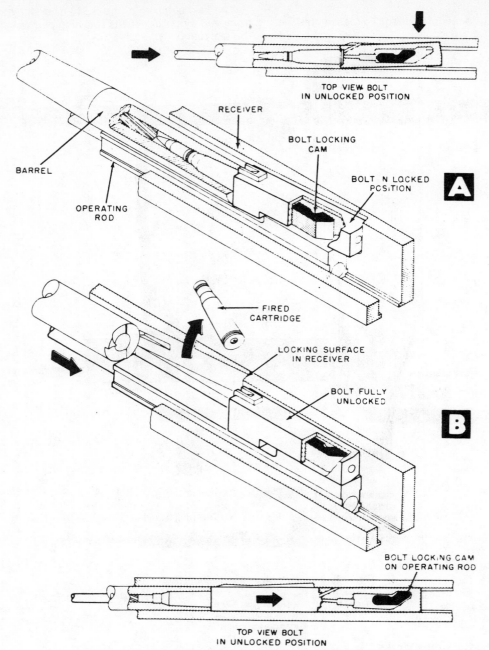

TOP VIEW BOLT
IN UNLOCKED POSITION

RECEIVER

BOLT LOCKING
CAM

BOLT IN LOCKED
POSITION

A

BARREL

OPERATING
ROD

FIRED
CARTRIDGE

LOCKING SURFACE
IN RECEIVER

BOLT FULLY
UNLOCKED

B

BOLT LOCKING CAM
ON OPERATING ROD

TOP VIEW BOLT
IN UNLOCKED POSITION

Lug on Operating Rod Cams Bolt Out of Side Locking Surface.

The extractor withdraws the fired case from the chamber. As the operating parts approach the rearward position, the ejector, a pin placed at an angle through the right side of the bolt to contact the base of the cartridge case, contacts the locking recess of the receiver. The ejector and the cartridge case are forced forward. The case, pivoted on the extractor, is ejected through the ejection port in the left side of the receiver.

If the trigger continues to be depressed, the firing cycle will be repeated. However, should the trigger be released, the sear will engage the bolt and hold it to the rear.

Notes on the Goryunov Machine Guns

The idea of a bolt whose rear end locked into the side of the receiver by being turned out of the line of axis of the bore was patented by John Browning many years ago. Browning never did very much with this idea in machine guns, but the Russians did. Goryunov, the Russian developer of this gun, died before his gun was put into service in the Soviet Army.

Since World War II, a modified gun, the SGM, has been adopted by the Soviets. The SGM has a longitudinally fluted barrel, and the barrel lock has been changed to incorporate a provision for headspace adjustment. The barrel lock has been changed by adding a scale, a slide and an Allen-screw type of lock and by having multiple grooves and ridges on the barrel lock and barrel. Thus, as the barrel and/or receiver wears, it is possible to unlock the slide, tighten it in the desired position (which can be determined from the scale) and relock it. This, of course, is not done with every barrel change but only after the components have had enough wear to make a significant difference in headspace.

THE 7.62mm PK/PKS MACHINE GUN

The Soviets have adopted a general purpose machine gun that will probably replace the 7.62mm RP-46 Company machine gun and the 7.62mm SGM battalion-level machine gun. When used on a bipod, this weapon is called the PK; when used on a tripod, it is called PKS. The PK stands for "Pulemet Kalashnikova"—machine gun Kalashnikov; the S, as in the other Soviet machine guns, stands for "Stankovy"—mounted. With the adoption of the PK, Kalashnikov now has a near monopoly of small arms designed by him in service at battalion and lower levels in the Soviet and many satellite armies. The PK is a clever combination of the basic operating principles of the AK with some apparently original design on the feed mechanism. The operating system of the PK is basically that of the AK turned upside down, as was done circa 1955–56 by FN with the mechanism of the Browning Automatic rifle to produce the MAG. Gene Stoner did the same thing somewhat later to produce machine gun versions in his Stoner 63 system.

For additional details see Chapter 2.

NO BUTT REST

FLUTED BARREL

7.62mm PK Machine Gun.

NO SIGHTS

ELECTRIC TRIGGER

NO PISTOL GRIP

NO BUTT STOCK

7.62mm Tank Machine Gun; the tank version of the PK.

SMOOTH BARREL

BUTT REST

7.62mm PKM Machine Gun.

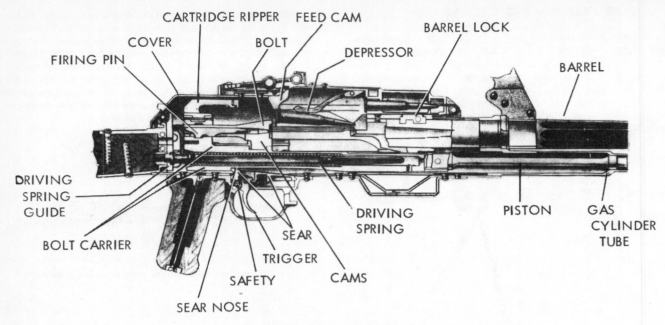

CARTRIDGE RIPPER   FEED CAM
COVER   BOLT   DEPRESSOR   BARREL LOCK
FIRING PIN   BARREL

DRIVING
SPRING
GUIDE   DRIVING
                                              SPRING   PISTON   GAS
BOLT CARRIER   SEAR   CYLINDER
                          TRIGGER   TUBE
                    SAFETY   CAMS
              SEAR NOSE

Section view of the PK Machine Gun.

How To Load And Fire The PK/PKS

Open cover by pressing in catch at top rear of cover and lifting cover. Lay cartridge belt in feedway so that first cartridge in belt is flush against the cartridge stop. Close cover and pull operating handle on right side of the receiver all the way to the rear. The weapon is now cocked and pressure on the trigger will produce fire. The safety is located on the receiver at the rear of the trigger. The barrel is removed by sliding out the barrel lock and pulling forward on the carrying handle; it is changed after 500 rounds of sustained fire.

How the PK/PKS Works

The bolt of the PK is similar to that of the AK; it has forward locking lugs and is cammed into and out of its locked position in the barrel by a raised cam lug on the slide. The body of the bolt is mounted in a tunneled-out portion of the slide post at the rear of the slide. The slide is in turn attached to the piston; for ease of disassembly, the slide-piston assembly is articulated. The firing pin is also mounted in the slide post; it rides in a hole in the bolt. The operating spring and operating spring guide, which are seated in the rear of the receiver, go into a hole in the rear of the

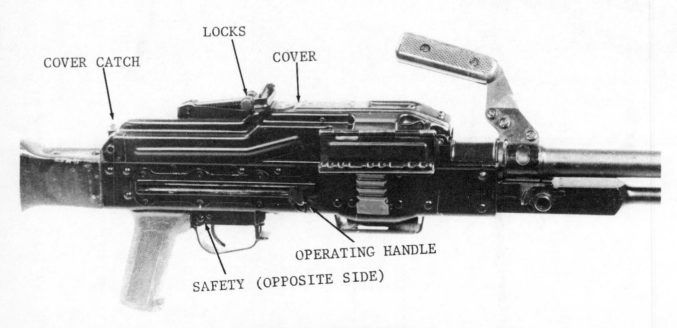

LOCKS
COVER CATCH   COVER

SAFETY (OPPOSITE SIDE)   OPERATING HANDLE

Receiver details of the PKM Machine Gun.

slide. The underside of the slide has a cut out section to engage the sear nose and hold the bolt-slide-piston assembly in cocked position. With the bolt in the cocked position, the following occurs when the trigger is pulled. The nose of the sear is lowered and the bolt-slide-piston assembly is forced forward by the compressed operating spring and rams a cartridge into the chamber. As the bolt goes forward, it is cammed in a circular motion into the locked position in the barrel by the action of a lug on the bolt body on the cam-way in the raised cam lug section of the slide. After the bolt is locked, the slide-piston continues forward a slight distance causing the firing pin, which is mounted on the slide, to continue through the bolt and strike the cartridge primer functioning the cartridge. At a point about two-thirds down the length of the barrel, gas is tapped off through a gas port and goes through the adjustable gas regulator into the gas cylinder where it impinges upon the gas piston forcing it to the rear. If the trigger is still held to the rear and there are cartridges in the belt, the gun will continue to fire.

Feed Mechanism: Although there are certain features of this feed mechanism that resemble the RP-46 and the Goryunov, for the most part the feed system appears to be original. The feed plate on this weapon is directly over the chamber as in the RP-46, and the cartridge must be withdrawn to the rear, then directed downward in a position to be rammed into the chamber by the bolt. The extractor, which pulls the cartridge from the link belt, is mounted on the hook-like piece that protrudes forward from the slide post. This piece, the slide post, and the bottom rear section of the piston resemble a square configured letter "C". When the bolt operating handle is pulled to the rear, the extractor pulls a cartridge from the belt and to the rear. In a fashion similar to the RP-46, it is forced downward by a spring-loaded lever mounted on the top cover and presses the cartridge down-

ward. In addition, the base of the cartridge runs into a cam track—called a cartridge stop—which is curved rearward and downward and causes the cartridge to travel in that position and end in an angular position with the bullet pointing toward the chamber; this piece also keeps the cartridge from travelling all the way to the rear with the slide. Like the SG-43, the PK has two covers—a top cover and a feed cover under that. The cartridge is held in the feed lips of this cover until it is engaged by the top of the bolt and rammed into the chamber. This system resembles that of a box magazine if the feed lever pushing down on the cartridge is thought of as a follower and the feed lips of the feed cover are thought of as the feed lips of a magazine. The means of moving the belt across the feedway appears to be original. A bow-shaped feed lever assembly is mounted in the receiver so that it is perpendicular to the receiver in the vertical plane and crosswise to the receiver in the horizontal plane. This feed lever assembly goes completely under the slide-piston-bolt assembly with its left-end engaging the left side of the slide. A roller on this end of the feed lever assembly engages a cammed surface on the slide causing the assembly to move up and down—left to right at the bottom and right to left at the top—in a rocking fashion, so that the left arm of the feed lever is under the slide when the top section—that which operates as a belt feed pawl—is pulling a cartridge on to the feed plate. A short arm of the feed lever—called the feed stud—engages a lip on the right side of the slide and functions as a pivot point for the feed lever. As mentioned, the top portion of the feed lever assembly rises and pushes the cartridge belt from right to left. A spring loaded belt holding pawl, mounted in the cover, then engages the belt and holds it in position. Both the feed and link ejection ports have dust covers. The dust cover on the link ejection port is opened when the bolt is pulled to the rear.

Disassembled view of the PK Machine Gun.

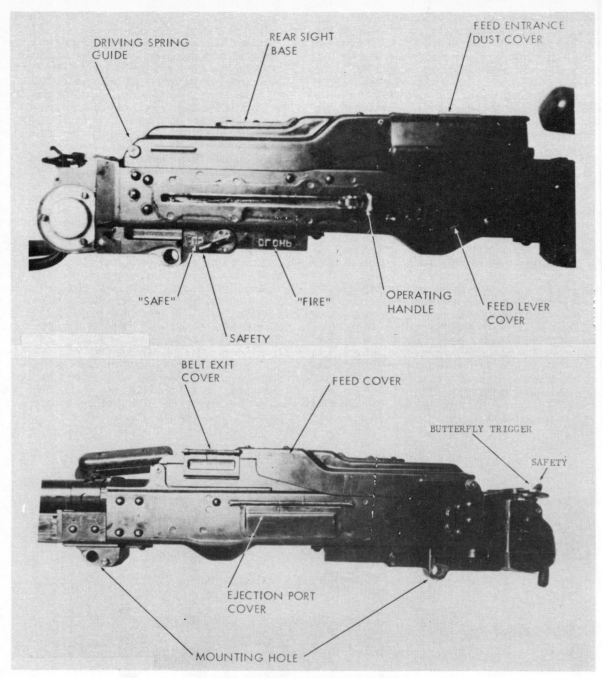

DRIVING SPRING GUIDE

REAR SIGHT BASE

FEED ENTRANCE DUST COVER

"SAFE"

"FIRE"

OPERATING HANDLE

FEED LEVER COVER

SAFETY

BELT EXIT COVER

FEED COVER

BUTTERFLY TRIGGER

SAFETY

EJECTION PORT COVER

MOUNTING HOLE

Receiver details of the PKT Tank Machine Gun.

Disassembly and Assembly

To disassemble the weapon:

Clear the gun but do not set at safe or close the cover. Remove the barrel.

Press in the driving spring guide at the rear of the receiver; then ease the guide and spring upward and out of the gun. Grasp the bolt carrier by the cartridge grippers and pull the entire unit rearward, then upward until it comes free of the receiver. Lift the bolt and carrier up and out of the gun.

Pull the bolt forward in the carrier, simultaneously twisting the bolt free of the cam until it comes free of the receiver. Lift the bolt and carrier up and out of the gun.

To reassemble the gun:

First seat the firing pin in its recess in the bolt. Seat the bolt into its hole in the bolt carrier twisting as necessary to engage the firing pin and the bolt with their recess in the carrier.

Start the piston into the gas cylinder tube until the slide can be seated in the receiver. The bolt must be pulled forward in the carrier prior to seating the slide. Pull the trigger and push the bolt carrier fully forward. Insert the driving spring into its tunnel in the slide, and press the guide forward against spring pressure until it can be seated against the rear wall of the receiver. Insert the barrel, slide the barrel lock into position and close the cover.

PKB Machine Gun designed for use as a flexibly mounted weapon on an APC.

Close-up of PKB spade grips and trigger.

PKM on convertible tripod that can be used for ground or antiaircraft fire.

PK quick change barrel.

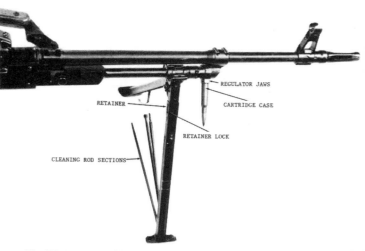

REGULATOR JAWS

RETAINER

CARTRIDGE CASE

RETAINER LOCK

CLEANING ROD SECTIONS

The PK cleaning rod is stored in the right leg of the bipod. Note also that the cartridge is used as the tool for adjusting the gas regulator.

THE 12.7mm DShK M1938 AND M1938/46 HEAVY MACHINE GUNS

The DShK is another of the Degtyarev series of weapons; its basic system of operation is similar to the other Degtyarev guns. The original DShK had a rotating block type of feed; the M1938/46 has a belt-feed lever type similar to the RP46's. These guns are chambered for the Soviet 12.7mm cartridge, which is almost identical in performance to (although not interchangeable with) the US cal. .50 cartridge. The M1938 was the primary Soviet heavy ground gun; in Korea it was frequently used by the North Koreans against aircraft. The weapon has been replaced in the Soviet Army in this role by the 14.5mm ZPU series of weapons. It is still used as antiaircraft armament on tanks and armored personnel carriers and is also used as co-axial armament on tanks. The ground mount for the DShK weapons is a wheeled mount, which can be converted into a tripod mount for AA fire.

Soviet 12.7mm DShK M1938 Heavy Machine Gun.

How to Load and Fire the DShK M1938

Push forward the feed cover latch located at the top rear of the feed cover. Lift the feed cover and place the feed belt on the revolving feed block so that the first round can be put in the upper recess of the feed block. Hold the free end of the ammunition belt with the right hand and press the feed belt against the revolving block. Rapidly rotate the block with belt as far to the right as it can go (the upper recess should rotate 120°). Close the feed cover. Pull reloading handle to the rear until the slide is engaged by the sear. Hold spade grips with both hands and press the trigger slowly with the index fingers of both hands; the weapon will fire. To put the weapon on safe, rotate the safety catch forward.

DShK 12.7mm M1938/46 Heavy Machine Gun.

How to Load and Fire the DShK M1938/46

Loading and firing of the DShK M1938/46 are the same as for the 7.62mm RP46.

Field Stripping the DShK M1938

Set the safety on fire and loosen (one turn) the latch of the machine gun mounting studs on the gun mount. If the bolt is to the rear, move it forward by pulling the trigger. Stand with back to the muzzle in front of the mount axle with the left foot resting on the axle. Grasp the gas piston tube with both hands and pull it as far forward as it will move. Then turn the tube clockwise with both hands until the support of the tube comes out of its grooves in the barrel. Push all the moving parts (bolt and slide group) to the rear until the recoil stop roller emerges from its recess in the receiver.

Unscrew the connecting screw of the rear machine gun locking bracket. Remove the backplate pin and tap the backplate lightly with a wooden mallet or a copper hammer to separate it from the receiver, meanwhile supporting it with one hand. Remove the trigger housing and then withdraw the bolt and slide group from the rear of the receiver. Remove the firing pin and the bolt and bolt locking flaps. To reassemble the weapon, perform the above steps in reverse order.

7mm DShK M1938/46, tripod set for AA fire.

How the DShKs Work

In general, both of the 12.7mm Degtyarev guns operate the same as the 7.62mm guns of this series. The M1938 has a circular type of feed mechanism that operates somewhat like the cylinder of a revolver. The feed lever, which is operated back and forth by the slide, turns the feed drum, which carries the cartridges in its recesses. As the cartridges are turned, their links are stripped, and in the final feed step the cartridge is aligned with the bolt, which rams it into the chamber. The feed system on the M1938/46 is basically the same as that on the RP46.

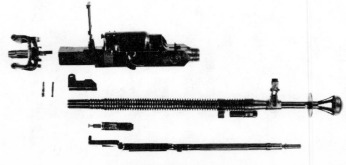

DShK, field stripped.

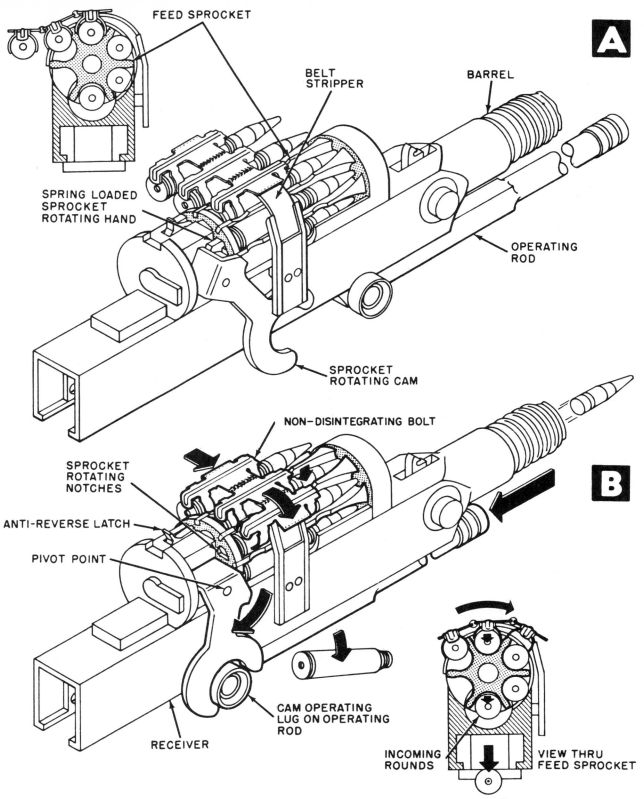

A

FEED SPROCKET

BELT STRIPPER

BARREL

SPRING LOADED SPROCKET ROTATING HAND

OPERATING ROD

SPROCKET ROTATING CAM

NON-DISINTEGRATING BOLT

B

SPROCKET ROTATING NOTCHES

ANTI-REVERSE LATCH

PIVOT POINT

RECEIVER

CAM OPERATING LUG ON OPERATING ROD

INCOMING ROUNDS

VIEW THRU FEED SPROCKET

Lug on Operating Rod Actuates Sprocket Rotating Cam.

DShK38 Machine Gun feed system from G. M. Chinn, *The Machine Gun.*

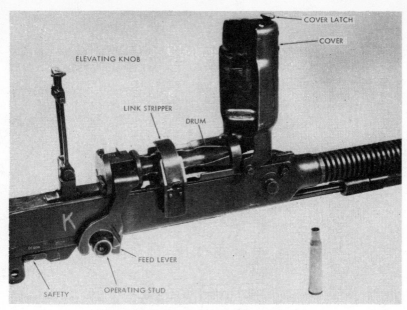

ELEVATING KNOB

COVER LATCH

COVER

LINK STRIPPER

DRUM

FEED LEVER

SAFETY

OPERATING STUD

Receiver details of the DShK38 Machine Gun.

CHARACTERISTICS OF PRE-WORLD WAR II AND WORLD WAR II SOVIET 7.62mm GROUND MACHINE GUNS

	Model 1910 Maxim (SPM)	Model 1939 DS	DP	DPM	DT	DTM	SG43
Caliber:	7.62mm.	7.62mm.	7.62mm.	7.62mm.	7.62mm.	7.62mm.	7.62mm.
Type of gun:	Heavy ground gun.	Heavy ground gun.	Squad automatic.	Squad automatic.	Tank gun.	Tank gun.	Heavy ground gun.
System of operation:	Recoil, automatic only.	Gas, automatic only.	Gas, automatic only.	Gas, automatic only.	Gas, automatic only.	Gas, automatic only.	Gas, automatic only.
Weight:	52.47 lb. w/water.	52.47 lb. w/water.	26.23 lb. loaded.	26.9 lb.	27.91 lb.	28.46 lb.	30.42 lb.
Mount Weight:	99.71 lb. w/shield.	99.71 lb. w/shield.					59.3 lb.
Length overall:	43.6 in.	46 in.	50 in.	50 in.	Stock extended, 46.46 in. Stock retracted, 39.76 in.	Stock extended, 46.44 in. Stock retracted, 39.76 in.	44.09 in.
Barrel length:	28.4 in.	28.4 in.	23.8 in.	23.8 in.	23.5 in.	23.5 in.	28.3 in.
Feed device:	250 rd.	250-rd. web belt or 50-rd. link belt.	47-rd. drum.	47-rd. drum.	60-rd. drum.	60-rd. drum.	250-rd. drum. metalic link belt.
Sights:							
Front:	Blade.	Post w/ears.	Post w/ears.	Post w/ears.	None on tanks On bipod: Post w/ears	None on tanks On bipod: Post w/ears	Blade.
Rear:	Leaf.	Leaf.	Tangent leaf.	Tangent leaf.	Aperture.	Aperture.	Leaf.
Cycle rate of fire:	500-600.	2 Rates: 500-600, 1000-1200.	500-600.	500-600.	600.	600.	600-700.
Muzzle velocity w/light ball:	2822 f.p.s.	2832 f.p.s.	2756 f.p.s.	2756 f.p.s.	2756 f.p.s.	2756 f.p.s.	2832 f.p.s.
Cooling:	Water.	Air.	Air.	Air.	Air.	Air.	Air.

NOTE: An aircraft version of the Degtyarev, the 7.62mm DA, was also used. It has been obsolete for some time. All use the 7.62 × 54mm cartridge.

CHARACTERISTICS OF SOVIET POST-WORLD WAR II MACHINE GUNS

	SGM	RP-46	RPD	RPK	PK/PKS	DShK M1938/46
Caliber:	7.62mm (7.62mm x 54).	7.62mm (7.62 × 54).	7.62mm. (7.62 × 39).	7.62mm. (7.62 × 39).	7.62mm (7.62 × 54).	12.7mm.
System of operation:	Gas, automatic.	Gas, automatic.	Gas, automatic.	Gas, automatic.	Gas, automatic.	Gas, automatic.
Length overall:	44.09 in.	50 in.	40.8 in.	40.9 in.	47.2 in.	62.5 in.
Barrel length:	28.3 in.	23.8 in.	20.5 in.	23.2 in.	25.9 in.	42.1 in.
Feed device:	250-round metallic link belt.	250-round metallic link belt.	100-round metallic link belt in drum.	75-round drum and 40-round box magazine.	100, 200 or 250-round metallic link belt	50-round metallic link belt.
Sights: Front:	Blade.	Post w/ears.	Post w/ears.	Post w/ears.	Protected post.	Post w/ears.
Rear:	Leaf.	Tangent.	Tangent.	Tangent.	Tangent w/notch.	Leaf.
Weight, gun:	29.76 lb.	28.7 lb.	15.6 lb.	w/empty drum: 12.3 lb. w/empty box: 11 lb.	19.8 lb. w/bipod.	78.5 lb.
mount:	50.9 lb.*	----	----	----	16.5 lb.	259 lb.
Muzzle velocity:	2870 f.p.s.	2750 f.p.s.	2410 f.p.s.	2410 f.p.s.	2700 f.p.s.	2822 f.p.s.
Cyclic rate:	600-700 r.p.m.	600-650 r.p.m.	650-750 r.p.m.	600 r.p.m.	650-700 r.p.m.	540-600 r.p.m.

*A 30.6 lb. tripod mount also exists.

The Egyptian Army uses the following weapons: the 9mm Beretta Model 1951 pistol, the 7.62mm Soviet SKS carbine, the 7.62mm Soviet AK assault rifle, the 7.62mm Czech Model 52 rifle, the 7.92mm Hakim (modified Ljungman rifle), the 7.92mm FN self-loading rifle and the 7.92mm Type D automatic rifle. Submachine guns used include the 9mm Port Said (Model 45 Swedish Carl Gustaf) and various models of the 9mm Beretta and 9mm Sten. Machine guns used include the 7.62mm Soviet RPD, the 7.62mm Czech Model 52, the 7.62mm Soviet

United Arab Republic (Egypt)

44

SG43 and SGM (Goryunov) machine guns, the 7.92mm Spanish Alfa machine gun and the Soviet 12.7mm DShK Model 1938/46 heavy machine gun. Many older British weapons may still be used by reserve and paramilitary forces.

Generally speaking, Egypt obtained all of her weapons from western nations prior to 1954, and most of the weapons from those nations were obtained before that time. In 1954, the UAR made the first of a series of extensive arms purchases from the Soviet Bloc. Egypt has developed a small arms industry of its own and is less dependent on imported small arms. This industry, which was established by Swedish technicians prior to the overthrow of the Egyptian monarchy, originally produced copies of foreign weapons. Of late, it has started development of native designs, which, although they are basically modifications or combinations of foreign designs, are definitely Egyptian in origin. Cartridges for all UAR service weapons are produced in that country.

EGYPTIAN PISTOLS

Egypt was originally equipped with British caliber .455 No. 1 Mark VI Webley revolvers and Enfield caliber .38 No. 2 revolvers. After World War II, Egypt adopted the 9mm Parabellum as the standard pistol and submachine gun cartridge. A modification of the Tokarev TT M1933, called the Tokagypt Model 58, chambered for the 9mm Parabellum cartridge, was developed in Hungary for Egypt, and limited purchases of this weapon were made. The Egyptian authorities were not too pleased with this weapon, and the usage has been confined to police work. The 9mm Beretta Model 1951—covered in detail in the chapter on Italy—is the standard service pistol.

The Egyptian small arms authorities, in conjunction with Beretta, developed a target version of the Model 1951. This weapon has an adjustable target type rear sight and a ramp mounted front sight, a longer barrel than the standard Model 1951 and target type stocks.

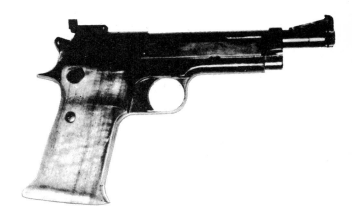

9mm Parabellum target type Beretta, Model 1951; developed for Egypt.

EGYPTIAN RIFLES

The Egyptians used the British caliber .303 rifle No. 1 Mark III and Mark III* rifle from the time of World War I until approximately 1949. At that time, the Royal Egyptian government purchased quantities of the FN self-loading rifle (also known as SAFN) chambered for the 7.92mm cartridge. These rifles can be identified by the Royal Egyptian crest on the receiver.

In this same time frame, a small arms manufacturing plant was set up in Egypt with the assistance of Swedish technicians. This plant manufactured by the 7.92mm Hakim rifle, a modification of the 6.5mm Ljungman Model 42, and the 9mm Parabellum

Port Said submachine gun. The Hakim differs from the Model 42 in having a full length hand guard, tangent type rear sight, enlarged charger guide, modified magazine catch and the shape of the muzzle brake/compensator. A number of training versions of the Hakim rifle are used by Egypt. Beretta made a caliber .22 version of the Hakim, and Anschutz made a 4.5mm air rifle version of this rifle for training.

In 1954, the UAR procured significant quantities of the Soviet 7.62mm SKS carbine and the Czech 7.62mm Model 52 rifle. The design of the SKS apparently appealed to the Egyptians in-

sofar as its shortness, lightness and permanently attached folding bayonet are concerned. These features of the SKS plus use of the Soviet 7.62mm Model 1943 "intermediate" sized cartridge were incorporated into the design of the Egyptian Rashid rifle.

The Rashid has a modified Ljungman action; the bolt retracting handle on the Rashid is mounted in the right forward section of the action; bolt retraction on the Ljungman is accomplished by pulling the receiver cover forward and to the rear. Very few Rashid rifles were made. The most common rifle in Egyptian service today appears to be the Soviet 7.62mm AK assault rifle.

7.92mm Hakim rifle.

Action of Hakim rifle, field-stripped.

7.62mm Rashid rifle.

EGYPTIAN SUBMACHINE GUNS

The Egyptians used British 9mm Parabellum Sten guns and also purchased various types of submachine guns in Western Europe, including the 9mm Parabellum Spanish Star Model Z-45 and the 9mm Parabellum Beretta Model 38/42 and 38/49.

As previously noted, Egypt was tooled to produce the 9mm Parabellum Swedish Carl Gustaf (Model 1945) submachine gun, which the Egyptians call the Port Said submachine gun. This weapon is covered in detail under Sweden.

EGYPTIAN MACHINE GUNS

British machine guns formerly predominated in Egypt, and prior to the overthrow of the Egyptian monarchy, some Spanish

ALFA 7.92mm M1944 machine guns were procured. Soviet machine guns now predominate in the Egyptian forces.

45
United States

US forces use the following small arms: caliber .45 Pistol M1911A1; caliber .45 Submachine gun M3A1; caliber 5.56mm Rifles M16 and M16A1; 7.62mm NATO Rifles M14 and M21; 7.62mm NATO Machine Guns M60 (several models), M73, M219 and M240; caliber .50 Machine Guns M85 and M2 Heavy Barrel; and 40mm Grenade Launchers M79 and M203. Weapons such as the caliber .30 M37 Machine Gun may still be found on older armored vehicles. The following weapons are now obsolete: M1 Rifle; M1, M2 and M3 Carbines; M1918A2 Browning Automatic Rifle; and all .30 caliber Browning Machine Guns.

UNITED STATES PISTOLS

The United States adopted the caliber .45 Browning-designed Colt automatic pistol in 1911. All manufacture of this pistol was originally carried on at Colt, but Springfield Armory was tooled to produce the weapon prior to 1914. At the time of United States entry into World War I, 55,553 pistols were on hand. During World War I, Model 1911 pistols were manufactured by Remington Arms and Colt. Springfield did not manufacture the pistol,

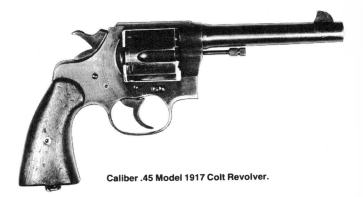

Caliber .45 Model 1917 Colt Revolver.

Caliber .45 Model 1911 Pistol made by Remington.

Caliber .45 Model 1917 Smith & Wesson Revolver. issue revolvers did not have checked stocks.

since top priority was given, at that arsenal, to the manufacture of Model 1903 rifles. Approximately 450,000 Model 1911 pistols were made during World War I by Colt and Remington. Colt was by far the largest producer; Remington produced only 13,152 pistols by the close of December 1918.

Owing to the shortage of Model 1911 pistols, orders were placed with Colt and Smith & Wesson for a heavy frame revolver chambered for the caliber .45 Model 1911 pistol cartridge. The revolvers chosen were the Colt New Service and the Smith & Wesson Hand Ejector models. Both had been in production, chambered for the .455 Webley cartridge, for the United Kingdom. Modifications were made to accommodate the rimless .45 Model 1911 cartridge. Three round, half-moon clips, which fitted in the cartridge case cannelures, were used with these weapons to allow case ejection by use of the ejector rod. They may be loaded and fired without these clips, but the individual cases have to be ejected one by one with a nail or pencil if half-moon clips are not used. These revolvers are conventional swing-out cylinder types; the cylinder latch is pushed forward on the Smith & Wesson to release the cylinder and is pulled back on the Colt. Colt manufactured 151,700 Model 1917 revolvers, and Smith & Wesson manufactured 153,311 of their Model 1917 revolver.

The Colt and Smith & Wesson revolvers were still in use by Military Police and security personnel during World War II but are no longer used in the United States armed forces or as a standard weapon in any army.

After World War I, the Colt automatic was modified. The modifications, adopted on 15 June, 1926, caused a change in nomenclature to: Pistol U.S. Caliber .45 Model 1911A1. The changes were as follows:

(1) The main spring housing of the 1911 is flat and smooth; that of the 1911A1 is arched beyond the line of the grip portion of the receiver and is knurled.

(2) The trigger of the 1911 is smooth and is longer than the serrated trigger of the 1911A1.

(3) The tang of the Model 1911A1 is longer than that of the Model 1911.

(4) The 1911A1 front sight is wider than that of the 1911.

(5) Finger clearance cuts were made on the receiver of the 1911A1 immediately behind the trigger;

these are not present on the 1911.

(6) Rifling and diameter were reduced, and land height was increased.

During World War II, the Model 1911A1 was manufactured by Colt, Remington Rand, Union Switch and Signal, and the Ithaca Gun Co. Approximately 1,800,000 pistols were made during World War II in addition to the 150,000 or so that were purchased by the United States prior to World War II. Added to the total of caliber .45 Model 1911 pistols made prior to and during World War II, over 2,400,000 .45 Colt Automatics have been made for the United States Government. In addition, hundreds of thousands have been made for commercial sale and export to foreign forces.

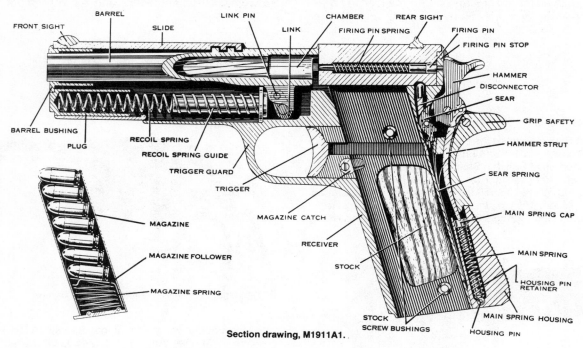

Section drawing, M1911A1.

Field Stripping the M1911A1 Pistol

While no stripping beyond that illustrated is ever necessary to clean and properly care for this pistol, the following instructions will be helpful to those who wish to master every detail.

To Remove Safety Lock. (1) Cock hammer. (2) Grasp thumbpiece of safety lock between thumb and index finger, pull steadily outward and at same time move back and forth.

To Remove Hammer. (1) Lower hammer—do not snap it. (2) Use safety lock to push out hammer pin, removing from left side. (3) Lift out hammer and hammer strut.

To Remove Mainspring Housing. (1) Using hammer strut, push mainspring housing pin out from right side of receiver. (2) Slide housing and its contained spring down out of its guides. (3) Push in on mainspring cap; at the same time push out mainspring cap pin.

To Remove Sear and Disconnector. Using hammer strut, push out sear pin from left side of receiver and remove sear and disconnector.

To Remove Magazine Catch. Press in checkered left end to permit turning catch lock a quarter turn to left out of its seat in receiver, using long leaf of sear spring. Catch, its lock and spring may now be removed. Be careful not to let spring jump away when released.

To Remove Trigger. Pull straight to the rear.

To Remove Slide Stop Plunger, Safety Lock Plunger and Plunger Spring. Draw straight to rear.

Notes on Assembling

Barrel link must be tilted forward and link pin properly in place before it will slide into place in the slide.

Put sear and disconnector together, hold by their lower ends, place them in the receiver, and replace sear pin.

Sear spring should be replaced after sear and disconnector are in place, care being taken that lower end is in its place in the cut in the receiver; upper end of left-hand leaf resting on sear.

Insert mainspring housing until lower end projects about one-eighth inch below frame. Then (1) Replace hammer and pin; (2) Grip safety; (3) Cock hammer and replace safety lock; (4) Lower hammer and push mainspring housing home, and insert pin.

Cock hammer. Insert end of magazine follower to press safety lock plunger home.

When inserting slide stop, make sure that its upper rear end stops on the receiver just below the small slide stop plunger. Then push stop upward and inward with the one motion. This will enable the upper round part of the stop to push the plunger back and let the stop snap into place.

In replacing sear and disconnector, hold the receiver as when firing, then tilt front end down. Insert the sear and the disconnector using the trigger bar as a guide to align the holes in these two parts with the receiver holes. Slight pressure may be applied on the trigger until the holes are properly lined up. When replacing the mainspring housing, it is important that the rear end of the hammer strut be in its place in the mainspring cap.

Instructions for Loading and Firing the M1911A1 Pistol

To remove magazine: Press magazine catch (button). Magazine will normally be ejected and should be caught with left hand. If spring is weak, it may come only part way; withdraw it from handle.

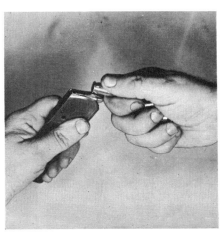

Load magazine: Holding firmly in left hand, press cartridge down in forward end of magazine follower (platform) and slide in under the curved lips of the magazine. Press following cartridges down as illustrated. Any number from 1 to 7 may be inserted.

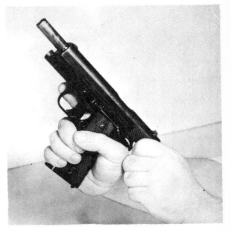

To load chamber: (1) Holding pistol at height of right shoulder and pistol 6 inches from shoulder, insert loaded magazine and press home until it locks with a click. (2) Grasp slide with thumb and fingers of the left hand, thumb on right side of slide pointing upwards and pull back slide as far as it will go. This compresses the recoil spring, cocks the hammer and permits the magazine spring to push the top cartridge into line with the breech block. (3) Release slide. The recoil spring will drive it forward and feed a cartridge into the chamber; barrel will be forced up on its link and will lock into slide; firing mechanism will engage ready for first shot.

To engage thumb safety: Unless pistol is to be fired at once, always push safety lock up into place as soon as chamber is loaded. A stud on the inner face of the thumb safety locks the hammer and sear when the safety is pushed up into the slide. It can be released by simply pushing down on the thumbpiece.

Slide stop: When the last shot has been fired, a section of the front end of the magazine follower, pushed up by the magazine spring, presses against the underside of the slide stop. This forces the stop up into a niche cut in the slide and holds the slide open as an indication that the pistol is empty.

Reloading from open slide: (1) Press magazine catch and extract empty magazine. (2) Insert loaded magazine. (3) Push down on slide stop with right thumb. This will release the slide to drive forward and load the chamber. Note: Slide stop cannot be released while an empty magazine is in the pistol. Slide will go forward only on a loaded magazine or when the magazine has been pulled part way out.

Field Stripping the M1911A1 Pistol

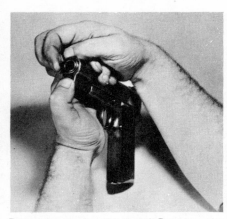

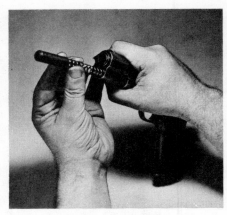

Remove magazine and examine chamber: (1) Press magazine catch and withdraw magazine. (2) Draw back slide and look into chamber through the ejection port to be sure the pistol is empty. Remember that even when the magazine is out, the pistol is still dangerous: there may be a cartridge in the chamber.

Release tension of recoil spring: (1) Press in on plug which covers end of recoil spring, using thumb or butt of magazine if it is too stiff. (2) Barrel bushing, freed from spring tension, may now be turned to the right side of the pistol.

Ease out plug and recoil spring: The spring is very powerful. Take care not to let it fly out of the pistol. Do not withdraw these parts from the pistol yet, as they serve to keep the recoil spring guide in place and make the next step easy.

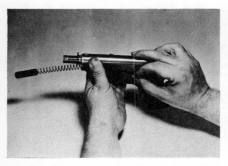

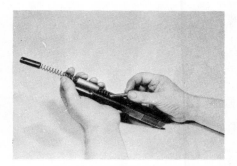

Remove slide stop. (1) Push slide back until the rear edge of the smaller recess in the lower edge of the slide is even with the rear end of the slide stop. (2) Now press from the right side against the protruding pin which is part of the slide stop. This pin passes through the right side of the receiver, then through the barrel link which holds the barrel, then through the left side of the receiver. (3) Now pull slide stop out from left side of pistol.

Remove slide and components: Pull slide forward on its guides in the receiver and remove. With the slide will come the barrel, barrel link, barrel bushing, recoil spring and recoil spring guide.

Remove recoil spring guide: (1) The recoil spring guide (on which the recoil spring compresses) may now be lifted out to the rear. (2) The recoil spring and plug are pulled out from the front. (3) The barrel bushing is turned to the left which unlocks it so it can be withdrawn.

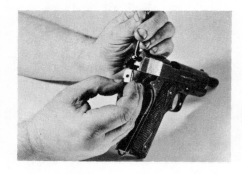

Remove barrel: Turn barrel link forward on its pin and withdraw barrel assembly from the front of the slide. Note: Normally no further stripping of this pistol is required.

To remove firing pin: (1) Should it be necessary, the firing pin may be easily removed by pressing the pin in against the tension of its spring, at the same time pushing down on the firing pin stop which holds the firing pin in place. This may be done with a nail, match or similar object. (2) Slide the stop down out of its grooves and ease out the firing pin and spring.

To remove extractor: When the firing pin has been removed the extractor, which is a long piece of spring steel inserted in a hole to the left of the firing pin, may be pried up and pulled out to the rear as illustrated.

Description of Mechanism

The pistol has three main parts: receiver, barrel and slide. The receiver is fitted with guides in which the slide runs. Its handle is hollow to permit insertion of the box magazine, which is locked by the magazine catch.

The receiver also holds the trigger whose front end projects through the trigger guard. The firing mechanism, made up of the hammer, sear, automatic disconnector, grip safety and safety lock, is at the rear of the receiver. Here too are the mainspring and sear spring. The mainspring is a coiled spring seated within the mainspring housing held by the mainspring cap pin. The mainspring cap and housing pin retainer are also in this housing.

The sear spring is a flat spring with a rib fitting into a slot in the rear wall of the receiver to prevent the spring from moving vertically. The mainspring housing bears against the rear of the spring, locking it into position to give it the required tension.

A bent metal piece called the hammer strut is fastened to the hammer by a pin in rear of its pivot, while its end rests in the mainspring cap. In a tube above the handle are the slide stop and safety lock plungers whose ends protrude from front and rear of the tube respectively, as well as the spiral spring plunger seated between the two that holds them in position.

The ejector, a solid piece of metal against which the head of the withdrawn cartridge case strikes, is fastened to the top of the receiver near the rear end.

The top of the receiver extending forward above the trigger guard forms a semi-tubular extension to provide a seat for the rear section of the recoil spring.

The barrel has two transverse locking ribs on its rear upper surface. They positively lock into corresponding slots on the inside of the slide when in firing position. The lower rear end of the barrel is attached to the receiver by a swinging link and pin. It can thus move a limited distance lengthwise and downwards.

The heavy slide mounts on the receiver from the front end, and the distance of its rearward movement is controlled by a tubular abutment, which absolutely prevents it being thrown rearward from the receiver.

In this abutment at the front end of the slide, rests the forward portion of the recoil spring and the plug that fits over its end, while the rear end of this spring is fitted over a removable guide supported by the shoulder at the front of the receiver.

A barrel bushing is inserted in the front of the slide over the barrel and locks when turned down into place. It serves to retain the recoil spring, and the plug and also supports the muzzle end of the barrel.

When the barrel and slide together are mounted on the receiver, the slide stop is in place, its pin passing through the receiver from side to side and through the barrel link, thereby positively locking slide, barrel and receiver together.

The exterior of the slide stop is provided with a checkered thumb piece to be pressed for releasing slide from the open position. When the safety lock is pushed into the upward position, it enters a recess on the slide; a stud on the inner face at the same time locks the sear and hammer when in the full cocked position. This safety can only be applied when the pistol is cocked.

The grip safety is a curved metal piece pivoted in the upper part of the receiver. It acts automatically to lock and release the firing mechanism without any attention on the part of the shooter.

The disconnector is a small lever, which when pressed down prevents the trigger mechanism from engaging with the sear and hammer in all positions except when breech is fully closed. This also prevents more than one shot following each pull of the trigger.

How the M1911A1 Pistol Works

A magazine holding any number of cartridges from 1 to 7 is inserted in the handle and pushed in until it locks. This locking is produced by the thumb-catch lock snapping into a notch cut in the upper front end of the magazine.

As the slide is drawn back for the opening movement, it compresses a recoil spring and forces the hammer back and down to full cock. Here it is held in position by the sear. As the slide goes back, the disconnector is pressed back, positively preventing the trigger from connecting the firing mechanism. When the slide is to the rear as far as it will go, it clears head of the magazine, and the magazine spring feeds a cartridge up in line with the breech.

The slide on being released is forced forward by the recoil spring, and the breech bolt face of the slide carries the first cartridge into the barrel chamber. As the slide nears its foremost position, the face of the breech bolt comes against the rear extension of the upper part of the barrel forcing the barrel forward and upward on the barrel link. When the slide and barrel reach the full forward position, the locking ribs are positively locked into the corresponding grooves on the inside of the slide.

The firing pin spring, firing pin and the extractor are located in the breech bolt section of the slide. As the cartridge is seated in the barrel chamber, the extractor, which is made of heavy spring steel, springs over the head and into the cannelure of the cartridge, thus preparing it to be drawn back during the rearward motion of the pistol for extraction.

The firing pin is a "flying" one. It is seated in the breechblock surrounded by its spring. It is shorter than the breechblock itself. Thus, if the hammer is lowered all the way down on the firing pin, it will push the pin inside the breechblock but cannot push it far enough to make it rest against the primer in the cartridge. The one way in which the firing pin can touch the primer is when it is struck a sharp blow by the hammer itself. As the hammer falls, it drives the firing pin ahead to strike the primer and is stopped by the face of the breechblock. The inertia of the firing pin causes it to fly ahead and strike the primer; then its compressed coil spring pulls it back into the breechblock.

The pressure of the powder gases driving the bullet down the barrel also drives the empty case back against the base of the breechblock, pushing the slide and barrel together rearward until the bullet is safely out of the barrel. At that point, the barrel swings downward on its pivoted link leaving the slide free to continue direct rearward motion in its guide in the receiver, extracting and ejecting the empty shell, cocking the hammer and compressing the recoil spring for the next forward movement.

Breech Pressure. When the .45 automatic pistol is fired, a pressure of 16,000 lbs. per sq. inch is generated in the firing chamber. Since the base of the bullet has an area of .159 square inches, a total pressure of 2,225 pounds is exerted against the base of the bullet, driving it forward down the barrel. The same total pressure is exerted back against the face of the breechblock driving it backwards.

The bullet, weighing only a fraction as much as the moving section of the pistol, gets under way much more quickly and utilizes most of the pressure as it travels down the barrel. The pistol's motion as compared to that of the bullet is inversely proportional to the weights of the pistol and the bullet.

Thus the bullet is well out of the barrel before the pistol has recoiled sufficiently to permit the locking mechanism to open. The pressure, of course, lasts only for a very small fraction of a second. However, in high powered military pistols of comparatively low weight, it is necessary that the breech be positively locked until the bullet has left the barrel. The locking principle on the .45 automatic pistol, model 1911, is among the best ever designed.

How the Slide Stop Works. The forward end of the magazine follower is split in two longitudinally for a short length. The left hand section is bent down below the level of the follower.

When the last cartridge has been stripped from the magazine, the follower rises under the influence of the magazine spring, and the bent section presses against the rear of the inside of the slide stop, thus forcing the projection on the top of the stop up into line with the large notch in the base of the slide into which it locks.

The slide will not go forward while the magazine is empty. If the empty magazine is extracted, pressing on the slide stop will permit the slide to run forward by pulling the stop down out of its locking notch. If a loaded magazine is inserted in the handle, then the magazine follower with its bent arm is in position below the cartridges on the inside of the magazine. Hence, if the slide stop is pushed down when a loaded magazine is in the handle, it will release the slide to run forward and load the chamber.

SPECIAL PURPOSE HAND GUNS

The United States forces have and do use various commercial pistols for specialized purposes, such as air-crew armament, issue to general officers and issue to security personnel. Among the weapons that have been or are issued for such purposes are the Colt caliber .32 and .380 automatic pistol, the caliber .38 Colt Detective Special Revolver, the caliber .38 Colt Police Positive Revolver, the caliber .38 Colt Special Official Police and the caliber .38 Smith & Wesson Military and Police Revolver. The above revolvers are all chambered for the .38 special cartridge; Smith & Wesson Military and Police revolvers chambered for the .38 S&W cartridge have also been used. Various commercial target type caliber .22 pistols and revolvers are also used for training purposes.

Rock Island Arsenal Caliber .45 General Officer Model Pistol, M15, (top) and older Colt .32 ACP Pistol formerly issued to Generals. More details in Chapter 4.

CHARACTERISTICS OF UNITED STATES SERVICE PISTOLS

	Colt Model 1917	Smith & Wesson Model 1917	Model 1911A1
Caliber:	.45.	.45.	.45.
System of operation:	Double-action revolver.	Double-action revolver.	Recoil, semiautomatic.
Length overall:	10.8 in.	10.8 in.	8.62 in.
Barrel length:	5.5 in.	5.5 in.	5 in.
Feed device:	6-round, revolving cylinder.	6-round, revolving cylinder.	7-round, in-line, detachable box magazine.
Sights: Front:	Blade.	Blade.	Blade.
Rear:	Square notch.	"V" notch.	Square notch.
Weight:	2.5 lb.	2.25 lb.	2.43 lb.
Muzzle velocity:	830 f.p.s.	830 f.p.s.	830 f.p.s.

UNITED STATES RIFLES AND CARBINES

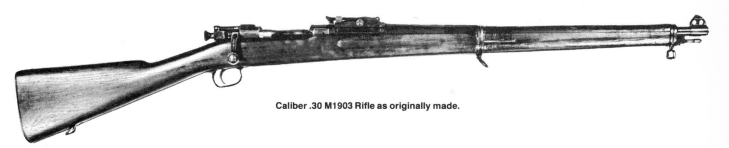

Caliber .30 M1903 Rifle as originally made.

HISTORICAL SUMMARY

In 1903, the United States adopted the caliber .30 Model 1903 rifle, commonly known as the "03" Springfield. The action is basically a modification of the Mauser Model 98 action. As made from 1903 to 1906, the Springfield had a tangent type rear sight, a cleaning-rod type bayonet contained in the stock under the barrel and was chambered for the caliber .30 Model 1903 cartridge (.30-03), which is longer than the .30 Model 1906 (.30-06) and uses a 220-grain bullet. The adoption of the Model 1906 cartridge resulted in the rebuilding of most of the rifles previously issued, and the Model 1903 appeared in the form that remained standard until the adoption of the Model 1903A1 in 1929.

The Model 1903A1 remained the standard rifle until the adoption of the M1 rifle in 1936. In 1940, the British government contracted with the Remington Arms firm at Ilion, New York, to produce caliber .30 M1903A1 rifles for British forces. Before production was started, however, the United States government took over the contract under Lend Lease, and plans were made for a simplification of manufacture. A few Model 1903A1s were made by Remington—production figures on the Springfield are given in the detailed section on that rifle—before production of the simplified M1903A3 was begun. A sniper version of the Model 1903A3, the Model 1903A4, was also developed and produced during World War II.

The entry of the United States into World War I found this country with a very limited number of M1903 rifles on hand—approximately 600,000—and only two plants tooled to produce the rifle, Springfield and Rock Island. The government also had 160,000 caliber .30 Krags on hand and purchased 20,000 caliber .303 Canadian Ross rifles and 280,049 Russian 7.62mm Mosin-Nagant rifles from New England Westinghouse and Remington Arms, who had been manufacturing this rifle for the Imperial Russian government. The Krag, Ross and Mosin-Nagant were not suitable for service with the American Expeditionary Force in France due to logistical problems and the type of war being conducted.

Three large gun plants—Winchester at New Haven, Conn., Remington Arms at Ilion, N. Y., and Remington Arms Union (later called Midvale Steel and Ordnance Co.) at Eddystone, Pa.—were completing large contracts for British-designed caliber .303 P14 (Enfield) rifles. (See the chapter on Great Britain.) The P14 had originally been designed, as the P13, for a rimless caliber .280 cartridge; it was not too difficult to modify the design to use the US caliber .30 M1906 cartridge. Additional modifications were made to simplify production and to standardize parts among the plants, and in this manner the US caliber .30 Rifle Model 1917 (or Enfield as it is commonly known) was born. This rifle was used by the United States for training purposes during World War II, and large quantities were sold to the United Kingdom in 1940, where for some reason, it was frequently referred to as "the Springfield."

The Model 1917 is a modified Mauser with frontal locking lugs that cock, as the British Lee Enfield, on the forward push of the bolt. Bolt removal is by means of a bolt-retaining catch, which also houses the ejector, on the left rear side of the receiver, and is similar to that of the Model 98 Mauser and its many variations. The bolt sleeve is held on the one-piece firing pin by interrupted threads, and its removal is rather complicated. The cocking piece is drawn to the rear and turned, by use of a piece of string looped over the sear nose, to allow the firing pin to go forward, thereby relieving the tension on the main spring and allowing the cocking piece to be removed. In the Army, various tricks such as inserting pennies between the cocking piece and bolt body while the bolt was forced forward with the safety in the "on" position were also used to achieve this purpose. Indeed, the possession of a penny was essential to the United States Army user of the Enfield. Since the Enfield did not have a cutoff, as did the Springfield, and the follower of the Enfield held the bolt to the rear of the magazine when empty, a penny was necessary to put in the top of the magazine to hold the follower down so that the bolt could be shoved smartly home during inspection arms.

Bolt disassembly excepted, the Model 1917 was a fine weapon and had better battle sights than the Model 1903. Total production of the Model 1917 was 2,202,429. Barrels, firing pins, main springs, stocks and various other parts were made for the rifle during World War II, but the last complete rifles were made after World War I. The Model 1917 is no longer used by any major power and is probably not used in significant quantity by any country.

The search for a suitable semiautomatic rifle began before World War I but became more urgent at that war's conclusion. After a series of tests in which the St. Etienne, the Liu, the Bang, the Thompson, the Hatcher, the Pedersen, the Garand and various other rifles were contenders, the Garand was chosen and standardized in 1936 as the United States Rifle caliber .30 M1. The M1 is covered in detail later in this chapter.

THE CALIBER .30 MODEL 1903A1, 1903A3 and 1903A4 RIFLES

The history of this rifle is given in the introduction to United States Rifles earlier in this chapter.

Differences in 1903 Models

The differences between the various 1903 individual models follow. The basic 1903 with straight stock has a leaf type rear sight and no finger grasping grooves in the fore-end of the stock. The bolt was originally bent straight down but after 1918 was given a slight bend to the rear. These bolts are stamped "NS" on the handle. These rifles were made by Springfield and Rock Island. Receivers made by Springfield with serial numbers below 800,000 are made of Springfield Class "C" steel and should not

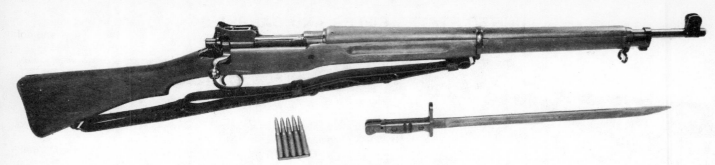

US Enfield caliber .30 M1917 Rifle.

be used with stepped-up loads. Later receivers made at Springfield are suitable for use with any factory-loaded .30-06 ammunition, except proof loads. Receivers of Rock Island manufacture up to number 285,506 were also manufactured of Class "C" steel and require similar precautions.

M1903 Mark I. This rifle was altered by the fitting of a new sear mechanism and changes in the cutoff; a slot was drilled in the left side of the receiver to accommodate the caliber .30 Pedersen device, which replaced the regular bolt and converted the weapon into a semiautomatic, firing the caliber .30 pistol cartridge. The Pedersen device, or "Pistol caliber .30 Model 1918" as it was known, was never issued, and the Mark I rifles were remodified to be used as standard M1903s.

M1903A1. A pistol grip "type C" stock with grasping grooves was fitted, the butt plate was checkered, and the trigger was serrated. This model was adopted in December 1929.

M1903A2. This is not a shoulder rifle; it is a barreled receiver used as a subcaliber rifle in various artillery pieces.

M1903A3. Adopted on 21 May 1942, this rifle was modified to simplify production. Stamped bands, swivels, butt plate and magazine trigger guard assemblies are used. A one-piece hand guard, simplified front sight and ramp type aperture rear sight, mounted on the receiver bridge, are also found on these rifles. Most of these rifles are fitted with straight stocks; however, a semi-pistol grip stock was also issued. Four, two and occasionally six land-and-groove barrels may be found. These rifles were manufactured by Remington Arms and the L. C. Smith Corona Typewriter Co. A total of 945,846 rifles were made. Remington also produced approximately 345,000 M1903 and M1903 (modified) rifles before production of the M1903A3 began.

M1903A4. This is the sniper version of the M1903A3; a full pistol grip stock is fitted. The bolt handle is cut away to clear the M73B1 (Weaver 330C) 2.5 power scope. No iron sights are fitted. This rifle was adopted in December 1942. Approximately 26,650 were manufactured.

Model 1942. This is a Marine Corps modification of the M1903A1. The rifle is fitted with a 10x Unertl scope.

Total production of the Model 1903 and 1903A1 rifles was ap-

Caliber .30 Model 1903 Rifle.

Caliber .30 M1903A1 Rifle.

Caliber .30 M1903A3 Rifle.

proximately 1,295,000 rifles at Springfield, Rock Island and Remington Arms.

Loading and Firing the Model 1903

As a Single-Shot Rifle. Check the magazine cutoff on the left side of the receiver, making sure that it is down and the word "Off" can be seen. Turn the bolt handle up as far as it will go. This will release the locking lugs from their recesses in the receiver, and permit the bolt to be drawn straight back. Now place a cartridge in the firing chamber, thrust home the bolt to seat the cartridge properly and permit the extractor to snap over the cannelure of the cartridge case, and turn the bolt handle down as far as it will go to lock the piece. Note: This rifle is cocked as the bolt is rotated clockwise. The knob on the cocking piece will project out of its casing when the weapon is at full cock. If desired, the safety lock may now be applied, by turning the safety lock thumb piece at the rear of the bolt over to the right as far as it will go, when the word "Safe" will be seen on its face.

If safety is not set, pressing the trigger will explode the cartridge in the firing chamber, which then may be extracted and ejected by turning up and pulling back sharply on the bolt handle.

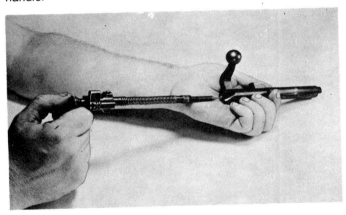

To Dismount Bolt. Holding bolt firmly in left hand, press in bolt sleeve lock with right thumb and unscrew, turning to the left. Bolt sleeve assembly can now be drawn back out of bolt.

Holding firing pin sleeve with left forefinger and thumb, pull back on the cocking piece with the right middle finger and right thumb, and turn the safety lock to the left with the right forefinger to release it. This will relieve part of the tension of the main-spring.

Resting the head of the cocking piece on a firm surface, pull back the firing pin sleeve and remove the striker. Firing pin sleeve, mainspring and firing pin rod may then be withdrawn.

Extractor is removed by turning it to the right and pushing forward.

Assembling Bolt. Holding bolt handle up in left hand, make sure that the extractor collar lug is in line with the safety lock on the bolt and insert the extractor collar lug in its undercut in the extractor, then push extractor until tongue comes in contact with bolt face. Now press extractor hook against a rigid surface to spring it into its groove in the bolt.

See that the safety is down and to the left, and assemble firing pin rod and bolt sleeve. Place the cocking piece against a solid surface, draw back the firing pin sleeve and attach the striker. The firing pin must be cocked before the bolt can be screwed on. This is done by pressing the striker point against a wooden surface (which must not be hard enough to injure it). Force the cocking piece back and engage the safety lock.

Assembled bolt sleeve is now replaced in the bolt and screwed until the bolt sleeve lock engages.

With cutoff still turned to center notch, insert bolt in its guide in the receiver, push down the magazine follower and push the bolt home. Now turn safety lock and cutoff down to the left, and press the trigger.

Stripping the Magazine. Turn rifle upside down, insert nose of bullet in the hole in the rear of the floor plate to depress the spring catch.

Retaining pressure, pull back toward the trigger guard. This will release the spring and the magazine follower, and permit them to be removed from the weapon.

Assembling the Magazine. When assembling the magazine, make sure the front end of the floor plate catches on the front end of the magazine opening and push it toward receiver and forward until the spring catch engages.

No further stripping of this weapon is necessary or desirable.

M1903A3, A4. Floor plate cannot be removed, follower is removed from the top of the magazine.

CHARACTERISTICS OF UNITED STATES BOLT-ACTION SERVICE RIFLES

	Model 1903	Model 1917	Model 1903A1	Model 1903A3	Model 1903A4
Caliber:			.30 US (.30-06)		
System of operation:			Manually operated turn bolt		
Length overall:	43.2 in.	46.3 in.	43.2 in.	43.5 in.	43.5 in.
Barrel length:	24 in.	26 in.	24 in.	24 in	24 in.
Feed device:			5-round, staggered row, non removable box magazine		
Sights: Front:	Blade.	Blade with protecting ears.	Blade.	Blade.	2.2X telescopic*
Rear:	Leaf with aperture, notched battle sight.	Leaf with aperture, aperture battle sight.	Leaf with aperture, aperture battle sight.	Aperture on ramp.	
Weight:	8.69 lb. with oiler and thong case.	8.18 lb. w/oiler and thong case.	8.69 lb. w/oiler and thong case.	8 lb.	9.38 lb.
Muzzle velocity: (M2 Ball):	2805 f.p.s.	Approx. 2830 f.p.s.	2805 f.p.s.	2805 f.p.s.	2805 f.p.s.

*Weaver 330 C (M73B1) usually used, some were fitted with the Lymann Alaskan (M73).

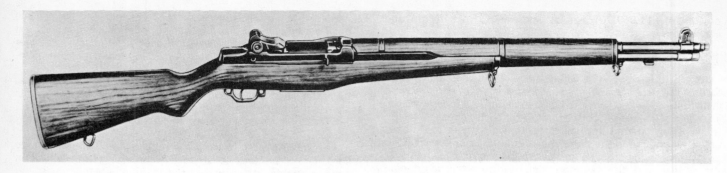

Caliber .30 M1 Rifle (Garand semiautomatic rifle).

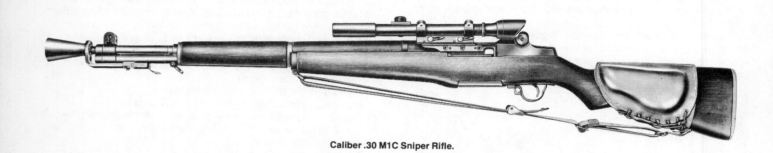

Caliber .30 M1C Sniper Rifle.

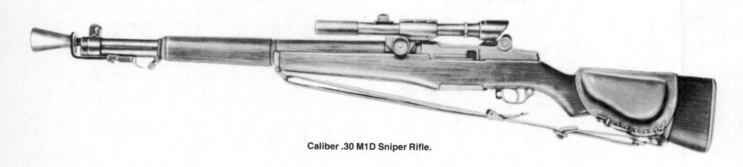

Caliber .30 M1D Sniper Rifle.

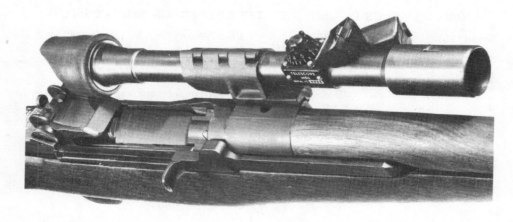

Caliber .30 M1D Sniper Rifle.

RIFLE CALIBER .30 M1

As noted in Chapter 1, the M1 Rifle is now obsolete in the US, but it is still used by a number of other nations and is very popular with US collectors and shooters. The M1D, equipped with the M84 telescope, is still a standard sniper rifle. National Match M1 Rifles, hand assembled with special barrels and fiberglass bedded stocks, are still found in the hands of some competitive shooters.

Loading and Firing the M1

Pull operating rod straight to the rear. It will be caught and held open by the operating rod catch.

Place the loaded clip on top of the magazine follower; with right side of right hand against the operating rod handle press down with right thumb on the clip until it is caught in the receiver by the clip latch.

Remove the right thumb from the line of the bolt and let go of the operating rod handle, which will run forward under the compression of the spring. Push operating rod handle with heel of right hand to be certain that bolt is fully home and locked.

Pressing the trigger will now fire one cartridge. Weapon will be ready for the next pull of the trigger.

If weapon is not to be used at once, set the safety. The safety is in front of the trigger guard. Pulling it back toward the trigger sets it on safe; forward is the fire position.

Note that the cartridge clip is reversible and may be fed into the rifle from either end.

Unloading the M1 (Garand) Rifle. First check to be sure that the safety is off.

Pull the operating rod back sharply and hold it in rear position. This will eject the cartridge that was in the firing chamber. With the left hand, grasp the rifle in front of trigger guard. Hold the butt against the right hip to support it. With the left thumb, release the clip latch.

The clip and whatever cartridges remain in it will now pop up into the right hand.

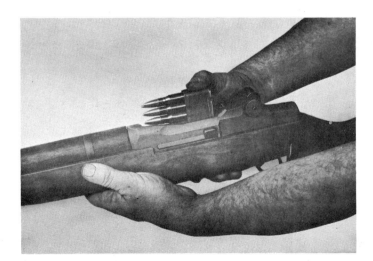

With the right side of the right hand held against the operating rod handle, force the operating rod slightly to the rear. With the right thumb, now push down the magazine follower and permit the bolt to move forward about an inch over the end of the follower.

Remove the thumb smartly from the follower and let go of the operating rod. The action will close under the tension of the spring. Now press the trigger.

If you wish to unload the firing chamber but leave the magazine loaded, pull the operating rod back as described above to eject the cartridge from the firing chamber; then pull the operating rod handle back past its normal rear position, force the clip down, ease the rod far enough forward to let the bolt handle ride over the top of the clip, then let operating rod go forward.

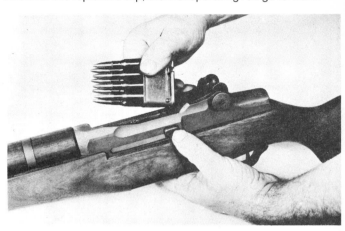

Field Stripping the M1

A thorough knowledge of field stripping is necessary in order to give the rifle the care essential to its correct operation.

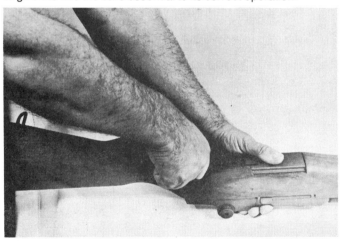

Start by placing the rifle upside down on a firm surface. Holding the rifle with left hand, reset the butt against the left thigh.

With thumb and forefinger, unlatch the trigger guard by pulling back on it.

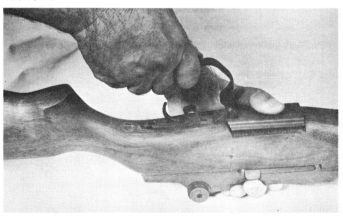

Continue the pressure and pull out the trigger housing group.

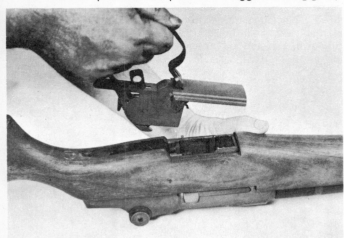

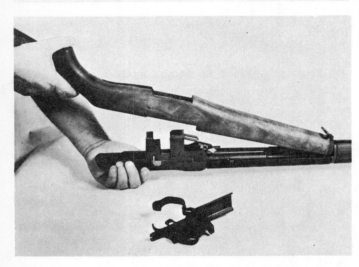

With left hand, grasp rifle over rear sight. With right hand, strike up against the small of the stock, firmly grasping it at the same time. This will separate the barrel and receiver group from the stock group.

To Dismount Barrel and Receiver Group, M1. With the barrel down, grasp the follower rod at the knurled portion with thumb and forefinger and press it toward the muzzle to free it from the follower arm.

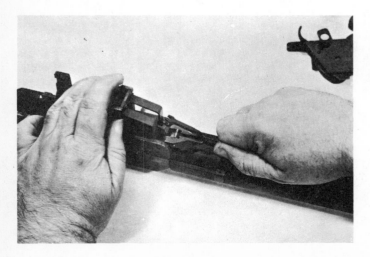

The follower rod and its compensating spring, which is attached, may now be withdrawn to the right. The compensating spring is removed from the follower rod by holding spring with left hand and twisting rod toward the body with the right hand and pulling slightly to the right.

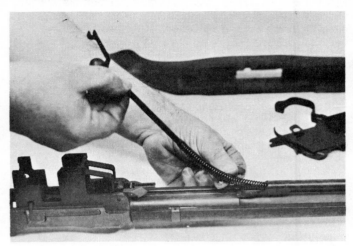

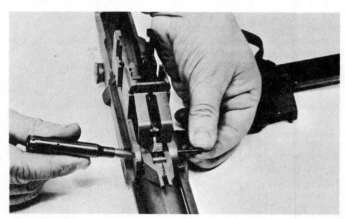

With the point of a bullet, push the follower arm pin from its seat and pull it out with the left hand.

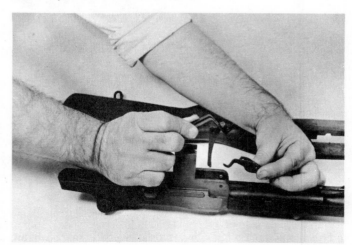

Seize the bullet guide, follower arm and operating rod catch assembly; draw these to the left until they disengage. The three separate parts may now be lifted out. Accelerator pin is riveted in its seat, so do not attempt to remove accelerator from operating catch assembly.

Lift out follower with its slide attached (do not separate follower from slide.)

Holding barrel and receiver assembly with left hand, grasp the operating rod handle with right hand and move it slowly to the rear, meanwhile pulling the rod handle up and away from the receiver. (This disengages operating rod from bolt, when the lug on the operating rod slides into the dismount notch of the operating rod guide groove.) When operating rod is disengaged, pull it down and back and withdraw it. (Note that the operating rod is bent. This is intentional. Do not attempt to straighten it.)

Slide the bolt from the rear to the front by pushing the operating lug on it, and lift it out to the right front with a slight twisting motion.

Note on M1 Gas Cylinder. A spline type gas cylinder is used in which the barrel protrudes beyond the cylinder. The front sight screw is entered from the rear of the sight and is sealed to prevent unscrewing. The combination tool must be used to unscrew the gas cylinder lock screw.

Unscrew the gas cylinder lock.

The gas cylinder is tapped toward the muzzle and removed from the barrel.

Gas cylinder assembly should never be removed except when necessary to replace the front handguard assembly.

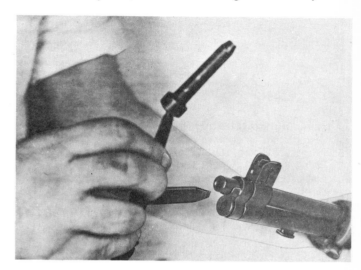

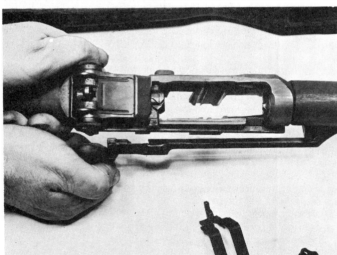

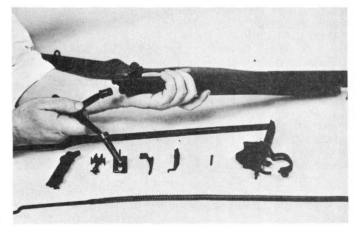

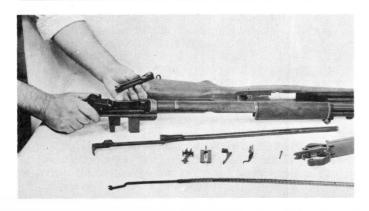

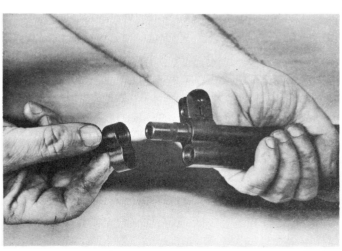

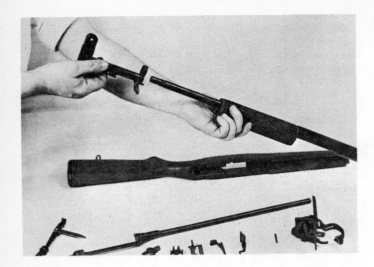

Assembling the M1 Rifle. Replacing gas cylinder, if it has been dismounted, is done by merely reversing the dismounting procedure.

To assemble barrel and receiver group, tilt the barrel and receiver assembly, sight up and muzzle to the front to an angle of about 45°.

Holding the bolt by the right locking lug so the front end of the bolt is somewhat above and to the right of its extreme forward position in the receiver, insert the rear end in its bearing on the bridge of the receiver. Switch it from right to left far enough to let tang of the firing pin clear top of the bridge. Next guide the left locking lug of the bolt into its groove just to the rear of the lug on the left side of the receiver, and start right locking lug into its bearing in the receiver. Now slide bolt back to its extreme rear position.

Turn barrel and receiver assembly in left hand until barrel is down.

Grasp operating rod at the handle and holding it handle up, insert piston head into gas cylinder about 3/8''. Be sure that operating rod handle is to the left of the receiver.

Hold barrel and receiver assembly in left hand and twist to the right until barrel is uppermost.

Adjust operating rod with right hand so that camming recess on its rear end fits over operating lug on bolt. Now press operating rod forward and downward until bolt is seated in its forward position.

With barrel and receiver assembly held barrel down and muzzle to your left, replace the follower with its attached slide so that its guide ribs fit into their grooves in the receiver. (The square hole in the follower must be to the right.) The follower slide rests on the bottom surface of the bolt when the follower is in the correct position.

With left hand replace bullet guide, fitting the shoulders of the guide into their slots in the receiver and the hole in the projecting lug in line with the hole in the receiver.

With left hand replace bullet guide, fitting the shoulders of the guide into their slots in the receiver and the hole in the projecting lug in line with the hole in the receiver.

With left hand replace follower arm passing stud end through bullet guide slot and inserting stud in proper grooves in front end of follower.

Place the forked end of the follower arm in position across the projecting lug on the bullet guide, with pin holes properly aligned.

Insert rear arm of operating rod catch into clearance cut in the bullet guide (be sure its rear end is below the forward stud of the clip latch which projects into the receiver mouth.) Line up the holes in the operating rod catch, the follower arm, and the bullet guide with those in the receiver; and insert the follower arm pin in the side of the receiver toward your body and press the pin home.

Insert operating rod spring into operating rod; assemble follower rod by grasping the spring in left hand and inserting follower rod with right hand, twisting the two together until the spring is fully seated.

Seize the knurled portion of follower rod with thumb and forefinger of left hand with hump down and forked end to the right.

Place front end of follower rod into operating rod spring and push to the left, seating the forked end against the follower arm.

Insert U-shaped flange of stock ferrule in its seat in the lower band.

Pivoting about this group, guide chamber and receiver group and press into position in the stock.

Replace trigger housing group with trigger guard in open position into the stock opening.

Press into position, close and latch trigger guard. This completes reassembly.

How the M1 Works

Starting with the rifle loaded and cocked, the action is as follows. The trigger being pressed, the hammer strikes the firing pin, exploding the cartridge in the chamber. As the bullet passes over the gas port drilled in the under side of the barrel, some of the gas escapes into the cylinder and blasts back against the piston and operating rod with force enough to drive the rod to rear and compress the spring.

During the first 5/16 inch of rearward travel, the operating lug slides in a straight section of the recess on the operating rod; after which the cam surface of this recess is brought in contact with the operating lug, which it cams up, thereby rotating the bolt from right to left to unlock its two lugs from their recesses in the receiver.

During the moment of delayed action, the bullet leaves the barrel, and the breech pressure drops to a safe point. The further rotation of the bolt then cams the hammer away from the firing pin and pulls the firing pin back from the bolt. The operating rod continues its backward movement carrying the bolt with it as the lug on the bolt has reached the end of its recess.

During this rearward motion of the bolt, the empty case is withdrawn from the chamber by the extractor positioned in the bolt until it is clear of the breech; at which point the ejector, exerting a steady pressure on the base of the cartridge case, throws it to the right front by the action of its compressed spring.

The rear end of the bolt at this point forces the hammer back, rides over it, compresses the hammer spring and finally stops in the rear end of the receiver.

As the bolt has now cleared the clip, the follower spring forces the cartridges up until the topmost one is in line with the bolt.

The operating rod spring comes into play at this point to pull the action forward.

Forward Movement of the Action. As the bolt moves forward, its lower front base strikes the base of the cartridge case and pushes it into the firing chamber. The hammer, pressed by its spring, rides on the bottom of the bolt. While it tends to rise, it is caught and held by the trigger lugs engaging the hammer hook, if trigger pressure has not been released. Otherwise, the trigger engages the rear hammer hook until letting go the trigger disengages the sear from the hammer. The hammer then slides into engagement wih the trigger lugs.

When the bolt nears its forward position, the extractor engages near the rim of the cartridge, and the base of the cartridge forces the ejector into the bolt, compressing the ejector spring.

The rear surface of the cam recess in the operating rod now cams the operating lug down and thereby twists the bolt from left to right until the two lugs lock into their places in the receiver.

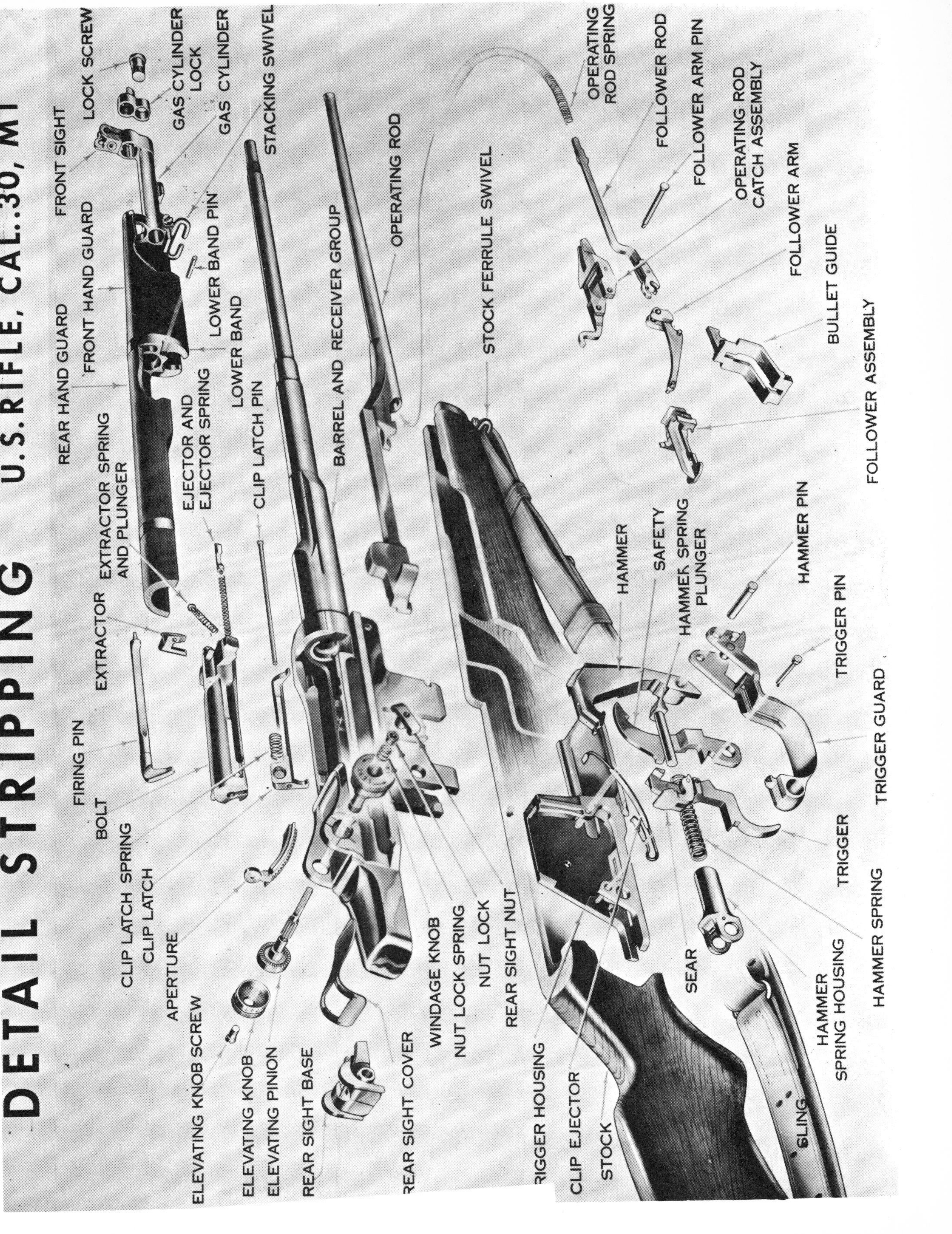

DETAIL STRIPPING U.S. RIFLE, CAL..30, M1

FRONT SIGHT
LOCK SCREW
GAS CYLINDER LOCK
GAS CYLINDER
STACKING SWIVEL
REAR HAND GUARD
FRONT HAND GUARD
LOWER BAND PIN
LOWER BAND
CLIP LATCH PIN
BARREL AND RECEIVER GROUP
OPERATING ROD
STOCK FERRULE SWIVEL
OPERATING ROD SPRING
FOLLOWER ROD
FOLLOWER ARM PIN
OPERATING ROD CATCH ASSEMBLY
FOLLOWER ARM
BULLET GUIDE
FOLLOWER ASSEMBLY
EJECTOR AND EJECTOR SPRING
EXTRACTOR SPRING AND PLUNGER
EXTRACTOR
FIRING PIN
BOLT
CLIP LATCH SPRING
CLIP LATCH
APERTURE
ELEVATING KNOB SCREW
ELEVATING KNOB
ELEVATING PINION
REAR SIGHT BASE
REAR SIGHT COVER
WINDAGE KNOB
NUT LOCK SPRING
NUT LOCK
REAR SIGHT NUT
HAMMER
SAFETY
HAMMER SPRING PLUNGER
HAMMER PIN
TRIGGER PIN
TRIGGER GUARD
TRIGGER
SEAR
HAMMER SPRING
HAMMER SPRING HOUSING
TRIGGER HOUSING
CLIP EJECTOR
STOCK
SLING

GRENADE LAUNCHER M-7 . . . PRECAUTIONS & FUNCTIONING
U. S. RIFLE, CAL. 30, M1

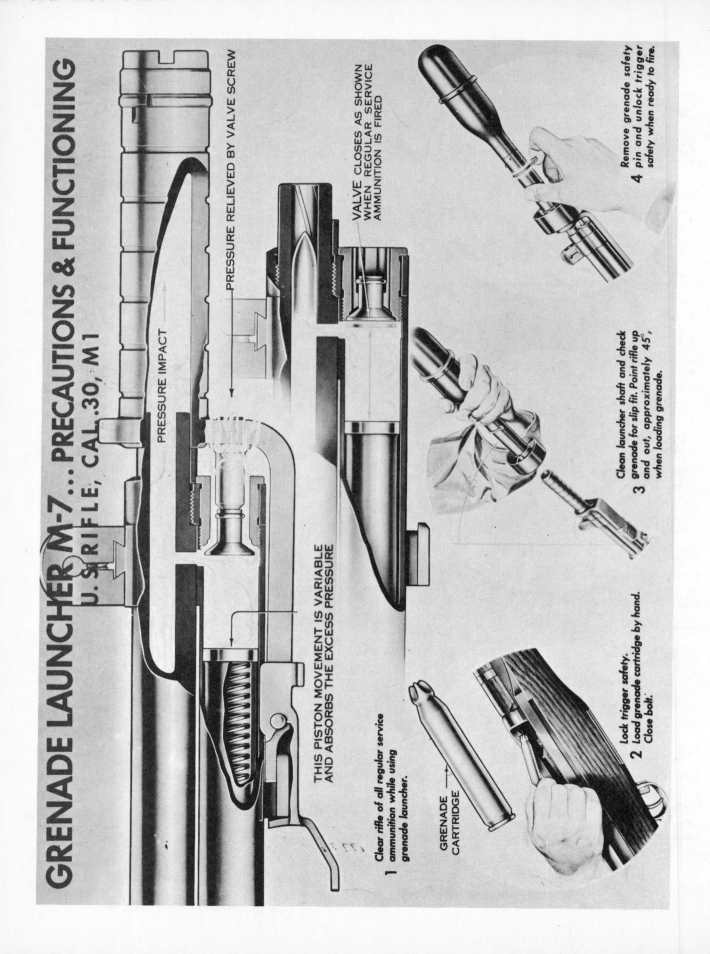

PRESSURE IMPACT

PRESSURE RELIEVED BY VALVE SCREW

VALVE CLOSES AS SHOWN WHEN REGULAR SERVICE AMMUNITION IS FIRED

THIS PISTON MOVEMENT IS VARIABLE AND ABSORBS THE EXCESS PRESSURE

GRENADE CARTRIDGE

1 *Clear rifle of all regular service ammunition while using grenade launcher.*

2 *Lock trigger safety. Load grenade cartridge by hand. Close bolt.*

3 *Clean launcher shaft and check grenade for slip fit. Point rifle up and out, approximately 45°, when loading grenade.*

4 *Remove grenade safety pin and unlock trigger safety when ready to fire.*

The operating rod drives ahead for another 5/16 inch. The rear end of the straight section of the operating rod recess reaches the operating lug on the bolt, which completes the forward movement and leaves the rifle ready to fire when the trigger is pressed.

This cycle continues as long as there are cartridges in the magazine and the trigger is squeezed.

Care of the M1 Rifle

The rifle must be kept clean and properly lubricated. Failure to do so may result in stoppages at a critical moment. The rifle should be inspected daily.

To Clean the Bore. A clean patch saturated with bore cleaner should be run through the bore a number of times. Plain water, hot or cold, may be used if bore cleaner is lacking. While the bore is still wet, a metal brush should be run through several times to loosen up any material that has not been dissolved by the water. Dry patches should then be pushed through the bore until thoroughly dry. The bore should then be coated with light issue gun oil. Also use the chamber cleaning tool to give the chamber the same attention. Remember that primer fouling in the bore contains a salt that rusts the steel.

To Clean Gas Cylinder. The carbon forming in the gas cylinder varies in amount in different weapons. When the deposit is heavy, the rifle is sluggish in action and may fail to feed. The carbon must be scraped from the exposed surface of the front of the cylinder and the gas cylinder plug and piston head after extensive firing. A knife or similar sharp bladed instrument should be used for this scraping process.

Gas cylinder plugs and grooves in the gas cylinder should be cleaned so they will feed correctly in the plug.

The gas cylinder lock should be removed, and the lock screw inserted in the cylinder far enough to break loose any carbon. Inside the cylinder must be thoroughly wiped clean and oiled at the conclusion of any extensive firing.

When firing is expected to be resumed the next day, tilt the muzzle down and place a few drops of oil into the cylinder between the piston and the walls of the cylinder. Then operate the rod by hand a few times to distribute the oil thoroughly.

Wipe the outside of the gas cylinder and the operating rod and then oil lightly. Should no firing be expected for a week or two, remove the rod and gas cylinder lock screw (or plug) so that the cylinder is open at both ends. Then clean cylinder with rod and patches exactly as the bore of the rifle is cleaned.

Hold the weapon so that no water gets into the gas port. Do not remove the gas cylinder for cleaning.

Piston head and rod should be cleaned with cleaner or with water and dried thoroughly, while the rod and cylinder should be oiled before assembling. Any carbon present should be removed. Do not use abrasive cloth if it is possible to avoid doing so; should it be used, take proper care that the corners of the plug or lock screw and piston head are not rounded.

Attention to Other Parts of Rifle. Graphite cup grease is used for lubricating bolt lugs, bolt guides, bolt cocking cams, compensating spring, contact surfaces of barrel and operating rod, operating rod cams and springs, and operating rod groove in the receiver.

All other metal parts should be cleaned and covered with a uniform light coat of oil.

Wooden parts must be treated with light coat of raw linseed oil about once a month.

The leather sling should be washed, dried with a clean rag and lightly oiled with neatsfoot oil while it is still damp, whenever the sling shows signs of stiffening or drying. Rust should be removed from the metal parts with a piece of soft wood and oil, never with abrasive. Screw heads must be kept clean to prevent rusting.

Be careful not to use too much oil, as any heavy coat will collect dirt and interfere with operation.

THE JOHNSON CALIBER .30 SEMIAUTOMATIC RIFLE M1941

How to Load and Fire the Johnson Rifle

Lift magazine cover; on right side of receiver below and parallel to ejection port, insert five rounds either on a Springfield-type charger (stripper clip) or singly. If using a charger, insert horizontally into charger guides in charging port. When last round is stripped or fed singly into magazine, magazine cover will close automatically. Raise the operating handle 20° and pull completely to rear; bolt will run forward, chambering a round. The rifle is now loaded and will fire if the trigger is pulled. When the last round is fired, the bolt will remain to the rear; load as directed above and pull bolt handle slightly to the rear and release it—the bolt will run home chambering a cartridge and the weapon is loaded. The Johnson can be loaded with single rounds or chargers with the bolt home on a loaded chamber. It is therefore easy to replenish the magazine at any time. The magazine can be emptied by depressing the magazine cover with the thumb of the right hand. The safety lock lever is located immediately in front of the trigger guard. When the free end of the lever is at an angle to the right of the axis of the barrel, the weapon is on safe. When the lever is to the left of the axis of the barrel, the weapon is on fire.

How to Field Strip the Johnson Rifle

Check rifle to insure that it is empty. With the point of a bulleted round (or a drift), push on the latch plunger of the hinged barrel latch found in the hole in the forward right side of the fore-end and push the barrel rearward. Raise the operating handle with the thumb of the left hand to the unlocked position and withdraw the barrel from the receiver. Disengage the bolt stop plate plunger with the point of a bulleted round and lift out bolt stop plate. Remove bolt stop and disengage the link from the main spring plunger. Raise the operating handle and retract the bolt about two inches. Grasp the knob of the operating handle spindle and pull it outward. Slide the operating handle forward until it is clear of the shoulders in the extractor recess and remove it. Lift out the extractor. Grasp the projecting end of the link and pull it to the rear, withdrawing the bolt through the rear end of the receiver. Rotate the locking cam counterclockwise and remove it from the bolt, remove the firing pin, and push out the link pin and remove the link. Disengage the hammer block pin and push it out with point of bullet; pull off the butt stock. Remove the ejector pin and ejector. Hammer should be

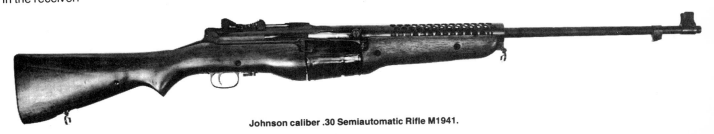

Johnson caliber .30 Semiautomatic Rifle M1941.

cocked before removing the butt stock group. Unscrew the front guard screw and the hammer block screw and lift out the hammer group from the stock. Unscrew the rear trigger guard screw and remove the trigger guard and safety assembly. No further disassembly is recommended. To reassemble, follow the above directions in reverse order.

How the Johnson Rifle Works

When the trigger is pressed, the sear disengages from the hammer. The hammer is driven against the firing pin, which protrudes from the rear of the locking cam, and the weapon fires. The barrel recoils against the tension of the barrel recoil spring and the main spring (transmitted through the bolt.) When the bullet is at the muzzle, the barrel has moved rearward about 1/64 inch; when the bullet is about 2 feet from the muzzle the barrel has recoiled about 1/8 inch. The camming arm on the bolt engages the camming face in the receiver and unlocking begins. The Johnson has an 8-lug bolt. When the bullet is about 5 feet from the muzzle, the barrel has recoiled its full 5/8 inch and the bolt has rotated 20° and is unlocked. The rearward motion of the barrel is stopped by a shoulder in the receiver. The bolt moves to the rear independently of the barrel due to inertia and residual pressure in the chamber. The extractor gives the empty case a sharp pull and the bolt receives a sharp blow from the locking cam, which taps the bolt rearward. The rearward movement of the bolt cocks the hammer, and the extracted case is brought into contact with the ejector, which throws the case clear of the rifle. The bolt is halted in its rearward travel by the forward end of the link bringing it up against the bolt stop, when the head of the bolt has passed behind the base of the top cartridge in the magazine.

As the bolt moves forward under the pressure of the main spring, the bolt face picks up a cartridge from the magazine and rams it into the chamber. The locking lugs enter the barrel locking bushing, and the locking cam rotates the bolt 20° to the locked position. Pressure on the trigger must be relaxed between shots. When the last round has been fired, the bolt remains open.

The Johnson is the only recoil-operated military shoulder rifle that has been manufactured in quantity. It appeared soon after the Army had adopted the M1, and at the time its backers claimed that it was far superior to the M1. A series of tests and demonstrations during the period 1939–40, however, indicated that the Johnson was not superior to the M1; Springfield Armory was already tooled up to produce the M1.

Quantities of the 1941 Johnson were used by the US Marines for a limited period of time, and significant quantities were made for the Dutch East Indies. The rotary magazine is the common version of the Johnson Rifle; however, a vertical feed version was made as well.

CARBINE CALIBER .30 M1, M1A1, M2, AND M3

The carbine was developed to replace the pistols in use by noncommissioned officers, special troops and company-grade officers.

Manufacturers of the carbine were:

Winchester: 809,451 M1 carbines, 17,500 M2 carbines, and 1,108 M3 carbines.

Inland Manufacturing Div. of General Motors: a total of 2,625,000 carbines including M1s, M1A1s, M2s, and a few M3s.

Underwood Elliot Fisher: 545,616 carbines.

National Postal Meter: 413,017 carbines.

Rock-ola Manufacturing Corp: 228,500 carbines.

Quality Hardware: 359,662 carbines.

Standard Products: 247,155 carbines.

Saginaw: 739,136 carbines.

IBM: 346,500 carbines.

There were more carbines produced than of any other United States weapon.

The variations of the carbines are as follows:

Carbine M1—semiautomatic, originally made with L type flip over sight, which was replaced with a ramp-mounted aperture adjustable for windage, sporter type stock.

Carbine M1A1—same as M1, but has folding-type metal butt stock.

Carbine M2—selective fire, usually found with fixed wooden stock.

Carbine M3—receiver grooved for Infrared "Snooper Scope," otherwise identical to the M2.

Loading and Firing the M1 Carbine

Load magazine exactly as for automatic pistol with 15 cartridges.

Thrust up into position in the trigger housing until it locks.

Pull back handle of operating slide on right side of gun as far as it will go, opening the action and allowing a cartridge to rise in the magazine in the path of the bolt, and cocking the weapon and compressing the return spring.

Remove hand and permit operating slide to go forward, loading the firing chamber. With heel of hand, push operating slide handle forward to be sure it is fully locked. The weapon is now ready to fire.

Push the button safety in the front end of the trigger guard all the way through to the right. This is the safe position. Pushing the button through to the left side as far as it will go releases the safety.

How the M1 Carbine Works

Starting with the gun loaded and cocked, the action is as

The Winchester caliber .30 Light Rifle—prototype of the US M1 Carbine.

follows: The trigger being pressed, the hammer is released to strike the firing pin and discharge the cartridge. As the bullet passes down the barrel, a minute quantity of gas behind it flows down through a very fine hole bored in the under side of the barrel and escapes into a sealed cylinder where it expands against the head of the piston-like operating slide. This operating slide moves back a short distance until a cam recess engages an operating lug on the bolt. During this time, the bullet has had sufficient time to leave the barrel, and it is safe for the action to open. The extractor fastened in the bolt draws the empty cartridge back to strike the spring-actuated ejector, which hurls it out to the right front of the weapon. The bolt is rotated out of its locking recess, simultaneously turning the hammer away from the rear of the firing pin and forcing the firing pin to draw back inside the bolt. This compresses the hammer spring. The rear-

Top view of the M2, shown without magazine. Full auto switch is seen at the receiver above the stock. Externally, the M2 resembles the Carbine M1.

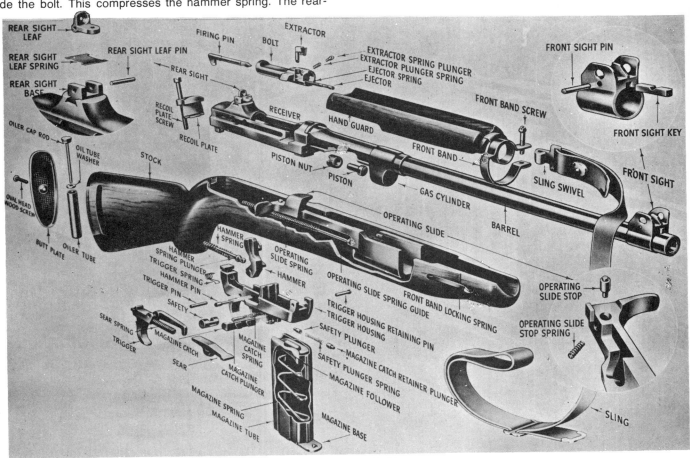

Parts of the M1 Carbine.

ward motion of operating slide is completed when rear end of its inertia block strikes against forward end of receiver. Bolt stops when it reaches the end of bolt hole in rear receiver. Boltway is now clear permitting the next round to rise in the magazine in line with the bolt. During this motion, the powerful operating slide spring has been compressed. It now drives the bolt forward loading the chamber. The cam recess in the operating slide again comes into play. Pressing against the bolt operating lug, it rotates it from left to right into its locking recess.

Forward movement of operating slide continues until the rear of its inertia block lodges against the piston in the cylinder. This action continues each time the trigger is squeezed until the last cartridge has been fired.

Field Stripping the M1 Carbine

Push the magazine catch to the left (it is positioned just in

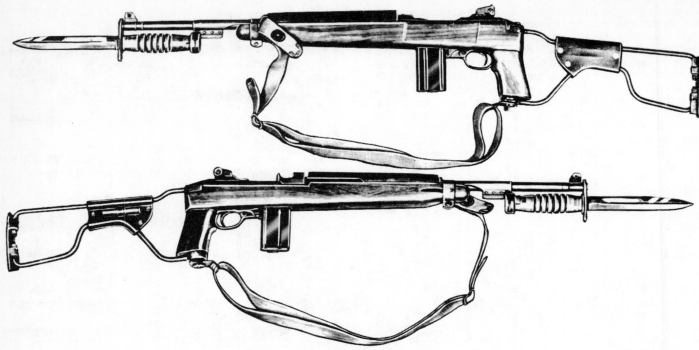

Caliber .30 M1A1 Carbine.

front of the trigger guard on the right side), and withdraw magazine from below.

Draw back bolt to examine chamber and make sure that the weapon is unloaded.

At the end of the wooden fore-end is a sling swivel. Push this back against the fore-end and loosen it by unscrewing the front band screw. A cartridge may be used as a screwdriver.

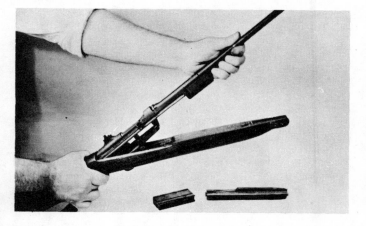

and receiver can now be pulled forward and lifted out of the stock; carrying the trigger housing group with them.

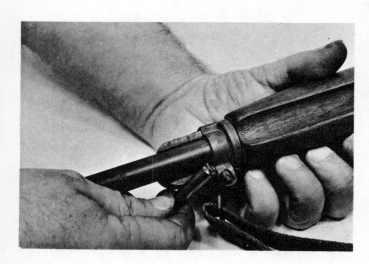

Press the front end of the lock spring toward the rear and slip the front band forward over its locking spring; it will not slip off the barrel unless the front sight is removed.

Now slide the wooden handguard on top of the barrel forward until its liner disengages from the undercut in the forward face of the receiver; it can then be lifted from the barrel.

Holding the stock firmly with the right hand, grasp the barrel near the front end with the left hand and raise it until the lug at the rear of the receiver clears the retaining notch on the face of the recoil plate (the plate just above the pistol grip). The barrel

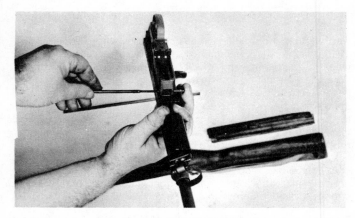

At forward end of trigger guard is the trigger housing retaining pin. Push it out until it clears the lug in the receiver.

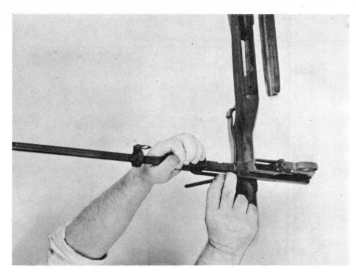

Pull back the operating slide spring guide a short distance until it is free of the operating slide. Pulling it forward and to the right permits it and its spring to be withdrawn.

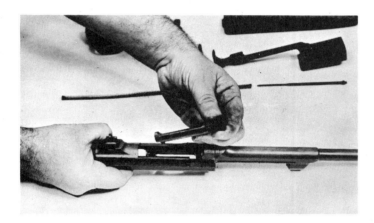

Take hold of the bolt and slide it to the rear until its face is behind the locking shoulder in the receiver. Twist the bolt from right to left, lift it to an angle of 45° and turn it bottom up. It may now be drawn forward and up out of the receiver.

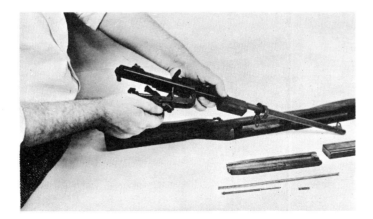

Pull the housing forward until it clears the grooves in the receiver, when it may be lifted out.

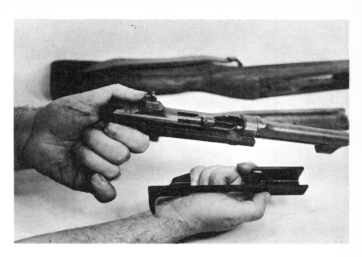

Pull the operating slide back until the guide lug at bottom of handle end aligns with dismounting cut in receiver. Lift handle up and to right until the guide lug clears the retaining cut in receiver and also disengages from the bolt lug. Then push slide forward until the left barrel guide lip aligns with clearance cut on bottom of left barrel guide groove. Rotating the slide body so as to free the left guide lip of the slide from its barrel guide groove will permit removing the slide from barrel.

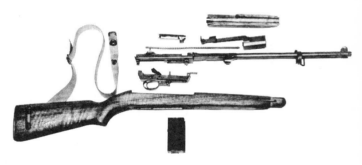

This completes field stripping. To assemble, reverse this procedure.

Caliber .30 M2 and M3 Carbines

The M2 carbine is the selective-fire version of the M1. Parts that differ from those of the M1 carbine are as follows: hammer, sear, trigger housing, operating slide, magazine catch and stock. Added parts are as follows: disconnector group, disconnector lever assembly and selector group. All M2 and M3 carbines and many M1 and M1A1 carbines are fitted with a front band assembly that incorporates a bayonet lug. These carbines use the bayonet knife M4.

The M3 carbine is an M2 with a receiver designed to accommodate an infrared sniperscope. It does not have a conventional rear sight.

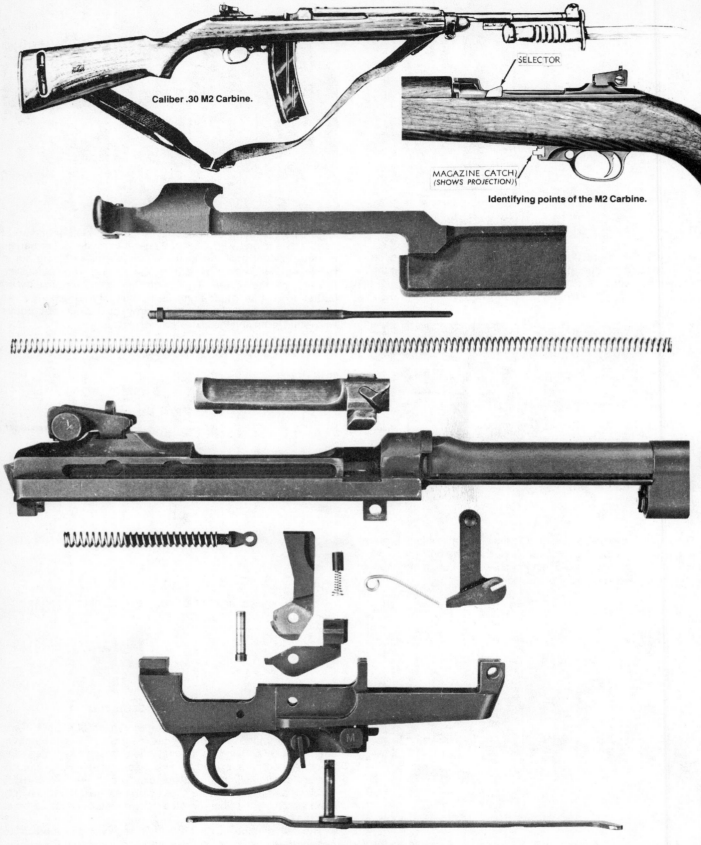

Caliber .30 M2 Carbine.

SELECTOR

MAGAZINE CATCH
(SHOWS PROJECTION)

Identifying points of the M2 Carbine.

Stripped action of the M2 Carbine.

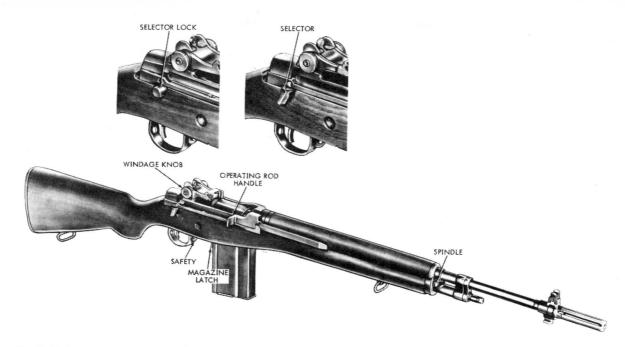

The M14 Rifle as initially produced at Springfield Armory with wood stock and wood handguard. Top left drawing shows blank selector lock, which prevents the rifle from being fired automatically. Top right drawing shows the selector switch that may be substituted to permit selection of fire mode.

Intermediate production version of the M14 Rifle equipped with wood stock, shoulder rest buttplate and ventilated fiberglass reinforced handguard.

Late production version of the M14 Rifle with fiberglass reinforced synthetic stock and unventilated handguard. M14 Rifles in the field are encountered with both wooden and synthetic stocks.

THE 7.62mm NATO M14 RIFLE

The M14 is a standard rifle of the United States Army. It was produced at Harrington and Richardson Arms Co., Thompson Products (TRW), at the New Haven (Winchester) plant of the Winchester-Western Arms Division of Olin Mathieson Corp. and at Springfield Armory. The M14 is capable of automatic as well as semiautomatic fire, and a certain proportion fitted with bipods serve as squad automatic weapons. The M14 rifle is no longer in production.

The M14 is an evolution of the M1 rifle; in the design of the M14 many of the shortcomings of the M1 have been eradicated. The basic action of the M1 remains, but the troublesome eight-round en bloc clip has gone. The hanging of the gas cylinder on the end of the M1 rifle's barrel gave some accuracy difficulties; these have been overcome in the M14 by moving the gas port and gas cylinder back about eight inches from the muzzle. The gas cutoff and expansion system used on the M14 lends itself to better accuracy because its action is not as abrupt as that of the M1. Various other changes were made to give the Army a basically better weapon than the M1.

How to Load and Fire the M14

Application of Safety. Place the safety in the safe position by cocking the hammer and snapping the safety rearward.

Loading of Rifle. Place the safety in the safe position.

Insert a loaded magazine into the magazine well, front end leading, until the front catch snaps into engagement; then pull backward and upward until the magazine latch snaps into position.

Pull the operating rod handle to its rearmost position and release; this allows the top round to rise and the bolt to move forward, thus stripping and chambering a round from the magazine.

Semiautomatic Fire with Selector Lock. With the selector lock in the rifle, it cannot be fired automatically. Load the rifle and release the safety. The rifle will now fire one round upon each pull of the trigger.

Semiautomatic Fire with Selector. Press in and turn the selector until it snaps into position with its blank face to the rear and its projection downward. The connector assembly is inoperative in this position since the connector is held forward and out of engagement with the operating rod.

Load the rifle and release the safety. The rifle will now fire one round upon each pull of the trigger.

Full Automatic Fire with Selector. Press in and turn the selector until it snaps into position with the face marked "A" to the rear and the projection upward. This rotation of the eccentric selector shaft moves the sear release to the rear into contact with the sear and moves the connector assembly rearward into contact with the operating rod.

Load the rifle and release the safety.

Pull and hold the trigger. The rifle will fire automatically as long as the trigger is squeezed and there is ammunition in the magazine. To cease firing, release the trigger.

Bolt Lock. When the last round of ammunition is fired, the magazine follower engages the bolt lock and raises it into the path of the retracted bolt; this holds the bolt in the open position.

Unloading the Rifle. Place the safety in the safe position.

Grasp the magazine, placing the thumb on the magazine latch, and squeeze the latch. Push the magazine forward and downward to disengage it from the front catch and remove the magazine from the magazine well.

Pull the operating handle rearward to extract and eject a chambered round, and to inspect the chamber. The rifle is now clear.

Gas Shutoff Valve. For semiautomatic and full automatic firing, turn the valve to the open position by pressing in and rotating. The valve is open when the slot in the head of the valve spindle is perpendicular to the barrel. The shutoff valve in the gas cylinder opens and closes the port in the cylinder between the barrel and the gas piston.

Stripping the M14

General Disassembly (Field Stripping). Unload the rifle, remove the magazine, and place the safety in the safe position.

Turn the rifle upside down with the muzzle pointing to the left.

Insert the nose of a cartridge into the hole in the trigger guard and pry upward to unlatch the trigger guard.

Swing the trigger guard upward and lift the trigger group from the stock.

Separate the stock from the rifle by cradling the receiver firmly in one hand and by striking upward sharply on the stock butt with the palm of the other hand.

Turn the barrel and receiver group on its side with the connector assembly upward. Press in and turn the selector until the face marked "A" is toward the rear sight knob and the projection forward (this step applies to rifles modified for selective firing.) Press forward on the connector with the right thumb until the forward end can be lifted off the connector lock. Rotate the connector clockwise, until the slot at the rear end is aligned with the elongated stud on the rear release. Lower slightly the front end of the connector and lift it from the sear release. **Note:** The connector assembly is a semipermanent assembly, it should not be disassembled.

With the barrel and receiver group upside down, pull forward on the operating rod spring, relieving pressure on the connector lock. Pull the lock outward, disconnect the operating rod spring guide, and remove the spring guide and spring. Turn the barrel and receiver group right side up.

Retract the operating rod until the key on its lower surface coincides with the dismount notch in the receiver. Lift the operating rod free and pull to the rear, disengaging it from the operating rod guide.

Grasp the bolt group by the roller and, while sliding it forward, lift it upward and outward to the right front with a slight rotating motion. The rifle is now field stripped, and basic assemblies such as the bolt and the trigger groups may be disassembled, if required.

Bolt Group. With the bolt in the left hand and the thumb over the ejector, insert the blade of a screwdriver between the extractor and the lower cartridge seat flange. Pry the extractor upward to unseat it. The ejector will snap out against the thumb. Lift out the ejector assembly, extractor plunger and spring. Remove the firing pin from the rear of the bolt. **Note:** No attempt should be made to disassemble the roller from the bolt stud.

Barrel and Receiver Group. Disassemble the rear sight as follows. Run the aperture all the way down and record the reading for use in reassembling the sight. Hold the elevating knob and unscrew the nut in the center of the windage knob. Withdraw the elevating knob. Unscrew and remove the windage knob. Pull the aperture up about one-half inch. Place the thumb

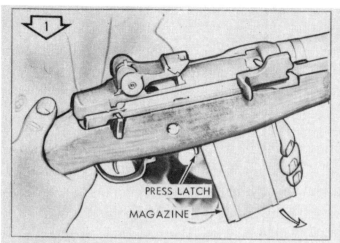

REMOVE MAGAZINE.

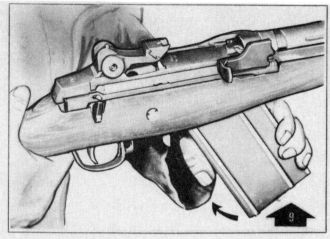

INSTALL MAGAZINE

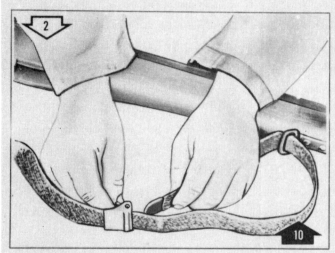

REMOVE/INSTALL SLING.

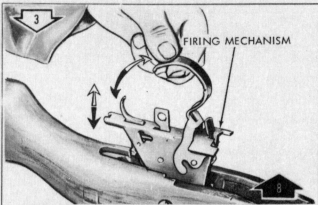

FIRING MECHANISM

CAUTION: OVER 90 DEGREES ROTATIONAL MOVEMENT, TOWARDS THE MUZZLE, CAN BE FELT WHEN THE COCKING STUD OF THE TRIGGER GUARD ENGAGES POINT AT BASE OF HAMMER, WORKING AGAINST HAMMER SPRING TENSION. THE FIRING MECHANISM SHOULD BE REMOVED BEFORE THIS POSITION IS REACHED. PARTIAL WITH-DRAWAL OF FIRING MECHANISM COMBINED WITH THIS ADDED MOVEMENT WILL CAUSE DAMAGE TO THE RIB OR KEEPWAYS ON SIDE OF FIRING MECHANISM HOUSING. THIS WILL RESULT IN DIFFICULT INSTALLATION AND REMOVAL OF FIRING MECHANISM.

REMOVE/INSTALL FIRING MECHANISM.

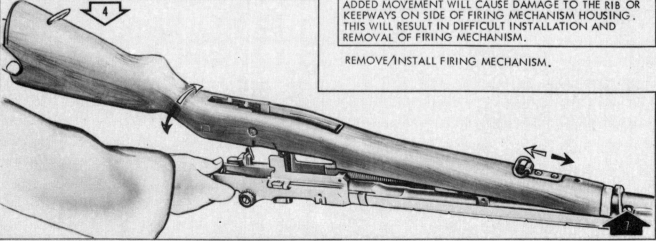

REMOVE/INSTALL STOCK WITH BUTT PLATE ASSEMBLY.

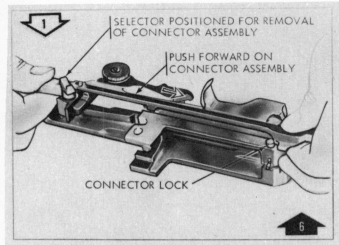

SELECTOR POSITIONED FOR REMOVAL OF CONNECTOR ASSEMBLY

PUSH FORWARD ON CONNECTOR ASSEMBLY

CONNECTOR LOCK

DISENGAGING/ENGAGING CONNECTOR ASSEMBLY.

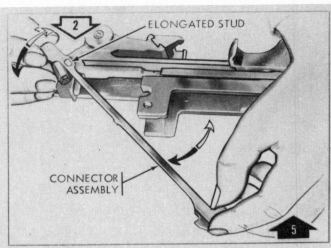

ELONGATED STUD

CONNECTOR ASSEMBLY

REMOVE/INSTALL CONNECTOR ASSEMBLY.

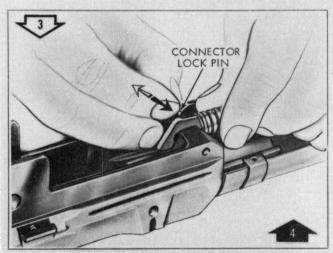

CONNECTOR LOCK PIN

DISENGAGE/ENGAGE CONNECTOR LOCK.

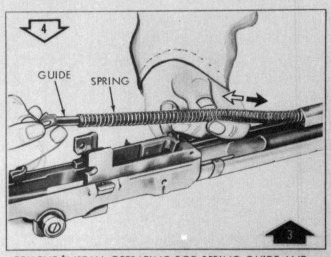

GUIDE   SPRING

REMOVE/INSTALL OPERATING ROD SPRING GUIDE AND OPERATING ROD SPRING.

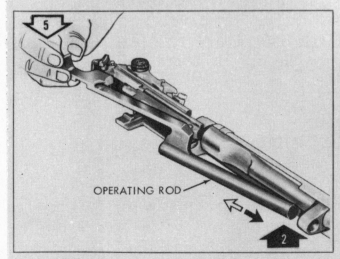

OPERATING ROD

REMOVE/INSTALL OPERATING ROD.

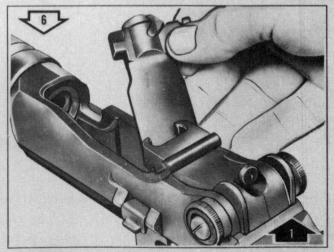

REMOVE/INSTALL BOLT ASSEMBLY.

RIFLE, 7.62 mm
SNIPER, XM21

The M21 Sniper Version of the M14 is used by the US Army. Existing supplies of this weapon are supplemented by the M1D. The US Marine Corps uses a special model of the Remington M700.

under the aperture and push upward and forward to remove the aperture, cover and base. Separate the rear sight cover from the rear sight base.

Loosen the setscrew in the base of the front sight lug on the flash suppressor. Unscrew the flash suppressor nut and slide the flash suppressor forward off the barrel.

Loosen and remove the gas plug, using the gas cylinder plug wrench. Tilt the muzzle down and remove the gas piston from the gas cylinder. Unscrew the gas cylinder lock and slide the lock and the gas cylinder off the barrel.

Slip the front band off the barrel. Push the handguard forward and lift it from the barrel.

Trigger Group. To disassemble the trigger group, close and latch the trigger guard. Squeeze the trigger, allowing the hammer to go forward. Hold the trigger housing group with the first finger of the right hand on the trigger and the thumb against the sear. Place the front of the trigger housing against a firm surface. Squeeze the trigger with the finger and push forward on the sear with the thumb. At the same time, using the tip of a cartridge, push out the trigger pin from left to right. Slowly release the pressure with the finger and thumb; this allows the hammer spring to expand.

Lift out the trigger assembly. Remove and separate the hammer spring plunger, hammer spring, and the hammer spring housing.

Push out the hammer pin from left to right, using the tip of a cartridge. Move the hammer slightly to the rear and lift out.

Unlatch the trigger guard. Push out the stud of the safety from its hole. Remove the safety and safety spring. Slide the trigger guard to the rear until the wings of the trigger guard are aligned with the safety stud hole. Rotate the trigger guard to the right and upward until the hammer stop clears the base of the housing. Remove the trigger guard.

Drive out the magazine latch spring pin with a suitable drift to remove the semipermanently assembled magazine latch and spring.

Assembly of M14. To assemble the rifle, reverse the disassembly procedure. However, the following instructions are provided to facilitate and to insure satisfactory assembly:

To assemble the hand guard, when the gas cylinder and related components are in place, position the front end of the guard in the front band and snap the rear band of the handguard assembly into the barrel grooves. **Note:** The handguard need not be reassembled prior to assembly of the gas cylinder and related components.

To assemble the trigger group to the stock and receiver, cock the hammer and swing the trigger guard to the open position. Insert the assembly into the receiver, and close the trigger guard.

To assemble the gas system, replace front band, gas cylinder and gas cylinder lock. Tighten the lock by hand to its full assembled position and then "back off" until the loop is aligned with the gas cylinder. Assemble the piston and the gas cylinder plug.

Special Note on the M14 Rifle

Although the M14 is a selective-fire weapon, most weapons in the hands of troops will have their selectors locked in the semiautomatic position. When desired, these weapons can be made to deliver selective fire by the removal of the selector lock. This feature has been added to the weapon since combat experience with the M2 carbine and troop tests with earlier prototypes of the M14 indicate that troops keep selective-fire weapons set on full automatic as a matter of course. This limits the effectiveness of the weapon at long ranges, since it is effective in off-hand automatic fire only at ranges up to about 100 yards. It also results in a great expenditure of ammunition with little in the way of results to show for this expenditure. Those weapons equipped with bipods for use as squad automatic weapons will not have their selectors locked and will be capable of selective fire at all times. Production M14s have aluminum butt plates with shoulder support and plastic handguards. Production of the M14 rifle ceased in 1964.

Variations of the M14 Rifle

There have been a number of variations of the M14 rifle produced. Two of these variations have steel folding stocks, one of which folds to the side similar to the M1A1 carbine stock—the Type V—and the other folds under the weapon in a manner similar to the stock of the German MP40 submachine gun and the Soviet AK assault rifle—the Type III.

The M14A1. The M14A1 is a variation of the M14 produced for use as a squad automatic weapon. It was originally developed by the United States Army Infantry Board, Fort Benning,

7.62mm NATO M14A1 Rifle.

7.62mm Rifle M14, fitted with bipod for use as a squad automatic weapon.

Georgia. Springfield Armory made various changes in the design to ease manufacture and maintenance. The M14A1 has a straight-line stock design with full pistol grip and folding forward handgrip. A compensator, which helps to keep the barrel down in automatic fire, is fitted over the flash suppressor. The stock has a rubber recoil pad and folding shoulder rest, and the M2 bipod has been modified by the addition of a sling swivel and a longer pivot pin. The Browning Automatic Rifle sling is used on this rifle. The selector lever is found on all M14A1 rifles so that they may be used for automatic or semiautomatic fire.

M14 National Match Rifle. A match version of the M14 rifle for use at the National Matches was developed as the result of a requirement set down in 1959. The M14 National Match Rifle cannot be fired full automatic; it has a hooded aperture rear sight, special sight parts, selected barrel and glass bedded action similar to the National Match Rifle.

The M14M Rifle. The M14M rifle was intended for issue to NRA affiliated rifle clubs, for sale through the Director of Civilian Marksmanship. This rifle was modified by welding the selector shaft and lock to eliminate automatic fire capability. The "M" in this rifle's designation stands for "Modified Service." Only a very few M14Ms were fabricated, and their distribution was equally limited.

The M21 Rifle. The M21 is the sniper version of the M14 rifle. It uses a Leatherwood type variable power scope. See Chapter 5 for further details.

7.62mm NATO M14 Rifle with Type V folding stock.

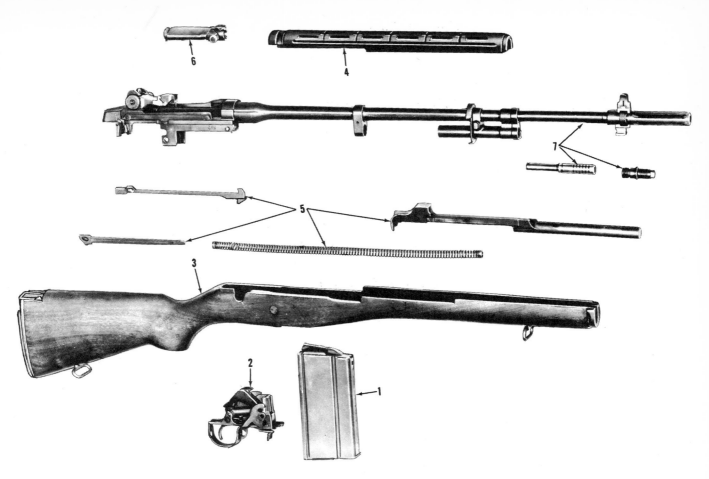

M14 Rifle, field stripped.
1. Magazine 2. Trigger assembly 3. Stock 4. Hand guard 5. Operating rod group
6. Bolt assembly 7. Gas piston, gas plug.

How the M14 Works

Semiautomatic operation:

The cycle of operation is broken down into eight steps.

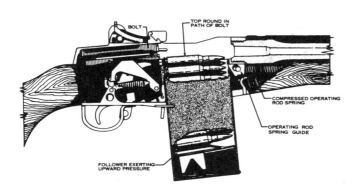

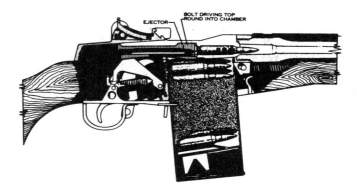

1. Feeding. Feeding takes place when a cartridge is forced into the path of the bolt by the magazine follower, which is under pressure of the magazine spring.

2. Chambering. Chambering occurs when a cartridge is moved from the magazine into the chamber by the bolt, which is propelled forward by the expanding operating spring. Chambering is complete when the extractor snaps into the extracting groove on the cartridge and the ejector is forced into the face of the bolt.

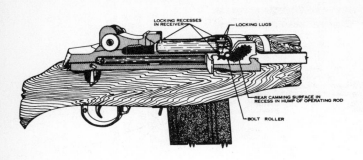

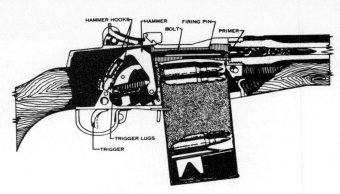

3. Locking. The bolt is locked by the rear camming surface in the hump of the operating rod forcing the bolt roller down. This turning action engages the locking lugs on the bolt with the matching recesses in the receiver.

4. Firing. When the trigger is pressed, the trigger lugs are disengaged from the hammer hooks. The hammer is released, moving forward under pressure of the hammer spring and striking the firing pin. As the firing pin moves forward, it in turn strikes the primer, which ignites the propellant.

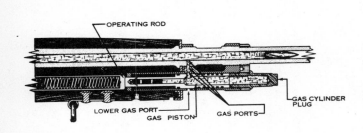

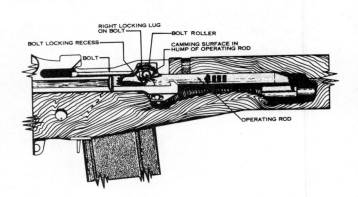

5. Unlocking. After firing, the unlocking cycle begins. As the bullet passes the gas port, a small amount of gas enters the gas cylinder/piston assembly (See fuller description of gas system below.). The gas inside the cylinder expands, and after enough pressure has built up to overcome the tension of the operating rod spring the piston starts its rearward movement. The operating rod travels rearward about

9.5mm (3/8 in.) before unlocking begins. The delay allows the projectile to exit and the residual gas pressure to drop. After the operating rod has moved that short distance, the camming surface inside its hump forces the bolt roller upward, disengaging the locking lugs on the bolt from the locking recesses in the receiver.

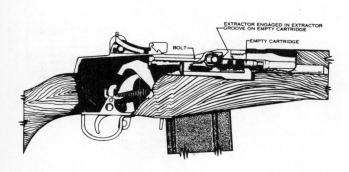

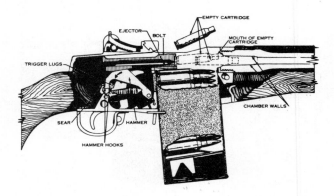

6. Extracting. As the bolt begins its rearward stroke, the extractor pulls the cartridge case from the chamber. The bolt and cartridge continue to the rear together.

7. Ejecting. As soon as the bolt has completely withdrawn the empty case from the chamber, the compressed ejector plunger pushes the bottom edge of the cartridge base away from the bolt face. As a result, the front (neck) of the cartridge case moves upward and to the right. In rapid succession, the case strikes the lower right

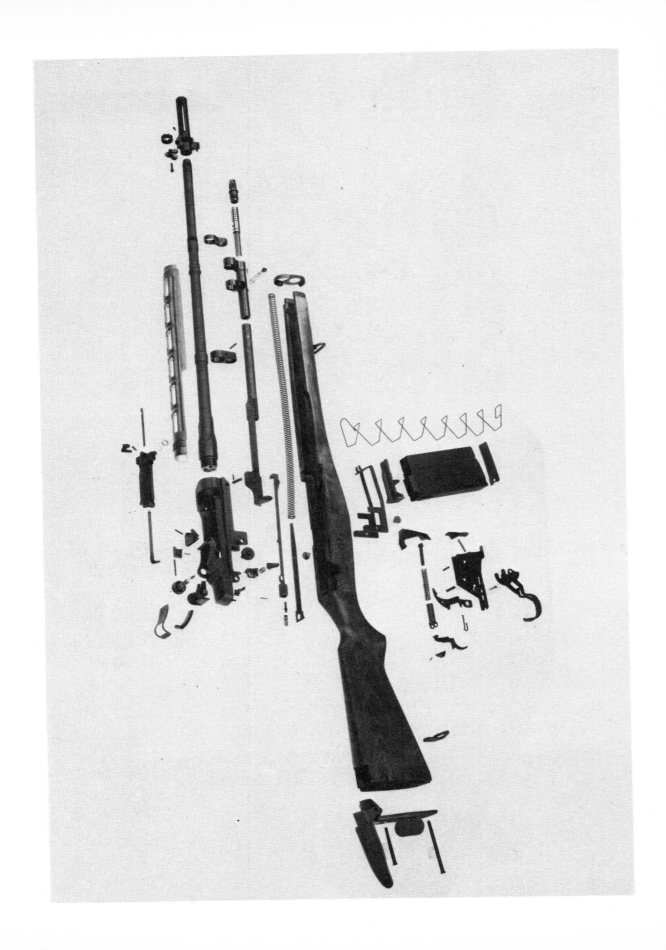

Detailed stripping of US Rifle, 7.62mm NATO, M14.

corner of the charger guide and the operating rod hump, which aids the right and forward motion of the empty case.

8. Cocking. Cocking occurs as the bolt continues to the rear. The back end of the bolt forces the hammer back and rides over it. The hammer is caught by the sear if the trigger is still held to the rear and by the trigger lugs if the pressure on the trigger has been released.

Automatic operation:

The basic cycle of operation is the same except that as the operating rod travels to the rear the connector assembly also moves rearward. That movement rotates the sear release on the selector shaft so that the flange on the sear release allows the sear to move forward into a position where it can engage the rear hammer locks. When the bolt drives the hammer to the rear, the sear engages the rear hammer hooks and holds the hammer in the cocked position.

After the bolt moves forward and locks, the shoulder on the operating rod engages the hook on the connector assembly and forces it forward. That movement rotates the sear release on the selector shaft, causing the flange on the sear release to push the sear to the rear, disengaging it from the hammer hooks. The hammer will then go forward to fire another round. This cycle will be repeated until the trigger is released or the magazine is emptied.

Operational system:

When the Springfield Armory engineers began work on the prototypes of the M14 Rifle, they sought a substitute for the gas impingement type operating system John Garand had incorporated into the M1 Rifle. That type of actuation had very high operating stresses since the propellant gases were admitted suddenly at relatively high pressures into the gas cylinder. The short time operating impulse of high intensity placed a great strain on the operating components, especially under adverse firing conditions. Earle M. Harvey adapted the gas cutoff and expansion system originated by Joseph C. White (US Patent 1,907,163) to the prototype M14 because it provided for a flexibility with which the operating power could be controlled as to magnitude, duration and rate of application.

Power to operate the M14 is derived from gas bled from the barrel into a hollow gas piston. The gas flows through ports in the barrel, gas cylinder and piston. Once the piston is filled with the expanding gas and begins its rearward stroke, the gas ports move out of alignment. The flow of additional gas is cut off. The piston, in contact with the operating rod, is driven fully to the rear (a 38mm [1.5 in.] stroke). As the piston nears the end of its rearward travel, the lower (exhaust) port in the bottom of the gas cylinder is uncovered, and the gases trapped in the closed system are vented. The gas system will continue to function in this manner unless the shutoff valve is closed. When that valve is closed, the gas system is rendered inoperative, thus requiring manual operation of the operating rod. The shutoff valve is normally only used when launching grenades from the rifle.

THE 5.56mm M16 and M16A1 RIFLES

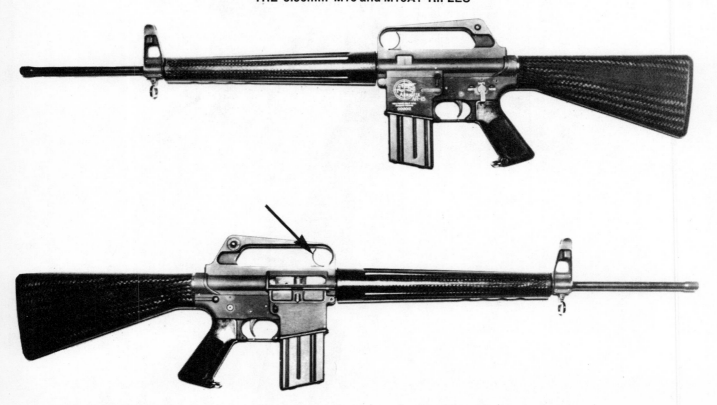

Early Armalite prototype of the AR-15 Rifle. Note the AR-10 type top mounted charging handle, the round handguard and the absence of a flash suppressor.

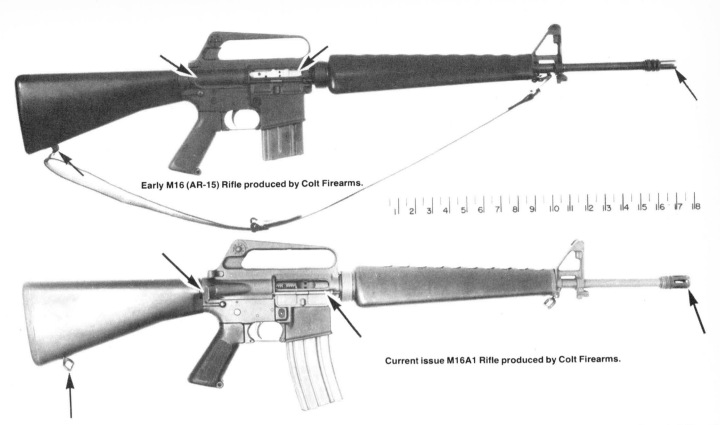

Early M16 (AR-15) Rifle produced by Colt Firearms.

Current issue M16A1 Rifle produced by Colt Firearms.

Note the differences in the above weapons: Left to right, the older models did not have a storage trap in the buttstock and they have a moveable rear sling swivel. Current models have a trap and non-moveable swivel. All M16 and AR-15 Rifles have no forward bolt assist. M16A1s have the bolt assist. Early production weapons have bright chrome plated bolts. Current production M16 and M16A1 Rifles have a dull parkerized bolt. Older weapons have the open flash suppressor, while the new ones have a closed suppressor.

Comparative length of the AK47 and Colt's M16 Carbine (Model 655) with a 14.5-inch barrel. Note the handguard, which is used only on the Carbine and the XM177 series.

Colt XM177 Submachine Gun.

Colt XM177E2.

There were three variants in the XM177 collapsible stock series. The XM177 had a 10-inch barrel and the basic M16A1 receiver with forward bolt assist. The XM177E2 had an 11.5-inch barrel to permit grenade launching. Absence of the forward bolt assist was the only difference between the E1 and E2,

which had that feature. Note: the flash suppressors have been determined to be noise suppressors by the US Bureau of Alcohol, Tobacco and Firearms, and as such, they are registerable and taxable items.

The XM177 series is now obsolete.

XM177E2 showing extended and retracted positions for the sliding buttstock.

Field Stripping the AR-15, M16, M16A1 Rifles

The M16 series of weapons all have the same basic components. The AR-15 Sporter will not fire automatically because it does not have the automatic fire components; the M16 and M16A1 differ mainly in that the latter has the forward bolt assist plunger on the right side of the receiver. Briefly described, the major components of the weapon are as follows.

Barrel Group. This group consists of the barrel and barrel extension, front sight assembly, flash suppressor, barrel nut and slip ring assembly and the left and right handguards. The front sight group includes the forward sling assembly, front sight and gas tube assembly and front sight post, which is adjustable for elevation. Inside the handguards are heat resisting shields.

Upper Receiver Group. This group contains the upper receiver, bolt carrier assembly, forward assist mechanism (M16A1 only), charging handle, ejection port cover assembly and mounting provisions for the barrel assembly. The top of the upper receiver takes the form of a carrying handle, which contains the rear sight and provision for mounting a telescope.

Lower Receiver and Buttstock Group. This group includes the lower receiver, pistol grip, lower receiver extension and buttstock. The lower receiver contains the trigger, fire control selector, bolt catch, disconnect, automatic sear and magazine catch. The receiver extension to which the buttstock is fastened contains the buffer assembly and return spring. Both the upper and lower receivers are machined from aluminum forgings. The buttstock and pistol grip are made of a high impact plastic material.

Bolt Carrier-Assembly. This assembly is made up of the bolt carrier, bolt, firing pin, firing pin retaining pin, cam pin, extractor and ejector. The rotary bolt locking system is one of the key mechanical features of the M16 series. Locking lugs on the bolt match up with locking recesses in the barrel extension to lock the weapon closed during the firing part of the operating cycle. The initial force of the cartridge explosion is absorbed by the barrel, barrel extension and bolt.

No special tools are required to field strip and assemble the M16. After clearing the weapon, return the bolt to the forward position, press out the rear takedown pin from the left to the right. Pull the pin until stopped by the detent. Hinge the upper receiver away from the lower receiver. Pull the charging handle to the rear (about 3 inches) and remove the bolt and bolt carrier from the upper receiver. Remove the charging handle by pulling down and to the rear.

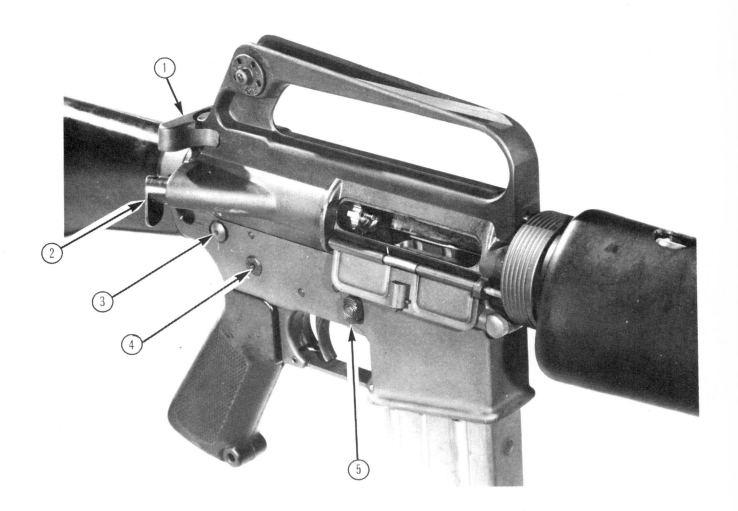

Main Features of the M16A1 Rifle

1. Charging handle
2. Forward bolt assist
3. Takedown pin
4. Selector switch pin
5. Magazine release
6. Magazine catch release
7. Bolt catch
8. Selector switch
9. Charging handle catch.

Main features of the M16A1 Rifle continued. Rifle shown is an early Model 602 made for military sales.

For more detailed stripping of the bolt, push out the firing pin retaining pin with the tip of a cartridge projectile. Drop out the firing pin. Rotate the bolt to the right until the cam pin is clear of the bolt carrier key. Rotate the cam pin one quarter turn and remove. Using the firing pin, carefully push out the extractor pin and remove the extractor. (Caution: The extractor is under spring tension.) *Do not* remove the extractor spring from the extractor.

To completely separate the upper and lower receivers, push the pivot pin to the right using the nose of a cartridge projectile. Pull out pin to detent. Separate the receivers.

To remove the buffer, push the buffer to the rear, depress the buffer retainer and slowly ease the buffer forward. (Caution: The buffer is under tension from the operating spring.) As the buffer is moved forward, depress the hammer to permit removal of the buffer and operating spring.

M16 hinged open for removal of operating parts.

M16 Rifle with charging handle pulled half way to the rear. Note bolt showing through the ejection port.

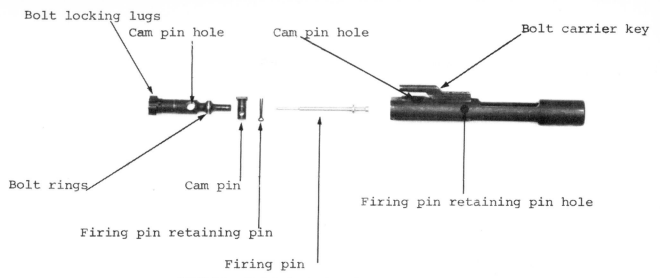

Bolt locking lugs

Cam pin hole

Cam pin hole

Bolt carrier key

Bolt rings

Cam pin

Firing pin retaining pin hole

Firing pin retaining pin

Firing pin

M16A1 Bolt and Bolt Carrier showing major components disassembled.

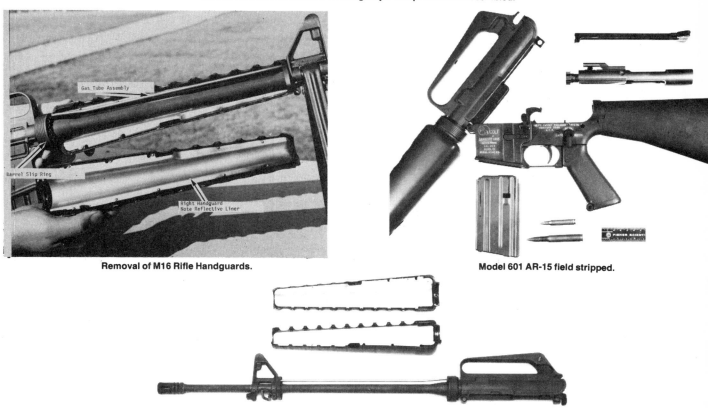

Gas Tube Assembly

Barrel Slip Ring

Right Handguard
Note Reflective Liner

Removal of M16 Rifle Handguards.

Model 601 AR-15 field stripped.

M16A1 disassembled view.

To remove the handguards, pull the handguard slip-ring to the rear until it clears the handguards. Remove the handguards by pulling them out and down.

How the M16 and M16A1 Rifles Work

The cycle of operation of the M16 and M16A1 Rifle is described as follows.

Cocking. The rifle is cocked before firing by pulling the charger handle rearward, which pulls the bolt carrier group to the rear. As the carrier moves rearward, it cocks the hammer. If an empty magazine is installed at the time of cocking, the magazine follower will actuate the bolt catch to hold the carrier to the rear. If a loaded magazine is installed in the gun or the magazine is removed, the bolt catch must be manually operated to hold the bolt to the rear.

Feeding and Chambering. To feed a cartridge into the chamber, the bolt carrier group must be pulled to the rear by the charging handle or held there by the bolt catch. With a loaded magazine installed, the charging handle or the bolt catch is released, and the action spring drives the carrier forward. As the carrier moves forward, the lugs of the bolt pick up a cartridge from the magazine and feed it into the chamber. As the bolt locking lugs enter the barrel extension, the ejector is compressed against the left side of the cartridge head, and the extractor snaps into the extractor groove on the right side of the cartridge.

Locking. When the forward motion of the bolt and cartridge are stopped by the chamber, the bolt carrier continues forward until it is stopped by contact with the rear face of the barrel extension. This last portion of the forward travel of the carrier rotates the bolt through the action of the cam slot in the carrier on the cam pin in the bolt. This engages the bolt lugs with the barrel extension lugs to lock the bolt in battery. The bolt, when so locked, is said to be "closed."

Firing. With the fire control selector, located on the left side of the lower receiver set to either "Auto" or "Semi," the rifle may be fired. When the trigger is pulled, it causes the sear to release the hammer. The hammer spring then drives the hammer against the firing pin, which then strikes the cartridge primer to discharge the chambered round.

Unlocking. As the pressure of the gas generated by the burning propellant drives the projectile down the barrel and past the gas port, a small quantity of the gas is bled off through the gas port, gas tube and bolt carrier key into a cylindrical section in the bolt carrier where it expands and drives the bolt carrier rearward. During the first rearward travel of the carrier, the bolt is rotated by the cam pin acted on by the bolt carrier cam slot. This rotation disengages the bolt lugs from the barrel extension lugs so the bolt is unlocked. The carrier then continues rearward with the unlocked bolt.

Extraction. As the bolt is moved rearward by the carrier, the extractor, which is engaged in the extractor groove of the fired cartridge case and is pinned to the bolt, withdraws the spent case from the chamber.

Ejection. As soon as the extractor has drawn the spent case out of the chamber, the spring loaded ejector, acting against the left side of the case head, pushes the spent case out of the ejection port located on the right side of the upper receiver.

Cocking (after firing). As the carrier group continues rearward to recoil, it compresses the action spring and cocks the hammer. Two different actions now take place dependent upon whether the fire control selector is set on "Semi" (semiautomatic) or "Auto" (automatic). These actions are as follows.

"Semi" (semiautomatic). When the trigger is pulled, the firing action of the rifle is so much faster than human reaction that it would be impossible to release the trigger quickly enough to prevent several shots being fired unless there were a device provided that would limit the shots fired to one. For this reason, a disconnect is used to catch and hold the hammer until the trigger is released and pulled a second time when the fire control selector is in the semiautomatic position. When the trigger is pulled, the disconnect is rotated forward by the action of the disconnect spring. As the hammer is cocked by the recoil action of the carrier group, the hook of the disconnect engages the upper inside notch of the hammer, holding it to the rear.

When the trigger is released, the trigger spring returns the trigger to its normal position rotating the disconnect back with it. The hammer is thus released from the hook on the disconnect. However, before the disconnect hook actually releases the hammer, the trigger sear surface has moved in front of its hammer notch so that the hammer drops from the disconnect sear to the trigger sear. The rifle is then ready for a second shot.

"Auto" (automatic). When the fire control selector is set on "Auto" and the trigger pulled, the trigger sear releases the hammer. The disconnect is prevented from moving forward to engage the hammer by a cam on the fire control selector. After the first shot, as the hammer is being cocked by the recoil action of the carrier group, the notch on the top outside edge of the hammer is engaged by the automatic sear. The hammer is then held in the cocked position by the automatic sear until the bolt carrier strikes the upper edge of the automatic sear in counter-recoil, causing it to release the hammer near the end of the forward travel of the carrier. The hammer then falls to fire the next round. This cycle repeats until the magazine is emptied or the trigger is released. When the trigger is released, the hammer falls from the automatic sear but is held by the trigger sear, thus ending the cycle of automatic fire.

Buffering. The rearward or recoil movement of the carrier group is arrested by the buffer assembly acting against the bottom of the receiver extension.

Counter-recoil. After buffering, the action spring forces the carrier forward toward the chamber.

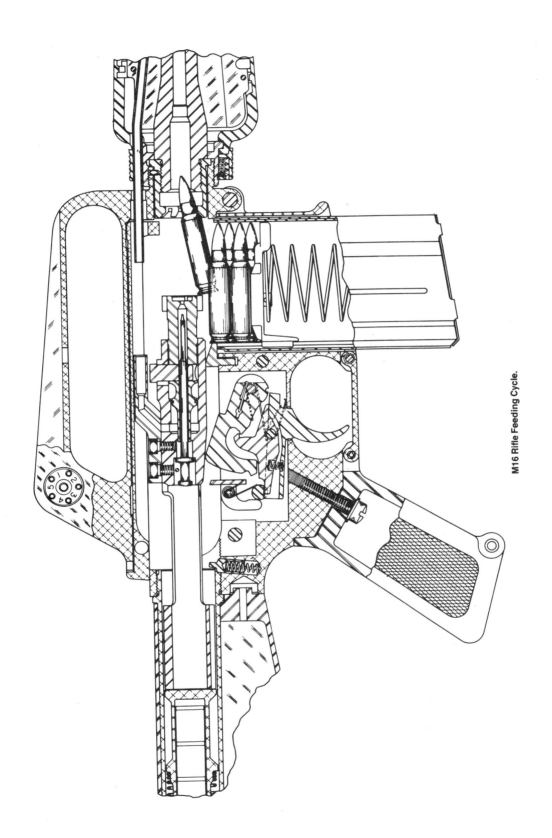

M16 Rifle Feeding Cycle.

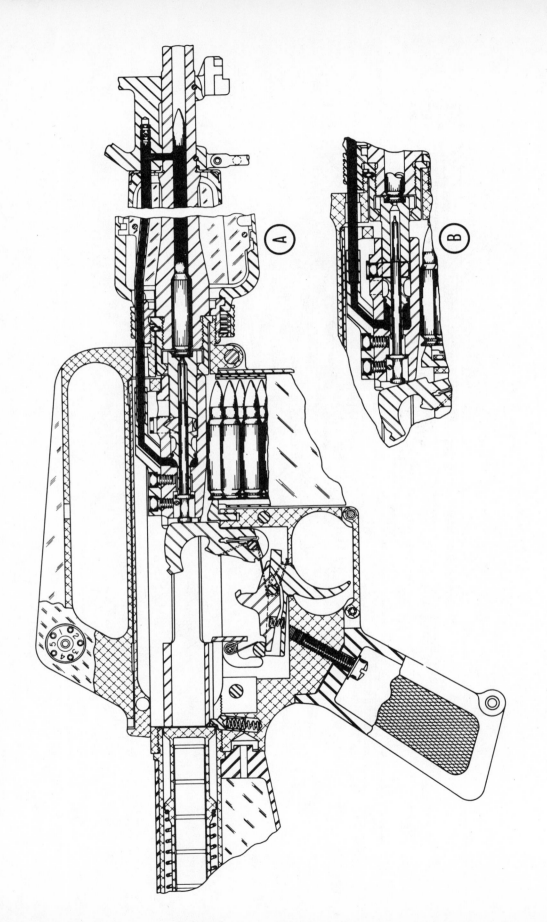

M16 Rifle Firing Cycle. In Figure A, note that the gas (indicated in black) has just begun to fill the cavity inside the bolt carrier as the projectile passes down the barrel. In Figure B, note that the expanding gas inside the bolt carrier is beginning to force the carrier to the rear.

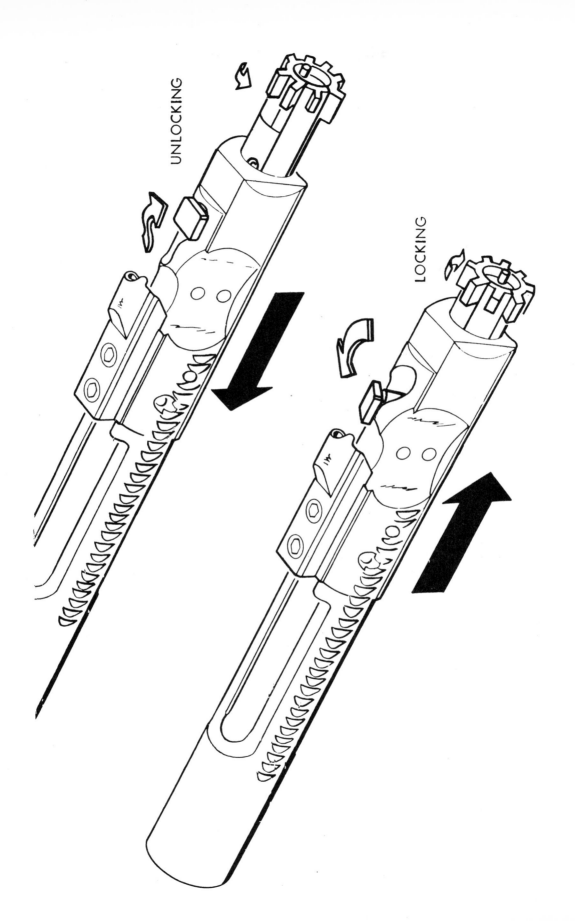

UNLOCKING

LOCKING

M16 Rifle bolt and bolt carrier showing the locking and unlocking movements of the bolt.

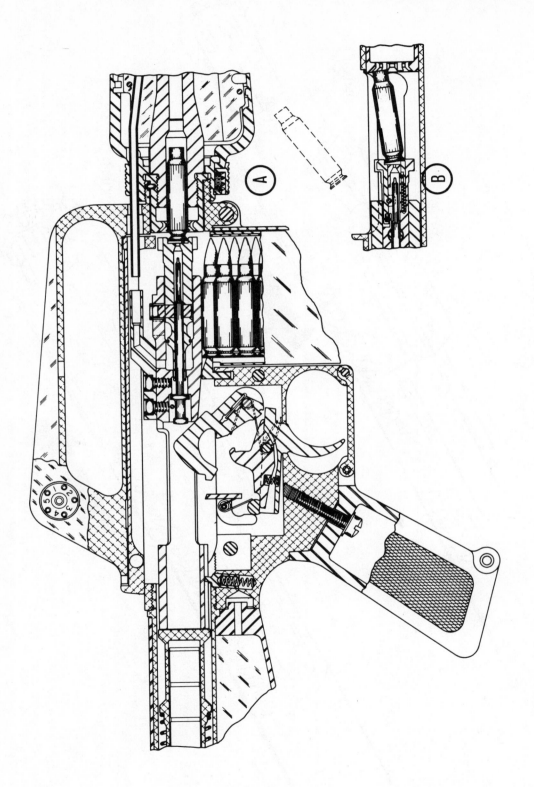

M16 Rifle Extraction and Ejection Cycle. In Figure A, extraction begins as the bolt and bolt carrier begin their movement to the rear. Figure B illustrates the ejection process as viewed from the underside of the magazine well. The ejected cartridge moves to the right.

Early M16 Rifle Buttplate without storage trap.

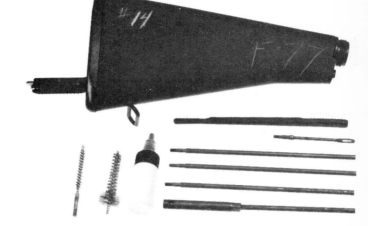

Current issue M16 Buttstock with storage for cleaning equipment.

Very early AR-15 flash suppressor. To the right the current closed suppressor and obsolete open suppressor are illustrated.

Current buffer with additional mass to slow the cyclic rate is shown on top. The obsolete original issue buffer is shown below.

To the right, the comic book style M16 Rifle maintenance manual that was issued after the initial maintenance problems with the M16 were discovered.

Maintenance

When the M16 was first introduced into service, the proper cleaning tools were not issued with it. This oversight was in part the result of publicity that indicated that the M16 series did not need to be cleaned as often as older weapons. But it was also the consequence of the rifle having been introduced without its having passed through the standard US Army adoption process. The M16s however, did get dirty, and this condition was aggravated by the use of ball type propellant issued by the Army, which left considerable residue in the gas tube, bolt carrier key and bolt carrier. The high humidity of the Southeast Asian theater of operation also led to considerable corrosion. Several major modifications were made to solve the maintenance problems.

1. A new buffer, designed by F. E. Sturtevant, to prevent bolt rebound also helped slow the rate of fire when ball type propellants were used. All M16 and M16A1 Rifles were retrofitted with this buffer.

2. A chrome plated chamber, and later chrome plated bores, reduced corrosion and hence extraction difficulties caused by rusty chambers.

3. A closed prong type flash suppressor reduced the possibility of water being attracted into the barrel. A plastic protective muzzle cap was introduced to keep dirt out of the barrel.

4. A cleaning and lubrication kit was introduced to facilitate maintenance. In addition, a new buttstock with a storage trap was fitted to the M16A1. More explicit cleaning and lubrication instructions were issued.

5. A new 30-shot magazine was introduced to replace the 20-shot feed device.

Early 20-shot M16 Magazine (left) with M1 (Garand) 8-shot clip.

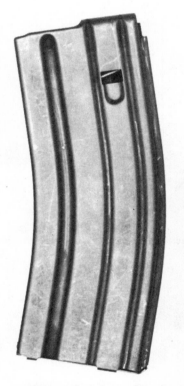

Current issue 30-shot M16 Rifle Magazine.

GAPCO 30-shot Zytel Synthetic magazine.

The past three decades have seen considerable improvement in small arms magazines. Whereas nearly all World War II feed devices were made from steel, Armalite and Colt have pioneered the use of aluminim magazines to reduce total weapon weight. Considerable experimentation has been aimed at producing inexpensive magazines made of synthetics. Such magazines were developed for the M14 Rifle years ago but were not reliable enough for the Army to adopt. The Soviets too have experimented with synthetic magazines for the Kalashnikov Avtomats. Recently, GAPCO of Wilson, North Carolina, introduced a much improved 30-shot plastic magazine fabricated from DuPont Zytel, a fiberglass-reinforced nylon resin. The GAPCO magazine has the advantage of being self-lubricating, and it contains a dye that will not fade, as the finish on aluminum magazines often does. This nylon magazine also demonstrates improved resistance to denting and bending. As Zytel claims higher resistance to temperature and humidity variations, the new GAPCO magazine may herald a new era in small arms magazine design.

62139

94004

61826 BOLT CARRIER AND KEY ASSEMBLY
61547 BOLT CARRIER KEY
92201 BOLT CARRIER SCREW
61548 BOLT CARRIER

61704
61547
92201
61826
61548

61826
61547
92201
61548

62114

61562
61568

62119
61681
61574

61580
61561

92601
61935 NO SWIVEL
62132 WITH SWIVEL

61700
61708
61755
61754
61703
95101

61563
61502

95111
62118

62116 BOLT ASSEMBLY CONSISTS OF:
61538 BOLT
61540 BOLT RING
61562 EXTRACTOR
61568 EXTRACTOR SPRING
61563 EXTRACTOR PIN
61564 EJECTOR
61569 EJECTOR SPRING
95102 EJECTOR PIN

90402
61658
61962
90403
61518
62112

61563
95102
61540
61538

61577

95101
61564
61569
61578
61579

61546

62120
90001
92701

61555
95107
61600

61702

61901
61902

62032
61582
61694

61692
61569
61970

61785
61569
95106

95105
61759

61657
61955
61925

61599
95601
61691
61699

62095

61645

61573
61606
61605
61959
61918
61697

62144

62087

62096

61706
61705
62068
62083

62117
61654
61622
61615

SHORT 62135
LONG 62140

61709
62070
62126

95108
62086
95105
61322

62119 ACTION SPRING GUIDE CONSISTS OF:
61580 ACTION SPRING GUIDE
61578 BUFFER RING-OUTER
61579 BUFFER RING-INNER
61577 BUFFER END RING
61576 BUFFER CAP
95101 BUFFER PIN

* THESE ASSEMBLIES MAY BE
  PURCHASED AS ONE UNIT OR
  AS SEPARATE PARTS.

Exploded view of 5.56mm M16 Rifle.

COLT AR-15, M16, M16A1 MODEL NUMBERS

Weapon Description	Feature	Model #	Model Name	Roll Marked (left)	Roll Marked (right)
Early Armalite AR-15	w/o forward assist	NA	AR-15	ArmaLite AR-15 Costa Mesa, Calif. USA Patents Pending 0000000	
Early Military Colt Version	w/o forward assist	601	AR-15	Colt Armalite AR15 Patents Pending Cal. .223 Model 01 Serial 0000000	
Early US Government Purchase	w/o forward assist	602	AR-15	Colt AR-15 Property of US Gov't Cal. .223 Model 02 Serial 0000000	
Present US Army Rifle	w/forward assist 20-inch barrel	603	M16A1	Property of US Gov't M16A1 Cal 5.56mm 0000000	
Korean Version of 603	w/forward assist 20-inch barrel	603K	M16A1	M16A1 K0000000	Made in Korea Under License from Colt's, Hartford, CT. U.S.A.
Present US Air Force Rifle	w/o forward assist 20-inch barrel	604	M16	Property of US Gov't M16 Cal 5.56mm 0000000	
Export Version of 616	w/o forward assist 20-inch barrel	606	HBAR	Mod 606 Cal 5.56mm 0000000	
Submachine Gun—Army	w/forward assist 10-inch barrel	609	SMG #1 XM177E1 Commando	Property of US Gov't Commando Cal 5.56mm 0000000	
Submachine Gun—Air Force	w/o forward assist 10-inch barrel	610	S.M.G. #2 XM177	Property of US Gov't SMG 5.56mm 0000000	
Export Version of 621	w/forward assist 20-inch barrel	611	HBAR	Mod 611 Cal 5.56mm 0000000	
Philippine Version of 611	w/forward assist 20-inch barrel	611P	HBAR	Made by Elisco Tool for the Republic of The Philippines M16A1 RP0000000	Made in the Philippines Under License from Colt's, Hartford, CT. U.S.A.
Export Version of 603	w/forward assist 20-inch barrel	613	AR-15	Mod 613 Cal 5.56mm 0000000	
Philippine Version of 613	w/forward assist 20-inch barrel	613P	AR-15	Made by Elisco Tool for the Republic of The Philippines M16A1 RP0000000	Made in the Philippines Under License from Colt's, Hartford, CT. U.S.A
Export Version of 604	w/o forward assist 20-inch barrel	614	AR-15	Mod 614 Cal 5.56mm 0000000	
Singapore Version of 604	w/o forward assist 20-inch barrel	614-S	AR-15	C I S Made in Singapore by Chartered Industries of Singapore Limited Under License from Colt Industries Hartford, Conn, USA Patented	
Heavy Barrel Auto Rifle US Government	w/o forward assist 20-inch barrel	616	HBAR	Property of US Gov't Mod 616 Cal 5.56mm 0000000	
Export Version of 609	w/forward assist 10-inch barrel	619	S.M.G.	Mod 619 Cal 5.56mm 0000000	
Export Version of 610	w/o forward assist 10-inch barrel	620	S.M.G.	Mod 620 Cal 5.56mm 0000000	
Heavy Barrel Auto Rifle US Government	w/forward assist 20-inch barrel	621	HBAR	Property of US Gov't Mod 621 Cal 5.56mm 0000000	
Submachine Gun—Army	w/forward assist 11.5-inch barrel	629	XM177E2	Property of US Gov't XM177E2 Cal 5.56mm 0000000	

Weapon Description	Feature	Model #	Model Name	Roll Marked (left)	Roll Marked (right)
Submachine Gun—Air Force	w/o forward assist ?-inch barrel	630	Not available		
Export Version of 629	w/forward assist 11.5-inch barrel	639	S.M.G.	Mod 639 Cal 5.56mm 0000000	
Export Version of 630	w/o forward assist	640	S.M.G.	Mod 640 Cal 5.56mm 0000000	
Submachine Gun—Air Force	w/o forward assist ?-inch barrel	649	S.M.G.	Property of US Gov't GAU-5/A/A Cal 5.56mm 0000000	
Colt Carbine	w/forward assist 14.5-inch barrel	651			
Colt Carbine	w/o forward assist 14.5-inch barrel	652			
Colt Carbine	w/forward assist w/sliding buttstock 14.5-inch barrel	653			
Philippine Version of 653	w/forward assist w/sliding buttstock 14.5-inch barrel	653P		Made by Elisco Tool for the Republic of The Philippines M16A1 RP0000000	Made in the Philippines Under License from Colt's, Hartford, CT. U.S.A.
Colt Carbine	w/o forward assist w/sliding buttstock 14.5-inch barrel	654			
Colt Carbine	w/forward assist standard stock 14.5-inch barrel	655			
Colt Automatic Rifle	Closed-Gas System M16 Variant 20-inch barrel	CAR-703	M16A2 (unofficial)		
Semiautomatic Commercial Sporter	w/o forward assist 20-inch barrel	R6000	AR-15	Colt AR-15 Cal. .223 Model SP1 Ser. SP00000	

Representative Receiver Markings of the M16 Rifle.

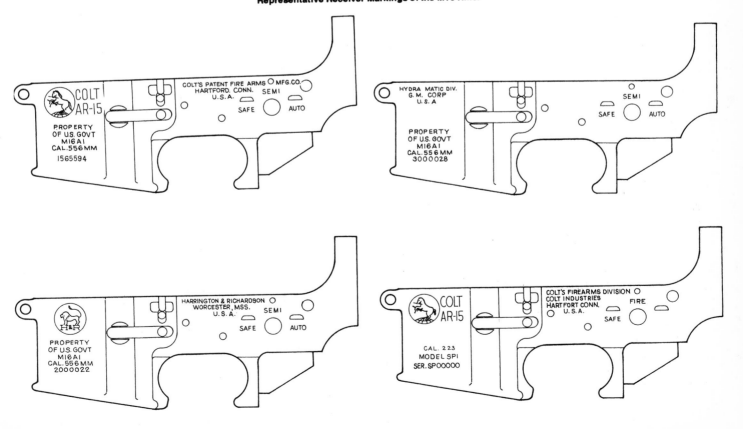

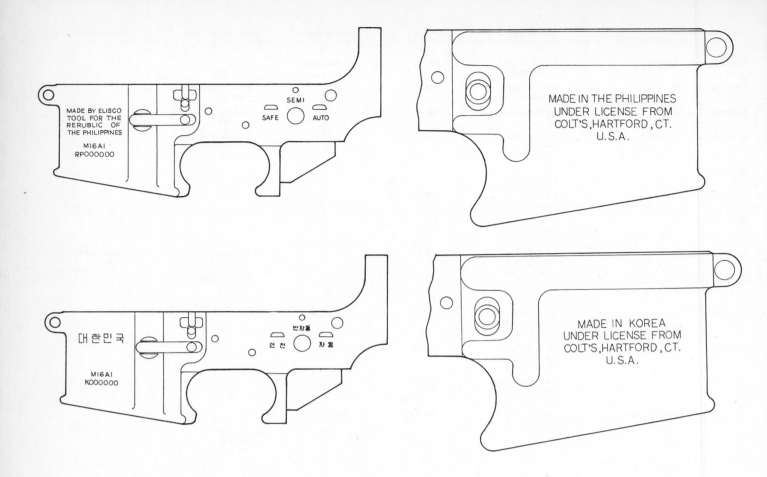

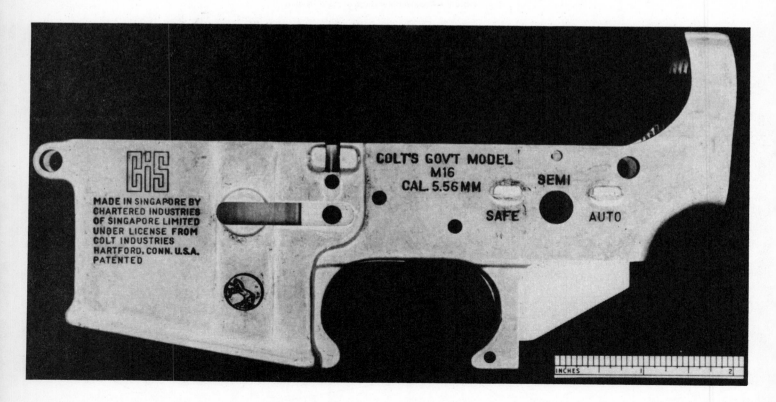

Conversion Kit, XM261
Caliber .22 Rimfire Adapter for the M16 Series

The appearance of 5.56mm (.223) caliber rifles has made it possible to use inexpensive .22 rimfire ammunition for training. This in turn reduces costs, increases the amount of training and familiarization and permits the firing of the M16 Rifle on indoor ranges. Several organizations have developed .22 caliber conversion units for the M16—Colt Firearms, Military Armaments, US Armament Corporation and Rock Island Small Arms System Laboratory. The US Army is currently testing the US Armament Corporation conversion kit as the XM261.

All the conversion units embody the same basic principle of replacing the standard bolt with a blow-back .22 caliber mechanism that has a forward extension that looks like the case of the standard 5.56 × 45mm cartridge.

To install the conversion unit, remove the standard bolt as outlined under the M16 above. Then insert the rimfire adapter unit in its place. The rifle is cocked and loaded in the standard manner. The 10-shot magazine adapter fits inside of the standard 30-shot magazine as shown in the illustration.

Caution: When the bolt adapter is not being used with the rifle, NEVER pull the bolt of the unit to the rear and load a cartridge into the chamber of the adapter. If the bolt is allowed to fly forward, the chambered cartridge could explode and thus either damage the adapter or injure personnel in the immediate vicinity.

The technical characteristics of the XM261 .22 Rim Fire Adapter Kit have not yet been released.

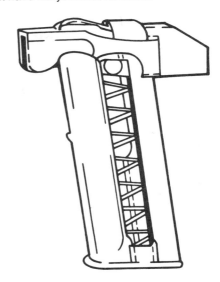

Ten-shot adapter which is inserted into the standard 30-shot magazine.

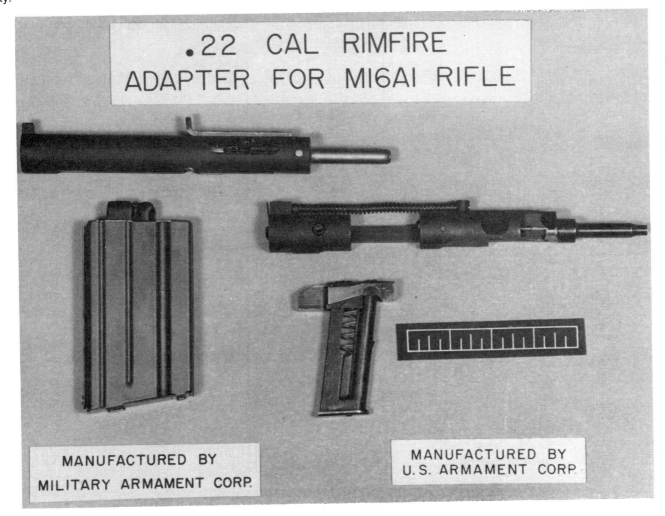

.22 CAL RIMFIRE ADAPTER FOR M16A1 RIFLE

MANUFACTURED BY MILITARY ARMAMENT CORP.

MANUFACTURED BY U.S. ARMAMENT CORP.

.22 Caliber Rimfire Adapter Units for the M16A1. The XM261 is on the right.

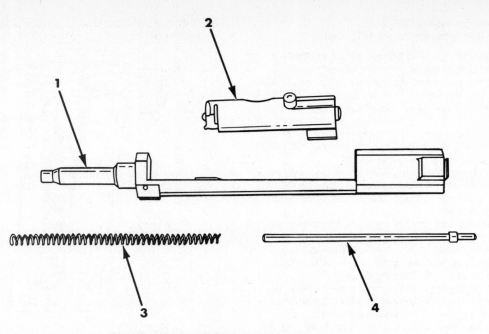

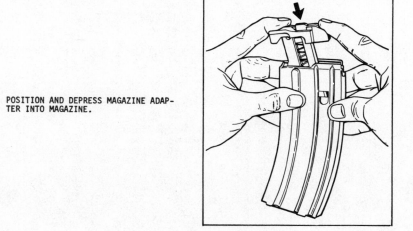

The XM261 Adapter Kit disassembled.
1. Barrel and receiver group. 2. Bolt. 3. Guide rod spring. 4. Guide rod.

1. POSITION AND DEPRESS MAGAZINE ADAP-
    TER INTO MAGAZINE.

2. TILT ADAPTER ON ANGLE, HOOK BASE OF
    ADAPTER UNDER MAGAZINE LIPS. THEN
    SLIDE ADAPTER ALL THE WAY IN.

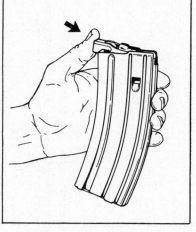

Installation of the 10-shot magazine adapter into the standard 30-shot magazine.

CHARACTERISTICS OF UNITED STATES SERVICE LIGHT SEMIAUTOMATIC AND AUTOMATIC RIFLES AND CARBINES

	M1 Rifle	M1C Rifle	M1D Rifle	M1 Carbine	M1A1 Carbine	M2 Carbine
Caliber:	.30 (.30-06).	.30 (.30-06).	.30 (.30-06)	.30 Carbine M1.	.30 Carbine M1.	.30 Carbine M1.
System of operation:	Gas, semiautomatic.	Gas, semi-automatic.	Gas, semi-automatic.	Gas, semi-automatic.	Gas, semi-automatic.	Gas, selective fire.
Length overall:	43.6 in.	43.6 in.	43.6 in.	35.6 in.	Stock extended: 35.5 in. Stock folded: 25.4 in.	35.6 in.
Barrel length:	24 in.	24 in.	24 in.	18 in.	18 in.	18 in.
Feed system:	8-round, staggered row, non-detachable, box magazine.	8-round, staggered row, non-detachable, box magazine.	8-round, staggered row, non-detachable, box magazine.	15- or 30-round, staggered row, detachable, box magazine.	15- or 30-round, staggered row, detachable, box magazine.	15- or 30-round, staggered row, detachable, box magazine.
Sights: Front:	Blade with protecting ears.	2.2X telescopic.	2.2X telescopic.	Blade with protecting ears.	Blade with protecting ears.	Blade with protecting ears.
Rear:	Aperture.			Aperture on ramp.	Aperture on ramp.	Aperture on ramp.
Weight:	9.5 lb.	11.75 lb.*	11.75*	5.5 lb.	6.19 lb.	5.5 lb.
Muzzle velocity:	2805 f.p.s. (M2 ball)	2805 f.p.s. (M2 ball)	2805 f.p.s. (M2 ball)	1970 f.p.s.	1970 f.p.s.	1970 f.p.s.
Cyclic rate:	----	----	----	----	----	750-775 r.p.m.

CHARACTERISTICS OF UNITED STATES SERVICE LIGHT SEMIAUTOMATIC AND AUTOMATIC RIFLES AND CARBINES (Cont'd)

	Johnson M1941 Rifle	M14 Rifle	M14A1 Rifle	M16 Rifle
Caliber:	.30 (.30-06).	7.62mm NATO.	7.62mm NATO.	5.56mm (.223).
System of operation:	Recoil, semiautomatic.	Gas, selective fire.	Gas, selective fire.	Gas, selective fire.
Length overall:	45.87 in.	44.14 in.	44.3 in.	39 in.
Barrel length:	22 in.	22 in.	22 in.	20 in.
Feed system:	10-round, rotary type, non-detachable magazine.	20-round staggered row, detachable, box magazine.	20-round staggered row, detachable, box magazine.	20-round staggered row, detachable, box magazine.
Sights: Front:	Post with protecting ears.	Blade with protecting ears.	Blade with protecting ears.	Post with protecting ears.
Rear:	Aperture.	Aperture.	Aperture.	Aperture.
Weight:	9.5 lb.	8.7 lb.	12.75 lb.	6.3 lb. w/o magazine.
Muzzle velocity:	Approx. 2770 f.p.s. (M2 ball)	2800 f.p.s.	2800 f.p.s.	3250 f.p.s.
Cyclic rate:	----	750 r.p.m.	750 r.p.m.	700-900 r.p.m.

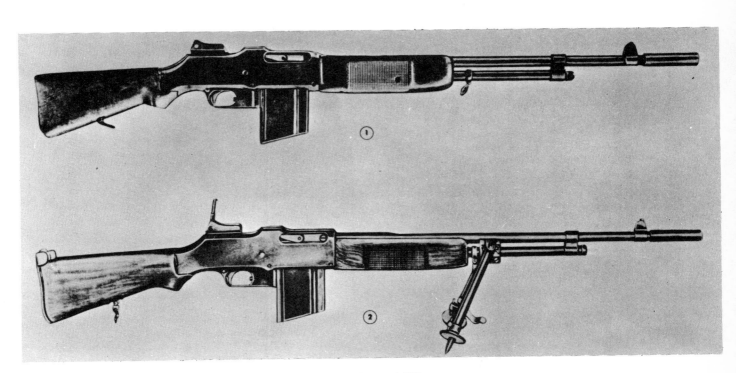

Caliber 30 Browning Automatic Rifles.
(1) Model 1918 (2) Model 1918A1.

THE BROWNING CALIBER .30 AUTOMATIC RIFLE
MODEL 1918, 1918A1 and 1918A2

This weapon was developed by John Browning in 1917 to meet the United States requirement for an automatic rifle for service in World War I. The M1918 was made during World War I by Colt, Winchester and Marlin Rockwell. These concerns made 85,000 weapons before the armistice concluded the war.

Basic BARs

There are actually four basic Browning Automatic rifles officially adopted by the United States. These weapons and their descriptions follow.

Model 1918. This weapon has no bipod, is capable of selective fire and is relatively light (16 pounds) compared with the later models. A simple tube type flash hider is used. There is no shoulder support plate hinged to the butt plate. The rear sight and butt plate are similar to those of the Model 1917 (Enfield) rifle.

Model 1918A1. This model has a shoulder support plate hinged to the butt plate and a bipod attached to the gas cylinder just forward of the forearm. It fires selective fire, has a tube-type flash hider and uses the same sights as the Model 1918. This modification was adopted in 1937.

Mode 1918A2. Adopted shortly before World War II, this weapon, as the Model 1918A1, was originally made up from Model 1918s and 1918A1s of World War I manufacture. The bipod, which has skid type feet as opposed to the spike type feet of the Model 1918A1, is fitted to the tube type flash hider. The forearm has been cut down in height around the barrel and shortened. As originally made, a removable stock rest, which fitted in a hole in the buttstock, was used with this weapon. It has a hinged shoulder rest attached to the butt plate as does the M1918A1, but the shoulder rest plate is shorter. There is a metal shield inserted horizontally in the forearm to protect the recoil spring guide from barrel heat, and right and left magazine guards have been attached to the front of the trigger guard body. The rear sight of the M1918A2 is similar to that of the M1918A4

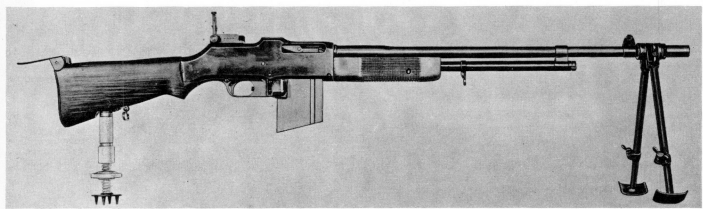

Caliber .30 Browning Automatic Rifle, Model 1918A2 as originally issued.

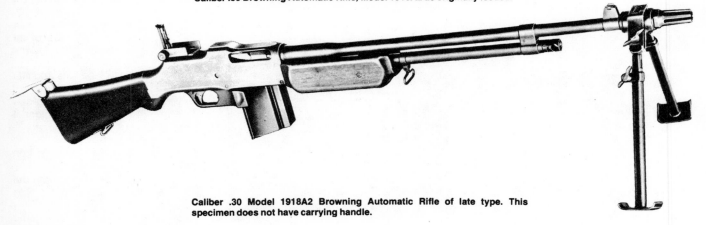

Caliber .30 Model 1918A2 Browning Automatic Rifle of late type. This specimen does not have carrying handle.

machine gun and the M1922 Browning Automatic rifle. It is adjustable for windage as well as elevation and uses micrometer screws for adjustment. The 1918A2 is not capable of semiautomatic fire. It has two rates of automatic fire and a rate-reducing mechanism.

The Model 1918A2 went through a number of modifications during World War II. Among these were the use of a shortened fore-end with grasping grooves, the abandonment of the stock rest, the use of plastic buttstocks and the development of a carrying handle for the weapon, which, due to the conclusion of World War II, did not see much service until the Korean war.

I.B.M. and New England Small Arms Corporation manufactured Browning Automatic rifles during World War II. During the Korean war, a prong type flash suppressor was adopted. Royal McBee Typewriter Corp. manufactured 61,000 M1918A2 BARs during this period. A gas cylinder regulator that can be easily turned by hand was also introduced during this period.

Browning Machine Rifle Model 1922. This weapon, which appeared in very limited numbers, was developed to give the horse cavalry of the twenties lightweight sustained-fire capability. It has a heavy barrel with radial cooling fins, butt swivel attached to the left side of the stock, a wide groove around the

CHARACTERISTICS OF UNITED STATES SERVICE BROWNING AUTOMATIC RIFLES

	Model 1918	Model 1918A1	Model 1918A2	Model 1922
Caliber:	.30 (.30-06).	.30 (.30-06).	.30 (.30-06).	.30 (.30-06).
System of operation:	Gas, selective fire.	Gas, selective fire.	Gas, automatic only.	Gas, selective fire.
Length overall:	47 in.	47 in.	47.8 in.	Approx. 41 in.
Barrel length:	24 in.	24 in.	24 in.	18 in.
Feed device:	20-round, staggered row, detachable, box, magazine.	20-round, staggered row, detachable, box magazine.	20-round, staggered row, detachable, box magazine.	20-round, staggered row, detachable, box magazine.
Sights: Front:	Blade.	Blade.	Blade.	Hooded blade.
Rear:	Leaf w/aperture battle sight w/aperture.	Leaf w/aperture battle sight w/aperture.	Leaf w/aperture adjustable for windage.	Leaf w/aperture adjustable for windage.
Weight:	16 lb.	18.5 lb.	19.4 lb.	19.2 lb.
Muzzle velocity:	2805 f.p.s.	2805 f.p.s.	2805 f.p.s.	Approx. 2700 f.p.s.
Cyclic rate:	550 r.p.m.	550 r.p.m.	Slow: 300-450 r.p.m. Fast: 500-650 r.p.m.	550 r.p.m.

buttstock for the butt rest clamp, a bipod that clamps around the barrel and a rear sight adjustable for windage and elevation similar to that used on the Model 1919 machine guns and the M1918A2 BAR. This weapon was declared obsolete about 1940.

T34 Automatic Rifle. This is a modification of the Browning Automatic Rifle for the caliber .30 T65E3 cartridge case (7.62mm NATO) initiated in June 1949. It is the last United States military Browning Automatic rifle.

The Browning Automatic rifle was made with cast steel receivers during World War II and was the subject of much experimentation in materials and methods of manufacture by the United States, since it is basically a difficult weapon to make and requires a great deal of material and machine time. It is, like so many of the weapons designed during its period, built to last a lifetime with commensurate disabilities in cost and tool expenditure.

Colt's Patent Firearms Manufacturing Company manufactured versions of the weapon for sale to police and foreign governments. The Colt Monitor had a shortened barrel and was widely used as a police weapon; another Colt model was the R75A, which had a quick change barrel similar to that of the Swedish Model 37 BAR. FN of Belgium also has produced a number of models of the Browning Automatic rifle, covered in the chapter on Belgium.

How to Load and Fire the Browning Automatic Rifle

Cock weapon by pulling operating handle, located on the left side of the receiver, to the rear. Push the handle back to its forward position—it will now reciprocate with the action. Put change lever on "S"—safe—marking. Insert magazine, rear end cocked up slightly, and slap smartly in with heel of hand. If using M1918 or M1918A1, setting the change lever on the letter "F" will give semiautomatic fire for each pull of the trigger. If using the M1918A2, setting the change lever on "F" will give slow rate—approximately 350 rounds per minute—automatic fire. If the change lever is set on "A", all models will fire automatic fire. To remove the magazine, push magazine release located on the interior front surface of the trigger guard.

Loading and Firing the BAR

If a magazine filler is available, place the wide end over the top of the magazine so the grooves fit over the magazine catch rib. Insert a clip of cartridges in the filler, and with the right thumb strip the cartridges into the magazine exactly as though they were being fed into a bolt action rifle. Single cartridges may be so loaded. If no filler is available, cartridges may be loaded singly into the magazine as for automatic pistol.

Insert magazine between sides of receiver in front of the trigger guard and push home until it locks. This will normally be done with the right hand. While the magazine may be inserted

with the weapon uncocked, it will ordinarily be done after the rifle has been cocked and set on safe.

Field Stripping the BAR

Pull the operating handle back to cock the weapon. Then thrust it fully forward.

Rotate the gas cylinder retaining pin (at forward left end of the receiver) and withdraw it from its socket.

Now pull forward the forearm and gas cylinder tube and remove from the rifle. Ease the mechanism forward.

Rotate the retaining pin at forward end of trigger guard and withdraw it. The entire trigger mechanism may now be withdrawn from the bottom of the rifle.

Remove the recoil spring guide. Press in the checkered surface on its head and turn it until the ends clear the retaining shoulders; ease out the guide and the recoil spring and withdraw. Withdraw the handle by lining up the hammer pin holes on the side of the receiver and on the right side of the operating handle. Insert the point of a bullet in the hole in the operating handle with the right hand. Press back against the hammer pin while pushing the slide backward with the left hand.

As the two holes register, the pressure of the bullet will force the hammer pin out of the large hole on the left side of the receiver and it may be withdrawn. This will permit the operating handle to be pulled straight to the rear and out of its guide.

Push the hammer forward out of its seat in the slide and lift it out of the weapon.

Pull the slide directly forward out of the receiver, taking care that the link is pushed well down so that slide can clear it. Remove the slide carefully to avoid striking the gas piston or its rings against the gas cylinder tube bracket female.

With the point of a bullet, force out the spring bolt guide from inside the receiver, then lift the bolt, bolt lock and link by pulling slowly to the rear end of the receiver and then lifting them out. The firing pin may now be lifted out of the bolt and the extractor removed by pressing the small end of the cartridge against the claw and exerting upward and frontal pressure. No further stripping is normally necessary or recommended.

How the Basic Browning Automatic Rifle Action Works

Starting with the gun loaded and cocked, the action is as follows. Pressing the trigger pulls down the nose of the sear, disengaging it and permitting the slide to move forward under the action of the recoil spring. The rear end of the slide contains the hammer, which is connected by a link to the bolt. The slide is pulled forward by the compressed recoil spring. During the first quarter-inch of travel of the slide, the front end of its feed rib strikes the base of the top cartridge in the magazine, driving it ahead toward the firing chamber.

When the cartridge has traveled about a quarter of an inch, the bullet strikes the bullet guide on the breech and is deflected upward toward the chamber. This action also guides the front end of the cartridge from under the magazine lip. When the head of the cartridge reaches the part of the magazine where the locking lips are cut away and the opening enlarged, the magazine spring forces it out of the magazine. The base of the cartridge now slides across the face of the bolt and under the extractor; if it fails to position correctly the extractor will still snap over its head as the bolt reaches its forward position. At the time the cartridge leaves the magazine, the bullet nose is so far in the chamber that it is guided from that point on.

When the slide is within two inches of its complete forward position, a circular cam surface on the bottom of the bolt lock starts to ride over the rear shoulders of the bolt support, camming up the rear end of the bolt lock. The link pin rises above the line joining the bolt pin and the hammer pin, so that its joint has a tendency to buckle upwards. As the attached bolt is now opposite its locking recess in the receiver, it pivots upward about the bolt lock pin. The link, whose lower edge is attached to the hammer pin, revolves upward and forces the bolt lock up; the rounded surface on the bolt lock, just above this locking face, slips over the locking shoulder in the hump of the receiver and provides a lever thrust, forcing the attached bolt home into final position.

The bolt lock is now above the position of the bolt, and locks firmly in the hump in the receiver as the hammer pin passes beneath the link pin. The firing pin is in the bolt, with a lug on its rear end buried in the slot at the other side of the bolt lock, making it impossible for the firing pin to be struck by the hammer at any time except when the bolt lock is in its recesses in the hump of the receiver. Thus when the hammer pin passes under the link pin, the head of the firing pin is exposed to the center rib of the hammer; as the slide still continues forward, the hammer drives the firing pin ahead and explodes the cartridge in the chamber.

The forward motion is now halted when the front end of the slide strikes against a shoulder at the rear end of the gas cylinder tube.

Return Movement of the Action. About 6 inches from the muzzle, a small port is bored in the bottom of the barrel. As the bullet passes over this port, a small amount of gas, still under high pressure, escapes through it and passes through similar ports in the gas cylinder tube bracket, the gas cylinder tube and the gas cylinder. The gas cylinder port is the smallest of these and acts as a throttle on the barrel pressure. The ports in the gas cylinder lead radially into a small well situated in the head of the gas cylinder. Through this well, the pressure is conducted to the gas system plug, through which it acts on the piston for the length of time the bullet is traveling the 6 inches from barrel port to muzzle. This results in a sudden, hard blow, backward against the piston plug.

The gas piston is assembled to the slide, and the sudden blow as it drives the gas piston back also forces back the slide and the parts attached to it and compresses the recoil spring seated in the slide.

After the piston has traveled back a little over ½ inch, bearing rings on its rear and corresponding ones in the gas piston plug pass out of the gas cylinder. The gas now expands around the gas piston head into the gas cylinder tube where it is exhausted into six portholes in the tube placed just at the rear of the gas cylinder tube brackets.

Two rings on the piston about 1-¼-inches from the head prevent most of the gas from traveling back through the gas

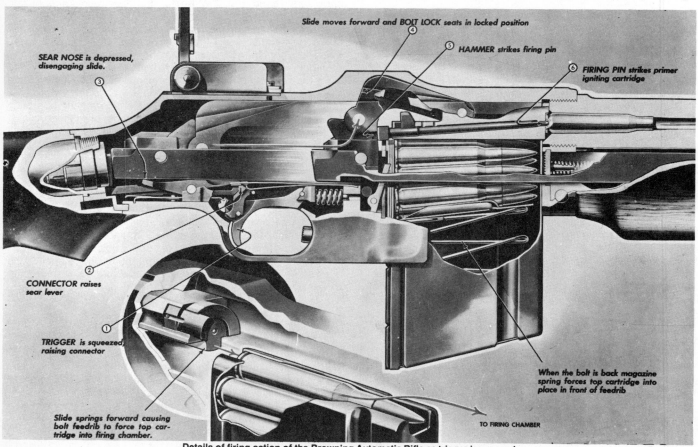

SEAR NOSE *is depressed, disengaging slide.*

③

Slide moves forward and BOLT LOCK *seats in locked position*

④

⑤ HAMMER *strikes firing pin*

⑥ FIRING PIN *strikes primer igniting cartridge*

CONNECTOR *raises sear lever*

②

TRIGGER *is squeezed, raising connector*

①

Slide springs forward causing bolt feedrib to force top cartridge into firing chamber.

When the bolt is back magazine spring forces top cartridge into place in front of feedrib

TO FIRING CHAMBER

Details of firing action of the Browning Automatic Rifle as trigger is pressed. Follow numbers to study action sequence.

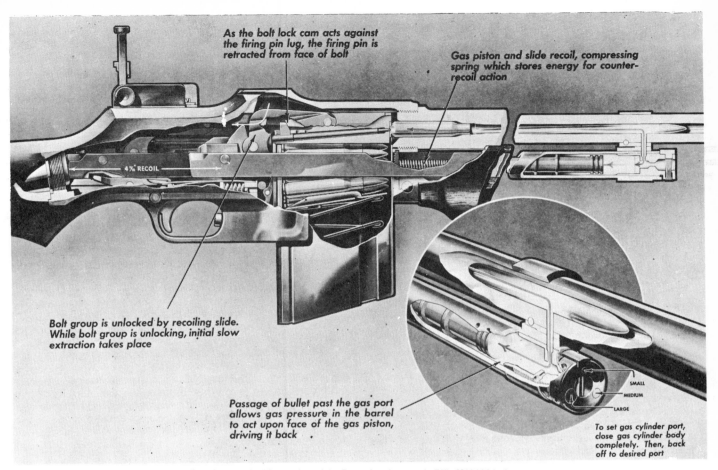

As the bolt lock cam acts against the firing pin lug, the firing pin is retracted from face of bolt

Gas piston and slide recoil, compressing spring which stores energy for counter-recoil action

4⅘ RECOIL

Bolt group is unlocked by recoiling slide. While bolt group is unlocking, initial slow extraction takes place

Passage of bullet past the gas port allows gas pressure in the barrel to act upon face of the gas piston, driving it back .

SMALL
MEDIUM
LARGE

To set gas cylinder port, close gas cylinder body completely. Then, back off to desired port

Recoil and unlocking action of the Browning Automatic Rifle M1918A2 showing action beginning as bullet passes over gas port and gas escaping into cylinder which starts the rearward action.

cylinder tube and also act as bearings to maintain the front end of the piston in the center of the gas cylinder tube after the piston has passed out of the cylinder.

Unlocking Action. As the hammer pin is slightly in advance of the connecting link pin, the initial backward movement of the slide carries the hammer back without moving either the attached bolt lock or bolt; when the movement has progressed far enough (about 1/5″) and the high breech pressure has dropped to safe limits, the unlocking action starts. The link is compelled to revolve forward about the hammer pin and so draw the bolt lock down out of a hump in the receiver and start it to the rear. The motion of the bolt and bolt lock is now accelerated as the lock is drawn completely out of its locking recess, locking the shoulders in the receiver.

As the bolt lock is prevented from revolving from below the line of backward travel of the bolt, further rearward travel of all moving parts is in a straight line. Meanwhile, however, during the unlocking motion, a cam surface on the slot in the bottom side of the bolt lock has come in contact with a cam surface on the firing pin lug and has drawn the firing pin away from the base of the bolt.

Also during the backward action, the circular cam surface on the lower part of the bolt lock, operating on the rear shoulders of the bolt support, has produced a lever action tending to loosen the cartridge case in the firing chamber. From that point, the slide and all its moving parts are traveling to the rear at the same speed, carrying along the empty cartridge case held in its seat in the face of the bolt by the extractor (the extractor is positioned in the upper right side of the bolt near the ejection port). Thus as the slide nears the end of its travel and the base of the empty cartridge case strikes the ejector on the left side of the bolt feed rib, the empty case is pivoted about the extractor and through the ejection port. As the front end of the cartridge case passes out of the receiver, it is so pivoted that it strikes the outside of the receiver about an inch to the rear of the ejection port and hence rebounds toward the right front.

The rearward motion is now completed as the end of the slide strikes against the end of the buffer and the sear nose catches in the notch at the underside of the slide and holds the weapon open and ready for the next pull of the trigger. (If the weapon is set for full automatic fire, the sear nose is held depressed, so that it does not stop the slide, which continues forward, firing the weapon in the full automatic cycle.)

The buffer is a tube in the butt of the rifle in which are placed a buffer head against which the slide stops, a friction cup slit to allow for expansion, a steel cone to fit into the cup, and four more cups and cones in series. Behind these is the coil buffer spring and the buffer nut, which is screwed into the end of the tube to form a seat for the spring.

As the rear end of the slide strikes the buffer head, it moves it to the rear, forcing the cups over the cones causing them to expand tightly against the tube, thus producing friction as the cups move back and the buffer spring is compressed. The rearward motion of the slide is therefore checked gradually, and practically no unpleasant rebound occurs. The friction mechanism is returned to its original place by the compression of its spring.

Notes on the BAR

A very important feature of this rifle is that the bolt, bolt lock and link mechanism start back comparatively slowly and do not attain the speed of the slide itself until after the period of high breech pressure passes. This feature is also important in that it does not subject the mechanism to undue strain as the gas pushes the piston back.

There are three different gas ports. The weapon will normally be set to operate on the smallest port. It is properly aligned by screwing in the gas cylinder with combination tool until the shoulder of the cylinder is one turn from the corresponding shoulder of the gas cylinder tube and the smallest circle on the cylinder head is toward the barrel. (To permit setting the regulator, the split pin must be pushed out sufficiently to permit the regulator to be turned on older weapons.)

If the rifle is sluggish from insufficient gas, the cylinder should be set one complete turn on each side of the original setting. However, it is to be noted that the larger ports are provided only for emergency use. They should be utilized only when through lack of oil or accumulation of dirt or carbon, the rifle is sluggish and conditions make it impossible to properly correct these troubles. It is therefore essential that the threads be kept cleaned and oiled and cylinder free to turn at all times.

In field service, at the first sign of insufficient gas, unscrew the cylinder a third of a turn, and line up the medium circle and port with the gas opening.

When gas is insufficient, the weapon may fail to recoil because the port is not properly aligned or is unusually dirty. A very dirty mechanism may also cause such a stoppage. Or the weapon may not recoil far enough to permit complete ejection, or the ejection may be weak. Under some conditions, although this is unusual, it may result in uncontrolled automatic fire.

On the other hand if the gas pressure is too high, the rifle will be speeded up too much causing a pounding, which will interfere with accuracy. This may also generate excessive heat in the gas operating mechanism.

How the Browning Automatic Rifle Model 1918A2 Works

The Model 1918A2 is a modification of the M1918A1 Brown-

ing Automatic rifle. The change lever spring and the carrier have been modified. Several new components have been added. These include a sear release stop lever, a sear, key and head buffers, sear release actuator and actuator spring, actuator stop and buffer head. The bipod is attached to the flash hider. A stock rest has been added and the forearm made lighter. A trap plate has been added between the barrel and the gas cylinder tube.

This gun has been modified to replace the single-shot mechanism. Single shots can be fired in this modified version only by pressing and releasing the trigger rapidly.

However, as a compensating factor, the gun has been designed to fire at a low and a high rate of speed somewhat in the manner of the British Besa Machine Guns.

When the change lever is at "F," the rifle is cocked in normal fashion and the sear engages in a notch in the slide. Pressing the trigger in the usual manner results in controlled automatic fire at a reduced rate, which will be delivered as long as the trigger is held back. There is a distinct difference noticeable when handling the gun when the mechanism is in operation and when it is firing full automatic without it. There is no provision made for semiautomatic fire in this model.

On pressing the trigger, the slide goes forward in normal BAR fashion firing the cartridge; then the slide starts on its rearward movement in the usual manner, driven back by gas expanding into the gas cylinder, but it picks up the sear release and strikes it on the front end. This forces the sear release to the rear until the slide reaches the face of the buffer head, while during this movement it also meets the front end of the actuator. The actuator tube is forced to the rear, meeting the actuator stop. At this point, the actuator reverses its direction of travel moving forward under the tension of the actuator spring, and the slide engages on the sear. The slide remains in engagement with the sear until the actuator reaches its extreme forward position. At that point, the actuator forces the sear release forward forcing it to move through the buffer head, while the foot of the sear release is in contact with the angle surface of the rear of the sear. This cams the sear out of engagement with the slide forcing the slide to go forward at this point to fire the cartridge.

The M1918A2 was the standard squad automatic weapon of World War II and Korea.

UNITED STATES SUBMACHINE GUNS

Although the United States was the third country in the world to develop a submachine gun, this type weapon was not adopted by the United States until about 1928 when it was first used by the Marines in Nicaragua and by the Coast Guard in their war with the rum runners of the prohibition period. The weapon used was the caliber .45 Thompson Model 1928. Developed by General John T. Thompson and the Auto-Ordnance Corp, it had made its first public appearance in earlier form in 1919. The first production Thompson was the Model 1921, and the "Tommy Gun" earned a reputation, probably unfairly and mainly due to movies, as a gangster weapon during the age of the "big gang wars" in the United States. The weapon was widely used by police forces, and the attitude seems to have been adopted both in the United States and the United Kingdom that the submachine gun was basically a police weapon. Be that as it may, the first submachine gun purchased by the United States Army was the caliber .45 Thompson Model 1928A1, purchased in limited quantities, principally for use by armored and reconnaissance units. The Thompson was being produced by Colt at this time; the patent owner—Auto Ordnance Corp.—did not have any manufacturing capability at the time and developed only a limited manufacturing capability during World War II. Colt produced approximately 15,000 Thompsons. In 1940, the British government gave large contracts to Auto

Ordnance Corp, for the Model 1928A1 Thompson. Auto Ordnance subcontracted most of this order to the Savage Arms Corp., then at Utica, New York. When Lend-Lease came into effect—1941—the United States government took over these contracts, and the Thompson remained in production until 1943. During the course of this contract, modifications were made in the Model 1928A1, and M1 and M1A1 models were produced. Savage made 1,501,000 Thompson M1928A1, M1 and M1A1 submachine guns. Many of these weapons made on the British contract did not make it across the Altantic because of the German U-boat campaign, at its height when shipments of the Thompson to the United Kingdom were at their greatest. The Thompson, while a reliable weapon, has several outstanding shortcomings. It is overly heavy in relation to its muzzle energy, and more importantly it is expensive in the use of materials, machine time and machine tools, all items that are in short supply during a large war. The Army therefore decided to find or develop a weapon to replace the Thompson. In 1941, a requirement was generated for a new weapon, and a number of guns were submitted in competitive tests to meet this requirement. Among these were the Hyde 109, first tested in 1939 by the Army and Hyde Inland, the ATMED—also designed by George Hyde—the Star, the Atlantic (also a Star design), the United Defense, the Reising 1 and 2, the Olsen, the Owen, the Sten

Mark III, the Austen, the Woodhull, the Suomi, the Turner, the Smith & Wesson semiautomatic carbine, the standard Thompsons, the Thompson T2, the German MP38 and Bergmann. The MP38 and the Bergmann were not official competitors but were under study.

The Hyde Inland was adopted as the "substitute standard" caliber .45 submachine gun M2 in April 1942. The M2 was never put in mass production, and the first production models reached Aberdeen Proving Ground for test in May 1943, five months after the M3 had been standardized.

The Reising Gun, in a fixed-stock version, the Model 50, and a folding stock version, the Model 55, was manufactured by Harrington and Richardson for the Marine Corps, the Home Guard and the British Purchasing Commission. Approximately 100,000 weapons were made. Many wound up in the armories of local police departments throughout the United States. It is no longer in military service.

The United Defense gun, known as the U.D. Model 42, was designed at High Standard by Carl Swebilius, and approximately 15,000 were made by Marlin for the United Defense Supply Corporation. This weapon, which was chambered for the 9mm Parabellum cartridge, was used by the OSS and air dropped to various underground organizations. The Dutch government also purchased a few. It was known in the UK as the Marlin.

The weapons that eventually developed into the M3 submachine gun were the T15, a selective-fire weapon, and the T20, an automatic only weapon, which could be converted from caliber .45 to 9mm Parabellum. This weapon was made of stampings with a minimum of machined steel parts and was at least partially the result of studies made of the British Sten. Mr. George Hyde did the basic design work, and the industrial

engineering was handled by Mr. Frederick Sampson of the Inland Manufacturing Div. of General Motors Corp. The M3 was adopted in December 1942. In December 1944, the M3A1, a modification of the M3, was adopted as standard.

THE THOMPSON CALIBER .45 MODEL 1928A1, M1, and M1A1 SUBMACHINE GUNS

The Model 1928A1 Thompson as originally manufactured has a Cutts compensator mounted to the muzzle and a leaf type rear sight adjustable for windage and a barrel with radial cooling fins. Before the end of production of the Model 1928A1, specimens had been produced without compensators, with a simple nonmovable "L" type rear sight and a smooth barrel. All Model 1928A1 Thompsons, however, have a top-mounted actuator, the brass "H" type lock, which operates on the theory of adhesion of different types of metal under pressure (the Blish principle), and breech oiler pads mounted on the receiver. The Model 1928A1 has a removable buttstock and, although usually found with a horizontal fore grip, may be found with a vertical fore grip.

M1 Thompson

The M1 Thompson designs were prepared for the simplification of the M1928A1, and in April 1942 the M1 Thompson was adopted. The Breech lock, actuator, breech oiler, compensator, radial cooling fins on the barrel and buttstock catch of the M1928A1 were all dropped in the M1 design. The bolt was made a bit heavier, as a result of not being hollowed out for the actuator, and a bolt-retracting handle was fitted into the right side of the bolt where it rode in a track in the receiver. A simple fixed aperture rear sight with sight guards was initially issued; at a later date, the sight guards were dropped. The M1 will not accept the drum type magazine used with the Model 1928A1. The buttstock of the M1 is permanently attached to the trigger housing (frame), and the design of receiver and frame are modified so that the frame slides over a protruding track located on both sides of the receiver and makes a noticable bulge at the bottom of the receiver, not present on the M1928A1.

The M1, with the exception of the locking and oiling processes, functions the same as the M1928A1. It has a spring-loaded firing pin and a hammer like the M1928A1.

Caliber .45 Model 1928A1 Thompson Submachine Gun.

Caliber .45 Submachine Gun M1.

M1A1 Thompson

The M1A1 differs from the M1 only in having the firing pin machined in the face of the bolt, thereby doing away with the firing pin assembly and hammers. The thirty-round box magazine was introduced at the same time as the M1 type guns.

To Load Box Magazine. Load as for automatic pistol magazine but support base of magazine against body or a solid surface if heavy spring tension makes it difficult to force cartridges down.

To Insert Box Magazine. Cock the gun, set the fire control lever for the type of fire desired. Put the safety on safe. Insert rib at back of magazine in its recess at the front of the trigger guard and push in until the magazine catch engages with a click.

Warning: Remember that when the bolt goes forward in this weapon a cartridge is fired. Hence, if the weapon is not to be fired and you wish to move the bolt forward to prevent straining the recoil spring, first press down the magazine catch and remove the magazine from the gun. **Note:** While it is possible to insert the box type magazine in this gun with the action forward (that is, uncocked), this procedure is not recommended. In so inserting the magazine, make sure that the magazine catch is fully engaged because the overhang of the magazine spring must be taken up before the engagement is securely locked.

Inserting a Drum Magazine. Cock the gun. Set fire control lever for single or full auto fire. Put safety on Safe. Hold magazine so that key spring is facing forward. Now insert the two ribs on the magazine into their horizontal grooves in the receiver and slide the magazine into the gun from the left side. Push in until the magazine catch clicks into place.

Warning: While this magazine may be inserted from the right side, it is unwise to do so as this may injure the magazine catch. Also, do not try to insert the magazine when the bolt is in forward position. The bottom of the bolt will strike against the mouth of the magazine and may injure it.

Loading and Firing the Thompson

To load the drum magazine raise the flat magazine key spring to disengage its stud and slide the key off via its slot.

Lift off the magazine cover. Insert 5 cartridges base down in that section of the rotor in which the magazine feed opening is cut.

Loading from right to left, place 5 cartridges in each section of the spiral track, taking care to load all outer spirals first.

Warning: Be careful not to insert any cartridges near the loops opposite the two sectors which hold five cartridges each; any cartridges so placed will jam the magazine when the rotor revolves. Now replace the magazine cover. Make sure that the large slot cut in it engages properly with the cover positioning stud. Slide the magazine key into place. Check to be sure that the stud on the spring correctly engages the center piece. Now wind the key from left to right. As it turns you will hear a distinct click. Count the number of clicks. Stamped on the magazine cover you will find the correct number of clicks necessary to indicate sufficient spring tension to work the magazine properly. (The normal number is 9 or 10 for a 50-shot magazine.) Note: If magazine is not to be used at once, wind up only two clicks to assure proper locking of the magazine and prevent straining spring.

When correctly loaded, the first four sectors starting left from the magazine opening will contain 10 cartridges each, while the last two will have 5 each.

Caution: Never rewind a partially empty magazine. This is unnecessary and may break the magazine mainspring.

Field Stripping the Model 1928A1 Thompson

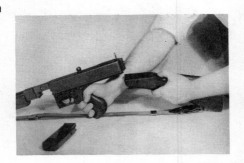

Remove magazine by pressing magazine catch up with the thumb and pulling 20-shot magazine straight down; or sliding 50-shot magazine out to the left.

Set safety on "Fire" and set fire control lever on "Full Auto." Remember this can only be done when the weapon is cocked.

Remove buttstock by pressing its slide catch down and pulling stock straight to the rear out of its guide.

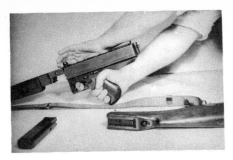

Hold firmly to actuator knob with left hand, pull trigger with right forefinger and ease bolt forward.

Turn gun upside down on table or knee. Push in the frame latch (the spring plunger on under side of frame behind pistol grip), and tap frame with right hand until it slides back a short distance.

Grasp the rear grip with the right hand and pull the trigger holding the receiver firmly in the left hand, and slide the pistol grip group off out of its grooves.

Remove recoil spring, as follows: With gun held firmly, turned upside down, grasp buffer flange with first and second fingers of right hand and pull out with upward and forward motion.

By pulling back on actuator knob, bolt is drawn back and can be removed to the rear.

Actuator is then slipped forward with lock, and lock removed through its grooves in the receiver.

Then actuator itself is removed by sliding it to the rear. This completes field stripping, no further dismounting is necessary.

Note: On earlier models of this gun a special tool is required to remove the recoil spring. In this type, the stripping tool is inserted into its hole in the front end of the buffer rod. Then it is pushed in as far as it will go in the direction of the bolt. The rear end of the buffer rod is thus withdrawn from its hole at the rear end of the receiver. By tilting this stripping tool, the buffer may be grasped by the hand, and the recoil spring, fiber buffer disc, and rod will come out with the stripping tool. Buffer rod and spring are to be securely held so they do not fly apart.

Assembling

Inserting the actuator knob at its rear position, pull it forward and replace the lock which must be placed in its recesses in the receiver, so that the word "up" stamped on it is in uppermost position and the arrow stamped on it is pointing in the direction of the muzzle. The crosspiece of the lock (the lock is called the "H-Piece" because of its shape) must fit into the jaws of the actuator knob.

Pull the actuator and lock back and insert the bolt. Be sure and insert its bolt-end first so that the inclined cuts line up with the side members of the lock. (Now push the assembly forward as far as it will go.)

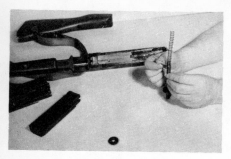

Compress the recoil spring over its rod, push it forward and down and push a nail or clip between the coils and through the hole in the rod.

Insert end of spring in hole in bolt; press rod forward until head of rod will slip into receiver and protrude through its hole to the rear; then withdraw nail.

Note: If the gun is the earlier model, put the recoil spring over its rod and push front end of spring into housing and rear of breech block. Compress recoil spring on buffer rod a little at a time. While partly compressed, hold spring on rod with left hand and insert stripping tool into hole and buffer rod to retain spring in position. Replace fiber buffer disc and insert loose end of recoil spring in its hole in the actuator knob. Now place rear end of the buffer rod in its hole at the rear end under receiver. Draw back actuator

knob until rear of bolt touches stripping tool. Recoil spring will now enter proper holes. Withdraw stripping tool.

Holding the frame by rear grip pull the trigger and slide the frame forward in its guide in the receiver. Remember that safety must be at "Fire" position and fire control lever at "Full Auto."

Insert undercut of the frame in the buttstock and slide the butt forward until it locks in place.

How the Thompson Gun Works

Starting with the gun loaded and cocked, the action is as follows. When the trigger is pressed, it moves the disconnector up to lift the sear lever. The sear lever raises the forward portion of sear, thus depressing the rear section and disengaging it from the notch on the bolt. The bolt is now free to be driven forward by the coiled recoil spring. If the fire control lever is set for semiautomatic fire, the rocker will act on the disconnector and sear lever to leave the sear free to lodge in the bolt on backward motion.

In its forward motion, the bolt strips the top cartridge from the magazine, forces it into the chamber and drives the lock downward into locked position. The forward end of the bolt is round to fit in the bolt wall of the receiver, and the rear portion is rectangular to fit into the receiver cavity.

The forward motion of the bolt is halted by the rectangular end abutting against the receiver. The lock is an H-shaped piece of steel with lugs on each side whose center is engaged by the actuator.

The hammer is pivoted in the bolt between the H-piece and the receiver bottom, and as the action closes the lower end of this hammer strikes the abutment somewhat in advance of the bolt so that as the cartridge is seated, the upper end of the hammer strikes the firing pin. (The hammer is made so it can strike the firing pin only when the bolt is completely closed.) The extractor snaps over the cannelure of the cartridge case, and the firing pin strikes the primer.

Return Movement of the Action. The residual breech pressure forces the empty cartridge case back against the bolt,

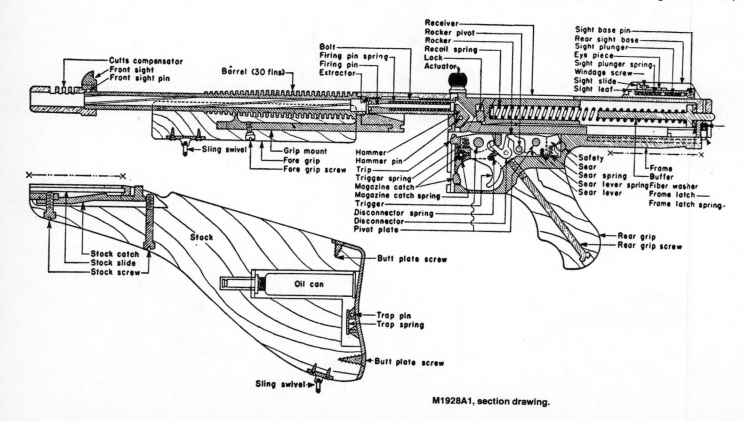

M1928A1, section drawing.

which in turn transmits the pressure to the H-piece locking device. This in turn transmits it to the locking surface of the receiver.

How the Lock Works. The lock, or H-piece, is situated in a 70° inclined slot in the bolt, with its lugs engaged in short 45° grooves recessed in the receiver. When engaged in the short 45° inclined slot with the H-piece offering resistance to the backward motion of the bolt, resistance to this lifting action is offered by the forward inclined base of the H-piece meeting the rear face of the 70° inclined slot in the bolt itself. The rising of this H-shaped lock is further resisted because its bridge is thrust up into the slot in the actuator knob, which is set at an angle of 10° from the vertical, pointed to the rear.

The general direction of movement of the locking piece, as a result of the movement of these several components, is upward and backward. Thus the bolt is prevented from moving to the rear while the chamber pressure is dangerous.

Because of the rapidity with which the pressure in the bore rises to its maximum on firing, the bolt is said to be supported by adhesion of the inclined surfaces until the pressure has again dropped materially, which acts as a breech locking factor.

For this adhesion lock to work, it is essential that the engaging surfaces remain constantly lubricated by the oil pads in the receiver.

Note. The actual value of this locking system is dubious. The necessity for constant oiling, incidentally, is a source of jams. Regardless of the real or theoretical value of the locking device, the fact remains that the weight of the parts themselves and the inertia of the recoil spring are sufficient to work the weapon safely and satisfactorily when the locking device is removed from the gun.

The forward end of the recoil spring is housed in a cavity in the actuator. The buffer forms a guide for the rear end of the recoil spring, permitting it to compress in a straight line as the action goes backward. A fiber washer is provided to absorb the shock of recoil, and oil pads in the receiver lubricate the locking lugs and bolt sides during the passage of those pieces.

The extractor, which is positioned on the right forward end of the bolt, draws the empty case out of the firing chamber until it strikes the ejector, which moves into a clearance cut in the bolt path and hurls it out of the ejection port.

If a box type magazine is in the weapon, the magazine spring forces cartridges up in line bringing the next cartridge into position for the forward movement of the bolt. If the drum magazine is being used, springs inside the drum twist the spiral and feed a cartridge into line.

Field Stripping the M1 and M1A1 Thompson Submachine Gun

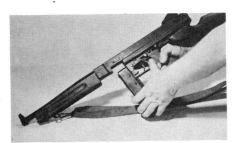

(1) Remove magazine by pressing magazine catch up with the thumb and pulling the box magazine straight down and out of its guide.

(2) With bolt forward, push in on receiver locking catch.

(3) Pressing trigger, draw frame straight back out of its guides in the receiver.

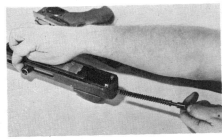

(4) Push the plug protruding from the rear of the receiver (the buffer pilot) in and draw the buffer pad up out of its seat.

(5) Holding the buffer pilot, pull the bolt back about half way. This will permit removing the recoil spring and the pilot from the rear of the receiver.

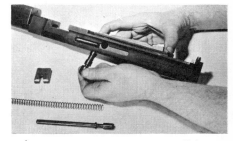

(6) Still holding the weapon upside down, lift the rear end of the bolt when the bolt handle is opposite the low cut in the center of its slot in the receiver.

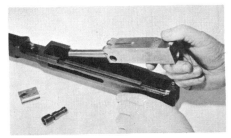

(7) Lift the bolt back and up out of the receiver.

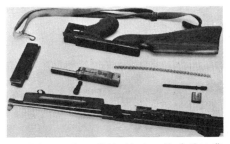

(8) This completes field stripping. No further dismounting is normally necessary.

Field Assembly. Assemble the buffer pilot to the recoil spring and holding the gun on the knee insert the recoil spring through the buffer pilot hole in the receiver from the outside, permitting the recoil spring to slide into the hole in the bolt.

Replace the bolt in the receiver so the bolt handle hole is in the center of the half circle in the receiver slot. Push the back end of the bolt up slightly out of the receiver. Push the hammer back against the shoulder of the bolt and the bolt handle can then be inserted. Then slide the bolt forward.

Now move the bolt halfway in the middle of the receiver, and assemble the buffer pilot with the recoil spring into the receiver and bolt.

When the end of the buffer pilot is flush with the outside of the receiver, the buffer pad can be placed over the buffer.

THE CALIBER .45 M3 and M3A1 SUBMACHINE GUNS

The M3 submachine gun was adopted in December 1942. It had a number of deficiencies that showed up in field service; these were corrected in the M3A1 submachine gun, standardized in December 1944.

The M3 submachine gun was designed so that by changing the barrel and bolt and adding an adaptor to the magazine, it could be used with 9mm Parabellum cartridges. There is a version of the M3 with silencer built into the barrel. Approximately 1,000 of these were made for the OSS during World War II.

Guide Lamp Division of General Motors Corp. produced approximately 646,000 M3 and M3A1 submachine guns during World War II.

A curved barrel was made for use with the M3A1 submachine gun after World War II, and a flash hider was developed for use with both the M3 and M3A1 submachine guns. Approximately 33,200 M3A1s were made by the Ithaca Gun Co. of Ithaca, New York, during the Korean War.

Differences Between M3 and M3A1

The principal differences between these weapons are as follows.

M3. The bolt is pulled to the rear by means of a spring loaded retracting lever assembly.

M3A1. The bolt has a finger hole in its right front side for cocking the gun. The magazine catch has a guard to prevent it being accidentally depressed. The ejection port and its cover are longer, and the safety lock on the ejection port cover is placed further to the rear. Disassembly grooves were added so that the bolt can be removed without removing the housing assembly. A stock plate and magazine filler were added to the stock, and a larger oil can is fitted inside the grip. The retracting pawl notch is eliminated, and a clearance slot for the cover hinge rivets was added. The barrel ratchet was redesigned to provide a longer contact surface for easier disengagement from the barrel collar.

M3

M3A1

COMPARISON
GUN, SUBMACHINE, CAL. .45
M3 AND M3A1

Modifications from M3 to M3A1

① LARGER EJECTION PORT

② RETRACTING HANDLE ELIMINATED

③ FINGER HOLE FOR COCKING

④ DISASSEMBLY GROOVES ADDED

⑤ STRONGER COVER SPRING

⑥ LARGER OIL CAN INSIDE GRIP

⑦ STOCK PLATE AND MAGAZINE FILLER
ADDED TO STOCK

⑧ GUARD ADDED FOR MAGAZINE CATCH

M3

M3A1

Loading, Firing, and Field Stripping the M3 and M3A1

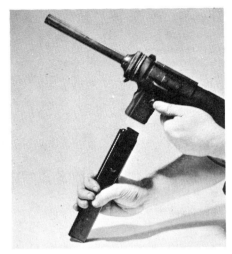

(1) A loaded magazine is inserted in the magazine housing from below until it locks. Pull the cocking handle back as far as it will go to open the ejection port cover to its full extent and draw the bolt back until it is caught and held by the sear.

(2) Release the handle and let it fly forward. If it is desired to carry the gun ready for use but on safety, push the cover down into place. Otherwise the gun is ready to fire on a pull of the trigger.

(3) With the magazine out of the weapon, push in the stock catch on the left side of the receiver above the pistol grip with the left thumb and pull the wire stock out of its grooves.

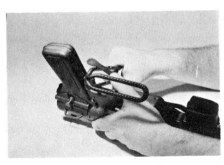

(4) Insert the shoulder end of the wire stock inside the trigger guard to provide a pressure point. Then press down on the lower end of the trigger guard until it springs out of its slot in the pistol grip. Handle this trigger guard carefully as it is of light gauge spring steel. Rotate it toward the muzzle of the gun. This will unhook it so it can be lifted out.

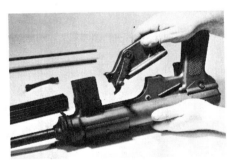

(5) Push down on the housing assembly unit a short distance, and then lift it to the rear until it can be lifted off. This should be done with care to prevent injury to the metal.

(6) Pull the ratchet catch back with the left thumb and unscrew the barrel assembly from left to right. The barrel and its collar will come out.

(7) Open the bolt cover and tilt the gun forward. The bolt and the two guide rods and their springs will come forward out the front of the receiver.

(8) No further stripping is normally necessary.

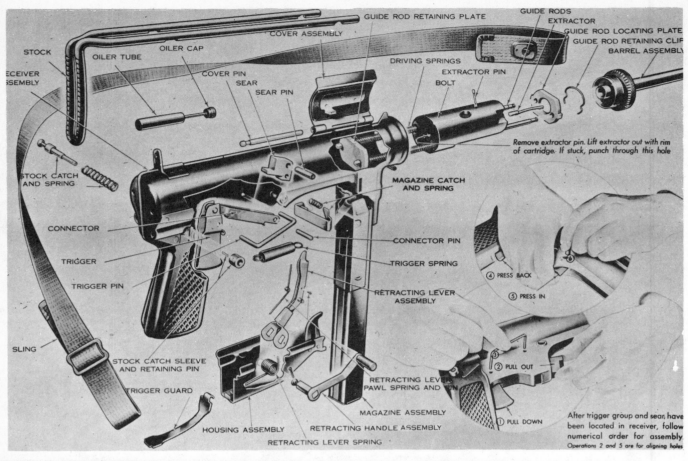

STOCK
OILER TUBE
OILER CAP
COVER ASSEMBLY
GUIDE ROD RETAINING PLATE
GUIDE RODS
EXTRACTOR
GUIDE ROD LOCATING PLATE
GUIDE ROD RETAINING CLIP
BARREL ASSEMBLY
RECEIVER ASSEMBLY
COVER PIN
SEAR
SEAR PIN
DRIVING SPRINGS
EXTRACTOR PIN
BOLT
Remove extractor pin. Lift extractor out with rim of cartridge. If stuck, punch through this hole
STOCK CATCH AND SPRING
MAGAZINE CATCH AND SPRING
CONNECTOR
TRIGGER
TRIGGER PIN
CONNECTOR PIN
TRIGGER SPRING
RETRACTING LEVER ASSEMBLY
④ PRESS BACK
⑤ PRESS IN
SLING
STOCK CATCH SLEEVE AND RETAINING PIN
TRIGGER GUARD
HOUSING ASSEMBLY
RETRACTING LEVER PAWL SPRING AND PIN
MAGAZINE ASSEMBLY
RETRACTING HANDLE ASSEMBLY
RETRACTING LEVER SPRING
③
② PULL OUT
① PULL DOWN
After trigger group and sear, have been located in receiver, follow numerical order for assembly. Operations 2 and 5 are for aligning holes

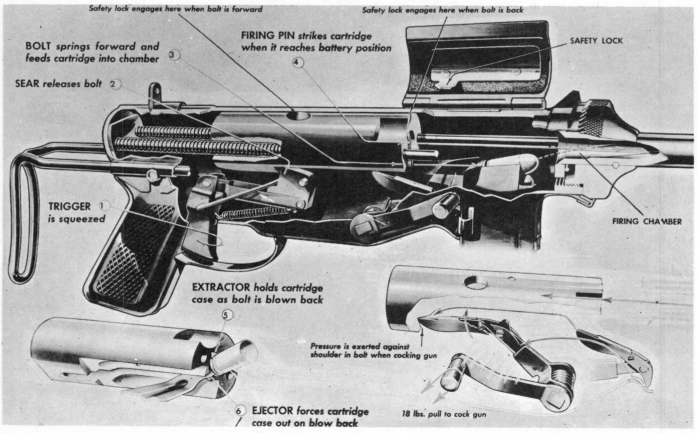

Safety lock engages here when bolt is forward
Safety lock engages here when bolt is back
FIRING PIN strikes cartridge when it reaches battery position
SAFETY LOCK
BOLT springs forward and feeds cartridge into chamber ③
SEAR releases bolt ②
④
TRIGGER ① is squeezed
FIRING CHAMBER
EXTRACTOR holds cartridge case as bolt is blown back
⑤
Pressure is exerted against shoulder in bolt when cocking gun
⑥ EJECTOR forces cartridge case out on blow back
18 lbs. pull to cock gun

How the M3 Submachine Gun Works

When a loaded magazine is inserted into the magazine housing and pushed upward until it locks, the cocking handle on the right side of the gun is drawn back to its full extent. This movement raises the bolt cover (which must be opened full to permit proper ejection) and also cocks the bolt against the tension of two recoil springs mounted in the receiver and extending one on each side into the bolt itself.

When the trigger is pressed, the sear releases the bolt. The driving springs force the bolt forward, and the feed guides machined into the bolt strike the rear of the topmost cartridge in the magazine and drive it ahead into the firing chamber.

As the cartridge enters the chamber, the bolt continues forward, and its extractor snaps over the head of the cartridge to fasten in the extracting groove.

The firing pin can now strike the primer and discharge the cartridge.

As the bullet moves out the barrel, the back pressure pushes the empty cartridge case out to the chamber and transmits its force to the bolt face pushing it to the rear.

The bolt assembly as it goes back takes the empty cartridge case with it. The case strikes against the ejector and is thrown out the ejection port.

The driving springs are compressed around their guide rods, and the bolt travels back on tracks in the receiver until the energy is absorbed and the bolt is caught by the sear.

The gun will fire as long as the trigger is held back and there are any cartridges in the magazine. If the bolt cover is pushed down in place when the bolt is back, it acts as a safety by holding the bolt off the sear and also interfering with forward travel. It is also a dust cover.

Special Note on the M3A1 Submachine Gun

The M3A1 is loaded and fired in the same manner as the M3 with the exception that the bolt is retracted by placing the right forefinger in the bolt finger hole and drawing the bolt back until it is engaged by the sear. Disassembly differs from that of the M3 in that the bolt and operating springs can be removed after the barrel is removed without removing the housing.

CHARACTERISTICS OF UNITED STATES SUBMACHINE GUNS

	Thompson M1928A1	Thompson M1 and M1A1	M3
Caliber:	.45.	.45.	.45.
System of operation:	Delayed blowback, selective fire.	Blowback, selective fire.	Blowback, automatic.
Length overall:	w/buttstock: 33.75 in. w/o buttstock: 25 in.	32 in.	Stock extended: 29.8 in. Stock retracted: 22.8 in.
Barrel length:	10.5 in.	10.5 in.	8 in.
Feed device:	20- or 30-round, staggered row, detachable, box magazine; 50-round drum.	20- or 30-round staggered row, detachable, box magazine.	30-round, in-line detachable, box magazine.
Sights: Front:	Blade.	Blade.	Blade.
Rear:	Leaf w/aperture notched battle sight.	Fixed aperture.	Fixed aperture.
Weight:	10.75 lb.	10.45 lb.	8.15 lb.
Muzzle velocity:	920 f.p.s.	920 f.p.s.	Approx. 920 f.p.s.
Cyclic rate:	600–725 r.p.m.	700 r.p.m.	350–450 r.p.m.

CHARACTERISTICS OF UNITED STATES SUBMACHINE GUNS (Cont'd)

	M3A1	Reising M50	Reising M55	U.D. M42
Caliber:	.45.	.45.	.45.	9mm Parabellum.
System of operation:	Blowback, automatic.	Delayed blowback, selective fire.	Delayed blowback, selective fire.	Blowback, selective fire.
Length overall:	Stock extended: 29.8 in. Stock retracted: 22.8 in.	35.75 in.	Stock extended: 31.25 in. Stock retracted: 22.5 in.	32.2 in.
Barrel length:	8 in.	11 in.	10.5 in.	11 in.
Feed device:	30-round, in-line detachable, box magazine.	12- or 20-round, in-line detachable, box magazine.	12- or 20-round, in-line detachable, box magazine.	20-round, staggered row, detachable, box magazine.
Sights: Front:	Blade.	Blade.	Blade.	Blade.
Rear:	Fixed aperture.	Adjustable aperture.	Adjustable aperture.	Adjustable aperture.
Weight:	8 lb.	6.75 lb.	6.25 lb.	9.12 lb.
Muzzle velocity:	Approx. 920 f.p.s.	Approx. 920 f.p.s.	Approx. 920 f.p.s.	1312 f.p.s.
Cyclic rate:	350–450 r.p.m.	550 r.p.m.	450–550 r.p.m.	700 r.p.m.

UNITED STATES MACHINE GUNS

HISTORICAL SUMMARY

The United States adopted its first true machine gun, as opposed to the hand-operated Gatling gun, in 1896. The Navy adopted the 6mm. Browning-designed, gas-operated machine gun manufactured by Colt. This weapon, because of its jointed gas lever, which swings in a vertical plane below the gun, was known popularly as the Colt "potato digger." The Army used the manually-operated Gatling in the Spanish American War. In December 1898, a joint Army-Navy Board recommended adoption of a common caliber—the caliber .30 Krag, or .30-40. The Navy Colt machine guns were rebarreled for the .30-40 cartridge and later rebarreled for the .30-06 cartridge. They were known as the Mark I in 6mm, the Mark I Modification I caliber .30-40 and caliber .30-06.

The Army did not officially adopt a machine gun until it accepted the caliber .30 Maxim Model 1904 manufactured by Vickers and Colt. Few of these guns were bought.

In 1909, the United States Army adopted the light Hotchkiss as the caliber .30 M1909 Benét-Mercié Machine Rifle. This striped weapon is essentially the same as the 8mm French M1908 light Hotchkiss and the caliber .303 British Mark I Hotchkiss. The weapon was manufactured by Colt, but only 670 Benét Mercié machine rifles were on hand at the beginning of World War I. There were also 282 Model 1904 Maxim guns, 353 Lewis guns and 148 Colt "potato diggers" on hand.

The Lewis guns were a windfall from a British contract with the Savage Arms Corporation for the manufacture of ground and aircraft type Lewis guns. The United States government bought 2,500 Lewis caliber .30 ground guns and 39,200 caliber .30 flexible Lewis aircraft guns from Savage by December 1918. Only the aircraft guns were used in action; the ground guns were used for training and later by the United States Marine Corps and Navy.

There were also 1,050 caliber .303 Lewis ground guns procured for training purposes.

The Army also purchased the caliber .30 colt "potato-digger," because it was in production for the Italian and Russian governments; 2,810 guns were procured. Marlin-Rockwell Corporation produced 38,000 Marlin aircraft guns and 1,470 Marlin tank machine guns through December 1918. The Vickers, as adopted by the United States, was the same as the British Mark I Vickers—chambered for the .30-06 cartridge. Colt manufactured approximately 12,125 Vickers ground guns, plus 2,476 Vickers caliber .30 aircraft guns. Vickers guns, which were under construction for the Russian government, chambered for the 7.62mm cartridge, were converted to 11mm for use as aircraft anti-balloon guns when the United States ceased deliveries to Russia.

With all these miscellaneous weapons available or on order, the United States had to purchase 5,255 8mm Hotchkiss Model 1914 heavy machine guns, 15,918 8mm Model 1915 (Chauchat) light machine guns and 19,241 caliber .30 Model 1918 (Chauchat) light machine guns and 19,241 caliber .30 Model 1918 (Chauchat) light machine guns from the French government. The first 12 divisions of the United States Army sent to France were equipped with French automatic weapons. The next 11 divisions to go overseas were equipped with the

Caliber .30 Model 1918 Flexible Lewis Machine Gun.

Caliber .30 Browning Model 1917 Machine Gun.

Johnson caliber .30 Model 1941 Light Machine Gun.

caliber .30 Model 1915 Vickers gun, but they also used the Chauchat in the light machine gun role.

Meanwhile, John Browning had developed the Browning Automatic Rifle and the .30 caliber Browning Machine Gun, Model 1917. That latter weapon was an improvement on his M1901 recoil operated weapon. The M1917 was produced by Remington, Colt and New England Westinghouse. A total of 56,608 weapons were manufactured through December 1918. The last 12 US divisions sent to France used the M1917.

After the First World War, the US Army continued to product improve the M1917. The aircraft version was used as the starting point for the development of a light machine gun. Originally designed for cavalry use, the M1919A2 was the predecessor to the A4 and A6 models, which saw service through the Korean conflict. The water-cooled M1917A1 was the standard batallion level machine gun until the mid-1950s. More than 820,000 caliber .30 Browning machine guns of all types were manufactured during World War II.

Despite extensive experimentation in the years between the two world wars, the Johnson M1941 machine gun was the only new design utilized in the 1941–1945 period by US troops. After World War II, the Ordnance Corps initiated design projects that ultimately produced the M60 and M73/219 machine guns (See Chapter 2.).

THE CALIBER .30 BROWNING MODEL 1917 AND 1917A1 MACHINE GUNS

All weapons of this type used during World War I were of the Model 1917 type. Wartime service indicated that the bottom plate was weak. This was modified by adding a reinforcing stirrup; 25,000 of these stirrups were mounted on weapons being placed in storage in 1920–21. In 1936, it was determined that further changes were necessary in the weapon, and a remanufacturing program was set up at Rock Island Arsenal. The modified weapon was designated the Model 1917A1.

The principal changes made at that time were:

   (1) Fitting of a new bottom plate.
   (2) Fitting of a new belt-feed lever.
   (3) Fitting of an improved cover-latch assembly.
   (4) Fitting of a sight leaf graduated for the caliber .30 M1 and M1906 ball ammunition.
   (5) Cover catch assembly that would hold the cover in a fixed position when opened.
   (6) The tripod was modified to produce the M1917A1 tripod.

Weapons of new manufacture made during World War II had additional modifications as follows:

   (1) A steel end cap was fitted in place of the bronze end caps used with the earlier guns.
   (2) A steel trunnion block was fitted in place of the bronze trunnion block used on earlier guns.
   (3) An improved steam tube assembly was used.
   (4) A new type bunter plate, similar to that of the Model 1919A4, was used.
   (5) An improved barrel gland assembly made of non-corrosive material was used.
   (6) A recoil plate was fitted in the face of the bolt, i.e., separate ring of steel around the firing pin, which can be replaced as firing pin hole wears, thus obviating the necessity of replacing the complete bolt body.
   (7) The sight leaf was graduated for caliber .30 M2 ball ammunition.

The Browning M1917A1 is not used in United States service, but can be found in the armies of other countries.

Loading the M1917A1 Machine Gun

Check the tripod to see that there is no unusual play, that it is firmly seated, that all its jamming handles are tight, and that the splayed feet of the legs are pushed securely into the ground. Check the water jacket and condenser. Make sure that both are

Caliber .30 Browning M1917A1 Machine Gun.

full. Then check to see there is no water leakage at the muzzle glands. See that rear barrel packing is water tight and oil or grease it heavily if it is not. Check headspace adjustment. Re-

member that this is a most important adjustment on this gun. If it is too tight, the gun will refuse to fire; too loose headspace will result in bulged or ruptured cartridge cases, which will jam the gun badly. Check that ammunition belts are loaded uniformly and correctly and that they are clean and dry. Check rear sight for vision and working order. See that all moving parts are lightly oiled and work smoothly by drawing the bolt handle back and permitting it to go forward. All mechanism should work smoothly and no unusual effort be required to withdraw barrel and recoiling mechanism to the rear. When bolt handle is released, it should position in its fully forward place and bolt should lock home properly. Bore should be inspected to be sure that it is clean.

With ammunition box securely locked in place on the left side of the gun and cover closed, insert the tag of the belt through the feed block as far as it will go to the right and pull the belt sharply to the right.

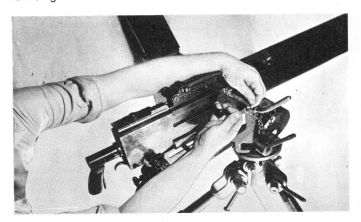

Pull the bolt handle to the rear as far as it will go. This will compress the barrel plunger spring and the driving rod spring, and when the bolt handle is released, these two springs will drive the action forward, moving the recoiling parts to their forward locked position, and half load the gun.

Now pull the bolt handle back a second time as far as it will go. Release it and let it fly forward. This completes the loading, leaving a cartridge properly positioned in the firing chamber and the weapon cocked and ready for firing.

Unloading the M1917A1 Machine Gun

Pull back the cover latch (this is the milled knob on top of the receiver to the rear of the rear sight). The spring controlled section will move backwards and permit you to raise the feed cover.

Lift the belt out to the left and replace it in its box.

Pull the bolt handle to the rear and look inside the bolt way to make sure there is no cartridge in the firing chamber or in the face of the breechblock.

Now push the extractor down to its seat in the front of the

breechblock and let go of the cocking handle, permitting the breechblock to go forward.

Snap down the cover and press the trigger.

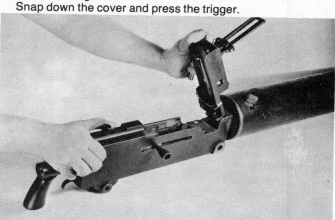

Stripping the 1917A1 Machine Gun

Raise the rear sight. Pull back the cover latch (the knob on top of the receiver behind the rear sight base) and raise the cover.

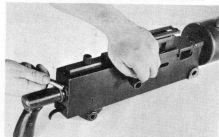

Draw bolt handle back as far as it will go and hold it firmly with the left hand. The driving spring rod protrudes through the back plate of the gun. Insert the base of a cartridge in the slot in the head of the rod. Push the rod in to compress the spring, and turn the rod to the right. This will lock the driving rod and its spring under compression inside the bolt.

Push the bolt handle forward a few inches to draw the driving rod out of the locking hole in the back plate. Then pushing the cover latch forward with the left thumb, raise the pistol grip up and out of its retaining slots in the rear of the receiver.

Pull the bolt handle as far as it will go to the rear, at which point it may be pulled to the right out of the bolt and receiver. Reach inside the receiver and grasp the driving rod; then pull the bolt directly to the rear and out of the receiver.

Insert the point of a bullet in the trigger pin locking hole in the lower right side of the receiver and push in the trigger pin against the tension of its spring. This frees the lock frame spacer and other recoiling parts and permits pulling them directly to the rear.

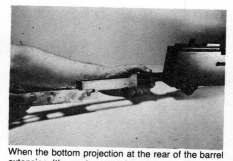

When the bottom projection at the rear of the barrel extension (the part screwed onto the barrel) drops below the bottom of the receiver, pull the combined lock frame spacer, barrel extension, and barrel directly to the rear out of the gun.

Grasp the lock frame spacer with the right hand, and with the left thumb, push forward on the turned up tips of the accelerator.

This will spring down and forward, separating the lock frame spacer (which holds the trigger and

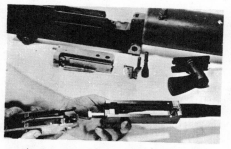

accelerator mechanism) from the barrel extension.

Push the accelerator pin out of the lock frame spacer and remove the accelerator (this is the curved piece of metal with two claws).

Insert head of cartridge in slit in head of barrel plunger at the left side of the lock frame. Twist it and ease it out. Remember that it is under strong spring tension (if necessary trigger pin may now be pushed out and spring and trigger removed).

Holding the barrel extension with the left hand, use the point of a bullet to start the breechblock pin from left side and remove it from the right, permitting the breechblock (the heavy wedge whose lower front end is beveled) to drop down out of the barrel extension. (Barrel extension may now be unscrewed from the barrel if necessary.) Turn the extractor (the swinging hook-shaped piece on the left forward end of the bolt) up as far as it will go and pull it out of its hole in the bolt.

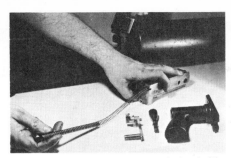

With the base of a cartridge, push in the head of the driving spring rod in the bolt and twist it to the left. Be careful of the very powerful driving spring which will now be free to fly out the back carrying the driving spring rod with it. Grip this firmly and ease it out gradually. Push out the cocking lever pin from the upper front left side of the breechblock and lift out the cocking lever.

Turning the breechblock upside down, push the sear up with the bullet to release the firing pin spring; turn the breechblock the right way up again and insert the bullet into the slot of the sear spring. Push over to the left, pry the sear spring into a locking recess and the sear drops out. When sear spring is pushed back into normal position its pin may be pushed up and it and the spring removed. The firing pin and its spring may now be dropped out of the back of the breechblock.

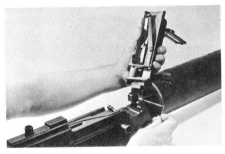

Use the point of a bullet to turn up the cover pin spring at the right side of the receiver just behind the water jacket. Pull the pin out to the right and lift the cover up out of the receiver. Pushing back on the nose of the split pin on the left side of the feed block, control the feed pawl with the left thumb and ease the

pawl and its spring up out of the receiver as the locking pin is pulled out. Insert point of bullet between the extractor cam and the long flat piece of metal on the side of the cover opposite the belt feed lever (this is the extractor spring) and pry the extractor spring out

of its seat in the cam, then lift it up and out. The feed lever and slide may be removed if necessary by turning feed lever pivot pin spring outwards. This completes stripping the Browning machine gun.

Assembling the M1917A1 Machine Gun

Start by screwing the barrel into the barrel extension, then insert the barrel and barrel extension into receiver. Slide slowly forward until the projection of the barrel extension (which holds the bolt back) is against the bottom plate of the receiver. Holding the lock frame in the right hand, place the accelerator claws between the rear face of the barrel extension and the forward faces of the T-lug extension and at the same time insert the forward projections of the lock frame into their grooves in the barrel extension. Give a quick thrust forward to the lock frame to tip back the accelerator claws and compress the barrel plunger spring; this locks the lock frame to the barrel extension.

Now push the lock frame attached to the barrel extension and barrel farther ahead in the receiver until the trigger pin on the lower right side comes against the side of the receiver. Push in the trigger pin against its spring tension, and the whole assembly can now be pushed fully home while the trigger pin will be forced by its spring into its slot in the right side of the receiver.

Now replace the bolt in the receiver being sure the extractor is in position and that the cocking lever projecting through the top is fully forward.

Insert the bolt handle in the end of the slot in the receiver and into its hole in the bolt; then push it forward far enough so that when the cover latch is pushed forward, the pistol grip and back plate may be slid down in their grooves in the receiver. Pull the cover latch back to lock the back plate in position; holding bolt handle back as far as it will go, insert the base of the cartridge

into the slit in the driving rod, push in and turn to the left to release the driving rod spring. Now permit the bolt to run forward under the thrust of the driving rod spring.

How the M1917A1 Machine Gun Works

Starting with the weapon loaded and cocked, the action is as follows. The trigger being pressed, the trigger bar disengages from the sear block and allows the striker to be driven forward by the spring in the bolt to fire the cartridge.

As the bullet goes down the barrel, the recoil drives back against the base of the cartridge base, which transmits the blow to the bolt face thereby starting the locked recoil action and barrel to the rear.

Locked together, the barrel, barrel extension and bolt recoil about ⅝ of an inch. For the first half of this travel, during the period of high breech pressure, they are securely locked together, and then the front projections of the lock frame (which are set against the sides of the pin passing through the barrel extension and the breechblock) force the breechblock pin down, drawing the breechblock down out of its locking slot on the underside of the breechblock. The bolt is thus released from the barrel extension and so can continue straight to the rear. As the barrel extension itself travels to the rear, the barrel plunger spring is compressed, and the rear of the barrel extension drives the claws of the accelerator back sharply, flipping the accelerator up and backwards on its pin.

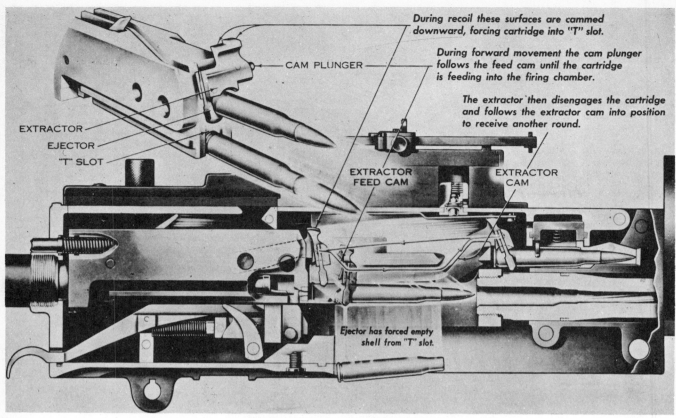

During recoil these surfaces are cammed downward, forcing cartridge into "T" slot.

CAM PLUNGER

During forward movement the cam plunger follows the feed cam until the cartridge is feeding into the firing chamber.

The extractor then disengages the cartridge and follows the extractor cam into position to receive another round.

EXTRACTOR

EJECTOR

"T" SLOT

EXTRACTOR FEED CAM

EXTRACTOR CAM

Ejector has forced empty shell from "T" slot.

Cross section of parts in firing position.

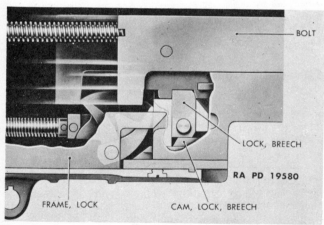

BOLT

LOCK, BREECH

RA PD 19580

FRAME, LOCK

CAM, LOCK, BREECH

Breech locked.

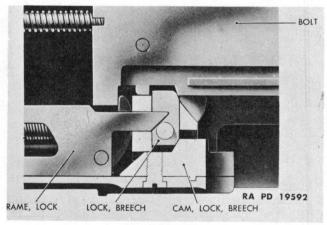

BOLT

RAME, LOCK

LOCK, BREECH

CAM, LOCK, BREECH

RA PD 19592

Breech lock beginning to open.

As the accelerator turns, the tips of its claws strike bottom projections on the bolt and thus accelerate the rearward motion of the bolt by transmitting to it the thrust absorbed from the barrel extension, which is now held in rearward position locked to the frame spacer slots. Speeding the rearward motion of the bolt, at the same time that the barrel is slowing up, permits the empty case to be extracted from the chamber without the sudden tug that would normally occur. (This makes special lubrication unnecessary.) The accelerator claws while engaging the shoulder of the T-lug firmly lock the barrel extension in the rearward position to the lock frame. A stop prevents the accelerator from going backwards too far and the barrel plunger spring is held compressed.

During backward motion of the bolt, the driving spring is compressed over the driving spring rod whose head is held securely in the back plate of the receiver. The extractor fitting over the top front of the bolt draws a loaded cartridge from the belt at the same time that the T-slot machined into the face of the bolt draws the empty cartridge case from the firing chamber. The extractor cam plunger (which rides along the top of the extractor cam and the extractor feed cam) is finally forced in by the beveled section of the extractor feed cam. The cover extractor cam thus forces the extractor down and the plunger spring out behind the extractor feed cam.

During the backward movement of the bolt, a stud on the belt feed lever (which is mounted in the front of the cover on a pivot) moves to the right in the cam groove cut in the top of the bolt. Thus the belt feed slide, which is attached to the lever, is moved to the left. The belt feed pawl (located on the under side of the cover above the belt) springs over the left of the first cartridge

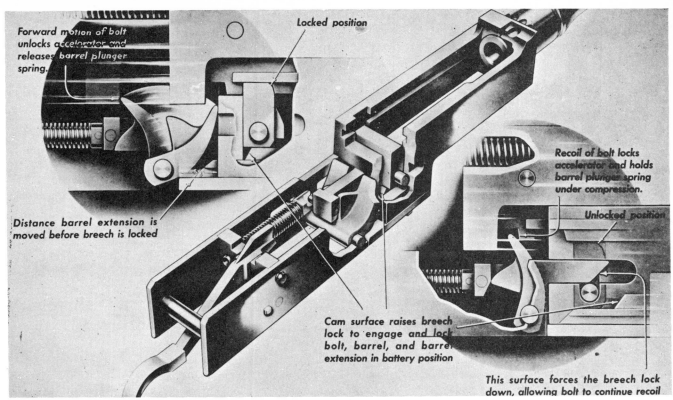

Operation of accelerator mechanism.

(which is being held in position by the belt holding pawl below the belt on the left side of the feed block) and supports the cartridge and the belt to prevent feeding trouble.

The cocking lever is fastened by a pivot pin inside the bolt, and its top protrudes through the top of the bolt and rests inside the top cover of the receiver. Thus as the bolt starts backwards, pressure on the lower part of this lever drives it back revolving it on its axis, and the firing pin spring is compressed drawing back the firing pin. The firing pin engages a notch in the sear (which has been pulled upward by the action of the sear spring).

The rear of the bolt strikes against the buffer plate mounted in the back plate at the upper part of the pistol grip, and the remainder of its energy is absorbed in friction and by the buffer disc. (A brass buffer ring is forced over a plug and expands against the inner wall of the grip.)

The driving spring in the bolt, now fully compressed, reacts to drive the bolt forward. During this forward motion, the upper end of the cocking lever is forced to the rear, thus pulling the lower end away from the rear of the firing pin. The extractor feed cam acts on the extractor cam plunger, forcing the extractor down so that the cartridge it is holding drops down the T-slot in the face of the bolt until it reaches a direct line with the firing chamber. The ejector strikes the empty case in the T-slot expelling it through the bottom of the gun and stopping the live cartridge when properly positioned.

Also during the forward motion of the bolt, the bottom projection strikes the top of the accelerator to swing it forward on its axis pin. This unlocks the barrel extension from the lock frame, permitting those two units to move forward as the bolt acts through the accelerator against the rear end of the barrel extension. The forward motion of the barrel extension and barrel is further assisted by a thrust from the barrel plunger spring as it uncoils. The force passed on by the accelerator from the bolt to the barrel extension is sufficient to guarantee proper timing of the locking action.

The actuating stud on the feed lever fits down in a cam groove in the bolt. Thus as the bolt goes forward, the stud rides in the cam and forces the lever on its pivot to the left; the forward end of the lever, which carried the feed slide, is thus pivoted to the right, bringing with it the belt feed pawl, the belt and the next cartridge. As the motion ends, the cartridge to be fed is held between the cartridge stops and the feedway. The next round to load is pulled over the belt holding pawl, which rises behind it. It is in position to be engaged by the belt feed pawl on the next movement.

The final action of the extractor during forward motion of the bolt is to rise under the influence of its plunger riding along the top of the extractor cam. As the ejector pivots forward, the extractor releases its hold on the cartridge, which is now well into the chamber. The extractor continues to ride upwards and over the base of the next cartridge in the belt in the feedway. Then the flat extractor spring in the top cover forces the extractor down and into the cannelure of this cartridge gripping it ready to pull it back on the next movement to the rear of the bolt.

The breechblock, mounted in the rear of the barrel extension, strikes a cam as the recoiling parts near the firing position and is forced up this cam and into a recess cut in the bottom of the bolt. Thus as the action comes to a complete close, the breechblock firmly locks the barrel extension (into which is screwed the barrel) to the breechblock.

Special Note on M1917A1 Adjustments

It is extremely important that the headspace on this gun be correctly adjusted before firing. To test the adjustment, pull the bolt handle back and let it run forward several times.

If the bolt does not go home fully and smoothly, it indicates too tight space between the face of the bolt and the face of the firing chamber. If the gun is put into use in this condition, it will fire sluggishly, or it may refuse to fire at all.

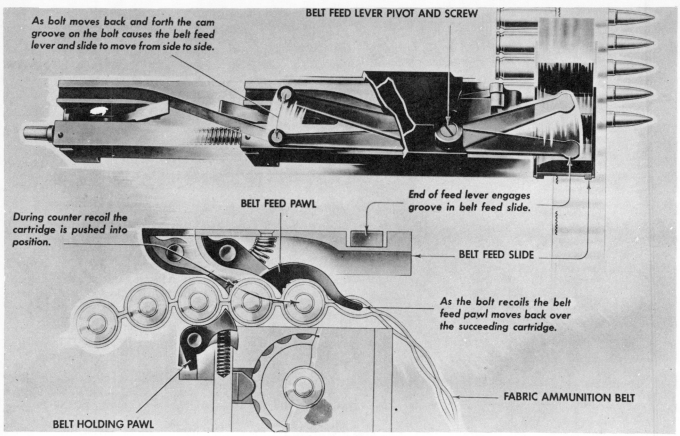

As bolt moves back and forth the cam groove on the bolt causes the belt feed lever and slide to move from side to side.

BELT FEED LEVER PIVOT AND SCREW

During counter recoil the cartridge is pushed into position.

BELT FEED PAWL

End of feed lever engages groove in belt feed slide.

BELT FEED SLIDE

As the bolt recoils the belt feed pawl moves back over the succeeding cartridge.

FABRIC AMMUNITION BELT

BELT HOLDING PAWL

Belt-feed mechanism.

To correct this condition, it will be necessary to strip the weapon and unscrew the barrel one notch, then assemble and test again.

To Test for Loose Headspace. Lift the cover and raise the extractor; then pull the bolt slightly to the rear. If the bolt moves back at all without carrying the barrel and barrel extension with it, then gun is too loose. Fired in this condition, the pressure of the gas in the firing chamber will bulge the head of the empty cartridge case (since it is not fully supported by the bolt), or may rip it off entirely, causing a serious jam.

To correct this condition, screw up the barrel one notch, then retest.

Adjusting Headspace. Screw the barrel into its extension and stop when the first clicking sound is heard (this click is caused by the barrel-locking spring).

Push the breechblock (minus extractor) fully forward on barrel extension.

Push the lock piece up from below to lock the breechblock to the barrel extension; and while holding it firmly, screw up the barrel until resistance is encountered.

Now check to see that barrel locking spring is in a notch and that the lock piece is solidly seated.

Now let go of the lock. If it drops freely, the adjustment is correct. This adjustment should be punched on the barrel, to save time when assembling in future.

Water Leakage. If water leaks from muzzle end, remove the muzzle gland. Wind packing around the barrel. Press it together with combination tool. Then push back on barrel and guide the packing into its seat. Screw the muzzle gland back on. Test by working bolt handle. If there is friction, packing is too tight. This will make a sluggish gun.

If water leaks from breech end, remove barrel and work oiled packing down into barrel cannelure with combination tool. Test

as before for undue friction and headspace.

CALIBER .30 BROWNING MODEL 1919A4 AND 1919A6 MACHINE GUNS

The M1919A4

Two types of the M1919A4 have been issued—the fixed gun and the flexible gun. The fixed gun was widely used on World War II armored vehicles; the flexible gun was mainly used as the infantry company level machine gun. The M1919A4 is used on the caliber .30 M2 mount as a ground gun. The mechanism of the M1919A4 is identical with that of the caliber .30 M1917A1 Browning gun. The principal differences between the M1919A4 and M1917A1 are as follows:

(1) The M1919A4 has a ventilated barrel jacket rather than a water jacket.

(2) The M1919A4 is normally used on a light mount with limited terrain command, classified as a light machine gun by the United States. The M1917A1 is normally used on a heavier mount with much greater terrain command, classed as a heavy machine gun; it was the battalion level gun.

(3) The M1919A4 has a much heavier barrel than the M1917A1 but has a lower sustained rate of fire than the water-cooled gun.

(4) The sights of the M1919A4 and the M1917A1 are different. There are other various minor differences between these guns. The M1919A5 is the same as the M1919A4, except that it has a bolt retracting slide and a different cover detent. These changes on the weapon were necessary to mount it in the World War II M3 light tank. The US Navy has a number of Browning Model 1919A4 machine guns converted to 7.62mm NATO.

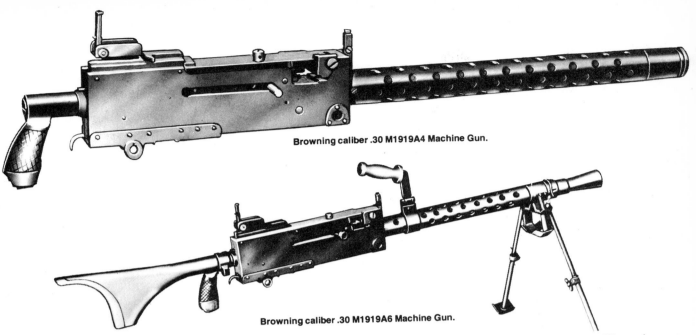

Browning caliber .30 M1919A4 Machine Gun.

Browning caliber .30 M1919A6 Machine Gun.

These weapons, fitted with a closed-prong type flash suppressor, are called Machine Gun 7.62mm NATO Mark 21 Mod. O by the Navy. A similar weapon is standard in the Canadian Army as the C1 7.62mm Machine Gun.

The M1919A6

The M1919A6 was a wartime modification of the M1919A4 to give the weapon more tactical flexibility. A bipod, shoulder stock and carrying handle were added to the basic Browning machine gun action to create a weapon that was easier to move and to get into action than the tripod-mounted M1919A4. The M1919A6 also has a lighter barrel and a different front barrel bearing than the M1919A4. The lighter barrel of the M1919A6 gives it a higher cyclic rate of fire than the M1919A4.

A post-World War II version of the M1919 Brownings (in addition to the M37) also exists; this is the M1919A4E1. This weapon also has a retracting slide similar to the M1919A5.

Loading and Firing; Field Stripping the M1919 Series

The method of loading and firing and the method of field stripping the M1919 series of guns is, in all essentials, the same as

that of the caliber .30 M1917A1 water-cooled Browning gun.

The M1919A4 and the M1919A6 may be used with M1917A1, M2, or M74 tripods but are normally used with the M2 tripod. The M1919A6 is also used on the bipod shown in the photo.

CALIBER .30 TANK MACHINE GUN M37

The M37 is basically a modification of the Browning M1919 series of weapons. It was designed to produce a weapon that would have more usefulness in tank mountings than the Browning M1919A4 and A5.

Notes on the M37 Tank Machine Gun

The principal differences between the M37 and the Browning M1919 series of guns are as follows.

The M37 can be fed from either the right or left side. The bolt has a dual track for the belt feed lever stud. By positioning two switches, the ejector and various feed components, the weapon can be easily changed to feed from either side. This arrangement is generally similar to that found on the Browning cal. .30 M2 aircraft gun and the cal. 50 M2 and M3 aircraft guns.

The cover catch has been changed so that it can be opened easily from either side.

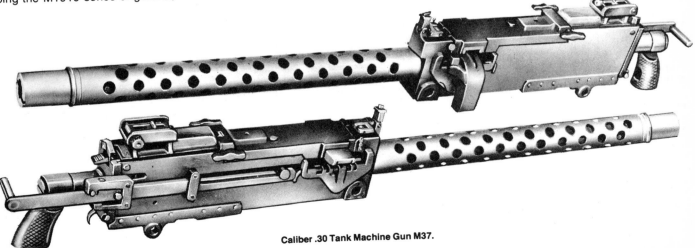

Caliber .30 Tank Machine Gun M37.

THE 7.62mm NATO M60 MACHINE GUN

The M60 is called a general purpose gun because it replaced the cal. .30 Browning light and heavy machine guns. The M60 is used on a bipod as a light machine gun, and on a tripod as a heavy machine gun. The M60 (T-161E3) is the result of a series of designs started at the end of World War II. The first of these was called the T44 and was essentially a combination of the belt feed mechanism of the German MG42 with the operating mechanism of the German automatic rifle FG42. A later design, which was considerably modified, was the T52; and from the T52 evolved the T161 series of guns.

The M60 therefore has, in a considerably modified form, the belt feed mechanism of the MG42 and the operating mechanism of the FG42. (See Chapter 2.)

Loading and Firing the M60 Machine Gun

Cocking. For all normal purposes this weapon, being fully automatic, should remain cocked at all times. The gun can be cocked only with the safety off or in "F" position. Pull the cocking lever handle, extending from right front of receiver, to its maximum rearward position, where the engagement click of the sear is heard. Return the cocking lever forward to engage its retaining latch. NOTE: Cocking lever will return to its latched position on the first shot, but this practice is not recommended, although it is not harmful if done occasionally. Return the safety lever to the "S" or safe position.

Loading. Rounds should be firmly assembled and positioned in their push-through links. Raise feed cover by lifting cover latch at right rear. Feed cover is retained vertically by a torsion spring and detent. The feed plate should remain in place on the receiver rails. Place the linked belt on the feed plate, links up, with the first round to be fired in the feed plate groove and held by the feed plate retaining pawl engaging the second round. An empty link ahead of the first round will help to position the belt, if desired. Close cover firmly, making sure the cover is latched securely.

Firing. With weapon positioned and aimed, push safety lever forward and up, out of the way, with right thumb. Visual examination will show the lever is directed toward the "F" symbol. When down, near the right thumb, the safety lever is directed toward the "S" symbol. Because of the low cyclic rate (550 r.p.m.) of this weapon, single rounds or short bursts can easily be fired. It is important that the trigger be completely released after each shot, to fire single rounds, or to interrupt firing at any time.

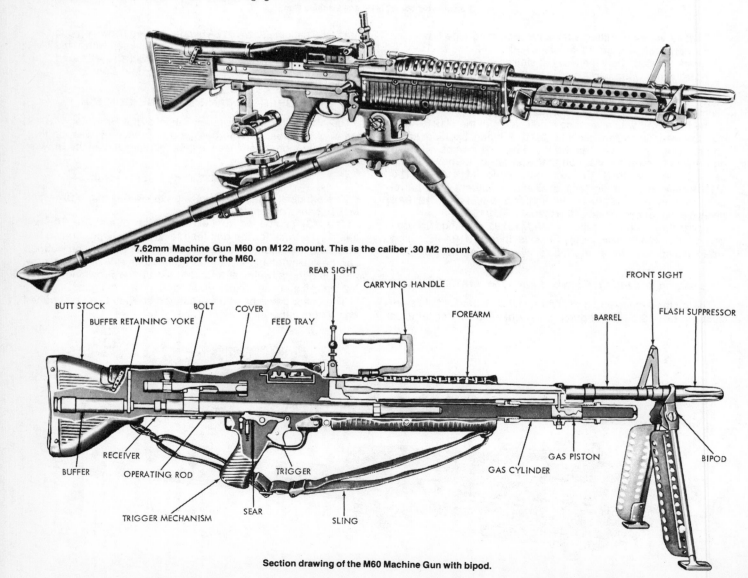

7.62mm Machine Gun M60 on M122 mount. This is the caliber .30 M2 mount with an adaptor for the M60.

Section drawing of the M60 Machine Gun with bipod.

Reloading. After firing, if the belt has been exhausted, the gun will be closed and must be cocked by hand to reload. The last link of the belt will remain in the feed plate. This link can be removed by the alternate method of loading described above; or, if a leading-link tab is provided, the link can be pushed through by utilizing the tab; or, finally, it can be removed when the cover is open for reloading.

Sights. The weapon as furnished is sighted in at 100 yards. A "quick adjustment" type of rear sight is provided. Barrels are zeroed-in by utilizing the lateral and elevating adjustments on the rear sight. For lateral adjustment, turn the knob at the lower left side of the rear sight. If additional lateral adjustment is required, the spring dove-tail (base) can be moved in its dove-tail on the receiver. The receiver should be restaked to retain the sight in the position permanently. For normal use, the spring action of the sight base is sufficient to hold the sight in its place.

For elevating adjustment, a scale slide is provided on the rear sight. Zero the barrel to the aperture; then, after this zeroing is accomplished, the scale can be lined up with the aperture by loosening the lower screw, sliding the scale to its desired location, and tightening the screw securely.

Barrel Changes. Barrels are changed by raising the lever found at the extreme right front of the receiver to the vertical position and withdrawing the barrel. Use the bipod as a handle. Assemble the barrel by inserting from the front, aligning the gas cylinder pilot nut with the receiver extension tube. Press the lock lever down and rearward to the full limit of travel.

Stripping the M60

For ease in cleaning, oiling and inspection, this weapon can be taken down as follows, using the cartridge as a tool. With gun in closed or fired position:

Unlatch and raise feed cover.

Remove butt stock by lifting shoulder rest and insert cartridge in exposed latch hole. Withdraw butt rearward.

Lift lock plate vertically for removal, holding the buffer to prevent drive spring from ejecting it. Withdraw buffer.

Pull operating rod drive spring guide and spring out of the rear opening. Withdraw operating rod and bolt assembly rearward with the cocking lever, pulling the bolt out of the receiver by hand the remaining distance. As the bolt rotating cam is exposed, insert lock plate in front of cam opening to hold firing pin back. The operating rod can then be withdrawn from the bolt.

CAUTION: Roller bearing and pin retainer are staked in place and should not be removed. These parts are normally also held in place by the firing pin; therefore, care should be exercised to prevent their loss.

Remove trigger housing assembly by pressing spring lock flat against the trigger housing at extreme front pin to unlock it from the pin. Rotate the spring lock down and away from the receiver to disengage it from the pin, and withdraw it. Remove the front pin from the left. Remove trigger housing by sliding it forward to disengage it from the receiver.

Feed cover removal is not necessary for field stripping but can be done if desired. With feed cover raised vertically, and feed plate in place on the receiver (at approximately 90° with cover), use bullet nose to remove cover pin spring, and withdraw cover pin spring and cover pin by hand, rocking cover slightly to aid disengagement. Cover and plate are free for removal. A torsional counterweight spring is also retained by the pin and is removable when pin is removed.

Remove barrel by raising lock lever to its vertical position and pulling the barrel out in a forward direction.

Handguard removal is not necessary for field stripping but can be done if desired. Grasp the handguard firmly. Insert a bullet nose in the hole provided at the bottom rear of the handguard.

Field stripped view of the M60 Machine Gun. 1. Barrel assembly. 2. Trigger assembly. 3. Butt stock assembly. 4. Handguard assembly. 5. Feed cover assembly. 6. Piston and buffer assembly. 7. Bolt assembly. 8. Receiver assembly.

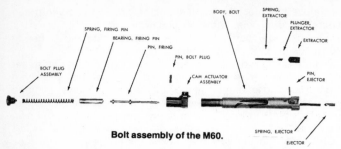

Bolt assembly of the M60.

Push cartridge to disengage spring lock. Slide handguard off to front. It is helpful to position the receiver vertically, with the front extension tube resting on a flat hard surface when disengaging the lock. After unlocking and sliding the handguard forward to disengage it from the receiver, tip the handguard to clear the tripod clevis and remove.

The weapon can be reassembled by reversing the order of the above steps.

How the M60 Works

With the gun loaded, in the cocked position, the following is the sequence of operation.

Release the safety and pull the trigger. The trigger raises the front of the sear, dropping the rear of the sear out of its engagement notch in the operating rod.

The operating rod, released by the sear, is propelled forward by the energy stored in the drive spring by the cocking operation. The bolt, engaged by the operating rod cam yoke, is carried forward with the rod, as is the gas piston, should it be positioned to the rear.

The bolt top locking lug strikes the rear edge of cartridge in the feed plate groove, where the cartridge is positioned by the belt link and the feed cover guides and springs. The bolt strips the cartridge from its link, carrying the cartridge forward out of the feed plate. The empty link is retained in the feed plate by the cartridge guide and the next round.

As the bolt enters the barrel socket, the round has been deflected downward and into the chamber by the front cartridge guide, the receiver feed ramps and the barrel socket feed ramp. The barrel socket lead cams impart clockwise rotation to the bolt sufficient to enter the locking lugs into the socket locking cam. At this point, the round is seated in the chamber, its base contacting the extractor and ejector. The forward motion of the operating rod and bolt compresses the ejector spring and moves the extractor out to snap over the rim of the cartridge.

The firing pin, held back by the bolt cam and its engagement with the operating rod, has also compressed its drive spring during cocking. As the bolt rotates, its rotating cam releases the firing pin. The firing pin spring now contributes its energy to the operating rod through the bolt rotating cam and aids the drive spring to complete the bolt locking rotation. The operating rod continues forward, carrying the firing pin with it until the pin strikes the cartridge primer and ignites it. The firing pin is stopped by its seat in the bolt at the pin front bearing spool, stopping the operating rod. The operating rod has also positioned the piston in its forward position.

After ignition of the powder charge by the primer, the bullet is forced down the bore by the gases released. At a point about 8 inches from the muzzle, the bullet passes the barrel gas port, allowing part of the gases under pressure to enter the gas cylinder and hollow piston through their respective ports, which are aligned with the barrel port.

Gas under pressure, bled from the bore by the gas port, fills the hollow piston until enough pressure is built up to overcome

the mass of the piston and operating rod and the load of the operating rod spring. The piston begins its travel rearward, propelled by gas pressure against the forward end of the cylinder. After a very short travel rearward, the piston ports and collector ring are out of line with the barrel gas port, sealing off a measured charge of gas under pressure in the cylinder and hollow piston. By this time, the bullet is well out of the bore, and gas pressure in the bore rapidly falls to help provide easy extraction of the spent round.

The piston, propelled rearward by the trapped expanding hot gases, forces the operating rod rearward to contact the firing pin rear spool. This compresses the firing pin spring withdrawing the firing pin from the cartridge primer as well as compressing the operating rod spring. Rearward motion of the operating rod continues in the "dwell" slot of the bolt rotating cam, until the rod yoke rollers contact the spiral or counterrotating part of the bolt cam.

The bolt now begins its counterclockwise rotation and unlocking, urged by the energy of the operating rod. At full unlock, the firing pin spring is fully cocked, the roller of the rod cam yoke contacting the rear of the bolt rotating cam.

Bolt and rod together continue to the rear, propelled by the energy of the expanding gas, withdrawing the spent cartridge from the barrel chamber. As the spent cartridge leaves the chamber, it is moved sideward in the direction of the ejection port; the ejector spins the case sideward to pivot about the extractor lip and disengage, allowing the case to be ejected with force out of the port, and against the ejection deflector which propels it downward.

In this interval, the piston has reached the limit of its travel. Spent gases are exhausted through ports provided in the gas cylinder, uncovered by the piston in its rearward travel.

Air behind the piston is exhausted through a set of ports near the rear of the gas cylinder, allowing escape of dirt and powder residue.

The bolt and operating rod continue rearward, propelled by stored energy and inertia, compressing the operating rod drive spring. As the drive spring is fully compressed, the operating rod contacts the buffer through the drive spring guide rod collar. Energy remaining in the rod and bolt is now transferred to the buffer. As the buffer plunger is forced rearward against its pads and preloaded springs, the rubber pads are compressed, acting as a high-rate spring. The rubber is forced to flow radially, to expand frictional surfaces tight against the buffer tube wall. Further rearward motion compresses the buffer return spring, and the sliding friction of the pads on the tube wall absorbs the remaining energy of the rod and bolt. The moving parts now come to rest, and the counter-recoil cycle begins.

The energy stored in the drive spring now forces the operating rod and bolt forward. The frictionally damped buffer springs return the buffer plunger to its initial position. The firing pin spring also contributes some force until it is halted by the front of the rod yoke, which stops the firing pin in the "cocked" position in the bolt rotating cam. As the rod continues forward with the bolt, if the trigger has been released, the sear is held up against the bottom of the rod by the sear spring. As the sear engages the sear notch in the rod, forward motion stops, and the weapon is held in cocked position, ready for fire. If the trigger has not been released, the weapon continues to fire until interrupted by the sear, or until the ammunition is exhausted. If the last round is fired and the trigger held down, the gun will close on an empty chamber and must be recocked manually.

Feed Cycle. For simplification of description, this portion of the operation is considered separately. As the bolt travels forward for firing, the feed cam mounted in the feed cover is engaged by the feed cam actuator roller attached to the rear of the bolt. Forward motion of the bolt and actuator causes the feed cam to swing to the right, forcing the front of the feed cam lever

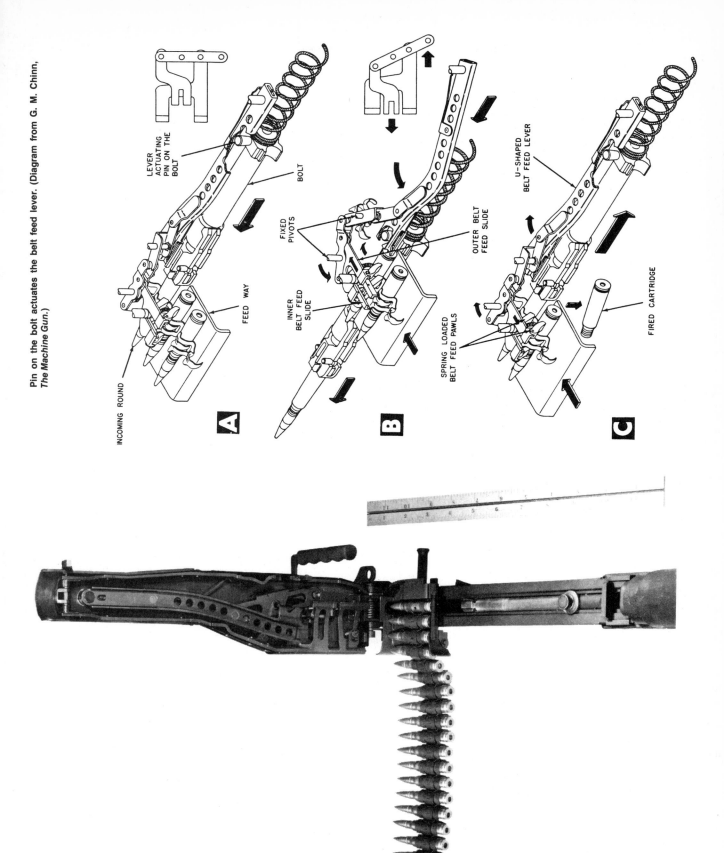

Pin on the bolt actuates the belt feed lever. (Diagram from G. M. Chinn, *The Machine Gun*.)

LEVER ACTUATING PIN ON THE BOLT

BOLT

FEED WAY

INCOMING ROUND

A

FIXED PIVOTS

INNER BELT FEED SLIDE

OUTER BELT FEED SLIDE

B

U-SHAPED BELT FEED LEVER

SPRING LOADED BELT FEED PAWLS

FIRED CARTRIDGE

C

MG42 Feed system adapted to M60 Machine Gun.

M60 Machine Gun feed system.

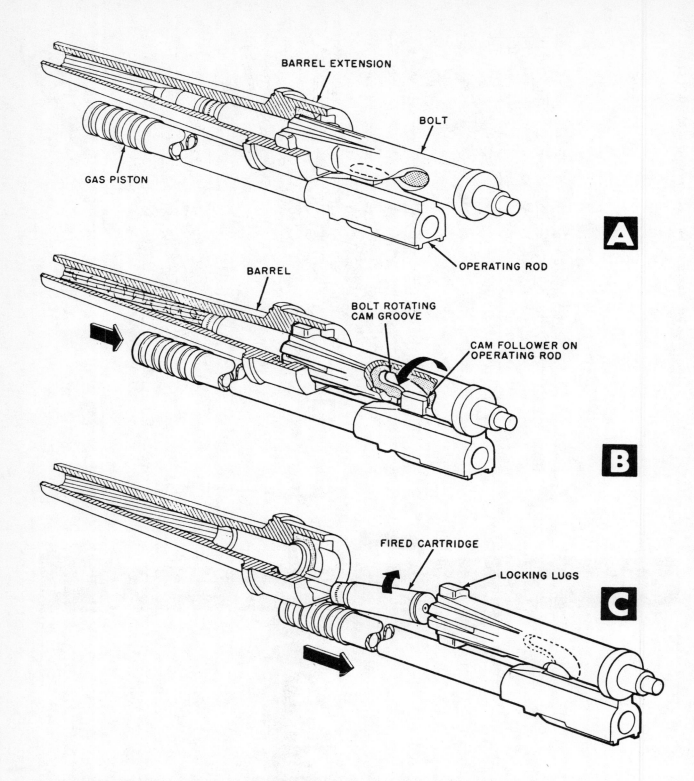

BARREL EXTENSION

BOLT

GAS PISTON

OPERATING ROD

A

BARREL

BOLT ROTATING CAM GROOVE

CAM FOLLOWER ON OPERATING ROD

B

FIRED CARTRIDGE

LOCKING LUGS

C

FG42 Bolt Mechanism adapted for use in the M60 Machine Gun. The bolt is unlocked by action of the operating rod on a cam groove in the bolt. Diagram taken from G. M. Chinn, *The Machine Gun*.

to the left. This carries the cartridge feed pawl plate assembly to the left where the pawls drop over and engage the next or second round for transport and remain there until the round in the plate is stripped and fired.

As the bolt recoils, the actuator forces the feed cam to the left, and the feed pawl assembly transports the round to the right into the feed plate groove. The round is forced down into the groove by the cartridge guides and their springs. The empty link left on the plate is pushed out the port in the feed plate by the new round as it is fed. The feed plate contains a spring-loaded retaining pawl that retains the belt, holding the second round when the first round is in the plate groove. Two anti-friction rollers help guide the belt in place and support the hanging belt. The weapon is provided with sufficient reserve power to lift a 100-round belt vertically under all normal operating conditions.

7.62mm M60E1 Machine Gun with barrel removed.

Special Note on the M60 Machine Gun

The M60 is the first United States machine gun to have a true quick change barrel. It was specifically designed for light weight, and components design was simplified for manufacture. Stampings or fabrications were used wherever possible. The quick change barrel, light weight and adaptability for use as either a heavy or light machine gun, as well as relative ease of manufacture, make the M60 superior to the Browning guns it replaces. The performance of the lined and plated barrel of the M60 in sustained fire is exceptional. An added factor of advantage in the case of the M60 versus the Brownings is that the M60, like most other weapons with a quick change barrel, has no head-space adjustment problem.

The M60 has been modified somewhat since original manufacture. The receiver has been strengthened by the addition of several pins, and the feed tray now has a hanger assembly pinned to it. The hanger assembly is used with a 100-round ammunition box, for some peculiar reason called a bandoleer in some publications. The box or bandoleer is merely slipped down over the hanger and makes it relatively easy to move the gun around with ammunition in place ready to fire.

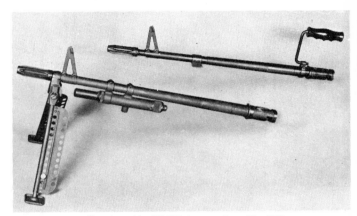

Top: barrel for M60E1; bottom: barrel for M60.

7.62mm M60E1 MACHINE GUN

A modified version of the M60 machine gun, the M60E1, has been developed. The principal reason for the development is to simplify barrel change and decrease the number of parts. This weapon differs from the M60 as follows: (1) The barrel does not have the bipod or gas cylinder attached to it. They are attached to the gas cylinder tube; (2) The bipod is attached semi-permanently to the rear of the gas cylinder; (3) The gas cylinder has been simplified and has no threads. It has a "U" shaped key to retain the gas cylinder extension; (4) The operating rod guide tube has a lug that retains the gas cylinder and bipod on the weapon and eliminates the gas cylinder nut; (5) The modified spool type gas piston has no holes; (6) The modified rear sight has the lateral adjustment increased by 20 mils; (7) The modified die-cast feed cover eliminates parts and allows the cover to be closed whether the bolt is in the forward or cocked position; (8) The modified feed tray eliminates parts; (9) The magazine hanger fitted to the left side of the weapon eliminates parts and can be used either with a modified magazine or a modified bandolier; (10) The new die-cast forearm eliminates parts and eases changing the barrel because the absence of the forearm cover allows the carrying handle to be fitted to the barrel; (11) The sling swivels have been relocated to the left side of the forearm and the top rear of the buttstock easing the carrying of the weapon; (12) The carrying handle has been increased in diameter.

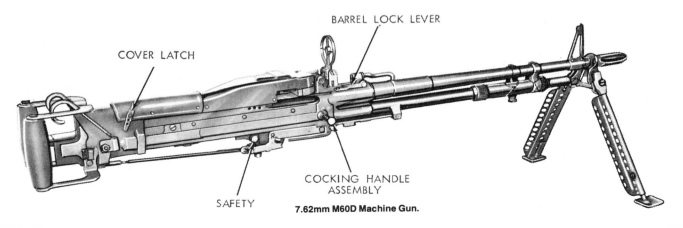

COVER LATCH

BARREL LOCK LEVER

SAFETY

COCKING HANDLE ASSEMBLY

7.62mm M60D Machine Gun.

M60C AND M60D

The M60C is a modification of the M60 machine gun for use on helicopter armament kits. The weapon has the stock removed and is remotely charged and fired. The M60D also has the stock removed and the pistol grip as well. The trigger has been relocated to the rear, and spade type grips have been fitted. This gun is used on flexible pedestal type and other mounts on helicopters and gunships.

M60E2

Maremont Corporation, manufacturer of the M60, also developed a tank version called the M60E2 (See Chapter 2.). This weapon has a barrel extension and gas evacuator tube that keep the propellant fumes from entering the interior of the tank.

ARMAMENT SUB-SYSTEM, HELICOPTER, 7.62MM
M.G., TWIN: M2
(INSTALLED ON OH-13 HELICOPTER)

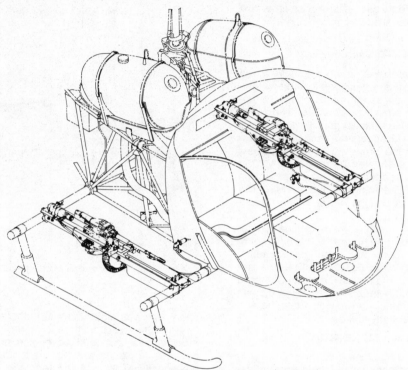

M60C on early helicopter armament system.

M60C on Helicopter Armament System M2.

M60D used as door gun.

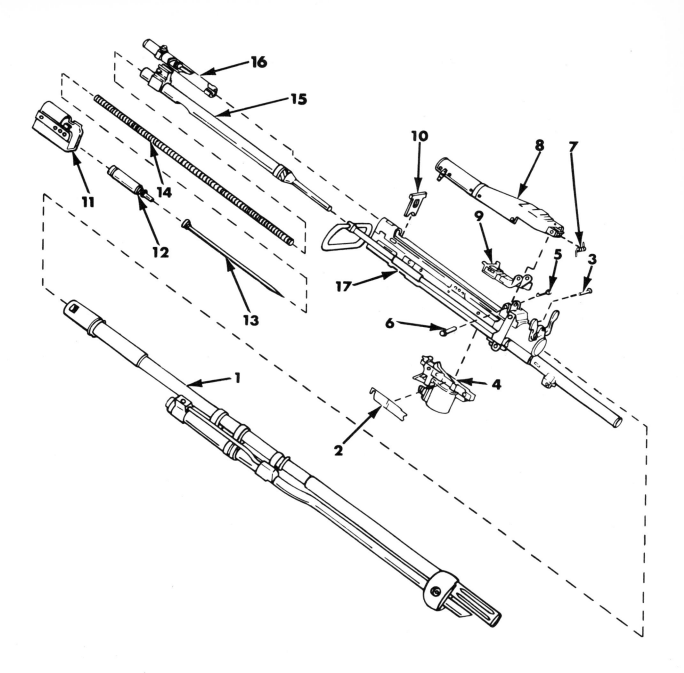

M60E2 Tank Machine Gun.

1. Barrel and evacuator assembly.
2. Leaf spring.
3. Pin.
4. Electric actuator group.
5. Latch.
6. Pin.

7. Spring.
8. Feed cover.
9. Feed tray assembly.
10. Yoke.
11. Backplate assembly.
12. Buffer assembly.

13. Buffer guide.
14. Drive spring.
15. Operating rod.
16. Bolt.
17. Receiver.

THE 7.62mm NATO M73 TANK MACHINE GUN

The development of the M73 (formerly known as the T197E2) was the result of the need for a rifle-caliber machine gun designed specifically for use in tanks. (See Chapter 2.) The M73 has a quick change barrel and can be fed from either side. The M73 uses the same link, the M13, that is used with the M60 general purpose machine gun. It can be charged and fired by either manual operation or solenoid. The barrel jacket of the M73 is to be attached to the tank in a semipermanent manner, and all the working components of the weapon, plus the barrel, can be removed from inside the tank for cleaning and repair.

How to Load and Fire the M73

Preparation for Firing. Open cover by pressing the cover latching rod on the side of the receiver from which the belt will be fed. Pivot the cover to an open position.

Retract the action to seared position, using the charging mechanism; make sure that the safety is at the "F" position. NOTE: Mount the charger on either left or right side of the receiver as determined by the mounting conditions of the weapon. Slide the charger connector to the proper side by pressing the retainer and sliding the connector manually.

Quick change barrel of M73.

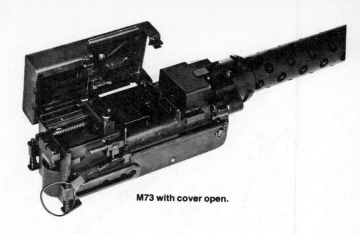

M73 with cover open.

Slide the safety to the safe position, exposing the letter "S" on the back plate.

Visually inspect the barrel chamber and inside of receiver for assurance against possible obstructions.

To load the weapon, insert the cartridge belt with the first round in the slot of the feed tray (open side of link loops facing downward).

Press the cover latch rod, close the cover, and release the cover latch rod to the lock position.

Firing. Slide the safety in the back plate to the fire position, exposing the letter "F" on the back plate ("S" for safe).

Actuate the solenoid for remote firing.

Press the trigger on the back plate for manual firing.

Immediate Action Procedure (to resume fire after a stoppage). When a stoppage occurs BEFORE COMPLETING A 200-ROUND SERIES (starting from a cool gun), perform the operations listed below in the given order. (If weapon starts after the first operation, do not perform the next, etc.)

(1) Charge weapon fully to sear position and fire.
(2) Repeat above twice if weapon does not respond.

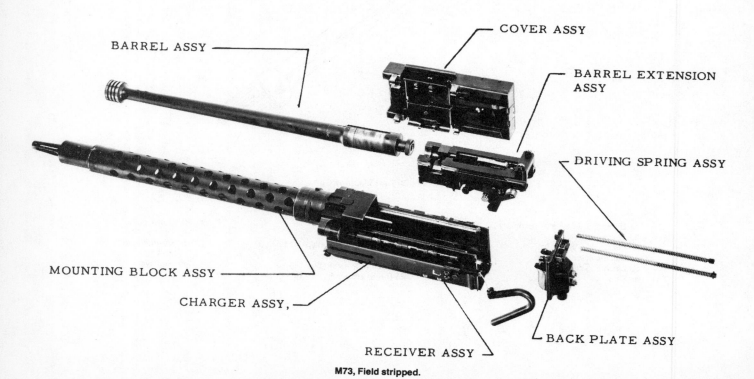

M73, Field stripped.

(3) Charge weapon fully and hold back on charger. Then—

(4) Open cover and remove belted ammunition.

(5) Open feed tray and remove live or spent cartridges from the action.

(6) Charge and hand-function weapon.

(7) Load and fire.

(8) If the weapon still does not fire, inspect for broken parts. NOTE: To prevent the possibility of an open-breech cookoff with the cover open, proceed as follows: When a stoppage occurs AFTER FIRING MORE THAN A 200-ROUND SERIES (starting from a cool gun), charge and fire three times. If weapon does not resume fire at this point, charge fully (do not open cover) and allow the gun to cool to near-ambient temperature before opening cover as above.

Feed Change. Observe the following instructions when changing from left-hand to right-hand feed:

Remove the cover assembly from the receiver.

Swing the feed tray to a vertical position relative to the receiver by disengaging it from one of the cover latching rods. Press the plunger of the round stop, and slide the round stop to engage the locating hole on the left side of the feed tray. In this position, the "R" on the round stop will be adjacent to the "R" on the feed tray ("L" and "L" for left-hand feed).

Follow operations listed below to convert the cover assembly from left to right.

Stripping the M73

Actuate the trigger to insure that the weapon is in the forward position.

Press the cover latch rod at either side of the receiver and raise the cover and feed tray assemblies to clear the latch rod. Release the cover latch rod and allow the cover and feed tray to rest on the rod. Press the second rod, and remove the cover and feed tray from the receiver.

With action forward, press and rotate counterclockwise the driving spring rods. Withdraw the driving spring and guide rod assemblies through the holes in the backplate.

Slide the backplate assembly vertically from the receiver housing.

Depress the buffer support lever at either side of the receiver and slide the barrel extension with the barrel to the rear, by pulling the charger handle. Remove the barrel extension and the barrel from the rear of the receiver. NOTE: An alternate method of field stripping is to pull on either receiver disconnector and pivot the receiver down and about the opposite receiver disconnector. Remove the receiver from the mounting block by withdrawing the second receiver disconnector. Proceed as above and withdraw barrel from mounting block assembly.

Assembly. Assemble the weapon by reversing the procedure given above.

Slide the feed support retainer away from the feed cam.

M73C Machine Gun on XM132 Tripod.

Slide the feed cam fully forward and lift it out, retaining it in hand.

Lift out the feed support and retain this in the same hand.

Remove the feed track and slide as a unit. Reassemble this unit to the cover after turning it end for end (180°). This will align the "R" of the feed track with an "R" in the cover ("L" and "L" for left hand feed).

Slide the feed support retainer fully to the opposite side of the cover.

Replace the feed support.

With the "R" side of the feed cam facing up, assemble to the cover in the fully forward position ("R" on cam adjacent to "R" on cover), picking up the feed slide roller during the operation. (Assembly notches prevent improper assembly.) Slide feed cam to rear of cover.

Slide the feed support retainer to the central lock position where it will secure the assembly. NOTE: In changing from right-hand to left-hand feed, reverse the foregoing procedure.

Reassemble the cover to the receiver by placing it in proper position and pressing the two cover latching rods.

How the M73 Works

Operational Power. The energy of recoil is supplied by the momentum of the recoiling parts and a muzzle booster driving the action rearward to buffer contact. Counterrecoil energy is supplied by the driving springs and the buffer spring that were compressed during the recoil cycle. The open-bolt action employs the driving springs alone and counterrecoil for the first shot from the sear position.

Recoil Movement. During the rearward movement of the barrel extension, the attached lever linkage actuates the rammer assembly by means of opening closing cams located in the sides of the receiver. The rearward movement of the barrel extension enables the sliding breechblock to move transversely to the right and away from the base of the chambered cartridge case. The extractor with the rammer grips the rim of the case and removes the spent round from the chamber, carrying it rearward to engage the round carrier grips. At this point, the spent case is transferred from the extractor to the round carrier grips. In the interim, the hammer, which is assembled to the barrel extension, is cocked by the cocking cam and is secured in the seared position by the sear assembly. At this stage of the recoil cycle, the ammunition will have been fed into the path of the retracted rammer assembly by the barrel extension and the connected feed cam in the cover assembly. The buffer assembly that is attached to the receiver trunnion block limits the rearward travel of the recoil mechanism.

Counterrecoil Movement. Energy of the driving springs and buffer return spring forces the barrel extension forward. During this movement, the rammer assembly strips and chambers the next round; the round carrier transports the empty case downward where it is dislodged by a fixed ejector; the breech assembly locks the next round in position; the rate control slide is released to actuate the hammer sear and allow the hammer to fall on the firing pin extension. The forward motion of the barrel extension is limited by the trunnion block in the receiver.

Firing will cease when the trigger is released and the barrel extension is engaged in the open-bolt position by the sear.

Special Note on the M73

As the result of field experience, a number of changes have been made to the M73 machine gun. They are as follows:

(1) A new front barrel bearing, jacket booster assembly and flash hider assembly have been fitted.

(2) New right-hand and left-hand round (cartridge) carriers have been fitted.

(3) A new case carrier link assembly has been fitted.

(4) A new retainer lock has been fitted.

(5) A new sear hammer has been fitted.

(6) Modified springs have been fitted to the barrel extension, the case carrier assembly and the trigger.

(7) The barrel has been modified.

(8) The firing solenoid lever has been modified.

(9) The trigger sear has been modified.

(10) The feed pawl has been modified.

(11) Rings and a washer have been added to the barrel disconnector to ease barrel removal.

7.62mm Machine Gun M73C on XM132 Tripod

This is the flexible version of the fixed M73 tank machine gun. It is basically the same gun as the M73, with sights and a pistol grip trigger added. The solenoid, which is normally used to fire the gun in a tank, is integral with the back plate and remains on the M73C. The weapon is loaded as the M73 and is fired as follows.

Slide the safety in the back plate to the fire position—letter "F" exposed. Push down on trigger.

The XM132 tripod mount is the caliber .30 M2 mount with a special adaptor for the M73C. This weapon exists only in prototype form.

7.62mm MACHINE GUN M219 (M73E1)

The M219 is a simplified, product-improved M73. The basic difference in design of the two weapons is in the ejection system. The ejection system has been simplified considerably in that the cartridge case carrier mechanism used in the case ejection cycle of the M73 has been replaced by fixed ejectors located on the underside of the feed tray. The rammer assembly, buffer rod, buffer support tension spring and receiver are modified to be compatible with the fixed ejectors. As indicated in Chapter 2, both the M73 and the M219 Machine Guns will be replaced by the M240 (the FN MAG tank version). The Marine Corps will use the M60E2 as their coaxial gun in the M60 series of Tanks. A complete discussion of the M240 Tank Machine Gun is presented in Chapter 9 (Belgium).

7.62mm M219 Machine Gun.

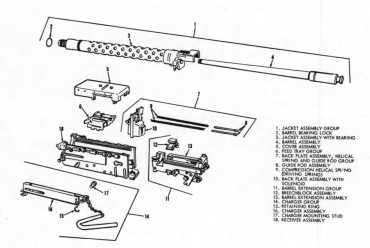

1. JACKET ASSEMBLY GROUP
2. BARREL BEARING LOCK
3. JACKET ASSEMBLY WITH BEARING
4. BARREL ASSEMBLY
5. COVER ASSEMBLY
6. FEED TRAY GROUP
7. BACK PLATE ASSEMBLY, HELICAL SPRING AND GUIDE ROD GROUP
8. GUIDE ROD ASSEMBLY
9. COMPRESSION HELICAL SPRING (DRIVING SPRING)
10. BACK PLATE ASSEMBLY WITH SOLENOID
11. BARREL EXTENSION GROUP
12. BREECHBLOCK ASSEMBLY
13. BARREL EXTENSION ASSEMBLY
14. CHARGER GROUP
15. RETAINING RING
16. CHARGER ASSEMBLY
17. CHARGER MOUNTING STUD
18. RECEIVER ASSEMBLY

Exploded view 7.62mm M219 Machine Gun.

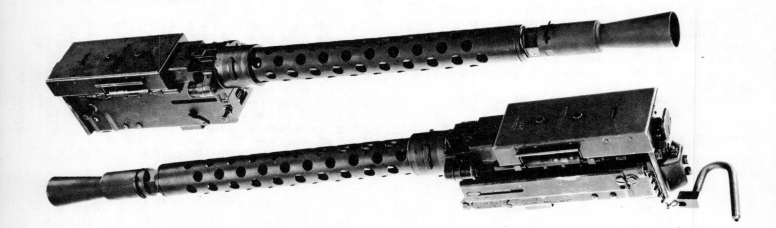

7.62mm Tank Machine Gun M73.

BROWNING CAL. .50 HEAVY BARREL M2 MACHINE GUN

The caliber .50 M2 Heavy Barrel is the ground gun of the M2 Browning series, which also include the aircraft and water-cooled antiaircraft guns. A turret type version of the M2 heavy barrel also exists; it was mainly used on multiple A.A. mounts. The aircraft and water-cooled antiaircraft guns are not too frequently encountered at present, but the heavy barrel is still in wide use throughout the world.

Caliber .50 Browning M2 Heavy Barrel Machine Gun.

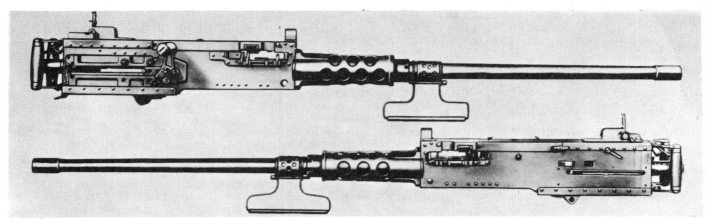

The M2, Heavy Barrel, Flexible.

Tripod Mount

A tripod mount is provided for the Browning machine gun caliber .50 HB M2. The tripod assembly weighs about 40 1/2 pounds, while the pintle and elevating mechanism assemblies weigh another 4 pounds.

Loading and Firing the M2

To provide for mounting in aircraft or in vehicles where position or space available require a right-hand feed, this gun is fitted with a bolt and feed mechanism that is inter-changeable for right- or left-hand feed.

Ammunition box is mounted on the side of the gun and belt fed through the feed block from the side set for feed. Pull belt through as far as it will go, and while retaining grip pull back retracting slide handle as far as it will go and permit it to run forward. This half-loads the gun. Pull the retracting handle back again as far as it will go and release to complete loading.

Note that in this gun the bolt latch release must be locked down before bolt is retracted for loading the gun.

Unlock the bolt latch release by pressing down on it. Pressure on the thumb trigger will now fire the gun. It should be fired only in short bursts.

To Unload the M2. Lift the cover and remove the belt. Pull back the retracting slide handle and look and feel in the feedway, the slot and the chamber to be sure the gun is unloaded.

Release the bolt and let it go forward and then lower the cover.

Press the trigger. If the bolt latch release is unlocked, alternately pressing the trigger, then the bolt latch release will fire the single shots.

If the bolt latch is locked down and the trigger pressed and held, the gun fires until the trigger pressure is released.

Field Stripping the M2

Grasp the barrel handle firmly and unscrew until the barrel is free from the barrel extension, then withdraw it to the front.

Release cover latch and raise cover as far as it will go.

Release back plate latch lock and also the back plate latch; this will permit the back plate to be lifted up out of the top of the receiver.

Push the protruding end of the driving spring rod forward and away from the slide plate and ease out the spring and the rod.

Pull the bolt back until the bolt stop lines up with the hole in the center of the slot in the side plate and then pull the bolt stud out to the right.

The complete bolt may now be removed from the rear of the casing. Driving spring unit need not be removed.

Insert the point of a bullet in the small hole at the rear of the right side plate to compress the oil buffer body spring lock. Oil buffer, barrel extension and the barrel assembly may now be taken back and out of the gun.

Pressing the accelerator forward permits the oil buffer assembly to be detached from the barrel extension.

This completes the field stripping. Cover should not be removed or dismounted except for repairs, as considerable force is required to compress the pawl spring for reassembly, making this a difficult operation.

Assembly of M2. Reverse the dismounting procedure.

Insert oil buffer into the oil buffer body from the rear, making sure that the cross groove in the piston is on the upper side where it can engage the shank of the barrel extension.

Assemble the buffer and buffer body to the extension. Holding the accelerator up under the barrel extension shank, start the breech lock depressors into their guideway in the barrel extension, and press forward permitting the shank of the barrel extension to engage the cross groove in the piston rod. Thrust sharply forward as far as oil buffer will go. The parts will now lock together and may be assembled into the receiver as a single unit. Press forward until the oil buffer spring locks in its recess in the right side plate.

Insert extractor in bolt and check that cocking lever is fully forward. Then insert bolt into rear of receiver. Press the rear end of the bolt down to elevate the front end just enough to clear the accelerator, otherwise the accelerator will be tripped and will not permit the bolt to be moved forward. When the accelerator has been cleared, raise the rear of the bolt to clear the buffer body. To do this it will be necessary to raise the bolt latch by reaching under the rear of the top plate with thumb or finger of one hand, while the other hand pushes the bolt forward. Bolt latch must be kept in raised position until rear of bolt passes in front of it. If this is not done, its spring will force it downward and engage the notch in the rear of the bolt preventing the bolt from going forward.

Push the bolt forward until the bolt stud hole lines up with the hole in the slot in the side plate; then insert the bolt stud until its shoulders are inside the side plate.

Insert the driving spring rod assembly and push the bolt all the way forward and keep the stud at the rear end of the driving spring rod at the recess in the right side plate.

Holding out the back plate latch lock, insert the back plate from the top. Press the trigger.

Make sure that the bolt is fully home, then close the cover. If the bolt is not fully forward, the feed lever will be forced down in front of the bolt which may result in malfunctioning.

Holding barrel by barrel handle, use both hands to insert it carefully in the front end of the barrel support. Guide the rear

end over the breech bearing until it contacts the threads of the barrel extension, then screw it in until definite resistance is met. Now back off two notches to make headspace adjustment.

Headspace Adjustment of M2

As in the case of the Browning cal. .30 machine gun, the headspace adjustment is the most important adjustment on this gun. It is not necessary to remove the barrel to make this adjustment on the caliber .50.

Remember that headspace means that space between the rear end of the barrel and the front face of the bolt; if this space is too wide the gun will function sluggishly or not at all and may pull the head away from the cartridge case causing serious jams; if it is too tight the recoiling parts will not go fully home and the gun may refuse to fire.

Screw the barrel up tight into the barrel extension, then pull back the slide and let bolt go forward to test the action.

If the action does not close fully, unscrew the barrel one notch. Then the test should be made again by pulling the bolt back and then letting it go forward.

The barrel may be unscrewed a notch at a time by pushing with the point of a bullet to rotate the barrel when the cover is raised and the bolt is in rearward position.

Work the bolt by hand several times, and if the breech does not close without effort, unscrew the barrel one notch.

Raise the cover and lift the extractor, then pull the bolt slightly to the rear. If it moves independently of the barrel extension, the adjustment is too loose. Screw the bolt up one notch and then repeat the test. When a dummy cartridge is in the chamber, there must be no rearward motion of the bolt independent of that of the barrel extension before the unlocking action takes place.

Headspace test should be made whenever gun is prepared for firing.

How the M2 Works

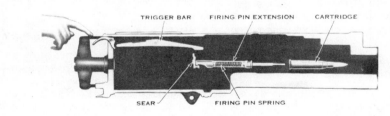

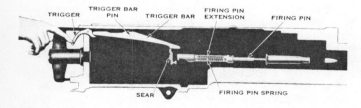

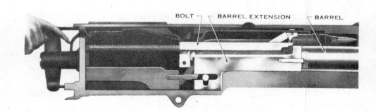

Starting with the gun loaded and cocked, the action is as follows. Pressing the trigger raises the back end of the trigger bar, which pivots on the trigger bar pin and presses its front end down on the top of the sear. The sear is forced down until its notch disengages from the shoulder of the firing pin extension. This permits the firing pin extension and the firing pin to be driven forward by the coiled firing pin spring. The firing pin strikes the primer of the cartridge and explodes the powder.

Recoil Action. As the bullet starts down the barrel, the rearward force of the recoil drives the securely locked recoiling

mechanism directly to the rear. During this initial motion, the bolt is supported securely against the base of the cartridge by the breech lock, which rides up from the barrel extension into a notch in the underside of the bolt.

After a travel of about 3/4 inch, during which time the bullet has left the barrel, the breech lock is pushed back off its cam. It is forced down out of its locking notch on the underside of the bolt by the breech lock depressors riding up and over the lock pin, which passes through the breech lock and protrudes on either side. This action unlocks the bolt.

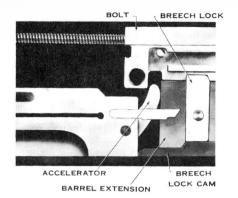

BOLT   BREECH LOCK

ACCELERATOR

BARREL EXTENSION

BREECH LOCK CAM

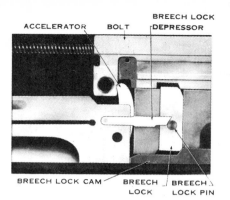

ACCELERATOR   BOLT   BREECH LOCK DEPRESSOR

BREECH LOCK CAM   BREECH LOCK   BREECH LOCK PIN

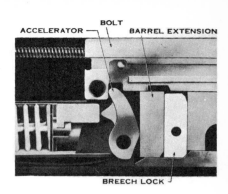

ACCELERATOR   BOLT   BARREL EXTENSION

BREECH LOCK

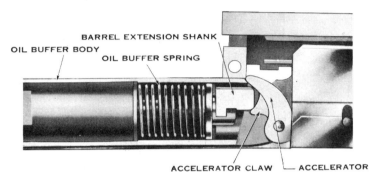

BARREL EXTENSION SHANK
OIL BUFFER BODY
OIL BUFFER SPRING

ACCELERATOR CLAW   ACCELERATOR

OIL BUFFER BODY

The barrel extension trips the accelerator up and to the rear of its pin. The tips of the accelerator striking the lower projection on the rear of the bolt accelerate its rearward travel. After a travel of about 1 1/8 inches, the barrel and barrel extension have completed their rearward travel. They are stopped by the oil buffer body assembly, whose oil buffer spring has been compressed in the oil buffer body by the shank in the barrel extension. The flipped-up claws of the accelerator lock the spring in compressed position as they are moved against the shoulders of the barrel extension shank.

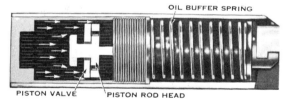

OIL BUFFER SPRING

PISTON VALVE   PISTON ROD HEAD

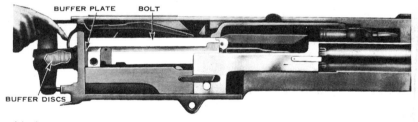

BUFFER PLATE   BOLT

BUFFER DISCS

Meanwhile a piston rod head in the oil buffer assembly is forced from front to rear end of the oil buffer tube, and presses against oil in the tube to absorb the rearward shock of recoil until the oil escapes through the front side of the piston. This oil flow is through notches between the edge of the piston rod head and the oil buffer tube. This cushions the recoil and brings the rear- ward motion to a complete stop when the recoiling functions have been completed.

As the bolt travels to the rear, the driving springs inside it are compressed, and its rearward motion is stopped when the rear of the bolt strikes the buffer plate.

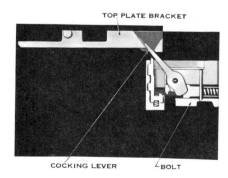

TOP PLATE BRACKET

COCKING LEVER   BOLT

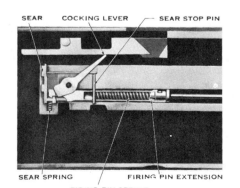

SEAR   COCKING LEVER   SEAR STOP PIN

SEAR SPRING   FIRING PIN EXTENSION

FIRING PIN SPRING

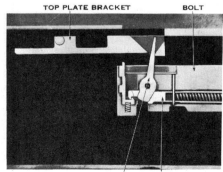

TOP PLATE BRACKET   BOLT

Cocking Action. The tip of the cocking lever protrudes through the top of the bolt where it lies in a V-slot in the top plate bracket. As the bolt starts to recoil, the tip of this cocking lever is pushed forward and its lower end is pivoted to force the firing extension rearward. This compresses the firing pin spring against the sear stop pin until the shoulder at the rear end on the firing pin extension hooks over the notch in the bottom of the sear under pressure of the sear spring.

When the bolt goes forward after the completion of the rearward motion, the tip of the cocking lever enters the V-slot in the top plate bracket, thus pivoting the bottom of the cocking lever out of the path of the firing pin extension to release the firing pin.

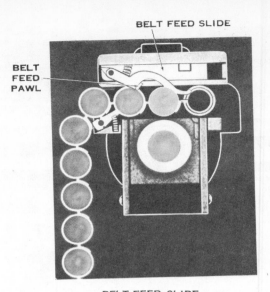

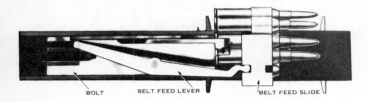

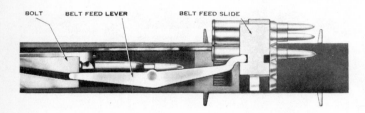

Feeding During the Rearward Motion. As the bolt moves to the rear, the stud at the rear of the belt feed lever is engaged in the diagonal groove on top of the bolt. This bolt stud thus serves to move the feed lever, which is pivoted near its center, and carry the belt feed slide at the front end of the lever out of the side of the gun where its spring snaps it down over the next cartridge in the ammunition belt.

The belt is pulled into the gun by the belt feed pawl attached to

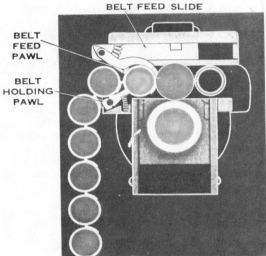

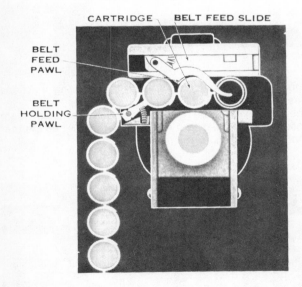

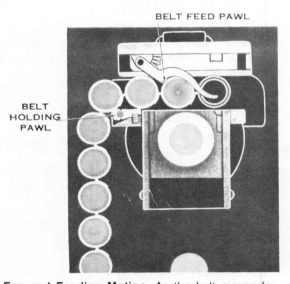

the belt-feed slide and ridges over the next cartridge.

As the recoiling motion is completed, the belt-feed slide has traveled far enough to permit the belt-feed pawl to be snapped down by its spring behind the next cartridge, ready to pull the belt forward into the gun on the next motion.

Forward Feeding Motion. As the bolt moves forward, the stud riding in its top pulls on the pivotal belt feed lever. The belt holding pawl is forced downwards as the cartridge is pulled over it and the belt holding pawl snaps up behind the next cartridge.

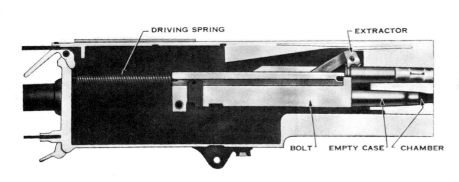

DRIVING SPRING · EXTRACTOR

BOLT · EMPTY CASE · CHAMBER

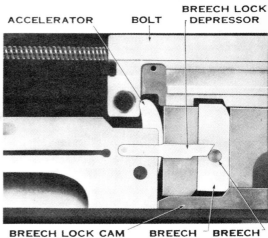

ACCELERATOR · BOLT · BREECH LOCK DEPRESSOR

BREECH LOCK CAM · BREECH LOCK · BREECH LOCK PIN

Extraction and Ejection. When the rearward motion starts, the extractor mounted in the side of the bolt and with its head above the bolt level snaps down into the cannelure of the cartridge in the belt, then draws the cartridge back out of the ammunition belt. The empty cartridge case is held in the T-slot in the front face of the bolt and the bolt withdraws it from the chamber.

The top front edge of the breech lock and the front side of the notch in the bolt are beveled to start withdrawals of the empty cartridge case slowly to prevent the case from being torn apart by the sudden jerking motion. As the breech lock is unlatched, the bolt pulls away from the barrel and barrel extension easily enough to prevent rupturing the cartridge case.

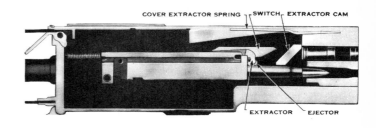

COVER EXTRACTOR SPRING · SWITCH · EXTRACTOR CAM

EXTRACTOR · EJECTOR

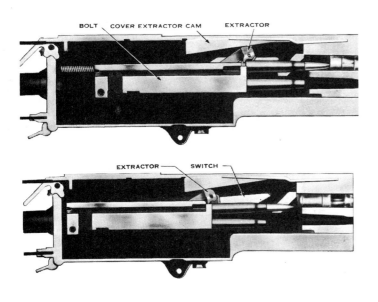

BOLT · COVER EXTRACTOR CAM · EXTRACTOR

EXTRACTOR · SWITCH

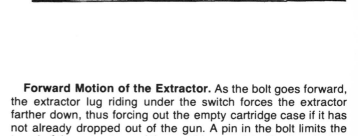

DRIVING SPRING · BOLT · ACCELERATOR

The cam on the inside of the cover forces the head of the extractor down, pushing the loaded cartridge into the mouth of the T-slot in the bolt. A lug on the side of the extractor rides against the top of the switch causing it to pivot downward at the rear; as the recoiling motion comes to an end, the lug on the extractor overrides the end of this switch, permitting it to snap up into normal position.

During this movement, the empty cartridge case drops down out of the T-slot and is expelled through the bottom of the gun.

Forward Motion of the Extractor. As the bolt goes forward, the extractor lug riding under the switch forces the extractor farther down, thus forcing out the empty cartridge case if it has not already dropped out of the gun. A pin in the bolt limits the travel of the extractor and the cartridge, assisted by the ejector, is fed directly into the firing chamber.

When the cartridge is nearly chambered, the extractor rides up its cam compressing the cover extractor spring and is snapped into the cannelure of the next cartridge.

Further Action During Forward Movement. After the recoiling motion has been completed, the compressed driving spring and the compressed buffer disc force the bolt forward. The bolt travels about 5'', when the projection on its bottom strikes the tips of the accelerator, rolling the accelerator forward on its pin.

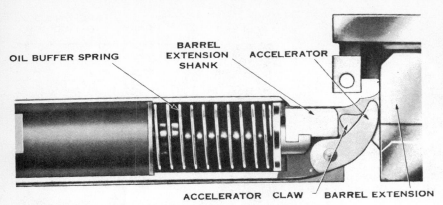

OIL BUFFER SPRING

BARREL EXTENSION SHANK

ACCELERATOR

ACCELERATOR CLAW — BARREL EXTENSION

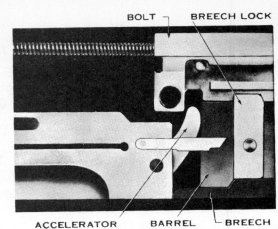

BOLT ⌐ BREECH LOCK

ACCELERATOR   BARREL EXTENSION   BREECH LOCK CAM

The accelerator claws are pulled away from the shoulder of the barrel extension shank, releasing the oil buffer spring. This spring now shoves the barrel extension on the barrel forward.

As the barrel extension goes forward, the breech lock strikes its cam and is forced upward on its pin. At that moment, the bolt has reached the position where the notch on its underside is directly above the breech lock; the breech lock rides up its cam and engages in this slot in the underside of the bolt. The bolt is locked to the breech end of the barrel just before the recoiling section reaches firing position.

Oil Buffer. As the action moves forward, additional openings for oil flow are provided in the piston rod head of the oil buffer assembly. The piston valve is forced away from the rod head as the parts move forward to uncover these openings. Thus the oil is permitted to escape freely from the opening in the center of

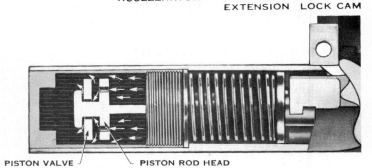

PISTON VALVE   PISTON ROD HEAD

R. S. ELEVATING SCREW KNOB
R. S. SLIDE   R. S. COVER PLATE AND SCREW
R. S. LEAF   R. S. BASE SCREWS
R. S. WINDAGE SCALE, AND SCREWS   R. S. BASE
R. S. BASE SCREW   TELESCOPIC SIGHT CLAMP AND SPRINGS
R. S. WINDAGE CLICK PLUNGER, AND SPRING   R. S. LEAF STOP
R. S. WINDAGE KNOB PIN   R. S. WINDAGE SCREW
R. S. WINDAGE SCREW KNOB
TELESCOPIC SIGHT CLAMP SCREW, HANDLE, AND SPRING
RETAINING PIN
REAR SIGHT BASE SPRING
BOLT LATCH PLUNGER AND SPRING
BOLT LATCH STOP SCREW AND NUT
TRIGGER (AND BOLT LATCH RELEASE) SPRINGS
SPADE GRIP BACK PLATE ASSEMBLY
BACK PLATE LATCH AND TRIGGER PIN
BOLT LATCH RELEASE
TRIGGER
ADJUSTING SCREW PLUNGER, AND SPRING
BUFFER TUBE SLEEVE
ADJUSTING SCREW
22 (OR MORE) BUFFER DISCS
BACK PLATE LATCH LOCK, PIN, AND SPRING
BACK PLATE LATCH, AND SPRING
BUFFER PLATE
BACK PLATE LATCH LOCK PIN, AND COTTER PIN

BOLT LATCH
BOLT LATCH ROD
BOLT LATCH PIN
BOLT LATCH BRACKET
BOLT LATCH SPRING
RETRACTING SLIDE BRACKET BOLTS
BOLT LATCH ROD NUT, AND COTTER PIN
BACK PLATE LATCH PIN

BARREL CARRIER HANDLE ASSEMBLY
BARREL CARRIER BOLT HEAD, AND PIN
FRONT SIGHT COVER AND PINS
FRONT SIGHT BLADE
BREECH BEARING LOCK SCREW
BARREL CARRIER BOLT, AND SPRING
BARREL CARRIER SLEEVE ASSEMBLY, AND BOLT PIN
BARREL
BARREL SUPPORT
BREECH BEARING
TRUNNION BLOCK SHIM
RETRACTING SLIDE PLUNGER, AND SPRING
RETRACTING SLIDE PLUNGER PIN
RETRACTING SLIDE GRIP ASSEMBLY
RETRACTING SLIDE NUT, AND COTTER PIN
RETRACTING SLIDE STUD WASHER
RETRACTING SLIDE LEVER
RETRACTING SLIDE SPRING
RETRACTING SLIDE STUD
RETRACTING SLIDE BRACKET NUTS
RETRACTING SLIDE BRACKET
RETRACTING SLIDE ASSEMBLY
RETRACTING SLIDE BRACKET SCREW (3 EACH)

M2 Browning Heavy Barrel Machine Gun.

the piston valve as well as at the edge of the valve near the tube wall, and so prepare it for the rearward motion.

Oil Buffer Adjustment. The oil buffer provides a method of regulating the speed of fire of this gun. Fire rate may be regulated by turning the oil buffer tube the required number of clicks. Turning the buffer tube to the left opens the oil buffer and permits oil to pass through the large ports, increasing the rate of fire. Turning the buffer tube to the right tightens up the oil buffer allowing it to absorb more recoil and reduce the rate of fire. This tube may be turned by inserting a screwdriver in the slot in the rear of the buffer tube.

Automatic Fire. If the trigger is pressed and held down, the sear is depressed as its tip is pressed against the cam surface of the trigger bar by the forward motion of the bolt just before it completes its forward motion. The notch in the bottom of the sear releases the firing pin extension and firing pin, automatically firing the cartridge as the forward motion is completed and continuing the action as long as the trigger is held and cartridges are fed into the gun.

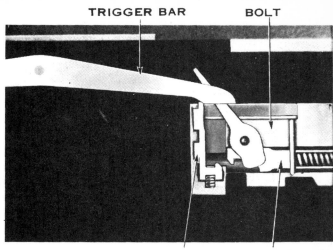

CALIBER .50 TANK MACHINE GUN M85

The M85 was developed by the Aircraft Armaments Corp. of Cockeysville, Md., as the T175E2 machine gun. It fills a requirement of the Armored Forces for a cal. .50 weapon suitable for co-axial or cupola mounting, having a dual rate of fire and quick change barrel and being shorter and lighter than the cal. .50

Browning. This weapon is not yet in service.

The requirement for a dual rate of fire originated from the desire to have a high rate of fire for use against low-flying aircraft, and a low rate of fire for use against ground targets. While the cal. .50 Browning M2, HB, has an almost ideal rate for use against ground targets, its rate of fire for use against modern attack aircraft leaves something to be desired.

Caliber .50 Tank Machine Gun M85.

How to Load and Fire the M85.

Open the cover and visually inspect the chamber to assure that chamber is clear. The bolt must be in the battery (closed) position before the ammunition belt is set in the feedway. Place the first round in the belt inboard of the two belt holding pawls. The belted ammunition must be placed in the gun with the open side of the links downward. Close the cover; the gun can be loaded without opening the cover if necessary. Pull bolt to the rear with the hand charger. Place safety on safe position. Set the rate selector lever to the proper position for the desired rate of fire. For high rate of fire, turn the lever completely to the left. For low rate of fire, turn the lever completely to the right. Do not change rate selector while firing a burst. Release the safety and fire the gun electrically by depressing the electrical trigger switch or manually by pushing forward on the manual trigger.

How to Field Strip the M85

Check to see that gun is not loaded. With hand charger control, allow the driving spring to slowly return the bolt to battery as follows:

(1) Pull back and hold hand charger.
(2) Depress trigger.
(3) Allow the driving spring to slowly return the charging handle to the original position.

Remove the barrel. Transversely depress the lock on the barrel latch, full depress the barrel latch, rotate the barrel 90° until the head of the "unlock" arrow is in line with the head of the arrow on the barrel support, and pull the barrel forward out of the barrel support. Remove the cover and tray assemblies. Open the cover, withdraw the quick release pins by inserting the rim of a cartridge case in the annular groove at the top of the pin; using the cartridge case as a lever, pry out the pin; withdraw the tray. Depress the latch lock on the lower left side of the back plate, then depress the back plate latch and lift the back plate straight up off the receiver. Remove back plate slowly for the first inch as the preload on the driving spring may cause the buffer assembly to jump out. CAUTION: Do NOT attempt to disassemble gun with bolt in the REAR position. The driving spring is then heavily loaded and may cause injuries. Remove the bolt buffer assembly from the rear of the receiver. Depress the sear block detent, visible through the right side of the receiver, with the nose of a cartridge and withdraw the sear assembly out of the rear of the receiver. Remove the feed and ejector assembly; withdraw the front and rear quick release pins, which fasten the feed and ejector assembly to the receiver. Remove the feed assembly by first pulling its front end out from the side of the receiver, then pull the assembly forward out of the receiver. Pull the barrel extension assembly, with the bolt in it, out through the rear of the receiver. Withdraw the quick release pin from the side of the receiver and lift the accelerator assembly straight up out

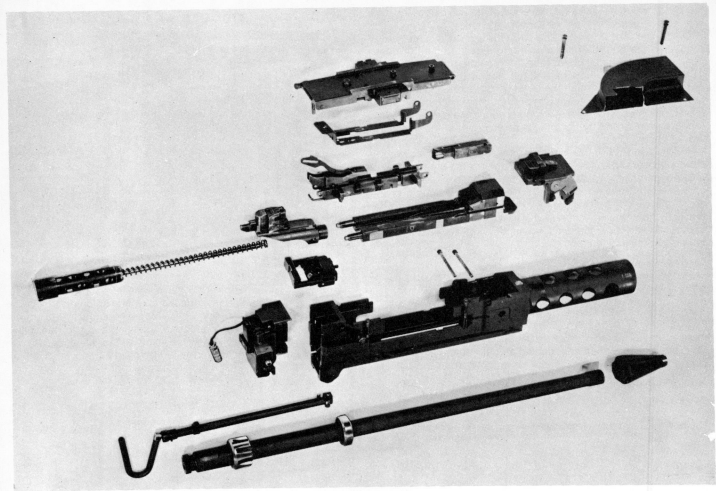

M85, field stripped.

of the receiver. Disengage the detent from the receiver by pulling on the knurled knob at the front end, and slide the hand charger forward. To reassemble, reverse the procedure given above.

Cyclic Operation—High Rate of Fire

Charging the Gun. To begin the cycle, the loaded gun must be hand charged. During the charging stroke, the feed mechanism is actuated by the bolt, positioning a round on the center line of the gun, in the forward path of the bolt.

The bolt is held in the open-bolt position by the sear, with the bolt-driving spring compressed.

Stripping and Chambering of Round. When the firing switch is depressed, or the hand trigger is pressed, the solenoid plunger pushes the sear actuator forward about its pivot, camming the sear up and out of the bolt notch.

The bolt is driven toward battery position by the compressed bolt-driving spring.

The round in the feedway is picked up by the stripper on the bolt, is stripped through the belt link by the action of the bolt, and is deflected downward into the chamber by the chambering ramp.

Locking and Firing. The forward motion of the bolt block is arrested by the base of the chambered round, and the bottom extractor engages the extraction groove at the rim of the cartridge.

The bolt slide continues forward, wedging the bolt locks in place.

As the bolt slide completes its forward motion, the firing pin protrudes through the bolt block and strikes the cartridge primer, firing the round and initiating the recoil stroke.

Recoil Stroke. The feed mechanism, operated by the recoiling barrel extension through a feed spring and a feed cam, is actuated at the beginning of the recoil stroke.

As the barrel and the barrel extension begin to recoil, the barrel actuates the accelerator, thereby driving the bolt slide rearward at an accelerated speed.

As the bolt slide starts to move rearward, it cams the bolt locks inward, releasing the bolt block, which moves toward the rear, pulling the spent cartridge case out of the chamber and compressing the bolt-driving spring.

Ejection. The ejector mechanism is actuated by the action of the recoiling bolt on the ejector lever.

Just before cartridge ejection, the bottom extractor is disengaged from the extraction groove of the cartridge by the cam grooves in the barrel extension.

As the bolt continues rearward motion, the springloaded stripper is depressed by the income round.

The barrel group and the accelerator now start their return to battery position, driven by the barrel return springs and accelerator return springs.

As the ejector strikes the cartridge case, the case rotates about the side extractor and is thrown clear of the gun.

Bolt Buffing and Counterrecoil. As the bolt nears the end of its recoil stroke, it compresses the bolt buffer spring, which stops the rearward motion of the bolt.

By this time, the barrel group and the accelerator have returned to their battery position.

The compressed bolt buffer spring reverses the direction of the bolt, starting the counterrecoil stroke, and the cycle is repeated.

Firing will continue as long as the solenoid plunger remains forward, holding the bolt sear up, providing that ammunition is supplied.

The velocity of the counterrecoil stroke of the bolt is much higher on those cycles following the initial cycle because the force of the buffer spring adds to the force of the bolt-driving spring.

Cyclic Operation—Low Rate of Fire

Initial Action and Bolt Recoil. The rate selector lever is set for the low rate of fire, positioning the striker in the path of the bolt so that it is ready to actuate the time-delay drum.

The gun is loaded, hand charged, and initially fired, and the bolt recoils at the same velocity as during the high rate of fire.

Bolt Actuation of Time-Delay Drum. Near the end of the bolt recoil stroke, the bolt block extension contacts the striker, causing the time-delay drum to start rotating.

The drum rotation cams the yoke rearward, retracting the solenoid plunger.

The retraction of the solenoid plunger releases the sear actuator and the sear is forced down to locking position by its return spring. Drum rotation continues, winding up a torsion spring.

Bolt Searing and Time Delay. The bolt starts its counterrecoil stroke because of the action of the bolt buffer and driving springs, but is stopped by the sear.

During this time, the time-delay drum continues to rotate until it strikes a stop. Drum rotation is then reversed by the action of the wound torsion spring.

Bolt Release. The drum returns to its original position, driving the striker forward in preparation for the next bolt recoil stroke.

The yoke cam rollers fall into notches on the periphery of the drum, releasing the solenoid plunger.

The solenoid plunger moves forward, operating the sear by means of the sear actuator, and thus releasing the bolt. The bolt is driven forward on the counterrecoil stroke only by the driving force of the bolt-return spring.

This cycle is repeated as each round is fired.

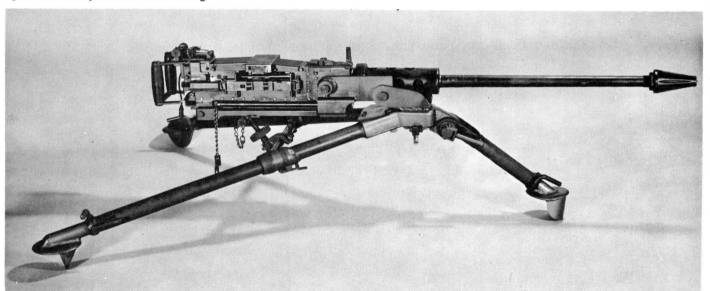

Caliber .50 Machine Gun M85C.

CHARACTERISTICS OF UNITED STATES SERVICE MACHINE GUNS

	Colt M1917	Browning M1917A1	Vickers M1918 Aircraft	M1919A4
Caliber:	.30.	.30.	.30.	.30.
System of operation:	Gas, automatic.	Recoil, automatic.	Recoil with gas assist, automatic.	Recoil automatic.
Length overall:	40.8 in.	38.5 in.	44.19 in.	41 in.
Barrel length:	28 in.	24 in.	28.4 in.	24 in.
Feed device:	250-round, fabric belt.	250-round, fabric belt or disintegrating link belt.	250-round, fabric belt or disintegrating link belt.	250-round, fabric belt or disintegrating link belt.
Sights: Front:	Blade.	Blade.	none— aircraft type fitted to the weapons as required.	Blade.
Rear:	Leaf.	Leaf.		Leaf.
Weight: Gun:	35 lb.	41 lb. w/water.	25 lb.	31 lb.
Mount:	61.25 lb.	53.15 lb. (M1917A1).		14 lb. (M2).
Muzzle velocity:	Approx. 2800 f.p.s.	2800 f.p.s.	Approx. 2800 f.p.s.	2800 f.p.s.
Cyclic rate:	480 r.p.m.	450-600 r.p.m.	800-900 r.p.m.	400-550 r.p.m.

CHARACTERISTICS OF UNITED STATES SERVICE MACHINE GUNS (Cont'd)

	M1919A6	M2 Aircraft	M37 Tank	M60	M73 Tank
Caliber:	.30.	.30.	.30.	7.62mm NATO.	7.62mm NATO
System of operation:	Recoil, automatic.	Recoil, automatic.	Recoil, automatic.	Gas, automatic.	Recoil, w/gas. assist, automatic.
Length overall:	53 in.	39.9 in.	41.75 in.	43.75 in.	34.75 in.
Barrel length:	24 in.	23.9 in.	24 in.	25.6 in.	22 in.
Feed device:	250-round, fabric belt or disintegrating link belt.	Disintegrating link belt.	Disintegrating link belt.	Disintegrating link belt.	Disintegrating link belt.
Sights: Front:	Blade.	None permanently attached to gun.	Blade.	Blade.	None permanently attached to gun.
Rear:	Leaf.		Leaf.	Leaf.	
Weight: Gun:	32.5 lb.	21.5 lb.(fixed gun). 23 lb. (flexible gun).	31 lb.	23.05 lb.	28 lb.
Mount:	14 lb. (M2)			15 lb. (M122)	
Muzzle velocity:	2800 f.p.s.	2800 f.p.s.	2800 f.p.s.	2800 f.p.s.	2800 f.p.s.
Cyclic rate:	400-500 r.p.m.	1000-1350 f.p.s.	400-550 r.p.m.	600 r.p.m.	450-500 r.p.m.

CHARACTERISTICS OF UNITED STATES SERVICE MACHINE GUNS (Cont'd)

	Johnson M1941	M1921A1 Antiaircraft	M2 Aircraft, Basic	M2 Heavy Barrel
Caliber:	.30.	.50.	.50.	.50.
System of operation:	Recoil, selective fire.	Recoil, automatic.	Recoil, automatic.	Recoil, selective fire.
Length overall:	42 in.	56 in.	56.25 in.	65.1 in.
Barrel length:	22 in.	36 in.	36 in.	45 in.
Feed device:	20-round, in line, detachable box magazine.	250-round, fabric belt or disintegrating link belt.	Disintegrating link belt.	disintegrating link belt.
Sights: Front:	Blade.	Hooded blade.	None permanently attached to gun.	Hooded blade.
Rear:	Adjustable folding aperture.	Leaf.		Leaf.
Weight: Gun:	Approx. 13 lb.	79 lb. w/o water.	61 lb.	84 lb.
Mount:				44 lb. (M3).
Muzzle velocity:	2800 f.p.s.	2840 f.p.s.	2840 f.p.s. (M2 ball).	2930 f.p.s. (M2 ball).
Cyclic rate:	400-450 r.p.m.	Approx. 500 r.p.m.	750-850 r.p.m.	450-550 r.p.m.

CHARACTERISTICS OF UNITED STATES SERVICE MACHINE GUNS (Cont'd)

	M2 Antiaircraft	M3 Aircraft	M85
Caliber:	.50.	.50.	.50.
System of operation:	Recoil, automatic.	Recoil, automatic.	Recoil, automatic.
Length overall:	66 in.	57.25 in.	54.5 in.
Barrel length:	45 in.	36 in.	36 in.
Feed device.	Disintegrating link belt.	Disintegrating link belt.	Disintegrating link belt.
Sights: Front:	Hooded blade.	None permanently attached to gun.	None permanently attached to gun.
Rear:	Leaf (may be found without rear sight).		
Weight: Gun:	121 lb. w/water.	68.75 lb. w/recoil adaptor.	61.5 lb.
Mount:	401 lb. (A.A. M3).		
Muzzle velocity:	2930 f.p.s. (M2 ball).	2840 f.p.s. (M2 ball).	2840 f.p.s. (M2 ball).
Cyclic rate:	500-650 r.p.m.	1150-1250 r.p.m.	Low rate: 450 ±50 r.p.m. High rate: 1050 ±50 r.p.m.

GRENADE LAUNCHERS

40 mm GRENADE LAUNCHER M79

The M79 grenade launcher is a shotgun type weapon designed to fire a high explosive grenade considerably more accurately than a grenade can be fired from a rifle grenade launcher.

Characteristics of M79 Grenade Launcher

Caliber: 40mm.
System of operation: Single-shot, break-open type.
Weight of launcher (loaded): 6.45 lbs.
Length of launcher: 28.78 in.
Length of barrel: 14 in.
Muzzle velocity: 250 f.p.s.
Sights: Front: Protected blade.
      Rear: Leaf, adjustable for windage.

How to Load and Fire the M79

Move barrel locking latch FULLY to the right and break open breech. Moving latch fully to right automatically puts the weapon on "safe." Insert cartridge in chamber until the extractor contacts the rim of the cartridge case. Close the breech, push safety to forward position exposing the letter "F." Pressure on the trigger will now fire the weapon.

How to Field Strip the M79

Under normal conditions, it should not be necessary (for maintenance purposes) to do more than break the weapon using the barrel locking latch. The firing pin retainer in the face of the standing breech can be tightened up from time to time by use of the lugs on the combination wrench supplied with the weapon. If the weapon has been immersed in water or snow, the following procedure should be followed. Remove the fore-end assembly by taking out screw that passes through the rear mounting hole of the front sling swivel. Pull front end of fore-end away from barrel until lug on the rear sight base is clear of the hole in upper surface of fore-end bracket. Keeping lug clear of hole, pull forward on fore-end assembly until it is free of receiver assembly. Operate barrel locking latch and open breech, holding the stock and receiver stationary, move the barrel rearward in the receiver until it is disengaged from the fulcrum pin. Separate barrel from receiver group. From bottom of stock, near front end, remove machine screw, lock washer and flat washer, which secure stock to receiver. Separate stock from receiver. To reassemble, perform the steps listed above in reverse.

40mm Grenade launcher M79.

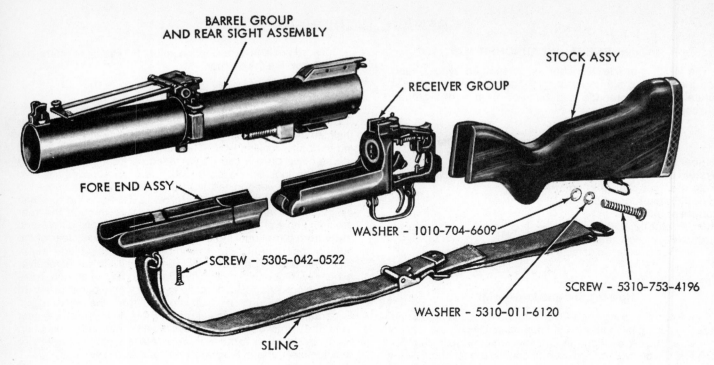

BARREL GROUP
AND REAR SIGHT ASSEMBLY

RECEIVER GROUP

STOCK ASSY

FORE END ASSY

WASHER - 1010-704-6609

SCREW - 5305-042-0522

SCREW - 5310-753-4196

WASHER - 5310-011-6120

SLING

40mm Grenade launcher M79, field-stripped.

40mm GRENADE LAUNCHER XM148

Now obsolete, the XM148 was developed by Colt Firearms to be attached to the M16 and other rifles. This launcher was loaded by sliding the barrel forward, inserting the grenade cartridge and retracting the barrel. The launcher was cocked by pulling the cocking handle to the rear. While the XM148 was well received due to the extra fire-power it gave to the rifle squad, the launcher itself was not considered reliable, simple nor safe enough for type standardization.

Characteristics of XM148

Caliber: 40mm.
System of operation: Single-shot; slide-open type.
Weight of launcher (loaded): 3.5 lbs.
Length of launcher (front of barrel to rear of extended trigger): 16.5 in.
Length of barrel: 10 in.
Muzzle velocity: 250 f.p.s.
Sights: Quadrant sight mounted on adjustable sight slide.

40mm GRENADE LAUNCHER M203

In the spring of 1967, development of a new rifle-attached grenade launcher was begun by the Department of the Army. Called Grenade Launcher Attachment Development (GLAD), this project led to the testing of designs produced by AAI Corporation, Ford Aerospace and Communication Corporation and Aero-Jet General. The AAI launcher, XM203, was standardized as the M203 in August 1969. an initial production contract was carried out by AAI. Beginning in January 1971, Colt has been the sole production source for the M203.

Field Stripping the M203

There are two methods for removing the forward moving barrel assembly.

First, depress the barrel latch and slide the barrel assembly forward. From the muzzle of the M16A1, count back to the fourth hole on the left side of the handguard. Insert the end of a section from the cleaning rod into the fourth hole, depress the barrel stop and slide the barrel assembly off the receiver track.

The XM148 Grenade Launcher attached to the M16A1 Rifle.

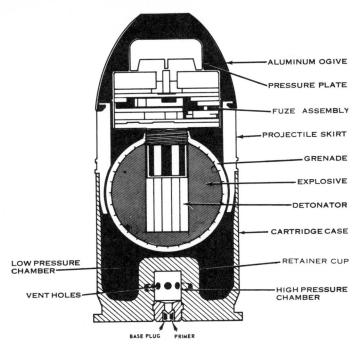

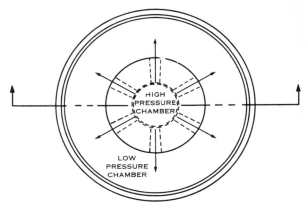

WHEN IGNITED BY THE PRIMER, THE PROPELLANT ENCLOSED IN THE BRASS POWDER CHARGE CUP (HIGH PRESSURE CHAMBER) RUPTURES THE CUP AT THE VENT HOLES AND IS VENTED INTO THE REMAINDER OF THE CARTRIDGE CASE (LOW PRESSURE CHAMBER)

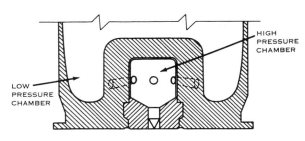

Typical 40mm High Explosive (HE) Grenade Cartridge for the M79 and M203 Launchers. Right; Operating principle for the high-low pressure chamber of the 40mm Grenade Cartridges.

*The ogive is the nose end of the cartridge.
**Not authorized for use with M203 Grenade launcher.

40mm CARTRIDGE IDENTIFICATION

Cartridge	Body	Color identification Ogive*	Lettering
40-mm, HE, M381 and M406	Green	Gold	Yellow
40-mm, HE, M386 and M441	Green	Gold	Yellow
40-mm, HE, M463 (smokeless, flashless)	Green	Black	Yellow
40-mm, HE, M397 (airburst)	Green	Gold	Yellow
40-mm, HE, M433 (dual purpose)	Green	Gold	Yellow
40-mm, practice, M382 and M407A1	Green	Silver	Yellow
40-mm, multiple projectile, XM576E1	Green	Black (SABOT)	White
40-mm, multiple projectile, XM576E2	Green	None	White
40-mm, green smoke parachute, XM658	Green	Green	Black
40-mm, white star parachute, XM583	White	White	Black
40-mm, red smoke parachute, XM659	Green	Red	Black
40-mm, white star cluster, XM585	White	White	Black
40-mm, yellow smoke parachute, XM660	Green	Yellow	Black
40-mm, violet smoke parachute, XM669	Green	Violet	Black
40-mm, tactical CS,XM651E1	Green	Gray	Black
40-mm, yellow smoke streamer, XM696	Green	Yellow	Black
40-mm, green star parachute, XM661	White	Green	Black
40-mm, green smoke streamer, XM697	Green	Green	Black
40-mm, red star parachute, XM662	White	Red	Black
40-mm, orange smoke streamer, XM698	Green	Orange	Black
40-mm, green star cluster, XM663	White	Green	Black
40-mm, red smoke streamer, XM699	Green	Red	Black
40-mm, red star cluster, XM664	White	Red	Black
40-mm, brown smoke streamer, XM700	Green	Brown	Black
40-mm, yellow smoke canopy, XM676	Green	Yellow	Black
40-mm, violet smoke streamer, XM701	Green	Violet	Black
40-mm, green smoke canopy, XM679	Green	Green	Black
40-mm, white smoke canopy, XM680	Green	White	Black
40-mm, violet smoke canopy, XM681	Green	Violet	Black
40-mm, red smoke canopy, XM682	Green	Red	Black
40-mm, riot control CS, XM674 (E24)**	Gray	N/A	Black
40-mm, riot control CS, XM675 (E25 RS)**	Light Green	N/A	Black
40-mm, orange star parachute, XM695	White	Orange	Black

A second alternative method involves removal of the handguard and front sight assembly. Push down on the M16A1 slipring and remove the handguard. Then depress the barrel latch and barrel stop in sequence as above.

Further disassembly or removal of the launcher from the rifle is not recommended. Additional maintenance should be carried out by an armorer.

How the M203 Works

Unlocking. Depress the barrel latch and slide the barrel assembly forward.

Cocking. As the barrel and barrel extension assembly is moved forward, the cocking lever, with which the barrel is interlocked, is forced downward forcing the spring loaded firing pin to the rear. The spring loaded follower moves forward with the barrel extension. As the barrel assembly continues its forward movement, the barrel extension disengages from the cocking lever. The follower holds the locking lever in the down position. When the barrel assembly is moved to the rear, the follower is also forced to the rear. The cocking lever again engages the barrel extension, and the firing pin moves slightly forward and engages the primary trigger sear. The weapon is then cocked.

Extraction. As the barrel assembly is opened, a spring loaded extractor keeps the spent cartridge seated against the receiver until the barrel is clear of the cartridge case.

Ejector. When the barrel is forward, the spring loaded ejector pushes the cartridge from the receiver where it is being held by the extractor.

Loading. While the barrel is open, a cartridge is manually inserted into the breech end of the barrel.

Chambering. This step takes place when the barrel is closed. As the breech end of the barrel assembly closes, the extractor contacts the rim of the cartridge. The round is firmly seated.

Locking. As the barrel assembly closes, the barrel latch engages the barrel assembly, and the cocking lever engages the barrel extension so that it cannot be moved forward along the receiver assembly.

Firing. As the trigger is pulled rearward, the primary trigger sear is disengaged from the bottom sear surface of the firing pin, releasing the spring driven firing pin and causing it to be forced forward against the primer of the cartridge.

HIGH-LOW PROPULSION SYSTEM

A high-low propulsion system is required to propel a 40mm projectile from a shoulder fired weapon. This system functions as follows: when the firing pin strikes the primer, the primer flash ignites the propellant that is contained within the brass powder-charge cup inside the high pressure chamber. The burning propellant creates a pressure of 35,000 pounds per square inch within the high pressure chamber, causing the brass powder-charge cup to rupture at the vent holes. As the vent holes rupture, the gases flow into the low pressure chamber (interior portion of the cartridge case). As the gases enter the larger area, the pressure is reduced to 3,000 pounds per square inch, which is sufficient to propel the projectile through the barrel and to the target. The grenade leaves the barrel of the launcher with a muzzle velocity of 250 feet per second and a right-hand spin of 37,000 revolutions per minute. The spin stabilizes the grenade during flight and provides rotational forces necessary to arm the fuze.

M203, 40mm Grenade Launcher attached to the M16A1 Rifle.

46

The army of North Vietnam was equipped with the basic inventory of Soviet small arms of both Soviet and Chinese manufacture. With the fall of the Saigon government of South Vietnam in 1975, the Socialist Republic acquired a large inventory of US material, which had been shipped to Vietnam during the Americans' two-decade involvement there.

North Vietnam (Socialist Republic of Vietnam)

NORTH VIETNAMESE SUBMACHINE GUNS

7.62mm MODIFICATION OF THE FRENCH MODEL 49 SUBMACHINE GUN

The French apparently lost considerable quantities of 9mm Parabellum Model 49 (MAT49) submachine guns. The Vietnamese forces used this weapon as issued until their stocks of captured ammunition ran low. They then rebarreled the weapon for the Soviet 7.62mm Type P pistol cartridge (Chinese Type 50 pistol cartridge). The rebarreled MAT49 has a noticeably longer barrel than the original weapon but in other respects appears the same as the MAT49.

This weapon is loaded, fired and field stripped in the same manner as the MAT49, which is covered in detail in the chapter on France.

7.62mm Modified MAT 49 Submachine Gun.

7.62mm Modified Type 50 Submachine Gun.

MODIFICATION OF THE 7.62mm TYPE 50 SUBMACHINE GUN

This weapon, which appeared in the hands of the Viet Cong as well as the North Vietnamese, is a modification of the 7.62mm Chinese Type 50, a copy of the Soviet Model PPSh M1941. The weapon is made up of components of the Type 50, some of the Type 56 (Chinese copy of the AK) and the wire stock of the French MAT49.

The pistol grip and front sight are the same as those of the 7.62mm Type 56 assault rifle; the receiver and magazine are the same as those of the Type 50 submachine gun. The barrel jacket of the Type 50, reduced in length, is also used.

Characteristics of the Modified Type 50 Submachine Gun

Caliber: 7.62mm (Type 50 cartridge).
System of operation: Blowback, selective fire.
Length overall: Stock extended: 29.75 in.
Stock retracted: 22.56 in.
Barrel length: Approx. 10.5 in.
Feed device: 35-round, box magazine.
Sights: Front: Hooded post.
Rear: "L" type aperture.
Weight: 9 lbs.
Muzzle velocity: 1640 f.p.s.
Cyclic rate: Approx. 900 r.p.m.

SOUTH VIETNAMESE PISTOLS

Prior to the establishment of the Diem government in South Vietnam, there were a number of dissident groups that had, in effect, private armies. The Cao Dai were one of these groups and manufactured arms in rather primitive workshops. Two of these weapons, a copy of the FN Browning Hi-Power and the US Colt .45 Model 1911A1—both chambered for the 9mm Parabellum cartridge—are shown here. The finish on these pistols is surprisingly good considering the circumstances under which they were made. The quality of the metallurgy is questionable.

Copies of the US caliber .30 M1 rifle were also made by dissident groups. It is not certain that all the parts for these weapons were made in Vietnam, some parts may have been of US manufacture and obtained from stocks of parts originally held by the French.

Although Cambodia is not part of Vietnam, it is geographically contiguous. Therefore, this chapter will include a weapon of Cambodian manufacture. The Cambodians have manufactured a 9mm weapon that combines features of the French M1950 and the USM1911A1 pistols. The Cambodian pistol, although shaped like the French M1950 and having its safety mounted on the slide, has a barrel bushing, recoil-spring-plug-arrangement similar to that of the US M1911A1.

Cao Dai 9mm Parabellum copy of US M1911A1.

Cao Dai 9mm Parabellum copy of FN Browning Hi-Power.

Cambodian 9mm Pistol.

Yugoslavia uses the following weapons: the 7.62mm Pistol Model 57, the 7.62mm Rifle Model 59/66, Model 59, Model 64, Model 64A and Model 64B, the 7.62mm submachine guns Model 49 and Model 56, the 7.62mm light machine guns Model 65A and Model 65B, and the 7.92mm general purpose machine gun Model 53. US caliber .50 Browning machine guns are also used as is the Soviet 7.62mm SGMT.

Older weapons such as the 7.92mm rifle Model 48 and various World War II Soviet and German weapons may still be held in reserve.

47

Yugoslavia

YUGOSLAV PISTOLS

Yugoslavia inherited quantities of Austrian 9mm Model 12 Steyr pistols when the State was established at the end of World War I. The new state adopted the FN Browning 9mm short (.380 ACP) Model 1922 pistol prior to World War II.

After World War II, Yugoslavia had quantities of 9mm Parabellum Luger and P38 pistols taken from German forces and Beretta pistols captured from the Italians. The Tokarev 7.62mm TT M1933 pistol was adopted in the late forties.

Yugoslavia manufactures a copy of the Tokarev called the Model 57.

The Yugoslav Model 57 differs from the Tokarev in that it has a nine-round magazine rather than an eight-round magazine. The Yugoslavs also manufacture a copy of the Tokarev in 9mm Parabellum called the Model 65 and the Model 70. It also has a nine-round magazine.

FN Browning M1922 caliber .380 (9mm Short) made for Yugoslavia prior to World War II.

Yugoslav 7.62mm Model 57 Pistol.

YUGOSLAV RIFLES

Yugoslavia obtained many Austrian Mannlicher rifles and Turkish Mausers at the time of its foundation. Few of the 7mm Serbian Mausers (Serbia became part of Yugoslavia), the Model 1889, 99/07, 99/08 or 1910 survived World War II, and they were never a major factor in Yugoslav armament. Austrian Model 1895 Mannlichers were converted to 7.92mm and called Model 95M; Turkish Model 1890 and 1893 were also converted to 7.92mm, the conversion being called the Model 90T. French 8mm M1886M93, M1907/15 and Model 1916 rifles and carbines were also procured.

The Czech ZB 7.92mm Model 24 rifle was adopted as standard, and weapons were manufactured at Kragujevac in Yugoslavia, in addition to purchases made from Czechoslovakia. This rifle is the same as the Czech Model 24 rifle, which is covered in detail in the chapter on Czechoslovakia.

After World War II, the Yugoslavs had quantities of 7.92mm Kar 98ks and some Italian rifles. They also were furnished with 7.92mm Model 1944 carbines and Model 1891/30 rifles by the Soviets.

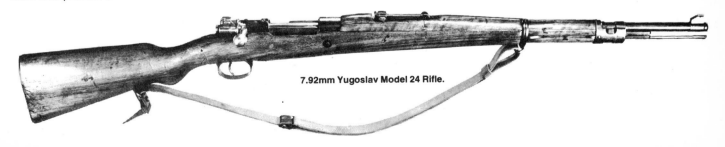

7.92mm Yugoslav Model 24 Rifle.

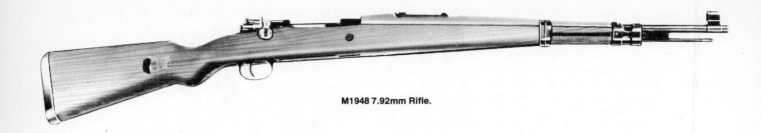

M1948 7.92mm Rifle.

THE YUGOSLAV 7.92mm RIFLE MODEL 1948

The Yugoslavs adopted a slightly modified copy of the Kar 98K as the Model 1948.

The Model is loaded, fired and field stripped in the same manner as the Kar 98K.

Characteristics of the Model 48 Rifle

Caliber: 7.92mm.
System of operation: Manually operated bolt.
Weight: 8.62 lbs.
Length, overall: 42.9 in.
Barrel length: 23.3 in.
Feed device: 5-round, integral, staggered-row box magazine.
Sights: Front: Hooded blade.
  Rear: Tangent w/ramp.
Muzzle velocity: 2600 f.p.s. (approx.).

YUGOSLAV 7.62mm MODEL 59/66 RIFLE

The Model 59/66 is a modified copy of the Soviet SKS. Like the SKS, it is chambered for the 7.62 × 39mm intermediate sized cartridge. The major differences from the SKS are the presence of a gas shut-off valve on the gas cylinder and integral grenade launcher fitted to the barrel. A grenade launcher sight is mounted on the front top of the barrel. The grenade launcher sight pivots upward from the front sight base. As a matter of interest, the diameter of the grenade launcher is 22mm, the same as that of the grenade launchers in service in the Western World but is not the same diameter as the grenade launchers in service in Poland and some of the other Communist countries. The Model 59/66 has a rubber recoil pad fitted to the butt, and its blade type bayonet is slightly longer than that of the SKS. It also has night sighting aids fitted to the front and rear sights. Yugoslavia advertises this weapon for export. With the excep-

tion of the gas shut-off valve, which in the on position-turned up-is used for launching grenades, loading firing and functioning of the Model 59/66 is the same as that of the SKS.

YUGOSLAV 7.62mm MODEL 64, MODEL 70 (64A) AND MODEL 70A (64B) ASSAULT RIFLES

These weapons are all essentially modifications of the Soviet AK assault rifle. They are in the Yugoslav FAZ family of weapons, which includes two light machine guns, the Models 65A and 65B. The Model 64 is essentially the same as the AK but has a longer barrel. As with all the rifles of this series, it has a built in grenade launcher sight that pivots on the gas cylinder. The Model 64 uses a 20-round magazine as opposed to the 30-round magazine normally utilized in AK type weapons. Since the FAZ family of weapons has a bolt stop—bolt holding open device—which works on a notch cut in the magazine, the standard AK magazines cannot be used with these guns.

The Model 70, which was previously called the Model 64A, is essentially the same as the standard wooden stocked AK except for grenade launcher sight and magazine. The Model 70A, which was previously called the Model 64B, is the same as the Model 70 but has a folding steel stock. All of these weapons can be fitted with a 22mm grenade launcher or a short compensator/muzzle brake.

Characteristics of the Model 59/66

Caliber: 7.62mm (7.62 × 39mm)
System of operation: gas, semi-automatic only.
Weight: 9.36 lbs.
Length overall: 43.9 in.
Barrel length: 19.7 in.
Feed device: 10 round, staggered row, integral box magazine.
Sights: Front: hooded post.
  Rear: notched tangent.
Muzzle velocity: 2411 f.p.s.

CHARACTERISTICS OF THE MODEL 64, MODEL 70 AND M70A RIFLES

	Model 64	Model 70	Model 70A
Caliber:		7.62mm (7.62 × 39)	
System of operation:		gas operated selective fire	
Weight:	8.6 lbs.	8.3 lbs.	8.2 lbs.
Length overall: stock fixed:	40.9 in.	37.7 in.	37.7 in.
stock folded:			27.2 in.
Barrel length:	19.7 in.	16.3 in.	16.3 in.
Feed device:	20 round detachable box	30 round detachable box	30 round detachable box
Sights: Front:		hooded post	
Rear:		tangent with notch	
Muzzle velocity:	2395 f.p.s.	2297 f.p.s.	2297 f.p.s.
Cyclic rates:		600-650 r.p.m.	

KALIBAR 7,62 MM
MODEL 59/66
PUNI SE OKVIROM OD 10 METAKA
BRZINA GAĐANJA U BORBI 30 METAKA U MINUTI
DUŽINA PUŠKE S OPRUŽENIM NOŽEM 1,255 METARA
TEŽINA PUŠKE OKO 4 KILOGRAMA
TEŽINA METKA 17 GRAMA

POLUAUTOMATSKA PUŠKA

Yugoslav 7.62mm Model 59/69 Rifle.

YUGOSLAV SUBMACHINE GUNS

7.62mm Model 49 Submachine Gun.

Yugoslavia adopted the 9mm Parabellum Vollmer Erma in the mid-thirties. After World War II, quantities of the German 9mm Parabellum MP38 and MP40 were available, as were Italian Beretta submachine guns and British Sten guns. The Soviet Union supplied their 7.62mm PPD and PPSh41 submachine guns to Yugoslavia.

YUGOSLAV 7.62mm SUBMACHINE GUN MODEL 49

Yugoslavia developed a submachine gun of native design chambered for the 7.62 × 25mm Soviet cartridge. The Model 49 is similar in appearance to the PPSh M1941 but differs internally. The bolt is similar to the Beretta Model 38A, and the

7.62mm Model 56 Submachine Gun.

buffer is considerably more complicated than the plastic or rubber piece found on the PPSh M1941. The buffer of the Model 49 has a spring, separate from the operating spring, and split ring assembly which is retained by a collar on the end of the operating spring tube guide. The Model 49 is field stripped by twisting the receiver cap a quarter turn and removing the buffer, operating spring, and bolt assembly.

YUGOSLAV 7.62mm SUBMACHINE GUN MODEL 56

The Yugoslavs have developed a new and somewhat less complicated gun called the 7.62mm Model 56. The Model 56 has a folding stock similar to the German MP40 and uses a knife-type bayonet. The Model 56 submachine gun is now being made in 9mm Parabellum as the Model 65. It is essentially, except for caliber, identical to the Model 56.

YUGOSLAV MACHINE GUNS

7.92mm ZB30J Machine Gun.

Yugoslavia has used the 8mm 07/12 Schwarzlose, the 7.92mm Maxim Model 8M—a conversion of Serbian 7mm and Bulgarian 8 × 50mm Maxim guns to 7.92mm—the 8mm St. Etienne, and various models of the Madsen gun. The principal light machine gun, prior to World War II, was the 7.92mm ZB30J, a slightly modified version of the ZB30. The principal noticeable difference between the ZB30 and ZB30J is the presence of a knurled ring on the barrel just ahead of the receiver on the ZB30J. This shows up clearly in the photograph above. This weapon was made in Yugoslavia as well as in Czechoslovakia.

After World War II, Yugoslavia had 7.92mm MG34 and MG42 machine guns and various Italian machine guns. They were supplied with some 7.62mm DPs and Model 1910 Maxims by the Soviets. They tooled up for the manufacture of the 7.92mm MG42, which is called the Model 53 or "Sarac" in Yugoslavia. This is the current standard machine gun.

THE YUGOSLAV 7.62mm MODEL 65A AND 65B LIGHT MACHINE GUNS

These guns are part of the Yugoslav "FAZ" weapons family. They, as the rifles covered earlier, are based on the Soviet AK in so far as basic design is concerned. The Model 65A and 65B are essentially the same in all basic respects except one: the 65A has a finned, quick change barrel. Both guns have bipods and flash hiders.

CHARACTERISTICS OF YUGOSLAV SUBMACHINE GUNS

	Model 49	Model 56
Caliber:	7.62mm.	7.62mm.
System of operation:	Blowback, selective fire.	Blowback, selective fire.
Length overall:	34.4 in.	Stock extended: 34.25 in.
		Stock folded: 23.25 in.
Barrel length:	10.5 in.	9.84 in.
Feed device:	----------------------32-round, detachable staggered row magazine ---------------------	
Sights: Front:	Hooded blade.	Hooded blade.
Rear:	L-type with "U" notch.	L-type with "U" notch.
Weight:	9.44 lb.	6.61 lb.
Muzzle velocity:	Approx. 1700 f.p.s.	Approx. 1700 f.p.s.
Cyclic rate:	Approx. 700 r.p.m.	570-620 r.p.m.

CHARACTERISTICS OF THE 7.62mm MODEL 65A AND 65B LIGHT MACHINE GUNS

	Model 65A	Model 65B
Caliber:	---7.62mm (7.62 × 39)---	
System of operation:	---gas, selective fire ---	
Weight:	12.3 lb.	11.4 lb.
Length overall:	--- 41.5 in. ---	
Barrel length:	---approx. 20 in. ---	
Feed device:	---30 round, staggered row detachable box ---	
Sights: Front:	--- hooded post---	
Rear:	---notched tangent---	
Muzzle velocity:	--- 2411 f.p.s. ---	
Cyclic rate:	---600-650 r.p.m.---	

48

Modern military small arms are generally capable of firing several different projectiles. To cover in detail all the variants of military cartridges would require several hundred more pages. This two-page chapter is designed to provide the reader with only a quick guide to contemporary military cartridges.

TABULAR AMMUNITION DATA

Shown below are charts of pistol cartridges, rifle cartridges, and heavy machine-gun cartridges. In each of the three charts there is shown, opposite each cartridge (and case type) listed, the following data: complete round weight, bullet weight, and propellant weight; and complete round length, case length, bullet diameter, and case diameter. Also shown for each cartridge are some common synonyms and the best known weapons in which each cartridge is used.

The dimensions and weights given are approximate. There are many variations insofar as weights are concerned due to the different bullets used with type variations within a given caliber and the differing propellant weights among different types. Weights given are for the basic ball round in each type. Diameters given are for the point of maximum diameter of bullet and cartridge case.

The data given in the charts should NOT be used as a guide in the reloading of cartridges. There is considerable variation in the performance of the various propellants in use throughout the world. Therefore no presentation such as that given here can serve as a guide to handloading unless the specific military or commercial model designation for the propellant is given.

PISTOL CARTRIDGES

Cartridge and Case Type	Complete Round Weight	Bullet Weight	Propellant Weight	Complete Round Length	Case Length	Bullet Diameter	Case Diameter	Some Common Synonyms	Best Known Weapons in Which Used
7.62mm Pistol Rimless Bottlenecked	167 gr.	87 gr.	7.71 gr.	1.36 in.	.97 in.	.307 in.	.39 in.	7.62mm Type P (Soviet) 7.62mm M48 (Czech)	TT M1933 Pistol, M34/38 SMG, PPD 40 SMG, PPSh 41 SMG, PPS 43 SMG (All Soviet) SMG and M52 Pistol (Czech) and various satellite copies of Soviet pistol and SMGs, can also be used in weapons chambered for 7.63mm Mauser cartridge.—Note that Czech cartridge has a heavier charge.
7.65mm Browning Straight Semi-rim	121.0 gr.	73 gr.	2.47 gr.	.98 in.	.68 in.	.308-.311 in.	.354 in.	.32 ACP, 7.65mm Browning short	Colt Automatic, Walther PP & PPK, (German & various copies), Browning M1910 & M1922, large numbers of pocket automatic pistols throughout the world.
7.65mm Long Rimless Straight	132 gr.	85-88 gr.	5.0 gr.	1.19 in.	.78 in.	.309 in.	.335 in.	7.65 Longue Pour Pistole et Pistolet Mitrailleur .30 cal. Pistol Cartridge M1918 (Pedersen Device Cartridge)	French M1935A and M1935S Pistols and M1938 SMG.
7.65 Luger Rimless Bottlenecked	160.0 gr.	93 gr.	5.2 gr.	1.17 in.	.85 in.	.308 in.	.392 in.	Cal. .30 Luger	Swiss M 06/29 Pistol, some Pre-W.W. II Bergmann and SIG SMGs.
8mm Jap Rimless Bottlenecked	177.5 gr.	102 gr.	5.0 gr.	1.23 in.	.83 in.	.320 in.	.411 in.	8mm Type 14	Japanese Type 14 and Type 94 pistols and Type 100 SMG.
8mm Lebel Rimmed Straight	194.5 gr.	120 gr.	14.0 gr. black powder 11.5 gr. smokeless	1.44 in.	1.07 in.	.323 in.	.408 in. (Rim)	8mm M1892	French M1892 Revolver.
9mm Short Rimless Straight	148.8 gr.	95 gr.	3.5 gr.	.98 in.	.68 in.	.356 in.	.372 in.	9mm Browning Short, 9mm Kurz, 9mm Corto, .380 A.C.P., 9mm Court	Colt automatic, Walther PP and PPK and various copies, Hungarian M37, Italian M34 Beretta.
9mm Parabellum Rimless Straight	164. gr.	115 gr.	5.6 gr.	1.17 in.	.76 in.	.356 in.	.457 in.	Pistolen Patrone 08, 9mm M1, 9mm Mk1, 9mm M38, 9mm M39, 9mm Luger	German P08, P38, MP38, MP40, British Browning No. 2 Pistol, Sten SMGs and L2A3 SMG, French M50 Pistol and M49 SMG. Belgian Browning HP Pistol and Vigneron SMG, Swedish and Finnish Lahti Pistol and Suomi SMGs. Swedish M45 SMG, Israeli Uzi SMG, Madsen SMGs. Beretta M38, 38/42, 38/49, 5 & 12 SMG, Beretta M951 Pistol.
9mm Largo Rimless Straight	192 gr.	124 gr.	6.6 gr.	1.32 in.	.91 in.	.354 in.	.385 in.	9mm Bergmann Bayard	Spanish Super Star Pistol and Star Model Z45 SMG.
9mm Makarov Rimless Straight	156 gr.	94 gr.	3.7 gr.	.97 in.	.71 in.	.363 in.	.389 in.		Soviet Makarov and Stechkin pistols.
.380 MK II Rimmed Straight	246.5 gr.	181 gr.	5.0 gr.	1.22 in.	.76 in.	.357 in.	.435 in.	.38 S&W and .38 Webley Scott	British Pistol No. 2 (Revolvers) in all Marks, Webley Mark IV Pistol, S & W .38/200.
.45 M1911 Rimless Straight	327. gr.	230 gr.	5 gr.	1.275 in.	.91 in.	.452 in.	.480 in.	.45 ACP, 11.43mm, 11.25mm, 11mm M40	U. S. Pistol M1911 and M1911A1, M1928 A1, M1, M1A1, M3, and M3A1 SMGs. Norway—pistol M1914. Argentina-Ballester.
.455 Webley Rimless Straight	324.0 gr.	224 gr.	7 gr.	1.22 in.	.91 in.	.455 in.	.502 in.	.455 Webley auto.	Webley Automatic Pistol.
.455 Revolver Rimmed Straight	350 gr.	265 gr.	7.5 gr.	1.22 in. to 1.26 in.	.76 in.	.455 in.	.532 in.	.455 Webley revolver .455 in. Mark II	Pistol No. 1 Marks 4, 5, & 6.

RIFLE CARTRIDGES

Cartridge and Case Type	Complete Round Weight	Bullet Weight	Propellant Weight	Complete Round Length	Case Length	Bullet Diameter	Case Diameter	Some Common Synonyms	Best Known Weapons in Which Used
5.56mm Rimless Bottlenecked	182 gr.	55 gr.	25 gr.	2.26 in.	1.76 in.	.224 in.	.378 in.	.223 5.56mm M193	U.S. M16, M16A1, and AR-18 rifles, Stoner 63 System.
6.5mm Dutch Rimmed Bottlenecked	356 gr.	156 gr.	37 gr.	3.03 in.	2.11 in.	.263 in.	.526 in.	6.5mm Rumanian 6.5mm M93 6.5 x 53mm R	
6.5mm Italian Rimless Bottlenecked	350 gr.	162 gr.	35 gr.	3.01 in.	2.06 in.	.2655 in.	.447 in.	6.5mm Mannlicher Carcano, 6.5mm M91-95	Italian M91 rifles and carbines Breda M30 MG.
6.5mm Jap Semi-rim Bottlenecked	326 gr.	139 gr.	33 gr.	2.98 in.	2.00 in.	.262 in.	.476 in.	6.5mm Type 38	Japanese Type 38 rifle, Type 38 and Type 44 carbine, Type 11 and Type 96 MG.
6.5mm Mauser Rimless Bottlenecked	363 gr.	139 gr.	36 gr.	3.15 in.	2.17 in.	.264 in.	.478 in.	6.5mm M94, 6.5mm Norwegian, 6.5mm Swedish, 6.5 x 55mm	Norwegian M94 rifle and M12 carbine. Swedish 94 carbine. M96, M38 and M42 rifles, M21 and M37 automatic rifles (used in some Swedish MGs as well).
7mm Mauser Rimless Bottlenecked	377 gr.	172 gr.	38 gr.	3.00 in.	2.24 in.	.284 in.	.474 in.	7 x 57mm	Spanish M93 rifle and M95 carbine.
7.5mm French Rimless Bottlenecked	363 gr.	139 gr.	44 gr.	2.99 in.	2.13 in.	.307 in.	.484 in.	7.5mm M1929	French M 07/15, M34, M36, M49, M49/56 rifles and M1924M29 automatic rifle. M31 and M52 MG.
7.5mm Swiss Rimless Bottlenecked	404 gr.	174 gr.	49.35 gr.	3.05 in.	2.18 in.	.308 in.	.496 in.	7.45mm Swiss 7.5mm M11 7.5mm Schmidt Rubin	Swiss M11 rifle and M11, M31, M31/42 and M31/43 carbines, M57 assault rifle. M11, M25, and M51 machine guns.
7.62mm NATO Rimless Bottlenecked	375 gr.	150 gr.	48 gr.	2.80 in.	2.01 in.	.308 in.	.496 in.	7.62mm Ball M59 7.62 x 51mm 7.62mm M1954 7.62mm OTAN .308 Winchester 7.62mm Ball M85	U.S. M14 rifle, M60 and M73 machine guns. British L2A1 rifle, Belgian FN FAL rifle and FN MAG. M.G. Canadian C1 rifle and C2 LMG. W. German FN and G3 rifles.
7.62mm Russian Rimmed Bottlenecked	348 gr.	148 gr.	50 gr.	3.03 in.	2.11 in.	.311 in.	.564 in.	7.62mm M1908 type L 7.62 x 54mm	Soviet Mosin-Nagant rifles and carbines, Simonov M36 and Tokarev M32, M38, and M40 rifles and carbines. Maxim M1910, DP, DPM, DT, DTM, DA, ShKAS, SG-43, SGM, and RP-46 MGs. Soviet Satellite copies of these weapons.
7.62mm M43 Rimless Bottlenecked	253 gr.	122 gr.	25 gr.	2.20 in.	1.52 in.	.311 in.	.45 in.	7.62mm Russian Short 7.62mm M1934 Type PS 7.62 x 39mm	Soviet AK assault rifle, SKS carbine, RPD LMG.
7.62mm M52 Rimless Bottlenecked	293.7 gr.	132 gr.	27 gr.	2.35 in.	1.77 in.	.310 in.	.442 in.	7.62mm Czech Short	Czech M52 Rifle and LMG.
7.65mm Mauser Rimless Bottlenecked	390 gr.	174 gr.	38.6 gr.	2.95 in.	2.11 in.	.310 in.	.472 in.	7.65mm M30 7.65 x 54mm	Belgian M89 rifles and carbines, M35 and 36 rifles. Argentine M91 and M09 rifles. Turkish M91 and M03 rifles.
7.7mm Rimless Jap Rimless Bottlenecked	415 gr.	182 gr.	43.13 gr.	3.14 in.	2.25 in.	.310 in.	.47 in.	7.7mm Type 99	Japanese Type 99 rifle and LMG.
7.7mm Semi-rim Jap, Semi-rim Bottlenecked	429 gr.	200 gr.	44.18 gr.	3.14 in.	2.25 in.	.310 in.	.49 in.	7.7mm Type 92	Japanese Type 92 MG.
7.92mm Mauser Rimless Bottlenecked	408. gr.	198 gr.	47 gr.	3.15 in.	2.24 in.	.323 in.	.468 in.	7.9mm SS 7.9 x 57mm 7.9 IS 7.9 JS 8mm Mauser .315 Mauser rimless 8 x 57mm M98	German M98 rifles and carbines, MO8, 08/15, 08/18, 15, 17, 34 and 42 MGs. FG-42. Czech M24, M33 rifles and carbines, M26, M30, M30J and M37 MGs. British BESA MGs, Chinese-Brens MK 2.
8nn Austrian Rimmed Bottlenecked	437 gr.	244 gr.	42 gr.	3.00 in.	1.99 in.	.323 in.	.554 in.	8mm M1893 8 x 50mm R	Austrian M90 rifles and carbines, M07/12 MG, M95 rifles and carbines.
8mm M31 Rimmed Bottlenecked	441 gr.	208 gr.	55 gr.	3.02 in.	2.21 in.	.330 in.	.55 in.	8mm M30S 8 x 56mm R	Hungarian M35 rifle and M31 MG. Austrian M30 MG, rebarrelled M95 Mannlichers.
8mm Lebel Rimmed Bottlenecked	429 gr.	198 gr.	43 gr.	2.95 in.	1.98 in.	.328 in.	.629 in.	8mm M1886 D(AM)	French M86M93, M1890, M92, M07, M07/15, M16, M17, M18 rifles and carbines. M14 and M15 MGs.
Cal. .30 Carbine Rimless Straight	195 gr.	110 gr.	14.5 gr.	1.67 in.	1.28 in.	.308 in.	.356 in.	Cal. .30 M1 Carbine	U.S. M1 and M2 carbines.
Cal. .30-06 Rimless Bottlenecked	396 gr.	150 gr.	50 gr.	3.33 in.	2.49 in.	.308 in.	.469 in.	Cal. .30 M2 Ball Cal. .300 Browning 7.62 x 63mm	U.S. M03, 03A1, 03A2, 03A3, 03A4 Springfield rifles, M17, M1, M1C, M1D rifles. Browning automatic rifle M18, M18A1, 18A2. Browning M17, 17A1, 19A4, 19A5, 19A6, M37 MGs.
Cal. .303 Rimmed Bottlenecked	384 gr.	174 gr.	37.5 gr.	3.04 in.	2.21 in.	.311 in.	.53 in.	.303 in. Mark 7 .303 British	British No. 1, MKs 1, 2, 3, 3*, 4, 5, 6, No. 3, MK 1, 1*, No. 4 MK 1, 1*, 2, No. 5 MK 1, 1* rifles. Lewis MG, Hotchkiss MG, Bren MKs 1, 2, 3, and 4 MGs. Vickers MK 1 MG. Canadian Ross M05 and M10 rifles.

HEAVY MACHINE GUN CARTRIDGES

Cartridge and Case Type	Complete Round Weight	Bullet Weight	Propellant Weight	Complete Round Length	Case Length	Bullet Diameter	Case Diameter	Some Common Synonyms	Best Known Weapons in Which Used
Cal. .50 Rimless Bottlenecked	1800 gr.	709 gr.	240 gr.	5.45 in.	3.90 in.	.511 in.	.804 in.	Cal. .50 Ball M2 Cal. .50 Browning	U.S. M2, M2HB, M3 MGs.
12.7mm Soviet Rimless Bottlenecked	2160 gr.	788 gr.	271 gr.	5.76 in.	4.25 in.	.511 in.	.85 in.	12.7mm	Soviet DShK M38, DShk M38/46 and UB MGs.

49   Sporting Arms

SPORTING RIFLES

Although *Small Arms of the World* is basically devoted to military firearms, this chapter on centerfire civilian and sporting arms is presented to outline the relationships and divergences in these two realms of gun design. Until the end of World War II, virtually all forms of cartridge era rifles, pistols and revolvers were originally developed for military use and subsequently adapted to sporting purposes—target shooting, hunting and plinking. In the world of rifles, the introduction of military self-loaders in the post-1945 period has altered patterns of rifle production. And in more recent years, the Gun Control Act of 1968 (GCA 68) and the growing numbers of shooters and collectors have had an impact on the sporting rifle market. A closer look at these contemporary developments will benefit both the student of military arms and the users of sporting rifles.

The single most important rifle mechanism, in terms of popularity and quantities produced, has been Peter Paul Mauser's Model 98 bolt action rifle. In addition to the tens of thousands of military Mausers, Springfields and M1917s that have been converted to sporting rifles, a substantial number of Mauser type actions have been and continue to be manufactured. When the 1968 gun control law forbade the further importation of surplus military rifles into the United States, companies such as Interarms arranged for production of modernized versions of the Mauser action. The Mark X rifles and actions, which incorporate a sliding safety mounted on the right rear of the receiver, are marketed by Interarms and manufactured in Yugoslavia. Other companies such as Champlin, Colt-Sauer, Steyr, Mauser and Sturm-Ruger have introduced new designs and manufacturing technologies to the rifle scene during the last decade. One of Ruger's important technological contributions has been the use of investment castings for rifle receivers and other important components. In an era when machining finished parts from forgings has become increasingly costly, investment casting has provided a quality alternative. Thompson-Center Arms and Plainfield Arms have also used this technique in the manufacture of their sporting arms.

In addition to the traditional bolt, lever and pump action rifles, two distinctive classes of sporting rifles have emerged since 1945—military self-loaders and new versions of older patterns. As standard semiautomatic military rifles have increased in price due to their collector appeal and as the newer selective fire weapons have qualified as registerable "firearms" (i.e., automatic weapons) under GCA 68, manufacturers have sought to market "look alike" weapons and semiautomatic versions of military weapons. Chief among the "look alikes" is a semiautomatic-only copy of the M14 Rifle produced by Springfield Armory Inc. (a private firm, not to be confused with the national armory, which was closed in 1968) and

A. R. Sales Co. When it became clear that only limited numbers of the National Match M14s would become available to a few DCM qualified shooting organizations, Springfield Armory Inc. began production of their MIA, and A. R. Sales introduced their Mark IV Sporter. Both Plainfield and Universal have manufactured copies of the US M1 Carbine for commercial and police markets.

Among the commercial sporting versions of military rifles, the leader by far is the Colt AR-15. More than 300,000 of these semiautomatic M16 Rifles have been sold since Colt began to market the sporter model in the early 1960s. Subsequently, Armalite produced the AR-180 version of the AR-18, while Heckler and Koch has sold the HK91 and HK93 models of their G-3 and HK33 rifles. CETME has made the CETME Sport variant of the Spanish military rifle. SIG has marketed a sporterized Model 57 assault rifle, and Beretta has produced limited quantities of semiautomatic BM59 Rifles for sale in the US. Ironically, the semiautomatic version of the Fabrique Nationale FAL has been kept off the American market because the Bureau of Alcohol, Tobacco and Firearms has determined that it has been designed as an automatic rifle. The same point could be argued for the other rifles listed above, but the sales agencies for those guns have been more successful in devising semiautomatic-only sporting models of their military rifles. Sturm-Ruger has taken a different approach with their 5.56mm Mini-14, initially marketed as a semiautomatic rifle, by subsequently introducing military, selective fire, rifle and carbine versions. The Valmet M62S sold by Interarms is the only sporterized military rifle produced to fire a non-standard American cartridge. Chambered for the Soviet 7.62 × 39 M43 cartridge, the M62S is basically a semi-automatic AK47 of extremely high quality manufacture. A newer version with a stamped steel receiver and chambered to fire the US 5.56 × 45mm cartridge is being sold by Interarms as the M71S.

Included in the second class of rifles, the newly manufactured versions of old models, is a group of replicas of 19th century guns. The originals are such valued collectors' items that they are no longer used as shooters. Leading the list of these replicas are the Harrington & Richardson reproduction of the Springfield 1873 Trapdoor Rifle and the Navy Arms Company Remington type dropping block and Martini-Henry type dropping block rifles. In addition, several small companies have introduced copies of Sharps, Sharps-Borchardt and Winchester M1885 High Wall rifle actions, while Sturm-Ruger has produced their classic style No. 1 and No. 3 single-shot rifles as the demand has increased from shooters for such high quality specialty firearms.

In rifles, only one design form has a purely sporting heritage—the slide or pump action, which is manually actuated by a sliding fore-end. Slide action rifles offered today generally have the same actions as existing self-loading models. Only the method of applying the actuating power is different.

A few words need to be said about rifle ammunition. Traditionally, military cartridges have been altered by the adoption of special projectiles for both match target and hunting purposes. Whereas the US .30-06 and German 8mm (7.92 × 57mm) cartridges were extremely popular in the early decades of this century, the .308 Winchester (civilian version of the 7.62 × 51mm NATO) and .223 Remington (5.56 × 45mm) currently enjoy wide usage on the sporting scene. As noted in Chapter 1, Gene Stoner started with the .222 Remington cartridge when he began his search for a small caliber military round. At about the same time, Earle M. Harvey at Springfield Armory began work on a modified version of the .222 Remington. That cartridge, the Springfield .224, was subsequently marketed as the .222 Remington Magnum. As with weapons designs, the sporting world has been and will continue to be influenced by military ammunition development.

Following is a representative sample of those sporting rifles popular with shooters today.

BOLT-ACTION RIFLES

BSA (BIRMINGHAM SMALL ARMS CO.), UK

The BSA Monarch action is essentially a modified Mauser type with dual opposed locking lugs at the bolt head. It utilizes a counterbored bolt face and a short spring-loaded hook extractor let into the counterbore. Firing pin and cocking system are typically Mauser; however, the bolt sleeve completely encloses the head of the firing pin, and the safety has been transferred to the trigger assembly and protrudes alongside the rear receiver tang. A fully adjustable single-stage trigger is fitted, as is a hinged magazine floor plate retained by a pivoted latch in the front of the guard bow. Functioning and manipulation are identical with that of other Mauser type rifles.

Characteristics of BSA Monarch Rifle

Caliber: .222 and 7mm Remington Magnum; .243, .270, .308 Winchester; .30-06.
Barrel length: 22 in.
Overall length: 41 in.
Weight: 7⅛ lbs.
Magazine capacity: 5 rounds; 3 in belted magnum calibers.

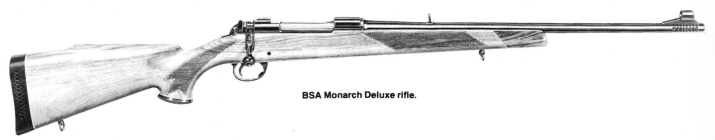

BSA Monarch Deluxe rifle.

BROWNING

Browning distributes an extensive line of high-power, bolt-action sporting rifles in the US though it does not produce those guns in this country. The bulk of the Browning models are simply the FN rifle manufactured to Browning's own particular specifications of finish, weight, and stock. Browning rifles for cartridges of the .30-06 and larger class are the FN. The so-called "short-action" Brownings are manufactured by SAKO of Finland to Browning specifications.

CHAMPLIN FIREARMS INC.

Champlin produces several variations of a single basic model built upon a massive action of original design. The large-diameter bolt is characterized by three equally spaced lengthwise ribs running its full length. The ribs are interrupted to form six locking lugs—three front, three rear. The ribs between the lugs function as bolt guides, sliding in corresponding slots in the receiver. The bolt face is deeply counter-bored to shroud the case head and is fitted with a hook type extractor. At the rear, the bolt is closed by a streamlined, Weatherby-style bolt sleeve completely enclosing the cocking piece. The receiver is octagonal in section through its upper half, the bottom being square and fitted with a conventional Mauser type recoil lug. The manual safety is located shotgun-style on the rear receiver tang. The trigger assembly is characteristic of the modern, single-stage, fully adjustable type with pivoted sear. The trigger guard/magazine assembly is typical of the Mauser M98, fitted with a hinged floor plate secured by a pivoted latch in the front of the guard bow.

Champlin rifles are essentially custom built with many optional features, finishes and dimensional and weight variations. In view of this, there are no standard specifications. Prices begin in the $1700 range. Loading, firing and manipulation are as for Mauser type actions.

COLT-SAUER

In collaboration with J. P. Sauer & Sohn, W. Germany, Colt introduced the rear-locking Colt-Sauer rifle in late 1972. It is of unusual design, having a non-rotating bolt locked at the rear of the receiver by three retractable locking lugs actuated by a rotating cam on the bolt handle. This new mechanism is very smooth and fast operating. Another key feature of the Colt-Sauer is its patented split receiver, which contributes to the rifle's strength and accuracy. After the barrel is threaded into the split receiver ring, two transverse machine screws are torqued into position, locking the receiver around the barrel. This exclusive attachment method makes the barrel and receiver act as one solid piece of steel. Some additional features include a tang safety that mechanically locks the sear and trigger mechanism; a fully adjustable trigger; an exclusive loaded chamber indicator that shows the hunter when a round has been chambered.

The Colt-Sauer has not been mass produced. Only about 7,000 have been produced annually in this joint venture. Currently there are four models available.

Characteristics of Colt-Sauer Rifle

Caliber: .25-06; .270; .30-06; 7mm Remington Magnum; .300 Winchester Magnum; .300 Weatherby Magnum.
Operation by: Manual; rotating bolt handle.
Barrel length: 24 in.
Overall length: 43¾ in.
Weight: 7¾ to 8½ lbs.
Sights: None; drilled and tapped for scope mounts.
Magazine capacity: 3 round detachable magazine

Characteristics of Colt-Sauer Short Action Rifle

Caliber: .22-250; .243; .308 Winchester (7.62mm NATO).

Operation by: Manual; rotating bolt handle.
Barrel length: 24 in.
Overall length: 43 in.
Weight: 7½ to 8¼ lbs.
Sights: None; drilled and tapped for scope mounts.
Magazine capacity: 3 round detachable magazine

Also available are the Grand Alaskan in .375 H&H Magnum and the Grand African in .458 Winchester Magnum. The latter has iron sights; wind and elevation adjustable rear; hooded ramp-style front.

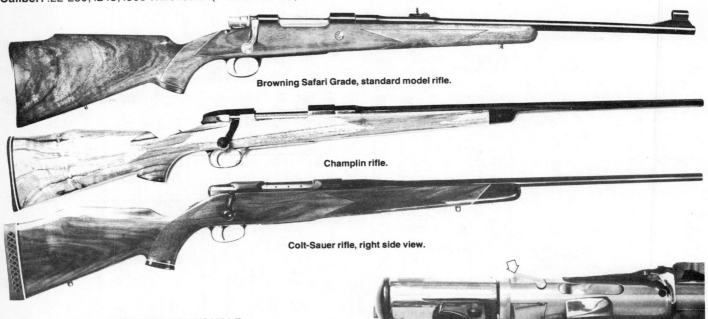

Browning Safari Grade, standard model rifle.

Champlin rifle.

Colt-Sauer rifle, right side view.

FABRIQUE NATIONALE

Fabrique Nationale has manufactured Mauser rifles of various types continuously since 1889. Following WW II, this firm began producing M98 Mauser type sporting rifles for sale throughout the world. The first such rifles were identical in all respects to the M98 rifles produced by FN during the war except for stock and sights. However, a distinct sporting variation soon developed. It consisted of the basic M98 barrel, bolt, and trigger guard fitted with a single-stage fully adjustable sporting trigger containing a manual safety which protruded at the right side of the rear receiver tang. The bolt sleeve was streamlined and stripped of the original military-style safety. The magazine is fitted with a hinged floor plate retained by a catch in the front of the trigger guard bow. Functioning and manipulation of FN rifles is identical to the standard M98 Mauser, which see.

The FN action is widely used by other makers to produce Mauser type sporting rifles under a variety of names. At the present time, Firearms International is the exclusive US distributor of FN rifles and actions and utilizes the latter in its own style rifle called the "Musketeer," which is assembled in this country.

Colt Sauer rifle with bolt open. Arrows indicate locking lugs.

FABRIQUE NATIONALE-SAUER

FN has recently begun to manufacture their own version of the rear-locking Sauer rifle action. It differs from the Colt-Sauer mainly in the incorporation of a light-alloy frame to which the barrel and receiver are fixed. This design requires the use of a two-piece stock.

Characteristics of the FN Rifle

Caliber: Most popular US sporting from .222 to .458.
Operation by: Manual: Mauser type rotating bolt.
Barrel length: 22 in. to 24 in.
Overall length: 42½ in. to 44½ in.
Weight: 7¾ lbs.
Sights: Open, adjustable.
Magazine capacity: 5 rounds; 3 in belted magnum calibers.

Characteristics of the FN-Sauer Rifle

Caliber: 7 × 64mm; .270 Winchester; .30-06; 7mm Remington Magnum; .300 Winchester Magnum; and 8 × 68mm.
Operation by: Manual; rotating bolt handle.
Barrel length: 24 in.
Weight: 7.8 lbs.
Sights: Open, adjustable; can be fitted with a scope.
Magazine capacity: 3 rounds detachable magazine.

Fabrique Nationale Musketeer rifle.

FN-Sauer rifle, right side view.

Whitworth Express rifle.

MARK X MAUSER RIFLE, w/
MODEL 4x40,

MARK X MAUSER RIFLE, w/
MODEL 3-9x40 VARIABLE

a) Mark X Mauser rifle with Model 4×40.
b) Mark X Mauser rifle with Model 3-9×40 variable.

HARRINGTON & RICHARDSON

During the early 1960s, Harrington & Richardson added a high-power, bolt-action sporting rifle to its extensive line. This rifle is designated as Model 300, 301, or 330, depending upon finish, barrel and stock. All are built around the SAKO Mauser type action by Harrington & Richardson. Particulars given under "FN" are applicable. In addition, Harrington & Richardson builds a .17 caliber wildcat rifle on the SAKO L-461 action, for which particulars will be found under "SAKO" elsewhere in this volume.

INTERARMS

Interarms currently imports a number of centerfire sporting rifles. The Churchill "One of One Thousand," which has been the top of their line for several years, is available in very limited numbers since sales have nearly reached the 1000 mark. Replacing the Churchill is the Whitworth Express Rifle-African Series. Assembled in the UK using Mark X Mauser actions, the Whitworths are barrelled to handle the heavy bullets of the 7mm Remington Magnum, .300 Winchester Magnum, .375 H & H Magnum and .458 Winchester Magnum. Interarms also markets five versions of the Mark X Rifle.

Characteristics of Mark X Rifles

	Rifle	Mannlicher Carbine	Cavalier	Viscount	Alaskan
Caliber:	.22-250; .243; .270; .308; .30-06; .25-06; 7 × 57mm; 7mm Rem. Mag.; .300 Win. Mag.	.270; 7 × 57mm; .308; .30-06.	Same as rifle.	Same as rifle.	.375 H & H; .458 Win. Mag.
Operation by:	Manual; rotating bolt handle.	Same.	Same.	Same.	Same.
Barrel length:	24 in.	20 in.	24 in.	24 in.	24 in.
Overall length:	44 in.	40 in.	44 in.	44 in.	44¾ in.
Weight:	7½ lbs.	7½ lbs.	7½ lbs.	7½ lbs.	8¼ lbs.
Sights:	Open; hooded front.	Same.	Same.	Same.	Same.
Magazine capacity:	5 rounds.	5 rounds.	5 rounds.	5 rounds.	5 rounds.

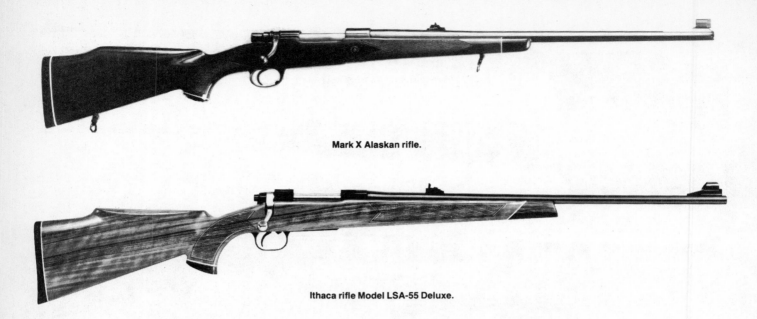

Mark X Alaskan rifle.

Ithaca rifle Model LSA-55 Deluxe.

ITHACA GUN COMPANY

Ithaca first entered the centerfire rifle field in 1969. At present, two models, the LSA-55, in Standard and Deluxe versions, and the Ithaca/BSA CF2 are available. The LSA-55 is essentially a modified Mauser type, bolt-action rifle of conventional style and configuration. It utilizes a recessed hook type extractor rather than the long leaf type of the M98. A manual safety is pivoted on the right side behind the bolt handle, and the hinged floor plate is secured by a latch inside the trigger guard bow. Integral male scope-mounting dovetails are machines in the receiver ring and bridge. The LSA-55 series is manufactured in Scandinavia.

Characteristics of Ithaca LSA-55 Rifle

Caliber: .243 and .308 Winchester; .22-250 and 6mm Remington.
Operation by: Manual; rotating bolt.
Barrel length: 23 in.
Overall length: 42$\frac{1}{2}$ in.
Weight: 6$\frac{1}{2}$ lbs.
Sights: Open, adjustable.
Magazine capacity: 4 rounds.

Characteristics of Ithaca/BSA CF2

Caliber: 7mm Remington Magnum; .270; .300 Winchester Magnum.
Operation by: Manual; rotating bolt handle.
Barrel length: 24 in.
Overall length: 43 in. (approx.)
Weight: 7$\frac{3}{4}$ lbs.
Sights: Hooded, adjustable.
Magazine capacity: 3 rounds.

MAUSER, WEST GERMANY

In 1966, Mauser Werke introduced a radically new, rotating bolt, manually operated, bolt-action magazine rifle. The entire action design is a complete departure from previous Mauser practice. The design is not as new as the date of introduction might indicate; a quite similar prototype was produced by the Mauser plant in WW II. The action is unusually short, measuring only 4 1/2 inches in length. The receiver, as we know it, does not

exist. It is replaced by a simple frame containing guide tracks for the bolt and a mortised seat for the quick-detachable barrel. The short bolt body is fitted with a conventional handle near its front end and carries dual, opposed locking lugs. The lugs engage abutments inside a barrel extension, thus locking the bolt to the barrel proper instead of joining the two by a receiver ring as in past practice. The bolt body is largely enclosed by a sliding, non-rotating sleeve engaging tracks on the receiver.

In unlocking, the bolt is first rotated independent of the sleeve; then the two are drawn rearward and thrust forward as a single unit to accomplish extraction, ejection, feeding, chambering, locking and unlocking. This extremely short action requires that the double-column box magazine be sandwiched between the trigger assembly and the receiver. This results in an unusually shallow magazine with the capacity of only three rounds of .30-06 class cartridges and two rounds in the belted magnums. This also makes it necessary to route the trigger-sear linkage around the magazine box. Single-stage and double-set triggers, both fully adjustable, are offered. The barrel attachment method is unique.

The barrel proper is fitted with a barrel extension that contains locking abutments to engage the locking lugs of the bolt. The lower surface of this extension carries ribs fitting very closely in corresponding grooves in the receiver. And the barrel assembly is secured by a clamp screw. Since the bolt locks into the extension, which is rigidly attached to the barrel, there is no longitudinal stress upon the receiver, so little strength in that direction is necessary. However, accurate alignment is quite important. This method of barrel attachment makes possible quick interchange of barrels in different weights and/or calibers. In fact, the Diplomat Model is supplied cased with barrels of three calibers. Interchangeability of calibers is limited only by magazine shape and size and bolt face dimensions.

Characteristics of the Mauser 660 Rifle

Caliber: Most popular US, from .243 Winchester through .458, and European cartridges.
Operation by: Manual; rotating telescoping bolt.
Barrel length: 20-25$\frac{1}{2}$ in.
Overall length: 38-43$\frac{1}{2}$ in.
Weight: 6$\frac{5}{8}$-9 $\frac{7}{8}$ lbs.
Sights: Open, adjustable.
Magazine capacity: 3 rounds; 2 in belted magnums.

Mauser Model 660 rifle.

The Mauser Model 3000 represents what might be called the ultimate Mauser development of the original M98. It utilizes the same general style of bolt, but with a recessed hook type extractor and plunger type ejector recessed into the bolt head. The firing pin is of two-piece construction, and cocking and primary extraction are accomplished by cams in the same manner as the M98. A fully adjustable single-stage trigger is fitted, and the trigger guard and magazine are of typical Mauser construction. The bolt sleeve is streamlined in Weatherby fashion, and the large bolt stop has been replaced by a simple plunger. The manual safety fitted to the right side of the bolt sleeve is pressed upward to engage, down to prepare for fitting. Operation and manipulation of the Mauser M3000 is essentially the same as for other modern Mauser type bolt rifles.

O. F. MOSSBERG & SONS

After having been in business since 1919, Mossberg introduced its first centerfire bolt-action rifle in 1965-1966—the M800. It utilizes a rotating bolt with six locking lugs positioned in three rows of two each, and the lugs are of the same diameter as the body. The bolt face is deeply counterbored to shroud the cartridge head and is fitted with a narrow, recessed hook extractor and plunger type ejector. The firing pin is unusually slender in its front half, the larger rear portion being counterbored after the fashion of the Japanese Arisaka to accept a relatively short mainspring. The rear of the bolt is closed by a threaded bolt sleeve, which sweeps downward to join the curve of the stock. The sliding manual safety is installed on the rear slope of the sleeve; it moves rearward to engage and forward to make ready for firing. The receiver is tubular and utilizes the Remington type recoil lug clamped in place by the barrel. The trigger mechanism is housed within an upward extension of the plastic trigger guard. The double-column box magazine is fitted with a hinged floor plate, the latter secured by a sliding latch ahead of the guard bow. Several variations of the M800 are offered, ranging from a full-stocked carbine to a heavy barrel varmint rifle.

Characteristics of the Mossberg M800 Rifle

Caliber: .243 and .308 Winchester; .22-250.
Operation by: Manual; rotating bolt.
Barrel length: 20-24 in.
Overall length: 40-44 in.
Weight: $6\frac{1}{2}$-$9\frac{1}{2}$ lbs.
Sights: Open.
Magazine capacity: 4 rounds; 3 in .22-250 caliber.

PARKER-HALE, UK

This is a straightforward design, consisting of a Spanish-made Mauser M98 type receiver and bolt to which Parker-Hale adds the remaining parts of its own manufacture. It differs from the basic military M98 mechanically only in that an adjustable, single-stage trigger assembly, incorporating a manual safety lying alongside the receiver tang, is used. The magazine and trigger guard are typically Mauser, and the floor plate is hinged, secured with a catch inside the trigger guard bow. Functioning and manipulation are as for other Mauser type rifles.

Characteristics of the Parker-Hale Rifle

Caliber: .243, .270 and .308 Winchester; .30-06; .308 Norma Magnum.
Operation by: Manual; rotating Mauser type bolt.
Barrel length: 22-24 in.
Overall length: $42^{13}/_{16}$-$44^{13}/_{16}$ in.
Weight: $7\frac{1}{2}$ lbs.
Sights: Open, adjustable; folding rear.
Magazine capacity: 5 rounds; 3 in belted magnum calibers.

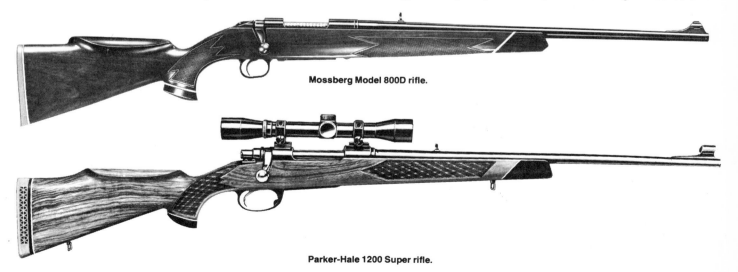

Mossberg Model 800D rifle.

Parker-Hale 1200 Super rifle.

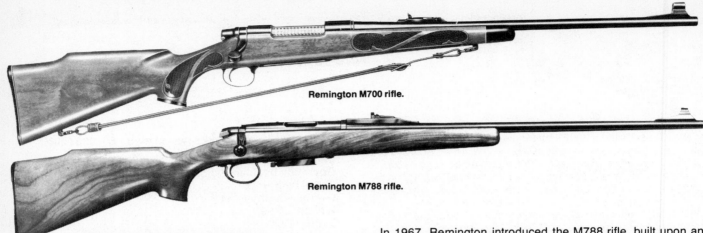

Remington M700 rifle.

Remington M788 rifle.

REMINGTON ARMS COMPANY

The Remington M700 rifle is simply a logical improvement of the M721-722 series introduced in 1948. The M700 makes full use of design features and production techniques that were considered quite advanced, if not almost revolutionary, in sporting arms in '48. Other manufacturers who first decried such things have since adopted many of the features and techniques introduced at that time by Remington. The bolt is essentially Mauser in character with dual opposed locking lugs at the head and helical cocking cam at the rear. However, it utilizes a spring-clip type extractor, fully enclosed in a recess inside the bolt face. The extractor design permits complete enclosure of the head of the cartridge case within a counterbore within the face of the bolt. The ejector is a Garand type, spring-loaded plunger in the bolt face. The receiver is round in section, the traditional integral recoil lug being replaced by a barrel bracket protruding downward, sandwiched between barrel and front face of receiver ring.

The magazine is of Mauser type, though simplified by utilizing a separate sheet metal box, sandwiched between floor plate and receiver. The fully adjustable single-stage trigger assembly of the M700 is considered by many to be the best offered on any commercial sporting rifle, and the assembly incorporates a manual safety that lies closely alongside the rear receiver tang and does not interfere with scope mounting.

Characteristics of the Remington M700 Rifle

Caliber: All popular US.
Operation by: Manual; rotating bolt.
Barrel length: 22-26 in.
Overall length: 42$\frac{1}{2}$-46$\frac{1}{2}$ in.
Weight: 7-7$\frac{1}{2}$ lbs.
Sights: Open, adjustable.
Magazine capacity: 3-5 rounds.

The M40X series of bench-rest and target rifles are built upon the basic M700 action in both single-shot and magazine form.

There is also the M660 Carbine, which possesses all of the basic design features of the M700 but is made shorter to accommodate smaller cartridges and to achieve maximum weight reduction. This model also utilizes a one-piece plastic magazine box/trigger guard.

In 1967, Remington introduced the M788 rifle, built upon an entirely new action designed for maximum rigidity and accuracy and for the most economical production of advanced techniques. The bolt is designed for screw machine production and carries nine small locking lugs in three rows of three just forward of the bolt handle. The balance of the bolt design is mechanically identical to that of the M700. The receiver is simply a thick-wall, steel tube containing ejection and feeding cutouts and abutments against which the locking lugs bear. The trigger and safety mechanism are virtually identical to that of the M700. However, a detachable sheet metal box magazine and stamped trigger guard are utilized. Aside from the differences in location of locking lugs, functioning and manipulation are the same as in the M700. Both the M700 and M788 rifles are available in left hand versions, and the Model 700 Safari is available in .375 H&H and .458 Winchester Magnum.

Characteristics of the Remington M788 Rifle

Caliber: .222, .22-250, 6mm Remington; .243; .308.
Operation by: Manual; rear-locking bolt.
Barrel length: 22-24 in.
Overall length: 41$\frac{1}{2}$-43$\frac{1}{2}$ in.
Weight: 7-7$\frac{1}{2}$ lbs.
Sights: Open, adjustable.
Magazine capacity: 4 rounds; 5 in .222 caliber.

SAKO, FINLAND

SAKO rifles are produced in Finland and distributed exclusively in the US by the Garcia Corporation. The action is a slightly modified Mauser type, utilizing dual opposed locking lugs at the bolt head, combined with a recessed spring-loaded hook extractor on the right side of the bolt. The balance of the bolt is a typical Mauser design; the manual safety is incorporated in the adjustable, single-stage trigger assembly. The SAKO receiver is tubular in section and carries integral tapered scope-mounting dovetails on its upper surface. The bolt stop is original in design and functions quite well. Magazine and trigger guard are of typical Mauser construction except that the box proper is a separate sheet metal part clamped in place between the guard and receiver. The floor plate is hinged, secured by a latch inside the forward portion of the guard bow.

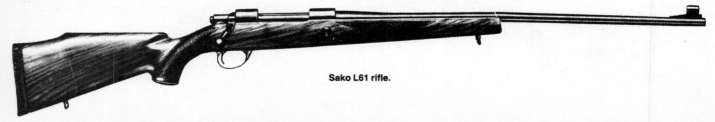

Sako L61 rifle.

A wide variety of SAKO rifles are produced on the above described action; however, the action is made in three lengths. All major parts of the three different actions are dimensionally different so that there is actually a single action design produced in three different sizes—not simply minor variations of a single size to accomodate cartridges of different lengths. Shortest of the series is the 6$^{1}/_{2}$-inch L-461 (Vixen) action, weighing 2$^{1}/_{8}$ pounds; the L579 (Forester) is 7$^{3}/_{8}$ inches, weighing 2 pounds; and the L61 (Finnbear) is 8$^{3}/_{8}$ inches, weighing 2$^{3}/_{4}$ pounds. SAKO is the only firm producing so complete a line of actions tailored specifically to different cartridge lengths. Essentially the same style rifles are offered built on each of the actions.

Characteristics of SAKO Rifles

Caliber: Most popular US from .222 upward.
Operation by: Manual; rotating bolt.
Barrel length: 20-24 in.
Overall length: 40-44 in.
Weight: 6$^{1}/_{2}$-7$^{1}/_{2}$ lbs.
Sights: Open.
Magazine capacity: 4 rounds; 3 in belted magnums.

SAVAGE ARMS COMPANY

In 1958, Savage introduced the Savage Model 110, a highly modified, Mauser type bolt-action rifle. The bolt contains an unusual number of parts; the body alone consists of the head, front and rear baffles, friction washer, retaining pin and handle—all separate pieces. The firing mechanism consists of 10 parts, exclusive of the sear. All parts are, however, designed for maximum production economy and result in low overall cost. The design is noteworthy in that there are two baffles to obstruct the rearward flow of gas should a case or primer rupture. The Savage extractor is similar in principle to the Remington enclosed type but is fitted in the outside of the bolt head, with the claw entering the bolt face counterbore through a slot. The cocking piece is housed completely within the bolt, and a pin protrudes from it to engage a Mauser type cocking cam in the side of the bolt body ahead of the handle. The unusual sear protrudes upward on the right side of the bolt to engage the cocking-piece pin and has an external projection, which serves as a cocking indicator and also as a bolt release.

The receiver is tubular, essentially Mauser form, fitted with a separate recoil lug in Remington fashion. The barrel screws into the receiver, sandwiching the recoil lug between the two, but it is also fitted with a threaded lock nut. The barrel proper does not screw up tightly in assembly as in other makes; final clamping of all parts is accomplished by drawing up the barrel lock nut tightly. The trigger assembly is of single-stage type, and the

manual safety is situated on the rear receiver tang in shotgun fashion. The trigger guard and magazine floor plate are of multiple-piece construction while the double-column magazine box is attached directly to the receiver. The Savage 110 series includes the 110E, 110B, 110BL (left hand), 110C and 110CL (left hand). The more expensive M111 Chieftan and 112-V Varmint Rifle have evolved from the 110 series.

Characteristics of Savage Model 110 Rifle

Caliber: .243, .270, .308 Winchester; .30-06; 7mm Remington Magnum.
Operation by: Manual; rotating reciprocating bolt.
Barrel length: 20-22 in.
Overall length: 40$^{1}/_{2}$-45 in.
Weight: 6$^{3}/_{4}$-8 lbs.
Sights: Open; folding rear.
Magazine capacity: 4 rounds; 3 in belted magnums.

Savage also produces the Model 340, an economy-priced centerfire rifle of distinctive design. The bolt utilizes a single large locking lug at its head, and the bolt handle functions as a safety lug by virtue of being seated deep into a recess in the receiver. Cocking and extraction are accomplished in Mauser fashion, and the receiver is tubular, requiring a minimum of machining. A pivoted manual safety is fitted to the right rear of the receiver. The trigger is a simple, single-stage design. A detachable, single-column box magazine is installed ahead of the trigger guard.

Characteristics of Savage Model 340 Rifle

Caliber: .22 Hornet; .222 Remington; .223; .30-30.
Operation by: Manual; rotating single-lug bolt.
Barrel length: 20-22 in.
Weight: 6$^{1}/_{2}$ lbs.
Sights: Open; folding rear.
Magazine capacity: 3 rounds; 4 in .222 caliber.

SCHULTZ-LARSEN, DENMARK

The Shultz-Larsen design is one of the few not based on the Mauser 98. It has been produced in Denmark for many years, and the action has long been highly popular in Europe for building best quality target rifles, including those for international competition. The bolt consists of a massive cylinder with four large locking lugs equally spaced around its circumference several inches back from the bolt face. It is thus what we commonly call a rear-locking bolt. The lugs engage corresponding

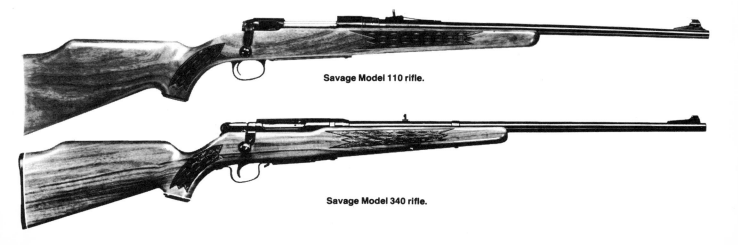

Savage Model 110 rifle.

Savage Model 340 rifle.

abutments in the ring of the massive tubular receiver, and a thick bolt handle root also doubles as a safety lug by turning down into a notch in the receiver. Multiple gas-escape ports are drilled in the bolt body, exposed in the ejection port, and the bolt face is deeply counterbored to surround the cartridge-case head. The firing mechanism and cocking method follow Mauser practice closely. A fully adjustable single-stage trigger is fitted, as is a hinged floor plate, on the magazine. Aside from the unusually short bolt lift, occasioned by the four locking lugs, functioning and manipulation are identical with Mauser type rifles.

Characteristics of Schultz-Larsen Rifle

Caliber: Most popular US and foreign.
Operation by: Manual; rotating reciprocating rearlock bolt.
Barrel length: 24 in.
Overall length: 44 ½ in.
Weight: 7 ½ lbs.
Magazine capacity: 4 rounds; 3 in belted magnums.

STEYR-MANNLICHER, AUSTRIA

Mannlicher sporting rifles have been produced at Steyr Daimler Puch in Austria since the early 1900s. The basic sporting rifle is based upon the military M1903 model described in Chapter 22. Numerous improvements have been made on the original action, and the current production model is the Steyr-Mannlicher introduced in 1968. This is a lightweight design intended to follow in the tradition of the Mannlicher-Schoenauer carbine, both in styling and in the more desirable mechanical features. The locking system consists of six rearward lugs locking into the receiver bridge. Cocking is accomplished in the Mauser manner. Only minimum cutouts are made in the receiver to permit ejection and feeding, and the rear of the bolt is closed by a streamlined sleeve, which blends into the lines of the receiver. A detachable rotary type magazine is employed. A fully adjustable single-stage trigger is offered with a European styled double-set trigger optional. Particularly unusual is the appearance of the barrel, which is hammer-forged around a rifling mandrel. The forging marks on the exterior are retained, resulting in a many-faceted surface, rather than the usual polished barrel finish. The models SL and L are based on a short action suitable for cartridges from the .222 Remington to the .308 Winchester. Two other lengths are being produced—the Model M for .30-06 class cartridges and the Model S for the larger cartridges up through the .375 and .458 Magnums.

Characteristics of the Steyr-Mannlicher Rifles

Caliber: Most popular US and European rifle cartridges.
Operation by: Manual; Mannlicher style bolt.
Barrel length: 20-25½ in.

Overall length: 40-46 in.
Weight: 7¼-8½ lbs.
Sights: Open; hooded ramp front.
Magazine capacity: 5 rounds.

STURM, RUGER AND COMPANY, INC.

Introduced in 1968, the Ruger M77 was the company's first entry in the bolt-action field. On the surface, it looks more like a cleaned-up M98 Mauser than anything else, but several advance design and production features are incorporated. The bolt is typically Mauser, including the long non-rotating extractor and bolt-guide rib. The firing pin and cocking system is also typically Mauser. The safety, however, is eliminated from the bolt sleeve and placed on the rear receiver tang in shotgun fashion. The receiver is somewhat slab-sided and intricate in contour and carries a Mauser type bolt stop at the left rear.

Scope-mounting dovetails are formed integrally with the top of the receiver, and Ruger supplies rings to match. The single-stage trigger is quite crisp and is fully adjustable. The trigger guard/magazine assembly resembles the Winchester M70 and is held in place by three guard screws. An unusual feature is that the head of the forward guard screw is angled rearward so that tightening it not only pulls the receiver down into the stock, but rearward, seating the recoil lug solidly in the wood. The magazine floor plate is hinged and held in place by a quick-release latch in the front of the trigger guard bow.

Characteristics of Ruger M77 Rifle

Caliber: .22-250; 6mm Remington; .243, .308, .284 Winchester; 6.5mm, .350 Remington Magnum.
Operation by: Manual; rotating reciprocating bolt.
Barrel length: 22 in.
Overall length: 42 in.
Weight: 6½ lbs.
Sights: None; furnished with scope bases.
Magazine capacity: 5 rounds; 3 in magnum calibers.

WEATHERBY INC.

The first proprietary Weatherby rifle design, the Mark V, was introduced in 1958. At that time, it represented a radical departure from current action design. The bolt body is a massive cylinder, carrying three small locking lugs, each on a reduced diameter portion at the head. Lugs and bolt body are both of the same major diameter. The body contains longitudinal flutes, which reduce weight and friction and provide escape areas for dust and dirt. The bolt face is deeply counterbored to completely surround the cartridge-case head. The only opening into the counterbore is a slot for the recessed hook extractor. The rear of the bolt is closed by a streamlined sleeve, which completely en-

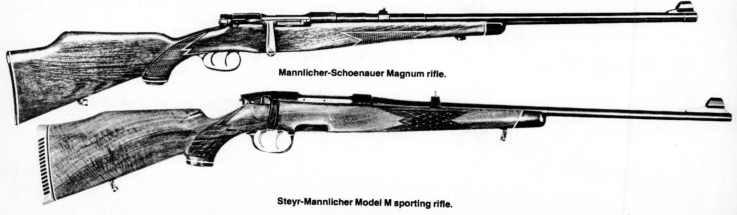

Mannlicher-Schoenauer Magnum rifle.

Steyr-Mannlicher Model M sporting rifle.

Weatherby .300 Magnum Mark V rifle.

Winchester Model 70 Target.

Winslow Plainsmaster rifle.

closes the cocking piece, except for an indicator tongue that protrudes from underneath the sleeve when the gun is cocked.

A manual safety is pivoted to the right side of the bolt sleeve. A sheet metal box magazine is held between the receiver and Mauser style trigger guard, to which is fitted a hinged floor plate. The trigger is of single-stage design and is fully adjustable. Weatherby rifles are characterized by high-gloss finishes and unusual stock wood. Also, they are generally chambered only for the Weatherby proprietary cartridges. The Mark V action is made in two sizes, the smaller being adapted to cartridges of the .224 Weatherby and .22-250 class; the larger action handles all other calibers.

Characteristics of Weatherby Mark V Rifle

Caliber: The full line of special Weatherby cartridges; any other on special order.
Operation by: Manual; Weatherby rotating bolt.
Barrel length: 24-26 in.
Overall length: 42^1/$_2$-46^1/$_2$ in.
Weight: 6^1/$_2$-10^1/$_2$ lbs.
Sights: None.
Magazine capacity: 4 rounds; 3 in .378 and .460 calibers.

WINCHESTER REPEATING ARMS COMPANY

First introduced in the middle 1930s, the Winchester Model 70 underwent minor evolutionary improvements until 1964, when a completely redesigned version was introduced. It is considered by some to be the most popular American bolt-action rifle. The design is relatively straightforward, utilizing the Mauser type cocking system. A plunger type ejector and sliding/hook type extractor are let into the bolt face. The receiver is typically Mauser, containing locking abutments at its front and threaded for barrel attachment. The magazine is of basic Mauser type and is considerably modified for economy of fabrication. The trigger mechanism is adjustable. Variants of the Winchester Model 70 include the Model 70A, Model 70 Target rifle, Model 70 African and Model 70 International Army Match Target rifle.

Characteristics of Winchester M70 Rifle

Caliber: All popular US.
Operation by: Manual; rotating bolt.
Barrel length: 19-24 in.
Overall length: 39^1/$_2$-44^1/$_2$ in.
Weight: 7^1/$_2$-8^1/$_2$ lbs.
Sights: Open, adjustable.
Magazine capacity: 5 rounds; 3 in belted magnums.

WINSLOW ARMS

Winslow Arms takes existing actions, domestic barrels and assorted woods and accessories and assembles them into unusual and often highly ornate sporting rifles on a semi-production basis. The FN action is used for the larger calibers, the short SAKO L-461 for the shorter and smaller calibers.

It is primarily in the matter of style and finish that Winslow rifles differ from those assembled by other makers of the same actions. Stock styling, for example, is quite unique, incorporating such features as extra long, hooked pistol grips, fluted foreends, extra large roll-over combs and sweeping curves not encountered in other makes. In addition, exotic inlays, checkering patterns and carvings are found on the more costly models. Considering the fact that some models cost up to $4,000, the result is often quite striking. Virtually any caliber, barrel length or weight may be ordered.

GENERAL

In addition to the individual makes and models of bolt-action rifles already listed and described, a number of firms import rifles marked with their own name but manufactured abroad as minor variations of existing models. These rifles are normally based on one of the basic Mauser M98 type actions. In some instances, actual assembly takes place in the US. The actions may be of new European manufacture, refurbished military actions or commerical actions purchased in partly finished condition. Generally speaking, these rifles are identical in characteristics, operation and loading and firing procedures to the M98 or FN Mauser or their variations. Some names under which these rifles may be encountered are Colt, Reinhart Fajen, Herter's, L. A. Distributors, Smith & Wesson and Dan Wesson Arms.

LEVER-ACTION RIFLES

BROWNING

One of the newer, and hence more modern, lever-action rifles is Browning's BRL, which features a rotating bolt head with multiple locking lugs, recessed bolt face and side ejection. For safety, the rifle has a three-position hammer, trigger disconnect system and inertia firing pin.

Characteristics of Browning BLR

Caliber: .243; .308.
Operation by: Swinging finger lever; reciprocating bolt.
Barrel length: 19$^7/_{16}$ in.
Overall length: 38$^5/_8$ in.
Weight: 7 lbs.
Sights: Open, adjustable; tapped for scope mounts.
Magazine capacity: 4 rounds, detachable.

MARLIN FIREARMS

The design for the Marlin M336 originated in 1889, making it the oldest still produced in the US. It has undergone considerable improvement but has remained little changed since 1948, when the breech bolt was changed from square to round section. The M36 then became the M336. It utilizes a solid receiver, vertical sliding lock and reciprocating bolt, side ejection, tubular under-barrel magazine and a two-piece stock. Operation is by a swinging finger lever forming the trigger guard. An unusual feature is the two-piece firing pin, which is aligned by the locking block to prevent firing when the breech is not fully locked. Since 1972, this rifle has also been made in .45-70 as the M1895.

Characteristics of Marlin M336 Rifle

Caliber: .30-30 Win.; .35 Rem.; .444 Marlin; .45-70 (M1895).
Operation by: Swinging finger lever; reciprocating, rear-locked bolt.
Barrel length: 20-24 in.
Overall length: 38$^1/_2$-42$^1/_4$ in.
Weight: 7-7$^1/_2$ lbs.
Sights: Open, adjustable.
Magazine capacity: 5-7 rounds.

The Marlin 1894 is actually a new (1969 introduction), modernized copy of the original M1894 once made for the short .44-40 cartridge.

Characteristics of Marlin M1894 Rifle

Caliber: .44 Magnum.
Operation by: Swinging finger lever; reciprocating bolt.
Barrel length: 20 in.
Overall length: 37$^1/_2$ in.
Weight: 6 lbs.
Sights: Open, adjustable.
Magazine capacity: 10 rounds.

Mechanically, physically and functionally, the M1894 differs from the M336 only in bolt section (square) and its full length bolt slot in the receiver wall. Operation and handling are as described for the M336. Also available are the Marlin 1895 in .45-70 caliber and the M444 in caliber .444.

O. F. MOSSBERG & SONS

In 1973, Mossberg introduced a traditional Western style lever-action carbine design, the M472. In both appearance and design, it greatly resembles the Marlin M336. It is the only exposed-hammer lever-action rifle that utilizes a separate manual safety instead of a safety position on the hammer. It also uses a vertical rising block locking system similar to the Marlin & Winchester and functions generally the same.

Characteristics of Mossberg M472

Caliber: .30-30 Win.; .35 Rem.
Operation by: Manual; finger lever.
Barrel length: 20 in.
Weight: 7$^1/_4$ lbs.
Sights: Open.
Magazine capacity: 6 rounds.

FN-made Browning Lever Action rifle.

Marlin M336 rifle.

Marlin M1894 rifle.

SAKO, FINLAND

The SAKO Finnwolf is the only European high power lever-action rifle manufactured. First introduced in 1962-1963 and produced in only relatively small quantities primarily for sale in the US, it is of solid-frame, hammerless construction, using an unusual system of rack and pinion gears to translate lever movement into bolt movement. A curved rack inside the receiver rotates a gear segment on the lever connected by crank and links to the bolt carrier. The bolt is of the reciprocating type with a separate rotating head. The stock is one piece, and a detachable box magazine is fitted.

Characteristics of SAKO Finnwolf Rifle

Caliber: .243; .308 Win.
Operation by: Swinging finger lever; reciprocating rotating bolt.
Barrel length: 22 in.
Overall length: 42$^1/_4$ in.
Weight: 7 lbs.
Sights: Hooded front only; integral scope-mount bases on receiver.
Magazine capacity: 4 rounds.

SAVAGE ARMS

The Savage M99 has been in continuous production since its introduction in 1899, and many minor improvements have been made during that time. Actuated by a swinging finger lever, the M99 has a solid receiver, tipping, rear-locked reciprocating bolt and rotary magazine. Many minor variations have been produced, and the current M99C utilizes a detachable double-column box magazine. Also currently marketed are the Savage 99-A and 99-E.

Characteristics of Savage M99 Rifle

Caliber: .243; .284; .308; .358 Win.; .300 Savage.
Operation by: Swinging finger lever; tipping reciprocating bolt.
Barrel length: 20-22 in.

Overall length: 39$^3/_4$-41$^3/_4$ in.
Weight: 6$^1/_4$-6$^3/_4$ lbs.
Magazine capacity: Rotary, 5; box, 4; .284 caliber, 3.

WINCHESTER REPEATING ARMS COMPANY

In 1965, Winchester introduced the M88 as the first really new lever gun since the 1890s. The action is quite similar to that of the M100 semiautomatic. It utilizes an entirely different firing mechanism combined with a finger lever. Bolt movement is obtained by the lever, rather than by an operating slide as in the M100. Considerable parts interchangeability exists between the two. It is currently out of production.

Characteristics of Winchester M88 Rifle

Caliber: .243; .284; .308 Win.
Operation by: Swinging finger lever; reciprocating bolt.
Barrel length: 19-22 in.
Overall length: 39$^1/_2$-42$^1/_2$ in.
Weight: 7-7$^1/_2$ lbs.
Sights: Open, adjustable.
Magazine capacity: 4 rounds; 3 in .284.

Introduced in 1894 and produced virtually without change until 1964, at which time the design was revised, the Winchester M94 continues in production. In the minds of most shooters, it typifies the "American style" lever-action arms developed only in this country during the last half of the 19th century. It is built around a solid receiver, two-piece stock and tubular magazine. The reciprocating bolt is locked at the rear, ejecting fired cases upward. Operation is by swinging the finger lever.

Characteristics of Winchester M94 Rifle

Caliber: .30-30 Win; .44 Magnum.
Operation by: Swinging finger lever; reciprocating bolt.
Barrel length: 20-26 in.
Overall length: 37$^3/_4$-43$^3/_4$ in.
Weight: 6$^1/_8$-8 lbs.
Sights: Open, adjustable.
Magazine capacity: 6-10 rounds.

Savage M99 rifle.

Winchester M88 rifle.

Winchester Model 1894 Lever Action rifle.

PUMP-ACTION RIFLES

REMINGTON ARMS COMPANY

Introduced in 1952 to replace the earlier M14 and M141 pump rifles, the Remington M760 was the first such action capable of handling full power cartridges in the .30-06 class. It remains so. Except that power to operate the action is supplied by manual reciprocation of the forestock, it is identical mechanically, physically and functionally to the Remington M742. Most internal parts are interchangeable between the two.

Characteristics of Remington M760 Rifle

Caliber: 6mm Rem.; .243, .270, .308 Win.; .30-06.
Operation by: Reciprocating forestock; rotating bolt.
Barrel length: 22 in.
Overall length: 42 in.
Weight: 7 1/4 lbs.

Sights: Open, adjustable.
Magazine capacity: 4 rounds.

SAVAGE ARMS

Introduced in 1971, the Model 170 is a lightweight, slide-action hunting rifle offered only in .30-30 Winchester caliber. It is of very simple, hammerless, locked breech design and construction and priced quite low.

Characteristics of Savage M170

Caliber: .30-30 Win.
Operation by: Slide-action.
Barrel length: 22 in; carbine, 18 in.
Overall length: 41 1/2 in; carbine, 37 1/2 in.
Weight: 6 3/4 lbs.
Magazine capacity: 3 rounds.

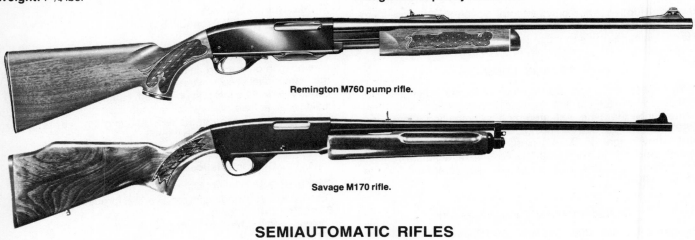

Remington M760 pump rifle.

Savage M170 rifle.

SEMIAUTOMATIC RIFLES

BROWNING

In 1967, the US Browning firm introduced its first centerfire self-loading rifle in this country, the Browning BAR. It is produced by Fabrique Nationale. The design utilizes a short-stroke gas system with a two-piece reciprocating bolt and a characteristically Browning double-hook firing mechanism. It uses a solid receiver, two-piece stock and an unusual hinged box magazine. Present models have the distinction of being the only self-loading design chambered for belted magnum cartridges.

Characteristics of Browning BAR

Caliber: .243, .270, .308 Win; .30-06; 7mm Rem. Mag.; .300 Win. Mag.; .388 Win. Mag.
Operation by: Gas; reciprocating rotating bolt.
Barrel length: 22 in.; 24 in. for magnum calibers.
Overall length: 43 1/2 in; 45 1/2 in. for magnum calibers.
Weight: 7 3/8 lbs; 8 1/2 lbs. for magnum calibers.
Sights: Open, adjustable.
Magazine capacity: 4 rounds; 3 in belted magnums.

HARRINGTON & RICHARDSON

During 1966, Harrington & Richardson announced its Ultra M360 full caliber, self-loading rifle. It is modern in style, operated

by a short-stroke gas piston. It uses a rear-locked, tipping, reciprocating bolt, one-piece stock and detachable box magazine. The design is relatively simple for a self-loader, and the bolt somewhat resembles that of the Reising SMG once made by Harrington & Richardson.

Characteristics of H&R Ultra M360

Caliber: .243, .308 Win.
Operation by: Short-stroke gas; tipping bolt.
Barrel length: 22 in.
Overall length: 43 1/2 in.
Weight: 7 1/2 lbs.
Sights: Open, adjustable.
Magazine capacity: 3 rounds.

HECKLER & KOCH, GERMANY

Building upon their growing family of roller-locked military rifles and pistols, Heckler and Koch has added two semiautomatic, Monte Carlo walnut stocked rifles to their sporting line—the 630 and the 770.

Characteristics of HK Model 630

Caliber: .22 Hornet; .221; .222; .223.
Operation by: Delayed recoil; roller lock.

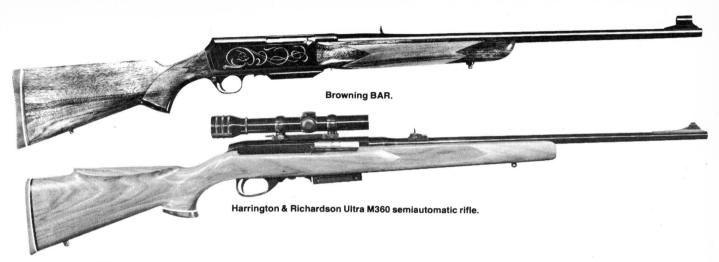

Browning BAR.

Harrington & Richardson Ultra M360 semiautomatic rifle.

Overall length: 39⁷/₁₀ in.
Weight: 7³/₁₀ lbs. (cal. .223).
Sights: Open, adjustable; telescopic.
Magazine capacity: 4 rounds.

Characteristics of HK Model 770

Caliber: 6.5 × 57mm; 7 × 57mm; .243; .308.
Operation by: Delayed recoil; roller lock.
Overall length: 42½ in.
Weight: 7⁷/₁₀ lbs. (cal. .308).
Sights: Open, adjustable; telescopic.
Magazine capacity: 4 rounds.

REMINGTON ARMS COMPANY

The Remington M742 was the first successful full power and the first gas operated semiautomatic to be offered on the American market. It was introduced in 1955 as the M740 and subsequently redesignated the M742 in 1960 as improvements were added. It utilizes a typical under-barrel gas cylinder and piston; the latter connects to twin operating rods that carry a two-piece, reciprocating, multiple-lug bolt at their rear. It utilizes a solid receiver with side ejection and two-piece stock.

Characteristics of Remington M742 Rifle

Caliber: 6mm, .280 Rem.; .30-06; .243, .308 Win.
Operation by: Gas; reciprocating rotating bolt.
Barrel length: 20-22 in.
Overall length: 40-42 in.
Weight: 7½ lbs.
Sights: Open, adjustable.
Magazine capacity: 4 rounds.

STURM, RUGER AND COMPANY

The Ruger .44 Carbine is the only semiautomatic rifle chambered for the .44 magnum revolver cartridge. Introduced in 1961 as a short-range deer rifle, it is gas operated, utilizing a short-stroke floating piston, heavy operating slide and short one-piece rotating reciprocating bolt. Uniquely, it is the only centerfire self-loader using a tubular, under-barrel magazine. It is styled after the US M1 Carbine, capitalizing on that gun's popularity.

Caliber: .44 Rem. Mag.
Operation by: Short-stroke gas; rotating bolt.
Barrel length: 18½ in.
Overall length: 37 in.
Weight: 5²/₃ lbs.
Sights: Open, adjustable.
Magazine capacity: 4 rounds.

The Ruger 5.56mm Mini-14 semiautomatic rifle is described in Chapters 1 and 45.

"MEDVED" [THE BEAR], USSR

A product of M. T. Kalashnikov's Design Bureau, the "Medved" is a well made, high quality, gas operated sporting rifle. Unlike its military counterpart, the Dragunov (Chapter 43), the Bear, chambered for a larger caliber, has a conventional sporting type wood stock and a smaller capacity magazine—five shots instead of 10. The soft-nosed, jacketed 9mm bullet (.354 in.) is fired from the 7.62 × 54R case, which has been enlarged to take the larger diameter projectile. Traveling at an instrumented velocity of 2120 f.p.s., the 231.5-grain bullet is quite accurate at normal hunting ranges.

Characteristics of "Medved"

Caliber: 9 × 54Rmm
Operation by: Gas; rotating bolt (Kalashnikov type).
Barrel length: 20⁴/₅ in.
Overall length: 43³/₈ in.
Weight: 7¼ lbs.
Sights: Open, adjustable; telescopic, 3½ ×.
Magazine capacity: 5 rounds.

WINCHESTER REPEATING ARMS COMPANY

Winchester introduced the gas operated Model 100 in 1960. It has unusually clean, smooth lines and is a thoroughly modern design, exploiting mass production techniques, including stampings and weldments. It utilizes an under-barrel gas cylinder, twin-armed operating slide/gas piston, two-part rotating reciprocating bolt and pivoted hammer firing mechanism. The stock is a one-piece design, and the detachable box magazine holds four rounds. When assembled, the rear of the receiver is closed by a solid steel recoil block attached permanently to the stock in M1 Carbine fashion. This model is out of production.

Characteristics of Winchester Model 100

Caliber: .243; .284; .308 Win.
Operation by: Gas; reciprocating rotating bolt.
Barrel length: 19-22 in.
Overall length: 39½-42½ in.
Weight: 7 lbs.
Sights: Open, adjustable.
Magazine capacity: 4 rounds; 3 in .284.

Remington M742 semiautomatic rifle.

Ruger Carbine with "Built-in" receiver sight .44 magnum caliber.

Soviet Medved 9×54 Rmm semiautomatic rifle.

Disassembled view of Soviet Medved rifle.

Winchester M100 semiautomatic rifle.

MISCELLANEOUS MAKES AND MODELS

Armalite AR-180: Semiautomatic version of Armalite AR-18 5.56mm military rifle. See Chapter 1.

Beretta BM59: Commercial semiautomatic version of the Italian Army 7.62mm BM59. See Chapter 28.

CETME Sport: A very slightly modified semiautomatic version of the CETME rifle adopted by the Spanish Army. See Chapter 39.

Colt AR-15 Sporter: Semiautomatic version of US M16 5.56mm rifle. See Chapter 45.

Heckler & Koch HK91 Sporter: Semiautomatic version of G3 7.62mm NATO rifle. See Chapter 20.

Heckler & Koch HK93 Sporter: Semiautomatic version of HK33 5.56mm rifle. See Chapter 20.

SIG/AMT: Commercial semiautomatic version of the Swiss Army Stgw. 57. See Chapter 41.

Universal M1 and Ferret Carbines: Identical to US M1 Carbine. See Chapter 45.

Valmet M62S; Commercial semiautomatic version of M62 7.62 × 39mm rifle. See Chapter 17.

Valmet M71S: See Chapter 17.

SINGLE-SHOT RIFLES

HARRINGTON & RICHARDSON

A very basic single-shot caliber .30-30 rifle, the Topper Model 158 is based upon the standard H&R break-open, exposed-hammer, a single-shot shotgun. It has no distinguishing or unique characteristics other than its economy and utility. A .45-70 version is available.

Characteristics of H&R Topper Model 158

Caliber: .30-30.
Operation by: Hinged frame; top lever.
Barrel length: 24 in.; optional 20-gauge barrel.
Overall length: 37½ in.
Weight: 5½ lbs.
Sights: Open.

STURM, RUGER AND COMPANY, INC.

A completely modern (introduced in 1968), single-shot rifle of top quality, the Ruger No. 1 is designed in the classic style, utilizing modern manufacturing techniques. Even the receiver is produced in virtually finished form by investment casting. The action combines features of many others but most resembles the British Farquharson. It features a separate bar to support the forestock, a two-piece stock, a through-bolted buttstock, a ¼-length barrel rib containing telescope bases, an internal hammer firing mechanism, a cocking indicator, a selective ejector-extractor, a powerful extraction and adaptability to any centerfire sporting cartridge. A .45-70 version is available as the No. 3 rifle.

Characteristics of Ruger No. 1 Rifle

Caliber: Any standard US centerfire on special order.
Operation by: Falling-block; under-lever actuated.
Barrel length: 22-26 in.
Overall length: 42 in. (26 in. bbl.).
Weight: 6¾-8½ lbs.
Sights: None; fitted for telescope bases.

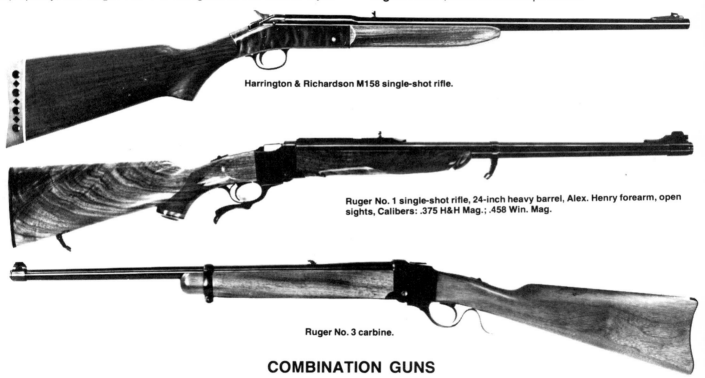

Harrington & Richardson M158 single-shot rifle.

Ruger No. 1 single-shot rifle, 24-inch heavy barrel, Alex. Henry forearm, open sights, Calibers: .375 H&H Mag.; .458 Win. Mag.

Ruger No. 3 carbine.

COMBINATION GUNS

COLT-SAUER

Colt has reintroduced the premier grade, 3-barrel (drilling) combination gun to the US market. Prices start at about $1750.

Characteristics of Colt-Sauer Drilling

Caliber: 12 gauge over .243; 12 gauge over .30-06.
Operation by: Hinged frame; top lever; box lock.
Barrel length: 25 in. (modified and full choke).
Overall length: 41¾ in.
Weight: 8 lbs.
Sights: Open; front, bead; rear, folding leaf.

FABRIQUE NATIONALE EXPRESS RIFLE

Built upon a 20 gauge FN-Browning shotgun action, the FN Express over and under rifle is individually crafted in a special workshop which reflects the time honored craftsmanship of the Liege gunmakers.

Characteristics of the FN-Browning Express Rifle

Caliber: 7 × 65Rmm and 9.3 × 74Rmm.
Operation by: Hinged frame; top lever.
Barrel length: 27 in.
Sights: Undercut rib; rear sight with a plate that can be folded, fore sight with gold bead.

FERLACH, AUSTRIA

Prices for this high quality, custom order drilling begin at about $2100.

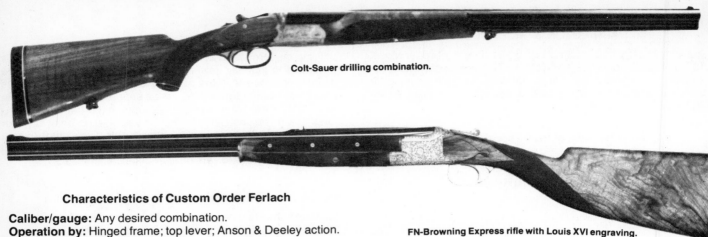

Colt-Sauer drilling combination.

Characteristics of Custom Order Ferlach

Caliber/gauge: Any desired combination.
Operation by: Hinged frame; top lever; Anson & Deeley action.
Length: To customer's specifications.
Weight: To customer's specifications.
Sights: To customer's specifications.

SAVAGE ARMS COMPANY

Savage produces several different model combination guns based on essentially the same action. All are in the M24 series, and most are chambered for the .22 Long Rifle or .22 MRF in the top barrel, and .410 or 20 gauge in the bottom barrel. The most recent development, the Model 24V series, is chambered for the .222 Remington and the 20 gauge shotshell. All are of external hammer, break-open, hinge-barrelled design and utilize pivoted locking blocks seating in a wedge-shaped recess in the rear face of the barrel under lug. All utilize a pivoted top lever for unlocking and opening, except the 24S and 24SM series in which the design is somewhat modified to utilize a pivoted side lever. The M24V is generally of more robust construction and has barrels of larger diameter to accommodate more powerful cartridges. Barrels of the M24V are separate and are inserted into a single barrel block at the chamber; however, the less powerful models have both barrels machined from a single block of steel. Barrel lengths in all models are 24 inches; weight is 6³/₄ pounds.

TIKKAKOSKI OY, FINLAND

Tikkakoski produces a rather unusual shotgun/rifle combination sold in America by Ithaca as the "Turkey Gun." One unique

FN-Browning Express rifle with Louis XVI engraving.

feature of this gun is the muzzle attachment, which is brazed securely to the shot upper barrel and surrounds—but is not attached to—the muzzle of the rifle barrel. This permits the rifled tube to elongate freely as it heats. The latter is shorter than the shot barrel, permitting the attachment to function as a muzzle brake by means of the eight gas-escape slots machined in its sides. The chamber ends of both barrels are silver-brazed into a solid steel block, which contains a recess into which a conventional double-bite locking block seats when the action is closed. Unlocking is accomplished by a typical shotgun type pivoted top lever. A conventional exposed hammer is utilized, and its impact is transmitted to the upper or lower firing pin as desired by means of a sliding block controlled by a button on the left side of the receiver. The receiver itself is also quite unusual in that instead of being machined or cast as a single unit, it is formed by brazing together pre-cut laminations of steel to form the necessary internal cavities. After brazing, the exterior of the receiver is shaped.

Characteristics of Turkey Gun

Caliber: 12 gauge and .222 (5.7 × 43mm) Rem.
Operation by: Hinged frame; top lever; manual cocking.
Barrel length: Shot, 26 in.; rifle, 24¹/₂ in.
Weight: 7¹/₄ lbs.
Sights: Open, adjustable.

Savage Model 24V combination gun.

SHOTGUNS

Shotguns, since the beginning of the cartridge era, have developed completely apart from military arms. While they do have limited military use—notably guard duty and riot control—such requirements are normally met by procuring standard or slightly modified off-the-shelf sporting guns. The standard shotgun in the US Army today is the Winchester Model 1200, while the Marine Corps uses the Remington Model 870. The following shotguns will be found in limited numbers in the US inventory: Winchester Model 12 and Stevens Models 520-30, 620A and 77E.

Repeating shotgun mechanisms are generally quite similar to those used in rifles of the same type, modified only as necessary to accomodate the lower chamber pressure and the larger size shot shells.

The traditional double-barrel shotgun exists in such widely diverse forms and designs that it is impossible to be specific. The basic design types solidified well before the turn of the century and are produced in countless makes and models all over the world. Because of the diversity, it is not possible to cover them in this publication.

Ithaca Turkey combination gun.

PUMP-ACTION SHOTGUNS

ITHACA GUN COMPANY

In 1937, Ithaca introduced its M37 "Featherlight" shotgun. At that time, it was the lightest 12 gauge repeating gun available—and at 6¹/₂ pounds, still compares very favorably with the most modern lightweight developments. The design is unique in that fired cases are ejected downward through the same port utilized for loading. This makes the gun excellent for use by left-handers and also avoids having ejected cases strike a shooter nearby. A tipping bolt locking system is utilized, and the firing mechanism is not fitted with a disconnector, meaning that the gun will fire if the trigger is held down as the action is closed on a loaded cartridge. Overall, the design is simple, straightforward and contains a relatively small number of parts.

Characteristics of Ithaca M37 Shotgun

Gauge: 12; 16; 20.
Operation by: Manual; reciprocating fore-end; tipping bolt.
Barrel length: 26-30 in.
Weight: 5³/₄-6¹/₂ lbs.
Sights: Bead; open, adjustable on slug-gun models.
Magazine capacity: 5 rounds.

MARLIN FIREARMS

Characteristics of Marlin Model 120 Magnum

Gauge: 12.
Operation by: Manual; reciprocating fore-end; tipping bolt lock.
Barrel length: 26, 28, 30 and 40 in.
Overall length: 50¹/₂ in. with 30-in. barrel.
Weight: 7³/₄ lbs.
Sights: Bead; open, adjustable on slug models.
Magazine capacity: 5 rounds.

O. F. MOSSBERG & SONS

Mossberg produces a number of variations on its basic, economy priced M500 pump gun. This gun is conventional in design, construction and appearance. It utilizes a non-rotating bolt locked to the receiver by a pivoted locking block passing through a recess in the center of the bolt. A single action bar connects the sliding fore-end to a bolt slide, which functions in a conventional manner. Mossberg currently markets the 500, 500AS Slugster, 500AR, 500AMR and 500E versions in this series.

Characteristics of Mossberg M500 Shotgun

Gauge: 12; 20; .410.
Operation by: Manual; reciprocating fore-end; non-rotating bolt.
Barrel length: 24-30 in.
Overall length: 43¹/₄-49¹/₄ in.
Weight: 5³/₄-6³/₄ lbs.

Sights: Bead; open, adjustable on slug models.
Magazine capacity: 5 rounds; 4 in 3-in. Magnums.

REMINGTON ARMS COMPANY

In 1950, Remington introduced the M870 pump gun to replace the Model 31. The new design bears considerable resemblance to the old, but it incorporates many improvements and more modern production methods. It utilizes a non-rotating bolt locked into the barrel extension by a pivoted block swinging vertically through the center of the bolt. Dual action bars connect the reciprocating fore-end to an action slide, which contains cam and engaging surfaces to actuate the bolt and bolt lock. The firing mechanism is conventional in design and with only minor exceptions, it is virtually identical to that of the M742/M760 rifles. Most parts will interchange. Remington offers the 870 in nine models: Wingmaster; All American; TB Trap; SA Skeet; D Tournament; Brushmaster Delux; Magnum; Premier; and Small Gauges.

Characteristics of Remington M870 Shotgun

Gauge: 12; 16; 20; small-frame version also in .410 and 28.
Operation by: Manual; reciprocating fore-end.
Barrel length: 20-30 in.
Overall length: 40¹/₂-50¹/₂ in.
Weight: 6¹/₂-7 lbs.
Sights: Bead; open, adjustable on slug guns.
Magazine capacity: 5 rounds.

SAVAGE ARMS COMPANY

The Savage Model 30 series pump shotguns represent the current development of a long line of similar designs. The design is relatively conventional and straightforward and utilizes a non-rotating tipping bolt locking system that incorporates a number of well proven principles. A single action bar connects the reciprocating fore-end (which slides on the magazine tube) to a slide that transmits movement to the bolt and performs locking and unlocking functions.

Characteristics of Savage Model 30 Shotgun

Gauge: 12; 16; 20; .410 in M77 version.
Operation by: Manual; reciprocating fore-end; tipping bolt lock.
Barrel length: 26-30 in.
Overall length: 45¹/₂-50 in.
Weight: 6¹/₄ (.410) - 8 lbs.
Magazine capacity: 4 rounds; 3 in 3-in. length.

SMITH & WESSON

Smith & Wesson has introduced two models of their 916 pump gun—the Eastfield and the 916T takedown model. The latter has an interchangeable barrel capability.

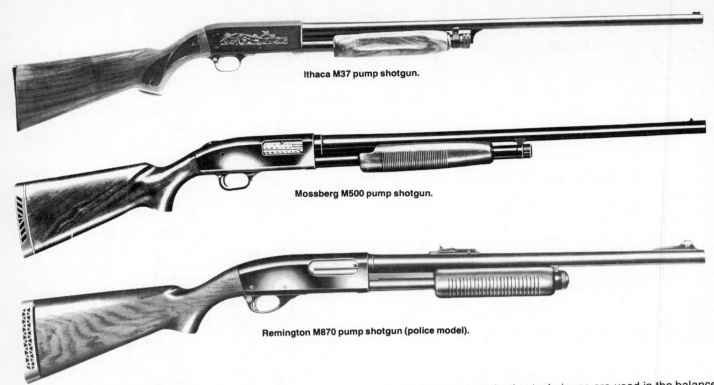

Ithaca M37 pump shotgun.

Mossberg M500 pump shotgun.

Remington M870 pump shotgun (police model).

Characteristics of S&W 916 Series

Gauge: 12 (916 Eastfield also in 20).
Barrel length: 20–30 in.
Weight: 7$\frac{1}{2}$ lbs (28-in. barrel).
Sights: Ventilated rib with bead.
Magazine capacity: 5 shots.

WINCHESTER REPEATING ARMS COMPANY

In 1963, Winchester introduced the successor to its justly-famed M12 pump gun—the Model 1200. In external appearance, the new gun is virtually identical to the old. However, internally, it differs vastly. The bolt is a two-part unit, consisting of a heavy rectangular carrier and a separate rotating bolt head carrying four short locking lugs spaced in pairs around its perimeter. An extension screwed solidly to the barrel contains abutments behind which these lugs lock. This arrangement, whereby all the longitudinal stress of firing is taken up within the barrel extension, allows simple takedown and/or barrel interchangeability. A ring on the barrel slips over the magazine tube, and a nut is screwed on after it to hold the barrel in place. All major structural parts are made of machined forgings, and modern low-cost production techniques are used in the balance of the gun. Some parts previously produced by costly machining are replaced by sophisticated stampings and precision castings. The rotating bolt locking system is much stronger than that of its predecessor, and the dual action bars make for very smooth operation. The M1200 (and companion) is the only production gun available with a recoil-absorbing mechanism built into the butt stock, called the "Winchester Recoil Reduction System," offered only on 12 gauge guns.

In 1972, Winchester reintroduced its famous M12 pump shotgun.

Characteristics of Winchester Model 1200 Shotgun

Gauge: 12; 20 (including 3-in. Magnum).
Operation by: Manual; rotating bolt; sliding fore-end.
Barrel length: 20–32 in.
Overall length: 40$\frac{5}{8}$-51 in.
Weight: 6$\frac{1}{2}$-8$\frac{1}{4}$ lbs.
Sights: Bead; open, adjustable on slug guns.
Magazine capacity: 2 rounds.

Winchester M1200 pump shotgun.

AUTOMATIC SHOTGUNS

BREDA, ITALY

The Breda Mark II was introduced in 1957 by Breda Meccanica Bresciana, Brescia, Italy. The design is essentially a highly modified form of the original Browning long recoil system, which has been widely copied since the early 1900s. While functioning remains essentially the same, the Breda utilizes a two-part bolt and a vertically sliding, rather than pivoted, locking block. The Browning friction ring system is utilized in conjunction with the recoil spring and requires adjustment when switching between light and heavy loads. In outline, the Breda is quite similar to the Browning except for a rounding off of the upper rear corner of the receiver. None of the Breda parts will interchange with the Browning; however, functioning, manipulation, loading and firing are essentially the same.

Characteristics of Breda Mark II Shotgun

Gauge: 12; 2¾-in. only.
Operation by: Long recoil; Browning system.
Barrel length: 26–28 in.
Weight: 7¼ lbs.
Sights: Bead.
Magazine capacity: 3 rounds.

BROWNING

The Browning Automatic was introduced in Europe shortly after the turn of the century. In both that form and as the Remington Model 11, it became the first commercially successful self-loading shotgun in the world. The Browning Automatic has been produced continuously since, making it the oldest repeating shotgun still in production. It is a long recoil type, the barrel, barrel-extension and bolt recoiling several inches as a unit first, then unlocking to allow the routine functioning cycle. This design results in a rather massive receiver of rectangular outline, which has earned it the nickname "Humpback." As a result of its success and durability, this design has been widely copied—both line-for-line and in varying modified forms. Among the names that will be encountered on Browning type designs are Breda, Franchi, Savage Arms, Sears Roebuck, Stevens Arms, Tradewinds and Universal.

Characteristics of Browning Automatic Shotgun

Gauge: 12; 16; 20.
Operation by: Long recoil; rising block lock.
Barrel length: 24–32 in.
Weight: 7–8¼ lbs.; lightweight models from 6⅛ lbs.
Sights: Bead; open, adjustable on slug guns.
Magazine capacity: 3–5 rounds.

As was its long recoil ancestor in 1903, the Browning 2000, by Fabrique Nationale, is well ahead of its time today. Evolved from the Browning Automatic Shotgun described above, the B.2000 is gas operated and has a versatility not often found in automatic weapons with interchangeable barrels. Four basic models are currently produced by FN; Standard, Superlightweight, Skeet and Trap. While the last three are available in 12 gauge only, the Standard is also made in 20 gauge.

Characteristics of the FN Browning 2000 Shotgun.

Gauge: 12 and 20.
Operation by: Gas; piston below the barrel.
Barrel length: 24–32 in.
Sights: Bead and ventilated rib standard.
Magazine capacity: 5 2 ¾-in. shells.
  4 3 inch shells.

NOTE: The super lightweight cannot safely use the 3 inch chambered barrel.

FRANCHI, ITALY

The Franchi semiautomatic shotgun is manufactured by Luigi Franchi, Brescia, Italy. Essentially, this design may be considered a highly modified form of the Browning. It utilizes the long recoil system, and the bolt and locking mechanism are identical in principle and extremely similar in outline to the Browning. None of the parts will interchange with the Browning; however, all perform the same functions and are similar in outline. The interior of Franchi barrels are chrome plated to resist corrosion and leading. The outstanding feature of this design is its usually light weight.

Characteristics of Franchi

Gauge: 12; 16; 20 (2¾-in. shells only).
Operation by: Long recoil; rising block lock.
Weight: 6¼ lbs. in 12 gauge; 5⅛ lbs. in 20 gauge.
Magazine capacity: 4 rounds.

INTERARMS

Interarms currently imports for the American market a semiautomatic shotgun produced by Manufrance. Of fairly conventional design, this gun utilizes a non-rotating bolt fitted with a rising locking block. Styling is conventional, and the gun is relatively lightweight.

Characteristics of the Manufrance Semiautomatic Shotgun.

Gauge: 12 (2¾ in.)
Operation by: Gas.
Barrel length: 26–30 in.
Weight: 6¾ lbs.
Sights: Bead.
Magazine capacity: 3 rounds.

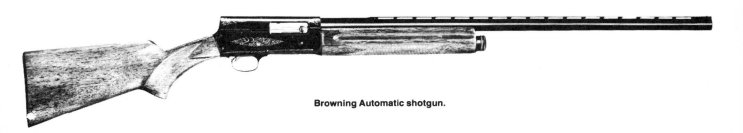

Browning Automatic shotgun.

ITHACA GUN COMPANY

In 1968, Ithaca introduced its M300 semiautomatic shotgun, climaxing a development program that expanded the line to include shotguns of all basic types. The M300 is also offered in a deluxe version, the M900. This is essentially the original Browning long recoil design, streamlined in appearance, simplified somewhat and adapted to more modern production techniques. The squarish profile of the Browning receiver has been changed to a pleasing curve that blends with the stock; aside from that, the appearance is essentially the same. Functioning, manipulation, loading and firing are essentially identical to that of the Browning.

Characteristics of Ithaca Semiautomatic Shotgun

Gauge: 12 (2³/₄-in.); 20 (3-in.).
Operation by: Recoil; Browning type.
Barrel length: 26–30 in.
Weight: 6¹/₂-7 lbs.
Sights: Bead.
Magazine capacity: 4 rounds.

Ithaca also introduced in 1972 an excellent gas operated autoloading shotgun, designed M51. It utilizes a rotating bolt with three locking lugs actuated by a self-regulating gas system, which handles light and heavy loads without adjustment. It has been rated highly by reviewers.

Characteristics of Ithaca M51

Gauge: 12 (2³/₄-in.); 20 (3-in.).
Operation by: Gas.
Barrel length: 26 or 30 in.
Weight: 7¹/₂ lbs.
Sights: Bead.
Magazine capacity: 3 rounds.

REMINGTON ARMS COMPANY

In 1962, Remington introduced its first gas operated semiautomatic shotgun, the M1100. This design carried forward the original concept of maximum interchangeability of parts initiated with the M870 shotgun and continued through the M740–42 and M760 rifles. Essentially, the action of the M1100 is the same as that of the M870, modified only as necessary to permit a gas piston and cylinder to supply the power for operation. Bolt and locking mechanism remain the same; however, the dual action bars are combined into a single unit with the action slide. A separate action bar sleeve is attached to the action bar and encircles the magazine tube. The forward end of the sleeve enters the gas cylinder (attached to the barrel) and functions as an annular piston.

Characteristics of Remington M1100 Semiautomatic Shotgun

Gauge: 12; 16; 20; small frame versions also in .410 and 28.
Operation by: Gas; non-rotating bolt.
Barrel length: 22–30 in.
Overall length: 42–50 in.
Weight: 6¹/₄-7¹/₂ lbs.
Sights: Bead; open, adjustable on slug models.
Magazine capacity: 5 rounds.

SMITH & WESSON

Smith & Wesson has also entered the automatic shotgun field with the gas operated Model 1100.

WINCHESTER REPEATING ARMS COMPANY

In 1964, Winchester introduced its gas operated M1400 semiautomatic shotgun. In external appearance, the M1400 is virtually identical to the M1200 pump gun. The action is also

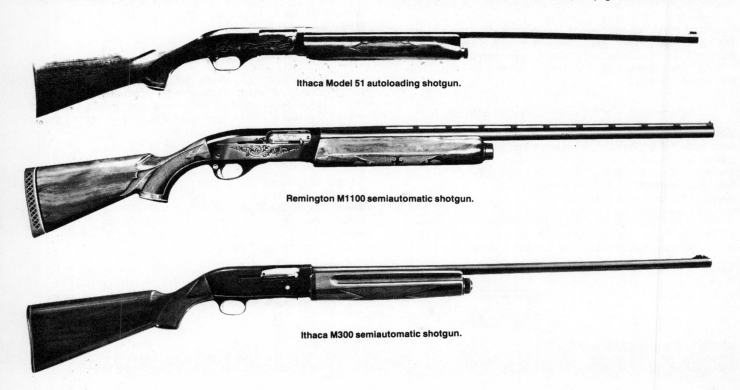

Ithaca Model 51 autoloading shotgun.

Remington M1100 semiautomatic shotgun.

Ithaca M300 semiautomatic shotgun.

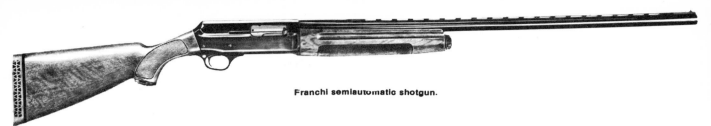

Franchi semiautomatic shotgun.

only slightly changed, and a very high degree of parts interchangeability exists between models. The difference lies only in that the M1400 has been modified so that a conventional gas piston and cylinder provide the power for operating the action. Dual action bars are attached to the gas piston, and at their rear extremities they are identical to the action bars of the M1200. The forward portion of the magazine tube functions as the gas cylinder, and the action bars are attached by means of a pin protruding through a slot in the tube. The magazine cap, which holds the barrel in position, contains a gas relief valve to bleed off gas over and above the designed operating level. This permits use of light, heavy and magnum loads through the same

mechanism without adjustment. The action release of the M1200 is replaced by a bolt latch activated by the magazine follower. After the last round is fired, the bolt is locked to the rear. Pressure on the magazine follower disengages the latch, allowing the recoil spring to drive the bolt forward. This makes it necessary for some slight change in loading procedures. With the action open, drop a round in the ejection port. Then either depress the follower by hand or with the cartridge being inserted in the magazine. All other functioning, manipulation, loading and firing procedures are essentially identical to those of the M1200 pump gun. Specifications and characteristics are identical.

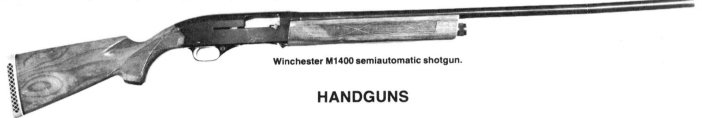

Winchester M1400 semiautomatic shotgun.

HANDGUNS

As in the case of rifle development, many handguns originally appeared as military sidearms. Basic patterns such as the Colt M1911, Colt M1917, Walther P38/P1, FN Browning High Power, SIG 210 and SIG 220 are described under the country of their origin in Part II. More recent military developments, some of which have target applications, are discussed in Chapter 4. The

text below presents representative handguns currently available to the sporting public. While some shooters and small arms companies continue to experiment with new calibers, the standard revolver and pistol cartridges of the past two decades still hold sway.

REVOLVERS

CHARTER ARMS

Charter Arms introduced its Undercover Model in the mid-1960s in an effort to capture part of the revolver market held by Colt and Smith & Wesson. Their revolver is a solid frame, swing-out cylinder, double/single action revolver of minimum weight and size. The design dispenses with a frame side plate, access being provided by removing the trigger guard. It is unique in that the cylinder may be unlatched by either pressing a thumb piece forward or pulling forward on the extractor rod. In 1973, a .44 Special version was introduced. A .357 magnum target revolver and a .32 Undercoverette were added to the line subsequently.

heritage. Their 11 1977 center-fire revolvers are built on four frame types—P, D, I and J. For convenience, the Colt revolvers will be described by variations within frame type.

Characteristics of Charter Arms Undercover

Caliber: .38 Special; .32 S&W Long; .44 Special.
Operation by: Manual; double or single action.
Barrel length: 2–3 in.
Overall length: 6¹/₄-7¹/₄ in.
Weight: 16–17 oz.
Sights: Open, fixed.
Cylinder capacity: 5 rounds; 6 in .32.

COLT INDUSTRIES

The Firearms Division of Colt Industries is one of the oldest revolver-makers in the world, and their handguns reflect that

Charter Arms revolver.

Model P Revolvers

Known variously as the Colt Single-Action Army, the Peace-maker and the Frontier Six-Shooter, this revolver has been in production in its present form since 1873. The basic action design dates before 1850, and the Model P in .45 Long Colt was the standard US Army sidearm for many years. Produced in 36 calibers during its long career, the Peacemaker is currently manufactured in only two calibers—.357 Magnum and .45 Colt. Colt offers two variants of the Model P—the Single Action Army, which has the classic lines of the 1873 model, and the New Frontier Single Action, which also has adjustable target sights. The latter revolver is available only in 5½- and 7½-inch barrels.

Characteristics of the Colt Single-Action Army Revolver

Caliber: .357 Magnum; .45 Colt.
Operation by: Manual, single-action only.
Barrel length: 4¾ in. to 5½ in.; 7½ in.
Overall length: 10¼ in. to 13 in.
Weight: 36 to 43 oz.
Sights: Open, fixed.
Cylinder capacity: 6 rounds.

The basic popularity of the Model P is reflected in the many copies that have been produced in the past three decades. Those still in production include:

Cattleman—Made for LA Distributors in West Germany, this is a single-action revolver of solid-frame, rod ejection "Frontier" style identical to Colt and Ruger models. Operation and loading-firing instructions for those guns apply.

Characteristics of the Deputy Revolver

Caliber: .22 RF; .22 MRF; .357 Magnum; .44 Magnum.
Operation by: Manual; single-action only.

Barrel length: 4¾ in. to 7½ in.
Overall length: 10¾ in. to 13½ in.
Weight: 30 to 42 oz.
Sights: Open, fixed. Target type on some versions.
Cylinder capacity: 6 rounds.

Hawes Western Marshal—.357 Magnum/9mm; .44 Magnum/.44-40; .45 Long Colt/.45 ACP.
Sturm, Ruger Blackhawk: See below.
Virginian Dragoon—Now made by Interarms in Midland, Virginia, this revolver was formerly manufactured in Switzerland. It is available in .357 Magnum, .44 Magnum, and .45 Colt. Barrel lengths available vary with caliber but include 5-, 6-, 7½- and 8-inch.

Model D Revolvers

There are six variations of this .38 Special caliber solid-frame, swing-out cylinder, double/single-action revolver—Detective Special, Cobra, Agent, Diamondback, Viper (new 1977) and Police Positive (new 1977 version). This design dates before 1900, and although it has been product improved from time to time the basic frame and lock work remain the same. The most significant mechanical change was the addition of a safety hammer block during the 1920s. (A bar is interposed between hammer face and frame except when the trigger is held fully rearward. This prevents the firing pin from reaching a cartridge or in rebounding-pin models prevents the hammer from reaching the firing pin.

In 1972, Colt altered the barrel profile of its D Model revolvers, adopting a heavy Python style barrel, which has an ejector rod enclosure and ventilated rib.

Characteristics

	Barrel length	Overall length	Weight	Frame
Detective Special:	2 in.	7 in.	22½ oz.	Steel
Cobra:	2 in.	7 in.	16⅝ oz.	Aluminum alloy
Agent:	2 in.	6⅞ in.	16⅜ oz.	Aluminum alloy
Diamondback:	2½–4 in.	7½–9 in.	24–27½ oz.	Steel*
Viper:	4 in.	9 in.	20 oz.	Aluminum alloy
Police Positive:	4 in.	9 in.	26½ oz.	Steel

*Looks like a scaled down Python.

Pre-1972 Colt Detective Special revolver.

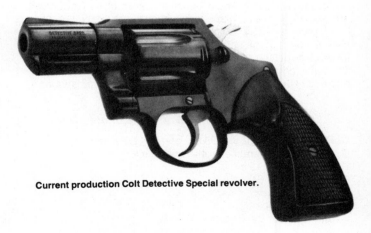

Current production Colt Detective Special revolver.

Model I Revolver

Built upon the .41 caliber big brother of the Model D frame, the .357 Magnum caliber Python is one of the leading police handguns in the United States. Available in 2½-, 4- and 6-inch barrel lengths, this steel frame pistol ranges in weight from 33 oz. for the shortest barrel to 43½ oz. for the longest barrel.

Model J Revolvers

Two versions of the Model J are currently marketed by Colt—the Lawman Mark III and the Trooper Mark III. Introduced in 1969, this revolver action contains completely redesigned lock work, which in detail functions differently from other standard models. The bolt is of the Smith & Wesson type actuated by a forward projection on the trigger; rebound action and trigger return are furnished by separate springs instead of the old style lever. All springs except that of the hand are the coil type. Loading and firing procedures are identical to other Colt models. Various hammer, trigger and grip options are offered.

Characteristics of the Colt Trooper Mark III Revolver

Caliber: .357 Magnum; .38 Special
Operation by: Manual, double- or single-action.
Barrel length: 4 in. to 6 in.
Overall length: $9\frac{1}{2}$ in. to $11\frac{1}{2}$ in.
Height: $5\frac{5}{8}$ in.
Weight: $38\frac{1}{3}$ oz. to 42 oz.
Sights: Open, micrometer-adjustable target type.
Cylinder capacity: 6 rounds.

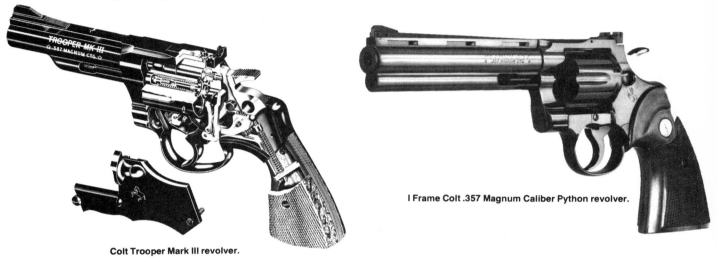

Colt Trooper Mark III revolver.

I Frame Colt .357 Magnum Caliber Python revolver.

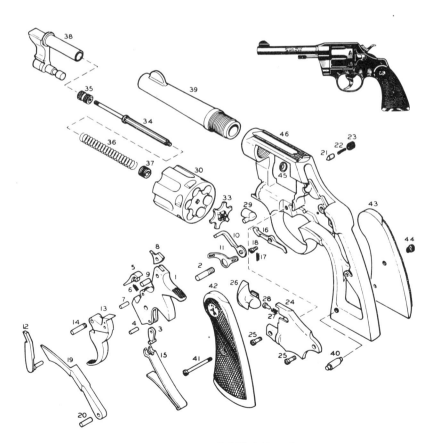

Exploded view of typical Colt Model I revolver.

SMITH & WESSON

Smith & Wesson solid-frame, side-swing, exposed-hammer, double/single-action revolvers are known and respected throughout the world. The basic design is identical in virtually all models, except the Bodyguard and Centennial. The design dates to the turn of the century in the 1902 Military and Police Model with relatively minor improvements in the late 1920s and early 1950s. The various models are produced on three different size frames—the .32 size of the 5-shot guns; the .38 size of the 6-shot guns through .38-.357 caliber; and the .44 size Magnum frame of the 6-shot .41, .44, .45 and heavy .357 guns.

The basic design as represented by the US M1917 .45 revolver and the .38/200 K200 "Victory Model" is covered in Capters 45 and 10. Present commercial models differ only in minor areas, such as the shortened hammer fall introduced in 1950, micrometer-adjustable sights on target models and frame mounted rebounding firing pins in the rimfire models. Most of the .32 and .38 frame models are available as "Airweight" with aluminum alloy frames.

Smith & Wesson is a pioneer in the development of stainless steel handguns. S&W introduced the M60 "Stainless Chief" in 1965 and in 1972 began delivery of the M64, M66 and M67 revolvers, stainless steel versions of the M10, M15 and M19 respectively. Specifications are identical with their plain steel counterparts.

Characteristics of the Smith & Wesson Revolvers

	.32 Frame (1)	.38 Frame (K) (2)	.44 Frame (M) (3)
Caliber:	.22; .32; .38.	.22; .32; .38; .357.	.357; 44; .45; .41.
Barrel length:	2 in. to 6 in.	2 in. to 8³/₈ in.	3¹/₂ in. to 8³/₈ in.
Overall length:	6¹/₄ in. to 10¹/₂ in.	6¹/₈ in. to 12⁷/₈ in.	9³/₈ in. to 13³/₄ in.
Weight:	*17 to 20 oz.	*28 to 42¹/₂ oz.	42 to 51¹/₂ oz.
Cylinder capacity:	5 rounds.	6 rounds.	6 rounds.

*Airweight models weigh approximately ⅓ less in 2-in. barrel length.
(1) Terrier, Chief Special, Kit Gun.
(2) M&P, K22-32-38, Combat Masterpiece, Combat Magnum.
(3) .357, .41, and .44 Magnums; .44 Mil; .45 Target; .38/44 Outdoorsman.

S&W Bodyguard, Model 38

Built on the .32 frame and differs from the basic model only in that frame side-walls are extended to surround the hammer. The hammer is altered in profile and the checked spur protrudes through a slot just enough to permit single-action cocking, if desired. It is intended primarily for double-action use.

Characteristics of the S&W Model 38 Pistol

Caliber: .38 Special.
Operation by: Manual; double- or single-action.
Barrel length: 2 in.
Overall length: 6³/₈ in.
Sights: Open, fixed.
Weight: 20¹/₂ oz.; Airweight 14¹/₂ oz.
Cylinder capacity: 5 rounds.

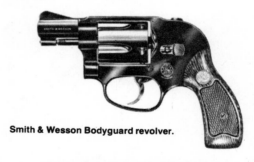

Smith & Wesson Bodyguard revolver.

Smith & Wesson Stainless Steel M67.

STURM, RUGER AND COMPANY INC.

Ruger Blackhawk

This is a modern center-fire revolver of traditional American single-action "Frontier" styling. In appearance and manipulation, it is identical to the Colt SAA. Mechanically, however, it differs considerably. The grip frame is a one-piece casting rather than a two-screw assembly of parts. The lock work, while quite similar and functioning the same as in the Colt, is redesigned to use coil and torsion springs throughout. The entire gun in all versions is designed for modern production techniques, especially precision casting and screw-machine fabrication.

In addition to the Blackhawk, there is a smaller-frame version made for rimfire cartridges and designated "Single Six."

Characteristics of the Ruger Revolvers

	Single Six	Blackhawk
Caliber:	.22 RF; .22 MRF.	.30 Carbine; .357; .41; .44 Magnum.
Operation by:	Manual, single-action only.	
Barrel length:	5¹/₂ in. to 9¹/₂ in.	4⁵/₈ in. to 7¹/₂ in.
Overall length:	10⁷/₈ in. to 14⁷/₈ in.	10¹/₄ in. to 13³/₈ in.
Weight:	36 to 38 oz.	38 to 48 oz.
Sights:	Open, fixed*	Open, adjustable target type.
Cylinder capacity:	6 rounds.	6 rounds.

*Super version has target-type adjustable sights.

Ruger Blackhawk revolver.

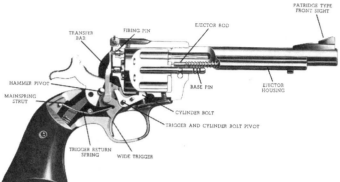

Ruger New Model Super Single-Six. Action cutaway—mechanism shown with trigger pulled and hammer beginning to fall. Transfer bar is held in firing position, between hammer and firing pin. Cylinder bolt is engaged in cylinder locking notch.

Ruger New Model Super Single-Six. Action cutaway—mechanism shown at rest. Transfer bar is not in line between hammer and firing pin. This is the normal carrying position. All six chambers may be loaded.

Ruger New Model Super Blackhawk. Caliber .44 Magnum, 7½-inch barrel.

Ruger produced the Blackhawk (.357 Magnum) and Super Blackhawk (.44 Magnum) revolvers from 1955 and 1959 respectively until 1972. The New Model Blackhawk and Super Blackhawk revolvers, introduced in 1973, have the same outward appearance as the earlier pistols. The internal mechanism, however, has been redesigned for greater safety. Although only the .22 rimfire Single Six is illustrated below, the figures and descriptions are valid for the Blackhawk and Super Blackhawk revolvers as well.

In the Ruger New Model single-actions, the hammer has only two positions—all the way forward, or fully cocked. In the first illustration, the hammer is shown fully forward; it rests directly on the frame. There is no "safety" notch, nor is there a "loading" notch. In this figure, the trigger has been released, and the transfer bar, which is pivoted at its lower end to an arm of the trigger, has been lowered, removing any possible connection between the hammer and the firing pin. In this position, the hammer surrounds but cannot touch the firing pin, and the revolver can be carried with all six chambers loaded.

The second illustration shows the revolver with the trigger pulled and the hammer beginning to fall. The trigger is in its rearmost position, and the transfer bar is raised so that its upper tip is immediately behind the firing pin. When the hammer falls, it will drive both the upper end of the transfer bar and the firing pin forward to ignite the cartridge. As the hammer is cocked, it cams the trigger almost to its extreme rearward position. It is this motion of the trigger that raises the transfer bar. Unless the trigger is held to the rear as the hammer falls, the transfer bar will automatically lower, preventing the revolver from firing.

The firing mechanism of the New Model includes a component usually found only in the double-action revolver—the transfer bar. It is the medium through which the energy of the hammer blow is transmitted to the firing pin to strike the cartridge primer. The hammer itself never touches the firing pin, which, as in all Ruger revolvers, is mounted in the cylinder frame.

The transfer bar is pivoted at its lower end to the trigger. When the trigger is held to its rearmost position, the top of the transfer bar is in line between the hammer and the firing pin. Therefore, unless the trigger is held to the rear, the hammer blow (or in the case of a fall, a blow to the hammer) is not transmitted to the firing pin.

When the hammer is down, the top of the transfer bar is interlocked with the hammer face so that the trigger cannot be pulled until the hammer is drawn to the rear.

The transfer bar system provides an unprecedented measure of security against accidental discharge, and the New Model Revolvers can under all normal conditions be carried will all six chambers loaded.

The New Model revolvers meet the proposed US governmental requirements for hammer safety drop tests.

Ruger Double-Action Revolvers

Ruger introduced a new revolver, their first double-action design, in 1972, aimed at the police market, which was dominated by Colt and Smith & Wesson. (This was the third new police revolver since 1965 when Charter Arms entered the field; Dan Wesson Arms began marketing their contender in 1970.) The Ruger Security-Six has a standard square butt, while the Speed-Six has a round butt. Both are available in blued steel and stainless steel. The Speed-Six is available with only 2¾- and 4-inch barrels, while the Security-Six has a 6-inch barrel option. Wide use of investment castings, a Ruger trademark, and the absence of screws (A coin is all that is required for disassembly.) contribute to an excellent design. As with the Ruger single-action revolvers, the transfer bar concept in the trigger mechanism makes the weapon very safe to handle.

Characteristics of the Ruger Security-Six

Caliber: .357 Magnum
Operation by: Manual, single/double-action.
Barrel length: 2¾, 4 and 6 in.
Overall length: 8, 9¼ and 11¼ in.

Weight: 33 oz. (4-in. barrel).
Sights: Open, adjustable.
Cylinder capacity: 6 rounds.

There is a third variant in this family of revolvers—the Police Service-Six. Like the Speed-Six, it has fixed sights and is available in .38 Special and 9mm Parabellum calibers.

Ruger Speed-Six, full right view.

DAN WESSON ARMS

The double-action revolver introduced in 1969 by Dan Wesson Arms, Inc. of Manson, Massachusetts, is the third new revolver to recently appear on the US market. Dan Wesson, a direct descendant of Daniel B. Wesson of the original Smith & Wesson firm, has no tie with the Springfield, Massachusetts, company. Conventional in appearance, the Dan Wesson revolvers differ considerably from other pistols available today.

Most unusual is its rapid interchange of barrels. Whereas changing barrels on revolvers has heretofore been a task for a gunsmith, the Dan Wesson people have made it a relatively simple procedure. The barrel proper is a simple, thin-walled, rifled tube threaded on both ends. It is screwed into the receiver against a feeler gage laid across the cylinder face. The gage insures proper cylinder/barrel gap. A separate housing is slipped over the barrel to butt against the frame, and a muzzle nut is tightly turned on the barrel to lock both barrel and housing securely in place. Barrels of 2½-, 4-, 6- and 8-inch lengths, each

with its own housing, may be freely exchanged on the same gun in about one minute. As in the current line of Colt revolvers, the ejector rod is protected by the barrel housing.

Dan Wesson revolvers also differ in that the cylinder latches at the front of the frame. The latch moves vertically to act directly on the swing-out crane. Having been designed primarily for double-action work (though capable of single-action), the distance the hammer travels is 25% less than in other contemporary designs.

There are two basic series of Dan Wesson revolvers—.38 Special and .357 Magnum calibers. The standard service revolver model in .38 Special is Model 8 and in .357 Magnum Model 14. The target model in .38 Special is Model 9 and in .357 Magnum Model 15. Model 14–22 designates the .357 service revolver with a 2½-inch barrel. Model 15–28 equals the .357 target model with an 8-inch barrel.

Characteristics of the Dan Wesson Model 14

Caliber: .357 Magnum.
Type: Solid frame, swing-out cylinder, double- and single-action, manually operated.
Barrel length: 2½, 4, 6, 8 in.
Overall length: 9¼ in. with 4-in. barrel.
Height: 5¾ in.
Weight: 34 oz. with 4-in. barrel.
Sights: Open.
Cylinder capacity: 6 rounds.

Model 14 Dan Wesson revolver with four interchangeable barrels.

Foreign Copies of Domestic Models

There are numerous foreign manufactured revolvers that are either outright copies or only slightly modified versions of basic modified models. They include copies of both Colt and Ruger single-actions as well as Smith & Wesson and Colt double-actions. Some are encountered regularly in the United States, others not often. Generally speaking, there is sufficient resemblance to domestic models that they are readily recognized. Some are of good quality, others are not, and each should be examined and judged on its own merits.

SEMIAUTOMATIC PISTOLS

Beretta

With the exception of the Brigadier and M90, all Beretta pistols are based on the M1934 design, described and pictured in

Chapter 28. Manipulation and functioning of the Jaguar, Puma and Sable are essentially the same as for the Beretta 9mm Model 1934.

Characteristics of the Beretta Pistol

	Jaguar	Puma	Model 76 Sable	Model 70S*
Caliber:	.22 L.R.	.32 ACP.	.22 L.R.	.380.
Operation by:	Blowback.	Blowback.	Blowback.	Blowback.
Barrel length:	6 in.	6 in.	6 in.	3⅝ in.
Overall length:	8¾ in.	9½ in.	8¾ in.	6½ in.
Sights:	Open, adjustable rear.	Open, adjustable rear.	Open, adjustable rear.	Open, adjustable rear.
Weight:	19 oz.	19 oz.	26 oz.	n/a
Magazine capacity:	10 rounds.	10 rounds.	10 rounds.	7 rounds.

*A similar model called the Cougar cannot under existing laws be imported into the US.

Beretta Brigadier

This is a simply a commercial version of the 9mm M1951 pistol adopted by the Italian Army. It is chambered for the 9mm Parabellum (Luger) cartridge and is described and pictured in detail in Chapter 28.

Model 90

In 1971, Beretta introduced a very modern double-action .32 caliber pocket-size autoloader designated M90. Of blowback design, it features a stainless steel removable barrel, concentric recoil spring and exposed hammer. With a 3⅝-inch barrel, it is 6¾ inches overall. The magazine holds 8 rounds.

BERNADELLI

When the 1968 Gun Control Act imposed new standards on imported handguns, this Italian firm introduced two versions of a new centerfire pistol for the US market—the Models 80 and 90. Externally similar to the Walther PPK, these guns have the following characteristics.

Characteristics of Bernadelli Automatic Pistols

	Model 80	Model 90
Caliber.	.22 L.R.; 32; 380.	.22 L.R.; 32; 380.
Operation by:	Blowback.	Blowback.
Barrel length:	3½ in.	6 in.
Overall length:	6½ in.	9 in.
Weight:	26.8 oz.	25.6 oz.
Sights:	Open, adjustable rear.	Open, adjustable rear.
Magazine capacity:	10 rounds, .22 L.R. 8 rounds, .32 ACP. 7 rounds, .380 ACP.	10 rounds, .22 L.R. 8 rounds, .32 ACP. 7 rounds, .380 ACP.

Model 90 Bernadelli .380 caliber pistol.

Colt Industries

In their 1977 line, Colt offered four variants of the M1911A1 automatic pistol—two Commanders and two Mark IV/Series '70 handguns. See US M1911A1 Pistol for mechanical and functional details.

Colt Commander

Introduced in 1951, this is essentially a shortened version of the .45 Government Model. Initially available with an aluminum alloy frame as a spinoff from experimental models developed for the US Army (See Chapter 4.), a steel frame Commander was subsequently introduced. Except for the slide, barrel and recoil spring, parts interchange with those of older models.

Colt Lightweight Commander in .45 caliber.

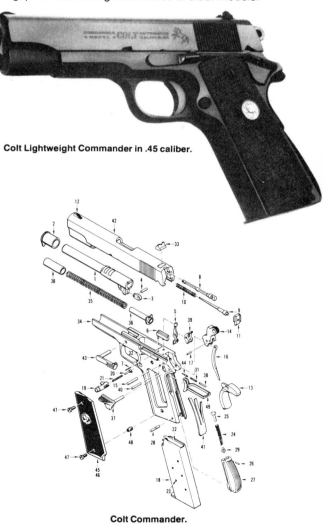

Colt Commander.

Characteristics of Colt Commander Pistols

	Leightweight Commander	Combat Commander
Caliber:	.45 ACP.	9mm Parabellum; .38 Super; .45 ACP.
Operation:	Recoil, Browning system.	Recoil, Browning system.
Barrel length:	4¼ in.	4¼ in.
Overall length:	7⅞ in.	7⅞ in.
Height:	5½ in.	5½ in.
Weight:	27½ oz.	36 and 37 oz.
Sights:	Open, fixed.	Open, fixed.
Magazine capacity:	7 rounds.	9 rounds, 9mm Parabellum. 9 rounds, .38 Super. 7 rounds, .45 ACP.

In 1970, Colt introduced their Mark IV/Series '70 versions of the standard government model. Basically identical to the M1911A1, it has an improved collet-type barrel bushing and reverse taper at the end of the barrel to provide a tighter fit when the pistol is ready to fire, thus providing greater inherent accuracy. A match model, the Gold Cup National Match MKIV/Series '70, replaces the older Colt Gold Cup match model, which was dropped in 1970. The MKIV/Series '70 Gold Cup has adjustable target sights, wide, adjustable trigger and target barrel.

Characteristics of Colt MKIV/Series '70 Pistols

	Government Model	Gold Cup National Match
Caliber:	9mm; .38 Super; .45 ACP.	.45 ACP.
Operation:	Recoil, Browning system.	Recoil, Browning system.
Barrel length:	5 in.	5 in.
Overall length:	8½ in.	8½ in.
Height:	5½ in.	5½ in.
Weight:	39 and 40 oz.	39 oz.
Sights:	Open, fixed.	Open, adjustable.
Magazine capacity:	9 rounds, 9mm. 9 rounds, .38 Super. 7 rounds, .45 ACP.	7 rounds, .45 ACP.

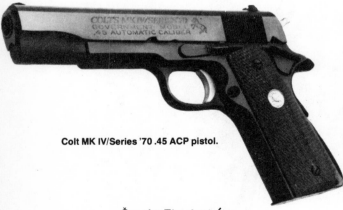

Colt MK IV/Series '70 .45 ACP pistol.

Čzeska Zbrojovká

This Czechoslovakian firm has recently introduced two new pistols into the world market. The 9mm M1975 military type pistol is described in Chapter 4. Their second handgun is the Model 70 7.65mm Automatic Pistol, similar in operation to Walther's PPK pistol.

CZ Model 70, left side.

Characteristics of CZ Model 70 Automatic Pistol

Caliber: .32 ACP.
Operation by: Blowback.
Barrel length: 3²⁵/₃₂ in.
Overall length: 6 ¹¹/₁₆ in.
Weight: 24³/₄ oz.
Sights: Open, fixed.
Magazine capacity: 8 rounds.

Fabrique Nationale

In addition to their 9mm Parabellum High Power described in Chapter 9, the FN commercial line includes the Browning "Baby" automatic pistol, the Model 125 and the new FN Browning Model 140 D.A.

Browning "Baby" Automatic Pistol

Introduced by FN in 1906, this pistol has not been imported into the United States since the 1968 Gun Control Act went into effect. With the exception of the grips, factory markings and sights, the "Baby" is mechanically the same as the Colt .25 ACP vest pocket automatic that was discontinued in 1941.

Characteristics of FN "Baby" Browning Auto Pistol

Caliber: .25 ACP.
Operation by: Blowback.
Barrel length: 2¹/₈ in.
Overall length: 4 in.
Weight: 7 oz.
Sights: Open, fixed.
Magazine capacity: 6 rounds.

FN Browning "Baby" automatic pistol.

FN Browning Model 125 pistol.

FN Browning 140 D.A. automatic pistol.

Browning Model 125 Automatic Pistol

Basically the M1922 Browning Pistol equipped with adjustable target sights, the Model 125 is still very popular in the world handgun market.

Characteristics of FN Browning Model 125 Automatic Pistol

Caliber: .32 ACP.
Operation by: Blowback.
Barrel length: 4³/₈ in.
Overall length: 7 in.
Weight: 24 oz.
Sights: Open, adjustable rear.
Magazine capacity: 9 rounds.

Browning 140 D.A. Automatic Pistol

A very recent addition to the FN product line, the Model 140 D.A. is FN's attempt to capture part of the world military, police and sporting handgun market held by the Colt Commander and the Smith & Wesson Model 39 alloy frame automatic pistols. Like the Model 39, it combines the aluminum alloy frame with a steel slide. This double-action newcomer will undoubtedly make its mark on the handgun world as have FN's other pistols.

Characteristics of FN Browning 140 D.A. Automatic Pistol

Caliber: .32 ACP (7.65mm Browning); 9mm Parabellum.

Operation by: Recoil.
Barrel length: Approx. 4 in.
Overall length: 6 ⁷/₁₀ in.
Weight: 22 ¹/₄ oz.
Sights: Open, fixed.
Magazine capacity: 12 rounds, 7.65mm.
13 rounds, 9mm Parabellum.

Heckler & Koch

HK-4

An unusual design, the HK-4's most distinguishing characteristic is that it is sold as a complete 4-caliber set with barrels, springs and magazines for firing .22 L.R., .25 ACP, .32 ACP or .380 ACP. The need for separate slides for each caliber is avoided by a dual purpose firing pin and extractor; the former must be switched from centerfire to rimfire and back again. The extractor automatically adjusts to the different diameter cartridge cases.

Essentially, the HK-4 is a highly refined version of the pre-WW II Mauser HSc 7.65mm pistol. It is constructed by modern methods, the slide being a welded assembly of castings and stampings. The frame is of a light alloy precision casting. The first round may be fired double-action by first lowering the hammer. Disassembly is also unique; depressing the latch in the trigger guard allows the slide and barrel to be lifted off after moving it ¹/₈ inch forward.

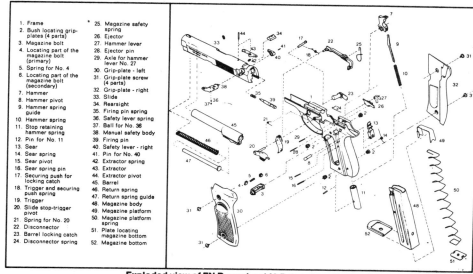

1. Frame
2. Bush locating grip-plates (4 parts)
3. Magazine bolt
4. Locating part of the magazine bolt (primary)
5. Spring for No. 4
6. Locating part of the magazine bolt (secondary)
7. Hammer
8. Hammer pivot
9. Hammer spring guide
10. Hammer spring
11. Stop retaining hammer spring
12. Pin for No. 11
13. Sear
14. Sear spring
15. Sear pivot
16. Sear spring pin
17. Securing push for locking catch
18. Trigger and securing push spring
19. Trigger
20. Slide stop-trigger pivot
21. Spring for No. 20
22. Disconnector
23. Barrel locking catch
24. Disconnector spring
25. Magazine safety spring
26. Ejector
27. Hammer lever
28. Ejector pin
29. Axle for hammer lever No. 27
30. Grip-plate - left
31. Grip-plate screw (4 parts)
32. Grip-plate - right
33. Slide
34. Rearsight
35. Firing pin spring
36. Safety lever spring
37. Ball for No. 36
38. Manual safety body
39. Firing pin
40. Safety lever - right
41. Pin for No. 40
42. Extractor spring
43. Extractor
44. Extractor pivot
45. Barrel
46. Return spring
47. Return spring guide
48. Magazine body
49. Magazine platform
50. Magazine platform spring
51. Plate locating magazine bottom
52. Magazine bottom

Exploded view of FN Browning 140 D.A. automatic pistol.

Characteristics of HK-4 Automatic Pistol

Caliber: .22 L.R.; .25 ACP; .32 ACP; .380 ACP.
Operation by: Retarded blowback.
Barrel length: 3 11/32 in.
Overall length: 6 3/16 in.
Weight: 16 9/10 oz.
Sights: Open, fixed.
Magazine capacity: 8 rounds, .22 L.R.
                 8 rounds, .25 ACP.
                 8 rounds, .32 ACP.
                 7 rounds, .380 ACP.

Heckler & Koch also produces a large locked-breech 9mm Parabellum military and police type autoloading pistol designated P9 (single-action) and P9S (double-action) similar in appearance and construction to the HK-4. The frame and slide are of stampings and weldments, and part of the frame is overlaid with plastic. Locking is by the cam and roller system of the G-3 Rifle. See Chapter 20.

Llama (Gabilondo & Cia)

These Spanish Llama large-frame pistols in .45 ACP and .38 Colt Super Automatic calibers are extremely close copies of the Colt Government Model described in Chapter 45. The more recent models have ventilated sighting ribs and other minor variations, but the resemblance to the Colt is so great that many parts will interchange. A reduced size version weighing only 20 ounces is produced in .380 ACP but is mechanically and functionally identical to the big guns. An apparently identical Llama in .32 ACP has the locking system deleted and functions as a blowback. It is otherwise identical to the .380, and most parts will interchange.

Characteristics of Llama .380 and .32 ACP Pistols

Caliber: .32 ACP; .380 ACP.
Operation by: Blowback, recoil; Browning system.
Barrel length: 3 11/16 in.
Overall length: 6 1/4 in.
Height: 4 3/8 in.
Sights: Open, fixed.
Weight: 21 oz; 20 oz.
Magazine capacity: 8 rounds; 7 rounds.

In addition, premium priced, adjustable sight versions of the .45 and .38 models are offered.

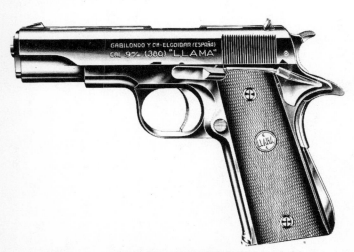

Llama .380 semiautomatic pistol.

M.A.B. (Manufacture d'Armes Automatiques Bayonne)

M.A.B. P.15

This is France's most modern pistol design and matches the largest magazine capacity, 15 rounds, of any currently produced handgun. It is of conventional style and construction but uses an unusual rotating barrel locking system. In appearance, it is quite similar to the Browning M1935 and does, in fact, use a magazine identical—except for length—to the Browning. See Chapter 18.

Mauser

HSc Automatic Pistol

In 1968, the famous West German Mauserwerke again entered the commercial handgun market with a newly produced version of the original HSc pistol. The highly advanced double-action, pocket-size autoloader made its debut during the late 1930s, and hundreds of thousands of 7.65mm specimens saw service in WW II. The new version is offered in .22 L.R., 7.65mm (.32 ACP) and 9mmK (.380 ACP) calibers. Except for the slight differences in the added calibers, the new HSc is as described in Chapter 20.

Mauser HSc automatic pistol.

Parabellum

Also in 1968, Mauser introduced newly manufactured Parabellum pistols in 7.65mm (.30 Luger) caliber. This model is identical to pre-World War II "Luger" pistols, but that name cannot be applied to Mauser's weapon since Stoeger Arms owns the name copyright. The new gun is actually made on original Swiss arsenal tooling utilized to produce the M1929 pistol for the Swiss before WW II. The Parabellums are available in 7.65mm Luger in a 6-inch barrel and 9mm Parabellum in a 4-inch barrel. The original design is described in Chapter 20. All Mauser pistols are distributed in the US by Interarms.

SIG (Swiss Industrial Co.)

SIG P210

This series of commercial pistols is based on the Swiss SP47/8 (M49) service pistol. A blowback .22 L.R. conversion unit and glossy finished target models are offered. See Chapter 41.

SIG-Sauer P220

See Chapter 4 for a description of this new pistol.

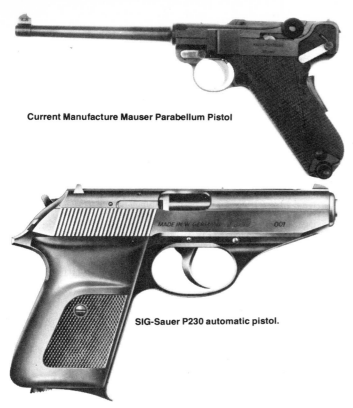

Current Manufacture Mauser Parabellum Pistol

SIG-Sauer P230 automatic pistol.

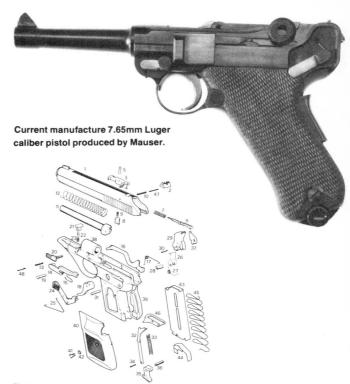

Current manufacture 7.65mm Luger caliber pistol produced by Mauser.

Exploded view of the SIG-Sauer P230 pistol.

SIG-Sauer P230

A companion to the military P220, this pocket automatic is available in three calibers—.22 L.R., .32 ACP and 9 × 18mm police. The design is notable for its lightweight alloy frame, decocking lever and double-action trigger mechanism. Both the P220 and P230 are manufactured in West Germany.

Characteristics of SIG-Sauer P230 Automatic Pistol

Caliber: .22 L.R.; .320 ACP; 9 × 18mm police
Operation by: Blowback.
Barrel length: 3 3/5 in.
Overall length: 6 3/5 in.
Weight: 18 oz. in 9 × 18mm police
Sights: Open, fixed.
Magazine capacity: 10 rounds, .22 L.R.
8 rounds, .32 ACP.
7 rounds, 9 × 18mm police

Smith & Wesson

Smith & Wesson M39

As described in Chapter 2, the Model 39 was designed in the early 1950s for US Army lightweight pistol tests. The M39 was introduced commercially in 1954 after those tests were terminated. It is a modern, locked breech double-action, self-loading pistol built on an aluminum alloy frame. It contains a magazine safety and a means of dropping the hammer from full cock without firing. It utilizes a single column box magazine in the butt and is available only in 9mm Parabellum.

Characteristics of S&W M39 Pistol

Caliber: 9mm Parabellum.
Operation by: Recoil; modified Browning system.
Barrel length: 4 in.

Overall length: 7 7/16 in.
Weight: 26 1/2 oz.
Sights: Open, rear adjustable for windage only.
Magazine capacity: 8 rounds.

In 1973, Smith & Wesson introduced an improved version of the M39 pistol, designated the M59. Otherwise the same, it is modified to accept a 15-round, double column magazine in the butt, making its fully loaded capacity 16 rounds. Empty it weighs 30 ounces, loaded 37.

Smith & Wesson M52

This is a longer, heavier version of the M39 intended purely for target shooting. Mechanically and functionally, it is identical to the M39, though much more closely fitted and adjusted. It carries micrometer-adjustable target sights and is chambered only for the .38 Special Wadcutter cartridge.

Characteristics of S&W M52 Pistol

Caliber: .38 Special Wadcutter.
Operation by: Recoil; modified Browning system.
Barrel length: 5 in.
Overall length: 8 5/8 in.
Weight: 41 oz.
Sights: Micrometer-adjustable, target type.
Magazine capacity: 5 rounds.

Smith & Wesson M59

Described in Chapter 5 under the Hush-Puppy silenced pistol project, the M59 was introduced commercially in the early 1970s. The M59 is similar to the M39 in that it has a steel slide and alloy frame, but it has a double row magazine, which holds 14 rounds instead of 8 as in the M39.

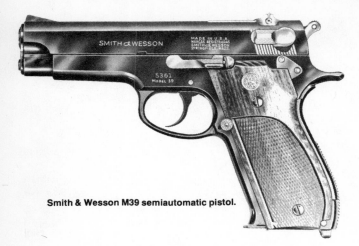

Smith & Wesson M39 semiautomatic pistol.

Smith & Wesson M59 9mm Parabellum automatic pistol.

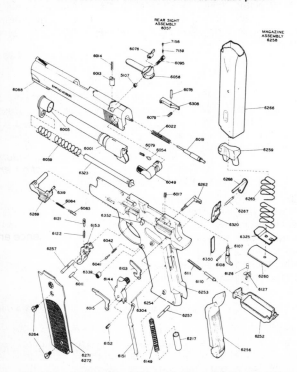

Exploded view of the Smith & Wesson M59 pistol.

Characteristics of S&W M59 Pistol

Caliber: 9mm Parabellum.
Operation by: Recoil; modified Browning system.
Barrel length: 4 in.
Overall length: 7 $7/16$ in.
Weight: 27 oz.
Sights: Open, fixed front; adjustable rear.
Magazine capacity: 14 rounds.

Star (Bonifacio Echeverria & Cia)

Large caliber Star pistols are described in Chapter 39. Commercial models of the A, B and P are sold widely, especially in the Americas. In addition, a reduced scale version in .380 ACP and .32 ACP is available commercially. Called the S and SI, this model duplicates all features, including the locking system of the larger guns. Smaller Star blowback type pistols are offered in .22, .25, .32 and .380 caliber but are no longer available in the US due to government restrictions.

Characteristics of Star Pistols

Caliber: .32 ACP; .380 ACP.
Operation by: Recoil; Browning system.
Barrel length: 3 $3/4$ in.
Overall length: 6 $1/2$ in.
Height: 4$3/4$ in.
Sights: Open, fixed.
Weight: 22 oz.
Magazine capacity: 8 rounds, .32 ACP.
                        7 rounds, .380 ACP.

Star "SI" Model semiautomatic pistol.

Carl Walther Sportwaffenfabrik

Walther pistols are distributed in the US by Interarms. The P38 is available in its military configuration and finish and in a glossy finish commercial model. Both are identical to the aluminum frame military model described in Chapters 20 and 21. The P38 is also furnished commercially in 7.65mm Parabellum (.30 Luger).

More recent is the .22 rimfire P38. It is identical to the others except for a light alloy slide and elimination of the locking system, which converts it to blowback operation.

Walther also now offers the PP Sport Model in .22 L.R. It is simply the basic PP fitted with a 6-inch barrel protruding from the slide and carrying its own removable front sight. An adjustable target type rear sight is fitted, and the hammer has a spur for easier thumb-cocking. See Walther PP in Chapter 21.

50 Selected Bibliography

As interest in the study and collecting of small arms has grown during the past three decades, so has the number of books on specific weapons and weapon groups. Since it has become impossible to describe all of the small arms of the world in a single volume, the editor and publisher decided it would be useful to add a selected bibliography to this edition. For the most part, only newer books have been cited. Readers who wish to locate older volumes are referred to Ray Riling's excellent book, *Guns and Shooting: A Selected Chronological Bibliography,* New York: Greenberg, 1951. Reader recommendations for additional entries to the bibliography that follows, especially European titles, will be appreciated.

Journals for students of small arms:

Armies and Weapons (Interconair, via G. Brentain 7, 6900 Lugano, Switzerland).

International Defense Review (Interavia SA, P. O. Box 162, 1212 Cointrin, Geneva, Switzerland). Published in English, French, German and Spanish editions.

National Defense (American Defense Preparedness Association, Union First Bank Building, Washington, D.C. 20005).

Books:

Archer, Denis H. R., ed. *Jane's Infantry Weapons, 1976.* London and New York: Macdonald and Jane's Publishers, Ltd., and Franklin Watts, 1976.

Belford, James N., and Dunlap, Jack. *The Mauser Self-Loading Pistol.* Alhambra, CA: Borden Publishing Co., 1969.

Boothroyd, Geoffrey. *The Handgun.* New York: Bonanza Books, 1970.

Breathed, John W., Jr., and Schroeder, Joseph J., Jr. *System Mauser: A Pictorial History of the Model 1896 Self-Loading Pistol.* Chicago: Handgun Press, 1967.

Campbell, Clark S. *The '03 Springfields.* Philadelphia: Ray Riling Arms Book Co., 1971.

This revised and updated version of Campbell's 1957 volume is a very helpful guide to the 1903 Springfield family of weapons.

Chinn, George M. *The Machine Gun.* 4 vols. Washington: Government Printing Office, 1951–1954.

These volumes are essential reading for any individual who wishes to understand the history and design characteristics of the world's machine guns.

Datig, Fred A. *The Luger Pistol (Pistole Parabellum); Its History and Development from 1893–1945.* Revised and enlarged edition. NP: Borden Publishing Co., 1962.

Federov, V. G. *Evolyutsiya strelkovogo oruzhíya* [Evolution of infantry weapons]. Moscow: unknown, 1938–1939.

This volume is in two parts. Part I is titled "Razvitie ruchnogo ognestrel'nogo oruzhiya ot zaryazhaniya s dula i kremnevogo zamka do magazinnikh vintovok" [The development of hand-operated weapons from muzzle loaders and flintlocks to magazine rifles]; Part II is "Razvitie avtomaticheskogo oruzhiya" [The development of automatic weapons]. With a German introduction, this book was reprinted in 1970 by the Biblio Verlag of Osnabruck, Germany. A classic study, it deserves to be translated into English.

Götz, Hans-Dieter. *Die deutshen Militärgewehre und Maschinenpistolen: 1871–1945.* Stuttgart: Motorbuch-Verlag, 1974.

German text.

Greener, W. W. *The Gun and Its Development.* 9th ed. New York: Bonanza Books, 1910.

Hackley, F. W.; Woodin, W. H.; and Scranton, E. L. *History of Modern U.S. Military Ammunition, Vol. I, 1880–1939.* New York and London: Macmillan, 1967.

Hackley, F. W.; Woodin, W. H.; and Scranton, E. L. *History of Modern U.S. Military Ammunition, Vol. II, 1940–1945.* Highland Park, NJ: The Gun Room Press, 1976.

Hatcher, Julian S. *The Book of the Garand.* Washington: Infantry Journal Press, 1948.

An overview of the development of the M1 Rifle.

Hatcher, Julian S. *Hatcher's Notebook.* 2d ed. Harrisburg: The Stackpole Co., 1957 and 1962.

Hicks, James E. *Notes on French Ordnance, 1717 to 1936.* Mt. Vernon, NY: author, 1938.

Hicks, James E. *Notes on German Ordnance for the Collector, 1841 to 1918.* 2d ed. New York: author, 1941.

Hicks, James E. *U.S. Firearms, 1776–1956. Vol. I, Notes on U.S. Ordnance.* La Cañada, CA: James E. Hicks & Sons, 1957.

Hobart, F. W. A., ed. *Jane's Infantry Weapons, 1975.* London and New York: Macdonald and Jane's Publishers, Ltd., and Franklin Watts Inc., 1974.

Hobart, F. W. A. *Pictorial History of the Machine Gun.* London: Ian Allan, 1971.

Hobart, F. W. A. *Pictorial History of the Sub-Machine Gun.* London: Ian Allan, Ltd., 1973.

Hogg, Ian V. *German Pistols and Revolvers, 1871–1945.* New York: Galahad Books, 1971.

Honeycutt, Fred L., Jr., and Anthony, F. Patt. *Military Rifles of Japan, 1897–1945.* Lake Park, FL: F. L. Honeycutt, 1977.

A very useful and well illustrated guide to this subject.

Hughes, James B., Jr. *Mexican Military Arms: The Cartridge Period, 1866–1967.* Houston: Deep River Armory, 1968.

A helpful guide to the small arms used by the Mexican armed forces.

Johnson, George B., and Lockhoven, Hans Bert. *International Armament: With History, Data, Technical Information and Photographs of over 400 Weapons.* 2 vols. Cologne: International Small Arms Publishers, 1965.

Johnson, Harold E. *Small Arms Identification and Operation Guide—Eurasian Communist Countries.* DST–1110H–394–76. Charlottesville, VA: US Army Foreign Science and Technology Center, 1976.

The latest edition of this series is a very handy guide to foreign small arms.

Johnson, Harold E. *Small Arms Identification and Operation Guide–Free World.* DST–110H–163–76. Charlottesville, VA: US Army Foreign Science and Technology Center, 1976.

Jones, Harry E. *Luger Variations.* Vol. I. Los Angeles: author, 1959.

Catalogue of the many variations of Luger pistols.

Krcma, Vaclav. *The Identification and Registration of Firearms.* Springfield, IL: Charles C. Thomas, 1974.

Leithe, Frederick E. *Japanese Hand Guns.* Alhambra, CA: Borden Publishing Co., 1968.

Identification guide to Japanese handguns through WW II.

Lugs, Jaroslav. *Firearms Past and Present: A Complete Review of Firearms Systems and Their Histories.* 2 vols. London: Grenville, 1975.

This previously little known volume is an invaluable addition to the English language literature on small arms. Of particular significance are the biographies and bibliography contained in Vol. I.

Lugs, Jaroslav. *Handfeuerwaffen: Systematischer Uberblick über die Handfeuerwaffen und ihre Geschicete.* 2 vols. East Berlin: Deutscher Militarverlag, 1962.

German text.

Lugs, Jaroslav. *Rǔcni palne zbraně.* 2 vols. Prague: unknown, 1956.

Czech text.

Mathews, Joseph Howard. *Firearms Identification.* 3 vols. Madison: University of Wisconsin, 1962–1973.

Musgrave, Daniel D., and Nelson, Thomas B. *The World's Assault Rifles & Automatic Carbines.* Vol. II of the World's Weapons Series. Alexandria, VA: T. B. N. Enterprises, 1967.

The first in-depth look at this subject.

Neal, Robert J., and Jinks, Roy G. *Smith & Wesson, 1857–1945.* Cranbury, NJ: 1975.

Nelson, Thomas B., with the assistance of Hans B. Lockhoven. *The World's Submachine Guns* [machine pistols]. Vol. I. Cologne: International Small Arms Publishers, 1963.

The single most comprehensive book on the subject through the date of publication.

Office of the Chief of Ordnance, Research and Development. *Record of Army Ordnance Research and Development.* 3 vols. Washington: OCO, 1946. Part of Vol. II, Book 1, *Small Arms and Small Arms Ammunition,* has been reprinted as *American Small Arms Research in World War Two. Vol. I: Hand and Shoulder Weapons, Helmets and Body Armor.* Wickenburg, AZ: Normount Technical Publications, 1975.

Olson, Ludwig. *Mauser Bolt Rifles.* 3d ed. Montezuma, IA: F. Brownell & Son, 1977.

Owen, J. I., ed. *Brassey's Infantry Weapons of the World, 1974–75.* New York: British Book Center, 1974.

Owen, J. I., ed. *Brassey's Infantry Weapons of the World, 1975.* New York: Hippocrene Books, 1975.

Pender, Roy G. III. *Mauser Pocket Pistols, 1910–1946.* Houston: Collectors Press, 1971.

Rankin, James L., with the assistance of Gary Green. *Walther Models PP and PPK, 1929–1945.* Coral Gables, FL: author, 1974.

Rankin, James L., with the assistance of Gary Green. *Walther Vol. II. Engraved, Presentation and Standard Models.* Coral Gables, FL: author, n.d.

Reynolds, E. G. B. *The Lee-Enfield Rifle.* London: Herbert Jenkins, Ltd., 1960.

Schneider, Hugo *et al. Handfeuerwaffen System Vetterli.* Zurich: Stocker-Schmid, AG Dietikon, 1972.

Descriptions and illustrations of the many Vetterli variations. German text.

Sharpe, Philip B. *The Rifle in America.* New York: Funk & Wagnalls Co., 1947.

Useful reference source on American rifles through WW II.

Simone, Gianfranco; Belogi, Ruggero; and Grimaldi, Alessio. *IL91.* Milano: Ravizza, 1970.

A basic introduction to the Model 1891 Carcano Rifle; well illustrated, with a good bibliography. Italian text.

Smith, W. H. B. *Mannlicher Rifles and Pistols: Famous Sporting and Military Weapons.* Harrisburg, PA: The Stackpole Co., 1947.

Smith, W. H. B. *Mauser Rifles and Pistols.* Harrisburg, PA: The Stackpole Co., 1972.

Smith, W. H. B., and Smith, Joseph E. *The Book of Rifles.* 4th ed. Harrisburg, PA: The Stackpole Co., 1972.

First published in 1948, this volume provides an encyclopedic reference on the subject of rifles.

Smith, W. H. B., and Smith, Joseph E. *The W. H. B. Smith Classic Book of Pistols and Revolvers.* rev. ed. Harrisburg, PA: The Stackpole Co., 1968.

This companion to *The Book of Rifles* was first published in 1946. It is a basic reference work for individuals interested in the world's handguns.

Textbook of Small Arms, 1929. London: Holland Press, Ltd., 1961.

US Army Foreign Science and Technology Center. *Small Arms Ammunition Identification Guide.* FSTC–CW–07-7-68. Charlottesville, VA: US Army Foreign Science and Technology Center, 1969.

Wahl, Paul. *Carbine Handbook.* New York: ARCO, 1964.

White, Henry P., and Munhall, Burton D. *Cartridge Headstamp Guide.* Bel Air, MD: H. P. White Laboratory, 1963.

White, Henry P., and Munhall, Burton D. *Center Fire Metric Pistol and Revolver Cartridges.* Vol. I, Cartridge Identification. Washington: Infantry Journal Press, 1948.

Whittington, Robert D. III. *German Pistols and Holsters, 1934–1945: Military–Police–NSDAP.* Dallas: Brownlee Books, 1969.

Williamson, Harold F. *Winchester: The Gun That Won the West.* South Brunswick, New York and London: A. S. Barnes and Co., and Thomas Yoseloff, Ltd., 1952.

Wilson, R. K., with Hogg, I. V. *Textbook of Automatic Pistols.* rev. ed. London, Harrisburg, PA, and Schwäbisch Hall: Arms & Armor Press, Stackpole Books, and Deutsche Waffen Journal, 1975.

First published as *Textbook of Automatic Pistols: Being a Treatise on the History, Development and Functioning of the Modern Military Self-Loading Pistol—Its Special Ammunition—and Their Evolvement into the Sub-Machine Gun Together with a Supplementary Chapter on the Light Machine Gun, 1884–1935.* Plantersville, SC: Small-Arms Technical Publishing Co., 1943.

Index

better coverage of the psychological data than did dissonance theory. In the free choice simulation, the locus of most of the action was in the re-evaluation of the rejected alternative in the difficult condition. This was indeed what Brehm (1956) found, although he did not comment on the discrepancy from strict dissonance theory predictions.

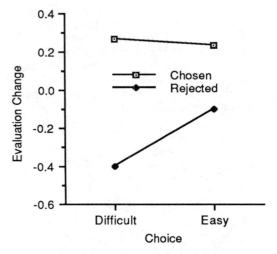

Figure 4. Results for Brehm simulation.

We have found similar instances of the constraint satisfaction model fitting psychological data from other dissonance experiments better than dissonance theory does. These superior fits derive from the capacity of constraint satisfaction models to deal with variables other than those unique to dissonance theory and the increased precision that is inherent to computational formulations.

The present simulations were conducted with a minimum of parameter adjustment. Network weights were positive, negative, or zero; resistance was high or low; and initial levels of activation were either high or low. Additional experimentation revealed that these effects were robust against parameter variation, and that the default parameter settings were applicable to a variety of other dissonance simulations.

The present simulations began with some units having initial, non-zero activation values. More conventionally, constraint satisfaction programs start all units at zero activation and provide some units with external inputs. Activations then gradually build up from zero as a function of both external input and internal network input. This conventional scheme did not seem appropriate for cognitive dissonance phenomena because it yielded results indicating a gradual increase in consonance, but no dissonance. To ensure that the networks modeled dissonance, we initialized some unit activations in conformity with procedures in the psychological experiments.

Although connection weight values can be learned for constraint satisfaction models (e.g., Anderson & Mozer, 1981), there was no such learning in the present simulations. This reflects the fact that the typical dissonance experiment is not an occasion for learning. Instead, acculturated, experienced subjects enter a situation in which they commit themselves to some behavior under the influence of a few salient, experimentally engineered cognitions. These cognitions, the behavioral commitment, and existing knowledge act as constraints on the subject's subsequent re-evaluations. Thus, the typical dissonance experiment capitalizes on past learning, but does not involve much in the way of new learning. The principal thing a subject in a dissonance experiment might learn is how he or she feels about something.

Indeed, there is a sense in which cognitive dissonance phenomena are antithetical to learning phenomena. In both contexts, subjects behave in a way that is less than ideal. In some cases, subjects are able to learn to change their behavior to improve their payoff. But that avenue is closed in dissonance experiments by the fact that subjects remain committed to their behavior. Reduction of cognitive dissonance by re-evaluation is an exercise in coping with behavior that cannot be undone.

Cognitive dissonance phenomena have traditionally been considered as distinct from less counter-intuitive psychological phenomena. But since constraint satisfaction models also account for a wide variety of other phenomena, there is considerable scope for novel theoretical unification.

Cognitive dissonance theory is but one of a number of theories in social psychology emphasizing that people try to achieve consistency among cognitions (Abelson, Aronson, McGuire, Newcombe, Rosenberg, & Tannenbaum, 1968; Abelson & Rosenberg, 1958; Heider, 1958). Although these consistency theories have enjoyed considerable success as verbal formulations, the underlying reasoning mechanisms for establishing consistency have not been precisely specified. It may be that connectionist constraint satisfaction models could serve as a general modeling technique and explanatory device in these areas (cf. Holyoak & Spellman, 1991).

Acknowledgements

This research was supported by a grant to the first author from the Social Sciences and Humanities Research Council of Canada and a grant to the second author from the U. S. National Institute of Mental Health.